The French Writers' War

1940–1953

POLITICS, HISTORY, AND CULTURE
A series from the International Institute at the University of Michigan

Sponsored by the International Institute at the University of Michigan and published by Duke University Press, this series is centered around cultural and historical studies of power, politics, and the state—a field that cuts across the disciplines of history, sociology, anthropology, political science, and cultural studies. The focus on the relationship between state and culture refers both to a methodological approach—the study of politics and the state using culturalist methods—and a substantive one that treats signifying practices as an essential dimension of politics. The dialectic of politics, culture, and history figures prominently in all the books selected for the series.

The French Writers' War

1940–1953

Gisèle Sapiro

Translated by
VANESSA DORIOTT ANDERSON
and DORRIT COHN

DUKE UNIVERSITY PRESS DURHAM AND LONDON 2014

La Guerre des écrivains by Gisèle Sapiro,
© 1999 Librairie Arthème Fayard.
English translation © 2014 Duke University Press.

Printed in the United States of America
on acid-free paper ∞
Designed by Amy Ruth Buchanan
Typeset in Garamond by Westchester Books

DUKE UNIVERSITY PRESS GRATEFULLY
ACKNOWLEDGES THE BOOK DEPARTMENT OF
CULTURAL SERVICES OF THE FRENCH EMBASSY
IN THE UNITED STATES, HEMINGWAY GRANT
PROGRAM, WHICH PROVIDED FUNDS TOWARD
THE TRANSLATION OF THIS BOOK.

Library of Congress Cataloging-in-Publication Data
Sapiro, Gisèle.
The French writers' war, 1940–1953 / Gisile Sapiro ;
translated by Vanessa Doriott Anderson and Dorrit Cohn.
pages   cm — (Politics, history, and culture)
Includes bibliographical references and index.
ISBN 978-0-8223-5178-8 (cloth : alk. paper)
ISBN 978-0-8223-5191-7 (pbk. : alk. paper)
1. France—Intellectual life—20th century.
2. Intellectuals—France—History—20th century.
3. France—Cultural policy—History—20th century.
I. Title. II. Series: Politics, history, and culture.
DC33.7.S27 2014
840.9'3584053—dc23
2013045006

In memory of my father

Contents

Acknowledgments

Gisèle Sapiro wishes to thank Jasmine Deventer for her help revising the translation.

Dorrit Cohn wishes to thank three people who have helped with the preparation of this translation. Richard Ingram, who assisted me with my computer and was immeasurably useful in checking my spelling; Professor Susan Suleiman, who set me straight on the French educational system and helped with the idioms; and François Proulx, who was my main source of information on French idioms.

Vanessa Doriott Anderson wishes to thank Alice Kaplan, for her advice on the logistics of presenting French culture and history to an American audience; Gisèle Sapiro, for her generous assistance with certain very specific details of the manuscript; Courtney Berger, for her guidance throughout the project; and John Anderson, for his superhuman patience and support over many months.

Introduction

In occupied France, the national cultural heritage was at stake for the acting forces. This is why they vied for the big names. Having failed to attract André Gide, the collaborators flaunted Louis-Ferdinand Céline, Henry de Montherlant, and Jacques Chardonne. The homegrown (especially Communist) Resistance retorted with Louis Aragon, Paul Eluard, François Mauriac, and Jean Paulhan. At the beginning of 1944, Charles de Gaulle added the names of oppositional writers in exile to those of Gide and Mauriac: Georges Bernanos and Jacques Maritain. The Vichyist contingent had its own stars, from Henri Pourrat to Charles Maurras, through Henri Massis. With more or less success, each camp thus claimed literary legitimacy in this ideological war. Why and how did writers respond to this demand?

My goal in this book is to demonstrate what is specific about the behavior of French writers under the Occupation, in light of the representations and practices proper to the literary world. The political positions taken by these writers obeyed logics that were not simply motivated by politics. The writers themselves rarely differentiated them from their professional practices: their tendency to engage depended on the way they viewed their craft. And they usually became engaged as artists or intellectuals. But the question of writers' conduct during the "dark years" surpasses that of engagement. The working conditions associated with the craft of writing changed drastically during this period and, as a result, the social signification of individual and collective practices was modified. The very meaning of professional practices and aesthetic options— from art for art's sake to invective—became a site of struggles involving individuals, groups, and institutions. I will analyze the effects of this crisis on the literary world, and what the proposed answers owe to its history.

Writers' engagement during the Occupation has most often been approached from the perspective of a politically focused intellectual history. Cultural practices and institutions are generally dealt with in studies of "daily life" or "cultural life" under oppression. This division leads, on the one hand, to an over-politicized and strongly individualized view, one that tends to focus on extreme figures (Céline, Pierre Drieu La Rochelle, Robert Brasillach, Lucien Rebatet) at the expense of more moderate examples. On the other hand, it leads to a depoliticized view that underestimates the ideological dimension of the most apparently "neutral" cultural activities. Faced with the tendency to disassociate these two questions, my book aims to shed light on each, using the other. I will reinscribe them in a more global approach to literary milieus and the way they worked during this period.

The achievements of the historiography of the "dark years," especially in the field of cultural production, made this approach possible.[1] Still, by adhering to the geographical and political divisions imposed by the specificity of the issues and the mechanisms of constraint, works devoted respectively to Vichy, to the Collaboration, and to the Resistance remained segregated for a long time. It is not by chance that studies attached to different cultural domains—whether literature, artistic creation, or theater—helped shatter these walls:[2] the cultural hegemony of Paris, which was largely maintained despite the forced emigration of the government to the Southern zone, forced a reevaluation of the weight of the demarcation line; political divisions appeared less clearly in those milieus, since corporative and professional solidarities sometimes won out over ideological divergences. Recently, a parallel interest has developed for the characteristics of behavior in social groups, professions, or milieus.[3] From the viewpoint of the historiography of the Occupation, this book is linked to the latter perspective, although it privileges a sociological approach.[4] Rather than working from geographical (Northern zone/Southern zone) and political divisions, I will take a given professional milieu, its practices and institutions, as my point of departure, in order to examine the crisis's repercussions within it. I will limit myself to metropolitan France, where the majority of the struggles for redefinition of the literary stakes played out.

➤ "The strange defeat," according to Marc Bloch's expression, that brought an end to the "Phoney War" through the occupation of two-thirds of the territory and the signing of the armistice on June 22, 1940, at Rethondes, would open up a real crisis of national identity. Writers did not escape from the logic of struggle and payback that seems to be the lot of every community caught up in a crisis of what Durkheim called collective consciousness. But the writers' war was not simply a reflection of the civil war. Like any other professional milieu, the literary world has its own codes, references, rules, and principles of division.

It may seem paradoxical to add this study to an approach targeting professional milieus, given that the literary profession is the most individualistic, the least regulated, and the least organized (to the extent that its professional status is called into question): no technical training prepares writers for their trade (unlike musicians, for example) and there are no official requisites mandating entry. The literary world is nonetheless ruled by laws and value hierarchies that are relatively autonomous, to the extent that they cannot be reduced to external social determinations, as Pierre Bourdieu has shown.[5] Confronted with political, religious, and economic demands, the literary field has affirmed its autonomy, by instituting the primacy of peer judgment as proof of legitimacy: thus, when the book market was industrialized in the nineteenth century, while a large-scale circulation network was developing under the rule of market logic and oriented toward short-term profits, a network of small-scale circulation emerged concurrently, one in which peer recognition outweighed economic criteria. Tension resulted between a pole that was more disposed to respond to external demand and a pole that was more oriented toward the defense of specifically literary values. This tension structured the literary field. What happens to literary autonomy in a period of crisis, when economic constraints are doubled and subject to political stakes? In what forms does it survive, and how does it resist external pressures?

Subject to the double mechanism of constraint imposed by the Nazis and Vichy, surrendered to the different attempts to harness its power, the literary field witnessed the abolition of those conditions that had assured its relative independence, particularly freedom of expression, during the Occupation. But in spite of its objective destructuration, which was amplified by the confusion born of the debacle, in spite of the manhandling of its channels of diffusion, a form of autonomy survived in the way that this now-shattered space functioned.

Whether exiles or stars of the collaborationist Parisian in crowd, underground or counselors to the prince, politicized or aestheticizing, silent or verbose, writers indeed continued to discuss, debate, and judge each other, above and beyond the geographical, political, and legal frontiers. Gossip and rumors were a powerful vector of group cohesion and self-regulation at a time when standard reference points were in upheaval. While the rumor-mill flourished, payback was in fashion: Pierre Drieu La Rochelle and Aragon traded accusations; Robert Brasillach and Lucien Rebatet tore into François Mauriac for having joined the anti-Fascist camp. When it did not consume them, the crisis exacerbated preexisting divisions that owed more to the history of the literary field than to the historical conjuncture: Henri Massis thus pursued a fight begun twenty years earlier with André Gide and *La Nouvelle Revue française*. Ideological divergences do not sufficiently explain the principles of division that underpin the struggles surrounding the redefinition of the stakes: although appearing in the specific form they adopted during the dark years, they still contain the constants of generational rifts and opposition between forces of autonomy and heteronomy. These principles, which acted in tandem without necessarily overlapping, were at work in both public polemics and institutional struggles.

While generally speaking, we can differentiate "dominant" from "dominated" writers according to their degree of notoriety (an opposition that often coincides with the rift between "old" and "young"), we can also differentiate between them according to the type of notoriety they enjoyed: on one hand, notoriety of a temporal order (institutional consecration, sales figures, high print runs); on the other, notoriety in the symbolic order (peer recognition). How did these factors of differentiation influence their political choices and the behaviors they adopted during the Occupation? Based on these factors, and according to the forms of dependence that they imply with respect to external demand (of the acting powers, the market, the press, or political parties), I will identify four types of social logics that coexisted in the literary field, and that induced different relationships to literature and politics.

At the temporally dominant pole, near the fractions that wielded economic and political power, the trend was toward a worldly respectability that allied "good taste" with a sense of one's responsibilities, and coincided with what we might call the state logic. Here, politics were considered "vulgar" and took the form of a morality to which art should remain subordinate. At the pole of large-scale production, close to journalism, the media logic prevailed. Privileging the current, the event, the sensational, it tended to impose itself via public scandal in order to stay connected to "public opinion." The aesthetic logic prevailed at the pole of limited production, especially among authors who enjoyed a strong symbolic notoriety. In keeping with the precepts of art for art's sake, this logic gives priority to style and form, and tends to distance itself from politics as well as from morality. Finally, at the temporally dominated avant-garde pole, literature's subversive dimension was brought to the fore. This often led the avant-gardes to align themselves with the political forces of opposition.

These different logics, which obviously never exist in a pure state, are more or less embodied in practices and institutions. The four institutions that I will examine here—the French Academy, the Goncourt Academy, the *Nouvelle Revue française*, and the Comité national des écrivains—illustrate them in their most typical manifestations. The forms of dependency that they imply with respect to different social spheres allow us to understand the internal mechanisms that favored the process of autonomy loss during the Occupation. I will pay particular attention to the ways in which the factors of heteronomy conveyed by the literary field's own authorities participated in this process, and to what extent they resisted.

▰▶ The method that I have favored here is that of a structural history, one that shows not only the coexistence of different logics but also of different temporalities—meaning forms of inertia and rhythms of evolution in the long and short run—in a given state of the literary field: the rapidity of the defeat and the events that followed contrasted with the inertia of representations and the (variable) slowness of readjustments; literary activity was generally slowed by the material difficulties and other dysfunction brought about by the Occupation; finally, the relationship to time varied according to institutional logics (specific inertia), just as it varied among groups and individuals.

In the first part, I examine the literary logics behind writers' engagement. Although it is tempting to interpret attitudes and political choices as direct "reactions" to the event—even more so when the event (defeat, foreign occupation) invades the private sphere and has effects on the most routine daily actions—we must seek out the social mediations that helped orient them. I am less interested in the decisional processes than in the set of factors that overdetermined them at the group level, and especially those factors linked with the mediation of the literary field.

A situation of national crisis such as the Occupation, in which politics carry more weight than usual and all the more so for professional writers, constitutes an ideal-typical case for studying the relationship between writers and politics due to the heightened constraints exerted on their choices. However, while the modalities of writers' engagement are more legible, the interweaving of literary and political logics becomes simultaneously more "transparent" and more difficult to untangle. More transparent, because in times of crisis, tacitly regulated competition becomes a struggle for the symbolic, if not physical, destruction of the adversary, to borrow the terms of Max Weber.[6] This is what Georges Duhamel, from an "indigenous" point of view, said about the crisis of the 1940s:

> I hardly dare confess that literary rivalries have always seemed to me to lack
> great venom, because they have the benefit of a natural emunctory: they are

settled in public with the aid of strokes of the pen and floods of ink. It has needed the disorders of the present times, when politics can be discerned everywhere under the guise of literature, for me to find enemies in the very place where I was determined to see only competitors or interlocutors.[7]

More difficult to untangle, also, for two major reasons: first, the shuffling of reference points, due to social upheaval; second, over-politicization, which attributed political significance to conducts beyond what was intended by the agents (this is why, even today, the attitudes of writers under the Occupation are generally understood from a strictly political point of view).

The crisis of representations engendered by the defeat and the redefinition of the space of possibles offered to writers in the new conditions of cultural production will first be presented from a synchronic perspective. Starting with the constraints that were specific to the situation, I will move on to the factors that were specific to the literary field, grasped through a quantitative study concerning the trajectories of 185 writers who were active in 1940.[8] The factorial analysis that I conducted as the basis of this study illuminates the literary field's structuring principles during the Occupation. These principles, which I will later return to in more detail, shed light on the writers' attitudes during the "dark years," as well as the forms of their political engagement.

But these forms of politicization and the relations that they maintain with the categories of literary understanding cannot be grasped without an (at least partial) historicization of the representations that were associated with them, especially those that touch on the "responsibility" of the writer. Centered on the key moments in their crystallization, the diachronic perspective shows the persistence of the representations and the systems of opposition that preceded the crisis. From Agathon's (pseudonym of Henri Massis and Alfred de Tarde) polemics against the New Sorbonne to the attacks on André Gide and *La NRF* after the Great War, along with mobilization for the "defense of the West," it was the representations forged twenty, even forty years earlier that reemerged at this time of national crisis, tirelessly renewed by the same actors (Henri Massis played the starring role) or their successors, while adapting them to the contemporary atmosphere. They were mobilized during the "bad masters quarrel," a key moment in the redefinition of the stakes and the redistribution of positions under the Occupation. The relationship to politics is considered here from the vantage point of discursive practices, which tend to differentiate themselves according to the four logics mentioned earlier: "good taste," "scandal," "art for art's sake," and "subversion."

The literary logics of engagement will be considered, thirdly, through the comparison of two singular trajectories, those of two Catholic novelists belonging to the French Academy, Henry Bordeaux and François Mauriac. While the former was a champion of the new regime, the latter was the only "immortal," as the members of the French Academy are called, to enter the literary Resistance. Centered on the relationship between dispositions, positions, and position-takings, in this case my analysis will privilege the opposition between the types of notoriety, temporal and symbolic, and its implications for the political evolution of these two writers.

The process of redefining the stakes was also driven by institutional struggles. After highlighting the systems of opposition that generally ground the divisions of the literary world under the Occupation, I will examine in the second part how they are embodied in four institutions: the French Academy, the Goncourt Academy, *La NRF*, and the Comité national des écrivains, and how they operate distinctively in each one. Neglected by literary history, the "institutions of literary life," as Alain Viala has designated them, constitute "the best linkage between the structures of the field and those of the social sphere in which the field is located [. . .]. Their role is crucial, for they serve as spaces for potential dialogue and conflicts between the literary space and political, financial, and religious powers."[9] In this respect, they are a good indicator of the forms of autonomy and heteronomy that coexist in that space. As authorities of the literary field that regulate literary life, they help ensure its relative autonomy. They are one of the means by which the peer group exerts control over its members. However, in their conditions of existence and in their very mode of functioning, they bear principles of heteronomy, whether it is a question of dependency on the state, on those who hold temporal power, on the political field and the parties, on the laws of the market, or even on the media. These principles of heteronomy are fully revealed under an authoritarian regime, when the question of institutional survival enters more or less into contradiction with that of maintaining literary autonomy.

In a period of destructuring and representational crisis, these authorities constituted tangible reference points that guided writers' orientation. While a number of forums disappeared, while certain literary juries, such as the Femina or the Interallié interrupted their activity, both academies and *La NRF* illustrate the literary field's modes of survival at an institutional level. Ensuring continuity between the previous state of the field and its current state, they allow us to distinguish effects proper to the crisis from changes that were the result of a morphological evolution or previous conflicts. But above all, in a period of ideological war and national identity crisis, these institutions became a stake in the struggle between the acting forces. And this is all the more true since they all claimed to play a national role that justified their survival. Instruments of literary power in their role as legitimizing authorities, they were also ordinarily powerful instruments of mobilization—to gather petition signatures, group memberships, and so forth—and potential instruments of propaganda, which the different political camps would try to exploit thanks to the crisis. One of the effects of the crisis was precisely the appearance of a new organization, the Comité national des écrivains, which was the principal organization of the literary Resistance.

Taken at once as full-fledged *agents*—endowed with a corporate name and an identity—and as codified groups of positions, these four authorities illustrate the state, media, aesthetic, and political logics that were at work in the literary field. In each one of them, intergenerational struggles, the opposition between forces of autonomy and forces of heteronomy, and ideological stakes had specific repercussions. These characteristics will be examined through a brief reminder of the conditions of their founding, a study of their morphology,[10] and an analysis of their position, as well as of the conflicts that affected them from the 1930s to the Liberation. For clarity's sake, and also to highlight their proper institutional logics, which allow us to better understand their modes of functioning under the Occupation, I have dealt with them separately, while still accounting for the relations between them (the competition between the French Academy and *La NRF*, for example) and with other authorities (thus I will mention the Renaudot Prize in reference to the Goncourt Academy, when appropriate). The schism within *La NRF* team following its takeover by Drieu La Rochelle, who turned it into a "showcase" of the Collaboration, has led me to study the struggles to reappropriate its heritage that punctuated the recomposition of the literary field. They provoked a veritable war of reviews that transcended the demarcation line, and a fratricidal combat between Drieu and Aragon, the great orchestrator of "contraband literature" in the small reviews of the Southern zone. Illustrated by the relationships between its founders (Aragon, Jean Paulhan, Jacques Decour), the alliance between the Communists and non-Communists would make it possible, thanks to literary and militant solidarities, to set up the Comité national des écrivains and constitute a real underground literary community that was able to impose norms of conduct on writers starting in 1943.

The effects of the crisis were not limited to the Occupation period. They largely determined the modes of restructuring the literary field at the Liberation, which is the subject of the last part. Social upheaval favored the crystallization of a new generation that established itself starting in September 1944, particularly through the CNE and the confrontations surrounding the purge. The notion of the "responsibility of the writer" was at the heart of these struggles. Having emerged from the shadows, the CNE claimed to inaugurate a new deontology for the writer's profession. But its power of excommunication was quickly contested. Rocked by internal divisions, the enterprises born of the Resistance also found themselves confronted with the traditional authorities, which intended to regain their place and take part in the national reconstruction. These institutional conflicts, through which the process of "normalization" began, will be sketched out in the last chapter. They culminated in 1953, date of the second amnesty law, after which the issues that the crisis raised, without disappearing, ceased to dominate literary life.[11]

The choice to found my analysis of writers' attitudes under the Occupation upon the logics proper to the literary world and its institutions, rather than upon preconceived categories of political history, has the merit of reevaluating the relative significance of some actors, to make others emerge, and to establish the share of continuities and ruptures in the collective and individual lives of the members of this atypical social group. A contribution to the social and cultural history of the "dark years," this book also helps to better determine the place of those years as a turning point in contemporary literary history, while shedding a different light on the forms of imbrication between literature and politics in what has been called a "literary nation."[12]

PART I

The Literary Logics
of Political Engagement

CHAPTER 1

Choices under Constraints

For those of our townsfolk who risked their lives in this predicament the issue was whether or not plague was in their midst and whether or not they must fight against it.
—Albert Camus, *The Plague*

In order to pose the question of writers' political choices under the Occupation, we must first ask ourselves what the stakes were and how they were perceived by the literary community. But these stakes were not immediately clear. Of course, for those who heard it, the appeal of June 18 offered an alternative: defeat was neither foregone nor irreversible; the armistice was a political and military error. But who was this upstart young general who dared to rise up against the hero of Verdun? How much credit should be given to this military man, who had declared himself the head of the "Free France" government without any other formality? In the beginning, Vercors tells us, "Everyone believed that the government had authorized the general to speak, since he had just served as minister under Reynaud."[1] This illusion was quickly dispelled. Two attitudes now became possible: acceptance or refusal of the German Occupation. But even if it were enough to sum up the range of choices possible at that particular conjuncture, which obviously isn't the case, this alternative remains purely theoretical. How did it translate into practice? The question is even more pressing since writers, just like the rest of the population, had to confront practical and material problems. The faculties of critical thinking that we attribute to writers as intellectuals—that is to say professional thinkers—should not mask the fact that these faculties are exercised from a given and necessarily limited point of view. Nor should we forget that, even if these faculties are not forged by and for practice, they are no less inscribed in the practical conditions of life, at both group and individual levels. Thus the principles that informed the modes of perception of the issues at stake, as well as the attitudes and the conducts adopted, need to be related to the specific conditions under which these issues appear in the literary field.

The Redefinition of the Stakes and the Space of Possibles

The apparatuses that both the Nazi occupant and the Vichy government put in place to control cultural production generated an obvious loss of autonomy and a real destructuring of the literary field. Repression, proscriptions, censorship, control of the means of production (notably through the distribution of paper), propaganda: French literature had never known such constraints, even under the Second Empire. Moreover, the division of the territory into two zones and the exodus of a number of writers who sought refuge either in the unoccupied zone or abroad led to the loss of the very geographic centralization that had been one of the conditions of the autonomization of the French intellectual field and its ability to compete with power during the Dreyfus affair.[2] The crisis of representations caused by the upheaval of reference points further weakened the literary field's mechanisms of resistance to heteronomy. Finally, loss of autonomy translated into the subordination of the literary stakes to the political stakes: whether or not to publish in these conditions became a political issue. The most apolitical attitudes thus took on political significance.

The over-politicization of the literary stakes is directly linked to the transformation of the conditions of production. But it also arises from the eagerness of an entire fraction of agents (institutions and individuals) to serve the new powers. Thus, loss of autonomy also occurred according to the literary field's own logic. If the promotion of internal agents like Drieu La Rochelle to enact collaborationist politics in the cultural domain initially emphasized the blurring of reference points, it ultimately contributed to the solidarity of Resistance writers in their struggle to reclaim autonomy.

THE UPHEAVAL OF REFERENCE POINTS
AND THE REIGN OF RUMOR

After the debacle, confusion was great. The defeat, the occupation of more than half the country by a foreign power, the scuttling of the Republic, the construction of an authoritarian regime, a whole month-long chain of events that occurred at breakneck speed—while scattered families were still trying to reunite and scarcity led to an obsession with material matters—generated a deep confusion and feeling of disorientation, of "floating," while awaiting clarification of the issues.[3] "I float like a cork," Roger Martin du Gard wrote to Maria van Rysselberghe on July 22, 1940, "[...] and for the moment it is on the most stinking, the most fermented sludge that I float ... Vichy is something that exceeds all the images one can make of it."[4]

Before the war, the shuffling of political reference points had increased confusion, due to the back-and-forth maneuvers that led a large fraction of the nationalists to adopt neo-pacifist positions—against sanctions for Mussolini's Italy as a result of the invasion of Ethiopia, for the Treaty of Munich, against France's entry into the war—whereas the anti-Fascists rallied the hawks. It was also the result of a schism on the left, between full-fledged pacifists and anti-Fascists, a schism that began to appear during the Spanish Civil War. The Blum government's politics of nonintervention—supported by the moderate or pacifist fractions against the Communists and proponents of the anti-Fascist cause—created divisions that were solidified by the Treaty of Munich and the invasion of Czechoslovakia. Finally, it was the result of the pact between Germany and the Soviet Union, which sounded the death knell of the union of the left realized under the Popular Front and excluded the Communists from the political playing field. The rise of the Vichy regime increased confusion. As Robert Paxton says, "It was not clear in the south whether anti-Germanism meant opposing Vichy or rejoicing in its simulacrum of independence and its nationalist rhetoric."[5]

This confusion translated into hesitations, doubts, and about-faces. On July 14, the day the Germans entered Paris, André Gide found Marshal Pétain's speech—claiming that "the spirit of enjoyment" had won out over the "spirit of sacrifice"—"admirable." He changed his mind two days after the armistice when he heard the marshal's new speech, suspecting "some infamous deceit": "How can one speak of France as 'intact' after handing over to the enemy more than half of the country? How to make these words fit those noble words he pronounced three days ago? How can one fail to approve Churchill? Not subscribe most heartily to General de Gaulle's declaration?"[6] Roger Martin du Gard, a sworn pacifist and in favor of Munich, apologized in December 1940 for having "renounced" his "deep convictions" in 1939 and "thought that there was no other solution than war, and that, *this time*, this war was 'just'"[7]—which would, by the way, have no effect on the attitude of withdrawal that he adopted. In the unoccupied zone, Paul Léautaud, whose initial anti-German reflex would not long resist the occupant's politics of seduction, was astonished from the month of September on by the sudden reversal of institutional writers' positions:

It is a nice contrast, and rather unexpected: the reactionary writers, the conformist, official academicians, celebrating homeland, patriotism, honor, great sentiments, writers such as Abel Hermant, Pierre Benoit, Abel Bonnard [...] have collaborated from day one with the papers published in Paris, with the authorization and under the surveillance of the Germans. Writers who are somewhat marginal, "resistant" as they are called, like Descaves (a little) and myself, if I dare to name myself, are saying: "Not on my life."[8]

For writers, the new powers' "call for bids" opened, despite an apparatus of constraints, a new space of possibles that did not offer itself up to immediate decoding. In the autumn of 1940, solicitations were the order of the day. Meant to ensure the literary legitimacy of these new ventures, they at first fed the illusion of a large and diversified supply, at least for those who weren't immediately excluded because of their origins or opinions. This illusion masked the restriction of possibles within the framework of the new conditions of production. Appointed by the ambassador Otto Abetz to revive *La Nouvelle Revue française* under his direction, Pierre Drieu La Rochelle urged writers to associate themselves with his project. During his September stay in Vichy, he summoned the former director of the journal, Jean Paulhan, and then the literary columnist of *Le Figaro*, André Rousseaux, a Catholic who had been an editor at *Action française* in the 1920s. Like Jean Paulhan, André Rousseaux declined. He would still be approached by Jean de la Hire and Jacques Chardonne, who wished to see *Le Figaro* return to Paris.[9] Roger Vailland, a journalist at *Paris-Soir* who had withdrawn to the Southern zone along with his newspaper, met with his former professor, Marcel Déat, in Vichy. Déat was editing the revived *Œuvre* in Paris and asked Vailland to join him there. After long hesitations, Vailland declined the offer.[10]

Senior writers were solicited first and most frequently in an effort to legitimate these enterprises. Their hesitations contributed to the loss of reference points during the first months of the Occupation, since younger authors usually situated themselves in relation to their elders, either in alignment or at a distance. But for the younger generation, these hesitations also inspired hope, at a time of social upheaval, that positions would become available, a hope that the extolling of the youth by the Vichy regime could only nourish. For the youngest ones, the cost of abstaining, of retreating from public life, a stance the writers of "refusal" would soon assume, could moreover appear greater, as this quote by Henri Membré, reported by Vercors, illustrates: "In fact, it's easy for a Gide, a Duhamel, to publish nothing under German domination; their work is done, it is famous, they will have no trouble finding their audience after the Liberation, whereas I, with just one well-received novel and another that came out too late? In five years, in ten years, I will be forgotten; I'll have to start over from scratch."[11] For older writers, meanwhile, the threat of a takeover by the younger generation inspired a feeling of being cast aside, which likely played a part in André Gide or Paul Valéry's initial decision to lend their prestige to Drieu La Rochelle's project—although they would quickly change their mind. Roger Martin du Gard expressed this feeling in his typical form, that of "incomprehension"; harassed by pressing questions—"Why are you silent? People like you who have gained some credit for their work have a duty to light the way!"—and exiled in Nice, he felt he had even less "right to say a word" because he seemed "to have lost contact with the up-and-coming generation": "Do we even have a common vocabulary anymore? When I happen to hear young people hold forth, discuss, I am often struck by the feeling that I no longer speak the same language. That we no longer use the same words to mean the same things."[12]

The politicization of literary issues, the political meaning now attached to publication in *La NRF*, for example, wasn't immediately perceptible, especially for those residing on the other side of the demarcation line. Doubled by geographical dispersion, the *hysteresis* effect meant that the space of possibles was still viewed as it was before the war, as writers' hesitations again show us. Should we publish in Drieu La Rochelle's *NRF*, the writers asked themselves? Jean Schlumberger, Michel Leiris, and Raymond Queneau flatly refused, but André Gide offered up his "leaflets," which appeared in the first and third installments (December 1940 and February 1941), although he continued to waffle until several letters, including those of Francis Crémieux (the Jewish literary critic Benjamin Crémieux's son), who accused him of treason, and Jean Wahl, who blamed him, called him back to order.[13] Solicited by Drieu La Rochelle to resume his theater article in *La NRF*, Paul Léautaud immediately thought to suggest that his *Journal littéraire* appear there, since the *Mercure de France*'s disappearance suspended its publication. Jacques Bernard, the director of the *Mercure*, opposed this plan for reasons of competition. Still, Léautaud expressed his worries about the journal's publication conditions to Drieu, who assured him that he ran it in complete freedom. He rebelled upon discovering that the journal was subject to German censorship, then allowed himself to be reassured upon learning that Gallimard was paying the collaborators and that he had refused the entry of German capital into the house.[14] Must we publish in *La NRF*? Jean Grenier asked Armand Petitjean, André Fraigneau, and François Mauriac. "Why not write for *La NRF*?" Armand Petitjean replied in April 1941. This former journal contributor, who had been mutilated in the Phoney War, continued: "Drieu is weak, but sincere. As for myself, I'm going to publish an article in it in May, and I don't have any lessons to learn from the French after what I saw of them in June 1940."[15] "It's a duty to write in *La NRF* to show that the French civilization continues,"[16] retorted the novelist André Fraigneau. François Mauriac, who was "very happy with its reappearance and [who had] congratulated Drieu, before having read it" but saw in the first issue "the opposite of what [he] expected: a pure space, a summit reserved for poetry, for pure literature, for ideas..." still retained "a small weakness for this review";[17] he could still answer Jean Grenier in November 1941, when he was on the verge of committing himself to the first underground writers' committee: "But yes, of course, it is necessary to contribute to *La NRF*. Unnecessary to tell you that I'm not at all with Drieu, but I am not outraged by his attitude. Such is the position of France, today, that nobody has the right to cast stones at anybody. For who could be sure of taking the best side?"[18]

Slowly, a kind of "cooperation" fell into place among the scattered writers. Correspondence, soon limited by the creation of interzonal cards, was replaced by generalized word of mouth spread by newsmongers, especially those who legally or clandestinely crossed the demarcation line. "We had just been admitted into the vast information system that was developing day by day and made word of mouth a much more powerful news vector than Radio-Paris," Jean Lescure recalled.[19] Jean Paulhan was one of these newsmongers. Thanks to the position of "power behind the (literary) throne" that he had acquired during the interwar period, thanks to the breadth of contacts that he was probably alone in maintaining among the scattered authors, he was the "hub" that more or less preserved the unity of this fragmented field. From summer to winter 1940, whether through an abundant correspondence or chance encounters, he spread the writers' news and informed them, from day to day, of the conditions in which *La NRF* would reappear. He was also an indispensable mediator, "taking the pulse" of the authors vis-à-vis the renewed publication of *La NRF*, with which he was no longer involved. Even better, as we will see, he directed the authors, gave them advice and tips, and played the role of an oracle, since the verdicts he handed down—depending on whether or not they were heeded—predicted the authors' future in literary "eternity." He would be one of the pillars of the recomposition of the pole of limited production in the struggle to regain literary autonomy.

In a time of censorship and information control, word of mouth replaced official information channels which, reduced to propaganda, found themselves discredited. Marc Bloch, who noted this phenomenon for the Great War, quoted a comedian: "The prevailing opinion in the trenches was that anything could be true except for what was allowed to be printed."[20] Things were no different during the four years of the Occupation. As Paul Léautaud observed in his *Journal*: "We are surrounded by lies, exaggerations, biased arguments on both sides. The coryphaei of the newspapers stamping them with their tremolos and their command tirades. How do you find the truth in all that, how do you know which side it's on? Anyone who gets worked up for either side is a naïve fool."[21]

But the network of informal information was also an amazing network spreading idle gossip, false news, and rumors. The war, German oppression, social upheaval, terror, denunciations, the muzzled press, outrageous propaganda, the police-state character of the Vichy regime associated with its instability, with its changing leaders, could only give free reign to rumors at every level of society, the outlet of all social fears. "[French opinion] obeys anonymous commands and propagates wild rumors that spread from one end of the country to the other like wildfire. We hadn't seen that since the Great Fear of 1789," Alfred Fabre-Luce described.[22] The rumor of the "synarchic plot" is one of the most famous examples of this phenomenon.[23]

In the literary world, dispersion and the loss of reference points consolidated the reign of malicious gossip and backbiting which, practiced in a playful or polemic mode, are normally the essential vectors regulating internal power relations. As Norbert Elias has shown,[24] gossip is a practice that aims to reinforce or perpetuate group cohesion. It exerts a vital function since only the word, whether of praise or criticism, has the power of making something *exist*, and since the worst punishment a writer can receive is the silence of his colleagues. Nothing demonstrates this fact more clearly than this anecdote related by Raymond Queneau in his journal written in 1939:

> Gide's *Journal* was just published. In Paulhan's office, everyone bustles about and looks for his name. Benda arrives. Paulhan says: "We'll see what Gide has to say about you." Benda agrees. We look: Gide only has good things to say. But Paulhan says: "Look, Benda, p. 250 (f. ex) ... p. 1250 ... he went 15 years without talking about you!"[25]

Under the Occupation, gossip was at once a vector of cohesion that contributed to the restructuring of the literary field, a weapon used to exhume old grudges, and a channel for redistributing alliances. At a time of shifting allegiances, rumors and false news proliferated in fertile ground. "Unpleasant rumors were circulating about him [Daumal]. It's difficult today to imagine how those times of whispers, of monitored words were times of rumor, insinuation, false information, endless repetitions, hidden meanings, and often self-interested lies.

The various tragedies that we experienced hadn't discouraged the 'pals' from their gossip-mongering," Jean Lescure recalled.[26] "False news," Marc Bloch has said, "is the mirror in which the 'collective consciousness' observes its own features."[27] Rumors "justified," a posteriori, all of the old disagreements that then took on an aura of premonition—the "ah! I knew that we couldn't count on him," "ah! I told you so," and so forth—and had the double virtue, in those troubled times, of reassuring everyone in their position while retroactively giving them a clear conscience. André Breton thus made use of the rumors stating that Louis Aragon—with whom he had broken ties in 1932 after denouncing "Front rouge" as a circumstantial poem—had become a champion of the new regime. "Sincerely, I don't see myself cozying up to Déroulède's disciple, the new Lavedan, the libertine who sleeps with Joan of Arc," he answered Pascal Pia, after Pia asked him to contribute to the review, *Prométhée*, that he was planning to launch in the Southern zone with Aragon's participation.[28]

The conjuncture of civil war and institutional distrust gave these types of rumor an immediate effectiveness. Rumors had to be taken seriously by the Resistance, given the necessary precautions it had to take while recruiting (semi-) clandestinely. "Tzara—Ribbemont-Dessaignes. Yes, if necessary. La Tour du Pin, better not. His liberation occurred under mysterious conditions,"[29] the Swiss mediator François Lachenal wrote to Jean Lescure, editor of the semi-legal review *Messages*, in the summer of 1943. One year later, Paul Eluard expressed his reservations about Arthur Adamov's possible contribution to *Messages*, since he was supposedly an agent of the Romanian Fascist organization OFRA. Meanwhile, Jean Lescure was quietly reproached for including Raymond Queneau in the journal, since the ambiguities of his novel *Un rude hiver*, published by Gallimard in 1939, made him appear suspicious.[30]

While spontaneous cooperation, calls to order, and readjustments ultimately ensured some last measure of autonomy for the literary field, the transformation of the conditions of production and the over-politicization of literary issues that followed contributed to the shuffling of reference points. Moreover, literary life was widely disrupted following the debacle and the division of the country into two zones. Literary prizes weren't distributed in 1940. Returning to literary activity meant fulfilling administrative requirements for the occupying authorities, such as the request for a pass, in keeping with the exception allowed by paragraph 8 of title V of the August 28, 1940, ordinance allowing selection committees to meet, and a dispensation of the ban forbidding publications from circulating between the two zones, so that the members who had withdrawn to the Southern zone could receive the new publications. The attribution of the Femina and Interallié Prizes would be suspended for the duration of the Occupation. The Goncourt Academy and the Renaudot jury would resume their activities in 1941. But the modalities of this return to activity did not meet with the Goncourt committee members' unanimous approval. Why shouldn't they award the Goncourt Prize in Lyon rather than Paris?

Decentralization quickly became a site of struggle: it opposed, at either end of the new dominant ideology, those who "wanted to keep Paris going" and those who favored a decentralization that was better adapted to the circumstances, preferring to situate themselves under French authority alone. The problem was even more urgent when it applied to the two very Parisian sites of consecration, the French Academy and the Goncourt Academy. In the official press, the fate of the two academies and the dispersal of their members were a continual source of preoccupation. The "immortals" who, unlike the Goncourt committee members, could not vote by correspondence or delegation, were regularly called upon to return (only a dozen Academy members attended the weekly dictionary meetings during the entire duration of the Occupation) and asked to conduct elections to replace the members who died during this period.

Publishing houses, traditionally concentrated in Paris, returned to activity under the conditions imposed by the occupier. Should publication continue "under the boot" in order to maintain "the French spirit" as some insisted, or should it cease given the risk of playing into the hands of the occupier, who was trying to normalize cultural life under its heel? Was it legitimate to contribute to the Parisian press, or the Vichy press? The answers to these questions were not unequivocal. They were not posed in the same manner for those in different positions in the literary field. Nor were they determined by solely political considerations. It was also a matter of literary survival, and sometimes material survival, when it wasn't a question of seeking profit in both areas.

While some hesitated about the proper behavior to adopt, others immediately adhered to the "National Revolution" and/or the Collaboration, an adhesion that was also often the chance to enact a coup de force in the literary field. Yet between abstention and ideological adhesion, there was a wide array of attitudes and self-justification strategies, from those who minimized, not without bad faith, the political effects of their choice to continue publishing in a subjugated press, to those who, without openly declaring their support of the conqueror, nonetheless didn't have a hard time resigning themselves to the yoke of an occupant who appeared less awful than expected. Vercors relayed a conversation with André Thérive, a critic at *Le Temps* before the war: "'After all,' he says to me, 'it's my job. A waiter will serve a beer to a German, so why couldn't a journalist publish an article?'"[31] For his part, Jean Guéhenno observed in his *Journal des années noires*:

The republic of letters is decidedly none too rich in character. X . . . is pre-paring his conversion. Naturally, he avoids sweeping declarations, as is his habit, but if you ask him about Germany, he explains that it has made huge progress over the past twenty years and has become more . . . democratic. As for America? It has also changed a lot. It's no longer the colonial and still young America of 1909, but a cowardly country from which we can no longer expect anything . . . He leaves you the task of drawing, from his statements, the resigned conclusions that they bear. He is himself resigned to once again, and as quickly as possible, having his plays performed in Paris.[32]

Let's not forget that the restriction of the possibles wasn't one-way, even if it was much more severe for writers who refused to compromise with the acting forces. Thus, while it may seem atypical, the attitude of someone like Paul Léau-taud was no less significant; he refused to give a fragment of his journal to *Le Figaro*, which passed for a refuge of the opposition in the unoccupied zone, because he was afraid of upsetting the occupier! A few days later, having learned that Léon-Paul Fargue and Paul Valéry had been denied the *visa de censure** (the decision would later be reversed), and fearing for his own volume of theater ar-ticles that was due to be published by Gallimard, he congratulated himself on his decision: "Here's something that really proves I was right to give up contributing to *Le Figaro*."[33]

The new powers, whether German or Vichyist, turned to projects to har-ness French cultural heritage that would not have been as successful had they not matched interests on both sides: from the logic of survival, to the turn to-ward political authorities to overthrow the power relations that constituted the prewar literary field, the redefinition of possibles and the conduct that was adopted cannot be understood from a solely ideological viewpoint. In the heart of the literary world were found the factors of "accommodation" of the Occupation situation that Philippe Burrin has identified. He differentiates be-tween three categories according to their form and degree: a form that is "a structural one imposed by the need to have public services that continue to function and an economy that does not collapse," a more willful form that "was chiefly motivated by a desire to defend or promote interests of either a personal or a corporative nature, in a situation of uncertain outcome," and fi-nally simple "political accommodation," the search for an agreement with Nazi Germany.[34]

---

* Official permission to publish.—Trans.

THE NAZI APPARATUS OF CONSTRAINT AND
THE SITES OF LITERARY COLLABORATION

The double apparatus of constraint and the workforce that it required, joined with the new powers' eagerness to ensure the continuation of cultural activities in order to "normalize" life under the Occupation, actually match up with the corporative or individual, economic, professional, or ideological interests of cultural agents and producers (publishers, press bosses, authors), generating a chain of participation in the structures of Collaboration. The economy's subordination to the political sphere contributed greatly to the political significance that the stakes related to the pursuit of cultural activities assumed, even though this political meaning was not necessarily intended. Meanwhile, the crisis situation and the demand for legitimation emanating from the German and Vichyist powers created a true "call for bids" among those producers of collective representations otherwise known as intellectuals. This double movement had a direct impact on the power relations that structured the literary field, favoring their reversal to the benefit of those who yielded to the most heteronomous logics.

Judging by the occupier's efforts to monitor French cultural production, this was a sizeable economic and ideological stake. Gérard Loiseaux arrived at the same conclusion while taking stock of the 1,073 people employed by the Propaganda-Abteilung alone: "The Propaganda's means in terms of personnel translate the importance that Nazi Germany attributed to psychological action in France."[35] Three different services shared this task.

The Propaganda-Abteilung, placed under the control of the occupied zone's military administration, the Militärbefehlshaber in Frankreich (MBF), but taking orders from Joseph Goebbels, was tasked with the suppression of anti-German protests and the creation of pro-German propaganda; it also monitored public opinion and managed an intelligence service, in conjunction with German espionage services. It saw to the strict application of policy from the Ministry of Propaganda of the Third Reich, whose object was to weaken France's "cultural imperialism." Until December 1940, the Gruppe Schrifttum (literature) of the Paris Propaganda-Staffel was directed by the Sonderführer Friedhelm Kaiser; after, by the Sonderführer Gerhard Heller.

The German Institute, affiliated with the Reich embassy for the German military administration in France, was directed by Doctor Karl Epting, the former director of the office of German university exchanges in Paris. The Institute worked toward the development of a cultural collaboration between Germany and France. In the cultural field, it enacted the policy that earned Otto Abetz, an expert on French affairs for the minister of Foreign Affairs Joachim von

Ribbentrop, his ambassadorship. This policy sought to maintain the illusion of a possible Franco-German collaboration for the purpose of building a "New Europe" even as it worked surreptitiously to divide the French and destroy France's influence abroad: "In exactly the same way that the idea of a peace was usurped by national socialist Germany and served to weaken French morale without damaging the combative spirit of Germany itself, similarly the European idea could be usurped by the Reich without prejudicing the claim to primacy in Europe, a primacy that national socialism has anchored in the German people."[36] Aside from its support of certain French authors, the Institute established lists of translations of German books into French: Epting's adjunct, Karl Heinz Bremer, had forty German works translated between January 1940 and January 1941, and in February 1941, Epting created a "Franco-German translation committee" that, in conjunction with French editors and authors, drew up a list of more than 1,000 German titles to be published in France.

Finally, the Amt Schrifttum, a subsidiary of Alfred Rosenberg's office (Alfred Rosenberg was Hitler's delegate for the intellectual and ideological education of the Nazi Party members), which starting in 1941 designated the "Office of the Reich for the promotion of German literature," was an example of "expertise" intervening after publication. Its vocation was to "decontaminate" and "sanitize" literature, and maintained branches in occupied countries for this purpose.[37]

Despite their close collaboration, these three departments would be rivals throughout the Occupation, fighting over jurisdiction and disagreeing on the means to employ. Drawing on the strength of his seduction strategy, which consisted in making the French work for German interests, Otto Abetz tried to extend his sphere of influence into the cultural sphere, and, moreover, into the political sphere. He did not manage to reduce the Propaganda to a censorship department, or obtain the closure of the Rosenberg unit in Paris; the latter, following a close competition with the embassy, would monopolize the pillage of artwork; still, he won a half victory against the former when, in July 1942, the Propaganda Ministry and the Ministry of Foreign Affairs reached an accord regulating the division of labor, limiting the Propaganda's spheres of influence in favor of the Institute. Yet the conflicts continued. In the aftermath of the accord, Gerhard Heller would be assigned to the embassy. In its summary of November 1943, the Reich's Security Service would judge the various strategies of both the embassy and the Propaganda equally deficient—a deficiency that we might describe as relative.[38]

The apparatus of repression took hold in the summer of 1940. The Denoël and Sorlot publishing houses were shut down, the Hachette distribution services requisitioned. The system created to apply political and racial censorship was rapidly put in place. The first list of forbidden books, called the "Bernhard list" and including 143 titles, led to the confiscation of more than 700,000 books between the twenty-seventh and thirty-first of August.[39] On October 4, the "Otto list," created by the Propaganda in conjunction with the embassy and including 1,060 works pulled from the shelves, appeared along with a censorship agreement signed by the publishers' union. This agreement presented the principle of self-censorship as a condition of resuming activity in the publishing houses of the occupied zone. In 1942, new measures would reinforce censorship and the monitoring of production: paper rationing began in January, while an authorization number was required for all publications in the occupied zone beginning in March. The Otto list would undergo two new editions in January 1942 and May 1943, whose supplements would notably include a list of 739 "Jews writing in French" in the latter edition, thus systematizing the application of racial policy in the cultural domain.

The reopening of publishing houses, occurring under the constraints of self-censorship that the publishers chose to accept, also involved negotiations of an economic and ideological order. Despite Vichy's vigilant defense of French economic interests, Abetz worked toward the influence of German capital in publishing and the press. Thanks to the billion-franc credit it received from the embassy, the Hibbelen trust would control nearly fifty periodicals by 1944, that is to say 45 to 50 percent of the Parisian press.[40] The book community was generally more anxious to defend its interests, while still making necessary, and sometimes overzealous, concessions in order to secure advantageous conditions. In addition to the Aryanizations, particularly those of Calmann-Lévy, Ferenczi, and Nathan, which culminated in either a German participation or the nomination of a subservient administrator, the Germans bought up shares of the Denoël and Sorlot publishing houses. The Denoël house, suffering from financial difficulties, would extract a great benefit from this collaboration: at the beginning of 1942, it would increase its capital from 365,000 to 1,500,000 francs.[41] But Gallimard would not allow the Germans to acquire shares in the company.

The orientation of French cultural production was not solely repressive. Promotional campaigns encouraged collaborationist literature. In 1941, the Propaganda drew up a "List of literature to promote" that included 189 works, some authored by notorious champions of extreme collaboration: Pierre Drieu La Rochelle, Jacques Chardonne, Lucien Rebatet, and Robert Brasillach; but also Pierre Benoit, Marcel Arland, Henry de Montherlant, Paul Morand, Jean Giono, Roger Vercel. It served as a "veritable multimedia publicity operation" targeting print journalism, radio, and bookstores.[42] The following year, the luxurious catalogue "Mirror of Books 1941–1942" would appear, copublished by the Propaganda and fourteen French publishers, including Gallimard, Grasset, and Denoël. The Propaganda authorities increased solicitations of, and favors for, the "promoted" authors: trips to Germany, translations, film adaptations. While the politics of censorship severely limited translation into German, eleven authors, including Alphonse de Chateaubriant and Jean de La Varende, benefited from this new, exceptional form of promotion.

The press was influenced more directly. Having taken possession of the Havas agency offices and created the French Agency of Press Information (AFIP), which became an intermediary for the official information agency of the Reich (which also funded private agencies like Inter-France), the German authorities organized a twice-weekly orientation conference aimed at the managers and editors in chief of the occupied zone. In December 1941, eleven periodicals were selected for priority paper allocation: *La Gerbe, Comoedia, Je suis partout, L'Appel, Le Journal de la Bourse, Le Rouge et le Bleu, Jeunesse, L'Atelier, Au pilori, La Révolution nationale, Le Franciste.*[43] The first three on the list were politico-literary weeklies with a high concentration of writers, or aspiring writers. They were the principal platforms for the literary press in the occupied zone and were representative of the different options and tendencies; while *Comoedia's* literary page claimed non-involvement, *La Gerbe* and *Je suis partout*, each in its own way, set the tone for intellectual collaborationism, as we will see.

Like certain publishing houses, a number of newspapers, whether preexisting or newly created in honor of the conjuncture, immediately began to go with the flow, forecasting the Germans' demand. For their staffs, this was a chance to take the place of the two-thirds of Northern zone periodicals that had ceased publication,[44] such as *L'Aube, L'Intransigeant, L'Ordre*, and *Le Populaire*, or moved to the unoccupied zone, like *Le Figaro, Le Temps, Paris-Soir, L'Action française, La Croix, Gringoire*, and *Candide*. For instance, *La Gerbe*, a politico-literary weekly that claimed to represent "the French will," founded in July 1940 by the writer Alphonse de Chateaubriant, replaced the two great right-wing weeklies of the 1930s, *Gringoire* and *Candide*. Its circulation, which reached 140,000 copies in 1943,[45] made it one of the chief sites of intellectual collaborationism; according to Lucien Rebatet, it represented the "conformist and academic-leaning" pole.[46] This position was reinforced by its proximity to the Collaboration group, founded and chaired by Alphonse de Chateaubriant; its honor committee, born in part of the very official prewar Comité France-Allemagne, united leading figures of the intellectual world, including five members of the Institute, four of whom were members of the French Academy.

Financed by the German embassy, advised by the Gruppe Schrifttum of the Propaganda-Staffel, *La Gerbe* advocated an active collaboration in order to insert an agricultural France into the "European order," and quickly distanced itself from a Vichy regime that it considered not collaborationist enough. Taking as its model the "religious act" of self-effacement vis-à-vis the community that was accomplished by National Socialism, *La Gerbe* sought to work toward the "recovery" of a France that had been abandoned to the "slavery" of the machine, capitalism, and individualism. Anti-Semitism ruled, along with repeated invectives against the Freemasons and the suggestion that they be confined to concentration camps. Contrasting the obsolete era of the "political" with the "organic" era founded on the eternal laws of nature, the paper did not initially identify with any party,[47] but it would draw closer to Marcel Déat's Rassemblement national populaire (RNP). Some of the RNP's members participated in conferences organized by the "Gerbes françaises" and funded by the Office of the Secretary of State for Youth.[48] In 1944 *La Gerbe* would launch a campaign for a single party; the leaders of the RNP and Jacques Doriot's Parti populaire français (PPF) would be interviewed for this purpose. The editorial staff also received representatives of the Légion des volontaires français contre le bolchévisme (LVF), which included Chateaubriant on its board of benefactors,[49] and would see two members join its ranks (including its former manager Marc Augier, future Waffen-SS).

La Gerbe rallied elements that came to support Nazi Germany for a variety of different reasons—PPF, Action française, regionalism—but were joined in visceral anti-Republicanism and anti-Bolshevism. Its sixty-three-year-old director, Alphonse de Chateaubriant, had authored novels that retraced the geste of his ancestors, the fallen landed gentry. These novels had earned him the Goncourt Prize (1911) and the French Academy's Prize for the Novel (1923), as well as the respect of regionalists. He then committed himself to an antimodernist campaign that led him to seek the archaic sources of a mysticism beyond Catholicism; he would find this mysticism reflected in National Socialism.[50] This "Breton-mystic-Hitlerophiled novelist," according to the portrait traced by Lucien Combelle, had published "a book of astonishing fervor, *La Gerbe des forces*, with Hitler as Saint George confronted by the Muscovite dragon; the swastika, a recasting of the Christian cross in Toledo steel" in 1937.[51] Among the paper's regular participants, Bernard Faÿ, professor at the Collège de France and Freemasonry specialist who was promoted to the administration of the Bibliothèque nationale after Julien Caïn's dismissal, served as the designated historian; ethnology professor Georges Montandon filled its pages with his theories of eugenics, calling for the separation of "individuals [who are] ethnoracially foreign" and their exclusion from the right to reproduce.[52] The race theorician Arthur de Gobineau's grandson, Clément Serpeille de Gobineau, brought his personal touch to the paper. The writings of Pierre Drieu La Rochelle and Abel Bonnard, a member of the French Academy, appeared conspicuously on the political "front page"; they would be joined in 1944 by Robert Brasillach, following the latter's departure from *Je suis partout*. Camille Fegy, a former Communist militant who had joined Doriot's PPF, became the journal's editor in chief in 1941. Until 1942, sections such as "peasantry" and "youth" could still be found, along with a social and women's page that offered to return woman to her state of maternal "dignity," and in which countless articles were devoted to the premarital examination.

From a literary point of view, *La Gerbe* distinguished itself from collaborationist periodicals by devoting a considerable amount of space to regionalist production, thanks to its columnist Gonzague Truc, a Maurrassian Catholic critic, and Henry Poulaille, the leader of "proletarian literature." While the former represents, along with Camille Mauclair and François Navarre, the self-righteous criticism that dominated *La Gerbe*, the latter's presence at first seems incongruous. This heterogeneity was the result, notably, of the few volunteers among established writers, which favored an alliance of minorities. The young Lucien Combelle, who began offering his services in 1940, remembers that "the first and second knives[†] were lined up on the kitchen table, in complete equality, simplicity, in the winter of 1940, there was no crowd, aside from the 'diehards,' it was enough to show up. I show up, immediately hired for the literary page, my devil."[53] He would manage to add a more anticonformist touch to the page. Ramon Fernandez, *La NRF* critic won over to the Collaboration, wrote columns on political books. Charles Péguy, Céline, and Montherlant were set up as models of an aesthetic conception deriving from the Middle Ages, while the literary pages regilded by such famous figures as Paul Morand, Marcel Aymé, and Jean Giono published mainly populist or regionalist authors like Jean Rogissart and Pierre Béarn. The theater section, edited by André Castelot and H.-R. Lenormand, initially benefited from the appearance of Jean Anouilh, Charles Dullin, and Jean Cocteau.

Belonging to the Grasset network united some of these writers who, from Chateaubriant to Poulaille by way of André Fraigneau and Cocteau, had very diverse literary and ideological sensibilities (we can hardly consider Poulaille an

---

[†] This is an idiomatic expression corresponding to the idea, in English, of first and second string. A *second couteau* could also be translated as "second fiddle."—Trans.

admirer of National Socialism).[54] The Grasset house was, indeed, overrepresented at *La Gerbe*, whether by past or current authors.[55] Furthermore, in his collection "À la recherche de la France," Bernard Grasset gathered the most engaged essays by collaborationist writers who were not—or were no longer—part of his "stable." These included Abel Bonnard's *Pensées dans l'action*, Pierre Drieu La Rochelle's *Ne plus attendre*, and Henry de Montherlant's *Le Solstice de juin*, and notably collected authors that had been published or, like Montherlant, "taken"—by Gallimard, his chief rival. Like Ramon Fernandez (a Gallimard author who had additionally published with Grasset), these authors were also the stars of the new rendition of *La NRF*.

La Gerbe soon found itself competing with two other publications that were resurrected in 1941: *Je suis partout* and *Comoedia*. Lead by a team that was both younger and more ideologically homogeneous, *Je suis partout* billed itself as the "revolutionary" and "avant-gardist" pole of intellectual collaborationism. It was launched in 1930 by the Arthème Fayard publishing house, which was already publishing *Candide*, in order to discuss international politics. *Je suis partout* had united Pierre Gaxotte, its editor in chief, with a team of young Maurrassians (Robert Brasillach, Lucien Rebatet, Claude Jeantet, Thierry Maulnier, Claude Roy) whose turn toward Fascism at the time of the Popular Front victory led to the journal being abandoned by its publisher and handed over to an anonymous society whose principal shareholders were Charles Lesca and André Nicolas.[56] Though it had yet to embrace doctrinaire racism, the new editorial staff, including Alain Laubreaux, made *Je suis partout* one of the forums for triumphant anti-Semitism in the years preceding the war. Pulled between the Germanophobic nationalism that they had inherited from their master and the seductive power of Nazi Germany, the contributors called for a French version of Fascism that they would not find in the Vichy regime. This was all the more true since the members of the team who had taken refuge in the Southern zone—Rebatet, Laubreaux, and Henri Poulain, who had become writers for the radio—were quickly regarded with suspicion at Petain's headquarters, as much for their pro-Nazi fervor as for their blatant *arrivisme*.[57] At the end of 1940, they decided to return to Paris, where they resumed publication of *Je suis partout* in 1941. The journal's publication had been suspended in May 1940 for its antiwar attitude.

The team reunited, minus some of its members, including Pierre Gaxotte, Thierry Maulnier, and Claude Roy, representatives of the nationalist line who disassociated themselves from the enterprise (in fact, following the arrest of Lesca and Laubreaux for attacking state security, Thierry Maulnier and Pierre Varillon had published a final issue in June 1940 without commenting on the fate of their colleagues, which earned Maulnier the reputation of a "sniper" and a "Gaullist" in the collaborationist press).[58] Although Brasillach sought the approval of Maurras, the latter rejected those of his offspring who had crossed enemy lines. Still, Brasillach reunited with his colleagues after his release in the spring of 1941, along with Pierre-Antoine Cousteau. They appointed new writers, including the inevitable Abel Bonnard, who wrote editorials in the spring of 1941; Lucien Combelle; Noel B[ayon] de la Mort, who produced the column on prisoners, "Nos prisonniers"; Morvan-Lebesque. The permanent secretary of the French Academy, André Bellessort, maintained a literary column there, alternating with Georges Blond until Bellessort's death in January 1942; Alain Laubreaux served as theater critic. Laubreaux, who meant to take advantage of the circumstances by reigning over theatrical life, aspired to the administration of the Comédie-Française, a position that he almost attained after the resignation of Jean-Louis Vaudoyer in March 1944.

Having become a "major political and literary weekly," *Je suis partout* competed with *La Gerbe* for the few fashionable writers who did not balk at giving texts to the collaborationist press (Marcel Aymé, Jean de La Varende, Anouilh), all the while promoting its own editors, longing for literary recognition, in its columns (it published, for example, novels by Laubreaux and Brasillach). Like *La Gerbe*, the journal staked a claim to Péguy, Céline, and Montherlant, but while a conformist criticism and self-proclaimed subversiveness coexisted at *La Gerbe*, *Je suis partout* claimed exclusive adherence to the second category in order to build a "European," "virile," and "healthy" literature; in a word, a "Fascist" literature.[59] More than *La Gerbe*, where some of its editors ended up, the *Je suis partout* team sought to distance itself from the conventional moralism of the traditionalists surrounding Marshal Pétain, like Henry Bordeaux, and the backward-looking neoclassicism of their former master, Charles Maurras. Céline's publisher, Denoël, opened its doors to the most virulent among them, Rebatet and Laubreaux.[60]

Whereas, at Brasillach's initiative, the paper momentarily appeared deferential toward the head of the French state, its hostility toward the Vichy regime became plain once it was revived, and this hostility would grow. The already seriously undermined nationalism of its collaborators effortlessly transformed into an unconditional support for Nazi Germany and the unification of Europe under its leadership. Setting aside the tireless exhortation to form a single party, the editors were less concerned with the elaboration of a program of "national and social revolution" than with denunciation—of the dead Republic, the prewar literary establishment, Bolshevism, Gaullism, England, Freemasons, and especially Jews—and the calls to murder that were their specialty.[61] Far from disarming them, the turning point of the war would lead them to harden their positions, provoking a split within the team after the fall of Mussolini in the summer of 1943 and the departure of Brasillach, followed by Georges Blond and Henri Poulain.[62] Those who stayed would radicalize their engagement by joining the militia or the PPF.

A true "pressure group,"[63] the *Je suis partout* team also filled the principal forums of the collaborationist press, notably *Le Petit Parisien* which, with a circulation of 500,000 copies in 1943, was by far the most widely disseminated Parisian newspaper. The profits were not just symbolic. Although they generally remained secondary in initial motivations, the economic profits that editors, papers, and authors could draw from an active collaboration partially explain the amount of goodwill and zeal that some displayed. The different forms of support that the German propaganda services offered the writers and distribution authorities seem to have been fruitful. In a situation where salaries were frozen while prices climbed, leading to a 37 percent decline in real salary between 1938 and 1943,[64] we can imagine the relative rise of profits linked directly or indirectly to collaboration, with the help of a few examples.

With a print run of 65,000 copies, Lucien Rebatet's *Les Décombres* [The Ruins], published in 1942 by Denoël, was one of the best sellers of its time. It earned its author 500,000 francs, or approximately twice his annual income as a journalist,[65] a considerable sum at a time when Paul Léautaud saw his secretarial salary at Mercure de France reduced by 25 percent, bringing his income to 1,000 francs a month.[66] *Je suis partout* doubled its prewar circulation of 50,000 copies, and would even reach 200,000 copies. Having become a booming business, it could supplement its contributors' freelance wages, which amounted to a share of the business's profits according to Brasillach himself. His salary of 8,000 francs a month as editor in chief was supplemented by 20,000 francs in 1941, 90,000 in 1942, and 20,000 in 1943.[67] Certainly, the sum of 20,000 francs that Brasillach received for the publication of a novel in *Je suis partout* seems ridiculous in light of the payments that the Anglophobic and anti-Semitic weekly *Gringoire* (relocated to Marseille) was then offering Pierre Benoit and Jean de La Varende, two very popular authors. These payments for their novels reached 200,000 francs.[68] But as I have said, the growth in profits was relative. With a circulation of 600,000 copies, *Gringoire* was the leading weekly before the war, and it maintained its status under the Occupation, with 330,000 copies. It could therefore richly reward those bestselling authors that German support and the eviction or voluntary retreat of competitors had helped make into stars.

The conditions under which *Comoedia* (a theater daily that had ceased publication in 1937) reappeared in 1941 with the agreement and under the direct control of the German Institute illustrate these different forms of compromise.

The journal, now a weekly, was required to demonstrate its "European" objectives through the creation of a "Know Europe" page and the insertion of a number of pro-German articles. Since its director, René Delange, cannot be accused of Germanophilia, according to the German censors themselves, there remains the prickly question of the growth of the *Comoedia* company's capital, which went from 500,000 to 4,000,000 francs after the paper was acquired by the anonymous company "R. L. des Journaux et Publications modernes."[69] As we have seen, this weekly also appeared among the eleven periodicals that received preferential paper allocations from the German authorities at the end of 1941, which would allow it to reach a relatively modest circulation of 48,000 copies. The fact that its allowance was reduced a month later, while those of *La Gerbe* and *Je suis partout* were increased, can likely be explained by the new measures of restriction applied from the beginning of 1942. *Paris-Soir* and *Le Petit Parisien*, despite operating under German control, also suffered (they were forced to reduce their circulation by 150,000 copies).[70]

Comoedia's artfully maintained ambiguity allowed it to attract the prestigious signatures of writers who were little-suspected of sympathy with the occupant, like Jean Paulhan and Jean-Paul Sartre, into its cultural pages directed by Marcel Arland. Paulhan, the former director of *La NRF*, had been solicited by René Delange to take on the literary direction of the weekly when it was launched. Having declined, he recommended Marcel Arland.[71] The informal role that Paulhan played by directing authors to *Comoedia* made it seem like an outpost of an *NRF* that had been progressively abandoned since Drieu La Rochelle was named its director. Competing with *La NRF* for the role of platform for "art for art's sake," *Comoedia* became the principal publication site for Gallimard authors who had remained in the occupied zone without engaging in ideological collaboration.[72] The question of whether to publish in its pages led to debates within the literary Resistance, pitting Jean Paulhan, who unwaveringly defended it on principle, against François Mauriac and Jean Guéhenno who were resolutely opposed. The inversion of positions between *La NRF* and *Comoedia* (the weekly being, despite its ambivalence, progressively perceived as more "autonomous" than the review, a perception encouraged by Paulhan, as we will see) illustrates one aspect of the shuffling of reference points: the blurring of the opposition between the pole of small-scale production and the pole of large-scale production, toward which the weekly nonetheless tended due to the political and economic rationales to which it submitted. This shuffling largely resulted from the takeover of *La NRF*.

If we compare the evolution of the weeklies, on the one hand, and the reviews, on the other, taking them as rough indicators of the opposition between the poles of large-scale production and small-scale production, we can see that the first pole was clearly less affected by the crisis than the second. The principal politico-literary weeklies survived the defeat, sometimes at the cost of emigrating to the Southern zone and printing significantly fewer copies. More fragile ventures, the reviews experienced a veritable slaughter starting with the "Phoney War," for reasons that were, in most cases, not political (only the Communist cultural reviews, like *Commune*, where banned as a consequence of the German-Soviet pact).[73] While most of the ephemeral small reviews disappeared definitively between 1939 and 1940, the more established ones, those that, thanks to their circulation, their readership, their nonspecific character, and the networks of politico-social relations to which they belonged had more in common with the pole of large-scale production, like the *Revue des deux mondes* and the *Revue universelle*, reemerged in the unoccupied zone. Between these two poles, the fate of major literary reviews attached to a publisher, like *Le Mercure de France* or *La NRF*, that by their circulation (two or three times lower than that of the *Revue des deux mondes*, which printed close to 50,000 copies on the eve of the war) and their primarily literary vocation, remained nearer the pole of small-scale production, confirms that this pole was the most disturbed by the new conditions of production.

Wishing to normalize French cultural life, Otto Abetz, well versed in French culture, paid special attention to symbolic issues. Upon his arrival in Paris, he is credited with quoting Paul Bourget as follows: "I know in France only three powers: the bank, Communists, and *La NRF*."[74] From the end of August 1940, he started negotiations to begin republishing the prestigious review under the direction of his friend Pierre Drieu La Rochelle. *La NRF* would be the only review authorized for republication in the occupied zone, to the great displeasure of Marshal Pétain who, according to a rumor spread by Jean Paulhan, apparently tried to obtain this favor for the very academic *Revue des deux mondes*, where he himself was a contributor (let us recall that he was a member of the French Academy): "They have banned *all* the other reviews. Even the *2 Mondes*, despite the insistence of the Marshal. It is after all retrospectively flattering," the former director of the review wrote to André Lhôte, with a hint of bitter irony.[75] Certainly, although it had been resolutely anti-Munich, *La NRF* had never been anti-German, unlike the *Revue des deux mondes*. But this does not adequately explain its unique privilege. Making ideological pledges to the occupant would prove useless: Jacques Bernard would wait in vain for authorization to pursue publication of the *Mercure de France*, and neither Lucien Combelle nor Georges Pelorson would attain it to create new reviews.[76]

During the summer Jean Paulhan, who was staying with Gaston Gallimard in Villalier, near Carcassonne, at Joë Bousquet's house, attempted to convince the editor to publish *La NRF* in the unoccupied zone. Gallimard wanted nothing to do with it. As he wrote to André Gide in early October, he thought that "accommodations" with the Germans would be "easier than with the Vichy government."[77] Drieu La Rochelle had recently sought him out to inform him of Abetz's proposition; raised the specter of a German takeover of the Gallimard publishing house; assured him that the review would be republished anyhow; presented himself, in short, as the house's savior. This is in any case the version that Gaston Gallimard broadcasted among his authors to gain their consent—he would visit André Gide on the night before he returned to Paris, October 21—and the version that Jean Paulhan adopted at the Liberation to justify his publisher.[78]

Of course, the Gallimard house did not have a good reputation with the Occupation authorities. It appeared anti-Nazi, under Jewish influence, infiltrated by leftist writers and included the highest number of books banned by the "Otto list," with 140 works pulled from the market. Not coincidentally, it was shut down on November 9, by an order of the Propaganda-Staffel dated October 9, although Pascal Fouché suggests that this was a blunder.[79] Drieu La Rochelle explained the affair to Jean Grenier, who had come to see him on November 20: "The house has just been closed . . . because German officers billeted at the Gallimard castle in Mirande where the latter had sent editions had been scandalized by the anti-Hitler books they found. It is on their report that the Paris office was closed. But the German civilians have not been consulted and an important German will come to Paris today who will undoubtedly reopen it."[80] This closure was presented to Gaston Gallimard, summoned by Dr. Kaiser to Propaganda on November 23, as a warning for all French publishers. Since Gallimard had refused a German firm the right to acquire capital in his publishing house, the negotiations to reopen it were now resumed with the embassy, represented by Councilor Rahn. The right to reopen was granted on November 28, as Kaiser notified Gaston Gallimard, on the condition of "reserving for a duration of 5 years to Mr. Drieu La Rochelle [. . .] powers extended to the totality of the execution of the intellectual and political production of [the] house."[81]

Could the "important German" that Drieu mentioned be Gerhard Heller, in Paris since November 9, who convinced him during their meeting at the end of the month that he was responsible for the reopening of the Gallimard publishing house (even though negotiations were already in progress with the embassy)? In any case, on December 1 Kaiser was called back to Berlin, due to his conflicts with Dr. Epting of the Institute, according to Gerhard Heller,[82] who replaced him "temporarily" and could easily reopen Gallimard himself. Are we to relate, as chronological proximity suggests, Kaiser's dismissal with the "blunder" committed at the initiative of the Propaganda-Staffel, a blunder that thwarted Abetz's plans? The fact that Drieu was informed of Kaiser's dismissal seems to confirm this.[83] Heller saw it as the translation of the political opposition between the Ministry of Propaganda and the Ministry of Foreign Affairs, and their respective subsidiaries: the Propaganda and the embassy. Was this Abetz's chance to promote his old friend within the competing department? In any case, Heller would occupy this position until his transfer to the German Institute after an agreement in July 1942 limiting the Propaganda's oversight of cultural matters. This transfer served as a promotion. Meanwhile, the director of the Institute, Epting, would be called back to Berlin.[84]

Jean Paulhan, whom Drieu had summoned to Vichy in October, had refused to serve as coeditor of the review. The Occupation authorities opposed it, moreover, criticizing Paulhan for his article "L'espoir et le silence" [Hope and silence], which appeared in the last issue of La NRF in June 1940. "In the end," he wrote to the Belgian critic Franz Hellens, "even if I had agreed to it and the Germans had accepted me, I could not have stayed in a review where the Jewish collaborators (Benda, Suarès, Wahl), and the anti-Nazis (Bernanos, Claudel, Romains) that I had called there were driven out."[85] On October 1, Jean Giono had informed André Gide of a letter from Drieu La Rochelle announcing, to his great surprise, that La NRF would now be published under his direction, with an editorial committee composed of Eluard, Céline, Gide, and Giono.[86] During his visit with Gide, Gaston Gallimard floated the idea of an editorial committee composed of Drieu, Eluard, Giono, André Malraux, and Antoine de Saint-Exupéry. Gide declined—and we are to believe that the project failed for lack of volunteers, since La NRF reappeared on December 1, 1940, without an editorial committee—but Gallimard managed to extract a promise that Gide would contribute to the review's first issue.

The links of interdependence between authors and publishers, which brought external constraints into the very heart of professional practices, thus constituted one of the essential links in the chain of involvement in the structures of the Collaboration. Added to these mechanisms of the process of loss of autonomy were the effects induced by the Vichy regime's apparatus of constraints. Far from preventing it, the latter intensified the former due to its authoritarian nature and its competition with the powers of occupation over the authorities of cultural production.

Because of the concentration of publishing, cinema, and theater in the capital, the French state exercised only limited control over the majority of means of cultural production, with the exception of the press.[87] The Occupation forces did not miss an opportunity to remind the Vichy government of its limited oversight in this domain. Thus, in April 1941, the Propaganda suspended, in the name of "artistic freedom"—but really to declare its monopoly on censorship in the occupied zone—the ban on staging Jean Cocteau's *La Machine à écrire* at the Hébertot theater; the French government delegate to the Occupation authorities, Fernand de Brinon, had pronounced this ban in the name of "morality."[88] But unlike the occupant who had no desire to import German cultural models into France, the Vichy regime had a political program, the National Revolution, that accorded a significant space to "intellectual and moral reform," although this program would be gradually abandoned due to the evolution of the war and the whims of internal rivalries.

To carry out this program, Vichy built an apparatus of control and propaganda that reached the height of centralization with the plan of "total supervision" instituted by Secretary of State for Information Paul Marion starting in 1941. In the literary domain, a moral censorship began to rage; this, undoubtedly more than political censorship, worried a number of writers and publishers, including the Parisian collaborationists. Two pro-German observers, Alfred Fabre-Luce and Paul Léautaud, expressed this concern:

> The free zone "does virtue." The bookstore windows blossom with works on Péguy. The windows flourish with works on Péguy. (He is no longer here, thank God, to get bogged down in this circumstantial success.) Newspaper editorials are in a moralistic vein. (In a state of armistice, discretion is necessary on many subjects; homily is sometimes only the welcome means to darken a white column.) Zealous municipalities purge their city libraries. A "vamp" on the cover of a magazine arouses emotion in the office of the Secretary of State for the Family. But censorship operates above all inside consciences. "I'm writing a romantic comedy," a playwright says, "but, given the circumstances, my heroes don't sleep together." Actually, if you want to have a play performed, obtain paper, earn the favors of the government, it is preferable to celebrate virtue. But from the moment virtue brings these advantages, it no longer distinguishes itself from the previous corruption. Thus it will soon be systematically bled dry by some groups. [89]

It is even accredited, on our side of occupied France, even by the publishers, that if you have to publish a book that is a bit daring in this sense, even a bit immoral, you have to take advantage of the presence of the Germans, who only exert their censorship on politics and the war, a regime of Moral Order being what probably awaits us after peace and their departure, unless a political reversal and change of government occurs. [...] In any case, it is said that *Tartuffe* has been banned in the free zone, *Tartuffe* that Louis XIV allowed to be performed.[90]

The apparatus of monitoring and propaganda was coupled with an apparatus of exclusion and repression. It was put in place at the advent of the regime, with the measures decreed in August 1940 against Freemasonry (dissolution of secret societies), then with the first Statute on Jews promulgated in October, which excluded them from any activity having an impact on cultural life. To these measures, we must add the ban on the Communist Party, maintained by the decree of September 1939 that pronounced its dissolution as a result of the German-Soviet pact (this ban was not repealed, unlike the government decree of April 21, 1939, forbidding hate speech in the press, that would be annulled on August 27, 1940). Such a legislative arsenal had, as in other domains, an immediate effect on the literary landscape, since a certain number of signatures disappeared: while Julien Benda, André Suarès, and Léon Werth were reduced to silence because of their Jewish origins, Communists such as Georges Sadoul and Léon Moussinac published under pseudonyms in the reviews of the Southern zone during the entire Occupation.

At the same time, the efforts of the Vichy government to retain oversight over cultural production and increase its domain of intervention ended up serving the politics of the occupant, who was only too happy to meet its goals through a discipline of self-censorship. Vichy's efforts also resulted in the consolidation of the chain of involvement of cultural agents in the structures of the Collaboration, by making this chain official and perfecting it. The development of the Office of Information and of the State Department for Youth, as well as the creation of organisms to oversee the publishing industry, offered in any case a new slate of jobs to those authors more or less devoted to the regime's ideology.

The relative subordination of the publishing industry to the Vichy political apparatus was achieved through the distribution of paper. To this end, measures were taken from the summer of 1940 that resulted in the creation, on May 3, 1941, of the Comité d'organisation des industries, arts et commerces du livre [Organizing Committee of Industries, Arts, and Commerce of the Book], attached to the Ministry of Industrial Production. The government's concern was twofold: to safeguard French prerogatives over cultural production and to give that production an orientation that conformed to its ideological line. These concerns encountered the corporative and individual interests of cultural agents, publishers, and authors.

The new measures of control and the corporate structures put in place by the French state thus awakened age-old claims concerning the defense of literary interests.[91] Writers from different sides returned to a project that had already been planned before the war, the creation of an organism or an official position that would represent literature in the government.[92] "We must create a Department of Literature, or even better, a Ministry of Literature and Art," Alphonse Séché exclaimed in Jacques Doriot's daily, *Le Cri du peuple*,[93] calling for state intervention to provide for the needs of writers. *Le Figaro*'s literary critic, André Billy, formulated the same wish in the summer of 1940, as he worried about the fate of literature in the new regime :

> First, what will be the legal and social status of the writer? Will the literary corporation be regulated? We hear again of a journalistic professional order: will there be an equivalent for writers and what will be the conditions for admission? Will anyone be able to write? Will this right be refused, not only to foreigners, but also to certain categories of the French?
>
> And above all, what will we be able to write? There will obviously be a censorship of books and periodicals, and by the way, it has been happening for a year. Will they be satisfied with maintaining it by enlarging its orders? [...] Laws exist with the aim of punishing insults to morality by means of printed publications. They could suffice if it was decided to apply them, but insult to morality is only a weak aspect of the risk implied by the word literature alone under an authoritarian regime. It seems that a preventive censorship will remain indispensable since it will bear, for the writer as well as for the power, both the greatest chances for agreement and the greatest respective guarantees of security.[94]

And yet, the prospect of a "directed literature" caused profound concern in the literary world. In *Le Figaro*'s inquiry in the autumn of 1940 asking, "What will literature be tomorrow?" the majority of writers, including those who considered that literature had "taken a wrong turn" before the war, according to the phrase used in the questionnaire, spoke against this prospect; they invoked, among other things, the risk of conformity that would result.[95]

There would be neither a department of literature nor a corporation of writers. A commission was nonetheless created and charged with studying the needs of the writers' corporation. From 1942 to 1944 this commission would include two members of the French Academy, Georges Duhamel and Paul Valéry, and it would in fact reexamine the project of a Caisse nationale des écrivains,[96] envisioned since 1928.[97] Meanwhile, a form of compromise was reached to satisfy the demands of the literary publishers and writers who did not benefit from the new Comité de l'organisation du livre. On June 9, a book council was created under the direction of the State Department for National Education and Youth; this new council was responsible "for all the questions concerning the intellectual orientation to give the production of books, the development of public reading, and the diffusion of the French book."[98] Under the presidency of the new general administrator of the Bibliothèque nationale, Bernard Faÿ, the permanent secretary of the French Academy, André Bellessort, represented the corporation of writers with the expectation that it would be created. Other members included five authors: Octave Aubry, Pierre Drieu La Rochelle, Paul Morand, André Siegfried, and Jean Vignaud; an illustrator, André Dunoyer de Segonzac; four publishers including Grasset; and two representatives from the Comité de l'organisation du livre: its director, Marcel Rives, and the president of the publishing group, René Philippon.

Paul Marion, who had suggested creating the book council, would try in vain to obtain its affiliation with the General Secretariat for Information. As far as books were concerned, he would have to be satisfied with censorship or promotion. The Department of Information could thus ban books in the Southern zone that were authorized in the occupied zone, like Céline's *Les Beaux Draps*, or encourage publication by buying copies that they then distributed, especially in prison camps; this was the case for André-Paul Antoine's *Mémorial de France* (100,000 copies) and Robert Vallery-Radot's *La Franc-maçonnerie vous parle* (10,000 copies).[99]

The new paper restrictions adopted by the Propaganda-Staffel in early 1942, which threatened to extend German control, and the attitude of certain publishers who did not hesitate to deal directly with German censors, led to the creation, in April 1942, of the Commission de contrôle du papier d'édition [Commission for the Control of Publishing Paper]. When, at the end of the month, a German ordinance took effect requiring every publication to have an authorization number, an agreement between the Comité de l'organisation du livre and the Propaganda allowed the new commission to make its own selection of manuscripts deserving to be published, according to the quantity of paper allotted each month, a selection that it would then submit for authorization by the Propaganda.[100] Composed of the president of the Conseil du livre, Bernard Faÿ; the director of the Comité de l'organisation du livre, Marcel Rives; the president of the publishers' union, René Philippon; and two authors, Paul Morand and Louis de Broglie, with Madame Robert Antelme (Marguerite Duras) as secretary, the commission used about forty readers for its purposes, including Ramon Fernandez, Dionys Mascolo, Brice Parain, and André Thérive. A growing involvement, then, of cultural agents in the apparatus of control over cultural production, but also a concentration of responsibilities in the hands of "reliable" men: like Bernard Faÿ, a professor at the Collège de France, as well as an anti-masonry advocate; and Paul Morand, who held, as we saw, positions in the Conseil du livre and the commission (he would later be named ambassador to Bucharest, then to Bern).

The authoritarianism of the regime would hit the Southern zone particularly hard; until the German invasion of November 1942, this zone was under Vichy's sole control. To exert its authority, the government could rely on the war measures taken in 1939, but as Philippe Amaury explains, "the regime of censorship of the press and publications, established in 1939, compatible with the freedoms of opinion and expression even though setting unusual limits for them due to the exceptional circumstances, bec[ame] a 'regime of orientation' that suppresse[d] those freedoms[. . .]."[101] Control of information at the source by means of the official news agency, the French Office of Information (OFI); daily memoranda of information; instructions that go so far as to dictate the typography of titles; censorship and suspension, temporary or sine die, of newspapers; the centralized apparatus of supervision, which was founded by Paul Marion in 1941 and boasted its own training structure for propagandists, the École nationale des cadres civiques, only appeared to weaken after Laval's return in April 1942 and the nomination of René Bonnefoy as general secretary for information in December. Actually, supposing propaganda to be more effective in a more diversified press, the latter passed an agreement in January 1943 that substituted the general instructions with a commitment on the part of newspaper editors to unfailingly support the politics of the government; this was the institution of self-censorship.[102] Furthermore, the Propaganda disposed of substantial credits. Worried about the possibility of their return to the capital, the government subsidized the nine dailies and thirty Parisian newspapers that were somehow being published in the Southern zone. *Action française* was one of the few periodicals to decline this offer, despite its support of the regime.[103] In fact, while the rightist weeklies *Gringoire* and *Candide*, published in Marseille and Clermont-Ferrand respectively, experienced only a relative decline—the first went from a circulation of around 600,000 copies before the war to 330,000, the second from more than 400,000 to 180,000—the sales of *Le Figaro* and *Le Temps* fell to 15,000 copies for the former, half as much for the latter, during the winter of 1940–1941.

The elaboration and diffusion of the ideas of the National Revolution mobilized an entire fraction of intellectuals promoted by the regime. The creation of the Musée des Arts et Traditions populaires as well as commissions of regionalist propaganda favored the involvement of specialists in the program of restoring and diffusing folklore.[104] In the literary domain, the cultural project of Vichy translated into a celebration of regionalism that culminated in the creation, in July 1942, of the Sully-Olivier de Serres Prize aimed at "encouraging, supporting, and rewarding literature devoted to peasant life."[105] Whether they occupied an official function, like Henry Massis, Joseph de Pesquidoux, and the future minister of education Abel Bonnard at the National Council, or René Gillouin and Gustave Thibon at the Centre français de synthèse; whether they were "counselors to the prince" like Charles Maurras and René Benjamin; or whether they simply put their pen to the service of his glory, like Henry Bordeaux, Henri Pourrat, and José Germain, a good number of writers were organically linked, through their past or present engagements, to the authoritarian regime that aroused the "divine surprise" of Maurras, and that they all helped legitimate. In chapters 4 and 5 we will examine the nature of these links, through the example of two official literary institutions, the French Academy and the Goncourt Academy, along with the role of mediation that they were able to play between Vichy and Paris during this period.

Representing the traditionalist or reactionary side of the National Revolution, these literary notables reunited to purge the dead Republic and preach repentance while praising the head of state in the old structures that survived the debacle by emigrating to the Southern zone. Such publications included the very academic *Revue des deux mondes*, now a quasi organ of the regime under the direction of André Chaumeix; the *Revue universelle*, a forum for the Catholic intellectuals linked to *Action française* and directed by Henri Massis; or the weekly *Candide*, of a Maurrassian tendency. On the literary plane, they promoted a moralizing conception of literature that participated in the program of "intellectual and moral reform" called for by Marshal Pétain. A number of them, like Henry Bordeaux, Jean Guitton, Jacques Madaule, or even the Catholic critic of *Action française*, Robert Havard de la Montagne, would also contribute to the Catholic weekly *Demain*. Under the direction of Jean de Fabrègues, its mission starting in February 1942 was to gather Catholics of every opinion around the marshal.[106] Among the old structures, the extreme-right populist weekly *Gringoire* displayed an Anglophobia and violent anti-Semitism that brought it close, in style and ideas, to the Parisian collaborationist press where it was indeed well received. (*Gringoire* was the only weekly from the Southern zone that found favor with *Je suis partout*, which had distanced itself from *Candide* despite originally sharing close ties both on an ideological level, and because of its editorial team.)[107]

New forums were created with the support of the Ministry of Information, circumstantial like *Demain*, or more doctrinaire and with a "revolutionary" pretense. The review *Idées* is a good example of the latter; a self-described "laboratory of ideas" for the National Revolution, it was also subsidized by the regime.[108] *Idées* was launched in November 1941 by a group of intellectuals who had belonged to the Young Right of the 1930s, animating the reviews *Combat*, *L'Insurgé*, and *Réaction*. In the wake of Paul Marion, representative of Vichy's Fascistic circle, they would find themselves opposed to the traditionalist or reactionary wing surrounding Pétain. Let us note that being "freed from the meritocratic constraints which had until then formed the basis of civil service,"[109] the new administrations, the Department of the General Secretary for Youth, the General Secretary for Information, or even the Commissariat général aux questions juives (CGQJ), offered favorable conditions for the recruitment and advancement of those who had not followed the regular routes traditionally opening access to the state nobility: the *grandes écoles*† and civil service entrance exams.[110] It is not surprising, then, that a number of young intellectuals and writers were drawn to this unexpected chance to attain high levels of responsibility.

A number of the contributors to *Idées*, promoted by Marion, thus held official positions in the regime's propaganda apparatus. René Vincent, its editor in chief, who had been part of Marion's cabinet since June 1941, became the head of the censorship department in late 1941. This was a position that he would hold until August 1944. Maurice Gaït, a graduate of the École normale supérieure§ in philosophy who aided the review, was the first director of the École nationale des cadres civiques du Mayet-de-Montagne, which was created by Paul Marion in October 1941. In April 1942, he would become chief of staff to Abel Bonnard, the minister of national education, and then general commissioner for youth in February 1944. François Gravier, a member of the editorial staff and a certified professor of geography, succeeded him as the director of the École du Mayet-de-Montagne in January 1942, having left, like Jean Maze, the Office of the Secretary of State for Youth in order to follow Marion to Information. Jacques Laurent-Cély (Jacques Laurent) was still at Information; writing as Jacques Bostan in the review, as director of the research and development department he prepared "notes of orientation" meant for the press.[111] Pierre Dom-

---

† The *grandes écoles* are the most competitive and prestigious institutions of higher learning in France.—Trans.
§ The École normale supérieure, located in Paris, is a *grande école* in science and the humanities. Its students are known as *normaliens*.—Trans.

inique, a writer and journalist, was named director of the Office français d'information in May 1941 after having been the head of the department of the press and censorship. Charles Mauban, a novelist, was a delegate for youth in Lyon, then director of the General Secretariat for Youth. Armand Petitjean, a literary critic and contributor to both the prewar NRF and its incarnation under Drieu La Rochelle, who also published regularly in *Idées*, codirected the propaganda bureau in the Office of the Secretary of State for Youth; then, after resigning in December 1940, was a leader in the Compagnons de France. He was Paul Marion's candidate to take over the Compagnons in May 1941 (he lost to a Catholic candidate),[112] before trying, again with Marion's support, to create the Jeunesses légionnaires.

They were joined by Jean de Fabrègues, a former contributor to the reviews *Réaction* and *Combat* who directed, as we have seen, the Catholic weekly *Demain*. Writers like Pierre Drieu La Rochelle and Jean de La Varende occasionally lent their prestige to the review. Experts like Louis Salleron, the theoretician of agrarian corporatism, who served on the Commission nationale d'organisation corporative [National Commission of Corporative Organization] from January to September 1941, exposed their views there; and the director of the Institut de formation légionnaire, Yves Urvoy, was invited to express himself in its columns.[113]

The review understood the National Revolution as the realization of a synthesis, eclectic if nothing else, that the Proudhon Circle had tried to sketch out at the beginning of the century[114] between Joseph de Maistre, René de La Tour du Pin, Charles Maurras, Frédéric Le Play, Pierre-Joseph Proudhon, and Georges Sorel, a synthesis that Jean de Fabrègues thought he recognized in Pétain's speeches.[115] "The split between *Action française* and revolutionary syndicalism, whose alliance constituted before 1941 about the only chance for a fertile revolutionary explosion, was never reconsidered seriously in what followed, even by ventures like the Faisceau of Georges Valois. Certainly, we have had remarkable theorists of the Revolution like Proudhon or Sorel, of the Reaction like de Maistre, Le Play, or Maurras, and of the national popular like Péguy," Armand Petitjean proclaimed.[116] While his colleagues at *Idées* flatly rejected parliamentarianism, capitalism, liberalism, egalitarianism, individualism, and materialism, they equally denigrated the "moral order" that Vichy's traditionalists tried to establish, the same order that banned Colette and alcohol, a "caricature of the Christian spirit," "personalist imagery illuminated in Saint-Sulpice."[117] They refused to call it revolutionary— "[Paul] Bourget was not revolutionary and this order is purely bourgetian"[118]— contrasting it with "a moral of order" fueled by "virile virtues," by "greatness and heroism," whose roots reached to the Christian Middle Ages as well as the Revolution.

Taking inspiration from, among other things, the works of "experts" like the economist François Perroux, the review thoroughly developed the theme of "natural communities" in the framework of an organic society hierarchized on a corporatist basis, in which "the State must now be understood and served as the organ of a community."[119] Reflecting on "popular representation," Jean Maze considered that the real question was not one of delegation but of the "mode of creation of new elites and their progressive participation in power." Evoking the single party that constituted, in the twentieth century, a solution to the problem of the conduit "between the Executive and the masses, that the Parliament has shown itself incapable of ensuring," he nonetheless specified that this solution should be sought once the "revolution" had been accomplished.[120]

Understandably, the education of youth and the new "elites" was one of the review's major preoccupations. Although it defended free education, along with the traditionalists, wishing that its representatives would sit on exam juries, it nonetheless demanded that education be placed under the control of the state and that its personnel hold a state-issued diploma.[121] On the other hand, declaring their rivalry with the state nobility issued from the *grands corps* of the senior civil service as well as the technocrats who triumphed under Vichy,[122] these newcomers asked for a reform of the system of grandes écoles.[123]

For those "revolutionaries" who did not separate "thought" from "action," the civic elites and political executives should be recruited from among the militants.[124] On this question of the recruitment of elites, *Idées* converged with other "revolutionaries" who expressed themselves, for example, in the columns of *France, revue de l'Etat nouveau*, born in 1942: "The principal enemy of the National Revolution is this: competition. Are we to believe that revolutionaries will be recruited from the stables of the State Council or the benches of Sciences Politiques?" wrote Michel Mohrt,[125] a young law school graduate (he was not yet thirty) descended from a family of merchants in Morlaix. He jumped into essay writing with *Les Intellectuels devant la défaite, 1870* (Corrêa, 1941), before becoming a critic and novelist (starting in 1952, he would be a reader at Gallimard). Here these revolutionaries converged with the program of Drieu La Rochelle, who noted in his *Journal*:

> Purge the French Academy, suppress the Goncourt. Purge the whole Institute. Suppress Normale and the Agrégation.** Reduce secondary education,

---

** Teaching certification exam.—Trans.

suppress all means of exams, of grants, of compensation. Move the grandes écoles and the Sorbonne to the provinces. Suppress several universities. Crush the spirit of the Polytechnique and the Inspection.[††][126]

I will return at greater length to the anti-intellectualism that these "revolutionaries" shared with the Parisian collaborationists in the next chapter, in reference to the survey on "Intelligence and Its Role in the Polis" launched by *Idées* in February 1942. The nomination of Abel Bonnard as minister of national education in April 1942 can be considered a victory for anti-intellectualism. This period, marked by Pierre Laval's return to power and the death of the National Revolution, was also marked by a radicalization of the collaborationism of these "revolutionaries" without a revolution who, disappointed by the regime's achievements in terms of internal politics, from now on pinned their hopes on a "new Europe." As Marc Olivier Baruch has noted, "the border was then tenuous between the collaborationist journals and an organ like *Idées*."[127]

Despite a constraining system, the Southern zone offered a larger and more diversified choice. Unlike the occupied zone, a number of literary reviews were authorized there and were able to survive in a semi-legality that included fewer risks, even after the invasion of German troops in November 1942. Proximity with nearby French-speaking regions opened up possibilities and alternatives that were not available to writers on the other side of the demarcation line. National sovereignty, although purely formal, also made participation in the literary press less compromising in the eyes of reluctant writers, and it was in the Southern zone that an opposition movement would be organized, speaking openly but in code.

THE CHOICE OF ARMS: "THE FRENCH SPIRIT" AT STAKE

In this state of over-politicization of the literary field, where freedom of expression was suppressed, where the majority of the authorities of diffusion and recognition were subject to political dictates, and where the subjugation of literature was supported by internal agents, what was the range of possibles offered to writers who refused compromise? Was the option of "art for art's sake" as a mode of detachment from political and social constraints, and thus an affirmation of the writer's autonomy, still legitimate, as the contributors to *La NRF* claimed, calling in its name for undecided or reluctant writers to emerge from their cloak of silence? Writing against voluntary abstention, *La NRF*'s con-

---

[††] Polytechnique is a *grande école* offering training in the sciences and management. Inspection is a school that trains tax inspectors.—Trans.

tributors constantly invoked either the cause of art or the need to maintain the "French spirit." An entire fraction of the literary field, including the *attentistes* but also the authors who made the best of the occupant's presence without openly proclaiming their position, would need no other pretext to justify the pursuit of its activities without any distinction of forums and regardless of the transformed conditions of cultural production. Collaborationist publications, like *Le Petit Parisien* or *La Gerbe*, could thus take advantage of brilliant contributions: Marcel Aymé, Anouilh, Léon-Paul Fargue, and others.

But this was precisely why the writers of "refusal" criticized them. Jean Guéhenno judged his colleagues mercilessly:

> The man-of-letters species is not one of the greatest human species. Incapable of living long in hiding, he would sell his soul in order for his name to be *published*. A few months of silence, of disappearance have done him in. He can't go on. He quibbles only with the importance, with the size of the type in which his name will be printed, on his place in the table of contents. It goes without saying that he is full of good reasons. "French literature," he says, "must continue." He thinks he is French literature, French thought, and that they would die without him.[128]

Michel Leiris made the same observation:

> For several weeks already I have been reflecting on this true malady of "literary people" who do not conceive of the possibility of staying silent and for whom no longer publishing is equivalent to a kind of annihilation.[129]

Didn't such a choice actually mean playing into those German cultural politics that aimed to normalize the situation of occupation? This position would be denounced by the underground press. The director of *Les Lettres françaises*, Claude Morgan, thus tried to demonstrate that this assessment was accurate, taking as his example the political meaning that a harmless article on Burgundy that Colette gave *La Gerbe* took on when placed next to an article by Dr. W. Reimer entitled "Land between Rhine and Rhone."[130]

We can assert that the minimum code of conduct on which the writers of "refusal" agreed, implicitly or explicitly, was to not contribute to the Parisian press, with the notable exception of *Comoedia*, where opinions diverged. The maximum position would have few followers. Represented by the uncompromising code of conduct that Communist intellectuals, reduced to secrecy, tried to impose in 1941, it was summed up in the formula: "legal literature means literature of treason."[131] This position would soon be relaxed, moreover, at Aragon's initiative, as we will see.

Despite the self-censorship agreement that the publishers' union had signed, the fact is that the question of book publication proved to be delicate. Few writers, in fact, abstained from all legal publication; they included Roger Martin du Gard, André Malraux, André Chamson, Jean Guéhenno, and René Char. Michel Leiris, who would publish *Haut Mal* in 1943, admittedly in the limited-edition collection "Métamorphoses" that Jean Paulhan directed at Gallimard, wrote in his journal on January 31, 1941:

> At no time in my literary life did the idea come to me to "officialize" myself. Now is therefore not the time to begin.... The essential meaning that I attach to my poetic activity is that of a refusal. There is thus no question for me of publishing in conditions that would represent for me, implicitly, an acceptance of what is happening now in the political realm.[132]

This position was delicate for at least two reasons. Would not the meaning of such an individual stance seem ambiguous, when it did not go unnoticed? In his *Journal*, Roger Martin du Gard evoked the difficulty of staying this course:

> Even though I am constantly harassed to take, in present-day France, a definite political attitude, and some even try to intimidate me by calling me an *attentiste*, which in modern vocabulary means not only abstentionist but "without character, cowardly, prudently opportunistic," etc., I do not manage to weaken in myself the firm intention that I formed to remain silent, to not attach one more voice to the confused cacophony of the "partisans." [...] I do not know what the future holds for me, and if this private—essentially private—attitude will be possible to maintain if, tomorrow, the passions of the parties, which are only at the beginning of their agitation, tear apart and devastate my country. I will hold off as long as possible. If one day I have to, I do not say "choose" but "declare my choice," I will do it, at any risk. If one also has to bend before the violence of the strongest, I think I will be able to bend also [...].[133]

And still today, Malraux is more often charged with his successive refusals of both the literary and the armed Resistance before going underground in 1944 than praised for his choice to publish nothing in France as long as the Occupation lasted.[134]

The second reason is that for a number of "writers of refusal," the struggle to maintain the "French spirit" was also at stake, but a struggle to maintain it honorably, that is to say without compromising their principles (this is what separated them from the attentistes and those who were complacent). Rather than not publish anything, they wanted to maintain a presence—legal but covert—that made their retreat from certain places like *La NRF* and their refusal to write for the collaborationist press the more obvious, by contrast. The idea that this could be only a form of self-persuasion seems to me without interest insofar as it is above all important to assert, against the thesis of "bad faith," that belief in the power of *esprit* is, by definition, one of the principles that the producers of symbolic goods must interiorize in order to enter the game, to take it seriously. Even if they come to doubt it, they need all the hindsight of a François Mauriac approaching death to be able to state, after the fact, that is to say after having played the game, that "the resistance of the intellectuals was useful first of all to them, and that is not insignificant after all."[135]

Let us note that, except in the case of those who were entirely condemned to forced silence, suppressing the freedom of expression did not in itself constitute a reference point susceptible of guiding conduct. When Michel Leiris enjoyed the banning of *L'Afrique fantôme* by the Ministry of the Interior in 1941—"Setting aside the fact that this could end up provoking practical inconveniences, I can only enjoy this decision, that objectively situates me. 'Objectively,' that is to say: without my being at all involved, by the very essence of things"[136]—it was because this ban reinforced a choice he had made a year earlier by refusing to contribute to authorized reviews. In contradistinction to this attitude, censorship, or fear of censorship, could lead others to multiply their tokens of good will toward the occupant, as we saw earlier in the case of Léautaud, who refused to publish in *Le Figaro* so as not to offend the German censors.

Furthermore, self-censorship did not represent only disadvantages for these writers who were specialists of a game with formal rules and constraints. The experience of history has moreover proven it, as Drieu La Rochelle explained in *La NRF* (October 1942): "The good literary periods are periods of censorship: the spirit is condemned to thinness."[137] There is no reason to doubt his good faith, especially since he developed this idea privately at the same time, as Jean Follain reported: "In the period where one can say anything, Drieu said (around 1928), words lose some of their value, some of their weight. Eras when governments have monitored literary productions while encouraging them (patronage) have seen flourishing literature."[138] And if we still doubted his impartiality, the reflections that André Gide published on the subject in *La NRF* (February 1941) confirm that this was a widely shared view:

> If tomorrow, as must be feared, the freedom to think, or at least the expression of that thought, will be refused to us, I will try to persuade myself that art, that even thought, will lose less by this than in an excessive freedom.

We enter a period where liberalism will become the most suspect and the least practicable of virtues. But I try to persuade myself that it is during non-liberal periods that the free spirit reaches its most lofty virtue.[139]

The recourse to coded language, to winks and insinuations, which became generalized after 1941 on the literary page of *Le Figaro* and in the young reviews of the Southern zone and the nearby French-speaking zones, illustrates the playful character—"Oh! We were having fun" Pierre Seghers would write at the Liberation[140]—that the efforts at getting around censorship would take on, establishing a new complicity with the reader that could only reinforce literary belief. It is no coincidence that this practice would first be developed by poets.

Definitively, what would circumscribe these stakes was not so much censorship itself as the use that the writers most inclined to heteronomy threatened to make of it, in order to silence rivals that they loudly denounced. François Mauriac thus wrote to Drieu La Rochelle in July 1941: "[. . .] but, Drieu, recognize that in any case they [my friends] don't have the occupier behind them, *they do not seek to put the occupier in the service of their vengeance.* That is what is unforgivable."[141] From then on, denunciation would constitute a reference point.

With all the precautions that the interpretation of retroactive testimony requires, we might quote Simone de Beauvoir's summary of the code of conduct adopted by writers of "refusal" (with the caveat that we might harbor a doubt concerning Radio-Vichy, where she herself contributed, in order to make a living after her dismissal from national education in the summer of 1943):

> The writers on our side of the zonal border had tacitly formulated certain rules and stuck to them. No one was to write for any journal or magazine in the Occupied Zone, nor to broadcast from Radio Paris. On the other hand, it was permissible to work for the press in the Free Zone and to speak on Radio Vichy: here it all depended on the content of the article or broadcast in question.[142]

In fact, with some rare exceptions, the question of refusing to publish books was never really posed, despite what Édith Thomas suggests: "I resolved not to publish it [the novel that she had just finished]. I would have had to send press copies to the critics who had accepted to work at French-language Nazi newspapers, ask for their opinion and thereby prove them right for having put themselves in the service of the invader. Others, like Elsa Triolet who published *Le Cheval blanc* at that time, did not have the same scruples."[143] In reality, her novel had been rejected by Gallimard.[144] This case matters less as an anecdote than for its exemplarity: for many of those engaged in underground endeavors, legal non-publication was not a choice. The choice that Jean Guéhenno made to keep silent, which must be relativized due to his status as a high school teacher (he did not live off his writing), still remains meaningful in comparison with Jean-Paul Sartre, another teacher. Also meaningful were the choices made by Roger Martin du Gard and Malraux, who published *Les Noyers d'Altenburg* in Switzerland and not in occupied France. They were exceptions.

On another level, René Char (like Malraux) made an exceptional choice by preferring armed to literary resistance—the few (rare) other writers who engaged in active Resistance also participated in the intellectual Resistance. These limit cases traced the contours of possibles on the side of "refusal." One of the artisans of the literary Resistance, Jacques Debû-Bridel, would summarize, although after the fact, what was at stake in these different choices, from the viewpoint of those who chose the weapons of the mind:

> The best and most qualified of French thought could only answer by their abstention, by their silence or some private endeavors. Was this haughty and courageous dignity enough to safeguard the influence and renown of French thought in a world that, delivered from Nazism, was to strike down the new barbarism at the cost of harsh sacrifices? Would it not soon be forgotten, if it were ever known? More than the treason of a dozen writers engaged in the ranks of the enemy, the too-general renouncement of semi-complicity threatened to greatly endanger French literature, the intellectual [*spirituel*] influence of France.[145]

For most of the writers on this side, the issue concerned the defense of the values of the spirit [esprit]. The first issue of *Confluences* that came out after the Liberation began with this theme: "It was a matter then of opposing the venture of systematically enslaving the mind, by the Nazis and their servants, with the silent, but effective action of free thought."[146] In its political version, it can be summarized as follows: this war being an ideological war, the opposition took the form of a defense of the universal values of the spirit [esprit] against racist particularism and the enslavement of thought. These universal values of the spirit [esprit] came from a French humanist tradition born of the Enlightenment and those siding with the new powers attempted to misappropriate them in favor of the "European ideal," or discredit them in favor of a particularist nationalism that drew from the sources of counterrevolutionary tradition. This is why, in its more spiritual and more patriotic version, which was the one that drew the most followers, the struggle took the form of a defense of national cultural heritage and an effort to reappropriate the "French spirit" through the themes and symbols misused to the advantage of the new dominant ideologies, from Joan of Arc to Péguy. Faced with the proclaimed patriotism of nationalists supporting the National Revolution, it was easy to respond: "Strange patriotism sometimes when it calls for revolution without worrying about independence."[147] Faced with those who intended to exploit the defeat in order to flout the values of the national heritage by denouncing the past faults that supposedly led to disaster, according to the rhetoric of contrition inaugurated by the head of state, the motto of "not disowning oneself" following the title of an article published by François Mauriac in *Le Figaro* of July 23, 1940, became the rallying cry for the opposition: "And, for example, there is no point in blushing for having cherished freedom, but only for having defended it badly [. . .]. And similarly, there is no reason to blame ourselves; we must, on the contrary, be proud of ourselves for having the cult of the human being."[148] Voices in exile, who said openly what could only be inferred in metropolitan France, came to the aid of the opposition. On August 17, 1940, Mauriac was harangued by Maurice Schumann on the London radio waves between two of General de Gaulle's appeals.[149] In New York—where several had taken refuge, including André Maurois; Jules Romains; Julien Green; the editor Jacques Schiffrin, who published works in French there; and a number of teachers including Georges Gurvitch and Claude Lévi-Strauss—the Catholic philosopher Jacques Maritain wrote *À travers le désastre*, which circulated illicitly in the Southern zone as early as 1941, before being reissued the following year by the underground Éditions de Minuit. It constituted an accusation of the Vichy regime and an indictment of the culture of disavowal: "It is utterly irrational to see in the sins of the French the direct and decisive reason for that defeat when the sins of their conquerors cry to heaven."[150] The moral censorship that raged in the Southern zone raised fears of the worst attacks against cultural heritage: "The hardest will be to give up Stendhal," declared René Lalou, pleading for the great works of the past in the literary pages of *Le Figaro*.[151] But it was above all the accusation launched in the summer of 1940 against the "bad masters," namely the recognized writers from the interwar period, rendered responsible for the defeat, which provoked a veritable outcry among the targeted authors, their critics, and their allies. Since they could with good reason equate the defense of their works to the safeguarding of the national heritage, they were all the more disposed to convert their personal indignation into an active opposition.

Formed around the literary page of *Le Figaro* and a group of newer reviews—*Poésie 40, 41* in Villeneuve, *Fontaine* in Algiers, followed in 1941 and 1942 by *Confluences* in Lyon, *Les Cahiers du Rhône* in Switzerland, and *Messages* in Paris—on the side of small-scale production, a struggle was engaged to regain literary autonomy. The conditions of occupation lent this struggle the form of a reaffirmation of national tradition ("French spirit") like a universalism, in the tradition of the Enlightenment. It was the exercise of thought and art that took on a patriotic value in the struggle against the obscurantism and barbarism of the forces destroying thought. In Algiers, the issue of the review *Fontaine* published in July 1940 was seized. It opened with these lines:

> The French victory is to be able to answer with names. Are we conscious enough of our poets? [. . .] At an hour when the confusion of planes attains an abusive power, France, to be worthy of its mission, has a duty to reestablish the true hierarchy. What makes its pure greatness has not been vanquished, and could not be vanquished except if, by ignorance of itself, by the misdeeds of a repentance not without phariseeism, and also by the action of those who have long called out against the heights of its arts, for the only reason that they can't reach them, it came to disown itself [. . .].[152]

These newer reviews, which played a subversive role, would contribute to the symbolic reunification of the shattered literary field, giving voice to the writers of "refusal" and to banned authors (writing under pseudonyms) or those who were exiled like Bernanos (*Fontaine* would thus reproduce fragments of his *Lettre aux Anglais* in the November–December issue, during the coup d'état in Algiers). At the instigation of Aragon in particular, they formed networks that would promote recruitment for the literary Resistance, without the move underground being automatic.

The struggle for the reappropriation of the "French spirit" would be the banner of the intellectual Resistance, from the Communists to the Catholics, by way of the humanist generation that discovered patriotic feeling. It made possible the alliance between Communists and non-Communists that characterized clandestine recruitment: *"French thought must become legal in France"* demanded the underground Communist review *La Pensée libre* in February 1941.[153] "We will save the honor of French literature with our writings. We will castigate the traitors sold to the enemy [. . .]. We will defend the values that have made the glory of our civilization," declared the manifesto of the Front national des écrivains, future Comité national des écrivains (CNE).[154] The defense of the national cultural heritage would also be the vocation of the underground Éditions de Minuit, in order to signify that "to be French is before all else a state of mind," according to James Steel's expression. On this subject he would evoke the library of the uncle and niece in the first novel published by Minuit, *Le Silence de la mer*, which describes the silent refusal attitude of the niece in front of a German officer, a "true pantheon of French culture, in the face of which the German officer billeted at their house is amazed."[155] In protest of the use that the flatterers of the National Revolution made of the author of

Jeanne d'Arc, the Éditions de Minuit published selected excerpts showing that "the intransigent and revolutionary patriotism of Péguy had discerned with an extraordinary lucidity the capitulations to which the spirit of cowardice can lead a government of treason."[156] Rallying in the name of maintaining the "flame of French thought," while claiming universal values that established France's prestige in foreign lands—"Once again France has *her word* to say. Her word: Liberty," wrote Forez alias François Mauriac in *Le Cahier noir*[157]—also offered the advantage of reconciling different political tendencies. The editorial project of the Éditions de Minuit, as analyzed by Anne Simonin, was thus inspired by an "idealistic and ideal" vision of the fatherland which,[158] thanks to the primacy of the unitary line and the common designation of Vichy as the enemy, allowed for a compromise between two conceptions of the Resistance: the attitude of "non-violent refusal" faced with the occupant that belonged to the humanist and pacifist generation, and the armed struggle advocated by the Communists.[159]

The Literary Foundations of Political Allegiance

While the conjuncture of national crisis and the literary field's loss of autonomy led to a redefinition of the stakes, that redefinition did not appear ex nihilo. It operated largely according to rationales that predated the crisis and were specific to the literary world. The tendency of writers to intervene on the political scene, the internal struggles, and their underlying structural opposition were not born of the defeat. The statistical approach—and especially factorial analysis—will allow us to understand all that writers' political attitudes during the Occupation owed to a field effect.

THE STRUCTURAL FACTORS BEHIND WRITERS' POLITICAL MOBILIZATION

The over-politicization induced by the circumstances should not mask the fact that writers' engagement under the Occupation also depended on endogenous factors of the literary field's "politicization" that preceded it. The ethical responsibilities that were associated, on both the right and left, with the figure of the intellectual since the Dreyfus affair, as well as the experience of the first worldwide conflict, during which the influence of Action française in intellectual circles reached its peak, contributed to the relative discredit of art for art's sake, and its corollary, the "ivory tower." I will come back to the debates surrounding the responsibility of the writer in the next chapter. In the absence of comparable data for earlier periods, it is difficult to know if writers' degree of involvement in public life really increased during the interwar period. Historians and witnesses nonetheless agree that the 1930s, especially after February 6, 1934, were a moment of widespread mobilization. Yet this mobilization is often explained by the raising of the international stakes, to the detriment of structural factors: the conditions of production, conditions of professional practice, the political supply, morphological evolutions, and the repertoire of representations were all transformed. The widespread mobilization of writers had, in fact, no equivalent among artists or musicians. Montherlant explained the constraint weighing on writers: "A painter, a sculptor, a composer of music is not expected to always *say his piece* on everything and nothing [...]. But a writer, yes. If there is reluctance, he will be reputed to 'shirk his duty.'"[160] Even though existing works, notably on the conditions of writers' professional practice, do not yet allow me to draw conclusive arguments, I will propose here an initial assessment of the convergence of these different factors, based on a few observations.

We can list multiple signs of this "politicization" of the literary field, and its accompanying radicalization of options. On the left, it runs from the reconciliation in the late 1920s between the surrealist group and the Communist Party, followed by alliances and divisions, to the position taken in favor of Communism by Gide, the archetypal intellectual hidden in his ivory tower, in 1932. On the right, it can be illustrated by the political hardening of the conservative right, which rallied the neo-pacifist camp, as well as by the political evolution of the young generation of Action française that sought out more "revolutionary" routes including Fascism. In 1930, Marcel Arland noted:

> I don't see a lesser danger in the contamination that politics imposes on literature today. The attacks of Mr. Julien Benda [*La Trahison des clercs*, 1927] don't change anything. A writer, whether he wants to or not, is forced to contend with political parties. He cannot write a book that is not immediately judged to be on the right or the left."[161]

In fact, as during the Dreyfus affair,[162] politics became a way of defining positions in the literary field. The time of literary schools had passed. While they still experienced a real profusion during the Belle Époque, few lasted. Even though it formed against the symbolism that had produced some of its contributors, *La NRF* defied any affiliation with a school from its creation in 1909. The adoption of an aesthetic concept defined by formal procedures and privileged thematics, which had characterized group strategies of distinction throughout the nineteenth century, was now almost entirely limited to the avant-gardes; even then, it was no longer enough: cubism and Dadaism certainly marked the period of the Great War, but the surrealist group would affirm its identity and establish itself in the 1920s through an ethical engagement.[163]

In the disappearance of literary schools, we can see the effects of the novel's domination; at the end of the nineteenth century, it had ousted poetry (this domination should itself be related to the expansion of the book market and the decline of the traditional forms of patronage). Literary schools made way for movements that united new or marginal writers on the basis of identity: the regionalist literature movement, the "Catholic literary Renaissance" movement, the populist literature movement, the proletarian literature movement.[164] While these forms of categorization most often expressed unfortunate power relations within the literary field—writers from the province who could not manage to establish themselves on the Paris scene, newcomers more or less deprived of the economic, social, and/or cultural resources necessary to attain the most prestigious authorities of legitimization such as *La NRF*, or even gain entrance to salons and society—they also included ethical, even political claims that gave them greater visibility and allowed them to take their place in editorial production by targeting a specific audience. Evidence of this includes the multiplication of specialized literary anthologies—*Le Nouvel âge littéraire* (1930) by Henry Poulaille at Valois, *L'Anthologie de la renaissance catholique* (1938) by Louis Chaigne at Alsatia, the numerous anthologies devoted to regional literature or rural life and so forth—the creation of reviews, collections such as the "Roseau d'or" at Plon or "Romans de la vie nouvelle" at Valois, and specific authorities of consecration such as the Province Academy (1924) or the Populist Prize (founded in 1931 and reinstated in 1939).

The appearance of politico-literary weeklies and of reviews, groups, and circles oriented toward the construction of a new world and with which writers were largely associated (including *Europe, Commune, Esprit, Réaction, Ordre nouveau, Combat*, etc.) constituted another indicator of this process of "politicization."[165] They competed on one hand with general interest reviews like the *Revue des deux mondes* and on the other with big literary reviews like *La NRF*. The growing space allotted to current events in *La NRF* starting in the 1930s, due to pressure from Gaston Gallimard and André Gide, is significant in this regard.[166] Politics had indeed become a mode of demarcation and differentiation in the literary field.

The launching of the politico-literary weeklies, where writers played a leading role, was closely linked to the strategies of the publishing houses: it followed transformations in the publishing market, increased competition, and the search for new advertising methods[167] to reach a cultured audience who had grown thanks to generalized instruction.[168] In 1924, to counter *Les Nouvelles littéraires*, created two years earlier with the support of the publisher Larousse, and whose links with *La NRF* worried competitors, Fayard founded *Candide*. Directed by the Maurrassian Jacques Bainville, *Candide* set itself apart from its rival through its treatment of current events alongside its cultural pages, and through its avowed political coloration; its innovative formula would meet with great success. It reached 265,000 copies in 1930 and saw its circulation peak at 465,000 in 1936.[169] Following this model, the Éditions de France launched *Gringoire* in 1928. This weekly of the extreme right with populist accents was directed by Horace de Carbuccia and would reach a circulation of 650,000 copies in 1938. Its two star writers were Henri Béraud and Roland Dorgelès. *Je suis partout* first came out in 1930; also by Fayard, it united Pierre Gaxotte with the young Maurrassian guard who would evolve toward Fascism (see above). In 1932, Gallimard launched *Marianne* under the direction of Emmanuel Berl; he wanted a left-leaning review to compete with the two large weeklies on the right, but this project would fail (after maxing out at 120,000 copies, circulation decreased, and Gallimard did away with it altogether in 1937).[170] Meanwhile, Plon responded with an extreme-right version the following year, with the participation of Maurice Bardèche, Brasillach, Abel Bonnard, and Henri Massis (named after the current year: *1933, 1934,* and so forth). Finally, in 1935, the weekly *Vendredi* was founded and directed by two writers, the radical-Socialist André Chamson and Jean Guéhenno, an SFIO (French Socialist Party) sympathizer; they were soon joined by the journalist and Communist sympathizer Andrée Viollis. *Vendredi* meant to embody the union of the left against Fascism in the intellectual field.[171] Thanks to the participation of renowned writers like André Gide, Romain Rolland, Alain, and Julien Benda, it printed 100,000 copies.

On both the right and the left, contributions were brilliant, and social recruitment showed that substantial socioeconomic and educational resources were necessary to join them. The writers who contributed to these periodicals were most often born in Paris, or they emigrated there at a younger age than most of their cohort.[172] They were more likely to have attended the grandes écoles than their colleagues (one out of three versus one writer out of four for the whole of our population). *Je suis partout* attracted the highest number of École normale supérieure (ENS) graduates (six, or twice the average of the other weeklies), for whom criticism and journalism were potential careers.[173] Failing their *agrégation* exams was not the only factor that determined these students' turn toward the literary field: it is hard to know the extent to which the failure of someone like Robert Brasillach was due to his decreased involvement in favor of literary journalism (he had just begun contributing to *Action française*). As Robert Smith has shown, ENS students' move away from education was most frequent (about a third) in the fraction of sons best endowed in economic capital (their fathers were property owners, senior civil servants, in the liberal professions), especially those of Parisian origin. This is a sign of the devaluation of teaching careers with the new competition from the universities, but also a sign of the resources necessary to plan on a career that was at once more prestigious and more risky, in the case of the literary field (Jules Romains and Jean-Paul Sartre would only leave teaching when their literary career was settled, while Jean Guéhenno would stay his whole life). These relatively atypical properties of ENS graduates who moved away from teaching[174] perhaps explain the phenomenon, already described,[175] of the connections that a number of them maintained with the politico-social networks of the right and with the French Academy, where they constituted a quarter of the membership. Let us remember that this was a period when the ENS passed for a bastion of Republican ideology.

The politico-literary weeklies' new editorial supply reinforced the introduction of a journalistic logic into the literary field, at the very moment when journalism was undergoing increased professionalization. Widely practiced in the nineteenth century, the recourse to journalism as a means of subsistence and as a stepping stone toward a literary career was disavowed by those writers who came from the most privileged segments of society. At the turn of the century, fictional representations of journalists oscillated between sordidness and venality.[176] Unlike the traditional, "noble" press that regularly hosted great writers, the emergence during the Second Empire of the "little press," the cheap popular press that recruited a new category of journalists with more modest origins, had deepened the divide between journalists and literary men. Starting at the end of the nineteenth century, "among the famous journalists, from now on one out of three ha[d] nothing in common with the literary man, versus one out of five thirty years earlier" according to Marc Martin.[177] The relative decline of traditional literary journalism (criticism and column) in the daily press was nonetheless compensated by two phenomena: on one hand, the appearance of in-depth reporting as a literary genre, in which writers like Joseph Kessel, Paul Morand, Pierre Mac Orlan, and Roger Vailland would distinguish themselves; on the other hand, the development of cultural weeklies that invited writers to comment on events. Big Parisian dailies like *L'Écho de Paris*, *Le Figaro*, and the *Journal des débats* continued, moreover, to attract articles by academicians and high-society writers like André Chaumeix, André Bellessort, Abel Hermant, Abel Bonnard, Henry Bordeaux, and François Mauriac. The opinion press also had its stars: Charles Maurras, Léon Daudet at *Action française*; Aragon and Jean-Richard Bloch at *Ce Soir*, starting in 1937.

Journalism therefore remained both a means of accessing the literary field and a means of subsistence, whether mediocre for the writers of news items and other "articles" who did not benefit from a fixed income, or substantial—often exceeding royalties—for established writers, due to the great disparity in salaries.[178] Half of our population of 185 writers contributed regularly to a daily (*Le Temps, L'Écho de Paris, Action française, Le Figaro, Paris-Soir, Ce Soir*, etc.) and nearly two-thirds wrote more or less regularly for the major outlets. Journalism was the main source of income for one out of four writers.

Thus if editorial and journalist supply and working conditions seemed to elicit writers' intervention in public affairs, the phenomenon of solidified political oppositions in the 1930s was also, more broadly, a social phenomenon that would be exacerbated by international issues. We must also take into account the generational effect, at a time when the "generation of fire" was establishing itself in French society: "In 1930, veterans constituted most of the men between 30 and 60 years old," explains Antoine Prost.[179] In the politico-literary weeklies, this generation was overrepresented (two-thirds of our writers who contributed to *Candide, Gringoire*, and *Je suis partout* were born between 1880 and 1899, whereas they represent 40 percent of the overall population studied). This observation coincides with Bernard Laguerre's assessment of the weeklies *Marianne* and *Vendredi*, where the "generation of fire" was the best-represented age group in both cases (more than half for *Marianne*, a little less than half for *Vendredi*).[180] Moreover the theme of "action" was privileged by veterans' associations, even if it never resulted in concrete political content.[181] In the intellectual field, the banalization of this theme doubtless favored the rejection of the "ivory tower," already amply encouraged by Maurrassism through its critique of idealism and the "gratuitous games" of the mind.

But what characterized perhaps even better the morphological transformation of the literary field during this period was the newfound recognition of writers emerging from the second "generation of fire," those who experienced the first war when they were very young and were mobilized after patriotic fervor had died down, according to the distinction established by Robert Wohl.[182]

This was the generation—of Aragon, Breton, Eluard, Drieu La Rochelle, Montherlant, Céline, and Giono—who had not mapped out their career before being mobilized; the war was their first socialization in the adult world. Making their entry into the literary field during the 1920s, they established their presence in the 1930s. Their aesthetic project was marked by the search for a frame of reference, for an ethical system, in order to analyze the event as writers.[183] Whereas the war experience formed the basis of the surrealist revolt,[184] it also inspired Montherlant's aesthetic of "virility" (*La Relève du matin*, 1920; *Le Songe*, 1922) and Drieu La Rochelle's thematics of "action," which furthermore allowed him to generalize his individual (familial) experience of social decline through the leitmotif of French "decadence," widespread in the discourse of the right since the beginning of the century (*Mesure de la France*, 1922). It also formed the stylistic violence and the nihilist philosophy of Céline (*Voyage au bout de la nuit*, 1932), the integral pacifism of Giono and his condemnation of the misdeeds of industrial civilization (*Le Grand Troupeau*, 1931). This generation would contribute to the politicization of the literary stakes and give direction to junior writers who, jealous of their elders' wartime decorations (those same elders initially seemed like their brothers), compensated for their lack with political escalation.

Evidence of the establishment of the "generation of fire" could be found in publications on the war, especially novels and narratives, that appeared around 1927–1928, and peaked in 1930.[185] This new production on the war distinguished itself from the first wave of witness literature that broke between 1914 and 1922–1923 by its historical spirit,[186] its will to understand the past in order to prepare the future. The intrusion of History into individual destinies by means of the war made it a fruitful theme for the bildungsroman in the 1930s. Starting in the late 1920s, the novel of analysis and manners, still predominant at the beginning of the decade, gave way to an exploration of contemporary history that proposed both a philosophical, historical, or psychological interpretation of the era's sociopolitical conditions, and an attitude toward them. Massive social frescoes marked the literature of those years: *Les Thibault* (1922–1940) by Roger Martin du Gard,[187] *Les Hommes de bonne volonté* (1932–1946) by Jules Romains, *Le Monde réel* (1934–1944) by Aragon. Whereas, from Henri Barbusse's *Le Feu* to Céline's *Voyage au bout de la nuit*, the experience of modern industrial war had discredited the epic and heroic genre in favor of derision, civil war with a revolutionary vocation offered a favorable frame for the rehabilitation of war heroism, thanks to both its ideal of fighting for justice and the original nature of its urban guerilla warfare.[188] Rehabilitated by a newcomer who did not fight in the war of 1914, André Malraux (from *Les Conquérants*, 1928, to *La Condition humaine*, crowned by the Goncourt Prize in 1933), novels of war heroism found a new source of inspiration in the Spanish Civil War, for both the left and the right, paired with the author's engagement. Examples include *L'Espoir* (1937), a report-novel by Malraux and *Gilles* (1939) by Drieu La Rochelle.

In a shifting literary field, the reconversion of André Gide, which began in 1927 with *Le Voyage au Congo*, no doubt owed something to his concern over maintaining his position there. This was all the more clear since it coincided with the end of a properly literary production, an effect of the twin processes of social aging and consecration: in 1932, his collected works began to appear, and Gide began dedicating himself almost exclusively to his autobiographical writings and, occasionally, to political essay (*Retour de l'URSS*, 1936, and *Retouches à mon "Retour de l'URSS,"* 1937, marking his break with Communism). Gide's statement of support for Communism in 1932 stupefied the literary world. It led to an indignant uproar from his friends—"[it is] strange to see them all, those great bourgeois of *La NRF* [. . .] throw themselves into the mouth of the Bolshevist Eugène," wrote François Mauriac[189]—and this strange "public trial" at the headquarters of Union de la vérité, where he agreed to appear in order to justify himself to his peers. The tendency of the new generations toward political radicalization largely determined the engagement of a writer who was always concerned about cutting himself off from young people, whose expectations he sensed. His peers' exhortations certainly influenced his decision as well. Léon Daudet, who held Gide in high esteem, "predicted" during the very year of his engagement that he would soon find a cause worthy of his gifts.[190] Such injunctions seemed to multiply at that time, indicating the politicization of the literary field. After his election to the French Academy in 1933, François Mauriac was heralded as a future journalist, both in a tribute by Daniel Halévy, and by André Chaumeix, who returned to this theme in his response speech during Mauriac's reception.[191] Paradoxically, these injunctions emanating from the intellectual right would end up creating his most formidable adversaries. Gide's engagement would, in return, contribute to the legitimation of the "prophetic" model—both for François Mauriac, who started making his turn toward anti-Fascism in 1935, and for Ramon Fernandez who, after having almost followed Gide in 1934, made a radical turn the following year to join Drieu La Rochelle on the path to "Fascist Socialism," then into the ranks of the PPF—and, more specifically, the practice of fellow-traveling that people like Louis Martin-Chauffier, Jean Cassou, and Jean-Paul Sartre would illustrate into the 1950s.

In the end, we must relate this evolution to the transformation of the political supply, which simultaneously favored the realization of the "prophetic" option in the literary field and the solidification of ideological oppositions. The rising generation found fuel for its tendency toward political radicalization in the modern ideologies of Communism and Fascism. The ephemeral reconciliation between the surrealists and the PCF (French Communist Party) in 1927 turned into a lasting engagement in the party ranks for people like Aragon and Georges Sadoul, while Breton turned to Trotskyism. At a time when the leagues' rise to power embodied the ambient anti-parliamentarianism that exploded on February 6, 1934, the PCF's line of openness to the intellectuals, facilitated by the Communist International's reversal of tactics in 1935,[192] enabled new forms of engagement that required neither submission to party discipline nor support of its program. The party encouraged or initiated mobilization efforts in the struggle against capitalism and Fascism, such as the Association des écrivains et artistes révolutionnaires (AEAR), and took an active part in anti-Fascist intellectual movements like the Comité de vigilance des intellectuels antifascistes (CVIA) and the Congrès pour la défense de la culture.[193] Among writers, at least one out of ten was a member of the AEAR, and almost as many belonged to the CVIA. Between 1930 and 1934 the proportion of fellow-traveling writers doubled in comparison with the 1920s (from 2.7 percent to 5.4 percent); after 1934, it was the number of party members that increased (from 3.2 percent between 1930 and 1934 to 5.9 percent between 1934 and 1939), at a time when the PCF experienced tremendous growth (from less than 30,000 at the end of 1933 to 87,000 at the end of 1934, then 328,000 in 1937) and unprecedented electoral successes.[194] The call for bids created by the union of the left after February 6, 1934,[195] and especially by the struggle against Fascism, which Hitler's rise to power presented as a threatening danger, favored a much more widespread mobilization of intellectuals around the Congrès pour la défense de la culture, held at the Mutualité in July 1935, and around the weekly *Vendredi*: anti-Fascism and "the defense of culture" were immediately declared a universal and nonpartisan cause.

On the right, as the Action française league became more academic and formed alliances with conservative fractions, its prestige was diminished in the eyes of the new literary generations. After February 6, 1934, young militants from Action française left a Maurras who was at once too lyrical and too nostalgic to be the spokesman for Fascism in France (which also recruited from the left). At this time, the Fascistic circle of influence represented between 5.4 percent and 8.6 percent of our population, depending on whether we include the leagues of the extreme right (excluding Action française, which totaled 4.3 percent of the whole). But the advent of the Popular Front, the Ethiopian war, and the Spanish Civil War would unite the intellectual forces of the conservative right and the extreme right in a neo-pacifist struggle for the "defense of the West" against an anti-Fascist movement led by other intellectuals. The formation of these two well-defined camps, each of which assembled about a quarter of the whole of our population (meaning that one out of two writers was directly involved in this confrontation), simply revealed the constitutive structural oppositions of the literary field, whose foundations—as we will see—were as much literary as political. Despite the shuffling brought about by the dissensions surrounding the politics of nonintervention in Spain and surrounding the Munich agreement, then the German-Soviet pact, these were essentially the same two camps that existed under the Occupation. One side rallied to the new powers, while the other formed the literary Resistance.

THE RELATIVE WEIGHT OF SOCIAL PROPERTIES

While they do not, by themselves, account for the political choices of writers under the Occupation, the global distribution of social properties (age, social origins, educational capital) among different political possibles offers an initial template for the relationships between dispositions and political tendencies. Thus, close to two-thirds of the sixty-four writers of our population who were engaged in civil or armed Resistance were less than forty years old, and almost the totality (90 percent) were less than fifty years old in 1940. On the other hand, more than two-thirds of the Vichyist writers were then over fifty years old, and almost half were over sixty (they represent between 14 percent and 20 percent of our population depending on whether we include those who would eventually develop a more favorable attitude to the Resistance). These figures only reconfirm the relationship between social aging and conservatism on one side, between youth and protest on the other, along with the propensity for taking risks (clandestinity, in this case) which decreases with age. The writers who were more or less involved in the Collaboration (forty-four, or 24 percent of our population) occupied, from an age standpoint, an intermediary position between these two extremes: half were between forty and sixty years old, the average age for reaching the peak of one's literary career, while the rest were equally divided between the other age groups.

To a certain extent, we can also socially characterize each of these three positions, keeping in mind that intermediary zones subsisted between the extremes. Thus, among the Vichyists, the sons of senior and mid-level civil servants (including military but excluding teachers) were overrepresented (at close to a third, their rate was twice that of our entire population), whereas they were underrepresented among the resisting writers (6 percent). A minimal interpretation of this statement could translate an inherited disposition toward allegiance to the state as the ultimate guarantor of order, and thus a lesser propensity for dissidence among those writers with a civil service background.[196] According to a maximal and more historical interpretation, comparing this characteristic to the age of the people concerned and to the fact that they were also more likely on average to have provincial origins than their colleagues (two-thirds versus half of the whole of writers),[197] we can view these writers as the direct heirs of those former "elites" who used to form the "France of the notables" and that the Third Republic had deprived of social and political power in favor of the new Republican "elites."[198] Nostalgic for a rural France and for the local ecclesiastic power with which their fathers were allied, they chiefly constituted the traditionalist extreme of the Vichy regime. The first definition could apply to someone like Georges Lecomte, the son of a postmaster in Mâcon, descended from an old Burgundian family; and the second to someone like Charles Maurras, the son of a very Catholic civil servant from Martigues, descended from an old Provençal family; both men were over seventy years old in 1940. But these examples have only a general indicative value: the extreme case of Maurras clearly shows that family values were not reappropriated wholesale by sons who did not follow in their fathers' social footsteps, especially for intellectuals who, out of scholastic habit as well as their propensity to stand out, subjected these (reappropriated or rejected) values to a rationalization and a systematization that made them unrecognizable.

The Resistance writers were, on the other hand, most often the product of intellectual and artistic fractions, including teachers (this was true of almost one in three Resistance writers, versus one in four for the whole of the population), whereas these social fractions were represented three times less often among the writers close to the Collaboration. While the latter were the most Parisian of writers (since their childhood), they were globally less well endowed in all kinds of assets, especially inherited or acquired cultural capital. They were most often recruited from the petty bourgeoisie (a third as compared to a little more than a quarter of the whole of writers); almost a quarter of them held a degree inferior to the baccalaureate, which is twice the rate of the whole group (they were also twice as likely to have attended an upper primary school or to have had no post-primary education—16 percent versus 7 percent). Among them, 41 percent had no higher education, versus 30 percent of the whole group; finally, they were more likely to have had an "incident" during their academic career. Whether for material reasons, health reasons, or due to a relative academic failure, this statement applies to 40 percent of them (with 18 percent experiencing an academic failure) versus less than 20 percent of the Resistance writers and 30 percent of the whole group (who experienced academic failure at the rate of 9 percent and 13 percent, respectively).[199] This phenomenon would probably have been more pronounced if our sample included those numerous collaborationist journalists with literary pretentions but no body of work and who were therefore situated on the edge of the literary field, like Henri Poulain. The son of a locksmith, he was a secretary at *Je suis partout* who distinguished himself in the newspaper's literary pages during the Occupation before retiring along with Brasillach in 1943; in his memoirs, Rebatet described him in these terms: "The only one on our team who was talentless as a writer, a Normand, nitpicky, curlicued, animated by a proletarian hatred toward Lesca [the administrator of *Je suis partout*]."[200]

The relationship to school partially explains the development of anti-intellectualism among a number of collaborationist writers, particularly the "disinherited" heirs, that is to say those who deviated from the career their family intended for them due to an academic failure. They tended to contrast the "intellectualism of 'ace test takers'" with the aristocratic values of action, the cult of the body, and sports, which were favorite themes in the works of writers like Montherlant or Drieu La Rochelle.[201] Their propensity for anti-intellectualism was undoubtedly inspired more by the relationship between an academic failure and a declining family situation, as in the two cases cited, than by the academic failure itself, since this was a relatively frequent step on the path leading to the writing profession.

Among the intellectuals of the first generation, whose loss of status came from above, anti-intellectualism could be born of confrontation with certified agents of authorized language, and from the feeling of inferiority it engendered. Born in 1913 in Rouen to a working-class family (on his father's side, he was the grandson of a manual laborer who was also a militant Socialist; on his mother's side, of a bistro owner), Lucien Combelle, who described himself in his memoirs as "a kid with a primary school degree whom Maurras, the Sorbonne, and Gide united to disorient," evoked both his fascination and his uneasiness with respect to those whom he thought—although he was usually wrong (notably about Petitjean)—to be graduates of the ENS:

> Ah the guys, how could I forget them? Those captivating normaliens, fascinating products of a hypertrophied intellectualism, with sophisticated mechanisms catapulting them right and left [...]. But how do I look, talking like this about a "caste," when some of its members have tolerated my presence? For they knew that I was not one of them, not even the hardworking fuddy-duddy from the neighboring Faculty! [...] But this is how, thanks to them, I learned at my expense what it cost to love rhetoric, especially when it is seasoned with plebeian words.[202]

A former Camelot du roi who was repelled by Maurrassian neoclassicism, he turned to Gide and Rémy de Gourmont, adopting the position of "art for art's sake" in the review *Arts et idées*, which he founded in 1936 while attending the Sorbonne and working as a teacher in a private high school, before becoming Gide's secretary from 1937 to 1938. "Art without labels" quickly proved to be an illusion, or at least an untenable position for a young pretender during this period, as suggested by the reference to Malraux that Combelle made while reconstructing his career: "But Malraux still makes your pen tremble, which proves that politics prowls around your little chapel of *Arts et idées*. Gourmont and Léautaud are alibis, aristocrats that placed you more to the right than the left, anti-democratic diplomas; with them, you were sure to find the Republic vulgar."[203] An anti-Communist and anti-Semite, filled with resentment toward his class of origin, he was hardly receptive to Gide's influence (although he would remain very grateful to him);[204] he found his prophet in Céline, who reconciled him to his awkward position in the social circles that had adopted him and which he would hold responsible for his political evolution toward Fascism. The desertion of the Parisian scene under the Occupation gave him the unhoped-for chance to stand out: he grew closer to Drieu La Rochelle, contributed to *La Gerbe* and *Je suis partout*, and obtained first the chief editorship, then, in June 1942, the direction of *La Révolution nationale*, voice of Eugène Deloncle's Mouvement social révolutionnaire (MSR), which had become a "political and literary" weekly.[205]

Social properties in the form of dispositions thus seem to have had a certain influence on political attitudes. But their weak contribution to polarization in factorial analysis, aside from age, illustrates the effect of refraction exerted by the literary field. In fact, they only act through the mediation of positions occupied within the field.

POSITIONS AND POSITION-TAKINGS

Indicators of the social, literary, and political trajectories of the population of 185 writers who were active during the war were submitted to Multiple Correspondence Analysis (MCA).[206] It reveals the structure of the literary field under the Occupation, which was organized around four clusters (see figures 1.1 and 1.2): writers who enjoyed notoriety in the temporal order (on the left), writers who had achieved notoriety in the symbolic order (on the bottom), avant-garde writers (on the right), and writers who were weakly endowed with symbolic capital (on top). Factorial analysis also sheds light on the homology between positions occupied in the field and political position-taking. We will work to understand this homology by interpreting the two first factors of MCA, which present its major tendencies.

The first factor of the analysis refers to the volume of notoriety in the temporal order. It opposes the writers occupying a temporally dominant position to the writers occupying a temporally dominated position, an opposition that merges on this (horizontal) axis with the split between a pole of large-scale production and a pole of small-scale production. This opposition is specified on four levels, according to the indicators that contributed the most to the axis's formation: age, place of publication, literary genre (novelists vs. poets), and type of recognition; or rather, the degree of institutional consecration (from the most academic to the least academic extreme).

On one side, we find the fashionably exotic or regionalist novelists: Claude Farrère, Louis Bertrand, Henry Bordeaux, Joseph de Pesquidoux, André Demaison, and Jean de La Varende, who published in the old houses that aimed for short-term profitability, that is to say rapid sales, large print runs and popular collections (especially Flammarion and Albin Michel).[207] Otherwise, they published with the more "academic" editors, mainly the Catholic Plon, but also Fasquelle or Perrin (see figures 1.1 and 1.2). On the other side, we find poets formed by the surrealist movement like Paul Eluard, or newcomers seeking new forms of poetic expression that would surpass surrealism, and who were mentored by Pierre Jean Jouve, Pierre Reverdy, or Max Jacob; these included the poetic realism of Francis Ponge or Eugène Guillevic, the lyric poetry of Jean Tardieu, Michel Leiris, or André Frénaud, the metaphysical poetry of Pierre Emmanuel, and the École de Rochefort. They were admitted into the small publishing houses born under the Occupation, especially Seghers and, in some cases (Emmanuel, Ponge, Leiris, Tardieu) into the "Métamorphoses" series that Jean Paulhan ran at Gallimard.

Whereas these young poets published in the small poetry reviews created right before the war or under the Occupation (*Les Cahiers du Sud, Poésie 40, 41* . . ., *Messages, Fontaine, Confluences*), the successful novelists often contributed, before the war and/or under the Occupation, to the very "academic" *Revue des deux mondes*, or to the politico-literary weeklies with a large circulation such as *Candide, Gringoire,* and *La Gerbe.* The representatives of this pole of large-scale production also contributed to the great dailies of the right like *Le Temps, L'Écho de Paris,* and *Le Petit Parisien* (which welcomed a number of academicians and Goncourt jurors during the Occupation). By contrast, the opposing pole groups writers who did not write for the mainstream press, with the exception, for some, of the weekly of prewar Fascist writers, *Vendredi* (see figure 1.2).

The variables concerning political position-taking, pro-Vichy and collaborationist on one side, pro-Resistance on the other, also strongly contributed to the formation of the first axis. The opposition between the pole of large-scale production and the pole of small-scale production intersects on this first axis with the political cleavage between those who supported the acting forces and those who aligned with the opposition,[208] a (partial) intersection resulting

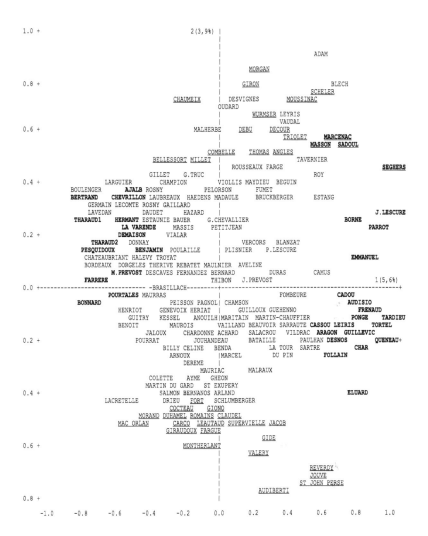

Fig. 1.1 The literary field under the Occupation: the writers. Multiple Correspondence Analysis. Plane of the first and second axes of inertia: the space of writers. (The individuals corresponding to the strongest absolute contributions have been indicated in bold for the first factor, and underlined for the second, underlined and bolded for both.)

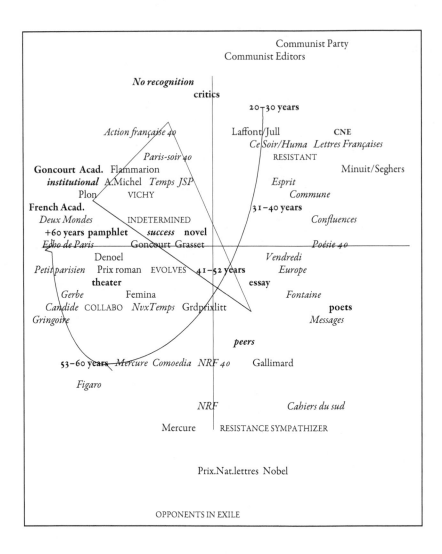

Fig. 1.2 The literary field under the Occupation: positions and position-takings. A simplified representation of the Correspondence Analysis (the space of properties). *Note*: This graph was reconstructed based on the one that represents the variables on the planes of the first and second axes of inertia of the analysis of multiple correspondences, which can be found in appendix 2. Periodicals are in italics. Age is bolded. Types of recognition are in italics and bolded. Political position-takings are in CAPS. Publishers and literary prizes are in plain type.

from structural factors: since the pole of large-scale production was closely tied to the economic field and the media space, it was caught up in the chain of participation in the structures of the Collaboration that I described earlier.

The relationship between a position and political position-taking appears clearly through the lens of literary genre (see figure 1.2). While a third of the novelists in our population (and almost half the dramatic authors) opted for Collaboration, while no renowned novelist or playwright aside from Mauriac participated in underground activity, nearly two-thirds of the poets engaged in a literary Resistance that did not radically alter, for them, the conditions of production. Accustomed to limited printings, to thin booklets that circulated only among the members of a coterie, it was as though their practice predisposed them to clandestinity and secrecy. Yet just as circumstantial factors (like the politics of Nazi propaganda authorities that promoted political books to the detriment of novels, or the uncertain conditions of life that diverted from steady projects) do not offer sufficient explanations, no intrinsic link between literary genre and engagement can be established. The literary Resistance had its novelists, from the mysterious Vercors to André Chamson, along with Édith Thomas, and the Collaboration had its poets, including André Salmon who went so far as to declare his support for the Legion of French Volunteers against Bolshevism (LVF). The relation between genre and political choice was the expression of a particular state of literary power relations. These power relations were expressed through a combination of criteria—age, religion, sex, social position, notoriety—that were retranslated according to the logic proper to that space of production of symbolic goods called the literary field.

If genre immediately appears as a factor structuring this space, it is because it was one of the determining factors of social position, both in the literary field and in the field of power:[209] strong differentiated conditions of professional practice were associated with each genre, from the best-selling novelist who received a monthly paycheck from his publishing house and supplemented his income with prepublication serials in periodicals with large circulations, to the poet who had to resort to a day job (or exercise another profession) in order to survive. The opposition between poets and novelists thus looks like a variant of another one: the opposition between the pole of small-scale production and the pole of large-scale production, which constitutes a first matrix of political attitudes in this crisis situation.

This structural opposition can be further nuanced through institutional affiliation. Two authorities strongly contributed to the formation of the first axis: the French Academy on one hand and the Comité national des écrivains (CNE) on the other (see figure 1.2). Like the reviews, these two authorities embodied the association between the three kinds of variables that formed the opposition on the first axis: age, position in the literary field (genre and place of publication), and aesthetic and political position-taking. The fact that the opposition between a pole of institutional consecration (the Goncourt Academy is situated near the French Academy) and a "nonacademic" pole intersects with the split between "old" and "young," with, on one side, authors over sixty, and on the other, those under forty, is not surprising. More interesting here is the imbrication of literary and political variables that emerges from the simple comparison of an institution with a cultural vocation (the French Academy) and an organization with a political vocation (the CNE). The fact that this opposition between a nonacademic pole and an academic pole is superimposed, on the first axis, with the political split between dissidence and support of the acting forces (Vichy or the Collaboration) is significant. The partial redundancy between age and institutional affiliation appears in this light as sociologically significant: in a situation of national crisis, the intergenerational struggle that ordinarily opposes the young pretenders to the literary establishment takes on a political form.

It is the French Academy's particular position in the literary field as the guardian of an orthodoxy close to the demand of the fractions holding economic and political power that disposed it to play a political role. Conversely, at the other pole, the over-politicization of the literary stakes led to the formation of an organization with a political vocation (the CNE) around a set of *de-crystallized* positions, either because they were situated on the margins of the field (young pretenders or Communists), or due to the schisms of established groups (like *La NRF*) and the (self-) exclusion of a number of writers (Aragon, Paulhan, Mauriac, Eluard).

As a product of the crisis, the political association of these de-crystallized positions reveals, a contrario, the relative homogeneity of social positions at the institutionalized pole.[210] Whereas for the young writers of the CNE, being a writer was a way of life ("artistic" or "bohemian"), for the academicians, it was a social status. Whereas one group collected literary distinctions and honors (prizes, institutional consecrations, Legion of Honor) along with academic titles (diplomas), the other group often chose to give up their social status, without, however, ceasing to soak up all sources of knowledge, from the classical humanities (literature, philosophy) to the young social science disciplines (psychology, sociology, ethnology), the new tendencies of German philosophy (Husserl, Heidegger), and even the occult sciences. "I didn't want to take exams. I was part of that Gidian generation that wanted life without security, like that, difficult . . . the slightly stupid side of Lafcadio. But I worked a lot [. . .]. It had given me a reputation as a philosopher. You know, Paris is bizarre," Jean Lescure said to me in an interview; he also wrote in his memoirs, "We were formed in a certain idea of literature that excluded considering it as a profession. Or in any case earning our living at it. For material needs, we would have to look elsewhere."[211] "It is not from the literary point of view that surrealism interested me, but as a way of life. It was the total revolt. At the time, I did not want to become a writer. For me surrealism represented everything," Raymond Queneau would declare.[212] From 1932 to 1939, after distancing himself from surrealism, he followed the teachings of Alexandre Koyré and Alexandre Kojève on Hegel at the École pratique des hautes études and participated, with Michel Leiris and Georges Bataille among others, in the Collège de Sociologie experiment, all while immersing himself in the works of René Guénon on Eastern thought and traditionalism. On the eve of the Phoney War, he noted in his journal "that if war broke out, I would *personally* (affecting me, as a little individual) find quite funny that it be so at the time when, crowning 6 years of psychoanalysis [...], I will finally 'earn a living'—and when the publication of my novel in the N.R.F. might resemble a 'recognition.' That a modest success might escape me *thanks* to a war would be quite delightful."[213]

Conversely, far from the romantic image of the damned creator, the academicians were "set up" at a very young age under the control of their families, often exercising a profession which they would only leave once they were sure of making a comfortable living from their writing. Living in the upper-class neighborhoods, associated with members of high society and the salons where "good taste" was developed, they were its authorized guardians and participated, as official representatives of French culture, in the circles of politico-social reflection and the authorities of power: Cercle Fustel de Coulanges, Comité franco-allemand, Comité France-Amérique, Conseil national de Vichy, and so forth.

At the academic pole, the association between institutional affiliation and political position-taking suggests the mediating role played by most authorities of consecration between the Vichy regime and Paris collaborationism. It is not by chance if, among the individuals who most contributed to the formation of the axis, we find precisely those who played this role of mediator at an institutional or ideological level, including Abel Bonnard, Abel Hermant, and Louis Bertrand for the French Academy, and René Benjamin, Jean Ajalbert, and Jean de La Varende for the Goncourt Academy. At the other pole, the superposition suggests a hypothesis that I will develop later, concerning the affinities of position underlying the clandestine alliance between Communists and non-Communists. The pivotal role of Eluard and Aragon, who combines all the properties characteristic of this pole—surrealist affiliation; threefold affiliation to *La NRF*, Gallimard, and the Communist Party; contribution to small literary reviews; underground engagement—becomes obvious here, illustrating the charismatic attraction that these older writers exerted over the young generation of poets that emerged under the Occupation (despite being past their forties, they figure among the authors who helped form the axis).

The literary field was thus structured, first of all, around the opposition between a temporally dominant pole, formed by institutionalized writers who accumulated all kinds of capital (economic, educational, social) and enjoyed a "worldly" notoriety in high society, and a temporally dominated pole, chiefly composed of young pretenders in social ascension, deprived of economic resources but endowed with an important cultural capital that was both inherited and acquired; they pursued the recognition of peers and symbolic profits. The partial superposition between this structural opposition and the principal political opposition illustrates the homology between political attitudes and the positions occupied in the literary field. While the majority of representatives of the first pole rallied around the new powers (the Vichy regime and/or Collaboration), most of the representatives of the second engaged in underground action. It is this opposition that Jean Paulhan expressed when he wrote to Guillaume de Tarde in October 1940: "Let us say nothing of [Alphonse de] Chateaubriant. He is half mad. But (in spite of the distrust I may have for writers "of good company"), I would not have thought that Mr. A[bel] Hermant, Mr. [Jacques] Boulenger, and Mr. [Abel] Bonnard could go so far into filth."[214]

SYMBOLIC POWER AND TEMPORAL POWER

This first model of analysis must, of course, be nuanced. All positions are far from being represented. The second axis of MCA, which does not correspond to a political split, gives us a better grasp of the principles of hierarchization of this space. Formed by the indicators of contemporary and long-term recognition, (inclusion in literary histories and dictionaries),[215] it indicates the volume of retained symbolic capital.[216]

This axis sets up a constellation of recognized writers from the interwar period—which almost exactly corresponds to the Gallimard catalogue— dominated by the group that founded *La NRF*: André Gide, Jean Schlumberger, Paul Claudel; and by poets and dramatic authors: Saint-John Perse, Paul Valéry, Pierre Jean Jouve, Pierre Reverdy, Jacques Audiberti, Montherlant, and Jean Giraudoux, opposing them to a minimally cohesive group of individuals who share a lack of participation in *La NRF* and enjoyed no form of literary recognition, at least at that time. They define the limits of the literary field. They were, without the slightest pejorative connotation, "activists" of the literary field, review-makers, text smugglers, columnists, go-betweens, and as such they played an important role as mediators. Chiefly critics, but rather "militant" critics situated at the extremes of the political scale (Maurrassians, like André Bellessort, or Communists like André Wurmser), and thus endowed with a weak power of symbolic consecration; often critics "by default" or authors whose creative project was aborted (Claude Morgan, Édith Thomas). More difficult to characterize socially (the absence of notoriety makes their biographical information much less accessible), they seem to have little in common, apart from the fact that a number of them occupied an "outsider" position with respect to the literary field, because they more often came from foreign countries and/or arrived late to the capital. There we can identify (in the upper-right quadrant) those Communist writers who form a subset, and whose strong representation is due to the central role they played in forming the literary Resistance. Let us note that Aragon and Eluard are better defined by their literary characteristics, which situate them at the pole of small-scale production (see figure 1.1, lower-right quadrant) than by their membership in the Communist Party.

On the whole, the first factor of MCA opposes the pole of small-scale production, where peer recognition is the predominant principle of appreciation, and the pole of large-scale production, stratified according to two modes of recognition, social success and high sales. Representative of the modes of consecration proper to the intermediary sector of publishing (sales figures, literary prizes), high sales lie between the temporally dominant pole (institutional and social consecration) and the temporally dominated pole (specific consecration), on the diagonal running from the lower-right quadrant to the upper-left quadrant. Along with the modality corresponding to the absence of recognition, which is situated on the second axis (at the top), this diagonal forms a triangle, the triangle of recognition (see figure 1.2). The interaction between the first two factors of MCA thus differentiates between two types of notoriety: notoriety in the temporal order and notoriety in the symbolic order, which opens the way to posterity, notably shedding light on the gap between temporal authorities of consecration (the academies) and the distinctions that mark the process of canonization, like the Prix national des lettres and above all the Nobel Prize (see the bottom of figure 1.2). At this pole of strong symbolic notoriety, far from all forms of militancy, we find Resistance sympathizers who adopted a position of "refusal," like Gide, Valéry, Schlumberger, Martin du Gard, Jouve, and exiled opponents like Saint-John Perse, Jules Romains, Bernanos, and Maritain.

The second axis introduces, moreover, a dynamic that simultaneously reconstructs a state of the field in transition and the historical forces that generated this structure. Those who knew momentary success in a previous state of the field saw themselves, at this period of its history, relegated to oblivion, and those who, too young or too marginal, were still or had already been eliminated from play, were both sent to the top of the graph. A hierarchy appears at the pole of small-scale production (centered in the lower-right quadrant), between writers endowed with an important symbolic capital who were undergoing canonization (Gide, Valéry, Claudel), and an avant-garde on the road to recognition (Sartre, Tardieu, René Char, Francis Ponge; see figure 1.1). This stratification of the pole of small-scale production, which represents both a state of power relations and its history, follows a curve parallel to that of age and moment of entry into the field (see figure 1.2).[217] The Mercure de France (with its eponymous review) and the small publishing houses that represented the pole of small-scale production at the beginning of the century would be succeeded by Gallimard and the team of *La NRF*, whereas the young pretenders gathered around small, often ephemeral reviews. This stratification expresses the transformation of the hierarchy of genres: theater and poetry, both still very legitimate at the turn of the century, gave way to the reign of prose, novel, and (philosophical or moral) essay;[218] this reign, however, was soon limited by the phenomenon of poetic renewal led by the avant-gardes (this phenomenon was not just a product of the crisis situation, even though the crisis revealed it and made it highly visible: the contestation of the novel was already part of the surrealist project).

The position of Valéry, Mauriac, and Duhamel, who are better defined on the second axis than on the first, is significant. It reflects their belonging to a literary generation that established itself in the 1920s around *La NRF*. Far from merging with biological age, the generational factor interferes here with other variables, like place of publication and aesthetic choices, along with the type of notoriety. While Pierre Benoit, born like Mauriac and Duhamel in the 1880s, is closer to the "academic" pole, the latter two are more aptly characterized, like their elder Paul Valéry, by their symbolic notoriety than by their membership in the French Academy.

The formidable effect of Gallimard's concentration of symbolic capital visible in MCA is inseparable from the power of consecration that *La NRF* acquired during the interwar period. The interaction between the first two factors of MCA presents the principles of hierarchization that operated at this point in the history of the literary field, through a comparison of the consecration authorities that dominated the two poles of this space, the French Academy and the Goncourt Academy on one side, *La NRF* on the other. If this polarization intersects with the oppositions between "old"/"young" and the poles of large-scale production/small-scale production that are invariables of this space's structure, it is not only because the two academies were structurally (but differently) predisposed, by their proximity to the temporal powers, to convey principles of heteronomy. It is also the historical effect of the accumulation of symbolic capital and competing power of consecration, in the "intellectual" [spiritual] order, by *La NRF*.

Nonetheless, the position of *La NRF* near the center of the first axis also reveals the effect of its growing institutionalization which led, after the defeat, to the splitting of its team. While the review's young guard (and the Gallimard avant-garde: Sartre, Queneau, Leiris, Tardieu) followed Jean Paulhan to the CNE, the "established" critics of *La NRF*, like Ramon Fernandez, and authors on their way to consecration, like Marcel Jouhandeau and Marcel Arland, remained with the review under Drieu La Rochelle's leadership. Without entering here into the details of this split which will be studied later, we can, through the phenomenon of institutionalization, conceptualize the intermediate zones between the poles of small-scale production and large-scale production.

To the extent that it is accompanied by a growing notoriety, social aging is a factor that helps bring together, socially, the writers on the side of small-scale production—especially novelists and playwrights—and those who emerged more through the logic of large-scale production, their symbolic notoriety ultimately yielding temporal profits (in terms of print runs as well as monthly payments from the publisher). It was not by chance that collaborators were recruited from the circumscribed space between worldly success and specific recognition on the one hand, between the age brackets of 41–52 years and 53–60 years on the other (see the lower-left quadrant of figure 1.2). They are those who, already prizewinners and having won an audience, were solicited by the press and had to choose whether to accept or refuse distinctions and temporal successes rather than seek them out. The constraint of publicly taking a political position, whether through direct solicitations or the expectations inscribed in their position, weighed the most heavily on them. This is why, just like what happened during the Dreyfus affair,[219] the intermediate sector between the temporally dominant pole and the temporally dominated pole (where the pole of small-scale production partially intersects with the pole of large-scale production) found itself divided between those who chose to align themselves with the new powers, and those who, more predisposed by their position to defend the autonomy of the literary field, settled into a more or less wait-and-see "refusal." On one side, Roger Martin du Gard, Georges Duhamel, François Mauriac,

André Gide (after his break from Drieu La Rochelle's NRF in April 1941), who chose "refusal." On the other, Paul Morand, Henry de Montherlant, Jean Cocteau, Marcel Aymé, Henri Pourrat, Jean Giono.

The example of Montherlant is eloquent. Could his political positions before the war have been sufficiently ambiguous for the anti-Fascist writers assembled around *Vendredi*, and notably Aragon, his former classmate at Sainte-Croix de Neuilly, to have momentarily hoped to rally the author of *Service inutile* (1935) to their cause?[220] At a time of strong bipolarization of the literary field, Montherlant contributed simultaneously to the *Revue des deux mondes* and *Commune*, the review of the AEAR, to *Candide* and *Vendredi*. He even went so far as to give an article to *Ce Soir*, the Communist daily directed by Jean-Richard Bloch and Aragon. None of this kept the Comité France-Allemagne from inviting him, in 1938, to preside over a conference by Otto Abetz (but he declined the invitation to the Nazi Congress in Nuremberg). This ambivalence translated the oscillation of a moralist between traditionalism and nonconformism. It also expressed the position that he occupied between two poles of the literary field: while his inherited dispositions drove him toward the "academic" and high-society pole that honored him with the Grand Prize for Literature of the French Academy in 1934, his nonconformism and a high standard of intellectual work that kept him from taking the easy way out held him to the pole of small-scale production where he enjoyed the high esteem of his peers,[221] notably André Gide and his NRF colleagues. This knowingly maintained duality allowed him to accumulate symbolic and temporal profits.

L'Équinoxe de septembre (1938) passed for an anti-Munich book. In the 1976 edition of the "memoir" that he drafted at the Liberation to justify his positions under the Occupation, he presented it as "a book that could not be more 'anti-Munich.'"[222] We have two versions of this memoir available, one dated September 13, 1944 (at the time when Montherlant learned he appeared on the "black list" of "undesirable" writers established by the CNE, the first version of which was published in *Le Figaro littéraire* on September 9). The other version was sent in October 1946 to the Comité national d'épuration de gens de lettres. Whereas in the second version, *L'Équinoxe de septembre* is presented as an "anti-Munich" book, the version dated September 1944 was much less categorical:

> The horror that every reasonable man has of war was balanced in me by the belief that we had to put an end to it, to stop "retreating" continuously, and also that in the war (a widespread idea) France would find its virtues and its fraternity again; at the time of the Munich agreement the two tendencies

were balanced in me: this is the symbol contained in the title of the book that I published then (equinox: date when the night is equal to the day). Later, between 38 and 39, I leaned toward war.[223]

Certainly, in the context of the widespread consensus that greeted the Munich agreement, *L'Équinoxe* offered arguments for the anti-Munich contingent. Its author had moreover signed the call to national unity published March 20, 1938, by *Ce Soir*; he was one of thirteen authors including Aragon, Bernanos, Malraux, Maritain, and Mauriac, which placed him in the anti-pacifist camp.[224]

A correspondent for *Marianne* during the "Phoney War," Montherlant settled in the Southern zone after the defeat and would stay there until May 1941. He supported the armistice.[225] Siding with the Vichy regime out of contempt for democracy and sympathy for its authoritarianism, he detached from it as he noticed the increasingly conformist and moralizing tone of the National Revolution. The "intellectual and moral reform" that it called for was not the one he wanted. His aristocratic morality demanded the betterment of the "human quality." French decadence, according to him, was caused by "the pathological perversion of taste," by the "invasion of crudeness," and he called for a censorship of the press and of cinema that would prohibit mediocre and vulgar products.[226]

Back in Paris, he continued contributing to Drieu La Rochelle's NRF and gave articles to the collaborationist press (*Le Matin, Aujourd'hui, La Gerbe, Comoedia, Deutschland-Frankreich* and so forth).[227] He could now more freely express his criticism of the Vichy government: "My opposition to Vichy, which drew attention to me while I was in the free zone, was the rule in the occupied zone and my arrows against the French State,†† which in the South made me look like a subversive spirit, were nothing but banalities in Paris."[228] *Le Solstice de juin*, which was published in the autumn of 1940, was first banned, not by the Germans, as he claimed, but by the Vichy government, due to the attacks leveled against it.[229] The directors of the German Institute, Karl Epting and K.-H. Bremer, who were his friends from before the war—the latter was his translator into German—intervened in his favor. The book, which concluded with an acceptance of the defeat and the conqueror's yoke, appeared on the Propaganda list of "literature to promote" and in the "Miroir des livres" catalogue. Montherlant would justify this position by his conception of the war which drew on both athletic competition ("fair play") and chivalry: when you are

---

†† "L'État français" was the expression which replaced that of "French Republic" under the Vichy regime and became associated with it.—Author.

beaten, you bow down before your adversary.[230] This is why, according to him, *Le Solstice* was a continuation of *L'Équinoxe de septembre*. This acceptance also revealed his conception of "alternation," symbolized by the "solar wheel." The German victory of 1940 answered the French victory of 1918. The armistice was signed on June 24, date of the summer solstice: "The swastika, which is the solar wheel, triumphs in one of the festivals of the sun."[231] In the German army, he admired the pagan and virile forces whose "mission" was to "ruin the bourgeois and ecclesiastical morals, from the banks of the Atlantic to the steppes of Russia." In comparison, the Christian army cut a sorry figure (for Montherlant, Christianity lay at the origin of French decadence and of that "bimbo morality" that he was already denouncing before the war).[232] While most of his writings from that time, including in the press, remained ambiguous enough to lend themselves to contrary interpretations, he nonetheless took a stand expressly in favor of the "new Europe":

> This Europe is to come into being historically and politically; it is to be constructed. A struggle has begun: struggle of the heroic elite of the great adventurers of the new European civilization against average Europeans (average is, here, a polite word for base: it is a matter of base Europeans), struggle of creators against creatures, struggle of harmony against chaos. [...][233]

Whereas the inexactitudes, the omissions, the modifications that are part of the "memoir" attest to a certain bad faith, we can believe Montherlant when he lists his refusals of a number of solicitations; they show that his participation was sought out because of the prestige associated with his name, but also that he was identified as favorable to the Collaboration: thus he declined an invitation to the Congress of "European" writers at Weimar along with several publication offers, he refused to sign copies of his books at the pro-German Rive Gauche bookstore, and he did not belong to any political group.

We can also believe him when he claims to have "no greed where money is concerned."[234] But he did not scorn temporal gratifications. During their first meeting in October 1940, Martin du Gard sketched a striking portrait:

> [...] it is obvious that the disaster touches him quite little, less than a toothache or a threat of appendicitis. He seems naturally armored against the attacks of any collective cataclysm by a premeditated egoism, haughty, irrefutable. The important thing is not that France escape servitude and its population, famine, but that Montherlant maintain solid health, eat his fill, have enough money to live as he wishes, pursue his work and his pleasure in

total independence. He must excel, moreover, in using noble pretexts to justify the satisfaction of his deep instincts [...]

[He] takes care of his affairs and his legend, organizes the development of his work and the commercial expansion of his notoriety in the best possible way.[235]

The temporal profits that can, in the long run, be gained through symbolic prestige are flagrant in this case. Under the Occupation, Montherlant earned an average of 2,000 francs for an article in the press (he wrote forty-seven between December 1940 and November 1942, followed by twelve in the press of the occupied zone, and 9 in the press of the unoccupied zone, bringing him 132,850 francs overall),[236] 5,000 francs for two conferences, and 6,604 francs for six talks on national radio at the beginning of 1942. The royalties that Gallimard paid him in January 1943 and June 1944 totaled 743,107 francs, exceeding the sum paid to Lucien Rebatet for the current best seller, *Les Décombres* (and not counting his publications with other editors). Finally, he received 47,000 francs in advance payment from a German publisher for the rights to reproduce and stage *La Reine morte* in Germany (the play was never performed; he donated this money to the Swiss Red Cross).[237] *La Reine morte*, which was first staged in November 1942 at the Comédie-Française, and *Fils de personne*, first presented in December 1943 at the Théâtre Saint-Georges, were performed 400 times between 1943 and 1944. Financial gain was certainly not his motivation. Martin du Gard's expression about his concern for "the commercial expansion of his notoriety" translates quite well the not solely material considerations and expectations that might enter into the work of consolidating his position at a time in his career when he had already achieved notoriety. His abstention would have inconveniently disrupted this work, which no doubt prevented him, along with his fascination for the cult of force that Nazi Germany symbolized, from seeing that the heroism and patriotism he had always advocated were perhaps on the side of those underground soldiers he preferred to ignore.

Multiple Correspondence Analysis sheds light on the homology between the space of positions occupied in the literary field and the space of political position-taking. The crisis situation had a revelatory effect. The subordination of the economic field to the political field shows the propensity of writers situated at the pole of large-scale production to sacrifice the rule of art's autonomy to heteronomous logics, whether economic, political, or media-related, and to ally themselves with the fractions that possess temporal power to defend or restore "social order." On the other hand, it is when its autonomy is threatened that the pole of small-scale production reveals its subversive potential. This structural opposition, which MCA represents in a static manner through statistical trends, assumes specific forms at different levels and manifests itself in the struggles where different conceptions of literature and the writer's social role confronted each other. These struggles, where the complex intertwining of ethical, aesthetic, and political dispositions can be read, and the dynamic of collective assignation of positions (annexation, stigmatization, labeling, calls to order) have a distinctive history that we will now study.

CHAPTER 2

The Responsibility of the Writer

Is it because its gratuitous, if not "futile" character threatens literature with removal from the public scene that in a period of national crisis questions regularly return regarding its social role? In any case, such periods favor the imposition of a moralistic point of view that confronts the writer with his responsibilities and duties. Testifying to their over-politicization, the redefinition of literary issues under the Occupation was thus marked by a debate over intellectuals' responsibility for the defeat. "Bad masters," "bad enchanters," troublemakers, and warmongers, the recognized writers from the interwar period, notably *La NRF* team, were accused by their adversaries of committing the wrongs that led to defeat. They were turned into "public enemies." Under the particular conditions of the Occupation, those accusations took a denunciatory turn that would contribute to knitting together those who tried to resist the importation of heterogeneous logics in a struggle for the reconquest of the literary field's autonomy. Faced with the problem that was imposed on them, reaffirming the autonomy of literary and intellectual values was initially achieved by denying their social impact. At a second stage (without this shift being automatic), they reversed their stance by assigning to these values, in roundabout or covert phrases, an intrinsic universal bearing, by equating the defense of the values of the "spirit" to the struggle for liberty. Such would be the meaning ascribed to the intellectual resistance and the foundation of its legitimacy.

Although the conjuncture conferred a new significance upon the "bad masters quarrel," as André Rousseaux of *Le Figaro* called it, the arguments of the dispute were not born of the defeat. The schemes of perception and evaluation that they mobilized have a history of their own. Writers confronted the debacle armed with representations forged from previous struggles. In the first part of this chapter, I will sketch the socio-genesis of the systems of opposition that underpinned these representations, while paying special attention to the social construction of the category of "bad masters." These systems of opposition had partly crystallized at the turn of the century during the struggles generated by the morphological transformations of the intellectual field and the development of Republican education. They were transposed in the literary and political debates that rocked the literary field during the interwar period. By examining three of these debates—classicism and romanticism, moralism and literature, West and East—I will offer an overview of the evolution and redefinition of the stakes from one war to the other.

In a space governed by permanent symbolic struggles for the maintenance or the transformation of power relations, these quarrels are modes of regulating and redefining positions, oppositions, and alliances. They provide us with a condensed view of the dynamic of discursive readjustments, the logics of attraction-repulsion, and the collective work of assigning positions. Thus the attacks against André Gide are what drove the author of *Corydon* to radicalize his position. Finally and above all else, the quarrels offer a privileged vantage point for observing the process of universalization of the passions which is at work in literary propheticism, emblematized by the act of making adversaries into "public enemies."

We will approach these complex academic disputes, each of which deserves a separate study, less for themselves than for what they reveal about the discursive logics of the scholarly debate surrounding the responsibility of the writer and the ethical categories of literary understanding at this time. It was through these ethical categories that political categories were imported into the literary debate, and, conversely, that literary categories entered the political discourse of the writers. The attack on romanticism, renewed at the end of the nineteenth century by the dissident symbolists, became the keystone of Charles Maurras's doctrinal edifice. Reactivating the debate after the Great War as the centennial of romanticism approached, its condemnation in the name of the classical values that embodied "French genius" essentially set the conceptual framing of the debate on moralism in literature, provoked by the attacks against André Gide and *La NRF*. It would also provide the framing for the debate surrounding "the defense of the West" that would be the spearhead of the right's neo-pacifist campaign in the 1930s.

Based on the analysis of these debates, I identified four types of critical discourse, which of course do not exist in a pure state, but rather are distributed, by the play of homologies, according to the positions writers and critics occupy in the literary field. They can be ordered around two axes. On the first axis, they go from the most to the least "academic" discourse. The more dominant the position of the writer, the more he tends to adopt a euphemized and depoliticized "academic" discourse—in form—according to the rules of polite intellectual debate. Conversely, the more dominated the position of the writer, the more his discourse is likely, by struggling against the dominant points of view, to denounce academicism as a form of conformism, and to become politicized. This polarization largely intersects with the opposition between the old and the young in the literary field, between established writers and young pretenders or "failed" writers. On a second axis they spread between two poles. At one pole we find the discourses where attention to the form and style of the work prevails, an expression of the logic of autonomization and of growing reflexivity in the fields of cultural production that were more and more oriented toward the search for "culturally pertinent distinctions,"[1] to quote Pierre Bourdieu. At the other pole lie discourses that tend to focus on the work's content.

Thus, according to this second structuring factor, we see an opposition between two types of discourse at the dominant pole. On one side, legitimate discourse concerned with style and form prevails at the symbolically dominant pole. On the other, at the temporally dominant pole, discourse privileges content over form and tends to apply a moral, indeed moralizing judgment to works by worrying about their social effects. It is at this pole, where "good taste" is cultivated, that the notion of the "responsibility of the writer" was developed against "disturbing" writers by figures ranging from Paul Bourget to Henry Bordeaux. Here the function of literature as an instrument to reproduce a social "elite" and uphold the social order was the most clearly stated, despite the work of euphemization that forced these arbiters of "good taste" to endow themselves with a social philosophy, even a metaphysics (as we will see in regards to Henri Massis), or risk looking like mere spokesmen for conservative and conformist moralism. In response to the moral judgment of works, legitimate critics, from Paul Souday to *La NRF* team, were led to reaffirm the preeminence of "talent," of "originality," of "style." Against the conception of literature as an instrument of the symbolic power of conservative forces, they promoted the critical function of intellectual activity, the function of literature as a form of research, and the universal values of Thought, as illustrated by *La NRF*'s response to Henri Massis's attacks. This is why, at the symbolically dominant pole, moralism tends to take the form of a defense of "truth" and "justice," in opposition to the "common good" or to "reasons of state" put forward by their adversaries, an opposition that the Dreyfus affair had consecrated.

At the dominated pole, we must also distinguish between two types of discourse on literature. The subversive strategies of the avant-garde often led them to lend a political significance to their protest (this was true for the surrealists in the 1920s), but they remained focused on the redefinition of the aesthetic and stylistic possibles in a given state of the field. In contradistinction to the defenders of "good taste," they advocated the subversive vocation of literature. On the other hand, those who did not possess the cultural resources (inherited or acquired in the course of their education) that were necessary to enter the literary debate or to contest it based on its own categories tended to reduce critical discourse to a political and social criticism that had the greatest chance of being heard if it resorted to the logic of public scandal, as Henri Béraud's attacks on *La NRF* will show.

These four types of discursive practices are thus differentiated by their relationship to literature. We can therefore identify four logics: "good taste" (related to the sense of social "responsibilities"), "scandal," "art for art's sake," and "subversion." These logics imply different types of mediation between literature and politics. They are more or less embodied by historical forces, individuals, groups, and institutions. We will return to them later, through the institutions that represent them in an ideal-typical manner.

The tendency to introduce political and ethical categories into aesthetic judgment becomes higher as we move, on the second axis, toward discourse that privileges content. It is here where one also slides more easily from a work's morality to the author's morality, and where a writer tends to make his opponent into a "public enemy" in order to disqualify him. In this process of constructing "public enemies" out of rivals, we can read the double work of adjustment to the circumstances and euphemization according to the rules governing the field in question, whether literary, scientific, or artistic.[2] These two operations may seem contradictory, but they are the condition for effectuating the transubstantiation of individual passions (rivalries, hostilities, or elective affinities) into universal causes, by making them appear disinterested. The work of euphemization operates through reference to the scholarly tradition that produced those categories which lend discourse its legitimacy and universal bearing. Notions like humanism, civilization, and classicism are thus at stake in permanent struggles for their reappropriation. The work of adjusting to circumstances, which we cannot satisfactorily reduce to a term like "opportunism" (even though bad faith, which allows for a clear conscience at a low cost, plays a significant part in both logics), relies on scholarly myths that can by definition be readapted at will, as in the opposition between North and South, the representations of national "characters," and so forth. During both wars, the nationalists were all the more able to impose the problematics of national interest on the literary field since "French genius" was a category of literary debate at that time.

The "French Genius"

It was very largely in the name of the "French genius" that the struggles structuring the literary field in the first half of the century were conducted. This category of literary understanding owed its legitimacy along with its social effectiveness to a range of exogenous and endogenous factors. I will limit myself to naming the exogenous factors that emerged from the recomposition of the "national conscience" with the dawn of the Third Republic; the humiliation of the defeat of 1870 gave this event a dramatic tone. Nationalism, still the prerogative of the Republicans until its reappropriation by the new right at the end of the century, was closely associated with instilling a civic morality through education.[3] The debates on Republican morality and the violence of the confrontations surrounding the question of education, between the defenders of the Republican system and the partisans of a "free" education (referring to confessional schools, most of them Catholic), in the context of secularization and the separation of church and state, defined the entire period up to the defeat of 1940. They also marked the educational politics of the Vichy regime, which tried to destroy the Republican educational system.

Moralism was thus closely linked to the national question during this entire period, revived by the experience of the Great War and the threat of new conflicts in the 1930s. This association was essentially transposed in the literary field, where "French genius" constituted a category in the debate over the moral responsibility of the writer. A tributary of the Enlightenment heritage that, by affirming the universality of French culture and its language, provided an essentialist justification of its dominant position in the circles of enlightened European elites, "French genius" always appeared, on both the right and the left, as a category of the universal rather than an expression of the particular. Associated in the repertoire of national representations with "humanism" and "civilization," it legitimized a messianism that became an imperialism of the universal. This is why the nationalist new right would work to reappropriate these universalist categories by redefining them: it opposed an elitist conception of man to a humanism founded on the philosophy of human rights. Only the agents of the "eternal" values of "the" civilization, that is to say the heirs, could lay claim to this title.

The struggles to lay claim to "French genius" can be fully understood if we relate them, on one hand, to the competition that occurred between writers and scholars, the new "prophets" of the universal, who appear as authorized agents of a specialized knowledge at a time when the recruitment of intellectual fractions experienced an unprecedented expansion.[4] On the other hand, these struggles must be linked to the educational war that pitted the defenders of the classical humanities against the partisans of modern instruction in secondary education. Through these confrontations that peaked at the turn of the century, when most writers who would take part in the "bad masters quarrel" during the Occupation were socialized, a number of representations were forged that would be imported into the polemics internal to the literary field, more or less euphemistically.

These confrontations, which were ultimately concerned with the mode of social reproduction (the Republican meritocratic ideal having disrupted the play of direct transmission of heritage), conferred all their social importance to the literary quarrels that would otherwise have been limited to strictly scholarly debate. One example was the condemnation of romanticism, accused of having perverted the essentially classical "French genius." But more profoundly, the issue of the mode of social reproduction lay at the heart of the interpenetration of literary and political logics, just as it lay at the heart of the shifting meanings that allowed one to import the categories of political discourse into the literary discourse, and vice versa. The conception of "man" or the "person" developed by Henri Massis, the Catholic thinker of Action française, during the interwar period was merely the generalization of a particular scholastic condition, that of a social elite trained in the classical humanities. It was mobilized both in Massis's literary attacks on André Gide and his ilk and in his "defense of the West." I have chosen Massis as one of the touchstones of my genealogy of the quarrel of "bad masters," not only because he led all of the battles but also for the exemplarity of his discourse in this regard.

THE SCHOLAR AND THE WRITER

In a French tradition inclined to recognize as well founded the independent writer's claims, to propheticism and universalism,[5] "French genius"—embodied in a language that had conquered the courts of Europe during the Enlightenment[6]— was largely identified with literary values. But since the rise of the Third Republic, the hegemony of literary culture was threatened by scientific culture. The new legitimacy captured by the figure of the scholar opposed certified competence to the writer's charisma as the foundation for the exercise of symbolic power. Embodied in its highest degree by Louis Pasteur, it was no longer limited to the natural sciences: Hippolyte Taine and Ernest Renan had based their intellectual magisterium on the application of scientific methods to the social, psychological, and literary fields. The fact that science had become a source of inspiration for the two principal novelistic currents of the period, naturalism and the psychological novel, was, as Christophe Charle has said, "the best proof of the emergence of this new symbolic model of intellectuals."[7] And Rémy Ponton has shown that the birth of the psychological novel, the genre that gave the novel its prestige and helped it dethrone poetry—as demonstrated by the massive admission of psychological novelists into the French Academy starting in 1890—was indebted to the reconversion of scholarly competences in the literary field, through which psychological novelists, posing as the heirs of Taine and Renan, marked their distance from "vulgar" naturalism.[8]

The expansion of the Republican university under the banner of this new scientific belief would nonetheless exacerbate competition between writers, confronted since 1860 with a market logic that widened the gap between literature and a scholarly career, and the new agents of a state-sanctioned knowledge who fought them for symbolic power. This rivalry was grafted onto the traditional opposition between creator and professor that opposed *auctor* and *lector*, invention and repetition (or imitation), intuition and reason, gift and application, genius and skillfulness, elegance and pedantry, the innate and the acquired.[9] This opposition was aggravated due to the competition between independent literary criticism and scholarly criticism which played a decisive role in the process of perpetuating and canonizing works since its institutionalization as an academic discipline at the end of the nineteenth century.

According to Renan, it was German universities rather than schoolteachers that had won the war of 1870.[10] Since the 1860s, French academics had called for university reforms based on the German model, which privileged scientific culture and erudite research. It would be the task of liberal Republicans to begin these reforms. They were marked by the development of the humanities and science faculties starting in 1877 (with the creation of scholarships for the *licence* and agrégation,* which led to an increase in the number of students), the importation of the model of German research (with the creation, in 1896, of the New Sorbonne as a specialized research institution; Émile Durkheim, Gustave Lanson, and Charles Seignobos were its principal representatives), and the affiliation of the ENS with the reformed Sorbonne in 1904.[11] A reform of secondary education began at the same time. The Ribot Commission was appointed to

---

* The *licence* is a three-year university degree that corresponds roughly to the American bachelor of arts. The *agrégation*, as already mentioned, is a competitive national exam for high school teachers; those who pass are guaranteed entry into the French civil service.—Trans.

examine the question of integrating special instruction (sciences), known as modern instruction since 1891, into secondary education. This reform provoked a vast polemic that opposed the defenders of the classical humanities and of Latin as an educational barrier to the partisans of modern reform, including Durkheim and Lanson. The reform was inaugurated in 1902 with the creation of four courses of study for the baccalaureate, including section D: science-languages, which allowed access to the university without Latin. These reforms would inform Durkheim's argument in favor of specialization in his introduction to *The Division of Labor in Society* (1893):

> This general culture, formerly lavishly praised, now appears to us as a loose and flabby discipline. [...] The praiseworthy man of former times is only a dilettante to us, and we refuse to give dilettantism any moral value; we rather see perfection in the man[†] seeking, not to be complete, but to produce; who has a restricted task [...].[12]

By stigmatizing general culture and the dilettantism of the *honnête homme*, the partisans of modern reform provoked a veritable outcry. The arguments for the defense of the humanities and against the sciences largely coincided with those that promoted the genius and universality of the writer against the pedantry of the professor, the specialization of the scholar cut off from the "real."[13] "Literary" values were invoked in order to affirm the superiority of "disinterested" general culture (Latin) against the "utilitarianism" of the sciences and against specialization, which was equated to "intellectual egotism." The "classical" spirit, guarantor of the capacity for synthesis and general ideas, was promoted against the "lowest common mentality" and against pedagogy, which was judged "useless."[14] It was in the name of personal development, imagination, invention, intuition, and originality that the Republican model of "instruction" was unfavorably compared to an "education" that would form taste, character, and will, all qualities that specialized knowledge avoided as the generator of that double calamity: materialism and individualism. In the end, it was "French genius" and its favored mode of expression, rhetoric, along with taste, "esprit de finesse" (shrewdness), French order, and clarity that found themselves threatened by a foreign model, that of German erudition and science, characterized

---

[†] The French text makes a clear distinction between the *honnête homme*, which Durkheim's translator has rendered as "praiseworthy," and the "competent" man of modern times. The term *honnête homme* refers to a man of culture, a gentleman. Durkheim opposes broad eighteenth-century literary culture to specialized knowledge. For the purposes of this study, I will retain the French expression.–Trans.

by its "esprit de géométrie" (systematic thinking), its heaviness, it pedantry, its obscurity.

In order to understand the violence of these confrontations, we must relate the antinomies between creator and professor on one side, between humanities and science on the other, to a third antinomy symbolized by the opposition between heirs and scholarship holders, the *boursiers*, in the social imagination. This representation of the social differences between writers and professors that Albert Thibaudet would sanction in *La République des professeurs* (1927) was not without social foundation. Compared with scholarly recruitment, the recruitment of writers was more elitist.[15] Confronted with a new, school-mediated mode of reproduction,[16] writers, as heirs to the traditional "elites," could only display their contempt toward degree holders, those "upstarts" of the intellectual field. This contempt was fueled by the resentment that academic failure or the devaluation of academic titles (diplomas) inspired in these "disinherited" heirs, thanks to the expansion of higher education. The opposition between heirs and scholarship recipients made the previous debates seem like manifestations of the struggle between old and new "elites" over the mode of social reproduction at a time when the Republic outlawed congregational schools, developed the scholarship system within the new science and literature curricula, and suppressed the social barrier of Latin. The figure of the boursier would fuel the long-established myth of the "intellectual proletariat" as an instigator of social disorder.

These three antinomies are interwoven in two famous novels. *Le Disciple* by Paul Bourget, which was published in 1889 and enjoyed great commercial success (22,000 copies sold in a month), featured a scholar cut off from the real world whom society held accountable for his moral responsibility: he was held up as a bad master insofar as he was a master of abstraction and specialized knowledge. In someone from a modest background who had abandoned his class of origin, his unused faculties risked erupting in the form of uncontrolled passions, thus threatening the social order.[17] This theme of the harmful effect of abstract instruction on a pupil deprived of the social and economic conditions of disinterest and incapable of controlling his passions would be taken up again by Maurice Barrès in *Les Déracinés* (1897). According to the conception popularized by this work, scholarship recipients were socially displaced. Secondary school gave them hopes of social ascension that they could not achieve without the economic and social capital required to establish themselves. Uprooted from their region under the influence of a bad master, torn from their original social sphere, instilled with abstract Kantian universalism, they could only serve to increase the masses of the "intellectual proletariat." Gnawed with resentment, they would then turn against the society that deceived them by becoming criminals. Forty years later, the same reasoning would authorize René Benjamin to put the following words in a doctor's mouth: "In Paris there are three hundred qualified female lawyers who are selling themselves on the streets."[18] Albert Thibaudet would write about *Les Déracinés*, "For the first time, I believe, we had a literary example of the dramatic spectacle of the professor judged by the student."[19] Against the philosophy of his master, Jules Lagneau (one of the models for Bouteiller in *Les Déracinés*, who had "made Kant's watchword his own, according to which there are two enemies of education: the government and parents"), the student Barrès developed a "philosophy of inheritance."[20]

This philosophy of inheritance was implicit in the concept of "education," now opposed to "instruction." In an article that appeared in the *Revue des deux mondes* in 1895, the critic Ferdinand Brunetière, who was answering Durkheim indirectly, argued that instruction did not guarantee "morality." Specialized, it strived only for utility, to the detriment of "disinterested culture" and "general ideas," and developed individualism, the enemy of education and the social order. Brunetière warned against a purely scientific education ("Metaphysical truths, moral truths, historical truths, aesthetic or critical, if I can say so, there are truths that scientific methods cannot reach") and refused to recognize the critical spirit of the scientist.[21] The defense of the humanities and of Latin would be just as explicit regarding the necessity to maintain the barrier between the education of the leading classes for whom secondary and higher education should be reserved, and the middle class, whose education must be confined to practical orientation, or risk displacing them socially.[22] Above and beyond this affirmation of the superiority of "literary" values, or rather through it, was fear of the devaluation of titles traditionally reserved for the dominant classes, along with fear of competition from the new "elites" promoted by school, that penetrated the discourse on numbers and on overproduction of graduates. Such fears formed the basis of the alliance between the Catholic right and the nationalist right for the defense of the "natural" elites.

The Dreyfus affair crystallized these oppositions that would help structure the intellectual field, in a conjuncture of expansion and crisis in this space, with the crisis in the book market on one side, and the discourse on overproduction of graduates and the "proletariat of baccalaureate holders" on the other.[23] Barrès, in his attack against the intellectuals who supported Dreyfus, suggested that most of them were obscure degree holders who were obeying their professors.[24] Put differently, these troublemakers who threatened the social order were none other than the "intellectual proletariat." And the intellectual partisans of the revision of the verdicts were identified with the reformed Sorbonne. Echoing Barrès, Brunetière denounced pro-Dreyfus intellectuals who used competence in their specialty to justify their intervention in an issue that they were actually not competent to judge due to their very specialization: "They only talk authoritative nonsense about things they are not competent to judge."[25] Erudition and science didn't equate to intelligence, and could even be opposed to it insofar as specialized knowledge was "limited" and thus "narrow-minded," unlike "general ideas." Intelligence itself was not a substitute for "experience," "firmness of character," and "energy of will." As a result, science offered no "titles to govern one's fellow creatures," and scientism served "only to hide the pretensions of *individualism*, which is itself a principle of anarchy."[26] Durkheim responded by distinguishing individualism based on the philosophy of the rights of man from the egoistic utilitarianism of Herbert Spencer, the latter in fact serving as a sign of anarchy; the individualistic morality, which should be the new religion of humanity, was based on respect for the rights of the human person. It was because those rights had been scorned that "intellectuals" assumed, not the right to judge by themselves, but to put "their reason above authority," and this not in the name of their competence, but as men, although they were "accustomed by the practice of the scientific method to reserve their judgment as long as they don't feel enlightened; it is natural that they yield less easily to the practice of the crowd and the prestige of authority."[27] And he reminded Brunetière of his position as an amateur writer.

The representation that the anti-Dreyfus camp gave of its adversaries, the "intellectuals," thus helped codify the opposition between the literary field and the scholarly field, and institute a lasting form of anti-intellectualism at the heart of the literary field. This anti-intellectualism would appear all the more legitimate by reaffirming the preeminence of literary qualities and values over those of instruction and research. In *L'Évolution pédagogique en France*, Durkheim noted the alliance between humanism and the Church starting in the nineteenth century.[28] The waves of conversion to Catholicism in the literary field from the end of the nineteenth century to the mid-1930s owed something to this antimodernist reaction to the threat that science, under the double figure of the professor and the scholar, posed to writers' claim to the universal.[29] This threat was increased by the conditions applied to the writer in the modern capitalist world.

Thus the opposition between creator and professor was solidified in this configuration of relations between literary field and scholarly field, in a new and accentuated form. It is nonetheless necessary to distinguish between two expressions of this opposition. On one side, the attacks against professors emanating from the "left" of the literary field (from Zola's attacks on the "pions" of the ENS,[30] consecrated as authorized censors by the French Academy during this period, to Nizan's Marxist critique in *Les Chiens de garde* (1932), along with Péguy's anarchist critique) more traditionally targeted the orthodoxy of the guardians of the temple. They were inscribed in the defense of freedom of creation against all forms of academicism and routinization. On the other side, the figure of the intellectual bureaucrat who propagates an individualist moral code thanks to the sinecures of the Republic, immortalized by the character of Bouteiller in *Les Déracinés*, became the symbol of the irresponsible upstart, master of decadence, for the "right" of the literary field. This representation, based not on the defense of the rights of creation but rather the stigmatization of the new Republican elites, informed the incriminations of the "Republic of Professors" under the Cartel des Gauches,[†] then against Léon Blum and the intellectuals of the Popular Front. This kind of grievance would be hugely successful during the Occupation. Although it is necessary to distinguish between these two traditions, they are far from mutually exclusive. While the first group did not fail to denounce, for diametrically opposed reasons, those state intellectuals who put their knowledge to the service of power, the second group, of chief interest to us here, did not abstain from using the arguments of the first. Indeed, they quoted Péguy, in order to give their social critique the form of a defense of the rights of "genius."[31] This was a social critique that included a stigmatization of "the foreign" in the name of defending "French genius," threatened with "decadence."

Much contributed to the nationalist withdrawal of a whole fraction of the literary field in reaction to these new prophets of the universal who contested their authority and described them as dilettantes: the alliance of scholars with the Republic, the promotion of new elites recruited from religious minorities (Protestant and Jewish), and the particularly strong ties between internationalism and the university that took on a novel form due to the diffusion of Socialist internationalism, notably among the sociology graduates of the ENS.[32] Traditionally linked to the "national" through language, they now turned to a nationalism founded on tradition, French "civilization," and "race," in the sense of a people's "genius." The crisis that scientific optimism and the belief in progress underwent at the beginning of the century created a veritable "call for bids" on prophecies about "decadence."[33]

[†] A coalition of left-wing political parties, namely the Radical-Socialist Party and the Socialist party SFIO, which was formed after World War I and won the elections in 1924.—Trans.

At the time Maurras was developing his theory of four confederated states (Jewish, Protestant, Freemason, and Mediterranean) on the basis of victorious Dreyfusism, Combism, and the separation of church and state, the literary attacks against the New Sorbonne teemed with anti-Semitic and anti-Protestant intimations. In the series of conferences he held in 1908–1909 at the Institut d'Action française, and that formed the basis of his book, *La Doctrine officielle de l'Université* (1912), Pierre Lasserre, a philosophy professor with roots in Bern, author of a thesis on *Le Romantisme français* that he defended with some difficulty at the Sorbonne in 1906, accused the New Sorbonne of having succumbed to a leftist plot stirred up by Protestants and Jews. Shortly thereafter the inquiry by Agathon, pseudonym for Henri Massis, a literature graduate, and Alfred de Tarde, the son of sociologist Gabriel Tarde,[34] a law graduate, appeared in the press. Apparently inspired by the conferences of Pierre Lasserre, equally marked by anti-Semitism,[35] their work was collected in a 1911 volume under the title *L'Esprit de la Nouvelle Sorbonne: La Crise de la culture classique; La Crise du français.* Later, in *La République des professeurs*, the Protestant Albert Thibaudet, himself divided between the literary and scholarly fields, would lend credence to the image of scholars as a "pastorate," pointing out the affinities between the "Protestant world and this world of the high university that, from 1885–1905, directed the three orders of instruction in France, and created and organized the educational program of the Third Republic: Buisson, Rabier, Pécaut, Stecg, all Protestants, almost all sons of pastors, all *agrégés* in philosophy, entered the university as though it were a more flexible and liberal pastorate."[36]

Besides the 1902 reform of the baccalaureate and the affiliation of the ENS with the New Sorbonne, Agathon's attacks were motivated by the reform of the literature degree in 1907, which planned to suppress the tests common to the four literary courses of study (Latin theme or Latin and French dissertation), and ultimately suppressed only the French dissertation. They also targeted the Diplôme d'études supérieures (DES), which was now a prerequisite for agrégation; the implementation of Durkheim's pedagogy course as an obligatory step in preparing for the agrégation; and the decrees of 1910, which established certain equivalences between primary (the École normale de Saint Cloud, which trained primary school teachers) and secondary diplomas. The special diplomas that benefited foreign students—whose proportion doubled in Paris between 1897 and 1909, going from 9.3 to 17.7 percent[37]—also seemed like an attack on the prerogatives of the French "elite," as Agathon's xenophobic remarks show:

Well! I don't know whether we shouldn't prefer the old Sorbonne, where a few enthusiasts came to be instructed, to this modern Babel, where foreigners of every language jostle each other; they are attracted, flattered, and seduced, a cosmopolitan crowd in the midst of which the French students, disoriented, lost, no longer feel at home.[38]

Scientism was then experiencing a crisis that rendered these attacks effective. This is all the more clear if we consider that, in the literary field, they first emanated from a graduate of the ENS, a Socialist, a Dreyfus supporter, disappointed with Dreyfusism which he accused of having betrayed a mystic: Charles Péguy. In reaction to the New Sorbonne, Péguy developed a critique of the scholar endowed with divine attributes and undertook a reflection on genius—unique, inimitable, unclassifiable—that did not emerge from an explanatory model. This reflection led him to a form of anti-intellectualism—"All the intelligent people we know, and this trash swarms in Paris, France, fatally hate genius and the works of genius"[39]—and to examine the links between genius and the supernatural. Agathon would not fail to note that the youth at both ends of the political spectrum, Socialists and monarchists, agreed in their disapproval of the methods of the Sorbonne. Just as the future fellow-traveler of Action française, René Benjamin, would quote Georges Sorel from the *Indépendance* in his satire on life at the Sorbonne that appeared in 1911 under the title *La Farce de la Sorbonne*: "By admitting their aesthetic incompetence, the 'Sorbonnards' render a notable service to literary men."[40]

Agathon's inquiry, like Pierre Lasserre's book, argued in favor of the honnête homme and disinterested general culture, and against the utilitarianism of specialization. The schemas of perception that were mobilized were generally tributaries of the antinomies mentioned earlier. Against historicism, positivism, patient observation, fact-gathering, quantitative measures (nomenclatures), "ingrate erudition," the mechanical work of memory, patient labor, minute research, bibliographies, the collection of files, "method" that required technical competencies, and the skill of the "science worker," they meant to reestablish the rights of judgment and taste.[41] Agathon contrasted the German "esprit de géométrie" (systematic thought) of those whom Anatole France called "the 'illiterate stuffed with letters' of the Sorbonne"[42] with the French "esprit de finesse" (shrewdness):

> If all dissertations have been suppressed, it is because the most fearsome intellectual qualities unfolded there with too much ease. The work of the mind heads more and more toward the automatism of manual labor. Still talent is less valued, in the Sorbonne, than the skill of a worker in a factory. [...][43]

Faced with the threat of a "domination of the lowest common mentality" in which the *Journal des débats* saw the "insolence of the upstarts,"[44] they posited "the necessity of an elite." Because of the reforms, "the clientele of secondary education and the Faculties, more and more recruited from humble families, is more and more incapable of understanding all the nuances of literary education […]."[45] "The utilization of the mediocre" contained a threat of despotism. Literary studies, which implied the formation of taste and judgment, served as a bulwark against this threat. Taste was "one of the lookouts that preserved the humanity of humankind," explained Pierre Lasserre.[46] Massis and Tarde would be recruited as secretaries of the league for the defense of humanities and classical culture, the "League for French Culture" that formed in 1911 under the patronage of thirty-six academicians.

While Agathon's attack differed from that of Lasserre in its defense of the individual against the tyranny of the group, and in its anti-determinism, the basis of argumentation was less different than it might appear. Action française condemned the philosophy of clear ideas in Cartesian rationalism, which signified access to ideas for all; in the philosophy of the rights of man, they condemned the individual right to think.[47] The despotism feared by Agathon was a mass despotism enabled by universal suffrage and the Republican school; it was less an issue of defending Liberty through free will than of defending the liberties of the dominant classes. Their common defense of taste, general culture, and speculative unity won out over their differences. Distancing himself from Péguy and Henri Bergson, Henri Massis would, as we will see, waste no time in following the path traced by his elders: Barrès, Maurras, and Henri Vaugeois, who also started out as unapologetic anarchist individualists.

Against mysticism, the pressure of irrationalism, and against a subjectivist philosophy of becoming spread by Bergsonian neo-spiritualism, Action française constructed a social philosophy that lay claim to scientificity, in line with Barrès.[48] Maurras remembered the teachings of Paul Bourget who was the first and almost the only person to answer Maurras's inquiry on the monarchy by saying that "the monarchist solution was the only one conforming to the most recent instructions of science"; his goal was to "take science from the revolutionaries."[49] Founded on heredity, continuity, and race, Maurras's organizational empiricism claimed to be a "political science" or rather a realistic "scientific politics" based on the observation of facts, in the tradition of counterrevolutionary thinkers like Louis de Bonald and de Maistre, Le Play's sociology, Comte's positivism, and Taine's environmental determinism. He opposed "experimental" science to deductive rational science that applied ideas and systems a priori while ignoring tradition (the Revolution). His goal was to found a normative pseudoscientific determinism that claimed an association with "realism"— namely the interiorization of social limits within the framework of "natural hierarchies"—against romanticism and utopia. His brand of determinism also promoted the experience of history (rather than history itself) against idealist abstraction.[50]

By proposing this synthesis between traditionalism and science—on which the Catholics applied a spiritual damper ("the unknowable" for Bourget, which reappeared again in René Benjamin's notion of "mystery")—Action française killed two birds with one stone: it used the pretention to truth inscribed in scientific belief to its own advantage, by transposing it with politics, even as it generalized its defense of classicism forged in the literary struggles of the late nineteenth century in order to emerge as the guardian of "French genius." It thus constructed a doctrine that was at once aesthetic, social, and political, founded on a neoclassicism and an intellectualist realism that would rely on the Thomist doctrine then accredited by the Church. The neo-Thomist Jacques Maritain, who had converted to Catholicism in 1905 and become the quasi-official philosopher of the Church, was linked with Action française after the Great War (he would cut ties with it after the pope's condemnation of integral nationalism in 1926). "What our classical culture has lacked is a philosophy founded on reality. It has had Descartes, that is to say the father of modern idealism and subjectivism," he explained in a discussion with Frédéric Lefèvre.[51]

CLASSICISM AND ROMANTICISM

By announcing the premises of a "classical renewal" in the last decade of the nineteenth century, at the very moment when the notion of "classicism" received its scholarly consecration, the "École Romane" that assembled the dissidents of symbolism around the figure of Jean Moréas, and for which Charles Maurras served as theoretician, produced a symbolic revolution at the heart of the literary field.[52] This revolution was much less the result of a restrained and muted poetic production than of the categorical condemnation of romanticism in the name of the principles decreed to be classical, such as harmony of composition, subordination of the parts to the whole, and perfection of form, which it turned against the symbolist school. According to Albert Thibaudet, "The new school [the neoclassical movement] almost succeeded in marking the word Romanticism with a pejorative significance for the current language, as though it were a type of sickness."[53]

If, for an entire fraction of the literary field, the classicist injunction fulfilled expectations of an ethical and political order in a euphemized form, it also had an impact of a purely aesthetic nature: it imposed a specific problematic on the symbolist generation and its successors. When La NRF reappeared at the end of the Great War, Jacques Rivière, its new director, also announced a "Classical

Renaissance" that *La NRF* intended to wrest from Moréas's disciples.[54] In an interview in 1921 with Émile Henriot, Gide proclaimed himself "the best representative of classicism" of the day.[55] But by equating this fight against romanticism with the defense of the French "genius," the neoclassicists linked to Action française brought the question of national moralism and the social responsibility of the writer to the very heart of the critical debate.

Without entering into the conditions of this symbolic revolution, let us recall here the principal terms of the charges against romanticism. Mastery of feelings through reason, ordering impressions and ideas through style, harmony based on a hierarchy of the elements; such were the principles of the "human" and "Beauty" that were developed by the classical tradition, from antiquity to the French "Great Century," and that romanticism perverted. By sacrificing reason to animal sensibility, by dividing the "self" in favor of a relativist subjectivism that exalted the passions, by underestimating the art of composition in its frantic pursuit of originality, romanticism had introduced a principle of "decadence" whose effects, it was suspected, would not be limited to the aesthetic order. The attack against individualism, which was assimilated in the counter-revolutionary tradition to the philosophy of the rights of man, lay at the core of the indictment of romanticism, whose initiator was none other than Rousseau. By cultivating the insatiability of "selves," sentimental individualism created a terrain that was favorable to the "revolutionary messianism" in the France of 1830, as Pierre Lasserre explained in the *Revue de L'Action française* articles that formed the thesis he would publish under the title *Le Romantisme français*.[56]

French romanticism was, according to Pierre Lasserre, the result of a combination between "German pantheism," which, unlike Platonic tradition, considered it possible to reach the divine through emotions rather than reason; and "revolutionary messianism."[57] For Maurras, the transgression of classical rules was "barbarism." Through a learned attempt to recast history and the map of the world, he found its origin in Alexandria, and its development "under the Christian frock in Rome and in Africa," then in "Byzance," and finally in modern Europe, especially Germany, where it was imported by Judaism and the Reformation.[58] It was a matter of redefining the opposition between the North and South, rooted in scholarly tradition, although it was a poor fit for the urgency of a French "recovery" vis-à-vis Germany. Theorized in Montesquieu's theory of climates, codified in Madame de Staël's literary criticism (*De l'Allemagne* promoted the modernity of German romanticism versus French classicism), the scholarly myth of the superiority of the Nordic "races" had known a sad avatar in *L'Essai sur l'inégalité des races* (1855) by Gobineau; the text met with great success in Germany. Fueled by the same mythical coherence,[59] Maurras's division opposed a West ruled by the "masculine" principle of order and self-mastery, now based in the Provençal South, heir to Greco-Latin tradition, and an East ruled by the "feminine" principle expressed through romanticism.[60] This vision of the world was at the foundation of the new nationalism that emerged at the end of the nineteenth century, and which Maurras would soon lead with the doctrine of "integral nationalism." Conceived by the children of the defeat of 1870 who were brought up with the German romanticism against which it defined itself, while constantly drawing inspiration from it,[61] this doctrine turned its gaze toward the "internal enemy."

As I have already stated, the indictment of romanticism would prove to have lasting effects. Classical aesthetic theory opened the door to a national(ist) conception of literature that would radiate beyond the circle of Action française, as well as a moralizing conception that took on the signs of literary legitimacy (in spite of Maurras who privileged politics over morality). From 1902 to 1904, Jean Carrère, a former symbolist poet allied with the École Romane—a "Southern Lamartine" according to Jules Renard's expression[62]—now a critic and journalist, published a series of articles in *La Revue hebdomadaire*. After the Great War, he would collect them in a book called *Les Mauvais Maîtres* (1922). Seeking to determine the responsibility of the great writers of the last century for "the state of intellectual trouble, moral weariness, and public worry" that reigned among the young men of his time,[63] he located it in the romantics. According to him, they had corrupted the classical values of balance and harmony, force and clarity, action and heroism, and instead abandoned themselves to their egotistical passions and their sensuality, sources of trouble, confusion, and helplessness. He applied the romantic label not only to Rousseau, initiator of this "unhealthy" current, and Chateaubriand, Stendhal, George Sand, Musset, Baudelaire, and Verlaine, but also to Balzac, Flaubert, and Zola, and denounced their harmful influence even more firmly because he recognized their genius. Against the "male spirit" that characterized classical literature, they made themselves the propagators of "the female spirit, nocturnal, troubled, and unhealthy," a factor of "decadence" which, in both its excess and its passivity, "sacrifices order and the necessity of the state to its exorbitant individuality" and destroys itself "in oriental fatalism."[64]

The war had contributed to the diffusion of the classical directive in literature, art, and music.[65] More than ever, individualism was condemned in the name of affirming national identity and the "return to order." At the same time, Action française, emerging victorious from the war, saw its intellectual magisterium peak, and the question of the writer's moral responsibility was timely; romanticism, equated with the hereditary enemy, Germany, was once again put on trial. In 1918, the Catholic weekly *L'Univers* published a series of articles entitled "The Intellectual Criminals," which featured severe portraits of Madame de Staël, Lamartine, Vigny, Musset, and Hugo by Abbé Delmont.[66] The rationalist Julien Benda's condemnation of the romantic *Belphégor* in the name of "Minerve" led a fraction of Catholics to indict intellectualism and rehabilitate romantic mysticism as a principle of religiosity (for example, Abbé Brémond's argument for romanticism in *Pour le romantisme*, published in 1923), and a number of writers tried, in numerous studies, to highlight the positive contributions of romanticism. As a response, in *Les Chapelles littéraires*, Pierre Lasserre turned his criticism of romanticism against Péguy, Francis Jammes, and Claudel.[67] In 1922, while the French Academy gave its Grand Prize for Literature to Pierre Lasserre for his body of works, Léon Daudet reopened the case with his *Stupide dix-neuvième siècle*, which considered Hugo and Michelet as "two perverters of men's minds, and that they were almost as pernicious as Rousseau"; *La Tentation de Saint Antoine* as "a *Faust* for primary schools"; and Zola's naturalism, which reduced man to his animality, as "the romanticism of the sewer."[68]

Despite the conjuncture of the war's end, or perhaps in reaction to the conformist patriotic moralism of the immediate postwar period, critics were far from unanimous in their adoption of the moralist position. But the debate was the order of the day. Strengthened by its resonance in a self-righteous audience, recognized as legitimate in a whole fraction of the literary field (including its opponents), not only could the moralist position not be ignored, but it also condemned its opponents to either deny the social importance of art or fight on its turf.

"MORALISM AND LITERATURE": THE ATTACK ON *LA NRF*

In this period of reconstructing national identity, "French genius" was the banner under which literary struggles between competing factions were led (with the exception of the Dadaist and surrealist avant-gardes). Each of them sought to simultaneously reappropriate and use it to disqualify the adversary. Classicism, equated here to "French genius," furnished the debate's conceptual frame, in its most intellectualized form. The arguments against romanticism—individualism, Protestantism, (German) foreign influence—haphazardly fueled the offensive first launched in 1921 against the group that then tended to hold the monopoly over literary legitimacy: *La NRF*.

The attacks that, according to Gide, had "made [him] more famous in three months than [his] books had done in thirty years" emerged,[69] and for good reason, from the two extremes against which the NRF aesthetic had defined itself: "good taste" and "vulgarity." Both their virulence and their determination testify to the legitimacy won by the NRF group at a time when the review still had only a limited audience: in terms of its average circulation, 5,500 copies,[70] it resembled an avant-garde review. "If it had no aesthetic value, we would not even bother with it," Henri Massis answered Frédéric Lefèvre in *Les Nouvelles littéraires*.[71] The spectacular rise in the number of subscribers beginning in 1923,[72] although not entirely attributable to the attacks, was undoubtedly related, as André Gide suggested.

The offensive that Henri Béraud launched against *La NRF* in September 1921, and whose first version would remain a dead issue, owed its fortune to an interview that the author of *Martyre de l'obèse*, winner of the Goncourt Prize in 1922, gave at the beginning of 1923 in *Les Nouvelles littéraires*. In his first attacks, Béraud had notably attempted to discount André Gide by criticizing his grammar usage, a criticism that had not passed the bar of publication.[73] He retreated to an argument that was both more credible and more fruitful, accusing *La NRF* authors of benefiting from a level of foreign distribution that the modest sales of their works in France did not justify, thanks to their supporters at the Quai d'Orsay (where Jean Giraudoux worked). This argument had the advantage of lying outside the realm of ideas, and within that of public scandal, which forced Jean Giraudoux to respond.[74] Around this accusation arose a series of slanders that actually constituted the root of the attack. It was the "Huguenot snobbism" of this cohort, its "scholarly" and "bookish" asceticism, that was called into question and that placed them outside French genius:

> Against the spirit that is ours, the grace, the pleasure, the sun, the feasts, the laughter, the living word, French taste, good wine, pretty women. Of these hatreds, these aversions, of that lack of appetite and dyspepsia, they made a literature that they feed on after their works. It is not surprising that this literature is indigestible to our stomachs. But much more surprising is the fact that, through official attention, this literature is presented abroad as the triumph of our gastronomy and after long hesitations and legitimate worries they try, at present, to force us to ingest it.[75]

In short, Protestant "pions," homosexuals, "richer in money than in faith," threatened the French genius. This extraliterary and typically populist rhetoric that married anti-intellectualism, social criticism, and criticism of the mores of "bourgeois" writers was written in the same pamphleteering vein in which Béraud would distinguish himself in politics. This rhetoric was characteristic of the resentment that privileged writers who did not need to cash in on their work inspired in the writers most deprived of economic, cultural, and social resources, who saw themselves condemned to turn to journalism and submit to market laws by banking on high sales. For them, it was a matter of survival. A thirty-six-year-old journalist at Gustave Téry's *L'Œuvre*, Béraud was a baker's son from Lyon who had abandoned his secondary studies and practiced numerous professions even as he attempted to imitate Gide. At the time of his attack, he had just published two novels in a naturalist vein, *Vitriol de la lune* (1921) and *Le Martyre de l'obèse* (1922), which earned him the Goncourt Prize and high sales. His attack on *La NRF* was a milestone in his evolution toward a populist extreme right; the future polemicist of *Gringoire* would become a spokesman of this political tendency in 1934. Béraud rallied a constellation of literary men, described by Gide in his journal: "The pack he groups around him is made up of those who have been refused by the *N.R.F.* He [. . .] quotes ten names of which eight belong to authors we have blackballed."[76]

In November 1921, two months after Béraud's first attack, the theoretician of the Catholic version of the Maurrassian aesthetic, Henri Massis, editor in chief of the *Revue universelle*, launched after the Great War by Jacques Bainville and Jacques Maritain, opened fire by describing Gide as "demonic."[77] This son of an insurance agent from Montmartre, who was Alain's student at Condorcet, had rejected the literary tastes of his youth, which ran toward Zola's naturalism, just as he had denigrated his master at the New Sorbonne and the school's rigorous scientific methods in the inquiry that he and Alfred de Tarde had written under the pseudonym of Agathon. Impatient as he was to situate himself in the literary field, this young pretender had, under the influence of Péguy and a then-popular Bergsonism, redeployed his philosophic training that was late to emerge in a novel as a weapon against scientism. His defense of "literary" qualities, of the rights of "judgment" and "general ideas," followed by Agathon's inquiry on "the young people of today," born of an aborted plan for a novel, gave him a reputation that he could now use to shore up his authority as a critic. Having converted to Catholicism in 1913, this disciple of Barrès was won over to Jacques Maritain's neo-Thomism and joined the ranks of Action française.[78]

For the Catholics who did not wish to appear to yield directly to the constraints that dogma exerted on art so as not to be excluded from the literary field, but whose ethical and aesthetic dispositions, more than competition, led them to reject the work of someone like Gide or Proust who inspired them with nothing but disgust—Henri Massis wrote to Jacques Rivière that *Les Caves du Vatican* had so profoundly "disgusted" him, "I cannot find another word"[79]—a work of euphemization was necessary. Maurrassian aesthetic theory came to their aid. Henri Massis would occupy himself with this kind of work; his attacks were taken more seriously by his adversaries than those of Béraud and his ilk. Aside from the doctrinaire Catholics, the proponents of "good taste," and especially the "academic pole," could easily recognize themselves in them. His literary *Jugements* and *Défense de l'Occident* [*Defence of the West*] were recognized by the French Academy in 1929 with the Grand Prize for Literature. Although he was a candidate for the Academy starting in 1936,[80] Massis would only enter it in 1960, his membership having been deferred due to his pro-Vichy engagement during the Occupation.

The attacks of Massis and Béraud had some common themes: "the boredom," "the frightful moroseness" that Gide's work emitted were contrary to "life"; as much as this aesthete exalted life, he did not love it.[81] The "aesthetic Puritanism," the "Protestant rigor" of this "reformer" were denounced along with the "immoralism" of this "Nietzschean nauseated by God."[82] Ultimately, this literature was foreign to the "French genius." But Massis's argumentation, unlike that of Béraud, was clothed in philosophical rigor, borrowing its arms from the indictment of romanticism; these were the proven weapons of a still-timely debate of ideas. Moreover, although Massis refused the separation of the word and the flesh, of the spirit and the body, in the name of the religion of incarnation, for him the word "life" did not include the "jovial" and "bon vivant" meaning that Béraud assigned to it. Reason's grasp of reality, which Maurrassian realism advocated, and which Maritain's neo-Thomism had ennobled, set itself clearly apart from the "vulgar" realism and naturalism that the doctrinaires of Action française identified with "materialism."

Did Gide's work indeed withstand the attacks of a formal nature that were leveled against romanticism? Massis saw in it only one more attack against the classical conception of literature, since this refusal of "individuality of form" was only a subterfuge "to make the underlying individualism triumph all the better, in order for the dignity of monsters that hide there to grow."[83] The classicism that Gide claimed to best represent was, in his case, only hypocrisy, the mask behind which he hid his "morbid nature." This is why Gide was "demonic." The accusation of "divorce of thought and form" that Massis leveled against the twentieth century was precisely due to this dissociation between classic art and the classical—or "Western"—conception of man, between the order of language and the order of thought that must, according to this conception, respond to the same exigencies of balance, harmony, and discipline. By advocating the "gratuity of art," Gide avoided his "responsibility"; he "only [sought] to crush logic, to ruin the Western conception of man, to escape the risk of thought and action."[84] This social philosophy of immobility that opposed "improvement" to "progress" and swept aside history in the name of eternal values was constructed both to denounce the perpetual search for the new in art,[85] and to condemn the altogether romantic admiration for the "irrational period of the human existence," namely puberty, and the philosophy of becoming, imbued with Bergsonism, that grounded it.[86]

Young literature, under the influence of Gide, Proust, and Freudian psychology, was reduced to individualism, to "philosophical subjectivism." Massis drew on a parodic phrase by Henri Ghéon, a member of the first *NRF* group that had converted and aligned with Action française. He had said that this literature was "in search of the lost object." Deprived of an object, the subject became its only object. "For Mr. Jacques Rivière and the neo-Proustians [. . .] it seems that the only events are interior, the only reality is psychological; the self, this is the only object, the only reality that is knowable."[87] In his attack against this current, Massis's literary conservatism broke through: he blamed these writers for being critics rather than creators, because their works were "without events, without characters: nothing happens there." They could not claim "to enrich our humanity," which was the essence of classicism. In the case of Jacques Rivière, with whom he had once sympathized and whom he had momentarily hoped to win over, Massis specifically targeted the apologist of the Dada movement, one of the "most anarchic attempts that the 'gratuity of art' had ever generated."[88]

For lack of scholarly arguments, the pamphleteering rhetoric of someone like Béraud drew its weapons from social stigmatization in order to translate his resentment of symbolically dominant authors. In contrast, the rhetoric of the proponents of a conception of literature as an instrument for reproducing the social elite, illustrated here by Henri Massis, euphemized the social issues behind the critical discourse by arming themselves with the categories and forms of literary culture. The former did not call for a response according to the rules of scholarly debate (unless it called for an armed response or when it managed to engage the powers or the public "opinion," according to the logic of scandal). The latter, which targeted writers who "disturbed," necessarily had effects on their public position-takings, to the extent that it applied a social image to them that they would then have to confront. Mentioned in reference to a work's morality (*L'Immoraliste*, Lafcadio's gratuitous act,[§] Proust's amorality, Dada's "demolition project"), redefined within *La NRF* which established a distinction between moralism and dogmatism, but where the oppositions that structured the literary field were retranslated, announcing the split that would divide its team, the polemic shifted imperceptibly, in regards to the man who represented the

---

§ Lafcadio, a character in André Gide's novel *Les Caves du Vatican*, commits an infamously gratuitous act when he pushes another character from a moving train for no apparent reason.—Trans.

headmaster of the young generation, toward the morality of the author whom it made into a "bad master." Gide's strategy encouraged this dynamic, as his only response to the attacks targeting him was a radicalization of the position assigned to him. He would make *Corydon* public and publish *Si le grain ne meurt* in 1924, before beginning an evolution that would lead this aesthete to commit to the Communist Party. In the meantime, politics had actually become the principal means of defining positions within the literary field.

THE DEFENSE OF THE WEST

Action française and its imitators had done their share to discredit the "retreat" to the ivory tower. From 1913, Agathon's inquiry on "the young people of today" had made a "taste for action" one of the characteristics of the rising generation.[89] The experience of the war and the patriotic effusion that reached almost all the intellectual milieus could only be favorable to the wide diffusion of the Maurrassian slogan of not separating "thought" from "action."

La NRF managed, nonetheless, to defer, if not definitively ward off, this new constraint that the right tried to inscribe in the definition of the social role of the writer. On the contrary, it gave itself the objective of "making this constraint cease, that war still practices on intelligence,"[90] a constraint that made its mark on all literary production. "As a whole, we are not people of action," declared Jacques Rivière, turning disinterest of thought and creation into a patriotic duty to safeguard the prestige of France. Nevertheless there was to be no retreat into an ivory tower, he insisted, testifying to the devaluation of this option. Rather, it was a matter of separating literature from politics, which *La NRF* did not intend to abandon. Despite this precaution, Rivière's text, which he had not submitted to the founders of the review beforehand, was the object of a lively internal polemic in which Gide supported his junior colleague against the protests of Henri Ghéon and Jean Schlumberger. "It is the Dreyfus Affair all over again," Rivière proclaimed in the text that he had prepared in his defense for a July 3, 1919, meeting with the team of founders on the orientation and direction of the review.[91] In it, he invoked the antithesis forged by Péguy between the mystical and the political in order to oppose the "politics first!" of Ghéon and Action française: "Ghéon represents (whether he is successful or not) the political point of view, and tries to introduce it into the review. My entire temperament resists it. I am a mystic of truth. I am a *dreyfusard*."[92] For Rivière, there was no "opposition between two manners of thinking. But an opposition between thought and action."[93] The discord was revealed to the public the following year by Gide himself who, after having defended Rivière, seemed to disown him publicly. His cutting remark against the young director whom he would have preferred to see secretary under his own direction expressed not only the rivalry between master and disciple, but also the very ambivalence of Gide's position. His wartime sympathy for Action française was not entirely diminished, and he continued, at the very least, to define himself with respect to it: "Could or should the French spirit still claim an impartiality, a serenity that seemed at first sight to avoid real service?" he wrote in *Le Gaulois* to evoke the problem that arose at *La NRF* at the end of the conflict. "Personally, I kept myself from taking part in the debate, for fear of aggravating it, but more than ever a discreet place seemed to me necessary, a place where, without fear of deformation, the clear face of France could gaze at itself."[94]

Thus, the war had allowed the nationalists to establish themselves as moralists and impose their problem on the defenders of pure literature. And, according to a recurring schema, it was in the interest of literature's autonomy against the politicization advocated by the nationalists under the guise of national interest that the defenders of pure literature were led to oppose this politicization. Thus they mobilized the representations forged during the Dreyfus affair: the search for truth as a moralism of the universal, which was more important than national interest. Julien Benda would codify this opposition in *La NRF* with *La Trahison des clercs* (1927), which opposed Justice and Truth to partisan passions. Nevertheless, the separation of literature and politics would prove more and more difficult to maintain as the review became institutionalized on the one hand, and the politicization of literary debates was accentuated on the other. While the discredit cast on the "ivory tower" was the heritage of previous struggles, the generalization of recourse to politics was one of the characteristics of the 1930s. The shift from aesthetic debate to political polemic occurred in the form of an ethical debate, through the struggle to reappropriate the categories of the universal. The definition of notions like humanism, civilization, and culture was at stake in the struggles that structured the literary field during this period.

The concept of "civilization," soon equated with "the West," formed the ideological core of the social philosophy around which Maurras would manage to gather very diverse fractions of the intellectual field between the wars, even after the Vatican's condemnation in 1926 of "integral nationalism." "I adhered to no party, I yielded to civilization," Jacques Laurent-Cély would write about joining Action française in the 1930s, while he was finishing his secondary schooling.[95] Presenting itself as a "humanist" philosophy, this conception drew its symbolic efficacy in the literary field from the idea of necessary defense of a Western culture founded on the classical humanities, embodied by the French "Great Century." This defense was promoted at a time when this culture saw itself threatened on all sides: by the romantic tradition that lingered, in art, through its idealist and materialist offspring (symbolism and naturalism); by the harm the Republic had done to "free" instruction, and the classical humanities, in introducing modern instruction into secondary education and claiming to unite the primary and secondary curricula; by the "utilitarian" cult of science, a foreign (German) import that claimed to replace metaphysics, and by Eastern mysticism; by the idealist and subjectivist tradition of Cartesian rationalism and of Kantism, adapted through Republican instruction, and by Bergsonian intuitionalism. Although to its credit, the latter called scientific determinism and mechanism into question, it resulted in a metaphysics of change "as deadly to reason as Hegel or Fichte,"[96] not to mention Marxist materialism. Finally, this Western culture was threatened by the social philosophy of the rights of man in its liberal form (capitalism) and its collectivist form (Socialism). According to this conception, in fact, the "unrealistic dogma" of the rights of man engendered anarchism as well as collectivism: on one hand, the abstract idea of freedom exalted individualism at the expense of the social order, founded on the so-called natural hierarchies; on the other, egalitarianism reinforced the centralizing power, with the help of romantic passivity (mechanism) and determinism (fatalism).[97] Similarly, on another level, it engendered both idealism (abstraction, disconnection of ideas from reality) and materialism (egoistic instincts).

This conception could attract the heirs of the traditional "elites" who found their prerogatives threatened. It could also attract the defenders of the classical humanities, that is to say, of a literary and philosophical culture that they doubly controlled by virtue of their education and their belonging to the literary field. It might appeal to the proponents of a moralizing or populist aesthetic conservatism or the rear guard marginalized by new literary currents; provincials that the Parisianism of the literary field had immediately relegated to the margins or who were in a hurry to make a place for themselves there; or young pretenders who hastened to establish themselves by asserting their talents as polemicists. In this list, which is neither exhaustive nor exclusive—several of these traits were expressed concurrently in the same position—politics in the strict sense are deliberately absent. Such was the effect of mediation exerted by the structure of the literary field that, while ethical and aesthetic dispositions influenced the initial orientation of those who tried to participate, they could be redeployed as a result of the confirmations or sanctions that this orientation received. The political option could, in certain cases, be one of the manifestations of this reception. It then often seems like an interpretation which illuminates in the eyes of its adopter his own trajectory or position in the field by rationalizing it and endowing it with a universal coherence. Evoking his entry into *hypokhâgne*** at Louis-le-Grand, where his fellow students included Thierry Maulnier, Bardèche, Roger Vailland, and Jean Beaufret, and where he experienced the charisma of André Bellessort who taught Latin and French there, Robert Brasillach wrote in *Notre avant-guerre*:

> My first political thoughts came into contact with "L'Action Française" and Maurras; they haven't wandered far from these influences since then. Suddenly, I was presented with a world of reason, clarity, and truth. I admit that I hadn't the least idea of all this before I came up from the provinces […] It is in the courtyard of Louis-le-Grand that my friendship with "L'Action Française" began.[98]

The attack on "civilization" could be brandished against adversaries and competitors whom it made into public enemies. Since the end of the Great War, the struggle to defend "civilization" had been fueled by the exploitation of social fears rekindled by the Bolshevik Revolution in 1917, symbolized by the poster of "the man with the knife between his teeth" that was used in the National Bloc's campaign; the Bloc's victory in 1919 was largely due to this propaganda.[99] In the collective imaginary, the Bolshevist replaced the terroristic anarchist of the turn of the century.

In 1919, Henri Massis had written the manifesto "Pour un parti de l'intelligence," answering Henri Barbusse's call for the formation of "Clarté" or the "International of Thought" (May 1919), as well as the "Déclaration de l'indépendance de l'esprit" by Romain Rolland, which blamed intellectuals for having put their art and science in the service of governments and called on them to honor "truth" alone, joining in solidarity with "the People—unique, universal—the People of all men, all equally our brothers."[100] Massis responded by equating the cause of France with that of the "spirit." Fighting his competitors, in the name of "the Classical spirit," for this "international of thought that the Bolshevists of literature want to monopolize," the "party of intelligence" set the two-part goal of the *restoration of public spirit in France by the noble pathways of intelligence and classical methods,* [the] *intellectual federation of Europe and the world under the banner of victorious France, keeper of all civilization.*" By serving the interests of France, he claimed to serve the "interests of the *species*," those of "humankind." He opposed these interests to both the "industrial modernism" that "claims to

---

** *Khâgne* and *hypokhâgne* are courses of study that prepare students for advanced literary studies, usually at the ENS.—Trans.

rebuild a society without worrying about *man*" by eschewing general philosophy and the male authority held by the Church alone; and "this Bolshevism that, from the start, attacks spirit and culture, in order to better destroy the society, the nation, the family, the individual."[101] This manifesto marked above all the alliance of a large fraction of Catholic intellectuals, who supplied almost a third of the signatures, and Action française. Paul Bourget, with his title of member of the French Academy, headed the list.

The notion of "the West" did not appear in this manifesto but was already present, as we saw, in Maurras's writing. It would be mobilized from the beginning of the 1920s, in response to the prophecies of the decay of the West that were spread thanks to the wave of orientalism that swelled in a defeated Germany at the initiative of Oswald Spengler, Hermann von Keyserling, and Hermann Hesse. The literary historian Ernst Robert Curtius hinted at the threat it held for France.[102] The (temporary) reconciliation between Rollandian internationalism and the "panhumanism" of the Indian writer Rabindranath Tagore under the banner of pacifism could only heighten this threat, in the eyes of the right. Paul Valéry's famous line in *Crise de l'esprit* (August 1919 *NRF*)—"We civilizations, we now know that we are mortal"—took on a prophetic meaning. In the interview that they gave in October 1923 to *Les Nouvelles littéraires*, Jacques Maritain and Henri Massis denounced those tendencies that took advantage of the German defeat to open the door to "Asian mysticism": "The future of the West is once again in peril. Since the end of the war, we have witnessed a wave of Orientalism that originated in Germany and threatens to lead us back to Tibet following Nietzsche and Tolstoy [. . .] Thanks to the Germano-Slavic despair, the worst Asiatic ferments begin to dissociate our culture, to *dewesternize* us," explained Massis, and Maritain would go one step further with "the abdication of the vocation proper to the West."[103] These arguments reveal the representations underpinning the notion of "defeatist literature" that the detractors of the "bad masters" would employ in 1940: the (German) "mentality of the defeated," which grounded "Eastern fatalism," found fertile ground in France in the tradition of subjectivist individualism. The literary youth's infatuation with these "calls from the East," from the surrealists to André Malraux (*La Tentation de l'Occident*, 1926) and Paul Morand (*Bouddha vivant*, 1927), would confirm it.

Let us note that the system of oppositions was more complex and blurred than my outline implies. If the cultural relativism and irrationalism of someone like René Guénon made him look suspicious, his traditionalism, his condemnation of Cartesian rationalism, of specialization, of the utilitarian belief in progress, of modern materialism in the name of a principle of superior spirituality, and his utopian vision of an ordered and hierarchized society under the control of an intellectual elite that had not suffered the "deformation" of specialized education could not completely displease the detractors of modernism and democracy.[104] An essentialist approach to this debate would not allow us to understand the principles of position-takings, which derive all their meaning from the dynamic of power relationships between competing factions and the strategic uses of representations of the East and West. Here I will analyze only one aspect.

The evolution of the national and international stakes, with the arrival of the Cartel des Gauches into power and the Franco-German reconciliation, favored the transposition of the debates over East and West into the register of contemporary politics. This opened up a veritable editorial market. The equation of Germanicism and Asiaticism on one side, between Bolshevism and Asiaticism on the other, formed the basis of the rhetoric that viewed France as the repository of the universal values of the West, rooted in Greco-Latin civilization and Roman Catholicism. Against the dominant discourse on the supremacy of Western civilization, the myth of the Orient served, in 1925, as a "catalyst for the Surrealist revolt," as Marguerite Bonnet has shown.[105] The surrealists and the contributors to the review *Clarté* came together under the banner of the East; along with the group "Philosophies," they cosigned the petition started by Barbusse against the Rif War. This engagement conferred an anticolonialist bearing on the surrealist myth of the Orient, thereby exhausting it, and marked the beginning of their attraction toward Communism.[106] Here also Drieu La Rochelle's break from the surrealists became a reality. He criticized them for their infatuation with the East, having included "this awakening of the East that fascinates the Germans and the Russians" among the factors of "decadence" that he listed in *Mesure de la France* (1922). Still, this would not prevent him from later ceding to the same attraction.[107] Barbusse's declaration, borne by the fractions of a literary and political avant-garde that was noisy enough to awaken the concern of their elders, provoked a counterpetition entitled "Les intellectuels aux côtés de la Patrie" (*Le Figaro*, July 7, 1925). By its defense of colonialism and the civilizing mission of France, it recruited very largely from the ranks of the intellectuals—from Paul Valéry and Henri Massis—even though the majority of the 175 names that followed belonged to the right.[108] The assimilation of the threefold Germanist, Bolshevik, and anticolonialist threat would give Henri Massis's fight to defend the West all its social and political bearing.

As we have seen, Massis turned his "Western" conception of man into the weapon of his inseparably literary and political struggle. The study that Gide had published in 1923 on Dostoevsky gave Massis an occasion to develop this theme. Under the influence of the Russian master, the Gidean doctrine had undertaken the dissolution of the "human person." "In this doctrine, the Eastern graft flourishing on the Protestant and Germanized terrain led to the blossoming of that bizarre product of Manicheanism and Gnosticism, which he presents to us as the true evangelical doctrine."[109] *Défense de l'Occident* was the title of the essay, published in 1927, that Massis devoted to "this new assault by the East on the Latin inheritance." Its analysis, inspired by Maurras's *Kiel et Tanger* and Gonzague de Reynold's *Civilisation et catholicisme*, returned to representations that were already widespread in France and Germany: Johann Gottlieb Fichte's conception of "Germanism"; Keyserling's importation of orientalism; and Bolshevism, less characterized by its Marxist borrowings than by its Asiatic origins, significant in the Slavic nationalism which it represented, along with Dostoevsky's nihilism. All of these joined forces, thanks to the "secret complicity" between the Orthodox Church and Protestantism, to destroy a Western civilization founded on Catholicism and Latinity.[110] Although this argument for Roman Catholicism derives all its meaning in relationship to the struggles that then divided Catholics faced with the ecumenical movement,[111] I will only refer here to the aspects that allowed Action française and its Catholic fellow-travelers to pose as defenders of Western civilization and, on this basis, make their adversaries into public enemies.

In these confrontations that I will not detail here, *La NRF*'s position was, as always, ambivalent; even as it appropriated the terms of the debate, it put them at a distance. After Paul Masson-Oursel's learned historicization of the intellectual and political stakes that lay beneath the representations of the East-West antithesis (1926)[112]—a historicization that revealed its share of arbitrariness—*La NRF* had published a critical review by Ramon Fernandez under the title "Retour à l'Occident." This review dealt with a group of essays, including *La Tentation de l'Occident* by Malraux. For Fernandez, the dialogue between a French philosopher and a Chinese philosopher staged by Malraux was "an exchange of nihilisms." To the lyricism of Malraux, he preferred the way Paul Morand treated the "miserable compromise" resulting from the exchanges of "impurities" between East and West in *Rien que la Terre*. Yet according to Fernandez, the attraction that the East exerted revealed the search for feelings—feelings like the Cornelian hero's sense of heroism that Cartesian rationalism had obscured: "Our technique of truth radically excludes these 'powers of feeling' which in other ages contained their share of truth."[113] It was, on the other hand, André Malraux who was entrusted with the review of Massis's *Défense de l'Occident* the following year. Returning to Massis's intellectual trajectory, Malraux showed that in Renan, France, Barrès, Gide, and in Asian culture, Massis fought what was offered to him as so many temptations, leading to their de-monization by this man who was actually trying to escape them. Through them, Massis fought against the spirit of knowledge and research which implied "this idea that the nature of man is such that all experiences are possible." For Malraux, "the East helps deliver us from a certain academicism of spirit." In terms of this academicism, Massis's attachment to the "*fixed* elements" of thought seemed, through Malraux's writing, like a caricature.[114] Here we find again the opposition between two conceptions of intellectual activity, one that makes it into a perpetual search, the other that, wanting to find in it a confirmation of established values, turns those who shake their certitudes into bad masters.

An inquiry on Gide's influence over French and foreign authors was undertaken in honor of the sixtieth birthday of the author of *Nourritures* by the review *Latinité*, subtitled *Revue des pays d'Occident*. This review claimed as its models the *Revue critique des idées et des livres* (the Maurrassian review from before the war) and *La NRF*, even though it blamed the latter for having "fallen back into individualism, into anarchy" after the war.[115] In the inquiry, the arguments both for and against Gide lay largely in the realm of moral values. Through Gide, it was the definition of humanism, classicism, and Western values that was at stake. For his defenders, including Drieu La Rochelle, he was the very incarnation, and this in an entirely French tradition, of the humanist, classical, European, even universalist values that were contested to him, and to which writers like Barrès and Maurras, encased in their national particularism, could lay no claim. The adversaries' position drew largely from the Maurrassian argumentation of Massis. Thus Camille Mauclair, for whom the foreign success "of a man who is hardly French any more except for his style," testified to "this hate, sly and admitted, that unites the Germano-Jewish-Slavic forces against Latinity, and since 1918 has sought the revenge of the Kultur against the Mediterranean spirit." His success was "the very indication of our necessary moral defense," and Gide was decreed "the 'worst master' of this time of moral fall."[116]

Mauclair did not know how right he was. The following year, again radicalizing his position against all expectations, Gide declared himself favorable to Communism. In the eyes of those who recognized themselves in the analysis proposed by Massis, it was as though this position-taking constituted the materialization of their prophecies of doom: the anarchic individualism favored by capitalism intersected with collectivism; idealism led to materialism; from the ivory tower to submitting to collective forces; from internationalism of spirit to bowing before foreign powers. Comparing Gide's support for Maurrassism during the Great War and his present support for Communism, Massis analyzed them as a choice of the "priority of the political." He thus turned against Gide the principal criticism aimed at Action française. Gide's choice allowed this reformer to escape moral demand and the "Western" conception of man. "He made his reform starting from the individual."[117] Less "philosophical," the reaction of Camille Mauclair was in continuity with the fight that he had led in conjunction with Henri Béraud, mixing the pamphleteer style with the moralizing register and the critique of the bourgeois writer: "A famous propagandist of homosexuality, rich, eager, filled with success and favors by the bourgeoisie from which he descended, hating the family, the property he enjoys, the religion he has long claimed, proclaims his piercing support of Sovietism."[118]

In the second half of the 1930s, the "defense of the West" became the watchword of the neo-pacifist organization against the anti-Fascist intellectuals who for their part posed as defenders of the "Culture" threatened by Fascism. Born of the congress held at the Mutualité in July 1935 under the patronage of André Gide, the International Association of Writers for the "Defense of Culture" was formed in November 1935 thanks to the union of the radical, Socialist, and Communist left. Engaged in a strategy of national legitimization symbolized by its participation in the majority of the Popular Front, starting in 1937 the Communist Party tried to reappropriate the values of French tradition. The reaction of the intellectual right was marked by the double alliance, under the banner of the "defense of the West" and the "anti-Bolshevik crusade," of the conservative right with Action française, and the proponents of "good taste" with the populist right.

The eruption of Action française in the French Academy starting in 1935, which culminated in Charles Maurras's reception in 1938, illustrated the first of these alliances; we will return to this later. They were solidified by the neo-pacifist struggles in favor of suspending the sanctions against Mussolini's Italy during the invasion of Ethiopia, then in favor of Francoism. At the bottom of the manifestos, the signatures of academicians neighbored those of Action française intellectuals (Maurras, Daudet); representatives of the movements of the "Catholic literary renaissance" (Robert Vallery-Radot, Gaëtan Bernoville, René Johannet, Henriette Charrasson) associated with those of the Fascistic new guard (Drieu La Rochelle, Brasillach) and with the spokesmen for the populist extreme right like Henri Béraud and Camille Mauclair.

The Western notion of "man" justified "the colonial work," and the sanctions that the League of Nations (La Société des Nations, or SDN) had pronounced against Italy, "on the pretext of protecting in Africa the independence of a mixture of uncultivated tribes," were not only "a crime against peace, but an unpardonable assault against Western civilization, that is to say against the only valid future that, today as yesterday, is open to the human species." The "defense of culture" was invoked to justify intellectuals' duty of engagement in favor of this cause. Henri Massis was the editor of this manifesto for the lifting of SDN sanctions, which appeared simultaneously in the *Journal des débats* and *Le Temps* dated October 4, 1935, under the title "For the defense of the West." The next day, *L'Œuvre* published the response of anti-Fascist intellectuals, who denounced the abuse of the "notion of the West and that of 'intelligence'" that Massis's manifesto "tries to distort, for the benefit of war in its most odious form, the war of aggression, the love of our people for peace." André Gide and Romain Rolland notably expressed solidarity with the signers. They also headed the list of writers who signed the "Declaration of Republican intellectuals about the events in Spain," which called for the reestablishment of commercial relations with the Spanish government following the violation of the pact of nonintervention by Italy and Germany.[119] In the name of the "defense of culture" threatened by Fascism, the anti-Fascist intellectuals fought their adversaries for the "defense of the West":

> And you, you who are the defenders and continuators of human thought, you who have inscribed the new and resounding words of *Defense of Culture* at the threshold of these years, recognize in the Spanish people, in this people whose songs, dances, and even prayers summarize the authentic depths of the European West, recognize in it the heroic, blazing avant-garde of this culture, which will disappear if it disappears.[120]

But, while its defense of the principle of colonization and its will to not inflame relations with Italy allowed the manifesto "For the defense of the West" to recruit largely from the conservative and Catholic right, the Spanish war raised much more complex issues.

In fact, even if the Frente popular could only inspire hostility in them, the alliance of conservative intellectuals with the Francoist cause was curbed by the fear that it was the Trojan horse of Fascist, or worse, Nazi ideology in Spain. Certainly, they were opposed to French intervention in favor of the Republicans. But Franco seemed like a pagan, and the creation of a single party in April 1937 did not reassure any more than the Germano-Italian intervention that conflicted with the Germanophobic feelings of the nationalists as well as Catholic beliefs. The Vatican put off making a statement, despite the tone of its condemnation of Communism:[121] Rome still refused diplomatic exchanges with the national state. It would take all the art of persuasion deployed by the spokesmen of Francoist propaganda in France, and above all the official position-taking by the Spanish bishops in favor of the National Movement in July 1937, as well as the pledges given by Franco to both the Vatican and French Catholics starting in the autumn of 1937, for this alliance to be forged with the support of Catholics close to Action française or the extreme right. The latter groups chose sides much more rapidly, as illustrated by the publication in October 1936 of the *Cadets de l'Alcazar* by Robert Brasillach and Henri Massis; 50,000 copies quickly sold.[122] Henri Massis would be received by Franco in 1938 and would become one of the propagators of the idea that a Germanic influence was impossible in Spain.[123]

French stakes largely determined the rallying of the conservative right to Francoism, an alliance that prefigured the dissociation between conservatism and nationalism that the German Occupation would ultimately expose. It seemed like a double reaction to the split of the Christian Democrats, suspected of complicity with the Popular Front, and the strong mobilization of anti-Fascist intellectuals in July 1937, in the context of the Congress for the Defense of Culture that met in Valencia, Madrid, Barcelona, and then Paris. The massacre perpetrated by the nationalists in Badajoz in August 1936 and the Basque problem, with the execution of autonomist priests in the autumn of 1936, had, in fact, divided the Catholics. In the articles that he wrote from Majorca, and which prefigured *Les Grands Cimetières sous la lune* (published in 1938), Georges Bernanos evolved toward a denunciation of Francoist repression. Even as they advertized their political neutrality in order to distinguish themselves from the anti-Fascist camp, a fraction of intellectuals close to the Democratic Christian circle, which had already regrouped around Jacques Maritain with the support of François Mauriac to protest Mussolini's aggression in Ethiopia, rose up against the bombings of Durango and Guernica in May 1937 in a manifesto entitled "For the Basque people."[124] Faced with these Catholics who were more or less allied with democracy, the conservative intellectuals would overcome the fears that Fascism still inspired in them.

The reestablishment of diplomatic relations between the Vatican and the Spanish nationalists, theoretically decided in September 1937 and immediately transmitted by the members of the French ecclesiastical hierarchy,[125] left the field open for a true pro-Francoist campaign in France. On November 3, the *Journal des débats* published the letter of Cardinal Baudrillart, rector of the Catholic Institute of Paris and member of the French Academy, to the anonymous author of *La Persécution religieuse en Espagne* which was prefaced by Paul Claudel, a supporter of the Francoist cause. At this time, while Franco was trying to establish diplomatic relations with France, the Spanish nationalists multiplied their propaganda aimed at the intellectuals of the French right, and in particular the Catholics, on the theme of "Franco-Spanish friendship." They notably insisted on the fact that Franco distinguished "real France" from its government of the moment, the despised Popular Front. It was also during this period that Franco adopted the term "crusade."[126] On the French side, a number of intellectuals, including several members of the Academy, would contribute to this Franco-Spanish connection.

The beginning of October was marked by the publication of a book by Maria de Cardona, *La Terreur à Madrid*, the text of a conference given in June 1937 at the Union interalliée and published by "The friends of the new Spain." It notably included a description of the destruction of the palace of Liria. It was prefaced by Louis Bertrand, of the French Academy. Without guaranteeing the absolute exactitude of the facts, Louis Bertrand affirmed that "the accent of the witness does not deceive" and that the experience of horror "can only confirm [her] in [her] hatred of all revolutions, whatever they be, beginning with French revolutions [...] Revolution is never anything but organized spoliation and murder," he explained, reactivating the old counterrevolutionary cliché of "failed literary men [who] are the seed of torturers and executioners." A specialist of Spain, for several months Louis Bertrand had been developing the theme of "Eternal Spain" [L'Espagne de toujours] in the *Revue universelle* directed by Henri Massis, and in a presentation of *L'Espagne* (the country's geography, civilization, and history) aimed at a general public; Flammarion entrusted him with the project for an illustrated popular edition.[127] "Eternal Spain" was the crucible of Western civilization that had always resisted the call of the East; it resisted the Muslim invasion and now resisted the new assault of "Asiatic barbarity" reincarnated in Bolshevism. On one side lay the defense of "civilization," of the "human person"; on the other barbarity, tyranny, terrorism. But "Eternal Spain" was above all the strong intertwining of religious and national feeling. It was actually a matter of lifting the concerns raised by Germano-Italian interference by demonstrating that "while they momentarily tolerate foreign intrusion or intervention, [Spaniards] will never submit to foreign domination."[128]

On October 7, probably at the invitation of the Francoist *Prensa y propaganda*, Claude Farrère of the French Academy and René Benjamin met in San Sebastian. In November, a series of articles by Farrère on "Spain today" appeared in *L'Écho de Paris*. They consisted of the story of his trip to a Spain conquered by the nationalists, written in response to *Retour d'Espagne* by André Chamson, codirector of the anti-Fascist weekly *Vendredi*. He would turn this material into a book, *Visite aux espagnols*, which he would address to Franco and for which he would be thanked by the Caudillo.[129] In this narrative, Farrère, who claimed to be impartial, made himself the spokesman of Francoist propaganda in France. To the "Marxist terror," to the massacres perpetuated by the government, to the looting and destruction of places of worship and art objects, he opposed the return to "order, liberty, abundance, and peace" in nationalist Spain,[130] showing a happy Spanish people who were largely allied with Francoism, even the Basques. Received by Franco in Burgos, he loyally transmitted his message to the French: Franco appealed to Germany only because he was constrained and forced by the attitude of the Popular Front government, which in spite of the "hypocrisies of nonintervention" lavished material on the "Communists" against whom he fought, not in a civil war but in a holy war; and he knew that "true" France was on his side.[131]

At the end of the month, the ministry of Francoist propaganda based in Salamanca created the bimonthly *Occident*,[132] with the help of several French writers. Directed in Paris by the Majorcan Joan Estelrich,[133] it was meant to prepare for France's diplomatic recognition of the nation-state by promoting "the Franco-Spanish friendship," and to rally the still-hesitant Catholics. Proof: versus one article attacking André Chamson's "unnecessary trip" and another the "despair" of Malraux,[134] we find, among the twenty-six issues that appeared from October 1937 to December 1938, no fewer than ten articles directed against the Catholic intellectuals allied to the Christian Democrats, Mauriac in particular (five articles devoted to him alone), Maritain and Bernanos, which evolved from the "open letter" to variations on the theme of "error" and "treason." On the other hand, the journal promoted the most prestigious Catholic writers converted to the Francoist cause: Claudel and Francis Jammes. Claude Farrère gave an interview on his journey in which, boasting about his military experience, he asserted against all evidence that in Guernica everything was exclusively destroyed by dynamite rather than bombardments. Having undoubtedly been criticized on this point, he would add in his book that it was also burned down, and would maintain that "the ingeniousness of photographers" transformed the image of Guernica into a bombarded town.[135]

The review's luxurious appearance—photos of ecclesiastics and famous men rallied to the Francoist cause along with architectural masterworks destroyed or threatened with destruction were included to concretize the idea of civilization against barbarity—was nonetheless balanced by the poverty of its original intellectual production. The editorials were signed "Occident"; the news articles were anonymous. In fact, it was mostly fueled by quotations from pro-Francoist intellectuals, their concentration giving the impression of a broad consensus for the cause of "civilization." Next to some occasional articles by Spanish intellectuals, the recurrent signatures were those Catholics close to the extreme right: the Catholic graduate of the ENS, Maurice Legendre, assistant director of the Institut culturel français de Madrid; the historian Bernard Faÿ, professor at the Collège de France and, like Legendre, a great promoter of the Francoist cause in

France;[136] Jean-Pierre Maxence, representative of the "Jeune droite" or Young Right; sometimes Robert Havard de la Montagne, Catholic columnist of *L'Action française*; the Catholic essayist René Johannet; the poet Francis de Miomandre. To these were added the occasional contributions of Henry Bordeaux of the French Academy, Jacques-Émile Blanche of the Institut de France,†† and Mario Meunier, contributor to the *Revue des deux mondes*, all of whom brought academic credibility to the review.

In his article on "Spain in Our Literature" published in January 1937, Henry Bordeaux, always quick to put literature to the service of politics, invoked the great space that Spain and its culture occupied in French literature to "wish so ardently for the triumph of old religious and national Spain over the barbarity of foreign importation."[137] From the Cid to the officers of the war of 1914, Bordeaux saw a great French lineage of heirs to Don Quixote. Unlike Prosper Mérimée, who latched onto a minor incident, and whose invincible "Carmen" did not reflect the "Spanish race," Barrès and René Bazin knew how to evoke the "true" Spain. Thus we can read between the lines to find the complicity between "true" Spain and "true" France, those that belonged to Latin and Catholic civilization.

In December 1937 an intellectual Committee of Friendship between France and Spain was formed. It launched a "Manifesto for Spanish Intellectuals" published in the *Journal des débats* of December 9, 1937, and in the bimonthly *Occident* of December 10. Claiming to place itself "above all politics," the manifesto called for "fraternity" rather than "hate" between classes, the "freedom of persons," the rights of national independence, willing "the reestablishment of an order founded on morals and the respect of the notions of liberty, authority, and property," the triumph "of what actually represents civilization against barbarity, order and justice against violence, tradition against destruction, guarantees of the human person against the arbitrary."[138] One hundred and four signatures would be collected between December and January. At the end of February, the committee, coordinated by Maurice Legendre, numbered 176 members:[139] nine members of the French Academy, nine members of the Institute, twenty-six politicians, eighty-three writers and publicists, forty-nine scholars and doctors (divided roughly in thirds between doctors, scholars—usually literary scholars—and representatives of private instruction).[140] In June 1938, a "French association for the restoration of sanctuaries, hospitals, and orphanages of Spain" was created under the presidency of Bernard Faÿ. Baptized

---

†† The Institut de France comprises the five academies; the Académie française, the Académie des Sciences morales, the Académie des Inscriptions et des Belles-Lettres, the Académie des Sciences, the Académie des Beaux-Arts.—Trans.

"Solidarity of the West," it asserted its fidelity "to that Christian spirit and to those traditions which have made France and the other Western nations."[141] Benefiting from "the high approval" of Cardinal Verdier and Cardinal Baudrillart,[142] it numbered ten members of the French Academy on the honor committee, presided by Paul Claudel. Maurras had just been elected French correspondent to the Royal Academy of Moral and Political Sciences of Spain and made a trip to the peninsula "to show that real France is not behind the red army of murder," according to Robert Havard de la Montagne's comment in the *Revue universelle*.[143] Franco's reception of the leader of Action française, who had tirelessly preached Germanophobia, testified to "Latin brotherhood" as Francis de Miomandre exclaimed in *Occident*.[144] It constituted a pledge with respect to the orientation of the Francoist regime and its distance from Hitlerism. In his work *Chefs*, Henri Massis established a distinction between the Latin dictators, "defenders of the human person," and the materialist dictator, Hitler.[145]

But at the same time it gained respectability with the election of Maurras to the French Academy in June 1938, before becoming one of the sources of inspiration for the Vichy regime's program of National Revolution, this dichotomous vision founded on the conception of Latinity was already called into question by a fraction of the intellectual generation born at the turn of the century, and established in the 1930s. Thanks to the resurgence of a romanticism that found something in Fascism to fuel its fascination for Hitler's power, some of these newcomers reactivated, under the influence of Nazism, the myth of the superiority of the Nordic races and Aryanism that racist theories then "supported." The strong increase in anti-Semitism that France experienced in the 1930s, and that would crescendo up until the war, fostered by the secret funds with which Germany supported certain movements like Louis Darquier de Pellepoix's Anti-Jewish Rally, provoked an escalation of verbal violence which nonetheless tried to endow its discourse with a coherence drawn from the old mythical oppositions readapted to contemporary issues.[146] Borders were blurred between the anti-Semitic arguments naturalized since the nineteenth century in *La France juive* by Édouard Drumont, who had made a "synthesis between Christian anti-Judaism and critics of the left against Jewish plutocracy," and the racist anti-Semitism that Hitler's Germany gave the force of law. The latter was propagated in France by youth or men in the prime of life.[147] According to the sociological portrait painted by Ralph Schor, the leaders of anti-Semitic groups belonged most often to the upper-middle class of Northern France; many of them had fought in the Great War and, disappointed by the unfulfilled hopes and ambitions they had harbored as a result of willing sacrifice, they found the reinforcement of their social resentment in this traditional scapegoat. Among writers, Drieu La Rochelle and Céline belonged to this generation. The young Fascistic faction of *Je suis partout*, educated at a school that challenged racial anti-Semitism in favor of a state anti-Semitism, hesitated to call itself racist, contenting itself to declare the inassimilable nature of Jews. Meanwhile, it participated significantly in this escalation, praising Céline's pamphlet, *Bagatelles pour un massacre* (1937), and publishing in February 1939 a special issue on "Jews and France" which alluded to the role that Action française had played in the "anti-Jewish struggle."[148] Unlike their elders who had been raised with an obsession for revenge, these children of the victory of 1918, having inherited the fear of French decadence without the Germanophobic urge being as strongly rooted in them, were seduced by the German recovery. In his memoirs, Lucien Rebatet would write:

> The systematic Germanophobia of the Southerner Maurras always made me shrug my shoulders. If the occasion offered itself, I would have no doubt begun in literature around 1923, when I had just arrived at the Sorbonne, with an essay that was three-quarters written on the ridiculousness of Maurrassian pseudo-classicism, with Papadiamantopoulos, the drummers of the Félibrige and the starched false collar alexandrines of the École Romane, opposite the immortal works of the Nordic spirit that he claimed to oppose.[149]

Whether they opposed the virile virtues of German paganism to Christianity as a source of decadence (Montherlant), or on the contrary promoted the pagan sources of Christianity and the "virile Christianity" of the Middle Ages (Drieu La Rochelle); whether they found in it the culmination of their lyric momentum (Brasillach) or a justification for their social resentment (Rebatet), Nazi Germany offered these writers—who, whether they fought or not, shared the war as a frame of socialization, along with an elitist vision of society—a kind of inverted image of a French "decadence" whose extent was revealed by the Popular Front. This regime, with its "vast trampling of enormous crowds" obediently assembled "around the fishermen with the anti-Fascist line" had been headed by the hated symbol of the "Republic of Professors," Léon Blum, a Jew and an ENS graduate; it represented the triumph of "the lowest common mentality," "in ascendance everywhere."[150]

The "Bad Masters"

As the defeat approached, the question of the social role of literature and the moral responsibility of the writer was reactivated. "Have we loved literature too much?" André Billy asked in *Le Figaro*, criticizing writers' disinterest for political action, to which Maurras responded that "a certain literature" had been too well-loved, an "escapist literature."[151] And Gide would rebel in his journal as early as June 11, 1940, against the indictment of literature and against the contrition of intellectuals.[152]

For those who had made themselves the prophets of France's "decadence" for the past twenty years, the defeat seemed like the implacable consequence of the "sins" they kept denouncing. The "hypnosis of the punishment," as Marc Bloch called it in *L'Étrange défaite*, was cleverly orchestrated by those producers of salvation goods who, thanks to the rise to power of their vision of the world, classified the program of National Revolution as a "redemption" for errors, and the defeat as their atonement.[153] Literature did not escape this denunciation of past mistakes. In fact, starting in the summer of 1940, interwar literature was made into a symbol of this "spirit of pleasure" that had won out over the "spirit of sacrifice," to use Pétain's expression. In short, the writers who were accused of being "bad masters" for the past twenty years were now rendered responsible for the defeat.

The importation of the rhetoric of contrition into the literary field obviously relied on representations forged in the course of internal struggles that preceded it. It responded to specific issues and interests, conferring an authority and an immediate social bearing on the grievances that the accusers, who posed as righters of wrongs, had long been developing against their competitors. In both the Northern and Southern zones, the repeated slanders against the recognized writers from before the war, *La NRF*, and the intellectuals of the Popular Front were the occasion, for their detractors, to assimilate the ills of the spirit to the flaws of the Republic, or vice versa. At this pole of relatively high heteronomy, the critical discourse tended to reduce literary oppositions to social oppositions, giving free reign to the mixture of literary and social resentment. According to the interwoven logics of the gossip of stigmatization and the universalization of passions, social categories (professors, Jews, Freemasons, etc.), converted thanks to the influence of politics and the restriction of possibles into vague political categories detached from their referent, served to make competitors into "public enemies," enemies of the established order or rather of an order to be reinstated.

But while the arguments supporting the indictment of literature had little or nothing new, except that they were readapted to current circumstances, they weighed more heavily on the new conditions of cultural production, which were subjected to the double apparatus of Nazi and Vichy constraints. Two observers, Alfred Fabre-Luce and Thierry Maulnier, although close to collaborationism and Vichyism respectively, denounced this escalation of literary payback that involved the public powers as arbiters of the literary field's internal relations:

> In Paris, since June 15, 1940, a power of exception is suspended over private lives. How delightful it would be to make this blade fall on some old comrades! Some display the enthusiasm and orthodoxy to make us recognize their right to work the machine. Faced with these judges, it is not enough to be blameless. If we hold up a pen and don't use it against the impure ones, we are classified as suspicious. It's a movement that comes closer and closer to Jacobinism, up to the point that it suffocates its initiators themselves . . . A known writer, if he dares to publish a novel or have a play successfully performed? They will recall that he did not oppose the war, they will insinuate that he wished for the triumph of England, they will count on the "Embassy" or the "Institute" to ostracize him, rather than abandon "their true friends." But these authorities, most of the time, contemplate the maneuver with disgust.[154]

> As for those who, in the time of the former regime, were left justly unknown, because they had no talent, they taste the hope for revenge and think that a revision of values has some chance, if not to give them glory, at least to diminish the glory of those who make them jealous, which would in their eyes not be a negligible result.[155]

The fact that these self-proclaimed judges of their peers relied on the acting forces and their repressive methods in order to reverse the power relations constituting the literary field is characteristic of the heteronomous logic. By casting moral and social discredit on their colleagues, some to impose a moralizing conception of literature that resonated with the cliché of the "moral recovery" dear to the new dominant ideology of the "National Revolution," others to take over positions and impose their Fascistic visions of the world, they also satisfied an old desire for revenge, with no regard for the rules of the literary game. That is why their show of force inspired an acute defensive reaction on the part of a whole fraction of the literary field, including those who were more or less won over by the ideology of the National Revolution, triggering a vast polemic. Launched in the Southern zone, the "quarrel of the bad masters" reached the Parisian press in the autumn of 1940 and would remain at the forefront of the literary scene up until the summer of 1942. Its echoes could be found in the press of the Southern zone until March 1943. Renewing the tradition of putting intellectuals on trial in the summer of 1941, it led to a broader debate on intellectualism. Since the history of the debate and its principal arguments have already been analyzed by Wolfgang Babilas,[156] we will refer here only to the principal milestones (with some additions), with the intention of using it to understand the redefinitions of the literary stakes under the Occupation and the rhetoric of denunciation, bringing to light the divisions that lay beneath position-takings.

The accusatory discourses can be divided between the two poles that we have already identified. At one pole, the moralizing and apparently depoliticized discourse of the proponents of "good taste," who held dominant positions in terms of temporal power. They included members of the French Academy and "organic intellectuals" from the traditionalist wing of the Vichy regime. Despite the work of euphemization and theorization that they were forced to do in order to respect the rules of scholarly debate, we can still recognize their rhetorical process. It was characteristic of conservative ideological discourse, which consists in depoliticizing their own vision of the world by reducing "the public to the private, the social to the personal, the political to the ethical, and the economic to the psychological"[157]—we might add the aesthetic to the moral. It did this by accusing politics (that is to say the Republic and the social philosophy attributed to it) of being the origin of all evils, by asserting, finally, the "social decomposition" caused by legitimate literature from the interwar period. At the other pole was the over-politicized discourse of the pretenders who sought to differentiate themselves from these champions of moral order and their academic conformism. At the moralizing pole, it was André Gide who looked like the "bad master" par excellence, whereas at the other pole, François Mauriac was made into the symbol of the consecrated bourgeois writer who, through his "unhealthy" influence and his endorsement of warmongering positions, had a share in the responsibility for the nation's misfortunes. This polarization partially intersects with the struggles that opposed the Collaboration extremists and the traditionalist wing of Vichy, but it took on a specific form, as we will see, in each of the zones. The defenders of the stigmatized writers responded to these attacks, according to the aesthetic logic that prevailed at the autonomous pole, by denying the "responsibility" of the writer and asserting the rights of literature.

LITERATURE RESPONSIBLE FOR THE DEFEAT

It was first in reference to the education of youth that on July 9, 1940, on the eve of the vote of full powers for Pétain, an unsigned article in *Le Temps* condemned the "harmful influence" of André Gide.[158] At the end of the month in *Le Journal de Genève*, Guy de Pourtalès resumed Pétain's discussion of the Republic's purportedly disastrous shortcomings, in order to denounce the "bad masters" who had been "deceiving" youth for twenty years; he called for their punishment. Prominently among the politicians, journalists, and instructors, he questioned certain literary figures:

Here, the bad master has exercised the most fearsome influence of all. Intelligence has striven to kill conscience. [...] Look through the bookshelves of your library: pessimists, defeatists, immoralists, and corydons (many with an incontestable talent) will inform you of the depth of "intellectualist" evil. "It is not with good feelings that one makes good literature" one of the most famous among them has said. Writers have abused a false truth that has all the advantages of what is easy, and pleasant like a paradox. We have silenced reason in order to better hear the voice of enchanters. We smiled at the Surrealists, crowned the Bolshevists, applauded the futurists, unanimists, Fustigists. We said: *After us, the deluge.* But deluge came before and more quickly than we expected.[159]

The need for explicit redefinition of the positions in a period of disruption of the reference points was probably at the origin of the vast echo that greeted these attacks from the margins.[160] *Le Figaro*'s literary page made itself into a defense team. Its critics' argument had all the more bearing as they shared certain presuppositions with the accusers in regards to their vision of the world, and they were far from hostile to the new regime. André Billy responded that "the calamity of intellectual anarchy" was not new, and that the influence of the "bad masters" having "only touched an elite," the military defeat could not be attributed to them.[161] André Rousseaux, after having responded ironically, took the matter seriously, arguing that quite on the contrary, the denounced literature knew, by its "passion for truth in a world sullied by lies," how to take "a sort of tragic consciousness of the terrible moral, not to say theological crisis that crisscrossed our world in such a way that its material collapse was bound to come" and he warned against the confusion between "moral order" and "conformism."[162] At the end of September, at the initiative of Pierre Brisson, *Le Figaro* launched an inquiry entitled "What will literature be tomorrow?" The topic would fill its columns until November 1940. To the questions "Did our literature take a wrong turn, according to you, before the turmoil?" and "Does a recovery, in this case, seem necessary to you? In what form?" the majority of authors consulted, from André Gide to Roland Dorgelès, would answer in the negative.

Meanwhile, an unsigned article by Henri Massis in *Le Temps* revived the issue: No one can reasonably imagine that our disaster has come from an insufficiency of physical culture in our country. *The French defeat is largely due to a weakness of intelligence.* The moral reform itself, so important, should be accompanied by an intellectual reform in order to be profound and last-ing. It is advisable to never forget the primacy of the mind.[163]

Massis would use this "acknowledgment" of the "weakness of intelligence" as his main argument in the preface of his book, significantly entitled *Les Idées restent*; it was published in January 1941, and included the articles he had writ-ten on Gide since *Jugements*. Massis had been slightly preempted by the acade-mician Henry Bordeaux. In *Les Murs sont bons*, an appraisal of the causes of the defeat, Bordeaux devoted a chapter to the misdeeds of literature, reminding it of its duties and expressing the wish that it play its role in the "recovery" of France.[164] Hailed by his colleagues at the French Academy, the historian Louis Madelin and the critic Edmond Jaloux,[165] the book was criticized by André Rousseaux who retorted:

> When Mr. Bordeaux reveals to us what he prefers in literature, he shows us at the same time the weaknesses from which we must preserve our taste [. . .] In the end, there are not two literatures, the good and the bad. There is only one: the one that exists, the one that merits the name of literature because it is literature.[166]

In the *Journal*, Maurice Constantin-Weyer, close to Action française,[167] made the "corruption of intelligence" a legacy of symbolism which, through the "snobbism of the nebulous and the 'abstruse,'" had perverted the simplicity and clarity of the French language. He denounced the "ravages made on French in-telligence" by the work of Gide and the "destructive values" cluttering French literature, even as he reaffirmed "the role of intelligence" in the "national resur-rection."[168] At this beginning of the year 1941, Charles Maurras himself became involved in the debate.[169]

Since the month of October, the wave of denunciation of "bad masters" had reached the Northern zone. Later, we will examine these articles, which belong to another vein. For now, I will only cite Camille Mauclair's article, "Pour l'assainissement littéraire" [For a purification of literature], which appeared in January 1941 at *La Gerbe*. Close in style to the pamphletary rhetoric of Henri Béraud, with whom he had formerly shown solidarity, Mauclair nonetheless borrowed certain arguments from the proponents of the moralizing concep-tion of literature. He occupied, as we saw for the interwar period, an intermedi-ary position between the two poles. According to Mauclair, writers did not know how to profit from the victory of 1918, instead devoting themselves to a "literature of the defeat," cultivating talent as an end in itself and not as "a means whose use constitutes a moral and social responsibility, and can be as disastrous as useful in the formation of the soul of generations."[170] Valéry, Gide, Mauriac, and Cocteau were called into question. This article would have a certain echo in the Southern zone, as shown by the reaction of André Rousseaux in *Le Figaro*; his response unmasked the resentment of the embittered and envious author behind the invocation "of morals, the interest of the state and society."[171] The following week, *Le Figaro* published an article by François Mauriac entitled "L'honneur des Lettres" [The honor of literature]. In it he contested the responsibility of "the writers worthy of that name" who "touch only an elite of insignificant number, and isolated from the mass," and warned against "the fools, the envious, the deceitful who claim to demand a ready-made moralism from the writers of France."[172]

For its part, the weekly *Gringoire* launched an inquiry on the theme "Does literature bear any responsibility for our disaster?" The points of view that emerged were divergent. Léon Daudet, from the Goncourt Academy, and Marcel Prévost, from the French Academy, challenged the accusations against literature. On the other hand, the "counselor to the prince" René Gillouin, a Maurrassian and representative of the traditionalist wing of Vichy, came to lend a hand to the accusers, followed by Henry Bordeaux who reiterated the arguments that he had developed in his book.[173] Despite these divergences, *Gringoire* assumed a resolute stance in the lead-in to Gillouin's response, thus marking the alliance between the proponents of "good taste" (Bordeaux and Guillouin) and the populist extreme right (Béraud). It recalled the arguments of Maurras and Massis against the "escapist literature" that they considered "the greatest cause of the moral and mental disarmament of France," then quoted a Parti populaire français journal article by Jacques Doriot, who took François Mauriac to task:

> Such challenges are not to the taste of François Mauriac. By the position that he has taken, notably during the Spanish Civil War when his sympathies went to the disinterrers of the Carmelites, Mr. François Mauriac, in fact, has his share of responsibility in the disorder of the minds. Very opportunely, Mr. Jean-Loup Dulac recalls in *L'Émancipation nationale* some texts of "Monsieur Mauriac the warmongering hypocrite."[174]

In addition, while in *Le Figaro*'s inquiry, Henri Béraud was content to condemn the cowardice of those who "refuse to 'Take a stand,'"[175] this did not prevent him at all from continuing in his newspaper to practice payback with his old literary enemies on the margins of the "quarrel of the bad masters." The conjuncture was favorable, for example, for reviving his vendetta against Jules Romains, who had fled to the United States and was stigmatized by the collaborationist press as an "emigrant."[176] *Gringoire* thus mediated between the poles of traditionalist Vichy and Parisian collaborationism.

Finally, in *France 41*, the summary and program of "the constructive National Revolution," the permanent secretary of the French Academy, André Bellessort, a member of Action française, would paint a portrait of the degradation of French literature following the Great War, at a period when society, "corrupted" by its institutions, experienced a grave "moral disruption." Feminist and working-class demands, "fever of pleasures," lure of profit, agony of a traditional bourgeoisie "crushed by taxes": society had "abandoned itself to the foul influences of the regime and an invasion of foreigners that has cluttered our administrations, our university, our legal profession, our medicine, our industry, our factories."[177] At the end of a study entirely dedicated to the content of works and their moral implications, as we shall see, he invited the writer to rediscover the meaning of his "social responsibility."

In fact, the offensive emanated not from the young rising generation but from yesterday's competitors. They were the "rejects of *La NRF*," to borrow Gide's expression, those who had been subjected to the criticisms of a Thibaudet or a Paulhan, or those whom *La NRF*'s symbolic show of force after the Great War had simply offended, who revived from its ashes a debate in which they were the protagonists, twenty years earlier. In the accusers' camp at this point in the "quarrel of the bad masters," the average age was over sixty years. It was fifty-four years in the defenders' camp.

The accusers' camp gathered the spokesmen of the Academy's right wing (Henry Bordeaux, Edmond Jaloux, Louis Madelin), writers, poets, and critics who represented the Catholic wing of the Action française circle, most of whom contributed to the *Revue universelle* (Henri Massis, Henri Ghéon, Robert Havard de la Montagne, Camille Mauclair, Tristan Derême), Goncourt Prize winners who were close to this circle of influence (Maurice Constantin-Weyer, Guy Mazeline, and the regionalist writer Henri Pourrat, who would win the prize in 1941), Charles Maurras himself, then a member of the French Academy, and critics from conservative newspapers like *Le Temps* or *Jour-Écho de Paris* (Jean Fernand-Laurent). It expressed the alliance between the conservative Catholic right, the reactionary extreme right and the populist extreme right that marked the recomposition of the intellectual field after February 6, 1934, upon the rise of the Popular Front government. This alliance was solidified by the neo-pacifist fights for the "defense of the West." A number of the "bad masters'" detractors were involved (Bordeaux, Madelin, Massis, Maurras, Mauclair, Ghéon, Guy Mazeline, Maurice Constantin-Weyer, Henri Pourrat, and Paul Claudel, who joined this camp during the Spanish Civil War), although the political split did not correspond exactly to the literary split. Thus Léon Daudet, in the *Gringoire* study, invoked Maurras's "politics first" in order to assert that literature was not a social cause but "an effect, a historical resultant."[178] Faithful to his principles, the son of Alphonse Daudet did not hesitate to praise André Gide in the very columns of *L'Action française*, saying that his "thoughts [have] known neither weakness nor failure in the series of events."[179] Ideological divisions therefore do not suffice to account for the positions taken in this quarrel. It is necessary to relate them to "field effects," and notably to two principles of opposition: the struggles between literary generations to impose a legitimate definition of literature (from this viewpoint, the debate was a culmination of struggles begun twenty years earlier), and the struggles that opposed the defenders of the autonomy of literary values to the "moralists."

The crusaders against legitimate literature from the interwar period criticized its spirit of individualism, its aesthetic amorality, its decadence. Their arguments nonetheless betrayed the double concern of evading the label of conformist moralism that their adversaries applied to them with good reason, and of answering the criticisms of the latter, who opposed truth to moralism. The Maurrassian neoclassical aesthetic provided them with the necessary conceptual tools. The simplistic version of this conception was outlined by Henry Bordeaux. The identification of the Beautiful, the Good, and the True allowed him to reply to Gide's famous expression, "good feelings are not a matter for literature": "But they are the honor of masterpieces," even as he abstained from attaching literature to morality. He quoted Maurras who, inspired by Plato, "sees in beauty the principle for perfecting the soul and the body" to state: "The enemies of the Good seek in vain to shield themselves behind the True that proposes to them the infinite diversity of human decays."[180] Similarly, Henri Massis asked himself: "On the pretext of painting man, must we show the impure and the dishonest?"

It was in fact a question of the writer's "material," as Maurras explained in his response to the article that Mauriac published in *Le Figaro* under the title, "The Honor of Literature." Maurras agreed with Mauriac about the risk that literature would run with a "ready-made morality": "True Beauty is not a slave of utility, even moral and national utility." It was not a matter of submitting aesthetics to ethics, but of questioning the "material" used by the writer. Together with "order" (the relation of the parts to the whole) and "movement" (the expression), material was one of the three conditions for the quality of a work of art. Maurras blamed a certain literature of the interwar period for having rejected material "of purity and grandeur" for "base and vile" material, "purity and grandeur" referring to the "national feeling" numbed by "a long century of revolutionary denial and Romantic folly." But the writer's material was his soul, Maurras explained. The "puny and poor natures, the feeble ones whose vices submerge virtue" could not attain the "mental and moral sublime [that] is the native element of superior souls." By elaborating his aesthetic theory from the assumption that grounded his social philosophy, namely the existence of "natural hierarchies," Maurras could then do without a transcendent morality. He established a distinction between the "elite" of writers, represented by people like Péguy and Barrès, and the average, and particularly the below-average whom he claimed recruited "more and more, with a growing facility [. . .] the army of intellectual crime."[181]

Far more than Catholics like Bordeaux and Massis, Maurras was always careful to distance himself from moralizing discourse. His social philosophy avoided the moral question. For him, "if we want to avoid an individualism that only suits Protestants, *the moral question becomes a social question again*: no morals without institutions. The problem of morals must be brought back under the dependence of the other problem, and that last one, all political, reestablishes itself in the foreground of reflection of the best."[182] In this aesthetic debate, he substituted "private interest," namely "the good of persons," and "public interest," namely "the good of society and of the State," for morals. From this standpoint, he joined Massis and Bordeaux; for them, the question of content—"material"—raised the question of its social effects.

In the tradition of Paul Bourget, they considered that it was the writer's duty to do the work of a social clinical practitioner.[183] Thus, Henry Bordeaux did not deny literature "the right to paint monsters," on the condition that, like Balzac and Paul Bourget in *Le Disciple*, it assumes its responsibilities, consisting in the search for causes and proposition of remedies for the ills of society. He opposed them to "those sickly contemporary novels where no general observation can be gleaned that denounces the evil of man or of society and discovers the causes if not the remedies for them."[184] Bordeaux quoted Captain Jean L'Hote who asked himself: "Who is the one who makes us grow and tears us from our worries and our egoisms, when he tells us stories of madmen, of unbalanced people, of unsexed people?"[185] Under the influence of Proust and Freud, André Bellessort explained, literature after the war "was dominated by sensuality, pathological cases, the indecision of characters, the attraction of physiological and moral misery and human degradation that was translated by the benevolent curiosity of the filthy and shady milieus" to the detriment of "the willful, powerful, generous energy, the active goodness, the heroism and sacrifice." For young writers, "the unconscious [. . .] was only the unexpected and disconcerting awakening of animality." Never had one met with as much non-willfulness in the French novel. This complete absence of moral self-control, of self-domination exposes the individual to fall to the power of any pressing suggestion from his innermost self or from the outside. It puts him at the mercy of the worst incentives and the worst instincts. Our novels are full of murders that are only sudden reactions or blind impulses of the animal awakened in man, unless they are gratuitous crimes like the one that is described to us in *Les Caves du Vatican*.[186]

Henri Massis denounced this "unhealthy psychologism that ends in the dissociation of personality." He blamed Gide for his lack of concern that "his work brings trouble to other people, engenders pestilence."[187] While he refrained from putting Gide on trial for immorality, he blamed him for having presented himself as a reformer, substituting his own laws to the laws of nature.[188]

The link of cause and effect between this literature and the military defeat remained to be proven. Against those who, like André Billy and François Mauriac, denied the influence of literature on the masses or disagreed that its effect on the morale of combatants could be measured, the critic and academician Edmond Jaloux responded through *Le Figaro* inquiry, alleging that "zero on the masses, the influence of the writer is, however, liable to exert itself over the semi-elite that trains the *managers*." While the influence of a "bold and 'progressive' literary man [...] is without danger for the intellectuals of his race," it could be harmful for the "naïve people who do not have the experience of ideas. [...] Democracy, by multiplying the pseudo-well-read, creates unforeseen responsibilities for the writer."[189] This argument, which returned to the theme of the "intellectual proletariat" and the "socially displaced," was taken up again by Massis in the preface to his book, then by Robert Havard de la Montagne in *L'Action française*.[190]

According to this conception, literature was not a simple reflection of the "health" of the social body. It was also a social cause. The justification for the "unhealthy" effects of literature relied implicitly on a semi-scientific theory of energy that was based, like Montesquieu's climate theory and the learned myth of the North and the South,[191] on the schemas of the sexual division of the world (soft/hard, loose/sturdy, cowardly/courageous). Nascent social psychology (Gustave Le Bon's theories on crowd psychology or Gabriel Tarde's theories on the spread of ideas through imitation) had given this theory a new authority. Thus, according to René Gillouin, artistic production, through its pacifist inspiration or its "morbid eroticism," had greatly contributed "to the intellectual and material disarmament, to the loosening of social bonds, to the weakening of energies, to the diminution of moral health, to the discrediting of spiritual values, which all, as it were, augured our defeat."[192] Responding to his critics in an article entitled "The Responsibility of the Writer," Henry Bordeaux claimed the authority of "three excellent judges of effects and causes: a great doctor, a great historian, a politician of genius," whose argumentation he offered in support of his own: the professor Pierre Mauriac, brother of the writer, dean of the Faculty of Medicine at Bordeaux and a member of Action française, along with his colleagues from the French Academy, Louis Madelin and Charles Maurras. Far from condemning the whole of literature from the interwar period, Bordeaux explained that he limited himself to "denounc[ing] the bad currents that threatened to turn youth away from national life as from the conservative powers of individual and social life." He argued that literature was not only an effect but also a cause, to the extent that it "projects into the brains of an elite or a crowd, according to its credit, images that uphold the energies or weaken them."[193]

On the side of the defenders of literature from the interwar period were mainly writers who established themselves during that period. Thus it was, from the viewpoint of the principal figures in this debate, a confrontation between generations. *Le Figaro*'s inquiry had given a platform to writers who were more or less directly targeted, particularly André Gide, Georges Duhamel, Roger Martin du Gard (along with François Mauriac, André Maurois, and Jules Romains, they would seek refuge in the United States, the whipping boys of the collaborationist press in Paris). They would be seconded by two Goncourt jurors (Francis Carco, Roland Dorgelès), and critics like Alexandre Arnoux and Gérard Bauer. They refuted on principle an evaluation of the work in virtue of its social or moral role, denied the influence of literature on social and political reality (it was only a consciousness-raising tool for the realities it reflected), and emphasized the importance of the interwar period in French literary history. In short, against the moralists, they invoked the values of pure literature. "Without freedom, no art. We are not suppliers," proclaimed Francis Carco.[194] "Reform literature? Why? Was it twisted?" his colleague Roland Dorgelès asked ironically.[195] And André Gide made a demonstration through the absurd: "By engaging literature so much, those who accuse ours today would have us believe that it was necessarily inferior to that of all victorious nations."[196] These arguments were supported by the young review *Poésie 40*, which reproduced large excerpts.[197]

Between these two quite well-defined camps, the attitudes of Paul Claudel and Jean Schlumberger, representatives of the moralist side of *La NRF*'s founding team, reflected the ambivalence of the positions they occupied in the field. Without refuting the principle of the writer's moral responsibility and social role, they turned it around against their direct competitors, thus destabilizing the play of settled positions. If Jean Schlumberger challenged didactic literature, it was not in the name of the autonomy of art, but because "with its forced optimism, [it] is the least able of all to build character," he explained. On the other hand, he condemned the novelistic "miserabilism," an expression that targeted, through accusations of nihilism, "complacency for what is most sordid in life" and "abandonment to nausea," the most representative author of Gallimard's young guard, Jean-Paul Sartre.[198] For his part, Paul Claudel hastened to accuse writers of "complacency toward the worst perversions," "dryness," and "lack of charity," even as he rushed to praise writers such as Duhamel, Jules Romains, and Romain Rolland ("whatever you think of his tendencies") who were out of favor with Vichy as in Paris. Only the name of André Gide, his great rival, directly targeted by the attacks, was not pronounced.[199]

The fact that this debate was also the culmination of the struggles between the two literary generations that asserted themselves before and after the Great War, respectively, was confirmed a contrario by the distance between the positions taken by the young generation of Action française and their masters. It was not enough, actually, to share a belief in the Western conception of "man" and in the need for a National Revolution to line up automatically on the same side as those who accused literature of being responsible for the defeat. One also had to believe that literature could be a cause and not just an effect, and grant it a moral role that not everyone who shared this vision of the world was ready to concede, not only because they did not drink from the same spiritualist sources as the conservative or reactionary Catholic fraction, but also because such a position was costly on the literary plane. This was all the more true for the ideologically marked young pretenders. Such was the case for Kléber Haedens, Claude Roy, and Thierry Maulnier, the most promising critics of *L'Action française* (the latter two having, as we saw, separated from the team of *Je suis partout*); the example of Léon Daudet offered them an alternative. Representatives of the young generation formed at a time when André Gide and the NRF team had established themselves as the bearers of literary legitimacy, they showed a certain deference to those masters, all the more so since two of them (Haedens and Roy) had reached the columns of the prestigious review in 1939. In response to *Le Figaro*'s inquiry, Kléber Haedens wrote: "To undertake the recovery of a literature that includes writers like Claudel, Maurras, Valéry, Proust, Gide, Giraudoux, and Montherlant is a ridiculous pretension. We had not had a similar flowering of talent and genius since the 17th century."[200] Mocking, moreover, the "champions of the moral order," in an article entitled "The National Revolution and Literature" Kléber Haedens invoked the example of the "most absolute sovereign of our history" who had defended Molière against "the proponents of conventional morals" before concluding: "When the State is strong, writers are free."[201] In the tradition of André Rousseaux's reaction to Camille Mauclair's article and François Mauriac's warnings against "the fools, the envious, the deceitful," Thierry Maulnier—who was himself, let us remember, under attack in the collaborationist press by his former colleagues at *Je suis partout*; he had broken away from them on the eve of the debacle—denounced "the assault of the mediocre": "The greatest, happiest, and most fatal changes are almost always received with joy by the mediocre, to whom they seem to offer hopes of revenge."[202]

Like the defenders of the "bad masters," Thierry Maulnier would reassert one of the fundamental principles of the autonomy of the literary field, namely that the value of a work was "independent of the utility or uselessness that it may have," and pay tribute to the literature from the interwar period.[203] His analysis, which was meant to help redefine the terms of the debate, will be examined later.

The literary cost that adhesion to the authoritarianism of the regime represented for these young pretenders, and their will to distinguish themselves from the proponents of the moral order, were legible in their rhetorical precautions, which testified to their discomfort in occupying the position of moral censor. A typical strategy consisted in anticipating supposed objections, as the following citation by Jacques Bostan alias Jacques Laurent illustrates: "I know that despite my 'precaution,' to quote Gide, I will be treated like Clément Vautel.†† I want to set military rules for literature: in "redresser" [to set right], there is "dresser" [to drill]. In short, the just response given to Henry Bordeaux. Nonetheless, I want so little to set petty rules for our literature that the fear of it is the impulse for my worry," he wrote, to introduce his argument in favor of a regime's right to practice political censorship by alleging the double nature, spiritual and temporal, of the work of art. "If this temporal nature is the matter of its success, it is also the very matter where state authority is exercised. From the moment that a work uses the means of distribution that society puts at its disposal, it tacitly recognizes its jurisdiction."[204] On this basis, Jacques Laurent said he was favorable to the banning of works that had "harmful effects," even as he stated that those effects were often independent from their author's intentions.

The ambivalent relationship that the young pretenders, whether pro-Vichy or collaborationist, maintained with censorship due to the incompatibility of

---

†† A conservative journalist and popular novelist who became the symbol of reactionary morality.—Trans.

their double allegiance to political authoritarianism and literary values made discursive developments and adjustments necessary in order to justify the conservative revolution they endorsed. The contradictory position that Jacques Laurent adopted two months later was a sign of these difficulties of adjusting to the new conditions of production:

> We are confused at having to endlessly repeat that it is not by burning Rabelais, by expurgating Molière and by forgetting Gide that we will revive our virtue [. . .] that if there is a French baseness it is not in the cynicism of Montherlant but in the idealism of the romans bleus[§§]; that if there is a French degeneration it is not attributable to the freedom of its arts but to the incontinent stupidity of a sometimes conformist press. [. . .][205]

Between 1941 and 1942, a generational shift in the dominant positions of the literary world occurred. This change can be illustrated by a comparison of the official assessment of the literature from the interwar period drawn up by André Bellessort in *France 41* with the one presented the following year by Daniel Halévy, Marcel Arland, and Thierry Maulnier in the album of the *Nouveaux destins de l'intelligence française*, which appeared in 1942 under the auspices of the Office of the Secretary of State for Information. The texts were gathered by Henri Massis and Maximilien Vox, and an unabridged version was published the following year by the publisher Sequana under the title *La France de l'esprit*. The attacks by André Bellessort, Henry Bordeaux, or Charles Maurras, all members of the French Academy, were like the culmination of the struggles begun in the 1920s, at a time when a whole new literary generation asserted itself, under the banner of their fellow writer and old rival André Gide. Upon the death of André Bellessort at the beginning of 1942, one of the figures of this postwar generation, Georges Duhamel, would succeed him as permanent secretary of the Academy. Marcel Arland was also a representative of this generation. In his article, Bellessort noted the disdain of the young writers returning from the front for the writers that his generation had admired: Guy de Maupassant, Ferdinand Brunetière, Jules Lemaître, Pierre Loti, Bourget, France, Barrès. Among the writers from the interwar period, only his colleagues from the Academy were spared: Pierre Benoit, Georges Duhamel, and François Mauriac. Although Arland joined Bellessort in his condemnation of the "escapist literature" of the postwar period and its misguided "ramblings of the *self*," he still

---

[§§] Blue novels, or a series of popular novels published by Tallandier and intended primarily for women.—Trans.

considered that "the novelistic literature of the interwar period is one of the richest and most curious that we have seen blossom," and applied a more nuanced judgment to this production. Gide—whom the Christian philosopher Gustave Thibon nonetheless filed, in the same volume, among "our false prophets" along with Rousseau and Hugo[206]—Proust, and Giraudoux appeared as the masters of that generation.[207] In his appraisal of French poetry, Thierry Maulnier would also hail a remarkable "poetic flourishing" and respond to the detractors of the "bad masters":

> The fact that the French literary genius had the strength to remain vivacious and fertile in the darkest days of our political and social decomposition should not lead us to draw the conclusion—as some do today—that it has been complicit, that it bears its flaws, and that a new society, more austere and tougher, has as its first duty to scorn and destroy the only of our riches that society has spared.[208]

These revelations mark, if not the end of the debate in the Southern zone, at least its marginalization after the Riom trial,*** which was like the tragicomic culmination of "the hypnosis of punishment." Meanwhile, the debate had moved on to a question that exceeded the "bad masters," concerning the responsibility of "intelligence" in the defeat. We will return to this question after studying the redefinition of the stakes caused by this debate in the Northern zone.

THE RHETORIC OF STIGMATIZATION

More than the conformist moralism of academicians in decline (despite the official role that was bestowed upon them in the new regime) and whose arguments were refuted with relative ease, it was the offensive launched in the Northern zone that would solidify the stakes of the debate. Assimilating the writers they condemned with the social groups targeted by the occupant (Jews, Freemasons, Communists), the rhetoric of denunciation took a far more threatening turn than in the Southern zone. The situation of occupation conferred a new meaning on common forms of literary payback such as malicious gossip, disparagement, and slander. At such a conjuncture, and in the words of those agents most inclined to heteronomy, what was ordinarily only a regulatory practice slid toward denunciation and designation to the acting forces. This

---

*** Through the Riom trial, launched in 1942, Pétain sought to prove that the leftist leaders of the late Third Republic were responsible for France's defeat.—Trans.

time the practice was illicit, according to the principle of autonomy, because it had recourse to external powers in order to overturn internal power relations.

The invective, as a literary genre, had experienced a new vitality under the Third Republic, from Léon Bloy to Céline, along with the surrealists. This genre, related to the pamphlet, owes its credibility, like the pamphletary speech analyzed by Marc Angenot, to the production of a solitary, unauthorized person who demonstrates intellectual courage by raising his voice to shout in indignation against a scandal, "truth" versus an instituted "lie."[209] Unlike established writers whose discourse is authorized by institutions (like members of the French Academy), or by a group endowed with a capital of recognition, the pamphleteer draws his legitimacy from his isolation and the objective risks he takes—proof of his good faith—while fighting a dominant ideology or its representatives. The break with the linguistic and discursive conventions of urbane discourse is the mark of its anti-conformism and gives this speech a subversive potential that can prove gratifying.

After the defeat, thanks to the generalized anomie that favored the transgression of the discursive norms proper to the literary field, the rhetoric of the invective spread throughout the collaborationist press. By taking as its target the prewar literary establishment, just like the politicians, the Republican institutions, Jews, and Freemasons made into occult powers, it declared itself subversive, eliding the transformations of the conditions of production that not only authorized it but conferred a real performative power on its practitioners. This negation of the conditions of discourse exposed their bad faith. Even when they turned this violence against the Vichy regime, not "revolutionary" enough for their taste, their credibility found itself undermined by their complicity with the occupying forces. This was precisely what, in the eyes of the most legitimate fractions of the literary field (which also often provided victims for invective writers), not only discredited this politico-literary coup d'état, but universally justified the sometimes quite personal indignation of those victims faced with the disgrace heaped upon them. From this standpoint, the generalization and institutionalization of defamatory practices would help designate the places and, for the victims of these attacks, favor the conversion of indignation into an active opposition.

Although the demarcation line did not trace a clear divide between the discourses of stigmatization—as we saw in the case of *Gringoire* and Camille Mauclair—the division of France into two zones nonetheless accentuated the difference between the moralizing discourse on the academic side and the overpoliticized discourse of the pretenders or embittered authors. This was all the more true since such discourses were readjusted in keeping with the expectations that prevailed according to the dominant ideology in each of the zones. Despite a clean break in style, behind the avalanche of invectives that Paul Riche poured on "Gallimard and its 'lovely team'" in the anti-Semitic weekly *Au pilori*, we nonetheless find accusations of the same order as those emitted in the Southern zone against the "bad masters," notably "aggression against the French spirit" and the "slow moral decomposition" for which the Gallimard house was supposedly responsible: "Assassin of the spirit. Gallimard! Corrupter Gallimard! Leader of the criminals, Gallimard! The French youth vomits you."[210] Reproducing these sentences, the young semi-legal review *Messages* would ironize, "we wonder how old Mr. Riche is."[211] Similarly, in Jacques Doriot's daily *Le Cri du peuple*, whose strategy in the fall of 1940 was still to declare its allegiance to the National Revolution, Alain Janvier attacked André Gide in the name of public morality and taste:

> The public mind has let itself be informed by the most subversive philosophies and debilitating theories. The *Faux Monnayeurs* made a fortune, but those who cashed in on fraudulent currency without controlling its title nor its effigy are now dumbfounded in the face of the fraudulent inflation of ideas and the ruin of their traditions.
>
> The example of André Gide is typical from this viewpoint. In 50 years, no writer has enjoyed such an uncontested prestige [. . .] This is because, at the same time, the *moral sense* was anesthetized in a large number of Frenchmen: the mind gave up, the will gave in.
>
> How else to explain the extraordinary flowering of the novel of "bad morals" where filth and talent were combined?[212]

The previously quoted article by Camille Mauclair haphazardly revived Massis and Béraud's old accusations, adapting them to contemporary taste. Mauclair criticized Valéry, just as Massis used to blame Gide, for masking his "nihilism" under "the charms of the form," and for having introduced the "soul-destroying notion of 'poetry in a pure state'" into the poem and the essay. In his words, André Gide devoted "his eminent gifts and his specious dialectic to the demolition of religion and family, to the intoxication of youth by doubt, to the argument for homosexuality. This great Bolshevizing bourgeois, versatile and devious, was a sower of weeds, responsible for the disarray of many souls." François Mauriac, for his part, "painted in his novels only perverse, cruel, and sometimes monstrous figures."[213] Mauclair thus crudely stated the presuppositions of Massis or Bordeaux's masked and euphemized discourse.

The work of adjusting discourse to the circumstances in order to make the adversary into a public enemy is legible in this first series of Parisian attacks against the NRF team. Inscribing themselves in the pamphletary vein of Béraud, the team's faultfinders no longer applied the stigma "Huguenot" (respect for the occupant *oblige*!), but that of "Jewified" [*enjuivé*]. Gallimard thus became, in the words of Paul Riche, a "Merchant of Jews!"[214] whereas Camille Mauclair adapted Béraud's old arguments to the circumstances: "This more or less skillful and rotten production was presented in foreign countries as the supreme expression of the taste and aspirations of French people after the war by the harmful NRF of the Jew Hirsch, and other organizations." He made Paul Valéry into the "poet laureate of the Masonic Republic," and François Mauriac into a "more than strange Catholic, taking sides, with the sugary Maritain, with the hangmen of priests and the exhumers of nuns in Spain."[215]

The escalation of the stigmatization and the attempt at disqualification led to spreading the stigma's field of application by metonymy or potentialities (elective affinities, traits of character, etc.), according to the tendency toward amalgam characteristic of pamphletary logic, which wanted "the enemy to have *only one head*," as Marc Angenot reminds us.[216] In *L'Appel*, for example, François Mauriac, who cannot plausibly be made a "Jew," became, in the words of "Dr. Guillotin," "a good zealot of Israel. He was not a Jew, but how he would have deserved to be one!"[217] By playing off of two possible interpretations—"Jew" as a metonymy for those who received a "deserved" punishment, and "Jews" as an "essence"—without worrying about the contradictions between the second meaning and the biological foundation of racist theory (couldn't one become "Jewish" by contamination?),[218] and by introducing potentiality, the author rendered rhetorically "acceptable" an infringement on the logical rule according to which a phenomenon cannot have an attribute and its opposite (Mauriac cannot be Jewish and not Jewish at the same time). Such a procedure was characteristic of the rhetoric of invective, in which all blows were allowed. But if this typical procedure was rhetorically "acceptable," it was because it was socially "acceptable" for an entire fringe of the intellectual field (the most marginal, to be sure) that did not stop at the logic or conventions of scholarly debate when it was a matter of pouring out one's hatred or resentment with respect to recognized authors. The social effectiveness of this kind of discourse, which was served by every means, resided in the fact that it could claim the immediate support of an audience that took anti-Semitism for granted, and indicate its new scapegoats by taxing the established competitors with suspicion of complicity with the stigmatized population. This suspicion strengthened, and was reciprocally reinforced by, the representation of the "Judeo-Masonic plot" purportedly enacted by the Third Republic. This rhetoric was thus a double blow: on the one hand it allowed its practitioners to make the targeted writers responsible for the misfortunes of France, notably by having subscribed to a "warmongering" carried out by Jews to the detriment of the national interest. On the other, it undermined the purely literary foundations, the integrity, the validity of a reputation acquired under, if not aided by, a regime abandoned to foreign and evil powers. Thus Mauriac, according to Jacques Dyssord, had obtained the creation of his play *Asmodée* at the Comédie-Française "as a reward for his scandalous campaigns in favor of the Spanish Marxists."[219] Even when they evaded the second kind of accusation, and even when they made ideological pledges, they incriminated themselves, like Jean Giraudoux, whose "style [. . .] is very distant from the decadent French style furnished by Israel," and who cannot be suspected of "warmongering," but who, as minister of information, had agreed to "second the Jews in 'their' war":

> In spite of himself, and this proves the cunning and danger of the Jews, Jean Giraudoux was carried away in the ranks of the frizzy-haired snipers of the Continental and became their right-hand man.
>
> However, Jean Giraudoux is no longer a child: if he obeyed Mandel, if he accepted into his departments too many Jews who controlled the spiritual life of a nation at war, he is after all a little bit responsible.[220]

This rhetoric of the invective was the most pervasive thing in the press of the occupied zone. It was the literary weapon of writers and journalists who had little in common, aside from their extreme collaborationism, but their will to dethrone consecrated authors. They had fought side by side in the battles for the "defense of the West," and they had distanced themselves at the same time from Maurrassism to become the sycophants of a Europe under the Nazi banner. Still, everything seemed to separate someone like Camille Mauclair, almost seventy years old, who during the 1930s had transformed his fight against the avant-garde painters into a denunciation of the "métèques" (aliens), who threatened French Art,[221] from the young guard of collaboration extremists. The first issue: their relationship to conventional morality.

The moralizing posture was indeed violently denounced by one of the spokesmen of this young guard. André Gide's former secretary, Lucien Combelle, never disparaged his former master. His panning of *Les Murs sont bons* by Henry Bordeaux was quite characteristic of the double political and literary criticism of the young Fascistic and pro-European collaborationists in regards to the reactionary Vichyites who defended bourgeois, moral, religious, and French values. On the literary plane, Combelle expressed the opposite of Henry Bordeaux's indignation concerning the Gidian motto, "it is with good feeling that one produces bad literature":[222] "Of course! This malicious colleague thought of Henry Bordeaux's literature, which being stuffed full of good feelings nonetheless becomes immoral from dullness and ugliness."[223] In *Je suis partout*, he addressed this theme in an article significantly entitled "The Honor of Our Profession." Setting himself apart from the moralizing posture of people like Henry Bordeaux or Camille Mauclair, he shifted the debate. Quoting Jacques Dyssord who before the war, in *L'Intransigeant*, accused writers of having become too "conciliating" (complacent), Combelle called for the severity of authors and their public. He recognized the freedom to write, as long as writers took their responsibilities seriously:

> Bad pastors! my friend who descends from Sirius and takes me for this poor Camille Mauclair will tell me, asking to purify our arts with the brush of Henry Bordeaux. Why should there be bad pastors? Because they are less elegant than the others? Less courageous? More pink or less red.
>
> No, dear threader of pearls, no. Bad pastors because they are dishonest. Dishonest because they are today guiding one herd, tomorrow another; they guide without taking their job seriously. They guide like a game, seeking to satisfy vanity and envy [...] we have stopped judging our comrades with the honesty and severity that such a job demands.[224]

This tension between the young collaborationist guard and the Vichy regime was heightened by the turn that "the intellectual and moral reform" of the National Revolution took, thanks to the concessions Pétain made to the traditionalist and Catholic wing of the government. Again in *Je suis partout*, an article by Jean Servière entitled "The Literature of Good Feelings" expressed these fears. Relying on Gide's phrase to declare, "It is not enough to be right-minded to think right," he drew a parallel between the question of the relationship between the politician and the priest and that of literature and morals:

> The call comes from all sides for a new, virile, healthy literature. And we are also in agreement to ask for something other than Mr. Chardonne's splitting of hairs or Mr. François Mauriac's dance hall confessions. But we grow wary when we see the first results of these calls and these demands. In the same way, firmly persuaded of the ignominy of the anti-Catholic fights, we think that the people should not be able to say: "the National Revolution is the priests!" (And there are many blunders committed on that side.) Similarly, we think that the call for virile virtues must not dissolve into right-minded literature, and sickly sweet novels.[225]

Céline's work was cited as a model: "Even if we were to quibble over certain points, it is a vigorous work, thus healthy [...] Much healthier and much more useful than that of the recently dead Mr. Marcel Prévost."[226] The banning and (partial) seizure of Céline's *Beaux draps* in the Southern zone at the end of 1941 would show that these fears were not groundless.

The politicization of discourse is thus a means of euphemizing a moralizing rhetoric in the literary field, through an inversion of the logic that prevails at the academic pole. The call to violence, the stylization of violence, is another means to set oneself apart from the posture of someone like Henry Bordeaux by giving the principles of obedience to order and authority the appearance of heterodoxy and subversion. It translated the over-politicized vision of the world embraced by the young Maurrassian or Fascistic guard, raised in the shadow of glorious elders who fought during the Great War. They were more convinced by Maurras's "politics first" and an aesthetic theory that did not separate thought and action than by the aestheticizing moralism that the Catholic wing of *Action française* displayed. The "virile" aesthetic of people like Montherlant, Drieu La Rochelle, Bernanos, or Céline, who belonged to this generation of veterans, showed them the way.

Between these two poles where we find the opposition between moralizing discourse and politicized discourse refracted within *Action française* itself, Maurras occupied an intermediate position. Concerned with distancing himself from the moralizing position, as we saw, Maurras subordinated morality to politics, which he enobled with a scientific and especially aesthetic aura. This clerical atheist who saw the Church as a necessary institution, but thought religion should submit to politics; this defender of "integral nationalism" brought upon himself the wrath of a Pope who had condemned Action française in 1926. But the compromises he had to make in order to renew the alliance with the Catholics; the negotiations conducted by Catholic French personalities with Rome to suspend the condemnation in light of his election to the Academy, which resulted in his submission; his academic consecration; and finally the social aging of the leader and his team contributed, with the advent of the Vichy regime, to making the once-subversive *Action française* into a quasi-orthodox organ of the regime. In any case, Maurras, unlike Léon Daudet, found himself on the side of the moralists in the "quarrel of the bad masters." This was yet another reason for his young followers, Haedens and Maulnier in the Southern zone, Brasillach and Rebatet in the Northern zone, to set themselves apart, the former by rallying the camp of defense of the "bad masters," the latter by reaffirming the primacy of politics and advocating an aesthetics of action. Besides, hadn't the *Je suis partout* team that had broken away in order to ally itself with Fascism blamed its master, on February 6, 1934, not only for failing to take action, but for having slowed "the momentum of his own troops"?[227] While

Maurras had been "lucid in the face of democracy," *Action française* remained "incapable of thinking of the revolution of tomorrow as anything other than a reaction," explained Jean-Pierre Maxence in Drieu La Rochelle's NRF, in reference to *Les Idées restent* by Massis. Massis had the merit, in his eyes, of having recalled "the necessary unity of intelligence and the heart," the "danger of idealist 'confusions,'" but his horizon was not "a profoundly, fundamentally revolutionary horizon." He let "an entire section of the real" escape, namely the social and economic problem raised by the failure of capitalism.[228]

The European perspective, Fascism, allowed the Collaboration extremists to pose as "revolutionaries" in response to the nostalgia of their former master, with his conservative nationalism. From an aesthetic point of view, they continued to subscribe to the notion of art's social utility, but they established a distinction between the "healthy" and the "moral."[229] Thanks to a Nietzschean vitalism and a pantheism that drew from pagan sources, they promoted the Dionysian principle over the Apollonian principle, instinct over reason, the body over the mind.

Céline was the symbol and the avant-gardist guarantee of the "revolutionary," "virile," and "healthy" aesthetic that they promoted. This imprecator, who reconciled their political ideas with a style that made the surrealists green with envy, was their "prophet," according to the expression that Rebatet, Brasillach, and Combelle each used in turn.[230] "If the thought, the attitude, the reactions are revolutionary, the style itself disrupts the grammar. We are in a full verbal hurricane. Compared to that audacious expression, the attempts of the surrealists are no longer anything but wails," Lucien Combelle wrote.[231] This style, which was attributed with both Rabelaisian qualities and an "enormous vitality" that authorized the comparison with Nietzsche, as Lucien Combelle explained after Ramon Fernandez, was not to the taste of those who were "mediocre" or "delicate": "Célinian excessiveness wants the reader to have a good stomach and a good mind. His genius touches the mind and the body. That is why it is healthy despite its mud."[232] Here we find the digestive metaphors of an Henri Béraud type. This author, who passed for "obscene," was truly obscene "in form, but how *healthy* in substance," François de la Mésanchère claimed in *La Gerbe*. Faced with "the surrounding stupidity," Mésanchère prized this popular frankness even as "all [his] education—familial or literary—leads [him] to prefer the manner of Abel Bonnard."[233] The abundance, the "vividness of the language," was for the critic of *Au pilori*, André Gaucher, "first a marvelous sign of physical balance, of vital power. It's because the form of the idea, that is to say the word, in suggesting the idea does not only caress our brain."[234] This biologization of literary criticism, which was in perfect harmony with doctrinaire racism, marked a clean break with the spiritualism of the conformist moralists. While for the latter, the medical metaphor could not be pushed beyond the limits set by spiritualism, here it was reduced to its literal meaning: physiology determined thought; the health of the body determined the health of the mind. Moreover, wasn't Céline a doctor? His fans never missed a chance to remind everyone. The medical metaphor could thus be fully restored. Dr. Destouches, with the help of the "sure scalpel" that was the French language, had proceeded to the "vivisection" of the Jew, a product of the hideous crossbreeding "of Asiatic barbarians and negroes" and reaffirmed the "biological superiority of the Aryan," André Gaucher continued. Breaking with a Cartesianism that had sacrificed the "heart" to the mind, along with a scholarly and academic tradition that had frozen the French language, Céline had rediscovered its medieval sources, lyricism, sensibility, "to communicate with the quasi-dead body of the poor French people" whose "resurrection" he announced.[235] In that, he was the personification of the "French genius." But such were the implicit presuppositions of his discourse; Céline, antiacademic, anti-conformist, antibourgeois, was a man of the people, who spoke "with his guts" and expressed popular "common sense" which had been perverted by the rationalist tradition and the democratization of instruction. Unlike the complacency of bourgeois writers for the "people," Céline made an "authentic" and well-informed diagnosis of "proletarian baseness," thus strengthening the elitist vision of the world, the class racism and the biological racism of these pseudo-revolutionaries, as this quotation from Robert Brasillach illustrates:

> [...] this book is one of the most perfect books by insubordinates in our literature. Our writers have always been bourgeois: it is the bourgeois Hugo who is the author of *Les Misérables*. Vallès, an authentic rebel, is nothing compared to Céline. Céline is in a fight with the entire universe, he knows bourgeois crookedness, he knows proletarian baseness, he has no illusion about any class, about any being [...] The *Voyage* is a total act of accusation, and the continuation of the works of Céline is only a series of fragmentary accusations against the Jew, against society, against Moscow, against the Republic. What an irony to think that he could have been pressed into service in spite of himself for the petty bourgeois hack writers of the Popular Front![236]

If Céline was their prophet, François Mauriac was their whipping boy. Even more than the writers of the Popular Front, whom they nonetheless showered with their disdain, he offered an antithetical image of the author of *Bagatelles pour un massacre*. By attacking the author of *La Fin de la nuit*, they killed two birds with one stone: first, denouncing the Catholic moralist and academician, already panned by Sartre in 1939, rather than the creator of Lafcadio, cleared them of any suspicion of orthodoxy. It was easy, in the same stroke, to double this literary criticism with a social criticism of the bourgeois writer allied with anti-Fascism. What Massis blamed on Gide was turned against Mauriac.

It was not by chance that the attacks came from the "left" wing of the Collaboration. Jean-Loup Dulac, in *Le Cri du peuple*, and Jacques Dyssord, in *La France au travail*, first set the tone in the fall of 1940. In *La France au travail* Jacques Dyssord created a special column called "Baudruches," where he sketched a series of satirical portraits of institutionalized writers[237]—Giraudoux, Duhamel, Mauriac, Maurois, Louis Gillet, all members of the French Academy with the exception of the first. By denouncing the academic conformism of these "bourgeois" writers and their involvement with the "former regime," he gave these portraits an air of social criticism that matched the objectives of a populist newspaper launched to spread National Socialism among workers.[238] Mauriac thus appeared in Dyssord's words as the archetype of the bourgeois writer who "possessed all that is needed to belong to the Forty [members of the Academy]. From his first book—a book of poems—conforming to the sensibility of his social caste—that of the shameful profiters—he had received the investiture of Maurice Barrès." To illustrate the "unhealthy" and "obscene" character of Mauriac's work, he juxtaposed two semantic fields, the religious and the scatological, making sexual allusions, according to a typical rhetorical device:

> He's a sexton who wants to give himself the airs of an officiant. He loves to scandalize the old devout ones and the children of Mary, by sliding gallant images in his book of prayers.
>
> If only these were attractive! But we might say that they are obscene graffiti drawn on the bathroom walls in an ecclesiastical school.
>
> When he speaks of love in his books, Mr. François Mauriac speaks of it in the manner of a school kid with rings around his eyes from bad habits [...]
>
> The unhealthy works of Mr. François Mauriac release an odor of fever and dirty linen that make us think of a poorly run dispensary in a leprous suburb.[239]

The denunciatory rhetoric expounded by Mauriac's detractors consisted, in a vitalist vein that was probably meant to be Nietzschean, of inferring from the "pathology" of fictional characters the moral and physiological degeneracy of the author, "himself badly screwed-up, scrofulous, looking like a chamber pot that is too full" in whom "everything [...] is troubled, vile, false, satanic, degenerate, stinking."[240] We could multiply the examples of this illicit rhetoric. For instance, during a June conference at the Théâtre des Ambassadeurs around the theme "Mauriac, agent of French disintegration," Fernand-Demeure revived the "analysis" he had already developed before the war in a medical review, on the "pathology of Mauriac's heroes."[241] Lucien Rebatet went one step further in *Les Décombres*, pushing the juxtaposition of the religious register with the scatological and sexual to its limit: "[. . .] the rich bourgeois with his baleful face of a false Greco, his decoctions of a Paul Bourget macerated in rancid cum and holy water, these oscillations between the Eucharist and the homosexual brothel that form the unique drama of his prose as well as his conscience, is one of the most obscene rascals that has grown in the Christian manure of our era."[242] Robert Brasillach would denounce Mauriac's themes for their "signs of a malaise both physiological and moral" before concluding: "The conquest of Mauriac, an academician and conformist, by intellectual anti-Fascism, is a victory of the midlife crisis."[243]

This campaign of stigmatization was likely the product of a concerted plan: a report by Gerhard Heller dated June 14, 1941, mentioned a meeting with Brasillach and his *Je suis partout* colleague Henri Poulain, where it was said that "young literary critics will also lead attacks against Mauriac because they do not agree with the attitude and style of this man."[244] Even as they served Nazi objectives, indeed as they overflowed with an excess of zeal (this was the case here), these anathemas thrown down from the heights of collaborationist forums were in any case deeply motivated by literary payback. The campaign against Mauriac was thus accompanied by a boycott of *La Pharisienne*, which appeared thanks to the agreement his publisher Grasset had obtained, to Lucien Rebatet's fury, from the director of the German Institute, Karl Epting (despite the fact that the Nazis considered Mauriac's art to be "decadent").[245] This concerted boycott, most probably instigated by Robert Brasillach, serves as an exemplary illustration of the strategy of "literary assassination" that mobilized extraliterary weapons, taking advantage of the heteronomous situation of the authorities of diffusion: "We were," wrote Lucien Rebatet, "censors more fierce than his compatriots" (he meant Karl Epting). "We asked him vehemently to ban the awful twisted neck François Mauriac, who could, to our great disgust, publish new books."[246] Indeed, these "revolutionaries" did not intend to limit themselves to the power of words. When Lucien Combelle wrote of Aragon that he had, like so many others, "mainly gained the right to be quiet," when he listed, proof in hand, the "criminals" that "France can no longer afford the luxury of keeping" (besides Aragon and the review *Poésie 41*, which "gives honorability back to the shameful Jews of the old NRF," as well as the review *Fontaine*, they notably included the anti-Fascist Catholics, Stanislas Fumet, Mauriac, Marc Beigbeder, whose *Mémoires d'un âne* contributed to the ban on the review *Esprit* in the Southern zone), it was not merely a stylistic device.[247] It was truly a matter of fighting for symbolic—if not physical—suppression of the adversary.

THE INTELLECTUAL, "BAD PRIEST OF INTELLIGENCE"

The wave of denunciations of "bad masters" in the two zones was related to the anti-intellectualism that grounded the Vichyites and collaborators' view of the world. Anti-intellectual discourse relied on a series of normative presuppositions that set limits on the exercise of thought: intellectual activity must not be its own aim (it was then nothing but "gratuitous games" of the mind); thought must not be separated from action; "intelligence" must not be dissociated from "character" and "will"; it must submit to the laws of "nature." The opposition between "intellectuals" and "intelligence," forged during the Dreyfus affair, was a recurrent figure in the discourse of the intellectual right until the 1940s (let us think, for instance, of the manifesto "For a party of intelligence" launched by Massis in 1919), even if we see the progressive generalization of the noun "intellectuals" in the interwar period, and its adoption by the right.[248]

The exploitation of the defeat against those who were qualified as "bad masters" found its justification in the theory that France had been lost by "false ideas." This theory, which reappeared in the writings of René Benjamin, Henri Massis, and Jean de Fabrègues,[249] established the urgency of the "intellectual and moral reform" that Pétain had called for in the National Revolution. Blame was assigned to the regime headed by intellectuals, from the "Republic of Professors" to the Popular Front.

While they did not agree on the proper remedies, Vichyites and collaborationists joined in a common rejection of the Republic, democracy, and parliamentarianism, and identified the intellectuals of the Popular Front as their principal enemies. Ramon Fernandez could thus observe that

> with a singular consistency, in perhaps the most intelligent country of the world, it is always intellectuals who have hindered our progress and our lives. Remember the Popular Front [. . .] Remember, remember above all that Mr. Léon Blum offered the image of the pure intellectual who "threw himself into the brawl." We would have thought that the intellectual, who had become a solid bourgeois, would have remained with the French people when the brawl became serious [. . .] But Mr. Léon Blum had bank accounts that French workers don't have [. . .] Nonetheless Mr. Léon Blum "was" an intellectual.[250]

Similarly, Lucien Combelle evoked elections that brought to power "an aesthete who plays at being a statesman, a writer who should have settled for making Goethe converse with Eckermann and writing a refined and sugared prose for a good hundred lecherous fans" and who went off to "make speeches to the people with a imperfect subjunctive every three lines," before observing: "The era is placed under the sign of the Intellectual. There are intellectuals everywhere and intelligence becomes a watchword. [. . .] intelligence 'is on the left, always on the left'—a writer [. . .] told me this huge joke with a comical gravity [. . .]."251

At the foundation of anti-intellectualism, there was resentment for the new mode of reproduction with its educational component, that is to say the Republican meritocracy that allowed for the promotion of new elites. The educational stake, often neglected in studies of anti-intellectualism, was nonetheless omnipresent in the discourse of its representatives. In a conference that took place in 1941 entitled "Formation of an Elite," the academician Abel Bonnard made "the indictment of an intelligence that had become common: intelligence that excludes character" and denounced "the intellectual, 'this bad priest of intelligence.'" Author of an *Éloge de l'ignorance*, the future minister of National Education attacked, in this conference, degree holders: "It was said: they are the smart ones! Nothing frightened me more than this expression. Their value was based on their brilliant entrance and exit from the grandes écoles [. . .] The notion of Elite, disengaged from the sterile contract that is the diploma, is therefore a thing that is measured by realities [. . .]."252 Likewise, Ramon Fernandez lamented that the intellectuals of the Popular Front "[made us] believe that a diploma was equivalent to a contract. They wanted to make us believe that the institution that allowed science or grammar to progress authorized each one to choose for France the government that suits him."253

The belief in school was, in their eyes, the illusion supporting the democratic "error." It was the principal obstacle to the expression of "natural hierarchies" and therefore to the social order. By feeding the "people" with an abstract knowledge without giving them a sense of the limits that were "naturally" assigned to them, school promoted individualism and material utilitarianism. The old theme of the "intellectual proletariat" spontaneously reappeared in the youngest writers, a sign of the persistence of representations created at the turn of the century and their reappropriation by successive generations. Jean-Pierre Maxence, born in 1906, wrote for instance:

> [. . .] In this inhumane society, the poorest was taught that instruction was enough to make him live, that it should be his sole ambition, his only faith,

and this actually created an immense proletariat of bachelors and degree holders, more disarmed in the face of life than the proletariat of workers.[254]

Jean de Fabrègues posed the problem of "the relationship of the mind and the body" in order to affirm that the "cult of the mind" that had characterized France since the end of the nineteenth century was in truth only a "reverence for material success, an expectation of pleasure." "For science," he explained, "[is] the domination and the possession of the world." Scientism and the attainment of diplomas were nothing more than two expressions of the "materialism" that was the necessary result of the "cult of the mind." The responsibility lay with Cartesian rationalism, and notably an interpretation of the philosophy of "clear ideas" that, dictated by the "desire to please," let it be supposed that "the mind thus resolved in propositions that were easy to formulate and understand was within reach of anyone."[255]

This resentment of the Republican school was one of the essential links in the chain that joined, in social representations, two types of "bad masters": writers and professors. The commonality of themes that gave substance, on all sides, to the content of these attacks (individualism, anarchy, removal from the real), as well as the stigmatizing use that was made of teaching-related categories ("ENS graduate," "professor") to disqualify a writer, shows the close relationship between these two types. The back-and-forth between the two was mediated, as we saw earlier, by the socially constructed system of oppositions— creator/professor, honnête homme/specialist, heir/scholarship recipient, person/individual—and by a repertoire of more or less formalized representations, such as "the intellectual proletariat" or the "Republic of professors," which made the terms used in a pejorative sense, "pion," "ENS graduate," and so forth immediately intelligible to contemporaries. Under the Occupation, Jules Romains thus appeared as the incarnation of the "bad master" par excellence: was he not the product of the ENS where "all [minds] have been touched by a kind of dialectical dryness," was he not the very expression of this "intelligence" as opposed to "emotion"?[256] About Romain Rolland, Drieu La Rochelle wrote in his journal: "What an ignoble style! What vulgar thought. Another normalien. What low trash," and about the former director of La NRF, Jean Paulhan: "a little pion, a little bureaucrat, pusillanimous and shifty, oscillating between hysterical surrealism and stupid rationalism of the Republic of Professors."[257]

For its opponents, the Popular Front reactivated the figure of the intellectual bureaucrat, a socially displaced upstart, tied to the "stipends" that the Republic granted him and typically represented by the professor. "For the artificial revolution of 1936 was indeed an intellectuals' revolution. Having rushed to obtain lucrative sinecures, they produced nothing from them but reports and propaganda," wrote Robert Brasillach. And, further on: "It was clownish and stuffy, with the primary school mentality in ascendance everywhere."[258] Powerlessness and sterility of pure thought associated with the satisfaction of material interests—the leitmotif of "stipends" being a metonymy of "materialism" in its double vulgar and philosophical meaning—such was the stereotypical image of these intellectuals:

> What was most shocking in these intellectuals of the Popular Front is that they constantly mixed up moral and material interests. In other words, generously remunerated by a complacent and somewhat naïve State, receiving relatively considerable salaries (more considerable in any case than the money received by the nationalists they denounced as corrupt), they gave themselves both the glove of purity and the bag of stipends.[259]

Finally, the metaphor of the fair to designate the Houses of Culture and the meetings of anti-Fascist intellectuals was recurrent: it constructed the negative image of the cultural policy of the Popular Front that "sells off cheaply" an imitation of culture and the organized disorder of parliamentarianism.

In his preface to the very official album *Les Nouveaux destins de l'intelligence française* (1942), Charles Maurras listed the "diminutions inflicted on intelligence," including "the existence of a class devoted to the type of remunerated exercise called study or teaching," which "naturally" tended toward the "greediness of the mind" and "the fertile mind of certain races, Jewish among others, which, passing for practical, or posing as such, are in reality very apt to treat thought like a commercial and artificial beverage" which "is not a simpler abandonment of facility, nor training, nor laissez-aller: a perfidious will gets mixed up in it to organize, undertake, prepare, cultivate in the sciences, the arts, the trades, shameful inversions and perversions that confound everything, aim and means."[260] The texts collected by Henri Massis and Maximilien Vox covered the principal domains of intellectual life. Next to relatively distant articles of scientific synthesis, engaged texts proposed a biased assessment. Albert Rivaud, professor of philosophy at the University of Strasbourg, member of the Institut de France, and the first state secretary for public instruction in the Vichy regime, thus condemned "the invasion of foreign influence, of the spirit of criticism and demand, the chimerical plans for social reform, the always-reborn obsession of a ready-made science put within reach of all in an encyclopedia, the indiscreet call to sentiment" that had destroyed the classical equilibrium between "the taste for experience, the scorn for appearances, simplicity, order, reason, the will to serve God, the State, and men." Against scientism, positivism, materialism, one must, he wrote, return the sciences to their limits and reestablish the place of religion and morality, tasks to which Henri Bergson and especially Charles Maurras had devoted themselves, the latter having restored the principles of order and necessary social hierarchies.[261] Likewise, Gustave Thibon, a philosopher very much in favor at Vichy, hailed the resurgence of the Christian spirit in a number of thinkers and writers of this century against "a rationalist, skeptical, or scientific tradition" which in France remained, according to him, "a superficial phenomenon."[262] For Louis Madelin also, history escaped this scientism "so contrary to all natural aspirations of the French mind" and renewed its relationship with "art," despite the efforts of people like Charles Seignobos, a representative of the New Sorbonne.[263] Needless to say, the names of Lucien Febvre and Marc Bloch were not even mentioned. For his part, Alexis Carrel, a renowned doctor and author of the best seller *L'Homme cet inconnu* (1937), exposed the project—put in place with the creation in 1941 of the Foundation for the Study of Human Problems—of a human science that would reunite the knowledge scattered across the different domains of human and natural sciences in order to "reconstruct men following natural laws, and give them a milieu where they could adapt without degenerating."[264] The volume ended with a text by René Benjamin, entitled "Hope," that paid homage to Pétain for having presented "the mirror of a magician" to a battered France, and for having shown it its past virtues which had been lost under the influence of false ideas.[265]

We must differentiate between two types of anti-intellectual discourse, the "elitist" and the "populist," which certainly shared some solutions. In fact, these two anti-intellectualist positions joined in a common rejection of the tradition of Cartesian rationalism and the philosophy of the Enlightenment, as well as in their will to impose restrictions on the exercise of thought in the name of greater interests, a will that grounded their heteronomous character. While they joined together in the same battle against the tradition of critical thought (just as they teamed up, as we saw, to denounce legitimate literature), they distinguished themselves by their relationship to the school.

The writers situated at the academic or institutional pole, close to the field of power and the state, where we find the greatest concentration of individuals educated in private Catholic schools and in the grandes écoles, tended to denounce the Republican school, the democratization of education and access to culture for all, pitting "instruction" against "education," specialization against general culture. They saw in this educational system, which disrupted the simple mode of social reproduction and produced socially displaced intellectuals, the origin of the "failure of intelligence" that led to defeat, according to Henri

Massis's expression. These allies of the dominant fractions of the dominant class sought to impose limits on thought (whether scientific or creative), notably moral or religious limits.

On the other hand, the intellectuals of the first generation or the heirs "disinherited" by the mode of reproduction with an educational component (those who "deviated" from their trajectory due to an academic failure, notably) tended to borrow schemes from the ideology of the "creative genius" and creative freedom valued in the literary field. Not without populist demagogy, they did so in order to disqualify degree holders en masse, and more particularly the elitist system of the grandes écoles. The populist wing of the Collaboration thus easily cited Balzac in order to declare the failure of the system of grandes écoles:

> In the grandes écoles issued from the movement of 1789, he [Balzac in *Le Curé du village*] mainly criticizes specialization. "Aren't special schools," he writes, "the great factories of incapacities?" A terrible question that seems to have its answer in the outcome of the war criminally engaged by our normaliens and lost by our Polytechnicians. Balzac adds: "[...] When the geniuses appear suddenly like this from the social milieu, pushed by their vocation, they are almost always complete; man, then, is not only special; he has the gift of universality."[266]

Still in the columns of *La France au travail*, Jacques Dyssord went one step further: "Intellectual workers, my brothers, before the painful end of this crazy war, didn't our innocence consist in believing that the rules of the game were those we had been taught on school benches, when in fact the dice were loaded and the cards beveled?" before rejoicing at the end of "the rule of the starchy rhetoricians and the abstracters of quintessence that a tam-tam of a fairground hut claimed to impose on a public badly defended against itself."[267] In reference to Vichy's suppression of the Écoles normales devoted to training primary school teachers, Dyssort wondered: "When will they in turn suppress the École Normale Supérieure, secular seminar of the surly rue d'Ulm, for which the nearby Pantheon serves as a snuffer?"[268] The suppression of the ENS was also part of the reform program imagined by Drieu La Rochelle.[269] The figure of the "quintessential abstracter," of the "secular seminarist of the rue d'Ulm" appeared, in Dyssord's "Baudruches" portraits, in the guise of a Jean Giraudoux, ashamed of his monocle and displaying an "affected simplicity." As for his work: "What to say of these laborious graces that claim to leave out the work that they have cost; of this false spontaneity; of these tiresome classical references that smell like their *collège* from twenty yards away; of this careful preciosity; of this Gongorism [...]."[270] Here anti-intellectualism took on its most common form: according to the opposition already mentioned between creator and professor, intuition and emotion were opposed to "soul-destroying" reason and intellectuality; spontaneity and "freedom" were opposed to labor and diligence; the living letter was opposed to the dead. Unlike spiritualism, which remained predominant at the elitist pole, vitalism led here to a condemnation of the "intellectualist disdain for the body," according to Drieu La Rochelle, who saw the loss "of the sense of the body" as the source of the decadence that had led the French to defeat. He specified that "[if he] speaks of the body, [he] speaks of the soul": "A soul only specifies itself, only realizes itself by its body. Christians knew it well—before the Bolsheviks and the Nazis. But our professors, our intellectuals had forgotten this old chestnut of life. Arrogance of the poorly made, knock-kneed intellectual, who nonetheless claims to know the laws of nature."[271] The postulate of a Catholic such as Henri Massis, situated close to the academic and elitist pole, was just the opposite: "No one can reasonably imagine that our disaster came from an insufficiency of physical culture in our country. The French defeat was due in large part to a failure of intelligence."[272]

This postulate justified, as we saw, the attacks against the "bad masters." That was why in this trial, their defenders were led to counter the prosecution with the weak influence of intellectuals, or even their "impotence," according to the expression of Thierry Maulnier, who blamed society in an article entitled "Are 'Intellectuals' Responsible for the Disaster?"[273] Published in June 1941 in *Candide*, the article, which answered Massis indirectly, modified the terms of the "quarrel of the bad masters" in the Southern zone: "The trial of French intelligence has been opened by the defeat," stated Thierry Maulnier. This article was followed by a serial in three parts on "The Future of Literature" that Maulnier published in *L'Action française* from August to September of the same year. Maulnier differentiated between the responsibilities of intelligence and those of intellectuals in order to clear the latter: intelligence (politics, diplomacy, strategy) was to blame, and beyond that, social causes ("demographic weakening, alcoholism, social struggles"). If literature participated in the "decomposition" produced by "intelligence," it was due to "the powerlessness of the mind" rather than the opposite. The blame belonged to a society that sometimes pushed literature to a withdrawal into "idealism"—represented by symbolism—to which "the classic notion of truth remains foreign." Delighting "in its own game," this resulted in the "ivory tower," a source of decadence. Sometimes, meanwhile, society pushed literature toward "materialism"—represented by realism and naturalism—where it denied itself by becoming the expression of interests and forces.[274] The cause resided in the divorce between mind and matter for which society was to blame: "At the beginning of the 20th century, general culture was so gravely hit that the only way of touching the crowd seemed to be vulgarity or banality, and the only way of touching the elite, artifice or scandal."[275] Although he exonerated the "intellectuals" of their perceived responsibilities for the defeat, by making them into the victims of a political and social system, Maulnier's analysis relied on the presuppositions of his political family.

In February 1942, the review *Idées* launched a study of "Intelligence and Its Role in the Polis." Five questions were asked: Did intelligence have any responsibility for the defeat? Was interwar France characterized by an abuse of intelligence? Was it not proper to distinguish between a society, shining through its writers and artists, and a state separated from the spiritual life of the nation? Didn't intelligence for its own sake that refused to contribute to the good of the polis fail its vocation? What was the role of intelligence in the new state (the question contained a section on the condition of the writer and the artist, and another on the relationship between intelligence and the state)?

From March to July 1942, responses appeared from Edmond Jaloux, Emmanuel Berl, Pierre Gaxotte, Pierre Dominique, Daniel-Rops, Gabriel Boissy, Charles Plisnier, René Gillouin, Jean Paulhan, Jacques Chardonne, Jean-Pierre Maxence, René Tavernier, and Henri Massis. The average age—forty-seven years in 1940—was lower than in the first period of the debate. Most of these writers belonged to generations that asserted themselves between the wars. Jean Paulhan's name stands out in this list of intellectuals allied with the National Revolution, including some of the regime's public personalities (Gillouin, Massis, Dominique, Berl). His brief response, colored by a hint of irony—"But no, it is the lack of intelligence rather, I suppose . . . ," "But your questions seem to bear their own answer quite well"—where he quoted the Zohar to say that one must "leave in wisdom some room for stupidity, and in good works some (small) place for the devil," was no doubt published as the work of a man of the young, prewar NRF review, or so the introductory paragraph suggested. The Maurrassian Pierre Gaxotte held to an equally terse response in saying that "it would be more equitable to incriminate *stupidity*."[276] All were concerned with exonerating "intelligence" of its purported responsibility for the defeat, and this was, in fact, the goal of the study. For most of them, however, intelligence was inseparable from "feeling" and "intuition."[277] There had been no abuse of intelligence during the interwar period, but rather of "pseudo-intelligence."[278] It was the intellectuals, and not intelligence, who had a large share of responsibility in the defeat: they had "betrayed" through their "withdrawal into art" and their "cult of pure ideas";[279] they had separated themselves from reality due to an individualism that had brought about a "failure of reason";[280] "they opened up like women to all available influences."[281] This derailing of "intelligence" was blamed on growing specialization,[282] "an educational system that never tries to develop human value, but a single aptitude,"[283] "the democratic university" that, through "an altogether analytic, critical conception of intelligence had ended up producing this people of masters for whom the meaning of life, power, character, and effort did not exist anymore."[284] With the exception of René Gillouin, representative of the traditionalist wing of Vichy, and Edmond Jaloux, who evoked the too-common examples of "the infatuation and the general ignorance of the Intellectual" to distance them from politics in favor of "informed specialists and prudent counselors who have a wide experience of men and events, the sense of the past and a courageous confidence in the future,"[285] all affirmed the role of intelligence in the polis and its necessary contribution to the "rise" of France. In his conclusions, "the inquirer," satisfied that the inquiry had demonstrated "the inanity of the debate that some wanted to hold on a poorly stated subject" by incriminating intelligence, quoted Barrès who made of it "a little thing at the surface of ourselves" in order to argue that "Intelligence and Action cannot oppose each other without disorder."[286]

Since the nomination of Abel Bonnard, at the very least, the task of "national interest" that the secretary of state for public instruction had taken on could be summed up by a formula, as the leadership of the general studies section explained in May 1944 in a letter to the French Academy: "to struggle against intellectualism, if we understand, in a general matter, intellectualism as the forgetting of human qualities, physical and spiritual, which are given by action." It was time to replace this negative definition with a positive one. That is why the general studies section had prepared, with the plan of consulting the entire country on this issue—while this country was being pillaged—a press and radio release that it submitted to the French Academy. Only a few weeks before the allied landing, the permanent secretary of the Academy, Georges Duhamel, surely ignored the request.[287] We do, however, have the plan for this press release, and it is worth quoting:

> Some have frequently, and not without reason, pointed to *intellectualism* as mainly responsible for humbling our country. It is thus particularly important to define what is understood by "intellectualism," when this accusation is made against it, in order to fight effectively against this calamity. The definitions given by the dictionaries don't seem satisfactory, because they don't allow us to understand how intellectualism can become a true national peril. It seems evident, in particular, that an individual or a people could in no case be too intelligent.

The General Superintendent of General Education and Sports has therefore decided to organize a national consultation on the following theme:

"To give a definition of intellectualism" [...].[288]

But this "intellectualism" that the cultural and educational politics of the regime sought to fight even without managing to define it was none other than the exercise of critical thought, and its subversive potential, as Jean de Fabrègues explained in his article quoted earlier:

> University philosophy is limited to what it calls the reflective mind, that is to say the mind's view of itself, conscious of not being able to get out. Taken down a notch, it will settle for what it will call "the critical mind," or an "ironic" view of all thought considered in the true sense of the word as *improbable*. Still one step further down, the critical will simply become the constant will to refuse, since nothing can be held by the mind as existing in truth. The refusal itself is then the very place of the mind: to say *no* is the sign of intelligence, the kingdom of the spiritual.[289]

Fabrègues summed up in a formula the presupposition that grounded the cultural and educational politics of the regime: "The separated mind is assured everywhere of a necessary failure: we command nature only by obeying it."[290] It was precisely this refusal, this ability to say no, this capacity for revolt, that was being asserted by the intellectual Resistance, and that writers like Sartre, Camus, and Vercors would later theorize as the foundation of human freedom.[291]

"THE JUDGES JUDGED"

In the general confusion, the culture of denial and the denunciation of the "bad masters" as public enemies exposed the restriction of possibles and the bipolarization of the issues masked by the struggles between Vichyites and collaborationists and by the nationalist discourse of the former.[292] The quarrel of the "bad masters" showed writers not only their potential allies, but also their proper place. It was in part because they were constrained, in the name of "art for art's sake," to defend their literature against the heteronomous logics that the supposed "bad masters," from André Gide to François Mauriac, from Roger Martin du Gard to Georges Duhamel, and their defenders, namely their critics (especially those writing in *Le Figaro*, André Rousseaux, André Billy, Alexandre Arnoux, etc.) were led to choose their camp—that of "refusal." François Mauriac best expressed, after the fact, this process of assigning places:

> The glorious name of Pétain resounded in my home as in the homes of all Frenchmen [...] But at the same time I reacted instinctively, without calculation, without reflection toward the Resistance—or rather I found myself on that side *without even having to choose it*; *my enemies*, much more numer-

ous and vigilant than I could have imagined, *had designated my true place to me by their insults*, from the first day.[293]

In this sense, aesthetic position-takings in the "quarrel of the bad masters" generally announced both the literary and political attitudes that would be adopted later. They show the reworking of alliances caused by the crisis situation. Placing the writers closest to the Collaboration and/or the Vichy regime on the side of the accusers, they simultaneously—through an effect of repulsion and according to the logic of choice restriction in a crisis situation—made the defenders of the rights of literature into the objective (and, for some of them, effective) allies of those who would soon commit their pens to the service of the fatherland in the context of an intellectual resistance that reaffirmed, in the tradition of Enlightenment philosophy, the supremacy of critical thought and its universality.

These themes, which had already been developed before the war by the anti-Fascist intellectuals and the Communists, notably Georges Politzer, in order to fight Nazi obscurantism in the context of the new Thorezian line of a national Communism, would be the spearhead of Communist propaganda and the mobilization of the intellectual Resistance. Whether they lay the blame on society, the regime, or the "bad masters," Vichyists and collaborationists considered that those they pejoratively called "intellectuals" had betrayed their mission. But the intellectual Resistance would turn this weapon against them. The theme of the failed intellectual, borrowed from the counterrevolutionary tradition to designate revolutionary intellectuals, was taken up against the collaborationists. In an underground article entitled "Literature, That Freedom," Sartre denied the writers of the Collaboration all literary legitimacy:

> The other day, in an article of pure denunciation, Rebatet proudly opposed the names of the "traitors" Gide and Jules Romains to those of the "great writers" of the collaboration. Oh surprise, these tenors of *La Gerbe* or *Je suis partout* are almost all lacking in talent, whether they have lost the little vigor or charm they once had, like Céline and Montherlant, or whether, like Thérive and Brasillach, they never had anything to say. We could not have hoped for more: at first sight, in fact, it would not have seemed that talent and character were linked and we might have imagined that a novelist of value, but cowardly, envious, or greedy, would collaborate with inspired newspapers. That is not so and, upon reflection, could not be so. [. . .] And, if we must finally explain this paradox, it is clear that they do not love writing, they even hate literature, because they know, at the bottom of their hearts, that they have no talent.[294]

"Lure of profit," "cupidity," cowardliness, lack of character, "poor blood," femininity, "homosexuality," "self-hatred," and "hatred for men," "hatred for literature" and the mind, the judges would be judged according to their own criteria.[295] Except that, in the rhetoric of the new judges, intellectual values would come first. Traitors of the mind before becoming traitors of the nation, or rather traitors of the nation because they were traitors of the mind, such was the accusation that the dissident writers turned against them. The crime for which they would be tried, "intelligence with the enemy," was, in the eyes of the literary community, only the corollary of the "crime against the mind," to borrow the title of an underground text by Aragon where, under the pseudonym of "Witness to the martyrs," he related the martyrdom of French intelligence.[296] This role reversal between accusers and accused sheds a significant light on the debates on the responsibility of the intellectuals at the Liberation, which must therefore be resituated in the perspective of this long tradition of the social construction of the "bad masters." It was in this role reversal that the Sartrian theory of "engaged literature" was sketched out. In the article cited above, Sartre wrote:

> We do not write to the winds and for ourselves alone: literature is an act of communication [. . .] Therefore literature is not an innocent and easy song that can accommodate all regimes; but itself poses the political question: writing is to claim freedom for all human beings; if the work is not to be the act of a freedom that wants to make itself recognized by other freedoms, it is only a vile chatter. Thus, outside even his feelings as a patriot, every writer conscious of his craft finds in his very literary activity a political duty: he must struggle to deliver his country and his compatriots, to give back to them this freedom that, alone, will give their value back to his writings; there is a time when literature itself demands silence and combat.[297]

The Phoney War and the defeat favored the imposition of the problematic of national moralism into the literary field. But the situation of occupation and the Vichy regime's politics of official collaboration produced a dissociation between nationalism and conservatism (or reaction), which had been closely linked since the end of the nineteenth century. The culture of disavowal and the charge against legitimate literature from the interwar period actually revealed the deep motivations of the euphemized discourse of the "moralists," who were also the proponents of "good taste." These motivations consisted in the preeminence of the defense of "order" over patriotic sentiment, and the struggle against the agents of "disorder" over the fight against the occupant. Among the agents of "disorder," the writers whose work contained a subversive potential and critical intellectuals ranked highly, as we have seen. The dissociation between national-ism and conservatism was brought to its climax by the Collaboration extrem-ists. Despite everything that separated them from the Vichy traditionalists, there was some continuity between these two tendencies, embodied on one side by the established writers of the Collaboration like Abel Bonnard, and on the other by the young generation of Action française that had been won over by Fascism (the *Je suis partout* team), and which readapted the Maurrassian heritage according to the redefinition of the space of political possibles.

Because it violated the elementary rules of literary debate, especially that of its autonomy, the generalization of the discourse of social stigmatization that accompanied the accusations against the "bad masters" in the occupied zone led to an almost parodic unveiling of the presuppositions underlying the cate-gory of the "responsibility of the writer," imposed by the proponents of "good taste" in the name of national moralism. As a result, whereas the first reaction to the moralists' attacks in the Southern zone consisted in denying the writer this responsibility in the name of "art for art's sake," the defense of literary au-tonomy would soon coincide with the attempt to reappropriate national mor-alism, through a fight for the defense of "the French spirit." The disrepute that the option of "art for art's sake" suffered very rapidly resulted, as we will see later, from the way the "distinguished" pole of Collaboration, Drieu's NRF, used it to attract writers into the review's columns. The reconquest of national au-tonomy appeared all the more like a condition of the reconquest of literary au-tonomy, as the opponents' illicit recourse to the acting forces in order to regulate power relations internal to the literary field made literary "treason" and national "treason" seem like two sides of the same coin. In this fight, which could be waged only in "contraband" or clandestinely, literature would redis-cover all its subversive power. Before seeing how this dynamic was driven by institutional struggles, we will examine it through the comparison of two exem-plary trajectories, those of François Mauriac and Henry Bordeaux. They illus-trate the articulation between the generational split, the opposition between autonomy and heteronomy, and ideological divergences.

CHAPTER 3

Literary Salvation and
the Literature of Salvation

François Mauriac and Henry Bordeaux

I wish for freedom in salvation.
—Arthur Rimbaud, *A Season in Hell*

Henry Bordeaux and François Mauriac were two protagonists in the "quarrel of bad masters," the first as a prosecutor, the second as a defense attorney before finding himself the main defendant. While Henry Bordeaux represented the traditionalist camp that surrounded Pétain, François Mauriac rapidly evolved from a seemly Marshalism to an opposition to the regime that led him to join the underground struggle. This atypical evolution—Mauriac was the only member of the French Academy to join the literary Resistance—owed a great deal to the dynamic generated by the quarrel. But Mauriac would not have become the whipping boy of collaborationist writers without his previous engagements, which made him the symbol of the "treason" of Catholic writers allied with anti-Fascism.

Analyzing the trajectory that led the young bourgeois, Catholic, and conservative writer, then "the immortal," to break, at over fifty years of age, with the positions doubly assigned to him by his class of origin and his initial orientation in the literary field illuminates the "field effects" that helped change its course. The comparison of this statistically unlikely trajectory to that of his Academy colleague, Henry Bordeaux, shows an ideal-typical opposition between two logics of the literary field that we have already seen at work. The first is governed by extraliterary principles (economic, social and/or ideological); the second, proper to the pole of small-scale production, postulates the primacy of specific (aesthetic) demands over economic, moral, or political constraints.

This antagonism largely grounded the political divergences between these two Catholic novelists, both members of the French Academy, which everything seemed to bring closer together: their social trajectories, their vision of the world, even their privileged objects of observation—the mores of the provincial bourgeoisie—which often earned them the labels of "moralist" or "regionalist."[1]

These "field effects" are even more discernible when they generate oppositions between writers who are otherwise close in social space. As I have already emphasized, such is the effect of refraction exercised by the literary field that social properties only act through the mediation of the logics proper to that universe. From this point of view, although they exert an overall effect in the form of dispositions, as the statistical tendencies reveal, none of these properties bear a direct causal relationship on the aesthetic or political position-takings—neither social and geographic origin, nor education, nor religion, nor biological age. It is the relationship between trajectory and field that will be emphasized here, to clarify what the opposition between Bordeaux and Mauriac owes to their respective positions in the literary field, and what the distance between those positions reveals, in return, of a profoundly different relationship between ethical and aesthetic dispositions for the two writers, which would make their social destinies diverge.

First, I will focus on the comparable aspects of both careers, in order to better illustrate everything that opposed the novelist of the family and "honest people," artisan of a didactic literature, with the painter of social "monsters" who did not hesitate to deprive his character Thérèse Desqueyroux, who poisoned her husband, of salvation—"In truth, these consoling pages have been written then torn: I did not *see* the priest who was to receive Thérèse's confession"—reminding us "that a true novelist would not be able to introduce an element that strikes him as arbitrary into his work, even to illustrate his moral convictions," as the critic René Lalou has written.[2] All of which further opposed the fashionable novelist to the writer consecrated by his peers, the prolific writer of numerous best sellers first printed in serial form in the *Revue des deux mondes*, then published with Plon, sometimes with Flammarion, and often reedited in popular collections, to the NRF contributor who even in his finest hours obtained more modest printings, but for whom the prestigious publisher of the interwar period, Gallimard, tried at a certain point to compete with Grasset. (Let us note that Henry Bordeaux produced twice as many titles as François Mauriac: seventy-three novels among some 150 titles, or two to three a year, as opposed to twenty-five novels and around forty essays.)

The quarrel of the "bad masters" was also, at least in its first phase, as we have seen, the culmination of a struggle between two literary generations, that of the children of the defeat of 1870 who came together to form the new nationalist right around Bourget, Maurras, and Barrès and who established themselves in the first decade of the twentieth century, and the so-called generation of 1885, born under the banner of the liberal Republic, mobilized during World War I, which asserted itself around André Gide and *La NRF* in the aftermath of the Great War. The fact that they were socialized in two different states of the literary field, and thus confronted with different models and problematics, partially explains what helped separate the social destiny of the younger from that of the elder, despite everything that brought them together socially. But the generation gap does not suffice to account for this "deviation" in Mauriac's trajectory.[3] His peer Henri Massis, a disciple of Barrès, like Mauriac, and converted to Catholicism, would choose to join the camp of Action française as opposed to *La NRF*. Mauriac would waver between these two options for a long time.

At first glance, the social properties of François Mauriac (born in 1885) predisposed him to reproduce, one generation later, the position that his elder, Henry Bordeaux (born in 1870) occupied in the field. While at the avant-garde pole, positions are always yet to be made and forms of sociability to be reinvented, at the worldly pole, literary socialization occurs without great variation following the ritual of entry into "high society," in accordance with the mechanisms of social reproduction. Young people from good families came to Paris for their higher education; after a brief period of hesitation linked to their encounter with different intellectual milieus, they followed the stages of socialization that led them toward the French Academy.

YOUNG PEOPLE FROM GOOD FAMILIES

Henry Bordeaux and François Mauriac both came from the rising provincial bourgeoisie through the paternal line, liberal professions on one side, landowners and merchants on the other. But the proximity of their original positions was especially due to the familial strategies of reproduction that, favored by the cultural resources of a mother belonging to the bourgeoisie in both cases, were oriented toward the acquisition of educational capital, the only guaranteed way to access the field of power in these "troubled" times of the nascent Republic. This was all the more true since both families had experienced the hazards of private enterprise: the paternal grandfather of Henry Bordeaux, who managed a tannery, had gone bankrupt, and the refinery of François Mauriac's grandparents had been destroyed in a fire. Lawyer's sons, the five Bordeaux brothers (among eight children) aimed for the professions traditionally reserved for the bourgeoisie: one made a career in the army, becoming a general; two others were trained as engineers at a grande école (Polytechnique and Mines). A bachelor at sixteen years old, the future writer saw himself granted the possibility of fulfilling his literary ambitions only on the condition of studying law in conjunction with his literary degree at the Sorbonne. After a family council, it was decided that he would attend university rather than prepare for the ENS "that led to a professorship": "They had to recognize for me some right to leave the habitual careers proposed to young men of our milieu: the grandes écoles that trained cavalry men, infantry men, artillery men, sailors, engineers, law with magistrates, lawyers, notary publics, the Faculties of Medicine, the newly-created Colonial School. And journalism? Journalism, little-honored in our bourgeois families, was condemned in advance. As for literature, it was admitted that it could not keep a man alive, except for certain consecrated novelists, an Alphonse Daudet, a Zola whose printings then seemed outrageous."[4] Having received his law degree, he interned with his father in Thonon, then obtained, thanks to his father's intervention, a civil service position—a true sinecure—with the Compagnie Paris-Lyon-Méditerranée. The ministries were closed to him because his father, who had taken up the defense of the outlawed congregations, was thought to be hostile to the Republic.

A merchant, Mauriac's grandfather was a landowner who had capitalized on the vineyards and acres of pine that his own father, a barrel manufacturer then an importer of wood, had acquired in the Gironde. The first accumulation of a cultural capital also occurred for the Mauriac family at the level of the father's generation, this father struck down at age thirty-five; his sole activity, aside from his passion for books, consisted in managing the family fortune. His brother, a magistrate, would help the young widow administer the bequeathed goods. The shadow of this passion for books—whose traces subsisted in the family library—surely had some influence on the Mauriac children's aspirations to a more "spiritual" than "temporal" power. Certainly, medicine and law guaranteed a comfortable social position. Raymond was an attorney, Pierre became a doctor, and their older sister married a professor of gynecology at the University of Bordeaux. But spiritual quest and intellectual ambition showed through in the literary whims of Raymond who published, under the pseudonym of Raymonde Ousilane, two novels with Grasset (he won the prize for a first novel for *Individu*). They would also appear in the intellectual and political activities of Dr. Pierre Mauriac, a militant of Action française, whose younger brother, François, would open the doors of the *Mercure de France* and *La Revue hebdomadaire*;

their brother Jean, close to Marc Sangnier's Sillon, a democratic Catholic movement, took orders and would be named vicar of a Bordeaux parish. As for François, initiated in poetry by his elder brother Raymond, he chose the École des Chartes after earning his literature degree from the University of Bordeaux, which provided both the pretext to "go up" to Paris and the guarantees of a civil service future compatible with creative activities. He would in fact resign as soon as he was sure of having a sufficient private income to devote himself to literature.[5]

The two family histories were marked by the encounter between a dominant anti-Republican tradition and a Republican tendency swept aside by the process of intergenerational transmission. The clericalism and anti-parliamentary conservatism of Mauriac's maternal family would not be tempered—at least in appearance—by the agnostic and anticlerical Republican heritage of the paternal line, which disappeared with the father's premature death and whose only representative would be the children's uncle-guardian, a Dreyfusard reduced to silence in matters of education by the devout widow. Likewise, the monarchist conviction of Henry Bordeaux's father, which was moderated by a resignation to the regime commanded by the sole prudence of assuring his progeny's future,[6] was not more counterbalanced by the maternal grandfather's Republican tendencies, annihilated by the piety of the mother. The sons of both families followed the teachings of the Marists: the annex of the collège Stanislas that the Marists had opened in Thonon-les-Bains and that closed after the last of the Bordeaux brothers had finished his schooling; the École Sainte-Marie, then the collège Grand-Lebrun, run by the Marianites in Bordeaux, where the Mauriac brothers studied. François Mauriac would reach the public high school, or *lycée*, only after two failed attempts at the baccalaureate. Strengthened by this religious education that opened doors for them, Henry Bordeaux and François Mauriac first honed their critical and creative skills in Catholic literary reviews.

Henry Bordeaux's first study, devoted to Villiers de l'Isle-Adam, appeared in *Magazine littéraire*, a Belgian Catholic review that published Maurice Maeterlinck. Bordeaux contributed to it for five or six years before getting in to *Le Petit Journal* and the *Revue générale* of Brussels. His first book, *Âmes modernes* (1891), a collection of critical essays published by the Librairie Académique Perrin, was hailed by *La Revue blanche*, the *Mercure de France*, and *L'Écho de Paris*. A contributor to *La Revue hebdomadaire*, he would become its theater columnist in 1907.

As for Mauriac, after having published his first short story in *La Vie fraternelle* (the organ of the Bordeaux Sillon) and contributed to the *Revue Montalembert*, the monthly of the Marist-run family boarding house for provincials where his mother sent him in Paris, he spent three years in charge of the poetry column at the modest *Revue du temps présent* founded by Pierre Chaine and would participate in the efforts to promote a Catholic literature started by *Les Cahiers de l'Amitié de France*.[7] "Launched" by Barrès after the self-publication of his first collection of poetry, *Les Mains jointes* (1909), he saw the doors of the mainstream press open to him starting in 1912 via *La Revue hebdomadaire*.

Having entered into literature under the banner of Catholicism, both authors built a position for themselves by following the social path prepared for them by their bourgeois origin. Immediately introduced into literary salons, Mauriac in those "parallel academies" that were the salons of Madame Daudet and Madame Mühlefeld, Bordeaux in the salon of the academician José-Maria de Hérédia, they seemed destined, from the very beginning, for the supreme social consecration of the French Academy. Bordeaux was a regular contributor to the *Revue des deux mondes* and in 1925 Mauriac won the Academy's Prize for the Novel for *Le Désert de l'amour*. "It is curious that, no sooner had I arrived from my province, I smelled the atmosphere of the quai Conti* around me," wrote the latter.[8] And it was Bordeaux himself who would organize Mauriac's election, although not without first having "plotted" against his candidacy with Paul Bourget (and unbeknownst to Paul Valéry who wanted Mauriac to become a member and thought that he could "necessarily and naturally" count on the votes of these two Catholic novelists).[9]

These contradictory attitudes are revealing not only of the relationship of rivalry that the older writer maintained with respect to a competing younger peer, but also of the divided feelings about a body of work in which the distance between their respective ethical and aesthetic dispositions showed through, despite the apparent proximity of their Catholic intellectual positions. Witness Bordeaux's comment on the speech that André Chaumeix gave for Mauriac's reception at the Academy, which alludes to the divided feelings: "André Chaumeix does not do him enough justice. *Just criticisms for pessimism and light heresy.* But he has extinguished this consuming fire of disgust and desire that devours him, disgust for men and desire for God."[10]

THE SUBVERSIVE TEMPTATION REPRESSED

The convergence of their principal political positions in the 1920s and the beginning of the 1930s resulted from this worldly socialization appropriate to their education. Both more preoccupied, at the beginning of their trajectories,

---

* The location of the French Academy.—Trans.

by their literary career than by politics—"What was politics for me next to literature?" Henry Bordeaux asked[11]—they briefly let themselves be "seduced," around age twenty, by ideas "from the left," despite an elitist disposition that did not take long to manifest itself in their disgust at the attitudes of "subversive" intellectuals. Despite everything that separated the intellectual milieus that they encountered then, the literary milieus for Bordeaux, the Sillon for Mauriac, the analogy reveals what might look like an "indecision" (or a "subversive temptation") when viewed retrospectively from the point where their trajectories met up again, at the time of Mauriac's election to the Academy in 1933. Their inherited ethical dispositions would soon subdue these impulses, characteristic of the position of "young" or "newcomer." Both experiences are also comparable in what they reveal of the "sense of place and of placement" that guided both authors according to their dispositions, and came to reinforce the image that the intellectual milieus where they entered reflected back to them.[12]

Not having taken part in the Boulangist crisis[†] that rocked the capital where he was studying, Bordeaux said that he wavered, under the influence of the literary milieus, between individualism and Socialism. "Patriotism, in my literary generation, was no longer in fashion. Indifference had followed the fever of revenge that followed the disaster of 1870, when it was not a quasi-anarchic bravado, or the sneering of narrow-minded patriots like Déroulède."[‡13] Here we are very far from the Henry Bordeaux for whom all society relied on the land, the family, the fatherland, and religion, work, and authority. It was his return to Thonon where, armed with his law degree, he helped his father as an intern, which seems to have helped set his conservative positions, fueled by readings of Joseph de Maistre, Hippolyte Taine, Numa Denis Fustel de Coulanges, and Frédéric Le Play. In 1893, he accepted in any case the position of editor in chief at the newspaper *Réveil de Savoie*, which the committee of the local Republican right offered him in order to run the electoral campaign of its candidate. But it was mainly upon the death of his father in 1896 when, momentarily sacrificing his literary career, he decided to take charge of his father's law office for the next five years—enough time to train his younger brother to replace him—and repay the family debts that Bordeaux became rooted in his condition as a nota-

---

[†] Georges Boulanger (1837–1891), a general and politician, inspired a populist uprising that threatened to culminate in a coup d'état and dictatorship in 1889.—Trans.
[‡] Paul Déroulède (1846–1914), co-founder of the Ligue des patriotes, advocated for France's revenge against Germany following the Franco-Prussian War. He was also well-known for his patriotic poems.—Trans.

ble and sharpened his conservative convictions. His wait-and-see attitude during the Dreyfus affair—solicited by the Ligue de la patrie française, where he had friends like Paul Bourget or Charles Maurras, he declined—seems to owe more to a prudent professional strategy with respect to the Bar than to a true political stance. While he claimed to have been moderately in favor of the revision from a legal point of view, he still maintained a certain reserve with regard to Dreyfus's defenders, "deploring that the Dreyfusards used honor as a springboard to beat down the lively forces of the nation."[14] He would not take a position publicly. This was a last hesitation before aligning resolutely with those to whom he was objectively, and felt himself subjectively, close. His contributions, before World War I, to both *Le Figaro* and *L'Écho de Paris* with Barrès attest to it, as do his later positions.

The experience of the young Mauriac was fundamentally different. It was, he said, due to the questions raised for him by the bourgeois pharisaism of his family, and through the mediation of his brother Jean, that he joined Marc Sangnier's Sillon in 1905—even as he declared his admiration for Barrès and regularly read *L'Action française* (remember that his brother Pierre was a follower). The testimonies that Mauriac left about his break with the Sillon clearly evoke a feeling of uneasiness and rejection, due to the discrepancy between his social position and his ethical and aesthetic dispositions: "[...] a little Barrèsian of my kind wasn't welcome in a 'working class' milieu [...] none of my qualities applied, whereas my faults as a nascent literary man and 'rich people's kid' inspired horror there."[15] We thus find Mauriac, once his notoriety was established, at *L'Écho de Paris*, that same bastion of the militant right were Bordeaux had seconded Barrès before and after the Great War (Mauriac had asked Barrès to introduce him there in 1919, in vain).[16] He contributed to it until 1933, then moved to the more liberal *Figaro* that Pierre Brisson had just relaunched. Had he not, from 1919 on, agreed to write the column offered to him by *Le Gaulois*, that "headquarters of academicians," to borrow Jean Lacouture's expression, that gathered together Barrès, Bourget, René Bazin, and so forth?

Captivated by the intellectual milieus of the right who, recognizing them as potential allies, opened up their salons, their newspapers, their academy—and this was all the more significant, in Mauriac's case, since his work was accused of immorality by the Catholic establishment and the spokesmen of the conservative Catholic bourgeoisie, such as the newspaper *La Croix*[17]—these two disciples of Barrès were thus in agreement from 1919 to 1934 on the terrain of anti-parliamentarianism, elitism, and visceral anti-Bolshevism. At the request of his colleague at the Academy, Mgr. Baudrillart, Bordeaux would preside at an international novel contest organized by the Académie d'éducation et d'entr'aide sociale at the Vatican's instigation in January 1933, on the "danger the progress of Communism presents for Christian civilization."[18]

Their positions also converged in the ambiguous relationship they maintained with Action française. They would both plead its case to the pope, Mauriac in 1935, Bordeaux in preparation for Maurras's election to the French Academy in 1938 (Bordeaux would also protest against Maurras's imprisonment in 1936, in the weekly *Candide*).[19] A rallying point, at the threshold of the thirties, between the traditional right and the extreme right, the struggle against Communism reinforced the sympathy of the two Catholic novelists for the leader of Action française. They saw him as the leader of the "anti-Bolshevik crusade." While their ethical dispositions and the presence of the anti-Republican model in the familial milieu (paternal for Bordeaux, fraternal for Mauriac) could only sensitize them to the antidemocratic message of Maurras and his elitism, without yet making their political convictions shift from traditional conservatism to the revolutionary extreme right, it was above all their Catholicism that prevented a true endorsement of integral nationalism.

Despite the seduction that the royalist tendency of the interwar period was able to exert on Bordeaux,[20] his allegiance to the Church, associated with the feeling that a return to monarchy was illusory, made him adopt a certain reserve with respect to Action française. Still, this did not trouble the friendship, founded on aesthetic as well as ethical values, which had linked him to Maurras since his entry into literature (he was also close to René Boylesve and Moréas). It was he who would run the electoral campaigns for Maurras's two candidacies at the Academy, in 1923 and 1938.

Describing these campaigns in his memoirs, Bordeaux explained his relationship to Action française in order to justify an action that he wanted to seem "disinterested" on the political plane—with the exception of an alliance against Communism that, for a conservative Catholic, transcended the political stakes since it called into question the very principle of his vision of the world, namely his religion,[21] and thus motivated mainly by aesthetic considerations: "I have a very old friendship for Maurras, much less so for Action Française. Although I belong to a family of Royalists, I don't believe in the return to royalty and in response to Charles Maurras's survey on the monarchy (1924), I stated that the Republic would get by with us if it had recourse to the elites."[22]

A zealous reader of *L'Action française*, Mauriac had nonetheless confronted the partisans of integral nationalism, a majority in the family boardinghouse where he resided upon his arrival in Paris, which led to him being thrown out of the house. That the idea of fatherland constituted an end in itself was unthinkable for the young Catholic: it should be subordinated to God and justice. This essentially Christian conception implied a relationship to religion that was different from Bordeaux's allegiance to the Church as an institution regulating the social order, a relationship that would manifest itself in his work as in his later position-takings. Starting in 1916, his conservative dispositions would nonetheless bring him to more firmly applaud Maurras's denunciation of the "leveling" worked by democracy:

> It is the individualist in myself who is attracted by Maurras. I hate what Maurras calls consular equality, that is to say the work of Napoleon, as much as he does. If he were to carry it off, the individual would be saved from leveling, intelligence from the uniform rudiment of the universities, France from uniform administrative ugliness [...] Whether he means to or not, Maurras subordinates the Church to a party, which matters little to him since Catholicism is in his eyes only one necessary element of the fatherland. But for us . . .[23]

And he was never as close to Action française as when he was going through a religious crisis (between 1926 and 1929), and when he wrote *Souffrances du Chrétien*, published in 1928. His conversion, that year, would be marked by the writing of *Bonheur du Chrétien*, which came out in 1929, and by his canceled subscription to *L'Action française*, two years after the papal condemnation.[24] Let us note that the intellectual influence of Action française was then at its height: André Gide himself had come close to it in 1916, as Mauriac would not fail to mention in his introduction to the new edition of *Journal d'un homme de trente ans* in 1948.[25] Mauriac's true break with Action française nonetheless occurred later, since in 1935 he could still intervene in its favor at the Vatican.

But, it was precisely on the subject of Maurras's candidacy at the French Academy that, five years after Mauriac's reception, the two novelists would confront each other in the famous showdown during which Mauriac violated custom—he stood up—to contest this candidacy. What happened?

THE DOUBLE PLAY

Unlike Bordeaux who, after a few initial fumblings, found himself sent back to a position that he would have no trouble adjusting to, Mauriac never lost his ambition to be recognized by *La NRF*, even though the cost—twelve years of "trampling"—was very high. Moreover, he was endowed with a sense of placement that allowed him, through a subtle double play, to "navigate" between two logics and accumulate their respective profits—the social consecration of the Academy on one side, and the recognition of peers on the other.

A few years after the publication of *Âmes modernes*, Bordeaux began to forge a position as a best-selling author. Whereas Mauriac would learn, during his studies, that his inheritance would be enough to ensure him a certain financial ease, Bordeaux discovered the debts and decline that threatened his family upon his father's death. Success thus came at the perfect time, and Bordeaux would know how to cultivate it. Received in society, Bordeaux composed his first novel, *Le Pays natal*, in 1900, wrote for the mainstream press and was accepted into the *Revue des deux mondes* starting in 1903; there he would publish part of his work in serial (*L'amour en fuite*, 1903; *Les Roquevillard*, 1906; *Les Yeux qui s'ouvrent*, 1908; *La Maison*, 1913, etc.). These were novels of manners in the moralizing tradition, fueled by his experience as a lawyer in Thonon, often anchored in the provincial scenery of his native Savoie, and centered on the couple or the French bourgeois family. Some of them would achieve dazzling sales figures: *La Robe de laine*, published in 1911, had a print run of 600,000 copies, and the printing of *La Neige sur les pas*, published in 1912, surpassed 700,000 copies in 1920, not counting reeditions in popular collections after the war.[26] As a point of reference, despite the difficulties inherent in the comparison of printing figures, note that Mauriac's most successful novel, *Le Nœud de vipères* (1932), was printed at a rate of 45,000 copies a year.

This didactic literature was soon paired with an ideological struggle. Following a survey on marriage that he conducted in *L'Écho de Paris* after the Great War, Bordeaux evaluated the ravages of the war on this threatened institution and started a fight for the defense of the family against the "social danger" represented by divorce, feminist demands, and the drop in birth rate. His opening shot was *La Crise de la famille française*, which appeared in the collection "Les Bonnes Lectures" that the academician Georges Goyau and Georges Viance edited for Flammarion.[27]

In response to the criticisms accusing him of enlisting his art in the service of a doctrine, and of erecting a monument a priori, established criticism countered with the disciple of Le Play "who is conscious of having sought to reach general conclusions only thanks to a patient observation of particular facts," and hailed the "sound and conscientious art, full of an ardent and serious faith in life, books of an upstanding writer and good French man," the "audacity" to have proven "that one does not create a society merely with monsters."[28] Faced with those who mocked the "family novelist," it sang the praises of the "social novelist," indeed of the "sociologist." The Catholic critic Gonzague Truc's assessment of Bordeaux's work in his *Histoire de la littérature catholique contemporaine* is, in this regard, eloquent because it reveals the target audience and extraliterary function of that work:

To a class in disarray and afraid of the future, he has proposed a more reassuring image of itself, he has strengthened its foundation and persuaded it
of the legitimacy of its privileges as well as the authenticity of its virtues.
All this in a language that was not at all too subtle. The result, for him, was
another bourgeois glory that strengthened him in turn, and also moderated him.[29]

The list of critiques of his production up to 1930 also offers evidence of the
reception channel for his work:[30] for about twenty novels published up to that
date, the majority of articles (more than forty) were divided between Catholic
reviews—Maurrassian like the *Revue universelle*, or doctrinaire like the *Revue
des jeunes*—and the mainstream press of the conservative or liberal right (*L'Écho
de Paris, Le Temps, L'Opinion, Le Gaulois, Le Figaro, La Croix, L'Illustration, La
Revue hebdomadaire, Journal des débats*), as opposed to four articles in *Mercure
de France*, four others in *Les Nouvelles littéraires*, and none (according to the inventory) in *La NRF*. In reality, Albert Thibaudet had, since 1914, disavowed Bordeaux's style in *La NRF*, in reference to *La Nouvelle Croisade des Enfants*:

> It is true that Mr. Bordeaux is, in many respects, a weak author [...]. He is
> weak [...] by lack of will, of discernment, of discipline, not by lack of natu-
> ral means, of invention, and of observation. What would be needed to make
> this page exquisite? [...] decision, sacrifice,—crossing out, deleting. Sup-
> press, without adding anything, all dull filling, all flour sauce [...] Mr. Bor-
> deaux's page, put on a diet of grilled meats, and melted, with the fat cut off,
> rejuvenated, immediately gives you a little spicy and savory air of Jules Re-
> nard. I would like for this Renard, potential in his case, to serve Mr. Bor-
> deaux as a kind of literary conscience, a living remorse [...] But that is not
> true style [...][31]

Having entered literature at the birth of *La NRF*, Mauriac, as a passionate
reader of Jammes, immediately aimed for the recognition of this new Church he
made his own—"It was the Law and the Prophets"[32]—and whose "pope," André
Gide, along with Paul Claudel, would remain his masters and models. He was
initially disappointed in this ambition due to the rejection he encountered,
which all the marks of recognition that the Barrès, the Anna de Noailles, and the
Cocteau of the world lavished on him could not make up for, in his eyes:

> It was the era when the first installments of the *Nouvelle Revue française* ap-
> peared. I read it each month, including the announcements. In literature, it
> was my *gospel*. The young writers of today will hardly be able to imagine [...]

when Alfred Capus reigned over Paris and the great writers of the Academy only gloried in "serving," the *prestige* of this *pure* little group around a review that was *modest in appearance,* and how we were captivated by its *scruple* with respect to the work of art; this *revision of values* that was achieved there, that *rigorous* putting into place of each one seemed to me unquestionable. *Now, I did not exist for Gide's friends* [. . .]. *It wasn't much to be excluded by them,* but I thought myself *despised* by them.[33]

Propelled to the forefront by a survey on youth that *La Revue hebdomadaire* entrusted to him in 1912, Mauriac mixed criticism with his praise of René Bazin, Henry Bordeaux, Maurice Barrès, and Paul Bourget, and also *La NRF* for "preaching" nothing. In a reply published by the *Paris-Journal,* Alain-Fournier, spokesman for *La NRF,* countered with young Mauriac's poetry on the side of "obedience," "wisdom," "cleanliness," and "order," little-prized qualities in a literary field whose values had relied on permanent contestation as a first condition of "innovation" since its autonomization in the nineteenth century. "It is the poetry of a rich child [. . .] who does not get dirty playing," who has the means to do without worry and to have "ineffable" memories, Alain-Fournier said ironically.[34] "So it took me twelve years [. . .] to finally join the literary group that I best agreed with [. . .]"[35]

Condemned to twelve years of "trampling" and "fumbling" before arriving at a mastery of his art, Mauriac in fact only saw the "front door" open to him after 1920: in that year, Gide shared his admiration for *La Chair et le Sang*; in 1922, *Le Baiser au lépreux,* published in the prestigious series of "Cahiers verts" that Daniel Halévy edited at Grasset, raised him to the top rank—his printings passed from 3,000 to 18,000 copies—ensuring him the recognition of his elders ("Even Valéry finds it good")[36] and an advantageous contract with Grasset.[37] At the end of the same year, *La NRF* finally praised *Le Fleuve de feu.* The "cost" of this trampling appeared in his journal: "The *Mercure* refuses my manuscript. Enormous difficulties of the career of a literary man. Why not have the courage to imitate Rimbaud and free myself of the obsession to 'arrive'? Base stubbornness, how persistent you are in me! The four corners of the world are on fire and I worry more about the fate of a lost manuscript at the *Mercure* than the fate of Verdun."[38] Thus, in Mauriac's trajectory, investment at the temporal pole of the literary field seemed like a refuge position while waiting for true literary "salvation."

We understand why, at the time of his political conversion, Mauriac had retrospectively rationalized this worldly "choice" by reconciling, in the Barresian manner, this submission to an extraliterary logic with his ethical principles: "Possess everything in order to obtain the right to scorn everything. Suppress the temporal obstacles between God and ourselves, but by surmounting them; get rid of the obsession with earthly honors, but by assuming them: these ideas of Senecus retouched by Barrès flashed through the head of the attentive and respectful little guy from Bordeaux [. . .]." Evoking the autonomy that his material comfort allowed him, he attributed a conscious cynicism to this strategy that no doubt owes more to the combination of elapsed time and his conversion: "It was decided: I would not enroll among the gendarmes of tradition, who already addressed complicit smiles to me; I would never belong to this old immobile guard except by education, the customs of high society, and the need to not be swindled. Since I had the luck of being materially independent, I would not agree to be subordinate anywhere." He nonetheless acknowledged the social malaise generated by this double game, condemning him to an awkward position: "I led then the most stupid existence and, *on the pretext of not choosing*, the most *hypocritical*: I wrote nothing that was mediocre or base, but I hardly lost the feeling of living beneath myself."[39] Mauriac's self-reflexive analysis reconstitutes what this "worldly" strategy actually owed to family expectations, profoundly inscribed in the appreciation schemes of evaluation that dictated the initial orientation of his career as a writer: "[. . .] a little provincial of my kind who arrives in Paris has his family to convince, and, to say the word, amaze [. . .] He leaves for Paris to make literature: Ah! Ah! Ah! . . . Well! after all! What a pity! This poor idiot! Etc., etc. Then, the family, the provincial family, demands proof [. . .] I remember, when I won the Academy's Grand Prize for the Novel: Ah! But . . . Ah! nonetheless! . . ."[40]

Two moments illustrate Mauriac's double game and sense of placement. Telling Jacques Rivière that he would not write an article on Paul Bourget—maker of literary reputations and influential member of the French Academy—for *La NRF*, Mauriac allowed a glimpse of "cynicism" to appear in his letter (a privileged moment when the strategies of placement are only immediately outwardly visible because they appear as such in the very consciousness of the individuals): "It seems to me that I would be able to write a good article on him in a ferocious genre—but for once my duty and my interest are in agreement to set me against it. If you would like it, I retain in advance his obituary. . . ." He added, however: "I write you these things so that you will despise me: there are actually some of these calculations within me—and yet (how to explain this?) paired with a secret and desolate indifference, a total detachment. But the rules of the game impose themselves on me, as if, engaged despite myself in a match, I had to avoid mistakes, like it or not."[41] Now, if he could allow himself to refuse an article on Bourget once he had gained the recognition of *La NRF*, he had also been able, as early as 1921, to take up the defense of André Gide against Henry

Massis's attacks, knowing "that he cu[t] himself off that way, for a long time, from that academic and worldly right that [had] done so much for his nascent reputation and on which his future [could] depend."[42]

Beyond the trampling, this double play would have a lasting literary "cost." Contrasting "regular clergy" and "secular clergy," Jean Lacouture recalled that despite his aspiration to be recognized by the NRF team, and despite the warm reception that the prestigious circle would ultimately reserve for him, Mauriac would never become part of the "family." In the eyes of the "hermits of the Port-Royal of the rue de Grenelle," Mauriac would remain "he who has dined out and frequented socialites his whole life," the "writer praised by the bourgeoisie, while waiting on the Academy."[43] On the other hand, his political "conversion" would only take place after his election to the "immortals," after he had drawn all the profits he could reasonably expect from this worldly logic.

From Literary Salvation to Prophetism

As Pierre Bourdieu writes, "[. . .] the art of estimating and seizing chances, the capacity to anticipate the future by a kind of practical induction or to take a practical gamble on the possible against the probable, are dispositions that can only be acquired in certain [. . .] conditions, that is certain social conditions."[44] Those conditions remain to be determined. Yet Mauriac attained recognition in the field of small-scale production at a time when, in his novels, a "tear" became clear. It would run through his whole work, translating a conflictual relationship to religion, source of this "spiritual worry" that was very much in vogue in the milieu of the "regular priests" of *La NRF* in the 1920s. Much of the team converted to Catholicism during those same years, including Henri Ghéon, Jacques Copeau, and Charles Du Bos, who, with Mauriac's help, would try in vain to convert their "pope," André Gide.[45]

Far from being a mere figure of speech under the pen of this Christian grappling with bourgeois pharisaism, the use of the term "Gospel" to designate *La NRF* assumes all its meaning if we make the hypothesis that his perception of the literary field is simply the transposition of his ambivalent relationship to religion. The opposition between Catholicism and Christianity, the Church and the Gospel, thus seems to ground Mauriac's grasp of the opposition between "worldly" logic and "ascetic" logic that dictated his orientation in the field. This situation resulted from the interweaving of ethical and aesthetic dispositions that had been determined by certain decisive experiences. By managing to transpose into the fictional universe and stylize this conflictual relationship to religion and the perpetual quest for salvation, Mauriac fully inscribed himself in the problematic of the tension between ethics and aesthetics that *La NRF* was constructing during this period. And it was above all in and by this relationship to religion that François Mauriac set himself apart from Henry Bordeaux. Academic and Catholic critics would not fail to criticize it, suspecting him of "Jansenism."[46] Whereas at the pole of heteronomy embodied by Henry Bordeaux, the relationship to the Catholic institution never appeared to contradict the literary logic, the reconciliation of ethical and aesthetic dispositions was a permanent preoccupation at the pole of autonomy represented here by François Mauriac. Literary autonomy was maintained through a subtle play with the margins tolerated by Catholic orthodoxy, which verged on heresy. This game overdetermined Mauriac's break with the Church in the name of Christianity during the Spanish Civil War.

ETHICAL AND AESTHETIC DISPOSITIONS

Without the very principle of faith being questioned, the ghostly shadow of an anticlerical father and the weight of the unsaid that could only be accentuated by the Dreyfusard uncle's "silent" reprobation very probably fueled this conflictual relationship with religion.[47] It is illustrated by the contradictory models of the two brothers: Pierre, the partisan of Action française, and Jean the Sillonist. This is also to say that the relationship with the father, his presence for Bordeaux, his absence for Mauriac, marked an additional difference between the two authors. An event—the death of the grandmother, which would become the framework of *Nœud de vipères*—crystallized, for Mauriac, the progressive consciousness of the "disparity between words and thoughts" proper to bourgeois pharisaism and founded on this "unwritten law of the Church [...] that the bourgeoisie knew without its having been taught": the "bourgeois duty" of accumulating and transmitting family wealth, "to which all morality remained subordinate, and even the word of God."[48]

Mauriac accounts for a third decisive factor: his experience of the contradiction between the double intellectual and aesthetic demand, and blind submission to the moral rules dictated by the Church. Mauriac has mentioned the eye-opening role played by his professor of rhetoric at Grand-Lebrun, Abbé Péquignot, who initiated him to Pascal and Racine, and forbade the use of Abbé Blanloeil's literary manual that had been imposed by the establishment.[49] The fact that his studies with the Marianites ended in failure at the baccalaureate and that his move to the lycée as a second-year student in philosophy was marked by a "shameful" experience—when the professor, Mr. Drouin, Gide's brother-in-law, had asked for a manual, Mauriac had proposed Father Lahr's manual used by the Marianites, which incited the mockery of the class—is enough to determine the conditions through which he became conscious of the contradiction between aesthetic demand and religious demand. This contradiction would be amplified by the Church's rejection of modernism.[50] Still, we must resituate his adhesion to intellectual values in the relationship that opposed them to the values common to the social world of the "sons" of the upper bourgeoisie in the Chartrons neighborhood of Bordeaux. Mauriac associated with these sons of the "aristocracy of wine" in collège, but his family did not belong to their milieu. The Mauriacs were of "rustic origin" except on his maternal grandmother's side (his mother frequented the legal milieu, "which was at that time, in Bordeaux, extremely brilliant"). The sons of the "aristocracy" of wine valued athletic (riding, tennis) and social qualities, "all those virile and noble virtues that I lacked when I was fifteen years old, for which I had no dispositions." He admitted to having experienced a "feeling of envy" toward them.[51]

The oscillation between the worldly logic and the specifically aesthetic logic that prevailed at the pole of small-scale production could thus, in Mauriac's case, only take on the form of a dilemma where ethics and aesthetics were inextricably interwoven. In the Gidean aesthetic, didn't he recognize the "Jansenism" that tormented his Christian vision of the world, without modifying his way of life? The fact that he experienced a religious crisis shortly after attaining the long-awaited literary "redemption" can only reinforce this hypothesis. The crisis first manifested itself in literary form with *Thérèse Desqueyroux* (1927), which marked "the limit, at least provisional, of his distance from Christianity,"[52] before expressing itself directly in the *Souffrances du chrétien* (1928). Without a doubt, the attacks that the Catholic establishment leveled against his work were part of the root of this uneasiness: "So I continued to work within Catholicism—an object of mistrust and even of contempt and reprobation to my fellow-Catholics. It seemed to me that they accepted me as one of them for the sole purpose of being able to judge and condemn me."[53]

The writing of the *Souffrances* coincided with that of a biography of Racine that examined the contradiction between literary and religious demands. *Dieu et Mammon* (1929) would be the response to a letter from Gide (published in *La NRF* on June 1, 1928) who saw in this *Vie de Racine* (1928) the search for a compromise: "In fact, what you are searching for is [...] the *permission* to be a Catholic without having to burn your books [...] and you are not Christian enough to cease to be a writer." Mauriac would refuse to opt for a "reassuring" compromise, giving this contradiction the form of a profound moral dilemma: "The conflict between the disinterestedness of the artist and what I called the utility-sense of the apostles soon broke out in me [...] It is true that the defender of a sacred cause, the soldier of God, demands that everyone should serve; and by serve he often means: write nothing which is not immediately useful."[54]

This crisis was also the occasion for him to look back on his origins and to denounce the religious practice of his childhood—as he did explicitly in the preface to the new edition of *Les Mains jointes* and in *Dieu et Mammon* (1929). And was it not literature—*Ce qui est perdu* (1930), *Le Nœud de vipères* (1932), *La Pharisienne* (1941)—that would give him the means to "exorcize" this constitutive pharisaism constituting his *habitus*, and overcome his conflictual relationship to religion after his mother's death? The expectations generated by his peers' view of him were not indifferent to this process. With his typical "sociological" lucidity, Mauriac paired literary salvation and rediscovered grace by attributing them to a single person: Charles Du Bos, a representative of *La NRF*, who had contributed to the specific consecration of Mauriac in an article published in 1925. Du Bos had just converted to Catholicism: "Perhaps without them, I would have plunged into the outer darkness of the Boulevard and Academism, if there hadn't been some at the N.R.F. who liked a certain tone in my work and who perceived that a certain question had been raised in it. Du Bos understood that the time had come for me to give an answer."[55]

An answer to the crisis and to the disparagement—marked by his break with Action française—of this bourgeois pharisaism that had informed his ethical and political dispositions, religious conversion appeared, in this light, as one of the preliminary conditions of political conversion, that is to say a break with the values of his class of origin and the attitudes dictated by his position as a result of his (partial) submission to the "worldly" logic.[56]

A HERETICAL ACADEMICIAN

Mauriac's redeployment to political journalism owed, certainly, a great deal to "literary aging." If it could only take place after his election to the Academy, it was also an effect of this consecration. On the eve of his redeployment, Mauriac no longer produced anything but "minor" works, *La Fin de la nuit* (1935) and *Les Anges noirs* (1936). His exhaustion of the novelistic vein led him first, at the instigation of his friend Édouard Bourdet, who had just been named administrator of the Comédie-Française, to try his hand at theater, which often capped off the career of a consecrated prose writer. The laborious collective effort of rewriting, in which Bourdet and Jacques Copeau took an active part, undoubtedly helped turn Mauriac away from this path. Sartre would become the spokesman of the young guard that was then starting to impose new novelistic devices, proclaiming the author's "literary death" in a famous article of 1939 titled "M. François Mauriac et la liberté."[57] As a consequence, Mauriac considered no longer writing novels.

This process of "sterilization" associated with literary aging was not specific to academic consecration. Witness the example of Gide, whose position-taking in 1932 in favor of Communism corresponded, remember, to the end of his properly literary production. The fact that politics were an option for redeployment in those years marked by the rise of a new literary generation was, as we saw, the result of a field effect. In return, Gide's engagement legitimized the "prophetic" model as such for the intermediate generation—called the generation of 1885—to which Mauriac belonged. The whole relation of fascination-rivalry that Gide's rebel disciple maintained with his master corroborates this hypothesis, despite both the indignation that the nature of Gide's engagement aroused for this right-leaning Catholic who was resolutely hostile to Communism,[58] and the distance that resulted between the two friends (they would only reconcile after the publication of Gide's *Return from the USSR*, when Mauriac was making his own political conversion). Or, at least, the Gidian model may have confirmed him in the route that his entourage opened up for him, from the "predictions" that foretold Mauriac's fate as a lampoonist when he was elected to the Academy,[59] to the injunctions and the growing influence of his Catholic friends—Henri Guillemin, a close friend of Marc Sangnier; Jacques Maritain and Father Maydieu, contributors to the review *Sept* run by the Dominicans of Juvisy—who would push him, during the war in Ethiopia, to break with the positions of his class of origin in the name of Christianity. By this very act, they gave him the means to distinguish himself as a Catholic intellectual.

For Mauriac, the event that epitomized the contradiction between the worldly logic and the aesthetic logic was the unsuccessful candidacy of Paul Claudel at the Academy. Claudel was defeated in 1935 by Claude Farrère, author of exotic novels and notorious admirer of Mussolini: "There are times when disgust turns to bile and fills your mouth: Lecomte! Bertrand! Prévost! Farrère! What a crusade against Claudel!" Mauriac wrote to the loser.[60] And in his memoirs:

> This academic right, by daring to elect Claude Farrère against Paul Claudel, showed that it was master of the terrain. The literary aspect of this scandal, this shame of having preferred Farrère to Claudel, if I felt it in my guts, it is because I had discerned from that moment that it was less the poet that they loathed in Claudel (even though he embodied everything that Henry Bordeaux or Abel Bonnard hated) than the civil servant of the Third Republic [...] In their eyes, he embodied the animal to slaughter [...].[61]

The priority that the majority of the assembly accorded to political consideration to the detriment of aesthetic values or, worse, the assimilation of the former to the latter in the worldview of the academic right, constituted for Mauriac a double heresy, as the quotation implies—since it struck in him both the Christian poet and the representative of *La NRF*. This heresy would succeed in dissociating him from the "worldly" fraction of the literary field. As we will see in the following chapter, the stakes of the Academy's internal struggles had a decisive effect on Mauriac's trajectory. Forced to defend the principle of literary autonomy against the camp of the "academic right," he found himself sent back to a position homologous to that of the left in the intellectual field, by a double reversal. It was indeed Mauriac's double game that enabled this conversion, which was perceived as "rare" from an emic point of view: "What is rather rare with him, is that success tends to liberate him, to tear him from his prejudices—or who knows, from his lie. Once at the Academy, he seems close to defrocking himself. But then, he throws himself toward the prejudices of the left. It was not a haughty liberation," commented his former friend, Pierre Drieu La Rochelle, who had become a ferocious adversary.[62]

This is how, despite a first favorable reflex toward Mussolini's regime and to Francoism, Mauriac ended up adopting a position diametrically opposed to that of the academic right, led in part by Henry Bordeaux. This shift occurred during the wars in Ethiopia and Spain. While the academic right allied itself with the Maurrassian and Fascist extreme right to form the neo-pacifist camp that demanded the suspension of sanctions against Fascist Italy after Mussolini's aggression in Ethiopia, Mauriac joined with a few Catholic intellectuals to denounce, in the October 18, 1935, *Aube*, the "sophism of the inequality of races" in the name of an egalitarian Christian justice. During the Spanish Civil War, as we saw, they represented the two contrasting Catholic camps, conservative on one side, Christian Democratic on the other. While Bordeaux brought his endorsement as an academician and a Catholic writer to pro-Francoist propaganda, Mauriac, alongside Maritain and Bernanos, allied himself to the Catholic dissidence emanating from the Christian Democratic sphere of influence that condemned the machinations of the Spanish nationalists against the Basque people, and engaged his talent as a polemicist—unpaid, in accordance with the prophetic stance—in the progressive Catholic review *Temps présent*.

Let us note, however, the concern that Catholic intellectuals, estranged from their political camp, showed to differentiate themselves from their peers close to the Popular Front. The contempt that Mauriac expressed for the "herd of civil servant writers," "the Chamsons, the Cassous, the Jean-Richard Blochs," "stools" at the feet of Malraux, reminds us what still drew him to the worldly pole.[63] It allows us to grasp the stakes of Mauriac's adhesion to the literary Resistance, among those same writers whom he had disparaged only recently, just as it retrospectively revealed the impossibility of preserving this Catholic specificity in a crisis situation.

THE DESIGNATION OF A PROPHET

By modifying power relationships, Mauriac's political conversion produced, in part, the field effect that would, in return, overdetermine his choice under the Occupation. In September 1940, he wrote to Georges Duhamel: "I believe *despite everything* that we have to support Pétain in spite of what he is *obliged* to do," and in a letter to Henri Guillemin dated December 9, he "declare[s himself] entirely persuaded that there is, for France, no other politics possible except collaboration," despite the repression targeting Jews, which conflicted with his Christian ethics.[64] But, on August 17, he had been heckled on the radio in London by his former comrade at the reviews *Sept* and *Le Temps présent*, Maurice Schumann, allied with de Gaulle.[65] This shows the stake that the French cultural heritage then constituted for the acting forces; everyone was trying to turn that heritage to his own profit. It also shows the necessity of relying on intellectual power in order to establish the legitimacy of a political power that, although it claimed to be legal, had no immediate foundation except charisma. As much as his recent conversion to a prophetic stance helps explain it, the fact that the appeal was addressed to Mauriac is no less an illustration of the phenomenon of designation or election by which the powers and/or the intellectual field encouraged a consecrated intellectual to come to the fore, to occupy the position of prophet in order to legitimize a political venture. As Pierre Bourdieu writes: "The prophet is the man of crisis situations, where the established order topples over and the future is suspended."[66] But what is the circuit of legitimation or conspiracy that authorizes the prophet to feel designated?

Schumann's appeal would be echoed, in the intellectual field, by the solicitations of Mauriac's entourage—the young Socialist and Catholic instructor Jean Blanzat and Father Maydieu, who both gravitated around the former director of *La NRF*, Jean Paulhan—to obtain his adhesion to the first organization of literary Resistance. This organization, the Front national des écrivains, was created at the instigation of the underground Communist Party. Compared with the categorical refusal of his colleague at the Academy, Georges Duhamel, who was nonetheless originally closer to leftist circles, Mauriac's agreement to work with the sworn enemies of yesteryear, the Communists, seemed like a transgression. The stakes of this adhesion to the literary Resistance are doubly significant if we take into account the real risk—it was characteristic of this crisis situation to have transformed the symbolic risk associated with position-taking into a life and death risk—that it implied for this man whom the appeal from London had already designated by name to the German and Vichyite authorities, and who had also become the target of ultra-collaborationist writers, as we saw.

Designation simultaneously involved a positive procedure of "election" and a negative procedure of "stigmatization." Mauriac himself said twice that his "true place" had been designated for him by his literary and political enemies. I have already quoted the first instance. I will quote the second here: "[...] there was not really a choice on my side, as I was the whipping boy, and I was from the beginning the whipping boy of the 'collaborationist' press, even if I could have asked myself the question in the beginning, I found myself completely isolated, treated as an enemy. I am grateful to them for it because they helped me become conscious of what I was [...]."[67] Certainly, what may appear as a retrospective lucidity undoubtedly owed more to Mauriac's position-taking, at the Liberation, against the purge in literature. Minimizing his own initiative, he retroactively rehabilitated those who were "led astray."

It remains that the chronological proximity of the stigmatization campaign led against him by the extremists of the Collaboration, beginning in June 1941 with the publication of *La Pharisienne*, and Mauriac's adherence to the first underground committee of writers shortly after its creation in the autumn of 1941,[68] tends to confirm the link between this double process (positive and negative) of designation and Mauriac's choice. It also illustrates the logic of allocating positions by an effect of repulsion, and the radicalization that could result. Driven by personal indignation in the face of the disgrace cast on him, and that he could rightly consider as a double attack on the rights of literature and the rights of the person, Mauriac was ready to shift from a position of "refusal" to underground action, even if the latter would only truly become real for him eighteen months later.

Between the time when the attacks against his person culminated, in June 1941, and his theoretical adhesion to the first underground group, an article was published in *La NRF* in September 1941. This article was written by Drieu La Rochelle, his former friend, who was the only one to disregard the general order calling for the boycott of *La Pharisienne*—not to praise it, but on the contrary to pan it. Of course, there was a clear difference in tone between the ad hominem invectives of the collaborationist press and this article which was meant to be a piece of literary criticism in form. But by its claim to literariness, the article on the contrary revealed its extraliterary impulses. Firstly, it echoed, in the form of pastiche, Sartre's "assassin" article. As far as properly literary (that is to say formal) criticism was concerned, Drieu limited himself to repeating (for lack of citing it) the Sartrian criticism of the narrator's omnipresence, without mentioning the fact that Mauriac had precisely accounted for his younger colleague's lesson by opting for a first-person narrator. In response to the Sartrian formula, "[...] there is no more place for a privileged observer in a real novel [...] M. Mauriac has put himself first. He has chosen divine omniscience and omnipotence," Drieu's attack: "The author is too close there, not holding himself back from intervening, with his moralist's brilliance. Not dreamy enough, not effaced enough. Calling Pascal's maxims, Racine's harp strokes to his aid. This explains the twisted construction of several of his novels, his predilection for the device of the narrator who is there and who is not there, or for the device of the hero keeping his journal."[69] All the rest of the article was a moral criticism of the content (notably the choice of the bourgeoisie as an object) that Drieu tied to a more general accusation against an author complicit with his object and embodying the intellectual exalted by a parliamentary democracy that was incapable of producing "men of action." This was a device that allowed him to put himself forward, to make himself look good at the expense of his victim: "I have no sense of sin, even though I was raised in a Christian way—and even by Marists like Mauriac. [...] But, not being Christian in the sense of Mauriac [...] I am when all is said and done an optimist, I believe ugliness is curable by human, social, religious means."[70] This article, which marked a milestone in the importation of generalized defamatory and denunciatory practices into the very heart of this NRF that had embodied the place of "pure" literature—and to which Mauriac, remember, had hesitated to contribute before refusing after Drieu assumed its leadership—could only justify the author of *La Pharisienne* in his indignation. All the more so as its publication coincided with the intensification of repression. In a letter to Jean Paulhan where he mentioned this article in a postscript (the juxtaposition is eloquent)—"And this article by Drieu! There is someone who speaks without 'weighing his words'! Poor Drieu"— Mauriac measured the distance between the realities he witnessed in spite of himself and the representations that were instilled in him during childhood:

How many pages could be written on the word "hostage"! In my childhood, it only designated Monsignor Darboy and the priest of the Madeleine, some other ecclesiastics, with hair on their neck, and blessing their executioners (in *Le Monde illustré*). No one ever spoke to me of the thousands of poor people that had to be gunned down to appease this "hungry for justice" class, which is ours. It is now that I think of them—and of those who today join them to satisfy another "justice."

"Suffer, o heart full of hatred, hungry for justice. ..."[71]

At the end of this same year, the Christian's indignation seemed to reach its apogee: "[...] Enough! Enough! And Pétain who drafts lists of proscriptions and piles up Jews in labor camps because there are assassination attempts, at night ... Enough! Enough!"[72] The police raids and the Obligatory Work Service in Germany would end up transforming indignation into revolt.

The stakes of Mauriac's adhesion to the literary Resistance were significant in several respects. The first consecrated writer to enter it, he brought literary legitimacy to the underground venture.[73] From 1943, he also gave his literary endorsement to *Les Lettres françaises* as well as the underground Éditions de Minuit with the publication of *Le Cahier noir*, under the pseudonym of Forez, in August 1943. "They would be the most beautiful pages of Éditions de Minuit": such was the reaction of Jacques Debû-Bridel upon reading the manuscript.[74]

The definitive version of *Le Cahier noir* kept the trace of the notes taken successively during the years of occupation—the "stammerings of rage"—where growing indignation against the culture of denial and against repression can be read. We also find the juxtaposition of personal and universal indignation (empathy for victims):

> You pretend to believe that the people demand the search for and punishment of the responsible parties, to cover the horrible necessity of satisfying the hatred of the victor.
>
> And if you were of good faith, History will accuse you of having served the vengeance of your masters. Of having looked to win them over through slaughter ... But do not hope that the Jews crucified by your police exempt you from paying the victor up to the last smallest offering.
>
> Slanderers of France, you who have never triumphed except thanks to its humiliation and its shame! Doctors take advantage of the sick man being tied up and clubbed to make him gulp down your remedies!
>
> These press items each day, in which a masked colleague denounces me, designates me with a trembling finger ...
>
> The hatred that mounts from the pierced heart of Paris is silent, but its cry covers the horrible whisper of the editing rooms all the same ...[75]

And later: "Those who insult me are also those who are dying of joy because the Republic is dead (because they think it is dead)."[76] The evolution from the personal to the universal is still legible in the work of rewriting that led from the individual examination of conscience that was originally *La Lettre à un désespéré pour qu'il espère*, marked by the use of the familiar "tu" form that the writer used to address himself, to the examination of collective conscience in

Le Cahier noir: the adoption of the "*we* of solidarity" was, in this sense, significant.[77] From now on, the prophet would call for such an examination in his role as spokesman for the national conscience against the false "prophets of doom [who] go up to the Capitoline hill with the conqueror whose arrival they had announced—prepared," to rehabilitate "the martyrs [who] give testimony to the people."[78] In this text that evoked the biblical prophets—apostrophy, imprecation, exhortation, repetition (not to yield to the contempt of man, not to yield to despair), defense of a morality superior to temporal forces, doctrine of salvation—despair progressively gave way to hope, rage to application and demonstration, supported by the Pascalian dialectic, as Jean Touzot has shown. The polemicist, elevated to the rank of national prophet, bearer of a universal message of belief in man, gave here his entire measure.

As for the famous phrase from *Le Cahier noir* (whose author had been immediately identified):[79] "Only the working class *in its mass* will have been faithful to a profaned France,"[80] far from being purely conjunctional (the alliance with the Communists), it should be read as the culmination of the process of breaking with his class of origin, begun before the war, and of the examination of individual conscience, which shed new light on the traditional values that still grounded him. New disenchantment was overcome here by a dialectic inversion: the hopeless one who saw the entire bourgeois system of values collapse still found, in the working class, reasons to believe in man. The surprise that this phrase created in the world of literature was reminiscent of the surprise that greeted André Gide's statement of solidarity with the Communists in 1932.[81] Did François Mauriac feel himself called to fill the prophetic position that his older colleague had assumed in the 1930s? The fact that he had often been associated with Gide by their common detractors as symbols of "bad masters" would tend to validate this hypothesis.

The specificity of the crisis situation made Mauriac's membership in the French Academy, which in a "normal" state of the literary field would have been of little importance (or a disadvantage) for his attainment of this prophetic position, become an issue in a struggle founded on competing claims on the "French spirit." The triple issue of literary legitimacy, the alliance of tendencies on all sides against the "powers of evil," and the claim on the national spiritual heritage are summarized in this testimonial from Jacques Debû-Bridel: "It was for us, in light of his personality, his talent, his political situation, a great victory, a great comfort; the only, the sole academician of the CNE until 1944."[82] Louis Parrot also remembered "the name of the intellectuals who distinguished themselves in the Resistance and helped raise the prestige, badly compromised, of the academicians and the great institutions of State. In the first place the French Academy, and above all, François Mauriac."[83]

The transgression represented by Mauriac's political evolution stood out even more in comparison with Bordeaux's stated positions; the latter illustrates, as we will see later, the majority tendency of the French Academy and, more generally, at the pole of the proponents of "good taste." In continuity with his previous engagements, they do not require the kind of explanation we have proposed for Mauriac. Pro-Munich even though he was a Germanophobe—*Les Étapes allemandes*, published in the *Revue des deux mondes*, then with Grasset in 1940, in which he expressed surprise at the "prodigious rise accomplished by Hitler" but denounced the state's control over man and child, crime and persecution, would be pulped by the occupier—at the end of 1940, Bordeaux published his assessment of the disaster, *Les Murs sont bons*. The title of the book borrowed the phrase of an old peasant observing, during the other war, the collapse of his home's roof. Bordeaux quoted this line in his speech-response to Charles Maurras at the French Academy as a symbol of popular good sense and wisdom. The structure of the narrative is characteristic. The first part, entitled "From the Bottom of the Abyss," retraced the states of the fiasco and the exodus as seen from on high, that is to say by the generals and men of power. Bordeaux, as Germanophobic as he was, did not neglect to signal in passing the discipline and "correct behavior" of the German soldiers, in keeping with a representation widely broadcast by the partisans of the armistice.[84] Under the title "Our Errors and Our Faults," the second part summarized the causes of the defeat in an assessment that was paradigmatic of the National Revolution traditionalists' rhetoric of contrition. Social causes included the marriage crisis and lowered birthrate along with crises in work and civil authority, hastened by the government of the Popular Front; political causes included the deficiency of the state, due to the "dupery" of universal suffrage that dismissed experienced notables in favor of "lamentable mediocrities," "oscillating between impotence and absolutism,"[85] coupled with diplomatic shortcomings; finally, moral causes: crisis in religion and morality, crisis in instruction (scientism, lay instruction, suppression of "free" instruction) and, in conclusion, a chapter devoted to the deviation of literature echoing the "bad masters quarrel." In a third part, entitled "Our Hopes," Bordeaux adopted the role of exegete for the "program of reparations" of the "National Revolution," in particular the return to the land that was meant to ensure the return to a hierarchical social order based on the family.

The book's reception illustrates the issues of the hour. The ambivalent critique from the director of the Amt Schrifttum, Dr. Payr, who criticized its lack of realism in *Phönix oder Asche*, along with its obsession with "the past," the "prejudices of a vision of the world closely linked to religion," and its omission of the "fatal role of Jews in France" ("it is only occasionally that Bordeaux releases a few words about undesirable 'foreigners'"), points to the ideological distance between a Catholic conservatism that recognized itself in the project of a National Revolution and the "European" Nazi program, but also shows how the occupant intended to accommodate it.[86] Praised in *Le Petit Journal* by his colleague at the Academy, Louis Madelin, the book was, as we saw, panned by André Rousseaux and Maurice Noël in *Le Figaro*, and by Lucien Combelle (*La Gerbe*) at the other extreme, that of the extremists of the Collaboration, due to its positions on literature.

The following year, with *Images du Maréchal Pétain*, Bordeaux made his contribution to the construction of Pétain's golden legend. "Every house, every cottage should be lit up by that face," he wrote as early as November 1940 in *Paris-Soir* in order to demand that Pétain's portrait be hung in every public and private place.[87] Denouncing the "decadence" of the Popular Front that had "not officially but shiftily and actively supported Spanish Communism in its struggle against the national revolution of General Franco," the "anarchic revolution of Social Democracy before the arrival of Chancellor Hitler,"[88] he hailed a conservative revolution which applied the values that he had ardently defended for more than twenty years—race, family, land, the "natural" hierarchies, corporatism, paternalism. This idyllic vision of "recovery" deserves to be cited at length and does not require commentary:

> With large strokes, he knocked down the rotten wood and suppressed the parasites that wrap around the beautiful trees and take their sap, by striking speculation, suppressing freemasonry, parliamentarianism, by imposing a status on Jews. Land, family, school, work were restored. No more wastelands, no more forced division, but honor to the peasant and protection of his dwelling. The family relieved of its charges, and rights of succession according to the number of its children and restored as the true social cell. Primary teaching brought closer to the realities of working and agricultural life and secondary education returned to the humanities [...] Work becoming a right and a duty together, reorganized in the craft industry, corporation and the union of the classes. That was the beginning of a program of recovery whose application little by little will bring order back to a country where carelessness was generalized.[89]

Whereas for Henry Bordeaux, hope was born of the arrival of traditional values to power, even if it occurred thanks to the defeat and the submission to

Nazi order, for Mauriac, who was just as attached to these values, this was the principal reason to despair: "This drama particular to our country, this fatality that links the triumph of traditional principles to military disaster and the domination of the enemy. . . ."[90] And he only found hope again when, refusing to yield to the contempt of man that the degradation "of a false elite and of everything that teems at the surface" and the triumph of Machiavelli's animal law both inspired in him, refusing also detachment from the world—"To hold oneself above the melee? To look down on the tortured multitudes? In any case, no higher than the cross. One must stay at the height of the gallows [. . .]"—he recognized in "those who have chosen to sacrifice themselves" the reasons to believe in man: "But we have made our choice; we bet against Machiavelli."[91]

Henry Bordeaux followed a political evolution appropriate for the young people of his class, from "anarchy" and "individualism" to conservatism and the sense of "social responsibilities," to which he subordinated professional practice. The break that François Mauriac enacted upon attaining consecration was, on the contrary, socially improbable, and it is not by chance that we find other typical examples at the most autonomous pole of the intellectual field.[92] Indeed, while at the pole of relatively high heteronomy the effect of refraction that the literary field exercises on inherited dispositions is weak and temporary, at the pole of autonomy it is susceptible of influencing trajectories to the point of reversing social determinisms, as much by a dynamic of repulsion with respect to the worldly pole as by the strong control that the group of peers imposes on the writers it admits. It was for reasons that were as literary as they were political—by opposing the subordination of literary stakes to a political worldview of the academic right, for whom Henry Bordeaux was a figurehead—that the author of *Dieu et Mammon* was led to break with this academic right that had admitted him, and join the camp of the "academic left," all without ever becoming a true man of the left. Against the writers of earthly salvation, François Mauriac would, in his quest for redemption, find literary salvation.

If the crisis situation accelerated and accentuated Mauriac's break, which he had already begun before the war, it was because, faced with the threat that weighed on the literary field, the internal struggles tended to concentrate around the opposition between forces of autonomy and forces of heteronomy. This dynamic, set in motion during the quarrel of the "bad masters," was embodied by institutional struggles that contributed to the redefinition of the stakes and to the reworking of alliances that would give rise to the literary Resistance.

PART II

Literary Institutions and

National Crisis

In the ideological war that tore apart occupied France, the literary institutions, like the writers, constituted a stake for the acting political forces, as potential instruments of legitimation, even of propaganda. These attempts to harness them were expressed in the press and through direct pressures emanating from political powers (as we saw in the case of *La NRF*), and they were relayed within the field by certain members who confronted each other in a struggle to define the identity of the institution and the role it should play in these times of national crisis. The confrontations were all the more violent because in these times of social upheaval, those among them that resumed their activities, like the French Academy, the Goncourt Academy, and *La NRF*, or those that emerged from the shadows, like the Comité national des écrivains (CNE), were reference points that guided the writers. These institutions' more or less marked tendency to respond to external demand must be related to their history as well as their modes of survival, which were differentiated according to the state, media, aesthetic, and political logics that they embodied according to their most typical traits.

"Good taste" prevails according to the first logic, which allies a sense of "duty" and worldliness: in this view, politics is scorned in favor of morality, to which art should be subordinated. The proponents of "good taste" and the "distinguished" writers describe the second logic as "vulgar." "Scandal" is its mode of existence and its most secure means of survival. The third logic makes aesthetics and the demands of intellectual work its supreme morality: distinction is its privileged mode. Finally, the last logic makes literature into a subversive weapon. Representative of the temporally dominant pole, the French Academy embodies the logic of respectability that suits its official status as a state institution. Its junior, the Goncourt Academy, closely tied to events and news through the prize it awards, is close to the media logic that imposed itself right after the Great War in the intermediate sector of large-scale production. La NRF had incarnated the aesthetic logic to the highest degree during the interwar period; this was the logic at the pole of small-scale production. The formation of the CNE, founded on the alliance between the avant-gardes and the forces of opposition (in this instance, the Communist Party), illustrates the enactment of a political logic that conceived of literature as action.

The comparative analysis of these four institutions reveals the sociohistorical and cultural foundations of these different logics. The unequal distribution of resources, which in large part determines orientation in the literary field, can be grasped through a comparative analysis of the trends in terms of social recruitment displayed by these institutions, taken as groups of codified positions. Designating the social meaning of collective and individual conduct, "sense"—"sense of duty," "sense of scandal," "sense of distinction," and "sense of subversion"—also refers to the "sense of orientation" of individuals and groups in the social space and, more specifically, in the literary world. It implies different relationships to politics. The institutional approach thus allows us to understand how the dispositions and the distribution of inherited or acquired resources weigh globally on political attitudes at the different poles of the literary field. Spaces of mediation between political dispositions and choices, the institutions are also instruments of mobilization and places where group control is exercised.

I will nonetheless nuance this institutional approach. While it has the merit of illustrating these four logics, it also masks their possible coexistence even in a single individual. I will compensate for this by analyzing the internal struggles that crisscrossed each of these institutions. Generational divisions, tensions between autonomy and heteronomy and political oppositions are refracted in each, according to its own process. The institution is understood here as a heterogeneous group of individuals who agree not to call its existence into question—except in the limited case of La NRF when it was taken over by Drieu

La Rochelle in the autumn of 1940—but who confront each other over the definition of its literary and social vocation. Internal divisions and the alliances and conflicts through which they were manifested show the antagonistic forces between which these authorities were caught,[1] revealing the specific constraints that they brought to bear on their members.

By exacerbating these divisions, the crisis situation tried the esprit de corps that ensured the relative autonomy of the institution, along with its chances for survival. Of course, the capacity of these authorities to resist external pressures depended on the intensity of the esprit de corps, but it also depended on the social and legal foundation of the body. The French Academy's status as an official body thus kept it, more than the Goncourt Academy or *La NRF*, safe from the vicissitudes of the hour. If, as full *agents* of the literary world, these literary institutions contribute, through what opposes them or brings them together, to the determination of the stakes specific to the field, the esprit de corps, via the solidarity it institutes, more or less tends to neutralize the effects that the field itself bears upon their internal dynamics.[2] But, as it happened during the Occupation, institutional survival could be in contradiction with the survival of the literary field as a relatively autonomous space, revealing as a result the factors of heteronomy conveyed by these institutions. In that sense, academies, like *La NRF*, each in their own way fully participated in the process of losing autonomy. But ultimately, the institutional struggles also favored the gathering of rebels around semi-legal reviews and at the Comité national des écrivains.

CHAPTER 4

The Sense of Duty

The French Academy

The French Academy, which makes people smile and which thoughtless people
believe to be a matter of caricature, has in truth been one of the places where our
destiny was prepared between 1918 and 1940.
—François Mauriac, "Histoire politique de l'Académie française"

Of the four institutions that we will study, the Academy is the one that partici-
pates most directly, through its members, in official political life. François Mauriac was not mistaken when he attributed a political role to it in the preparation
of the Vichy regime. This role was due to the position it occupied in the field of
power and its social recruitment, which made it, as an institution, one of the
surest allies of the forces of conservatism, indeed of reaction. The affinity
between the French Academy and the Vichy regime thus proceeded from a
"preexisting harmony."[1] In the interwar period, a number of its members took
an active part in the struggles against the advances of the Republican left in
matters of educational politics, social politics, and foreign politics. This engagement became radicalized with the advent of the Popular Front and the rise
of international tensions. The writers of the Academy, with the exception of a
small minority, were at the forefront of this combat that led them to support
the project of the National Revolution in its traditionalist form, when they did
not contribute directly to its development.

A symbol of this French particularity that is the place literature has held in
the definition of national identity, the Academy was an essential place of mediation between literature and politics. While its foundation originally participated in the literary field's process of autonomization, starting in the nineteenth
century the Academy instead represented a source of heteronomy, conveying

extraliterary interests from the preservation of the moral order to the defense of the social order when it was "threatened." As the guardian of a literary orthodoxy, the Academy was positioned against the movement that, since romanticism, had imposed a vision of literature as a permanent revolution. Structurally linked to the dominant fractions of the dominant class, it was the very embodiment of the place where those fractions exerted their control over the literary field, always suspected of generating "social disorder," with the complicity of those writers most disposed to fulfill this role due to their position. This is the meaning of the writer's "social responsibility" such as it was redefined by Paul Bourget and defended by Henry Bordeaux. The radicalization of the political engagement among writers in the Academy must therefore be linked to the struggles that opposed them to the subversive fractions of the literary field, against whom the proponents of "good taste" constituted themselves as the defenders of a conception of literature as an instrument for reproducing a social "elite." It must also be linked to their confrontation with oppositional intellectuals since the Dreyfus affair, and, more generally, with the new Republican "elites," notably in the university.

A State Literary Institution

The "immortals" constitute a very particular body of representatives. While the official role allotted to the Academy consists in the codification of the French language, registering its evolutions and setting its usages, as well as in the distribution of official rewards to those who, through their conduct or their works, have served the nation well, its effective power is not limited to this role. A symbol of national continuity above and beyond regimes and political changes, it plays a role in the reproduction and perpetuation of "national conscience." A place of negotiation between the temporal and spiritual powers, it also consecrates the "elites" of the nation. Despite the diversity of roles that it represents, its esprit de corps relies on a relatively homogeneous social recruitment. Finally, as a representative of official French culture, it plays a major role in the elaboration and imposition of "good taste." To police the uses of language, to abolish the subversive power of words, such was the vocation of an institution where the political and social were denied as such, and where the performative discourse of conservatism appeared in the guise of the "neutral places" of common sense that gave it a universal bearing by naturalizing it. But it was also because this policed discourse barely masked its conception of culture, and a fortiori of literature, as an instrument of the symbolic power of conservative forces, that it exposed the contradictions between the "worldly" logic and literary autonomy in the eyes of the academicians who were most independent with respect to the institution. And it was because this discourse was mainly political, despite its depoliticized form, that the stakes of the Academy's struggles tended to be posed in political terms, more than for other literary authorities.

A DELEGATED POWER

By the history of its founding and the roles that were assigned to it, the French Academy was tightly linked to the formation of the state and the emergence of national identity. Its founder, Cardinal Richelieu, gave it the mission of setting the usages of the vernacular, and he endowed it with a particular status: that of a state body. Its establishment in 1635 through patent letters signed by Louis XIII implied, in return, that serving the government would figure among its fundamental obligations. In 1672, the king became its protector, increasing its prestige and authority.

This foundation, which first liberated literary men from patronage, marked the developing literary field's formal entry into the field of power. This took place at a time when literary production began to differentiate itself from other intellectual activities.[2] The first debates over the writer's "social image" arose then, confined to a narrow circle of producers, while writers began to struggle with the acting powers for recognition of their status, notably through their claim to royalties. Specific authorities were institutionalized, like best writers awards and the academies, culminating in the granting of official recognition to the French Academy.

This official recognition, by opening the doors of "immortality" to literary men, gave them the power to legislate in matters of linguistic norms. A power of literary consecration would soon be added: starting in 1671, the Academy awarded an annual prize for eloquence; then, starting in 1701, a prize for poetry. Contributing to the linguistic and political unification of seventeenth-century France, this function served the centralizing project of an absolute monarchy. Allied with Court society, some notable representatives of which were among its members, the Academy dethroned clerics and scholars, full of erudite knowledge and specialized in scholarly language. In so doing, it brought about the victory of a worldly and French literary order that was accessible to "honnêtes hommes," "well-bred people," whose good sense it illustrated, against the old erudite and European order.[3] A site of mediation between the Court and the City, after 1760 it escaped the double control of the throne and the Church by appointing a majority of *encyclopédistes*, to the point of seeming like a force of opposition.

Dissolved by the Revolution as a "literary aristocracy" and replaced by the grammar and poetry sections of the new Institute,[4] then rehabilitated as a second class of the Institute by Napoleon, who allowed it to resume some of its pomp and customs, it was truly reestablished in its title and prerogatives only after the Restoration. An ordinance in 1816 restored its functions in return for the expulsion of several members. Having regained first rank inside the Institute, it alone depended directly on the head of state who, even today, ratifies the election of each of its members.

This ratification is not a mere formality. The head of state's veto right had been exercised several times under the Ancien Régime, twice by notice before the election for authors of licentious writings, four times by temporary refusal following election, and only twice by definitive refusal following election, for two Jansenists.[5] François-René de Chateaubriand, elected by order of the emperor who accepted him, was not admitted, his reception speech having displeased the protector of the Academy. When Charles Maurras was elected in 1938, several newspapers called for his non-validation, but the president, Albert Lebrun, who had vetoed his candidacy two years earlier when Maurras was in prison, now immediately dispelled Henry Bordeaux's fears, judging that it was not his right to control the Academy's choices. Charles de Gaulle, on the other hand, twice manifested his hostility toward a candidate: Paul Morand in 1958, who would only be elected ten years later (I will come back to this), and Saint-John Perse whom he criticized for not having joined his cause in 1940.[6]

Certainly, these cases are rare, and no authority interferes between the head of state and the Academy. This allows its members to affirm the Academy's full independence with respect to the political field. And it is true that as an official body, the Academy enjoys an undeniable autonomy in the field of power, which protects it from the vicissitudes of the temporal order. It nonetheless remained concerned, as we will see, with endorsing, beyond the head of state, the spiritual power from which it originally drew its authority: the Church. But the Academy needs no directives to exercise its role as the guardian of orthodoxy: its esprit de corps is enough, in that it places itself above the contingencies of temporal power to ensure the continuity of national culture by consecrating and perpetuating the symbolic power of the "elites" that successively illustrated it. By its very existence, it founds this power in prestige and legitimacy.

In the literary order, the Academy's inertia, proper to institutions that serve as guardians of orthodoxy, increased with the transformations of the literary field during the second half of the nineteenth century.[7] Liberalism's gains legitimated demands for autonomy from political and religious powers in terms of freedom of expression. The development of the publishing market, which progressively liberated literary production from the constraints of state sponsorship and patronage, created a new pole of dependency that spurred struggles to affirm the symbolic value of literary works, and to promote the judgment of peers over the verdicts of the lay public. A pole of small-scale production, confined to the peer audience, differentiated itself and became autonomous from the pole of large-scale production, ruled by sales figures. The multiplication of authorities of consecration specifically appointed to designate which works were worthy of interest and guide the taste of the public—reviews, clubs, literary criticism in the press, academies, literary prizes—deprived the French Academy of the quasi monopoly that it had enjoyed up to this point. Finally, in conjunction with the growth of the market, progress in the division of intellectual labor favored the professionalization of writing as an occupation, inciting literary men to challenge the influence of the salons that made and broke reputations, along with the amateurism of socialites. The founding of the Goncourt Academy as a counter-academy was an expression of this.

The creation, following the model of the Goncourt Prize, of a Grand Prize for Literature in 1912 and a Prize for the Novel in 1914, in addition to the numerous prizes that it already distributed—prize for eloquence, for poetry, for virtue, random prizes whose donors intended them for literary and historical works or morally "useful" works, and so forth—testifies to the will of the French Academy to continue monitoring the production of literary taste. In this light, its marginalization during the interwar period was due less to competition with the Goncourt Academy than to the power of consecration attained by La NRF.

THE SOCIAL FOUNDATIONS OF "ESPRIT DE CORPS"

"It is one of the charms of the Company that it is not a pure collection of literary men," assured Paul Valéry on the 300th anniversary of the Academy.[8] The fact that the most specifically consecrated writers who served there were led, making a virtue of necessity, to justify the heterogeneity of the assembly or present it as an advantage, even as a source of its "mystery" (Paul Valéry), indicates the negative value that was associated with this heterogeneity from the standpoint of the literary field. For Georges Duhamel, "Whether we want it or not, the French Academy meets a necessity. It represents the very physiognomy of the nation through the variety of its choices [. . .]."[9] It would be more appropriate to speak of a "physiognomy of the field of power."[10] A look at its morphology in the 1940s allows us to understand its principles of membership. This study will focus on the trajectory of forty "immortals" who were members between 1940 and 1944, to whom I will occasionally add—notably to illustrate the evolution of recruitment—the eighteen members elected between 1944 and 1947.

The Academy has traditionally granted a certain number of seats to the different "elites" who embody or have embodied national "greatness" in the temporal and spiritual order: nobility, the clergy, diplomacy, politicians, the army, the university mingled with literary men. Through a subtle balance, the Academy distributed its seats among the dignitaries of an outdated order and the new forms of notability that it knew how to assimilate, marking at once its function as a guardian of national memory and its ability to adapt, although belatedly, to the transformations of the social space. It took stock of the rule of the notables in the nineteenth century and annexed this new state nobility trained in the grandes écoles, especially the graduates of the ENS who, with fourteen representatives elected from 1874 to 1895 versus three from 1830 to 1874, subsequently constituted around a quarter of its membership.[11] The liberal professions, especially lawyers and physicians, found or regained their welcome when they organized themselves into professional bodies. While the Academy did not neglect the art of politics, it showed its preference for diplomacy.

The presence of the military, which had precedents in the eighteenth century, was characteristic of the interwar period: consecrating the nation's heroes was part of the Academy's assigned mission. Marshals Foch, Joffre, and Lyautey were followed in 1929 by Marshal Pétain, elected unanimously, and whose reception by Paul Valéry "took on the dimensions of a national event,"[12] as well as General Weygand in 1931 and Marshal Franchet d'Espérey in 1934. Admiral Lacaze, elected in 1936, represented the colonial empire after Lyautey.

Scientists held two chairs in 1940: the duke Maurice de Broglie, a former navy officer who would succeed Paul Langevin as the chair of general physics at the Collège de France in 1942, and the mathematician Émile Picard, a graduate of the ENS and professor at the Faculty of Science and the École Centrale, member of the Academy of Sciences and president of the International Council for Scientific Research.

Faithful to its tradition, which had opposed it to scholars, the Academy recognized erudition less than worldly notoriety. While a number of its members took the university cursus honorum, passing through the ENS, agrégation, and the doctorate, they could above all boast of the prestigious positions that capped off their careers. These included directing the École française de Rome (art historian Émile Mâle) and teaching at the Collège de France (Henri Bergson, professor of philosophy, member of the Academy of Moral and Political Sciences; and Paul Hazard, professor of modern and comparative literature). They could also point to their quality as orators, their international influence, and the contribution of their work to the safeguard of threatened values. Bergson's Jewish origins were thus forgiven due to his major contribution to the renewal of spiritualism against materialist positivism.[13]

Of historians, "the Academy has always asked [. . .] that art was never sacrificed to science. Clio has not ceased in our Company, as on the Parnassus of the *Chambres*, to remain near Apollo and smile at him."[14] Ignoring the epistemological rupture through which history was founded as a discipline in the nineteenth century, it consecrated illustrious representatives of the tradition of narrative history that survived outside the walls of the university. These elected historians included the Duke de La Force: one of the youngest to join its ranks (at forty-seven), the author of works on the age of Louis XIV and on Richelieu (in collaboration with Hanotaux), he joined forces with the "party of the dukes." Next to him, scholarly history had a single representative in the person of Louis Madelin, agrégé in history, former student of the École des Chartes, doctor, member of the École française de Rome, specialist on the Revolution and the Empire as well as the military history of the Great War. He was also a delegate from the Vosges department between 1924 and 1928.

To the "intellectual proletariat" formed by the Republic of Professors, the Company preferred the older model of scholarly notability, and to the Sorbonne reborn as a research institution it preferred the old Sorbonne where oratory qualities prevailed. It was only after the Liberation that the number of professors would grow, even double, in the Academy: although they had other titles to grant them entry, the inclusion of seven professors among eighteen Academy members elected between 1944 and 1947 finally echoed the morphological transformations of the intellectual field. Joining the only survivor of five academics who were seated there before the war, they then formed almost a quarter of the assembly. The election in 1946 of Édouard Herriot, one of the most illustrious representatives of this Republic of Professors that brought him from the ENS to the government as head of the Cartel des Gauches in 1924, was so atypical that it alone suffices to illustrate the extraordinary character of recruitment at the Liberation, made possible by the temporary weakening of the "academic right."

Literary men, who most interest us here, held half the seats in the assembly. The overrepresentation of the novelistic genre—twelve to fifteen seats in 1940, according to whether or not we count multi-genre authors—marked prose fiction's resounding revenge after it had been banished from the Mazarin palace until the end of the nineteenth century. A popular genre with a feminine reputation, the novel was held in contempt. Despite the rhetorical efforts that he deployed in order to inscribe his work in the moralist tradition, and the marks of notability that he otherwise accumulated, Balzac was kept at arms' length, like Zola, who would later be rejected twenty-four times. It was in the "ennobled" and edifying form of the psychological novelists, advertising their distance from the vulgar naturalist materialism that professed the theory of observation "without any concern for beauty and morality,"[15] and posing as the heirs of Taine and Renan, that the novel invaded the Academy at the turn of the century.[16] After the navy officer Pierre Loti, who was sought out to ensure the rejection of Zola's candidacy, Paul Bourget, elected in 1894, opened the march of the novelists into the Academy. This author of the *Disciple* also had the *Essais de psychologie contemporaine* to his credit. He was followed by André Theuriet, Anatole France, René Bazin, and Maurice Barrès. In less than forty years, the number of novelists would triple, to the detriment of dramatic authors (or rather, writers of light comedies) who went from six in 1903 to two in 1940 (Henri Lavedan and Maurice Donnay), and especially of poets, who would now have only one representative in the person of Paul Valéry. Meanwhile, as we have said, the Academy founded its own Prize for the Novel.

In this way, the Academy confirmed the triumph of the novel, now the dominant genre, in the interwar period. Light reading had always been welcomed there: very fashionable during this period, adventure and exoticism (Pierre Benoit, Claude Farrère, Jérôme Tharaud, Louis Bertrand), along with social satire (Georges Lecomte, Marcel Prévost, Abel Hermant) held the role that had previously been played by theater. In the moralist lineage, we find the psychological novel (Édouard Estaunié, Jacques de Lacretelle), the novel of manners (Henry Bordeaux, François Mauriac), the cyclic novel (Georges Duhamel, then Jules Romains after the Liberation), as well as the noblest florets of the regionalist novel (Joseph de Pesquidoux, then Maurice Genevoix after the Liberation). This classification, arbitrary like all generic classifications, is given here only as an example. The different novelistic subgenres gained recognition less for themselves than for the nobility of the object they examined—and the values they contained. Roger Martin du Gard, for example, even though he won the Nobel Prize (in 1937), was disdained by the Academy because of his affiliation with naturalism and the subversive potential of his *Thibault* cycle.[17]

The immortalized novelists had moreover proven themselves in nonfiction genres, which were more traditionally prized by the Academy than fiction. André Maurois, for example, served there more as an observer of British manners and a "renewer of the biographical genre,"[18] like François Mauriac, author of *Vie de Jean Racine*; Georges Lecomte, biographer of Adolphe Thiers who opportunely rehabilitated the bloody Commune fighter; or else André Chevrillon, the biographer of his uncle Hyppolite Taine. Through studies, travel narratives, paintings of the "characters" of people, and journalism in its noblest form (reporting), the writers consecrated by the Academy had traveled the world and opened new horizons on foreign civilizations to the French public. Among those civilizations, we find the United States (Hermant, Maurois, and Duhamel who, in his *Scènes de la vie future*, which appeared in 1930, condemned machinism), England (Maurois, Chevrillon), Germany (Valéry), Spain and Italy (Bertrand, Lecomte, Lacretelle), North Africa (Bertrand, Chevrillon, the Tharaud brothers), the Middle East (Benoit), and the Far East (Bonnard, Farrère). Some writers made themselves into the chroniclers and memoirists of society life (Hermant), when they were not rediscovering the traditions of the land (Pesquidoux). Moralists, essayists, they examined the contemporary problems and the crisis of values: Paul Valéry revealed the crisis of "Western civilization," Georges Duhamel studied the crisis of humanism, Henry Bordeaux inquired into the marriage crisis, and Charles Maurras denounced the role of money in the literary world; he also defended "Western civilization" through his critical work that rehabilitated classical values against romanticism, through his traditionalism and foreign policy. Grammarians took on the problems of the French language (Hermant, Duhamel). Exploring the soul, others produced meditations, reflections on the problem of consciousness or on art (Mauriac, Lacretelle).

Between exegesis and censorship, the elaboration of classificatory schemes and the production of taste, criticism entered quite naturally into the preoccupations of an assembly whose role was the codification of language and the regulation of its proper usage. Illustrated at the Academy by Charles-Augustin Sainte-Beuve, literary criticism had become a genre in itself, insofar as it became professionalized and distinguished itself from the university criticism that developed at the end of the nineteenth century. Edmond Jaloux, like Émile Henriot later, entered the Academy more in his quality of critic rather than as a novelist, even though his novelistic work was award-winning. André Bellessort, André Chaumeix, and Louis Gillet had a place there by right.

The heterogeneity of the intellectual specialties at the Academy masked the relative homogeneity of its social recruitment. The French Academy truly tended to consecrate "elites," associating social status and intellectual prestige. The academicians most often belonged, by their origins and by their social positions, to the dominant fraction of the dominant class, and to civil service.

Of the fifty-eight "immortals" who served between 1940 and 1948, one-quarter came from a wealthy background, or had fathers ranked highly in the civil service; close to two-thirds originated from the middle bourgeoisie, from legal professions, from intellectual sectors, or from mid-ranking civil service sectors (about 15 percent for each category). Only seven out of fifty-eight came from the relatively affluent petty bourgeoisie: Marshal Pétain, for example, was the son of affluent farmers. Civil service was dominant: more than half (thirty-one) of all members came from it, and the level of recruitment from the senior civil service (17.2 percent) was as high as that of senior civil servants in their own category (16.9 percent).[19] Almost half of the members had attended a grande école (fourteen at the ENS) and almost one-quarter among them were agrégés (13). They included eight doctors of letters (including one in theology as well), three doctors of science, three doctors of law (two of whom were also doctors in letters), three doctors of medicine, and thirteen who held a licence. Only three among them had not had any higher education.

Perpetuating a dynasty of members of the Institute,[20] from good society or having risen in society, besides the role they played in the illustration of the language and the values dear to the Academy, they also shared traits of distinction that designated them as representatives of national culture. These included civil service; the titles and laurels they had accumulated—titles of nobility, academic titles (grandes écoles, doctorate), rank in the ecclesiastical hierarchy, honorific distinctions (Légion d'honneur), academic consecrations, literary prizes; their notoriety as public figures on the national and international scene—from the successful novelist to the national hero, or from the fashionable philosopher like Bergson to the minister; and a bodily ethos and a lifestyle that had been inherited or acquired by frequenting society and salons, associated with a certain cosmopolitanism[21]—from the ambassador to the traveling writer who embodied the romantic model of the artist free from social constraints and accumulating exotic experiences, along with the sailor, or rather the officer of colonial campaigns.

LITERARY MEN OR SOCIETY MEN

Comparing the social recruitment of literary men in the Academy with that of the literary field during the same period demonstrates very clear differences that show that their predispositions to become the guardians of orthodoxy cannot simply be viewed as an effect of age (the majority were between sixty and eighty years old).[22] They testify to the "double inversion" that brought the writers from economically and politically powerful backgrounds to the temporally dominant positions of the literary field (which itself occupies, let us remember, a dominated position in the field of power).[23]

The writers who oriented themselves toward academic consecration were the fashionable society authors, close through their works, like their acquaintance, with the people of society and the salons where "good taste" was developed. This "good taste" was construed as style in the *Revue des deux mondes*, otherwise known as the "anteroom of the Academy" according to Léon Daudet's expression.[24] Unlike the bohemian, for whom writing was a way of life, for them it was a social status. They collected literary distinctions and honors (prizes, institutional consecrations, Légion d'honneur) in the same way that they accumulated academic titles.

Due to their social origins, the immortalized writers were situated midway between the literary field and the senior civil service.[25] Slightly more likely to come from a wealthy background, from senior civil service, and from legal sectors than the whole of writers, two or three times less likely to come from intellectual sectors and the petty bourgeoisie or popular classes (the categories from which writers were most often recruited, about one in five and at least one in four respectively), the "immortals" were much more frequently heirs of public service members. More than one Academy writer out of three was the son of a senior or mid-level civil servant versus barely one out of ten of all the writers included in this study, academicians excepted (see table 1 in appendix 2). Three of the four Academy writers from the petty bourgeoisie, Paul Hazard, Jules Romains, and Marcel Pagnol (the latter two would be elected only after the Liberation) were the sons of primary school teachers—an origin that, at the end of the nineteenth century, was a factor in social elevation. Two of the fathers would go on to become school principals.

These differences can also be observed in the relationship between geographical and educational trajectories (see tables 2–5 in appendix 2). The weight of French cultural centralization made proximity to the capital a condition of access to the literary field. Issued from a more provincial notability—two-thirds of the Academy's writers spent their childhood in the provinces versus half of the whole of nonacademic writers; a quarter of the former grew up in Paris versus a third of the latter—the "immortals" emigrated toward the capital during their secondary schooling twice as often as their provincial colleagues who would reach Paris only at the age of their entry into adult life or higher education (at this time of life, 70 percent of the writers in our total population were established there).

While this recruitment testifies to the Academy's allegiance to the "provinces" since the nineteenth century,[26] the strong geographic mobility of future academicians during secondary school reveals the weight of familial education strategies. At least two out of five of these writers, versus one out of three for the whole of the population, attended a major lycée in Paris—or the École Alsacienne in one case—either for the duration of their schooling (one in five) or after having been schooled in a provincial lycée or collège (nearly one in four). The others most often attended a Catholic secondary school—nearly one academic writer out of three versus less than one out of five for the whole of writers.

The Academy's writers were distinguished mainly by the amount of their overall educational capital: half of them attended a grande école or a preparatory class (ENS, Polytechnique, Centrale, the École des Chartes, or the École libre des sciences politiques, which prepared careers in diplomacy), versus less than a quarter of the whole of writers, who were a bit more likely to have attended university (a third versus a quarter of their academic counterparts). Only one in ten academic writers did not attend an establishment of higher education versus one in three for the whole of writers. Finally, while they were less likely to have finished their studies than the other "immortals," academic writers globally held more degrees than the whole of writers: more than three-quarters of them held a degree equal or superior to the licence, versus fewer than half of their counterparts.

Little inclined to the bohemian way of life, academicians often exercised a profession while working to stabilize their literary career—almost half of them had been professors, conservators, or civil servants versus one non-academic writer in five, which reinforces the remark on their proximity to the civil service—but they ultimately lived off their writing and elected to reside in elegant neighborhoods (the sixteenth arrondissement in Paris was a favorite). As an illustrative example, the salary received by Henry Bordeaux just for his contributions to the *Revue des deux mondes* reached an average of 33,600 francs per year between 1934 and 1938, giving him access to an executive retirement. This was roughly equivalent to the annual returns of *La NRF*'s director, Jean Paulhan, who also held several roles at Gallimard, and Bordeaux's wage was higher than the money Paul Léautaud earned for his secretary job at the Mercure de France, which reached 1,500 francs per month.[27]

Large print runs, prepublications in serial, a vast body of work: the pole of large-scale production was best represented at the Academy. To take the most extreme cases, besides that of Henry Bordeaux which has already been discussed, *L'Atlantide* by Pierre Benoit (Albin Michel), crowned by the Academy's Prize for the Novel in 1919, reached 150,000 copies in eighteen months.[28] Bordeaux published seventy-three novels, Benoit about forty, assuming what François Mauriac called "the shame of the annual novel."[29] This overproduction did in fact earn them the mockery of some of their colleagues and of critics, who suspected them of sacrificing quality to economic gain: "serial . . . in three months . . . for money," sums up the major accusations leveled against Pierre Benoit.[30]

Often award-winning—most of the Academy's novelists had won one of the main prizes for the novel, Goncourt, Femina, the Academy's Prize for the

Novel, or the Grand Prize for Literature, when they did not accumulate several, like Edmond Jaloux and Jacques de Lacretelle, winners of the Femina and then one of the Academy's two prizes, or the Tharaud brothers, winners of the Goncourt and then the Grand Prize for Literature—their works met with widespread success and opened the door to notoriety, and even notability for those who were the least socially endowed (Georges Duhamel, Jules Romains).[31] The temporally dominant position that they had achieved in literature can also be discerned in the places where they published. They were most often edited by the old houses of the nineteenth century, who counted on rapid sales and successful authors: Flammarion in particular, but also Albin Michel; or by ultraconservative houses, mainly the very Catholic Plon, as well as Fasquelle and Perrin, where André Bellessort, a member of Action française, directed a collection. They contributed to the major periodicals with large printings, like *La Revue hebdomadaire*, linked to Plon, as well as the large dailies of the right, like the *Journal des débats*, *L'Écho de Paris*, *Le Temps*, and *Le Figaro*.

The Academy's "esprit de corps" was thus founded on the relative homogeneity of its members' social properties, which made them the expression of the interests of the fractions with economic and political power. Guardians of literary orthodoxy and national values, they tended to make themselves into guardians of the social order.

GUARDIANS OF THE SOCIAL ORDER

Paul Bourget counted the French Academy among the four European fortresses of defense against revolution, next to the House of Lords, the Vatican, and the Prussian General-Staff. The strong politicization of the French Academy during the interwar period, led by the writers who served there, illustrates the alliance of the conservative right and the extreme right, symbolized by Charles Maurras's election in 1938.

It was customary to distinguish between a "right" and a "left" at the Academy. Two analyses, offered by direct witnesses who aligned with the so-called left camp—we owe the first to André Siegfried, it seems,[32] and the second to François Mauriac—agreed in their identification of the "academic right" with the political right, while they both refuted the assimilation of the "academic left" with the political left:

> [...] A member of the academic left does not necessarily align with the political left, but the academic right appears most often as an aspect of the political right: it is not essentially either royalist, or clerical, or capitalist, or nationalist, but as these traits are eliminated, there is still a remnant of pure

right, all the more significant since it is made of the most authentic attachment to the principle of authority, such as it is descended from the most orthodox Ancien Régime. It is a state of mind, an attitude, a reaction of resistance to the most inadmissible pretensions of the modern world. [...] By opposition, the academic left is assuredly and necessarily neither Republican, nor radical, nor socialist: it is characterized, rather, by a sort of humanist liberalism, issued from the Renaissance and from the 18th-century Enlightenment.[33]

The public believes that, at the French Academy, there is a left and a right. And for the right, it is not mistaken. Here is perhaps the last French "high place" where an authentic right subsists. And this is not saying enough: where the right subsists in a pure state. As for the left ... "Another Communist," sighed Marshal Pétain when Georges Duhamel was declared elected. That says it all. Even in this very benign form, I deny that there is a left at the Academy. There are some writers there who would wish [...] to have certain other writers enter it.[34]

This lack of symmetry was due to the homology between the structures of the assembly and the dominant class, where the intellectual fractions who possess cultural capital occupy a dominated position and define themselves in opposition to the temporally dominant factions, who hold economic and political power.[35] André Siegfried thus classifies "the dukes, the society men, such and such right-minded historians who did not claim the methods of the Sorbonne" on the right, and "lawyers, doctors, professors" on the left.[36]

In the nineteenth century, the opposition between the academic "left" and "right" seemed to coincide with the split between "professional" writers and "amateur" society men.[37] The Dreyfus affair would provoke a redistribution of the cards. The "birth of intellectuals" as an oppositional social group,[38] which resulted from the morphological transformations of the intellectual field, led to a new polarization inside the literary field, forcing the "intellectuals of the right," "at risk of being excluded from the field [...] to distance themselves from the primary truths of conservatism, but return to them all the more strongly at the end of the polemic against the 'intellectuals of the left,' " as Pierre Bourdieu has explained.[39] The French Academy took an active part in this restructuration, as twenty-two academicians, writers included, almost immediately joined the Ligue de la patrie française.[40] This was followed by the Academy's election of illustrious representatives of the new nationalist right, René Bazin and especially Maurice Barrès, who ensured a majority for the "academic right." By a double inversion, the new "academic right," which now claimed the majority of writers in the assembly, constituted itself as such against the intellectuals "on the left," or even just the intellectuals.

From then on, the Academy's writers were divided. On one side, the writers most inclined to heteronomy through their alliances with the agents of political and economic power, who, like Henry Bordeaux, owed the maintenance of their position in the literary field to the institution, and thus could be called the "oblates." On the other side, those writers who enjoyed a greater independence with respect to the institution; because they were recognized by their peers, they owed it only a part of their legitimacy and could join forces to defend literary autonomy against the heteronomous logic promoted by the "oblates." Such is the meaning of François Mauriac's knowing analysis, since his ideological break with the right following his election to the Academy exemplifies this dynamic of attraction-repulsion. In times of crisis, it could lead the most independent writers of the Academy to align with the subversive fractions of the literary field in their struggle against the acting powers.

The right-left split at the Academy that, from the beginning of the century, posed itself in terms of anti-Republicanism for the "academic right," had been temporarily set aside during the Great War thanks to the Sacred Union. The formation of a pacifist and internationalist intellectual left around Barbusse and Romain Rolland on one side, and the establishment of *La NRF* around André Gide on the other, would favor the French Academy's retreat to the defense of national, and soon "Western," values. This reaction, in the double sense of the term, and the ensuing politicization of the stakes, was more particularly conducted by the writers of the assembly.

The primary role that a number of writers played in the politicization of the institutions must be related to the structure of the literary field during the interwar period, and notably to the marginalization that the French Academy experienced due to *La NRF*'s concentration of the power of symbolic consecration. In 1930, one of the most well-known critics at *La NRF*, Albert Thibaudet, could thus respond to Paul Bourget: "Since 1914, the great Prussian General Staff is on the floor, the House of Lords bends and pales, the French Academy . . . let's move on!"[41] For François Mauriac, a privileged witness due to his double belonging to the Academy and *La NRF* (where he contributed without really being integrated into the team, let us recall), the opposition was clear:

> The political battle that resulted in the domination of the extreme right at the Academy simultaneously occurred on the literary plane. Between the two wars, the continuous electoral defeat of the right was paired in literature, after 1923, by a continuous rise in the values defended by *La NRF* and a no

less continuous descent, followed by a total collapse, of those that the French Academy and the *Revue des deux mondes* advocated.[42]

While we cannot subscribe to the direct relation that Mauriac established between literary and political history, his somewhat hasty assimilation of the political and literary stakes is important in terms of what it reveals about the "emic" principles of perception, and we can confidently attribute it to the "academic right" that Mauriac contested.

Against the "worldly" logic, *La NRF* had actually achieved the tour de force of imposing a purely intellectual principle of asceticism, which made it less a school than a counter-academy. This challenge was far more threatening than the mischief of the Goncourt jurors. It emanated from a group that represented, by the social origins of its members, by their preponderantly Parisian anchoring, by the significant amount of their educational capital, an elite that was not only social, but also intellectual (see chapter 6). And yet, a number of them, and some of the most famous, were Protestant. In 1919, the *Revue des deux mondes* had refused to publish André Gide's *La Symphonie pastorale* because of its "confessional character."[43] Denied worldly honors, the man called the "Protestant Barrès" also resembled Barrès because of his individualism, and his religion, which made him pass for the heir to that dangerous social denigrator, Jean-Jacques Rousseau, and beyond that, to the Reform. Coupled with his Protestant origins, his avowed homosexuality succeeded in excluding him from high society. Had he not, in *Corydon*, revealed his true face by claiming to reform the laws of nature? Furthermore, while everything brought the founders of *La NRF* and the academicians closer in terms of their social and educational resources, everything separated them from a literary point of view: unknown authors who had long been reserved for an audience of initiates, they had transposed their rigorist dispositions into a high aesthetic demand that lent their works a certain austerity, little prized in social circles. This high demand was all the more condemnable since they made it into a weapon against those who had rejected them, the worldly and academic poles. Henry Bordeaux had been panned by Albert Thibaudet, Pierre Benoit by Benjamin Crémieux who accused him of writing badly and enumerated the errors of style that he committed.[44] This surely helps explain the "hate" that Pierre Benoit reserved for *La NRF*, according to François Mauriac. "Pierre Benoit, a novelist, and a good novelist, has been, like Henri Béraud although more secretly, one of the sworn enemies of the Gidian revolution and *La Nouvelle Revue française*," Mauriac wrote.[45] This attitude made Benoit one of the surest allies of the "academic right." Others, like Abel Bonnard, had to settle for ironic and scornful allusions of this type: "A[ction]

F[rançaise] unanimously sings the praises of Abel Bonnard . . . author of rhymed bits on domestic animals."[46]

Finally, resisting the heteronomous logic that nationalist intellectuals were trying to impose on literature in the name of the Sacred Union and the defense of national interest, La NRF presented itself at the end of the Great War, as we saw, as a bastion of "pure" literature, albeit without neglecting politics. La NRF was one of the places to reflect on the Franco-German reconciliation just as it was to become, in the 1930s, one of the places to recruit anti-Fascist intellectuals, which did not prevent it from maintaining a subtle balance between the viewpoints of the right and the left within its ranks. But Gide's resounding endorsement of Communism in 1932 could only make it a Marxist bastion, in the eyes of the peaceful bourgeois of the Academy.

With Paul Valéry in 1925, the Academy had elected one of the only acceptable members from within the NRF team: Valéry had given proof of his "responsibility,"[47] through both his anti-Dreyfusism and his reflections on La Conquête allemande (the article, published in 1896, was republished as a booklet in 1915 at the Mercure de France) and the crisis of civilization. Familiar with the salons and the politico-social circles of the postwar period, he had just entered the International Committee on Intellectual Cooperation of the League of Nations and was to become one of the strongest supporters of Aristide Briand's peace politics in the intellectual world. He did this all without disavowing his concern for the national interest: in July 1925, he had joined a number of academicians in showing solidarity with intellectuals who were indignant about Henri Barbusse's declaration against the Rif War.[48] Still, he owed his election to the nonliterary academicians: politicians, military men, and scientists, rather than to literary men. He counted a few supporters among them—Eugène Brieux, Robert de Flers, Édouard Estaunié, Maurice Donnay, Henri Lavedan—but also enemies grouped around Paul Bourget, who rejected his supposed hermeticism.[49]

Another contributor to La NRF could legitimately stake a claim to academy membership, having allied a poetic and dramatic body of work marked by a profound Catholicism with a career as an ambassador: Paul Claudel. But the writers on the "academic right" did not see things that way. In their concern to defend literature at the Academy against a new political candidate, Maurice Paléologue, a group of writers identified with the "academic left" sought out Claudel in 1927 to fill the vacant Jonnart chair. Henry Bordeaux, fearing that the Academy would be accused of neglecting pure literature, suggested to René Doumic that he be opposed by Paul Morand rather than Maurice Paléologue.[50] Claudel did not run and Paléologue was elected. In 1935, as we have said, he failed against the navy officer and novelist of the sea Claude Farrère. Despite Georges Duhamel's insistence, with the complicity of Paul Valéry and François Mauriac, he would refuse to reapply the following year: "I made one mistake; I will not make two. I have nothing in common with all those people. Why go sit with them. Yes, I know, there is you, Mauriac, Valéry, a few others [...] Farrère was preferred to me, it is intolerable."[51] For François Mauriac, his failure would solidify the contradiction between the worldly logic and literary autonomy, as we saw in the last chapter. And along with Paul Valéry, Georges Duhamel, and Louis Gillet, Mauriac would be part of the minority of writers who would oppose Charles Maurras's entry into the Academy.

Delayed by the pope's condemnation of "integral nationalism" in 1926, the arrival of Action française at the Academy looked like a reaction to the mobilization of intellectual anti-Fascists and the coalition of the left after February 6, 1934. These events catalyzed the alliance between the conservative fractions and the reactionary extreme right under the banner of the "defense of the West" and the "anti-Bolshevist crusade." In 1935, the year when the Academy celebrated its 300th anniversary, it was marked by the triple election of the Maurrassians Jacques Bainville and André Bellessort, and of Claude Farrère, a league sympathizer and admirer of Mussolini. On that day, Louis Bertrand, then laboring at a work in praise of Hitler that led to his break with the still-Germanophobic Maurras,[52] supposedly greeted some of his colleagues with "Long live Hitler! Down with the Soviets," according to an anecdote reported by François Mauriac.[53] While it had escaped no one, the political meaning of this election appeared clearly in Pierre Benoit's speech at the reception of Farrère, which alluded to the assassination of President Paul Doumer at the Association des écrivains combattants book sale in 1932, during which Farrère, who accompanied the president of the Republic in his role as president of the association, had been wounded: "We have laws to banish the heirs of our kings, the kings of France! We don't have any to deal with the hideous international underworld that comes to our country to play at bombs and daggers to its satisfaction."[54]

The international tensions, the Italian aggression in Abyssinia, the arrival to power of the Popular Front government, then the war in Spain would succeed in welding this alliance based on a neo-pacifism of the right. Reviving the large anti-Dreyfus mobilization of the "immortals," sixteen academicians, mainly writers, cosigned Henri Massis's neo-pacifist manifesto, along with intellectuals from Action française and the Fascistic right. This manifesto, "For the Defense of the West," spoke out against the sanctions that the League of Nations had inflicted on Mussolinian Italy as a result of the invasion of Ethiopia. The first list included the names of Maurice Donnay, Abel Hermant, Pierre de Nolhac, Henry Bordeaux, Louis Madelin, Georges Lecomte, Édouard Estaunié, Louis Bertrand, André Chaumeix, Abel Bonnard, André Bellessort, and Claude Farrère; Cardinal Baudrillart and Henri de Régnier would soon add their approval.[55] In 1936, Henry Bordeaux presided over the committee of national action that was created to lift those sanctions.

A few days after the electoral victory of the Frente popular in Spain, Louis Bertrand wrote to René Doumic, permanent secretary of the Academy and director of the *Revue des deux mondes*: "Here we are three-quarters Bolshevized," before brandishing the threat of a civil war and an invasion.[56] The fears raised since the advent of the Second Spanish Republic by the prospect of a "secularizing and socializing" politics were largely expressed in the *Revue des deux mondes*, which reflected the majority tendency of the French Academy rather well. The military coup d'état in July 1936 and the civil war appeared in the review as the inevitable consequence of the Frente popular, which resonated all the more since the Popular Front government had just formed in France.[57] The conservative fractions of the Academy and the *Revue des deux mondes* supported Gil Robles, the leader of the conservative and Catholic party called the Spanish Confederation of Autonomous Rights. From January 1937, the *Revue des deux mondes* discreetly manifested its preference for the nationalists. But it was only starting in the autumn of 1937 that the academicians openly endorsed the Francoist cause, when, with the blessing of members of the French ecclesiastic hierarchy, the diplomatic reconciliation between the Vatican and the Burgos government was sketched out. Nine "immortals," as we saw, signed the "Manifesto to the Spanish Intellectuals" published in the *Journal des débats* and the review *Occident* in December 1937: Louis Bertrand, Abel Bonnard, Abel Hermant, Édouard Estaunié, and especially Henry Bordeaux, Georges Goyau, and Louis Madelin, who brought their Catholic endorsement; and Admiral Lacaze and General Weygand, who served as military endorsements.[58] If we add Claude Farrère, the author of *Visite aux espagnols*, and Cardinal Baudrillart, who gave the official Church endorsement, more than a quarter of the Academy had at this point publicly taken a stand for the Francoist cause, versus a single member, François Mauriac, for neutrality. Two other signers, Charles Maurras and Jérôme Tharaud, would soon enter the Academy. But the cause of the Spanish nationalists already benefited from an even broader sympathy at the Academy, which we can assess at close to half its members. André Chaumeix, André Bellessort, Duke de Broglie, Duke de La Force, Léon Bérard, and Maurice Paléologue, none of whom signed the manifesto, would actually join their colleagues on the honor committee of the association "Solidarité d'Occident," founded with the high approval of Cardinal Baudrillart in June 1938. This committee would include ten academicians.[59]

At the same time, Charles Maurras was elected to the Academy as a replacement for Henri Robert in the first round with twenty-three votes out of thirty-six voters. Released from prison a few months prior after serving his term for having incited to murder some members of the Popular Front government, he was returning from a trip to Spain where, as a French correspondent to the Royal Academy of Moral and Political Sciences of Spain, he was received by Franco. In February 1939, the Academy would congratulate one of its members, Léon Bérard, for his assigned mission in Spain. The following month, it would express its best wishes to another of its members, Marshal Pétain, for his nomination as ambassador to Spain.[60] The Academy thus played a role of mediator in the legitimation of the Francoist cause, presented as inseparably national and religious in French conservative opinion. It was concurrently working toward a reconciliation between Action française and Rome, preparing for the rise of Maurras's ideas to power.

POLITICS AND RESPECTABILITY: THE ELECTION
OF CHARLES MAURRAS

The leader of Action française had already applied to the Academy in 1923. Henry Bordeaux had then run his campaign with great diplomacy, but as he specified in a letter to Maurras, the Academy demanded in return, not that *L'Action française* should adopt a new orientation, but that it "change its tone slightly." The "terrible Daudet" had "finally understood," having deprived himself of some "precious victims," namely the academicians that he was used to targeting, like Henri Lavedan, René Doumic, and Gabriel Hanotaux. This argument was used in the two electoral campaigns in favor of Maurras. *L'Action française* was asked to behave, to institutionalize itself, to renounce its "revolutionary" accents and devote itself essentially to forming the dominant class by instilling ultraconservative values, as the letter from Bordeaux to Maurras implied: "*L'Action française* enters its maturity: it exerts its influence over the new generations, it can influence them on politics and the direction of the country." Faced with the reticence of the permanent secretary, René Doumic, Bordeaux had promoted "the work of social organization" that Maurras had constructed, "from which we all benefit on the whole, since it saves us from the Communist danger. And then, we have to reckon with the youth, even with a newspaper that determines the thought of a large part of the French bourgeoisie. We also need to be defended, we who represent a great traditional force [...]."[61]

The conditions that Bordeaux set for Maurras tell us something that usually needs not be stated, but is implicitly inscribed in the academic position: to be an academician is above all to abolish the subversive power of words, even reactionary words. It is to undergo the depoliticization that allows, by the act of distancing and by apparent neutrality, the transmutation of conservative commonplaces into "eternal truths," presented as the "neutral places" of common sense.

Maurras failed against the Republican candidate Charles Jonnart, ambassador to the Vatican, who successfully led the delicate negotiations to resume relations between the Republic and the Holy See, interrupted since 1904. The reaction of the Action française militants—in Maurras's absence, they had published the ballots of the academicians who were favorable to their master: Bourget, Barrès, Bazin, Bordeaux, Marshal Foch, without anyone knowing where they got them—and then the pope's condemnation helped put off the election for close to fifteen years.

When, at the death of Bainville in February 1936, Henry Bordeaux again envisioned Maurras's candidacy during the latter's imprisonment, the permanent secretary René Doumic shared his reservations:

> Nothing is more legitimate than the idea that one day or another, under normal circumstances, Mr. Maurras will apply for our vote as a writer. It would be a literary election, in accordance with our traditions, and no one could complain because of it. But an election in response to an imprisonment would clearly have the character of a political display. This is not the Academy's role at any time, but least of all today. . . .[62]

President Albert Lebrun had moreover made it known that he would not sign the decree ratifying the election.[63] Two years later, Henry Bordeaux, then acting director, sought him out to ask him to ratify the election. He was armed with documentation showing the rarity of recourse to the veto right and the existence of precedents regarding the election of previously incarcerated candidates: Voltaire, André Morellet, Joseph-François Michaud, François Roger, Charles Nodier, Paul-Armand Challemel-Lacour. Despite pressure from certain journalists who called for non-validation, particularly Georges Bidault in the Catholic progressive newspaper L'Aube, President Lebrun determined this time that it was not his prerogative to interfere in Academy elections.

During the June 8, 1937, assembly at the Vélodrome d'hiver meant to celebrate Maurras's release from prison, André Bellessort, Abel Bonnard, and André Chaumeix came to pay their respects.[64] A few months later, Henry Bordeaux participated by letter in the commemoration of the anniversary of the Action française leader's entry into prison on October 28, 1937:

> It is a date, in fact, that we are right to remember. There are honorable condemnations, imprisonments preferable to the freedom of which they are the outraged protestation. You had denounced the responsibility of politicians who believe they can unleash war without personal risk. As long as this irresponsibility lasts, we will be in internal and external danger. The best title of honor of our dear Paul Bourget has been to recall, in *Le Disciple*, the too-oft-forgotten principle of intellectual, moral, and political responsibility.[65]

In order to elect Maurras while the Roman condemnation was still in effect, the Academy had to obtain the endorsement of Pius XI, which attests to the Academy's deliberate submission to the temporal and spiritual powers that guarded tradition. Henry Bordeaux, who had been the instigator behind Bainville's election and one of the principal artisans behind that of Maurras, intervened. To Maurras, he counseled: "[. . .] The Pope's role has grown since then by resisting Hitler. He becomes one of the last defenders of the human person vis-à-vis State control invading from all sides; you will know how to say this in *L'Action française*."[66] At the same time, he intervened with the pope. This step was part of a collective venture aimed at favoring the reconciliation of Action française and Rome. It had been started in 1936 as much by "immortals" like the Catholic historian Georges Goyau and famous Catholic intellectuals like Henri Massis, as by certain members of the French ecclesiastical hierarchy, including Cardinal Verdier and Father Gillet.[67] André Chaumeix, René Doumic's successor at the helm of the *Revue des deux mondes* in 1937, also played a role in these negotiations, according to François Mauriac. "[. . .] I had seen with my own eyes," Mauriac related, "the obstacles the conspirators had to overcome in order to achieve this master stroke, even lifting Rome's ban on *L'Action française*."[68]

During the audience that he accorded to Bordeaux, Pius XI supposedly told this man who insisted on Maurras's writerly qualities: "Submitted to the Church, he would be greater. His election, *even though it is outside our plan*, will cause me no pleasure. It would have been, on the contrary, very agreeable later, when he will have submitted."[69] The clause allowed Bordeaux to state that the pope had recognized that this election lacked religious significance. To Cardinal Pacelli, secretary of state of the Vatican, he would again specify that the election would not be an attack on the respect for the Papacy, targeting only the great writer. As the election approached, he repeated the conditions set for Maurras: to modify the tone and form of criticism that *L'Action française* could formulate with respect to the members of the Academy and the head of state, to show respect for the Vatican. Maurras answered that if he were elected, he would not add his new title to his signature in his newspaper. He kept his promise.

At the stormy meeting of June 2, 1938, that preceded Maurras's election, when several opponents tried to postpone it, François Mauriac intervened in a way that scandalized as much by its form (he stood up, against custom, to read his requisition) as by its content (he opposed the election). He made two objections: the insults directed by *L'Action française* toward certain members of the Academy, Hanotaux in particular, and the reservations that the pope had expressed to Henry Bordeaux on the subject of this candidacy. Bordeaux, director of the assembly, avoided the first question by saying that he had consulted with Hanotaux who did not submit a personal veto and, considering it inappropriate of Mauriac to refer to a private conversation he had had with the pope, which concerned an entirely different question, he deferred to Cardinal Baudrillart on the second question. The cardinal made known that while he would not personally vote for Maurras, since he was himself held to the Roman ban, he thought he did not have any right to a veto: he therefore did not put his resignation in the balance, like Mgr Dupanloup when Émile Littré was a candidate. This gave the Academy free reign. Only Louis Gillet raised his voice to defend Mauriac's point of view.[70] With Georges Duhamel, Paul Valéry, André Chevrillon, and Marcel Prévost, Mauriac and Gillet represented only a minority of writers who were hostile to this candidacy. And it was the literary men who ensured the triumph of the Action française leader on June 9, 1938, by giving him fourteen of the twenty votes that elected him. "You avenge Balzac," his companion in arms Léon Daudet wrote to him, "you who, in contempt of all obstacles, and by the sole prestige of your obstinacy, have destroyed the work of the Encylopedists and shown France, bowed by democracy, the route to salvation."[71]

Without it being possible to exactly determine the complete distribution of votes for or against Maurras, since the ballot was secret and the tally in analyses and testimonies was in some cases contradictory,[72] we can reconstitute part of the two camps by cross-checking. It is significant that the writers are the easiest to pinpoint. In the camp favorable to Maurras, we can count André Bellessort, Pierre Benoit, Louis Bertrand, Abel Bonnard, André Chaumeix, Henry Bordeaux, Maurice Donnay, Claude Farrère, Abel Hermant, Jacques de Lacretelle, Georges Lecomte, and Joseph de Pesquidoux. The principal opponents to Maurras's entry were François Mauriac, Georges Duhamel, Paul Valéry, and Louis Gillet, along with André Chevrillon and Marcel Prévost.[73] Although Georges Duhamel classified Édouard Estaunié among the opponents, Eugen Weber situated him among the partisans, which seems very probable in light of the evolution of the author of *L'Empreinte*. This novel, in which he painted a severe portrait of the Jesuits who had educated him made him, in 1923, a candidate of the "academic left," but Estaunié had since rediscovered his faith and aligned himself with the camp of the "academic right" by signing the pro-Francoist manifesto that appeared in *Occident*. Estaunié had returned specifically for the vote. According to *L'Action française*, ill, he had insisted on bringing his support to Maurras.[74] Edmond Jaloux, who was mentioned in none of the analyses, also very probably gave his vote to Maurras.

The two prelates, Mgrs Baudrillart and Grente, had abstained so as not to engage the Church beyond "tolerance" with respect to the still insubordinate spokesman of the competing doctrine, and although, as Eugen Weber said, "they would have cast their vote for Maurras in twelve months' time."[75] For the same reasons, Georges Goyau who, as we have seen, participated in the negotiations with Rome to rehabilitate Action française, had also abstained. Eugen Weber also classified Émile Mâle among the four abstainers, while Duhamel situated him in his own camp.

Curiously enough, the military provoked the most divided opinions, maybe, for some, because of the recent condemnation of Maurras by the Count of Paris. Henry Bordeaux counted Marshal Pétain and Admiral Lacaze, along with Duke de La Force, among the "strong partisans," while Georges Duhamel classified Marshal Pétain among the abstainers, with Franchet d'Espérey, and Lacaze among the opponents (along with Duke de La Force). If we rely on Weber's tally, which only confirms Duhamel's tally in the case of Lacaze, three of the four military men voted in favor of Maurras: d'Espérey, Weygand, and Pétain (who had congratulated Henry Bordeaux after the preparatory session of June 2).

Léon Bérard let no doubt linger: "Of course I voted for him. One does not often have the chance to vote against the Republic, against the King, and against the Pope, all at one and the same time."[76] Maurice Paléologue, whom Duhamel placed among the opponents, probably gave his vote to Maurras. To the six opposing writers were added Gabriel Hanotaux and the two scientists, Émile Picard and the Duke de Broglie. That leaves three uncertain votes that Weber placed in the opponents' camp: Lacaze, Joseph Bédier (an Action française correspondent nonetheless claimed that Bédier had confided in him that he had voted for Maurras), and Louis Madelin, whom Bordeaux classified among the "benevolent approvers" of Maurras's foreign policy. Madelin might have been the fourth Catholic abstainer, rather than Émile Mâle, who may have belonged to the opponents' camp.

What these ambiguities reveal, above all, is that the "academic right" then counted more votes than we would suspect from the twenty ballots in favor of Maurras. The abstention or opposition of the Catholic conservatives masks mere respect of the Roman ban or, at the most, a traditional defiance with respect to the irreligion of the Maurrassian doctrine, as in the case of Louis Madelin. It is not by chance that Duhamel did not count them among the opponents: whether they were or not, Duhamel's tally reflects his perception of the camp on the right, and if he deceived himself on some whom he mistakenly believed to be allies, he made no mistake about his adversaries.

For his reception speech, Maurras, who had corresponded since 1937 with the Holy See through the intermediary of the Carmel of Lisieux in order to find a compromise, envisioned a "pontifical apologetics." He did, however, set a condition with Henry Bordeaux, who was tasked with welcoming him: this point would not be addressed in the response, so as not to seem to condemn the Catholics of Action française who had not submitted. This condition provoked a great agitation at the Academy. Henry Bordeaux decided to withdraw from his task. Who would receive Maurras? It was out of the question to designate Bellessort or Bonnard, who would have given the session the character of an Action française protest. Paléologue was suggested; he would speak of Maurras's foreign politics. Faced with this hardly tempting prospect, the author of *L'Étang de Berre* withdrew his condition, and was received on June 8, 1939, by Henry Bordeaux. He appeared between Marshal Franchet d'Espérey and Abel Bonnard, who were, according to reports, "the best royalists of the Academy."[77] Critics noted the moderation of tone that the recipient adopted. The formidable pamphleteer had submitted.

Georges Goyau, named permanent secretary in replacement of René Doumic, undertook negotiations with the intervention of Father Gillet, in order to achieve the reconciliation with Rome before Maurras's reception, "in the interest of French Catholicism and of France."[78] While the redefinition of international stakes, starting with the invasion of Ethiopia, and still more during the Spanish Civil War, had helped defeat the final resistances of many members of the French Catholic hierarchy, the task was not simple. Despite the Church's official support of the Francoist cause, Pius XI remained inflexible. It was only after his death, when Cardinal Pacelli, with whom the negotiations had been conducted, succeeded him that the lifting of sanctions against *L'Action française* was pronounced in July 1939. In exchange, the managing committee of the league was to send a letter of submission. Made public on July 15, following the Republican holiday, this reconciliation was only one more step in the reworking of alliances that prepared the organized suicide of the Republic and the rise of an authoritarian regime. By electing Maurras and working toward the reconciliation of Action française with the Vatican, the Academy legitimized the synthesis of Maurrassism and the social doctrine of the Church that would fuel the project of National Revolution.[79]

Between Engagement and Wait-and-See

Because the French Academy was bound by its regulations to hold meetings in Paris, the debacle and dispersal of its members would disrupt its operations. On June 14, the day German troops entered Paris, Mgr Baudrillart was the only one to sign the attendance sheet. On July 11, the day after the vote of full powers for Marshal Pétain that sounded the death knell of the Republic, the Academy decided to resume meetings: there was property to manage, and prizes to distribute that could bring precious support in the present conditions of scarcity. Nonetheless, during the Occupation, only twelve to fourteen members would more or less regularly attend the weekly session on the dictionary. Up until 1942, among the members who remained in Paris, active participants included Mgr Baudrillart, André Bellessort, Abel Bonnard, Maurice Donnay, Georges Duhamel, Duke de Broglie, Mgr Grente, Abel Hermant, Admiral Lacaze, Maurice Paléologue, Émile Picard, Jérôme Tharaud, Paul Valéry, and, starting in the autumn of 1941, Paul Hazard (back from the United States), Georges Lecomte (back from the Southern zone), André Chevrillon, and Jacques de Lacretelle. Pierre Benoit and Claude Farrère made a few appearances, as did Henry Bordeaux, Louis Madelin, and François Mauriac when they were in Paris. Some, called to their government functions like Marshal Pétain or General Weygand, and others who had retreated to the Southern zone, like André Chaumeix with the *Revue des deux mondes* (in Royat) and Charles Maurras with *L'Action française* (in Lyon), or hidden away in their provincial properties, attended no sessions,[80] despite the entreaties of the collaborationist press.

"To make Paris go on" was, as I said, at once a significant cultural and ideological stake for the collaborationists, since it was a matter of making the population accept the idea that the war was over and peace took the form of a Franco-German agreement whose foundations had been laid during the meeting in Montoire. The suspension of elections, despite the numerous deaths that had struck the Academy, was an attack against the process of normalizing cultural life that drew criticisms heavy with insinuations. In the weekly *Aujourd'hui*, Noël Bayon de la Mort wondered why the Academy waited for peace to fill its seats when "all France, having laid down its arms, turns toward a peaceful activity."[81]

But strengthened by its status as an official body, its secular prestige, and its esprit de corps that, unlike other literary authorities such as the Goncourt Academy, protected it from social upheavals and exposed it less to external pressures (especially from the press), the Academy could ignore the threats of the Collaboration extremists. The desertion of the assembly, associated with internal divisions that exacerbated the situation, contributed to its *attentiste*, or wait-and-see attitude. This attitude would allow it to survive the twists and turns of the situation, including the Liberation, unscathed or almost. This institutional wait-and-see policy had as its counterpart the great individual mobilization of the academicians, adorned with their title, in the construction of a new order. Seized by the National Revolution, in which a number of them would play a leading role, they also included a minority of activists in the Franco-German collaboration who sought the creation of a new "European" order. But the opposition that these activists would encounter inside the institution from another active minority grouped around Georges Duhamel, Paul Valéry, and François Mauriac led to a reversal of internal power relations in favor of the latter, translated by the designation of Duhamel as temporary permanent secretary in February 1942.

A PLACE TO RECRUIT THE VICHY ELITES

The conservative or reactionary nationalist and antidemocratic fractions of the Academy could only applaud the victor of Verdun's rise to power. They also hailed the arrival of a regime that they had largely helped prepare, having tirelessly preached the values of authority, tradition, the Church, family, nationalism, and rural France against modernity. The Academy was one of the places where the political and intellectual elites of the Vichy regime were recruited. The promotions and nominations in the political field are eloquent, beginning with Pétain himself; General Weygand, Vichy's delegate to North Africa in 1940; Léon Bérard, French ambassador to the Vatican during the entire Occupation; the writers Joseph de Pesquidoux and Abel Bonnard, named members of the National Council created by Vichy in January 1941; and Abel Bonnard yet again, promoted to minister of national education in April 1942 as part of the Laval government. Count Joseph de Pesquidoux, a folklore specialist and author of *Pour la terre* (1942) who represented the "peasants" at the National Council, would also serve on the jury of the "Sully-Olivier de Serres" literary prize. This prize was founded on July 23, 1942, by the state secretary for agriculture and supported by Marshal Pétain.[82] Counselors to the prince like Charles Maurras, these academicians participated in power. Whether ideologues of the regime or sympathizers, beyond their official duties they brought it charismatic legitimacy, taking part in the assessment of the "decadence" of prewar French society and the denunciation of the "bad shepherds" according to Claude Farrère's expression.[83] They did so in order to better exalt the new leaders and, in particular, "the providential man, designated for the salvation of our country," according to the expression of Henry Bordeaux.[84]

The *Revue des deux mondes* thus became a mouthpiece of the government. It reproduced the speeches of the head of state, published the educational reform programs of the state secretary for instruction, Albert Rivaud, and made itself the interpreter of government policy under the pen of its director, André Chaumeix. It applauded the end of the Republic and the disappearance of the despised parliamentary regime, hailing the reforms introduced in the framework of the National Revolution: "Without a word, without a clamor, without a polemic, the Marshal has conceived of a true revolution. France lived under a dilapidated regime, where the numbers game was everything, and where the search for votes that form the numbers provoked all the failures, including the worst crimes."[85]

In its pages, Louis Madelin explained that "what France has suffered from most cruelly for more than a century is the lack of a Leader, the disappearance of true Authority," and he searched in the lessons of French history for the foundations of the "true authority" that Marshal Pétain summed up in two sentences: "The leader is the one who knows how to make himself obeyed and loved at the same time. It is not the one who imposes, but the one who is essential."[86] The lack of authority, which the reserve officers had not practiced in civilian life since 1936, forced as they were to negotiate with the unionized delegates who replaced them, was one cause of the defeat. It was associated with pacifist defeatism, the corruption of the national sentiment, and with a deceitful ideology that made this war into a war against Nazism and not against Germany, according to the analysis of the novelist Robert Bourget-Pailleron, who would receive the Academy's Prize for the Novel in 1941.[87] "Alas! They have so loudly insisted to him that it [France] was capable of governing itself, that it had reached the age of majority and that its worst problems were within the grasp of its primary school teachers—when hardly a true leader is born, once in a century, a leader of men, in a people of fifty million civilized human souls!" Claude Farrère said in *La Gerbe*.[88]

In the columns of the *Revue des deux mondes*, Joseph de Pesquidoux and Henry Bordeaux developed the myth of the peasantry as a safeguard ensuring the continuity of the race and eternal values. By "peasant," Pesquidoux reminded the reader, we are to understand the etymological meaning of "man of the soil, man of the ancestral birthright [. . .] a peasant is someone who lives from the earth and for it": the owner of a manor is thus a man of the soil like the farmer. A rampart against individualism and the reign of personal interests, a bearer of wisdom and good sense acquired in the repetition of age-old rites, the rural world knew how to stand firm against the rioters who tried to put it on strike, "aside from three or four thousand seasonal workers, mostly foreigners who crossed their arms and drew a crowd." But during the interwar period, "a bad wind blew on the peasantry of France":

> It has been circumvented from all sides, it has been the prey of coffee house and bare boards orators. It has heard the praises of the forty-hour work week, paid vacations, a fixed schedule outside of which no one owes anything to anyone […] Then, still not wanting to despoil, the peasant deserted the soil.[89]

"Peasant spirituality," "peasant mysticism" inherited from an ancient pantheism that Christianity humanized, this was what was understood neither "by the great Balzac in *Les Paysans*—which is too bad—nor by Zola, nor Maupassant, narrow-minded as they were, nor by most of the novelists that examined the land," Henry Bordeaux assured.[90] Their uprooting was closely tied to the diminishment of religious feeling and the drop in the birth rate.[91] By preaching individualism, the secular and free school was one of the factors of dissolution that strained family ties and the attachment to the land. The defense of marriage, family, and the land were among the urgent tasks of the government.

These themes that fueled the ideology of the traditionalist wing of the regime were regurgitated by the same people and by others in the Southern zone, notably in the weekly *Candide*, which concentrated a good number of Academy writers.[92] The democratic regime was thus judged responsible for the "weakening of the elite" and "the lowering of the public spirit," "each believed he had the *right* to receive without acknowledging the *duty* to give," "the appetite for pleasures"—what Pétain called "the spirit of enjoyment"—associated with the "relaxation of manners" that had, "by debasing characters […] weakened brains."[93] Materialism, growing venality, a suicidal political passion, had invaded everything, aided by "the voluntarily destructive action of foreign countries," commented Edmond Jaloux in his review of *Les Murs sont bons* by Henry Bordeaux.[94] While Joseph de Pesquidoux tirelessly hailed the virtues of a return to the land that developed the "sense of heredity" in man,[95] Louis Madelin called for the reestablishment of the reign of the notables: "Democracy has killed notables. Already the Revolution had cast them aside; it is because the jealousy of mediocre people finds excellent arguments against the good ones."[96]

The very official France-Amérique Committee, founded in 1909 by Gabriel Hanotaux to encourage the relationship between the two peoples, and where close to half of the "immortals" served along with other notables and official representatives of the government such as Lucien Romier, became a mouthpiece for regime propaganda. Successively presided over by Marshal Pétain in 1937, Léon Bérard in 1939, Admiral Lacaze in 1940, André Chaumeix in 1941, and Louis Madelin in 1942, in 1942 it counted Duke de Broglie as vice president, and its managing council included Henry Bordeaux, André Chaumeix, Maurice Donnay, Georges Duhamel, Marshal Franchet d'Espérey, Louis Gillet, Admiral Lacaze, Louis Madelin, Paul Valéry, and General Weygand, who rubbed elbows with the writers Jean Giraudoux and Paul Morand, along with members of the Institut de France such as André Siegfried, ambassadors of France such as the marquis d'Ormesson, and other personalities of the political, economic, and intellectual world.[97] Hanotaux, Bordeaux, Bellessort, Mauriac, and Gillet were part of the commission on the French book; Cardinal Baudrillart, Paul Hazard, and André Maurois were members of the commission on teaching. From 1940 to 1941, the France-Amérique Committee devoted three "Notebooks on Foreign Policy," published in English and Spanish versions, and four "Notebooks on National Policy" to Pétain's official publications on the armistice, the new regime, national education, and the reconstruction of France; the second series also included *Le Paysan français* by the writer Henri Pourrat.

The National Revolution would occur not only through political and social reforms. It was also necessary to embody it in the realm of the mind. As we saw, the "immortals" widely participated in the denunciations of the "bad masters" and "false ideas" that had lost France: Cartesian rationalism, skepticism, scientism, positivism, materialism, individualism and its manifestations in Republican instruction; and in literature, romanticism. They sought to reestablish the "true" sources of the French spirit and morality, which they drew from the counterrevolutionary tradition, Roman Catholicism, and Maurrassian neoclassicism. They contributed to the official publications of the National Revolution, *France 41* for André Bellessort (1941), *Nouveaux destins de l'intelligence française*, prefaced by Charles Maurras, for Louis Madelin and the Duke de Broglie (1942).

As a counselor to the prince, Charles Maurras yoked himself to the reestablishment of "order" and to France's "recovery" according to tried-and-true methods. During his trial at the Liberation, the charges would concern his practices of informing and the anathemas that he cast down from the heights of his newspaper, demanding in May 1942 "a perfecting of the legislation established against them so that no Jew could escape the agents of Darquier de Pellepoix," repeating in 1943 his calls for the immediate execution of the Communist hostages and for the use of capital punishment against the Gaullists, going so far as to demand the execution of their families, all the while applauding Laval's organization of the "Relève," which sought to enroll French workers in the German forced labor service.[98] He would be one of the staunchest supporters of the militia upon its foundation. But what is most striking in contrast to this violence against the regime's scapegoats and enemies is the alignment of *L'Action française* with the government's official politics—despite its refusal to receive a subvention—and the numbing of the critical spirit and the daily polemic against the acting powers that had made the newspaper's fortune in the intellectual field. This was clearly a "divine surprise." He went so far as to abandon the topic of foreign policy, which had earned him a large part of his success, and which he now decided to leave to the government's sole jurisdiction, deeming the latter the only competent authority on this matter. From now on, he would devote himself to repressing his Germanophobic and vengeful impulses.

The pro-Vichy majority of the assembly nonetheless remained reserved with regard to Parisian collaborationism that collided with a Germanophobia-fueled nationalism, all the more so since Germany had signed its infamous pact with their sworn enemy, the USSR, which was maintained during the first year of the Occupation. The fate of the Empire was also at stake. The conflict between the two camps surfaced in the polemics that opposed Action française with its young ultra-collaborationist dissidents on the *Je suis partout* team, baptized by Maurras in 1942 as the "clique of Ja." The contradiction between this nationalism and support of Pétain's politics of collaboration, coupled with the condemnation of "those who deliver the Empire" to England[99] (Anglophobia winning out over Germanophobia), thus endangering French unity, was one of the more significant ambiguities among these ideologues of the regime. This contradiction was moreover one of the factors that contributed to the attentiste position that the Academy seemed to adopt as an institution. Didn't the Germanophobic dispositions of these academicians make them more reluctant to go to Paris for their meetings, under the auspices of the German authorities, in the very place that symbolized the entire tradition of the "French spirit"?

THE "NOTABLES" OF THE COLLABORATION

Some academicians would nonetheless stand out as mediators between Paris and Vichy and, with some of them won over to the new "European" order, they would embody the regime's politics of collaboration in the realm of the "mind." They were among those we might, with Philippe Burrin, call the "notables" of the Collaboration.[100] Four academicians, Pierre Benoit, Abel Bonnard, Abel Hermant, and Mgr Baudrillart, were actually members of the honors committee of the Collaboration group, which extended the France-Allemagne Committee that Jules Romains had left in 1938 and of which Louis Bertrand was a member at that time. The struggle against the common enemies of the "French state" and Germany, Bolshevism and England, also appealed to these academicians. Three of them, Abel Bonnard, Abel Hermant, and Mgr Baudrillart, would enter the patronage committee of the anti-Bolshevist Légion des volontaires français (LVF). Abel Bonnard, Abel Hermant, and Maurice Donnay would sign the "Manifesto of French intellectuals against British crimes" that appeared in *Le Petit Parisien* on March 9, 1942, a few days after the bombing of the Renault factories in Boulogne-Billancourt. Next to people like Alphonse de Chateaubriant and José Germain, Abel Bonnard and Abel Hermant were also counted among the literary men on the honors committee of the "European Circle," an association created in December 1942 for the explicit purpose of organizing the Cercle français de collaboration économique européenne. This association, subdivided into three areas of study—economic collaboration, cultural collaboration, and the propaganda center for French youth—emerged from a friendly circle founded in October 1941 where "intellectuals, scientists, industrialists, merchants, economists, writers, technicians [. . .] who [were] destined to form the European elite" would exchange their views.[101]

Among these promoters of Franco-German understanding, Pierre Benoit and Maurice Donnay were the least engaged ideologically. While Pierre Benoit did not become a sycophant of the new Europe like his colleagues, he did play the role of mediator as a member of the Collaboration group and through his participation in the festivities of the collaborationist Parisian in crowd. Notably, he hosted a lunch at the fancy restaurant, Ledoyen, in honor of the official sculptor of the Reich, Arno Breker, who was a close friend of Hitler's.[102] Furthermore, Pierre Benoit was one of the writers actively supported by the Propaganda-Staffel and appeared in the *Miroir des livres* catalogue, publicity that he undoubtedly owed to the occupant's interest in seeing a widely known writer affiliated with the Collaboration group. He was, as we saw, one of the best-diffused and best-paid authors during the dark years. Invited by Gerhard Heller to the Congress of European Writers at Weimar in 1941, it is true that he would prudently decline the offer.

The octogenarian Cardinal Baudrillart's engagement in favor of the Collaboration is still surprising. Georges Duhamel's thesis that that old man let himself be influenced by Abel Bonnard is contradicted by Paul Christophe's study of the cardinal's *Carnets*.[103] These documents show the rector of the Catholic Institute's full and complete support of a politics of collaboration that he soon found insufficient. They also demonstrate his will to guide public opinion toward the construction of a new "European" order under the banner of Nazi Germany. He refused to give up until his death in May 1942, despite the indignant reactions that his public position-takings would inspire,[104] and despite an intervention by the archbishop of Paris in the autumn of 1941.[105]

The *Carnets* show that the cardinal was won over in July 1940 by the pre-Nazi theses that Alphonse de Chateaubriant developed in his weekly *La Gerbe*, and by his demonstration, in *La Gerbe des forces* (1937), of the compatibility between Nazism and Christianity. To impute this reversal merely to fear of Bolshevism—at a time when the German-Soviet pact fueled Catholic arguments against two pagan ideologies—seems insufficient. The fear of a revolution, which rekindled in him the memory of the Commune, unquestionably dictated the attitude of the cardinal, to the extent that he did not hesitate to put seventy years of warnings about Germany firmly behind him on the pretext that "at this time we need the Germans in our country to reestablish a certain order."[106] The concern to reestablish a hierarchical and authoritarian social order, even at the cost of submitting to a foreign power and to Nazi ideology, thus won out over nationalism. Despite its atypical character, the evolution of Cardinal Baudrillart was, in this light, exemplary.

On November 8, he agreed to meet one of Hitler's personal envoys, the doctor Ruchl, an Austrian Catholic "officially attached to Hitler's chancellery, and *unofficially* sent by him to activate the politics of 'cooperation' and to achieve it specifically in the intellectual order."[107] On November 12, 1940, a little after the head of the "French state" had declared his commitment to collaboration following the meeting at Montoire, the cardinal made his own declaration to Agence Inter-France, under the title "To Choose, to Want, to Obey!" It was widely diffused in the collaborationist press, then published as a brochure (with a print run of 5,000 copies), and finally republished the year of his death, in 1942, under the title *Le Testament politique d'un prince de l'Église*, preceded by a tribute from Abel Bonnard. Evoking his memories of the defeat in 1870, the rector of the Catholic Institute expressed his fear of a "revolution more lasting than that of the Commune due to a civil war." He preached to the "souls of a sickly sensibility" who were displeased by the words "cooperation" and "collaboration" pronounced by Marshal Pétain, and enjoined the French to obey the savior who "offered himself as a victim" and follow him on the path of collaboration.[108] In 1941, the cardinal multiplied his public declarations. After the offensive of Hitler's troops against the USSR in June 1941, he made a declaration to the newspaper *Toute la vie* in which he said "the time of anger" had finally come and spoke of "sweeping away and purifying":

> The Christian and civilized world draws itself up in a formidable burst to defend and save our ancient Christian society. What will be the attitude of France, its effective and definitive attitude? Let us not concern ourselves with the political contingencies of special interest. Let us envision only the general good. As a priest and a Frenchman, in so decisive a moment, will I refuse to approve the noble common venture, directed by Germany, susceptible of delivering France, Europe, the world, from the most dangerous illusions, to establish between people a holy fraternity revived from the Christian Middle Ages?[109]

More and more critical of the government's "timorous" politics, he met Pierre Laval in July 1941 and became a follower of the former vice president of the council. Solicited by the ambassador Fernand de Brinon, he agreed at the end of November 1941 to join the committee of patronage of the Legion of French Volunteers against Bolshevism; he had hailed its creation in his notebooks in July 1941.

A member of the same patronage committee, his former classmate at the ENS Abel Hermant also evoked, in *Une vie, trois guerres*, his childhood memories of the Commune, and notably "the nightmare of the red specter."[110] Inherited reactionary dispositions had quickly taken over with this son of a City of Paris architect, who had fled the stifling atmosphere of the rue d'Ulm to make a career in literature. After having made his start in a naturalist vein, notably with his famous antimilitarist novel *Le Cavalier Miserey* (1887), and having joined the Dreyfusard cause, he had become the painter of cosmopolitan manners in society and the satirical observer of the bourgeoisie. Antidemocratic, he thought France's ills lay in the Jacobin spirit that secreted its "toxin" through "its essential principle, the prejudice of equality."[111] It was this prejudice that, according to him, had made the bourgeoisie into "an artificially privileged class," improper to serve as the ruling class. Self-absorbed, focused on the preservation of its material privileges, it was fundamentally conservative. Although chauvinistic nationalism was never the concern of this self-proclaimed cosmopolitan, the defense of "Western civilization" would appeal to his inner grammarian defending "good taste," and his obsessive elitist: he participated in all the neo-pacifist struggles of the 1930s. To those for whom this Anglophile's attitude after the defeat seemed like a reversal, he responded with an apology of change against bourgeois conservatism and against the *attentisme* of mediocre people. During conferences and in the collaborationist press, the octogenarian, concerned like his comrade

Alfred Baudrillart with retaining a say in the matter, would preach adhesion to the new European order. He identified Madame de Staël and Renan as its illustrious predecessors, explaining many times over that the "French genius" would not dissolve there.

Abel Bonnard theorized the contempt for conservatism of a bourgeois class attached to the selfish defense of its material interests, the parliamentary regime, and an artificial intelligence shortly before the advent of the Popular Front in his essay *Les Modérés* (1936). This work was a milestone in the hardening of the intellectual right steeped in Maurrassism and obsessed by the so-called fact of French "decadence," and who now turned toward Fascism. Abel Bonnard was the very definition of a mediator. As Jacques Mièvre has shown, his migration from the circle of influence of Action française to "European" ideology, with a pass through Doriot's PPF, remained incomplete. Essentially focused on the idea of collaboration with Germany, he remained anchored in the ideal of a rural France, without integrating all the aspects of Fascist ideology, and unlike the young collaborationist guard, he would not disavow the Vichy regime.[112]

To restore a social order founded on "natural" hierarchies rather than the "artifice" of the Republican meritocracy: such was the objective to which this notable would devote himself. He was the son of a director of prisons in the Vienne region, educated at the best Parisian lycées, Louis-le-Grand and Henry IV, then at the École du Louvre. An admirer of Valéry and Claudel in his youth, after some rather unsuccessful efforts (and despite the crowning of *Les Familiers* (1905) with the brand-new Prix National de Poésie), he had given up poetry for prose, then literature for the political essay. In 1925, *En Chine* earned him the Grand Prize for Literature from the French Academy. He was the author of an *Éloge de l'ignorance* published in 1926, and an activist in the Cercle Fustel de Coulanges, set up the same year to fight the foundations of the Republican school and the democratization of instruction. (The Cercle, which would produce official thinkers on education for the Vichy regime,[113] included current or future academicians like Louis Bertrand, André Bellessort, Marshal Lyautey, and General Weygand). This brilliant talker who was highly valued by the salons meant to reestablish the aristocratic values of character, courage, honor, good sense, and judgment versus intelligence. At the time when, according to Jérôme Carcopino, he schemed with the complicity of Otto Abetz to replace Jacques Chevalier as the minister of public instruction, he attacked the system and graduates of the grandes écoles in a conference entitled "Constitution of an elite" that we have already cited, putting "intelligence that excludes character" on trial.[114] Pétain, personally hostile to him it seems, preferred Jérôme Carcopino, and Bonnard had to await Laval's return to the government the next year before getting the job.

Approaching his sixties, Abel Bonnard was part of the new generation of "immortals" who fought for academic power, along with Pierre Benoit, Georges Duhamel, and François Mauriac. Evoking the Academy's state of "anarchy" since the death of Doumic in 1937—his successor Georges Goyau having "more virtues than authority"—and the loss of interest of former influential members such as André Chaumeix, now needed by the direction of the *Revue des deux mondes*, Louis Madelin who was often absent, and Henry Bordeaux who was tied to his work, a journalist predicted in 1938 "that this very influential circle of writers [would] soon leave some of the powers that they held to a new generation in which Mr. Pierre Benoit and Mr. Georges Duhamel [would] be called, in diverse capacities, to exert an important academic influence."[115] In reality, this struggle would play out between Abel Bonnard and Georges Duhamel after the defeat, when the Academy was abandoned by nearly two-thirds of its members. Abel Bonnard's ostentatious ultra-collaborationism was influential in his rival's success, despite the distrust that Duhamel could inspire in the most conservative fractions of the assembly.

THE OPPONENTS

The evolution of a small fraction of writers within the French Academy from a seemly Marshalism to Gaullism and their growing sympathy for the Resistance illustrate the dynamic that led the writers who were most independent with respect to the institution to ally themselves to the rebellious ones, or even to the subversive fractions of the literary field. This occurred under the double effect of a principle of repulsion with respect to the writers most inclined to heteronomy and of the control exercised by the group of peers favorable to autonomy. This dynamic was driven on one side by the stigmatization aimed at a number of them, Mauriac and Duhamel in particular, by the Collaboration extremists who were more concerned with overturning the power relation that structured the literary field during the interwar period than with constructing the new order. It was driven on the other side by the powerful network of informal dialogue, exchanges of information, advice, and calls to order through which the literary community recomposed itself at its relatively autonomous pole. The engagement of these oppositional academicians was characterized more by their adoption of an attitude of "refusal" and by the indirect support that they offered to the opponents than by a full-fledged underground undertaking. François Mauriac was the sole exception; his precocious adhesion to the literary Resistance was as atypical as it was paradigmatic, as we have seen. But in light of the stakes of the war such as they were echoed in the Franco-French crisis, this academic fraction would not delay in situating itself in clear opposition to the pro-Vichy and collaborationist groups within the assembly.

Among the most active, we again find the core group of the principal opponents to Maurras's election: Mauriac, Duhamel, Valéry. The voluntary abstention of the first two, whose names did not appear in any periodical of the occupied zone, did not go unnoticed. "Duhamel, Mauriac, save honor," Jean Guéhenno wrote in his journal.[116] The critic Louis Gillet who had aligned with them, as we saw, occupied an intermediary position between the two academic poles: in charge of the "foreign literature" column in the very conservative *Revue des deux mondes*, he nonetheless represented the only pole that was liberal and relatively open to avant-gardes there, having written about James Joyce, for example, unbeknownst to the director, his father-in-law René Doumic, who was totally ignorant of foreign languages. An enthusiastic Marshalist, it would seem that he only evolved toward Gaullism in November 1942. According to Louis Parrot, he was in contact with the leaders of the Resistance until his death in July 1943.[117]

Paul Hazard and Jérôme Tharaud would follow the same path. They both allied themselves with the opposition led by Georges Duhamel at the Academy. During the Phoney War, Paul Hazard had been the head of French propaganda abroad at the General Commissariat of Information. The experience of life in occupied Paris contributed to the evolution of someone like Jérôme Tharaud. Like Georges Duhamel and Paul Valéry, in the months that preceded the Liberation, the Tharaud brothers would give their support, in principle, to the Comité national des écrivains, a Communist initiative, to which François Mauriac had belonged since 1941.

Paul Valéry's variations at the end of 1940 show that decisions were far from set at that point for those writers pulled between competing appeals. Drieu La Rochelle and Gaston Gallimard thus managed to attract the theoretician of "pure poetry" and great partisan of the Franco-German reconciliation during the interwar period to *La NRF*, where he published his "Cantate du Narcisse" in the second issue (January 1941). But he did not follow up on this contribution. An old friend of Marshal Pétain whom he had received at the Academy, Valéry agreed to write, at the request of the City of Paris, a tribute to the head of state for the ceremony of restitution of the ashes of the Aiglon* in December 1940.

---

* The remains of Napoleon II, otherwise known as the *Aiglon* or "little eagle," were returned to France as a gift from Hitler.—Trans.

The speech was never given, Pétain having skipped the ceremony organized by Laval.[118] Shortly before, though, Valéry had opposed the Academy's position-taking in favor of the politics of Collaboration decreed in Montoire; I will come back to this. In January 1941, his eulogy for Bergson at the Academy was considered an act of resistance.[119] Solicited to participate in Franco-German manifestations, he adopted from then on a position of withdrawal. The Vichy regime would ultimately remove him from his position as administrator of the Centre universitaire méditerranéen in Nice. His old friendship with Pétain was of no help to him. Valéry looked like an opponent. Along with Duhamel, Mauriac, and Paul Hazard, he would soon make his contribution to the volu-minous anthology *Domaine français*, which was published by the Éditions des Trois Collines in Geneva in December 1943 and assembled fifty-six writers of "refusal."

A pacifist who had worked toward a Franco-German reconciliation in 1932, Georges Duhamel had condemned, in the articles he published in *Le Figaro* in 1939 (collected in *Positions françaises*), integral pacifism, the concessions made to Nazi Germany (the Munich "arrangements"), rejecting the choice between Hitlerism and Communism brandished by neo-pacifists on the right.[120] Under the Occupation, his work was banned. He chose to fight "with an uncovered face" inside the Academy;[121] he would ensure the institution's survival as tempo-rary permanent secretary starting in 1942. Approached several times to organize the literary Resistance, which proves that he was considered as a possible re-cruit, he refused to work with the Communists. The director of the under-ground journal *Les Lettres françaises*, Claude Morgan, son of the academician Georges Lecomte, who had been hiding his membership in the Communist Party from his father since 1937, was among those who approached him. But Morgan was not wholly mistaken about his father's friend, whom he knew well. Without going undergound, Duhamel gave considerable support to the resist-ing writers. He established liaisons; forwarded texts to *Les Lettres françaises*, notably the narrative of the massacre of Oradour; and had prizes and subven-tions distributed to authors who were hostile to the regime and to semi-legal ventures. How can we explain the fact that, unlike Mauriac, he did not fully commit?

Born to a large family in perpetual movement because of his father's career changes (his father became a doctor at the same time he was beginning to study medicine), Georges Duhamel had followed a haphazard educational course: lycée Buffon, lycée de Nevers, Institution Roger-Momenheim. His description of his birth family is charged with this feeling of "social vertigo" that emphasizes the search for stability undertaken by the author of *Chronique des Pas-quier*, at the end of a heady social ascension, in the bourgeois way of life:

> [. . .] our family, I say, did not seem to me particularly representative of a defined social order. The spectacle that it could give to the improbable observer was that of a great effort of instruction rather than construction, of movement rather than balance. It was, without even really knowing it then, completely concerned with changing social levels. Whence its nomadic spirit and the feeling that we had to live, not in a well-established house ruled by ancient laws, but under a kind of tent, and always ready to seek a new horizon.[122]

His literary aspirations led him first, in 1906, to engage with Charles Vildrac and René Arcos in the communal experience of the Abbaye de Créteil. His individualism, anchored in the prestigious intellectual model of the "scientist" who, through the figure of the physician, at that time still concentrated all the hopes of social ascension through education, could nonetheless only make the Abbaye a temporary experiment. Having finished his studies in 1909, he worked in an industrial laboratory even as he launched a literary career. As his theatrical works were being performed at the Odéon, he was entrusted, in 1912, with a review column at the *Mercure de France*, and the publishing house opened its doors to his future work. He would direct it for two years following the death of Alfred Vallette in 1935. By that time, finally freed from the tutelage of a wildly antiacademic editor-master, he had achieved worldly consecration. Assigned to surgical ambulances during the Great War, Duhamel transposed his painful experience into two collections of short stories: *Vie des martyrs* (1917), which sold very well, and *Civilisation*, published under his real name, Denis Thévenin, which earned him the Goncourt Prize in 1918. The following year, he left his profession to devote himself to literature and joined the group "Clarté," which he soon left on the pretext that Henri Barbusse had used his signature without his knowledge at the bottom of a manifesto.

Brought, due to his atypical trajectory, to traverse a plurality of social spaces, he was one of the rare writers to have been approached by both the Goncourt Academy and the French Academy. Having been Lucien Descaves's candidate four times before 1929, he went to him to say "that he would be happy if the Goncourt Academy did not pay any more attention to him."[123] It was the author of naturalist narratives on the atrocities of war, of plays performed at the Théâtre des Arts and the Comédie des Champs-Élysées, of the novelistic cycle *Vie et aventures de Salavin* undertaken in the 1920s, that Descaves wanted to recruit to the Goncourt. The "right" side of the jury, led by Léon Daudet, had no doubt rejected him as a member of "Clarté," author, in 1927, of a travel narrative about Moscow where, in a judgment that prudent critics nuanced, he bowed before the work of the revolution. This was a position that he would soon revise. It was, on the other hand, the traveler, the humanist essayist, the defender of the conception of "civilization" founded on Western and especially French superiority, the detractor of "machinism," of cinema, the columnist at *Candide* (starting in 1931), the explorer, finally, of the crisis of modern society through a family history (that of the Pasquier family; the first three volumes appeared between 1933 and 1934) inspired by his own, that the French Academy consecrated, at the time Duhamel started at *Le Figaro*. He would soon be elected to the Academy of Medicine in 1937, then to the Academy of Moral and Political Sciences in June 1944. The tribute that François Mauriac offered him upon his death in 1966 is a precious testimony to the transformation of the "social image" of the writer and a fine analysis of this "bifurcation." A trace of irony seeps through the text, as the upper-bourgeois writer considered the petty-bourgeois "ostentation" of his colleague. It deserves to be quoted at length:

> It seemed to us that the inheritance of Romain Rolland was promised to Georges Duhamel. This is when he branched off, certainly not by ambition, or by immoderate taste for money—but for reasons that the readers of the chronicle of the Pasquier family will have no trouble identifying. Georges Duhamel had suffered too much in his childhood and in his youth from everything that "bohemian" means, to not have had the ambition, as soon as he had acquired the means, to build a real house, a real home, to found a family in the most traditional sense. Not only did he not share bourgeois hate and contempt, so widespread among writers and artists since the Romantic times, and which modest bourgeois writers did not deny themselves, but he knew from experience that the bourgeois vices, they too, were only the opposite of the bourgeois virtues and that there is nothing in the world worse than disorder and the torment of a life without rules and without brakes. He attached himself thus, with a little ostentation maybe, and bravado, to everything that it is customary to despise in this old world: even the honors, and even the academies [...] Of this contrast between the writer of the left, the heir to Romain Rolland that was Georges Duhamel in the beginning, and the permanent secretary of the French Academy that he became in so few years, a personage was born for the public who was very different from the poet of the Abbaye, from the novelist who invented Salavin and the Pasquier family.[124]

The trajectories of Duhamel and Mauriac crossed: the first, ascending on the social plane, inclined toward institutionalization and conservatism; the second, in a state of rupture following wordly consecration, inclined toward subversion and prophetism. Mauriac would say this about his ally after the Liberation: "too 'academic' and . . . believes too much in this asylum of ghosts."[125]

A CIRCUMSTANTIAL ATTENTISME

Unlike the official policy that was adopted, for example, by the Academy of Moral and Political Sciences in favor of the regime, the French Academy adopted, as an institution, a much more prudent attitude. At the solemn meeting of November 6, 1941, Baron Seillière, permanent secretary of the Academy of Moral Sciences who had chosen to speak about the "moral recovery" that occurred after the events of 1848, officially enlisted his academy:

> Around an illustrious soldier who took the destinies of a country, we are now making [. . .] an energetic effort to repair our errors of direction that, in my view, have lasted at least two centuries [. . .] Our Academy will testify to its involvement in this astonishing newness of language and gesture: first by its warnings of long ago; and—since the change of our governmental regime—by the action of those of its members who have been called to collaborate with the head of State [. . .].[126]

Nothing similar at the French Academy. Its attentisme was the combined result of the lack of quorum, due to the dispersal of its members, and the internal struggles led by the minority fraction that was hostile to the regime against the pro-Pétain or collaborationist fractions.

At the session of October 31, 1940, Abel Bonnard, who presided, proposed that the Academy state its approval of the message that Marshal Pétain had addressed to France the night before, in which he announced the new politics of collaboration decided at Montoire. Strengthened by the support of the permanent secretary, André Bellessort, Cardinal Baudrillart, and Abel Hermant, he consulted the other academicians present. The Duke de Broglie, Maurice Paléologue, Paul Valéry, and Georges Duhamel expressed their reservations in turn, agreeing that it was not the Academy's habit to pronounce upon political events. Maurice Donnay abstained. At this point, Émile Picard arrived to tell the assembly about the previous day's arrest of one of their colleagues at the Institute, Paul Langevin. Questioned about the proposed letter to the marshal, he found the moment badly chosen. Bellessort suggested that Bonnard give up. Scandalized by the attitude of his colleagues, Cardinal Baudrillart intervened, as he reported in his *Carnets*: "As a result of not wanting to pronounce on anything, of not taking any responsibility, of giving no directive, for fear of being suppressed, we suppress ourselves, until the day when we are suppressed by others without being missed by anyone."[127] Then the discussion was closed: "We take the dictionary up again and for half an hour we discuss the words 'ajuster' and 'ajustement.' What a pity at such a time," the cardinal said indignantly.[128] Their scattered colleagues would also criticize this attitude.

At the November 14 session, Henry Bordeaux, who was returning to the Academy for the first time since the armistice, obtained, thanks to an intervention by Pierre Benoit, the task of personally addressing the sympathy and confidence of the members of the assembly to the head of the "French state." In a letter that he wrote to Pétain to tell him about it, he did not fail to mention, without naming them—but were they not easily identified?—"the coldness of a certain number of our colleagues" when he had informed them of his talk with the marshal, and "a brief intervention" in spite of which the motion for unofficial well wishes was passed, at his instigation.[129] He simultaneously signaled the names of the other faithful members of the assembly: Pierre Benoit, Mgr Grente, and Maurice Donnay. He deplored, finally, that the name of Paul Valéry appeared at the Freemasonry exhibition at the Petit-Palais—"It would have been preferable that they not designate any of ours"—a regret that was obviously a device to designate one of those "enemies" whose identity he had chivalrously masked in the previous line. François Mauriac, who then lived in Malagar and was therefore absent, was alluding to this session when he wrote to Georges Duhamel: "Your repugnances are mine, and if I had attended this session at the Academy, you know whose side I would have been on."[130]

The internal tensions at the Academy were soon known in the intellectual milieus. Abel Bonnard, little concerned with protecting the secrecy of the assembly's discussions, hurried to spread the word. Jean Grenier learned it from Ramon Fernandez, who himself found out from Bonnard.[131] It was probably the same source who told the services of the political police and German security (SIPO-SD). In April 1941, they would inform the German military administration in France that in the course of a secret vote at the Academy, Duhamel, Valéry, Émile Picard, and Duke de Broglie opposed Pétain's politics of collaboration.[132] André Gide would mention Valéry's opposition during his meeting in June 1943 with General de Gaulle in Algiers: "The general was thoroughly informed about it all."[133] On November 24, 1941, Paul Léautaud noted in his journal: "They say that, in the Academy, there are three members who are 'Gaullists': Duhamel, Valéry, and another one whose name could not be found for me. The others would be rather inclined toward the collaboration."[134]

The rumor probably fueled the violence of the attacks directed at several academicians, opponents and attentistes, in the collaborationist press. From the winter of 1940, some "immortals" were vigorously stigmatized by the left wing of collaboration, contempt for bourgeois and institutionalized writers mixing with the denunciation of warmongering Anglophile and philosemitic "traitors." In *La France au travail*, as we saw, Jacques Dyssord took issue with Georges Duhamel, François Mauriac, Louis Gillet, and of course André Maurois.[135] In *La Gerbe*, Lucien Combelle would devote long articles to the "academic buffoon" Georges Lecomte and to the "plagiarist" André Maurois.[136] "Warmongers in the pay of the Jews of Prouvost-Soir [*Paris-Soir*], the bearded Gillet and the upper bourgeois Chaumeix, the Tartuffe Mauriac, are afraid of Paris. Is this a reason for the Academy not to meet, among well-bred people, this time?" Robert Jullien-Courtine flung out in the anti-Semitic weekly *Au pilori*.[137]

It was easy to accuse the Academy of its complicity with big Jewish capitalism. For Jean Drault, in *Au pilori*, it had "become an annex of the synagogue, subjected to the exclusions of Rothschild and the Consistory, as the failure of Drumont prove[d], beaten by a Marcel Prévost, a novelist for Jewish baronesses like Paul Bourget."[138] Hadn't it gone so far as to receive Jews within its ranks?[139] Wasn't André Maurois still a member? In *Paris-Midi*, René Pernoud was in a hurry to know whether Maurois, born Herzog, he specified, and currently living in the United States (from where, in fact, he gave considerable support to Marshal Pétain) was "yes or no stripped of French nationality," and astonished that the Academy, "decidedly maternal," had not taken "measures" against him: "The National Revolution, as has been said and drummed into us a thousand times, should begin with the elites."[140] François Mauriac and Georges Duhamel were the most stigmatized of the "immortals." The slander against Mauriac culminated, as we saw, in June 1941. Nonetheless, esprit de corps won out at the Academy; the institution protected its members. Maurois would not be denaturalized, Bordeaux intervened so that Valéry's name would disappear from the exhibition on Freemasonry, and Bellessort rehabilitated Mauriac and Duhamel.

On the occasion of the annual solemn meeting of the five academies on October 25, 1941, the speech made by Abel Hermant, "The Province and Provincialisms," answered the question that the proposed National Revolution could not fail to ask the authority that embodied the cultural and linguistic unification of France: the renewal of the provinces would not call French cultural and political centralization into question:[141]

If, thanks to our continual coming and going, even differences in pronunciation are hardly more than a memory, it is all the more true that it has been a long while now since the provinces abandoned particularistic spelling. French unity has in any case been achieved and will be maintained. We can thus without fear revive the provinces, or give their name back to groups of departments: there is no longer any danger that the Basques, for example, will take advantage of it to start speaking French again like an impertinent proverb claims they speak Spanish.[142]

Yet the speech given two months later by Jérôme Tharaud, on the occasion of the annual meeting of the Academy, already announced the transition. He rose up against the indictment of France for its "present and past mistakes" and against the culture of denial:

> It is not only a collapsed regime that is being attacked, it is France, its very soul. Its trial is held; it is tied to the stake. It is reminded, with relentlessness and I don't know what strange pleasure, of its present and past mistakes. To be conquered is not enough for us. We want to be the accused, the guilty ones. We disown the Frenchmen of tomorrow. This thirst for repentance, renunciation, humiliation that has seized so many among us is, I confess, for me the most intolerable, the most hated aspect of our misfortune. Our journalists, our literary men have suddenly and in an unexpected way taken the tone of the prophets of Israel in order to berate France.[143]

In January 1942, the permanent secretary, André Bellessort, died. Georges Duhamel, then acting director, raised the question of the conditions under which the services of the Academy would operate until the election of the next permanent secretary—when the quorum would meet, it was understood. At the next session, on February 5, 1942, Admiral Lacaze returned to this question. The Company decided, by a show of hands, to designate a temporary permanent secretary. They immediately proceeded with voting. Georges Duhamel was elected by twelve votes out of thirteen. There was one blank ballot marked with a cross, a sign of hostility, that we might plausibly attribute to Abel Bonnard. Those who voted for him thus probably included Paul Valéry, François Mauriac, Jérôme Tharaud, André Chevrillon, Georges Lecomte, Maurice Donnay, Admiral Lacaze, Maurice Paléologue, Abel Hermant, Cardinal Baudrillart, and Mgr Grente.

The vote was obviously prepared by the camp of opponents. Duhamel had been its candidate since the death of Georges Goyau: in January 1940, he had collected nine votes against André Bellessort who was elected by seventeen votes; Henry Bordeaux and André Chaumeix had received only one vote each and there was one blank ballot.[144] Faced with the activism of Abel Bonnard who threatened to sweep the Company toward an overt collaborationism, the core group composed of Duhamel, Valéry, and Mauriac found allies in the writers who remained in Paris: Jérôme Tharaud, André Chevrillon, Georges Lecomte; scientists like Émile Picard and Duke de Broglie; the scholar Paul Hazard, who added his support to this camp following his reception in the autumn of 1941; and nationalists like Admiral Lacaze and Maurice Paléologue. The stakes were not only political, as proven by the votes Duhamel received from Cardinal Baudrillart and Abel Hermant. Duhamel had shown his determination to become involved in an institution he believed in, unlike Mauriac. Diplomatic, respectful of the rules of the game, he knew how to maintain good relations with his colleagues and play the role of a mediator. The disaffection of the majority of academicians, including many who were hostile to him, allowed him to impose himself. The absence of Abel Bonnard, called to his governmental functions starting in the spring of 1942, cleared his path.

THE ACADEMIC TURN

The permanent secretary wields real power. Whereas the director and the chancellor are elected for only a trimester, he is the only official to ensure the continuity of the institution. Named for life, he administers the Academy's property and legally represents it. "He alone is a little bit the Academy itself," as Roger Giron wrote.[145] Under the Occupation, this power was reinforced by the fact that in the absence of two-thirds of the "immortals," every member present participated in the different commissions (on the dictionary, the literary prizes, the prizes for virtue, etc.). Georges Duhamel's temporary designation therefore had an immediate effect on the life of the institution.

In 1941, the Grand Prize for Literature had been given to Gabriel Faure and the Prize for the Novel to Robert Bourget-Pailleron for *La Folie d'Hubert*. Paul Léautaud's commentary: "Grand Prizes of the Academy: Gabriel Faure, Robert Bourget-Pailleron. What a pity! This is literature. Gabriel Faure's confectionary."[146] Born in 1877 in Tournon (Ardèche), Faure had abandoned law for literature. He had established himself in one literary genre, "passionate pilgrimages" as he called them, situated at the intersection of the travel narrative, the essay, and criticism. Abel Hermant credited him with the genre's invention.[147] A contributor to the *Revue des deux mondes* (since 1907), *La Revue hebdomadaire*, the *Revue de France*, *Le Figaro*, *Le Temps*, and *L'Illustration*, he was a specialist on Italy and had notably edited a collective work, *Visages de l'Italie*, published in 1929 at Horizons de France with a preface by Mussolini. The volume assembled texts by academicians like Henry Bordeaux, Paul Bourget, Georges Goyau, Pierre de Nolhac, Henri de Régnier, and other authors belonging to the academic and society milieus.

Bourget-Pailleron was André Bellessort's candidate. A year earlier, the permanent secretary of the Academy had written an enthusiastic critique of his novel in *Je suis partout*, insisting on everything that separated the moralist's literary treatment of good taste from the treatment that a "novelist enraged, like so many of our Realists, against the human species" would have given the same subject.[148] It was moreover as a moralist that the author, great-grandson of the founder of the *Revue des deux mondes*, Charles Buloz, had made his debut in literature. Winner of the Interallié Prize in 1933, recognized by the Academy in 1937 (Calmann-Lévy Prize), he frequented the milieus of Action française. Member of the editorial staff of the *Revue des deux mondes*, he had applauded, as we saw earlier, the advent of the Vichy regime which reestablished a hierarchical social order against the hated regime of universal suffrage. Also rewarded that year were Maurice Bardèche for his thesis on Balzac (Dumarest Prize for philosophy); Henri Pourrat, "who recently wrote the history of peasants across countries and ages […]" in *L'Homme à la bêche* (Muteau Prize, reserved for writers "whose work the Academy is pleased to mention");[149] and a prisoner, the Catholic philosopher Jean Guitton, author of *Le Portrait de M. Pouget* (Vitet Prize) whose *Fondements de la Communauté française*, published the following year with a letter-preface by Pétain, would be a reference work for the regime. In 1940, the Vitet Prize was awarded to the Catholic anti-Masonic writer Robert Vallery-Radot. The two Budget Prizes for prose in 1941 had a theme of "a travel impression" and "family life"; the theme of the Budget Prize for poetry, which was postponed to the following year, was "Land of France."

In 1942, the Grand Prize for Literature was awarded to Jean Schlumberger, founding member of *La NRF*, who had kept his distance from the review since it reappeared under the direction of Drieu La Rochelle. Jean Blanzat received the Prize for the Novel for *L'Orage du matin* (Grasset). Both candidates had been proposed by François Mauriac.[150] The prize awarded to Schlumberger, aside from the fact that it consecrated the work of a largely censored author, was a prize of abstention: "Be sure that, on this side [of the demarcation line], everyone understands the meaning of this display that exceeds myself," the grateful prizewinner wrote to Mauriac.[151] As for Blanzat, whom Mauriac had befriended, he was one of the members of the very first core group of underground writers that formed in the autumn of 1941 around Jacques Decour and the former director of *La NRF* Jean Paulhan, and whom Mauriac had joined. Jean Paulhan, who had just published *Les Fleurs de Tarbes*, himself received a Dupau Prize the same year; this prize was reserved for writers who had served literature well, and was endowed with 20,000 francs. One of the three prizes in poetry went to the young review *Poésie 42* that Pierre Seghers directed in Villeneuve-lès-Avignon; it assembled the regime's opponents. Through Eluard, Paulhan suggested in return that he reward Aragon or Pierre Emmanuel, but they were undoubtedly too marked as representatives of opposition to the Vichy regime (and Aragon as a Communist).[152] Whereas his predecessor had ignored the phenomenon of poetic renewal, Duhamel noted in his report on the literary competitions "the admirable effort" exerted by French youth, "in this troubled period, in the middle of disconcerting and heartrending events that carry us off [. . .] to rediscover the sources of poetry, to refresh and soak them in again."[153] The Academy chose this subject for the 1943 Budget Prize for French prose: "Poetry is deliverance (Goethe)."

At the time of the German capitulation at Stalingrad, Duhamel was setting up projects with François Mauriac, acting director for the first trimester of 1943, and probably with the chancellor Paul Valéry. They thus thought for a time to propose Antoine de Saint-Exupéry for the Grand Prize for Literature for 1943. Winner of the Academy's Prize for the Novel in 1939, Saint-Exupéry had sought refuge in New York. His book *Pilote de guerre*, which had obtained the censor's authorization to everyone's surprise and was published in December 1942, had provoked such an outcry in the collaborationist press—Brasillach, among others, saw it as "the apotheosis of Judeo-Bellicism"—that it was quickly banned.[154] But Mauriac changed his mind, fearing that this candidacy would be taken by their colleagues as a provocation and thus compromise their longer-term projects; Duhamel agreed.[155] And to make a more reasonable proposition to the temporary permanent secretary, one that would be "well-received by literary men": Alain. It was in fact more reasonable. Alain had not renounced his pacifism and he contributed to Drieu's *NRF*. Mauriac had consulted Jean Paulhan, who had answered that it would be "a great choice," but Duhamel proved reticent: "The poor old man has been more or less mixed up in various troubled and unfortunate things" (he was speaking of *La NRF*, of course).[156] They finally decided on Jean Prévost, whose thesis on Stendhal had just been published under the title *La Création chez Stendhal* (Sagittaire, 1942). This choice would reveal itself a posteriori to be much more audacious. This graduate of the ENS who had established himself in the literary world with an essay on sports and who had become a novelist, moralist, and critic at *La NRF* as well as a journalist, notably at *Paris-Soir*, belonged to a group of underground writers that formed at the same time in the Southern zone under the name Comité national des écrivains; Mauriac may have been aware of this fact. Under the name of "Captain Goderville," he would play an important role in the organization of the Vercors Resistance network from the end of 1943 to the summer of 1944, before being shot in August 1944 at the age of forty-three. We can assume that he collected the votes of Duhamel, Mauriac, Valéry, Tharaud, Chevrillon, Lacretelle, Lecomte, Hazard, de Broglie, Paléologue, and Lacaze. Of the other four academicians present, Farrère, Hermant, Madelin, and La Force, two also gave him their vote, one

(Madelin?) voted for the Catholic critic René Dumesnil, a specialist of Flaubert, and another submitted a blank ballot.[157]

The Prize for the Novel was awarded that year to J.-H. Louwyck, author of *Danse pour ton ombre* (Gallimard), by eight votes against two to Maria Le Hardouin and five blank ballots. *Les Cahiers du Sud*, directed by Jean Ballard in Marseille, was at that time publishing authors who were hardly appreciated by the regime like André Breton and Saint-John Perse, and the young Catholic poet Luc Estang, a contributor to *La Croix*, who would also belong to the underground group of the Southern zone. These *Cahiers* were awarded a poetry prize. Henri Guillemin, professor in the literature department at Bordeaux, a progressive Catholic and friend of Mauriac who had to leave the occupied zone in July 1942 following a denunciation by Robert Brasillach (he had accused him of Gaullism in *Je suis partout*) and who currently lived off of a teaching position that Marcel Raymond had created for him at the University of Geneva,[158] received the Paul Flat Prize (criticism and novel) for *"Cette affaire infernale": Rousseau-Hume*. The subject of the Budget Prize for poetry in 1944 would be "Silence." The page from Renan that Duhamel quoted in December 1943 in his report to summarize the Academy's activity left no room for ambiguity: "[...] but if you want to call 'resistance' the moral protestation that, in some periods, is the first duty of those who do not want to be complicit in the debasement of characters and minds, it must be said that the Academy has nobly resisted."[159]

In June 1944, the winner of the Grand Prize for Literature was *Le Figaro* critic André Billy, who had taken up the defense of interwar literature in the "bad masters quarrel," and who was currently one of the targets of the collaborationist press. Based on the proposition of Abel Hermant and Mgr. Grente, the Prize for the Novel went that year to the journalist Pierre Lagarde, author of a historical novel entitled *Valmaurie* (Baudinière), against the advice of Mauriac who considered the work unworthy of the prize and its publisher too compromised.[160] But the Duhamel-Mauriac clan compensated by having one of the Dupau Prizes awarded to Louis-Martin Chauffier, member of the Comité national des écrivains, the Comité national des journalistes, and the editorial team of *Les Cahiers de Libération*.

Duhamel did not stop there. Following the French Academy's initiative, the Institute took steps with the general distributor of industrial production so that the French book would be accorded an exceptional ration of paper; this plan came to fruition on December 24, 1942.[161] The permanent secretary also worked to distribute prizes to the prisoners, and through the association Au service de la pensée française, over which he presided, he raised a sum of 50,000 francs, which was put to the service of increasing the number of prizes awarded by the Academy in 1944. This is why Duhamel could affirm at the Liberation that "those who are still present know what the life of the Academy was like in those times of trial. Our Company pursued its reports, played its moral role within the nation, served French literature and intelligence to its best ability at a time when the effort of the enemy tended to oppress them."[162]

The man of the hour, Duhamel had thus saved the honor and the social image of the institution. At the beginning of 1943, the underground *Lettres françaises* moreover praised the Academy, which had "remained faithful to its mission since June 1940," congratulating it for its latest literary prizes (those issued to Blanzat, Paulhan and Seghers), and assuring that "the old lady [would] emerge greater from the ordeal."[163]

The Academy, under the leadership of Georges Duhamel and his accomplices, had achieved two things. First, it had rehabilitated the legitimate literature from the interwar period, especially the old NRF, attacked from all sides since the defeat. Second, it had brought considerable aid to dissident writers and semi-legal ventures, thus contributing to the struggle to reconquer the autonomy of the literary field. Through the prizes distributed after the nomination of Georges Duhamel as permanent secretary, we see that a new alliance was formed between the new leaders at the Academy and the old NRF team, thanks to the rise to power of the younger generation of academicians who had made their career at a time when *La NRF* claimed the monopoly on consecration, and whom it had helped promote, although without integrating them into the "family" (this was the case for Mauriac and Duhamel). In this new alliance, we must see the premises of their great reconciliation, envisaged since the Liberation, that would only truly be solidified twenty years later with the election in 1963 of Jean Paulhan to the Academy. But in 1942, this alliance also had its limits. Just as the Academy could, without transgressing its role as guardian of the orthodoxy, consecrate the most classic and least subversive pole of *La NRF* (Jean Schlumberger rather than André Gide), it remained reticent in regards to the currents of the literary avantgarde. Before choosing candidates for the Prize for the Novel for 1942, François Mauriac consulted with Jean Paulhan, who had suggested *L'Étranger* by Albert Camus, and in second place, *Le Pain des rêves* by Louis Guilloux.[164] Louis Guilloux was probably too marked by his affiliation with the proletarian literature movement. As for Camus, Mauriac had expressed to Paulhan the repugnance that *L'Étranger* had inspired in him. He invoked, to Paulhan (who suspected religious reasons), "technical reasons," its "borrowed manner" and American inspiration: "America irritates me in its imitators. The least concerted art becomes a formula for them."[165] Thus, the very people who fought the ultraconservative fractions of the Academy transformed themselves by instinct, by a quasi-visceral rejection, into upholders of academic literary orthodoxy.

While the Academy pursued its dictionary meetings, its distribution of prizes, and its reports, it did not proceed with elections, despite the twelve deaths that culled its ranks during the four years of occupation.[166] From 1939 on, voting had been deferred due to the circumstances. As during the Great War, it seemed both difficult and inappropriate to proceed with public receptions. Since newly elected members could not participate in their colleagues' work without having given a reception speech, according to article 18 of the regulations, and the academicians had rejected the possibility of asking the president of the Republic for a decree that would suspend this obligation during the war, it seemed useless to elect new members as long as the most recently elected had not been received: so they voted for the status quo. But, on the other hand, since nine vacancies had opened up that would only be filled in 1918 or later, they came to fear a reduction in ranks such that the electoral quorum could no longer be assembled. And so to avert the precedent set by the Great War, a vote was taken on January 11, 1940; Paul Hazard was elected, but his reception, which was scheduled for June 27, was canceled due to the circumstances. For the same reason, the election of Henri Lavedan's successor was canceled. Lavedan had died in September 1940, and the election should, according to the rules, have taken place within three months following the declaration of vacancy. This cancelation created the precedent for differing elections. It was not for lack of candidates: Baron Seillière, permanent secretary of the Academy of Moral and Political Sciences, and René Peter, author of a *Vie secrète de l'Académie* had declared their candidacy in October. In August 1941, a solution was adopted, at the initiative of Admiral Lacaze, to allow Paul Hazard to join in the work of the Academy: the reception speech would be heard by the Commission de lecture. Paul Hazard could thus be seated starting in October 1941, reinforcing Duhamel's camp.

The dispersal of the "immortals" after the debacle had created a new difficulty. According to the rules, the sessions had to be held in Paris. The rules also required the presence of twenty members to proceed with voting, and voting by mail was not allowed. During the four years of occupation, never more than sixteen members were seated, and the quorum was not met. So lack of quorum, along with institutional inertia, is the primary reason for the continued suspension of elections, despite the demands of the collaborationist press which were nonetheless becoming more pressing, and became downright threatening after the election of Georges Duhamel as permanent secretary.

After the death of a fourth "immortal" at the end of 1941, the Academy stopped declaring vacant seats, as a precaution. There was a rumor that the French Academy and the Goncourt Academy might fuse, which Georges Duhamel denied.[167] In 1942, the situation became critical. The question seems to have been debated in the different sections of the Institute: the Academy of Sciences thus held, on March 30, 1942, a secret committee that would vote on the opportunity to resume elections. Did a ban from the marshal intervene? If we believe Henry Bordeaux's account of an intervention that Duhamel made during a post-Liberation meeting, of which no trace survives in the Academy's minutes just as there were no discussions on this subject, Duhamel noted a directive from Marshal Pétain that had been transmitted to him orally by André Chaumeix, aiming to prevent elections.[168] Was it, as Bordeaux suggested, because the hand of the occupier could be seen in them, or did the marshal fear the reinforcement of the camp that he had been told was hostile to him? Duhamel had then specified, still according to Bordeaux, that the suspension corresponded to his will. Each camp thus feared the reinforcement of the other and, as elections required everyone to take measures contrary to custom—vote by mail, or the reduction of the quorum[169]—institutional inertia favored the reciprocal neutralization of the opposing camps in this respect.

In July 1942, in order to deny the announcements made in the press, the Academy publicly announced that it was upholding its decision not to fill its vacant positions. At this point, nine seats were empty. Shortly before, Duhamel had refused in the name of the Company the offer that had been made by the Academy of Mâcon to allow use of its space at the hotel Sanaci in case the "immortals" preferred to meet in the "free" zone. According to the press, voting by mail had been considered, which made "the traditionalists howl."[170]

And yet the candidates multiplied, and names circulated unofficially. Among the most often cited (most of them would be elected in the two decades following the Liberation) were Baron Seillière; Father Gillet; Pierre Brisson, director of *Le Figaro;* Édouard Bourdet, former administrator of the Comédie-Française and his successor Jean-Louis Vaudoyer; Henri Mondor; André Siegfried; and for the writers, Henri Massis, Paul Morand, Henry de Montherlant, Marcel Pagnol, and Henri Pourrat, whom Joseph de Pesquidoux supported. It was said that "those who have the best chances are not those who most want to obtain a seat." Was this an allusion to Paul Claudel, who had sworn not to run again, and to Roger Martin du Gard? Neither one declared their candidacy, although their names were cited. But they belonged to the "ideal Academy" composed by Mauriac on a sheet of paper that Jean Touzot found,[171] and they would be approached by Duhamel and Mauriac after the Liberation.

In March 1943, the Academy decided to resume tradition and publish the candidates retained for the four seats declared vacant, those of Lavedan, Prévost, Bergson, and Louis Bertrand.[172] But three days later, on March 11, 1943, the

Academy judged that, under the circumstances, there was grounds for postponing the press release of the candidates' names until it decided to resume elections. Did the head of state's ban intervene in the meantime? Or must we see the hand of the temporary permanent secretary at work? The question of elections would not be raised again until the Liberation.

⬤➤ The French Academy was a place for elaborating and legitimating the ideas of the National Revolution and a place to recruit the "elites" of the regime. But its role as guardian of the "French spirit," which it assumed to maintain national cohesion and the lasting quality of the "national conscience," could not make it, as an institution, an auxiliary of the "hereditary enemy" in the besieged capital. Faced with the maneuvers of Abel Bonnard who attempted to make it adopt a pro-collaborationist stance, the Company, rebellious to external pressures, transferred—certainly thanks to the absence of its most pro-Vichy members—its confidence to Georges Duhamel, who took advantage of his nomination as permanent secretary to bring precious aid to the writers of the opposition. Devoted to the institution, this man of great moral rigor, who strongly opposed the regime born of the defeat, would, with the help of Paul Valéry, François Mauriac, and a few others, halt the Academy's drift just in time and thereby save its honor. Because of institutional inertia, this coup d'état would nonetheless have no bearing on the life of the institution beyond the first year of the Liberation. Elected fully permanent secretary in October 1944, Duhamel would resign in January 1946, after seeing his plans for reform fail and the "academic right" regenerate before his very eyes.

The dispersal of academicians and neutralization of antagonistic forces within disrupted, for the entire Occupation, the functioning of an institution that did not like scandal, reducing it to an attentiste attitude. Definitively, this attitude allowed it to safely cross through the turbulences that ensued from the changes in regime, twice in four years. Institutional inertia always worked in its favor. The esprit de corps, which protected the regime's opponents during the Occupation, would also protect the pro-Vichy academicians at the Liberation. The official status of the French Academy as a state institution, its age, and its formal prestige made it project itself in the long term, only needing to let its own inertia act in order to *be*. In this light, its mode of survival during a time of national crisis distinguished itself from the literary authorities that, threatened with (symbolic or real) death, like the Goncourt Academy or *La NRF*, had to adapt to the circumstances in order to continue *existing*.

CHAPTER 5

The Sense of Scandal

The Goncourt Academy

Unlike the French Academy, the Goncourt Academy's adjustment to the new dominant ideology of the Vichy regime did not proceed from a "preestablished harmony." An economic and media stake, the Goncourt Prize became an ideological stake when the first two logics found themselves subordinated to an authoritarian political power, which is what happened in the 1940s. In this sense, the Goncourt Academy illustrates the functioning of the large-scale production sector and reveals the processes of importing heteronomous logics into the heart of literary practices.

More dependent on the verdicts of the wider public than its elder counterpart, and thus more exposed to media pressures, the Goncourt Academy was also less animated by the "esprit de corps" that would have set it above contingencies. Whereas the French Academy had only to let its own inertia act in order to *be*, the Goncourt, which was linked to "public opinion," current events, and the short term, experienced the influence of current stakes much more strongly. It had to adapt to them in order to continue *existing*. "As strange as it may seem in the troubled times we are in, the Goncourt brothers and the Academy that bears their name hold what it is agreed to call the spotlight," observed a journalist in 1942.[1] In contrast to the wait-and-see attitude that its elder counterpart would adopt as an institution, the Goncourt Academy would distinguish itself by a politics of presence more dictated by its struggle for survival than by the preservation of the values it safeguarded, sometimes even to the detriment of those values. This explains what may first appear as a reversal of attitudes between the authority delegated by the field of power, where the literary stakes were strongly politicized, and the one whose original vocation was to compete with its elder in the name of literary autonomy.

But the influence of the press or of economic and political powers was never directly exerted over the choices of the Goncourt jurors, no more than the ideological stakes had an immediate effect on the electoral game. We must look for the mechanisms that enabled its quasi-spontaneous adjustment to the new dominant ideology in structural factors—its position as an *agent* of the literary field and its morphology—and in the play of the individual and collective strategies of its members with respect to institutional stakes.

A Counter-Academy

At first sight, the Goncourt Academy seems like the embodiment of a true principle of literary autonomy in the face of an expanding market. Acting as a hinge between the pole of small-scale production and the pole of large-scale production, its primary vocation was to defend literary legitimacy against the laws of the market by guiding the public's taste through a selection based purely on literary criteria and the judgment of peers.

Founded as a literary society in 1902, its public utility recognized in 1903, it explicitly constituted itself as a counter-academy, less conservative and more open to the literature of its time. Just like its elder counterpart, it was an assembly uniting a permanently-set number of lifetime members, ten in this case, on whom the sole fact of membership conferred an authority and a power of consecration. Contesting the age-old monopoly of the forty "immortals," it immediately positioned itself as a competing authority of consecration.

Unlike the power of the French Academy, that of the Goncourt Academy did not emanate from its recognition by the state, but in the capital that its founder, Edmond de Goncourt, bequeathed it, giving the Goncourt a certain economic and legal independence. Its particular aim, according to the model of academic prizes of the Ancien Régime adapted to the new capitalist market of the novel, was to award an annual prize of 5,000 francs to the "best work of imagination in prose," preferably the novel. Faithful to the values of originality and innovation that romanticism had established as criteria of literariness, the donor expressed his wish that "this prize be given to youth, to the originality of talent, to the new and daring attempts of thought and form."[2]

Only professional writers would have the authority to legislate in this domain. To be part of the society, "it will be necessary to be a literary man, nothing but a literary man; *neither great lords, nor politicians* will be received there," the testament indicated.[3] By making itself the expression of the process of professionalization of the writer's occupation, the society clearly distanced itself from the French Academy. It was moreover immediately clarified that "every election to the French Academy will lead by rights to the abdication of this member and the renunciation of the annuity." Banishing "society men" and "amateurs" liable to let extraliterary motivations guide their judgment, the society must be a circle of literary men freed from the influence of the salons. It opposed to them, according to the model of Stéphane Mallarmé's "Tuesdays" or the Evenings at Médan, the conviviality of an occasional dinner or lunch meant to favor "the formation of an intellectual and moral bond among its members, holding them to tighter relations of collegiality, and uniting them in the common taste for literature."[4]

By ensuring them a life annuity of 6,000 francs, or the equivalent of the salary of a certified professor with several years of experience, Edmond de Goncourt intended to protect the ten members from the ups and downs of a writer's life: "We want to free our academicians from bureaucratic tasks or the low work of journalism."[5] This material independence, which freed them from any extraliterary constraint, was meant to guarantee the conditions of disinterest necessary to literary work as well as to the autonomy of jurors' aesthetic judgment.

Still, structural factors predisposed these new producers of taste to fail in their role and yield to extraliterary pressures. The transformation of the annual prize into a media event rapidly made it an economic stake for the publishing field. It simultaneously made the Academy into an authority of official consecration. Caught between the pressures of the press, those of publishing, and the imperatives of this official position, which generated a tendency toward literary orthodoxy that was increased by the effect of institutional inertia, the jury tended more and more to match its choices to the presumed "public opinion."

THE MEDIA LOGIC

A ferment of heteronomy resided in the very principle of the prize. Its impact actually depended on its recognition by the publishing houses, the media, and, finally, the public. The transformations that the world of publishing experienced after the Great War, with the establishment of new sales circuits and the introduction of marketing tools at a time when the reading public grew thanks to the generalization of instruction, would render the Goncourt Prize an economic stake.

The prize was first of all a means of attracting press attention. The youngest publishing houses, Gallimard and Grasset, quickly understood the publicity advantage that they could draw from this principle of distinction, in a situation characterized by an overproduction and increased competition. This was true to the point that Grasset, whose authors won two consecutive Goncourt Prizes in 1911 and 1912, created a Balzac Prize of 30,000 francs in 1922, thanks to the generosity of a sponsor.[6] Although the Balzac Prize was immediately discredited after being awarded to two "in-house" authors, Émile Baumann and Jean Giraudoux, who split the reward, the scandal that it provoked in the press surely succeeded in providing free publicity to the prizewinners and their publisher. This media coup caused Grasset to be sanctioned by the Goncourt Academy in favor of its direct competitor, who knew how to be more discreet. From 1922 to 1935, Grasset received a single prize (in 1925) to Gallimard's seven.[7]

With twelve prizewinners, or half the total prizes distributed between 1919 and 1943, Gallimard looked like the great favorite of the Goncourt. Let us note that the house consecutively won the three prizes distributed under the Occupation: this had never been seen before! It would not be until after the war, however, that the publishers would find a surer means of winning, as illustrated by the election of four Gallimard authors to the Goncourt jury between 1944 and 1951, in addition to the fact that for the first time, a representative appointed by a publishing house (Raymond Queneau) joined the Ten. This precedent would be repeated. All this inaugurated a new era in the Academy's history: from now on, publishing houses would exert a direct influence on the electoral game.[8]

Up until 1928, the attribution of the prize earned its recipient, aside from the reward of 5,000 francs (a considerable sum before the Great War), only an additional print run of about 500 copies. This equated to a symbolic recognition rather than an economic advantage (from which the publisher also profited). Starting in 1928, the attribution of the prize brought with it an increased print run for the distinguished work, up to 100,00 copies. "While the monetary value of the 'Prize' itself is mediocre, the advantages that its attribution confers are enormous. It is always an admirable springboard, frequently the certitude of an advantageous printing, sometimes a fortune," explained a journalist in 1941.[9] From then on, the authors and editors' interest in obtaining the prize was not limited to a purely literary recognition. A media stake, the prize also became a sizable economic stake for publishing. In 1958, Armand Salacrou, member of the Goncourt Academy, observed:

> Yes, the Goncourt Prize is only a check for 5,000 francs offered to one writer by ten other writers. Yet the choices made each year for over fifty years [...] have been known from year to year to gather such an audience that along with the check for 5,000 francs, the prizewinner receives the assurance of a printing that will yield his editor a sales figure varying between 100 and 200 million francs [...] We are far from discreet aid given discreetly by literary men to another literary man.[10]

In the press, it was less often a question of the publisher's profits than those of the prizewinner, who became a star. In this way, the prize contributed to the concentration of the public's attention on the author as a personality, on his life. This was a new means of showcasing literature, expressed by the series of interviews with writers conducted by Frédéric Lefèvre for *Les Nouvelles littéraires*, starting in 1924. With the complicity of the jury, on whom the prize's impact was a reflection, the press helped strengthen the image of this distinction as a way of accessing notoriety through the front door.

The creation of the Goncourt Prize helped enduringly modify the rules of the game of consecration and, consequently, the structure of the relationships between the pole of small-scale production and the pole of large-scale production in full expansion. This fact was demonstrated by both the French Academy's adoption of these new rules (with the creation of the Grand Prize for Literature in 1912, then of the Prize for the Novel in 1915) and the multiplication of competing authorities of legitimation that defined themselves in relation to the young academy. From 1904, under the banner of the magazine *Vie heureuse* that was replaced by the review *Femina*, twenty-two literary women founded a prize to protest the misogyny of the new academy, without however reserving it exclusively for female writers. The sum of 5,000 francs, first collected by the affluent ladies who formed the jury, was soon provided by the publisher of *Vie heureuse*, Hachette. A few years later, Judith Gautier left the feminine assembly to join the Goncourt jurors. Correcting the choice of the Goncourt was the objective of the honorific Théophraste-Renaudot Prize, created in 1926 by journalists, and to demonstrate this mission, the new self-proclaimed jurors awarded it the same day, at Drouant, place Gaillon, where the Ten had gathered since 1914, but on the lower floor. The Interallié Prize, also honorific, was born in 1930 in the same conditions as the Renaudot, like a hoax destined, this time, to kill time while awaiting the declaration of the Femina Prize. Composed mainly of journalists, the Cercle Interallié honored a journalist-novelist. A sign of the extension of the field of large-scale production, the institutionalization of these new authorities reveals the growing intervention of journalism in literary life and the interpenetration of the circuits of diffusion and legitimation.

Media pressure on the Goncourt jurors was exercised not only through the escalation incited by the approaching date of the lunch at Drouant. On the one hand, the visibility of the prize had to be maintained, even through scandal. On the other hand, while the academicians drew more notoriety from the prize's impact, the devaluation of the life annuity condemned them to the very journalism that Edmond de Goncourt wanted to free them from. "Today, only the winner of the Goncourt Prize benefits from such a springboard that he finds himself at once freed from all financial worry for several years, while most of the academicians are obliged to earn their living in journalism,"[11] commented the Agence française d'information de presse in 1941. Increasing the influence of the press over the jury, the devaluation of the annuity tended to reinforce its submission to the media logic.

THE SOCIAL RECRUITMENT OF THE NEW TASTE-MAKERS

To the diversity of intellectual specialties represented at the French Academy, the Goncourt opposed a relative professional homogeneity: it gave priority to writers earning a living from their writings, preferably novelists. Its predilection for the novel and for the realist and naturalist vein, which also distinguished it from the more eclectic French Academy, reinforced this homogeneity on the properly literary plane.

In the guise of opposing the "lords" and the "amateurs" of good society to the true professionals of the pen, the Goncourt had in fact consecrated all the survivors of the naturalist school, the very ones that the French Academy had spectacularly banned in the person of the unfortunate eternal candidate that was Émile Zola. The disgust or contempt that naturalist "vulgarity" inspired in the proponents of "good taste," especially in Zola's case despite his talent that they agreed to recognize, was obvious in both the academic critic Ferdinand Brunetière's indignant howling, qualifying his creative project as "ignoble,"[12] and the judgment cast on him by Maurice Barrès in his reception speech at the French Academy: "[...] an irresistible vulgarity condemned [him] to the subordinate ranks, [and he] raged to transform best sellers into literary glory."[13]

What seemed like the stunning revenge of those whom the French Academy had refused was in no way premeditated. The successive lists established by Edmond de Goncourt attest to it, including Flaubert, Jules Barbey d'Aurevilly, Jules Vallès, Loti, and Bourget, among others. But aside from the numerous deaths (the case for the first three) and disgraces for personal reasons, there were those who, like Loti and Bourget, had been elected to the rival academy. Zola himself was crossed off the list for having applied there. With the exception of Alphonse Daudet, the faithful friend who refused to apply to the forty "immortals" but died before the creation of the Goncourt Academy, there remained, among the regular visitors of the Auteuil attic, the dissident naturalists that Edmond de Goncourt, suffering from a lack of disciples while Zola was acting head of the school, had attracted.

The broad representation of naturalism in the new academy can therefore be explained mainly by the configuration of the literary field during this period.

The naturalist school, identified with the sector of large-scale production, occupied an intermediary position between the dominant pole, represented by the French Academy, and the dominated pole of the avant-gardes.[14] The social composition of the group and its target audience placed it in a dominated position with respect to the novelistic schools that distinguished themselves from it, such as the psychological novel, destroying any chance of consecration at the French Academy. With Roland Dorgelès, elected in 1929, it was the Montmartrian bohemia of the Lapin Agile that made its entrance into the Goncourt, followed in 1937 by his old friend, the novelist-poet Francis Carco. Pierre Mac Orlan would not join them until 1950. The war, the milieu of the Paris underworld, so many themes tied them to the naturalist model, like the personal experience from which they drew their material. Like their predecessors of the naturalist school, the second generation of the Goncourt jurors was most often recruited from the pole of large-scale production. Most of them published in the old houses that counted on rapid sales and successful authors, particularly Albin Michel and Flammarion.

The young academy also distinguished itself from its elder by its social recruitment, more representative of the average of active writers at the time.[15] Less elitist by vocation, it recruited more often from modest milieus. A quarter of the thirty-four jurors who were seated from 1903 to 1951 were the sons of small shopkeepers, artisans, or employees: this rate, roughly equivalent to the share of writers from the petty bourgeoisie and the popular classes in the literary field of that period, was two times higher than at the French Academy. While from the standpoint of social origins, civil service (one in five), and particularly senior civil service, was slightly overrepresented there with respect to the whole of writers, at least in its early years, it was two times less so than at the French Academy. No diplomat's sons were to be found at the Goncourt. The two sons of generals, Léon Hennique and Paul Margueritte (whose father left the ranks), were orphans. Francis Carco, the son of a high-ranking official, was estranged from his family.

The weak educational capital held by its members as a whole, in comparison with their colleagues at the French Academy, marked the new literary jury's fidelity to the opposition between "creators" and "professors." Only a quarter among them had completed their higher education, and half of them had not even begun to pursue it, a breakdown that roughly corresponds to the distribution of educational resources among writers at the end of the nineteenth century.[16] Until at least 1950, the Goncourt Academy would recruit neither teachers nor graduates of the Écoles normales. One of its members out of five was a civil servant, versus almost one writer out of two at the French Academy. By contrast, it privileged writer-journalists, who represented half of the assembly. Four times higher than at the French Academy, this overrepresentation of writers who resorted to journalism to make ends meet is a sign of the relative precariousness experienced by members of the Goncourt Academy at the beginning of their career with respect to their colleagues at the French Academy, who used their academic titles to guard against the risks of a writing career. The comparison emphasizes the opposition between what we might call a "state" pole and a "media" pole within the literary field.

This weak educational capital was counterbalanced by a very marked Parisianism and inherited cultural and relational advantages. One Goncourt juror out of three was born in Paris versus one writer of the French Academy out of five. Even though the provincials' move to Paris occurred later, a sign of lesser family resources, and corresponded more to an individual orientation, almost all the future jurors were Parisian by the time they entered adulthood. To the predominantly economic and political capital of the "immortals" and to their academic titles, the members of the Goncourt Academy opposed cultural and artistic heritage. While there was only one son of a legal practitioner versus four at the French Academy, one Goncourt juror out of four came from intellectual and artistic fractions, versus barely one writer of the French Academy out of ten. To evoke only direct affiliation or affiliation by marriage with writers or journalists, the list is eloquent: Léon Daudet, son of Alphonse; Judith Gautier, daughter of Théophile; Émile Bergerat, his son-in-law (Estelle's husband); Courteline, son of the humorist Jules Moineaux; Gérard Bauer, son of the *Intransigeant* journalist Henry Bauer, who was the theater critic at *L'Écho de Paris*; without counting Sacha Guitry, son of the famous actor and theater director Lucien Guitry. This overrepresentation illustrates the weight of specific social capital in the principles of membership, which was openly claimed: the intimates or familiars of the Goncourt attic who had not been consecrated by the rival assembly, and their descendants, had preference there. Based mainly on a principle of exclusion that targeted the affluent, amateurs, and titleholders (titles of nobility and state nobility, scholastic titles linked to teaching), the recruitment practices of the Goncourt Academy in the first half of the century privileged personal relations and, to a lesser degree, aesthetic affinities founded upon a certain fidelity to realism.

Nevertheless, whereas the heterogeneity of intellectual specialties at the French Academy masked the relative homogeneity of its members' social properties, the apparent homogeneity of the Goncourt Academy was not based on an equally stable social recruitment. Since the Academy was attached to a literary conception rather than to marks of social distinction, its principles of membership varied according to the successive states of the literary field.

The study of the evolution of its recruitment, based on a comparison of the social properties of the twenty members who served between 1940 and 1951 with the first generation of the Goncourt, calls for two observations,[17] despite reservations imposed by the small numbers. In the first place, a growing overrepresentation of writers from the most modest backgrounds: they doubled, going from four to eight. This was the translation, in recruitment terms, of the principle of fidelity to naturalism: the epigones had fewer sociocultural advantages. Christophe Charle had already noticed this about the second generation of naturalists, whose representatives at the Goncourt Academy were still there in 1940 (the Rosny brothers, Lucien Descaves, Ajalbert). The effect of the death of the first generation, better socially endowed, was increased by the recruitment of the Montmartrian bohemia: Dorgelès, Léo Larguier, then Mac Orlan (Carco alone was an exception due to his privileged social origins). This imbalance between the first and second generation of Goncourt jurors perhaps explains why, sociocultural advantages accumulating with the prerogatives of seniority, the "old" ones were able to continue running the electoral game up to the eve of World War II, to the detriment of the assembly's newcomers.

On the other hand, against this general tendency, the very marked elitism of recruitment between 1938 and 1943 broke with the tradition of the Goncourt. The high, unprecedented proportion of writers coming from wealthy backgrounds—one out of five between 1940 and 1951 (René Benjamin, Sacha Guitry, Jean de La Varende, André Billy)—was, as we will see in more detail, a direct consequence of the institution's dysfunction in a time of crisis. The result, during this period, was a strong polarization at the Academy between the best endowed and the most impoverished in social resources, which, thanks to the circumstances, favored the reversal of power relations to the benefit of the newest members, this time. The violence of the confrontations under the Occupation was in part due to this configuration of internal power relations.

The slight educational capital globally held by the twenty jurors who served at the Goncourt Academy from 1940 to 1951, when compared with our sample of writers, would tend to confirm the observed tendency toward the relative decline of the level of social recruitment at the Academy. And yet this phenomenon, which helped weaken the position of the Goncourt Academy in the literary world, resulted less from the evolution of recruitment than from the effect of the institution's social aging. Situated, due to the advanced age of more than a third of its representatives, halfway between two states of the literary field from the viewpoint of the distribution of educational capital, the Goncourt found itself in an awkward position in the literary field of the 1940s, in light of its acquired cultural resources. The higher education level of future writers had doubled since the end of the nineteenth century, rising from 37 percent to 70 percent, proportional to the overall growth of the number of students in France.[18]

From the viewpoint of their secondary education, the members of the Goncourt Academy were not distinguished from the writers who were active at this time. They most often did their secondary studies in a provincial lycée or collège (this was the case for eight jurors out of twenty). One member in four had attended a prestigious Parisian lycée versus almost half the writers of the French Academy, and they were less often placed in a religious establishment; those who were all came from wealthy backgrounds. They included Sacha Guitry, who transferred to Sainte-Croix de Neuilly after being expelled from the lycée Janson-de-Sailly; André Billy, schooled by the Jesuits; and Jean de La Varende. But the Goncourt academicians were two times less likely to have reached the baccalaureate than the writers who were active during this period (20 percent versus 10 percent had not obtained the baccalaureate). Having more rarely undertaken postsecondary studies (half of them versus more than two-thirds of the whole of writers), they were also globally less degreed than their contemporaries: a quarter of them held a postsecondary degree, versus almost half the writers. Of the five members who had undertaken studies in law, literature, or medicine, only three finished them. The only juror to come from a grande école, Pierre Champion, who studied at the École des Chartes which trains librarians, was elected (like La Varende who attended the École des Beaux-Arts) under the extraordinary conditions of the crisis, against the will of part of the assembly.

This lesser endowment in educational capital was only partly the result of the overrepresentation of writers from the petty bourgeoisie among the Ten. Certainly, at least four of the twenty members, all from modest backgrounds, had an educational path that was disrupted by financial difficulties (this was the case for Lucien Descaves, the Rosny brothers, and Mac Orlan). But at least four others, originating from the dominant class, had experienced a relative educational failure, which represents a rate two times higher than at the French Academy. Affected members included Léon Daudet, who barely failed the entry exam for medicine; Francis Carco, who failed his first baccalaureate; Sacha Guitry, who did not finish his secondary studies; and finally René Benjamin, son of an industrialist, refused at a Sorbonne competitive examination by Seignobos.[19]

The relatively weak level of higher education among the Goncourt jurors must finally be reassessed in light of the generational effect. Seven of the ten members who served at the Goncourt Academy in 1940 were born before 1880. Among them, five had not undertaken postsecondary studies, and only one completed them (Ajalbert). By the same token, of the fourteen members who died before 1940, only three had obtained a law degree. On the other hand, only five members out of thirteen representatives of the second generation, or a little more than a third, had not attended an establishment of higher education, a level equal to that of the global population of contemporary writers. It was thus definitely the effect of social aging that, before all else, placed the Goncourt Academy in an awkward position in the new state of the literary field during this period.

A DENIED POLITICIZATION: TO MAKE
OR REFLECT PUBLIC OPINION?

The transformation of the prize into a media event would rapidly make it into an ideological stake. The example of the French Academy hardly predisposed its younger counterpart to resist the temptation of seeing its national role recognized. Born during the era of production of "public opinion" and organized competition for the victory of "numbers," the Goncourt Academy distinguished itself once more from its model by borrowing proven weapons from the journalistic and political fields, still not clearly differentiated. To enlighten opinion: this calling initially conceived by the Goncourt brothers as an instrument of struggle against the logic of the market, or rather as a means of influencing its flow, would quickly exceed the entirely literary meaning it originally had. While this process was in part the product of the internal struggles created by the more or less deliberate importation of ethical and political dispositions into the literary judgment of the jurors, it also resulted from the tendency of the press to perceive cultural stakes according to the political categories of left and right, at a time when the Dreyfus affair provoked a strong political polarization of the intellectual field. This was all the more true when it was a matter of a public, rather than a secret vote like those conducted at the French Academy. We should trust neither the depoliticized representation that the jurors gave it— Lucien Descaves wrote, for example, to Gustave Geffroy: "I vote to the left for my candidate of the right (so it is said): *Georges Courteline*"[20]—nor the overpoliticized vision imposed by the press. The tight imbrication of literary and political stakes, mixed with the conflicts of interest and struggles for influence typical of this kind of institution, the exchanges of votes, rivalries, and oppositional alliances, make them difficult to disentangle.

The affiliation to naturalism, the avowed opposition to the French Academy, and the social position of its members seemed to predispose the newcomer to lean to the left. This was in any case the image it evoked at the time of its creation. Zola's stunning position-taking for the review of Captain Dreyfus's trial was not insignificant, masking the division within the naturalist school that had actually been caused by the Dreyfus affair. Octave Mirbeau, Lucien Descaves, Jean Ajalbert, and Gustave Geffroy, who sided with Zola, opposed Alphonse and Léon Daudet, Léon Hennique, Henri Céard, and maybe Joris-Karl Huysmans (the attitude of J.-H. Rosny the Elder was ambivalent). This division reflected the intermediary position of the naturalist school between the dominant pole of the literary field, chiefly anti-Dreyfus, and the avant-gardes, rather pro-Dreyfus.[21] Léon Daudet's adherence to Action française in 1904 undoubtedly helped establish the idea that the Goncourt Academy was divided into two camps, the political left having a choice spokesman there in the person of Lucien Descaves. Passionate about the Commune and a notorious antimilitarist, Descaves had been put on trial for his novel *Sous-Offs* (1889). Despite the real effects of this image that the press made of the jurors, ideological stakes openly prevailed over literary stakes only exceptionally at the Academy.

This was the case when Julien Benda was a candidate for the 1912 Goncourt Prize, promoted by the leaders of the camp identified with the left, Lucien Descaves and Gustave Geffroy, which aroused a strong opposition from the camp on the right, led by Léon Daudet. Daudet refused to vote for a Jew.[22] During the first three rounds of voting, he ostentatiously gave his vote, alone, to his Action française comrade Pierre Lasserre, author of a virulent lampoon called *La Doctrine officielle de l'Université* in which he accused the New Sorbonne of having succumbed to a plot stirred up by Protestants and Jews.[23] To counter Benda's candidacy, the opponents transferred their votes to *Les Filles de la pluie* by André Savignon, which won in the seventh round with five votes. The testament stipulated that in the case of a tie, the vote of the president (Léon Hennique at that time) would count double.

A similar dissension arose nine years later around the candidacy of René Maran, a civil servant in the colonial administration, who denounced its abominations in *Batouala*, subtitled *Véritable roman nègre*. The same balance of votes got the better of the opposition this time (Henri Céard, tired of being identified with the right despite being anxious to please Léon Daudet who got him elected, had switched sides). Presidential privilege, which had belonged to Gustave Geffroy since the Benda affair, now benefited the "left."[24]

The event was sufficiently unusual that twenty years later, it could be cited as a failure of the Academy by a spokesman for racist theories, Alain Laubreaux:

The following year, the Goncourt Prize further surpassed the fame that it had just founded. It was given to a Negro.

Not a Negro in a literary or figural meaning that designates the obscure collaborator of some prince of literature,* nor even a half-Negro, with simply tan skin in the manner of Alexandre Dumas, but a true Negro of Africa, a Negro black like Erebus. This time, it was pandemonium. The Negro writer colonized Paris, France.[25]

Similarly, the exclusion of Jews from the Goncourt Academy, which was attributed to the anti-Judaism of Edmond de Goncourt, a friend of Édouard Drumont, would be cited, to his credit, by the representatives of the doctrinaire anti-Semitism of *Au pilori*. They deplored, in turn, that this was not the case of the French Academy, quoting with satisfaction a declaration made by Courteline when Tristan Bernard was a candidate: "The Goncourt Academy will remain French."[26]

Herein lies the entire ideological stake of the prize. It was all about "French literature." It was "French literature" that was to be represented. Although it had never been defined, nor did it figure among the conditions posed by Edmond de Goncourt, this concept entered into the more or less conscious considerations that dictated the jury's choices. Through it, the schemes of ethical and political appreciation could slip into aesthetic judgment. Everything depended, of course, on the meaning given to the word "French." But we can suppose that the political divergences on this question did not exclude a background of common representations strongly anchored in the literary milieus of the period, to which a number of spontaneous rejections attest (it took until 1937, for example, for a writer of foreign origin, the Belgian Charles Plisnier, to win the prize for the first time).

In a period of conflict, the Goncourt Academy could only take its national mission seriously. War was moreover one of the themes of predilection for the realist and naturalist novel (*La Débâcle* by Zola), as was military life (*Sous-Offs* by Descaves). In the novelistic production devoted to the Great War, realist and naturalist techniques would be widely used to transmit a lived experience, the preeminence of which likened the war novel to testimony or travelogues when it did not completely merge these genres, as in *Ceux de 14* by Maurice Genevoix (1918–1923).[27] Offering testimony on the war nonetheless required a revision of the techniques of the novel, traditionally centered on the individual. Next to

---

* This use of *nègre* corresponds to the English "ghostwriter."—Trans.

works that remained faithful to the epic tradition (exaltation of noble and virile virtues) and were full of patriotic feeling like *L'Appel du sol* (1914) by Adrien Bertrand, the first war novels, delivered in the heat of battle so to speak, were thus framed as a sequence of notable episodes in the life of a soldier, and the characters, multiplied or highlighted to ensure the unity of the whole, were subordinated to the phenomenon that they served to explain: the war.[28] Dialogue played a preponderant role, spiced up with military slang, whose comic effect contrasted with the naturalist (and often picturesque) description of the brutish, unsanitary conditions of life, of the physical realities of death. Another particularity linked to the new character of this war that remained, on the whole, elusive: the adoption of a realistic scale of observation, often confined to a limited point of view, like that of a squad. If a certain picaresque comedy was exploited for its own sake in the "pompier" genre (as Albert Thibaudet describes it) represented by René Benjamin (*Gaspard*, 1915), it allied itself with horror in the naturalist vein to mock epic heroism and open the way for pacifist protestation. This demythification of wartime heroism associated with the denunciation of false patriotism, whose multiple incarnations included *Voyage au bout de la nuit* (1932) by Céline, was inaugurated by Barbusse's *Le Feu* (1916), first published in serial, in a censored form, in Gustave Téry's *L'Œuvre*. It drew some of the highest sales with 200,000 copies sold in two years.

Having looked in vain for a prose work by Charles Péguy, killed at the front, that would have been published during the year, the Goncourt jurors decided to postpone the awarding of the prize for 1914. The next year, they unanimously honored *Gaspard* by René Benjamin. By simultaneously awarding the prize for 1914 to Adrien Bertrand for *L'Appel du sol* by nine votes and the prize for 1916 to Henri Barbusse for *Le Feu* with eight votes in spite of violent opposition from Léon Daudet and Élimir Bourges, partisans of extreme war against Germany, the Goncourt Academy displayed less a collective position-taking than a concern to reflect the evolution of "public opinion": the patriotic outpouring of 1914, which marked Adrien Bertrand's novel was followed by a feeling of disillusionment that the success of *Le Feu* confirmed. This compromise—the attribution of the prize for 1914 to Bertrand—had no doubt been found to appease the furor of Daudet and Bourges against the candidate supported by Descaves and Geffroy, Barbusse, who won the prize for 1916. In 1917, another book about the war was honored, *La Flamme au poing* by Henry Malherbe, and in 1918, *Civilisation*, a testimony on hospitals of the rear guard by surgeon-poet Denis Thévenin alias Georges Duhamel, won with six votes against *Koenigsmark* by Pierre Benoit. In 1919, Léon Daudet finally found a sizable candidate to oppose the "pacifist" camp. Gustave Geffroy himself supported his choice. The prize accorded to Marcel Proust for *À l'ombre des jeunes filles en fleurs*, to the detriment of a new war novel hailed by the pacifists, *Les Croix de bois* by Roland Dorgelès, provoked a general outcry in the left-wing press: Proust was regarded as a candidate of the right.[29] Albin Michel had a headline printed on the cover strip of *Les Croix de bois* that read "Prix Goncourt" in large characters, with " 4 out of 10 votes" written in a smaller font, which caused him to be sued by Proust's publisher, Gaston Gallimard. This resounding failure, which was alleviated by the Vie Heureuse (Femina) Prize, was not insignificant in the vast success of *Les Croix de bois*. Thanks to the rebalancing of its internal power relations, the Goncourt Academy had, for its part, given preference to an author defending the primacy of the aesthetic logic. This was an unusual choice.

Instead of molding public opinion, the Goncourt Academy conformed to it. Or rather, through its choices it registered the fluctuations in public opinion such as they were reflected in the press and thus made itself the expression of a supposed consensus, supported by the academic majority. This trait reveals the principle of structural heteronomy inscribed in the Academy's position between the pole of small-scale production and the pole of large-scale production: fulfilling the public's expectations (as they were reflected through the press) was a way of confirming the credit that its audience gave it. Concretely, this apparently consensual position was acquired by rallying the "swing" votes to the electoral leader who would best represent "public opinion" in the politico-cultural situation of the moment. If we study the internal power relations of the institution, we notice that these "swing" votes belonged to the members of the assembly who were the most devoid of cultural and social advantages. I will return to this point later.

The identification of the prize with "public opinion" and its media impact could only make it an ideological stake for the acting powers. This position reinforced the young academy that, imbued with its national mission, lent itself willingly to the game and aspired to a more official status. At the end of the war, it obtained from the Ministry of the Interior that the Goncourt elections and prizes be included in the *Journal officiel*. On January 18, 1919, it addressed, like its elder counterpart, a double message of congratulations to Raymond Poincaré and Georges Clemenceau for the "victory of the right by arms." Recalling the principles that were at the foundation of the counter-academy, Élimir Bourges had at first protested: "the Goncourt Academy would leave its role with such displays," but he finally came around.[30]

TOWARD AN ACADEMIC CONFORMISM
This officialization reinforced the effect of inertia (*hysteresis*) already inherent in the processes of institutionalization. In a universe ruled, since romanticism,

by the principle of permanent revolution, the effects of institutional inertia are increased, most often condemning the authorities of consecration to confirm values that are considered outdated by avant-garde tendencies and thus inducing a systematic gap between their verdicts and the dynamic of the literary field.

In the beginning, the Goncourt Prize was meant, let's remember, to sanction the "new and daring tendencies of thought and form." Was this intended to limit risks? Edmond de Goncourt had stated his wish that "aside from three or four famous names, the Academy [would be] accessible to young literary men that the whims of fortune, the necessities of life put in an inferior situation and oblige to accept any kind of job."[31] This wish would not be respected. Aside from the first generation of jurors, whom Edmond de Goncourt had designated, the membership age was rarely under fifty and, since academicians were elected for life, the majority among them were between sixty and eighty years old, which referred back to literary careers launched thirty or forty years earlier. This social aging of the institution did not favor its adjustment to the transformations of the literary field. In addition, other factors impeded the assembly's accomplishment of such an adjustment, such as its traditional predilection for the novel in general, a genre already contested in the 1920s by the surrealist avant-garde, and for naturalism in particular, a preference still recently confirmed by François Nourissier:

> An unwritten law: this Naturalist tradition that means fantastic or futuristic literature, or science fiction for example, very rarely appears in our selections [. . .] while there is no "Goncourt style," the taste that dominates among us is francophone, Naturalist and even populist, rather than cutting edge, avant-gardist, and worldly.[32]

The Goncourt Academy had been suspected of orthodoxy from the start. "When you are afraid of making a mistake, you return to traditions and, by rewarding the work of the little Tharaud brothers, the Goncourt brothers' Academy has quite simply done what its older sister, the French Academy, would have done," Estienne complained in *Gil Blas* in 1906.[33] The critic was not mistaken. Jérome and Jean Tharaud, rewarded by the French Academy's Grand Prize for Literature in 1919, would be elected to that institution in 1938 and 1946 respectively. There they would increase the ranks of the Goncourt Prize winners, along with Claude Farrère (1905) and Georges Duhamel (1918), both received into the Academy in 1935, and Maurice Genevoix (1925), elected in 1946. Certainly, the gap between the dates of winning the prize and becoming a member reminds us of what the evolution of these trajectories owes to social aging. But it is also the sign of the progressive convergence between the two rival authorities, confirmed by the fact that two of those prizewinners, Duhamel and Jean Tharaud, to whom we must add Georges Lecomte and Paul Claudel, were approached to enter the Goncourt Academy before going to serve at the rival institution. The fact that their names were just proposed (Georges Lecomte), or that they did not obtain enough votes (Paul Claudel, Georges Duhamel), or that they refused because they rightfully sought a seat among the forty "immortals" (Jean Tharaud), or that they also shared (with the exception of Claudel) an ascending social trajectory that led them to seek a social position associated with the writing profession, changes nothing. This connection emerged from a converging movement. On the one hand, the high rate (eleven out of thirty-one, or a third) of writers who had won one of the main prizes for the novel at the French Academy was a consequence of the modification of the rules of the literary game induced by the creation of the Goncourt Academy, and more particularly of the increasing exposure of literary life to the media, a process I analyzed earlier, which made the prize into a means of gaining notoriety. Aside from the French Academy's own prizes, the Goncourt Prize had the greatest impact. On the other hand, whether by prudence or conformity, the Goncourt Academy's propensity for orthodoxy led it to honor authors who sustained justified hopes of institutional consecration.

The official position that the Goncourt Academy aspired to could only increase its tendency toward orthodoxy. This tendency nonetheless collided with the strong opposition of those of the Ten who intended to save the Company from the academicism that threatened it, and respect the wishes of Edmond de Goncourt. This concern could unite longtime political adversaries Lucien Descaves and Léon Daudet, who moreover fought for influence over the electoral game. The Céline affair is one of the most famous illustrations of this split that opposed the proponents of anti-conformism and the defenders of literary orthodoxy at the Academy.[34]

In 1932, Descaves proposed the candidacy of an unknown, Louis-Ferdinand Céline, for his *Voyage au bout de la nuit*. Descaves thought he could count on six votes that appeared favorable during the preparatory meeting. On the day of the vote, he obtained only two, from Léon Daudet and Jean Ajalbert. With six votes, Guy Mazeline won the prize in the first round for *Les Loups*. Furious, Descaves publicly accused "some" of being "sold" and sparked a violent scandal in the press that ended up in court. His accusation was aimed at the president, Rosny the Elder, who had just published a serial novel in *L'Intransigeant*, a weekly where the prizewinner was a contributor. At the advice of Pol Neveux, the Goncourt Academy, "indignant over the slanderous campaign led against its venerated president, Rosny the Elder," showed solidarity with him, giving him "the fervent testimony of its admiration and respect."[35] It "warmly" approved the measures that Rosny the Elder and Dorgelès took against the director of *Le Crapouillot*, Jean Galtier-Boissière, and against Maurice-Ivan Sicard for slander. The ejection of Lucien Descaves was considered. Descaves ended up retracting his accusations. In response to the presiding judge who asked him if the testament permitted the attribution of the prize to a work including foul language, Rosny the Elder answered: "The Goncourt Academy, being of public interest, has the duty to respect certain conventions."[36] Léon Hennique had also declared himself shocked by the audacity of the writer. Thus, invoking its official position, the Goncourt Academy practiced self-censorship! But this argument masked the aesthetic dispositions of the academic majority, dispositions that led it to reject the audacities of someone like Céline. The Renaudot jurors rushed to reward the unsuccessful candidate.

Inseparable from the young Academy's desire to be officialized and play a national role, the concern for respectability thus reinforced the logic of institutional aging that led toward an academic conformism. Along with the media logic that predisposed it to become the expression of the fluctuations of "public opinion" such as they appeared through the press, in order to ensure the impact of the prize, and along with the relative weakness of the sociocultural resources globally held by its members, this logic weakened the resistance of the Goncourt Academy to the external pressures that threatened the very literary autonomy it was at first called to protect. In fact, those who leaned toward conformism in literary matters were also those who tended to support the representatives of the current dominant ideology inside the assembly, as happened during the Occupation. Let us note in addition that while opposition to the conformism of the academic majority could favor the alliance of people like Descaves and Daudet in the name of fidelity to the testament, it was also the ambiguity of the reception of *Voyage au bout de la nuit*, which both the left and the extreme right tried to claim when it was published, that had made this alliance possible.

THE STRUGGLES FOR INFLUENCE BETWEEN
SENIOR MEMBERS AND NEWCOMERS

Another principle of division could cause similar alliances that transcended ideological divisions. These were the struggles that opposed the more senior members with the assembly's newcomers for the conservation or overthrow of the former's supremacy. Such are the stakes that determined René Benjamin's election in May 1938. Following on the heels of the Anschluss and the fall of the

Blum government, the election of this ultraconservative warrior against the Republican regime, and an admirer of Mussolini, upon his return from Rome where he had attended Hitler's reception by the Duce, was to have serious consequences for the Academy.

The candidacy of Tristan Bernard for Raoul Ponchon's seat was well advanced. Léon Daudet, who contested it—Tristan Bernard was Jewish—had declared that he would vote for René Benjamin in all rounds.[37] At the next meeting, Tristan Bernard's candidacy was definitively removed. René Benjamin, made more famous by his activity as a lampoonist than by his properly literary production, was not an outsider. He was a winner of the Goncourt Prize for 1915, and four of the jurors who had elected him were still members: Daudet, Descaves, and the Rosny brothers. His name, promoted by Léon Daudet and J.-H. Rosny the Elder (he also obtained the support of Raoul Ponchon), had been regularly mentioned since 1926, even though he hardly collected more than two votes. He had failed for the fourth time against Francis Carco in 1937.

Benjamin was elected in the first round with five votes (Daudet, Rosny the Elder, Ajalbert, Larguier, and Descaves) versus two for Mac Orlan (Dorgelès and Carco), one for Alexandre Arnoux (Pol Neveux), and one for Marius Leblond (Rosny the Younger). In the press, it was hypothesized that the jurors had much less voted for René Benjamin than against Roland Dorgelès who, strengthened by his victory with the election of Carco the year before, supported the candidacy of his Montmartrian friend Pierre Mac Orlan (Jean Ajalbert had declared himself hostile to an "Académie du Lapin Agile," after the name of the famous bar in Montmartre).[38] Descaves's alliance with the Daudet camp was not as unexpected as it might seem. Descaves had encouraged Benjamin at the beginning of his literary career, and it was he who had backed *Gaspard* for the prize for 1915. In addition, Descaves, who was again excluded since the Céline affair, could only oppose Dorgelès whom he had battled on this subject. Threatened in their prerogative by the newcomer Dorgelès (elected in 1929), who was trying to establish himself as an electoral leader, the old guard had rallied around Léon Daudet to bring Dorgelès down.

This configuration of alliances shows the weak echo at the Goncourt Academy of the confrontations between the neo-pacifist right and the anti-Fascist left that rocked the intellectual field during this period. While Jean Ajalbert's pacifism was perhaps ready to compromise with the neo-pacifism of the extreme right as represented by Léon Daudet and René Benjamin, this was not the case for Lucien Descaves, who figured, along with Aragon, Malraux, and Mauriac, among the thirteen signers of the call to national unity that appeared on March 20, 1938, in the Communist daily *Ce Soir*. Benjamin's election shows that specific institutional logics could trump ideological divisions even in periods of strong politicization of the literary field.

From the first vacancy in 1939, the new juror established himself as an electoral leader, making his friend Sacha Guitry replace Pol Neveux; Guitry was elected seven to one against Alexandre Arnoux, whose lone vote belonged to Descaves. Ajalbert, who was opposed to Guitry because of an old grudge, had submitted a blank ballot. "When Benjamin, in his turn [after being elected], spoke to me of Sacha Guitry as a successor to Pol Neveux, I agreed with a sort of enthusiasm. Sacha Guitry is our Calderón," wrote Léon Daudet.[39] Lucien Descaves did not calm down. The reception of an actor, very affluent and living moreover quite luxuriously, was for him an insult to the memory of the Goncourts and a violation of the testament. Descaves went so far as to accuse Benjamin of having counted on this election to favor the reception of his *Vie de Balzac* at the Comédie-Française.[40]

Sacha Guitry, meanwhile, supposedly hinted to some of the jurors that he might bequeath his mansion on the Champs de Mars, and the priceless collections that it contained, to the Goncourt Academy. When Guitry publicly announced his intentions in January 1942, a promise that would make much ink flow on the theme "from the attic to the palace,"[41] the underground press would rush to revive the rumor that he had bought his election. The gift would in fact quickly turn into a simple dinner invitation. A meeting was actually held at his house on December 11, 1943, in the sole presence of René Benjamin and... himself. At the Liberation, Maurice Noël would describe, in *Le Figaro*, a letter from October 1941 that had been discovered by "Free France." In it, Guitry invoked the future meetings of the Goncourt Academy at his home to ask for thirty tons of coal destined to heat his mansion![42] True or false, what these echoes and rumors tell above all is the illegitimacy of Guitry in the literary field. Descaves's indignation translates rather well the feeling that this election aroused in the world of literature, tarnishing the image of the Academy. In response to Pierre Benoit who spoke to him disdainfully of "this Goncourt Academy that elects a Sacha Guitry," Paul Léautaud said: "It has become the sort of place you don't want to be in."[43] Descaves would have other opportunities to regret his support of Benjamin. Guitry's election was only the first in a series of extraordinary elections in the annals of the Academy.

For the attribution of the prize for 1939, in the midst of the Phoney War, Benjamin chose his candidate: Robert Brasillach, author of *Les Sept Couleurs*, who was mobilized at the front. Didn't the Academy have the duty to reward a writer-soldier? But Brasillach was also the editor in chief of *Je suis partout*, the weekly that assembled the young dissidents of Action française who had converted to Fascism. His weekly displayed an offensive anti-Semitism and found itself torn, since the declaration of war, between a pro-Hitler tendency represented by Alain Laubreaux, and Charles Lesca's nationalism tempered with neo-pacifism. "What confusion among the sons of Abraham if the Goncourt Prize were attributed to the editor in chief of *Je suis partout!*" Laubreaux jubilated when René Benjamin announced his intentions to him.[44] Benjamin advised him to write to Larguier to tell him about the book. Laubreaux also campaigned to Sacha Guitry: he visited him and . . . above all rushed to publish an article praising him.[45] Benjamin and Guitry, his new ally, this time met with defeat: Brasillach earned only three votes in the first round. Rosny the Elder, president of the assembly, joined them, then transferred his vote to Philippe Hériat, a writer assigned to censorship as part of his military service, who won the prize for *Les Enfants gâtés.* They did not even obtain the support of Léon Daudet, who voted for Madame Simone. Was Daudet intractable because he condemned the pro-Hitler orientation of *Je suis partout* or because, faithful to his image, he would defy expectations by setting himself apart from his political camp through his literary preferences? In any case, the events were to help shift power relations in their favor.

AN UNEQUAL POWER RELATIONSHIP

The different logics of opposition that we saw at work at the Goncourt Academy, "right" versus "left," conformism versus anti-conformism, old guard versus newcomers, acted conjointly without necessarily intersecting. A glance at the individual trajectories of the jurors who composed the Goncourt Academy in 1940 and their life during the Occupation will allow us to better assess the power relations within the assembly. They shed light on the resources mobilized by the actors during internal struggles and let us perceive the part played by individual strategies in the principles of collective adjustment in a period of crisis.

Up until the defeat, the power relation was favorable to the old guard, not only due to the authority they had acquired and the sociocultural resources at their disposal in comparison to the new generation with fewer such advantages, but also because they constituted the largest group and were able to prevent the growth of the "Montmartrian" camp of Dorgelès and Carco. But several factors helped call this power relation into question at this decisive moment in history, further weakening the Academy's resistance in the face of external pressures. The death of Rosny the Elder in 1940 reduced the ranks of the old guard, which now numbered four: Daudet, Descaves, Rosny the Younger, and Ajalbert.

Dispersal and shortage, which hit the senior members harder, in their seventies or even their eighties, contributed to their loss of power within the institution, to the benefit of the newcomers. Benjamin and Guitry, in their fifties, not only benefited from the help of the acting powers (which was not the least advantage under conditions of censorship and repression), but also were disposed of substantial economic resources and were thus less touched by the decline in the standard of living. Finally, the strong politicization of the literary stakes divided the old guard: Léon Daudet, one of the influential members of the Academy, was closer ideologically to René Benjamin than to Lucien Descaves.

"An existence devoted to the invective always takes its source in the cemetery of aborted works [...] on the cadavers of his novels and his plays," François Mauriac wrote of Léon Daudet.[46] Born in 1867, the oldest son of Alphonse Daudet had followed the Republican cursus honorum. Educated at Louis-le-Grand, then at the faculty of medicine, this intimate of Jean-Martin Charcot who was regarded as a future "big boss" failed the very selective internship entrance exam by a very slim margin. Justified or undeserved, as he thought, this failure fueled a resentment equal in measure to his disappointed ambitions. He poured this rancor into a harsh satire of the medical milieu, Les Morticoles (1894), which was praised by Barrès. After some novelistic efforts, Léon Daudet had to redeploy the important cultural and social advantages that his father bequeathed him into a career as a critic and polemicist.[47] This pampered child of the Republic, whose alliance with Victor Hugo's granddaughter consecrated one of the first civil marriages of the regime, would pair his new professional orientation with an ideological conversion. It was sealed by his passage from anti-Boulangism to virulent "rationalization," during the Dreyfus affair, of an anti-Semitism that had recently infiltrated the intellectual milieus (Drumont was a friend of the family, and he introduced Léon to La Libre parole). It was also sealed by his divorce, and his second marriage with his cousin Marthe Allard, a fervent royalist, this time in the Church. In 1904, he joined Action française, newly founded by Charles Maurras, and became one of its leaders. This was a completely political engagement (as we saw, he vigilantly distinguished himself from Maurras by his literary tastes) that the famous lampoonist, great orator, and elected deputy to the "Blue Horizon" Chamber from 1919 to 1924 would never disavow. Léon Daudet experienced the same "divine surprise" that struck Maurras at the advent of the Vichy regime:

> To this incontestable and uncontested hero came the conviction that he would save his country by going back to the beginning, restoring the peasant virtues that are the primordial virtues; awakening the drowsy feeling of

honor, of respect for work, for the fatherland, for the family; chasing the merchants from the Temple; imposing himself to his conqueror through the respect of his commitments. In a few months, Marshal Pétain, served by Providence, has achieved a task as vast and as healthy as King Henri IV.[48]

This "task" was for Léon Daudet both the status that Action française had long demanded for the Jews, and the "return of God in School," a return to "traditional morals" that he considered the most essential of projected reforms.[49] It also meant limiting the practice of medicine, a subject he held dear, to persons born to French parents: "Foreigners and Jews belonging to different races substituted themselves in this way for natives and little by little transformed the professional spirit by the vulgar lure of money at any price [. . .]."[50] He called for the punishment of troublemakers (notably applauding the punishment levied against Jean Zay at the Riom trial).[51] Having retreated to Lyon with his newspaper, adopting, like Maurras, an attentiste position with regard to Pétain's foreign policy, the reformed polemicist now saved the last outbursts of his verve for the conventional causes of the National Revolution, and for his memoirs. At his death in July 1942, the critics on the right praised him as a Renaissance man.[52]

Everything separated Léon Daudet from his great rival of the Goncourt Academy. Born in Petit Montrouge in 1861, son of a reputed line engraver who encouraged him in his literary calling, Lucien Descaves had abandoned his studies at the Lavoisier school to become an apprentice in a bank.[53] He worked at the Crédit Lyonnais while starting his literary career with a collection of short stories published in 1882 by Henry Kistemaeckers, the publisher of young naturalists and members of the Commune, who was linked to his father. Having opted for journalism, he entered the *Revue moderne* as a critic; there he became linked with the second naturalist generation and soon saw himself admitted to the Goncourt attic. With his friends Paul Bonnetain, Rosny the Elder, Paul Margueritte, and Gustave Guiches, he signed the "Manifesto of the Five" in 1887 against *La Terre* by Zola, denouncing their master's "exacerbation of the obscene note." His four years of service inspired short stories, *Misères du Sabre* (1887), and one of the first antimilitarist novels, *Sous-Offs* (1889), which earned him both the recognition of peers and a resounding trial that ended in his acquittal. A manifesto in his favor, signed by renowned intellectuals like Zola and Alphonse Daudet, completed the establishment of his career. In 1892, Séverine brought him to the nascent *Journal* where he submitted "morning notes." He would be entrusted with its literary direction in 1919 and would hold it for twenty years while serving as theater critic for *L'Intransigeant*.

Participating in the experiment of Antoine's Théâtre-Libre, he signed, or co-signed with Bonnetain or Georges Darien, plays with social themes and literary inspiration that caused a scandal (notably *La Cage*, 1898) before beginning a fruitful collaboration with Maurice Donnay that would produce *La Clairière* (1900) and *Les Oiseaux de passage* (1904). A columnist at *L'Écho de Paris*, he was required to choose between *L'Écho* and *L'Aurore* where he engaged in the pro-Dreyfus struggle. A libertarian Socialist, he gathered important documents on the Commune and conducted a study based on numerous witnesses. At the Goncourt Academy, he established himself as an electoral leader, and notably enabled the elections of Jules Renard and Judith Gautier. Under the Occupation, he would lead an active opposition against the Benjamin-Guitry clan, without ever leaving his home in Senonches.

In interpreting the voting tactics of J.-H. Rosny the Younger at the Academy, no one neglected to mention his concern to distinguish himself from his brother. Rosny the Younger (born in 1859) had never achieved the recognition bestowed on his older brother (born in 1856), an author of futuristic novels and scientific fantasy, with whom he had previously written collaborative works including the prehistoric epic *Les Xiphébuz* (1887).[54] His position as the younger made him into the shadow of his brother, who seems to have concentrated all the family aspirations of social ascension through education. These aspirations were disappointed due to the premature death of the father and the material difficulties that this modest family of Brussels haberdashers experienced from then on (Rosny the Elder had to give up his studies before taking the baccalaureate). Rosny the Younger was in his eighties when, in March 1940, he replaced his dead brother as president of the Academy. The relative weakness of his cultural and social advantages was at the root of what Lucien Descaves would interpret as his "inertia" as president, an interpretation that was only a way to clear his old colleague who was actively allied with the camp of the "strong ones." Still, this interpretation has the merit of expressing the weakening of institutional mechanisms of resistance to the pressure of events:

> If Rosny the Younger has let himself be circumvented by his wicked assistants, he does, after all, have some excuses. With no experience (at his age!), he allowed his role of president to be reduced to that of a nonentity. His consorts took advantage of his long stays in Brittany to substitute their influence to his and prepare the elections [...] The inertia of Rosny the Younger served Benjamin admirably.[55]

To these representatives of the old academic guard, we must add Jean Ajalbert, born in 1863 at Clichy-la-Garenne, in Auvergne. Though he was elected in

1917, he belonged to the same literary generation. Son of an agricultural farmer and wine merchant, a lawyer by education, he had fought for the revision of the Dreyfus trial. After a mission to Laos, he became the curator of the Château de Malmaison, then director of the tapestry workshop of Beauvais. The author of travel narratives and exotic novels considered as the precursor of colonial literature, he was above all the adapter of *La Fille Élisa* by the Goncourt brothers for the Théâtre-Libre, and a close friend of Lucien Descaves (he was one of the few that the latter addressed by the familiar "tu"). A little-known author, in the 1920s he fought actively for the diffusion of regionalist literature in tourist networks.[56] In 1933, he was pushed to retire (his position was eliminated), and he saw his salary shrink away.[57] After the defeat, the anarchist of another century, withdrawn to Nice, would lend his voice to the injunctions to "return to the land" and engage in "moral recovery" in a call for the "redemption of the horrible past toward a future of spiritual greatness and inner morality, which escapes all foreign forces." In 1942, when he was nearly eighty, he would join Jacques Doriot's Fascist Parti populaire français (PPF). While this position-taking had an effect on his literary choices as a juror, it still did not lead him, as we will see, to join the camp of Benjamin and Guitry: his status as a senior member and his hatred for Guitry would cause him to fight against the new jurors.

Among the members of the second generation of the Goncourt jurors, Léo Larguier (1878–1950) and Roland Dorgelès (1885–1973) were closer, by their modest social origins, to Rosny the Younger than to Francis Carco. Representative of this second generation of jurors who were less socially well endowed than their elders, they, like Rosny the Younger, owed the maintenance of their position, indeed of their existence, in the literary field to their membership in the Academy. Named respectively vice president and secretary-treasurer of the association's board upon the death of Rosny the Elder, they represented the "swing votes" that, under the Occupation, allowed the majority to shift to the side of presumed public opinion. Larguier, born in La Grande-Combe in Languedoc, came from an old Protestant family from Cévennes. He was raised by his grandmother, who kept sheep but held a certificate of competency and taught him to read.[58] Settled in Nîmes after the defeat, the chronicler of artistic and literary life gave *Paris-Soir* evocations of the daily life of old through current themes like food rationing.[59]

Dorgelès, born in Amiens, was the grandson of a woodworker and the son of a fabric factory sales representative who transmitted a certain cultural capital to him, notably initiating him in the reading of Courteline.[60] After a disjointed educational career due to his family's many moves, he entered the École des arts décoratifs. A notorious figure in the nascent Montmartrian bohemia, he became its chronicler-humorist, all the while disparaging the avant-garde that was forming there. He was the author of a farce on the painting by the Lapin Agile donkey, whom he baptized Boronali for the occasion (this was an anagram of Aliboron that, due to its Italian sound, evoked the futurists), and whom he consecrated as leader of the school of "excessivism." He pursued his journalistic career at the *Journal*, where he would remain until 1941. Mobilized in 1914, he returned from the front with *Les Croix de bois*, a book that established his renown. The Goncourt Prize slipped from his grasp in favor of Proust, and the ensuing polemic reinforced the success of the loser, who was consoled by the Vie Heureuse (Femina) Prize. The Goncourt Academy made amends by admitting him ten years later, when he also attained the presidency of the Association des écrivains combattants. A traveling reporter, in 1937 he published *Vive la liberté!*; relating observations made during stays in the USSR, Germany, Austria, and Italy, he condemned their dictatorial regimes outright. While he saw Bolshevism as the most imminent danger because it had already survived its leaders, his aversion for Nazism did not shake his pacifism, all the more "noble" in his eyes as he was assured of a German defeat.[61]

During the Phoney War [*drôle de guerre*], as he named it, he was an army correspondent for the weekly *Gringoire*. His tale of the debacle, *Retour au front*, was banned by German censors along with *Les Croix de bois* from the beginning of the Occupation. He would refuse to excise his attacks against Germany and the word "boche"[†] when the Sonderführer Gerhard Heller offered to reedit it.[62] This account, which recorded military absences and demoralization within the ranks, would nonetheless earn him criticism after the Liberation for having lauded the heroism of two masked robbers, including Joseph Darnand, the future head of the militia. Having followed the editorial staff of *Gringoire* to Marseille, he resigned in September 1941 due to the increasingly collaborationist and anti-Semitic tendency of the weekly, which affected his wife and friends. His nationalism and his faithfulness as a veteran led him to write articles for the glory of the marshal and the "return to the land," without however approving the anti-Semitic laws decreed by Vichy. He would later say that he'd hoped de Gaulle's appeals would one day join the "reassuring comments of the old Vichy hostage" to announce the "resurrection" of France.[63] The apolitical stance of a man who described himself as a "Christian anarchist" and had long refused to vote, coupled with a fervent patriotism, a certain moral conservatism, and a growing nostalgic attitude, led him to adopt positions that were sometimes

---

[†] A pejorative name for Germans during this period.—Trans.

equivocal and often poorly adapted to the current stakes. His ideological ambivalence was characteristic of the state of mind of those who sought to "accommodate" themselves to the situation as best they could.

Unlike his friend and sponsor, Francis Carco, who led the academic opposition against the Benjamin-Guitry clan, had more resources to counter the newcomers to the Academy. Son of a senior official of the penitentiary colony of New Caledonia, Francis Carco (1886–1958) had disappointed the family ambitions that destined him for a career in the Registration,[64] and he had broken with his bourgeois origins to become an "eccentric" poet-songwriter in *cafés-concerts*, then a novelist, a painter of manners in the Pigalle underworld. Having retreated to Lyon after the defeat, he gave literary articles to *Le Figaro* and *Paris-Soir*. In them, he made concessions to the regime and to censorship that lend themselves to a double reading, such as the evocation, entitled "Return to the Land" of a poetic French tradition attached to "nature," a Rousseauist pantheism that the ideologues of the National Revolution did not find to their liking.[65] Meanwhile, he did not hesitate to praise writers hated by the regime, André Gide in particular.[66] In Carco, René Benjamin found a formidable adversary, who would establish himself as an influential member as soon as political power relations would swing back again, at the Liberation.

The new electoral leader of the assembly, René Benjamin, was born in Paris in 1885 to a family that had experienced a sudden social rise. The grandson of a line engraver, he was the son of a businessman.[67] The happy relationship that he seems to have maintained with the educational institution had as its counterpart a much less successful socialization among his colleagues at the collège Rollin: "I spent ten years of my life in fear of the first bell that announced recess, and hoping for the second that ended it." This was surely one of the defining factors in his fervent elitism: "The school, like all institutions and all laws, has been established for the masses, thinking of the most mediocre."[68] The ambitions that pushed this first-generation intellectual to perfect his family's social ascent by acquiring degrees would however be dismissed due to a failure during his postsecondary studies at the New Sorbonne. His resentment for the Republican educational system, which his inherited reactionary dispositions helped convert to a condemnation of the democratic regime as a whole, would unceasingly fuel his pamphletary verve during the course of his entire life, from *La Farce de la Sorbonne* (1911) to *Vérités et rêveries sur l'éducation* (1941). After a first novel that went unnoticed, he found his way in satire, began working for *Gil Blas* in 1910, and contributed to *L'Écho de Paris*. A protégé of Lucien Descaves whose salon he visited on Sundays, he composed at Descaves's urging a war novel, *Gaspard*, that earned him the Goncourt Prize for 1915. Having tried his hand at the novel and theater without great success, he undertook a series of satires of the regime: *Valentine ou la folie démocratique* (1924), an allegory of the electoral system and the versatility of public opinion presented in the guise of a woman; *Aliborons et démagogues* (1927), a ferocious diatribe against the teachers and defenders of the secular school; *Les Augures de Genève* (1929), in which he attacked the League of Nations. He also published portraits of Barrès, Maurras, Clemenceau, and a *Vie de Balzac*. A contributor to the *Revue des deux mondes*, friend of Léon Daudet and Élimir Bourges, mixed in with the Maurrassian milieu, he was part of the ultraconservative elite that gathered at the home of Countess Joachim Murat. Allied with the "defenders of the West," signer of the neo-pacifist manifesto against the sanctions inflicted on Italy by the League of Nations as a result of the aggression in Ethiopia, in 1937 he wrote *Mussolini et son peuple* for the glory of the Duce and his Fascist regime, which he considered the regime of true freedom. In October 1937, he went to Spain at the same time as Claude Farrère, at the invitation of those responsible for Francoist propaganda. For him, as for so many others, France expiated the "sins" of the Republicans by its defeat; he developed this theme in *Le Printemps tragique* (1941).

An "organic" intellectual of the Vichy regime, he passed for having been the adviser to the marshal, whom he accompanied in his tours[69] and about whom he published three consecutive tributes.[70] On December 15, 1940, he attended the ceremony marking the arrival of the Aiglon ashes at the Invalides, along with Abel Bonnard and Sacha Guitry. He obtained permission to go preach the good word in Morocco and Switzerland—in Geneva where he announced, shortly after the defeat, radiantly, that with Pétain, "Maurras's ideas are now in power," and in Neuchâtel on February 9, 1943, where after a conference on the Goncourts, during lunch, he justified the German invasion of the Southern zone as a result of the American landing in North Africa.[71] He contributed to *Le Petit Parisien*, the *Journal*, and the new series of the *Revue universelle*, directed by Henri Massis. He further composed an essay on education where, by virtue of the opposition between education and instruction—"instruction, which was to remain neutral, was no more than an abstention, a vindictive silence before all the big problems, religion, fatherland, morality, family"[72]—he condemned the unified educational system which allowed pupils to pass from primary to secondary school, secularity, free instruction, leveling out from below. Nor did he neglect the idea of progress and science, source of all evil since it claimed to solve the "mystery" that belonged to God alone.

Sacha Guitry had returned to the capital after the debacle and reopened the Théâtre de la Madeleine starting in July with *Pasteur*. He would see two of his plays censored, *Mon auguste grand-père* and *Le Dernier Troubadour*, but would be able to have three staged, including *N'écoutez pas Mesdames*, which was first performed in May 1942. Although he was held in suspicion by Propaganda—he would have to furnish proofs of his "Aryanness" after a press campaign that denounced him as Jewish—he was named a member of the Comité d'organisation des entreprises de spectacles founded in 1941 by Vichy. There he would fight against the state control of the regime.[73] Protected by the German Institute, a star of the Parisian in crowd who hurried to Franco-German social events, dinners, cocktails, receptions at the German embassy, meetings in honor of the sculptor Arno Breker, he also poured himself into philanthropic endeavors like the gala of the Union des artistes on July 8, 1942.[74] His film production group was one of the eleven French companies authorized in 1943–1944. While the relationships he cultivated with the occupier served above all his personal interests, he also knew how to use them to benefit his colleagues in distress, like Tristan Bernard or Colette's husband Maurice Goudeket, arrested as Jews. Along with other colleagues, he would intervene on their behalf with the occupying authorities (both would be freed). Neither anti-Semitic nor Fascist, he was also not a convinced Pétainist. But he knew how to harmonize his interests with the "duty" of allegiance to power, for example by editing the volume *De Jeanne d'Arc à Philippe Pétain*, a luxury work in which members of the two rival academies united with other renowned intellectuals to celebrate the French leader.[75]

Faced with two powerful newcomers, René Benjamin and Sacha Guitry, who had an "in" with the Vichy and German authorities, the old guard, divided and weakened, had few advantages to boast of, while among the members of the second generation of jurors, only Carco stood out as an opponent. Benjamin and Guitry would thus easily manage to reinforce their camp, by bringing members to the Table of Ten who were as atypical as they were in the Academy's tradition, whether by their social position, their titles, and/or their fortune.

Scandal as a Mode of Survival

The Goncourt Academy resumed its activities in December 1941, thanks to the steps taken by the president and Sachy Guitry with respect to the occupying authorities. Extraordinary in the history of the Academy, the results of the ensuing ballots, whether for the prize or the election of new members, provoked a series of internal conflicts that caused a scandal in the press. Stated in terms of fidelity to the testament or its violation, they sometimes let us glimpse the generational rivalries, ideological divergences, collusions of interest, and individual strategies that grounded them. The historical conjuncture and the over-politicization of literary stakes that resulted actually favored the inversion of the internal power relations to the advantage of the newcomers, the Benjamin-Guitry clan. Having become electoral leaders, René Benjamin and Sacha Guitry would have no trouble rallying a majority to choices that obviously contradicted the clauses of the testament. Yet, the vehemence of the opposing minority's reaction was symptomatic of the effects of the crisis that exacerbated conflicts and transformed the members' ordinary quarrel into a veritable schism. This minority, constituted by Lucien Descaves, Francis Carco, and Jean Ajalbert, was organized not on ideological bases, but against the violation of the testament, and above all against this takeover by the newcomers.

Caught in the constraints imposed on them by an anomic situation, the Goncourt jurors still pursued a single goal, albeit by different means: the survival of the institution at any price, which meant, for them, the resumption of its activities and the maintenance of the prize's symbolic value. It was a matter of its very existence, as the critics already implied. The recourse to scandal, which had already revealed itself to be an effective way of keeping the attention of the press, became a mode of survival. It allowed the jurors, whom the new conditions of production and geographic distance had deprived of power over the institution, to call the public as a witness to the hijacking of the heritage that the newcomers performed in the guise of continuity. But the latter had the support of the powers and the collaborationist press on their side. These allies also had a word or two to say about that heritage, which had become public property and, as a result, an ideological stake. Before even resuming activities, the mere suggestion, made by members who had retreated to the Southern zone, to decentralize the Goncourt Academy and award the Goncourt Prize for 1941 in Lyon provoked an outcry.

Worried that Parisian hegemony might be called into question, the collaborationist press multiplied its exhortations, insinuations, and sometimes open threats. The Goncourt Academy thus attracted the fury of *Les Nouveaux Temps* where the principal terms of the conflict were exposed under the pen of its editor in chief, Guy Crouzet:

> We will not receive this decentralization of the most Parisian of literary events without stupor. Does the Goncourt Academy, many of whose members, and dare we say the most famous? are in fact presently in Paris [a reference to René Benjamin and Sacha Guitry], consider itself an organ of the government, the equal of the National Council? Who has had the right to make this decision in its name, and on what authority, at a time when, in the hardest material conditions, everyone is trying *to make "Paris go on,"* whether it is a matter of commerce of things or ideas? [...] The Goncourt Prize in

Lyon is a resignation [...] By exiling itself, the Goncourt Academy would deprive us less of the tradition it represents than it would distance itself from the continuities of today, the rejuvenation of tomorrow.[76]

Strengthened by the support of the occupant and the monopoly it now held over the Northern zone, the collaborationist press had the power to threaten the Academy with symbolic death. It also had the power to shift the internal power relation in favor of Benjamin and Guitry, through insinuations directed at dissident jurors, making them doubly traitors—traitors to the Academy's heritage and traitors to the nation—and bringing them to the attention of the public powers.

A TOPICAL ACADEMICISM

After numerous postponements that provoked great tension in the press, the long-awaited lunch was held on December 20, 1941, at Drouant. It assembled only four guests: the president Rosny the Younger, the assistant secretary René Benjamin, Sacha Guitry, and the secretary-treasurer Roland Dorgelès who was the only one to have crossed the demarcation line. He wielded the power of the vice president, Léo Larguier. Rosny the Younger was Francis Carco's delegate, while René Benjamin spoke for Léon Daudet. The president reminded the group of the events of the war and the armistice that prevented general assemblies from being held. Even board meetings had been forbidden. Only three members had been able to meet (Rosny the Younger, Sacha Guitry, René Benjamin). The president and the assistant secretary, the only board members present in Paris, had thus managed the society's goods and taken steps toward resuming activities. For 1942, the board would be renewed by one member, Dorgelès, who left his place to Sacha Guitry.

The assembly then proceeded to the election of Rosny the Elder's successor. In the press the names of André Billy (candidate of Lucien Descaves), Jean Ajalbert, and Francis Carco; Blaise Cendrars, sponsored by Léon Daudet; Pierre Mac Orlan, supported by Roland Dorgelès, but who had announced in his *Nouveaux Temps* column that he would refuse any candidacy; and also those of Alexandre Arnoux, Maurice Genevoix, and Henri Pourrat had all been mentioned.[77] To everyone's surprise, it was an outsider who won against *Le Figaro* critic André Billy: the archivist and historian Pierre Champion, son of the bookseller, was an affluent notable, mayor of Nogent-sur-Marne. An unsuccessful candidate at the French Academy in 1939, he had been a member of the Academy of Moral and Political Sciences since 1940, and had just been named to the Conseil national established by the Vichy regime.[78] Conforming little to the testament and the tradition of the Goncourt Academy, this choice incited the fury of Descaves, Ajalbert, and Carco, who criticized his titles, "the more unquestionable because they have already been officially recognized by another assembly!"[79] Ajalbert denounced them as a mark of academic conformism: "With men like himself [Champion], I foresee that the day will come when the Ten will arrive at place Gaillon in carriages with revolutionary cockades to exchange general ideas and award the most conformist prize over the course of a classic lunch."[80]

The election had been carefully planned. Pierre Champion won in the first round by six votes: Rosny the Younger, Benjamin, Guitry, Daudet (who had clearly changed his mind), Larguier, and Dorgelès, versus three for André Billy. According to Lucien Descaves's version, Benjamin had deferred the assembly's meeting to eliminate the serious candidate who was André Billy. Benjamin and Guitry's aversion for Billy resulted less from ideological dissensions (even though Billy, treated by the collaborationist press as a "grotesque pencil pusher and notorious warmonger,"[81] had evolved from a seemly marshalism to a more distant wait-and-see attitude) than from literary payback aimed at the legitimate criticism from the interwar period. This fact would be proven when his election was not confirmed in 1943; I will return to this episode. The candidacy of Pierre Champion, meanwhile, had been proposed by Sacha Guitry in order to ensure a permanent majority for his camp, although Champion would only fill this role for one vote, since he would die six months later.[82]

Two days after the election of Pierre Champion, the general assembly continued its meeting at Drouant to award the Goncourt Prizes for 1940 and 1941. It was decided that the prize for 1940 would be reserved for a writer in captivity and would be given only after the return of the prisoners (Francis Ambrière would receive it in 1946 for *Les Grandes Vacances*). The prize for 1941 was given to Henri Pourrat, candidate of Benjamin, Guitry, and Rosny the Younger; Dorgelès, Larguier, and Champion transferred their votes to him in the second round. He won against Guy des Cars, who earned three votes from Descaves, Ajalbert, and Carco. Contrary to the traditions of the Goncourt Academy, the prizewinner was a writer who had already been widely consecrated. About sixty years old, the cantor from the Auvergne had received the Prize for the Novel from the French Academy for *Gaspard des Montagnes*, and the Forty had just awarded him the Muteau Prize for *L'Homme à la bêche* (1941). Furthermore, despite its subtitle "novel," *Vent de mars* (published by Gallimard and dedicated to Jean Paulhan) was not a work of fiction, but rather a booklet of notes taken between 1938 and 1940, with philosophical and historical meditations on the peasantry scattered throughout: "The deep history of France is in this meeting.

The alliance of earthly law and Christian law explains the French peasant; the peasant explains France [...]."[83] But Henri Pourrat was mainly "the official writer of Pétainism," as Anne-Marie Thiesse writes.[84] Author of *Paysan français* (1941) in addition to *L'Homme à la bêche*, in the *Revue des deux mondes* he had celebrated "the French leader" who, holding "his authority from his submission to the real,"[85] knew how to end politics and the rule of money in order to restore meaning to the true human and French values, those of the peasantry and Christianity.

Certainly, the ruralist vein, inasmuch as it was a ramification of naturalism, had always been honored in the Goncourt choices: it suffices to cite the names of Émile Moselly, Louis Pergaud, Alphonse de Chateaubriant, and Ernest Pérochon among the prizewinners. The expansion of the regionalist movement during the interwar period had helped establish ruralist literature in the literary field, as Anne-Marie Thiesse has shown: from then on, a chapter would be dedicated to it in the "Panoramas of Contemporary Literature." The Paris international exposition of 1937 devoted to arts and technology marked the national recognition of the movement.[86] In 1938, ruralist literature saw itself thrice consecrated by Parisian authorities; the Femina, the Renaudot, and the Interallié had honored rustic novels: *Campagne* by Raymonde Vincent, *Mervale* by Jean Rogissart, and *La Vallée sans printemps* by Romain Roussel. This recognition was echoed by the most prestigious reviews representing orthodoxy and the rear guard.[87]

As in the case of Pierre Champion, the Goncourt's acknowledgment of this well-known writer defied all the expectations of the Parisian press. It had put forward names like Paul Mousset (*Quand le temps travaillait pour nous*), Jean de Baroncelli (*Vingt-six hommes*), Pierre Béarn (*De Dunkerque à Liverpool*), Georges Blond (*L'Angleterre en guerre*), Yves Dautun (*La Batterie errante*), Roland Tessier (*Le Bar de l'escadrille*), Jacques Benoist-Méchin (*La Moisson de quarante*), and Maurice Betz (*Dialogue des prisonniers*). Most of these books were greatly appreciated by the collaborationist press, which saw them as the confirmation of its theses. Contrasting with this literature devoted to events was the also oft-cited *Thomas l'obscur*, the first novel by a former journalist of the extreme right who had converted to "pure" literature, Maurice Blanchot. "We were a little surprised by the choice," wrote Marcel Espiau in *Les Nouveaux Temps*: "In this way, it seemed that Mr. Henri Pourrat had no other laurels to hope for than a place in a large assembly. And it is 'the Goncourt'—the wartime Goncourt!—that falls to him."[88]

The first declaration delivered by the president Rosny the Younger to the press before the election foreshadowed nothing of this choice. While it clearly displayed the concessions made to the dominant ideology of the moment, it pledged allegiance to the collaborationist press by invoking the politics of collaboration, "European" construction, and the coming of a "European literature":

> At a time when France engages itself, following its leader, in this collaboration that should drive Europe to its highest power, it has been quite interesting to make the inventory of the nation's moral forces [. . .] In addition to the national literature, a European one will be born in France. Let us say that it has already been born [. . .].[89]

Meanwhile, the second declaration, ten days later, marked a reversal: "Among the books submitted to our jury, there are works by elders that show the path to follow toward a common recovery. Will we also reward those books? Will we offer them up as examples?"[90]

Between the two declarations, René Benjamin had returned to Paris. This reversal would also tend to confirm a rumor reported by Galtier-Boissière (whose testimony should nonetheless be handled with caution), who claimed that the choice of a writer "preaching the return to the land" was directly inspired by the Vichy government.[91] René Benjamin's closeness to the head of state tends to substantiate this hypothesis. Like the fact that in the Southern zone, with information taken from Benjamin, the public was better informed: in the *Paris-Soir* prospective, Henri Pourrat was cited at the head of the list of possible prizewinners, even though some of the jurors, notably René Benjamin, were thinking of him to succeed Rosny the Elder rather than for the prize.[92] While the Goncourt Academy demonstrated yet again its ability to adjust to the new dominant ideology, the fumbling is there as a reminder that the conditions for maintaining a position orchestrated with the Vichy regime in the heart of the capital were not obvious.

In exchange for the right to pursue its activities in the capital, had the Goncourt Academy become Vichy's ambassador in Parisian literary milieus? Certainly, the theme of "return to the land," while it did not correspond to the expectations of the young collaborationist guard intoxicated by the "European" perspective, was not about to displease the occupying authorities whom Céline's prose hardly inspired. Didn't the "Germano-European" aesthetic ideal exalt the pantheism of "those writers of the fertile land and of the blessed earth and who were treated scornfully as regionalists, when precisely, in this 'regionalist' literature was born this new sense of contemplation of oneself and of life that, after the military defeat, has begun to show the nation the path it was to follow?"[93] as Karl Rauch explained in the *Cahiers franco-allemands* that same year. And all the less since it harmonized perfectly with the agricultural vocation that conquering Germany assigned to France in a Nazi Europe.

In any case, the declaration of the secretary upon the announcement of the result of the vote leaves no doubt about the national role that the Goncourt Academy assumed by this choice. It foregrounded its concern to meet the expectations of "public opinion" while guiding it:

> At an exceptionally pathetic time, when France looks for itself and aspires to find itself, the Goncourt Academy has preferred to increase the notoriety of an already-known writer whose book of the year, by expressing some of the noblest French values, seems to respond to the desire of a public opinion where the most anxious ones are looking, in a work of art and thought, for a guide and a support.[94]

This consecration would earn the prizewinner a ceremony of honor under the patronage of the marshal: it was held on February 8, 1942, at the Chamalières social hall, in Puy-de-Dôme, in the presence of the minister of agriculture and regional dignitaries.[95] The prize thus brought a literary endorsement to his promotion as official writer of the Vichy regime. He would be named a member of the "Sully-Olivier de Serre" literary jury, founded in 1942 by the state secretary for agriculture and supported by Pétain. Joseph de Pesquidoux also served there, representing the regionalist current of the French Academy.

"Correcting" the Goncourt Prize, as was its habit, the Renaudot Prize went to the journalist Paul Mousset for *Quand le temps travaillait pour nous*, a war novel published by Grasset that reinforced the Anglophobe theses of Vichy. Immediately translated into German and considered by the head of the Amt Schrifttum, Bernhard Payr, as the "best war novel that has appeared in France until now," it would allow its author to become one of the writers actively sustained by the Propaganda-Staffel.[96] Having sold 48,000 copies, its success was less stunning than Pourrat's *Vent de mars* that neared 200,000 copies, but it still led the list of Grasset best sellers during the dark years.[97]

The quasi-spontaneous adjustment of the authorities of consecration to the new values advocated by the Vichy regime, preferably in harmony with German cultural politics when it was a matter of the very Parisian literary prizes, the Goncourt and the Renaudot, illustrates the process of importing heteronomous logics into the heart of the literary field. As hinge authorities between the pole of small-scale production and that of large-scale production, caught between media, editorial, and (due to their quasi-official position) governmental pressures, the literary juries had the difficult task of reconciling the expectations of Vichy with those of a Parisian collaborationist press that increasingly advertized its distance, even its hostility, with respect to a regime that wasn't "revolutionary" enough for its taste. The compromise that they adopted by rewarding authors who designated the zones of agreement, Anglophobia and the "return to the land," suggests the mediating and regulating role that these authorities were able to play, on the cultural plane, between Vichy and the Capital.

A NOISY DISSIDENCE

The reaction of the three protesting men, Descaves, Ajalbert, and Carco, to this new heresy was not long in coming: in a Lyon café, they awarded a "Goncourt free zone" prize to their candidate, Guy des Cars, author of *L'Officier sans nom*. A sign of the crisis situation, the minority of jurors thus found in the circumstances of division into two zones and decentralization a means of legitimating the Academy's schism.

Noisier than the discreet opposition led by Duhamel among the immortals, this dissidence was also less effective, the main objective being to survive on the public scene by maintaining the attention of the press through the use of verbal provocations, noisy protests, and threats of trials. The interpretation of the testament was a public cause that aroused the interest of both legal professionals and journalists. Following Pierre Champion's election, Ajalbert had addressed a letter of protest to the president Rosny the Younger, threatening to pursue legal action in the Conseil d'État. Rosny the Younger replied that "the will of the Goncourt brothers does not exclude the nomination of a member of the Institute, on the condition that he is not an academician from the quai Conti."[98] The authorized literary press took a stand; lawyers were consulted to find out if the cause could be pled. It could, according to Fernand Plas and Maurice Garçon, but before which jurisdiction could the case be brought? The debate raised the question of the Academy's legal status and its vocation. Fernand Plas, for example, recalled the meaning of Edmond de Goncourt's testament:

> We can say with certainty that their will was to create a society absolutely independent of all power and all official institutions by the choice of its members and by its activity [...] it aimed to assemble and help men who lived only for and by literature and whose mission was to promote an independent and "pure" literature as they said then. This was only possible, according to the testators, by erecting the distrust of institutions and powers as a dogma [...] At first, the election of Mr. Pierre Champion looks like a major heresy [...] He is a member of a section of the Institute, has just been named National Counselor, and has been distinguished several times by aca-

demic institutions. We would ignore the fact that he is the mayor of his land, in memory of Jules Renard who was the mayor of his, but we cannot cite more than one fictional work for this historian whose merits are unquestioned. It is contrary to public interest to violate a testament that led to the establishment of an association recognized for its public interest.[99]

Unlike Maurice Garçon, however, Fernand Plas still thought that the Conseil d'État had no rightful jurisdiction over such matters, and that only the courts of law were competent in regards to associations recognized for their public interest. According to Maurice Garçon, future lawyer of the Goncourt Academy, the Conseil d'État was competent if the Goncourt was considered an association, but if it were considered, along with its prize, as the execution of the Goncourts' testament, only the civil court was competent.[100] We must believe that Ajalbert gave up on presenting his petition since I cannot find any trace of a trial in the archives.

If dissidence at the Goncourt had less weight than at the French Academy, it was also because it had no ideological foundation. Ajalbert's political evolution serves as evidence of this, as it threatened to shatter the alliance of the protesters, all without pushing him into the camp of his adversaries at the Academy. This is a sign that the old resentments and particular individual logics trumped ideological complicities.

Initially won over to the new moral order, Ajalbert, a lifelong pacifist, former Briandist, and old partisan of the Franco-German reconciliation, was soon converted to Laval's politics. In Nice at the beginning of 1942, he chaired a talk given by Abel Bonnard.[101] He signed the "Manifesto of French Intellectuals against British Crimes" that appeared on March 9, 1942, in *Le Petit Parisien*. At the end of 1942, he returned to Paris for a Goncourt vote in a special PPF train and declared his support for Doriot's party.[102] Allied with the champions of "European thought," he gave articles to the collaborationist press and set himself apart from his colleagues through his votes at the Academy, without going so far as to betray his old allegiances. He announced that he would give his vote to André Billy and Alphonse de Chateaubriant, director of *La Gerbe*, or to Céline, which he would do, ultimately sacrificing Céline to Chateaubriant, then the latter to Billy. For the prize for 1942, he designated the best seller of the year, the virulently antidemocratic, anti-Semitic, and anticlerical lampoon by Lucien Rebatet, *Les Décombres*.

Ajalbert explicitly located the assembly's division on generational grounds. Since the death of Léon Daudet, he and Lucien Descaves were alone in representing the first generation of the Goncourt. When René Benjamin considered canceling the elections in 1942, Ajalbert settled his score with the new electoral leaders: "Room for the young! We made room for them, as Edmond de Goncourt wished. And now the elders must try to take the helm again and put the neglected ship back on course . . . No elections in 1942? Descaves protests and Francis Carco joins us."[103] Accusing Sacha Guitry of ignorance in the matter of modern novelists, he also did not neglect to recall Benjamin's comments on the eve of his election: he had advised his sponsors that while he would enjoy the oysters at the table of the Ten, he could never face 300 novels a year.

Was it this feeling of being cast aside by the young generation that pushed Ajalbert toward a final reconversion at eighty years old? Everything seems to confirm it, starting with the preponderant role that intergenerational relations played among his preoccupations then. In an article entitled "Long Live the Old! So That the Young Can Live," he made himself the apologist of age that responded to the then-omnipresent thematic of youth:

> Room for the young—or, for the truly young, not those who are old at birth, but room for the old ones who have aged normally, accumulating the treasure of experience and wisdom, that is not inherited in the cradle, and is acquired only in the slow commerce of men and the hard knocks of existence. But room for the old ones who remain young.[104]

Anti-conformism was a good means to stay young for an octogenarian, and his political conversion allowed him to display it. In an article justifying his vote for *Les Décombres*, Ajalbert placed himself on the side of "the avant-garde," in the tradition of Daudet and Descaves, and in the desire to remain faithful to the testament's demand for "originality," according to the split that opposed the extremists of collaboration to literary orthodoxy and Vichy conservatism. On this occasion, he returned to the matter of the prize awarded to Pourrat, without however contesting the literary value of his compatriot from Auvergne:

> All this to make you understand that it is not by a whim, a calculation to make myself singular when, so many times, I was the only cavalryman, separating myself from the majority group trembling before originality and boldness. This is how I voted for Henri Béraud, that I was for Céline, for his first book, with Léon Daudet and Descaves. When my vote, almost alone, went to the first works of Robert Brasillach and Alain Laubreaux, obviously I did not foresee that from pure literature they would leap with one bound to the avant-garde of the militants of *Je suis partout*, with Lucien Rebatet; but starting with the first page, I was not mistaken about first-class writers [. . .] With the war, how could we not push away the pale novel in light of the red

realities in the context of which, by the way, no worthy author has emerged? [...] With Francis Carco and Descaves, I proposed *L'Officier sans nom* by Guy des Cars, which was not without merit, with the luck of being the first [war book] to date. Our colleagues, to general derision, dared to crown Henri Pourrat, an experienced sixty-year-old—whose work of truthful peasantry rather designated to be seated among us—our Pesquidoux.[105]

THE KING, THE YOKEL AND THE "GENDELETTRES"

On December 17, 1942, Rosny the Younger, Benjamin, Guitry, and Ajalbert sat down together at Drouant. The society's financial situation was declared to be excellent.[106] The board was renewed without any change.

Two seats remained to be filled, formerly belonging to Léon Daudet and Pierre Champion, who had died in July 1942. The press released the names of André Billy, Pierre Mac Orlan, Alexandre Arnoux, Lucien Daudet, Henri Béraud, Jean de La Varende, Henri Mondor, Maurice Genevoix, and Henri Pourrat. Mentioned for the prize, among others, were Albert Camus (*L'Étranger*), Elsa Triolet (*Mille Regrets*, proposed by Francis Carco), Audiberti (*Carnage*), Marc Bernard (*Pareil à des enfants*), and Paul Haurigot, whose titles mainly included the fact that the secretary of state for information Paul Marion had tasked him this very year with a mission to study the problems surrounding the book.

The election of Jean Balthazar Mallard, Count of La Varende, to replace Léon Daudet, marked a new victory for the Benjamin-Guitry clan. Their candidate won with five votes, those that had supported Pierre Champion and Henri Pourrat, against Ajalbert and Carco's two votes for André Billy, and Descaves's vote for Lucien Daudet, Léon's younger brother, in tribute to his old brother-enemy. The fact that a royalist succeeded the celebrated royalist lampoonist was not at all surprising. But Jean de La Varende, a Norman nobleman, royalist, and Catholic who had never recognized the institutions or laws of the Republic, was for other reasons a very unorthodox recruit for the Goncourt. He admirably embodied the figure of the amateur "lord," and a wealthy one at that, such as Edmond de Goncourt had banished from his academy. René Benjamin exulted at the trick played on Descaves: "It is after all a master stroke. A rich man! A man in a castle! A lord! Everything that is forbidden in the testament read by Descaves."[107] When, the following year, Maurice Martin du Gard, a friend of Sacha Guitry, would unsuccessfully approach Paul Léautaud in advance about a candidacy to the Ten, he would give the following explanation: "It is because Sacha notices that with La Varende, another millionaire was named..."[108]

He owed his fortune more to literature than to his rents. Descended from a line of navy officers, grandson of the rear admiral Camille de Langle, La

Varende was born in 1887. Having lost his father at an early age, he attended the collège Saint-Vincent de Rennes; then, having followed his mother to Neuilly, he was received fifth at the École des beaux-arts. After his marriage in 1919, he reclaimed possession of his ancestral home, the manor of Bonneville-Chamblac, neighboring the domain of the Duke de Broglie, of the French Academy, whom he called his "lord." There, he occupied himself with writing, building a collection of model naval constructions, and personally restoring his crumbling castle. It was literary success that saved him from financial asphyxia. After having published tales in the *Mercure de France*, he met with eight consecutive rejections before seeing *Pays d'Ouche* printed at Mme Maugard, in Rouen, with a preface by the Duke de Broglie; the book would win the Vikings Prize in 1936. He accumulated three votes (from Daudet, Larguier, and Dorgelès) in 1937 at the Goncourt vote, for *Nez-de-cuir* (Plon), a huge best seller. The following year, he obtained the Prize for the Novel from the French Academy for *Le Centaure de Dieu* (Grasset).

His body of work, completely devoted to celebrating Ancien Régime society and to the nostalgic description of the decline of the caste of squireling, drew from the historical novel, the epic, legend, and the provincial novel. He intended it as "an homage to an entire race, to an entire unrecognized social class, to my province so deeply betrayed by Maupassant."[109] In *Les Manants du roi* (Plon, 1938), he also paid tribute to Action française because it gave new life to sentimental monarchism, and evoked the dilemma that Catholics felt after its condemnation by Rome. Despite the awkwardness of style unanimously recognized by critics, even the most positive,[110] Robert Brasillach could admire in the work of this "last feudal," whom he admitted to having initially resisted, "the familiar feeling of greatness," "the authentic tufa, the vigor, the muscular robustness," and Thierry Maulnier could praise "our writer who knows best how to attain poetry and epic simplicity in the painting of great souls, their violent and generous actions and their savage gentleness."[111] "Yes, in truth, Jean de La Varende is of the race of his heroes," Brasillach added.[112] The epithets referring to the corporal hexis, "magnificent," "superb," "flamboyant," "high elegance," used, by metonymy, sometimes to qualify the work, sometimes to trace the moral portrait of this character who seemed to have emerged from a history book, say a great deal about the fascination that the aristocracy exercised, above and beyond Action française, on the bourgeois and petty bourgeois "gendelettres."

Under the Occupation, La Varende was one of the most widely distributed authors and was among the eleven authors translated in Germany between 1941 and 1943. He published his prose in *Le Petit Parisien*, *Je suis partout*, and *Gringoire*, where he was, as we saw, one of the best-paid authors. After his election, he would give an article to the *Cahiers franco-allemands* in which he called on youth to accept the defeat with the humility of a sinner who atones for his sins and to restore, within the framework of the National Revolution, the values of honor and authority founded on the family and on "the accepted inequality [that] is generative of love."[113]

Didn't La Varende displace himself socially by sitting down with these petty bourgeois "gendelettres"? With the help of the "party of the Dukes," couldn't he legitimately aspire to a seat among the Forty? A letter from Mgr Baudrillart had nonetheless warned him that he would have an interest in limiting his production: "You must conserve its rarity, especially if you come among us."[114] A costly restriction for an author who had published no fewer than six books in 1938. Furthermore, according to his biographer,

> René Benjamin's proposition erased something in La Varende that he could not free himself from despite his successes: the feeling of being an amateur. The French Academy was the sure move, a foregone conclusion [...] the man of the dukes was worth as much there as the literary man, whereas the Goncourt Academy, so professional, made him smile despite himself: if it called him, wasn't it because it considered him a real writer?[115]

Was his election at the French Academy a foregone conclusion? History would prove the opposite when, in 1954, La Varende, who had resigned from the Goncourt Academy after the ratification of André Billy's election in 1944, could not gather more than eleven votes among the Forty with his candidacy.[116] Maybe he wasn't more than a squireling next to de Broglie, after all ... And then, he *had* been part of the Goncourt Academy.

The election to fill Pierre Champion's vacant seat was returned sine die after two ballots. The two rival clans had not succeeded in imposing their respective candidates. Paul Fort, the "prince of poets," was the candidate who the Guitry-Benjamin-Rosny the Younger trio had decided to oppose to André Billy this time. Billy, meanwhile, was still supported by Descaves, Ajalbert, and Carco. At the age of seventy, this friend of Lucien and of Sacha Guitry,[117] the author of *Ballades françaises* was bursting with activity: he published his poetry in Drieu La Rochelle's NRF, his prose in *Les Nouveaux Temps* and hosted a literary program on Radio-Paris. A member of the Académie Mallarmé, he was also part of the jury for the Prize of the *Nouvelle France*, founded in 1941, which assembled Pierre Benoit, Abel Hermant, Abel Bonnard, Sacha Guitry, La Varende, Mac Orlan, Drieu La Rochelle, and a few others. Jean Tharaud had declared the night before that he did not wish to be elected; while Dorgelès and Larguier had voted for him, because of this news, votes could not cluster around his name. During the first round, Pierre Mac Orlan obtained Carco's vote, and Alphonse de Chateaubriant, the director of *La Gerbe*, had garnered Ajalbert's.

On December 19, Marc Bernard managed to temporarily reconcile the opposing camps. *Pareil à des enfants* (Gallimard), a novel inspired by his working-class childhood, won the prize for 1942 with seven votes (Rosny the Younger, Benjamin, Guitry, La Varende, Carco, Dorgelès, and Larguier). This choice, which renewed the Goncourt tradition, satisfied the members in the Southern zone. Marc Bernard was part of the circle that met every evening at the Grand Café de Nîmes, with Léo Larguier and François de Roux, who had barely lost the Goncourt Prize for 1938. Descaves and Ajalbert continued to show their opposition. The first voted for a woman, Germaine Beaumont, for *Du côté d'où viendra le jour*. The second voted, as we saw, for *Les Décombres* by Lucien Rebatet.

Forty-two years old, originally from Nîmes like Larguier, Marc Bernard was the son of a miner and worked for the railroad and as a laborer before 1928, when Henri Barbusse opened the doors to journalism by hiring him at his weekly, *Monde*.[118] A former militant for the Communist Party, he was part of the Group of Proletarian Writers, along with Henry Poulaille, Tristan Rémy, Louis Guilloux, Eugène Dabit, and Édouard Peisson; this group differentiated itself from the Association des écrivains et artistes révolutionnaires (AEAR) of Communist inspiration.[119] After having received the Interallié Prize in 1934 for his novel *Anny*, he distanced himself from proletarian literature while continuing his anti-Fascist engagement. In 1937–1938, he was in charge of the "literary" section of Mai 36, the Socialist cultural organization that competed with the AEAR.

The Goncourt Prize, which allowed the Bernard family to leave Nîmes, saved his wife Elsé, of Jewish origin; the German police went to arrest her on the day after their departure.[120] The impoverished conditions in which the Bernard family lived were certainly known, at least by Larguier. But if Marc Bernard obtained the majority of the Ten, when he did not gain the approval of all of his peers, it was either due to an exchange of favors (didn't Larguier and Dorgelès give their votes to the Benjamin-Guitry candidates?), or because the author had offered them bribes. One of these does not exclude the other; on the contrary. Those who like Louis Guilloux and Elsa Triolet were more politically identified as aligned with the anti-Fascist left, and especially Communism, had little chance of being nominated under these political circumstances. For his part, Marc Bernard had broken off his Socialist engagements in 1940. After the armistice, he proposed in vain to Gaston Gallimard that he found a weekly entitled *Renaissance* in the Southern zone. He shared his views with Jean Grenier, whom he met in Nîmes in December 1940, views that he had moreover devel-

oped in three essays, "On Freedom of Thought," "On Inequality," "On Faith";
the second was published in *La NRF* in October 1941:

> [...] in July 40, he got a shock and felt his ideas solidify around the new re-
> gime. There is no need to hypnotize yourself with a feeling of fidelity. When
> you have recognized your error, you must change your opinion [...] Ine-
> quality is a necessary thing and the regime of castes is the only right one. The
> people desire only material satisfactions. Men who are part of the elite and
> who are born in the people are mistaken in thinking a social revolution neces-
> sary. This is a myth. There will always be castes, for example in the USSR.
>
> [...] The only problem that must be posed is how to make the best indi-
> viduals emerge from the people. Marc Bernard is thus not only very favor-
> able to the new government, but he even finds it too lukewarm and criticizes
> it for employing people who are, deep down, its adversaries.[121]

The Nazi terror, the massive arrest of emigrants, aided and abetted by the Vichy
police, and probably also the threat that weighed on his wife would extinguish
his infatuation for the new regime, as the letter he wrote to Grenier on September 23, 1942, would prove: "What barbarity! This is new, that a vanquished
country makes itself the executor of the menial tasks of the vanquishing country, dishonoring itself with the latter."[122] But this disengagement was certainly
not know to all the Goncourt jurors. Withdrawn to Saint-Julien, in 1944 Marc
Bernard would engage himself in the Resistant movement Francs-Tireurs et
partisans (FTP) and would write reports for their newspaper, the *Combat des
Patriotes*.

The Renaudot Prize for 1942 was given to Robert Gaillard for his romantic
novel *Les Liens de chaînes*, which was published by Colbert. Three votes went
to Marc Bernard and one to Audiberti.[123] Born in Saintes (Charente-Maritime)
of a geometrician father, Robert Gaillard, now thirty-three years old, had been
a journalist since 1927 and had been, among other things, editor in chief of
L'Ami du peuple, a daily with a very large distribution belonging to the perfume
manufacturer François Coty, leader of the Fascist party Solidarité française. A
disappointed member of the populist literature movement led by Léon Lemon-
nier and André Thérive, which competed with the "proletarian writers," Robert
Gaillard had left with Marcel Sauvage in 1939 in order to found the "vitalist
school." Criticizing populism for its use of slang and its ignorance of the peasant
novel, and naturalism for its scientific method, vitalism advocated a concrete
spoken language that would "marry the natural to the correction" and have recourse to folklore, the "great tradition of popular imagination" that contained
natural wisdom.[124] Imprisoned at the Stalag IX A, Robert Gaillard befriended

François Mitterand, whom he mentioned in *Mes évasions*. This book was published in 1941 by Debresse with a preface from the state secretary for information, Paul Marion. Freed from the stalag,[125] beginning in mid-1942 he wrote the "Prisoners" column in the weekly *Révolution nationale*. In 1943, Robert Gaillard would be entrusted with literary services at the general police station for prisoners. While the Renaudot jury hurried to beat the Goncourt Academy in rewarding the work of a prisoner, it also caught up with the Goncourt and even surpassed it in allegiance to the regime.

In this time of shortage, especially of paper, the impact of literary prizes was of course threatened. For an editor, winning the Goncourt Prize was then a "dreadful happiness," as *Le Figaro* critic Maurice Noël wrote; he had discussed this topic with Gaston Gallimard shortly after the designation of Henri Pourrat in 1941: the honored book's success threatened to exhaust the stocks of paper. "The Goncourt Prize is now priceless," a journalist would observe in 1942, after failing to procure a copy of Marc Bernard's novel.[126] The Goncourt Academy, in the person of its president, intervened at the beginning of 1943 with the prefect-delegate of the Ministry of the Interior in the occupied territories to obtain a special attribution of twenty tons of paper so that the book it had just awarded could be reprinted. Once notified, the organizing committee of the industries of art and commerce of the book approved the request, although it only granted 7.5 tons, in addition to the normal contingent attributed to Gallimard, and the publisher was authorized to proceed with a reprint of 25,000 copies.[127]

THE LAW OF THE FITTEST

The beginning of 1943 marked the turning point of World War II. Starting with the allied landing in North Africa, it was confirmed by the surrender of the German troops in Stalingrad in February 1943. Already, a number of those who had engaged in collaboration adopted a position of retreat. The rumor of reprisals to come was already spreading in the intellectual milieus. "There will surely be frictions between lots of people, in the case of an Anglo-American victory, between politicians and especially between writers. Now the E . . . , L . . . , Claudel, U . . . , will want to cast aside their colleagues who have been more or less collaborationist," Paul Léautaud wrote in his *Journal* on November 24, 1942.[128] "They will shoot all the 'collaborationists,'" Galtier-Boissière told him a few days later.[129] The threats didn't take long to concretize: the sending of small coffins, warnings in the underground press. One of those warnings, in the underground *Lettres françaises*, the forum for a group of underground writers that would take the name of Comité national des écrivains, was addressed to the Goncourt Academy after La Varende's election:

For a few years now, alas, the Goncourt Academy has enhanced publicity more than literature and the Ten are only there for scandal. But this year, the matter is much graver [...] the Ten have elected LA VARENDE, collaborator with the enemy. The Goncourt Academy will have to account for itself; this must be stated exactly from now on. Neither the two upright writers who have founded it, nor HUYSMANS, nor MIRBEAU, nor GEFFROY, nor ROSNY (the Elder and the only one) who were its former members would have allowed its influence to be used against French thought and against the soul of the nation.[130]

Vitriolic portraits of the incriminated jurors were traced in the "echoes" section of *Les Lettres françaises*.

ROSNY THE YOUNGER—With no more character than talent [...]

AJALBERT—Literary appraisal worthless. Parasite who lived off of missions begged for from Briand. Lacking works, he sold his vote for every Goncourt Prize, before selling his soul to Doriot.

René BENJAMIN—After having insulted the French in general, the teachers in particular, made himself the solemn and comical adulator of the worst enemies of our land. Has written of Mussolini that he was the greatest lyric poet of the century, of Maurras and Pétain that they are the honor of France.

Sacha GUITRY—[...] (who owed his seat at the Goncourt Academy to his promise that he would bequeath it his sumptuous mansion) is one of the active agents of the collaborating fraction of this Assembly.

And, under the title "Disqualified," the anonymous author specified:

[...] It is not acceptable that, after the victory, the men who lived in the spirit of betrayal during the enemy occupation can still have the least influence on the French public.[131]

It is in this context that we must resituate the new division generated by the secret debates surrounding Pierre Champion's replacement in December 1943. The minutes of the 264th meeting of the literary society were never recorded. Instead we find the minutes of the 265th meeting, which was held on December 11, 1943, at the home of Sacha Guitry, in the presence of only Guitry and Benjamin. Rosny the Younger and La Varende were represented. Despite article 8 of the statutes and article 14 of the internal ruling that "demands the presence or the representation of at least six members of the Assembly to validate the deliberations of the Assembly," the assembly declared itself "regularly constituted" by virtue of the law of February 5, 1943 (article 2, paragraph 1), that declared "exceptionally valid the declarations taken by the majority of the members present or represented."[132] The only recorded decision concerned adjourning the powers of the board members presently in office.

The election of Pierre Champion's replacement had nonetheless taken place. The vote was held by correspondence. André Billy won this time, with five votes against four for Paul Fort. The "swing votes" of Dorgelès and Larguier abandoned the Benjamin-Guitry camp, now reinforced by La Varende, instead shifting to the Descaves, Carco, and Ajalbert camp. Was it the warning of *Les Lettres françaises*, was it the evolution of "public opinion," one not excluding the other? It was those votes, belonging to the agents disposing of the weakest resources in the internal power relations during that period, that made the Academy evolve in a way that was very much adapted to the course of events. The attitude of Benjamin and Guitry, strengthened by the support of the occupying authorities, nonetheless shows that the conditions of heteronomous production were still ripe, which meant that anything was permitted to disqualify an adversary. The non-proclamation of the election of André Billy was a resounding demonstration of this.

It was once again the testament and the literary argument that had been emphasized during the debates that preceded the election. La Varende thus wrote to the president Rosny the Younger that Edmond de Goncourt had always wanted to keep critics out of his academy.[133] For his part, Benjamin had, as early as July 1943, warned Dorgelès of Guitry and La Varende's contempt for Billy, and had made him aware of his own antipathy. He specified: "Some of us (and Rosny agrees) will not allow even the thought of introducing a critic among us."[134] This clarification, which sounded like a threat, illustrates the universalization of passions. The structural resentment of writers with regard to critics could legitimately be converted into contempt, through a reversal that used the defense of the interests of creators, as a group, against their censors as an excuse. This is how the generalization of the particular experience of these authors whom the critic had formerly mistreated was accomplished.

Only the most informed initiates were apt to unmask this rhetoric, and they didn't hesitate to do so. The reduction of the adversary's arguments to special interests sufficed to disqualify them. Thus the game of representations was made and unmade, always in the mode of gossip and malicious rumor, and according to the rules of the game, the winner being the one who has the means to make his credibility prevail, either through the disinterest that his position presumes, or through the circuit of legitimation that he is able to mobilize. In the case that concerns us, the result of the election, kept secret from the public, was immediately known in the literary milieu. On December 22, André Billy wrote to Léautaud:

> No newspaper has told the truth yet on the little present-day Goncourt crisis. The truth is quite simply that I have five votes, against four to Paul Fort, and that I am virtually elected, but the President, who does not support me, has deferred the election on various bad pretexts and to please Sacha who, it seems, threatens to resign if my election is announced. It is as simple and as dirty as that. I criticized Sacha and La Varende a long time ago, and moreover Sacha must hold me responsible for the *Figaro* campaign against him.[135]

This was also the opinion of Lucien Descaves, according to whom La Varende had not forgiven Billy for a scathing criticism against him in *L'Œuvre*, with Benjamin holding a grudge against him "for having always misjudged his literary genius."[136] Certainly, Billy and Descaves were interested parties in the debate, but they were all the more able to accredit this version of the facts— which everything else also tends to confirm—since their adversaries were doubly suspect in the literary milieus. Suspect because of the relentlessness with which they disqualified a peer, without regard for the rules of the literary game and the law. Suspect also of sacrificing literary autonomy to ideological interests. This was the meaning of the short item that the underground *Lettres françaises* published on the affair before even knowing the outcome: "Discord reigns [. . .] at the Ten, whose President, Rosny the Younger, refuses to proceed with the election of the successor to Pierre Champion because his collaborationist fraction finds itself incapable of ensuring the success of its candidate, the anti-Semite Paul Fort."[137] And should we see a simple coincidence in the fact that a few months later, in May 1944, the French Academy awarded the Grand Prize for Literature to André Billy?

The fact that the news of the unannounced election did not filter into the press of the Northern zone was another consequence of the conditions of heteronomy that, as we know, favor payback. In November 1943, Galtier-Boissière attributed "to the resentment of authors whose books Billy found bad in his literary criticism, all the disagreeable notes that are published on him in the newspapers on this side."[138] We must relate these conditions to the virulent accents of the press at the Liberation; it would not neglect its turn to tarnish the image of the fallen masters of the hour, but for other reasons. The Billy affair, among others, gave them the raw material. While this election was the product of the reworking of alliances that began at the turning point in the war, only the reversal of power relations in the political field would be able to make the law triumph. André Billy's election was confirmed on December 23, 1944. Curiously, it was not five but six votes that were counted for him, the minutes clarifying that the president J.-H. Rosny the Younger had finally joined the majority! Everything tends to prove that this alliance followed the election (it is even very probable that Rosny the Younger had made his preponderant vote as president work in an abusive manner to block the election), and that it was very circumstantial. This would also be the case for the Goncourt Prize for 1944, awarded in 1945 to Elsa Triolet for *Le Premier accroc coûte deux cents francs*, which included a short story, "Les Amants d'Avignon," that had been published by the underground Éditions de Minuit (I will return to this). Wasn't it time to disprove the journalist of *Au pilori* who praised the Goncourt Academy in 1941 for having adopted as a rule: "No women and no Jews"?[139]

Even though the dominant ideology under Vichy was hardly favorable to it, critics had taken notice of what was then called the "feminine novel."[140] The names Elsa Triolet, Simone de Beauvoir, Dominique Rolin, Maria Le Hardouin, Alice Rivaz, and Marguerite Duras, and Dominique Bréjon de Lavergnée, among others, bore witness to this trend (Nathalie Sarraute's discreet entry into the literary field on the eve of the war would only be brought to the public's attention when *Portrait d'un inconnu* was published in 1948, prefaced by Sartre, after a period of forced silence because of her Jewish origins).[141] A consequence of the recent development of women's education,[142] this phenomenon was not viewed unfavorably by critics like Thierry Maulnier, on the condition that "feminine literature" remain confined to its particularism and that it did not become an instrument of emancipation.[143] An irony of fate, it was in reference to Simone de Beauvoir's *L'Invitée* that he made this reflection, congratulating her for not having fallen victim to this error:

> There is a feminine style in literature, a determinism of feminine nature and condition so powerful that, from Louise Labé and Mme de Lafayette [...] up to Colette, no one, to my knowledge, has escaped it, and the greatness of great female writers has consisted not in freeing themselves of this condition and this nature, but in bringing, by acuteness of intelligence, the intensity of felt and transcribed emotions, finally the beauty of language, the properly feminine problems above and beyond what they can have in themselves, in their ordinary forms, of the mediocre and the limited, to the level of universal anguish, of elementary pain and joy, of the eternal interrogation of destiny.[144]

There was quite some distance between this assessment and recognizing women's right to rise up as judges of their masculine peers. Lucien Descaves, a militant feminist during the interwar period (he had been vice president of the

Ligue française du droit des femmes), who had sponsored the election of the first female academician, Judith Gautier, had been trying for a long time to promote a female candidate for the prize, just as he had been trying to get Colette elected since the 1930s. He would succeed at the latter in 1945: women's newly obtained right to vote was finally a national event of sufficient scale for the Ten to go beyond their ancestral misogyny and double its echo! I must mention the fact that, since 1943, Colette's candidacy had been proposed by Claude Farrère at the French Academy, which for its part would wait until 1980 to welcome its first female member, Marguerite Yourcenar.

The name of Elsa Triolet, who began to publish her novelistic work in French in 1938, had already been mentioned for the prize for 1942, and she had received one vote for the Deux Magots Prize the same year. She collected one vote for *Le Cheval blanc* (Denoël), thanks to Carco, during the election for the prize for 1943; it would be awarded by correspondence, with three months' delay, to Marius Grout for *Passage de l'homme* (Gallimard), with five votes versus four.[145] She nearly paid for that vote with her life. That very day, March 21, 1944, the ss Heinz Röthke, one of the commanders of the Gestapo and of the Germany security service (SD) in France, sent the following order to the head of the Gestapo in Marseille: "Arrest immediately [...] the Jew Elsa Kagan known as Triolet, mistress of one named Aragon, also a Jew."[146] Fortunately, the couple had just left the region for Paris.

Another sign that the hour for recognizing women writers was approaching: in March, Simone de Beauvoir was approached by her publisher, Gallimard, to present her first book, *L'Invitée*, to the Goncourt jury. This effort was fruitless, but she was well placed for the Renaudot, which the doctor André Soubiran won a few days later. Through Sartre, she had received, on the condition of granting neither articles nor interviews to the press, the approval of the underground Comité national des écrivains (CNE).[147] Thus while the CNE had already established itself as an authority in the literary field, it still had to reckon with the traditional authorities, however compromised, or risk its exclusion from the game.

Reflecting the civil war that was raging, Carco's vote for Elsa Triolet had its counterpart, along with votes for two other women, Thyde Monnier (*Nans le berger*, Julliard) and Albine Léger (pseudonym of Albine Loisy, translator of John Dos Passos and author of *Elissa* published at Laffont): this was Ajalbert's vote, which went to the militia man Philippe Henriot (*Ici, Radio France*), named state secretary for information and propaganda in January 1944, at the Germans' insistence. Serving in a puppet government, he contributed to the advent of the milita state before being cut down by the Resistance on June 28.

Ajalbert would make a last tribute to the memory of this "martyr of European Thought" of whom "no one has been able to kill [the] thought that offers itself inextinguishably to history, in the collection of his 'talks,' from a writer worthy of the orator," and who would be "read like Demosthenes, Cicero, Bossuet." Ajalbert moreover congratulated himself for having voted for Henriot as he had voted for *Les Décombres*.[148] If not for the tragic circumstances of the civil war that saw the militia aid and abet the German troops in their struggle against the Resistance, the vote obtained by the first official propagandist of a state taken over by Fascism would seem like a burlesque avatar of the Academy's double ambition of being officialized and guiding opinion.

Between scandal and conformism, the attitude of the Goncourt jurors during the Occupation was, just like the situation of the Academy, torn between a media logic and the academicism toward which it tended, propelled by its propensity to become official. Its double concern of playing a national role and remaining involved in current events or risk seeing itself marginalized led it, in a time of crisis, to inscribe itself in the problematic of the hour and echo the dominant ideology. But the gap between the extreme and contradictory preferences of some of its members (Rebatet, Henriot on one side, Triolet on the other) and the compromises (which we might call "middling" or "median") that settle internal negotiations illustrates the common work of "neutralization" and "depoliticization." This work meant that the ideological meaning of the jurors' collective choices was never immediately perceptible. It was all the less so since the logic of alliances and oppositions arose more often from literary strategies and struggles for influence than from ideological stakes. All the less so, too, because the Academy sometimes honored a work less than its author, and that it was through a transfer of legitimacy—of a work that may appear politically, if not ideologically, "neutral" to its author, who was himself politically "situated"— that the mediation between literature and politics works here. In this respect, the Goncourt Academy greatly contributed to the legitimation of those writers close to or favorable to the regime. Whereas at the French Academy, the internal power relation was reversed as early as 1942, at the Goncourt Academy it was stabilized at the turning point of the war and wouldn't be reversed until the Liberation.

CHAPTER 6

The Sense of Distinction

The *"NRF Spirit"*

Otto Abetz paid a singular homage to *La NRF* by authorizing it, alone among all the reviews, to reappear in the occupied zone. The de jure ratification of the monopoly that the NRF had come to exercise de facto as an authority of consecration in the field of limited production could appear as the somewhat parodic culmination of its process of concentrating symbolic capital, were it not for the redirection of this capital to promote the normalization of the situation of occupation. The fact that in the name of "art for art's sake" the authority that had best embodied the principle of autonomy in the literary field for three decades would ultimately serve to reinforce the conditions of heteronomy imposed upon literature, in the very act of dissimulating them, was not the least of the paradoxes that the crisis situation exposed. This paradox would seem to bolster those who, like Aragon, then denounced in the very principle of "art for art's sake" those deceptive "clouds" that mask the material conditions of existence. Marx could not have imagined a more beautiful textbook case.

But a question arises: was Drieu's NRF actually *La NRF*? Certainly, Drieu La Rochelle took power at *La NRF* thanks to heteronomous conditions of production. It is thus possible to speak of usurpation. With one condition, however: that we remember that Gallimard encouraged the maneuver, that Drieu was not an illegitimate pretender to the editorial direction of the review, and that if he was a fraud, he was a well-founded fraud who won the consent of an entire fraction of the old team at the review. Upon the announcement of the reappearance of *La NRF*, the initial reaction of writers tended toward the thesis of usurpation, partly accredited by the eviction of its former director. Paul Léautaud, who would be a diligent contributor, told Jean Paulhan of his surprise to see the return of a review title belonging to Gallimard. Paulhan answered him: "Were the Germans ashamed to take *Paris-Soir*? Drieu La Rochelle proposed a differ-ent *Nouvelle Revue française* to them. They said yes, that's all."[1]

But unlike *Paris-Soir*, a forgery of the daily, now housed in the Southern zone, which the Germans launched in the occupied zone, Drieu's NRF was en-tirely "authentic." It was a pure "house" product, where no text was imposed by the acting powers, where the rules of the game were apparently respected (texts were published with their author's agreement), and that moreover offered itself the luxury, unequaled during that time, of enjoying a greater freedom on the condition of not saying anything bad about the Germans. Censorship inter-vened only very incidentally, according to the promise Abetz made to Drieu. The latter furthermore used this argument to convince the writers whom he approached, like Paul Léautaud, who recorded his conversation with the new director of the review:

> I ask him if he wouldn't be held to what we might call moral considerations. He laughs: "Not at all, never" [...] I ask him the Germans' conditions for him with respect to the review. He answers me: "Absolutely free. I have known Abetz for a long time; he is Hitler's ambassador, who has lived many years in France." (I held back from saying "Parbleu!") [...] "I told him: 'Here it is. I make the review appear, as a means of propaganda, but I alone am the master. You have nothing to do with it or impose on it. If not, I quit everything, and we will both be ridiculous.' "[2]

Drieu La Rochelle could also make the claim that Gallimard had refused the entry of German capital, and that the review's contributors were paid by its publisher.

Insofar as an entire fraction of the review's former contributors recognized themselves in its new version, and for a number of newcomers its identity went unquestioned, Drieu could rightfully plead the case of *La NRF*'s continuity. Just like when he inscribed the space allotted to current events and politics within the tradition of *La NRF* since the Great War. While he broke with the pluralism that had characterized the editorial line of *La NRF* in this domain at least until 1938, some imputed the responsibility for this break to Jean Paulhan himself. By making *La NRF* adopt an anti-Munich position, he supposedly gave it a political orientation before Drieu did. Support of the politics of collaboration would then be only the counterpart, and therefore the consequence of this orienta-tion. But it was here that the thesis of continuity faltered. The review's anti-Munich stance at a time when the Munich agreement was received by popular opinion with that "cowardly relief" that Léon Blum described was anchored in the critical tradition of *La NRF*. Can we compare it to a line that meant to be the embodiment of the politics of the acting powers, a "means of propaganda" as Drieu said? The question was not posed in exactly those terms, moreover. The conditions of production had changed. As Paulhan explained to Marcel Arland:

> [...] every judgment gets mixed up here with a prognosis. If victory and the German influence should last for six months, Dr[ieu]'s attempt is hateful: it is the *Gazette des Ardennes*. If we should have it for a hundred years, it is on the contrary ingenious, bold, necessary. Now Drieu believes, and has always believed, in the hundred years. (In what measure is hope a duty, this is another question, not very simple).[3]

In favor of the thesis of fraud, the writers of "refusal" rightly invoked the fact that the "art for art's sake" argument was exploited for extrinsic purposes, even though others' satisfaction with this argument echoed the tradition of elevating the artist above "vulgar" social conditions, as cultivated by *La NRF*. Deception was also present in the gap between the advertised claim of continuity with the previous review, and the obvious breaks that Drieu made with the successive editorial politics of Jacques Rivière and Jean Paulhan by transgressing some of the principles they shared: the preeminence of literary value over all other types of criteria, critical tradition, the principle of unity in diversity, perhaps also the Gidian principle of sincerity. Not that Drieu was insincere. Paulhan moreover proclaimed his sincerity to anyone who wanted to listen. In this, Drieu was a faithful imitator of André Gide, as he was also a typical product of this cult of originality at any price that *La NRF* brought to its paroxysm even in the political domain. But the manipulation that founded the review's project made it depart, in its very principle, from this role.

The reappearance of *La NRF* divided the review's team, and the literary field as a whole, between two stances. First, there were those who proclaimed themselves favorable to the pursuit of literary activity under duress, sometimes in the name of "art for art's sake," sometimes in the name of maintaining the "French spirit." They were opposed by the partisans of abstention, the writers of "refusal," who saw it as a means of legitimizing the situation of occupation. This principle of division surpassed political divisions: while the most engaged of the writers who participated in Drieu's venture were collaborationists, a number of those who figured in the table of contents considered themselves apolitical. This must be related to the positions occupied in the literary field, to the specific interests associated with each of the options, and to the very institutional logics according to which the *NRF* schism occurred. The choices were not completely settled when the review reappeared, either. The hesitations (of Jean

Grenier, François Mauriac, and André Gide), the precocious reversals (of Gide, Valéry, and Eluard), the later and more discreet departures (of Arland or André Rolland de Renéville), the new recruits, the young poets of the École de Rochefort, testified to an evolution that was neither linear nor one-dimensional. The ultimate failure of the venture cannot be read solely in the mirror of events. It was tightly linked to the fragmented literary field's mode of recomposition around the small semi-legal reviews that contested the NRF monopoly. They benefited in this from the support of those who challenged the hijacking of heritage realized by Drieu's NRF. At the pole of small-scale production that interests us here, this recomposition occurred on the basis of the defense of its autonomy. The reunification of the voices of dispersed writers was its first condition. It then passed through struggles for the reappropriation of the "French spirit." It was this vocation that these small reviews, allied in a common opposition to La NRF, would assume.

A Place of "Pure" Literature: La NRF

The power of consecration that La NRF had conquered was, as we know, the defining fact of literary life in the interwar period. Legitimacy and power to consecrate can be measured both by the reverence, even the veneration, that a school, a circle, a review inspires, and the vehemence of the attacks leveled against it. We would have to be able to cite all the metaphors, often borrowed from the religious register, that served to characterize La NRF: "In literature, it was my Bible" (François Mauriac); "I penetrated into the holiest of holies" (Jean Cassou); "the empyrean of literature" (Pierre Emmanuel); "It was [...] the sanctuary of literature, the Pantheon of living writers" (André Wurmser).[4] As for the attacks, whose substance we already saw in chapter 2, the sole acknowledgment of their persistence, over twenty years, along with the new passion of its detractors after the defeat, suffices to recall the intellectual hegemony it exercised. Those detractors, in fact, seemed to be revived by the shipwreck of the Republic and the concurrent sinking of the review.

But the review did not escape the process of social aging. While it managed to adjust to the transformations of the literary field and appropriate its most opposed currents almost to the point of embodying that field, its "spirit" had become routinized,[5] its power of consecration became institutionalized, to such an extent that it lost its specificity. Jean Paulhan's editorial policy on the eve of the war managed to temporarily halt this process: it largely determined the modes of restructuring the literary field under the Occupation and set a lasting new course for novelistic writing. But the resumption of La NRF by

Drieu La Rochelle and the conflicts that it generated (political conflicts and conflicts of succession) definitively accelerated the process: the review would not know how or would not be able to endow itself with any project that wasn't political, and saw itself condemned to record rather than dictate the new tendencies in literature. And if the hijacking of the symbolic capital formerly accumulated by *La NRF* in favor of the politics of collaboration was fraudulent, the failure of this venture is also an avatar of the process of institutionalization and social aging from which the review would not recover (*La Nouvelle NRF* that Jean Paulhan and Marcel Arland would launch in 1953 would regain neither the position nor the function that belonged to its ancestor).

THE AESTHETIC LOGIC

The symbolic capital accumulated by *La NRF* must be related, on the one hand, to its editorial policy and, on the other, to the properties of its contributors. The circle of little-known authors that formed, before the Great War, around André Gide drew its strength from a relative financial autonomy that allowed it, following the model of *Le Mercure de France*, to equip itself with substantial means of production: a review, and soon a publishing house.[6] Inversely, this relative financial autonomy and the power of consecration that the review rapidly acquired as the showcase and brand image of the publishing house that owed it its prestige conferred its team with a true power of negotiation susceptible to counterbalance the commercial logic within a business that experienced formidable expansion in the interwar period.[7]

Having reappeared at the end of the Great War under the direction of Jacques Rivière, *La NRF*, which then had a circulation of 5,500 copies, including 2,000 subscriptions, saw this number almost double in a few years.[8] While the number of subscribers was still far from the 8,000 that Jean Paulhan expected when he succeeded Jacques Rivière, who had died prematurely, in 1925, it continued to grow under his direction by nearly 1,000 a year (but would never reach 10,000).[9] In 1928, the review's circulation would reach about 12,000 copies, according to estimates, which situated it, like the *Mercure de France*, halfway between the avant-garde magazines, which hardly printed more than 3,000 subscriptions, and the pole of "academic" consecration represented by the *Revue des deux mondes*, which then printed about 40,000 copies.[10] From then on, *La NRF* tended to establish itself as the monopoly-holder for the power of consecration. It positioned itself as a competitor among the authorities whose role traditionally included this function, the French Academy and the Goncourt Academy, differentiating itself from them through its double rejection of "good taste" and "vulgar" Naturalism. It also eclipsed its principal rival, *Le Mercure de*

France directed by Alfred Valette, then, after his death in 1935, by Georges Du-hamel, sending it back to the rear guard. But the founders of *La NRF* belonged to the symbolist generation that had gathered around the *Mercure*: most of its famous contributors, André Gide and Paul Claudel in particular, cut their criti-cal teeth there, and in the beginning *La NRF* claimed to be as much against Symbolism as against Naturalism.

Fighting with the disciples of Maurras and Moréas to claim Classicism, *La NRF* did not mean to be a school, no more than it intended to erase the past. This was its strength compared to the ventures condemned to decline rapidly because they were too attached to a particular aesthetic conception. Its unity was based on a "literary morality" that consisted in a double refusal: the refusal of any complacency with respect to the public and of any instrumentalization of literature as a "means of arriving," a refusal of facility.[11] In other words, disin-terest and high formal demand were the primary conditions of literary creation.

The "classicism" of *La NRF*—what Jean Paulhan called its "orthodoxy"—chiefly consisted in the refusal of facility, of the romantic "letting go." This literary "orthodoxy" nonetheless aimed to go beyond the opposition between tradition and innovation by making room for the "bizarre," according to Jean Paulhan's terms. The "bizarre," which he also sometimes called the "quirky," was, for Paul-han, precisely what protected the review from both dogmatism and conformism. Rivière and Paulhan (who had assisted Rivière since 1920 as secretary of the re-view) had to impose it more than once against the opinion of their elders, notably Paul Claudel and Jean Schlumberger, often with the complicity of André Gide. This was the case for the benevolent welcome given to Dada and surrealism in 1920. It was again the case in 1935, when Jean Paulhan, upon the publication of a text by Raymond Roussel, was led to justify himself to Jean Schlumberger:

> Think of the dangers against which it was necessary to defend this ortho-doxy: after all *La NRF* has infinitely risked becoming too moralizing due to Pontigny, too Communist due to Gide, too metaphysical due to Benda; it could have slid with Maurois and Morand toward a rather dull conserva-tism; with Kessel toward a rather vulgar and garish novelistic style. And I do not say that it is perfect: at least it has conserved, precisely thanks to the "bizarre" and to literary experimentation, an opening toward young people and this kind of faculty for continuous renewal that means that even today, when a pamphlet or journal for younger people is founded—*La Bête Noire* or *Le Minotaure*—it calls on *NRF* contributors.[12]

Maintaining the review's preeminent position in the literary field up until the defeat of 1940 owed a great deal to *La NRF*'s ability to adjust to the transformations of the pole of small-scale production, which it registered even as it regulated them. The review was able to assimilate the contributions of the Dadaist and surrealist avant-gardes by forging a lasting (although hardly conflict-free) relationship with several of its most famous members like Aragon, Eluard, or, for the second generation, Queneau and Leiris. Or rather, it knew how to "receive the heretics" even as it refused the "heresies," to borrow another expression from Paulhan.[13] After having given its endorsement to the surrealist group, *La NRF* distanced itself as soon as politics were involved, opening its columns to dissidents. Here I will cite the first of three letters from Drieu La Rochelle to the surrealists, published in 1925, that criticized them for their engagement in favor of the USSR, and a note by André Rolland de Renéville (then allied with *Grand Jeu*) that the surrealists' reaction to the Congress for the Defense of Culture incited to "meditate on the conflict that seems unable to stop opposing the poet to the polis, even the future polis."[14]

This double work of adjustment and appropriation was also legible in the attention paid to the debates and polemics agitating the intellectual field, from the question of nationalism at the end of the Great War to that of anti-Semitism in the 1930s, along with the question of moralism in literature in 1924. Always prompt to harbor them, the review was careful to transpose them and impress its mark upon them. Primacy of the literary, or rather primacy, against all dogmatisms, of the aesthetic judgment of the work of art, could sum up the editorial line held by Jacques Rivière and Jean Paulhan. But *La NRF* kept itself from being locked in the position of "art for art's sake," or at least in what was stigmatized during this period (by Catholic and nationalist critics) as gratuitous games of the mind. Its successive directors did not intend to keep it at a distance from current events. "No ivory tower," announced Jacques Rivière when the review reappeared in 1919.[15] On the condition, he specified, of separating literature and politics. Also on the condition of respecting "this detachment from the personal, from the current, that constitutes the value of *La NRF*," as Paulhan would say.[16]

This detachment, through which it intended to distinguish itself from journalism as well as partisan passions, made the review into a place for dialogue and reflection where the divergent points of view confronted each other and critical thought prevailed over certitudes. Neither rationalist nor spiritualist, neither nationalist nor internationalist, neither radical-Socialist nor extremist, *La NRF* was a little of all that at once, reconciling the atheistic rationalism of Julien Benda with the spiritual concern of François Mauriac, the nationalism of Jean Schlumberger with the interest that André Gide or Paul Valéry shared for the emerging European cooperation, the radicalism of Alain with the pro-Communist engagement of André Malraux.

In the 1930s, at a time when politics invaded the intellectual field, the review was led, notably under pressure from Gaston Gallimard, and despite Jean Paulhan's resistance, to make increasingly more room for current events. The columns "L'air du mois," roughly translated as "today's trends," and "texts and documents" were created in 1933, the "bulletin" in 1937. Paulhan would nonetheless struggle to maintain a certain pluralism, at least until 1938. This was what made the review's singularity at a time when politico-literary ventures in search of new ideologies of salvation, like *Europe, Commune, Esprit*, and *Combat*, multiplied.

La NRF pushed the cult of difference and originality to its extreme, even into the political domain, while working to neutralize its effects through euphemization and distantiation, or conversely, exacerbation that confined them to the domain of the absurd. Or else, according to an art of balance that Jean Paulhan mastered, through the juxtaposition of opposites that, as a result, canceled each other out. In a radio presentation of *La* NRF in 1937, Jean Paulhan insisted on this pluralism to reaffirm the above-all literary character of the review: "*La* NRF is a literary review [. . .] It happens to address politics, but it is, in general, with contradictory meanings. And the reader who follows it faithfully should resign himself to being reactionary one month, and revolutionary the next; fascist in January and anti-fascist in March."[17]

Certainly, this image that its director tried to impose is misleading, and if those who opposed such a conception tried every bit as abusively to reduce the review to an organ of radical Socialism, they were not wrong about what made it their worst enemy: the heritage of the universalist humanism of the Enlightenment, the critical tradition, and the spirit of tolerance. Generally supportive of a Franco-German reconciliation until 1933 despite the Germanophobia of Julien Benda, after that date the review hailed studies on Hitler's Germany and invited different points of view, pacifist, anti-Fascist, and Fascistic, to express themselves. From then on, Paulhan had to deploy a wealth of ingenuity to temper political passions and partisan "excesses." In response to Marcel Jouhandeau, who rebelled against the publication of a virulent critique of Hitlerism by André Suarès, Paulhan, who built his position as a conciliator on his capacity to adopt his interlocutor's point of view, did not hesitate to answer: "But where would be the place for *all* these exaggerations, if not at *La* NRF?"[18] He also had to resist the influence of the Communist fraction of contributors, Brice Parain, Bernard Groethuysen, Malraux, and especially Gide, who was himself frightened by the emotion that his position-taking in favor of Communism in 1932 had aroused, along with its consequences for the review. Thus, in 1934, an essay by Trotsky, inserted in the review at Malraux's request, was counterbalanced by an "air du mois" from Drieu La Rochelle that appeared favorable to "fascist socialism."

Anti-Fascism nonetheless recruited quite heavily among the review's contributors, and above all found its figureheads there. As early as 1933, Gide and Malraux lent their support to the Association des écrivains et artistes révolutionnaires (AEAR), a Communist initiative; along with Paul Rivet and Paul Langevin, Alain supported the Comité de vigilance des intellectuels antifascistes (CVIA) founded in March 1934 (Ramon Fernandez was also a member of the CVIA staff when it was founded); in 1935, Jean Guéhenno, André Chamson, and Louis Martin-Chauffier launched the weekly *Vendredi*, a forum of the Cartel des Gauches against Fascism that foreshadowed the Popular Front, with contributions from Gide, Alain, Benda, Martin du Gard, Schlumberger, Giono, and so forth. In 1938, *La NRF* would adopt a resolutely anti-Munich attitude at its director's initiative—less, moreover, by anti-Fascism than by anti-pacifism.

These tendencies that definitively emanated from the review and helped situate it "on the left" in the intellectual field were less the expression of a deliberate bias (Paulhan refused this, and in 1940 it would be easy enough for him to point out to Drieu La Rochelle the anti-pacifist, antidemocratic, and anti-Republican views that he himself had expressed in the review)[19] than that of an intellectual ethos that must be related to the social properties of its contributors. While *La NRF* could be rightly identified by its enemies with the hated Republic, indeed with the Republic of Professors, it was not, far from it, because it was supposed to be the outlet for these new meritocratic elites emerging from the "people" that Barrès stigmatized in the figure of the uprooted scholarship student. The review's social recruitment was, on the contrary, more elitist and more Parisian than that of the literary field taken as a whole. Whereas nearly one writer out of three, for the whole of our population excluding NRF contributors, came from the petty bourgeoisie and the popular classes, this was the case for only one NRF contributor out of five. On the other hand, *La NRF* contributors more often came from the dominant fractions of the dominant class and from the mid-level bourgeoisie than did their colleagues.[20]

It was rather because of the overrepresentation of religious minorities, both Protestant and Jewish, among its contributors in comparison with the recruitment of the literary field during that period—they were twice as well represented at *La NRF*—and especially in comparison with the other authorities of consecration (especially the academies) that *La NRF* could seem like the expression of the new Republican elites in the literary world. A world that, up to that point, had remained much more closed to these minorities than the university (recall the rejection of Gide's *Symphonie pastorale* by the *Revue des deux mondes* in 1919).

Above and beyond the ethical dispositions inherited from family tradition, this overrepresentation of religious minorities had as its corollary the preponderance of Republican educational culture among the regular contributors to the review. For writers educated at a time when the conflict between public school and private religious instruction—the "two Frances"—established a lasting rift, educational culture induced profound differences of habitus. At the French Academy, for example, a third of the writers had attended a Catholic collège.

La NRF seemed like the product of the new mode of reproduction, which was characterized by its educational component. Better endowed with all kinds of inherited capital than the whole population of writers under study, its contributors also distinguished themselves by the level of their educational resources, making them the true competitors of academicians in the literary field. This formed the basis for the concentration of symbolic capital achieved by the review. More than half of its contributors had attended a major Parisian lycée (or the École Alsacienne), versus one academician out of three, and one writer out of four on average. Two-thirds among them held a degree superior to the baccalaureate, versus half of the whole of writers.[21] To the grandes écoles that they attended less often than their colleagues at the French Academy (one out of four versus one out of two), they opposed scholarly training, particularly literary training that began to develop in the 1880s, which a third of them pursued. This rate, three times higher than for the writers of the French Academy, could not be solely attributed to the generational effect, since it remained twice as elevated in comparison with the whole of writers.

This is what led *La NRF* and its team to find themselves accused by their adversaries, from Henri Béraud starting in 1923 to Robert Brasillach in 1938, of the stigmas that writers traditionally applied to the scholarly world: academicism, pedantry, routine, boredom, and fossilization, as opposed to "living literature." This rhetoric had the virtue of attributing a literary value to attacks that most often mixed social and political considerations with payback, as we have already seen. Thus Brasillach, whose last novel had recently been severely criticized by Jean Vaudal in the review,[22] described *La NRF* as "an annex of the rue Cadet [headquarters of the Grand Orient de France] and the Sorbonne." He would go on to say, "It gives us Mr. Benda, that circumcised diplodocus, and some agrégés flirting with the government."[23] In other words, he viewed *La NRF* as the emanation of that "Republic of Professors" so despised by literary men; thanks to the "Judeo-Masonic plot" it had been reincarnated in the figure of the Popular

Front. The fact that such a diatribe was written by an ENS graduate, by a renegade of the educational career, could only give it more weight in the literary
field—and more flavor for the outside observer.

In fact these attacks, although not new, were taken seriously by Jean Paulhan
in 1938, at a time when the director feared that the review was sinking into an
academic torpor. "No one had ever criticized *La NRF* of being glacial and gloomy
with more violence than in the past few weeks. Brasillach (among others) calls
us diplodocuses; and Jean Marteau, pedants," he wrote to a number of his contributors in 1938, soliciting their opinions and suggestions.[24] Paulhan was worried that the pluralism and diversity of the review had come to compromise its
unity, its "soul" as he said. According to him, this was the kind of unity behind
the strength of reviews like *Europe* and *Esprit*, certainly "at the price of a political and moral catechism" from which *La NRF* had always preserved itself. This
was a sign that the political now governed the modes of demarcation and differentiation inside the literary field. It was also a sign that, despite Paulhan's efforts, *La NRF* did not escape the effect of institutionalization and routinization.
The power of consecration that it had conquered was such that it no longer
managed to neatly outline its position, and its vocation seemed to be reduced to
an academic function rather than the affirmation of an identity.

REAFFIRMING "THE *NRF* SPIRIT": PAULHAN'S
EDITORIAL LINE (1938–1940)

To ward off this threat and retrace the outlines of "the *NRF* spirit," Paulhan's
approach was threefold. First, he promoted within the review a team of young
contributors who contested the established aesthetic canons. Then, he adopted
a decidedly anti-Munich position. Finally, he reaffirmed the primacy of the literary over the political. These three steps would determine very concretely the
modes of restructuration of the pole of small-scale production under the Occupation, as well as the formation of the literary Resistance.

The "notes" section was the initiatory exam for all new entrants into the review. Michel Leiris, Raymond Queneau, and Roger Caillois, who were then
grouped around the Collège de Sociologie (where Paulhan also participated),
had discharged this duty for some time. This was the section where Paulhan
first tried to create a greater unity in order to infuse new life into the review in
1938. Jean-Paul Sartre made his entrance there that year. One year prior, *La
NRF* had published one of his short stories, "Le Mur," which Paulhan had called
to Gide's attention: "Have you read Sartre's 'Le Mur'? He will be somebody."[25]
At the time, Paulhan and Pierre Bost were taking multiple steps to ensure that
Gaston Gallimard would accept two of Sartre's manuscripts: a novel called

Melancholia that had first been rejected and was rebaptized *La Nausée* [*Nausea*] at the request of the review committee, and a collection of short stories, *Le Mur*.[26] Their publication in 1938 established the writer, who was also cutting his critical teeth in the review notes he gave *La NRF* on the American novelists from whom he had borrowed new novelistic devices: Faulkner and Dos Passos.

One of the tactics that Paulhan imagined to revive the review in 1938 was to "emphasize the share 'of attack.'"[27] From now on, the review had to distance itself from the novelists that it had itself helped promote, and that had achieved institutional consecration, or risk lapsing into academic conformism. He informed Roger Martin du Gard that he was "trying to goad Sartre toward a 'novelistic offensive,'" in response to an article by André Rousseaux in *Le Figaro* dealing with Albert Thibaudet's *Reflections* on literature and the novel. Rousseaux criticized a former critic of *La NRF* for having neglected the work of François Mauriac, whom he called the "prince of the contemporary novel."[28] This offensive would be the famous panning of Mauriac, "François Mauriac and Freedom," where, applying the theory of relativity to the novelistic universe, Sartre decreed the device of the omnipotent and omniscient narrator obsolete, and with it, the realistic novel of the nineteenth century: "M. Mauriac has put himself first. He has chosen divine omniscience and omnipotence [. . .] God is not an artist. Neither is M. Mauriac."[29]

By taking this stand, *La NRF* was simultaneously in continuity and rupture with its tradition. Continuity of a Gide-inspired novelistic line that borrowed methods of exploring the self and subjectivity from the philosophies of the subject, psychoanalysis, and later from phenomenology. Radical rupture from the devices of the nineteenth-century novel, already declared moribund by the surrealists in the 1920s; this break confirmed the new formal research undertaken by the post-surrealist generation by opposing it to the elders who were still attached to this tradition (whether it was a matter of novels of manners, cyclical novels, naturalist novels, psychological novels, novels of apprenticeship, etc.). Those elders included consecrated novelists like Mauriac and Lacretelle, of the French Academy; Martin du Gard, winner of the Nobel Prize in 1937; but also Arland, Malraux, or Drieu La Rochelle, to mention only contributors to *La NRF*. Sartre's article was published in 1939, the year when Leiris's *L'Âge d'homme* was released by Gallimard, and *La NRF* delivered Queneau's *Un rude hiver* in serial form; his first book, *Le Chiendent*, had been published six years earlier at Gallimard. We must also consider the publication of Aragon's *Les Voyageurs de l'impériale*, starting in January 1940, as part of this editorial strategy, especially in light of the fact that a few months earlier Paulhan had refused to print the second part of *Gilles* by Drieu La Rochelle. To Gide, who was undecided, Paulhan explained:

> Aragon's plan seemed great to me. To write a novel that would be to psychological novels (from Feuillet to Bourget) what *Don Quixote* has been to chivalric novels—at once depleting them, completing them, making them (slightly) ridiculous, and yet drawing out of them a slightly desolate accent—Aragon never undertook a greater task.
>
> Whether he succeeded in doing this is another question. But isn't *La NRF* made to receive such a great project, even if it was aborted.
>
> This having been said, I am not sure that he failed [...].[30]

Above and beyond the effects that this editorial policy would have in the longer run on the transformation of the novelistic rules, it contributed to the formation of alliances that would support the recruitment of the literary Resistance. On the one hand, there was the reconciliation of Paulhan and Aragon (they had been at odds since 1931). On the other, the allegiance that a new literary generation swore to Paulhan; on his advice and to show their solidarity with the ousted director, they would desert the NRF of Drieu La Rochelle and follow Paulhan to the CNE.

Meanwhile, the broad consensus that greeted the Munich agreement gave the review an excuse to take a stand on events without abdicating its critical posture and without speaking out in favor of a political system. Paulhan took advantage of the review's pluralism in order to marshal anti-Munich points of view based on attitudes as different as anti-Fascism (Benda), nationalism (Schlumberger), and a sentimental patriotism (Petitjean). The authors had been carefully selected to represent both the successive generations of the review and the different religious traditions: "Petitjean—25 years—Catholic/Schlumberger—50 years—Protestant/Benda—70 years—Jewish."[31] The whole was completed by "airs du mois" that reinforced this unity in diversity, juxtaposing the arguments and impressions of Arland, Montherlant, Denis de Rougemont, Audiberti, and the "Declaration of the Collège de Sociologie on the international crisis" signed by Bataille, Caillois, and Leiris. Certainly, the viewpoint of the review's pacifists, Martin du Gard in particular, had been omitted. By this principle of composition, Paulhan wanted to do more than reaffirm "the NRF spirit"; he wanted to make it into France's guilty conscience. A few months earlier, in the April NRF, Armand Petitjean, another young contributor whom Paulhan was promoting within the review during this period, called for a "dictatorship of France on the French." Paulhan would revive this theme at the moment of the defeat in the famous article that opened the last issue of *La NRF*, published in June 1940, "Hope and Silence."

During the Phoney War, Jean Paulhan intended to invite writers to adopt a patriotic discipline, with *La NRF* serving as its instrument. In April 1940, he planned to publish one or two pages on the review's stance at the beginning of each issue. The first text, which would not be published, gave an idea of what this discipline should be. Entitled "For the Freedom of the Mind in a Time of War," it sought to be, in reality—we recognize here the taste of paradox proper to Paulhan—an "apology for brainwashing," against the fear of ridicule that dissuaded writers from joining the concert of patriotic voices in the manner of their predecessors during the other war, and from condemning the enemy in what Paulhan regarded as a just war. It was not a matter of judging a people by virtue of the "character" or "psychology" attributed to it, according to an intellectual tradition that Paulhan found "stupid," but, he said, "at least we can judge precisely a people who *takes a stand*."[32] He would develop this view shortly thereafter in his article "Hope and Silence:" faced with Nazi Germany, the "second Alliance of the Just," "a little inert still, no doubt," was rewarded in spite of itself. As he writes, "in the end, our enemy has had to take all evils upon himself: violence, but hypocrisy; deceit, but cruelty. And even those that might have admired its strength draw back before its bad faith." However, this was not the time for verbal escalation. *La NRF* suspended publication. And it was "the use of silence" that was now a sign of patriotic discipline:

> Certainly our Republic seems to have admitted, for the past twenty years, all the vices that its adversaries held against it. However, we fight for something that resembles the Republic: for people's freedom, against voluntary servitude. In truth, the problem has terms so clear that it would be crazy not to hope for a French reconciliation, if each one of us, from today on, poses and tries to resolve it in secret. In silence.[33]

"Hope" and "silence," these two words would reappear with great force in the discourse of the literary Resistance, and would soon acquire a prophetic meaning that Paulhan could not objectively suspect at the time of his writing. Not only because they founded the redefinition of patriotism and an attitude toward the occupant that served as its expression, but above all because they would symbolize exactly this "guilty conscience" of a France whose government had chosen "voluntary servitude."

A new way, then, of reaffirming "the NRF spirit," but also a reaffirmation of the literary autonomy in relation to politics, through which the review intended to maintain its singularity in a mutating intellectual field and to safeguard the interests of the literary faced with the growing injunction to politicize. And it was by remaining autonomous that literature would best serve France. In that, Paulhan stayed faithful to the tradition of the review: literature was irreducible to moral or political interrogations; it had its own laws that emerged in language and literary technique above all. Keeping it separate from politics implied not only a strict dissociation of those two domains in the review's table of contents, but also a distinction between the literary value of a work and the "morality" of its author, and particularly his political biases.

Paulhan ostentatiously put this distinction into practice in the midst of the war, by publishing Giono and Aragon in the review. The first had just been arrested for defeatism, and the second had just seen his party and its newspaper (*Ce Soir*) banned as a result of the Germano-Soviet pact. We can hardly suspect Paulhan of any ideological complicity. So little that, in line with his refusal to sign the petition against Aragon's charge for his poem "Front Rouge" in 1932, then to support a request for clemency in favor of Maurras during his imprisonment,[34] he imagined publishing a note in *La NRF* to say that it would be better to leave Giono in prison, "for security" if he was serious in "the precise *engagements* that he took for the cause of war," and if he was not, "for his honor."[35] A writer's speech engages him, and he must assume the consequences or risk seeing it discredited: "It is important that we can finally take seriously the word of a writer," he explained to Armand Petitjean.[36] But the director of *La NRF* changed his mind. If, according to Baudelaire's formula that Paulhan had adopted, the state should do its job as the writer did his, it was not for the latter to judge whether the state was "wise when it pu[t] Baudelaire in prison."[37] In January 1939, *La NRF* had published a short pacifist pamphlet by Giono accompanied by an equally brief commentary from Paulhan who, leaving aside politics and morals, limited himself to observing that it was not "very good Giono."[38] This was a way of saying that, in the columns of *La NRF*, the writer would be judged above all on the literary plane. It was also a way of showing contempt for his political engagements, as Paulhan recalled during the Phoney War:

> I am criticized for the space given to Aragon in the review. I answer (approximately) that a democracy like ours is absurd when it invites each writer, in spite of himself, to form a political opinion—when it makes the "great career" of a writer begin when he ascribes to a political party—that it is properly idiotic to wait for Giono or Aragon to utter the least sensible reflection on this subject—that the role of *La NRF* is, on the contrary, while showing what little respect we have for their opinions, to accept from them and place value on all the properly *literary* pieces, etc.[39]

We must keep in mind the principles of perception that, in times of war, subordinate all oppositions to the national stake in order to measure the audacity of Paulhan's editorial politics, which exposed him to the most contradictory criticisms. Roger Martin du Gard described the review as "profoundly warmongering, and perhaps not entirely innocent in the war with its Benda and its Petitjean." For his part, Jean Schlumberger considered "that deep down, it is defeatist and commits a sort of treason by printing Giono."[40] Neither the purely literary character of their contributions nor the anti-Munich bias of the review was enough, from now on, to make Giono or Aragon's signatures seem lacking in political significance.

It is in light of these stakes, then, that we must assess the "transgression" that the publication in *La NRF* of the man who made himself the defender of the German-Soviet pact as an instrument of peace implied. This was another way of reaffirming the principle of literature's autonomy with respect to political stakes, even though, in response to the indignant protests of Schlumberger and especially Drieu La Rochelle, Paulhan willingly invoked Aragon's status as a soldier, without failing to vaunt the merits of the poet. "France needed soldiers (even Communists) capable of battling *thoroughly*, like Aragon, and not bourgeois who were convinced in advance that everything was lost, like Drieu," he replied to Schlumberger.[41] In response to Drieu who resigned after criticizing Paulhan for having put him in the same table of contents as Aragon,[42] Paulhan insisted: "Do you want to tell me in what sense Aragon is 'more Communist than ever' today and, in particular, 'obeys the defeatist watchword.' I only know, for my part, that he is at the front, where neither you nor I are, and exposed." And he specified:

> He was never, in the Review, a political writer. But simply the poet that war has, up to now, inspired in the best and strongest way, out of all our poets. And (it seems to me at least) the novelist who took the most precise and broadest view of a whole period of the French novel [...] It is, of course, your right to leave the review. But do not seek to convince me that it is a matter here of the writer Drieu or of the political man Drieu. No, it is simply the personal enemy of Aragon who speaks.[43]

Try as Drieu might to use Schlumberger's opinion to prove his objectivity, if not his good faith, Paulhan was not fooled. Had he forgotten the story of this friendship that had abruptly turned to hate fourteen years earlier, which he had witnessed, he would have been reminded by reading the second part of *Gilles*, where Drieu commented on this quarrel publicly for the first time. A great deal of ink has been spilled on this friendship made of admiration and envy, of complicity even in sexuality and jealousy. Drieu's admiration and envy for the writer Aragon, "the first of [his] generation"[44] was fueled by a feeling of inferiority in which he delighted ("I violently enjoyed his superiority," he wrote to Paulhan).[45] It was as though he was calling forth (vanity of lucidity or masochism?) the contempt that he suspected Aragon hid from him. Aragon's admiration and envy for "the man covered in women," for the dandy who casually wasted the income that his first wife left him, and who lent him money at a time when the young surrealist was deprived. Nine years of friendship followed by a "divorce," according to Drieu's term, that the distance he took publicly with respect to the surrealists did not sufficiently explain. It has been established that a woman was involved, but here again, wasn't this more of a symptom than a cause? "Aragon, truly, there is nothing to say: it was a divorce for incompatible dispositions, an ineffable reason," Drieu would write in 1944.[46]

Aragon and Drieu had a lot in common. Raised in the heart of swanky neighborhoods in families that worked to maintain their rank, they both suffered from a feeling of social inferiority. Drieu's father, a lawyer short on clients, unhappy in business, who divided himself between two households, had wasted his wife's dowry. Aragon's mother, who passed for his sister—he was the illegitimate child of a deputy who served as his guardian—had run a family boardinghouse on avenue Carnot before settling in Neuilly. Whereas Drieu attended the collège Sainte-Marie de Monceau where he was preceded by Paul Morand, Aragon was a pupil at Saint-Pierre de Neuilly, where he met Montherlant, but he would finish his studies at the lycée Carnot. "My childhood was wholly poisoned by money worries around me, by the feeling that I experienced of not being at the level of my schoolmates," Aragon would recall. "I was at a school for rich boys, less rich, then poor because of my father. A petty bourgeois uncomfortable among high bourgeois," Drieu would write.[47]

They both concentrated the hopes of two families threatened with decline. Whereas the illegitimate child, forced to limit his ambitions, set off on the long path of medical studies that war would interrupt, Drieu, enrolled in the École libre des sciences politiques, aimed for a diplomatic career. The humiliation of his failure at the exit exam, when thirty-three out of fifty-six candidates were received, would be all the more keenly felt since it reduced to nothing all the hopes pinned on the young Pierre at a time when the family situation was critical, and especially because it transformed the father's misfortune into the son's destiny. "He won: we fell to his level"; thus ends, in *Rêveuse bourgeoisie*, the scene where Yves announces his failure to his family. His "bleeding, bloodthirsty" relations with his father had certainly something to do with his refusal of paternity,[48] although since *Mesure de la France* (1922), he had not stopped denouncing the decline in birth rate as a cause of decadence. In *Récit secret*, Drieu revisited the failure that would fuel his social resentment, his anti-intellectualism, and his obsession with "decadence," attributing it to his family's position:

> At age twenty, for a few days I thought about disappearing after a failed exam [...] It is necessary to say that I was refused at this exam for reasons determined by the authorities and not because of my insufficiency. It was the exit exam for the École des sciences politiques and they wanted to punish me for what appeared to be the dangerous disorder of my mind, and also to block the diplomatic career for me, which by the way was wise, since my family was ruined, and for a long time my timidity allowed me no mastery over my feeling of social inferiority.[49]

For Aragon, on the other hand, the meaning of the failure at his second doctoral exam in 1922 was less resounding: following the defining experience of the war, he went on to accomplish a brilliant literary debut (*Anicet* was published the previous year).

The relationship to their origins also differed for the two apprentice poets. Drieu, who enjoyed the effect that the particle of his name never failed to produce in intellectual milieus, unleashed "a dreadful anger" when he learned that Cocteau had discovered his uncle's pharmacy featuring the name Drieu La Rochelle.[50] Silent on the subject of his father-tutor, Louis Andrieux, a former prefect who had suppressed the Commune of Lyon, Aragon would become interested in another absent figure, his grandfather Fernand Toucas, who had deserted his home to live a life of adventures (the Pierre Mercardier of *Voyageurs*). An irony of fate, it was only after the completion of *Voyageurs* that Aragon learned, at the bedside of his dying mother, that Fernand Toucas had been implicated in the Commune of Marseille. On his side, Drieu, descended through his father from a line of soldiers of the Revolution and the Empire, grandson through his mother of an employee who was a national guard in Paris during the Commune, proclaimed himself "leader of the Republicans and the Bonapartists against the Royalists" at Sainte-Marie. Then, at the École des sciences politiques he signed on with the group of Republican students "which, in this atmosphere of official bourgeoisie, affluent and timid, was considered subversive," all the while initiating himself in the thinkers of the counterrevolution, from Maistre to Maurras, whom he discovered during this period (he also had a grandmother who supported the Vendée royalist current).[51] Whereas his teachers at Sainte-Marie—modernist Catholics, it seems—destined him to become a social apostolate, while still an adolescent he broke from his faith, like Aragon, but would conserve a base of spiritualism throughout his life. Occupying an awkward position in the milieu of his ultraconservative, even reactionary, fellow students, he was overwhelmed by a late discovery of modern literature, and could only be seduced by the abortive attempt at synthesis between Maurrassism and the revolutionary syndicalism of Sorel, which reconciled his contradictory ethical, aesthetic, and political dispositions.

His disagreement with the surrealists when they advanced toward political terrain, in their anticolonial stance during the Rif War, and in their attraction for the East (which Drieu would yield to only much later) exposed the ethical and political dispositions of the author of *Mesure de la France*, who had for several years hesitated between the surrealist dream and the "Western" elitism of Action française. This was no doubt why Aragon's break-up letter ("Well! my boy, go to them . . ."[52]) in response to his article on "The Real Error of the Surrealists" (*NRF*, August 1925) hurt Drieu deeply. To the point that he ended up declining the invitation that Maurras hurried to make.

Aragon would remain Drieu's most direct competitor, the one against whom he would measure himself all his life. On the political plane, his long-standing indetermination found its resolution in his adhesion to Fascism, after he had hesitated between revolution and reaction, then between Communism and Fascism. (Aside from the fact that his elitism and spiritualism turned him away from Communism, the place was already taken . . . by Aragon.) It is significant that he finally chose the ex-Communist Jacques Doriot, founder of the PPF, where he would be a member from 1936 to 1939, finally realizing his first ambition: to be "a counselor to the prince." On the literary plane, the writer who struggled to be recognized as a full-blown novelist by *La NRF*, where his qualities as an essayist were better appreciated, was irritated when Brasillach, under the slighting label of naturalism, compared *Rêveuse bourgeoisie* to Aragon's *Beaux quartiers*, which won the Renaudot Prize in 1937.[53] During the Phoney War, *La NRF*, which had rejected *Gilles*, would publish *Les Voyageurs*. And as if that were not enough, while *La NRF* was preparing to print the first poems of *Le Crève-cœur*, Drieu, without knowing anything about it, considered having his collection of poetry from the other war, *Interrogations* and *Fond de cantine*, re-edited, and thought about publishing his love poems. In September 1939, he wrote in his journal that he forgave Aragon; in January 1940, he was "furious to see Aragon harbored by Paulhan in *La NRF*. His verses, his novel reveal better than ever this ignoble sentimentality which disgusted me in him. This reeked of the languorous onanist."[54] And it was with an ill-tempered joy that he welcomed the German victory in the month of June:

As for *La NRF*, it will grovel at my feet. This mass of Jews, of homosexuals, of timid Surrealists, of freemason pawns, will be miserably distorted. Gallimard, deprived of his Hirsch [the house's commercial director] and some others, Paulhan deprived of his Benda, will rush away along the walls, their tail between their legs.[55]

By making himself (not entirely involuntarily) the arbiter of the brother-enemies, Paulhan did not measure the impact that his choice would ultimately have. "I have remained, in many circumstances of life, the *accomplice* of this man, even when diverse circumstances sometimes would have separated us, or it seems opposed us," Aragon would write upon Paulhan's death.[56] Accomplice in what and against whom? Rather than restrict ourselves to the metaphorical usage of the term, it is important to tease out the relationship it conceals, based on Aragon's reading.

Paulhan's death in the autumn of 1968 coincided with the relative failure that concluded Aragon's strategy for reaffirming his position in the literary field—a strategy that he had set in motion ten years earlier with the publication of *La Semaine sainte*, followed by renewing his relationship with his surrealist past and successively marking his distance, in his journal (*Les Lettres françaises*) from the aesthetics of Socialist realism and the politics of the party.[57] With this tribute to Paulhan, Aragon wanted to pledge his allegiance to the literary field: the notion of complicity implied both the "conflict inherent in obedience to regulations that contradict each other," as Max Weber puts it, and the constancy of a fidelity to the rules of art that he would never, despite everything, have sacrificed to the interests of the party.[58] His relationship with Paulhan was the guarantee.

Complicity refers to particular episodes in their trajectories during which, as Aragon said, "we have, he and I, each played several times for the other the funambulist role of the symbolic character of Destiny, in a sort of great spectacle in the Ubu genre that is politely known as our era."[59] For Paulhan, "Destiny" took on the face of Aragon when, at the end of 1919, the latter presented him to André Gide, who opened the doors of the Gallimard publishing house and *La NRF* to him. For Aragon, it took on the face of Paulhan in 1939 at a time when he was doubly banished from the national community and the literary community. Former accomplices because of their avant-gardism against the chauvinistic conformist consensus that hailed the victory, the two soldiers of the other war found themselves accused by their peers of complicity in antinational literary intrigues during the Phoney War, before finding themselves complicit in the crime of patriotism and the fabrication of illegal literary weapons under the Occupation.

"It was in 1939, the war had just broken out, my newspaper forbidden, my party illegal. Paulhan was surely not Communist. But he has always been on the side of the misfortunate."[60] Paulhan and Aragon had been estranged since 1931. It was through Elsa Triolet, who had given *La NRF* a fragment of her *Maïakovski, poète russe* that Paulhan asked about Aragon's "freedom" with respect to Denoël, his publisher since 1934, and solicited his new novel, *Les Voyageurs de l'impériale* for Gallimard (with whom he had been in court since 1934). After *Ce Soir* was banned on August 25, Aragon had taken refuge at the embassy of Chile, where he stayed until his mobilization on September 3. A few days later, Paulhan wrote to him: "[...] I think by the way that *Ce Soir* will reappear. But if not, you do know that *La NRF* is open to you, where I will be happy for you to submit a few pages (or a few lines)."[61] Paulhan would also serve as the mastermind of the reconciliation between Aragon and Gallimard.

Above and beyond the figure of deus ex machina that Paulhan assumed for Aragon, their complicity resided in a common literary problematic, in the compatibility between the poetic quest conducted by one, and the expectations of the other. They came together at a time when Paulhan sought to contest the novel's dominance not only by disparaging its devices (Sartre's article in *La NRF*), but also by favoring, for a chosen public, genres that the novelistic overproduction of the interwar period had eclipsed: poetry, tale, essay. Paulhan reserved his choice spots for them: the luxurious magazine *Mesures*, which succeeded the review *Commerce*, and the "Métamorphoses" series that he had founded in 1937 at Gallimard; Henri Michaux, Audiberti, Breton, Antonin Artaud, René Daumal, and so on were published there, mainly surrealists or dissenters from surrealism. "I am troubled that Aragon writes no more poetry. He absolutely must write some," Paulhan had written to Elsa Triolet in March 1939,[62] just as the writer, who had not published verses since *Hourra l'Oural* (1934), was immersed in research on medieval French poetry that would give rise to the theorization of a renewal of the rhyme ("La rime en 40") and the poems of *Le Crève-cœur*. The publication in 1941 of this collection, which "[would] make Aragon the most read, most famous poet of this period,"[63] in the series "Métamorphoses" sealed this complicity.

But complicity ran even deeper between these two writers who had abandoned surrealism, who tried to salvage classical forms from the Maurrassian neoclassicism that the French Academy had just consecrated en masse (rhetoric for Paulhan the grammarian, metrics for Aragon the poet), by readapting them to modernity. They were also united in their work on commonplaces (proverbs for Paulhan, rhyme such as it survived in old tunes for Aragon) that can also be found at that time in the work of someone like Raymond Queneau.[64] It was in this attempt to reappropriate a whole national tradition, which would encounter great success under the Occupation, that the secret understanding between Aragon and Paulhan took root during this period.

But Paulhan was not only the "accomplice" who established the poet in spite of everything. Because of his position as director of *La NRF* and his ideological distance from his protégé—his pacifism was as unambiguous as his anti-Communism—he was the one who had the power to produce a belief effect. Before even the publication of Aragon's poems in *La NRF* in December 1939, and *Mesures* in January 1940, he announced to all his correspondents that Aragon had given him "very beautiful poems."[65] Moreover, Paulhan took advantage of the opposition dictated by the state of war. The farther apart the positions (in this case, politically), the wider the channel of legitimation that grounds the production of belief. This, in effect, reinforced the power of imposition. The proscription of Aragon the political man gave Paulhan the chance to dramatically reestablish the poet.

"We were accomplices again," Aragon wrote, evoking the publication in *Le Figaro* of September 1940 of "Les lilas et les roses" that Paulhan had, unbeknownst to him, transmitted from memory—a ritual of mystification if there is one.[66] Recalling the conditions of isolation in which the couple found themselves at the beginning of the Occupation, Elsa Triolet would say about this publication that it "cleared Aragon a little bit with respect to the people. Up until that point, no one wanted to have anything to do with them, except Joë Bousquet,"[67] the poet who hosted a demobilized Aragon at his home in Villalier, where Jean Paulhan met with him and heard "Les lilas et les roses."

Paulhan's literary politics would have a twofold consequence: it established the legitimacy of the position of "national poet" that Aragon would construct under the Occupation, and simultaneously set the conditions for the poetic renewal that would be the defining literary event of the dark years. It largely determined the failure that Drieu La Rochelle would experience in his attempt to reappropriate the heritage of *La NRF*—to the profit of his greatest rival, Aragon.

A WELL-FOUNDED FRAUD: DRIEU'S *NRF*

Drieu's *NRF* would experience a double failure: it would not be able to reappropriate the heritage of the review, and it would not manage to create a literary project and identity. In the beginning, however, the venture presented itself in a false light of continuity. Drieu and Abetz insisted on keeping the title.[68] Drieu had, moreover, given up—at Gaston Gallimard's insistence?—on publishing, in its full original version, the opening text that he had initially written for the first issue of the review. He cut its most engaged passages, and those that distinctly set it apart from the old *NRF*: "Enough of this indirect, straight-laced, distinguished *NRF* language."[69]

By allowing for the continued presence of a number of former contributors, the choice to broadcast the review's continuity was initially misleading. But, by conditioning expectations, it also condemned Drieu's project to be judged by its predecessor's standard. The reappearance of *La NRF* first divided the literary field according to earlier literary cleavages. The collaborationist press thus found itself divided between those, like the contributors to *Je suis partout* and *La Gerbe*, who implicitly recognized the literary hierarchies from before the war while hailing the venture, and those, like the contributors to *Les Nouveaux temps* and *La France au travail*, who misunderstood them because of their own exclusion (they denounced the review's continuity with the old *NRF*). Among the former contributors, François Mauriac, who had congratulated Drieu on the announcement of *La NRF*'s revival, and who, without agreeing with his political articles, thought he was "alone or almost alone in being able to play, with dignity and without palinode, a role that is useful to all," shared his disappointment on reading the first issue: "No, it is not what I hoped for—I who dreamed of an 'uncurrent' review."[70] As for Jean Guéhenno, who had immediately refused to contribute, he found it "deplorable, to consider it even from a solely literary standpoint. The mind retaliates."[71]

Among the sixty-some writers who participated in Drieu's venture, more than half had already written in *La NRF* before the war. But it was above all the signatures of Gide and Valéry in the first issues that served as the guarantee of this continuity. And while politically, Drieu's *NRF* could give the impression of inscribing itself, above and beyond the anti-Munich "interlude," in the review's 1920s tradition of pacifism and of favoring the Franco-German reconciliation, this did not occur solely due to the presence of Alain in the table of contents. It was also because, next to the figure of the polite and correct "good German" who did not kill or plunder anyone, put forth by Chardonne,[72] or Fabre-Luce and Drieu's discourses on Europe,[73] the "leaflets" that Gide published were directly anchored in this tradition: "The risk is much larger, for thought, to let itself be dominated by hate."[74] And:

> We will have to pay for all the absurdities of the intangible treaty of Versailles, the humiliations, the unnecessary vexations, which turned my stomach in 19, but which it was unfortunately vain to protest; and the rather undignified abuse of victory. It is their turn to abuse now.
>
> Did we lack psychology, at this time when our triumph infatuated us! As if it would not have been wiser to hold out a hand to the vanquished, to help

THE SENSE OF DISTINCTION 315

him stand up again, instead of striving to debase him more, absurdly, and without realizing that, in so doing, we flexed his resentment and stiffened his energies?[75]

The distance that the review took with regard to the moralism of the "National Revolution" helped inscribe it in the continuity of "the NRF spirit." Marcel Jouhandeau and Henry de Montherlant ensured the maintenance of the individualistic and egoistical Gidian tradition abhorred by the Vichy regime. In an article on "Paternity and Fatherland," Montherlant certainly recognized, in accord with the "National Revolution," the family unit's importance to the nation as a protection against the materialistic and egoistical individualism of "the common man" (individualism should be reserved for an "elite"), but he warned against "the belief that the family spirit is enough [...] Because the good of the fatherland and the good of the family do not necessarily coincide," he explained. This allowed him to engage in a critique of bourgeois family love, maternal and thus feminine in its essence ("and," he said, "*it is in part by becoming bourgeois that we have been defeated*"), and to contrast it, according to a criterion of distinction that was dear to him, to the virile ethos of the martial aristocratic tradition.[76]

Against the Vichyites' injunctions for the moralization of art and the artist's awareness of his social responsibilities, *La NRF*, in line with its well-established tradition, also knew how to preserve creation from the external constraints that weighed upon it. It was a true argument in favor of "art for art's sake" that filled the pages of Drieu's NRF, although he was himself quite hostile to this posture.[77] In the text of a conference given in Lyon and Limoges in December 1940, Montherlant took the opposite opinion of the official discourse on art in the Southern zone: "The artist produces *for* nothing. He produces his work like the apple tree produces its apple, without aim and without responsibility, without worrying about a recipe so it can be used, nor the usage that will be made of it." Congratulating himself for the new conditions of production that were, according to him, favorable to creation ("In a word, no more of this impure and sordid commerce between artist and public"), he called, in the name of "freedom of the mind," for artists to pursue their work more than ever.[78] A similar concern also animated the young poet Armand Robin. In the name of "art for art's sake," he criticized the writers who had chosen to abstain, saying that they sacrificed the cause of art to the circumstances by ceding to political injunction:

> The truest reason for this will to abstain seems to be that, for a few years, many writers have asked themselves why they were writers or admitted to being writers only under cover of a political role [...] The proper nature of

thought and art is to continue. This gives the writer some fairly simple obligations: that of not making his activity depend on events, that of defending the civilization of his country, even if all the rest is lost; France is allowed to say: "Everything is lost except honor." Why refuse to proclaim: "Everything is lost, except beauty."[79]

Thus, in continuity with the editorial policy of Rivière and Paulhan, Drieu's *NRF* claimed to separate literature from politics. His main critics, Ramon Fernandez, André Thérive, and André Rolland de Renéville, abstained from professing their political thoughts. For the latter two, whatever their convictions, this restraint proceeded, certainly, from a general attitude. During the examination of his case in the professional purge process, André Thérive, who was criticized for his contributions to the collaborationist press (*Je suis partout, Les Nouveaux Temps, Aujourd'hui, Paris-Zeitung*), could allege their purely literary substance.[80] But the reverence of Ramon Fernandez, one of the regular critics of *La NRF* since the 1920s, who wrote pages of pure literary criticism without ever infusing them with the virulent tonality of the political articles that he disseminated at the same time within the collaborationist press, attests to this will of dissociation so dear to Jean Paulhan. Not that politics were absent from the review; Drieu, Fabre-Luce, Petitjean, and others took care of that. But then, they never had been since the end of the other war, and at the time of appraisal, Drieu could easily inscribe himself, here again, within an *NRF* tradition:

> Some have criticized me a great deal for doing *some* politics in the review. I prefer those who hate me for having done *a* certain politics. Thank God, in the old *NRF* agnosticism was never abused with respect to this human concern that is politics and that a true humanist should consider as much as the others. While the pre-1914 review showed its ignorance and disdain, Jacques Rivière and Jean Paulhan's versions, at least in these last few years, minded what was ultimately their own business. I have thus continued this tradition.[81]

Why, then, does this defense of "art for art's sake" ring false? It is not only because it ignored the eviction of a number of contributors to the old *NRF*, Jews and anti-Fascists, for political and racist reasons. It is because, to justify it, Montherlant believed it necessary to rely on the statements of a true "man of action," Hitler: "We cannot suspend the activity of the mind for a certain period without a regression of general culture and a definitive decadence," the Führer apparently stated in a speech to the National-Socialist Congress of 1935.[82] This procedure had the merit of betraying the true reasons for this argument in favor of "art for art's sake." By distancing *La NRF* from the moralism of Vichy, this

plea actually had another aim, which made it completely circumstantial: a sum-
mation addressed to the "writers of refusal" to abandon the silence in which they
had shut themselves. These writers were not duped: this argument for "art for art's
sake" masked the acceptance of the Nazi yoke and played into the hands of German cultural politics that aspired to normalize the situation of occupation. Concerning the publication of "La Cantate du Narcisse" by Paul Valéry in the issue of
January 1941, Jean Guéhenno noted in his journal: "We cannot help regretting
that he [Valéry] lends himself to this maneuver of the occupying forces that want
to make the world believe that everything in France continues as before."[83]

It was also a cover for Drieu's personal mission: "I hope to have compromised a certain number of people with La NRF who will be very badly viewed
and panned by the Aragons and the Bendas, when they come back as masters,"
he would write in his journal on November 9, 1942, on the day after the allied
landing in North Africa, which heralded the turning point of the war.[84] "Compromising" as many writers as possible, it was thus, from the moment he became conscious of his double literary and political failure, in wholly cynical
terms that Drieu would declare the stakes. And he would go so far as to try to
"compromise" the very man whose place he had usurped and who had deliberately distanced himself—at least publicly—from his venture. "Is it necessary to
say [...] that without Jean Paulhan my work would have been much more difficult, if not impossible," he slipped into the "assessment" he published in January 1943.[85]

THE SCHISM OF THE NRF TEAM

But this usurpation was precisely what inspired the initial distrust of a number
of contributors to La NRF, to such a point that Drieu had almost abandoned his
project, due to the excessive number of refusals. In November, Ramon Fernandez "searches for texts everywhere."[86] Certainly, Gaston Gallimard had ex-
tracted contributions to the first issue from Gide and Brice Parain, Gallimard's
secretary.[87] After being seduced momentarily, Gide publicly broke with the review in April 1941.[88] Drieu wouldn't stop soliciting Jean Paulhan's help; Paulhan played along rather unwillingly, as we will see. Let's remember that Paulhan
had declined to coedit the review with Drieu, refusing to approve the exclusion
of Jewish and anti-Fascist contributors.

The political conjuncture brought about a true scission inside the team of La
NRF. But it first happened according to internal principles of opposition and a
proper institutional logic that the events only solidified. A simple generational
observation indicates this. Whereas the generation of founders withdrew from
Drieu's NRF—Schlumberger immediately refused; Gide and Valéry reneged

after letting themselves be seduced; Claudel, initially kept at a distance, was hostile to it—a subset of the representatives of the intermediary generation took their place: those who were between forty and sixty years old in 1940, and who, having entered *La NRF* before Paulhan took over its direction, didn't owe this consecration to him. Plus, they rightfully considered *La NRF* as their "house," independent of its director.

On the other hand, those who swore allegiance to Paulhan, to whom they personally owed their introduction and their promotion within the review, showed their solidarity, or at least consulted with him before making their decision. Paulhan complied, undoubtedly at Gallimard's request, in probing the review's contributors. Raymond Queneau, who was part of the Obligatory Work Service contingent posted on site and who worked at Gallimard where he became general secretary in 1941,[89] responded to Paulhan about an article on Jules Romains that he had given him before the defeat: "What is more, I told G[aston] G[allimard]—with precaution, by the way, and circumlocutions—that I was not anxious to contribute to the review in question. Let us say f. ex. that I reserve myself, that I wait to see what it is. This is for you, naturally. In any case, I refuse (at least for the moment) any article. Thus, I ask you to send my Jules Romains back to me."[90] Paulhan, half-mischievous, half-sincere, also announced to Drieu La Rochelle that "Aragon and Pourrat *refuse* to contribute to the *nrf*. (I assure myself at least that it is not a friendship—unconsidered—for myself that compelled them. Aragon agreed to publish a follow-up: he does not want to give a poem)."[91] As he would explain later to Paul Eluard, "when the *nrf* was published again, some friends came to tell me that they would contribute only with my permission. It would have been pretentious and a little ridiculous to refuse this permission, which they desired to have. I gave it to them, as quickly as possible. Among them were Marcel Jouhandeau, Marcel Arland, and—it would not be exact to call him my friend—Jacques Chardonne."[92] Paulhan thus did not apply a veto to those of his close friends whose position at the review did not depend on him and whom he felt were holding back only out of courtesy toward him. But it was different for the youngest ones, it seems, as his severe tone with Rolland de Renéville shows.

The abstention of the young guard of *La NRF*—who also partially formed the avant-garde of Gallimard—Sartre, Leiris, Queneau, Tardieu, Blanzat, Vaudal, all under forty years old, is telling. All the more so since at the same time, Paulhan directed them to *Prométhée*, the review that Pascal Pia was trying to found in the Southern zone following the model of *La NRF*. Through Paulhan, they submitted the manuscripts that they had withdrawn from *La NRF*, but the review did not obtain publication authorization from the authorities.

Allegiance to Paulhan, associated with the generational split, was thus one of the principles that divided the NRF team. Armand Petitjean was one of the few, among the younger ones, to ignore Paulhan's opinion, which he would have reason to bitterly regret later on: Paulhan would sharply reprimand this young pretender who wanted to skip steps in disregard for the implicit hierarchy of the literary field, criticizing him for having yielded to ambition, pride, and the need to put himself forward.[93] Descended from the upper bourgeoisie of Paris, Armand Petitjean, then twenty-seven years old, his right hand amputated during the Phoney War, had changed his mind shortly after the defeat with regards to his warmongering positions of 1938. Won over to the myth of "French decadence" that he had once contested, he became a protagonist for the National Revolution, denouncing the drop in birth rate, the "desertion of the country by the peasant elite because our society no longer has natural foundations," and the class struggle, all the while opposing the Vichy traditionalists.[94] He entered the Office of the State Secretary for Youth, where he codirected the bureau of propaganda; then, after his resignation in December 1940, was one of the directors of the "Compagnons de France," and, recommended by Paul Marion to take the helm in May 1941, he failed against the Catholic candidate. He then tried, with Marion's support, to create the Jeunesses légionnaires. His circle, and especially Jean Paulhan, noted the contradictions of his engagements, which symbolized the paradox of the Vichy regime's revolutionary pretenses, and which betrayed, in Petitjean, personal ambitions. "Yes, the case of Petitjean is striking, and (no doubt) tragic. Can one make a revolution while being a minister?" Paulhan wrote to Drieu, who in turn took up his defense, pointing to the "situation" (at the Office of the State Secretary for Youth) that Petitjean had sacrificed to his revolutionary ideals.[95] "Deaf to the warnings of a few faithful friends, in the first place Jean Paulhan, like a sleepwalker I pursued my dream of a 'New French Revolution' extended to Europe, convinced that it was more important to struggle against the causes of the defeat than against its consequences," Petitjean wrote a half century later.[96] In the journal *Idées*, he developed his conception of the National Revolution as a synthesis between Maurrassism and revolutionary syndicalism, and in *La NRF*, his vision of a partnership between a regenerated France and Germany to construct Europe.[97] From the end of 1942, he searched with Angelo Tasca for a third way between Vichy and the Resistance,[98] and in September 1943, with the agreement of the government of Algiers, he took up the direction of the Équipes nationales before enlisting, in November 1944, in the army of General Leclerc.

Overall, *La NRF* was significantly rejuvenated. Three-quarters of its contributors were under fifty-two years old in 1940, and almost half were under forty.[99]

But the best-represented age bracket was 41–52, which totaled one-third of the contributors to Drieu's *NRF*. Whereas the authors under the age of forty were most often newcomers to the review, those who were over forty represented the intermediary generation. They were established critics like Ramon Fernandez, who had aspired, after Rivière's death in 1925, to the direction of *La NRF*; and André Thérive, the literary columnist for *Le Temps* who, unlike Fernandez, was not part of the editorial team and whose contributions to *La NRF* were more occasional. They were mainly postwar novelists: Drieu La Rochelle, Montherlant, Morand, Giono, Cocteau, Arland, Jouhandeau, who shared (unequally) a certain notoriety without being assured a place in posterity. Having entered *La NRF* in the 1920s, they found themselves crushed, at the end of the 1930s, between the still-predominant presence of the group of founders on one side, and on the other, the young guard promoted by Paulhan, which had nearly eclipsed them. The observation is especially valid for those who constituted the pillars of the review, and for whom it was, in return, the guarantee, if not the condition, for maintaining their position in the literary field: Fernandez, Arland, and Jouhandeau; to a lesser extent, Drieu La Rochelle, whose quarrels in 1939 with Paulhan we nonetheless saw.

Deprived of its authors of Jewish origin (Julien Benda, André Suarès, Jean Wahl, Benjamin Crémieux) and some of its pillars of Protestant origin (Jean Paulhan, Jean Schlumberger, André Gide after the break), the *NRF* under Drieu's direction also lost the political pluralism that constituted its originality among the journals of the 1930s, thanks to the withdrawal of the anti-Fascist influence. Certainly, the review's contributors came from the most diverse political horizons, from the pacifist left to Action française. But, aside from Alain and Giono who had not revisited their pacifism, the most famous authors of the new formula were distinctly situated at the far right of the political spectrum. Henry de Montherlant and Paul Morand were right-wing men. Ramon Fernandez had broken ties with the left in 1935 to join the ranks of the PPF in the wake of Drieu La Rochelle. Marcel Jouhandeau had proclaimed his anti-Semitism a few years earlier: the author of *Péril juif* (1937), whose first profession of faith, rejected by Paulhan, appeared in the columns of *Action française*, had led a fight since 1936 for the defense of "French culture" against the Jews and the "foreigners" who had taken "all our top places."[100] Among the youngest, Claude Roy and Kléber Haedens were from Action française; Lucien Combelle had gone from Action française to Fascism.[101]

At least a quarter of the contributors to Drieu's *NRF* had publicly declared their support for the politics of collaboration, in the review or elsewhere. Distinguishing itself from most of the collaborationist publications by a more measured, less quarrelsome tone, *La NRF* was not only one of the sites of the elaboration and legitimation of the "European" ideal on the basis of a Franco-German understanding,[102] but also a site where the situation of occupation was normalized and rendered banal.

Chardonne and Fabre-Luce's articles in the first issue, "Summer in La Maurie" and "Letter to an American" respectively, justified the politics of collaboration; and Drieu's article, "The Body," in the third, which blamed the "forgetting of the body" for the "decadence" of Western civilization since the Middle Ages, helped set the ideological orientations of the review. They incited waves of indignant protests. "Chardonne's Charente idyll and a certain frivolity of Fabre-Luce were hardly appreciated," Drieu wrote, euphemistically, to Mauriac, who responded: "What I think of the Chardonne/Fabre-Luce papers, is what the whole of France thought about them (as Saint-Simon said, for whom the whole of France meant a thousand people)."[103] One passage from Drieu's article had particularly shocked readers:

> When we think of those generations of knock-kneed lovers who exhibited their nudity in the beds of gallantry in the 19th century, when we think of a shirtless Baudelaire or Zola, we suddenly find the reason for the horrible Christian notion of sin [. . .] These exasperated and hacking lewd men were the exasperated children of rationalism, of intellectualism.[104]

The publication in serial of *La Bête à concours* by Georges Magnane, which dealt with poverty in the student milieu; Paul Gadenne's short story, "Simon Delambre étudiant" (January 1941), which opposed the scholastic universe to "life"; and finally Abel Bonnard's article, "A Change of Epoch" (March 1941), which denounced the break from "reality" that bookish culture had brought about, succeeded in giving a decidedly anti-intellectual tonality to the review. This anti-intellectualism fueled the antidemocratism and antiliberalism that grounded the Fascist stand *La NRF* had taken at the initiative of Drieu La Rochelle.

In his "assessment," Drieu had claimed that "if a single opinion was expressed [in the review], it was not up to [him] for it to be otherwise [. . .] I believe," he said, "that it would have been possible for some, at least if they had wanted it, to expose in a discreet but substantial manner, if not their refusal, at least a good number of the reasons that led them to these refusals."[105] This affirmation was contradicted by the veto he applied against the publication of a short story by Noël Devaulx, proposed by Paulhan, and deemed too "trendy."[106] In a letter to Paulhan, Drieu would criticize him for having lacked "tact" by sending him texts that he could not accept.[107] For lack of inviting divergent points of view to express themselves, according to the tradition of the review, Drieu's *NRF* was condemned, as we will see, to polemicize with those who expressed themselves outside it, particularly in the small magazines that were published on the other side of the demarcation line. It thus lapsed into the "dogmatism" that the old *NRF* had avoided, losing, at the same time, its ability to adjust to the transformations of the literary field and its double role of arbiter and beacon.

A REVIEW IN DECLINE

The review's rejuvenation was accompanied by a relative decline in social recruitment, which not only no longer distinguished itself from the average recruitment in the literary field but even showed a slight disadvantage with respect to social and cultural assets.[108] The proportion of writers from the upper or middle bourgeoisie was two times lower in Drieu's *NRF* than in the old review, while one contributor to the new *NRF* out of three (versus one out of five before) came from the petty bourgeoisie or the working classes. More often natives of the provinces (60 percent versus 50 percent), and thus more often educated in a provincial collège or lycée (one out of three versus one out of four), the contributors to Drieu's *NRF* had less frequently attended the major Parisian lycées (32 percent versus 39 percent). Finally, more than a third of them did not undertake postsecondary studies (versus a quarter of the contributors to the old *NRF*), and nearly one out of five had a level of studies inferior to the baccalaureate (versus one out of ten before the war).

This phenomenon was less due to the withdrawal or the eviction of former contributors than to the recruitment of newcomers. The examples of Montherlant, Fernandez, or Drieu himself show that it was not the socially-less-well-endowed who stayed; on the contrary, with the exception of educational capital that seems globally lower in comparison with the "abstentionists." Confronted with the order to abstain that spread through literary circles, recruitment had become, as we saw, difficult. Albert Camus, for example, who had just entered Gallimard, refused to pre-publish *L'Étranger* in *La NRF*. It was among writers who were not as well integrated in the best literary circles, those who had not yet gained entrance to the Gallimard house for example, that Drieu's seduction worked. Among the newcomers, we thus find a group of young poets that Drieu had attracted to the review so that it would not remain on the fringes of the poetic renewal movement undertaken by the small magazines published on the other side of the demarcation line. Although most often sporadic, their contribution to Drieu's *NRF* was significant at a time when many turned their back on it.

During the first months, poetry was represented in the review by Jacques Audiberti, Armand Robin, and Rolland de Renéville, who was responsible for poetry criticism. A poem by Paul Eluard—who had been approached in the autumn of 1940 to serve on the editorial committee and who had, it seems, accepted—was published in the second issue. This "incident" would not be repeated. All had contributed to the prewar *NRF*.

The evolution of the *NRF*'s list of contributors (chronology is telling in this regard) shows that the review no longer dictated the transformations of the literary field but, on the contrary, had to adjust to the new tendencies that emerged in the small magazines in the Southern zone (the poetic renewal) to maintain its position. The name of Eugène Guillevic appeared there for the first time in July 1941. That of Jean Follain reappeared in September and would return rather regularly. Starting in the autumn of 1941, the names of Fernand Marc, Luc Bérimont, Jean Bouhier, Michel Manoll, Yanette Delétang-Tardif were added; then in 1942, Maurice Fombeure, Pierre Guégen, and Marcel Béalu, while the older ones like Paul Fort, Léon-Paul Fargue, Jean de Boschère, and André Salmon made their return to the review. These young poets, who gravitated around the "Sagesse" group animated by Fernand Marc or around the nascent École de Rochefort, had not been formed in the surrealism school. With the exception of Fernand Marc (born in Paris in 1900), they shared rather modest provincial origins (often from the western part of France) and a secular education.[109] Having moved to Paris at the end of their advanced studies or having remained in the provinces, they would perhaps not have reached the very closed Parisian circle of *La NRF* without the particular conditions of the Occupation that provoked the abandonment of the Parisian scene by a number of its actors.

Though they were not wholly exempt from ideological ambiguities, a number of those who let themselves get caught up in Drieu's enterprise were imbued with political convictions. Unlike the former contributors to *La NRF*, the newcomers' participation in Drieu's venture proceeded more from misunderstanding the stakes such as they were then posed in the literary world than from an ideological stance. Among the elders who reappeared in the review's table of contents in 1942, André Salmon, a journalist, had taken a stand in favor of the Collaboration in *Le Petit Parisien* and had declared his support for the Legion of French Volunteers against Bolshevism.[110] Paul Fort accommodated very well, as we saw, the presence of the occupant. It was also true that, while they did not make any public endorsements, we can perceive ideological ambiguities in the works of Audiberti, Rolland de Renéville, and Armand Robin. The anarchistic Robin thus shocked his circle by the joy he displayed after the defeat: "Robin went back to Paris, so joyful that everyone was offended, and that Guéhenno threw him out," Paulhan wrote to Jules Supervielle.[111]

This was not the case for Eugène Guillevic. "He willingly presented himself as Communist. Preferably in the office of Drieu La Rochelle, no doubt out of kindness and to allow Drieu to make his little effect, presenting him to his German visitors, adding: *my* Communist," Jean Lescure reported.[112] Born in 1907, Guillevic was from a modest family of Breton peasants and craftsmen. His father was a sailor turned policeman, and his mother a seamstress. After studying at the collège Altkirch in Alsace, he was received at the supernumerary competition for the Registration in 1926, apprenticed as a financial civil servant, and in 1935 became an executive in the central administration. Having arrived in Paris at the age of twenty-eight, at the end of the 1930s he joined marginal literary circles, separate from surrealism, notably the "Sagesse" group that met at the Café Capoulade. There he met Yanette Delétang-Tardif, linked to the critic Edmond Jaloux; and especially Jean Follain, who published his first booklet, *Requiem*, in the Sagesse "Cahiers" at Tschann, and some of his poems in the review *Pont Mirabeau* directed by Henri-Philippe Livet. A practicing Catholic in his childhood, "rather theist" up until the age of thirty, he detached from the Church at the rate of the campaigns it supported (Ethiopia, Spain), was initiated to Marx, and ended up breaking ties with religion as he was won over to the cause of the oppressed.

Guillevic's contribution to Drieu's NRF (his poems appeared there in July 1941 and August 1942) while he was getting ready to join the underground Communist Party (a membership that certainly rehabilitated him) reveals the inertia of the schemes of perception that, for an outsider, dictated the orientation in the literary field according to earlier points of reference. Whereas for a number of the review's contributors, as we have seen, Drieu's NRF was a venture of usurpation, and thus not the "true" NRF, it conserved all its prestige in the eyes of the outsiders—those who were the least informed because the least integrated, and who had thus not readjusted their schemes of perception. "I am of my generation. *La NRF* counts. In 1930, when I was twenty-three, I waited impatiently for every issue of *La NRF*. It was my big reading of the month. I remained faithful to it. I publish in it roughly every year. I consider *La NRF* as my 'house' . . ." Guillevic would say later. The belief in the equivalence between the old and the new NRF was all the stronger since the blind spot on which it relied coincided with the position of the young poet in relation to the review. While Paulhan's NRF had rejected him, Drieu's NRF welcomed him via Marcel Arland, whom he had met after the armistice. Arland encouraged him to prepare his collection, *Terraqué*, and introduced him at Gallimard:

> Before the war, I had given some poems to Paulhan, who had not wanted them—according to him, they lacked "presence"—then I met Marcel Arland

during the war [...] It is thus through him that I entered Gallimard ... it did not work right away ... Paulhan was never very warm ... But my most surprising supporter, the most unexpected was Drieu La Rochelle [...] we were brother-enemies.[113]

Four years older than Guillevic, Jean Follain (born in 1903) had already made significant inroads in the Parisian literary milieus. Of Norman origin, he "affirmed and displayed his provincialism, but he knew Paris like few," as Guillevic would say.[114] Better endowed with cultural resources than his younger colleague—he was the son of a teacher and had studied at the collège Saint-Lô, then at the Caen Faculty of Law—and a lawyer by profession, he had married the daughter of the painter Maurice Denis, close to Action française, and he was linked to Léon-Paul Fargue, Max Jacob, Audiberti, and André Salmon, who had prefaced his collection of poems, *La Main chaude*, which was published in 1933 by Corrêa. He published in the most prestigious reviews of the period, *La NRF*, *Commerce*, *Europe*, *Les Cahiers du Sud*, and in 1939 won the prize awarded by the Mallarmé Academy.[115] At the Café Mabillon Wednesdays, where "Audiberti received visitors," according to Jean Lescure's expression, Follain met back up with Salmon and Roland de Renéville during the Occupation.[116] In the autumn of 1941, he renewed his ties with Drieu La Rochelle and they became friends.

It was in the spring of 1941 that Jean Bouhier, a pharmacist by profession, founded the École de Rochefort in Rochefort-sur-Loire, assembling among others the teacher René Guy Cadou; the bookseller Michel Laumonnier alias Michel Manoll; the bookstore worker Marcel Béalu; Jean Rousselot, an employee of the administration before becoming a literary journalist; and the journalist Luc Bérimont; they would soon be joined by elders who more or less gravitated around the "Sagesse" group: Maurice Fombeure, a graduate of the École normale de Saint-Cloud, which trained primary school teachers, and a teacher at the collège Jean-Baptiste Say; Guillevic; Follain; Fernand Marc; and Yanette Delétang-Tardif. These young poets, who were barely thirty, had started to make a name for themselves in the small provincial magazines, the best known being *Les Cahiers du Sud*. Some of them (Béalu, Cadou, Bérimont, and Rousselot) appeared in the table of contents of the magazine *Poésie 40 ...* edited by Pierre Seghers in Villeneuve-lès-Avignon. The *Cahiers de l'École de Rochefort* would appear regularly until April 1943 by predating their issues, a practice that the semi-legal magazines of the occupied zone would adopt starting in April 1942, when an authorization number became required for every publication.

And yet, these young recruits were not enough to restore the prestige of *La NRF*. The *Cahiers de l'École de Rochefort* was hailed by Rolland de Renéville in *La NRF* with a certain condescension. Even as he contested the group's designation as a school, Renéville conceded that "the poets who appear in these notebooks sometimes show some talent." As proof, he cited Yanette Delétang-Tardif, Maurice Fombeure, and "two certainly talented poets, Luc Bérimont and Michel Manoll, whose manner has already been revealed to readers by *La Nouvelle Revue française*."[117] *La NRF*'s claim of precedence over the *Cahiers de l'École de Rochefort* in the discovery of these young poets betrayed the competition to which it was reduced, even with a marginal publication. It also masked the fact that true competition was then playing out between the Northern zone and the Southern zone, where, Renéville noted at the beginning of the same article, poetic activity seemed very lively. When Drieu La Rochelle drew up the assessment of his venture at the end of 1942, in a final effort to redeem it with respect to its rivals from the other zone, he would not cite these young poets, but rather, with the exception of Guillevic, former contributors to *La NRF*:

> I am far from believing that *Fontaine* and *Poésie 41, 42* have presented more important lists of contributors than ours […] An altogether new generation of poets rose up in *La Nouvelle Revue française* as in *Poésie 41, 42* and *Fontaine*. In Paris, there were Audiberti, Guillevic, Rolland de Renéville, Follain, Fombeure, Henri Thomas, Armand Robin, Fieschi, who came to support Paul Fort, André Salmon […][118]

Nothing attests as clearly to the success of the symbolic takeover accomplished by these small magazines than the growing need that Drieu's *NRF* felt to define itself with respect to them. The failure of Drieu's *NRF* must therefore be related to the modes of recomposition of the literary field around these small magazines.

From Art for Art's Sake to the Defense of the "French Spirit"

The struggle to regain the autonomy of the literary field under foreign occupation happened through its symbolic reunification and the reaffirmation of its national particularism as a universalism. The struggle to legitimately define "the French spirit" or "French thought" would thus bring together very different writers in the same fight, from the believers in "art for art's sake" to the Communists, with some dissident Catholic poets and intellectuals thrown into the mix. This was a fight to reappropriate the themes and symbols hijacked by the ideologues of the National Revolution on one hand, and by the sycophants of "European" construction under the banner of Nazi Germany on the other: patriotic virtue, the elements of national identity, historical references (Péguy, medieval culture), up to the theme of "fidelity to the land," marked by the adoption of the names of French regions as underground pseudonyms; but also humanism, understanding between peoples, Europe, and so forth.

Lacking the means to collectively protest out in the open, dissidence was organized on two levels: contraband literature and clandestinity, which corresponded to a division in space and an evolution in time, which proceeded differentially in the two zones due to the differences between the modalities of constraint operated respectively within them. A group of small magazines, marginal in several respects (by their geographic position, the means at their disposal and/or their poetic project), were propelled to the forefront of the cultural scene and would assume a subversive role in both the ideological and literary orders. Founded shortly before the defeat or born of the crisis at the instigation of young pretenders, often coupled with an editorial support, the reviews *Fontaine* in Algiers, *Poésie 40, 41 . . .* in Villeneuve-lès-Avignon, *Confluences* in Lyon, *Messages* in Paris, then in Belgium and Switzerland, *Traits* in Lausanne, and *Les Cahiers du Rhône* in Neuchâtel, promoted an entire generation of young poets, and at the same time offered some of their elders a substitute for the instances of diffusion infiltrated by the Collaboration, *La NRF* in particular. The intergenerational alliance was one of the specific effects of the crisis, this "historical and literary fact" that Georges-Emmanuel Clancier evoked: "Between the Surrealist elders (like Aragon, Eluard) whom we admired, and us, there was no conflict, whereas if history had been different, there would have been."[119]

This intergenerational alliance would make it possible to call into question the monopoly of *La NRF* that the situation of occupation had initially allowed to materialize. It was in their common opposition to Drieu's *NRF* that the initially very different projects of these small reviews first converged. This was a sign that, despite geographic dispersion, *La NRF* (which was distributed in the Southern zone) remained a reference point, albeit repulsive. The specific circumstances meant that solidarity in the struggle against this powerful adversary won out over the spirit of competition that still remained active between all these small magazines. Pierre Seghers remembered, for example, having read a text by Henri Michaux, "La Lettre," "that [would] make [him] green with jealousy" in the issue of *Confluences* published in April–May 1943.[120] Although the circumstances made diffusion difficult, they also authorized a departure from normal publishing rules: texts circulated more than usual, from one magazine to another, and were republished in different places, a practice that would develop in clandestinity and that greatly favored the symbolic takeover that these magazines accomplished. This coup de force consisted in the reunification of the fragmented literary field, above and beyond the demarcation line and the established borders.

A CONTESTED MONOPOLY

It was less the initial vocation of these magazines than the conjuncture that led them to assume this role. For those newcomers ready to brave the censors, the situation of occupation and the resulting decentralization would, in a certain respect, have positive effects on their literary career. By offering substitute forums to confirmed authors who had been deprived of their own, they knew how to seize the double opportunity that presented itself, to compensate for their marginal geographic position with respect to Paris, and to ally themselves with the deposed elders. They had nothing, or little, to lose, unlike a preexisting structure such as *Les Cahiers du Sud* that Jean Ballard published in Marseille.

By the recognition that it had already achieved, *Les Cahiers du Sud* seemed predisposed to take up where the old NRF left off. "It seems to me that the *Cahiers du Sud* let the chance escape, that they had to a large degree, to become a very big review. Why didn't they call Aragon? And so many other omissions, or obstinacies," Jean Paulhan wrote to Joë Bousquet; to Roger Caillois he said, "These *Cahiers* moreover, apart from you, are quite lamentable: pushing prudence further than necessary."[121] The tradition of this magazine, which placed it, in the tradition of Valéry, at the pole of "art for art's sake," and the prudence of its director, Jean Ballard, so attached to assuring its survival that he practiced auto-censorship—in 1941 he rejected poems by Pierre Emmanuel and Loys Masson, and did not publish a text that Paul Valéry had sent—meant that it was quickly overtaken by its more audacious young competitors. It wouldn't be until 1942 that, trying to catch up with the movement that started without them, the *Cahiers* dared to print "Exil" by Saint-John Perse, who was living in the United States.

The principal competitor of *Les Cahiers du Sud* was, first, the magazine *Fontaine* that was published in Algiers. Starting in April 1939, under the direction of Max-Pol Fouchet, it had followed in the path of *Mithra*, where the young poet Charles Autrand had organized the first two notebooks. Born in 1913, son of a small-time Norman shipowner who had moved to Algeria for health reasons (he had been gassed during the Great War), schoolmate of Camus at the lycée d'Alger, Max-Pol Fouchet belonged to the young, Algiers-based intellectual milieu that met at Edmond Charlot's bookstore (he was Camus's publisher), read *La NRF*, and considered Gide as his "great awakener."[122] Whereas Camus joined with the Communist Party, Fouchet founded the "Socialist youth" in Algiers; he would later resign in protest of the politics of nonintervention in Spain.

After the defeat, *Fontaine* became one of the pivotal sites of the symbolic reunification of the fragmented literary field, due to its geographic position which allowed it to let the voices of exile be heard. Its July 1940 manifesto, "We are not vanquished," provoked the seizure of the issue. With Henri Hell as its editor in chief and Aragon's former secretary, Jean Roire, who would be arrested at the beginning of 1942 for being a Communist, as it administrator, the review soon gathered Jean Denoël, Georges-Emmanuel Clancier, Pierre Emmanuel, René Daumal, André de Richaud, and Jean Rousselot onto its editorial board; these were young authors, some of whom had debuted in *Les Cahiers du Sud*. Max-Pol Fouchet had tasked Georges-Emmanuel Clancier, who resided in Limoges, with procuring manuscripts for him in the Southern zone. Through Albert Béguin in Switzerland, they were transmitted to Georges Blin, then a scholar in Tangiers and a "pillar" of the magazine; he transported them to Algiers.

From 1941 to 1942, *Fontaine* would gather texts from exiled writers, Georges Bernanos, Jacques Maritain, Jules Supervielle (who submitted his "Poems of Unhappy France"), and texts from authors in the unoccupied zone, who could be found in the table of contents of *Poésie 41, 42 . . .* and then *Confluences*. They included Aragon, Pierre Jean Jouve, Pierre Emmanuel, Loÿs Masson, Pierre Seghers, André Frénaud, Louis Parrot, Claude Roy, Stanislas Fumet, and Jean Prévost. Henri Pourrat served as a "lightning rod," according to Max-Pol Fouchet's expression.[123] Paul Eluard, who lived in Paris, would appear in the table of contents in 1942. The elders would follow the example of the younger ones once the literary legitimacy of the enterprise was assured. André Gide, whom Max-Pol Fouchet had first contacted in July 1940, when he was trying to recruit the "writers who could help raise a combative awareness, because of their prestige," had put off "until later to join us because, he says in his response, he *did not know exactly where things were at, and where he was at himself.*"[124] But apart from an article in March 1941, it was only after his move to Algiers in 1943 that Gide would contribute to the magazine. Meanwhile, *Fontaine* had to suspend its activities for six months: while it had, until then, avoided a Vichyist ban, its paper ration was refused after the allied landing in Algiers due to an attack Bernanos had made against Charles Maurras, which was not to the liking of the nationalists surrounding Giraud! Before its suspension, *Fontaine*'s circulation, which initially attained a mere 500 copies in 1939, had reached 12,000 copies.[125]

Since the war, the aspiring poet Pierre Seghers had launched the magazine *P[oètes] C[asqués] 39, 40*, a forum for the "soldier-poets" published "in the armies."

It had a circulation between 300 and 500 copies. Having emigrated to Villeneuve-lès-Avignon in the autumn of 1940, it took the name *Poésie 40*. Born in Paris in 1906, Pierre Seghers was a newcomer to the literary world. He had self-published a first booklet in 1939. At that date, he held few advantages to establish himself in the closed literary circles of the capital. He was powerless on every plane due to the decline that his family had experienced on both sides. On the maternal side, his great-grandparents were wine merchants, but his grandparents, cloth makers, died prematurely. His father, a cabinet maker like his grandfather, had changed professions, becoming a chemist at a time when this specialty had been devalued, with the development of the engineering profession that was then becoming established in industry.[126] The family had to leave Paris for Carpentras, where Seghers did his secondary studies. Condemned to different day jobs for subsistence, he abandoned his law studies after two years. The printer Louis Jou, whom he met in 1932, encouraged his literary ambitions, but his collection *Bonne Espérance*, which Jou had confided to Bernard Grasset, was not accepted. He had it printed in 1939 by Maurice Audin in Lyon, who would also print *P.C. 39, 40* and then *Poésie 40* . . . which Seghers would create in Villeneuve after the defeat while taking charge of a family business, a small hotel supply venture.

Born under the sign of Guillaume Apollinaire and Péguy, *P.C. 39, 40* had benefited at its outset from the literary endorsement of Aragon who gave it "Les amants séparés" and "La rime en 40"; the kindness of André Billy, who published the advertisement announcing its publication in *Le Figaro*; and the active support of Jean Paulhan, who subscribed to it and supplied unpublished manuscripts by Apollinaire. When it reappeared in the autumn of 1940 under the title *Poésie 40*, the magazine had to ensure its survival beyond its founding conditions, tightly linked to the war. It was the necessary management of this "warrior" heritage—the capital of recognition acquired, as well as the stock of manuscripts it had to recycle—rather than an editorial choice, that made it appear subversive at first.[127] This heritage would also set it apart from *Les Cahiers du Sud*, well implanted in the region, allowing it to welcome the authors and texts that were rejected by the latter for being too audacious. Through Paulhan, it would moreover become a relay for texts rejected by *La NRF* as we saw earlier.

A former member of the Association des écrivains et artistes révolutionnaires (AEAR), and a diligent reader of *Commune* and *Mesures*, Seghers had every reason to get along with Aragon, whom he met for the first time in September 1940 in Carcassonne, when the Communist poet was still very isolated. Aragon's intervention with Seghers until November 1942 would be decisive in the subversive orientation of the magazine. Was it to renew ties with Aragon that Paul Eluard sent *Le Livre ouvert* to Seghers in November 1940? Eluard would immediately recognize the author of the unsigned note who assessed the work in the second issue of *Poésie 41*, putting twelve years of discord to rest. "Poetic Reconciliation—*Le Livre ouvert I* is made of topical poems—and political reconciliation for the resistance," commented Pierre Daix.[128] Eluard would appear in the table of contents of *Poésie 42*.

The magazine quickly became a center of attraction for young poets, Alain Borne and Claude Roy in *P.C. 40*; Pierre Emmanuel, Louis Parrot, Loÿs Masson in *Poésie 41*; then, in *Poésie 42*, André Frénaud, back from captivity, Francis Ponge, still a little-known author at this date (for the director of *Confluences*, René Tavernier, Ponge "at this moment was altogether unknown"),[129] and Henri Michaux, whom Gide's conference, banned by the Legion in 1941 in Nice and published under the title *Découvrons Henri Michaux*,[130] revealed that year to the literary public. *Poésie* thus largely contributed to the movement of "poetic renewal" and to the launching of this generation of young poets, taken over by the magazine *Confluences*: upon verification, none of the names that appeared in the table of contents of *Confluences* had not already figured in *Poésie 40,41. . . .* In 1942, the magazine's place in literature was assured; its audience now exceeded initiates and the Southern zone. After Gide's endorsement (no. 3), other consecrated elders agreed to sponsor it: Duhamel responded to a survey on Rimbaud (no. 7), Mauriac published his "Fragment d'Endymion" (no. 9), and that year they obtained for him a prize for poetry from the French Academy. Duhamel, moreover, ensured the magazine a grant of 10,000 francs from the Association "Au service de la pensée française" that he headed. At the Liberation, Gallimard would offer to take over *Poésie 44*, an offer that Seghers would decline.[131]

"The Union for Poetry": such was the motto of *Poésie 41*, distinguishing it, according to Seghers, from the project of *Fontaine*, journal of "New French Poetry": a "fundamental difference that ensures that our reviews complement each other instead of imposing on each other."[132] Between *Fontaine* and *Poésie 41*, a division of labor seemed to emerge: while the former sought to gather the voices of exile and those of the Southern zone, the latter set the goal of reuniting poets from both zones: "No, there are not two worlds, two zones: Poets of the North and South, you should know each other better, esteem each other, unite. You are the pilots; reconnect with the grand tradition above the line."[133] *Poésie 41,42 . . .* would render a constant tribute to *Fontaine*, even when it opposed it with respect to the special issue entitled "Poetry as a Spiritual Exercise," which confined poetry to a quest for the eternal and denied it the right to anchor itself in the event.[134] It would also know how to encourage the efforts of a newcomer, *Confluences*.[135] The mutual recognition of these small magazines was the condition of their legitimation. This solidarity, which won out over competition, founded their ability to establish themselves.

Paradoxically, it was the cultural voluntarism of Vichy that had initially favored a gathering that the conditions of dispersion in the Southern zone did not facilitate. Having returned from a trip to Paris in the summer of 1941, Aragon and Elsa Triolet were at Pierre Seghers's house in Villeneuve. "This summer 41 at Villeneuve has been very fruitful for the work of gathering writers: it could be said that it was to facilitate it that the Vichy government organized a sort of congress of writers at the Château de Lourmarin. On the way there and back, they passed through Villeneuve and came to see us."[136] Placed under the patronage of Vichy, the Rencontres de Lourmarin organized by Jeune France were held September 19 and 22, 1941. "Excellent way of utilizing the funds of Vichy for anti-Vichyist ends! Those who were there knew with what wood they were heated . . ." said Max-Pol Fouchet, who had come from Algiers in order to participate.[137] This retroactive vision is no doubt purged of the ambiguities that were then contained in the project of this Catholic association that was situated in the circle of influence of the journals *Sept* and *Esprit*. Created under the banner of the state secretary for youth, hosted by Pierre Schaeffer, it would experience an evolution and a fate similar to Emmanuel Mounier's journal, with its dissolution in March 1942.[138] A member of the administration council of Jeune France, Mounier was, with Roger Leenhardt, the organizer of these meetings. There, links were forged that would found the alliance with the Catholic writers, an alliance which would characterize underground recruitment in the Southern zone. Pierre Seghers, whom Aragon preferred not to join, met the young Catholic émigré poet from Mauritius, Loÿs Masson, who was accompanied by Pierre Emmanuel (they both contributed to the progressive Catholic weekly *Temps nouveau* directed by Stanislas Fumet), and offered him the secretary position at *Poésie 41*. Loys Masson then left Les Compagnons de France, the framing structure of the state secretary for youth. The next year, he would join the ranks of the underground Communist Party, just as Claude Roy would a little while later. Roy, a literary critic at *L'Action française*, also attended these meetings as the head of the literature, radio, and cinema sections of Jeune France.

A similar ambivalence characterized the evolution of the Lyon magazine *Confluences*, which moreover included Pierre Schaeffer among its contributors.

Opening with a profession of faith that refused the writer both the "ivory tower" and partisan engagement,[139] *Confluences* sought to be a less specialized cultural magazine than *Poésie 40* . . . , in large part imitating the model of the old NRF, whose tendency toward "art for art's sake" it did, however, condemn. It presented philosophical essays and critical studies on art and literature, as well as some prose and poetry (to which it still reserved an average of 20 percent of its space), paired with an important column of the "month."[140] Edited by Jacques Aubenques, the first issues of this magazine founded in July 1941 sometimes emitted clearly Vichyist notes: in the first issue, Pétain was defended against the "Anglomaniacs," "detractors," and "aggressive emigrants" who were trying to "demolish his prestige"; tribute was paid to the Portuguese dictator António de Oliveira Salazar and it was recommended to take a lesson from Henri Pourrat's *L'Homme à la bêche*.[141] Noteworthy supporters of Pétain made their contributions to the first issues: Kléber Haedens, Jean Guitton, Henri d'Hennezel, and Pierre Schaeffer. Even after its official takeover in October 1941 by René Tavernier, who gave it a new orientation, the magazine, now subtitled "Revue de la renaissance française" ("Review of the French Rebirth"), emitted some discordant notes, such as a study by Max Fortuit that glorified the modern myth as regenerator of a people, or Tavernier's own praise for the *Paroles aux Français* and their author, Marshal Pétain.[142]

René Tavernier was ten years younger than Pierre Seghers, and moreover everything separated them. Born in Paris in 1915, he came from the upper bourgeoisie of Lyon. Son of an industrialist and a translator of Italian literature, he studied at the lycée du Parc and the lycée Ampère in Lyon, then, after an interlude at Cambridge, obtained a diploma from the École libre des sciences politiques while pursuing a degree course in law and literature. His first two collections of poems, published in 1937 and 1938, earned him a warm note in *La NRF* thanks to Jean Wahl, who accepted to meet him at Gallimard. During the Phoney War, he left Paris for Lyon and settled there after the defeat. The war having interrupted his career plans, he threw himself, through his classmate Marc Barbezat, into *Confluences* where he could pursue his literary ambitions. His early education "in a traditional French milieu" undoubtedly meant that he at first felt in harmony with the orientation of a review that then seemed like the only possibility to realize those ambitions.[143] But the guardrails of a family ethos that had preserved him from the attraction that the Maurrassian and Catholic movements exerted in the lycées of Lyon, and the warm welcome that Paulhan's NRF had given him, helped determine his choices when, thanks to meetings with the Parisian milieus that had withdrawn to Lyon, he saw new options open up to him.

In the autumn of 1941, the *Confluences* team was still limited to a circle of friends and former classmates of René Tavernier, Marc Barbezat (who got Tavernier in at *Confluences*, before founding his own review, *L'Arbalète*), the ENS graduate Auguste Anglès, and the Communistic François Cuzin, assisted by the young *Esprit* contributor Marc Beigbeder. The magazine would soon be enriched by the young generation of poets "revealed" by *Poésie* (Pierre Emmanuel, Alain Borne) and, starting in 1942, Aragon (whose poem "Nymphée," which appeared in issue 12, in July, earned it a temporary suspension) and Eluard (no. 13, October 1942). In parallel, it came into contact with the milieu of the editors of *Paris-Soir*, withdrawn to Lyon. This contact was established by Roger Vailland, who had followed the editors of *Paris-Soir* to this city where he had met up with his former classmate, Jean Beaufret. A philosophy teacher at the lycée Ampère since the start of the academic year 1941–1942, Jean Beaufret was linked to the university milieus of Lyon gravitating around *Confluences*. He had introduced René Tavernier to Roger Vailland who, in turn, introduced the *Confluences* team to the "strongly envied club of *Chez Antoinette*," as his biographer Yves Courrière says of the canteen of *Paris-Soir* journalists.[144] Two of the newspaper's writers entered *Confluences*, Louis Martin-Chauffier starting in February 1942, then Jean Prévost in 1943. From January to June 1943, Aragon stayed with René Tavernier at Montchat, six months during which he brought considerable aid to *Confluences*. It was likely he who brought Joë Bousquet, Claude Roy, and Georges Sadoul alias Claude Jacquier there: they would be responsible for the book, theater, and cinema columns, respectively. In 1944, the circulation of *Confluences* would reach 5,000 copies, *Poésie 44* 4,800 copies, whereas *Les Cahiers du Sud* stagnated at 4,000.

The initiator of this practice of literary "contraband," Aragon was the great orchestrator of the poetic renewal. A text smuggler, he assisted Seghers, then Tavernier, and maintained contact with Max-Pol Fouchet, contributing significantly to the legitimation of their ventures. He also endorsed the young poets who gathered around him. Faced with this charismatic leader of a new generation of poets, Drieu, who secretly aspired to acquire his own disciples,[145] witnessed the collapse of the position he had won.

ARAGON, NATIONAL POET

In September 1944, in liberated Lyon, Paul Claudel would say to René Tavernier, "I would really like to meet Aragon, because he is a national poet."[146] Between the director of *Ce Soir* banished from the national community in September 1939 and this figure of national poet that Aragon assumed during the war, we can measure the distance: quoted by General de Gaulle in his October

31, 1943, speech in Algiers, Aragon would be compared to Victor Hugo in Guernsey. Aragon's national literary politics were inscribed in the line defined by Maurice Thorez in 1937 in Arles, during the Ninth Congress of the Communist Party where, to quote Aragon, "[the politics of *my* party] again found *the colors of France* (and gave them back to us), wedding the red flag of the worker movement to the tricolored flag of Valmy."[147] This Communist Party line nonetheless does not sufficiently account for the symbolic and practical forms that national politics took in the literary domain under the influence of Aragon.

The construction of this position of "national poet" can be approached in three ways: the foundations of legitimacy; the elaboration of appropriate symbolic forms; and the principles of recomposition of the literary field that marked the success of the poet's effort to gather writers around a certain conception of "the French spirit." The new legitimacy won by Aragon the poet was based on his "complicity" with Jean Paulhan, as I showed earlier. The publication of *Le Crève-cœur* in the "Métamorphoses" series edited by Paulhan in the spring of 1941 reaffirmed a legitimacy that had already been in large part earned. In July, Gide noted in his journal:

> A new issue of *Poésie 41* brings me some surprising poems by Aragon. This is the best I have read in poetry for some time and the most authentically new. I feel the need of writing this here, for I had not at all enjoyed his most recent books and feared he might henceforth be almost lost to us.[148]

First, I will discuss the symbolic forms elaborated by Aragon. Then, I will proceed to analyze the struggles that would culminate in a reversal of the power relations to the benefit of the young reviews.

Aragon's poetic work was, first of all, a work on form: it was, as his biographer Pierre Daix summarized, the "marriage of traditional metrics and a modern treatment of vocabulary and rhyme."[149] "I have invented a new way of rhyming," Aragon announced to Vladimir Pozner when he was discharged.[150] Published during the Phoney War, then resumed in *Le Crève-cœur*, this treaty of versification known as "La rime en 40" posed the conditions of such a renewal. "Freedom whose name was usurped by free verse takes back its rights today, not in carelessness, but in invention."[151] Relying on Apollinaire's definition of masculine and feminine rhymes, on medieval poetry and popular song—to which we must surely add Pushkin and Vladimir Mayakovsky— Aragon transgressed classical rules by making licit "the breaking up of enjambment": a fragmentation that, associated with complex rhyme, enriched the lexical possibilities of rhyme by allowing, notably, the use of *impair* words.[152] To those who protested, Aragon would reply that transgression was the very principle of literary magic, of "the alchemy" that produced literarity, both in language and prosody.[153]

Was rhyme the form of a poetry for all? Perhaps, but we must remember that the hope of reconciling the poet with the general public was not the prerogative of the Communist writers at this period: we find it notably with the man who, during half a century, had claimed to incarnate the true French classical tradition, Charles Maurras. Aragon intended precisely to fight him for this position by turning Maurras's weapons against him. In the autobiographical text he wrote in 1943, he said, "These words [France and fatherland] had become the exclusive property [...] of a social and political clique that monopolized patriotism [...] The *Everything that is national is ours* of the Maurrassians is a prime example of the total perversion of words [...]"[154] But unlike Maurras, Aragon adopted Isidore Ducasse's phrase, "poetry must be made by all," in a straight line, this time, from surrealism, and its echo in the work of Mayakovsky.[155]

Poetry was substituted for the novel in the route traced by Barbusse with *Le Feu* during the Great War, namely "the possibility to knock down the wall between the writer and the crowd of men" in the midst of "lies."[156] Under the title "Beauties of the War and Their Reflection in Literature," in December 1935 Aragon had published a critique of the "mystification of war" that Apollinaire, despite "a certain tone of voice [that], like contraband, reached in us this profound taste for the forbidden fruit" had practiced "with the cynicism of abstraction": "Neither blood, nor dead bodies [...] And I have to nonetheless say that Apollinaire lied." Against this lie, Aragon made Barbusse's sentence in *Le Feu* his own: "It would be a crime to show the beautiful sides of the war ... even if it had some."[157] By that time, however, the lie was no longer, for Aragon, the chauvinistic exaltation of the war that masked the horrors of the front, but Fascism. A text by Bertolt Brecht appeared in *Commune* in 1936, in which he reflected on the difficulties that "whoever wants to fight the lies and the ignorance" under the reign of Fascism must surmount: how to "have [...] the cunning to transmit to them the voice of truth" was one such difficulty that the Spanish poets confronted with Francoism (Antonio Machado, Federico García Lorca) would not delay in answering poetically.[158]

Aragon found the cunning in a poetic technique he borrowed from medieval poetry: the "trobar clus," this closed art that "allowed the poets to sing of their Ladies in the very presence of their Lord,"[159] put into practice from the moment the French Communist Party was banned in 1939, and which would spread under the Occupation. This art of contraband, this "language of complicity that has always served to speak among themselves, at the beard of the prison guards," as Jacques Gaucheron said about the slang that Robert Desnos used in his poems from *À la Caille* (satirical portraits of Collaboration figures that he signed as Cancale),[160] became one of the rules of the game that ensured the literary field a relative autonomy under oppression, and that only initiates would be able to decode—including initiates on the other side, like Drieu La Rochelle. It became a weapon to reaffirm this autonomy against the occupying forces and against the Vichy regime, and above all against those writers who, on the pretext of maintaining "the French spirit," played the game of the acting powers.

Through a critical return to the history of the genre, Aragon made himself the theoretician of poetic subversion under the Occupation in two essays that he published outside occupied France, in Algeria and Switzerland: "The Lesson of Ribérac or French Europe," published in *Fontaine* in June 1941, and "Arma virumque cano," the preface to *Les Yeux d'Elsa* that was published in March 1942 by the Éditions de la Baconnière in Neuchâtel, in the series "Cahiers du Rhône." Aragon made rhyme into the privileged instrument of the autonomization of poetry and the French language at their origin, in the twelfth century: "If the problem of rhyme is the first I wanted to address in 1940, it is because the history of the French verse begins where rhyme appears, it is because rhyme is the characteristic element that liberates our poetry from Roman influence, and makes it French poetry."[161]

This return to the history of French poetry was the occasion, for him, to counter themes imposed on one side by the partisans of "Europe" under the German banner, and on the other by the ideologues of the National Revolution. To reaffirm, first, French unity: it originated in the "fusion of North and South"—Provençal love and Celtic legend—realized by Chrétien de Troyes, "lesson of our unity" and proof "that there is no French race but a French nation, which is the harmonious fusion of races in this extreme West." To reestablish, then, the French sources of European culture: from the tribute rendered by Dante in his *Purgatory* to Arnaud Daniel, a nobleman from Ribérac who practiced the closed art and was the inventor of the sextine (customarily attributed to Italy), to courtly morality, which had "[invaded] Europe *poetically*," and to the wide reception of the works of Chrétien de Troyes, Aragon found evidence to support his conclusion: "France is the mother of European poetry, imitated by our poets."[162]

These texts by Aragon, like a number of the poems that he composed in 1941, can be read as so many replies to Drieu's NRF (just as *Aurélien*, which he also wrote during this period, responded to *Gilles*).[163] In January 1941, Montherlant's article on "Chivalries" was published in *La NRF*. For Montherlant, chivalrous morality was the expression of a martial civilization founded on a virile order to the exclusion of women, and was perverted precisely by women, gallantry having substituted "a morality of bimbos that, from then until our own days, by emasculating and distancing it from the real, has done so much harm to our France."[164] Aragon countered with the merits of "courtly morality," which was the vector of diffusing the "passion for justice, [the] taste for chivalry, [the] defense of the weak, [the] exaltation of high thoughts." The "cult of the woman" translated woman's attainment of a recognized social status, and even as he kept from making it a "watchword," Aragon recalled, for the benefit of the social reformers of the National Revolution, that this theme "in our day takes on a sense of protest"—at a time when women were denied access to public service and were meant to return to the home.[165]

And it was by responding to the critics who equated his poems to songs that Aragon developed his attack against the folklore that flourished under Vichy: "If I have looked, in the language of popular poetry, of old songs, for some gleam that erudite poetry does not give, it was in order to make an entirely metaphorical profit from it; and in no way to recommence folklore, which cannot be rendered at will or with a deliberate purpose."[166] This attack marked the dawn of his future reflection on the poetic usage of myths and legends, a metaphorical usage that employed symbols of national heritage to speak in coded language of the present. This reflection, which I will return to in the next chapter, was inscribed in the double context of the popularity of the question of myths in the literary milieus since the end of the 1930s, and the ideological combat that the Communist intellectuals led against Nazi obscurantism and its political usage of myths.

This ideological combat with poetic weapons was coupled with a literary combat against the "art for art's sake" that Drieu's NRF claimed to embody, and against the notion of "pure poetry." Outsmarting the trap that was laid for writers, the poetological poem entitled "Contre la poésie pure" thus responded to the publication of Paul Valéry's "La Cantate du Narcisse," again in La NRF in January and, more generally, the argument in favor of "art for art's sake" that appeared in the same issue thanks to Armand Robin.[167] This title evoked the old quarrel from the early 1920s between Abbé Bremond, a partisan of "pure poetry" in the manner of Paul Valéry, and Maurras, his detractor, who opposed "song" [chant] to "prayer." For Aragon also, poetry was song:

> The word chant translates the Latin Carmen which has also given the word charm, which makes both a magic and a musical image [...] It is in the sense of Virgil that I say I chant when I say it. Arma virumque cano . . .

"I sing [*chante*] of the weapons and the man . . ." This is how the *Aeneid* begins, this is how all poetry should begin [. . .] And my song cannot refuse to be; because it is a weapon also for disarmed man.[168]

At the end of "The Lesson of Ribérac," Aragon openly declared war on Drieu's review. He named his adversaries, who had all contributed to *La NRF*: "Shall I say that by frequenting Cligès, Yvain, Lancelot, Perceval, or Tristan, it seems to me that I move away from my time much less [. . .] than by reading the works of André Gide, Drieu La Rochelle, or Jean Giono," opposing Giono's "vivre à plat ventre" [*living prostrate*] to the verses of Chrétien de Troyes: "Il faut bien mourir / À l'honneur, qu'à honte vivre" [It is better to die in honor than to live in shame].[169]

THE BATTLE OF THE MAGAZINES

The growing place that poetry occupied in *La NRF* alone illustrated its alignment with the orientation of the semi-legal magazines. Starting in the summer of 1941, these were the magazines that set the tone for poetry. The shots they aimed at the new *NRF* soon constrained it, despite the respect it showed them, to go on the defensive, then the offensive. All the more so since, reduced to remaining only allusive on the political plane, they concentrated their criticisms on the literary plane and thus helped disqualify Drieu's review.

In the Southern zone, *La NRF*'s reception was lukewarm, as *Poésie 41* noted without sparing any irony: recalling the merits of the old review, it approached it from a strictly poetic angle to observe that "neither the unedited *Quatrains* by Péguy, published in December, nor *La Cantate du Narcisse* by Paul Valéry, published in January, add anything to the glory of Péguy or Valéry," and express amazement at the "critical method" employed by Drieu in his article on "the body": "Isn't what counts with a poet his poems, more than his calves? Such is not the opinion of Mr. Drieu, who no doubt gains by showing his legs."[170] The tone was set by André Billy in the literary page of *Le Figaro*, then by the magazine *Fontaine* that, via Henry Hell, missed the absent ones with whom "the very spirit of *La NRF* evaporated."[171] In the first issue of *Confluences* in July 1941, Marc Barbezat also missed them, but criticized their absenteeism. He congratulated the newcomers for having "chase[d] away the 'intellectual party,'" and "by the same token certain old sticks-in-the-mud, clerks clinging to their quasi-official position" (the allusion to Benda is transparent), but denounced the obstinacy of the new *NRF*, in continuity with Paulhan's version, to address current events.[172] The same arguments were revived in the next issue by Marc Beigbeder, who did however slightly correct the tone by noting that "the gesture of the writers who have withdrawn is beautiful," but that it had precipitated the decline of the current review, which he treated much more severely than Marc Barbezat.[173]

If, then, the condemnation of Drieu's *NRF* was unanimous among these small magazines, allied with *Le Figaro*, it was due to very different, even opposite motivations. But this common maxim was what originally drew them closer. Drieu's *NRF* would, on the other hand, meet with a warm reception at the Fascistic pole of the anticonservative and antiacademic young ideologues of the National Revolution, particularly in the columns of the journal *Idées*, where Drieu contributed. It was starting in the autumn of 1941, at the time when the magazines *Fontaine*, *Poésie 41*, and *Confluences* began to establish themselves and set the tone, that Drieu's *NRF* went on the offensive, or rather the counteroffensive. Up until then, Emmanuel Mounier's journal *Esprit*, which had just been banned in August 1941, constituted the principal adversary of Drieu's *NRF*, judging by a note in the July issue where the "fussy anarchism" of *Esprit* and its complacency toward the "Ancien Régime" were denounced. This was a reflection of the struggles between the Fascistic circle of influence, which called for a stronger centralized state as well as the formation of a single party and of a single youth, and the Catholics, who were attached to the pluralist claim, worried about Vichy's etatism.[174] The same note (which we can attribute to Drieu) hailed the magazine *Fontaine* even as it drew attention to the practice of "contraband": "In a general manner, the literary magazines of the other zone have, during the winter, been written with a strange tone of insinuation: fear of a German censorship that they supposed and a French censorship that they knew."[175] In September 1941, while Drieu was attacking Mauriac who had just published *La Pharisienne*, Rolland de Renéville could still list Aragon's *Le Crève-cœur* among the signs of the "vast poetic flowering" of 1941.[176]

The October issue seemed, on the other hand, like a response to the attacks on *La NRF* formulated in the June issue of *Fontaine*, which included the previously cited article by Henri Hell on *La NRF*, and above all "The Lesson of Ribérac or French Europe" by Aragon (this Algiers-based magazine's delivery time to metropolitan France was about two months). "The Lesson of Ribérac" was, as we saw, a declaration of war on *La NRF*. Drieu's counterattack (he had just published his *Notes pour comprendre le siècle* where he made the apology of medieval culture that did not separate the body from the soul) showed that the blow had hit its mark. By devoting a whole citation-strewn article to it, Drieu gave Aragon an unhoped-for publicity. As was Drieu's critical habit, the article mixed scholarly or so-called scholarly criticisms with personal attacks. Thus, in reference to the distinction that Aragon established, in response to Montherlant, between Christian morality and courtly morality, Drieu abusively equated courtly poetry with Cathar heresy:

> Aragon seems ignorant of the fact that the poetry of the troubadours was a poetry with a double meaning, secretly religious and which conveyed Albigensian doctrines under the symbols of Platonic love, which, for being no less Christian although abusively so, and spiritual although desperately so, since in the perspective of the accession of the Holy Spirit in the Gospel of Saint John and in the Apocalypse, they absolutely proscribed the flesh and propagated total depopulation.

And he would immediately reverse the argument by detecting in Aragon's apology of "courtly morality" and the cult of woman "the incapacity of the repented libertarians to acquire a virile morality."

But above all, the article marked the move from counterattack to denunciation. To understand the importance of this, we must remember that *La NRF* was among the rare publications whose distribution was authorized in the Southern zone. The article began with a categorical denunciation of the semi-legal magazines:

> What was improvised so recently [the new patriotism] still remains in that state, and in the young literary magazines of the other zone where political opposition to Marshal Pétain and the spirit of war at any price and any which way have taken refuge, we see some of our new patriots of the past few years occupy themselves by repolishing these strange weapons that served more to expose the fatherland than to defend it.

Behind the "heated adulator of the French Middle Ages and French poetry," Drieu identified the Communist—"And not just any Communist, but the militaristic and warmongering Communist of 1935–1939"—before concluding, "[. . .] all these coded appeals that Aragon spreads in the literary and poetic magazines, sewn with red thread, for resistance and hardening are not in the service of France [. . .] They will set it from Moscow, for sure, this dawn that knows no borders. And this Vermillion knight seems to me rather a red knight."[177] These magazines "sewn with red thread" were listed in a note in the same issue of *La NRF*.

By transgressing the dissociation that it claimed to maintain, in continuity with the prewar review, between literature and politics; by departing from the posture of "art for art's sake" that it advertized, Drieu's article unveiled the true position of *La NRF*. Drieu explained it in a footnote where, in accordance with what he had always defended, he challenged "literature in a vacuum." Drieu's scholarly apparatus, in the form of notes, was a good indicator of the objections raised by his stances: this was where, out of concern for respecting the rules of the game, he took them into account; and we can, by the same token, use them to decipher these rules and adjustments that the crisis situation made necessary. Thus, in the same note, Drieu would go so far as to justify himself to readers for making citations that they could not verify, alleging that the magazines of the other zone did not have any more scruples when they attacked a Parisian review (read: *La NRF*).[178] But by putting *La NRF* on the same level as these small semi-legal magazines, Drieu tried—with all the more bad faith since *La NRF* was distributed in the Southern zone—to obscure the conditions of production. While he resorted to the ordinary and altogether licit procedure of invective, a common form of payback that was, as I said, one of the regulatory practices of this symbolic universe, the circumstances gave this procedure a new meaning, that of identifying the target to the acting powers, that made it unacceptable according to the rules of the game because it relied on an extraliterary power relation. That is why this article would, in the literary field, have the opposite effect from what Drieu had intended.

Republished in *L'Émancipation nationale* on October 11, 1941, Drieu's article would serve unwittingly as an advertisement for those watchwords that Aragon had tossed out like a bottle into the sea. Denunciation sounded the alarm. In the general confusion, it served as a reference point. Pierre Daix's testimony on this subject is telling, all the more so since, not yet integrated into literary circles, he confirmed its echo in the most distant margins of the network of diffusion:

> In fact, this denunciation helped reveal the true position of Aragon, who was the subject of dishonoring rumors in Paris along these lines: "He writes for Pétain's newspapers." Among our students' groups—some of which were linked to the special organization that would shoot down a Nazi officer a few days later in Nantes [...] this article had an effect entirely opposite to the one Drieu had intended. Yes, there would be "a true French dawn." There were already new "vermillion knights" [...] Drieu had translated Aragon's lesson well.[179]

Aragon would emerge as the winner of this trial of strength with Drieu. "More Beautiful than Tears," Aragon's famous response to Drieu, appeared in *Tunis-Soir* on January 10, 1942, before being incorporated into *Les Yeux d'Elsa*: "By breathing, I keep certain people from living/I trouble their sleep with one knows not what remorse." Civil war made this competition into a life-and-death struggle, where each personified the enemy for the other, and where individual passions found their tragic justification in the universal cause. (Drieu's suicide in 1945—which happened only after he considered joining the Communist Party—would be its outcome, if not its consequence.)

After this first counteroffensive, *La NRF* displaced the struggle onto literary ground, by trying to discredit the movement of poetic renewal. In the issue of *La NRF* published in February 1942, Rolland de Renéville contested its literary value:

> It must be admitted that the postwar generation (but can we already speak of the postwar?) is far from displaying the richness, the seriousness, and the dynamism that was observed in the works of poets twenty years ago. Up until now we have only noticed, in the flood of booklets that in its size contradicts the aphorisms about the crisis of paper, pretense, facility, and absence of means—with very rare and fleeting exceptions. Let us wait.[180]

The strategy of disqualification would be concentrated on the man who was considered the emerging figure of this new poetic generation: Pierre Emmanuel. In the issue of *La NRF* published in April 1942, Maurice Chapelan wrote a long review of *Tombeau d'Orphée*, the first collection by this young poet published by the *Poésie 41* house (it was the first book edited by Seghers). Maurice Chapelan criticized Pierre Emmanuel, under cover of his "lack of sharpness in the conception and expression, of firmness in the outline, in sum of true force," for his audacity and his obscurity.[181]

On the publication of *Orphiques* in the "Métamorphoses" series that Paulhan edited at Gallimard, Drieu La Rochelle himself devoted not a note, but rather a long article to Pierre Emmanuel, in order to describe his art as "superficial." In this article, which included much discussion of Aragon, Drieu resorted again—for want of arguments?—to the procedure of denunciation. Based on a mass of errors and inexactitudes, this denunciation seemed almost parodic. He thus described Pierre Emmanuel as Jewish, an error that he had to correct (probably at the last minute) in a note, and said that he was an anarchist, in order to denounce the triple alliance between Catholics, Communists, and libertarians: "They have funny allies, the Catholics of the resistance; Pierre Emmanuel on one side, Louis Aragon on the other, whom they invite with Marshal Pétain to the second anniversary of the foundation of the *Compagnons* movement."[182] But in the end, Drieu was not entirely mistaken: the alliance between Catholics and Communists was indeed what would characterize the underground gathering of writers in the Southern zone a few months later.

It was nonetheless in this article published in October 1942 that Drieu made his famous statement of failure: "Almost the entire French intelligence, almost the entire French lyricism is against us. So what now?"[183] For several months, La NRF had been losing ground. In fact, attempts to rework the review's direction were sealed, in June, with failure.

THE STRUGGLES TO REAPPROPRIATE LA NRF

Since the beginning, Drieu La Rochelle had solicited Jean Paulhan's help, as we saw. Paulhan's refusal to assume the codirection of La NRF was not purely symbolic: he lost his position. He even had to think about looking for a job—he notably took steps at his former department, Public Instruction—before Gallimard entrusted him with the Pléiade series. It was primarily out of loyalty to the publisher that he accepted, unwillingly, to approach the former contributors to the review and ensure Drieu's transition, without, however, unduly facilitating his task.

Was Paulhan's refusal a choice in that, due to his previous endorsements, the German authorities did not wish for him to be involved? The problem must be posed in another way: we can suggest that, confirming his decision, the reservations expressed by the occupant in this regard above all freed Paulhan from his engagements toward Gaston Gallimard. This refusal, which seemed to come at a very high cost at the time, would prove to be profitable in the midterm, in many respects.

"A truly pivotal figure," according to Louis Parrot's expression, Jean Paulhan was then, due to his position and the extent of the contacts he was probably unique in having maintained with the dispersed writers, the man through whom the unity of the fragmented literary field was more or less maintained.[184] His article, "Hope and Silence," and his expulsion from La NRF, made him into the embodiment of that "guilty conscience" of the French writers for whom he had wanted La NRF to serve as the site of expression before the armistice. Less spectacular than Gide's later break, his refusal to coedit the review with Drieu was nonetheless, for his entourage, a moral reference point that discreetly sounded the alarm and, at a time when the stakes were still unclear, helped redefine the possibles. Paulhan's patriotism alone was not enough to explain this refusal, much less his political convictions; as a result of adopting the standpoint of his interlocutors, those convictions seemed piecemeal and resembled the "bizarre" that he held dear. For instance, following his disappointment with the Popular Front, he advocated a pseudo-monarchism which he opposed to the dictatorial principle as a "democratic" solution to the delegation of power.[185] Paulhan's choice during the Occupation must be related to a certain conception of the Republic of Letters that he had developed during his twenty years at La NRF. Its principle, as we saw, was the primacy of literary value over any extraliterary consideration, leading to the invalidation of any proscription on the basis of a moral or political criterion within the literary community.

Or at least the Protestant that lay within him—although he was not baptized, Paulhan came from a long line of Protestants from Nîmes[186]—then found in this principle the literary justification for his tendency to show solidarity with outcasts. For Paulhan, the rule of the literary game converged here with ethical dispositions that, for a number of fellow Protestants, were expressed during that period by solidarity with persecuted Jews: a solidarity that, according to Pierre Vidal-Naquet, was rooted as much in a collective memory of persecution as in what brought the Jewish and Protestant minorities closer together sociologically, namely "the concern for scholarly excellence [. . .] and solidarity with the Republican values to which they owed their own liberties."[187] Paulhan would again display his solidarity with the outcasts at the Liberation, now with regard to the former collaborators, for reasons that he would first intend as literary.

This son of a philosopher, who was rejected at the philosophy agrégation and who struggled to finish his own body of work (the thesis on the "Semantics of the Proverb" that he long refused to abandon),[188] had, making a virtue of necessity, developed a taste for secrecy. This was due to his long practice of effacement when faced with the egotism of the "creators" that he had often formed and oriented himself, with a sometimes "sadistic" severity but also with all the required discretion. Paulhan's "sadistic" reputation prevailed among the young writers, Jean Lescure remembered: "He terrorized us."[189]

Abandoning his job as the director of the review had a double effect on his trajectory. Freeing him from a heavy responsibility, it allowed him to complete the first part of his critique of criticism, *Les Fleurs de Tarbes, ou la Terreur dans les lettres*, emerging from his research on the semantics of the proverb, and which, when it was published in August 1941 in the "Métamorphoses" series, established him as a full-fledged author. Concurrently, by reinforcing his practice of collective literary work in the shadows, it could only sharpen the sensibility of the author of *Le Guerrier appliqué* with respect to another category of shadow "workers."

Anti-Munich, a notable opponent of collaborationism and a lover of secrets, Jean Paulhan was a choice recruit for the Resistance. One of the very first networks, known as the Musée de l'Homme, reached out to him, as Jacques Decour would do in the summer of 1941, when he would be charged with gathering writers in the underground. The fourth issue of the underground organ for the Musée de l'Homme network, *Résistance* (March 1941), published an unsigned article on *La NRF* to denounce the manipulation that, under cover of "the appearance of freedom," consisted in making the review and its great authors into the intellectual endorsement of collaborationism. Jean Paulhan—fearing Gallimard's wrath?—would deny authorship. In the same issue, three other notes by him attacked three Collaboration figures who had publicized their profession of faith in the first and third issue of *La NRF*: Chardonne, Fabre-Luce, and Abel Bonnard.

Arrested on May 6, 1941, while the Musée de l'Homme network was being dismantled, Paulhan was released a week later thanks to the intervention of Drieu La Rochelle, who supposedly threatened the German embassy that he would leave *La NRF*.[190] Drieu would take advantage of the debt that Paulhan now owed him. The former director of the review could no longer refuse his savior—the word is not too strong considering the fate reserved for members of the network—the help that he demanded. He sent him texts, gave him advice. In return, Drieu published two studies on *Les Fleurs de Tarbes* in *La NRF*, one by Ramon Fernandez in November 1941, the other by Rolland de Renéville in January 1942. Without being duped, and though he dreaded the consequences, Paulhan was not unmoved by this tribute. During this period, the solicitations from Drieu, who was beginning to take note of his own failure, became more and more pressing. Paulhan said he was ready to read the proofs, and recommended Maurice Blanchot to organize the notes, also suggesting that he ask Blanchot for a chapter from his second novel, *Aminadab*, which would be published by Gallimard that year.[191]

Aside from the debt of gratitude he owed Drieu, Paulhan was still sufficiently attached to what had been his work for more than fifteen years to have a hard time enduring its disfigurement. To his confidant, Monique Saint-Hélier, he wrote: "If he [Blanchot] asks me in turn for advice from time to time, I can't act badly in answering him, right? And for me, I can only return to *La NRF* when the Jews return. But all the same, I do not want it to become detestable."[192] Known for his prewar engagements on the extreme right, but having removed himself from the political scene since 1938, Maurice Blanchot was at once an acceptable recruit for Drieu La Rochelle—whom he had met before the war after having published an article on *Rêveuse bourgeoisie* and whom he had seen again at the beginning of the Occupation—and a man that Paulhan knew he could count on following the brilliant study he devoted to *Les Fleurs de Tarbes* under the title, "How Is Literature Possible?"[193] Paulhan therefore quite naturally thought of him when Drieu asked him to recommend a secretary. Maurice Blanchot would exercise this function from March to June 1942.

Paulhan's indirect help indeed proved insufficient. Canceled subscriptions multiplied. In March 1942, Drieu threatened for the first time to leave the review.

Invited by Gaston Gallimard to return as director, Paulhan declined. Drieu's threat seems designed to obtain Paulhan's official involvement in the review: "Paulhan is willing to make the review under my name without naming himself. But I don't want that. Since he writes to *Comoedia*, let him sign the review."[194] Breaking his silence, Paulhan had in fact given an article on Duranty to Marcel Arland in February for the literary page of *Comoedia*, which had already published an excerpt from *Les Fleurs de Tarbes* in August 1941.[195] These publications did not go unnoticed. Some people saw them as the endorsement of their own choice, like Rolland de Renéville who said he was morally "consoled" to see Paulhan publish in a weekly. "You can imagine that because of this fact, I felt less alone."[196] But Drieu was not mistaken. Paulhan's contributions to *Comoedia*, while he persisted in refusing to allow his name to appear in *La NRF*, made the weekly seem like a substitute for the abandoned *NRF* and contributed to the loss of the monopoly that the banning of the other journals in the occupied zone should have guaranteed. This was, moreover, the argument that Paulhan would invoke the following year to justify himself to François Mauriac: "I have not forgotten a time when Valéry, Claudel, or Vildrac's contributions to *C[omoedia]* signified quite precisely the refusal to continue contributing to *La nrf*."[197]

For his part, Gaston Gallimard feared the departure of Drieu, who was the guarantor of the publishing house with the Occupation authorities. This was all the more true since he had to deal with the new conditions placed on publishing in 1942: reinforced censorship measures and paper rationing were announced for April 1942; the establishment of a commission to control paper for publishing named by the Vichy government did not foreshadow anything good for those who, like Gallimard, were in the habit of bypassing Vichyist censors by directly addressing German censors. These worries materialized from mid-March: *La NRF* saw itself accorded only 34 pages instead of 128 a month in the new distribution, and Drieu La Rochelle, who took steps with the commission in April, met with refusal. *La NRF* would suffer from this restriction only temporarily, in its June issue, which numbered 63 pages instead of 128. Once more, Gaston Gallimard presented the review's maintenance as a means of rescuing the firm, which he said was threatened to be shut down if the review disappeared.[198] And in fact, without any evidence to support this threat, the Germans did not wish to see the end of *La NRF*, which would symbolize the failure of the politics of collaboration.[199]

The creation of an editorial board was considered. It would include Arland, Giono, Jouhandeau, Montherlant, and Paulhan, with Drieu officially maintaining his position as the director of the review. Torn between his resolutions—

not to appear by name in the review as long as its Jewish contributors were banned—and his attachment to *La* NRF, Paulhan set conditions. To mark the break with the orientations that Drieu had given it, the review had to become purely literary. This implied a change in form—the abandonment of the notes, brief notes, and "airs du mois," in a way that would reduce it to its anthological section and to the columns—and a change in leadership. Paulhan would agree to participate on the editorial board if a leadership council composed of the great elders was constituted concurrently, as Drieu also wished. Paulhan first solicited Paul Valéry, André Gide, and Jean Schlumberger. The latter having declined, fearing that the writers of "refusal" would lose "all the benefit of the abstention they practiced until now,"[200] Paulhan recruited Paul Claudel and Léon-Paul Fargue to replace him. At the same time, he probed possible contributors to the rebooted review: Groethuysen, Blanzat, Mauriac, Guéhenno, Duhamel. He had additionally asked the Sonderführer Gerhard Heller about the project's acceptability; his friends Marcel Jouhandeau and Marcel Arland had introduced him to Heller at the end of 1941 and they established cordial relations.[201] Claudel, Gide, and Valéry would be welcome; Mauriac and Duhamel would be tolerated; Aragon alone was "undesirable," out of respect for Vichy, Heller claimed.[202] Guéhenno and then Duhamel declined.[203] Gide, at first hesitant—as a result of a conversation with Malraux, in particular—ended up agreeing in principle if Paulhan obtained the agreement of "Eupalinos" (Valéry) and "Desqueyroux" (Mauriac), but he did not want "Contadour" (Giono) and Pincengrain (Jouhandeau) to participate in the project.[204] Valéry opposed the presence of Drieu, Montherlant, and Jouhandeau on the editorial board. Claudel accepted "on the condition that the traces of that revolting polecat Mont[herlant] are first disinfected."[205] Over the course of the negotiations, skillfully orchestrated by Paulhan, the project was modified. Paulhan thus whispered to Valéry to yield on the official attribution of the review's management to Drieu La Rochelle, but to remain "inflexible on what relates to the presence of Mauriac on the board."[206] Drieu La Rochelle refused this presence, just as he was not inclined to give up Montherlant and Jouhandeau, who represented the collaborationist tendency of the review, and whose elimination would put him in the minority. Valéry wrote to Gide: "As for the N.R.F., I have come to an agreement with Claudel by telephone. *We're standing fast.* Either *us* and us alone or nothing. Us means you, me, him, Mauriac, and some Fargue or other. In short, possible people. I have explained ten times that mixing these up with those means ruining everyone."[207]

The conditions of production were not yet favorable to an inversion of the internal power relation. Strengthened by the guarantee that he constituted for

the publishing house concerning the authorities of occupation, Drieu La Rochelle could apply his veto when he determined that the maneuver turned to his
disadvantage. The project failed. In June, Drieu again considered resigning,
then decided to return to the review at Gallimard's insistence, while his secretary, Maurice Blanchot, left. Yet the negotiations of the spring of 1942 exposed
the new alliances that were established at this date, especially the new relationship between the team of the old NRF and the refractory part of the French
Academy: Duhamel, Mauriac, and Valéry. They manifested themselves, as we
have seen, through the prizes that the Academy awarded that particular year—
for which Mauriac and Duhamel consulted notably with Jean Paulhan—and
their endorsement of the forums of opposition to the Vichy regime on the other
side of the demarcation line, the literary page of *Le Figaro* and the small magazines. The Grand Prize for Literature, awarded to Jean Schlumberger at François
Mauriac's initiative, was a reward for intransigence and "refusal." Alone on the
team of founders of *La NRF* to show himself completely intransigent, including
when the review's editorial board was being reworked, Schlumberger had exposed his fears to François Mauriac in a long letter where he asked him, as the
youngest member of the future council, to prevent drifting. To preserve the
moral benefit of the abstention of the four or five principal writers ("those
whom we hold dearest"), the distinction had to be clearly maintained between
them and the colleagues who "caused us painful disappointments [. . .] This
trench must remain clearly traced, and those who have crossed to the other
side cannot use any excuse to claim that it is only a question of more or less," he
explained.[208]

It was only a year later that Drieu would abandon *La NRF* to Paulhan. He
accepted first in May 1943 that Paulhan run the review in his name, with Jacques
Lemarchand as editor in chief. Thirty-four years old, secretary at *La Gerbe*,
which he left for this new position, Lemarchand had just published a novel
with Gallimard. To Henri Pourrat, whose "De la confiance" he published in the
June issue, Paulhan guaranteed that Drieu would no longer contribute political
columns and that the review would no longer address current events: "At last it
becomes, I think, altogether worthy of your contribution."[209] At this date, however, the rules of conduct were already to a large extent codified: this time, Leiris and Queneau refused to follow Paulhan.[210] In June, Drieu would seize the
pretext of a "bad article" that Paulhan had submitted to him, as he said—he
had in fact refused several texts, including Noël Devaulx's short story that
would be published in *Poésie 43*—and would definitively resign, this time. This
ultimately led to the dissolution of the review, Paulhan and Gallimard having
failed to reach an understanding with Gerhard Heller.

Drieu's disengagement, which grew as the failure of *La NRF* was confirmed, hastened the end. In September 1941, Drieu still enjoyed his hard-won position—"My passions have provoked and met those of others. Never had I been as much hated, negated, feared, appreciated as now"—but felt nothing but boredom in December 1942: "I put myself in a situation that bores me dreadfully: the review, the collaboration, all of it has annoyed me almost all the time since the beginning, and since it is all turning decidedly bad, I am infuriated by the role that I have to play until the end."[211] "I find no perverse pleasure in being almost alone," he wrote in the article on Pierre Emmanuel in November 1942, only to immediately correct in a note, "almost alone is a manner of speaking," before associating himself with the most prestigious figures of the Collaboration: Giono, Montherlant, Céline, Jouhandeau, Chardonne, Fabre-Luce, Fernandez, Morand.[212]

A SUBSTITUTE FOR *LA NRF* IN THE OCCUPIED ZONE: *MESSAGES*

The difficulties of communication between the zones until the total occupation of the territory in November 1942 meant that the writers of "refusal" who resided in the occupied zone were cut off from the forums of the zone said to be free, except for the elders who were the most solicited and whose mobility was facilitated by their notoriety, like Mauriac, Duhamel, or Valéry. André Rousseaux thus reported that his wife, having found an itinerary to illegally cross the demarcation line, had established a link that allowed *Le Figaro*, withdrawn to Lyon, to "publish the articles of writers, if not *résistants*, at least unsubdued by the Germans, who refused to write a single line in the publications of the occupied zone," like Duhamel and Valéry.[213] The younger ones stayed on the margins of the movement stimulated by the subversive magazines, even if they identified with it: "From the Southern zone some precious copies of *Poésie 41*, of *Fontaine* reached us, immediately devoured, copied, circulating like a thousand," Jean Lescure related.[214]

But, for these same reasons, Jean Paulhan found himself somewhat dispossessed of this movement of poetic renewal that he helped initiate by establishing Aragon the poet during the Phoney War, by lending his support to Seghers's *P.C. 39, 40*, and by publishing *Le Crève-cœur* in the "Métamorphoses" series in 1941. His attempts to resurrect the magazine *Mesures* were in vain. The project for the magazine *Prométhée* was aborted. The "Métamorphoses" series that he edited at Gallimard was, for the moment, the only place where he could continue to guide the tendencies of literature. It would consecrate the principal representatives of the new generation of poets that emerged in those years. "The

Métamorphoses series made everyone salivate," Jean Lescure remembered. "Emmanuel, when he announces to me that Paulhan has asked him for a text for 'Métamorphoses' [. . .] he is in seventh heaven and so am I."[215] In fact, Paulhan published *Le Parti pris des choses* by Francis Ponge there in 1942; it was the poet's first collection since *Douze petits écrits*, published by Gallimard in 1926 thanks to Paulhan. He also published *Orphiques* by Pierre Emmanuel the same year. In 1943 he published *Le Témoin invisible* by Jean Tardieu and *Haut mal* by Michel Leiris; they had been Gallimard authors since 1939. The "Métamorphoses" series was reserved for "tested" poets. Even though he had contributed to *La NRF* on the eve of the defeat, Emmanuel was not a house author, unlike Ponge, Tardieu, and Leiris. By confirming the verdict of the small magazines in the other zone and the new publishing house created by Pierre Seghers, Pierre Emmanuel's publication was a consecration that reflected on the movement of poetic renewal in the Southern zone to the detriment of Drieu's NRF. It was this publication that gave rise to Drieu's article, where he acknowledged his failure.

When Jean Lescure sought out Jean Paulhan at the end of 1941 to announce that he wanted to make an "anti-NRF" that he would name *La NPF* (*La Nouvelle Poésie française*), drawing the "f" in the style of the NRF acronym, he thought he would be thrown out. He was totally surprised to hear the answer: "Oh! That's interesting." "He clicked right away," he remembered.[216] Jean Lescure's astonishment shows how much Paulhan's reputation "terrorized" young writers. But it also reveals how much the particular circumstances of the Occupation made the improbable possible. The fact that this offer was welcome at a time when Paulhan was dispossessed of the literary forums where he used to rule as master was confirmed by his investment in this magazine. It finally assumed the title of the one that Jean Lescure had edited before the war, *Messages*, with the subtitle *Cahiers de poésie française*, and where, with his legendary discretion, he would assist in the task: "And there, at the relaunch, it is Paulhan who was truly my master."[217]

Jean Lescure was thirty years old at the time. Born in Asnières, the son of cinema owners, he had attended primary school at Saint-Joseph (Asnières), then pursued his secondary studies at the collège de Saint-Germain-en-Laye and at Sainte-Barbe. He then studied philosophy for one year at the Sorbonne, where he notably took Georges Dumas's courses in psychopathology, but refused to take the exams. This education earned him a reputation as a philosopher, which he put to work when the editor Walter Uhl, who published the magazine *Messages*, entrusting its direction to the young poet André Silvaire, called on him to take over and give it a more ambitious project.

During this period, a will to bring poetry and philosophy closer together appeared in certain literary circles. The surrealists had revalorized the romantic conception of poetry as a means of knowledge, against the art of pleasing dear to the classics. In his introduction to *De Baudelaire au surréalisme* (1940), a work that allowed the Geneva school to establish itself, followed by *L'Âme romantique et le rêve* by Albert Béguin, Marcel Raymond would acknowledge this new orientation:

> From then on poetry tended to become an ethic or some sort of irregular instrument of metaphysical knowledge. Poets were obsessed by the need to "change life," as Rimbaud puts it, to change man and to bring him into direct contact with existence. The novelty lies less in the fact than in the intention, which gradually emerges from the realm of the unconscious, of reconquering man's irrational powers and of transcending the dualism of the self and the universe.[218]

These tendencies, which were expressed by the current popularity of William Blake, were fed by the reflections of Heidegger on Hölderlein, according to Jean Lescure's testimony.

Jean Lescure proposed to Walter Uhl that he deepen this "poïétique" quest. The three issues of *Messages* published in 1938, under the direction of André Silvaire, gathered young poets, from the "Sagesse" group and the future members of the École de Rochefort, and recognized elders like Pierre Jean Jouve, Pierre Reverdy—two poets who were then the most important for Jean Lescure—and Jules Supervielle. The two issues that Jean Lescure edited in 1939, before the review's disappearance when war was declared, were devoted to William Blake and "Poetry and Metaphysics" respectively, with the contributions of Jean Wahl and Gaston Bachelard, among others. In his presentation of the Blake issue, Jean Lescure quoted Novalis: "Without philosophy, the poet is incomplete."[219]

During the Phoney War, Jean Lescure participated in meetings that assembled Georges Bataille, Jean Wahl, Georges Pelorson, Pierre-André Touchard, and Paul-Louis Landsberg at the home of banker Marcel Moré (an admirer of Léon Bloy who was close to *Esprit*). Marcel Moré and Georges Bataille had formed this group "to revive what remains of *Esprit, Volontés* and the *Collège de sociologie*," as Marcel Moré announced to Michel Leiris.[220] The journal *Volontés*, which Georges Pelorson had edited from 1938 to 1939, allied literature with social considerations. Alongside translations of Henry Miller, Pelorson and Raymond Queneau handled the literary section. Queneau notably published his "Technique of the Novel" where he exposed the mathematical structure of his novels and where his leaning for occultism and René Guénon's thought became clear.[221] Queneau's texts were paired with Pierre Guégen's reflections on the

"Metaphysics of the Machine," excerpts from the "Guiding Plan for a Reform of French Education" that Georges Pelorson would publish under the title *Éducation et Enseignement* at Denoël, and, in the "Will to Live" column, articles on urbanism (particularly Le Corbusier), on "peasant psychology" (Mara Thaon), on hygienism (Dr. Madeleine Violet).

Born in Belley in 1909, the son of a pair of instructors from the south of the Jura (his father had been promoted to inspector of primary instruction), Georges Pelorson had studied at the lycée de Beauvais, then Louis-le-Grand. Having passed the ENS entrance exam—he belonged to the class of 1928, like Brasillach, Bardèche, and Thierry Maulnier whom he had befriended—he left after receiving an English degree. He aspired to become a writer and poet, finally became a journalist, and from 1936 to 1939 directed the first bilingual school in France, where he had recruited Queneau as a teacher. In 1941, Pelorson was a member of the Parisian cell of Jeune France, before joining the office of documentation for the delegation of the Vichy government in Paris (he would be fired by Laval in February 1943). A contributor to *La Gerbe*, he would, at the request of Lucien Combelle, serve as theater columnist at *La Révolution nationale*. Charged with the literary section of Jeune France, Pelorson wanted to launch a review in Paris, planning to entrust its direction to Maurice Blanchot. He had appealed to Queneau and, armed with Queneau's agreement, to Michel Leiris, who flatly refused.[222] Georges Bataille had also agreed to participate: in response to Leiris, who had criticized him for it, he supposedly answered in substance: "What I always counted as essential comes from my inner life: I don't have to worry about *what is external to me* [*sic*]. In the present time, there will be no solidarity with those who are affected."[223] The review would not see the light of day, likely having failed to obtain the authorization of the occupant.

Still a very little-known author, Georges Bataille appeared at this moment, about 1941, as the figure who established himself among the young guard of the Gallimard house (where he published *L'Expérience intérieure* in 1943). Having met Maurice Blanchot via Pierre Prévost, who had participated in the meetings of the Collège de Sociologie, starting in the autumn of 1941 Bataille organized reading discussion groups at the home of Denise Rollin, rue de Lille, forming two distinct groups—only Blanchot participated in both, it seems—that gathered the members of Jeune France on one side (Pierre Prévost, Xavier de Lignac, Romain Petitot), and Queneau, Leiris, Michel Fardoulis-Lagrange on the other.[224] Jean Lescure and Raoul Ubac would take part in the second, thanks to relationships forged around the magazine *Messages*. Linked by bonds of friendship that were consolidated by their matrimonial unions (the Kahn, Maklès, and Kahnweiler families maintained close relationships), Queneau, Leiris, and Bataille were choice recruits for the magazine *Messages*. Dissidents of surrealism, they shared with Jean Lescure an interest in philosophy and the new disciplines of the human sciences: psychoanalysis, sociology, and ethnology, an interest that was embodied by the creation of the Collège de Sociologie. Having graduated with a literature degree and a philosophy specialization at the Sorbonne, in the 1930s Queneau followed Henri-Charles Puech's teaching on the gnosis and Manicheism, along with Koyré, and Kojève on Hegel at the École pratique des hautes études. Leiris, a scholarship holder at the National Center for Scientific Research (CNRS) where the human sciences section was in full development, and affiliated with the Musée de l'Homme, had just defended his thesis on *La Langue secrète des Dongons de Sanga* at the École pratique des hautes études (1938); he would be named a researcher at the CNRS in 1943. A graduate of the École des Chartes, Bataille had been initiated in anthropology by Alfred Métraux and took Marcel Mauss's courses.

Thanks to the 700 francs of income that his parents gave him, and the contributions of Paul Bodin and Georges Sonnier, Jean Lescure had managed to assemble the 3,000 francs necessary to launch the magazine. Jean Paulhan obtained funding for him. Jean Flory had found a printer, Mr. Gamon, in Thouars. With a circulation of 500 copies, the first issue of *Messages* appeared in March 1942. Entitled "Elements," it included, among others, texts by Pierre Emmanuel, Jean Grenier, Jean Follain, Guillevic, and Benjamin Fondane, the poet of Jewish Romanian origin who would be deported in 1944 to Auschwitz-Birkenau where he would die. The editorial board of the magazine was composed of Paul Bodin, Pierre Emmanuel, Jean Lescure, and Georges Sonnier, with Alexandre Astruc as secretary. Jean Lescure had befriended Pierre Emmanuel before the war via Pierre Jean Jouve. They had been back in touch through interzonal cards after the armistice. Pierre Emmanuel asked him for texts for *Poésie 40, 41* and for *Fontaine*. He agreed to enter the administrative board of *Messages*, giving himself the mission of being "the liaison between poets of O.Z and of Non O.Z."[225] In the Southern zone, Pierre Emmanuel nonetheless collided with the writers' distrust: "People are devilishly reticent," he wrote to Jean Lescure. Loÿs Masson nonetheless appeared in the table of contents in the second issue, along with Francis Ponge, whom Jean Paulhan had recruited. For his part, Guillevic, whom Jean Lescure had met through Jean Follain and who had resumed contact with him at the beginning of the Occupation, canvassed among the authors of the Gallimard house, including the contributors to Drieu's *NRF*. He thus obtained the full agreement of Jean Follain, Henri Thomas, and Jean Tardieu, and the agreement in principle, but not without hesitation, of Queneau and Leiris.[226] It was only after the publication of the first issue that Queneau sent the magazine a short story, "Dino," that appeared in the second issue. He then recruited Leiris and Bataille, who would contribute to the fourth issue. But Rolland de Renéville, whose name had been announced, would refuse to participate. The second issue, entitled "Dramatics of Hope," published a text by Paul Claudel without the author's permission. "We had to have 'big names,'" said Jean Lescure.[227] Paul Eluard, who figured in the table of contents of this issue, would become, with Queneau, a precious help for Jean Lescure.

The first issues of *Messages* did not yet distinguish themselves clearly from the project of the magazines *Poésie 42* and *Fontaine*, except by reuniting poets of both zones. The prewar project around "poetry and metaphysics" no longer fit the circumstances. "Poetry and liberty" was now the equation, and its resolution passed through the word "France":[228] another way of saying that regaining the autonomy of literature operated through the reaffirmation of its national character. *Messages* claimed a relationship with the semi-legal magazines of the other zone, to "attest here to the presence of a culture and what it implies of the will to create man and the world in the image of its demanding greatness," to attest to "the uninterrupted mission of France."[229] Poetry was a weapon to reaffirm "the French spirit" and maintain a space of liberty under oppression. A large part of the columns were devoted to *Fontaine* and *Poésie 42*: "These columns allowed us to introduce into the Northern zone, where they were forbidden, the complicit magazines of the Southern zone: *Poésie 41*, *Fontaine*, to quote the blacklisted poets, Aragon who was starting to be made into a kind of Zorro of oppressed poetry. Even those who were no longer read in Paris, for lack of welcoming publications or for other reasons: Daumal, Bertrand d'Astorg, Louis Emié, Lanza del Vasto, Lorca, Jouve, André de Richaud, Pierre Katz, Audisio . . ." Jean Lescure reported.[230] The "Color of the Times" section, imitating magazines of the other zone, resorted to irony to deride Collaboration figures: "Paris, February 1941—Monsieur Drieu La Rochelle professes that if the French have so well lost the war, it is because they have forgotten the *Body*," or again "Paris, November 1941—In the corridors of the metro, posters printed in all caps abound: ABEL BONNARD, FRENCH YOUTH."[231]

It was fearfully that Jean Lescure submitted the third issue of *Messages*, entitled "Exercise of Purity," to Jean Paulhan. Yet Paulhan, who had just received the special issue of *Fontaine*, "Poetry as a Spiritual Exercise," answered him: "The spiritual number of *Fontaine* is a horrible nightmare. Let *Messages* live more than ever"![232] This reaction attested not to a divorce—the time had not yet come—but a progressive differentiation of poetic projects, the literary "families" and ethical divergences regaining superiority over the common combat that the practice of "contraband" helped homogenize. *Poésie 42* was, as we saw, just as critical about this issue of *Fontaine*. While *Fontaine* then made itself the mouthpiece of a spiritual conception of poetry of Christian inspiration, while *Poésie 42* advocated an engaged poetry anchored in the world and in time, *Messages* would be the forum of "pure" literature, a substitute for Paulhan's *NRF*, even though Jean Lescure tried, in his presentations, to tie to the circumstances texts that were expected to include "a political position, that they did not express *at first*."[233]

The second issue, ready to appear at the beginning of the summer of 1942, had been predated—it bore a print date of "spring 1942"—to bypass the new dispositions of censorship that required an authorization number. This was a subterfuge that the surrealist publishers of the "Main à plume" employed for the printing of *Poésie et vérité 1942* by Eluard that appeared in the month of October, with a print date of April 3, 1942.[234] The third issue of *Messages*, "Exercise of Purity," came out in the same conditions, but the venture became more and more risky. "Exercise of Silence," the fourth issue of the review, which bore a print date of December 10, 1942, was printed in Brussels thanks to a young Belgian writer, Georges Lambrichs. Meanwhile, the editorial board had dissolved. With a circulation of 1,200 copies, this issue, which bore an epitaph by Bernanos, "To keep the silence. What a strange word! It is silence that keeps us," presented an impressive table of contents. Next to a letter from Baudelaire sent by Paulhan were Bachelard, Eluard, Jean Tardieu, André Frénaud, Roger Gilbert-Lecomte, Arthur Adamov, Fardoulis-Lagrange, Leiris ("La rose du désert"), Sartre (who submitted an excerpt from "La mort dans l'âme"), and Bataille ("Le Rire de Nietzsche"). If this table of contents was missing a name (Camus), it was not because they had not received some pages from him on the absurd, transmitted by Paulhan, but because they had received them too late.

Despite Paulhan's criticisms—"too many big names, big reflections between which there is no time to breathe (whoever deprives himself of 'gray parts' runs the risk of the whole becoming gray)"[235]—we can see this issue as the culmination of the literary project that he had formed at *La NRF* on the eve of the war: contesting the domination of the nineteenth-century novel by calling its techniques into question and promoting competing genres like poetry and the essay. It was Paulhan, as we saw, who promoted Sartre at *La NRF* and at Gallimard. It was he who advised Michel Leiris to read *Le Mur*, just as he had surely had *L'Âge d'homme* sent to Sartre during his mobilization.[236] In this, he was in large part at the origin of the "Sartre" phenomenon. Sartre "began to make waves [...] We had to have the signature," said Jean Lescure.[237] Anna Boschetti has shown how Sartre was predisposed to capitalize on the results of the research undertaken before the war by the avant-garde on its way to consecration.[238] Given his training in philosophy at the ENS, he was the best placed to reconcile literature and philosophy by combining the double heritage of Gide and Bergson. In addition to the importation of the techniques of the American novel and of Kafkaian devices, his reinterpretation of German phenomenology was capped off the following year by the publication of *Being and Nothingness*. Between 1942 and 1943, Sartre befriended Leiris, Queneau, and Bataille. He participated in the readings-debates at Bataille's home. It was this competitor, who established himself as the new head of a school, that Sartre would confront shortly after the creation of "Les Mouches" in June 1943. Under the title "A New Mystic," he published at the end of 1943, in *Les Cahiers du Sud*, an acerbic criticism of *Inner Experience*, denouncing the anti-intellectualist mysticism in which he saw "the product of a totalitarian thinking," philosophical approximation, and the quest for transcendence of this "shamefaced Christian" hidden by the Nietzschean.[239]

THE REUNIFICATION OF THE LITERARY FIELD

By attenuating the difficulties of circulation and communication between the zones, the invasion of the Southern zone in November 1942 favored the reunification of the literary field and allowed the more or less dispersed semi-legal ventures to accomplish a true symbolic takeover. Starting in 1943, the contents of *Poésie 43,44*, *Confluences*, and *Fontaine* reflected that movement: the signatures of Jean Tardieu, Michel Leiris, Jean Blanzat, and of course Jean Paulhan appeared in *Poésie 43,44* ... (Jean Lescure and Pierre Leyris had already contributed to *Poésie 42*), those of Jean Tardieu, Sartre, Paulhan, Jacques Debû-Bridel in *Confluences*, those of Queneau, Leiris, and Paulhan in *Fontaine*. It was of course Jean Paulhan who chiefly ensured the liaison with Paris.

But it was the fifth issue of *Messages*, "French domain," that best embodied this reunification. The project was ambitious:

> It was a matter, however, of bringing what passed for the expression of a group to broaden itself until it joined a conception of "French" literature as a fact of language and *anti-Nazi* society. In this idea, the "patriotic" nature of the activity of language should thus be present, its role in the formation of an identity, its reference to a History, its claim of a past, and the negation that this implied of the new order, the advent of which the totalitarian powers strove to impose.

What should then have figured as a manifesto was the great number of representative writers assembled. It was a matter of gathering everything that had a name in French literature, of everything that claimed the heritage of a culture […] Another idea had taken shape. The claim of a spiritual heritage.[240]

The question of the place of publication arose. The measures of censorship had been extended to Belgium. The Southern zone imposed the restrictions of Vichy censors. Publishing in Algiers would have given this project a meaning of political support for de Gaulle, which risked pushing away some contributors. For a long time, Jean Lescure thought about putting the issue out in Paris. During a trip to the Southern zone, he had tried to involve Pierre Seghers in the publication of the volume, but Seghers pulled out for financial reasons: printing a volume of 400 pages was a crazy venture. Switzerland offered itself providentially to Jean Lescure through François Lachenal, who introduced Pierre Emmanuel to him.

Since August 1940, when the Swiss Federal Council called for adapting to the "new Europe," François Lachenal had published a dissident literary and political semi-legal magazine, *Traits*, in French Switzerland.[241] Son of the head of the Department of Public Instruction, a "disinherited" heir to the Swiss-French elite of Geneva, François Lachenal was then twenty-two years old. Attached to the Swiss diplomatic service to Vichy from 1942, in January he inaugurated the new itinerary of manuscripts by French writers that had been transported to Switzerland, with two poems, one by Pierre Seghers, the other by Pierre Emmanuel, which appeared anonymously in the third issue of *Traits*: "We could not insert everything in the review (*Poésie 42* …). In Switzerland, *Traits* and *Lettres* published our most aggressive texts under pseudonyms," Pierre Seghers would say at the Liberation.[242] François Lachenal would thus nourish not only *Traits*, where texts by Aragon, Éluard, Vercors, and so forth appeared under pseudonyms, but also Albert Béguin's *Les Cahiers du Rhône* in Neuchâtel, *Ides et Calendes* in Freiburg, which published texts by Loÿs Masson, Pierre Emmanuel, and Pierre Seghers among others, and the journal *Lettres* that Pierre Courthion edited in Geneva, and in which Jean Starobinski and Pierre Jean Jouve participated. Lachenal would also work to reintroduce the published texts in France; sometimes they were repressed by Swiss censorship, sometimes by the censorship of Vichy.[243] The editor in chief of *Traits*, Jean Descoullayes, curator of the Musée des Beaux-Arts in Lausanne, also ran the Éditions des Trois Collines in Geneva, which hosted, in August 1943, *Domaine français* (the volume would only be published in December).

It was again Paulhan who obtained funding for the project. Georges Duhamel earned *Messages* 10,000 francs from the Association "Au service de la pensée française." "But more than an important debut to financing, what these letters brought to us was the support that we wanted from the *institutional* part of literature in France," Jean Lescure explains.[244] Paulhan worked to recruit the prestigious elders: Gide, Valéry, Claudel, Schlumberger, Benda, Duhamel, Mauriac, Paul Hazard, and André Rousseaux. According to Jean Lescure's account, he brought in about twenty texts, without counting, he specified, the authors that he had introduced at *Messages*. The contributors to the review represented another twenty-something names that figured in the table of contents. Eluard had brought about fifteen texts. The gathering did not occur without difficulty. Claudel had set conditions: "I would like just as well to be spared proximity to 'poets' like P. J. Jouve or Pierre Emmanuel."[245] Jean Lescure had for his part expressed reservations about François Mauriac, whom he relegated "into the shadows of provincial psychology." He nonetheless yielded to Paulhan's, then Eluard's pleas. "We placed, however, with a nice thick finesse, Mauriac immediately after: 'The one who believed in heaven, the one who did not believe in it' [Aragon]. I thought myself shrewd. It was in fact what they both wanted."[246]

Among the fifty-seven writers who figured in the table of contents of *Domaine français*, twenty-four had been contributors to the former NRF. If we add six authors from *La* NRF publishing house, what we might call the NRF-Gallimard network totaled more than half the contributions to the volume. The others were for the most part newcomers. The team of the founders of *La* NRF and the intermediate generations (Mauriac, Duhamel, representatives of the generation born in 1885; Aragon, Eluard, from the first surrealist generation) rubbed elbows there with the avant-garde of Gallimard, Sartre, Camus, Leiris, Queneau, Bataille, and the principal figures of the poetic renewal, Ponge, Emmanuel, Guillevic, and André Frénaud. The last was another figure that emerged from those dark years—"a great one, one of the greatest French poets," as Georges Meyzargues alias Aragon had introduced him in *Poésie 42*[247]— whose first collection, *Les Rois mages*, would be published by Seghers in 1943, and who would enter the Gallimard list in 1949. At the very moment when the last negotiations for the continuation of *La* NRF had just failed, Jean Paulhan had thus recreated, if not the prewar NRF, at least "the NRF spirit." By that time, a new role had already appeared for the review *Messages*: that of "recruiting agent" for the underground, according to Jean Lescure's expression.

Site of "pure" literature and intellectual debate, site of research and the conciliation of contraries, *La* NRF could not survive the defeat without betraying its heritage. Faced with its instrumentalization in the service of the politics of collaboration, its claim to represent "art for art's sake" exposed the obsolescence of this option in the new circumstances. Thanks to the intergenerational alliance, the very ones who cited it as a reference in order to defend the writers accused of responsibility for the defeat, now offered their endorsement to semi-legal ventures that put art to the service of the struggle to reaffirm the "French spirit," and some of them, like Paulhan and Mauriac, even went so far as to thereby lend their support to the underground ventures engaged in an open ideological struggle against the occupant and against Vichy.

CHAPTER 7

The Sense of Subversion

The Comité national des écrivains (CNE)

The Comité national des écrivains (CNE) was the principal authority of the literary Resistance. A literary group with a political vocation, it inherited the new forms of collective intervention for intellectuals since the Dreyfus affair, and more directly the structures of anti-Fascist mobilization in the 1930s. However, it was composed solely of writers, and its mode of intervention was specifically literary, by the means it employed (poetry, novel, criticism, echoes of the literary world), and its area of intervention: the collaborationist literary milieus were its principal adversary in this fight. This professional dimension played a part in its success. It was because the writers had the opportunity to fight with their own weapons that, reactivating the subversive dimension of literature, they ensured the prestige of the intellectual Resistance.

At the origin of the group that would take the name of Comité national des écrivains there was the encounter between writers dispossessed of their means of expression and the organizational and mobilizing structures of the underground Communist Party. The low probability of this meeting, as much as the unhoped-for success of this clandestine mobilization, which would be unequaled in the other intellectual committees encouraged by the French Communist Party, invites us to look for explanations elsewhere than in strictly political affinities.

Not that intellectual engagements close to or in the ranks of the Communist Party had been lacking before the war: there were, as we know, plenty of precedents. From Barbusse, Romain Rolland, Paul Nizan, and Aragon to Malraux and Gide, the Communist Party's power of attraction, still very marginal in the 1920s, had increased in the 1930s. Despite the stupor and protestations it aroused among his peers, André Gide's position-taking in 1932 would ultimately help legitimize the model of fellow-traveling, allowing intellectuals to salve their conscience without alienating their freedom of judgment. The line of opening from the Communist Party to intellectuals favored this form of engagement, through organizations like the Association des écrivains et artistes révolutionnaires (AEAR). The union of left-wing parties in the anti-Fascist struggle and the electoral triumphs of the party helped establish its political respectability. The victory of the Popular Front consecrated this union of left-wing parties, which the weekly *Vendredi*, directed by the radical-Socialist André Chamson, the Socialistic Jean Guéhenno, and the Communistic Andrée Viollis, embodied in the intellectual field. The will to maintain this alliance at all costs can be illustrated by the refusal of *Vendredi*'s directors to publish the preface to Gide's *Retour de l'URSS* and the public polemic that ensued between the weekly and the author.[1]

The union of the left-wing parties was nonetheless called into question during the Spanish Civil War, due to the divergences occasioned by the Blum government's politics of nonintervention, which the moderate and/or pacifist left supported against the Communists and the fractions where the anti-Fascist cause prevailed. It was then further shaken during the Munich agreement and the invasion of Czechoslovakia, which confirmed the split between integral pacifism and anti-Fascism. In the extreme-left milieus, the Moscow trials confirmed fears: "There, my innocence was taken away in one single stroke," Jean Lescure said.[2] Finally, the German-Soviet pact led to not only the dissolution of whatever remained of this union of left-wing parties, but, with the banning of the Communist Party, a veritable excommunication of Communist intellectuals. It would not be until the change of line of the clandestine Communist Party in mid-May 1941, that is to say a month before the German offensive against Soviet Russia, for the disarray that reigned in the ranks of the militants to dissipate—Paul Nizan bore witness to it shortly before his death at the front—and, by proving their patriotism in the underground struggle against the occupying forces, they were progressively cleansed of the suspicion of treason, thus regaining a moral credibility. The mutual suspicion between the writers and the party, temporarily overcome for the needs of the common struggle, subsisted in a latent state only to reemerge at the approach of the Liberation. The unitary politics would moreover not survive the ordeals of the purge and the Cold War.

The weight of past militant solidarities, the inscription of the representation and practices of unitary action in a preexisting repertoire can be observed in the recruitment of the literary Resistance: the writers who were engaged before the war in the ranks of the anti-Fascist secular left composed more than half the underground committee of the two zones combined. However, this static representation masks the difficulties that had to be overcome on both sides. Moreover, previous militant solidarities explain neither the recruitment in the Catholic milieus or on the right, nor the recruitment of the newcomers who were barely politicized before the war.

To the question of the foundation of these alliances, another question is added. Underground mobilization in the literary milieus would, as I said, experience an unequaled success. Why was it that in the most individualistic, least organized, and least regulated "profession," the formula of assembling on a professional basis was so successful? The question includes part of the answer. The weak professionalization of the occupation of writer, the absence of a competing organization, whether an order or a corporation—at a time when the Vichy regime worked to frame the corporative aspirations of numerous professions— the failure of traditional literary institutions (Société des gens de lettres, academies) to confront the abrupt transformation of working conditions, ultimately favored the implantation of this formula in the literary milieu. The new conditions of production, which suppressed the freedom of expression won at great cost at the end of the last century and which reduced certain writers to silence in the name of an ideological war, paired with the ostracism that struck certain recognized writers of the interwar period, held responsible for the defeat and designated to the authorities by their peers who subscribed to the National Revolution or collaborationism, emphasize the threat that once again targeted the "profession." The defense of autonomy was, as I have already suggested, one of the main motivations for collective mobilization at the pole of small-scale production in the literary field.

To these conditions, which are necessary but insufficient to explain the move to action and the form that this action took, we must add on one side the organizational formula that made this mobilization possible, and on the other the properly literary foundations of militant solidarity, which allowed writers to overcome traditional divisions of all kinds (ideological, generational, literary). In the Northern zone, the recruitment of the literary Resistance thus depended to a large extent on the split of *La NRF*, of which it seemed like a splinter group. In the Southern zone, the symbolic takeover accomplished by contraband literature favored a reworking of the alliances that would facilite underground recruitment.

The Literary Conditions of a Successful Mobilization

Like that of the National Front from which it emerged,[3] the history of the CNE did not follow a linear evolution. Its only principle of continuity resided in the politics of assembling writers around an underground journal, adopted by the directors of the Communist intellectuals during the summer of 1941 at Aragon's initiative. Interrupted by the arrest of Jacques Decour in February 1942, the project would not fully succeed until 1943. Meanwhile, the writers who had joined the first group continued to meet: Jean Paulhan, Jean Blanzat, Jean Guéhenno, and Jacques Debû-Bridel, notably, met in Paulhan's office at Gallimard. The first three writers, along with François Mauriac after his return to Paris at the end of 1942, also met at each other's homes. When Claude Morgan, designated by the party to replace Decour, managed to renew ties, he found a ready-made committee. Underground recruitment in the Northern zone relied on the Gallimard-*NRF* network, especially on the split of the *NRF* team; the magazine *Messages* was an expression of this. In the Southern zone, Aragon's task was to form an opposition to the Vichy regime around the semi-legal magazines. When, in 1943, he set out to assemble an underground committee of writers in the Southern zone, the networks were already formed there, too.

THE POLITICS OF THE NATIONAL FRONT

The shift that the underground Communist Party set in motion in mid-May 1941, after several months of fumbling and hesitations over the objectives of the struggle (the pursuit of "national liberation" being still largely subordinated to the aspiration for "social liberation"), was illustrated, in its version for the larger public, in the form of a tract, by the call "for the formation of a National Front for French Independence." Reviving anti-Fascist unitary politics and the national line defined by Maurice Thorez at the Ninth Congress of the Communist Party in Arles in 1937, the party called for the unity of the nation, "with the exception of the traitors and defeatists doing the work or playing the game of the invader," and extended a hand to "all Frenchmen of good will," even as it emphasized its primacy and denigrated its chief rival, the "de Gaulle movement."[4] While the rivalry did not exclude contacts in the field, the overture toward Free France would not be made official until the spring of 1942, when it paved the way for a reconciliation at the summit that would culminate in January 1943 with the delegation of Fernand Grenier as the representative of the party and the Francs-Tireurs et partisans movement (FTP) in London.[5] The relatively quick echo that the call met in milieus that had until then remained wary, even hostile, with regard to the Communists because of the German-Soviet pact, including the Gaullist milieus, was due to the efficacy and specificity of the organizational structures set in motion by the Communist Party.

The specificity of the underground structures implanted by the Communist Party in order to apply the line of the National Front resulted from its preexisting structures of mobilization and frames of action. Unlike other resistance groups that most often privileged an organization with a territorial base (region, department) or oriented around particular services (propaganda, direct action, etc.), requiring skills solely for the purposes of military action, the underground Communist Party activated its leaders at all levels of the system, including the specialized sectors: youth, women, peasants, traders and artisans, intellectuals, and so forth, thus forming the bases of an organized civil resistance, parallel to the development of its "armed" branch, the FTP.[6] While professional implantation was an issue for all resistance movements, the Communist Party was thus structurally predisposed to canalize the subversive potential of social and professional demands, to favor the generalization of the struggle against the Occupation, according to an operation that counterbalanced the state corporatism of the Vichy regime. In return, it ensured the reinsertion of its militants in the national community. The success of this form of mobilization varied according to whether it collided with the rivalry of more or less powerful preexisting organizations (the unions, notably). In the intellectual milieus, it would experience an original evolution, toward a "professionalization" into specialized branches.

In fact, the Communist Party's change of line allowed for the official adoption and implementation on a larger scale, in the framework of a politics of openness, of an initial project that preceded it. Thus, the notion of a "Popular Front from below" was more than a politics of assembling applied within the different sectors of social space: it translated the very principle that presided over the mode of constitution of the National Front, a principle that was rendered explicit, reappropriated, and ultimately generalized by the leadership of the Communist Party as soon as the new strategy of the Communist International allowed it. Starting in the autumn of 1940, the philosopher Georges Politzer, leader of the intellectuals and seconded by Danielle Casanova, had had "precisely the idea, for grouping scholars, to have a propaganda organization in order to develop the ideas of the struggle to wage against the occupying forces and against Vichy."[7] Pierre Villon was tasked with providing him the "technical apparatus to implement his project." This project produced *L'Université libre* in November 1940, then *La Pensée libre* in February 1941; the latter journal targeted the intellectual and literary milieus. The same team coordinated these two publications: the philosopher Georges Politzer and the physicist Jacques Solomon. They were joined at the beginning of 1941 by Jacques Decour, professor of German and a writer, who would soon be tasked with forming a "Front national des écrivains" or National Front of Writers. Arrested in February 1942 by the French police along with other directors of Communist intellectuals, then turned over to the Gestapo, they would be shot in May at the Mont

Valérien (the women, including Danielle Casanova, would be deported to Auschwitz where they would also die). Pierre Villon, who was himself imprisoned in October 1941 and escaped in January 1942, would be named by the party to succeed Politzer as director of Communist intellectuals. He would consequently be charged with reestablishing contact with the committees of the Front national des intellectuels; advised by Georges Cogniot, he would then become responsible for them.

Had the line of openness toward non-Communists on all sides already been considered in the autumn of 1940, according to the plan that Jeanne Gaillard, professor at the lycée Fénelon, attributed to Jacques Solomon?[8] It was not, in any case, really applied until after the call of May 1941.[9] As for its concrete achievements, they remained very limited at least until the renewed call for the constitution of a National Front in the spring of 1942, if not later, despite the proliferation of specialized committees. There was one exception, as we will see: the committee of writers. Aside from *L'Université libre* and *La Pensée libre*, in March 1941 the first issue of *Le Médecin français* was distributed, whereas *L'École laïque*, the teachers' newspaper, was first published in the month of June. It was not until the summer of 1941 that Jacques Decour would be tasked with forming a distinct committee of writers around a newspaper, *Les Lettres françaises*, as a result of the leadership's orientation at this time, which favored a specialization of committees. Between 1941 and 1942, other groups would blossom: a group of musicians including Roger Désormière, Elsa Barraine, and Roland-Manuel; a group of artists that published *L'Art français*; a group of engineers that published *Action*. The lawyers' journal *Le Palais libre* was launched by Joë Nordmann in May 1943. At that time, *L'Université libre* had a circulation of 5,000 copies, *Les Lettres françaises* and *L'École laïque* 3,000 or 4,000, and *Le Médecin français* 1,000. At the end of 1943, all the newspapers, previously roneotyped, were printed,[10] with the exception of *La Scène française*, *L'Écran français* (which had been published since December 1943), and *Le Musicien d'aujourd'hui*, which momentarily ceased publication. A sign of their relative failure, the first two would take their place in the pages of *Les Lettres françaises* starting in March 1944, under the direction of René Blech. Pierre Blanchard, Louis Daquin, Jean-Paul Sartre, and Georges Sadoul worked on the film pages, while Jean Fouquet, Pierre Bénard, Julien Bertheau, and Bernard Zimmer prepared the theater pages. The same occurred with *Le Musicien français*, whose contributors included Georges Auric; it was integrated into *Les Lettres françaises* in July 1944.[11]

In the Southern zone, the line of openness toward the intellectuals, applied by Aragon around the small literary magazines, remained limited to the legal domain until the invasion of the Southern zone by German troops in November 1942. Until then, only groups of local Communist intellectuals acted clandestinely. It was only after May 1943, while the National Front was becoming a full-fledged movement, the FN, that Aragon created the CNE of the Southern zone. Whereas in the Northern zone, the committees of intellectuals formed in a more compartmentalized fashion, in the Southern zone they branched out from the CNE. The project of a Union française des intellectuels, formulated by Aragon, would nonetheless be abandoned for tactical reasons.[12] Whereas in the Northern zone, committees were asked to join when the FN was forming, in the Southern zone, where the late-blooming committees had to face competition from previously formed Resistance movements, it was the autonomy of these groups that would be emphasized, to the advantage of unitary politics. "It cannot be said that these committees were organizations of the 'Front national'; they depended on it nonetheless, even as they extended beyond it," explained Aragon and Elsa Triolet.[13] Tasked since 1943 with the organization of the intellectual Resistance in the Southern zone, Aragon greatly contributed to the adoption of this solution.

FROM *LA PENSÉE LIBRE* TO *LES LETTRES FRANÇAISES*

The efficacy and specificity of the formula were necessary conditions for the success of the Communist Party's unitary politics, but they were not at all sufficient. In 1941, the principle of an alliance with the Communists was far from accepted in the intellectual milieus. Jean Lescure remembered that "the Communists, after the little episode of the German-Soviet pact, had trouble getting people to swallow their Frenchness, as we would say now, their nationalism and their patriotism. It was not very convenient. There were patriotic Communists, but Communism, for us, was still . . . a foreign land."[14] Georges Duhamel, approached several times, categorically refused to work with the Communists.

Inversely, the modalities of such an alliance, on conceptual and practical levels, still seemed very unclear until the end of 1941 and even later, both for the party leadership and its original masterminds. Sartre's offer of collaboration with the Communists in the autumn of 1941 was rejected,[15] and he would not be admitted to the committee of writers until 1943. The episode of the aborted attempt at openness of *La Pensée libre* illustrates the difficulties that the implementation of unitary politics confronted.

The underground heir to *La Pensée*, "journal of modern rationalism" launched in 1939, *La Pensée libre* followed the line developed in *L'Université libre* starting in the autumn of 1940 by Politzer, Solomon, and Decour, who were also the master builders of this ambitious project. The first issue, which was published in February 1941, numbered no fewer than ninety-six printed pages: it was the first underground publication of this size.[16] Far from being marginal within the Communist Party, the venture had received the leadership's approval and benefited from the production network of the official publications of the Communist Party as well as a large circulation (more than 1,500 copies).[17] Subtitled "Revue française," it announced the unitary politics and the national line that would not be officially adopted by the party leadership until May. The terms employed on the back cover, "the struggle for the freedom and independence of France," were adapted from Thorez's slogan in August 1936, "Front Français for the freedom and independence of France," revived in the calls for unity of the "People of France" in competition with the objective of social liberation; it would ultimately designate the politics of the National Front. Despite this orientation, the Marxist and anti-imperialist struggle still distinctly prevailed over the anti-Fascist struggle in this first issue, according to the still-predominant tendency to subordinate "national liberation" to "social liberation." In its editorial, the journal denounced "German imperialism and its vassal, Marshal Pétain," calling for the defense of French thought and culture.[18] Next to articles on science (Solomon, and perhaps Fernand Holweck), on "obscurantism in the 20th century" (Politzer), and a poem on Pétain (René Blech?), an article entitled "After the Death of Mr. Bergson" that Roger Bourderon attributed to Politzer accused the Bergsonian idealist philosophy of having created "a favorable terrain for the penetration of ideas that have directly served the ideological preparation of Fascism," while it recalled that the late philosopher had been subject to anti-Semitic laws.[19]

After the politics of openness became official, *La Pensée libre* was destined to become the forum for the union of intellectuals on all sides. The mission of recruiting non-Communist writers to prepare the second issue was entrusted to Pierre de Lescure, presumably via René Blech, former copy editor for the journal *Commune*, where Lescure had contributed before the war. Well-known in the literary milieus, Pierre de Lescure also had the advantage of already being initiated to underground action.[20] He turned to his friend, the illustrator Jean Bruller, the future Vercors, and after the latter's vain effort toward Duhamel, they set out to jointly prepare the issue that would overcome the reticence of the solicited authors.

According to the version related by Vercors, this issue's manuscript was destroyed during a Gestapo search at the printer, after which Pierre de Lescure was informed of a new project, "which was to replace the defunct magazine by a literary and therefore unpolitical paper, to be entitled *Les Lettres françaises*."[21] The novella that Vercors intended for the following issue, *Le Silence de la mer*, was consequently deprived of a medium. From this was born the idea of an underground publishing house, the Éditions de Minuit. The fact that the issue's manuscript was lost does not, however, suffice to justify the replacement of the review by another project. And if the technical matters of security—the necessity to return "to the prudent system of multigraphed sheets"[22]—alleged by the same informers were the sole reason for it, how are we to explain the existence of a second issue of *La Pensée libre*, of a similar thickness, which was published in February 1942 with a print run of 200 copies?[23]

In fact, the competing project for which this forum was, if not suspended, at least abandoned, in order to make an overture toward the non-Communist intellectual milieus, resulted from an intervention by Aragon. Up until the beginning of 1941, Aragon, settled in Nice, had lost all contact with the leadership of the clandestine Communist Party. This contact was reestablished by Georges Dudach alias André, who came to solicit his move to Paris in order to contribute to *La Pensée libre*. Arrested in June 1941 while they were illegally crossing the demarcation line, Aragon, Elsa Triolet, and Dudach arrived in the capital after ten days in jail. Housed by the painter Édouard Pignon in Jacques Lipchitz's studio, they met with Politzer and Danielle Casanova. "It is, by the way, on my exit from Tours prison that, once in Paris, I was able to persuade our friends to suspend the publication of a review where *some errors* had been committed, and I obtained the founding of *Les Lettres françaises* under the joint direction of Jean Paulhan and Jacques Decour," Aragon would recall much later.[24]

What errors? First of all, the still-too-pronounced political character of the journal. In the name of unitary politics, Aragon imposed the principle of a properly literary publication. In the notes taken by Elsa Triolet later, we read: "1941. Trip to Paris: Criticism of the first issue of *La Pensée libre* acceptance of the principle of making a work dictated by a com[munist] and non com[munist] Committee. The first one called—Paulhan."[25] In order to proceed with the recruitment of writers, Aragon thus designated Jean Paulhan in place of the "safe" man that was Pierre de Lescure. A choice that, while it should be read in light of the renewed "complicity" between Aragon and Paulhan, was not at all obvious, in the sole view of underground security rules. Even though he had already proved himself as a résistant in the Musée de l'Homme network, didn't Paulhan occupy the office next to Drieu La Rochelle at Gallimard?

Second error, the motto "legal literature means: literature of treason" in the first editorial of *La Pensée libre*, against which the author of *Le Crève-cœur*—which had just been published by Gallimard—made Politzer admit the principle of a legal "contraband" literature. Whereas the Communist Party wanted to keep him in Paris to take care of underground publications, especially *L'Humanité*,

Aragon obtained recognition for his "legal work" with the goal of assembling writers in the Southern zone, work that he had begun around *Poésie 40, 41 . . .* and *Fontaine*, and that he would pursue as soon as he returned to the Southern zone, during his stay in Villeneuve at Seghers's house. The publication in *L'Université libre* in the autumn of 1941 of the "Manifesto of Intellectuals in the Unoccupied Zone" testifies to this change. Probably written by Aragon, Elsa Triolet, Pierre Seghers, maybe Andrée Viollis, it referred to the contacts made at the Rencontres de Lourmarin organized by Jeune France between September 19 and 22, 1941, near Villeneuve (see chapter 6):

> In the course of Summer 1941, somewhere in the free zone, intellectuals from all the horizons of Science, Thought, and Art met regardless of their religious, philosophical, and political divergences. In solidarity with all those who, in both zones, resist in their heart, by their thought, by their actions against the enslavement of France, they declare themselves ready to defend the spiritual treasure of their country [. . .].[26]

The principle of this "legal work" was accepted by the leadership of the intellectuals on the condition that Aragon refrain from all underground activity in the Southern zone and that he exclusively reserve his illegal work for the Northern zone.

Spreading from *Poésie 41* and *Fontaine* to *Confluences* starting in 1942, Aragon's "legal work" would also be taken into consideration as such by Georges Cogniot, adviser to Pierre Villon after Politzer's arrest. In the notes taken by Cogniot from a "Report on Work among the Intellectuals in the Southern Zone" from April 1944, we find: "Legal work up until the beginning of 1943. Illegal organization since June 43."[27]

The third error that the first issue of *La Pensée libre* made in Aragon's eyes lay in the article that Politzer had published on Bergson, an error that Aragon, indignant, corrected in March 1943 in *Les Étoiles*, bulletin of the CNE in the Southern zone. In a text that honored a representative of each intellectual profession, it was Bergson, and not Politzer (shot in May 1942), who was chosen to represent a philosopher victim of the Germans.[28]

In order to convince Politzer of the necessity of the legal work of contraband, Aragon had given him "The Lesson of Ribérac or French Europe" that had just been published in *Fontaine*. The task was not easy. "I was, I confess, anxious about what this philosopher, who never separated thought from action, would think about it." Aragon presented his project to him: "to oppose the images of the Nation to the myths of race, thus taking up, in another domain, the lesson given by Maurice Thorez at one of the meetings of our party, at Montreuil, on the eve of the war."[29] Aragon's apprehensions lay in the use that he himself made of the myths of the national tradition. He rightly feared the reservations of the rationalist philosopher who had long worked to dismantle Nazi myths by opposing them to historical reality. This created the need, for Aragon, to explain himself after the Liberation with respect to the poetic use he made of history and legends, a metaphoric use that interpolated the national collective memory to speak about the present. And his reflection on "the historical inexactitude in poetry," inexactitude or lies (the myths) put to the service of contraband in order to tell the truth about the present, should be counted among the sources of the much later theory of "lying to tell the truth."[30] For the time being, Aragon settled for justifying this use of myths by their mobilizing function, and thus by their social efficacy: to awaken the epic sense, expression of the national sense, of the heroic tradition, such was the function of the myths that he consequently acknowledged having "put back on their feet."[31] By suggesting that he deepen the theme of the hero that was barely sketched in "The Lesson of Ribérac," Politzer had indicated this solution that he immediately put to work in his collection *Brocéliande* (1942).

On the other hand, Aragon would not concede the radical critique of the spiritualist tradition to Politzer. The necessities of unitary politics, and more particularly the outreach to Catholics of which he was the most fervent mastermind, would soon allow him to develop his conception of a universalist French humanism that indissolubly allies the materialist and Christian traditions. This would be the object of his contribution to the "Controversy on the Genius of France" in the issue of *Les Cahiers du Rhône* published in November 1942. Originally entitled "On a French Humanism," it appeared under the title "The ET Conjunction."[32] Opposing the ideologues who attempted to divide French heritage (he was aiming at Action française, among others), Aragon started from a very personal interpretation of historical materialism to reconcile these two traditions in the figure of the "French hero," which encompassed not only the war hero but also "civic courage" and "intellectual heroism."[33] While the theory was not entirely orthodox, this conception of heroism still corresponded to the line of the Communist Resistance that from then on called for all forms of resistance, from armed struggle to civil resistance.

These points of disagreement between Aragon and the leadership of the Communist intellectuals in the summer of 1941 no doubt translate the discrepancy, in terms of lived experience, between the occupied and unoccupied zones. This discrepancy generated tensions between the résistants in both zones, as evidenced by their testimonies.

But in this case, they also proceeded from their respective positions. The notion of "party intellectual" or "organic intellectual" could thus conceal different realities, brought to light by the zone of indetermination opened up by the conjuncture concerning the means of action and the hesitations: on one hand, Communist intellectuals who were doubly muzzled and threatened by the occupying forces and by Vichy (two of them, Politzer and Solomon, were Jews on top of everything else), assigned to their militant identity that they fully adopted—it would cost them their lives—and who, inclined to generalize their particular experience, attempted to impose stringent norms of conduct (the equation: legal literature = literature of treason); on the other hand, the poet who Jean Paulhan had consecrated who, at this time, published quite legally in the magazines of the Southern zone (whereas his comrades Georges Sadoul and Léon Moussinac hid behind pseudonyms), and who was published in the Northern zone under the strong protection of the Gallimard house (Gallimard would obtain German authorization and, not without difficulties, that of the Vichy censors for the publication of *Voyageurs de l'Impériale*, at the cost, it is true, of revisions and deep cuts that denatured the novel without its author's knowledge and gave it an anti-Semitic tonality: published in December 1942, it was removed from sale at the beginning of 1943 following an outcry in the collaborationist press).[34]

Between the philosopher Politzer and the writer Aragon, the difference of positions was coupled with the expectations, interests, and specific practices associated with their intellectual specialty. The "concessions" to Bergsonian spiritualism that the writer could allow himself were impossible for the official philosopher of the party, less because they were "prohibited" to him than because of his initial intellectual investments.[35] The son of a physician, Politzer had been a young Communist revolutionary in Hungary before emigrating to France in 1921, where he studied and passed the agrégation in philosophy without renewing ties with the party. Professor at a lycée, he was a member, in the 1920s, of the "Philosophies" group. It was due to the impasse which had resulted from his attempts to found a concrete psychology based on a critique of classical psychology and his precocious reading of Freud that he turned to Marxism. And it was when he was preparing to request membership in the Communist Party that he published *La Fin d'une parole philosophique, le bergsonisme* under a pseudonym (1929).[36] Rejecting psychology and psychoanalysis, he opted for political economics, which was then the noblest discipline in the internal hierarchy of the party.[37] Promoted to different leadership positions (member of the economic commission of the Central Committee, then, with Solomon, of the education section in the same committee), Politzer reconnected with his previous centers of interest at a time when Thorez decided to favor the return of intellectuals to their specialty in the framework of their militant activity. The rationalist philosopher would lead a fight against Nazi obscurantism, contrasting it to Enlightenment philosophy. His article on "Philosophy and Myths," published in the first issue of *La Pensée* (April–May–June 1939) attacked doctrinaire racism, but also denounced the idealist and irrationalist currents represented by Bergson, Heidegger, and Gabriel Marcel. Like the underground brochure, *Révolution et contre-révolution au 20ᵉ siècle—Réponse à 'Or et Sang' de M. Rosenberg*, that he published in 1941, the article on Bergson in the first issue of *La Pensée libre* placed itself firmly in the line of this struggle.[38] Certainly, he could have chosen to do without a discussion of Bergsonian philosophy in this context.

The national line adopted by Thorez at the Arles Congress, like the unitary politics that the Communist Party implemented under the Popular Front and that was reactivated with its call for the constitution of a National Front, found in Aragon an all the more fervent adept since they coincided with the specific investments of the writer in the literary field. In the name of a unitary politics, Aragon defended literary interests to the party. Strengthened by the position he had achieved in the literary world, he was able to alter, and even to transgress at a lower cost, the political constraints that weighed upon him, and to help redefine the line so as to ensure the maintenance of a relative literary autonomy. We have seen the symbolic forms that the national literary politics of Aragon took. By making them adopt the principle of the creation of a properly literary paper, his intervention helped push the line toward a professionalization of the Resistance, with the first successes "encourag[ing] the direction of the Communist Party in its frontist practices," in Daniel Virieux's words.[39] By designating Jean Paulhan to Jacques Decour, he guaranteed the successful mobilization of the writers: Paulhan was in contact with all the dispersed writers; he knew their positions and enjoyed an uncontestable authority among them; he would surely get along with Jacques Decour, whose first works he had published at Gallimard, and who had contributed to the prewar *NRF*.

THE GALLIMARD-*NRF* NETWORK

"Very quickly, we found ourselves *amongst ourselves* at the *Nouvelle Revue française* that Paulhan edited [...]": it was in those terms that Debû-Bridel evoked the formation of the first underground group in Paulhan's office at Gallimard.[40] If the alliance between Communists and non-Communists could be achieved from the autumn of 1941, it was because it relied on "elective affinities" in the literary order. The language of memory is eloquent: "complicity," according to Aragon's expression, "amongst ourselves," according to that of Debû-Bridel, or even the German term *Nebenmensch* that Jean Lescure used to speak of "the great proximity, a shared warmth, a joy in confidence."[41]

When, at the end of September 1941, Paulhan offered to put the nationalist Jacques Debû-Bridel, a Gallimard author, in contact with Jacques Decour, he took precautions: "'He is Communist, you know, but he would like to see you very much.' I knew," Debû-Bridel would say later, "that Decour was Communist because we sometimes discussed things at *La* NRF in Paulhan's office. But I also knew that against the common enemy, the Communists, like us, waged a war without mercy [. . .] It is *with joy*, thanks to Paulhan, that I seized the occasion to form *more intimate* relations with Decour."[42] The word "intimate," which in this context comes from the same semantic field as "accomplice," "friend," "brother," expressions recurring in later accounts, is here like a "lapse" revealing a complicity that exceeded militant solidarity.[43] Debû-Bridel would further attribute the success of Decour's project to his "friendship" with Paulhan: "He achieved it thanks to his tenacity and two advantages: his membership in the Communist Party on one side and the *friendship* of Jean Paulhan, on the other."[44] "We were all there openly,"[45] such would be, as a consequence of the public character of the profession of writer and its mode of co-optation through relational networks, one of the singularities of this underground group among the Resistance movement.

Paulhan was all the better placed to reunite since, as an authoritative critic and a courted decider, he was nonetheless the power behind the throne, so to speak, and was not in direct competition with "his" authors. Through him and thanks to the schism of *La* NRF, what I will call here the "Gallimard-NRF network" presided over the two principal phases of underground recruitment of the writers in the Northern zone, in the autumn of 1941 and throughout 1943. Implemented on different levels by writers who paired both memberships, to the Communist Party (or its circle of influence) and to *La* NRF (the publisher and/or the former review)—Aragon, Decour, then Eluard in 1943—the alliance between Communists and non-Communists operated through the complicity between authors belonging to the same house.

Paulhan already had a Resistance pedigree. In the autumn of 1940, one of the first nuclei of intellectual resistance had gathered around the Émile-Paul brothers under the cover of a literary society, the "Friends of Alain-Fournier," to write and distribute tracts. It included Claude Aveline, Jean Cassou, Marcel Abraham, Agnès Humbert, Simone Martin-Chauffier, and Jean and Colette Duval. Having entered into contact with a group from the Musée de l'Homme, they had agreed to form the editorial board of a four-page underground newspaper entitled *Résistance*. Aveline, Abraham, and Cassou were responsible for the last three pages of the leaflet; Agnès Humbert served as secretary. The board met at Simone Martin-Chauffier's house. On January 6, 1941, the linguist Boris Vildé, director of the Musée de l'Homme group along with the anthropologist Anatole Lewinsky and the librarian Yvonne Oddon, met Jean Paulhan at the home of mutual friends and recruited him for the editorial board of *Résistance*. Paulhan, who in 1938 had commissioned works from Lewinsky and Vildé for the NRF publishing house, and who moreover knew Aveline, Cassou, and Abraham, joined willingly with the underground enterprise. Assisted by Jean Blanzat, he installed the roneo in his apartment, where the third issue of *Résistance* was printed; it appeared on January 31.[46] After the publication of the fourth issue in March 1941, when a first wave of arrests had already clamped down on the network that would soon be wholly demolished, Paulhan had to decide, on Jean Cassou's advice, to get rid of the machine, which he dismantled and threw into the Seine with the help of Marguerite and Jean Blanzat, who was, according to Paulhan's expression, "strong as a lumberjack."[47]

Paulhan escaped the tragic destiny of the arrested members, whose trial, begun in January 1942, was sealed by seven of them being sentenced to death for spying. It was thanks to Drieu La Rochelle's intervention, as we saw, that he was liberated from prison. Shortly after his first meeting with the Sonderführer Gerhard Heller in November 1940, Drieu had told Heller that there were three people to protect: Gaston Gallimard, Jean Paulhan, and André Malraux.[48] Should we credit this "protection" that the Gallimard house exerted through Drieu for the fact that the committee of writers gathered around Paulhan was one of the rare underground enterprises in the Northern zone that had not been decimated? Certainly, the activity of the Musée de l'Homme network, the most directly comparable, had more "serious" goals than the production of a clandestine literature (it was an information network). What is more, there is no question of subscribing to the fallacious affirmations of Gerhard Heller, who retroactively claimed the merit of having protected Paulhan from a second arrest and, indirectly, the CNE.[49] Gérard Loiseaux has very meticulously demonstrated the strategy of Heller, from the publication of his memoirs after the death of the witnesses who could have contested his statements, up to the unverifiable character of the exploits he attributed to himself.[50] My intention here is rather to show a certain complicity that we can see at work between the two branches of the Gallimard-*NRF* network, the one that was oriented toward the intellectual resistance, and the one that was engaged, if not in the ranks, at least in the structures of collaboration via Drieu's review (they were moreover not airtight, as Eluard's passage from one to the other shows). This complicity took its source in the interests that united them in spite of themselves—Drieu needed Paulhan in order to make the review, while Gallimard needed Drieu to protect the house—and that Paulhan would express much later in a personalized manner:

> I am not without remorse with respect to Drieu. He knew how to save me, and I did not know how to save him. However, I did all I could. (He knew it and kindly thanked me, in a letter. But we did not see each other again: I thought he liked his solitude, and then I didn't know where he was hiding.) I at least managed to put off the charges for a long time. But suicide ... This is what I didn't know how to foresee. He was a straight, good, admirable man.[51]

In fact, while we can say that this de facto complicity protected the underground venture, it was probably less through interventions with the occupying forces—they were not at all systematic, as attested by Drieu's refusal to act in favor of Jean Wahl[52]—than due to the relative rarity of denunciations (which were practiced in other "regions" of the literary field).[53]

The first recruits of the underground committee were also linked to the "house." A Grasset author, Jean Blanzat "frequented the milieus of *La NRF* where he was very much linked to Paulhan,"[54] and would become a reader for Gallimard in 1942. Already initiated in a form of clandestine action with the affair of the roneo, he was one of the first to be solicited by Paulhan. While Jean Paulhan introduced the critic Jean Vaudal, who was a columnist at *La NRF*, to the new underground project, Blanzat recruited Grasset authors who had been closely linked to the prewar *NRF*. François Mauriac, the most prestigious of the recruits of the autumn of 1941, thus gave his commitment in principle to his young friend while he was in Paris, entrusting him with an article entitled "In the Present State of France" for the underground newspaper, probably with the "benediction" of that other intimate of Mauriac who was the Dominican Father Jean Maydieu. Paulhan had already let Maydieu in on the secret of Decour's projects.[55] Very close to Jean Guéhenno—he had contributed to the journal *Europe*, where Guéhenno was editor in chief from 1929 until its takeover by a Communist team in 1936—Blanzat proposed that the latter form a "cell" with François Mauriac, not without taking some precautions: "Would it annoy you if Mauriac were part of it?" he asked him. Guéhenno, who "ha[d] not had great relations with Mauriac,"[56] and justifiably so, Mauriac never having hidden his disdain for the "herd of bureaucratic writers,"[57] accepted. It was at Blanzat's home that the inaugural meeting was held for *Les Lettres françaises* around December 1941, in the presence of Decour, Paulhan, Debû-Bridel, and Charles Vildrac, an old Gallimard author and fellow-traveler of the Communist Party, who had been a member of the AEAR. The table of contents for the first issue was set during that meeting.

The role of mediator that Jean Blanzat played in the cohesion of the group, reconciling positions as opposed as those of Guéhenno and François Mauriac, found its source in the still-shaky position of this relatively deprived newcomer; the conjuncture offered him the chance to complete his integration into this milieu by allowing him to assert his militant dispositions. Close to Jean Guéhenno by his popular origins, he was, like his elder, a "miracle man" of the Republic: born in 1890, Guéhenno was the son of a shoemaker and a seamstress from Fougère, while Blanzat, born in 1905 in Domps, Haute Vienne, and descended from a peasant family, was the son of a postman. Both educated in a provincial collège, they went into public service, the elder through the "front door," ENS and agrégation in literature, the younger through the "back door," École normale for primary school teachers at Versailles. For the author of *Caliban parle*, the "royal road" had been paved with obstacles: despite his status as a scholarship recipient, the feeling of having betrayed his class of origin had led him to leave the collège at age fourteen to work as an apprentice shoemaker; self-taught, he had suffered two failures before finally obtaining the agrégation. More than the Socialist circle in which they both partook, it was a shared awkward in-between position that brought the brilliant *khâgne** professor closer to the young school teacher, due as much to their mutually bumpy social ascension as to the rarity and the contested legitimacy of teachers in the literary field.

More difficult to grasp is the affinity between François Mauriac, a member of the French Academy from bourgeois origin, and the young, Socialist school teacher, who met in 1938 during the reception of Spanish refugees. The position of the great writer, having lost his momentum and seeking disciples, probably partly explains Mauriac's attachment to this young Catholic (though also Socialist) pretender. Whatever the case, it was he who, in 1942, would help his protégé obtain the Prize for the Novel from the French Academy, writing to Blanche Duhamel:

> You should have gotten *L'Orage du Matin* by Jean Blanzat. I would like for you to read it to Georges and that it not be a chore for the two of you. I don't believe that I am mistaken in finding that this too "contracted" book is very rich—and I wish so much for my friend to have, at this time in his career, the encouragement and the consecration of the Prize for the Novel. I ask you to help me with this, by talking about him with the colleagues you see . . .[58]

Mauriac would intervene to have him named general secretary of Grasset in 1945,[59] and it was most likely he who got him into *Le Figaro* as a columnist during the same period.

---

* *Khâgne* and *hypokhâgne* are courses of study that prepare students for advanced studies in literature, especially the ENS.—Trans.

But the apprentice writer's true master was Jean Paulhan, who urged him to reconcile his "lumberjack" hexis with the excess of "grace" and "kindness" that were his shortcomings on the stylistic plane.[60] Without sparing his criticisms during their first exchanges, Paulhan recruited him in 1942 as a reader at Gallimard—"I was happy and proud to be near you at *La* NRF," Blanzat would say to him[61]—and at the Liberation he would encourage him to abandon his militant and teaching activities to devote himself more fully to writing. Having abandoned his functions at the NRF publishing house in order to enter Grasset at the Liberation, Blanzat would return to Gallimard in 1953, as a member of the very prestigious review board.

Linchpin of the first recruitment, the Gallimard-*NRF* network would enable not only the creation of the committee, but also the materialization of its existence through the creation of a true subfield of underground production, endowed with means of periodical (*Les Lettres françaises*) and editorial publications (the Éditions de Minuit, which, although independent, would maintain close relations with the underground committee, the liaison being ensured by the same network). In return, once its structure was constituted, the committee could play the role of a springboard with respect to the two "families" that founded it, whether entering the committee coincided with membership in the Communist Party, or it constituted, for the young poets, a center of attraction because by bringing them closer to Jean Paulhan, it increased their chances of reaching Gallimard without passing through the hated *NRF* of Drieu La Rochelle.

THE NATIONAL FRONT OF WRITERS:
A SELECTIVE RECRUITMENT

Although the conditions for assembling writers were in place from the autumn of 1941, the implementation of the project still met with many difficulties, including those that were evoked previously. On the writers' side, the resistances were not yet defeated. The steps taken conjointly by Paulhan and Aragon in the summer of 1941 (to "strike a great blow")[62] with Georges Duhamel had failed. Aragon responded to Paulhan who had shared his disappointment: "Upon reflection, I thought of Georges D[uhamel] without bitterness, with a certain regret, but all the while thinking that later he will think of us differently. I regret more not to have seen François [Mauriac]."[63] Later, when Claude Morgan, having succeeded Jacques Decour after his arrest, would go in turn to see Duhamel, a friend of his father, under his true identity, he would hear: "I admire those who, like yourself, risk their lives. But I cannot associate myself with your action. I have chosen to fight openly, in my role as permanent secretary of the

Academy. But while it is impossible for me to be among you, know that I appreciate courage and I think of you constantly."[64]

On the side of the party apparatus, Jacques Decour's veto of the proposition, made by Paulhan, to introduce Sartre to the underground project allows us to assess the weight of Communist censorship on recruitment practices.[65] While the Gallimard-*NRF* network was its matrix, recruitment was nonetheless submitted to severe oversight and a strict selection, as attested by Debû-Bridel:

> Then, minutely, we reviewed all those writers who were quiet and whose silence was a good omen. Decour, who was coming out of prison, was prudent, very prudent it seemed; not enough, however, as later events showed. And very often, for reasons of security, he dismissed such or such a name that Paulhan had proposed, not only out of distrust for the author that would have to be approached but on account of the milieus he frequented, of his chatter, also, let us say it, of his private life sometimes. The resistance had to necessarily be a school of virtue. The drunks and the cocaine addicts, all those who were not masters of their nerves constitute a danger for their comrades-in-arms in the fight, and it is a newspaper of struggle and combat that Decour wanted to create.[66]

During the same period, the party rejected the membership application of Roger Vailland, known for his drug use.[67] But the strict application of the rules of security, whatever its insufficiency as Decour's tragic end proves, still sometimes served as an alibi for principles of rejection proper to the party.

Pascal Mercier has noted Decour's pronounced aversion for Sartre.[68] This personal hostility most likely reflected his internalization of the party's position, but perhaps also a rivalry between the two Germanists and novelists in the intellectual field.[69] For the party, Sartre was a suspicious writer: suspect of complicity with Vichy due to his liberation from the prison camp, he was also suspect for his interest in Heideggerian philosophy, which would earn him a lampoon, published in the Southern zone, "where he is presented as a disciple of Heidegger *and consequently* as a henchman of National-Socialism," as Claude Morgan would relate.[70] But Sartre was also a friend of Paul Nizan who broke away from the PCF during the German-Soviet pact; he was the "pessimistic, decadent, petit-bourgeois" author of *Nausea*;[71] and above all the philosopher who participated in the collective work of introducing and reinterpreting German phenomenology in France, that is to say the idealist theory in most direct competition with Marxism in the intellectual field at the time. The aborted attempt to break with spiritualism and "set out from the Cogito and recuperate the world," an unavowed response to Marxist materialism that supported the approach of *Being and Nothingness*, as Anna Boschetti has explained,[72] clearly shows that even before the book's publication, Communists were not wrong to view Sartre as a major adversary.

To this still very selective recruitment was added the confusion, not to say the contradictions, that still seemed to reign at the level of the apparatus concerning the practical modalities of unitary politics. Had the principle of a properly literary paper, proposed by Aragon with Paulhan's agreement, actually been adopted in the summer of 1941? We might doubt it based on the testimony of Jacques Debû-Bridel: "We had first thought of a development of *L'Université libre* for which I had given, at Decour's request [. . .] some literary or political notes. But, by mutual agreement, and on the advice of Jean Paulhan, we thought it necessary to set up, however much it may cost and however much it is worth, a literary weekly."[73] Yet this project, which Decour described to Claude Morgan "with enthusiasm and pride,"[74] would only really succeed in 1943. This was not for lack of previous efforts to launch it as early as the winter of 1941. What became of the first issue of *Les Lettres françaises*, whose table of contents was fixed during the meeting held at Jean Blanzat's home?

All the witness accounts agree that the manuscript was lost at the time when the leadership of the Communist intellectuals was arrested at the beginning of 1942, but the divergences are troubling. Did the manuscript really disappear? Some elements leave room for doubt, especially the fact that two of the texts planned for this first issue of *Les Lettres françaises* appeared in the second issue of *La Pensée libre* in February 1942. Let's take a closer look.

According to one version reported in *Les Lettres françaises* after the Liberation, Jacques Decour's sister burned his documents on his instructions—including the manuscript for this first issue—when he was arrested by the French police on February 19, 1942, then handed over to the Gestapo.[75] This was a faulty version of events since Georges Dudach possessed the typewritten texts or manuscripts that he had given, on the day of his arrest, to Pierre Villon (who ensured the liaison with the person in charge of roneographing, the school teacher Pierre Maucherat). Pierre Villon, tasked with renewing ties with the intellectual committees after the arrest of Georges Politzer on February 15, was visiting Dudach when the police knocked on the door: Villon escaped through the window, leaving his overcoat with the manuscript in the pocket.[76] Who, then, told Debû-Bridel that the issue "was, it seems, under press" when Jacques Decour's arrest prevented its publication and "stopped the composition of the second"?[77] And how did it happen that the text of the "Manifesto of the National Front of Writers," written by Decour and intended for *Les Lettres françaises*, appeared under the title "We Will Save the Honor of French Literature" in the second issue of *La Pensée libre* in February 1942, along with the manifesto of the intellectuals of the unoccupied zone?[78] It was only in July 1942 that Morgan would resume contact with the head of the production department, Pierre Maucherat, who had meanwhile been promoted to Pierre Villon's liaison for all the intellectual groups, and who certainly holds the key to this affair. Maucherat would also put Morgan in contact with Villon.

Aside from Jacques Decour's manifesto, the "lost" issue of *Les Lettres françaises*, whose table of contents was reconstructed from memory, included a poem by Georges Limbour ("La Palissade"); an article on Montherlant, sometimes attributed to Pierre de Lescure, sometimes to Jean Blanzat; notes by Jean Paulhan and François Mauriac; book reviews by Jean Vaudal and Pierre de Lescure; a study on English philosophy by Jacques Debû-Bridel; and finally, a narrative of the death of the Châteaubriant hostages.[79] This narrative also appeared in the second issue of *La Pensée libre*. Only the properly literary texts had disappeared, then, like those that Pierre de Lescure and Vercors had submitted for the second issue of the journal.

The arrest of the leaders of the intellectual Communists would thus have called the very project of *Les Lettres françaises* into question, to the advantage of *La Pensée libre*, and the manuscripts meant for the former were partially recycled in the second issue of the journal, at the cost of a "censorship" of the too "literary" texts. This initiative might have been the work of the head of production, Pierre Maucherat, who was the only stable person involved, and as a result would see his responsibilities expand at this time.

After having renewed contact with the apparatus, but still cut off from the core of writers assembled around Paulhan, Claude Morgan, at the request of Pierre Maucherat, singlehandedly prepared a first issue of *Les Lettres françaises* that would be published in September 1942. Once more, the articles with a literary character were deleted at printing, due to technical difficulties, he said. The lone survivors were some "echoes" on the dying NRF ("*La NRF* was formerly a great French literary review. Since it fell into the hands of Drieu La Rochelle and Ramon Fernandez, it is nothing more than a corpse—that stinks"); on the Société des gens de lettres that had unfortunately agreed to create, in accord with the minister Scapini, three literary prizes devoted to the work of writers in captivity for the glory of "the new order"; and on Paul Morand's contact with German personalities. "I was," Morgan said, "[...] floored by the idea that this first issue was going to be distributed to the members of the committee and I begged the gods that Paulhan would never receive it. He received it, naturally, and judged it very bad, which it was."[80] Thus, the first issues of the journal that was to distinguish itself from the other underground publications by its literary specificity still barely distinguished itself from the literature of combat.

Must we see these successive "disappearances" as the mark of censorship at the level of the "apparatus," and more precisely as the hand of Pierre Maucherat, who alone held all the strings during this period? In the absence of sources, we are reduced to conjecture. But one thing is sure: in the autumn of 1942, a directive by Georges Cogniot, who had escaped from the Royallieu camp in June and was named as adviser to Pierre Villon by Jacques Duclos, announced a change of line. Disappointed by his reading of the second issue of *Les Lettres françaises*, although Morgan had worked to give it a more literary tone (with an article that condemned Paul Morand's book on Maupassant, in which the "cosmopolitan" writer disparaged the naturalism of the author of *Boule de suif*),[81] Cogniot signaled the need to "professionalize" the publications destined for the committees of intellectuals, in a letter to Pierre Villon in November 1942:

> [...] I believe that *Action* [newspaper for engineers] and *Les Lettres françaises* would gain from being written more in the "professional" style of *L'U[niversité]. L[ibre]*. [...] in the Lettres (next to the paper on Maupassant, excellent), the article "Notre Paris" takes up part of the "Crier la vérité" edito [by Édith Thomas] [...] It would be better, I think, to speak [...] more concretely to writers about literature, theater, the publishing market, etc [...] I think I can guess the difficulty: lack of connections, and consequently lack of contributions and information. In any case, there is one thing that should be possible: that is to follow the problems in the special newspapers and give our opinion. Perhaps you can find *one* technician and *one* man from the literary milieus to do this relatively easy work [...]
>
> F. ex. at the present hour, there is the question of publishing paper that everyone is talking about: French publishers used 3,500 tons of paper each month; the distributor announces that we can only count on 350 tons in the future. Good subject for commentaries!
>
> At the same time, following the theater scene, the new books, the conferences, the criticism, the actions of the censors. Unmasking, like before, but more methodically, the false writers and the prompted works.[82]

And it is only after this date that, almost miraculously, the threads came back together.

This chronology was the effect of the chain of arrests and executions of the main leaders of the Communist intellectuals, including Politzer, Solomon, Decour, and Dudach, which delayed the application of the new line of openness adopted in the spring of 1942 at the committee level. Even as the Communist Party launched a call for the union of all tendencies and all organizations of resistance in the struggle against the occupying forces, and it extended a hand toward "Free France," we observe, if not the hardening of a still very restrictive line, at least a form of inertia at the level of the committee leaders. Evidence: the reproaches that Pierre Villon launched beginning in the spring of 1942 against primary school teachers, physicians, architects, in the same spirit as the commentaries of Georges Cogniot on *Les Lettres françaises*.[83] Yet Villon, an architect by training, didn't understand anything about literary questions. So little that the ENS graduate Cogniot set about giving him lessons by correspondence, not without a certain paternalism (he went so far as to recommend that he read Daniel Mornet on the classical period), which said a great deal about the work of theoretical readjustment needed to enact the line of openness, notably the annexation of the French literary canons:

> As for the problem of Art and the People, there are magnificent pages by Jaurès on that, and very many others have treated it [...] You write to me that "the first issue will contain a tribute to the poets ... that already orients toward the observation that today, poetry exceeds the narrow milieu of amateurs and, rising up to the level of the requirements of the Homeland, addresses the people, responds to its aspirations."
>
> I think that your pen has betrayed your thought: we must not look like we are conceding to our Hitlerian enemies that French poetry, in the past, has only been a poetry of amateurs, a poetry for the elite, a poetry foreign to the people, whereas the Minnesingers, Herders and Goethes would always have been linked to the people and to the land! [...] There is perhaps no poetry as popular as the French, and this is what you must demonstrate, from the Chanson de Roland to the Symbolists [...].[84]

As for Claude Morgan, born Charles Lecomte, he could only be sensitive to Cogniot's remarks, he who so feared the judgment of Paulhan. Son of the academician Georges Lecomte, a former Dreyfusard whose wife hosted a literary salon, he was in fact particularly well placed to evaluate the literary sanction that threatened his solitary underground venture. But his familiarity with the Academy milieu, particularly Duhamel, Mauriac, Pierre Benoit, Dorgelès, Carco, and so forth also put him in an awkward in-between situation with respect to his literary generation: it was not by chance that he was "one of those rare writers who do not know Jean Paulhan," that he passed "in front of Surrealism without seeing it," and that he didn't even know Eluard by name.[85] Should we attribute his quixotic career (as he claimed in his memoirs) to the "deviation" of his trajectory following his brother's death during the Great War? In any case, although he was endowed with significant resources, Morgan did not stop accumulating "bad" placements. While he was simultaneously preparing the baccalaureate in elementary mathematics and in philosophy at Louis-le-Grand, he decided to become an electrical engineer like his older brother, passed the entrance exam at the École supérieure d'électricité, then managed to be sent to the front at the end of the war after a few months at the school of officer cadets at Fontainebleau. This "deviation" of his trajectory probably reinforced the discrepancy between his literary aspirations and the evolution of aesthetic problematics during the years when he found himself an engineer in a factory. "Seduced" until 1935 by Action française, an admirer of Mussolini, he signed the manifesto "For the Defense of the West" during the war in Ethiopia and began a literary career in marginal periodicals of the extreme right (*Rempart*, *Vendémiaire*), before converting to Communism at the age of forty. Having met Aragon through René Blech,[86] he contributed to Renaud de Jouvenel's anti-Munich journal, *Volontaires*, to *Commune*, and then he left his job to enter the editorial staff of *Ce Soir*. It was certainly his subordinate position at that time inside the Communist Party that explains his lack of initiative in the autumn of 1942: having returned from captivity in August 1941, he was only promoted after the arrest of Decour, whom he seconded, and initially depended on Maucherat before having direct contact with Villon.

Another sign of the fumbling to apply the new line of openness in the autumn of 1942 was the indecision surrounding the name of the committee. Decour's manifesto, published in the first issue of *Les Lettres françaises* in September 1942, was entitled "National Front of Writers." "Representative of all tendencies and all religions: Gaullists, Communists, democrats, Catholics, Protestants, we are all united to form the National Front of French Writers," the manifesto proclaimed. The last two paragraphs, omitted from *La Pensée libre*, announced: "Today, the signatories of this appeal create this journal, *Les Lettres françaises*, that is the very expression of the National Front. *Les Lettres françaises* will be its instrument of combat [. . .]." In the second issue, French writers were called to "form everywhere Committees of the National Front to fight for the independence and the freedom of France." But in the following issue, the editorial, entitled "November Eleventh," was signed for the first and only time until September 1943, "Comité national des écrivains." This editorial, which announced the next meeting at the summit between the Communist Party delegate Fernand Grenier and the leader of La France combattante, hailed "the volunteers of the Forces Combattantes who rose up at the appeal of General De Gaulle [. . .]." In

1943, the editorials only occasionally mentioned the committees "of" [*de*] then "of the" [*du*] National Front (thus referring either to it either as a line or as a movement), and the reference to the National Front dimmed, unlike the reference to the Soviet Union, legitimized by the victory of Stalingrad. The name "National Front of Writers" would reappear only once on the front page of the newspaper, in July 1943.

We lack the sources to determine whether this indecision concerning the name of the committee in the Northern zone, up until the Southern zone imposed the name of Comité national des écrivains in September 1943 at Aragon's initiative, was the sign of internal tensions or if it was deliberately kept vague in order to avoid creating any.

Claude Morgan followed the orders of Georges Cogniot. In the third issue of *Les Lettres françaises*, he mocked, in a long article, the delegation of collaborationist writers' second trip to Weimar, which looked "quite pathetic" in the absence of known writers; harshly criticized Daniel-Rops's book on *Psichari*; and wrote a note on Drieu La Rochelle "alone with the Gestapo" (concerning his acknowledgment of failure and the denunciation of Pierre Emmanuel). In the fourth issue (dated December 1942, it only appeared in February 1943 because the studio had fallen into the hands of the Gestapo), near three articles by Pierre Villon, Debû-Bridel presented a poem by Erich Kaestner, "Si l'Allemagne avait gagné la guerre," and short items were devoted to the unequal distribution of paper, which privileged the collaborators to the detriment of classical works, to the new list of banned books, to perspectives on the Goncourt Academy elections. *Les Lettres françaises* also strove to state the rules of conduct for writers. Publishing legally meant playing into the enemy's hands, as Morgan demonstrated with regard to an article on Burgundy by Colette in *La Gerbe*.[87] But abstention was no longer sufficient. In the first issue, a "Dialogue on Action" condemned abstentionism as a form of wait-and-see attitude, and called on writers to achieve their mission, that of "expressing themselves"—illegally, of course—by exalting the heroism of those who were fighting in the shadows. Yet the recruitment to *Les Lettres françaises* was slow.

THE APPRENTICESHIP OF CLANDESTINITY

A few months passed, in fact, between the time when the connection was reestablished between the core group of writers surrounding Paulhan and their presumed newspaper, and their effective collaboration at *Les Lettres françaises*. It was again thanks to the Gallimard-*NRF* network that this contact was established. In the summer of 1942, Claude Morgan met up with Édith Thomas, who had been his colleague at *Ce Soir*. Fellow-traveler of the Communist Party since

1934—she joined in September 1942—Édith Thomas had published her first novels at the NRF publishing house and slightly knew Paulhan. She contributed to the second issue of *Les Lettres françaises*, dated October 1942. Having become a liaison for *Les Lettres françaises*, for which she also managed distribution, starting in February 1943 she would host meetings of the underground committee at her home on rue Pierre Nicole.

Several signs indicate that the contact with Debû-Bridel began in the month of October. Morgan said he had asked him for an article on English philosophy for the November issue—this article would not be published—and had received short items on the trip to Weimar from Paulhan, which probably helped him write his article.[88] Debû-Bridel would contribute to the following issue. In a letter addressed to Georges Cogniot and dated October 9, the author, probably Pierre Villon, noted: "Among the writers, great sympathy also among the elements from the right and the Gaullist militants,"[89] characteristics that only applied to Debû-Bridel within the first core group of writers. He would be "the man of the literary milieus" whom Cogniot recommended that Villon find to pursue the work of *Les Lettres françaises*—"Jack [Debû-Bridel] finds number 3 of *Les Lettres* perfect," Pierre Villon wrote to Jacques Duclos at the end of December 1942[90]—before becoming a member of the managing committee of the National Front of the Northern zone. In the same letter, Villon announced that "Paulhan has promised personal memories of Decour [...]."[91] In December, everything was finally in place. Paulhan had obviously very concrete projects for the content and distribution of *Les Lettres françaises*, which he in all likelihood transmitted via Debû-Bridel. We find their trace in the notes taken by Cogniot from a report on the National Front of Intellectuals dated December 24, 1942:

> *Writers* 1 Committee. Activity suspended between March and September: arrest of Decourt [*sic*]. Composition very broad with influential personalities. 1 Manifesto "Les Lettres Franç." Printed at 1,000. Plan to spread distribution to former subscribers of literary reviews such as *NRF*. Plan to publish short stories and poems [...].[92]

The writers still needed to be convinced to contribute anonymously to the underground newspaper. "What's the use? they said."[93] Anticipating their reticence, Claude Morgan had staged the writers' dilemma in the "Dialogue on Action" quoted earlier: "What necessity do you see in my writing in your anonymous press, since it is impossible to sign what I write there. My support would bring you an efficacious help if it could be public. But not being public, it would bring you nothing and anyone could write the same articles in my place." Thus spoke writer X . . . To which the character of René Bastide, who played the role of the old sage, answered:

> [. . .] How modest you are all of a sudden! As though you didn't know that what everyone brings—even anonymously, is an enrichment. Must I flatter you by saying that few others would know, like you, how to tell the exploits of the young guerillas, the courage of weak women, to fill the reader with enthusiasm for the example of those who fight already and thus contribute by your talent to the mass uprising of the nation.[94]

The writers' reticence stemmed from various reasons linked to their professional ethics. Distrust with respect to "agitprop," refusal to turn to the ideological arms that they denounced in the writings of the enemy, for some; inability to write on command for others. "In the end, the anonymity of clandestinity made others grimace," remembered Jean Lescure. "I believe that some would have preferred to sign, at the risk of their lives, anti-Nazi texts rather than to not be acknowledged as their authors."[95] It was a question of deontology. Underground publication required them to alter their relationship to writing. This was all the more true since clandestine texts would be reviewed to ensure that the style did not betray the author. "[. . .] I remember having written, having helped write, since we corrected each other so that the styles did not reveal themselves too much, and I wrote for *Les Lettres françaises*—things that I would not be able to recognize," Jean Guéhenno testified.[96] Likewise, Jacques Debû-Bridel, who came to visit Mauriac to see the manuscript for *Le Cahier noir* that he intended for the Éditions de Minuit, advised him to make "some modifications of detail without which not so much the Germans, but the French writers in their pay, would have been able to recognize him too easily."[97] It was a question of symbolic efficacy also. What is a text without an author? By contrast, the conditions of clandestinity recalled—the "what's the use" is revealing here— what the recognition of the value of the literary product owed, at least since romanticism, to the symbolic capital accumulated behind the proper name of the author. The recourse to pseudonyms would, in addition, raise very concrete practical questions: thus Claude Morgan would explain to Jean Lescure that if his essay on Malraux appeared in *Les Lettres françaises*, he would not be able to sign his name to it in the Swiss journal *Traits* where it was originally meant to appear, at the risk of rendering "ridiculous the claim to anonymity that clandestinity imposes on *Lettres*."[98]

But a new phenomenon had just modified the conditions of literary production: an underground publishing house was born, whose first title, *Le Silence de la mer*, had appeared in the spring of 1942 at a time when the apparatus of censorship was tightened (an authorization number was now imposed on all publications). In the literary world, it was a success: an acceptable model for "engaged literature," the book met all the aesthetic requirements of literary publishing, both by the quality of presentation and by the content. Through the attitude of "nonviolent refusal" that it advocated, it "acclimate[ed] the idea of a civil resistance."[99] In fact, it was first of all an "organized" success. *Le Silence de la mer*, "that nobody sees since there exists one copy that no one has but everyone is talking about," as Jean Lescure remembered, was highly anticipated. It arrived already hallowed with an aura of mystery, which Jean Paulhan obviously encouraged: "It is Paulhan who talks about *Le Silence* in his usual fashion: 'you have not seen this book, it is very good you know, I haven't seen it but I've been told about it.'"[100]

Up until then, anonymity and recourse to a pseudonym had been only rarely attempted by writers who were not reduced to illegality like the Communist intellectuals. In January 1942, the Swiss journal *Traits* had thus anonymously published poems by Pierre Seghers and Pierre Emmanuel on the hostages of Chateaubriant. The creation of the Éditions de Minuit by Pierre de Lescure and Vercors accredited the possibility and the pertinence of a true underground literature that would not be reduced to agitprop. Far from damaging the singularity of the writer, pseudonyms, which signified to the reader that a "name" was hiding behind them, would only increase its value by mystifying it and arousing an entire game of enigma around the true identity of the writer. "Not knowing who this author, Vercors, was aroused all the more curiosity. All of that played a great deal in the literary success of this little novella," Vercors said.[101] The entire literary milieu engaged then in a guessing game: "Some spoke of Duhamel, others of André Gide and Roger Martin du Gard. I admit to having hesitated between Schlumberger and Marcel Arland. Then, certain details made me think of *Géographie de dix hectares* by Maurice Bedel [...]," evoked Debû-Bridel.[102] This practice would not soon be exhausted: "When and how was it revealed to us, the identity of Elsa Triolet and Jean Cassou composing in his prison the verses that he had to write? *L'Honneur des poètes* was a collection of poems that we read, recited. Louis Aragon and some of the authors were recognized," recalled Professor Robert Debré, who financed the underground publishing house via Paulhan.[103]

It was surely not a coincidence that the first to fully "play the game" had nothing to lose from anonymity: Jean Bruller was an illustrator and former contributor to *Vendredi* who had never published a literary work. Cofounder of the underground Éditions de Minuit, Vercors would dissimulate his identity until August 1944, making himself known to certain members of the committee of writers under the name Desvignes, as a clandestine publisher, but carefully hiding the fact that he was also the author of *Le Silence de la mer*. "The only true secret of the war," Aragon said.[104] More than a measure of security—wasn't it riskier to be a printer than a clandestine author?—the dissociation of the writer from the publisher seemed to proceed here from an implicit rule of the literary field: disinterest, which was both the first principle of the ethos of the profession of writer and the foundation of literary belief, bans self-consecration, and thus supposes relays in the network of legitimation.[105] This dissociation was all the more worth maintaining until an assured recognition was obtained, because the founding of the underground venture coincided with the expectations of an aspiring writer deprived of a medium, since his friend Pierre de Lescure had announced the abandonment of *La Pensée libre*. This journal, where he intended to publish his manuscript, was, as we saw, replaced by a newspaper: "The trouble so far as I was concerned was that my short novel could obviously not appear in the new paper for lack of space [...] I might as well admit that a drop of vanity, a whiff of slightly puerile romanticism played a role in this decision and project."[106] Another anecdote reported by Vercors tends to confirm that the rules of security were only secondary compared with the quest for recognition in this dissociation between the writer and the publisher. Anxious to have, in the absence of Pierre de Lescure, an opinion on his second book, *La Marche à l'étoile*, he had signed with another name, striving to transform his writing, and submitted it to Paul Eluard:

> When I came back to it the following week, surprise: the work was being printed! Eluard had told Yvonne [Paraf-Desvignes]: "I don't understand anything in the stories of Desvignes. What does he want me to say to him? It is a novella by Vercors to be put into press immediately! [...] When the work appeared, then, unlike Eluard everyone fell for it: if Vercors could write in two such different manners, either his pseudonym was a collective name, or—it was the opinion of Debû-Bridel—this absence of personality makes them rather doubt whether this Vercors had a true talent.[107]

This anecdote also illustrates the extent to which authors themselves were caught up in the game of anonymity. Anonymity became like the paradigm of disinterest, or rather of two types of disinterest that it fused together: one that founded the intellectual ethos, and one that founded the militant ethos. "Naturally, as everywhere else, there are some differences of opinion but, thanks to anonymity and the total disinterest of each, they can give way to no intrigue and no competition," Debû-Bridel would write.[108] Sacrificing their name to the cause that they served, the writers were definitively reinforced in the convictions that founded their professional ethics. As for "contraband," the mystery and play contributed to the cohesion of this small group of initiates and to their belief in the effectiveness of the project they pursued. This was a belief that the echo of clandestine literature beyond the limited circle and especially beyond the borders could only reinforce: the limited number of printed copies that circulated from hand to hand were recopied, sometimes reedited and/or translated, like *Le Silence de la mer* in London, Algiers, Quebec, Beirut, in America and even in Australia. "How not to feel the heartbreaking quality of these poems that today all of France recites in secret?" asked de Gaulle in his speech on October 31 at Algiers, citing verses by Aragon and "the complaint of Anne [Édith Thomas], a young woman dreaming in the Tuileries."[109]

Like *Les Lettres françaises*, the Éditions de Minuit was in search of authors. Since *Le Silence de la mer*, only the new edition of *À travers le désastre* by Jacques Maritain appeared there in November 1942; it was originally published in 1940 at the Éditions de la Maison française in New York. When, at the beginning of 1942, Pierre de Lescure had shared his plan for an underground publishing house with an incredulous Debû-Bridel, he had told him that "the most difficult [...] was to find authors."[110] Debû-Bridel had immediately suggested that he contact Jean Paulhan, who would serve as literary editor of the Éditions de Minuit starting in late 1942. This was how, in early 1943, the Éditions de Minuit became, almost at the same time as *Les Lettres françaises*, the place where members of the committee were published.

THE BIRTH OF AN UNDERGROUND LITERARY SPACE

The fifth issue of *Les Lettres françaises*, dated January–February 1943, "marked," according to Claude Morgan, "progress because several members of the Committee had brought their contribution to it. The Committee finally lived. The writers got used to the need for anonymous work. They began to be interested in the newspaper."[111] The first page of this issue featured a poem by Eluard, "Courage." In December, Claude Morgan had gone to see Eluard on the advice of Pierre Maucherat, who had told him about the publication of *Poésie et vérité 1942*. The collection opened with the poem "Liberté." When Morgan gave him the first three issues of *Les Lettres françaises* while asking for his contribution, Eluard "insisted on the necessity of increasing their literary character (we are not the newspaper of the FTP) [...]."[112] The Communist leader did not know that Eluard was already engaged, then, at Pierre de Lescure's request, in the preparation of an underground anthology of poetry for the Éditions de Minuit.

Since the spring of 1936, during a period when surrealism attained consecration with a first international exhibition in June, Eluard had been estranged from André Breton. Reticent on the distant attitude of the surrealists with regard to the Popular Front, "more and more tempted by a realistic and Communistic attitude" according to his biographer, he did not sign the declaration of September 3, "Comrades, more light!" that denounced the first trials in Moscow and, thanks to solidarity against Francoism, agreed at Aragon's request to publish in *L'Humanité* on December 17 the poem "November 1936" that he had entrusted to Louis Parrot.[113] "It's the first time that one of my poems has had a 450,000 run. I can guess what Breton will think of it. But, if I don't change my poetry, I don't see why I shouldn't rather contribute to *L'Humanité*, read by workers, than to the N.R.F. or elsewhere, read exclusively by the middle classes," he wrote to his lover Gala.[114] The publication of "Les vainqueurs d'hier périront" in *Commune* in May 1938, followed by the court of exclusion organized by Breton, consummated the definitive break.[115] This exclusion allowed Eluard to be welcomed at *La NRF* with open arms. In June, Jean Guérin alias Paulhan, with whom he had reconciled in 1937, granted him the title of "modern Petrarch."[116] The publication, in 1939, of *Chanson complète* and *Donner à voir* at Gallimard marked Eluard's consecration. And it was with a dedication to Jean Paulhan that the poem "Blason des fleurs et des fruits" appeared in Drieu's *NRF* in February 1941—"to console myself for your departure," he wrote to Paulhan.[117]

Isolated, Eluard agreed in 1941, not without a certain distrust, to support the group of young neo-surrealists of La Main à Plume, where *Poésie et vérité 1942* appeared in October 1942 with a print date of April 3. Engaged with Jean Lescure in the preparation of *Domaine français*, he broke with the Main à Plume group on May 2, 1943. After an attempt at reconciliation, they had just published a tract against *Messages* entitled "Nom de Dieu!" where *Messages* became "Messe à tous les âges" ("mass at all ages").[118] Eluard's presence at *Messages* was not insignificant in a quarrel motivated as much by rivalry as political reasons.[119] In April 1943, during Aragon and Elsa Triolet's brief stay in Paris to coordinate the writers' committees of both zones, the reunions occurred. Eluard had just joined the Communist Party. Had he intended to do this since the spring of 1942, as Lucien Scheler claimed?[120] According to Claude Morgan, when he approached him at the request of Pierre Villon, who really wanted it— he would go himself to get his membership—Eluard appeared reticent: "I will not be able to say what I want as a poet anymore and I could not stand it."[121] Morgan assured him that he would be left totally free in this domain. Morgan knew what he was saying. A poet who was now widely recognized and ready to become engaged without compromising his art, Eluard was able to set his own conditions. A letter dated February 1943 by Georges Cogniot should be added to the file of Eluard's return to the party. It deserves to be quoted at length and requires no commentary:

[...] I send back to you finally Poésie et Vérité 1942. In my opinion, the author is a real poet, probably even a great poet. I copied almost everything for my own enjoyment. The technique is very beautiful: there are magnificent verses of pure poetry such as

Gorge haut suspendue orgue de la nuit lente

and stanzas of a deeply mysterious resonance like

Aussi bas que le silence
D'un mort planté dans la terre
Rien que ténèbres en tête

Moreover, the intention, the inspiration is good, without question. The misfortune is that it would need a constant commentary for the general public, an explanatory article for each poem, five to ten times longer than the text. I don't say this to make fun of the author: he is, I repeat, really somebody; there are many artists—although they are never the most elevated, who require for the unfamiliar reader a presentation and a preparation. In sum: for the moment, it is a matter of using this among the intellectuals according to the general line of illustration of our cause by the men of high value who serve it;—later, we will look to bring the poet closer to the masses. As for insisting too much at present that he clarify himself, it would be indiscreet and probably ineffective, he could not yet [...].[122]

The allied landing in North Africa and the invasion of the Southern zone precipitated the implementation of a new politics of openness. The suppression of the demarcation line facilitated contact with the Southern zone. In December, Aragon asked for a liaison with the leadership of the party, who sent him Emmanuel alias Claude Morgan at the beginning of 1943.[123] Morgan brought back the "Chanson du franc-tireur," the "Prélude à la Diane française," and the "Ballade de celui qui chantait dans les supplices" for *Les Lettres françaises*.

In the Northern zone, the recruitment for the committee of writers was less selective. Sartre was finally admitted in January. Should we attribute the initiative for this recruitment to Aragon, as Claude Morgan suggested?[124] Simone de Beauvoir spoke of "certain members of the Communist intelligentsia" (that is to say François Billoux) who "invited Sartre to join the Comité National des Écrivains. He asked them if they wanted a spy in their ranks, but they all assured him they knew nothing about the rumors they had been circulating at his expense in

1941."[125] Still, unlike with Decour, it was not Morgan who decided on the recruitment.

Starting in February, the meetings were held at Édith Thomas's house and presided by Eluard. After Eluard and Sartre, Michel Leiris, Jean Lescure, and André Frénaud joined the initial group, introduced by Jean Paulhan.[126] These last, it seems, did not yet participate in the meetings at Édith Thomas's house (for his part, Leiris would never participate in them). For Jean Lescure, who along with Paulhan had transformed the review *Messages* into a "recruiting agent," "the true meetings of the CNE [which did not bear this name yet] were in Paulhan's office."[127] Meetings were also held at the home of Jean Blanzat, where René Tavernier, coming from the Southern zone, said that he saw Guéhenno, Paulhan, and Jean Lescure.[128] Yet this was not where *Les Lettres françaises* was made, as Jean Lescure confirmed. The texts were given directly to Claude Morgan, whom Jean Lescure wouldn't meet until the summer of 1943, when he would give him his essay on Malraux. The editorial councils were held in Claude Morgan's office in the Palais du Louvre. Nevertheless, the sixth issue made *Les Lettres françaises* seem like the organ of the committee. With the "Chanson du franc-tireur" by Aragon; the famous article by Sartre, "Drieu La Rochelle or Self-Hate"; and Leiris's article "Apollinaire, Citizen of Paris" that responded to a talk by André Salmon on Radio-Paris during which he had annexed the author of *Calligrammes* to "the European spirit"; with "Reflections on the Dead Queen" by Paulhan; and Jean Blanzat's column on *Pilote de guerre* by Saint-Exupéry that had just been banned, this issue looked good. Claude Morgan and Édith Thomas still edited most of the following issues, with the help of Debû-Bridel for the June issue (where the "Ballade de celui qui chanta dans les supplices" also appeared), and Eluard's help for the July issue.

The day after the dinner organized by Jean Lescure to celebrate the reunion, Aragon and Eluard met again to discuss the coordination of the two zones and the writers to solicit, in the presence of the poet-bookseller Lucien Scheler, who was then competing with Jean Lescure to "second" Eluard and who joined the Communist Party during this period. The names of Mauriac and Queneau were purportedly mentioned.[129] They joined the committee shortly after. Without knowing anything about Mauriac's theoretical support in 1941, Claude Morgan obtained a meeting with him thanks to Duhamel, who, while he still refused to participate in clandestine activities, regularly lavished advice on Morgan. First contacted by Paulhan, Mauriac had just promised Debû-Bridel a manuscript for the Éditions de Minuit, *Le Cahier noir*, that would be published in August 1943. He would say that he had decided to give his support to the National

Front (he would be a member of its directive committee at the Liberation) at the insistence of Debû-Bridel and Blanzat (Jean Paulhan, on the other hand, declined).[130] According to a report by Pierre Villon, Mauriac was a member of the National Front from May 1943: "Writ[ers]. Duhamel very good, gives advice; Mauriac joins the FN despite fears of 'materialism' and 'Marxism'; prospect of having Valéry. 'Éditions de Minuit' will publish a collection of short stories on the FTP and the hostages."[131]

The collection of short stories he mentioned was Édith Thomas's *Transcrit du réel*, the future *Contes d'Auxois*; Jean Paulhan had forwarded the manuscript, along with that of *Amants d'Avignon* by Elsa Triolet, to Yvonne Paraf-Desvignes during a meeting at Édith Thomas's home. From that moment on, the manuscripts multiplied at the Éditions de Minuit, which was catching up to *Les Lettres françaises*. The third volume from the Éditions de Minuit, *Chroniques interdites*, had been published at the same time as the sixth issue of *Les Lettres françaises*, in April 1943. In it we recognize Aragon's touch, and the aftermath of the Bergson affair already mentioned. While with this volume of *Chroniques*, the Éditions de Minuit didn't yet confirm their originality with respect to underground publications, they had already launched a more ambitious project, the anthology *L'Honneur des poètes* prepared by Eluard with the assistance of Jean Lescure; it was published with a date of July 14, 1943.

Eluard's entry onto the playing field as a new agent of alliance between the writers and the party was decisive for the articulation and coordination of the three underground ventures: the writers' committee, *Les Lettres françaises*, and the Éditions de Minuit. While the Éditions de Minuit retained a relative autonomy,[132] the CNE formed a sort of expanded committee of the underground publishing house: "For at the meetings of the CNE, we also prepared the *Éditions de Minuit*," Édith Thomas declared.[133] The connection was ensured at various levels by several members: Paulhan, who had taken on the role of literary editor at the end of 1942; he would be relieved in June 1943 by Eluard whom Pierre de Lescure had appointed to represent him in his absence; Debû-Bridel and Édith Thomas, both liaisons; and Yvonne Paraf-Desvignes, delegated by Vercors to represent the Éditions de Minuit at the meetings of the CNE. Here again, it was the Gallimard-*NRF* network at work. Yvonne Desvignes and Vercors were the sole authors not to belong to it: it was through Pierre de Lescure that contacts first passed to Debû-Bridel, and thus to Paulhan—"Debû-Bridel was truly the hinge, he knew all the writers and above all, he was in constant contact with Paulhan," Vercors recounted[134]—then to Eluard. In the summer of 1943, the membership of the writers' committee had doubled, going from seven to about fifteen members. With the exception of Lucien Scheler, recruited by Eluard, all were linked to Paulhan either through the Gallimard-NRF network, or the magazine *Messages* which, as we have seen, was a substitute for the writers of "refusal" in the occupied zone.

The announcement of the publication of *Le Silence de la mer* in the January–February *Lettres françaises* inaugurated a new division of labor between the three authorities. The fact that the exchanges in kind and recycling sometimes led to a "deviation" of the literary project of the Éditions didn't change anything: none of the three ventures would have survived without the others. After the first fumblings, the principle of exchange was put in place, which excluded neither rivalries nor internal conflicts; the committee solicited the authors, furnished manuscripts, discussed projects; the Éditions de Minuit selected a list that almost never betrayed the standards of a properly literary production; *Les Lettres françaises* commented on political and literary current events—public and underground—and contributed to the distribution of works that were published at Minuit, through book reviews on the one hand and the handling of part of the "distribution department" on the other.[135]

The exchange of services would also occur at the level of printing and production. Beginning with the tenth issue (October 1943), *Les Lettres françaises* would be printed on four pages thanks to Georges Adam, former editor of *Ce Soir*, whom Morgan had met up with again during this period. Thanks to his contacts with typographers of the CGT trade union (Confédération générale du travail), Adam had actually met the printer Antoine Blondin, who would now regularly print the newspaper. Its circulation, between 3,000 and 4,000 copies at the beginning of 1943, would reach up to 12,000.[136] It was at Georges Adam's home on place Adolphe Chérioux that the editorial councils for the newspaper were now held. The printer Blondin soon became the second printer of the Éditions de Minuit after Ernest Aulard, creating a distinct editorial network reserved for the "Témoignages" series, but also for the publications of Communist writers (notably Claude Morgan, *La Marque de l'homme*, and Georges Adam, *À l'appel de la liberté*). Conversely, the *Almanach des lettres françaises*, published in March 1944 with a print run of 5,000 copies, would be paperbound by the staff of the Éditions de Minuit. At the time this coordination was being put in place, toward the end of the spring of 1943, the project to reunite the committees of the two zones was just getting under way; it was prefigured by *L'Honneur des poètes* and symbolized, after Aragon's contributions, by those of Loÿs Masson and André Rousseaux in the issue of *Les Lettres françaises* published in September 1943.

When Aragon set out to assemble writers from the Southern zone in a committee parallel to the one in the Northern zone, he could rely on the networks that had already been formed around the subversive magazines. There is no doubt that contraband literature, for which it had been decided that Aragon's still-legal situation would be put to good use, had been considered by the leadership of the intellectuals of the party as participating in the fight against oppression. Based on a report in December 1942, Georges Cogniot noted: "Parallel committee in free zone having published a manifesto a year ago and whose members have had very courageous activity."[137] A report in April 1943 tried to theorize the role of these magazines: "It is a constant fact, pointed out by the historians of the Press, that in dictatorial periods, the literary publications enjoy, relatively, a certain freedom, due to the limited public that they address. This is a circumstance that has allowed some publications to adopt, with all sorts of precautions, a liberal or even oppositional position."[138] In the notes that Cogniot took on a "Report on Work among the Intellectuals in the Southern Zone," drafted in April 1944, he revels again in the work accomplished with the writers:

> CNÉcriv[ains]. The soul of the CN b[ecause] be[fore] w[ar], it is among the writers that our work had been the most fruitful and the legal work of three years was possible [thanks to] the weakness of the Vichy government, (liter[ary] pages of Figaro, of Mot d'ordre; literary magazines printed at 5–6,000 versus maximum of 3,500 for Europe after fifteen years of existence) [. . .].[139]

The study of the recruitment in the CNE of the Southern zone inclines me to relativize the first explanation that is given for this success, namely the direct link with the success of the prewar unitary politics among the writers, in favor of the second: the quality of the "legal" work orchestrated by Aragon.

Having gone underground after the total occupation of the territory in November 1942, Aragon, as we saw, asked for a liaison with the party leadership. At the beginning of 1943, he received the order to proceed with assembling the writers and was soon entrusted with the clandestine organization of the intellectuals in the Southern zone. Georges Marrane, who was a leader of the National Front there, paired him with Georges Sadoul and the "technical adviser" Georges Ternet. His connection to the leadership passed through Hubert Ruffe, "organizational" head of the party in the Southern zone. Up until then, Aragon had instructions to have contact only with the leadership of the Communist Party in the Northern zone. Did these instructions proceed from the partition of the different sectors within the apparatus? Did it correspond to a measure of security as the consequence of the repression that had decimated the leadership of the Communist Party in the Southern zone in 1941, then the organization of intellectuals in the occupied zone in the spring of 1942? Unless abandoning these instructions was meant to tighten control around this man who too often diverged from security rules. For Aragon did not trouble himself with precautions that he probably deemed superfluous, violating the rule of clandestinity that forbade a pair of résistants to live under the same roof, leaving his refuge in Dieulefit after two months to arrive in Lyon in January 1943, attracting the reprimands of Hubert Ruffe. In December 1943, Ruffe complained to the leadership that he had to "intervene quite often with 3 [Aragon] who still has too much of a tendency to practice 'political lunches' on too big a scale."[140] The leadership of the intellectual resistance would be entrusted to him on the condition that he go definitively underground: in June 1943, he left Lyon for Saint-Donat, in the Drôme region, with the means the party gave him.

This later order probably explains the temporal gap between the two zones when it came to writers' passage into clandestinity. It also corresponded to the particular situation of the Southern zone, which made the need less palpable in the literary milieus up until November 1942. The differences already evoked between the two zones in terms of the experience of the Occupation had an impact on attitudes on both sides. Lucien Scheler reported that during the meeting between Aragon and Eluard in April 1943, Eluard informed him of the behavior of the members of the committee in the Northern zone, "behavior clearly different from what Louis might have experienced moreover, for those that have lived under the yoke of the occupying forces for three years undoubtedly harbor an intransigence that often proves to be disconcerting for those of the Southern zone that Vichy has not maintained under its control for a long time, but on occasion still manages to dupe."[141]

Added to the later experience of the direct and daily confrontation with the occupying forces was a lesser exposure to the collaborationist press. René Tavernier claimed to have discovered the collaborationist press during his stays in Paris starting in November 1942.[142] More decisive was the existence of the subversive magazines that managed to hold up and appear regularly despite some problems with censorship, unlike in the occupied zone where they were rarer, lesser-known, and where their survival was more and more uncertain (this was the case for the magazine *Messages* that had to exile itself to Belgium and then Switzerland). The weekly *Temps nouveau* that Stanislas Fumet had launched in

Lyon at Christmas 1940—it took over for *Temps présent*—was indeed suspended in August 1941 by the Vichy government, at the same time as Emmanuel Mounier's *Esprit*, thus depriving the Christian Democratic circle of its forums.[143] But reviews with a purely cultural character could still serve as a refuge, by name or under a pseudonym, for the writers of "refusal" or banned authors, such as Jean Wahl, excluded from *La NRF* due to his Jewish origins, and who contributed to *Confluences*, or even Léon Moussinac and Georges Sadoul, Communists, who signed as Jacques d'Aymé and Claude Jacquier respectively in *Poésie 41 . . .* and *Confluences*.

Finally, the geographic position of the Southern zone provided authors with effective relays in Algeria and Switzerland: *Fontaine* and the Éditions Charlot in Algiers, Swiss journals like *Traits*, which welcomed the most subversive texts by writers in the Southern zone under pseudonyms. In 1942, *Les Cahiers du Rhône*, founded by Albert Béguin at the Éditions de la Baconnière that Hermann Hauser ran in the little town of Boudry, took over for the banned Catholic publications, *Esprit* and *Temps présent*. Albert Béguin, then a lecturer at the University of Halle, had been approached by Stanislas Fumet after the suspension of *Temps nouveau* "to pursue, in Switzerland, the gathering of all the good wills that risked dispersal."[144] He met Fumet and Mounier in the autumn of 1941, then, pushed by a group of Swiss and French students, created the series of *Les Cahiers du Rhône*. Starting in October 1942, the "blue" series that published collective compilations and works with a doctrinal and ideological character, and the "white" series, more literary, were joined by the "red" series, reserved for poetry. While the first series united progressive and conservative Catholics, pairing people like Stanislas Fumet and André Rousseaux, in March 1942 the second sealed the alliance between Catholic and Communist writers with the publication of *Le Poète et son Christ* by Pierre Emmanuel and *Les Yeux d'Elsa* by Aragon. This alliance would not be achieved without incidents and compromises, as shown by the (augmented) republishing in the "white" series of Eluard's *Poésie et vérité 1942* in February 1943; initially destined to ensure the prestige of the "red" series, it was redirected due to Eluard's request that the label bearing the motto of the Cahiers, "Dieu premier servy," be omitted.[145] René Tavernier, commercial agent of the Maison du Livre français in Lyon who helped *Les Cahiers du Rhône* enter France, recalled the importance of this Swiss "skylight":

> We had this extraordinary chance to receive Swiss newspapers, to listen to Swiss radio that was heard so easily, to be in contact with Swiss editors, for example Albert Béguin and his *Cahiers du Rhône* . . . That made a little

privileged corner. Geneva, Neuchâtel, Lyon, all were geographically close and it was possible to circulate. Naturally, after the denunciation of the armistice, the invasion of the Southern zone [. . .] it was no longer a question of going freely to Switzerland. Despite everything, we had—unlike in the Northern zone—the feeling of breathing through Switzerland, there was a little open skylight that brought us what Saint-John Perse, Maritain, Supervielle were writing abroad, works that came to us through the Éditions de *la Bâconnière* [sic], *Les Cahiers du Rhône*, *Les Trois Collines* . . . [146]

But before donning the yoke of occupation in their turn, the writers of the so-called free zone had also felt the effects of the tightening of censorship in the spring of 1942. In August, *Confluences* had been suspended for two months due to the publication of Aragon's poem "Nymphée." This suspension was meant to serve as an example, just as a letter of warning emanating from the Ministry of Information addressed to *Poésie 42* and *Fontaine* and threatening to begin sanctioning the procedure of contraband also signified. From now on, Aragon would publish under a pseudonym. The extension of Nazi jurisdiction to the Southern zone starting in November certainly helped weaken this relatively comfortable situation even more.

While the privileged conditions of the Southern zone help explain why the urgency of an underground organization was not felt until November 1942, we must also account for a negative factor. In fact, Parisian centralization and established forms of sociability (such as the day Paulhan hosted visitors at *La NRF*) probably favored a more rapid clandestine development in the capital, whereas in the Southern zone, the dispersal of the intellectuals would remain an essential fact of the conditions of organization and underground production until the Liberation, in spite of the frequent travels and the core groups that formed in some cultural centers, in Lyon, Avignon, Dieulefit, and Marseille, for example. "What was extraordinary in the Southern zone was the prodigious separation, we were very separated, the means of transportation very difficult. Thus our relations with Toulouse were almost impossible. Lyon had become a second capital [. . .]," René Tavernier stated.[147] It is significant, in this regard, that the work of assembling writers undertaken by Aragon had been favored, in the beginning, by the cultural voluntarism of Vichy, as we saw with the Rencontres de Lourmarin and the consecutive publication of the "Manifesto of Intellectuals in the Occupied Zone" in September 1941. It was just as significant that the CNE formed during Aragon's stay in Lyon from January to June 1943.

This dispersal also explains the organizational formula of grouping intellectuals of the Southern zone into five-pointed "stars," an organization with a territorial base unlike the professional organization that prevailed among their homologues of the Northern zone. "A Star is a group of five intellectuals, each of these is considered like a point of the Star, commits to forming another star and so forth, snowballing. According to the underground rule, the Stars are strictly isolated."[148] The operation had already been tried, it seems, with regards to the distribution in the Southern zone of the illegal publications that arrived from the occupied zone. The system of "stars," which gave its name to the clandestine bulletin that Aragon and Georges Sadoul launched at the beginning of 1943, would constitute the mode of recruitment for the committees of intellectuals in the Southern zone; they intersected, as a result: "We wanted to be dealing with people who were not from the same intellectual discipline, or in any case not from the same political milieu, so as to penetrate somewhere else, by each of these points, each thus being able to transmit to a point of another Star the material of information and agitation, thus distributed to the four other constituents of the Star, and from them to four other Stars. Thus an organization in layers was formed across the entire Southern zone," Aragon related.[149] Whereas in the Northern zone, the different committees of intellectuals had formed in a very compartmentalized manner, those in the Southern zone branched out from the CNE that was the first founded, before reorganizing themselves by "points" (without the territorial formula being abandoned). Louis Martin-Chauffier would thus be the link between the committee of writers and the committee of journalists, which he founded in August 1943 with Georges Altmann of Francs-Tireurs, René Leynaud from Combat (shot by the Germans), Audré Sauger from the FN, and Sadoul.

Taken in by René Tavernier whom he helped with the editing of *Confluences*, Aragon, during his stay in Lyon, brought about the convergence of Lyon's literary and university milieus grouped around *Confluences*, the Parisians who had retreated to Lyon, notably the editors of *Paris-Soir* (Louis Martin-Chauffier, Jean Prévost) and *Le Figaro* (André Rousseaux), and the network of young poets that had formed around *Poésie 40, 41* . . . From the beginning of 1943, the first "star" grouped Stanislas Fumet, Auguste Anglès, Henry Malherbe, and Jean Prévost around Aragon. Auguste Anglès, former schoolmate of René Tavernier, ENS graduate, newly received at the agrégation and assistant at the faculty of Lyon, was a contributor to *Confluences*. Catholic, he was furthermore linked to Stanislas Fumet, former director of *Temps nouveau*. Jean Prévost, ENS graduate, writer—a Gallimard author, he was a former contributor to *La NRF*—and journalist, had followed the editorial staff of *Paris-Soir* to Lyon. Henry Malherbe, winner of the Goncourt Prize in 1917 for *La Flamme au poing*, former president of the Association des écrivains combattants and former vice president of the

Croix de feu, had accompanied the editorial staff of *Temps* where he was the music critic. One month after a preparatory meeting attended by Seghers, the inaugural meeting of the CNE took place in July 1943 at René Tavernier's house in Montchat.

Since the month of February, a small typed bulletin called *Les Étoiles* already circulated clandestinely. The first issue included an "Appeal to the Intellectuals of France," a poem by Eluard, and a text by Péguy.[150] This appeal was diffused in the form of a tract entitled "To the Intellectuals." The reference to the Obligatory Work Service, instituted on February 16, 1943, situated it after that date. Was it really prior to the visit that Morgan paid Aragon in March, following the request for a connection that he had formulated to the leadership of the intellectuals in the Northern zone at the end of 1942? I am not able to pinpoint this. In any case, the tract called on the intellectuals of the Southern zone to form underground groups, on the model of the "Comité national des écrivains" of the Northern zone:

> [...] the intellectuals of France, following the example of the Comité national des écrivains that has formed in Paris, must form groups united among themselves, whose acting solidarity opposes the enemy's crimes against the mind and the Fatherland, supporting in particular the fight against deportation (where the physician, the priest, especially, can play a decisive role) [...].[151]

The fact that this name, which marked the relative independence of the committees with respect to the National Front, was claimed here while it appeared only once in *Les Lettres françaises*, inclines me to attribute its paternity, or at least its official adoption, to Aragon.

In June 1943, probably as a result of the preparatory meeting, *Les Étoiles* published "a document of prime importance: the manifesto of the Comité national des écrivains," which, under the title "The Comité national des écrivains Speaks to You ... ," "asks the writers of France, and around them all the intellectuals, to order the general mobilization of the mind against the Barbarians."[152] The reference to Bergson was marked with the Aragonian seal. Yet the July issue of *Les Lettres françaises* (no. 8) was subtitled for the one and only time "Review of the National Front of Writers." This was an echo of the transformations of the spring of 1943 that, thanks to the development of the structures for coordinating the different movements of the Resistance, notably with the creation of the Conseil national de la Résistance in May, saw the National Front transform into an individual movement among others, the FN. Did the FN movement attempt to reappropriate its offspring? In *Les Étoiles*, the reference to the National Front was absent. It was the Southern zone that set the name "Comité national," adopted by the Northern zone, as Aragon requested of Claude Morgan during the symbolic unification of the two committees in September 1943, because "it allowed us to hook people who did not want to be part of the F.N."[153] The first printed issue of *Les Lettres françaises* (no. 10), dated October 1943, was subtitled "Review of French Writers Grouped with the Comité National des Écrivains."

First published by the leading "triangle"—Aragon, Sadoul, Ternet—the bulletin *Les Étoiles* soon became the forum of the intellectual committees of the Southern zone, but would be edited by the CNE, whose members also contributed to the underground *Lettres françaises*. In August, starting with issue 10, the bulletin was printed and became a monthly. It would have several editions, in Lyon, Toulouse, Saint-Flour (with René Amarger who printed 1,000, then 1,500 copies), then in Marseille and Valence. Nineteen issues would be published up until the Liberation. Edited for a time by Pierre Emmanuel (presumably in 1944), it would count among its contributors Aragon, Auguste Anglès, Claude Aveline, Julien Benda, Father Bruckberger, Jean Cassou, Gabriel Chevallier, Paul Eluard, Luc Estang, Henry Malherbe, André Rousseaux, Georges Sadoul, Pierre Seghers, and René Tavernier. Still, the bulletin would remain, above all, a news bulletin; its literary quality did not reach that of *Les Lettres françaises*, which remained the true organ of the CNE after the unification of the committees of both zones under the same heading.

René Amarger, the printer in Saint-Flour who had been contacted by Eluard and Ternet, would publish the brochures of the Bibliothèque française, an underground publishing house common to all the intellectual committees of the Southern zone, which constituted a relay for the clandestine periodicals of the Northern zone—it printed the Southern zone editions of *L'Université libre* and *Le Palais libre*—and for the Éditions de Minuit; it reissued some of its volumes (*Le Silence de la mer*) in a low-priced "popular edition." Without ever attaining the literary importance of the house founded by Pierre de Lescure and Vercors, the Bibliothèque française, at the impetus of Aragon, attempted to surpass its prestigious competitor and promote a literature of combat starting in the autumn of 1942. Aragon alias François La Colère gave it the first pass at *Le Musée Grévin* (printed at 1,500 copies); he had already given the manuscript to the Éditions de Minuit. Under the pseudonym of Arnaud de Saint-Roman, he gave his novella *Les Bons Voisins* (which was part of the collection *Servitudes et Grandeur des Français* published in 1945); Eluard alias Jean du Haut gave his *Sept poèmes d'amour en guerre*. In 1944 it published *L'Arrestation* by Édith Thomas alias Jean Le Guern, *Yvette* by Elsa Triolet alias Laurent Daniel. *Le Père Milon* by Maupassant was republished there at 1,000 copies in the autumn of 1943; in 1944, *Hier comme Aujourd'hui*, collected poems by Paul Verlaine and Charles Cros.[154]

Like *Les Lettres françaises*, *Les Étoiles* publicized the Éditions de Minuit—notably giving an excerpt of *Le Cahier noir* by Forez alias François Mauriac in no. 13, November 1943—and created a list of underground publications, where "the beautiful volumes of the Éditions de Minuit" appeared alongside the "brochures of the Bibliothèque française" (no. 14, December 1943). But the relay was a one-way street. Whereas *Les Lettres françaises* included long reviews of Éditions de Minuit volumes, Bibliothèque française did not benefit from the same treatment. The critique of Aragon's *Le Musée Grévin*, which Claude Morgan published in the twelfth issue dated January 1944, did not mention the Southern edition. In reference to this column that he said satisfied him, Eluard, who seconded Aragon in his editorial venture in the Southern zone, wrote to Jean Lescure: "If the little booklets of the Bibliothèque franç[aise] can be reviewed as seriously, I will be at the height of joy."[155] Jean Lescure hurried to satisfy his "master" by reviewing his *Sept poèmes d'amour en guerre* in the following issue (no. 13, February 1944), but this article remained the exception. Was it due to Eluard's intervention that a paragraph by Georges Adam on the Bibliothèque française appeared in March 1944 (no. 14)? However, *Les Étoiles* would not be cited until May 1944 (no. 16)?

These "delays" cannot simply be blamed on difficulties of communication or distribution. The printings of the Bibliothèque française were no lower than those of the Éditions de Minuit, which did not exceed 1,500 copies, although this did not hinder their diffusion in the Southern zone. Revenge of the Northern zone on the Southern zone? "Capitalization" of the advantages of the anteriority of an underground struggle that was waged at the price of much higher risks?[156] Or reappropriation of the oppositional literary movement born in the Southern zone with contraband literature? In any case, there was an inversion here that announced the renewed victory of Parisian domination over intellectual life. Many a venture that the interlude of the Occupation years had filled with hope would suffer its effects immediately following the Liberation, as shown by the aborted attempts to establish some of them in Paris, including the Charlot publishing house, *Fontaine*, and *Confluences*.

THE SUCCESS OF UNITARY POLITICS
IN THE SOUTHERN ZONE

At a plenary meeting of the CNE in the autumn of 1943, during which a board was formed including Henry Malherbe, Aragon, Louis Martin-Chauffier, Georges Sadoul, and René Tavernier—Francis Ponge, who was not cited among those present, would be its secretary[157]—André Rousseaux counted about twenty people, including Jean Prévost, Stanislas Fumet, Pierre Emmanuel, Jean Cassou, Elsa Triolet, Andrée Viollis, Father Bruckberger, and Albert Camus. The last had gained entry through Pascal Pia, member of the directive committee of the National Front in the Southern zone, with whom he was engaged in the Combat movement. These members were joined by Claude Roy and Pierre Seghers (then visiting Paris).[158]

In November 1943, while the CNE had just held its third meeting with fourteen members present, it seemed like "the most active and the most important from the standpoint of influence."[159] Georges Ternet counted 300 writer members, "including all those at the forefront," attached to the 22 members of the directive committee "by individual connections" or forming "some small circles." The extension of recruitment nonetheless met with difficulties that were not remotely political:

> It would be necessary for us to form Committees in the big cities and penetrate among second-rung writers: the 800 or 900 members of the Societé des gens de lettres in the Southern zone. But we meet with difficulties due to rivalries between the great writers and the others: discredited beginners or scribers of the SGDL. And it is for us more important to influence the great writers.[160]

These "individual connections" left few traces. Elsa Triolet gave an account of the membership of Roger Martin du Gard and André Malraux, collected and transmitted by Georges Sadoul. Unlike the first who did not take part in any of the committee meetings, the second appeared at one of them, but we know the position of the author of *L'Espoir* who repeatedly refused all underground activity other than armed combat. As for Martin du Gard, he evoked in his journal the conditions of his membership, which attest to the difficulties of recruitment linked to the mode of functioning and the hierarchies proper to the literary field. In late 1942 and early 1943, Georges Sadoul came to see him, introducing himself as a friend of Jean Paulhan's. "'Some writers of the first rank,' he told me in substance, 'indignant over the collaborating attitude of the Parisian press and certain colleagues, are thinking of forming a small select committee of "intellectual resistance." They are Georges Duhamel, Paul Valéry, François Mauriac, and Jean Paulhan [...].'" And asked him in their name for his participation. Despite his reluctance to affiliate himself with a group and his decision to remain silent, Martin du Gard agreed, in a spontaneous move inspired by the names that Sadoul mentioned, to depart from the rule he had set for himself. During his third visit, Sadoul announced to him that the CNE of the

Southern zone had finally formed around the review *Confluences*, and invited him to take part in the plenary meeting. Disappointed by the first manifesto that Sadoul brought him (which "had an accent of political polemic, very well-intentioned, but whose virulent—and banal—tone only half-pleased" the pacifist that he was) and having the vague feeling that he had been duped, Martin du Gard, without withdrawing his support, did not go to the meeting and decided to remain a "passive 'member.'" As he put it:

> This movement remained eminently likeable. Nevertheless, I could not keep myself from having the impression that I had been somewhat toyed with . . . They had "got" me: by making me think that I would be part of a select committee, limited to some writers like Valéry, Mauriac, Paulhan, and Duhamel. In fact, I found myself the member of a vast resistance group, more or less directed by Aragon, and including everything that the Southern zone counted as "intellectuals" hostile to the politics of Vichy.

At the Liberation, when the list of CNE members was published, Martin du Gard would not be unhappy to appear on it with "a good number of friends and many eminent writers [. . .] In sum, I told myself, I was in excellent company . . ."[161]

While it is therefore difficult to reconstruct all of the contacts made—and this was all the more true since many of the members of the committee in the Southern zone were omitted from the list that appeared at the Liberation—we can nonetheless grasp the characteristics of recruitment in the Southern zone according to the composition of the directive committee. Almost as well represented, in the final analysis, as in the committee of the Northern zone (roughly half the members), the Gallimard-*NRF* network presided less over the modalities of recruitment of the CNE in the Southern zone, which relied principally on exiled Parisians and the preexisting networks surrounding the semi-legal reviews: those networks had already enabled the preparation of the anthology *L'Honneur des poètes* (published in July 1943 at the Éditions de Minuit) and the distribution of tracts or clandestine publications from the occupied zone. In fact, the CNE of the Southern zone mobilized Parisians (who represented two-thirds of its force) twice as often as local writers. And when it was a local, like August Anglès, student then teacher in Lyon, it was a matter of someone from Lyon who had been educated at the ENS. Rare—but their presence was significant—were the newcomers, like Pierre Emmanuel, Pierre Seghers, or Loÿs Masson, who benefited, thanks to the exodus, from a promotion that was accelerated by direct contact with the prestigious closed circles of the capital. Was this Parisian preponderance due, as a report on the intellectuals in the

Southern zone suggests, to the fact that having experienced the consequences of the exodus, the exiled writers and artists were quicker to manifest a feeling of indignation, accompanied by a growing distrust in the Vichy government that solidified throughout 1942, whereas the more sedentary intellectuals, scholars, professors, and physicians, who before the war mainly resided in what was to become the Southern zone, and who as a consequence "had not suffered from the war either in their person or in their goods, or in their families," underwent a later evolution, closely linked to the total occupation of the territory?[162] Or was it a consequence of the difficulties mentioned by Georges Ternet in the previously cited report of November 1943, namely the principles of hierarchization and election proper to a milieu where sociability operated through co-optation? I tend more toward the second hypothesis to explain this Parisian overrepresentation, which translated the persistence—through the established groups, and despite the undeniable effects of forced decentralization—of the capital's domination of literary life.

The specificity of the group in the Southern zone lay, among other things, in the reinforcement and diversification of political alliances. The premises of an alliance with the nationalists on the one hand, and the Catholics on the other, had been set by the recruitment of Debû-Bridel, Mauriac, and Father Maydieu, but this alliance would, in the Northern zone, be limited to just these representatives until the arrival in 1944 of Roger Giron and Georges Oudard, coming from the extreme right. The remainder were divided between Communists and other leftist tendencies. In the Southern zone, unitary politics would be stringently applied by Aragon, who would guarantee their success. On the Catholic side, we find in the directive committee Stanislas Fumet, Auguste Anglès, Pierre Emmanuel, Louis Martin-Chauffier, then Father Bruckberger (linked to the NRF milieu exiled to the Southern zone in 1940, he was brought to the committee by Albert Camus),[163] not counting Loÿs Masson, who at that time was a member of the Communist Party. On the right and extreme-right side, we find André Rousseaux and Henry Malherbe. Aragon "had attracted, either thanks to my review, or thanks to his personal contacts, a certain number of writers who were not Communists for the majority [. . .]," René Tavernier recalled, situating Stanislas Fumet, Jean Prévost, Henry Malherbe, Francis Ponge (who was a member of the Communist Party at that time), Pierre Emmanuel, and André Rousseaux "in Aragon's orbit": "Aragon was particularly happy with the presence of Malerbe [sic] which proved that the French of different opinions were united in the Resistance . . . just as he was very happy with the agreement of André Rousseaux, who represented a very Catholic and very conservative tendency."[164]

But these alliances owed more to the reorganization of the literary field in the Southern zone after the defeat than to past militant solidarities. Such solidarities mattered, of course, for Martin-Chauffier, former editor in chief of *Vendredi*, whose core group found itself almost completely represented at the CNE: Guéhenno in the committee of the Northern zone, Andrée Viollis and, through Martin-Chauffier, Jean Cassou and Claude Aveline in the Southern zone. But they did not concern newcomers like Pierre Emmanuel or Loÿs Masson, nor even the Christian Democrats like Stanislas Fumet, August Anglès, and Luc Estang, columnist at *La Croix*, who were anxious at the end of the 1930s to preserve their specificity with respect to the secular anti-Fascist left. They were even less meaningful for the literary critic of *Le Figaro*, André Rousseaux, a pro-Pétain Catholic on the right who, like many, evolved toward Gaullism.

The case of André Rousseaux once more illustrates the literary affinities that founded political alliances. Born in 1896, a doctor of law, the ex-editor of *Action française* who hid behind the collective pseudonym of Orion had entered *Le Figaro littéraire* in 1929 and had been the literary editor there since 1936. Despite his political conservatism, Rousseaux as a critic was open to the avant-garde: among the first to discover Sartre's *Nausea*, he led a fight against the salons and Parisianism, "for in the little war that opposed the Left Bank to the Right Bank and ended in the victory over the Boulevard, Rousseaux," Pierre Mazars recalled, "held out for the Left Bank, for the difficult authors and the courageous editors."[165] Exiled to Lyon under the Occupation, he frequented the social circles of *Le Temps* and *Le Figaro* that met "at the d'Ormesson house," milieus where, according to his account, the efforts of Free France were hardly discussed. Yet thanks to his wife, he had already established a clandestine liaison between *Le Figaro* and the dissident academicians, Mauriac, Duhamel, and Valéry. Urged several times by collaborationist leaders—Drieu La Rochelle, Jean de La Hire, Jacques Chardonne—to resume his place in the capital after the defeat, he had declined: his nationalism forbade him to work under the boot of the occupier. But despite a seemly pro-Pétain attitude, perhaps seduced by the traditional workmanship and the patriotic accents of Aragon's poetry, André Rousseaux had published in *Le Figaro* in December 1941 a serial on *Le Crève-cœur* that had made waves among the editors of the newspaper: "Brisson found that he went too far and wanted to make him publish a correction that he managed to reduce to very little." Upon which Rousseaux wrote to Aragon "to explain to him that the post-script had been imposed on him by precaution." Thus was born this complicity between Catholic critic and Communist poet that, when Andrée Viollis introduced them in 1943, brought him into the circles of *Poésie 40, 41 . . .* and *Confluences*, where he would contribute his work starting in 1943.

Approached in April 1943 to take part in the nascent CNE, André Rousseaux claimed to have "not at all understood why Aragon tried to convince him. He must have thought this necessary because the initiative was Communist, the organization Communist, but this did not at all bother A[ndré] R[ousseaux] who was then all naivety, all loyalty; he had been convinced for months of the need for a union without hesitation [. . .]"[166] He would be one of the first members of the committee of the Southern zone to contribute to *Les Lettres françaises*, from September 1943.

The premises of the alliance between Communists and Catholics, who constituted almost a third of the directive committee, were stated in the magazine *Fontaine*. It was the publication of Aragon's *Les Yeux d'Elsa* in *Les Cahiers du Rhône* that sealed it in March 1942. In the *Controverse sur le génie de la France* that *Les Cahiers du Rhône* (no. 5) published in November 1942, Aragon developed, under the title "The ET Conjunction," his conception of a universalist French humanism that allied the materialist tradition with the Christian tradition. Unlike *Les Lettres françaises*, *Les Étoiles* gave multiple signs of attention and recognition to the Catholics. Thus the principal document of the fifth issue, dated April 1943, was a pastoral letter from March 21, 1943, in which the Belgian episcopate protested the occupier's seizure of bells in all the parishes for the needs of the war industry. From *Le Cahier noir* by Forez alias François Mauriac, *Les Étoiles* would not quote the famous phrase that made Mauriac seem like a new fellow-traveler of the party, but an excerpt that ordered Christians to look for God in the victims of persecution, "Christians or pagans, Communists or Jews, for their resemblance with Christ is directly due to the insults they suffer: the spittle on the face authenticates this resemblance."[167]

The alliance with the Catholics was facilitated by the relative independence of the committee of intellectuals in the Southern zone with respect to the FN. In his postwar account, Aragon played off of his double position in the organizational chart, claiming that, as the head of the intellectuals' work in the Southern zone, he was under the direct supervision of Pierre Villon, now a member of the CNR, and not the leadership of the National Front of the Southern zone (Georges Marrane).[168] And in fact, this double position left him with room to maneuver, which he used to ensure the relative autonomy of the committees with respect to the movement.

But, in the Southern zone, the FN was rivaled on the ground by other movements, Combat, Libération-Sud, and Franc-Tireur, which had just merged to form the Mouvements de Résistance unis (MRU, future MUR); Martin-Chauffier and Cassou were two of the members. Another reason for Aragon to blur the reference to the FN. In September 1943, the newspaper *Libération* annexed the

Cahiers whose first issue, composed of texts by Emmanuel d'Astier de la Vigerie, Martin-Chauffier, Aveline, Seghers, and Maurice Noël, along with the unabridged version of the *Chant des partisans* by Maurice Druon and Joseph Kessel, was hailed by Maurice Schumann of the BBC; he called *Les Cahiers de Libération* "The *Nouvelle Revue française* of Tomorrow."[169] The second issue did not live up to the first. The leadership of the Communist Party in the Southern zone was no less worried. Hubert Ruffe saw it as a political reaction, which he asked Aragon to "denounce in advance as a gesture of division." Aragon was not at all convinced, and waited for the order to be confirmed by Pierre Villon two weeks later. It was then too late to prevent the publication of the new journal. Aragon nevertheless got the title changed to *Cahiers de la Libération*, no longer presenting itself as the organ of the MRU but as the organ "of all the intellectuals of the Resistance."[170] The third (February 1944) and fourth issues would in fact appear under this title, strengthened by the contributions of Paulhan, Eluard, Camus, Aragon, Guéhenno, Jouve, and so forth, and would be hailed in *Les Lettres françaises*.[171] The affair thus seemed settled, when Hubert Ruffe learned with stupefaction that in the meanwhile, Aragon, with Pierre Villon's approval, had made the CNE join with both the MRU and the FN at once! We can understand why he complained to the leadership of the party that Aragon "considers the last word to be from Paris."[172] Starting in December 1943, the line would be rectified. In May 1944, Pierre Seghers, a member of the directive committee of the FN in the Southern zone, would transfer the membership of all the groups formed by intellectuals to the FN.

An Underground Literary Authority

From September 1943, the date of the symbolic reunification of the CNE, while the history of the two committees continued to follow separate paths in terms of recruitment and the specific issues of each of the zones, it is no longer relevant to study their activity, nor their composition, separately: the circulation of people between the two groups, inaugurated by René Tavernier and Aragon in early 1943, became more frequent; common decisions were made after consulting both committees, or at least the delegate from the Southern zone at the meetings of the Northern zone, Pierre Seghers, and Aragon when he was in Paris. The members of the committee of the Southern zone started contributing to *Les Lettres françaises* (André Rousseaux, Loÿs Masson, Louis Parrot; then in 1944, Claude Roy, Camus, Cassou, and Seghers) as they reached the capital and swelled the ranks of the Northern zone committee (having gone underground, Seghers thus left for Paris in May 1944, and contributed to *Les Lettres françaises* in June 1944).

The organizational formula proposed to the writers thanks to the line encouraged by Aragon and the literary affinities that supported recruitment enabled the success of underground mobilization. We must still try to understand the sociological factors that favored the implantation of this formula in the literary milieu. Some elements of a response, as I have said, lie in the lack of organization of the profession of writer. The abrupt transformation of working conditions exacerbated an internal opposition that was already very pronounced between, on one end, those who lived comfortably from their writing, and on the other end poets, for example, for whom literature was an occupation that did not guarantee means of subsistence. The proximity of social positions could thus be associated, in a conjuncture of crisis, with shared specific interests (both corporative and literary) in order to transcend the traditional divisions of all types (generational, literary, ideological). The morphological analysis of the CNE, the most representative grouping of the literary Resistance, allows us in any case to confirm the relationship that existed between political position-takings and positions in the literary field during the period, a relationship that was mediated by these forms of solidarity that reinforced the group's influence over individuals.

AN ORGANIZATION WITH BLURRED BORDERS

Settling the question of the composition of the underground CNE involves a certain arbitrariness. Not only because of the lack of accounts, which were moreover sometimes contradictory, or the absence of older lists at the Liberation, or the difficulty of reconstructing the exact chronology of memberships. The difficulty also lies in the very character of this committee's blurred outlines, caused by its underground condition, its interaction with other authorities (*Les Lettres françaises*, the Éditions de Minuit, other intellectual committees), its strategy of openness, and its will to accumulate members. Finally, membership in the underground CNE became a stake at the Liberation, as much for the agents (to whom it gave a "certificate of Resistance"), as for an "institution" that was anxious to prove its legitimacy and its literary and national representativity. The list presented at the bottom of the "Manifesto of French Writers" that appeared in *Les Lettres françaises* on September 9 and 16, 1944, included seventy-five names, with some added at the last minute, while others were hastily omitted.[173] Rather than wonder about individual membership in the CNE, then, I will clarify, through the stakes associated with various modes of affiliation, the criteria retained to construct a representative sample of the committee with respect to its function, its objectives, and its activity under the Occupation; I will then tease out the principal morphological traits.

Claude Morgan's account allows us to establish a first criterion for hierarchizing the modes of belonging. He distinguished a directive committee, a "core group" produced by the initial (over-selected, as we saw) recruitment, which participated in the meetings:

> As the Comité National des Écrivains gained importance, the number of writers who attended the committee sessions became larger. We had been constrained by the very conditions of underground work to limit their number. There actually existed a directive committee that had formed around the initial core group, each member representing several writers who did not attend the sessions. There was naturally in our minds no idea of creating a hierarchy of the writers, all equal in rights, but the sole preoccupation of escaping the Gestapo.[174]

The denial of an internal hierarchy only reinforces it: the founding principle of the aforementioned directive committee lay in resistance *seniority*, which in return saw itself consecrated as the sole principle of hierarchization by this later subdivision: those who did not attend the meetings were the "latecomers."

The blurred borders also arise from the impossibility of determining the mode of formal recruitment or the principle of affiliation. Did contributing to one of the underground ventures (*Les Lettres françaises*, *Les Étoiles*, the Éditions de Minuit) lead to an "automatic" membership in the CNE, as some claimed? Eugène Guillevic, for example, whose name was never mentioned in the accounts as a member of the underground committee, said he belonged "quite naturally" to the CNE in the Resistance, without being able to date his membership, thanks to his relationship with Aragon and the team of *L'Honneur des poètes*: "We were in the CNE like that, there was no formal membership."[175] But belonging to the clandestine CNE was a proof for the poet. As a matter of fact, he needed to be "forgiven" for his work with Drieu's *NRF*, for which he was blamed until after the Liberation. Guillevic's membership in the party, the "protection" of Jean Paulhan, dazzled by his persona during their meeting in August 1942, would suffice to cast aside "doubt." He did appear on the list of CNE members published at the Liberation. The defensive position of the poet illustrates both the persistence of the feeling of "wrong" and the inertia of the logic of justification. Recalling his "wrong"—"I also did something that wasn't good, I published in Drieu La Rochelle's *NRF*"—he immediately specified:

But in these poems that I gave Drieu La Rochelle, there were camouflaged poems of Resistance. It is my own problem, I resisted all alone, I made things pass through like that. There are those who criticized me for publishing in *La NRF*. But I asked my friend Adler, who was my supervisor in the Resistance, if I should publish since Drieu La Rochelle had offered it to me. And my friend Adler said, "yes, yes, go get to know Drieu La Rochelle and you will bring back comments, gossip . . ." I was a double agent.[176]

We must compare the "accusations" that weighed on him—a competitor, Edmond Humeau, would revive them after the Liberation—with those that have been leveled against Sartre to this day.[177] For both of them, the dark years were a key moment for their promotion in the field. Suspected of having capitalized on this promotion to the detriment of their excluded colleagues, they had to account for their actions (while Eluard, for example, did not). Both would "make up" with a later political engagement. But while Sartre had also felt the need to promote early Resistance activities that left few traces (the Socialisme et Liberté group), the length of his membership in the committee and his contribution to *Les Lettres françaises* serve as proof.

The principle of "automatic" membership that Guillevic alleged may appear contestable in light of another case, that of one of the big names missing from the CNE, the former codirector of *Vendredi*, André Chamson. Chamson had been "dismissed for lack of courage," an underground report claimed.[178] We are even less able to explain the true reasons for this dismissal since the novelist of conscientious objection (*Roux le bandit*, 1925), a pacifist but resolute anti-Fascist (he had spoken out in favor of a French intervention in Spain), would, under the pseudonym of Commandant Lauter, join the Maquis du Lot and participate in the training of FTP leaders with Jean Marcenac, a member of the party.[179] And it was under the pseudonym of Lauter that he published an excerpt from his novel *Le Puits des miracles* (Gallimard, 1945) in the volume of *Nouvelles Chroniques*, published by the Éditions de Minuit with a print date of July 14, 1944. Whether it was a matter of personal dislike or an argument with Aragon, it remains true that Chamson, who would have actually been a choice recruit, did not appear in the accounts, nor on the list published at the Liberation.

The previously cited report, dated April 1944, noted the Tharaud brothers' membership in the committee of the Northern zone. It moreover discussed requests for membership in the Southern zone, for Mounier and René Laporte. Formal procedures for membership requests or recruitment therefore existed, at least as early as the spring of 1944. According to Pascal Mercier, Claude Morgan collected the memberships of Valéry, Duhamel, Gabriel Marcel, and Paul Hazard, and had them sign the "Manifesto of French Writers," in preparation for its publication to a wider public.[180]

In light of these difficulties, I have decided to create a sample that almost exactly corresponds to what Morgan called the directive committee, all zones mixed together, retaining presence at underground meetings as a first criterion, coupled with a mention on the first list published at the Liberation and/or the first list found in the archives of the CNE, the published list being full of holes, in particular concerning the members of the Southern zone who suffered the consequences of CNE recentralization in Paris after the Liberation. Following this criterion, although their inclusion would only have reinforced my observations relative to the social properties of the group, I have eliminated the two directors of the Éditions de Minuit, Pierre de Lescure and Vercors—who did not attend the meetings for security reasons but appeared on the list published at the Liberation—due to the autonomy of their initial venture in relation to the CNE and the specificity of their activity as underground publishers.[181] I have also eliminated those who, in some way, served as committee "liaisons" outside France, like François Lachenal in Switzerland, Gabriel Audisio and Max-Pol Fouchet in Algeria, as well as the occasional contributors to the underground *Lettres françaises* whose names were not mentioned among the meeting participants. On the other hand, regular contributions to *Les Lettres françaises* before 1944 (that is to say during the few months when the newspaper's contributors were directly recruited to the CNE), included on the list published at the Liberation, have served as a secondary criterion with respect to presence at the clandestine meetings, permitting the inclusion of Michel Leiris, who did not attend, but gave three articles to the newspaper starting in April 1943. Contributing to *Les Étoiles*—without distinction this time, since the bulletin's production was fully assumed by the members of the committee of the Southern zone—also constituted a secondary criterion. Finally, while I will take it into account in the qualitative approach, I have eliminated from the statistical analysis, for the validity of the comparison with writers belonging to other authorities, the members of the group who were not, properly speaking, writers, or at least did not first define themselves as belonging to the literary field: the two priests, Jean Maydieu and Raymond-Léopold Bruckberger, as well as Yvonne Desvignes, a translator, the Éditions de Minuit delegate to the CNE. There remain, then, fifty writers who comprised the directive committee of the two zones.

It is not by chance that the strict application of these criteria means eliminating all the great elders who appeared on the list published at the Liberation, with the exception of François Mauriac: Paul Valéry, Georges Duhamel, Paul

Hazard, Jérôme and Jean Tharaud, Alexandre Arnoux, René Maran, and Roger Martin du Gard. Except for the last, who remained a "passive" member as we saw, they all joined in the few months preceding the Liberation without attending meetings and without contributing to *Les Lettres françaises* or *Les Étoiles*. They were representatives of the consecrated rear guard—the first four were members of the French Academy, Jean Tharaud would join his brother there at the Liberation, Arnoux would enter the Goncourt Academy, René Maran was a former winner of the Goncourt Prize, Martin du Gard was a Nobel Prize winner—who did not "risk" themselves to "enter the game" except to a lesser degree, when both the literary and national legitimacy of the CNE had been acquired, and without engaging themselves beyond a kind of patronage. This patronage was solicited by the committee itself to confirm this legitimacy which, at the Liberation, would be exposed to all. One of the "corrections" published by *Les Lettres françaises* is revealing in terms of this strategy of inscribing the great names: "The difficulty of communicating with our friends in the Southern zone was the cause of a grave omission on our part in the Manifesto of French Writers published in our September 9 issue: that of Paul Claudel, who arrived in Paris this week [...]."[182] Claudel in the CNE? According to Father Bruckberger, he only agreed to be part of it after the Liberation, his membership surely obtained as a result of his meeting with Aragon, organized by René Tavernier in September 1944.[183]

AN INVERTED ACADEMY

From the standpoint of social recruitment, the CNE is entirely representative of the literary field of the period, the tendencies of which are therein exacerbated. Because of this, it looks something like an inverted image of the French Academy, which cannot be reduced to the opposition between "old" and "young" in the field (almost 90 percent of writer-academicians were over fifty-three years old in 1940, versus 10 percent of the members of the CNE). By contrast, the social properties of its members emphasize the differences that I have already noted concerning the recruitment at the Academy.[184] The members of the committee were two times less likely to have come from the dominant fractions of the dominant class than the writer-academicians, less likely also than the average of writers (12 percent versus 19.5 percent for the whole of our population).[185] Only two of them (4 percent) came from the legal professions, a level two times lower than for the whole of the population, and three times lower than in the French Academy (but equivalent to the Goncourt Academy). However, they were also recruited a little less frequently in the most impoverished sectors than the whole of writers (22 percent versus 27 percent).

While they thus came primarily from the middle class, their recruitment was distinguished, in this sense, by two notable traits that situated them opposite the writers of the French Academy: the underrepresentation of writers from a public service background (excluding the sons of professors) who were, as we saw, preponderant at the Academy (8 percent versus 38.7 percent, compared to 14.6 percent of the global population); and the overrepresentation of the intellectual fractions, underrepresented at the Academy (30 percent versus 9.7 percent, compared to 18.9 percent for the global population).[186] These differences are all the more flagrant since the two authorities share a member (François Mauriac) and a relation of kinship (Georges Lecomte). Here we measure the weight of the tradition of the intellectual field in terms of its competition with the fractions holding temporal power, and of its autonomization during the Dreyfus affair. Indeed, the CNE was, as a group, the expression of this principle of collective protestation. We also measure the heritage of the tendency toward contestation among the most politically engaged, for these second-generation intellectuals: Charles Vildrac, son of Henri Messager, a publisher and journalist deported after the Commune; Stanislas Fumet, son of an anarchist musician and Catholic convert; Louis Martin-Chauffier, son of a free-thinking doctor in a Catholic and monarchist family; Claude Morgan, son, as we saw, of the Dreyfusard Georges Lecomte, who had "settled down" with age and academic consecration, moving to the side of "order," while his son followed the opposite trajectory.[187]

The gap between the two authorities can also be observed from the perspective of geographic origins, which reveal an inverted relationship to their respective spatial positions: whereas the old Parisian institution showed a clear preference for writers from the provinces, the CNE, which recruited half of its members in the Southern zone, privileged the Parisian networks. While the geographic conditions of recruitment for the CNE are not expressed in the distribution of birthplaces (a third were born in Paris, like the average of writers; less than half were born in the provinces versus three-quarters of academicians), they are nonetheless legible in the fact that the members of the CNE were slightly less often Parisian at the time they entered adult life. For Pierre Emmanuel, Pierre Seghers, and Loÿs Masson, the establishment of the CNE corresponded to the time they began their career and constituted an unhoped-for "springboard" toward the capital.[188] These cases are nonetheless in the minority. In fact, the slight difference noted translates, for others, the handicap of late integration into the Parisian literary milieus, more frequent in the Communist fraction of the group: Georges Adam, Georges Sadoul, Elsa Triolet. Let us remember that Loÿs Masson joined the Communist Party during this period.

Pierre Emmanuel, who drew near it because of the circumstances, established this link in his *Autobiographies*:

> Moths attracted to the Communist flame, some among us bonded with a more intimate friendship perhaps, being less precise and often ambiguous, with these militants of the Communist intelligentsia, many of whom had passed through surrealism and remained avant-garde aesthetes through their multiple pasts. To be happy together, we multiplied Lamourette kisses:[†] I dreamed out loud in front of them, and soon like them through imitation. "They at least judge me as one of them," I told myself, a little too loudly perhaps to believe myself entirely convinced. It's easy enough to see how young I was. Provincial, as was not allowed, rather savage by nature besides, no "literary" contact had taken away my innocence yet.[189]

Unlike academicians, whose strong geographic mobility during adolescence corresponded to familial educational strategies, the stability of the members of the committee during their schooling testified to their lesser familial resources: we even see, with Seghers, a case of an inverted path from Paris to the provinces, due to the family's social demotion. Globally less endowed with academic titles than at the Academy, the members of the CNE were nonetheless representative, through their degree course, of the new literary generations who were better endowed, in this respect, than their elders of the turn of the century. The comparison with the Goncourt Academy is, in this sense, telling: three-quarters of the members of the CNE held a diploma that was equal or superior to the baccalaureate, versus half the Goncourt jurors.

Their secondary schooling, globally less "prestigious" than that of the writers of the French Academy or of the contributors to *La NRF*, conformed to the average of writers. A third of them were educated in a major lycée, and a fourth in a provincial lycée or collège; almost all had access to secondary education. The proportion who were educated in private institutions, relatively high at the CNE (one out of five), is explained by the presence of Catholics: Mauriac, Martin-Chauffier, Stanislas Fumet, Pierre Emmanuel, Luc Estang, André Frénaud (but also Aragon), among others, attended a Catholic establishment. This rate, in line with the average of writers but higher than at the Goncourt Academy or *La NRF*, seems to bring the CNE closer to the French Academy. This apparent relationship must be reinterpreted, taking into account the generation gap between

---

[†] The expression refers to a reconciliation attempt in 1792 by Antoine-Adrien Lamourette, who proposed that his colleagues at the Legislative Assembly kiss each other.—Trans.

the members of the two authorities. In fact, the rates do not conceal the same social realities:[190] all the members of the French Academy were born before 1899, and were thus educated either, for a third of them, before the secularization of the state educational system, or, for half, during the period of confrontation between the Republic and the congregations, which only a brief lull after the rallying of Leo XIII (1896–1900) separated from Combism[†] and the law of 1901 on congregations and religious establishments.[191] The education of a quarter of the academicians in a Catholic establishment at a time when, certainly, private school experienced an initial expansion due to the expulsion of priests from public school, but when the divorce from the Republic was being established, necessarily marked sensibilities. Inversely, for most of the writers of the CNE, the separation was a settled fact at the time of their first socialization. Moreover, two members of the CNE out of five were born after 1906, and were thus educated during the war of 1914, which marked a more durable lull, notably with the return of the exiled Jesuits and the reopening of collèges, authorized in August 1914 by a circular from the Malvy ministry.[192] The Christian Democrats were mainly recruited from this generation.

In accordance with the average of writers, only one member of the CNE out of three had not attended an establishment of higher education (versus one Goncourt juror out of two and, on the opposite end, one writer of the French Academy out of ten), and more than half of them obtained a degree equal or superior to the licence (versus a third of the Goncourt jurors and more than three-quarters of writers from the French Academy). To the grandes écoles, which they attended two times less often than the immortals (less than a quarter versus half), a third of them opposed a university education, in law or in literature (versus a quarter of the writers of the French Academy).

Their educational capital was coupled with an inherited cultural capital that was globally more important for these young dissident writers who were less close to the state and temporal power, as much by their origins as their educational trajectories, than the writers of the French Academy, and more representative of the literary field in spite of the heterogeneity of their group. Because of their young age, of the predominance of cultural resources to the detriment of economic capital (as their professional situation will show), of the weak degree of consecration that they enjoyed overall and their aspiration to a more sym-

---

[†] Refers to the prorepublican, anticlerical positions of Émile Combes, the government minister who fought for the separation of church and state at the turn of the century.— Trans.

bolic than institutional recognition, they occupied, contrary to the "immortals," a temporally dominated position in the literary field.

A PREMATURE LEGITIMACY

In terms of literary legitimacy and generational representativity, the image of a "national union" of the literary world that the CNE tried to give only very partially corresponded to what is revealed by studying the directive committee. In his memoirs of the "intellectual resistance," Vercors said that at the CNE "there were assembled against the occupying forces *all that was to count in Literature after the war* (Mauriac, Aragon, Sartre, Camus, Queneau, etc.), uniting, from the right to the left, *the best of national intelligence* in its resolution to think freely and to express, without compromising itself, what it deemed to be just, to be true."[193] Here we must emphasize the chronology of access to recognition ("after the war": in the quotation, retroactive legitimacy masks what postwar notoriety can precisely owe to belonging to the CNE) as well as what is covered by the abbreviation "etc." Far from being composed of consecrated writers, the CNE mainly assembled writers on their way to recognition (Sartre, Leiris, Queneau, Tardieu, and Camus for example), second-rank authors (Debû-Bridel, Édith Thomas), or else newcomers (Pierre Emmanuel, Frénaud, Loÿs Masson, Alain Borne, Seghers). Age as an indicator (a third of them were under thirty-five in 1940, and almost two-thirds of them were under forty at that date), which must be related to recruitment in this profession where precocity remains the exception, is reinforced by the indicator of the date of first publication. More than a third of them had published their first work in the 1930s, and one member out of five had not yet published in 1940.

They were gathered around what we might call the "organizing triangle," constituted by the prestigious elders (Paulhan, Aragon, and Eluard) who had actually experienced a relative demotion at the beginning of the Occupation: Paulhan deprived of his review and his other forums, Aragon banned as a result of the German-Soviet pact and reduced to semi-legality because he belonged to the Communist Party, Eluard excommunicated from the surrealist group and in an awkward in-between position with respect to the new surrealist generation of La Main à Plume. Let us note that those who were excluded from the first or second surrealist generation, estranged from Breton, formed a non-negligible contingent of the CNE: Leiris, Queneau, Tardieu, Ponge, Sadoul, among others, they were in total eight to have been socialized in the literary field at the school of the surrealist revolt, without counting the youth who, like Pierre Emmanuel, had been significantly marked by it.

Thanks to the "poetic renewal" that they had orchestrated, and strengthened by the legitimacy that Jean Paulhan ensured for them, Aragon and Eluard, the two poet-beacons of those years, attracted a number of young poets into the ranks of the committee. The poets formed roughly a third of the group, slightly more numerous in the committee of the Northern zone than in that of the Southern zone, as Seghers observed during one of his trips to Paris. If, as Seghers said, "between contraband and underground, the free zone only held by a thread," the poets of the Northern zone, for whom semi-legality proved less accessible and more risky, had crossed the line more often.[194] We notice, on the contrary, the absence of recognized novelists from before the war: Mauriac excepted, the only two renowned novelists who were involved with the CNE, without belonging to the directive committee and while maintaining a certain distance, were Martin du Gard and Malraux (under the Occupation, Aragon established himself as more of a poet than a novelist).[195]

Mauriac was the only great consecrated writer, and the only academician, to serve on the directive committee of the CNE. He represented, with Charles Vildrac, Henry Malherbe, and Jean Paulhan, the so-called generation of 1885. The veteran of the group, Julien Benda (born in 1867), was an author more recognized for his essays than for his novels; La NRF had maintained a forum for him until 1939, but under the Occupation he was banned due to his Jewish origins and forced to remain isolated and reclusive in his retreat at Carcassonne while his Paris dwelling was looted by the Germans. "I have the feeling," he wrote, "almost all my books being banned in France, the right to publish them there almost entirely refused to me, and everyone powerful taking my very name for a bogey, that I am totally suppressed as a writer, at least in my country, and could well be so until the end of my days."[196] His contribution to the Éditions de Minuit, in addition to the literary sociability he founded again with the CNE, and the support that the Communists brought him, in all likelihood via Andrée Viollis, were at the root of the debt of gratitude he owed to the party. He would repay this debt after the Liberation with an ironclad fellow-traveling. As for Andrée Viollis (born in 1879), more known as a journalist than a writer (she had written novels in partnership with her second husband Jean Viollis alias Henri d'Ardenne de Tizac),[197] her presence was likely due to her status of fellow-traveler and former codirector of Vendredi rather than to her literary activity. Linked to Louis Martin-Chauffier, with whom she often stayed during the Occupation, she probably established the contact between Aragon and him.

Thanks to their places of publication, periodicals, and publishing houses, the members of the CNE were situated mainly at the pole of small-scale production. From an editorial perspective, the Gallimard-NRF milieu was overrepresented:

half of all CNE members had published a work with Gallimard and/or contributed to the prewar *NRF*.[198] The other usually published with the small publishers born of the Occupation, like Seghers (one of five in total), and very rarely in the old houses representative of the pole of large-scale production like Flammarion or Albin Michel. Aside from the prewar *NRF*, along with the journal *Europe* and the weekly *Vendredi*, they represented the pole of the small subversive magazines, *Messages, Poésie, Confluences, Fontaine*, under the Occupation.[199] On the other hand, those who contributed to the major weeklies or "academic" journals like the *Revue des deux mondes* were rare.

This overrepresentation of the Gallimard-*NRF* milieu was not merely a generational effect; it was also, as we have seen, the expression of the committee's modes of co-optation. We must also balance what can be taken as a sign of the literary legitimacy of the group, by recalling that it included none of the great names from the interwar period: the only representatives of the house's "rear guard" were Benda and Vildrac. Among the Gallimard authors, we can distinguish at least three subgroups. The first was composed of "creators" who constituted the avant-garde of the house, on their way to consecration: Queneau, Sartre, Leiris, Tardieu, Camus, Ponge. A second group was formed of more or less versatile authors who, aside from Paulhan, were recognized as much for their critical work (rather than their properly creative work) as their militant action (anti-Fascist, in particular): Guéhenno, Cassou, Martin-Chauffier, to whom we should perhaps add the young Jean Blanzat and the critic and translator Pierre Leyris. A third group was constituted of authors who were poorly endowed with symbolic capital, whose situation at Gallimard was precarious and/or whose creative project had been aborted. In the committee, they established themselves more by their militant resources. Thus, the situation of Jacques Debû-Bridel (born in 1902), author of *Frère esclave* and *Jeunes ménages* who won the Interallié Prize in 1935, was not established at Gallimard, given that his *Duchesse de Longueville* was first rejected in 1938 for stylistic reasons (it would ultimately be accepted), and given the new rejection he faced with *Exil au Grand Palais* in June 1940.[200] This was surely the source of Debû-Bridel's propensity to emphasize, in his accounts, the complicity that united the authors of the house, unlike those who participated more closely and felt no need to advertize it. Similarly, Édith Thomas, who had already published three novels with Gallimard (one of them, *La Mort de Marie*, had won the prize for a first novel awarded by *La Revue hebdomadaire* in 1933), would try in vain, as we saw, to get the house to accept a new novel during the Occupation. She would switch to historical biography. Dead from an illness in 1953 at the age of fifty, René Blech, a former book columnist for the journal *Commune* where he also served as editorial secretary, was the author of a few novels with social overtones; the first two were published by Gallimard (1932 and 1934), and the third by the Éditions sociales internationales (1936).[201] We can also include in this subcategory Father Bruckberger, who had published *Rejoindre Dieu* at Gallimard in 1940, and Andrée Viollis who published reports there.

There remains a subset of authors who are more difficult to classify due to their premature death. The posthumous consecration of the first two was less literary than moral, due to the extent that their names symbolized the sacrifice of Resistance writers. Shot in 1942 at the age of thirty-two, Jacques Decour, the literary pseudonym of Daniel Decourdemanche, secondary teacher and German translator, was the author of two novels (*Le Sage et le caporal*, 1930; *Les Pères*, 1936) and a Prussian travelogue (*Philisterberg*, 1932), all published by Gallimard.[202] In his homage to Decour, Jean Paulhan implicitly criticized the author, whom he had appreciated, for having abandoned his literary production in favor of his militant activity.[203] Jean Prévost, who died in 1944 in the Vercors maquis at the age of forty-three, was a regular contributor to *La NRF* who became known due to his essay *Plaisir des sports*, published in 1925 by Gallimard. After having published several works, including a biography of Montaigne (1926), he embarked on a novelistic career with *Les Frères Bouquinquant* (1930), which allowed him to reach the general public, but, often categorized as "populist," earned him a lukewarm reception from his peers. His doctoral thesis on Stendhal was published shortly before his death. Jean Vaudal, born in 1900, an engineer by trade, had also contributed to *La NRF* and published two of his three novels with Gallimard. A member of the first team of *Les Lettres françaises*, in 1942 he entered the Resistance movement Organisation civile et militaire thanks to Jacques Debû-Bridel and led the resistance of Enghien-Montmorency before being deported and dying in 1944. In Vaudal's obituary, Jean Paulhan gave a laudatory analysis of his last novel, *Le Tableau noir*, although not without some reservations; he also criticized his first two books (*Démon secret* and *Portrait du père*) for being too "rigorous."[204]

Finally, the evolution of the publishing trajectories of the younger ones leads us to relativize the "smuggler" role that the CNE might have played with regards to the Gallimard house.[205] While the bonds that were forged under the Occupation determined future orientations, access to the Gallimard house was not automatic. Only André Frénaud would become a "house author" in 1949. Alain Borne, who died prematurely and whose work was fragmented between various editors, also published a collection with Gallimard in 1947 (*L'Eau fine*). Luc Estang, who had been publishing with Laffont, where he edited a series since the Occupation, switched to Seuil after the Liberation, but would reserve his poetry for Gallimard. Pierre Emmanuel, whose *Orphiques* was published in 1942 in the "Métamorphoses" series, also went to Seuil. Thus, above and beyond the affinities that could lead young Catholic authors to Seuil, the publishing houses born of the Occupation like Laffont, Seuil, Julliard, and Seghers seemed to open up more readily to these newcomers than their prestigious elder, committed to promoting those who already constituted the avant-garde of the house on the eve of the war. Jean Lescure and Auguste Anglès would only belatedly enter Gallimard, the first thanks to Queneau's intervention in 1960, the second in 1978 with his famous work, *André Gide et le premier groupe de la Nouvelle Revue française.*

Situated at the pole of small-scale production, the majority of the members of the CNE thus shared a still-precarious or unstable professional situation as writers, while the more established among them experienced a form of demotion due to the conjuncture (Benda, Paulhan, Aragon, Eluard, Guéhenno). An overview of their means of subsistence confirms this statement: almost a third of them exercised another profession at the time (nine were civil servants, including four teachers), except for journalists who represented a quarter of the group, and the six translators, readers, and series editors who were appointed by the publishing houses. Few of them lived, like Mauriac, off their literary production—and even Mauriac was a property owner who thus found himself less affected by the difficult conditions[206]—and the least privileged had to resort to day jobs when, like some of the youngest, they didn't benefit from a small income.[207] In total, a quarter of the members of the committee found or would find an outlet in publishing (series editors, readers), including Paulhan, Queneau, and Camus at Gallimard; Guéhenno and Blanzat at Grasset (and later at Gallimard); Pierre Leyris and Luc Estang at Seuil; Auguste Anglès at the Éditions du Chêne; Georges Oudard at Julliard; Raymond Millet at Calmann-Lévy; and Yvonnes Desvignes at Minuit.

Nevertheless, while they shared a temporally dominated position that grounded their alliance, this homologous position was due to the conjuncture—linked to the crisis situation on one side, to their inexperience in the profession on the other—and masked differing realities, as indicated by the analysis of Gallimard authors alone. The distinction between two types of dominated positions, the avant-garde on one side and marginal authors on the other (without counting the authors who had been "demoted" because of the conjuncture), is reinforced when we consider the signs of short-term or long-term recognition, based on their presence in literary histories and dictionaries. Only half of the committee members achieved literary recognition in their time and would live on in posterity,[208] and this by means of a more symbolic than institutional consecration, even though aside from Mauriac, three members of the committee would be (belatedly) "immortalized" by joing the French Academy (Paulhan, Guéhenno, Pierre Emmanuel), and two would enter the Goncourt Academy (Queneau in 1951, and Aragon who, elected in 1968, would resign almost immediately). While Camus would win the Nobel Prize in 1957, Sartre, as we know, would refuse it in 1964.

NATIONAL LEGITIMACY

The success of the unitary politics of the CNE was expressed in the repartition of ideological tendencies: Communists formed about a third of the group, a rate that barely exceeds Anne Simonin's inventory of the authors of a venture that was originally independent of the party, the underground Éditions de Minuit: eleven out of fifty-one (including eight who were also members of the CNE), or almost a quarter.[209] This rate is clearly lower than the proportion of Communists among the contributors to Les Lettres françaises, twelve out of thirty-one (if we were to measure by the number of pages, the Communist representation would be crushing), which confirms the intermediary position of the CNE between the Éditions de Minuit and the newspaper.

Moreover, out of the fifteen Communists counted in the CNE (including those close to the party who didn't have their card, like Elsa Triolet), five joined (or rejoined, in one case) during the Occupation, between 1942 and 1943: Eluard, Lucien Scheler, Édith Thomas, Loÿs Masson, and Claude Roy, newly repenting his attachment to Action française.[210] For them, entry into literary Resistance also coincided with membership in the party. The last two, and perhaps Eluard as well, were drawn there by the charismatic figure of Aragon, like Georges Sadoul a decade earlier. The oldest ones had contributed to the party's prewar cultural ventures in the wake of Aragon, to the daily Ce Soir, to the AEAR journal Commune, to the Maison de la Culture, and to the weekly Regards.

Globally, the Communists were the most deprived of resources in the group, whether due to their modest social origins (Georges Adam, Louis Parrot, and Léon Moussinac came from the working classes, Eluard from the petty bourgeoisie), paired with a weak educational capital (unlike, for example, Guéhenno and Jean Prévost, who were ENS graduates, or Queneau, who studied philosophy); or because their geographical origin and late insertion in the literary networks were coupled with a weak educational capital (Georges Sadoul, Loÿs Masson); or due to a less literary recognition (Scheler, Morgan); or because of the inequality in gender relations (the three women were Communistic). Aragon certainly seems like the best endowed in every respect, predisposed to play the role of the charismatic leader faced with this "emotional community" that in turn reinforced his position with respect to the committee as a whole.

While the representation of women was relatively high in the directive committee of the CNE (four women, including Yvonne Desvignes), whether in comparison to the leading authorities of the era or the literary institutions, particularly inaccessible to the second sex,[211] the fact remains that women occupied a dominated position there, recognized more for their status as liaisons, journalists, or even "wife of" (Elsa Triolet) than for their literary production, and reduced to silence.[212] It was not by chance that the first time a problem arose at the Éditions de Minuit about a manuscript, it concerned novellas by Elsa Triolet and Édith Thomas, set up as competitors at a time when the new house was actually still seeking authors. *Les Amants d'Avignon*, sent by Paulhan in the spring of 1943 at the same time as *Transcrit du réel* by Édith Thomas, was initially rejected by Pierre de Lescure (for his part, Paulhan preferred the former, despite having requested corrections). Eluard's intervention, which led to both being accepted, ultimately saved the publishing house from bankruptcy due to a lack of authors, as Anne Simonin has explained: it was actually only following the acceptance of Elsa's manuscript that they could add Aragon to their catalogue.[213] Communist solidarity thus allowed both of them to escape rejection, but the affair stirred up a rivalry that would reemerge regarding a report from the maquis that both would undertake in 1944.[214] This rivalry could only further weaken their position.

All in all, the writers affiliated with the secular left who had more or less committed to the anti-Fascist fight in the 1930s, including Communists, represented more than half of the group. While this number attests to the weight of past militant solidarity, as I have shown it also masks the tensions that flowed through them during the 1930s. The preexisting repertoire of unitary action also does not account for the alliance with Catholic and nationalist writers, nor the recruitment of a fraction of young authors who were minimally politicized before the war (seven including Sartre). The writers in the directive committee who were close to the Christian Democrat circle of influence numbered between six and eight, depending on whether we include Martin-Chauffier and Father Maydieu. With the exception of Martin-Chauffier, an active anti-Fascist militant, the elders came from Catholic fractions that had evolved toward a position that was hostile to Fascism, but tried to set themselves apart from the anti-Fascist left. These were the former contributors to *Le Temps présent*: Stanislas Fumet, François Mauriac, Father Maydieu; and to *Temps nouveau* for the younger ones, barely politicized before the war: Pierre Emmanuel and Loÿs Masson, who participated in the Jeune France circle at the beginning of the Occupation; the Sillonist Auguste Anglès; and Luc Estang, a contributor to *La Croix* and *Esprit*.

A third, non-negligible group emerged from the nationalist milieus, even from the extreme right. It fluctuates between six and eight members depending on whether we include Raymond Millet and Father Bruckberger, and counting Claude Roy. Note that Father Jean Maydieu (who has not been counted here), a former student at the École centrale, was also a former Camelot du Roi who joined the Dominicans of the CERF at *La Vie intellectuelle*, founded at the initiative of Pius XI after the condemnation of Action française. To Jacques Debû-Bridel, Henry Malherbe, and André Rousseaux, already mentioned, we must add Georges Oudard and Roger Giron. Georges Oudard was a former contributor to *Le Nouveau siècle*, an anti-Bolshevist, ultranationalist paper founded in 1925 by Georges Valois and supported by Action française, which initially presented itself as the mouthpiece of all the leagues. André Rousseaux and Roger Giron had signed the founding manifesto.[215] The latter, former head of the political department at *Éclair-Avenir* and contributor to *Le Nouveau siècle*, had then served as head of news and literary criticism at *L'Ami du peuple du Soir*, launched in 1928 by the "backer of fascism in France," the industrialist François Coty. It gave rise to the Solidarité française league that took part in the February 6, 1934, riots.[216] Raymond Millet had been a contributor to the prewar *Temps*; he would be the diplomatic editor of *Le Monde* from 1945 to 1950, then *Le Figaro*'s permanent special envoy in Rome. As for Father Bruckberger, engaged in the legion with Darnand since the beginning of the Occupation, he broke ties in September 1941, as he was being asked to pledge his fidelity to the regime, and would become the chaplain to the maquis.[217] While the first recruits from the right entered the CNE thanks to a literary complicity with their recruiters (Debû-Bridel, André Rousseaux, Claude Roy), the arrival of people like Georges Oudard and Roger Giron in early 1944 attests to the national legitimacy acquired by the committee at that point.

AN AUTHORITY OF ETHICAL ARBITRATION

What did the CNE's activity consist of? What happened during the meetings? The witnesses didn't remember. Jean Lescure recalls in an interview that Eluard, Guéhenno, Paulhan, and Frénaud spoke, along with Aragon during his Parisian visits. Vildrac also spoke, but Vildrac "was a man of the 19th century who spoke with discretion." Blanzat, on the other hand, "barely" spoke out.[218] "And all those Communists, let's say those umpteenth Communist knives,[§] were silent," Jean Lescure continues. The propensity to speak out was thus generally a func-

---

[§] Like an exaggerated version of the expression "second fiddle."—Trans.

tion of literary authority, with the exception of the Communist delegate, Claude Morgan, who spoke "with application" according to Jean Lescure—"the word application, I believe, suits him well because there was an applied side to him"—and with the assurance that his position granted him: "Morgan, of course, because Morgan always spoke in the name . . . You know, the Communist party was really extraordinary. You put ten guys together, among the ten guys there was a Communist: he had the majority. He alone spoke for everyone. It's unbelievable, those guys spoke with the authority of the Party."[219]

Aside from the information exchange that was not of little importance in a conjuncture where the means of communication were completely controlled, the essence of the CNE discussions seems to have concerned the establishment of a code of conduct for writers, the terms of which they were not able to agree upon, though. The CNE "spen[t] a considerable amount of time wondering whether it was appropriate to publish in authorized newspapers (to infiltrate them, it was said), or, on the contrary, to refuse, in order to unambiguously show their subservience to the enemy," Jean Lescure said.[220] At the very time that Brasillach was resigning as director of *Je suis partout*, when Ramon Fernandez was leaving the PPF, when Paul Morand was getting sent to Romania as an ambassador—unmistakable signs[221]—the question that had been posed to every writer in 1940 reemerged. Why?

Because, as the hour of victory approached, the CNE was already able to establish itself as an authority of arbitration for ethical questions related to the profession. We saw, for example, that Simone de Beauvoir, through Sartre, consulted the committee about the Goncourt Prize and found herself authorized to accept it in the case of a win, on the condition that she not give any interviews in the press. "The Goncourt Academy will have to account for itself," *Les Lettres françaises* had decreed a few months earlier.[222] The responses of the collaborationist or Vichyist press constituted that many marks of recognition. Thus, in the weekly *Présent* that was published in the Southern zone, the young Action française critic Kléber Haedens, observing the silence that had been established among the French writers for the past two or three months, argued that "our literature has many enemies." And insinuated: "It is possible that the foolish decisions of a mysterious *committee* aren't foreign to the new crisis of French booksellers," to which *Les Lettres françaises* had no problem retorting: "'Literature' is sometimes a very convenient refuge for he who fears that he will one day have to confront his duty as a man."[223]

Starting in the autumn of 1943, the CNE tried to establish its monopoly over the regulation of the profession, and therefore the power of excommunication; it would seek an official investiture from the leading authorities of the Resistance in order to exercise this power. In November 1943, the CNE, "after consultation with its groups in the Northern and Southern zones," thus addressed the Co-mité français de libération nationale (CFLN) that de Gaulle had created in June in Algiers, asking it

> to be authorized to form a commission seconded by a committee of jurists, like the Comité de la Presse, with the responsibility of examining, without prejudice to the legal measures that might be taken from another side against the people, the conduct of writers since June 1940 from a professional stand-point, in order to enlighten the legal action and set in place free working conditions for the profession in the future.[224]

While this project to monopolize legitimate violence within a profession sought recognition from the state apparatus put in place by the Resistance, it was not just to confirm its authority, but to safeguard the autonomy of the literary field by es-tablishing a specific authority in relation to the other authorities of the Resis-tance. *Les Étoiles* actually published a statement of warning to the résistants during the same time:

> For some time, the Press of the Resistance has published lists of writers and journalists offered up for national condemnation. Quite unfortunately, they too often put undeniable traitors on the same plane as men who are only guilty of thoughtlessness. They even contain errors that are difficult to cor-rect without endangering the people named [...] we draw their attention to the fact that this absence of Nuances serves the very people they attack.
>
> Here, we are partisans of a very serious purge. We fear that a too hasty denunciation detracts from the very seriousness of this denunciation, and its only effect on the day of the purge will be to give arguments to those, and we already see them coming, who intend to sabotage it.
>
> In the Resistance, there are a Comité National des Écrivains and a Comité National des Journalistes. Nobody will deny them their right to have their say. Perhaps we had better let them speak.[225]

As a result—and this is what explains the emergence of internal conflicts within the CNE during this time—the committee's decisions seemed like ver-dicts that were at stake not only because they targeted people, but also because they determined the reorganization of the literary field at the Liberation. This is what Jean Paulhan expressed in a letter to Jean Lescure, about a manuscript for a novel that Eluard had submitted: "Ah, the c[ommunists] are going to im-pose a funny kind of didactic literature on us: worse than that of the Nazis."[226] Ironic or not, the violence of this private statement has the particular merit of revealing the stakes as they appeared to the guardians of literary autonomy, even before the Liberation.

And yet it was not the Communists who formulated the project of a "black list" of compromised writers. The idea took root during a meeting that was held at François Mauriac's home on March 20, 1943, even before the underground committee had finished centralizing its various offspring, and thus occurred in its margins. Claude Mauriac's account of the meeting in his journal deserves to be cited at length:

> Yesterday afternoon at my father's house, ritual meeting of the three Jeans (Paulhan, Guéhenno, Blanzat), who were joined by Pierre Brisson [...] With an *inquisitive* air, they drew up *lists of proscription* "for the day of the victory." Jean Paulhan said (but with a certain irony) that there wouldn't be any need to change the law, the reference to "blatant treason" allowing the defendants to be tried rapidly and without an investigation. But it wasn't just a question of literary traitors: the Montherlants, whom one of them wanted to convict without any proof and about whom my father said: "it's true that they'll only be able to judge his tendencies. He didn't go to Germany"; the Chardonnes (whom my father wanted to acquit for "lack of discernment"); the X . . . ("That one," my father said, "will be sentenced to a confiscation of his property, because there could be nothing worse in his case"); the Maurrases ("For him, the punishment will consist in a definitive publishing ban").[227]

This state of mind, fueled by indignation and a feeling of revolt among our protagonists, was further expressed by Mauriac's phrase in a letter to Paulhan written one year earlier, during Abel Bonnard's nomination to the Ministry of National Education: "Bonnard the great master of the University! When everything will be back in order, we'll feed him to the teachers."[228]

If the split between Communists and non-Communists was most often emphasized by the CNE members themselves, it was because it best encapsulated the new threat of heteronomy that hovered over the literary field: the intervention of an outside authority in the arbitration of its internal relations. But this split, which tended to mask others, was actually just one of the principles of opposition that structured the struggles to redefine the hierarchies of values within the literary field. We will have the chance to verify this statement in reference to the debates surrounding the purge, but the *Comoedia* affair offers a preview.

The legal publication of books was more or less accepted and wasn't called into question, it seems, although the decrease in French literary production noted by Kléber Haedens cannot simply be blamed on the tightening of the censorship apparatus and the draconian constraints of paper distribution. It is as though the law of silence had become generalized, although this did not prevent Sartre, nor Elsa Triolet, nor Simone de Beauvoir from publishing between 1943 and 1944. The question of contributing to authorized periodicals in the Northern zone also seemed to have been resolved, with the opposite result, for the majority of notable cases. It only really arose in conjunction with Paulhan's two attempts to retake *La NRF*, and with the weekly *Comoedia*.

While the first attempt to retake *La NRF* in the spring unleashed an internal debate between the contributors to the old *NRF*, it avoided the arbitration of a committee that only survived then in Paulhan's wake. On the other hand, the second attempt, in May 1943, occurred at the very time that underground committee's life was becoming normalized. In the eighth issue of *Les Lettres françaises*, dated July 1943, an article written by Édith Thomas and Claude Morgan and approved by Eluard—unless Eluard endorsed it after the fact—on "The Agony of *La Nouvelle Revue française*" provoked a diplomatic incident with Paulhan. The article denounced the maneuver that tried to make *La NRF* into a purely literary review, and called Jacques Lemarchand into question:

> The truth is that after the failure of the "collaboration," *and at the hour when Germany has been forced to go on the defensive*, the goal of enemy propaganda has changed. It is no longer a question of winning "elites" over to the New Order, but only of anesthetizing the will of the people by neutralizing the intellectuals, by making them believe that there is currently a place for a neutral literature and art that enjoy a "certain" freedom.
>
> A so-called purely literary *NRF*, and especially if it really manages to become so, fulfills this goal. It is, by its very existence, insidious and dangerous [...].[229]

Paulhan let Édith Thomas know that the arrow hit its mark:

> [...] was it kind, was it loyal to show me so much distrust in the newspaper that I founded with J[acques] D[ecour]? It seems to me that you could have said to yourself [...] that as soon as I took over the review, either it would blow up, or it would prove itself *different* enough, from the first issue, for that difference to be obvious to everyone [...] But it blew up, and all is well.[230]

This incident would tend to confirm the polarization of conflicts between Communists and non-Communists. In reality, things were more complicated. If Paulhan was so sensitive to the content of this article, it was because his inner circle had disengaged from his project with Gaston Gallimard. Raymond Queneau and Michel Leiris refused to contribute to *La NRF* that Paulhan was trying to relaunch, as we have seen. Jean Guéhenno shared, with a great deal of tact but without ambiguity, the reasons for his reticence: he thought "—this caused too much debate between us—the fact that the freest and seemingly most daring review would have been the most harmful, being only a card from a game over which we do not hold control and that others take care of playing for us."[231] It was from the Southern zone that a "correction"—although we cannot say whether it was intended as such—was made to the version of the facts presented in *Les Lettres françaises*. It appeared in *Les Étoiles* in August 1943 under the title, "*La NRF* Is Dead: Long Live *La NRF*!" Directly informed by Paulhan of the conflicts with Drieu that led to the scuttling of the review, Aragon centered this account of the death of *La NRF* on Drieu's failure and censorship that he continued to exercise in the new version. For Aragon, unlike his Parisian comrades, the question was less one of knowing whether a legal literature was possible in the Northern zone than of condemning Drieu while handling Paulhan and the old *NRF* with care. The tone, if not the substance, was different:

> We knew that the sales of the Germanized *NRF* weren't going well [...]: but just like the readers refused to buy the review of Mr. Drieu and Mr. Abetz, French writers fled from the review of Mr. Drieu and Mr. Abetz, the writers fled every solicitation that tended to present a "reworking" of *La RNF* [acronym implying complicity with Déat's RNP] as a French victory. In the last attempt to date, under the direction of Mr. Lemarchand, Drieu remained the *manager* of the review (but in reality, its secret censor), consecrating the disrepute of the German Embassy's jack-of-all-trades and the contempt of his colleagues for this apologist of Oberleutnant Doriot, but it only culminated in a colorless issue, anthological, severed from any critical element, there won't be a second issue, Drieu having vetoed an insignificant article proposed by Mr. Lemarchand. As a result, *La RNF* died.
>
> Long live *La NRF* that will be reborn when victory will have cleared a space for it![232]

The *Comoedia* affair confirms that the principles of opposition cannot be reduced to a political division. It involved the most prestigious figures of the committee, and showed the control that the group of writers of "refusal" exercised over its members. This time, François Mauriac was at the origin of the polemic. Despite the missing documents in the file, we can re-create its principal stages. The problem first arose outside the CNE, it seems. A first exchange of letters between François Mauriac and Jean Paulhan mentioned a discussion on this topic in early 1943. To Paulhan, who made excuses for his contribution to *Comoedia*, Mauriac explained that his critics were not targeting him personally: "Everything depends on the person: you, for example, can do anything: contribute to *Comoedia* or spend time with Abetz, it's of no importance where you're concerned: you have moreover given your account: there is no mistake possible."[233] The question, however, would be raised about their common friend, Jean Blanzat. Solicited by Marcel Arland to contribute to *Comoedia*, he consulted Mauriac, whose violent reaction discouraged him: Mauriac proved "very strongly and very clearly against. I am actually frightened that he could see things from such a serious perspective. I had thought that there would at least be room for discussion," Blanzat wrote to Paulhan.[234] Paulhan, of course, had the opposite reaction, but he sought Guéhenno's advice. According to Guéhenno's response, we can deduce the argument that Paulhan used to counter Mauriac: the latter man judged the affair from the heights of his social position, that of a "billionaire" free from want. But Guéhenno took Mauriac's side, "although I am not a billionaire," he added, while remaining suspicious of his own "puritanism" and leaving Blanzat completely free to decide for himself: "[. . .] but I will regret bad company for Bl[anzat] because *Co[moedia]* is a bad company: too many people who are at least undecided—Arland himself—have 'collaborated' there. The virtue of a few has not sufficed to ensure its purity. Co[moedia] is, after all, only one more card in the hand of the real player [. . .]," he added.[235]

When and how did the polemic break out at the CNE meetings? Yvonne Desvignes mentioned a session during which the committee declared its opposition to contributing to *Comoedia*. Paulhan had raised opposing arguments, even as he said that he would bow to the committee's condition. "But it was impossible to mistake the emotion in this voice: the anxiety that choked it was clearly that of a child who is wrong—or right, what's the difference—but alone against the rest of the class."[236] We cannot give a precise date for this session, nor can we confirm that this is when the public confrontation between Paulhan and Mauriac occurred, but this confrontation did take place, very probably in the autumn of 1943. Jean Lescure remembered a "particularly heated" session, "rather sickening."[237]

The polemic was undoubtedly aggravated by the publication of a short news item, significantly entitled "*Comoedia* Like the Rest . . . ," by Claude Morgan in *Les Lettres françaises* in November 1943. "We all know that *Comoedia* concedes a 'European' page to Nazi propaganda every week," Morgan wrote. "That's why the newspaper is published and tries to gather eminent literary, artistic, and dramatic collaborations in its other pages." The item used the example of the inventory of an anthology of German poets published by Stock, which appeared in the weekly with the omission of Heine: "Heine was a Jew. And *Comoedia*, an 'independent' newspaper—or so it claimed in certain circles—an eminently literary newspaper that was perfectly impermeable to politics, had to bend like the others to abject racist guidelines."[238]

In a new exchange of letters between Mauriac and Paulhan, the stakes were set clearly, while each seemed to harden his position. From the beginning of the polemic, Paulhan had drawn a parallel between contributing to *Le Figaro* and contributing to *Comoedia*: "It seemed to me that I had contributed to the *Figaro* because Pierre Brisson was reliable—and because there was *Gringoire*. I thought I could contribute to *Comoedia*, because Delange [its director] and Arland seemed basically reliable to me—and because there is *Je suis partout*. (As it happens, neither *Je suis partout* nor *Gringoire* are fooled about it.)"[239] Mauriac resolutely refuted this comparison. "I don't like being my brothers' judge," he wrote—this was the first occurrence of this theme that Paulhan, whom Mauriac is probably borrowing from here, would make into his supreme argument in the debates on the purge—but the comparison struck him as "very forced" between *Le Figaro*, with its "unequivocal" attitude, and which "folded rather than suffer the direct control of the occupying forces," and *Comoedia* which "always hurried to submit to that control" (he recalled "Cocteau's despicable article" on the official sculptor of the Third Reich, Arno Breker, published in the literary section of the journal; and the invitation made to Lucien Rebatet to "sit on its juries"). And yet, he repeated that he had never been "scandalized" to see Paulhan himself contribute there. Paulhan also consulted him on the case of Marcel Arland who was, obviously, what most preoccupied him in this affair, since he was the one who had sent him to René Delange. Should he be advised to leave the weekly? Mauriac did not see the "advantage" that he would draw "by leaving *now*."[240] In his response, Paulhan developed his arguments at length, clearing Arland of having compromised himself, whether ideologically or for economic or symbolic purposes, repeating the comparison with *Le Figaro* from the point of view of submission to censorship, insisting on the difference between the literary page of *Comoedia* and the articles published on the European page, even on the front page—which, "by their obvious coarseness, were to my mind infinitely less dangerous than certain articles that the *Figaro*, also following orders, published on the front page"—finally arguing that Drieu and Fraigneau's attacks on *Comoedia* at the Weimar Congress, the reduction of the weekly's paper allocation, the threats leveled against its director, and its illustrious contributors (Claudel, Valéry, Vildrac, Eluard, Sartre) cleared it.[241] But these arguments were not sufficient to dispel Mauriac's apprehensions, although he nonetheless claimed to be touched by Paulhan's concern for his friend Arland.[242]

While Paulhan's eventual stance at the Liberation emerged in this polemic, the positions were far from settled at this point, as Mauriac's reversal in October 1944 would show. We can still deduce, at present, a first division that opposed those we might call "moralists" (Mauriac and Guéhenno, here), to the one who would soon situate himself, against the "moralists," as a defender of "art for art's sake," Jean Paulhan. According to this division, the positions of the Catholics and those of the former anti-Fascist militants could converge with those of the Communists.

A second principle of division would be added, linked to the different experience of the Occupation in the two zones, and the competition between committee members of the two zones to define their common line. Elsa Triolet's published version of her memories on this subject—"There were a few disagreements, the Northern zone more intransigent than us, the Southern zone"[243]—attenuated the violence that emerged from her unpublished notes:

> There was an established contact between the Southern and Northern zone CNE, decisions made together. I especially remember a meeting at the home of Édith Thomas in Spring 44. It was awfully cold . . . and there was something in the atmosphere that brought shivers. We bore a message from Southern zone CNE, a *proposition* for the attitude to adopt toward publishers aside from the activity of the purge, after the Liberation: reintegration of résistant and Jewish employees, back payment, expulsion of the collaborators, having replaced them. The Northern zone considered the proposal insufficient. There were violent interventions from Debû-Bridel, Guéhenno, Mauriac . . . We had to *hang* some publishers . . .[244]

In the eyes of the Northern zone, the members of the Southern zone were "less involved in the whole affair," according to Lucien Scheler, who confirmed in an interview the divergent points of view on the degrees of "compromise" with respect to the powers, Mauriac and even Paulhan were "much more involved" than André Rousseaux and Louis Martin-Chauffier.[245] But the tensions also emanated from a power struggle. In the eyes of Jean Lescure, Aragon's desire for "imperialism" was very clear.[246] Édith Thomas mentioned a confrontation between Aragon and Guéhenno about a prewar debate concerning the journal *Europe*, in the wake of which "Guéhenno, Blanzat, and Paulhan were ready to leave a group where they claimed to find 'perpetual bad faith,' the 'institutionalized lie' of the Communists," and were only prevented from doing so by the double intervention of Édith Thomas and Claude Morgan.[247] But the unification occurred, as we saw, to the detriment of the Southern zone. Among the signers of the Manifesto of French Writers, the list of the "forgotten" writers from the other zone was long. Neither René Tavernier nor Elsa Triolet was inventoried there. Aragon, who only returned to Paris at the end of September 1944, would have to regain his position within the CNE.

On the other hand, the dissensions with the Communists, which only really came to light at the Liberation, did not originally arise from the codification of the norms of writers' conduct, but rather from properly literary questions and the fear of Communist control over the different ventures that emerged from clandestinity. Prefigured by the internal tensions surrounding the underground catalogue of the Éditions de Minuit, which opposed the supporters of a didactic combat literature with the defenders of a more spiritual opposition to Nazism, they were also sketched around *Les Lettres françaises*. In December 1943, it had been decided, at the party's initiative it seems, that the direction of the newspaper (ensured by Morgan alone) would be replaced by a collegial direction composed of three Communists (Aragon, Eluard, Morgan), and three non-Communists (including Jean Lescure). According to Lescure, Eluard expected him to align with his own positions to ensure a Communist majority. The college never met, and the *Almanach des Lettres françaises*, published in March 1944, was presumably its only expression. But on the eve of the Liberation, the question of the status of *Les Lettres françaises* was posed in reference to its future as a nonclandestine publication. In a letter to Jean Lescure, Paulhan spoke of the meeting in these terms:

> Do you understand what happened yesterday? Here is my hypothesis. Fr[ançois] M[auriac] and Jean G[uéhenno] wanted to ask: "Will the C[ommunist]P[arty] finance the newspaper? Will the CP continue to control it?" And didn't dare ask. Paul E[luard] wanted the CNE to be at once very large and ineffective—thus bringing the CP the most brilliant and the least troublesome cover. And yet did not dare say it. In such a way that we could have had a much longer discussion.[248]

These tensions presaged the conflicts of the Liberation. Linked to the Communist Party by the conditions of its birth, the CNE would see this dependence confirmed when it emerged from illegality. While the Party provided dissident writers with the means to reaffirm their freedom with respect to the subjugated authorities of diffusion and the agents of heteronomy, this dependence was now perceived as a threat for the guardians of literary autonomy.

PART III

Literary Justice

The restructuring of the literary field at the Liberation was marked by a generational takeover. Jean Giraudoux, Romain Rolland, and Paul Valéry died between 1944 and 1945. Malraux was promoted to the position that Giraudoux occupied in 1939, that of minister for information. The position achieved by the CNE both reflected and contributed to the advent of a new literary generation.

The crisis of 1940 had privileged a rise to dominant positions on the part of the generation that had established itself after World War I: at the French Academy (Duhamel, Mauriac), the Goncourt Academy (Benjamin, Carco), *La NRF*. At that time, the struggle for influence pitted Aragon and Eluard on one side, against Drieu La Rochelle and Montherlant on the other, even though the elders (Gide, Valéry, Schlumberger) still had their say. But the crisis of the Occupation years and the experience of the Resistance (along with the opportunities for social promotion that it could inspire) also contributed to the crystallization of a new literary generation, its advent favored by the upheaval of the Liberation,[1] engendering competition with the elders. These struggles were all the more bitter inasmuch as they had been repressed until then for the sake of the alliances woven in the combat for literary autonomy.

Because it transformed the course of their existence and their social future, the experience of the Occupation was decisive for these younger writers, whose most famous representatives included Vercors, Sartre, and Camus. It also founded both their vision of the world as well as their authority to speak in its name. As we will see, it was precisely this "moral capital" that they seized upon in order to redefine the notion of the responsibility of the writer throughout the debates surrounding the purge. These debates appear as an aspect of the struggle for the transformation or conservation of the power relations that had structured the literary field prior to the war. While the debate is imbued with strong judiciary connotations, literary justice, far from submitting to judiciary or political logics, has a logic of its own, which depends on categories of literary understanding and on hierarchies that are specific to the literary world.

The longer-term effects of the crisis will be assessed through the institutional struggles that it engendered. The purge, the heritage of the Resistance, and the memory of the "dark years" lay at the heart of these struggles that divided the traditional literary authorities, the French Academy and the Goncourt Academy, and confronted them with their new competitor, the CNE. The two academies' modes of survival at the Liberation were similar to those that we saw at work under the Occupation. They allow us to sketch the process of "normalization," marked by the erosion of the unity of the Resistance and the marginalization of the CNE. Torn up by the divisions that crossed it, progressively identified with the Communist Party, on the threshold of the Cold War, the latter soon seemed like a fraud.

CHAPTER 8

The Literary Court

But now the hour has come
To love and join together
For their defeat and punishment.
Paul Eluard, "Un petit nombre d'intellectuels français s'est mis au service de
l'ennemi"

August 1944. Paris had been liberated. While a number of collaborationist
writers fled toward Sigmaringen, a press emerged from the shadows to fervently
comment on the national uprising. In *Combat*, Sartre wrote a series of articles
describing his walk through an insurgent Paris. Comprised of newspapers born
of the Resistance (*Combat, Libération, Franc-Tireur, Défense de la France*, etc.)
and some older, "uncompromised" titles like *Le Figaro, Le Populaire*, and
L'Humanité, the new press took over the deserted offices of the collaborationist
papers, which were banned.[1] Starting in September, the Parisian intellectual
field began to undergo a process of restructuration. The scattered writers slowly
returned to the capital. The authorities born of the crisis or promoted thanks to
forced decentralization left the Southern zone or nearby francophone countries
to settle there: the reviews *Fontaine, Arche*, and the publisher Charlot emigrated from Algiers; *Confluences* and *Poésie* from Lyon and Villeneuve. Yet the
euphoria of the first days was quickly followed by uncertainty and worry in the
face of an uncertain future.

Though power relations were reversed, the configuration of the relations between the intellectual field and the political field, which is proper to times of
war, notably subsisted through the control of cultural production: the Contrôle militaire des Informations drew up lists of "works of a collaborationist

nature" to remove from sale, counterbalancing the "Otto lists." At first, the restructuring of the literary field actually obeyed the logic that presided over the transformation of the political landscape. The establishment of the generation of the Resistance and the hegemony of the Communist Party were its two most characteristic traits. Their corollary was the affirmation of new values: patriotism, the "responsibility" of the intellectual, engagement, and the delegitimization of the ideological right, which the résistants could now fight for the monopoly of national moralism. In the tradition of the indictment begun during the interwar period, the devaluation of the option of "art for art's sake" had been precipitated by the crisis conjuncture and especially the exploitation of this theme by the partisans of the Collaboration. Along with the discredit cast on the ideas of the right, this devaluation consecrated the model of engagement on the left. The disappearance of *La NRF* and the launch of *Les Temps modernes* under Sartre's direction in the autumn of 1945 marked the end of the literary order that *La NRF* had brought about during the interwar period. Sartre opposed "engaged literature" to the now out-of-place "pure literature."

The CNE contributed a great deal to the establishment of these new values. Strengthened by the double literary and national legitimacy that it had earned in the underground struggle, the CNE, which strove to represent the Conseil national de la Résistance (CNR) in the literary world, established itself as a new regulatory authority in the literary field and played an important role in its restructuring. Its institutionalization was inscribed in the double context of the purge and institutional reform at the Liberation. Originally a group with a political vocation, the CNE now presented itself as an association devoted to the defense and regulation of the profession on an ethical basis. It was in this role, and in the name of the notion of "the responsibility of the writer," that it claimed the power of excommunication which would remain closely associated with its social image.

For those who challenged it, this power (symbolized by the "black list" of "undesirable" writers) was only the perpetuation, in an institutionalized form— and therefore even more serious, in their eyes—of the practice of denunciation that had developed under the Occupation. This argument was not the prerogative of the defeated. Jean Paulhan, cofounder of the underground CNE, made it into the driving force of his polemics with the committee members, which raised the question of the conditions of the literary field's autonomy in what looked like a new quarrel of the "bad masters," in certain respects and with an inversion of roles.

A detailed chronology of the polemics and position-takings with respect to the purge during the first few months of the Liberation will allow us to grasp the strategies, successive readjustments, and reversals that would ultimately engender a redistribution of the positions in the literary field. The oppositions were actually not as clear-cut as subsequent reconstructions would have us believe. Neither the "indulgents," as their adversaries called them, nor the "intransigents" stuck to their roles in every case. These oppositions were moreover far from set in the autumn of 1944. Attitudes evolved along with the events, polemics, and logics of assignation, as I will show more specifically in the cases of Jean Paulhan and François Mauriac. Similarly, alliances were not always founded on an affinity of worldview, but rather a common rejection—on potentially different bases—of the opposing positions. There again, they weren't immediately constituted, but were modified as the stakes shifted.

And yet we still find, in the particular form that they took at the Liberation, the principles of division already identified, namely competition between generations, the opposition between moralists and defenders of "pure literature," and the ideological split of right/left, along with the differing experiences of the Occupation (Northern/Southern zone, civil/armed resistance). This is why the conflicts that crossed the CNE starting in the month of September were in large part the expression of the intergenerational struggle that marked the rhythm of the recomposition of the literary field. Instead of focusing on fixed positions, I will try to grasp the dynamic of the process of redistributing positions by shedding light on some of its crucial moments, in order to lay bare the modalities through which the literary field transforms when the external constraints bearing upon it change.

An Institutionalized Power of Excommunication

As the first initiator of a purge in the literary milieu, the CNE looked like a "literary court" at the Liberation. While it is difficult to establish the role that the CNE played in the legal purge, we can still determine the role that it sought to play, at least at first, and the one that it effectively assumed in the professional purge and the reorganization of the literary field. The CNE was the first group of the intellectual Resistance to have established such a principle of boycotting. This initiative must be related, on the one hand, to the authority and prestige that the CNE had acquired in the underground, and on the other, to the specificity of the literary field, the least regulated and least codified of the fields of cultural production, the conditions of entry into its ranks being by definition undefined. Yet it was these rules of deontology, a "code of honor" of the writer's profession with its implied responsibilities, that the CNE tried to establish. And it was in the name of the moral capital collectively accumulated by its members in the Resistance that it assumed a power of excommunication.

In this self-regulated symbolic universe, excommunication was a common practice (the spectacular exclusions of the surrealist group were only its most ostentatious display). On the other hand, this practice was contested as soon as it relied on external authorities to regulate the internal power relations of the literary field, as we saw during the Occupation. This is why differences of opinion appear, not about the very principle of boycotting, but rather the relationship between the CNE and the state, justice, and the Communist Party.

THE INSTITUTIONALIZATION OF THE CNE

The Communist Party's hegemony in the intellectual field was, as I've said, one of the defining traits of the restructuration of the intellectual field. Its authority was reinforced by two factors, which effaced the memory of the German-Soviet pact and were inscribed in the wider framework of undermining collaborationist political and economic elites: "the Stalingrad effect" and the major role played by the Communists in the Resistance. It was this incontestable role that "the party of those executed by firing squad" would claim, demanding the right to take an active part in the reconstruction of France. It acquired this right, for our purposes, by attaining a number of key positions in the field of ideological production: widely represented in the new press (the authorized circulation of Communist and Communistic newspapers was 26.8 percent then versus 4.6 percent in 1939),[2] the party oversaw various cultural authorities, particularly the committees born of the intellectual Resistance, which were federated in the National Union of Intellectuals in June 1945. The results of the municipal elections in the spring of 1945 as well as the elections of the first Constituent Assembly in October, in which it won 26.3 percent of votes, would confirm the Communist Party in the national role that it demanded.

Although the membership of consecrated intellectuals and artists in the Communist Party remained relatively limited, it was no less significant. Aside from Aragon, the party's ranks now included Eluard, Picasso, and Fernand Léger. The extension of the practice of fellow-traveling, the attraction exerted by the party in student milieus, and the different position-takings of various ideological currents with relation to Communism or Marxism (from the Catholics, with *Esprit, Économie et humanisme*, to the existentialists gathered around *Les Temps modernes*) were so many expressions of its hegemony in the intellectual field,[3] also represented by the institutionalization of the CNE.

The position of the CNE actually reflected this hegemony as much as it reinforced it through its prestige, which remained unequaled among the other authorities born of the intellectual Resistance. Within the PCF, its institutionalization proceeded from the Thorezian line for the promotion of a national

Communism; Aragon was its chief representative in the cultural realm. Still, the links between the CNE and the party do not suffice to account for its at least partial success. From the viewpoint of the literary field, which is of primary interest to us here, the institutionalization of the CNE expressed not only the consecration of résistant writers, but also served as a key moment in the process of professionalizing the writer's trade. The role that the CNE played in the purge of the profession, which we will try to determine here, and the redefinition of its vocation as an authority for the defense of the corporative interests of writers, which we will examine in the next chapter, can in fact be read in this light. Its failure must be related to its relationship with a state that did not recognize the monopoly it claimed, dooming it to compete with the solidly established traditional authorities like the Société des gens de lettres and the French Academy. It must also be related to the field effects displayed in internal conflicts, which won out over an "esprit de corps" too closely linked to the crisis conjuncture that had fostered it to survive in its wake. The integration of the members of the underground CNE relied, as we saw, on fragile and situational alliances. While the first tensions were due to the intervention of new members who had arrived at the CNE just before the Liberation and were thus less integrated, beginning in 1944 the Liberation had the effect of exposing other, underlying tensions that only the feeling of solidarity born of the underground experience prevented from erupting; but these tensions bore the seeds of the coming fractures.

The Manifesto of French Writers, which was published in *Les Lettres françaises* on September 9 and included sixty-five names (ten others would be added the following week) was the founding act of the legal CNE. Besides Morgan's editorial, it was accompanied by three articles that illustrated its arguments: "The French Nation Has a Soul" by François Mauriac, "The Republic of Silence" by Sartre, and a "Eulogy for Jacques Decour" by Jean Paulhan. Strengthened by this prestigious company, the manifesto's title left no room for doubt: the CNE declared itself the official mouthpiece for French writers. We are to understand that these writers united, above and beyond generational, literary, and political divisions, in the name of the three principles that structured the manifesto: national interest, the defense of "civilization," and the "freedom of the mind," guarantor of truth and artistic creation. In that respect, the CNE reaffirmed the universalist vocation of the writer, intending to serve as its institutionalized expression. The CNE thus founded its assumed mission in the national reconstruction.

The first question posed by the history of this authority born of the underground is that of continuity. What role did the CNE aspire to play by maintaining its existence beyond the particular conditions of its creation? Does its change in status and new recruitment allow us to equate the legal CNE with the underground venture? Yes, to the extent that its members recognized themselves in it. From an internal point of view, the transition from clandestinity to public existence did, in fact, occur smoothly. At no time did the slightest discord arise, between August and September 1944, concerning the very principle of maintaining this association, nor what it represented. The only question raised during the first plenary meeting on September 4 concerned the social function reserved for the CNE. When Jean Paulhan claimed the "right to err" for writers, he contested the role of literary court that the CNE aspired to play, without calling the legitimacy of its existence into question. The turnover in membership— thanks to the Communist-initiated decision to open up the committee to recruitment—also modified neither the public image nor the identity of the CNE during this transitional phase. In fact, it was in the interest of the latecomers, including the great elders who joined right before the Liberation (Valéry, Duhamel, the Tharaud brothers) to be immediately identified with what the committee represented, a sign of the double legitimacy, both literary and national, that founded its authority.

While tensions began to appear in September, it was only at the end of the month that they emerged openly, if not publicly. Related more to questions of authority and form than objectives, these tensions opposed, as we will see, the latecomers to those who, thanks to their early membership in the CNE, benefited from the moral capital associated with Resistance seniority. On the other hand, for a fraction of the latter group, this was the moment that they started to question the relationship between the new institution and the underground organization. This is evidenced by a line from Jean Blanzat to Jean Paulhan, in a letter that we can situate toward the end of October 1944: "I don't know who this Committee is; if it's the real one or another."[4] From that point on, the question of the association's continuity with its underground precedent was at stake in the internal struggle. Those who had more power within the organization and gave it its internal orientation claimed this continuity, while the dissidents alleged that the association betrayed its original regulations. The question of maintaining the association would not be truly posed and put to a vote until the General Assembly of February 1946, when Aragon was proceeding with the legalization of its statutes in accordance with the law of 1901 on associations, as well as with its reorganization. Yet the struggles would continue until the 1950s, more precisely until the creation in 1956 of a competing authority that would claim true filiation with the CNE, Louis Martin-Chauffier's Union des écrivains pour la vérité. I will come back to this.

What literary and national role did the CNE aspire to play? It would take several months to decide. Drawing up a "blacklist" of writers considered "undesirable" because of their conduct under the Occupation, along with the role that the CNE played in the purge and the ensuing polemics, seems to have concentrated all the preoccupations of the association, at least at first. Meanwhile, the association was steadily growing, reaching more than 200 members in 1946.[5] According to the politics of openness determined just before the Liberation, membership was subject to sponsorship by two members, the publication of two to three works, and justification of a Resistance activity (in the absence of the last, the prospective member had to certify that he had "conformed to its spirit"). According to the CNE charter, membership involved a commitment to have no publishing relationship with the authors inventoried on the "blacklist." In the committee's internal information bulletin in June 1945, the objectives of the association were presented in a very general manner, through the first article of its statutes:

> The Association known as the Comité National des Écrivains, founded in 1943 under the German Occupation, has the goal of assembling patriotic writers, in order to defend and support French literature, to protect the independence and prestige of French art in the world, and to unite writers with all the forces of the nation that work for the recovery of France, on the path to this recovery.[6]

Still, the bulletin announced a plan for the CNE to participate in the États-généraux de la Renaissance française, in its role as a "professional representative" of the writers. From a financial point of view, aside from donations, the CNE had two main ways to fill its coffers: membership dues, and a "sale of manuscripts, rare works, luxury works, and signed books, with all profits going to our treasury."[7]

During this time, the life of the CNE was still closely linked to that of its organ, *Les Lettres françaises*, which had now become a weekly. The newspaper hosted the meetings of the directive board at its headquarters, rue de Courcelles, while the general assemblies were held at the Salle Pleyel. Claude Morgan, the director of *Les Lettres françaises*, was the general secretary of the CNE. He also served on the oversight commission of the CNE bulletin, along with two other *Lettres françaises* editors, Georges Adam and Loÿs Masson. L. Forestier, the secretary of the directive board of the CNE, served as its editor.

Aside from Claude Morgan, the directive board of the CNE, presided by Jacques Debû-Bridel, included Aragon, Claude Aveline, Jean Blanzat, Paul Eluard, Stanislas Fumet, Max-Pol Fouchet, Eugène Guillevic, Henry Malherbe, François Mauriac, Léon Moussinac, Raymond Queneau, Jean-Paul Sartre, Édith Thomas, Elsa Triolet, Yvonne Desvignes (for Vercors), and Charles Vildrac. All of them had belonged to the underground CNE. With eleven representatives out of eighteen members, the ex-committee of the Northern zone was clearly predominant. There was a total of seven Communists if we count Elsa Triolet, that is to say slightly more than one-third. Communist representation had thus slightly increased with respect to the underground version.

As we saw, the first tensions that had opposed Communists and non-Communists within the CNE just before the Liberation concerned *Les Lettres françaises*. Camus's resignation at the end of September 1944, a first for the committee, marked a turning point, less by creating a precedent—for a long time, the threat of resignation would be more often used as a means of persuasion or dissuasion—than because it concretized internal divisions that would soon overwhelm the feeling of solidarity. In Camus's resignation, personal grudges and rivalries mixed with mistrust of the Communist Party, which Camus knew from the inside out. The editorialist of *Combat* mainly addressed his criticisms to *Les Lettres françaises*. One of the reasons that he invoked for his resignation was that the weekly had not respected its commitment to not publicize. But Camus particularly criticized *Les Lettres françaises* for the critical commentary its editorial staff had added to his article in May 1944 about the death penalty pronounced in Algiers against the former Vichy minister Pierre Pucheu, in which he spoke out against the Vichy government's execution of prisoners.[8] The letter of resignation that he sent Paulhan expressed his discomfort in a climate where "moral independence is so poorly tolerated."[9]

Whatever the case may be, the question of the status of *Les Lettres françaises* as an organ of the CNE, rather than that of the "blacklist," was certainly first to inspire tensions between Communists and non-Communists. It would not be resolved until the dissociation of the committee and its organ in 1946. Announcing his resignation from the assembly in February 1946, André Rousseaux would serve as the spokesman for those who deplored the fact that the newspaper, which embodied the shared work of the underground movement, had become the organ of a party. He evoked the "brotherly friendship" formed then with the Communists, without politics ever entering into the debate.[10] The political division was nonetheless only one of the principles that divided the members of the committee. These divisions would be exposed during an internal polemic that was stirred up by the "blacklist."

THE "BLACKLIST"
We can read the stakes of restructuring the literary field through the tensions that shook the CNE in the aftermath of the Liberation. These tensions cannot be reduced to simple frictions between Communists and non-Communists.

They also resulted from the power relations between the members of the committees in the Northern and Southern zones, since their reunification occurred, as we saw, to the detriment of the latter. They especially resulted from a paradoxical configuration of the relations of legitimacy between senior members and newcomers within the committee. On the one hand, the most senior members, adorned with the moral prestige conferred by the seniority of their engagement in the underground, were relatively young and weakly consecrated from a literary point of view, with the exception of Mauriac and Paulhan. On the other hand, the new members, deprived of moral capital, intended to base their authority on the literary titles that they held. It is in light of this competition between two types of legitimacy that we must understand the first polemics surrounding the "blacklist." It was paired with an opposition between the "moralists" and the defenders of the rights of literature, represented by Paulhan in this debate.

Starting in late 1943, the CNE had initiated a purge of the profession, for which it had requested the investiture of the CFLN. During its first plenary meeting on September 4, 1944, the CNE voted a motion that was strongly inspired by the ordinance of August 26, 1944, instituting the crime of national indignity: it called for the government to bring charges against the writers who were members of the "Collaboration" group, political parties or paramilitary formations of "German inspiration," those who attended conferences in Germany, who received funds from the enemy, or who aided Hitlerian propaganda through their writing or their acts. The CNE specified that it would assist in carrying out these measures.[11] What type of assistance did the CNE intend to bring to the legal system? And what relationship existed between this offer of services and the "blacklist" of "undesirable" writers that the CNE set about establishing and that it would work to complete and correct during the first weeks of its legal existence? Through their charter, the committee members promised not to have any publishing relationship with the authors included on the list, meaning not even in the same collections, anthologies, or periodicals.[12] But in the beginning, the function of the "blacklist" was not limited solely to internal use. To clarify this ambiguity, we must closely follow chronology.

Twelve names were stated during this plenary meeting: Brasillach, Céline, Alphonse de Chateaubriant, Chardonne, Drieu La Rochelle, Giono, Jouhandeau, Maurras, Montherlant, Moran, Petitjean, and Thérive. The contributors to Drieu La Rochelle's *NRF* were favored here, with eight representatives out of twelve. This first list, which more or less coincided with the list of writers that *Les Lettres françaises* rewarded with an accusatory article, is significant. It translated the central place that *La NRF* of the defeat occupied in the spontaneous representations of literary "treason" or "dishonor," and in the feeling of indignation that they engendered. More generally, the list shows that the principle of literary legitimacy defined the boundaries of the category of writers who, as such, were the object of indignation. The vague notions of literary "treason" and "dishonor" were above all applicable to those who had once been recognized as members of the community of writers.

The symbolic significance of this spontaneous list becomes even more obvious when we compare it with the list published the following week, on September 16, 1944, in *Les Lettres françaises*. This time, ninety-four names were inventoried; aside from those already mentioned, they included Ajalbert, Bonnard, Bordeaux, René Benjamin, Pierre Benoit, Béraud, Combelle, Dyssord, Fabre-Luce, Fraigneau, Paul Fort, Guitry, Hermant, Jouhandeau, Laubreaux, La Varende, Mauclair, Maxence, Pelorson, Henri Poulain, and Rebatet, to cite only the best known. The product of a work of rationalization and systematization, this new list also included obscure pen pushers. This was because a commission was formed in the meantime to establish criteria. This commission included Jacques Debû-Bridel, Paul Eluard, Raymond Queneau, Lucien Scheler, Vercors, and Charles Vildrac. All had belonged to the underground committee of the Northern zone.

The publication of the integral version of the "blacklist" unleashed the first struggles within the CNE. It was the elders who were the latest to join the committee, those who thus had the fewest bonds of solidarity with the members of the underground committee, who proceeded to organize the opposition. In a letter that he sent to Jean Paulhan, the Christian existentialist philosopher Gabriel Marcel rebelled, not against the list itself, which he didn't contest in the case of Fabre-Luce, but against the process that the commission designated by the CNE had used to establish it. Instead of first submitting it to the approval of the assembly, they presented its members with a fait accompli. Informing Paulhan of the position of Jean Schlumberger, who shared his own, he formed the project of a collective protest.[13] Although he had been the only one to protest, during the plenary meeting on September 4, "that error, the risk of the mind, aberration (in the sense of the theologians) are the first right of the writer,"[14] Paulhan recused himself. Gabriel Marcel responded with regret that Paulhan would not be on his side, invoking the necessity of submitting the list to a serious examination and asking for its revision: "this list *exists* [...] it presents itself as a condemnation [...] Will you say: there aren't any vital consequences, nothing at all will happen? In this case we will have covered ourselves with ridicule and even *disqualified* ourselves. Which I cannot allow either."[15] Aside from Schlumberger, Duhamel, Mauriac, the Tharaud brothers, Alexandre Arnoux,

René Maran, and Pierre Bost joined the protest, while Blanzat and Guéhenno kept their distance, like Paulhan. The group of protestors was thus composed of "newcomers" to the committee (Mauriac excepted), who were also the elders in the literary field: "We represent what holds the most weight in literature," Jean Schlumberger wrote in his notebooks on this subject.[16] Their opposition did not take the very principle of a "blacklist" as its basis but, through the debates on the conditions of its elaboration and its "instructions for use," the power relations within the committee. Above all, they opposed the imposition of the rules of the game by their juniors, who held a large majority in the commission established to draw up the "blacklist" and formed more than half of the directive board. Some, moreover, were Communists.

The conflicts erupted during the meeting on September 30; François Mauriac presided. The group of protesters confronted the CNE purge commission. They proposed establishing two distinct lists based on the degree of guilt, one being a revised version of the list from September 16, and the other a list of the "major offenders." The criteria for incrimination were discussed. Duhamel having contested the criterion of fidelity to Marshal Pétain in reference to Henry Bordeaux, Aragon countered with a "coup de force." Here is Mauriac's account, as reported by his son:

> Yesterday, at the Committee of the purge of writers, an awkward intervention from the good Duhamel (my father tells), saying about Pétain, and referring to a private conversation that he had in my presence on this subject with De Gaulle: "The General, I know it directly from him, the General wants silence . . ." A snicker erupted, hateful, tragic: "Ah! Ah! the General wants silence!": it was Aragon.
>
> A little later, the question having been raised of whether the fact of having believed in Pétain was enough to deserve exclusion, the same Aragon had a paper passed to my father who was presiding, and left. My father read the text out loud; in it Aragon said that if this point, resolved once and for all, was put up for discussion again, he would resign and refer the matter to public opinion.[17]

In this "coup de force" by Aragon, we can read the political tensions between Gaullists and Communists: in Duhamel, Aragon was likely targeting the permanent secretary of the French Academy, suspected of solidarity with his colleague Marshal Pétain, and of complicity with the acting power. Let us recall that he had, moreover, refused to join the first underground writers' group out of hostility for the Communists. Yet it also demonstrates the power struggles within the committee. Aragon, who had just returned to Paris, had a position to regain within the CNE. The initiator of the project that had brought Decour and Paulhan together in the summer of 1941, he was partially dispossessed by the group of the Northern zone, which benefited from the reunification. The moral capital that Aragon could put forth to affirm his authority when faced with the members of the CNE of the Northern zone depended precisely on the condemnation of Pétainism, without which his semi-legal activity up until the invasion of the Southern zone in November 1942 lost its symbolic value in comparison with the illegal activity of the members of the first committee of the Northern zone and the risks that they ran much earlier than he did. Moreover, Aragon put all the more good faith in his "coup de force" because he had completely committed himself to the struggle against the Vichy regime (which was one of the watchwords of the Communist Party), unlike his colleagues in the Northern zone, for whom Vichy was only a far-off reality without any substance, compared to the German Occupation.

At the end of this meeting, a compromise was found between the different points of view. It was translated by the addition of two members to the purge commission of the CNE: Gabriel Marcel, spokesman for the group of protesting elders, and André Rousseaux, probably nominated by Aragon to express the viewpoint of the Southern zone and anti-Pétainism. The principle of two "blacklists" according to the degree of guilt, demanded by the group of elders, was adopted. It was decided that a delegation of the committee would be tasked with bringing a list of the "major culprits" to the Ministry of Justice. The delegation was composed of three prestigious figures from the literary world who represented different political sensibilities (Aragon, François Mauriac, Jean Schlumberger), who were joined by the president of the CNE, Jacques Debû-Bridel, who was also the spokesman for its purge commission and who, like Mauriac, was moreover a member of the directive committee of the National Front. Finally, in the wake of Aragon's intervention, the following motion was passed: "Support of the Maréchal's politics after the occupation of the Southern zone is considered a case of national indignity,"[18] which was actually only a half victory for the author of Le Crève-cœur. Above and beyond the conflicts, these decisions attested to the fact that the CNE still intended to oversee the legal purge and have an advisory role in establishing the criteria for writers' guilt.

But the "list of major culprits" would not be brought to the Ministry of Justice.[19] After the meeting, Paulhan, speaking with Claude Morgan and Paul Eluard, violently protested this new decision that favored Gabriel Marcel at his expense. He formulated his reservations in a letter to François Mauriac: "Are we really here to denounce those of our colleagues who haven't been arrested yet? Is there no honor among writers [. . .]?", adding that he "[wouldn't] like to resign from the Committee at this time."[20] The argument worked. Mauriac decided that he would not go to the Ministry of Justice. He also resigned from the honorary presidency of the CNE: "[...] we don't have cops' souls."[21] On his side, Jean Schlumberger, who had received a similar letter from Paulhan,[22] also refused to undertake any action with the ministry. In the meantime, Paulhan nonetheless sent his resignation from the CNE to Claude Morgan, who urged him to reconsider: "Don't leave us at this time, which is the most difficult the Committee has ever known."[23] Paulhan accepted, but asked to be "dormant." He won his claim: the project was abandoned.

In fact, it is clear that Paulhan rebelled not against the very principle of a purge, but against the institutionalization of the denunciation of writers by writers. "Neither judges, nor snitches," such was the principle that the members of the CNE had adopted during a clandestine meeting at the home of Édith Thomas. "That the first public act of the CNE would be to go ask the Justice Ministry to arrest other writers seems precisely horrible to me," Paulhan wrote to Debû-Bridel.[24] And to Eluard: "It's a matter of knowing whether the writer's honor allows him, orders him to denounce other writers."[25]

In the wake of these discussions, the CNE set about redefining its objectives, as evidenced by the successive readjustments of the arguments exposing the principles and use of the "blacklist." Starting in October, the committee distanced itself from the legal purge and affirmed the purely "moral" character of the sanctions it inflicted on the authors named on the list. On October 7, the CNE purge commission recalled for the third time the motion of September 4 urging the government to charge the compromised writers, but specified that the list "does not correspond to the preoccupations that inspired the above motion. This list was intended as one of writers whose attitude during the Occupation was such that the members of the CNE are loath to have any contact with them on a professional level [...]."[26]

A new, modified version of the "blacklist" was published on October 21 in *Les Lettres françaises*. It included 158 names, seventeen authors having been removed from the first list, versus eighty-one newly added. The introductory paragraph specified that the list was destined solely for internal use. It also indicated, thanks to the request of the group of senior members led by Gabriel Marcel, Schlumberger, and Duhamel, that the listed authors were unequally guilty:

> We insist on reminding [the reader] that, on this list that only tends to specify the personal attitude of the members of the CNE, writers appear who were very diversely and, as a result, unequally responsible for the misfortunes of our county. This is why the CNE again insists that all possible light be shed

on the degree of guilt of the "collaborators." It is important that more or less compromised writers not be confused with those who are liable under the law instituting the crime of "national indignity." Only this light can clarify the atmosphere of confusion and suspicion that risks dangerously serving the true culprits.[27]

The criterion of supporting Pétain's politics after the occupation of the Southern zone, demanded by Aragon, only had a limited bearing on this new version of the "blacklist." It allowed, as we can infer from the comparison of both lists, the continued inclusion of Charles Maurras and the addition of Henri Massis (the other identifiable authors among the eighty-one names added had all adopted collaborationist positions). Still, it did not prevent the elimination of Henry Bordeaux, at the request of Gabriel Marcel and Georges Duhamel who, although he belonged to the oppositional fraction of the French Academy, protected the honor of the institution in his role as permanent secretary; seven of its members were already being investigated. In November, a correction would add two names to this new list, reckoned to be definitive: Paul Morand and Armand Robin. Had Morand, who appeared on the list of September 16, been "forgotten" as the correction stated, or did Paulhan's remarks result in the reappearance of his name?

For, paradoxically, the disappearance of certain names, including Morand and Bordeaux, aroused the astonishment of the primary defender of the "right to err," Jean Paulhan who, in the letters that he wrote to François Mauriac, Claude Morgan, and Jean Schlumberger, rose up against the "protections": "Why were Bordeaux, Morand, Pilon (of the *Collaboration* group), La Varende erased? It's too obviously because they had friends in the CNE."[28] We could stop here and say that the passions (friendships, hostilities) and group interests, in this case the NRF team (Paulhan very probably had Jouhandeau and Giono in mind, as he would later ask for their removal from "the list") against the French Academy and the writers "of good society," would alone determine the positions taken in this debate. And certainly, those interests acted in conjunction with the division between senior members and newcomers to the CNE.

Paulhan's hostility with regard to the positions of Gabriel Marcel nonetheless translates another division, opposing the defenders of "pure literature" to the "moralists." Faced with the propensity of the latter to judge literature according to extraliterary criteria by appealing to authorities of arbitration or categories of the universal such as the law, the Church, the state, or the "common good," the former tended, as we saw, to deny its social effects and recall that it was above all a game with set rules, the first being that its players should not have recourse to extraliterary authorities. In the letter addressed to Schlumberger, Paulhan specified: "The justice system is, in these subjective questions, a pretext for cheating."[29] Paulhan's use of the word "cheating" here is revealing. While for a Christian philosopher such as Gabriel Marcel, if the "list" had no consequences the writers of the CNE would be discredited, it was precisely the systematization and officialization of what should be a "subjective" posture that made it intolerable in Paulhan's eyes. This was all the more true since the presence of Gabriel Marcel himself in the CNE purge commission reinforced and legitimized this "moralist" posture.[30] Thus he wrote to Jean Schlumberger about the correction of October 7: "No, I don't think that the introductory paragraph is progress. I don't see how the list would avoid seeming, let's say in ten months, ridiculous and vaguely disagreeable to us. It would still be ok if we could then tell ourselves, 'Those are the eccentrics of the group.' Alas, the moralists also put their touch on it."[31] Who are the "eccentrics of the group"? We can wager that, for Paulhan, they were yesterday's accomplices: Eluard, Aragon, Queneau, Debû-Bridel.

Despite the apparent coherence of Paulhan's arguments, the contradictions are legible on several levels. First, in relation to his prewar positions. We recall the attitude of the director of *La NRF* on the incarceration of Maurras and Giono: while it was not the writers' right to exclude their colleagues for political reasons—and on this point Paulhan remained faithful to himself—the writer's word engaged him, and he had to withstand its consequences, without which it could not be taken seriously. But the "right to aberration" that Paulhan argued before the "literary court" in the aftermath of the Liberation was only the beginning of an evolution that would lead him, by an effect of repulsion, to join the camp of the "indulgent" and condemn the purge outright in the *Lettre aux directeurs de la Résistance* (1952). This position was not yet fixed in September 1944, since Paulhan could still resent the "protections" that benefited certain authors listed on the first "blacklist."

The fact that the effect of repulsion of the members of the underground CNE with respect to the "moralist" newcomers to the committee was fully in play is also clear from the stance of someone like Jean Guéhenno. Like François Mauriac, he had also passed for a moralist in comparison with Paulhan a year earlier, during the *Comoedia* affair, and still wrote to his friend on August 17, 1944: "Currently, I feel that I will never be able to fraternize, it seems to me, whether in a review or a newspaper, with men whom I have constantly disdained for the past four years."[32] Yet Guéhenno refused to join the protest of Gabriel Marcel and Jean Schlumberger, aligning instead with Paulhan to the surprise of Jean Blanzat.[33] Underground solidarity was the predominant element here. Jean Guéhenno again expressed his "disgust" with the CNE to Paulhan, after the meeting on September 30, which he qualified as a session of "military courts." "It would be brave to resign," he would tell him in November.[34] Above all, this "disgust" reflected the sentiment of dispossession that members of the first underground committee felt with respect to their venture, which to a large extent dictated their progressive withdrawal, although their feeling of solidarity, still weighty, did not allow them to openly disown what the venture had become.

The relations between the CNE and the legal system revealed the ambiguous position of the former. The CNE aspired to be the institutionalized expression of the function of intellectuals as a group as it was defined during the Dreyfus affair. Born precisely of a confrontation with the justice system, this function materialized through an unprecedented manner of claiming the right of intellectuals to intervene in public affairs. Nevertheless, between the intellectual's right to protest and his recourse to political powers in order to regulate the functioning of the literary field, there was, as I have observed several times, a border that actually constituted the dividing line between the autonomous and heteronomous logics at work in the field. Paulhan's formula, "Neither judges nor snitches," traced its limits. And those were the limits that the CNE confronted in its attempt to become institutionalized as an authority of professional representation recognized by the state. Recourse to the apparatus of constraint monopolized by the state in order to impose new deontological rules on the profession was thus perceived, from the two opposing viewpoints that in large part structured the debates on the purge, as either a principle of professionalization (traced on the model of the press),[35] or as a source of heteronomy. At the CNE, this last point ended up winning out.

From then on, the committee would tirelessly repeat that the list only engaged its members. Thus in late 1946, when Pierre Benoit's name was removed from the list, the CNE would publish an update, recalling that

> the entirely moral sanctions taken by the writers of the CNE following the Liberation in their own field are absolutely independent of the legal decisions that may involve collaborationist writers. The CNE has not contributed to those decisions. It did not call for any of them. It limited itself to drawing up a list of writers with whom, following the very charter of the organization, the members of the CNE promise not to collaborate in any way.
>
> These moral sanctions are not adopted for a defined period. They are however subject to revision at any time by the CNE itself. These two attributes further distinguish them from legal sanctions [...].[36]

It would go on to specify that the authors named in the list were "variously guilty," the removal of names did not signify a "revision" of the list, but a limitation of these sanctions over time according to the gravity of the offending acts and the subsequent attitude of the author. In 1947, Vercors would publish a parable on this theme, entitled *Petit pamphlet de dîners chez Gazette*: the narrator refuses to sit down with a rapist of young girls. The introduction is explicit:

> I caught so much flack from a certain press! We all caught so much! "Police," they said to us, "Detectives," and "Where is the freedom of thought that you claimed to defend?" [. . .] I tried in vain to explain that it had never been about that. Never about forbidding others to write, but on the contrary about keeping us from writing with them; that, as a result, the newspapers were perfectly free to publish the writers of their choice, free to choose between them and us.[37]

According to Herbert Lottman "blacklisting was a moral sanction, with uncertain financial effects."[38] Yet, judging by the letters from newspapers, reviews, and anthology authors asking the CNE to send them the "blacklist" so as not to commit an indiscretion,[39] the "blacklist" had a real effect on the intellectual landscape. The professional boycott ended up excluding "undesirable" authors from the literary field. This was the implicit consequence of the committee members' refusal to maintain publishing relations with them, at a time when publishers and editors, worried about clearing themselves, rushed to announce the titles of Resistance writers. On the other hand, in 1947, when the credit of the Resistance had declined, the commitment made by the members of the CNE only hindered their own freedom to maneuver, limiting their publishing ventures to a few forums, including *Les Lettres françaises*. The fact that the moral sanctions inflicted on the "authors" had turned against the members of the CNE did not only result from the distance taken with respect to the legal purge, which deprived the "blacklist" of any status other than symbolic: it reflected, as we will see later, the CNE's loss of the power of excommunication after the departure of the great elders in December 1946.

THE PROFESSIONAL PURGE

The extension of the CNE's power of excommunication did not only find its first limits in the opposition of some of its members. The CNE did not obtain the monopoly it sought in the regulation of the profession. Still, its role was not limited to a moral sanction. It was represented among the authorities of the professional purge. And if its members felt the need to distance themselves from official procedures, it was because oversight over the purge very quickly escaped the writers.

In parallel with legal measures, a procedure of professional purge was put in place that fell within the jurisdiction of the Ministry of National Education.[40]

The ordinance of May 30, 1945, instituted a Comité national d'épuration (purge committee) for writers, authors, and composers, and another for artist-painters, illustrators, sculptors, and engravers. Societies of authors were mandated by the provisional government to file complaints with this committee: the CNE obtained a mandate, in the same way as authors' associations like the Société des gens de lettres, the Société des auteurs et compositeurs dramatiques (SACD), the Société des auteurs, compositeurs et éditeurs de musique (SACEM), the Société des orateurs conférenciers (SOC), and the Association des écrivains combattants. The ministry's general direction of arts and letters asked these six societies to elect representatives, twenty-four in total, who in turn elected twelve among themselves, six on the professional level, six résistants. The minister then named the six members who would compose the committee (three professionals and three résistants).

The CNE elected Claude Morgan, Jacques Debû-Bridel, Francis Ponge, and Gabriel Audisio. It was Audisio who would be chosen to sit on the Comité d'épuration de gens de lettres, which was presided over by Gérard Frèche, attorney general with the Paris Court of Appeals. It also included two representatives of the SDGL (Simone Saint-Clair and Francis Ambrière), one representative of the Société des auteurs, compositeurs, et éditeurs de musique (Joseph Szyfer), and a representative of the Écrivains combattants (General Bremond). Aside from Gabriel Audisio, official spokesman of the CNE, another of its members served on the Comité d'épuration: Charles Vildrac, delegated by the Société des auteurs et compositeurs dramatiques (he was, let us recall, a member of the CNE commission for the creation of the "blacklist").

In October 1945, the Comité d'épuration des gens de lettres announced that it had settled at 3, rue de Valois and asked that all complaints filed against writers be referred to it. The elected societies each had their own purge commission. Thus the SACD and the SOC had sent a questionnaire to their members regarding their attitude during the Occupation. Aside from a few definitive exclusions leveled against notorious collaborators who had fled to Germany (Alain Laubreaux, Jacques de Lesdain, Georges Oltramare) or those who had been found guilty by the courts, the Société des auteurs dramatiques had refrained from deciding its members' cases, and had sent the 564 questionnaires received to the Comité d'épuration. On the other hand, the SGDL had applied thirty-two sanctions in May 1945, and would record thirteen others in 1946, for a total of thirty-six definitive removals—including Abel Bonnard, Jacques Boulenger, Jacques Chardonne, Alphonse de Chateaubriant, André Demaison, Pierre Drieu La Rochelle, Alain Laubreaux, Camille Mauclair, André Thérive—five temporary exclusions, and four reprimands. Fifteen other cases, including those of Ajalbert, René Benjamin, José Germain, and Abel Hermant were pending in late 1945, mostly awaiting the results of the judicial investigation. By that time, the Association des écrivains combattants had also excluded twenty members, including Pierre Benoit, Jacques Boulenger, Paul Chack, André Demaison, Pierre Drieu La Rochelle, José Germain, Henri Massis, André Salmon, André Thérive; two members were suspended and ten others had pending cases. These lists were transmitted to the Comité d'épuration. For its part, the CNE sent the "blacklist."[41]

Starting in November, Gabriel Audisio consulted with the president of the CNE, Jacques Debû-Bridel, in order to know the exact position of the committee with respect to writers who were subject to sanctions and requested a reviewed and corrected copy of the "blacklist," according to the modifications planned during the last general assembly of the CNE (they had considered removing certain names from the list). Two weeks later, he expressed the desire to inform the CNE of his "scruples with regard to the purge." The CNE had decided, he recalled, to refuse to apply one of the sanctions planned by the legislative texts, which forbade an author to publish during a certain amount of time, but Audisio had not managed to rally the majority of the purge committee on this point. The Comité d'épuration des gens de lettres actually had the authority to temporarily ban the reedition of works that garnered the sanction, along with new works, articles, conferences, and so forth, and the collection of royalties or any other benefit drawn from cultural production. The sanctions were limited to two years, or, for authors sentenced by a court of law, to the duration of the sentence. The exchange of letters between Aragon and Audisio in March 1946 does not allow us to know the point of view adopted by the CNE, but it seems that the directive board was divided on this question.[42]

The fact still remains that the Comité d'épuration did not take Audisio's proposition into account since, out of fifty-six authors or composers whose cases were examined before the end of 1946, twelve would receive the maximum sentence of two years of banning (including Ajalbert). Twenty others would receive a lighter sanction, ranging from three to eighteen months (the suspension was, in several cases, mixed with the sanction given by other professional authorities, and sometimes served retroactively), including Montherlant, Paul Fort, André Thérive, while fourteen, including Pierre Benoit, Paul Morand, and Armand Petitjean, would have their cases dismissed (ten files were closed, five due to the committee's lack of jurisdiction, two due to death, three for other reasons).

In October 1946, Charles Vildrac informed the Comité d'épuration that he intended to give up his duties due to the length of his service and the weight of the task. He invited the other members of the committee to join him in this gesture. Called into service at the court, the president, Gérard Frèche, also announced that he intended to have his alternate replace him. The committee's work seems to have been interrupted at this point and would not recommence until 1949. On November 29, 1946, Gabriel Audisio also sent his resignation to the Comité d'épuration.[43]

The Ministry of National Education having asked the CNE to designate another member, the directive board tasked Paul Eluard with soliciting Raymond Queneau or Lucien Scheler.[44] At the insistence of Aragon and Elsa Triolet, Scheler accepted the mission, and having participated in one session, gave his resignation. The description that Lucien Scheler gave of this meeting deserves to be reported. The passion with which the witness delivered it more than forty years later, without having been questioned about this experience, attests to the mark that such experiences can leave. I transcribe approximately in free indirect discourse, on the basis of my notes. The commission summoned the person under investigation and questioned him about the motives of his "collaboration." They asked the author who was summoned that day why he collaborated. He said that he had had to leave Paris and did not have any work. He entered the local newspaper. After a half hour, the poor guy was trembling like a leaf, as if they were going to cut off his head. He was asked to leave the room so they could deliberate. A member of the commission suggested that he be banned from publishing for two years. But how will this guy eat, Scheler asked? It was an old guy who had done literary criticism; he hadn't written anything. They suggested six months. Scheler asked them to leave him alone. A member of the commission was astonished that Scheler, who was a Communist, was the most indulgent. Two others intervened to justify their presence. For the sake of principle, they would give him an official warning. On that note, the members of the commission agreed. They were ready to condemn, the wretches, Scheler concluded.[45]

While the "blacklist" served in the review of dossiers for the professional purge, the role that the CNE representatives played in the Comité d'épuration was thus, unlike the stereotypical idea of the CNE, all moderation. Let us note, moreover, that the inauguration of an official process helped diminish the impact of the "blacklist," and even discredit it.

According to Herbert Lottman, the limited nature of the list of authors sanctioned by the committee, in comparison with the "blacklist" of the CNE, can be explained, among other things, by the fact that the Comité d'épuration had decided not to hear matters concerning authors who were involved in the legal purge.[46] Thus, in a number of cases, the dossier was prepared, then frozen while awaiting documents from the trial. But in fact, only thirty-five names appearing on the "blacklist" were included on the list of 172 dossiers belonging to the Comité d'épuration, and eleven were subject to sanctions. Others, even though they appeared on the "blacklist" and were subject to legal investigation, did not even have their cases prepared: there is no file in the name of Marcel Jouhandeau, who was subject to legal action starting in May 1945, and who would be exonerated on December 1, 1945.[47] Furthermore, dossiers existed for authors who did not appear on the "blacklist," like Cocteau, Roland Dorgelès, and Paul Fort.

Should we attribute these gaps, or even these incompatibilities between the different types of sanction (moral, professional, legal), to a relative autonomy of the authorities with respect to each other, or to a lack of coordination due to the hasty, confused, and spotty nature of the preparation of dossiers, already observed by Herbert Lottman, and confirmed by the examination of the dossiers? Shortcomings, absence of incriminating evidence, lack of coordination between the legal and professional proceedings, stagnation:[48] so many hints of the confusion and the haste in which the first professional purge was conducted, and the inertia that characterized the second phase. The professional purge had to be quick. It confronted the inevitable difficulties and administrative delays and the weight of the task entrusted to its representatives. As I've said, the Comité d'épuration des gens de lettres would only return to its work in 1949, under the presidency of a lawyer named Milhac. From April to June 1949, twenty new—and final—sanctions were handed down, including nine that inflicted the maximum sentence of the totality of temporary bans for two years (this was the case for Alphonse de Chateaubriant and André Demaison, notably), and ten ranging from one to twelve months (only one person was exonerated).

THE STRUCTURAL LIMITS OF THE LITERARY PURGE

The heavy sanctions that hit the intellectual world have often been compared to the indulgence that benefited the economic sector, although it had furnished the material and technical means of the Collaboration. This contrast, as we will see later, shocked the literary milieus from the beginning of 1945 following the death sentences of Georges Suarez, Chack, Béraud, and Brasillach (only Béraud would be pardoned). It was not the raw statistics of the literary purge (which could not yet be predicted at that date), but rather the severity of the sentence to which intellectuals were exposed—death—that was its source. This first image of the purge of intellectuals would dominate the assessment that would later be given to it, independently of its evolution over time. Certainly, we know of at least twenty cases of writers and journalists who were condemned by the court of justice of the Seine department, among whom nine received the death penalty (four were executed). But if we consider, solely for indicative purposes, the population of my statistical study (in which only seven of the authors condemned by the court of justice of the Seine department figure), of the twenty-eight writers who were subjected to judicial inquiries and/or legal action (apart from deceased writers such as Drieu La Rochelle or Fernandez), fourteen, that is to say half of them, had their cases dismissed; five others were condemned in absentia (note that I included among the condemned not only those that appeared before a court of justice, but also two cases of national degradation pronounced by the Civic Chamber; for at least one of the other cases, the investigation was abandoned due to the death of the author in question). What remains, in fact, is the gravity of the sentence to which intellectuals were exposed.

The severity of the sanctions that struck writers was certainly not due to the actions of the CNE and the repeated exhortations of the literary generation born of the Resistance to punish the "traitors." Various hypotheses, of a practical or political order, have been proposed to explain these "excesses." First, for the punishment to be exemplary, it was necessary to condemn renowned collaborators, whose dossiers could be prepared quickly. The intellectuals fit the bill. Since the harshness of the verdicts decreased over the course of years, it is not surprising that they were among the most severely punished.[49] Moreover, the needs of the reconstruction on one hand (and probably the provisional government's will to counterbalance the rise of the Communists to numerous leadership positions), the support they could obtain from powerful people on the other (not to mention the organizations of professional defense), suffice to explain the indulgence that benefited industrials and magistrates. All in all, public and private institutions would be relatively protected in light of the sanctions that befell individuals.

We find this contrast within the literary world: while the purge struck individuals, it only partially affected the institutions of literary life, as we will see in the case of the academies. Similarly, it only moderately sanctioned press bosses and editors. "The structures are spared at the expense of the creator," Pierre Assouline has remarked.[50] While the press still experienced an important reorganization, overall publishing would not be more impacted by the purge than by the Occupation (only the "Aryanized" publishing houses were returned to their owners), in spite of the heavy charges that weighed against the publishers.[51] Or at least the relative cost of the purge decreased as a consequence of the degree of institutionalization.

The CNE still intended to oversee the publishing purge. In March 1944, it had sent the CNR a request along those lines. Voted by the committees of the Northern and Southern zones, it was simultaneously published in *Les Lettres françaises* and *Les Étoiles*. The CNE insisted that "the conduct of each Publisher or Director of a publishing house during the Occupation should be submitted, in conformance with the procedure established for the press, to an inquest by a Commission of jurists assisted by representatives from the Comité National des Écrivains in order to establish the responsibility of each, and to aid in the action of justice." The committee deemed indispensable that the publishers or directors who had "betrayed" the "duties for which they were responsible" be deprived of "any means of influence over French public opinion," and that they be "forced to indemnify the authors whose rights they had sacrificed, using the financial gains realized under the Occupation."[52]

At first, the CNE had even planned to apply "moral sanctions" to the publishers, similar to those it would adopt with respect to the writers. In the edition of *Les Lettres françaises* published in November 1943, which dealt with collaborationist writers, a "warning to editors," voted by the CNE of the two zones, was published. It was specified that this warning was not a charter of relations between writers and publishers, but that it had the "value of a solemn warning to them." This warning invoked, for the first time, the possibility of authors boycotting publishers, a "true writers' strike."[53] Herbert Lottman has aptly pointed out that in the CNE charter, which listed the types of "publishing relations" that the members of the CNE should refuse to entertain with the authors on the "blacklist," the publishing houses disappeared as such: it was no longer a question of anything but series, anthologies, and periodicals.[54]

It was actually in the material aspects of the profession that the preeminence of professional interests over writers' ethical positions became the clearest. The interdependence between author and publisher, while it guaranteed the functioning of this symbolic universe based on the denial of the economy, was also one of the structural limits of the relative autonomy of the literary field.[55] We have seen this principle at work under the Occupation. But we still should not forget that the authors of *La* NRF publishing house, for example, also pushed Gaston Gallimard to reopen his publishing house. Similarly, let us recall that the question of the legal publication of books had quickly been excluded from the debates on the norms of conduct that the Resistance writers were to adopt. In the summer of 1943, Jean Schlumberger, having revised his initial severity with respect to Gaston Gallimard's attitude and what he called "the *NRF* of the armistice," explained his position to Roger Martin du Gard, who congratulated him for this greater understanding:

> Believe me: a certain stiffness of attitude did not come from lack of understanding. I certainly saw the difficulties that Gaston had to deal with. But,

without the intimidation that we exerted over him, he would have made many more concessions. If we have, in general, managed to prevent the fall of literature, it is thanks to the stiffening of a few [. . .] The day will come when it will be quite useful for our friend to be able to point to us.[56]

And in fact, the list of witnesses who testified in the dossier created by Gallimard for his defense was impressive: Sartre, Camus, Queneau, Eluard, Father Bruckberger, Paulhan, Malraux, Martin du Gard, Chamson, Groethuysen, Joë Bousquet, Brice Parain, Pierre Brisson, Dionys Mascolo, Armand Salacrou, Henri Mondor, and others.[57] For their part, Aragon and Elsa Triolet would intervene in Denoël's favor; Mauriac and Lacretelle in favor of Grasset.[58] The fact that the Resistance writers hurried to testify in the defense of their editors says a great deal about these bonds of interdependence, which were not simply the result of immediate material interests, but also of actual solidarity.

The example of the purge commission for booksellers and publishing moreover shows how interdependence transformed into solidarity and complicity when professional interests were threatened from the exterior. Among the three members of the CNE who sat on the purge commission for publishing, Sartre, Seghers, and Vercors—the first two as official representatives of the committee, the third as a Resistance publisher—it was the two author-publishers, Seghers and Vercors, who were in favor of rigor, versus Sartre, a fervent defender of Gaston Gallimard, to the extent that he gave Seghers the impression of representing him "as much as—if not more than—the CNE."[59] In the account that he left on the purge in publishing, Vercors emphasized the bonds of friendship, a representation through which this outsider perceived, with a certain hint of bitter irony, the relations of complicity between author and publisher:

> While many among us, Pierre Seghers, Emmanuel Mounier, Francisque Gay, show themselves ready for a certain rigor, a few others are hardly ready. Sartre has too many ties to Gaston Gallimard, Mauriac with Bernard Grasset, to think of giving them even a light sentence. The effect of all this will be that the commission, obtaining nothing, not even its own recognition, will very quickly die out. And that the publishers, such as Grasset who offered himself to the Nazis as their "Gauleiter" of French publishing, or others who rivaled the signers of the "Otto list" to see who would obey the directives the most obsequiously, who would eat the most Jews, already shamelessly announce their new works including several, of course, on the resistance . . . [60]

Unlike Sartre, Seghers and Vercors were more competitive than complicit with regard to the prestigious NRF publishing house. Seghers, as we remember,

turned down the offer that Gallimard made to publish *Poésie 44.* . . . Bitterly
disappointed, Vercors saw the authors he had published in the underground
leave for Gallimard, attributing this departure to the material difficulties that
his young house encountered: "And that's why it was quite understandable that
the writers of the Éditions de Minuit, who had all pushed me to continue, well,
they ended up at Gallimard." Eluard's departure, in particular, had "affected"
him, he specified. The resolution of the government that made the paper quota
proportional to prewar production levels could only reinforce the feeling that
these newcomers to the publishing world had been the victims of an injustice.[61]
Yet as Anne Simonin has shown, the Éditions de Minuit benefited from an allocation of paper (although insufficient), obtained thanks to Malraux's intervention, and were given an office. In this sense they were privileged with respect
to a small house like the Éditions Charlot, which then emigrated to Paris.[62]

Seghers and Vercors resigned from the commission in the winter of 1944,
after having noted their incapacity to impose their views and contest institutionalized positions like those of Gallimard and Grasset. They did not leave
without having achieved a sizable victory: the suppression of *La NRF*, although
de Gaulle wished to see it reappear because of its prestige abroad.[63] Vercors,
who fought to ban it, remembered, in an interview I conducted with him: "[. . .]
I believe that I went with Seghers to find Sartre in his little hotel room, to persuade him, because he defended Gallimard with all his might. And we achieved
this compromise to not punish the house, but to punish *La NRF*."[64] *La NRF*,
which had been given to the occupant as collateral to ensure the proper functioning of the publishing house, was thus again sacrificed for the "safeguard" of
the house. This ban was all the more symbolic since, as Pascal Fouché has observed, the purge commission for publishing had no legal status.[65] The sacrifice
of *La NRF* traces the structural limits of the literary purge. It also shows that the
stakes of the internal struggles it inspired amounted to the conservation or the
transformation of the power relations that structured the prewar literary field.

A GENERATIONAL WAR

The sacrifice of *La NRF*, emblem of "literary treason," did not arouse much emotion among the writers of the new generation. Even as he defended his publisher and the interests of the house, and without allowing us to invoke a cynical
calculation on his part, Sartre would soon be able to profit from the compromise that had been reached, since the following year, in October 1945, a new review would appear at Gallimard under his direction. This review, *Les Temps
modernes*, would claim to occupy the vacant space left by *La NRF*. This succession
shows the reversal of the literary values that *La NRF* had helped establish during

the interwar period. Against "pure literature," Sartre's project promoted an "engaged literature." The break occurred within a continuity: Sartre hoarded the symbolic capital accumulated by the Gallimard house and especially *La NRF* in order to nullify the literary order that the review had instituted during the interwar period; but, increasing this capital by adjusting it to the new demand in the intellectual field, he simultaneously ensured the reproduction of the house's dominant position at the very time it seemed threatened.

The project had taken shape when it was decided to liquidate the review in the end of October 1944. It was first entitled *La Condition humaine* before being renamed *Les Temps modernes* in December 1944. It was clearly perceived by the old guard of *La NRF* as a challenge extended by the young generation that was progressively establishing itself at Gallimard. In November 1944, Jean Schlumberger thus wrote to André Gide: "Sartre's review, completely philosophical in principle, seems to want to encroach on private land. We will get off with inventing something new and crushing this rabble with our quality."[66] At the same time, Julien Benda was inquiring of Jean Paulhan: "Is it true that *La NRF* will continue under the name of 'la condition humaine,' director Sartre. In that case it would not often see my work."[67]

For his part, Jean Paulhan considered relaunching *La NRF*, at Gaston Gallimard's request. His maneuvers to take over the review in May and June 1943 had failed, as we saw. Shortly thereafter, while Aragon was putting plans together with Gallimard in order to revive the review, Paulhan had let him know that while he wished to join its editorial committee, he did not insist on serving as the director, preferring to devote himself to his own work, and moreover fearing—accurately—that a review like the one he had designed before the war was no longer possible: "And then, I have made, I would like to remake, I would only be capable of remaking one review: the one where Benda could appear next to Jouhandeau, Aragon with Audiberti. That review will be no more possible tomorrow (for the opposite reasons) than it has been for the last three years."[68] At the approach of the Liberation, Paulhan nonetheless ceded to Gallimard's will, but set his conditions. It was thus with bitterness that he learned he had been named liquidator of the review: "They have named me liquidator of *La NRF*. Perhaps this was a gesture. It seemed a bit bitter to me. It is, I suppose, a job without salary, honor, or work. And the ex-subscribers will be too afraid of a trap to raise the slightest complaint. Well, all of that is unpleasant."[69]

Pulled between the generation of the founders of *La NRF* and that of the pretenders, Paulhan agreed to be a member of the editorial board of *Les Temps modernes*, which would benefit from his long experience in producing a review.[70] He thus concretely achieved the work of heritage transmission. Yet this position in the shadow of the writer he had largely helped promote before the war hardly suited him. It suited him all the less since the project of *Les Temps modernes*, in the space it granted current events and the conception of an "engaged literature" that its director promoted, was the opposite of Paulhan's project. This is demonstrated by the *Cahiers de la Pléiade* venture that Paulhan began to envisage in March 1945, in continuity with the project of an "intemporal" *NRF* that he had been designing since 1942; the new venture took shape in April 1946. In the meantime, Paulhan had left the editorial committee of *Les Temps modernes*.[71]

Tensions, and soon open conflicts, with the new literary generation that established itself at the Liberation undoubtedly owed something to this relative demotion of the "éminence grise" of literature. Vercors thus attributed the distant relations he maintained with Paulhan to the role that he had played in suppressing *La NRF*:

> [With Paulhan] not much of a relationship either. All the more so since there was a big obstacle, there was this purge committee that I was a part of, and so I absolutely wanted to ban the publication of *La Nouvelle revue française*, at least for a few years, because *La Nouvelle revue française* had represented all French intelligence during the interwar period and could not have started representing it again after what it had been. And Paulhan never really forgave me for that. He never, how should I say this, violently held it against me but, obviously, he wasn't happy about it.[72]

Whatever the case may be, the marginalization of Paulhan's position, the disrepute cast on his conception of the Republic of Letters, according to which only literary motives justified exclusion, and the imposition of what seemed like a "didactic literature" to him—we saw that he dreaded it as the Liberation approached—helped exacerbate his opposition to this new generation and his move toward the academic pole of the literary field.

At the time of *La NRF*'s burial, the destitution of the great elders was playing out in parallel on another stage, that of *Les Lettres françaises*. It was the infamous "Gide affair," another key moment in the intergenerational struggle for the conservation or transformation of the power relations structuring the literary field at the time of the Liberation. Despite its parodic aspects, it marked a new defeat for the team of founders of *La NRF*, powerless to defend against the offensive that targeted one of their own.

As the organ of the CNE, *Les Lettres françaises* occupied the most prestigious position in the new literary press in the aftermath of the Liberation, uniting the great names of prewar literature like Mauriac, Paulhan, Duhamel, the now "national" poets Aragon and Eluard, and the best of the new generation born of the Resistance, Sartre and Vercors. Under the direction of Claude Morgan, it struggled to maintain and increase the symbolic capital acquired in the Resistance by pursuing the work of gathering "French writers" worthy of this name, above and beyond generational, literary, and ideological divisions. A sign of the recognition of the prestige that the committee and its journal enjoyed at that time, André Gide, who was still in Algeria, sent it a text on "The Deliverance of Tunis," announcing his membership in the CNE. A week after the publication of Gide's text, a protestation from Aragon appeared in *Les Lettres françaises*, in which he tried to deal him a lethal blow by making him a precursor of the Collaboration through his anti-Bolshevism, and quoting his journal from 1940 that evoked the possibility of "compromising with yesterday's enemy."[73] The ambiguous attitude of *Les Lettres françaises* with regard to Gide was very probably the expression of tensions between Claude Morgan and Aragon, of which other traces moreover exist (in 1947, Aragon would take over *Les Lettres françaises* and Morgan would be definitively ousted in 1953).

Prewar grudges surface in this offensive. Aragon had not forgiven Gide for his *Retour de l'URSS*, as indicated by the title of the article, "André Gide's Return." Its meaning did not escape anyone: "[. . .] the very title of the article of the 'man who used to cover the French army with shit' betrays the partisan: 'The Return of André Gide' . . . who had not been at all forgiven for 'Return from the USSR,'" Galtier-Boissière noted in his journal.[74] Aragon also probably held Gide's contributions to the first issues of Drieu's NRF against him as well. Strengthened not only by his position as a "national poet" and the charisma that he exerted over the young generation, but also the tacit support of a new ally, Paul Claudel—an all the more precious ally because he occupied a position that was very far from his own—Aragon could finally aspire to dethrone the "pope" of interwar literature.

The encounter between the "communist aristocrat" according to René Tavernier's expression, and the Catholic ambassador-poet with peasant shoulders— "that rocky massif of French thought"—definitely took place in September 1944, before Aragon's return to Paris. The reconciliation between the poet "who believed in heaven and the one who did not" had been very carefully organized by René Tavernier, assisted by Auguste Anglès, and in the presence of André Rousseaux. The lunch promised to be tense:

> The conversation floundered a bit because we were intimidated. What was Aragon thinking? What was Claudel thinking? They didn't really know how to catch hold of each other, how to speak to each other. A mistake was

made. One of us had the imprudence of saying the name of André Gide [. . .] Claudel and Aragon stood up suddenly like two devils coming out of a box and embraced each other across the table in a mutual hatred of the author of *Les Nourritures terrestres.* From that moment on, a frank gaiety reigned, the wine flowed, the conversation was easy and everything was wonderful.[75]

The two men, who had failed to convert Gide—one to Catholicism, the other to Communism—communed that day in their resentment for the invincible rival. It was following this encounter that on September 23, 1944, *Les Lettres françaises* published the statement mentioning the "omission" of Claudel's name from the list of CNE members. This new alliance thus gave a particular emphasis to the attack launched two months later against André Gide. The CNE, which included the chief representatives of the group of founders of *La NRF,* Valéry, Schlumberger, and Claudel, could allow itself—or so Aragon, at least, believed—to reject the membership of Gide, figurehead of the group, who more than his colleagues had continued to exert an influence over the young generations up until the war, a position that Aragon had since disputed. This rejection was a show of force that displayed the CNE's power of exclusion.

The Gide affair seemed to confirm the defeat of the elders, reduced to powerlessness, with respect to the rising generation that was establishing itself at the CNE. While Camus, estranged from the CNE, supported Gide, Aragon easily obtained the support of the committee's young pretenders. This is demonstrated by the attitude of Guillevic, the disciple that Paul Valéry fought over with Aragon, and whom Valéry ordered to choose between them. Engaged in the ranks of the Communist Party, won over by the new prophetic figures represented by Aragon and Eluard, Guillevic made his choice. "He [Valéry] died from it. He died four or six months later. I represented Aragon, the CNE, etc., and he said to me: I won't put up with you hanging around Aragon, you have to choose between Aragon and me. They hated each other, he and Aragon. They had a terrible hatred."[76] The non-resignation of the elders, particularly Jean Schlumberger, following this affair signified their defeat: it would take two more years for them to resolve to leave the CNE, after Paulhan's departure.[77] The letter that Schlumberger sent Gide on this occasion expresses their sense of helplessness well:

A very unanimous indignation answers the odious ambush of *Les Lettres fr(ançaises)* [. . .] The friends are still looking for the best line of conduct to display their disgust. It is probable that it will *not* be an article. A press polemic is exactly what the adversaries hope for. It would give them the means to fly into a greater rage and we are always at a disadvantage in the face of bad faith. In any case, it seems advisable that you not abandon a perfect disdain. Distant as you are, not in any state to counter quickly and discern the maneuvers, you would fall into the traps [...]

And as a postscript:

[Pierre] Brisson also thinks that silence is the cleverest. What is necessary is for us to manage to withdraw en masse from the CNE. Many are those who impatiently await a good opportunity. This article by A[ragon] would be a bad pretext.[78]

Paulhan, who was always fond of contradictions that, for him, constituted the primary rule of the game, giving it a breath of autonomous life, adopted an ambivalent position. Dissociating Aragon's attitude from that of *Les Lettres françaises*, which he implicitly assimilated to the Communists and blamed—wrongly, I think—for the affair (Paulhan had little sympathy for Morgan who looked like an intruder in this literary family), he wrote to Schlumberger: "Aragon criticizing Gide for having written that patriotism has its highs and lows, it's rather *joyous*. But what about the conduct of *Les Lettres françaises* in this affair? It's a pretty foul trap, attracting Gide to one's own turf (without having warned him), so as to better crush him."[79] In the letter that he sent to Gide, he compared Aragon to Henri Massis, before concluding: "It is less serious in itself—Massis knew how to do it better" (read: Massis respected the rules of the game better).[80]

While Aragon's offensive against Gide illustrates the collusion of the two principles of division that I have exposed, namely the intergenerational struggle and the opposition between moralism and "pure literature," the parallel with Massis also confirms the recurrent use that was made of moralism to reverse the power relations in the literary field: moral demands could serve as a weapon for the pretenders against the elders. But the parallel ends there. It is not a matter here of ratifying the equation between Action française and the Communist Party that Paulhan tried to establish, and which was only meaningful from his point of view, that of the defense of "pure literature" against moralism. The political and social configuration of the Liberation and the "revolutionary" atmosphere that reigned actually led to a total reversal of the frame of the debate over the "responsibility of the writer." Thanks to the struggles led during the Occupation, the new generation was in a position to impose its own conception of the "responsibility of the writer," redefined according to the stakes that grounded those struggles.

The Responsibility of the Writer

The writers who had taken part in the Resistance appropriated or were assigned a role in the reconstruction of what is typically called the national conscience. This made them stars in the new press: Albert Camus directed the daily *Combat*, François Mauriac was the editorialist at *Le Figaro*. New politico-literary weeklies born of clandestinity appeared, *Les Lettres françaises, Action, Carrefour, La Bataille, Gavroche*, taking the vacant space left by the disappearance of *Candide, Gringoire, Je suis partout, La Gerbe*. They were representative of the new political order.

Les Lettres françaises and *Action* were situated in the orbit of the Communist Party. As the organ of the CNE, *Les Lettres françaises* became a "great literary, artistic, and political weekly." Its first issue opened, as we saw, with the "Manifesto" of the CNE that called for remaining "united in victory" and for "punishing the traitors." The work of brilliant contributors (Mauriac, Duhamel, Maritain, Sartre, Paulhan, Queneau, Vercors, Benda, Cassou, Martin-Chauffier), added to the regular columns of Louis Parrot, Georges Sadoul, Georges Besson, Georges Pillement, and Henry Malherbe, made it the most prestigious of the forums born of the intellectual Resistance. Directed by Claude Morgan, it reached a circulation of 190,000 copies.

Also born of clandestinity, *Action*, "weekly of the French independence" with Maurice Kriegel-Valrimont as the political director and Pierre Courtade as the editor in chief, assembled a young team including Pierre Hervé, Victor Leduc, Claude Roy, Roger Vailland, Francis Ponge, Dominique Desanti, and Edgar Morin, who represented the new generation of Communist intellectuals. Its members often met at the home of Marguerite Duras, rue Saint-Benoît. "It was perhaps very useful to the Party that we made a living communist newspaper, free of jargon, that could publish Georges Limbour and Jacques Prévert, Simone de Beauvoir and Jean Duché, Alexandre Astruc and Raymond Queneau between Wurmser and Garaudy. But we didn't make an open newspaper out of craftiness," Claude Roy affirmed.[81] *Action* was soon printing 100,000 copies.[82]

Spearheaded by a team linked to the Christian Democrats (Émilien Amaury, Robert Buron, Félix Garas, and Yves Helleu formed its directive board), and close to the new Catholic party, Mouvement républicain populaire (MRP), *Carrefour*, which took over for the Christianity-inspired booklet *Cahiers du travaillisme français*, intended to be the "meeting place for patriots of good will" and the "support of a purged regime capable of ensuring [...] the structural reforms that are necessary [...] to give back to our country, exploited in the ordeal, a collective mystique and dynamism."[83] *Carrefour* gathered those of the academic and Catholic pole who had more or less converted to Gaullism: Jules Romains, André Maurois, François Mauriac, Georges Duhamel, the Tharaud brothers, Jacques de Lacretelle, Robert d'Harcourt, Henri Mondor, Georges Bernanos, Gabriel Marcel, and Denis de Rougemont. It was also open to former contributors to Drieu's *NRF*: Marcel Arland, Henry de Montherlant, Audiberti, and André Salmon. *Carrefour* quickly became a forum for anti-Communism, and soon, like *Le Figaro littéraire*, a place to go to for the dissidents of the CNE.

Thus, behind the surface unanimity of the Resistance, embodied in the literary world by the CNE, a new polarization emerged. Partially intersecting with the divisions of the political field where a rivalry between Gaullism and Communism slowly established itself, it opposed writers like Malraux and Mauriac to a young generation imbued with revolutionary values, Communist or other, although this opposition did not exhaust the stakes of the divisions of the literary field. The first divergences took shape in the polemics on the purge, which gave rise to the debate on the "responsibility of the writer."

The intergenerational struggle between the elders and the pretenders, the political division between right and left, and the opposition between the moralists and the defenders of "pure literature" structured, here again, the position-takings in this debate. But the specificity of the experience of the Occupation and of the conjuncture of the Liberation, lived like a revolutionary period, meant that these position-takings appeared inverted with respect to the forms that the debate on the responsibility of the writer had taken up to that point. In fact, the nationalist moralists like Henry Bordeaux who, in the wake of Paul Bourget, had used the notion of the "responsibility of the writer" to condemn the "bad masters," now found themselves in the camp of the partisans of indulgence, in the name of "national reconciliation," when it was not in the name of the rights of talent (this was precisely the argument that the defenders of the "bad masters" promoted). National moralism, which urged writers to assume their responsibility, seemed to have changed camps in turn, thanks to the redefinition of the stakes under the Occupation, namely the dissociation of conservatism from nationalism, and the work undertaken by the Resistance to reappropriate patriotic moralism: the struggle to regain literary autonomy operated, let us recall, through the reappropriation of "the French spirit."

FRANÇOIS MAURIAC, FROM FOUQUIER-TANVILLE TO SAINT FRANCIS OF THE ASSIZE COURT

"All in all, even if this period immediately following the Liberation was not revolutionary in its events, it was experienced as such in public opinion," Pierre Laborie has observed.[84] From *Action* to *Témoignage chrétien* along with *Combat* and *Franc-Tireur*, the revolutionary theme animated a large part of the new press, and even the most moderate agreed at least on the necessity to undertake social reforms.

The abundance of references to past revolutions to think through the recent past, the present, and the future fueled this revolutionary climate. In continuity with the counterpropaganda of the Resistance, the overhaul of the national conscience first operated through the reaffirmation of the values of the French Revolution that had been swept aside by Vichy. "The capitulation of the nation was only obtained by undermining and destroying the Republic, thanks to errors and lapses, by first acting against the ideal heritage of the great Revolution," Pierre Jean Jouve recalled, inviting his reader to "bring about the mystical reunion of all the forces of France" to finish "the monument of the Revolution."[85] Against the triptych of the National Revolution, "work, family, fatherland," the Republican motto was reestablished, revived by the Resistance: "Liberty, Equality, Fraternity . . . For us, it's no longer an empty formula written on official walls. This motto has been reincarnated, it has become flesh and blood: brothers equal in sacrifice gave their life so that France could be delivered. We will not forget it. Never," François Mauriac wrote.[86] From left to right in the Resistance camp, the résistants were identified with the soldiers of the year II. Against the National Revolution promoted by Vichy, the Liberation was inscribed in the line of 1789, 1793, 1830, 1848, even the Commune. While Georges Bernanos or Jacques Debû-Bridel privileged the liberal revolutions (1789 and 1830), François Mauriac did not hesitate to refer to 1793: "[. . .] the meaning of the nation was awakened in the militant people. The spirit of 93 finally lives again!"[87]

In 1944, the reference to 1793 had a purpose: it legitimized the purge. "And I will recall the arguments based in reason, and stripped of all sadistic sectarianism of Camille Desmoulins and Saint-Just, about the traitor Louis XVI, demonstrating that this criminal had to be judged *not as a citizen, but as an enemy*, for it was a matter of the salvation of the French people," Jean Cassou would write in July 1945, during the Pétain trial.[88] In the same spirit, Claude Morgan quoted Saint-Just: "The Republic is not founded on indulgence, but implacable rigor toward all those who have betrayed."[89] But the Terror was not a unanimously shared reference.[90] Mauriac's position-takings following the Liberation earned him the reputation of an "abject Fouquier-Tinville."*[91] He was moreover not the only one to be described this way. Paul Léautaud, who wrote to Paul-

---

* Antoine-Quentin Fouquier-Tinville (1746–1795) was named public prosecutor of the Revolutionary Tribunal during the Reign of Terror.—Trans.

han: "except for the guillotine—which may come—what we see is not far from 93," awarded Duhamel with the title of "little Fouquier-Tinville."[92]

Mauriac owes his image as a "righter of wrongs" to this reference to 1793 in "The French Nation Has a Soul," a text that appeared in the first legal issue of *Les Lettres françaises*, in which he wrote: "We now understand the meaning of the revolutionary motto that the timid republicans of the Second Empire had cut off from the essential: Liberty, Equality, Fraternity OR DEATH. Yes, or death."[93] Initially intended for the underground Éditions de Minuit, this text became particularly significant in the context of the purge. Mauriac further owed his identification with the "righters of wrongs" to his role as the honorary president of the CNE (a position from which he resigned, as we saw, in early October), and his place alongside the Communists on the directive committee of the National Front. On September 29, he sat at the Mutualité alongside Marcel Cachin, which shocked even his friends. And it was Jean Paulhan who then preached to him the doctrine of forgiveness that he would soon champion:

> [. . .] And, (on a related note) isn't it when a heresy threatens to triumph that we must refuse it more forcefully; when it is close to defeat that we must seriously consider pardoning the heretics? (The heretics. I certainly don't say the heresy. It's totally different. There was a time when people knew how to burn the heretics and still speak to them with tenderness before burning them. Actually, isn't it a Christian secret?).[94]

We cannot give any credit to the interpretation, with its defamatory accents, of Father Bruckberger, who accused Mauriac of having "encouraged" the "fraud of the Communists" out of fear. Father Bruckberger attributed it to Mauriac himself, based on a private conversation with Camus that the latter shared with him. In response to Mauriac who asked him why he had resigned from the CNE, Camus supposedly invoked a "Communist maneuver" and turned the question back to him: "—It's my turn to ask you why you don't resign.—Out of solidarity.—No, Mr. Mauriac, it's out of fear [. . .]—It's actually true, Mauriac admitted."[95] It is true that François Mauriac had great cause to worry about the fate of his brother Pierre, the ex-president of the council of the Order of Physicians of the Gironde under the Vichy regime, who was the target of Communist attacks, and who learned in February 1945 that he was liable to the court of justice. But no more than it justified Mauriac's presence at the CNE and the directive committee of the National Front, this familial anxiety does not suffice to explain the evolution of his positions on the purge.

Just as Mauriac had adopted a prophetic position as a Catholic intellectual during the Spanish Civil War, defying the official discourse of the Church but still speaking within its framework, under the oppression he had shattered that framework to raise his voice to a higher level of universality. The author of *Le Cahier noir* had thus gradually removed not only the anti-Communist accents but also the majority of Christian themes from the successive versions of the manuscript. Even though this action surely corresponded to an ultimately superfluous precaution (Forez's style was easily identifiable), it also gave his message a national bearing in which the different ideological tendencies could recognize themselves. It was definitely in his role as national prophet that Mauriac first intended, in his *Le Figaro* editorials or the articles he gave to *Les Lettres françaises* and *Carrefour*, to "capitalize" on the recognition he had acquired in the intellectual Resistance.

A man of crisis situations, the prophet is apt to legitimate a political power whose legality is still poorly established. We might say that Mauriac played this role in a certain manner with regard to de Gaulle during the two months of "normalization," up to the recognition of the provisional government by the Allies on October 23, 1944. After the legalization of the provisional government, the author of *Le Cahier noir*, while he pursued the prophetic mode, no longer worked in favor of but in conjunction with power, in his role as a Catholic intellectual, as demonstrated by his positions on the purge, his opposition to the Rassemblement populaire français (although his son Claude would be an "organic" intellectual there), his role at the head of the France-Maghreb committee during the Morocco affair (after he had obtained the Nobel Prize in 1953), and his denunciation of torture and his advocacy in favor of negotiations with the FLN during the Algerian War.[96] It was only in 1958, after de Gaulle's return to power, that the writer, then in his seventies, would agree to lay down his arms to receive the Grand-Croix of the Legion of Honor and become a "counselor to the prince."

For the time being, our Fouquier-Tinville began the turnaround that led him to join the camp of the "indulgents" and would earn him the nickname of "Saint Francis of the Assize Courts," with the publication on October 19, 1944, of an article entitled "Justice and the War." The change was clearly perceived in the intellectual milieus. On October 21, the critic Roger Lannes noted in his journal:

> Mauriac takes a violent turn, rises up against the crimes committed in the name of the Liberation. Speaks of a public opinion sickened by the tyrannical spirit of the resistance. It's on the orders of General de Gaulle, I know. But the whole press cries treason. In reality, Mauriac and the writers who, in the beginning were partially responsible for the abominable mess we find ourselves in resemble the sorcerers' apprentices of the fable.[97]

Was it on the orders of General de Gaulle, as Roger Lannes claimed to know? Mauriac did not need an explicit order from de Gaulle to calibrate his prophecy to that of the charismatic leader (with whom he had lunch on September 1, 1944, but whom he would never see alone until February 3, 1945). He had moreover not heeded the two calls to order that de Gaulle sent him through his son Claude, now the general's private secretary, concerning his presence on the directive committee of the National Front. After the Mutualité meeting, Claude Mauriac made a note of how "the General, unhappy about his presence yesterday at the Front National event, approached [his] father," and, at the end of October, he related the following comments from de Gaulle: "It's up to him, but he should know that he is part of an organism that works against France . . . It's not up to me to tell him what to do . . . But if he resigned, explaining himself in an open letter, he would be doing me a big favor . . ."[98] Yet even though, from October 13 on, Mauriac took a position against the National Front on the question of the single list of the Resistance,[99] he did not plan to leave the directive committee. He also continued to publish in *Les Lettres françaises*. And while he adopted the essential of Gaullist themes, the "advice" and "suggestions" on the question of the purge traveled in the opposite direction: starting on October 10, 1944, Mauriac thus intervened with de Gaulle through his son Claude so that Maurras would escape death. This was only the first in a series of steps taken in favor of the accused: his intervention to prevent the death sentence of Henri Béraud, the petition for clemency in Brasillach's favor that he himself presented to de Gaulle, and so on.

What, then, was the reason for this turnaround? The conflicts that rocked the CNE in early October, and in the wake of which Mauriac would resign from his honorary presidency, were not unrelated (let us recall that he refused to bring the list of the "major offenders" to the Ministry of Justice). Moreover, the prophet of the dark years had a position to maintain or to redefine when faced with a young generation that was seizing the key positions of the intellectual field: "I have my partner!" he had exclaimed on seeing Albert Camus's first article on the purge.[100] A résistant and editorialist for *Combat*, Camus occupied a homologous position to Mauriac, even as he was one of the most visible representatives of the new generation of writers that was establishing itself at Gallimard (we recall that Paulhan had recommended *L'Étranger* for the Grand Prize for the Novel in 1942, and that Mauriac had been reticent). Choosing Albert Camus as his interlocutor meant ignoring Jean-Paul Sartre, who in 1939 had decreed the symbolic death of the author of *La Fin de la nuit*.

Alone among the three great Catholic intellectuals who had risen up against the Church during the Spanish Civil War (Bernanos and Maritain had not yet returned to France), Mauriac tried to combine, for as long as possible, the different positions that allowed him to spread an always heretical message from one circle to another—the French Academy, the CNE, the National Front, the leader of the provisional government—and give this message a national bearing. But he was referred to his place as a Catholic intellectual by precisely that representative of the young generation he had chosen as an adversary, Albert Camus.

In the first polemical article that he had published after the few days of euphoria at the Liberation, François Mauriac already set the bases of what would be the major theme of his incessant sermons against the purge, "justice" swept aside by its upholders and abandoned to the rules of games of chance. Taking the French Academy, which had just voted to exclude Abel Hermant, as his target, he denounced the "recourse to the scapegoat" that, striking "the weakest," spared those who had a real responsibility: "What prevented the Academy from denouncing those of its members who were the guiltiest, even if they were absent from Paris?"[101] (Charles Maurras was the target here, of course.) But as Jean Lacouture has maintained, and whatever Claude Mauriac had to say about it, "'the Mauriac doctrine' in the matter of the purge [was] based less on Christian charity, as is always said, than on a very political vision."[102]

And, in fact, at the beginning of the famous polemic with Albert Camus, retroactively baptized "Justice or Charity," Mauriac explicitly guarded against possible accusations of "sentimentality" by situating himself on the plane of "national interest."[103] More, he articulated his intervention around the universal theme of "respect for the human being," common to the Marxists and the Christians, another manner of conciliating both positions of moral authority that he combined then, that of the Catholic intellectual and the one that he had won in the intellectual Resistance with regard to the Communists: "Thus, by various routes, we all arrive at this respect of the human being who, even guilty, even charged with crimes, must be punished without being debased."[104] The reference to the Terror would soon be reversed in his argument:

> But the times of revolution are recognized through other signs. Today, like then, it is the French who are hungriest for justice who risk being suspected of injustice. As early as 1792, the dreadful accusation of "moderantism" gave advance notice of the death sentence of André Chénier, who does not accept that the sword of justice strikes randomly.
>
> This, though, is what is happening. We want, we demand the punishment of the guilty—not that of the suspects.[105]

It was when Camus lashed out at de Gaulle—the General having called for "indulgence for those who erred"—that Mauriac resolutely sided with the

Gaullist thematic, invoking not "indulgence" but the necessity of a "national reconciliation."[106]

Yet Camus's first attack on Mauriac was not motivated by the latter's positions on the purge, but rather his critique of the uniformity of the Resistance press, which had offended the editorialist of *Combat*.[107] Opposing the maintenance of objectivity to the concern for "peace at any price," Camus challenged the Catholic intellectual: "There are times when each of us must argue with himself and sacrifice his emotional tranquility."[108] Mauriac clearly perceived the challenge as a reference to his position as a Catholic intellectual and, resolving to assume it, immediately changed the axis of his argumentation, which regained very clearly Christian accents (without, for all that, giving up the argument of "justice" that he reintroduced with the theme of the Dreyfus affair): "May the gentle not deprive this somber world of their gentleness! May the merciful not blush at the promise that was addressed to them one day on the Mountain of Beatitudes! There will always be enough cruelty on Earth."[109]

On October 23, the first death sentence was pronounced against Georges Suarez. Camus approved of the verdict, ascribing Mauriac with an opposing position that he had not taken, and flinging at him: "[...] the problem of justice essentially comes down to silencing what M. Mauriac calls 'mercifulness' when public truth is at stake [...] M. Mauriac will say that he is Christian and that his role is not to condemn [...] A Christian may believe that human justice is always supplemented by divine justice, hence that indulgence is always preferable."[110] Mauriac only responded to Camus on this point three weeks later: "We are not, in every case, opposed to the death penalty, but as far as youth is concerned, we are, in every case, against the pain of hopelessness."[111] When, in December, he protested against the death sentence of Paul Chack, it was the arbitrariness and inequality of treatment—in light of the attenuating circumstances that benefited Lucien Combelle—that he denounced.[112] During Henri Béraud's trial, he challenged the sentence: Béraud had not committed the crime of intelligence with the enemy for which he was condemned. And he then appealed to the solidarity among writers: "[...] all the same, a French writer belongs to our patrimony. It is not for us to devalue him. If Béraud had committed the crime for which he was condemned, his talent would not be an excuse in my eyes. But thanks to God and for the honor of us all, Henri Béraud did not betray."[113]

However, Mauriac no longer benefited from enough room to maneuver to escape the position that had been reassigned to him, that of a Catholic intellectual who only spoke from that particular point of view. His support of Béraud placed him in the category of the "indulgents." Try as he might to continue to deny himself any "sentimentality," Camus gained the upper hand by

reconstructing the polemic around the opposition "Justice" versus "Charity"—
"Whenever I have used the word *justice* in connection with the purge, M. Mauriac spoke of *charity*"—and by attributing the speech of a "writer who works by
feel rather than argument" to his adversary. He would once again go so far as to
anticipate the positions of Mauriac who, he said, "is meditating on the possibility of writing before too long a word he has yet to utter: pardon," before concluding: "[...] we will refuse to the end a divine charity that would frustrate
men of the justice they are due."[114]

And yet it was Camus who, revising his intransigent positions following Brasillach's death sentence, would soon align with Mauriac. Solicited by Marcel Aymé
to sign the petition supporting Brasillach's plea for clemency, he agreed after having gone back and forth all night. Out of "horror for the death penalty," he specified, and not "for the writer whom I consider to be nothing, nor for the individual
whom I despise with all my strength."[115] His repugnance with respect to the death
penalty still does not suffice to explain this attitude, since he had managed to
overcome it up to that point. Did a form of solidarity with a man of his generation
whose father had been killed a few weeks after his own in 1914 play a role? Did
Mauriac's arguments hit their mark? This is what Camus would admit later.[116]

Finally, the fact that this polemic was also a generational quarrel is shown by
Mauriac's famous reply to this young pretender who "from very high, from the
heights, I imagine, of his future work [...] allows himself to judge the author
of *La vie des martyrs*, of *Civilisation*, of the *Salavin* cycle and the *Chronique des
Pasquier*."[117] This call to order and the need that Mauriac felt to rush to the aid
of the permanent secretary of the French Academy, Georges Duhamel, betray
the poorly established position of the elders. Furthermore, Camus was not the
only one to take Mauriac to task. People like Claude Roy and Pascal Copeau
did the same in *Action*.[118] What is more, Mauriac's position was also contested
by the progressive Catholics of *Esprit*, who did not intend to leave him the monopoly over the Christian viewpoint. Observing that "among many today, the
call to charity is only the denial of justice," Jean Lacroix emphasized Mauriac's
"redoubtable privilege": "The disrepute in which those who should have spoken
and who remained silent have fallen means that he is the one who represents the
mass of Christians from now on, and who seems to engage all of Christianity in
his least comment." But Jean Lacroix did not intend to abandon the "notion of
charity" to the partisans of indulgence, denouncing its loss of meaning. For him,
there was no opposition between "justice" and "charity": "The *exemplary* punishment of those who where chiefly to blame or supportive of a treasonous regime—a
punishment necessary for the health and the very life of the country—was thus, is
thus in keeping with the highest charity."[119] While as an individual Camus would

end up seeing Mauriac's logic, on the public scene the confrontation still marked a defeat of the elders in the intergenerational struggle that was playing out in parallel at the CNE and within the Gallimard publishing house.

THE WRITER, A SCAPEGOAT?

Georges Suarez, Paul Chack, Lucien Combelle, Henri Béraud: the trials of collaborationist journalists had a big impact at the end of 1944.[120] The first two were sentenced to death and executed. Béraud was pardoned by de Gaulle, and his sentence was commuted to twenty years of hard labor. On January 26, 1945, Galtier-Boissière noted in his journal:

> In the purge, it's the journalist, that mangy scum, who serves as a scapegoat. They forget that some only had their pen to feed their family and only wrote innocuous columns.
>
> Are the Renault workers blamed for making tanks for the Wehrmacht? Wasn't a tank more useful to Fritz than a short item in the *Petit parisien*?[121]

More than its precedents, the death sentence of Robert Brasillach and his execution on February 6, 1945, left the literary world dumbstruck. At least this was the feeling that even the most intransigent would later ascribe to it. At the time, the list of those who signed the petition supporting Brasillach's plea for clemency only included, with the exception of Camus, representatives from the conservative pole of the literary field, including a number of academicians.[122] And the partisans of indulgence in the debate over the responsibility of the writer that this sentence incited most often belonged to the same pole. However, later accounts expressed a general discontent with regard to the legal purge. Was this an effect of professional solidarity faced with the interference of an extraliterary power over which writers quickly lost all control? Or a retrospective reconstruction by the witnesses who, with the passage of time, had qualified their intransigent view of the moment? Both effects undoubtedly combined to produce this resentment with respect to justice.

As I suggested earlier, this resentment was born of the death sentences, and more specifically those of Béraud and Brasillach, who unlike Suarez and Chack were considered to be writers. In comparison with the purge in the other sectors and at other levels of responsibility, the writer appeared in the eyes of the literary community as a scapegoat. Lucien Scheler, a member of the purge commission of the CNE, thus rebelled a half century later over the fact that Brasillach had been executed rather than Pétain ("Pétain deserved death a million times over!"), and evoked his responsibility in the deportations of Jews, the enactment of anti-Semitic laws even before the Germans imposed them, and which were harsher than those of the Germans, before concluding that while Brasillach had said "horrible things," he did not deserve death for all that: his trial happened too early.[123] In his memoirs, Vercors also expressed reservations about Brasillach's fate: "In truth, relatively few writers who had collaborated were investigated. We didn't wish for it and the lone execution of Brasillach hit us hard. Not that he wasn't the guiltiest; but because he paid for all the others."[124]

Surely, opinions still diverged between those who cleared the writer forced to live off his work and those who emphasized the notion of "responsibility." But the reasoning of the first only applied to the writers and journalists who published in the collaborationist press without endorsing the Collaboration, and who in any case were not sanctioned, since they did not fall under article 75 of the penal code that condemned "intelligence with the enemy," nor under that of the ordinance instituting the crime of national indignity. It was thus rather the degree of responsibility of writers in comparison to those who furnished the material means of collaboration that would be invoked as an extenuating circumstance. As early as 1943, Céline was proclaiming in *Je suis partout*: "Let them stop bothering us about traitors. The first traitors, then, are all those who earned a cent with the Germans."[125] After the Brasillach trial, the idea began to spread that the purge would hit the intellectuals harder than the industrialists. The argument would be taken up again in the petition supporting the clemency request of Lucien Rebatet in late 1946 (a request that was granted by Vincent Auriol). It was not by chance that the comparison with economic collaboration was privileged: the argument sought to be all the more fruitful by reactivating the structural resentment of writers with respect to the financial powers. It was based on the idea that venality was a greater crime than sincere support of reprehensible ideas, according to a hierarchy of values in force at the pole of small-scale production in the literary field. In his charge against the CNE, Paulhan would, however, develop a more legal argument: crime resided in acts and not in speech, responsibility lay with those who carried out the ideas rather than those who expressed them. It was the metaphor of the Atlantic Wall, which he first elaborated in June 1946 in *Les Temps modernes* (under the pseudonym of Maast) and would take up again in 1948 in *De la Paille et du grain* [*Of Chaff and Wheat*]:

A purge makes life hard for writers. Engineers, entrepreneurs, and masons who built the Atlantic wall now move among us in utter tranquillity. They're busy building new walls. They could be building walls for new prisons—for journalists who made the mistake of writing that the Atlantic wall was built well.

For Paulhan, writers were receiving a singular honor by being suddenly recognized for having such a responsibility: "Here's how we men of letters made a fortune three years ago. I'm talking about a moral fortune."[126] But it was precisely on this notion of responsibility, raised with respect to the execution of Brasillach, and increased in dramatic tonality by the suicide of Drieu La Rochelle shortly thereafter, that the discord within the literary world was founded. Vercors and Seghers thus held the responsibility of the writer as greater than that of the industrialist. Sartre wrote in *Qu'est-ce que la littérature*: "It is said nowadays that it was better to build the Atlantic wall than to talk about it. I don't find that particularly scandalizing [...] And I am not saying that this is just [...] But we ought to rejoice that our profession involves some dangers."[127] Evoking her refusal to sign the petition supporting Brasillach's plea for clemency, Simone de Beauvoir claimed in *La Force des choses* [*Force of Circumstance*] that she had never regretted her decision. And replied to Paulhan:

> People have condemned the weeding out of collaborationists for dealing more severely with those who talked approvingly about the Atlantic Wall than with those who built it. To me, it seems utterly unjust that economic collaboration should have been passed over, but not that Hitler's propagandists in this country should have been so severely dealt with. By trade, by vocation, I attach an enormous importance to words. Simone Weil used to demand that anyone who used writing to tell lies to men should be put on trial, and I understand what she meant. There are words as murderous as gas chambers.[128]

THE "INDULGENTS" AND THE "INTRANSIGENTS"

In September 1944, with respect to the deliberations of the CNE, Louis Parrot entitled an article that he published in *Action* "The Responsibility of the Writer."[129] "No more playing at literature," Charles Braibant decreed in *Gavroche* in 1944, claiming that the great moment of reconciliation between the writer and the people had finally come.[130] Who would dare contest it, after all those years of oppression? Nobody, not even Paulhan. The public debate surrounding the notion of the "responsibility of the writer" raised by Brasillach's execution concerned the degree and the limits of that responsibility. The weekly *Carrefour* launched a survey on this theme a few days later. The replies appeared there from February 10 to March 17. At that point, Marshal Pétain had not yet been judged. The debate would continue much longer. Culminating around 1946–1947, it would undergo new developments up until 1953.

The opposition between "indulgents" and "intransigents" generally intersected with the generational division and the political opposition between right and left, as illustrated by both the polemic between Mauriac and Camus and the list of those who signed the petition in support of Brasillach's plea for clemency. The average age of writers who signed it was fifty-eight in 1945. Among the signers, we find fourteen "immortals": Valéry, Mauriac, Duhamel, Bordeaux, Tharaud, Madelin, Henriot, Lecomte, Chevrillon, Farrère, Duke de Broglie, Prince de Broglie, Duke de La Force, and Admiral Lacaze. Dorgelès and Billy represented the Goncourt Academy. Paulhan, Schlumberger, and Gabriel Marcel joined forces with Marcel Aymé, Colette, Cocteau. Opposite them, the generation of the Resistance joined together, with the exception of Camus: it was forty-year-old writers who argued for the responsibility of the writer, without counting those CNE members who remained silent but did not think it any less, including a number of the youngest.

A second dividing line actually appears between those who adopted a public position as "moralists" and those who refrained from doing so, despite the stand they took within the CNE. Anne Simonin has reminded us that Vercors would be "one of the rare big names of the time, with the exception of Camus, to publicly defend the thesis of the intellectual's responsibility."[131] Sartre played a more cunning game, diffusing his ideas outside of France; Raymond Queneau, a member of the CNE purge commission, remained silent. Paul Eluard, who was also a member, would content himself with publishing a poem, "Les vendeurs de l'indulgence," [The sellers of indulgence] that appeared in *Les Lettres françaises* on March 17 and in the issue of *Ce Soir* dated March 18. He did, however, clearly take a stand in it: "There is no salvation on earth / As long as the executioners can be forgiven."[132] Eluard's "intransigence" was confirmed for us by the account of Eugène Guillevic, who insistently returned to the poet's rigor:

> And there, I insist on correcting the things that are commonly said [. . .] Aragon was not at all rigorous and severe. He was very indulgent [. . .] Eluard was very harsh [. . .] very rigorous, very harsh [. . .] It was his character, he was a very decisive man, Eluard [. . .] he was very anxious, a man of passion and . . . violence [. . .], not a little elegiac.[133]

Thus I can join Anne Simonin in saying that "by making his position public, [Vercors] seems like the official representative of the 'hard line' of the CNE."[134] We then immediately understand that he (unofficially) became Paulhan's target.

On November 11, 1944, while the polemic between Camus and Mauriac was at its height, Vercors published an article in *Les Lettres françaises* entitled "Forgiveness," in which he invoked the vow made to the dead.[135] The first to answer the *Carrefour* survey in February, Vercors proposed a distinction between shared responsibility in a conjuncture of free expression and the responsibility in a police state where, unable to be contradicted, the writer bore the consequences of his act. For him, the responsibility of the writer was unlimited: "To compare the industrialist to the writer is to compare Cain and the devil. Cain's crime was limited to Abel. The peril of the devil is limitless."[136] Paulhan, who ironically wrote to Vercors in the wake of his article, "I like your latest essays. It seems to me that your position as a moralist has gained in force and precision," sent a letter on the same day to Gérard Boutelleau, one of the directors of *Carrefour*, to recuse himself: "I must admit that the question does not interest me [. . .] I do not feel very moralistic," adding in a postscript, "that Vercors, all the same, what contempt for the readers (who defend themselves better than he thinks). In the end, I'm afraid I prefer Satan to Cain. But this is not to be said, especially now. And then, Cain can be condemned (and even executed). Not Satan."[137]

Who were the "moralists" who took a stand? Claude Aveline understood indulgence as an attack on the intellectual's honor.[138] Considering the war ideological and adopting not the viewpoint of national interest but rather that of the universal values (justice, freedom) flouted by the conflict, Max-Pol Fouchet argued for the responsibility of the writer if he took sides.[139] While Pierre Seghers considered the intellectuals as guilty as the economic collaborators, Emmanuel Mounier, even as he opted for responsibility, admitted that the former were more affected by the legal system than the latter: "May Themis thus verify its weight," he concluded.[140] The critic Émile Henriot insisted on national responsibility but, invoking "charity," suggested that "the law can absolve" without "pleading the right to error." "If the right to error were recognized," he specified, "literature would no longer look like anything but a game [. . .]."[141] Only Gabriel Marcel and Georges Duhamel applied restrictions to the notion of responsibility, the former setting the condition that the writer know what he was exposing himself to, and the latter maintaining that writing only engaged those who recognized its consequences.[142] Duhamel would reiterate his position in a response to Lucien Descaves diffused by *Les Nouvelles Épîtres*, in which he denounced the "redoubtable honor" that the law paid to literary men "in treating them harshly," while it was "benign for the great businessmen, for example." He asked for a revision of the "blacklist" so as to "lift all the measures of quarantine taken against the writers who were not subject to a judicial inquiry or who benefited from a dismissal."[143]

Discussing the "social role of writers" in the Socialist-leaning weekly *Gavroche*, René Lalou also remarked that "if, for a few months, writers have been the stars of the courtrooms, it is undoubtedly because the bankers and purvey-ors of munitions took refuge in a reserve that the law has very discreetly re-spected." Lalou did not argue in favor of a general amnesty, but it was necessary, according to him, to "signal more strongly that the victorious Resistance did not institute crimes of opinion, or even that it recognized this 'right to error' that Jean Paulhan talked about." Thus, he said, Béraud, Maurras, and Brasillach were not punished for their true crime, for which they deserved their sentence. "It comes down to saying," he continued, "at the risk of going against many prejudices, that the writer is a man among men, subject to the same laws, re-sponsible for his books or his articles as an industry leader is accountable for the interests that he manages."[144]

On the one hand, then, the elders who represented the institutional pole of literature, or rather those among them who were authorized to speak, François Mauriac, Georges Duhamel, and Émile Henriot (elected the following month to the French Academy), called for "indulgence" for different reasons, even though they did not claim Paulhan's principle of the "right to error." On the other, those representatives of the new generation that established itself at the Liberation tended to adopt an "intransigent" stand. But their propensity to publicly take part in the debate on the "responsibility of the writer" was all the stronger the less they were endowed with literary legitimacy, and they could al-ternatively promote the moral capital acquired in the struggle against the oc-cupying forces. In this respect, Vercors, Aveline, Fouchet, Seghers, and Mounier opposed Queneau, Sartre, and Camus, who represented the consecrated avant-garde of the Gallimard house, and who were certainly careful not to publicly confront Paulhan.

In this polemic, Gabriel Marcel and René Lalou occupied an intermediary position. Moralist due to his philosophical stand, Gabriel Marcel was, however, immediately hostile to the young generation of the CNE, infiltrated, he thought, by the Communists. The rhetorical contortions that he engaged in are telling: inverting the two conditions that determined his position, he was, as Anne Simo-nin has written, "practically in agreement with the existence of the blacklists, but metaphysically against."[145] Like most of the elders, he would not openly adver-tize his anti-Communism until the dawn of the Cold War, while the Commu-nist Party was doubly undermined in the intellectual field and the national space. The attitude of René Lalou also betrayed his own position, torn between Gide and Maurras. While he agreed with Gide for having recalled that "good literature is not always made with good feelings," he nonetheless subscribed to Nicolas Boileau's precept, "The verse always contains the baseness of the heart," before concluding that "today, the heart and the mind align to propose the same conception of the social role of writers."[146] He would be excluded from the CNE the following year for having breached the charter by publishing some of Maurras's poems in an anthology.

Jean Cassou's and Louis Martin-Chauffier's interventions in the debate, starting in the summer of 1945, lead us to introduce another criterion of judgment: the diversity of experiences under the Occupation. Like that of Camus invoking his dead resistance comrades against Mauriac, their speech carried greater weight and gave another accent to the voice of the "intransigents." The scope of the Nazi atrocities, exposed during the return of the deportees in May 1945 (no one spoke of the Shoah yet), conferred the notion of "responsibility" with a tragic meaning that it had never had before. "We still hear voices call for a writer's right to just be an artist," Martin-Chauffier observed. For him, it was only a means for those who had erred to try to get away with it. The act of writing engages the writer, and he, more than anyone else, has to account for himself. "The greater the writer and the more vast and deep his audience, the more he must consider his responsibility as much as it grows. Account for his actions? It does not say enough that he is subject to this law like the others. He makes it his law: if necessary, he would have promulgated it, it is his pride, like his risk."[147]

Certainly, Cassou and Martin-Chauffier, due to their past position-takings, and particularly their participation in the anti-Fascist struggle before the war, were immediately closer to the camp of the "moralists." But, above all, both engaged in the networks of the Resistance, they had a different experience of the risks of underground activity. Imprisoned for the first time in December 1941, then in 1942, detained in the Mauzac (Dordogne) and Saint-Sulpice La Pointe (Tarn) camps for a year, Jean Cassou had very nearly died in the fight for the Liberation. A delegate of the MUR to the directive committee of the National Front in the Southern zone, Louis Martin-Chauffier was arrested by the Gestapo in April 1944 and deported to Germany, first to the Neuengamme camp, then to Bergen-Belsen.[148] In the underground *Lettres françaises* of June 1944, Cassou concluded an article devoted to the temptation toward indulgence with these words: "*God willing, we will never have pity.*"[149] They were part of the minority of writers who took part in the active Resistance. Their voices could only resonate with those, silent, of people like Pierre de Lescure or André Chamson, whose withdrawal from the public scene introduced a discordant note in the good conscience of the representatives of the intellectual Resistance. Physical and moral exhaustion played a big role. This was the case for Pierre de Lescure. But his intransigence, both on the question of the purge and on the even more delicate one of the "monetization of the Resistance," also contributed, as Anne

Simonin has shown, to his marginalization: refusing to play the game, he "embodies, in a way, the 'living reproach' of an intellectual milieu that would show solidarity in putting him out of play."[150] For his part, André Chamson related how he was solicited by Sartre who wished for the former director of *Vendredi* to contribute to *Les Temps modernes*, considering him a precursor to existentialism. Grateful, but hit too hard by combat, Chamson said he had declined. "Sartre never forgave me."[151] And he continued by mentioning the article in *Les Temps modernes* that appeared shortly afterward, in which Sartre buried him with the famous writers from the interwar period who had died in the Resistance.[152]

Julien Benda's public support for the moralist camp starting in 1946 must also be related to the experience of the "dark years" and the rivalry with the new generation, which led him, unlike his peers, to escalate his intransigency. Benda had always been a moralist, and he was one more than ever at the end of those years, reediting his *Trahison des clercs* (supplemented by a preface calibrated to the circumstances) and his essay against romantic anti-intellectualism, *Belphégor*, publishing *La France byzantine*, a new charge against "the triumph of pure literature" in which he accused Mallarmé, Gide, Proust, and Valéry of having broken with the mores of intellectualism by only considering the literary fact in its relationship to form and language.[153] But this posture does not suffice to explain the fight in which he threw himself. Excommunicated under the Occupation because of his Jewish origins, dispossessed of his forum at *La NRF*, this fallen elder came up against fierce competition in the Gallimard house from a young, titled philosopher who combined the two positions that he himself had never managed to reconcile, that of a thinker and that of a writer, and who furthermore imposed a subjectivist philosophy against his universalist rationalism. As you may have guessed, this man was Jean-Paul Sartre. Allying himself quite naturally with those who had supported him during the Occupation, namely the Communists—who led a struggle during this time against the "philosophy of the absurd"—Benda, almost eighty years old, entered the melee one last time, choosing Jean Paulhan as his adversary.

In accordance with the moralist posture that had always been his, the author of *La Trahison des clercs* sought to dismantle the arguments of the partisans of "indulgence." Whether they invoked the safeguard of "thought" or the supremacy of "literary talent," none of these arguments was valid, according to Benda, in the cases at hand. The writer had the "right," and also the "duty," to "publish his moral conviction even if it tended toward the destruction of the State," but he had to accept the consequences and "drink the hemlock." Speaking of a "right to error" was an error of logic, since it concerned ideological positions that cannot be verified: "It is surprising to have to remind agrégés in philosophy about such elementary distinctions of ideas," he jeered in Paulhan's honor, whom he also targeted through an allusion to those who "suggest that the writer's propositions are pure games of the mind that should not be taken seriously in the realm of politics."[154] This offensive was only the first in a series of attacks. Benda would concentrate his fire on Jean Paulhan after the latter's resignation from the CNE in November 1946. Characterizing Paulhan's position as a "triumph of pure literature," he would support his demonstration by referencing Paulhan's writings that "exclusively discussed the literary problem and precisely literary language, as purely literary and outside of all kinds of considerations—moral, social, intellectual—that are normally involved in the study of literature."[155]

LITERATURE AND NATIONAL MORALISM

Under the Occupation, the reappropriation of the "French spirit" had been an essential stake in the struggle to regain the autonomy of the literary field. This explains the success of the national literary politics led by Aragon and the double legitimacy, both literary and national, of the CNE. Delighting in the fact that writers had finally abandoned the posture of "art for art's sake"—("art considered as the only source of morality")—Léon-Pierre Quint evoked the subversive dimension of art in *Les Lettres françaises*, namely the revolt against institutions as embodied by the surrealists. He congratulated himself, however, that they were able to abandon revolt for revolution at just the right moment to engage in the Resistance, and that today they took part in the leadership of the nation:

> Some may be surprised that formerly antinationalist poets who rebelled against society now sing "poems of love in war" [Eluard], that those who cried out in 1924: "Down with France!" today cry out: "I salute you, my France!" [Aragon]. But this contradiction is surely only superficial. It is the realities that have changed, and not these men. They always celebrated the word freedom, which only makes lowly slaves smile with a mocking air.[156]

This position would not long be tenable. While the Republican authorities had been fully reestablished, the double legitimacy of the CNE was contested. Not only because the Communist hegemony in the intellectual field now seemed like a new threat to the defenders of literary autonomy, but also because patriotic moralism was itself quickly considered incompatible with that autonomy. This is the meaning of *Le Déshonneur des poètes* that Benjamin Péret published in 1945 against the national poetry of Aragon and Eluard. Sartre's theory soon conferred the moralist injunction with an existential dimension that transcended the national question. Paulhan, for his part, would precisely turn this incompatibility into the argument of the polemic that he started with the CNE after his resignation in November 1946.

"I'm not a moralist. I don't know whether anyone has to be a patriot [. . .]." So begins one of the "Seven Letters to White Writers," written in 1947 and collected the following year in *De la paille et du grain*. In it, Paulhan identified the "betrayal" of an Alphonse de Chateaubriant with that of Romain Rolland who also supposedly "betrayed the cause of France" by his pacifism during the Great War. He then went back to Rimbaud who, in 1870, "wanted to see the Ardennes squeezed by our enemy." Hardening his commentary throughout the polemics with *Les Lettres françaises*—to the point that his name, listed as cofounder of the newspaper, would soon be removed from the banner—Paulhan pursued his game of analogy peppered with anti-patriotic quotations: Benda-Maurras, Eluard-Rebatet, Aragon-Drieu.

And it isn't, finally, Drieu La Rochelle who cries out:

"More than patriotism itself, which is one hysteria among others, what disgusts us most is the idea of the homeland, truly the most bestial, the least philosophical concept of all, where they try to invade our mind."

No. You've recognized Aragon [. . .].

Moreover, Paulhan would go so far as to insinuate that Chateaubriant had taken lessons in anti-patriotism from Romain Rolland, Drieu from Aragon: "Someone will say that no one ever took Aragon seriously for an instant. But I know someone who indeed admired Aragon, and perhaps took him all too seriously: the unfortunate Drieu La Rochelle."[157]

Was it a new "bad masters quarrel"? No. Paulhan did not criticize his former Resistance comrades for having "varied." These analogies conveyed the Gaullist representation of the "30 years war" with Germany, which challenged the specificity of World War II.[158] In response to Vercors who had corrected him on this point after his resignation, Paulhan, who claimed his experience in World War I against these newcomers, said:

Here you tell me that there was "nothing between 1914 and 1940 that is comparable in your eyes." And I don't understand you. Wasn't it the same war? Between 1914 and 1917, wasn't France a hair's breadth away from occupation? Wasn't it the same marshal who already wanted to admit defeat? Was he dealing with completely different Germans? And finally, what other feeling was common to all the members of the CNE, besides patriotism?[159]

The analogies also translated suspicion with respect to the triumphant patriotism of the Communists at the Liberation, a suspicion that grew stronger at the dawn of the Cold War. Moreover, for Paulhan it was a problem of language: it was the word "homeland" that varied. He would tackle it in *La Lettre aux directeurs de la Résistance*. At this point, these analogies had the main goal of reaffirming the rights of literature freed of all national moralism. Paulhan posed as the guardian of the memory of the literary field, which for him took precedence over the memory of the immediate past, whereas for the new generation, the latter was decisive and marked a break in history. Was it his propensity to show solidarity with outcasts that made him forget what he wrote in 1940 in "Hope and Silence," namely that some wars are more just than others? Just as before the defeat he had refused to exclude writers for political reasons, Paulhan now wanted to reorganize the Republic of Letters on the sole bases of this literary morality. But in the meantime, the war happened. The concern for "National Reconciliation" and its incarnation in the "Republic of Letters" that he had been calling for since 1938, his opposition to the conception of literature promoted by the new generation, an opposition that would take the political form of anti-Communism despite the fact that his political positions could not be reduced to that, would mainly have the effect of pulling him toward the academic pole, and to the right.

In continuity with the debates of the interwar period, but with the reversal provoked by the circumstances, the generation born of the Resistance inscribed this notion of "responsibility" in the ethical categories of literary understanding for the long term. The theory of "engaged literature" that Sartre developed starting in the autumn of 1945 was also a transposition of the notion of the "responsibility of the writer" in the metaphysical register, freed of the historical circumstances in which it was debated. By giving this notion of "responsibility"—which he attached to that of "freedom"[160]—its philosophical pedigree and a universal bearing, Sartre "capitalized" on the gains of the Resistance camp while taking advantage of its divisions. What is more, he made a dissociation between the notion of "responsibility" and the national moralism to which it had been closely linked since the end of the nineteenth century. "Thus, even aside from his patriotic feelings, every writer conscious of his trade finds a political duty in his literary activity itself," he wrote as early as 1944 in the underground *Lettres françaises*.[161] Now, he was denouncing the threat of "nationalization" that weighed on literature:

> Never has literature been threatened by a graver danger: formal and informal powers that be, the government, newspapers, perhaps even central banks and heavy industry have just discovered its might and are about to turn it to their profit. If they succeed, the writer will be able to choose—to devote

himself to electoral propaganda or to enter into a special section of the Ministry of Information. Critics are concerned no longer with appreciating his works but with calculating their national importance and effectiveness [...] That is not our understanding of literary commitment. There is no doubt that the written word is a social fact, and the writer before ever taking up his pen should be deeply convinced of it. He should, in fact, imbue himself with his responsibility. He is responsible for everything: lost or victorious wars, rebellions, and oppressions. He is the accomplice of the oppressors if he is not the natural ally of the oppressed. But not simply because he is a writer: because he is a man. He should live and desire that responsibility [...].[162]

With this condemnation, Sartre dispossessed the moralists born of the Resistance, and especially the Communists, of their chief asset, even as he took up, in a confrontation with Marxism, the goal of "social revolution" that had been their prerogative. Setting himself apart from the militant model embodied by Aragon and Eluard, around whom part of the young generation had gathered, he thus proposed a model of prophetic engagement that allowed writers, as Anna Boschetti has said, "to ease their conscience not only without joining the Communist Party or giving in to its pressures, but while reaffirming in an extreme form their predestined calling as the chosen few."[163] Of course, the bipolarization of the international stakes would not delay in making this position untenable. The failure of the Rassemblement démocratique révolutionnaire (RDR), that party of intellectuals formed in late 1947 that had Sartre and David Rousset as figureheads, proved this.[164] In 1952, Sartre would renew his fellow-traveling. The fact remains that in 1945, this theorization of engagement was a true symbolic coup de force. Like the surrealists in the aftermath of the Great War, but by reappropriating the notion of "responsibility" that they challenged, Sartre managed to overcome the opposition between "art for art's sake" and "the national interest" that continued—with a reversal of positions, as I've said—to structure the literary field, refusing to come out in favor of either the agents of "pure literature" or the spokesmen of patriotic moralism.

We can understand how, from that point on, Sartre became the target of both camps, although they did not succeed in contesting the dominant position he now occupied at the pole of small-scale production. Starting in late 1945, the Communists opened fire, reviving the attacks against the pessimistic subjectivism of "the literature of the absurd and of despair."[165] It would not be until 1951, when the first law of amnesty was on the verge of being passed, that someone like Jacques Laurent, converted to "art for art's sake"—remember his articles in Idées under the pseudonym of Jacques Bostan—tried a coup de force in his turn against the theorist of engaged literature in *La Table ronde*, which united a group of young novelists on the right, the "Hussards," around François Mauriac. In his famous article, "Paul and Jean-Paul," Jacques Laurent made a comparison between Paul Bourget and Jean-Paul Sartre, "both overproud of their university studies," who introduced scientific methods in the novelistic universe to demonstrate their theses.[166] Reactivating, in a new form, the old opposition between literary field and academic field, he got revenge for Sartre's harsh criticism of François Mauriac in passing. "At that time, communists and Sartrians combined their efforts to terrorize literature [...] That article [...] suited Mauriac all the more as it allowed me to refute all the arguments that Sartre had marshaled to try to demonstrate that the author of *Fin de la nuit* was not a novelist [...]."[167] Jacques Laurent was actually accusing the director of *Les Temps modernes* of having betrayed the work of *La NRF*, which had been created in opposition to the "ideological novel" (roman à thèse) and literature of good feelings in the style of Paul Bourget: "[...] through him [Sartre], Paul Bourget was given back the keys [to the house]."[168] "Art for art's sake" thus became, and for a long time, the shield that the redeployed losers, strengthened by the support that Paulhan's endorsements had conveniently brought them, would brandish against the heritage of the Resistance.[169] It remains for us to see how this heritage was assumed by the authorities of the literary field.

CHAPTER 9

Literary Institutions and National Reconstruction

The literary generation born of the Resistance established the notion of the writer's responsibility in a new sense, legitimating the model of engagement for the next two decades at the very least. But while the experience of the war left a lasting mark on the stakes proper to the literary field, while it contributed to the transformation of the literary landscape, with the marginalization of the writers on the extreme right on one side, and the establishment of the generation of the Resistance on the other, the reign of the ventures born of the Resistance would, on the other hand, not last long. Between 1945 and 1947, a reversal of the power relations occurred in favor of the traditional authorities, who regained the upper hand over these fragile ventures. Most of them disappeared. Those that survived either managed to do so at the cost of the eviction of their founders, for example in the case of the Éditions de Minuit, or at the cost of Communist Party control, as in the case of the CNE and *Les Lettres françaises*.

In 1945, consecrating the Resistance was not only a duty, it was a condition of survival for academies threatened by the purge. The internal struggles, the sometimes complicit, sometimes conflicted relations they maintained with the CNE, were revealing in terms of these institutional stakes, which were also competitive struggles for literary power. But the consecration of Resistance writers by the traditional authorities helped divest the literary Resistance of its original subversive charge. Good behavior, academic chairs, and official duties came at a price: the literary Resistance was absorbed, tamed, depoliticized. The "academization" of the Resistance also played out on its own terrain. While it was traversed by struggles that weakened its position and contributed to its loss of legitimacy, the CNE, by becoming institutionalized, participated in this phenomenon of routinizing the subversive logic, on the literary as well as the political plane.

From the viewpoint of writers' working conditions, the rise to power of the résistants accelerated, as in other areas of social life, the adoption of long-awaited reforms, particularly the creation of a Department of Literature at the Ministry of Fine Arts and the creation of the Caisse nationale des lettres, but it did not inspire a deep renewal of the literary institutions. The politics of the provisional government, which tried to preserve the traditional authorities at any price; the esprit de corps and inertia that weighed in their favor when confronted with ventures that were too closely tied to the conditions that witnessed their birth to be able to survive them; the transformations of the market and publishing interests; and finally the principles of opposition proper to the literary world, which would quickly gain the upper hand over the unity of the literary Resistance, were so many factors that contributed from 1946 to the reversal of the power relations at the expense of the Resistance writers. Having remained cautious during the first year following the Liberation, the Vichyist right soon began gathering its forces. This evolution can be clearly observed within the French Academy. The memory of the "dark years" became a stake in the struggle, the premises of which we noted in the previous chapter, and in which the literary institutions took part. While the Cold War, the revelation of the existence of Soviet concentration camps, and the Stalinian trials in Eastern Europe helped discredit ventures linked to the Communist Party and drain the remaining unity of Resistance writers, the literary rehabilitation of collaborationist writers was brewing. Without claiming to give an exhaustive view of the evolution of the literary field through 1953, I will outline its main steps here through an examination of the repercussions of the crisis within the institutions studied in this book.

The Tribute to the Victors

The suppression of *La NRF* might appear as a warning addressed to the institutions that pursued their activities in the capital under the more or less benevolent eye of the occupier. The CNE, as we saw, did not mince its words of warning to those, like the Goncourt Academy, that had adopted a conduct which seemed scandalous in light of the law of silence that a large number of recognized writers had adopted. The French Academy, spared by the underground committee, was in turn the object of attacks that went so far as to call for its dissolution following the Liberation. Moreover, starting in September 1944, several of their members were under investigation. The comparison of the purge of both academies, and of their attitudes with respect to the transformations of the national space, reveals the variable cost of institutional survival, which fluctuated according to their most typical social characteristics. It illustrates the structural limits of the purge, as well as the principles of inertia and the modes of reconversion typical of the two different—and sometimes incompatible—logics that prevailed at the pole of large-scale production: the state logic and the media logic.

Winning over the Resistance was a good means of survival. Actually, didn't the role that these two institutions claimed to play consist in consecrating, in their manner, the heroes of the nation? The prizes awarded by the two academies in 1945 serve as evidence: the Goncourt Prize was attributed to Elsa Triolet, the Grand Prize for Literature to Jean Paulhan. But while the Goncourt Academy recruited from the members of the CNE, the French Academy, despite the will of General de Gaulle and Duhamel's efforts, ignored Resistance writers. Should we see this as the origin of the struggles that the CNE engaged against the Academy starting in 1946? In any case, by becoming institutionalized, the CNE intended to compete with it for the title of official representative of France in the realm of literature.

A GONCOURT PRIZE FOR GOOD CONDUCT

While at the French Academy, the stakes and the strategies played out over the long term, at Drouant, where journalists feverishly gathered every winter, current events had immediate repercussions. Just as they had distinguished themselves by their respective attitudes under the Occupation, the two academies differentiated themselves by their reactions to the political and social transformations at the Liberation. While the French Academy refused to disown its two accused members, its younger sibling could not manage to get rid of the members whose presence was troublesome. While the assembly of the Quai Conti intended to win over the new acting power by electing a few notable Gaullists, even as it worked under the table to reform the "academic right," the Goncourt Academy did not hesitate to ally itself with the new dominant agents in the intellectual field, who also controlled the press: the attribution of the first prize of the Liberation to Elsa Triolet, the fact that two jurors (Carco and Dorgelès) joined the CNE, and the co-optation of three of its members into the academy (Alexandre Arnoux, Armand Salacrou, and Philippe Hériat) serve as proof.

The form that the liquidation of the repercussions of the crisis took and its duration also varied, just as the modes of managing the crisis during the Occupation had differed. While the Academy opted for the status quo, "moderation," avoiding measures that were too "hasty," bowing, with reticence of course, to the decisions of the courts without submitting to the pressures of "opinion" (attacks in the press, threats, etc.), while focusing on the long term, everything that was hatched among the Ten continued to be divulged in the press and by the jurors themselves, provoking the usual scandals. The scission generated by the crisis would culminate in a new "affair," with a role reversal, that would be settled by the courts.

Split in two, the Goncourt Academy did not manage to formally purge itself. According to the association's statutes, expulsion could only be declared with a majority of eight members, and four of the nine members who formed the group were then under investigation. Sacha Guitry, arrested at the Liberation, was released two months later. René Benjamin, also imprisoned, would only be freed in 1946. Jean Ajalbert was arrested in 1945. It seems that Jean de La Varende, also under investigation, quickly benefited from a dismissal.

Interviewed in *Le Figaro* dated November 4, 1944, the lawyer, Maurice Garçon, explained that if the members under investigation had been convicted of national indignity, their expulsion would have been automatic. But since the verdict had yet to be pronounced, the only way to resolve the problem would involve an intervention from the minister for public instruction to purge the Academy. In fact, although according to the law of associations of 1901 the "internal policing" was left up to the members, in the case of the Goncourt Academy the extent of the minister's authority was not defined and precedents existed that made such an intervention possible.[1] Given that the authorities did not follow Garçon's proposition, the Academy, which thus could not proceed with a legal expulsion, decided to remove from future meetings three members who were subject to legal action, and whose presence tarnished its prestige. For their part, those members could not agree to a resignation that might be interpreted as an admission of guilt.

The lunch in December 1944 did not take place. The Goncourt Academy contented itself with ratifying and publicly confirming the election of André Billy, which had been covered up the previous year. As a result, La Varende submitted his resignation, to the great relief of some members. Six votes were tallied for André Billy. But, remember, he had only obtained five. The well-informed *Lettres françaises* hurried to denounce the maneuver:

> A question comes to mind. Why didn't the Goncourt Academy announce the election when it happened? We are assured that it is because Mr. Rosny the Younger, far from supporting André Billy's candidacy a year ago as the press release indicates [...] only came around very recently, at the insistence of Roland Dorgelès, back from the Pyrénées.[2]

It was in March 1945 that the first post-Liberation lunch took place, in the presence of four members: Billy, Carco, Dorgelès, and Larguier. The following month, the Academy elected its new board: Descaves was its president; Rosny the Younger, the honorary president; Larguier, the vice president; Dorgelès was treasurer; and Billy, secretary. In May, Colette was elected unanimously by those present, as a replacement for the resigning La Varende. As with the two previous meetings, Ajalbert, René Benjamin, and Sacha Guitry were not invited. Maurice Garçon was invited to the June lunch. The vote to award the prize for 1944 was set for the month of July.

Going back to its tradition, the Goncourt Academy applied itself to consecrating works that fixed the memory of the immediate past. Echoing the five prizes distributed during the Great War, five of the six annual prizes awarded until 1949 went to novels that dealt with current events, unlike the "timeless" novels awarded under the Occupation. In both cases, it was the reflection of the new dominant ideology. The crowning of a consecrated representative of regionalist literature, Henri Pourrat, ratified the aesthetic principles promoted by the Vichy government. The prize for 1944 was awarded to Elsa Triolet for *Le Premier Accroc coûte deux cents francs*, a collection of short stories, two of which were published clandestinely: *Les Amants d'Avignon* (published by the Éditions de Minuit in 1943), and "Cahiers enterrés sous un pêcher."[3] Taking up a message transmitted by the BBC during the night preceding the D-Day landing, the title of the last piece gave its name to the collection, published by Denoël in 1945.

The first woman to win the Goncourt Prize, a résistante, a Communist of Jewish origin, Elsa Triolet was an author who testified to both the Resistance and the transformation of the conditions imposed upon women, without however breaking from the stereotypical literary representation of femininity.[4] Regarding the Resistance, contrary to the spiritual resistance symbolized by Vercors's *Silence de la mer*, she embodied the literature of combat, a war literature, according to the tradition dear to the Goncourt and from which the prize for 1941 had departed. Regarding the question of gender, it could not be a simple coincidence that the first Goncourt Prize ever awarded to a woman was granted the same year that female suffrage was instated in France. Indeed, the press did not neglect to make the connection: "The government of the Republic has recognized the rights of women, as we are aware. Did the virtue of such a high example influence the (purged) Goncourt Academy, which just gave two striking signs of its feminism, one after the other: the election of Colette and the awarding of the annual prize to Elsa Triolet?"[5] The Goncourt Academy showed once again that it knew how to stay in touch with current events. But Elsa Triolet was also the wife of Aragon, who called the shots at the CNE, now all-powerful in the literary field and to which it intended to apply ethical rules, at a time when the Academy needed badly to be pardoned. By awarding the prize for 1944 to Elsa Triolet, the jury took note of the Communist hegemony in the intellectual field.

This choice showed the reversal of internal power relations at the Academy, thanks to the transformations of the political field. It was Francis Carco, member of the CNE, a friend of Aragon and Elsa, who now called the electoral shots. Elsa Triolet had garnered five votes, those of Carco, who had already voted for her in 1943, Dorgelès, Larguier, Rosny the Younger, and Colette, versus two, those of Descaves and Billy, which went to *Amitiés particulières* by Roger Peyrefitte. The distribution of votes was significant: Carco rallied the "swing" votes of Dorgelès, Larguier, and Rosny the Younger, the very ones who, four years earlier, had tipped the balance in favor of Pourrat. Colette finally joined them. As for Descaves and Billy, they did not have to blame themselves for their attitude during the war and thus did not have to win over the masters of the hour. They simultaneously marked their autonomy with regard to Carco and the pressure that the new dominant ideology exerted indirectly.

Yet according to Carco, their candidate could not have been designated as the winner due to his suspension by the purge commission of the Quai d'Orsay—a civil servant, he had worked with the Vichy delegate to the Occupation authorities, Fernand de Brinon—a suspension that had caused his application to the CNE to be denied. This did not prevent the Renaudot jury from consoling the unsuccessful candidate. As for the Femina Prize, Vercors having made it known that he would decline, it was collectively awarded to the series "under oppression" of the underground Éditions de Minuit. With the Grand Prize for Literature that the French Academy awarded Paulhan, the literary Resistance was widely honored in 1945. But not for long.

While the press of the Liberation gave a favorable reception to the selection of Elsa Triolet, some insinuations slipped into the concert of praise that addressed the literary values of the work less than its value as an account.[6] The book was criticized for not being a novel, for having been published in 1945; Elsa Triolet was criticized for being Russian; the Goncourt jurors were criticized for having sided with the Resistance against "pure literature," realism against subjectivist intimacy, and for having displayed opportunism. It was also insinuated that the "particular friendships" were not as they seemed. But only the Catholic right-wing press displayed open hostility. While *La Croix* denounced "reasons of a political order," *L'Aurore* proved even more scathing:

> Let us mark this Goncourt with a white stone. For it is a pledge of Franco-Russian friendship, since it crowns a lovely writer who was born in the land

of the Soviets and who is, moreover, the wife of the poet laureate of the great party of the masses. It also shows the opportunism of the Ten; pardon, of the Five. For the lady of the Auteuil *grenier* aspires to recover a democratic virginity. Let us bet that the vote which, in the second round, ensured Elsa Triolet's success, was that of the guest whose signature was scrawled across *Gringoire* up until the arrival of the verdigris in the "nono" zone. The author of the *Route mandarine* strives to renew particular friendships on his left.[7]

However, it would be two more years before the anti-Communist journalist Jean Galtier-Boissière, who was then publishing a series of articles on "The Hypocrisy of the Purge" in *L'Intransigeant*, going after Aragon in particular, openly accused Dorgelès of having been "whitewashed" by Aragon in exchange for the attribution of the prize to his wife.[8] Whether or not it was founded, this accusation was related to the traditional attacks leveled against the Goncourt jury, to which Galtier-Boissière had never neglected to add his personal touch. But the chronological discrepancy illustrates the reversal of the situation between 1945 and 1947, and the disrepute that weighed on the CNE at that time. It also corresponded to a decline in interest for the war literature of which the ventures born of the Resistance, and their authors, bore the brunt starting in 1946. At the Éditions de Minuit, the sales of books related to the war fell by half.

The transformations of the demand had immediate consequences on the power relations within the Goncourt Academy, which turned to Carco's disadvantage. For the prize for 1945, the jurors' choice, which Carco did not support, was *Mon village à l'heure allemande* (Flammarion) by Jean-Louis Bory, a chronicle of the life of the inhabitants of an occupied village, destroyed by payback and old grudges, which multiplied the points of view and made the personified village into the first-person narrator. In the flood of more or less edifying narratives of the Resistance, the Interallié jury distinguished Roger Vailland's *Drôle de jeu* (Corrêa) the same year; its hero was a daredevil for whom the Resistance was above all a dangerous and exciting game. At the Goncourt lunch in December 1946, against the candidate whose campaign was led by Carco, Serge Groussard, author of *Crépuscule des vivants*, a narrow majority of four voices versus three voted for the candidate whose name had been passed along to Dorgelès by Pierre Benoit, Jean-Jacques Gautier, the author of *Histoire d'un fait divers* (Julliard) which, as its title indicates, had nothing to do with the war. The prize for 1940, which was set aside for the prisoners' return, was unanimously awarded to Francis Ambrière for *Les Grandes Vacances* (Éditions de la Nouvelle France), which the Goncourt jurors preferred to the witness account of David

Rousset, a survivor of the Nazi camps, in *L'Univers concentrationnaire* (the book had been published by the Éditions du Pavois, in the series edited by Maurice Nadeau). The Renaudot jury took this occasion to catch up on two fronts, by awarding the prize for 1940 to *L'Univers concentrationnaire* and the prize for 1946 to *La Vallée heureuse* (Éditions Charlot) by Jules Roy, which featured the pilots of the Royal Air Force. The Femina Prize for 1946 went to Michel Robida that year, for *Le Temps de la longue patience* (Julliard), the story of two brothers from the French bourgeoisie who were confronted with the Occupation and who, after some hesitations, made the right choices. Jacques Nels, meanwhile, won the Interallié for *Poussière du temps*. The following year, the Goncourt jurors voted against Carco again by awarding Jean-Louis Curtis's *Forêts de la nuit* (Julliard) with a margin of six votes; it was the distant painting of the intrigues in a small city in Béarn during the war. In *Les Lettres françaises*, Louis Parrot, who lauded the qualities of the author, nonetheless worried about what he perceived as an "adjustment" at the end of the book: "In fact, if we follow J.-L. Curtis' thought to its end, the resistance was just a matter of poor devils, of visionaries without great character, or of politicians without scruples, while the collaborators, or, to be more precise, the pro-Vichy faction, were always people of good sense, and, in the end, the only true patriots." According to Parrot, this last-minute adjustment "exactly corresponds to the triumphant return of the collaborationist spirit [...]."[9] The Renaudot jury distinguished itself once again from the Goncourt Academy by giving another prize to a deported résistant, the poet Jean Cayrol, a survivor of the Mauthausen camp, for two narratives that dealt with the difficulties of readapting to normal life, *On vous parle* and *Les Premiers Jours*, collected in *Je vivrai l'amour des autres* (Seuil), while *La Peste* (Gallimard) by Camus, an allegory of the Occupation experience, was crowned by the Prix des critiques.

Despite its seeming echo of the evolution of the image of the Resistance, the choice that their colleagues had made for 1947 definitely did not suit René Benjamin and Sachy Guitry. The undesirable members of the academy had been suspended while awaiting a legal decision. In 1946, René Benjamin had been freed from prison. In 1947, Ajalbert died and was immediately replaced by Alexandre Arnoux, a member of the CNE and of the purge commission of the Société des gens de lettres (SGDL), from which Ajalbert had been expelled. He was unanimously elected by the seven voters. A few months later, in the autumn of 1947, a dismissal was pronounced in favor of Sacha Guitry. Thus nothing prevented his return to the table of the Ten. But, invited to take part in the votes that would take place in the study of the academy's notary, Guitry and Benjamin stayed away. Considering the invitation to a notary's office as an "affront," Guitry decided, with Benjamin's approval, to choose their own candidate for the prize for 1947. Reproducing the scenario of 1941 in the opposite sense, Guitry and Benjamin thus awarded the "Jules de Goncourt Prize" to Kléber Haedens for *Salut au Kentucky*, with the complicity of the publisher Robert Laffont, who replaced the traditional green band with a red band bearing the inscription "Goncourt Prize" (in big letters) "from Sacha Guitry and René Benjamin" (in small letters). Once again, the Academy did not succeed in voting the expulsion of the two dissidents, one member of the eight having abstained. They were simply given a formal warning. A trial occurred, ending with Guitry and Laffont being sentenced to pay 700,000 francs in damages and interest. Benjamin, who was not in Paris during the affair (he had given his consent to Guitry by telephone), was not punished.[10]

Two days after the death of René Benjamin, which occurred in October 1948, Guitry resigned, thus preempting an exclusion that would have certainly passed in this vote. The same day, the Academy unanimously elected the late Rosny the Younger's successor: the journalist and essayist Gérard Bauer, son of the famous journalist of the Commune, Henry Bauer, who had been the friend of Descaves, of Alphonse Daudet. While the final aftereffect of the crisis was being liquidated, the academy had returned to its traditions. That year, it was the author of the "chant des partisans," Maurice Druon, who won the Goncourt for *Les Grandes Familles*, the first volume in a fresco of French society before 1940 entitled *La Fin des hommes*. It was the third consecutive Goncourt Prize won by his publisher, René Julliard, a newcomer to the world of publishing who was asserting himself with regard to Gallimard and Grasset (he had also won the Renaudot that year, following the Femina for 1946). The imbalance would be partially restored the following year in Gallimard's favor, with the distinction of a novel on the debacle in Flanders in the summer of 1940, *Week-end à Zuydcoote* by Robert Merle, which the Éditions Julliard had rejected.

In the meantime, the playwright Armand Salacrou and the novelist Philippe Hériat (winner of the Goncourt Prize for 1939) had sat down at Benjamin's and Guitry's place settings; both belonged to the CNE. In 1950, the Montmartrian friend of Dorgelès and Carco, Pierre Mac Orlan, was finally admitted to the Ten, and the following year, Raymond Queneau, member of the CNE, became the youngest member of the assembly at age forty-eight. His election to Larguier's place was contested: he was not only the fourth Gallimard author to sit at their table (with Salacrou, Hériat, and Mac Orlan), but also an influential member of the editorial board. It is true that Gallimard was once again the great favorite of the Goncourt jurors, and he would remain so for a long time (winning ten prizes out of thirteen from 1949 to 1962).

The attitude of the French Academy at the Liberation is a striking demonstration of an old institution's force of institutional inertia and capacities for resistance to the transformations of the literary field and political life. The Academy's age, the dominant position it occupied in the field of power, its prestige, its esprit de corps, are so many factors that helped limit its cost of survival. Not only did the Company refuse to disown two of its members who had been convicted and legally relieved of their duties, but it would also cause the failure of the head of the provisional government's renewal projects as well as the reforms of its permanent secretary, Georges Duhamel. Far from resolving in favor of the victors, the conflicts that had divided the assembly into two camps, at least since Maurras's election, would persist well beyond the period of reconstruction. The "academic right," whether pro-Maurras, pro-Vichy, or pro-Pétain, which observed an attitude of withdrawal during the first moments of the Liberation, would soon rear its head. Although this evolution exceeds the chronological limits of my analysis, it is necessary to evoke the longer-term repercussions of this crisis, which allow us to better understand its nature.

At the Liberation, seven "immortals" out of the twenty-eight survivors were investigated, amounting to a quarter of the assembly: Abel Bonnard, Abel Hermant, Charles Maurras, Marshal Pétain, General Weygand, Pierre Benoit, and Edmond Jaloux. Besides the five writers who were taken to court, the CNE "blacklist" included the name of Henry Bordeaux, which was removed, as we saw, at Georges Duhamel's request. As early as the meeting of August 31, 1944, the Academy had decided that in virtue of article 13 and article 10 of the regulations of 1635,[11] Abel Bonnard and Abel Hermant should abstain from participating in meetings from that point on. The examination of both these cases had been requested by the acting director, Jérôme Tharaud, following the speech he had given in front of the ten academicians present. Affirming that the Academy "did not cease fulfilling all its duties" during the long "ordeal" and that it had shown itself "worthy of its high mission" thanks to a "firm majority," he proposed that some "serious problems" be examined concerning the inner life of the Company.[12] At the following meeting, even as it confirmed his disbarment, the Academy approved Duhamel's request that the public powers release Abel Hermant. In October, the CNE sent a letter to the Academy about Marshal Pétain, as a result of which the Academy confirmed, in a press release, its decision to adjourn the debates concerning those of its members who were under legal investigation. This decision was made in September in reference to Charles Maurras.

On December 14, 1944, a confrontation took place between Henry Bordeaux, back in Paris since October, and Admiral Lacaze, then acting director, who with Paul Valéry's support asked that the temporary exclusion of Abel Bonnard and Abel Hermant be made permanent. Bordeaux suggested that the exclusion could be prejudicial to the members of the Company who were subject to legal action, and influence the verdict. Georges Duhamel, who had been elected permanent secretary on October 12, 1944 (he already occupied this position in a temporary capacity), revealed that the minister recommended maintaining the status quo while awaiting a legal decision, which put an end to the discussion. Four academicians out of the seven who were investigated would be convicted; the others would benefit from a dismissal.

On January 28, 1945, Charles Maurras was sentenced to life imprisonment and *dégradation nationale*.* In virtue of the ordinance of December 26, 1944, the sentence of dégradation nationale resulted ipso facto in expulsion from all official positions, orders, and distinctions. The assembly would settle for applying the letter of the law, which obliged the Academy to declare his seat vacant, and did not vote for expulsion. Henry Bordeaux agreed to participate in the meeting on the condition that he be allowed to speak to "say goodbye to our colleague," and he concluded his speech with these words:

> All the accusations of individual denunciations have failed pitifully. He could not be reasonably accused of complicity with the German that he never stopped fighting. It was necessary to turn to the campaigns that he led against our Allies, against communism. One of us recently entitled a wonderful article, "Every judgment will be judged." Such will be the case for this judgment.[13]

Jérôme Tharaud, Duke de La Force, and Louis Madelin shared in this good-bye. Louis Madelin then took the floor to recall a historical precedent, a law that, under the Bourbon Restoration, had led to the expulsion of about fifteen members from the Institute: "The law was applied, but a few years later, most of those members were reintegrated.—Maurras will be, the duke de La Force said quietly . . ."[14] These interventions perfectly illustrate the relationship to time and history that characterizes the academic vision of the world: regimes come and go, the institution remains. If it was necessary to momentarily submit to the diktats of the regime, the "immortals" would ultimately regain their institutional autonomy, letting the inertia that always weighed in their favor act while awaiting better days.

---

* *Dégradation nationale* was the penalty for the crime of "indignité nationale," that is national shaming. It involved the loss of civil rights.—Trans.

As in the case of Maurras, the Academy had to record the expulsion of Pétain and declare his seat vacant. But the Company decided that it was not necessary to register candidacies for these seats. Whereas the seats of Bonnard and Hermant were filled as early as 1946 without their successors, Jules Romains and Étienne Gilson, being required to deliver the traditional eulogy,[15] those of Maurras and Pétain would remain vacant as long as they lived. When Duhamel suggested naming two of the "illustrious dead" there, he was reminded "that an amnesty could intervene and that it was thus preferable to leave certain seats vacant in order to return them, on that day, to their former holders."[16] In 1948, a committee to free Marshal Pétain was formed; Henry Bordeaux would be a member. This committee would be outlawed.[17]

The loyalty of a number of academicians to Marshal Pétain and Maurras had not prevented the Company from continuing to assume its national role. On May 15, 1945, Duhamel addressed thanks in its name to General de Gaulle "for the work of salvation undertaken in distress, pursued in fervor and accomplished in glory."[18] The analysis that the historian and academician Robert Aron has made of this seemingly paradoxical attitude provides a good illustration of the logic of moderation, prudence, attentisme, and inertia that the Company tended to adopt in a period of social upheaval:

> [. . .] it's because the Academy was also concerned with not acting under the pressure of circumstances and, even as it declared its patriotic gratitude to the liberators, with not ceding to their influence [. . .] this patriotic impulse did not lead the Academy to skip steps in purging those of its members who had been compromised with Vichy.[19]

Moreover, de Gaulle had revealed on September 3, 1944, in response to the message that the Institute of France had sent him, that the provisional government of the French Republic counted on the traditional support of the five Academies of the Institute of France to assist in the work of diffusing French culture.

The Academy had all the more interest in winning over the new power as it quickly became the target of attacks and threats. De Gaulle mentioned the pressures he felt as the institution's protector, with some wishing for the assembly's renewal and others, its dissolution.[20] In a meeting on September 7, 1944, with Duhamel who, worried about the threats of dissolution, had come to consult with him, the general revealed that he wanted the Academy to survive in its traditional form, but proposed that the empty chairs be filled through an exceptional procedure that would suspend the rule of candidacy, calling eminent Resistance writers into service (as protector of the Academy, he himself declined the offer of the permanent secretary, who invited him to join the Company.) The list, drawn up by Gaston Palewski, of those whom de Gaulle wished to see serve at the Academy included the following names: Gide, Claudel, Maritain, Bernanos, Malraux, Eluard, Martin du Gard, Jules Romains, Aragon, Schlumberger, d'Ormesson, Fargue, Tristan Bernard, and Benda.[21] Strangely, this list assembled, with a few exceptions, the "ideal Academy" constituted by Mauriac on a sheet of paper found by Jean Touzot. It included five philosophers: Alain, Brunschvicg, Maritain, Benda?, and Paulhan?; six novelists: Bernanos, Schlumberger, Gide, Martin du Gard, Jules Romains, and Malraux?; three poets: Eluard, Aragon, and Claudel; two playwrights: Bourdet and Copeau?; two scientists: Prince de Broglie and Pasteur Vallery-Radot; one economist: André Siegfried; and two diplomats or statesmen: Massigli? and Noël? Had Mauriac composed the list at the general's request? In a private meeting with Mauriac, de Gaulle had wanted to know whether Gide would agree to enter the Academy. Jean Blanzat was probably correct in writing to Jean Paulhan that "in fact, it's the Ac[ademy] that doesn't want Gide. It cannot forgive self-proclaimed gays. It only accepts closet cases (Lacr[etelle], A[bel] H[ermant] etc . . .)."[22] Gide let it be known that he was willing to enter, but that he would immediately use his new title to diffuse *Corydon*, his book in defense of homosexuality, as he noted in his journal in January 1946:

> Academy? . . . Yes, perhaps, accept becoming a member if without solicitations, groveling, visits, etc. And immediately afterward, for my first deed as an Immortal, a preface to *Corydon* declaring that I consider the book as the most important and most "serviceable" (we have no word, and I don't even know if this English word expresses exactly what I mean: of greater usefulness, of greater service for the progress of humanity) of my writings.[23]

De Gaulle's suggestions met with an unfavorable reception from the academicians. And while the first elections aligned with the hopes of the permanent secretary, he was quickly disillusioned. Duhamel wanted to simplify the recruitment procedures, notably by suppressing the obligatory nature of the letter of candidacy and the visits, which were imposed by custom and not by regulation. The exemption from visits was only accorded to those candidates who ran in the first elections, which took place in October 1944. He moreover proposed naming the "illustrious dead" to the empty seats for a very brief time, by legal decision. He had notably obtained the agreement of Saint-Exupéry's widow. We have seen the objection that was made to him. As the academicians proved recalcitrant, Duhamel's efforts came to nothing, and in 1946 he resigned from his position as permanent secretary.

At the meeting where he presented his motives for resigning, Duhamel nonetheless obtained, with Mauriac's support, the Academy's agreement to suggest that Claudel run for a seat without having to take any official steps. Claudel had been enthusiastically approached by Duhamel starting in October 1944. The author of *Le Soulier de satin* had set as an essential condition that the measures of exclusion taken with respect to Bonnard and Hermant be extended to Charles Maurras, "much more guilty than them." "It was impossible for me to agree to be the colleague of that filthy scoundrel,"[24] he clarified to Paul Valéry. The press having announced his candidacy while he had not—for obvious reasons—received a response from Duhamel about the Maurras case, Claudel published a denial. During the preparation of Maurras's case, Claudel testified against him, accusing him of having denounced him twice. The literary quarrels entered the courtroom. Maurras devoted a long response to the complaints of his old literary and political enemy, unable to resist the temptation of slinging arrows at the "false and loose cadence called 'Claudelian verse,'" at his "style, stretched to greatness, [which] generally only attains bigness," and at the "pomposity" of his *Paroles au Maréchal* and the "vulgarity of tone" in his ode to de Gaulle.[25] In 1946, the Academy having recorded the exclusion of Maurras as a result of his conviction, Claudel finally accepted Duhamel's new offer and was elected.

Nineteen new "immortals" were elected between 1944 and 1946. At the meeting of September 7, 1944, at Paul Valéry's suggestion, the Academy had decided not to consider candidates whose "attitude or actions during the foreign occupation did not conform to national feeling and interests," a decision that was made public through a press release. The Academy had co-opted a few "patriotic" personalities or notorious Gaullists, like Pasteur Vallery-Radot, "boss" of the medical Resistance, André Siegfried, Édouard Herriot, and Maurice Garçon.

Duhamel's and Mauriac's attempts to elect Resistance writers, or at least those who had belonged to the camp of "refusal," were less successful. Of course, the Academy did award the Grand Prize for Literature for 1945 to Jean Paulhan, at their initiative. Thanks to the rapprochement that had occurred under the Occupation with the former team of *La NRF*, Duhamel and Mauriac hoped to see several of its representatives enter the Academy. They only succeeded with Claudel and Jules Romains. Roger Martin du Gard, who was approached, remained inflexible despite the persuasive arguments of Mauriac, who mentioned de Gaulle's wish to see him enter along with Gide, Claudel, Malraux, Bernanos, Maritain, Aragon, and others: "When the Academy will be *another* academy, there is no reason for you to avoid it."[26] Martin du Gard's reply to Duhamel illustrates well the incompatibility between the "ascetic" logic and the worldly logic:

It's then that, without any apparent trace of irony, you suggest that I formally deviate from the general direction of my life, that I act like a candidate, seek honors, take vows (and make speeches! . . .), take on semi-public duties, which would be heavier and more demanding than all those I have ever agreed to take on in private?[27]

But Mauriac and Duhamel's failure did not simply arise from the reticence of their candidates. André Gide, as we saw, was theoretically not opposed. Jean Paulhan had ultimately been convinced (see below). Jean Schlumberger, candidate for the Maurice Donnay chair, withdrew in the face of Marcel Pagnol. Their failure was also due to the fact that, faithful to the old rivalry with *La NRF*, the "academic right" opposed a strong resistance. Thus, François Mauriac and Henry Bordeaux confronted each other once again in early 1945. François Mauriac had mentioned the names Paulhan, Maritain, and Malraux for the succession to the Bergson chair. Bordeaux countered with the candidacy of a prisoner, Jean Guitton. Wary, Mauriac rebelled after thinking about it. As he wrote to Duhamel, he suspected that there was "Vichy underneath," solely because Bordeaux made the suggestion. He furthermore considered that "it would be too much to replace the greatest philosopher of modern times with a guy whose chief glory . . . is being a prisoner—*and whom we know nothing about.*" Finally, he contested the choice of "putting prisoners *before combatants and résistants* [. . .]: does the Academy want to elect resistance writers, or does it not?" To elect "an unknown prisoner" (for Mauriac) without his consent, and before his return, while "Malraux, Maritain, Paulhan, we know them," seemed intolerable to him. Tired of letting himself be "maneuvered" by Henry Bordeaux, he claimed to have decided to leave the Academy.[28] While Mauriac failed to elicit the hoped-for candidacies— undoubtedly because he failed to rally the votes of his colleagues—the threat would hit its mark, since Édouard Le Roy was elected to the Bergson chair, instead of Pierre Janet and Jean Rivain.

Meanwhile, the "academic right" slowly recovered. "While at the national level, the leaders of the Resistance ruined all the proffered chances one by one [. . .], the extreme right, quai Conti, did not commit a single tactical error and, as compromised as it seemed to be, would regain all its lost positions within a few months," François Mauriac commented, situating the turning point in 1946: "[. . .] already Baron Seillère and Jean Tharaud had slipped into the temple at the same time as them [the elected members of the academic 'left']."[29]

Led by André Chaumeix, the editor of the *Revue des deux mondes* (which reappeared in 1948), assisted by Pierre Benoit, from 1950 the "academic right" would constitute a powerful group that disposed of about a dozen votes. In January 1953, it had Duke de Lévis-Mirepoix elected to the chair of Maurras, who had just died. That very day, Maurras's former secretary Pierre Gaxotte was elected; he had been the editor in chief of *Je suis partout* up until the defeat, then had dissociated himself from its team. It would soon be the turn of Jean Cocteau (elected in 1955) who, having remained in Paris during the Occupation, had participated in the festivities of the collaborationist Parisian in crowd and published in the pro-German press, although he did not engage himself politically. It was most likely due to Aragon's protection that he did not appear on the "blacklist" and escaped judicial proceedings at the Liberation. On the same day, the historian of Christianity and faithful Pétain supporter Daniel-Rops entered the Academy; he had been awarded the Grand Prize for Literature in 1946. That year also witnessed the election of Jérôme Carcopino, former director of the École française de Rome, named director of the ENS by the Vichy government, then, following student protests on November 11, 1940, rector of the University of Paris where he replaced Gustave Roussy, before being promoted state secretary for national education from 1941 to 1942.[30]

It was in 1958 that a scandal would erupt with the candidacy of the famous writer Paul Morand, who had preferred not to return to France upon the Liberation, and resided in Switzerland where he had been the Vichy ambassador. The candidacy of Morand—who was criticized less, in spite of the dismissal of his charges, for his role as Vichy ambassador to Romania and then Switzerland than for "his conduct with respect to the occupier, in the middle of Paris"—could only be interpreted as a "pro-Vichy display, rising to its rank in a series of more and more overt displays by the Marshal's partisans."[31] A collective letter of warning in opposition to this candidacy, signed by eleven academicians and addressed solely to the "immortals" was quickly disclosed to the press, making the electoral campaign open to the public. The signers were Georges Duhamel, François Mauriac, Jules Romains, André Chamson, Fernand Gregh, Robert Kemp, André Siegfried, Pasteur Vallery-Radot, Maurice Garçon, Robert d'Harcourt, and Wladimir d'Ormesson. Mauriac seethed:

> It surely was about literature! An entire anti-résistant camp was mobilized and did not even try to hide it. Morand's personal friends, like Jacques de Lacretelle, had joined them. Morand would have a marshal's election [...] The other candidates were entreated to step aside for him, or risk losing all hope [...] Opposing Morand meant forever setting the powers of the academic right against oneself.[32]

Although the "academic right" managed to forge a powerful group, disposing of about eighteen votes, the opposition's camp ultimately succeeded by one vote. Having no candidate of their own for the reasons invoked by Mauriac, they resorted to blank ballots.

If it had taken place, Morand's election would have posed a problem regarding his investiture by the head of state. Indeed, de Gaulle, back in power, was hostile to the writer's candidacy. His exclusion lasted ten years. In 1968, Morand was elected. Meanwhile, two representatives of the pro-Vichy extreme right had entered the Academy: Henri Massis, elected in 1960, and Thierry Maulnier, elected in 1963. Among the writers that Mauriac characterized as "authentic," the Academy once again showed its preference for those on the right: Henry de Montherlant had been elected in 1960.

THE "HONOR JURY" OF LITERATURE: THE CNE VERSUS THE ACADEMY

The institutionalization of the CNE was inevitably inscribed in the cultural politics of the Communist Party and in its politics of rallying intellectuals. At the Tenth Congress of the party, which was held from the twenty-third to the thirtieth of June 1945, Georges Cogniot announced that all the underground organizations of the Northern and Southern zones that had merged by specialty (CNE, Union française universitaire, Mouvement national du spectacle, etc.), would form a National Union of Intellectuals. Cogniot then inventoried the renowned intellectuals in all realms of thought that the party counted in its ranks, in order to make it the "party of the elite and of intelligence," around which "intellectuals will unite to contribute to the profound renewal of democracy, which our Party prepares and advocates."[33]

To maintain the double legitimacy—literary and national—on which it intended to found its intellectual mastery, while respecting the constraints implied by the ideological line of the Communist Party, such was the issue at stake with regards to the CNE's survival, to the redefinition of its identity and mission. The illusion of a possible coexistence of literary, national, and Communist logics was a particularity of this period during which the country's national identity was undergoing reconstruction. It would prove indeed more and more difficult to preserve.

The prospect of the referendum in October 1945 meant to proclaim the Fourth Republic opposed the Communists and the Gaullists. While de Gaulle called for a yes-yes vote in response to the two questions posed, the first designating the elected national assembly as constituent, the second defining its role, the Communist Party advocated yes-no, in order to guarantee the sovereignty of the constituent assembly. De Gaulle's victory would only be partial. While the first "yes" was voted with a majority of 96 percent, the second majority was only 66 percent. In January 1946, de Gaulle left the government. The National Front experienced struggles that shattered résistant unanimity. For the Communist Party, it was then a question of regaining control over the authorities born of the Resistance. Jacques Debû-Bridel, director of the *Front national* newspaper, disagreed with the politics of the FN. He ran for election on a Fédération républicaine list that called for a yes-yes vote. In the meantime, a "Front national" society was formed, which effectively ousted Debû-Bridel from the newspaper that he claimed to own.[34] At the general assembly of the CNE in February 1946, Debû-Bridel was removed from the presidency by Aragon.

During that assembly, the very existence of the association seems to have been called into question, since Aragon, who led the discussion (without having been mandated) asked for an immediate vote, before any debate, on whether to maintain it above and beyond all differences. Debû-Bridel declared his agreement with its continued existence but asked that it state clear and precise goals. Aragon refused that the existence of the CNE be conditioned by anything. To ground their authority, both adversaries evoked their résistant past, a significant evocation that illustrates the persistence of the North-South division: Aragon cited his encounter with Paulhan, who had entered into contact with Decour, and cited the names of martyrs and members of the Southern zone who represented the most diverse tendencies (Jean Prévost, Henry Malherbe, Stanislas Fumet), while Jacques Debû-Bridel mentioned the inaugural meeting of *Les Lettres françaises* and cited the names of the members of the first committee in the Northern zone.

During the discussion regarding the relationship between the CNE and *Les Lettres françaises*, which part of the committee criticized for being a political newspaper, Claude Morgan maintained that the newspaper's politics had not changed, that they remained those of the National Front and of anti-Fascism, even if the struggle had changed forms. Debû-Bridel having replied that the politics of the National Front were no longer what they once were, invoking the resignations of François Mauriac and Father Philippe from the movement's directive committee as proof, Aragon intervened to contest his right to use this forum to put the politics of the National Front on trial, he who had appealed to the police against his former brothers-in-arms (he was likely referring to the affair of the *Front national* newspaper). And he went on to exclude him without further ado from the directive board of the CNE, with the support of an anonymous voice in the assembly that ordered Debû-Bridel to leave the gallery. A single protest was raised, that of Philippe Hériat, who asked the minister of national education, Marcel Naegelen, present at the meeting, to give the floor to Debû-Bridel. The latter refused to speak and withdrew. The ex-president of the committee was immediately replaced by Jean Cassou.[35]

On the other hand, Aragon conceded to the fact of the dissociation of the CNE and *Les Lettres françaises*. The CNE's survival was at stake. It seems that this dissociation was requested due to the campaign that the newspaper was then leading against François Mauriac. But it also served the party's work of reappropriating the publications that emerged from the Resistance, which would be marked the following year by the expunction of Jean Paulhan's name from the front page of the newspaper, then by the establishment of Pierre Daix as its editor in chief in place of Loÿs Masson. For the moment, it was agreed, at Aragon's suggestion, that the mention "organ of the CNE and member of the National Front" would disappear from the front page of the newspaper, and that a special page would be reserved for the CNE, with the title "The Comité national des écrivains Speaks to You." A column would also later be created in *L'Ordre*, Émile Buré's daily.[36] As the members of the directive committee who published in these columns had given up their freelance wages for its benefit, it became an additional source of income for the CNE coffers.

Aragon had drawn up a list of complaints against past management of the affairs of the committee, which he criticized for not suggesting "the bases of an action." Its only activity, according to the report of the general secretary, Claude Morgan, had been to draw up the "blacklist" of "undesirable" writers and the distribution of solidarity funds to the writers affected by years of war or to the families of victims. Aragon further criticized it for not having attained a legal status equivalent to that of the Société des gens de lettres, specifying that the blame did not lie solely with the directive board, but also with the public powers. Shortcomings in the administrative and financial management of the 1944–1945 staff would ultimately be noted at the exceptional general assembly held on May 28, 1946. They would be attributed to the "irresponsibility" of its then president, Debû-Bridel.

Aragon was clearly seeking to regain control; he actually became the general secretary of the committee—"irremovable," Paulhan would say[37]—under the presidency first of Jean Cassou, and then, starting in 1947, of Louis Martin-Chauffier. On this occasion, Aragon redefined the objectives of the CNE: in addition to its role as "honor jury of literature," which it assumed by maintaining the "blacklist," and through the "arbitration and defense of national honor," the committee should henceforth be "the cultural agent of France".[38]

After having affirmed the necessity of the CNE's permanence, the establishment of its official status (by making it the organ of consultation with the government for everything related to writers), and the reaffirmation of the charter [...] the program proclaims that the CNE is, in the literary realm, the cultural agent of France. That is to say that without waiting for its official recognition, it should enter into contact with the cultural attachés of all the foreign embassies in Paris; write to the writers of every country who defended France during our misfortunes and thank them for it; [...] establish connections that will allow us to make Paris and France into the confluence of international literary exchanges. The program of the CNE affirms that, to arrive at this result, we must present France abroad in the way that she is loved there, that is to say France the land of liberty, of traditional liberties, as well as the France of the resistance and of the reconstruction. This implies the essential duty of the CNE, which is to become the gathering place of the forces of creation and progress in French literature, against all national defeatism.[39]

It was for these reasons that the Socialist minister Marcel Naegelen, a member of the CNE, was asked for a "decent" office for the reception of foreign authors. It would be another year before this wish was realized. Following its separation from *Les Lettres françaises*, the CNE left the rue de Courcelles. At Elsa Triolet's initiative, the Agence Opera-Mundi placed an "attic" at 7, rue de la Paix at the disposition of the CNE. This is where Saturday receptions and the reception of foreign authors were organized, while the general assemblies were held at the Salle Pleyel. In November 1946, the committee had to move again: it was welcomed for several months by the Club Mallet-Stevens. The CNE also owed Elsa Triolet for finding a mansion on 2, rue de l'Élysée, occupied by the Americans, then by the English. Having become the "Maison de la Pensée française," the "House of French Thought," in April 1947 with the support of the public powers, it would host the National Union of Intellectuals and the groups that it federated, including the CNE.

The CNE, cultural agent of France? By becoming institutionalized, the CNE obviously intended to fight the French Academy for its role as official representative of French culture abroad. It was following the resignation of the permanent secretary Georges Duhamel, whose gesture he applauded, that Aragon engaged a campaign against the Company, explicitly targeting some of its members. The CNE, through its new general secretary, addressed two open letters to "one of the Forty" who apparently invoked, in its defense, the fact that the Academy was an old house that "couldn't be rushed," as well as the great prestige that it enjoyed abroad. Aragon's response is worth citing at length:

It is none the less true that at an essential moment in the national life, this Company demonstrated a shameful shortcoming, that it did not know how, nor did it want to show solidarity with the nation, that it refused to chase the traitors from its ranks, waiting for a court to make a decision about those of its members whose shame and infamy were public [...] The Academy's harm is a deep harm. Perhaps we have something to lose, in the eyes of our friends from the United States, by denouncing an institution that includes Claude Farrère, a frenetic friend of the Japanese soldiers who assassinated American pilots. Perhaps it is indispensable to French prestige in Patagonia to preserve the green outfit* of Louis Madelin, insulter of the French Revolution. Perhaps indeed, in Canada, Mr. Henry Bordeaux is still a great man, which can in any case only be true at France's expense [...]

Indeed, what is serious, the harm is not just that the Academy is ridiculed in song, it's not that it is a bunch (overall) of mediocre writers and people unrelated to literature, I would say more: it's not just that it waited for Charles Maurras, for example, to be judged before crossing him out of its records. It's much more: that it was possible for Maurras to be an academician, that a man whose whole work and life were devoted to perverting French words, to making them say the opposite of what they mean, could do so while claiming the authority of the Academy [...] If such is our prestige in the eyes of the foreigner, don't you think, my dear friend, that destroying the Academy would ruin nothing? On the contrary.[40]

An article by André David would follow in *L'Ordre* with the title "For a Republican Academy." Mauriac's response to this article testifies to the CNE's relative loss of legitimacy at this point, although it preceded the resignation of the great elders: "We certainly understand what this 'republican' means under the pen of this frantic neophyte, and that his new Academy would be nothing less than what our dear Comité National des Écrivains has already become: a lovely little abscess of Communist fixation."[41] Starting at the end of the year, the mass departure of the committee's elders would reveal the scope of the fracture.

The Literary Resistance Divided

Paradoxically, the CNE would not contribute less than the other authorities of the literary field to the depoliticization of the intellectual Resistance, divesting it of its original subversive charge. The story of the CNE is one of social aging,

---

* The *habit vert*, or green outfit, is the ceremonial garment of the French Academy.—Trans.

routinization, and the growing heteronomy of an authority that was formed in the struggle to regain autonomy. It is also the story of the successive ruptures that shook the unity of resisting writers. While routinization is part of the process of institutionalization, the acceleration of that process, despite the renewal of the committee's members, was due to the political constraints that the ties to the Communist Party brought to bear on the CNE, notably through Aragon. Routinization is thus closely linked here with growing heteronomy, which subordinated all the efforts of the leaders to a single objective: neutralizing the subversive vocation of the committee. While respect for political orthodoxy condemned the CNE to moral disrepute in the intellectual field, the national literary vocation that it claimed immediately condemned it to a form of academicism. Moreover, its professional aspirations were destined to fail.

Yet the story of the CNE also allows us to grasp the imbrication of the literary and political logics from another angle: that of the attraction that the Communist Party exerted over an entire generation of young pretenders. "It's not dodging the difficulty to affirm that it is not political reasons that push me to approach Aragon," wrote the poet Bernard Vargaftig, who joined the party in 1951 at the age of seventeen.[42] Bernard Vargaftig was not a member of the CNE. But this reflection probably applied to a certain number of aspiring poets who were attracted to the committee by the charismatic figures of Aragon and Eluard, the properly literary forms of socialization and sociability that the committee offered them, and the diffusion that it ensured them.

The CNE pursued its activities up until the end of the 1960s. We should not be fooled by this surprising longevity. While its literary and political role may have been modified over time, while its recruitment was diversified, its existence remained closely linked to the charisma of its principal leaders. The date of its suspension coincided with the distance that Aragon was taking with respect to the party during the same period. The CNE would not survive Elsa Triolet, who died in 1970. This decline did not happen overnight. Until 1953, we note the effective presence of an average of seventy members at the general assemblies. At the assembly of January 1962, they numbered less than half (32), out of the 166 enrolled members (36 others had delegated their power). At that point, the CNE was run out of the rue de l'Élysée. Its headquarters were again located at *Les Lettres françaises*. This history exceeds my analysis as well as my chronological framework. I will thus limit myself here to presenting an outline of the committee's evolution until 1953, date of the definitive fracture of the unity of the Resistance, by making, as with the French Academy, some forays beyond that date to give an overview of the aftermath of the crisis.

The reversal of power relations in the literary field to the detriment of the writers of the Resistance, which played out in the book market as well as within the authorities of consecration, was marked at the CNE by the departure of the great elders at the end of 1946. For more than two years, Jean Paulhan had been constantly postponing the moment of his departure. Having retracted his first resignation at the request of Claude Morgan, after his victory in the affair of the "list of major culprits" in October 1944, he had decided to distance himself. His close friends had also discouraged him. Jean Blanzat had written to him:

> I would be upset if you resigned. You have been the basis of everything, the original committee is your work. I think about the opinion of the resistance where there are so many great guys and also abroad [. . .] Montherlant will be thrilled and he's just waiting for our disagreements. All those who remain will look like bloodthirsty executioners and even the things that should be done will become impossible.[43]

Gaston Gallimard did not wish for this premature departure either.

Was it just because of solidarity that Paulhan put off his break for so long? Leaving is, of course, always more difficult than staying. His dissent with his former friends had moreover isolated the former director of *La NRF*. When he conceived of the project of the *Cahiers de la Pléiade* in March 1945, he notably informed Jouhandeau, whose contribution he immediately requested,[44] and Vercors, in order to ask him, strangely enough, his opinion on what he presented as a specific request from Gide and Gallimard. Vercors's response, no less strange, illustrates Paulhan's delicate position, constrained to submit his new project for the approval of the CNE (which he undoubtedly hoped to obtain with, precisely, the support of the author of *Le Silence de la mer*). Vercors emphasized the risk that an almanac of that type would be taken for a "disguised *NRF*." Pretending that he didn't know what to advise him, he implied that he would himself decline such a proposition, and that Paulhan's acceptance would in any case have a public significance.[45]

As long as Paulhan thought he could obtain the removal of his friends Marcel Jouhandeau and Jean Giono from the "blacklist," counting on their contribution for the *Cahiers*, he remained at the CNE. At the general assembly of May 28, 1946, two names were removed from the list: Pierre Andreu and Jean Vignaud. In the autumn of 1946, Paulhan announced to Jean Schlumberger that he intended to ask the CNE to remove Armand Petitjean and Pierre Benoit.[46] Invoking the dismissal of charges by the Comité d'épuration professionnelle that had just benefited Pierre Benoit, Paulhan first intervened on his behalf with Aragon.[47] At the meeting of November 12, Aragon presented Paulhan's request, saying he was in favor, and obtained the agreement of the members of the directive board, some of whom insisted, though, that other cases be examined at the same time. Nonetheless, with the support of Queneau, Aragon obtained a quick resolution to the Pierre Benoit case. In November, Paulhan asked Aragon for the removal of Giono and Jouhandeau while sending him his resignation.[48] This time, the break was definitive. It is true that on October 26, 1946, the court decided to close the Gallimard case. It is also true that 1946 marked a new phase in the history of the CNE, not only because of the reorganization Aragon began in February, but also because of the first implementation of a procedure of exclusion. After Debû-Bridel was expelled from the presidency, René Lalou was excluded for having violated the CNE charter.[49] Paulhan protested against this second exclusion to Aragon.

But it was less this exclusion than the update that the CNE published on the occasion of Pierre Benoit's removal from the list that appalled the defender of the "right to aberration." This update concluded in these terms:

> It is quite understandable that neither the execution of Brasillach or Paul Chack, nor the suicide of Drieu La Rochelle can erase their names from the blacklist, and that the CNE charter does not allow members of this association to publish a newspaper, a book, or a review, alongside men who can only have paid in the eyes of justice, but not the human conscience.[50]

In accordance with his initial positions, Paulhan resented the universal principles that the CNE claimed in order to establish its power of excommunication. This was all the more true since the Pen Club had just draw up its own "blacklist" in the summer of 1946 (a "blacklist" composed of the "blacklists" established in each country and destined to be applied at the European level) with Aragon's help. Announcing his resignation to Jean Schlumberger, Paulhan wrote to him:

> The exclusion of Lalou (guilty of having put a poem by Maurras in his anthology!) was simply ridiculous. But it seems to me that the last declaration of the CNE goes much further than ridiculousness. So we now give eternal rulings in the name of "human conscience"! I feel less and less like a benevolent judge (or policeman). I am sending, by the same post, my resignation to Cassou and Aragon [. . .] Too bad for them (I mean for the CNE).[51]

Too bad for the CNE? Paulhan knew what he was talking about. With his departure, the CNE lost its literary legitimacy, all the more so since Paulhan, who had just launched the *Cahiers de la Pléiade*, was then seeking the endorsement of the CNE's chief rival authority, the French Academy. Having obtained the Grand Prize for Literature the previous year strengthened his position. Recalcitrant until that point about a candidacy at the Academy that Mauriac and Duhamel had tried to elicit several times, Paulhan considered it starting in July 1946, and tried to convince Gallimard, who didn't like the idea:

> [...] Here is what seems more serious to me: my task of editing the *Cahiers [de la Pléiade]* seems to consist essentially in breaking this kind of iron circle that the Machiavellianism of some, the cowardice of the others has more solidly closed each day around a Jouhandeau, a Giono, and even a Montherlant (whom I hardly like) for the past two years. I hardly imagine, for example, a second issue of the *Cahiers* without some excerpts from the *Essai sur moi-même* [by Jouhandeau].
>
> I will have to break ties, then, with more than one friend—in any case with the CNE, with the UNI [union nationale des intellectuels], even with the Pen Club (which *only today* drew up its blacklist, and drew it up under Aragon's direction). I believe I will only lose a didactic literature, which I hardly prize. All the same, I wouldn't want to find myself abandoned by everyone overnight. (For myself, moreover, I don't give a damn; but it seems dangerous for the *Cahiers*; for the house [Gallimard] itself.) We need support here. I don't feel at all disposed to refuse—since they offer—that of the Academy; why not that of the *Revue des Deux Mondes* itself, which should reappear soon [...].[52]

Paulhan would have to wait over fifteen years more to enter the Academy. By resigning from the CNE, he anticipated the exclusion that would surely have been declared against him after the publication of the second issue of the *Cahiers de la Pléiade*, with a table of contents that included Jouhandeau. Paulhan had managed to get Gide to appear in the same volume, despite the latter's hesitations. "Of course I don't disapprove of you attempting this rehabilitation: you are admirably qualified to do it and your own record authorizes it. I will say as much for Malraux. But I am not in the same situation," Gide wrote him, a sign that Aragon's attacks in the autumn of 1944 hit their mark, and that they continued to produce an effect. But it was precisely this argument that Paulhan employed to convince him—"is it really you who want to give Aragon this triumph"—further reassuring him by mentioning that Sartre had also asked Jouhandeau for an article for *Les Temps modernes*.[53]

Paulhan's resignation was immediately followed by the resounding resignations of Schlumberger, Duhamel, the Tharaud brothers, and Gabriel Marcel, and the more discreet ones of Luc Estang, Dominique Aury, Denis Marion, and René de Solier (who had just joined in November). Only Mauriac abstained. Caught up in the struggles against the "academic right," he had just proclaimed his renewed solidarity with his Resistance comrades a few months earlier.

This wave of resignations illustrates the relations of legitimacy in the CNE. Despite their literary titles, the elders who had arrived late to the committee could not actually noticeably resign without Paulhan, the only one among them who held the moral capital linked to Resistance activity. Paulhan, who was more attached than his colleagues to the committee he had cofounded, hardly rejoiced at seeing himself assimilated with the "moralists." Viewed collectively, the resignation of the great elders masked precisely what opposed Paulhan to his so-called allies, and especially Gabriel Marcel. Paulhan thus wrote to Jean Schlumberger: "The Tharauds, after Duhamel, are resigning from the CNE (As for Marcel, I don't really see what right he has to leave the CNE, since his presence on the blacklist commission could only give that list more weight and authority)."[54]

It was neither the principle of the "blacklist" nor that of the purge that motivated the departure of these "moralists," but their position of dependency in relation to the new generation, and their anti-Communism, which could now be openly displayed. In a study on the subject, Gabriel Marcel explained himself publicly to Jean Duché, criticizing the CNE for its marked political tendency:

It has been a long time, he told me [G. Marcel], that I've been waiting for a chance to leave the CNE, which had become an instrument of political sectarianism. What did the CNE do from a professional standpoint other than draw up a blacklist? I don't contest that this work was useful at the Liberation. That it was poorly done is no less contestable. The list should have been revised: we were only able to obtain it for a few very rare exceptions. In my view, this list should only include a very small number of names, and the only criterion of accusation should concern informing. Any purely ideological exclusion is unacceptable when the war is over. But the political spirit plays such a role in the CNE that this work of discernment is impossible.

Jean Schlumberger invoked similar arguments, although more nuanced and more centered on the defense of literary autonomy:

[...] if the CNE had kept itself on the literary plane, if it hadn't tried to monopolize the Resistance for the benefit of a political party, I could have not approved of all its decisions, but I wouldn't have felt continually used to cover its displays, which have nothing to do with a good literary discipline

[. . .] The CNE's official organ is a periodical that is moreover very well done, very lively and interesting, but which is clearly a communist publication [. . .] I don't blame *Les Lettres françaises*, that's how they bring an important note into the concert of French voices. But I would appreciate them all the more if I didn't feel personally, through the CNE, engaged by what they publish.[55]

Like Gabriel Marcel, Jean Schlumberger did not oppose the principle of sanctions as such. In response to Jean Duché's question—"Are you for a general amnesty?"—he said, "No. I insist on stating that, for my part, while I believe it is time to give a more nuanced application to the principles that had united us at the CNE, I am not at all inclined toward a weak indulgence. I will never consider the writings that helped demoralize the French at a time when it was important to support their resolve at any price as simple games of the mind." This last phrase quite obviously targeted Jean Paulhan.

More than Paulhan's resignation, the late break of those who resigned in December 1946 only confirmed the central role that the CNE had played up to that point in the literary field. These resignations contributed to the loss of the double literary and national legitimacy that the committee claimed. On the verge of the Cold War, they exposed what had until then appeared to be demands specific to the literary field—founding the writer's working conditions on ethical bases—for what they really were: the diktats of a party. By reaffirming the autonomy of literature in relation to politics, they ultimately marked the beginning of a process of "normalization" of the literary field, which was completed in 1953.

Until December 1946, the charter of the CNE effectively functioned like an anathema: it excluded the banned authors of the "blacklist" from the literary field by depriving them of public forums. The charter largely drew its power of excommunication from its endorsement by the presence of Paulhan and the great elders. The engagement that the members of the CNE had made could thus easily be turned against them. This was the meaning that was immediately attributed to these resignations. It was formulated by a CNE spokesman who benefited from Resistance legitimacy without being identified with the Communist Party. The "Open Letter" from Vercors to those who had resigned was explicit:

You are great writers. As such, each of your acts is followed by consequences in proportion to your renown. Have you measured those that will follow your resignation? [. . .] unless you publicly and solemnly specify that your resignation does not in any way lead to the abandonment of this commitment [the CNE charter], it means that, in a few weeks, the dailies and weeklies that even yesterday were to refuse to publish anything by those writers who had no pity for the victims (but whose talent attracts readers) because it meant simultaneously depriving themselves of even bigger talents, will finally be relieved of this awkward dilemma, since you yourselves are lifting the ban [. . .] It means, as a result, that we are the ones, if we want to remain faithful to ourselves (and to the memory of those who died) that you simultaneously condemn to silence—or to denial.[56]

The CNE would still try to maintain its power of excommunication for as long as possible. Following the resignations and polemics surrounding the "blacklist," Aragon had suggested two brochure projects to the directive board: one would collect the articles, interviews, and letters related to the debate, while the other, an "anthology of the blacklist," would unite the most significant texts that earned their authors a place on this list. A revision of the "blacklist" was planned in correlation to the second project, Aragon having suggested that a removal was now necessary in the case of André Castelot, who, though an ex-contributor to *La Gerbe*, wrote articles that were not ideological. To my knowledge, neither of these two plans for brochures came to fruition.

On the other hand, a final exclusion from the CNE was declared in 1948, concerning François Mauriac. Mauriac had effectively violated the charter by contributing to *La Table ronde*, along with Marcel Jouhandeau in particular. Aragon, who presented the affair to the directive board, saw it as a "deliberate break" from the committee by Mauriac. "If we add that *La Table Ronde* is a publishing house that announces books by Edmond Jaloux, Bertrand de Jouvenel, Fraigneau, and Maurice Bardèche, we can only arrive at an organized venture."[57] This exclusion was the last: the "blacklist" was no longer heeded. From then on, it would be up to the CNE to readjust its principles according to the constraints of the literary field in order to ensure its survival and garner new memberships.

In 1949, Mauriac definitively settled his score with the CNE that had excluded him, in an article in which he accused it of usurping the "official advantages, beautiful rooms, and fresh gardens of the rue de l'Élysée": "What is a Comité national des écrivains that lacks almost everything that counts in literature today?" And he ironically mentioned the Congrès des écrivains pour la paix that met on the rue de l'Élysée:

What French writers? Gide? Claudel? Martin du Gard? Duhamel? Jules Romains? Siegfried? Maurois? Malraux? Sartre? Camus? Marcel Aymé? Gabriel Marcel? Schlumberger? Anouilh? René Char? Breton? Yes, I do indeed understand that around the illustrious Aragon-Triolet couple, living entries in History and legend, the Vercors and the Tzaras flocked, and that, a bit farther back, Paul Eluard, a true French poet, perhaps thought about those long dark days when, on those school notebooks, he wrote that word, "liberty"—that word that I challenge you to trace today on the panels of the Aragon palace [...].[58]

THE ACADEMY OF THE RESISTANCE

The establishment of the Maison de la Pensée française in an elegant space marked a new step in the institutionalization of the CNE: the "attic," which evoked the "Auteuil attic" of the Goncourts, strictly reserved for literary people unlike the high society salons, became a private club, following the model of the Pen Club. The Maison de la Pensée was first opened on October 16, 1947, for the book sale organized by Elsa Triolet in the name of the CNE, in the presence of the president of the Republic, Vincent Auriol, who would attend for several consecutive years.

During the 1948 sale, Vincent Auriol paid tribute to the CNE in these terms: "Your Comité national des écrivains is a double upholder, upholder of the spirit of the Resistance and also of the French spirit and French intellectual influence."[59] Guardian of the collective memory and organization of mutual aid in the style of the Association des écrivains combattants, a site for exercising intellectual power and site of sociability following the model of the Pen Club, the CNE also aspired, as we saw, to fight the French Academy for its role of "cultural agent of France." In fact, it would assume this role for the Soviet Writers' Union and for equivalent organizations in the other Eastern countries, which actually inspired it. Let us recall that the Soviet Writers' Union, founded in 1934 by the Communist Party, was not officially designated as a party organization (it was not necessary to be a member of the latter to join the former, although members of the Communist Party of the Soviet Union [CPSU] were in the majority there).[60] Aragon and Elsa Triolet attended its first congress in 1934. They were close to its first president, Maksim Gorky, and to Alexandre Fadeïev, who became its general secretary in 1946. While the CNE was far from concentrating a cultural power analogous to that of the union, it presented comparable characteristics: the autonomy claimed with respect to the party and the procedure of unanimous voting, for example.

The institutionalization of the CNE and its internationalization were accompanied by a relative loss of its moral authority and its legitimacy in the French literary field. This was all the more so since a crisis was shaking the literary ventures born of the Resistance during this period. They had established themselves at a time when military censorship, quarantine measures taken against collaborationist writers, threats that weighed on the traditional authorities of diffusion and consecration, and public demand left them almost unrivaled. Meanwhile, as early as 1946, publishing recorded, as we saw, a decline in interest for war literature. The impact of the "blacklist" waned as the traditional authorities regained the upper hand. In a letter intended for Paulhan and written after his resignation, Vercors complained about the fact that in booksellers' windows, there were more books by Montherlant than Vercors.[61] The magazines *Messages, Fontaine, Confluences*, and *Poésie* disappeared around 1947. *Les Lettres françaises*, on the verge of bankruptcy, were bailed out that very year by the Communist Party.[62] While the Éditions Charlot collapsed, the Éditions de Minuit saw their business figures cut in half between 1945 and 1947. They would only survive at the cost of a change in management. The financial aid given by the family of Jérôme Lindon saved the business from bankruptcy, but it led to the departure of Vercors following Lindon's rise to the head of the publishing house in 1948.[63] Fragile, barely hardened to the fluctuations of the market in a difficult conjuncture—particularly the book workers' strike, which ended with a 25 percent raise in salaries in October 1947—these businesses were the first victims of a crisis that touched all of French publishing. In 1948, Louis Joxe, general director of cultural relations at the Quai d'Orsay, reported a 50 percent reduction in exports in comparison with 1939, due to the excessive production cost of publications, the shortage of paper allotted to publishing, and the growing number of houses.[64]

In parallel, the total number of translations into French greatly increased, even doubled with respect to the prewar period.[65] Although they still represented just less than a tenth of the total production of French publishing, they were perceived as a threat for the diffusion of French books. This was such a concern that, during an interview with *Les Lettres françaises*, Georges Duhamel suggested temporarily reducing the amount of paper used to publish translations in favor of an exportation policy that would guarantee the diffusion of French books abroad and the upkeep of the French language in the world.[66] In its meeting on November 27, 1947, the French Academy expressed the wish, aimed at Louis Joxe, that French books be better distributed on the American continent.[67]

It was, of course, the penetration of American cultural products, books obviously, with the popularity of the detective novel, but also cinema, music, and comics, that primarily worried a large number of French intellectuals. On the verge of the Cold War, Communist intellectuals would turn what looked like an expression of American imperialism into the spearhead of their fight for the defense of French culture, around which they were able to rally progressive colleagues as well as representatives of the Gaullist academic pole like Duhamel. It was in this fight, led in parallel to the defense of peace, that the CNE, under the influence of Aragon and Elsa Triolet, would find the means to adapt its professional vocation.

"We are caught between our sense of the universal and our instinct for conservation," Aragon explained in a speech on "Culture and Its Diffusion," given at the National Union of Intellectuals (UNI) in April 1947. While he set himself apart from the "reactionaries" who asked that Henry Miller be banned in France, the author of *Aurélien* "[did] not think that freedom consists in organizing publicity for Millerism in France." For him, "the safeguard of the independence of a country [...] against a powerful imperialism" was at stake.[68] In March 1948, Elsa Triolet devoted a lecture at the CNE to this theme, in order to denounce the success of "a certain American literature" symbolized by the novel *Forever Amber*. Whether or not it was justified, the equation that she made on this occasion would found the rallying of Communist and non-Communist writers to the struggle to defend the French book: "In 1944, collaborators' books were replaced by the books of resistance writers. Little by little, the books of resistance writers were replaced by American translations, which were mixed with the works of collaboration writers."[69]

The lecture, which was excerpted in *Les Lettres françaises* and would be republished in the collection *L'écrivain et le livre*, gave rise to an investigation by René Lacôte on the French bookstore, concluding in the "proliferation of shopkeepers of the collaboration" drowning out the "professional booksellers."[70] The latter were victims of a diffusion network that, from criticism to distribution, was responsible for the "sabotage of French publishing." The investigation also ratified the postulate formulated by Elsa Triolet: "It's not the reader who refuses our books, it's the middlemen who hide them or keep them from the readers."[71]

Whether it regarded book distribution in France or abroad, this postulate was taken up by all the CNE writers who intervened in the debate. On the page of *Les Lettres françaises* that was reserved for the CNE, we find an article by the Communist writer André Wurmser on the influence of French books in South America which, in the absence of an exportation policy, was overtaken by the American influence whereas there was still very great interest for French culture there.[72] A year later, Henry Malherbe, former president of the Association des écrivains combattants, noted a disinterest of the French public for American novels, but recalled that the diffusion of French books still encountered obstacles of a material order, and hailed the initiatives taken by Elsa Triolet in this area.[73]

At first, the struggle would be led at the level of the middlemen between the book and the public, with the creation of the Comité du livre français, the French Book Committee. Eventually, it would go around the middlemen, directly to the public, through the "Battles of the Book."

After a preparatory meeting organized by Elsa Triolet, Vercors, and Pierre Seghers on May 4, 1948, at the Éditions de Minuit, the interprofessional committee of the book, called the "Comité du livre français," was created on July 5, 1948. In the meantime, the government had set up a Commission nationale du livre français, responsible for exportation policy: Elsa Triolet, who hoped to be named to it, would not participate. The "Comité du livre français" would thus devote itself to the diffusion of books in France. Under the honorary presidency of Georges Duhamel, the managing committee included Julien Cain, director of the Bibliothèques de France; M. Sarrailh, rector of the Université de Paris; representatives of publishing, printing, bookselling, and teaching. The memberships of about fifty writers and book professionals had been garnered beforehand; writers formed a significant majority. More than half of them were members of the CNE. In December 1948, Elsa Triolet, who succeeded Aragon as the general secretary of the association in October, obtained the CNE's support for the Comité du livre.

From March 25–27, 1949, a convention on French thought, convened by the National Union of Intellectuals (Union nationale des intellectuels or UNI) and the Confederation of Intellectual Workers (Confédération des travailleurs intellectuels or CTI), was held at the Maison de la Pensée française. The first portion of the meeting concerned "the material and moral condition of the intellectual." The second, placed under the sole banner of the UNI, was devoted to the defense of peace.[74] Elsa Triolet, René Jouglet, and Jean Proal served on the committee designated, in the name of the directive board of the CNE, to study and draft the response to the first questionnaire. Entitled, "On the Material Conditions for Freedom of Expression," this response was published on the CNE page.[75] It was centered on two themes: the defense of the book, in reference to which the work of the Commission nationale du livre with the Ministry of Foreign Affairs and that of the interprofessional association called the Comité du livre français were mentioned; and the status of the writer's profession, or rather its absence of status. In this respect, the CNE denounced the excess taxation that weighed on writers and called for them to be accorded a salaried status. Although they gave a more concrete content to the professional mission of the CNE, these interventions would have few repercussions.

A new project emerged in 1950, that of the "Battles of the Book," a good illustration of the cultural politics of the French Communist Party during the Cold War. After having invited Elsa Triolet to travel across France to present her books, in November 1949 François Billoux, head of the ideological section of the party, suggested setting up a "book week in Marseille."[76] For Elsa Triolet, the "Battles of the Book," which she initiated, according to Dominique Desanti, were inscribed in continuity with her previous combat:[77] she remained convinced that it was less public disinterest than the distribution network that was responsible for the slump in sales of progressive literature. Only Communist writers participated in the "Battles of the Book" put in place in 1950: Aragon, Eluard, Marcenac, Morgan, Wurmser, and others. The following year, as writers grew tired crisscrossing France, the Centre des BBL (Bibliothèques de la bataille du livre, or Libraries of the Book Battle) was founded. Intended to favor the creation of small lending libraries at work, it would bring the principle of the "book battle" together with the older plan for a "traveling library," which Aragon attributed to Jean-Richard Bloch. The CNE did not participate as such in these events organized by the Communist Party. They nonetheless illustrate the gratifications and benefits that writers would draw from their membership in the party, which offered them forums and distribution networks. Far from excluding political convictions, this convergence of interests between the party and its writers was based (more or less) on them. This point is essential to understanding the attraction that the CNE continued to exert, particularly over the new generations.

In literary life, the CNE played a triple role: site of intellectual sociability and, for newcomers to literature, of socialization, it ensured the diffusion of its members' works and their defense on the professional plane. Saturday meetings starring Aragon and Eluard, lectures, readings, exhibitions, receptions held in the honor of foreign writers like Elio Vittorini (before his exclusion from the Italian Communist Party), Adam Wazyk, José Mancisidor, Ilya Ehrenburg, Konstantin Simonov, John Steinbeck, Julius Illyès, Zoltan Szabo, and André Havas, the CNE was above all a site of literary sociability. Raised in the Russian school of the perpetual staging of literature, Elsa Triolet was the great organizer of these events. She was also at the origin of the Group of Young Poets, hosted in the columns of *Les Lettres françaises*. Again marginalized after the renewed favor it experienced with the public during the Occupation years, poetry found a privileged site of expression in the CNE. Young poets like Charles Dobzynski and Pierre Gamarra cut their teeth there. The CNE "Saturdays" were very popular with the young generation of Communist poets, attracted by the charismatic figures of Aragon and Eluard, who watched over their insertion in the literary field, opened up the forums of *Les Lettres françaises* to them, and commissioned work.

The new recruits of the CNE, Communists or non-Communists, were also attracted by the annual book sale, as Vercors has confirmed for us.[78] Modeled on the book sales of the Pen Club and the Association des écrivains combattants, but taking a more popular form, the CNE sale would be a literary and social event into the 1960s.[79] Hosted by stars like Gérard Philipe, Yves Montand, and Simone Signoret, it attracted a wide public, to the extent that the Maison de la Pensée location became too small to accommodate it. In 1951, it was transferred to the Palais d'Orsay and would be held at the Vél d'Hiv starting in 1952.[80] The gross sales receipts reached 750,000 francs in 1947, 1,736,000 francs in 1948, and 5,267,900 francs in 1952,[81] the year when approximately 30,000 people participated in the event. According to Vercors, writers sold about 200 copies, and Aragon managed to sell 600 or 700. Since the profits reverted to the committee, the authors' interest was symbolic rather than economic.[82] For the youngest, it was a chance to reach the general public and especially to mingle with the most prestigious writers.

It was in regards to the attraction that the sale exerted over the newcomers that the question of recruitment was first raised in 1952. The general secretary, Janine Bouissounouse, concluded her report on the sale in these terms: "We must therefore, in the future, find a way that allows us to admit only people of value and not second-rate writers with two published books." Aragon continued: "The CNE enters the second phase of its existence [. . .] It is clear that we are faced with a recruitment of youth. We need to find out how to limit things and only choose people who seem like professional writers."[83] The writers of the Resistance could only belong to the committee, and it was unlikely that those who were not there would join it now, explained Maurice Druon, then a member of the directive board. Aragon suggested working to obtain the membership of writers "worthy of interest." For the sale, a commission would be designated that would rule on each case.

This rejuvenation of the committee did not suffice to prevent any risk of academicism. This was all the more so since the traditional prosody that Aragon promoted at this time, in continuity with his search for a national poetic form opposed to pure poetry, whether avant-gardist (the surrealists) or academic (Valéry),[84] was now deprived of the subversive dimension that the practice of "contraband" had given it. Although it had a significant resonance with the new generation (Guillevic composed, for example, his *Trente et un sonnets* during this time), this poetic conception such as it would be recorded in the *Journal d'une poésie nationale* (1954) did not escape the effect of routinization, which annihilated its magical power.[85]

In the 1950s, the CNE added the role of literary jury to its duties. Indeed, in 1950, the creation of a CNE prize was proposed. Conscious of the threat of academicism that weighed on the committee, Aragon opposed the plan: "It's not a question of forming an Academy of the Resistance but of remaining connected to its spirit while going beyond it."[86] According to him, it was more within the committee's role to support its struggling members. The principle was adopted in the form of a poetry grant; René Guy Cadou was the first beneficiary, at Aragon's suggestion. In 1955, the Prize of Unanimity, which consecrated the work of a "writer of great renown" in virtue of its originality, would nonetheless be added to the two annual grants intended for young authors. Endowed with 250,000 francs, between 1955 and 1959 it would be awarded to Julien Benda, Gustave Cohen, Marie Noël, Francis Carco, and Pierre Mac Orlan. Mohammed Dib would be the winner in 1962.

A DIVERTED SUBVERSIVE HERITAGE?

The "academicization" of the CNE on the literary plane had its counterpart in the political field. It was the subversive political vocation of the CNE that had united its members in clandestinity. After the Liberation, the members of the CNE had united for the defense of the values of the Resistance, "respect, freedom, and the dignity of the human being," against all social discrimination and for freedom of expression.[87] But the cost of maintaining unity would be political neutralization, made official after the great fracture of 1953 that led to the departure of most of the former non-Communist underground comrades. To understand this fracture, we must make a detour through the stakes of the Cold War such as they reverberated in the camp of progressive intellectuals.

During the Cold War, the CNE was a site of mobilization for the Communist Party's ideological and cultural fights. The defense of culture and the fight for peace: these were the watchwords. They were general enough to allow a wide and diversified recruitment, especially among intellectuals of the left and progressive Catholics. Aragon worked in parallel to establish a literary genealogy of French humanist realism in its pacifist version, with Barbusse and Romain Rolland as its figureheads. At the CNE, which feared awakening ideological divisions, the president Louis Martin-Chauffier immediately presented the aspiration toward peace as a cause unrelated to politics.[88] At the initiative of Aragon and Elsa Triolet, the CNE took an active part in the peace movement. In June 1946, the CNE had already organized, with the Association des écrivains combattants, the French section of the Pen Club and the Société des écrivains de province, a Congrès des écrivains de la France in the context of the National Union of Intellectuals' congress on the theme, "French Thought in the Service of Peace." In February 1949, Aragon obtained the support of the directive board of the CNE for the "World Congress of Partisans for Peace," which was to be held in Paris from April 20 to 23, 1949, and which was already personally supported by Jean Cassou, Paul Eluard, Louis Martin-Chauffier, Elsa Triolet, and himself, all members of the directive board of the CNE. Elsa Triolet, Martin-Chauffier, and Jean Proal were named CNE delegates to the congress. Declaring herself unsatisfied, in her moral report for the 1949 staff, with the activity of the CNE in this fight, which had until then been limited to a theoretical agreement, Elsa Triolet asked it to "aid in the battle for peace with the arms that are our own, those of the writers."[89] In June 1950, she would garner the committee's support for the Stockholm Appeal.[90] At her initiative, the CNE addressed a letter in favor of peace to writers everywhere in the world. This letter was read by Henry Malherbe, CNE delegate, at the departmental peace meetings for the Seine, which were held October 28–29, 1950. At the general assembly of the CNE on March 10, 1951, President Martin-Chauffier would deplore the resignations due to the signing of the Stockholm Appeal—including two members of the directive board, Camille Marbo and Jean Proal—and would once more declare that peace was not a political matter.

Despite a few defections, the mobilization for peace did not truly divide the progressive camp. The tensions arose from the hardening of the Communist line, Zhdanovism, and especially the Stalinian trials. In their relations with their Communist colleagues, the fellow-travelers who emerged from the Resistance were in effect confronted with the problem of their freedom of expression. Aveline, Cassou, Martin-Chauffier, and Vercors, in particular, exposed their dilemmas in two collections, *L'Heure du choix* (1947) and *La Voie libre* (1951), in which they reaffirmed their attachment to Socialism and their fidelity to the struggle of the Communists, with which they were still united, but with conditions. The second collection, however, showed a difference in tone. The four years that separated them were marked by the political trials in Eastern Europe and the silence to which progressive intellectuals close to the party had been reduced in the forums controlled by the Communists. The dilemmas that Jean Cassou and Vercors were led to publish in 1949 in *Esprit*—barring their publication in *Les Lettres françaises*—in reaction to the Rajk trial and the Tito affair, were severely criticized by the Communists.[91] But while Jean Cassou denounced the "clearly clerical character of the Kominform," the imposition of "dogmas," the prohibition of free inquiry, the assimilation of the avant-garde's formal exploration to "heresies," all distinctive traits of a "Church"[92]—here Cassou took up a theme developed by Claude Aveline in *L'Heure du choix*—Vercors limited himself to condemning the dishonest character of the Rajk and Tito trials, to which the accused had contributed with their confessions, to deduce that "the people" were being "trick[ed]":

> Is this one guilty or innocent? The question is no longer posed since he confessed. One or the other: either his confessions are founded, Rajk has always

been what his confessions proclaim, the fierce adversary of the communist—and in that case there are contradictions in his confessions that are more than troubling: they are incredible. Or else these confessions themselves are dishonest. In both cases, Rajk lied: this is what matters.[93]

While in *La Voie libre*, the positions of Aveline, Cassou, and Martin-Chauffier were more critical, Vercors reiterated his condemnation of generalized dishonesty, asking what limits should be imposed on the justification of the means by the end.

These positions announced the new configuration of alliances at the time of one of the most serious crises that the CNE experienced. When the conflict erupted in 1953, Vercors had just accepted the presidency of the CNE, at the urging of Elsa Triolet and Maurice Druon, a newcomer to the directive board. This position was traditionally entrusted to a non-Communist. He replaced Martin-Chauffier, who found a pretext to resign from this role following Aragon's attack on Mauriac in *Les Lettres françaises*, shortly after the president of the CNE had offered his congratulations to the winner of the Nobel Prize. This was how Vercors would find himself confronted with his former allies, Cassou, Martin-Chauffier, and Aveline.

In his analysis of the endorsements of progressive intellectuals who were close to the party during the Cold War, the American historian Tony Judt affirms that "curiously, the worst trial of all, that of Slánsky and his associates in 1952, did not in fact produce many defections; most of those who could no longer find it in themselves to account for these things had already left the fold."[94] And yet, it was indeed on this occasion that the break initiated by the fellow-travelers was consummated, in a violent polemic published in the columns of *Le Figaro littéraire* under the title "Tempest in the CNE," from February 21 to April 25, 1953. Responding to a call from Serge Groussard who protested against the neutrality of the motion that the CNE had adopted on the anti-Semitic tone of the Prague trials, some twenty members of the CNE publicly resigned, including the non-Communist former comrades in the Resistance, namely Martin-Chauffier, Aveline, Cassou, and Vildrac.

Recalling that he had already taken to the press to protest the displays of anti-Semitism in these trials, Martin-Chauffier announced that he was withdrawing from the directive board. Charles Vildrac denounced the "partisan dependency" of the CNE and *Les Lettres françaises*.[95] Claude Aveline declared, "It is obvious that in the Slansky trial, racial discrimination was officially intended [. . .] Thus anti-Semitism in this case must fatally emerge from anti-Zionism (when they should actually have no relationship) [. . .]."[96] Jean Cassou offered his congratulations to Serge Groussard and, without naming him, accused Vercors of cowardice.[97] While he did not declare it publicly, his resignation was recorded in the committee's records. The others who resigned were André Chamson, Alexandre Arnoux, Armand Salacrou, Francis Ambrière, Pierre Bost, Edmond Fleg, Elian J. Finbert, André Obey, Lise Deharme, Henri Hetz, Jean Guirec, and Serge Groussard.

We might suppose that some other resignations were not made public. Indeed, given the names that were not rewritten or were crossed out on the lists of members and the address books of committee members, 1953 seems like a major fracture. Certainly, the many resignations were probably a chance to update previous defections. But the disappearance at this time of the names of other former underground comrades like Jean Guéhenno, André Frénaud, Pierre Leyris, and Yvonne Desvignes marks the depth of the break. Starting in 1953, the CNE counted almost no non-Communist members who had belonged to the underground committee.

What happened, then, for the press to have been so quickly informed of the conflict? In January 1953, Serge Groussard had sent a letter to the new president, Vercors, asking that the CNE vote on a motion condemning the anti-Semitic and anti-Zionist attacks launched by the Czechoslovakian authorities during the trials. The fact that the support of Zionism that Serge Groussard called for in this motion, by tying it to the condemnation of anti-Semitism, would pose a problem for the progressive intellectuals is not at all surprising. Claude Aveline's response, which I cited earlier, is clear on this point, and clearly shows that a large part of the fraction that joined in Groussard's appeal did not approve all of its terms. For Vercors, however, the motion that Groussard proposed was like a personal challenge: "This challenge is made within the CNE; if he [Vercors] is its president, it's largely because he is the author of *La Marche à l'Étoile*," or so it says in the minutes of the meeting of the directive board.[98] If he had thought that Serge Groussard's accusations were founded, Vercors explained, he would not have waited for him to protest. The directive board rejected his motion "which insults allied and friendly nations in its terms." Indeed, Vercors was satisfied that "the targeted governments had formally repudiated anti-Semitism," as it was said in the motion that the CNE finally adopted on this matter, and against which Groussard rebelled. In a very general manner, this motion protested "against any direct or indirect form of anti-Semitism and racism, and first of all when it is expressed in our own country" (the allusion targeted the reception speech in which André François-Poncet paid tribute to his predecessor, Marshal Pétain).[99] Vercors still promised Serge Groussard that he could explain himself in a few lines on the CNE page of *Les Lettres françaises*. But the editorial staff of the weekly vetoed this offer, and the CNE page in the forthcoming issue would be completely suppressed. Following this series of events, Serge Groussard communicated the affair to the French Press Agency.

It bears mentioning that Aragon and Elsa Triolet were then absent from Paris. Upon their return in February, Serge Groussard was invited to a meeting of the directive board. Those present included Marcelle Auclair, Janine Bouissounouse, Marie Lahy-Hollebecque, Elsa Triolet, Yves de Constantin, Stanislas Fumet, Claude Morgan, Léon Moussinac, Claude Roy, André Spire, and Vercors. According to the minutes from this meeting, Serge Groussard was ordered to provide evidence that had not been taken from the non-Communist press, which he seemed incapable of doing. He roundly criticized the Communist line of the CNE. Why, he was asked, didn't he inform the Pen Club, where he was also a member, of this matter? Elsa Triolet accused him of wanting to "liquidate the CNE." Aragon, who arrived at that moment, denounced the procedure. Ordinarily, the differences of opinion between its members were exposed outside the CNE, he explained. "But we find ourselves faced with the proposition of deciding together, as the CNE, on the Zion government. And public opinion was immediately informed of something under debate. Those are abnormal events. Moreover, it is typical that *Le Figaro*, the Tharaud brothers' newspaper, would accuse us of anti-Semitism," Aragon observed.[100]

For Vercors, in this affair Groussard was only an "instrument, the spearhead of an organized offensive that exceeded his person," and which sought to drain the authority of the CNE.[101] And in fact, taking advantage of the chance to ruin the prestige that the CNE still enjoyed, *Le Figaro littéraire* immediately took hold of it. Under the headline, "The Writers of the CNE Count Their Anti-Semites," the newspaper commented on the affair in these terms: "[. . .] Mr. Groussard was quite shocked by it and we hardly are: while the CNE continues to count non-communist writers among its members, the Stalinian positions have triumphed there for years with an unshakeable constancy."[102] The following week, the unsigned introductory paragraph that presented the investigation among the members of the CNE attacked Aragon:

> The Comité National des Écrivains was founded under the Occupation; it claimed to set the moral values that, beyond patriotism, ensured the Resistance. The Communists took a large part in this, but a number of non-communist writers found themselves associated with them. Did that give Mr. Aragon and the Stalinians the right to transform this group of great memory into an instrument and, when declared or latent anti-Semitism became a political expedient in Moscow, to resist raising the question?[103]

Louis de Villefosse, member of the committee, husband of Janine Bouissounouse who since 1951 had been its general secretary, confirmed the success of the intended effect by *Le Figaro littéraire* in his memoirs: " [. . .] from then on, CNE was no longer anything but an instrument of Muscovite propaganda, in the eyes of liberal opinion."[104]

The position-takings during these struggles in which the "identity" of the CNE was at stake are a good translation of the internal power relations. It was the members who were least dependent on the institution, because of their notoriety and the legitimacy they acquired in the Resistance, those who, having belonged to the clandestine committee, were also the most senior, Martin-Chauffier, Cassou, Aveline, and Vildrac, who gave this collective resignation all its weight. Aside from the "seniors," we also find the names of those other Resistance writers, André Chamson and Pierre Bost, among those who resigned, and the names of consecrated authors like Francis Ambrière, winner of the Goncourt Prize, and Armand Salacrou and Alexandre Arnoux, members of the Goncourt Academy.

Unlike Martin-Chauffier and Cassou, the two former presidents of the CNE, Vercors had not belonged to the underground committee. While at the Liberation, the cofounder of the Éditions de Minuit enjoyed the prestige that his activity in the intellectual Resistance had earned him, his literary legitimacy was less well established, in spite of the broad success of *Le Silence de la mer*: Vercors was an outsider in the literary world, who did not go through the ordinary networks of literary recognition. Since 1947, he had moreover been the target of attacks in certain literary circles, which would go so far as to minimize his role within the underground Éditions de Minuit.[105] In 1948, he had to abandon the publishing house to Jérôme Lindon. The restriction of authorized forums for the members of the CNE engaged by the "blacklist" since the departure of the great elders meant that he was reduced to publishing mainly in *Les Lettres françaises*. He owed the maintenance of his position in the literary field largely to the CNE. Hadn't Aragon, maker of literary careers, assured him in 1949, "Vercors, I would make you into the Romain Rolland of the 20th century"?[106] According to Vercors, nothing followed this "advance," due to the publication of his article on the Rajk affair in *Esprit*, which earned him attacks in *Europe*.

But this conflict also opposed two generations of progressive intellectuals: the writers of the humanist generation, engaged since the prewar period in anti-Fascist fights (Martin-Chauffier, Cassou, Chamson, Vildrac), and those for whom the war and the Resistance were the founding act of their engagement. The reactions of Jean-Paul Sartre and Michel Leiris serve as proof, as they hurried to fill the ranks disaffected by the former fellow-travelers. Michel Leiris had responded to Groussard in *Le Figaro littéraire* that he considered he did not need to make his personal position known on a question "with which a press release published in *Les Lettres françaises* already dealt, in the name of the association to which—you and I—belong."[107] To protest against the resignations, Sartre, who had no longer attended the CNE meetings for quite some time, returned to the directive board. Marking in this way his new fellow-traveling, which he made public at the writers' congress in Wroclaw in 1952, he would remain in it until 1956. Martin-Chauffier, who symbolized the alliance with progressive Catholics, was succeeded on the directive committee by Jacques Madaule, former contributor to *Le Temps présent* and MRP militant. From then on, the CNE recruited from the young generations that had not experienced the struggle against the occupying forces.

When Vercors had presented the affair to the directive board, Claude Morgan had observed that the question of anti-Semitism was not within the competence of writers. At the meeting on February 13, Elsa Triolet had gone one step further. Yves de Constantin, legal counselor to the CNE, having objected that supporting the peace movement could be considered as a political act, Elsa Triolet had responded that peace was not a political question. On April 16, 1953, after the twenty resignations had been recorded, Elsa Triolet proposed an amendment to the status, stipulating that the activity of the CNE should be limited solely to questions directly affecting writers. The amendment was adopted.

Unlike Vercors, Elsa Triolet refrained from intervening on the substance of the debate, situating herself solely on the formal terrain of the CNE's competences. Indeed, who was better placed than she to know the reality of the anti-Semitism that had been raging in the USSR since 1949? She was very probably a victim of it herself: approached to be elected to the Conseil mondial des partisans de la paix—after having participated in the congress of peace partisans in Vienna in December 1952—she was apparently rejected by Stalin because of her Jewish origins, according to confidences murmured to Aragon.[108] Her sister, Lili Brik, was directly threatened. By forcing the CNE to restrict itself to its professional vocation, she sought to preserve its existence without transgressing the party line during a turbulent period. Indeed, at that time, the Aragonian line was contested, in the cultural realm, by the workerist tendency that was growing stronger within the French Communist Party, under the leadership of Auguste Lecœur. Stalin's death sowed disarray among the Communists. In the absence of its leader, Maurice Thorez, the party cast opprobrium on Aragon due to the publication, in the memorial issue of *Les Lettres françaises* that was published on March 12, 1953, of Picasso's famous portrait of Stalin, which passed for scandalous.[109] It was prudent, at this time, to amend the statutes of the committee in order to avoid new turmoil, which risked not only definitively draining the credit from which the CNE still benefited in the intellectual field, but undoubtedly also that of Aragon within the party.

The codification of "apoliticism" in the statutes of the association only confirmed an existing state of affairs. For several years, in the name of safeguarding the unity of the Resistance, the CNE had been politically neutralized to thwart the action of the fellow-travelers who sought to turn the original subversive vocation of the CNE against the orthodoxy of the Communist Party (in reference to the Stalinian trials, in particular). The CNE was then reduced to a purely professional function. This public polemic seems to have been, for the "senior" members of the CNE, the long-awaited occasion to break with an association in which they no longer recognized themselves. In 1956, the revelations of the Khrushchev report and the invasion of Hungary by the Soviet troops sparked a crisis in the CNE like the one that had occurred in 1953, marked this time by the resignation of Vercors from the presidency and the cancelation of the annual sale as a result of the many withdrawals. Meanwhile, Louis Martin-Chauffier founded a competing association, "in order to reconstitute the CNE of the Liberation, freed from Communist control."[110] This association, which would take the name Union des écrivains pour la vérité, the Writers' Union for Truth, in tribute to the group founded by Paul Desjardins during the Dreyfus affair, assembled, out of a total of fifty writers, twenty-three former members of the CNE, of which a large part had belonged to the underground committee.[111] This splitting of the CNE was symptomatic of the struggles to appropriate the moral capital of the Resistance and, beyond that, of the Dreyfusard heritage, which grounded its pretension to hold "the truth." It was only starting in 1958, after de Gaulle's return to power and during the Algerian War, that the CNE would be able to (temporarily) return to its initial subversive vocation.

THE MEMORY WAR

The reference to the Dreyfus affair was omnipresent in the debates that had animated the intellectual field since the Liberation. "It's Dreyfus's revenge!" Charles Maurras had cried out when the verdict fell.[112] In the Resistance camp, on the other hand, Dreyfusard heritage was claimed in contradictory ways. "What do you want! The men of my generation grew up in a trembling and divided Europe because a Jewish officer atoned for another's crime in a penal colony," François Mauriac invoked in his polemic with Albert Camus on the question of justice.[113] André Rousseaux, on the contrary, saw the Pétain trial as a sad answer to the Dreyfus trial: "On one side, Dreyfus is accused because the innocent *had* to be a traitor. On the other, Pétain is defended because the traitor *has* to be an innocent." In both cases, he observed, it was "the demand for a certain so-called national 'order,' derived, must it be said, from 'the order' that claimed to be 'moral.'"[114] In *La Gazette de Lausanne* of September 14, 1946, André Gide published an article in which, considering that the events had proved him right versus Barrès, whose influence he had not ceased combating, he returned to the Dreyfus affair to accuse Maurras of having vindicated a "patriotic forgery" in the name of the false doctrine claiming that the end justified the means. Maurras's response, dated September 29, 1946, which *La Gazette de Lausanne* refused to insert, was printed by the "Friends of Charles Maurras" at the Éditions de "La Seule France" in 1948. Against Gide who denied the Maurrassian doctrine "its universal and human character," Maurras held that his "'politics first' was only established with the help of the most general truths, the same ones that the 13th-century Sorbonne used, notably its axiom that, *in the order of time*, the means came before the end." And he reiterated, to explain the meeting point between Barresian thought and that of someone like Frédéric Mistral, the canons of counterrevolutionary thought against "abstraction," the "lack of effectiveness," the "emaciated moralism that is aided by neither faith nor morals," all characteristics opposed to the French spirit and which were, according to him, the prerogative of "German transcendental Idealism," from Kant to Fichte, in which he found the sources of Nazism.[115]

The losers were far from pleading guilty. The events validated those who resisted, which is exactly what discredited them in the eyes of Maurice Bardèche. This argument was "a kind of confession," he explained in his *Lettre ouverte à François Mauriac*, since "it recognized that the Resistance actually was not founded on any essential necessity, but that *the event justifies it*." For Robert Brasillach's brother-in-law, the Resistance changed nothing about the course of the war. It "only added this fiction that France *did not lay down its arms*." In response to Mauriac, who viewed the purge as legitimate even though he denounced its injustices, Bardèche stated that it was a "crime."[116] The losers, pro-Vichy or collaborationists now reconciled in their common thirst for revenge, who first reorganized themselves in underground or semi-legal networks, plagiarizing the titles of Resistance authorities, "Éditions de Minuit et demi," "Éditions de Midi," "La Pensée libre" (where Maurice Bardèche's letter appeared), soon disposed of forums like *Aspects de la France*, the heir to *Action française* that was launched in 1947; and, starting in 1951, *Rivarol*.[117] They could now express themselves in a weekly like *Carrefour*. In their fight to proclaim the illegitimacy of the purge, they would find an unlikely ally in Jean Paulhan.

The cofounder of *Les Lettres françaises* also claimed Dreyfusard heritage in the struggle that, like Péguy destroying his former comrades in arms, he engaged in 1952 against the "directors of the Resistance."[118] The résistant, Paulhan wrote, thought that "he was once and for all on the right side: the side of Justice and the Law." He was wrong. The purge was an abuse of justice: "[. . .] Neither Maurras, Brasillach, nor Pétain were ever *judged*."[119] For Paulhan, article 75 of the penal code in the name of which they were condemned was applied in an illegal manner. The article stipulated that acts committed against France should be punished by death. But what was France? France, said another article of the penal code, was its legal government. There was only one choice: either the new government declared a revolution and repealed all the laws, or the sole legal government of France between 1940 and 1944, namely the Vichy government, was authorized to judge acts of treason.

The *Lettre aux directeurs de la Résistance*, published by the Éditions de Minuit, the Resistance publishing house, after having been rejected by Gallimard, *La Table ronde*, and the Gaullist journal of the Rassemblement populaire français, *Liberté de l'Esprit*, caused a scandal. None of the Resistance writers could follow Paulhan's reasoning. The numbers of purge victims that he used to support his demonstration were those claimed by the extreme right, from whom Paulhan also borrowed several arguments.[120] After the meeting at the home of Édith Thomas during which he read the text out loud, Jean Guéhenno asked him not to publish it, and François Mauriac shared his disapproval:

> [. . .] all the mistakes, all the errors, all the crimes even of what was called the Resistance don't change the fact that the Vichy regime 1) handed over foreign refugees who had believed in the word of France, to Germany, 2) arrested men like Reynaud and Daladier without a trial, throwing them into prison, 3) put the French police in the service of the Nazis so that we officially took part in the massacres of millions of Jews. I'm not even talking about direct responsibilities for the Militia crimes, the thousands of French youth who were killed because Vichy had ordered them to resist the American landing in North Africa, etc . . . etc . . .[121]

Upon publication of the lampoon, the press went wild. Louis Martin-Chauffier, Roger Stéphane, Elsa Triolet, and Pierre de Lescure took up arms against the "renegade."[122] In his "letter to a Resistance deserter," the president of the CNE, Louis Martin-Chauffier, violently denounced "the opportunism" of Jean Paulhan who published his text at a time when the collaborators "raise their heads and only aspire to vengeance," accusing him of having played off both sides during the Occupation; of having penetrated the milieu of the Resistance—all the while "soliciting" for Drieu's NRF—only to better discredit it later; of having understood "nothing about the résistants, neither their motives, nor their faith, nor their disinterest, nor the seriousness of their choice, nor the suffering that they experienced and often withstood, nor their death"; of having been, in a word, "a stranger amongst us."[123] In private, Mauriac also criticized him for playing the game of the extreme right:

> I no longer want to enter a debate where everything is defiled. You surely know that in substance I took a position close to yours starting in 44 ... And yet *you are wrong*—yes even when you're right. What subsisted of the Resistance, of the memory of what it was for us during the dark years, you came along and gave the coup ... *de l'ange.** You, the friend of Rebattet [*sic*], of Céline, you bring an unhoped-for assistance to *Aspects de la Fr[ance]*, to *Rivarol*, to the relentless children of Maurrassian hatred.[124]

Mauriac was well informed. It was in *Aspects de la France* that, on April 25, Paulhan published his final response to the attacks leveled against him, under the title "A Linguistic Error Betrays Injustice." Paulhan's opposition to the moralism of the new dominant agents of the cultural field, Communists and existentialists, would lead him, in the name of "art for art's sake," to make a deal with the extreme right. But Paulhan's attitude cannot be reduced to an individual strategy. The Gallimard catalogue now included Céline and Rebatet, whose novel *Les Deux étendards* had been supported by Paulhan for the Pléiade Prize. In January 1953, *La Nouvelle NRF* appeared under the joint direction of Jean Paulhan and Marcel Arland.[125] In the June issue, under the pseudonym Jean Guérin, Paulhan did not hesitate to sing the praises of Paul Rassinier, a former deportee who had just published the founding text of revisionism, *Le Mensonge d'Ulysse* (1950), for having "denounced the lies of 'concentration camp literature.'"[126] On July 24, 1953, the second law of amnesty was passed, concluding the long debates that had started in 1946 and formally putting an end to the Franco-French war: the measures taken at the Liberation were annulled. Shortly after, Jean Cassou's response to Paulhan, *La Mémoire courte*, was published by the Éditions de Minuit in the same collection as *Lettre aux directeurs de la Résistance*. In his response, Cassou, who had resigned from the CNE, restored the Resistance as "a moral action, absolute, suspended, pure. And to which, as a result, there is no need to return."[127]

---

* A play on words based on the expression, "donner le coup de pied de l'âne," which refers to the attack of a weak or cowardly person on an entity whose power he no longer fears. Here, Paulhan is attacking the very entity (the Resistance) that he himself embodies. The *âne*, or donkey, of the original expression has been replaced by *ange*, or angel.—Trans.

In this memory war started at the Liberation, and whose principal and lasting terms were set at this key moment, the French Academy played its role. While Gallimard was busy pulling the most famous collaborationist writers out of their purgatory, the French Academy rehabilitated the protagonists of the National Revolution. In 1952, Maurras died. At the Academy, Jules Romains, acting director, gave his eulogy. Only Claudel protested. Since Maurras was no longer part of the Company, he did not understand the meaning of the tribute that had just been made to him, and insisted on recording his disagreement in the minutes.[128] The successor to the leader of Action française, the Duke de Lévis-Mirepoix, would give a eulogy that contained only a discreet allusion to the Occupation years, declaring, with regard to the Liberation, that "he [Maurras] had to suffer, like Socrates, the anger of the polis."[129] In January 1953, the ambassador André François-Poncet, elected to Pétain's chair, gave his predecessor's eulogy with the necessary nuances, developing the famous thesis of the Pétainist "shield," which cast the blame on Laval. This speech, which the members of the directive board of the CNE cited, during the Groussard affair, as an example of "indirect anti-Semitism" (from the very fact of eulogizing Pétain) was considered "a model of historical method" by Robert Aron: "The Academy is indebted to the newcomer for having been the first French institution to express justice and truth."[130] The response by Pierre Benoit followed the theme of "reconciliation."[131] While the camp of the Resistance tore itself to pieces, the "academic right" rose up again. The French Academy had returned to its traditional vocation: ensuring national "continuity" by unifying past and present and erasing the dregs of history.

Conclusion

Never were we freer than under the German occupation.
—Jean-Paul Sartre, "The Republic of Silence"

A Paradise Lost

At the beginning of 1944, résistants and collaborators measured each other according to their literary legitimacy. In response to de Gaulle who "boasted of having the quasi-totality of 'French intelligence' with him," Lucien Rebatet listed, in *Je suis partout*, the "talents" that the Collaboration claimed: Pierre Drieu La Rochelle, Céline, Henry de Montherlant, Henri Béraud, Abel Bonnard, Alphonse de Chateaubriant, Jacques Chardonne.[1] He also mentioned the names of Marcel Aymé, Pierre Mac Orlan, Jean Anouilh, Jean de La Varende, André Thérive, and Marcel Jouhandeau, who, without engaging politically, were not reluctant to publish in the collaborationist press. "No, talent is not a monopoly of the 'resistance,'" he concluded, affirming that "with the partisans of the European order, we would make a new Academy, infinitely more brilliant and literary than the old one." Rebatet then took a closer look at the writers of the opposing camp—"the Academy of dissidence"—namely Bernanos, Maritain, Maurois, Gide, Mauriac, Jules Romains, Claudel, Duhamel, the Tharaud brothers, Malraux, and Aragon. Only Gide, whom he considered "the greatest [. . .] of living French writers" found favor in his eyes, and he saw in his Gaullism merely a "very negligible episode among those infinite variations" to which his successive political position-takings were subject. The others, some of whom were precursors of the Collaboration, according to him, because of their pacifism, were nothing but "traitors" to the nation and civilization. "Bolshevists," like Malraux and Aragon, "Judeofied" through their marriage, like Jules Romains or Maritain (not to mention Maurois), "social-democratic" like Duhamel or "Christian democratic" like Claudel, attracted by the "unhealthy and the equivocal" like Mauriac which resulted, in his eyes, from "*Psychopathia sexualis*," all united by their "Judeophilia," they had no competence to speak in the name of France and to give "lessons of patriotism." Not only had they "never shown the slightest concern for the French cause," but they had, on the contrary, "undermined the idea of homeland, professed antimilitarism, subscribed to the worst illusions of the universal International, heaped sarcasm on the national militants [...]" throughout their careers. Rebatet concluded with a threat:

> However, this time our indulgence has its limits [...] If Europe is saved [...] it will take a lot of leniency and a love of literature that we could not possibly expect of all the political leaders in order to forget that these honor-filled writers, engendered and nourished by our civilization, have betrayed their most natural mission by hatefully standing up against the heroic defenders of our civilization, that they gave arms to its mortal enemies.[2]

This article, which almost mechanically reiterated the outdated arguments of reactionary rhetoric on the theme of the defense of "civilization" and the writer's "responsibility" at a time when Europe had its feet held to the fire, and the Allied victory was only a question of time, had an obsolete quality, even if the threat that ended it had a very real foundation. But what is striking here is the will—just as obsolete at this point—to affirm the literary legitimacy of collaborationism up until the very end, even though Drieu La Rochelle had recognized his failure a year earlier.

In an unpublished text written in 1941—probably the article that he intended for the vanished first issue of the underground *Lettres françaises*—François Mauriac developed the theme of the "envious" who "breathed the sweet wind of the defeat." This was a theme that he had sketched out in January 1941, at the beginning of the "bad masters quarrel," in the conclusion to his article "The Honor of Writers," which ended with these words: "[...] in spite of their sublime principles, the writers of nothingness will not cease to belong to nothingness."[3] The violence of the unpublished text countered the violence that marked the second phase of the quarrel in the Northern zone. Giving in to a fit of rage, Mauriac borrowed some of his detractors' methods to deny their claims of legitimacy:

> All the trumpets of the Paris of 1941 proclaimed in vain that France possesses a new Rabelais in Mr. Céline, there isn't a single one of our readers who doesn't know how to tell the difference between this splendid springtime of

French prose, swollen with sap and juice, and this diarrhea of slang with which Mr. Céline embellishes his "sheets," this idiom of the brothel, this pathos of the penal colony.[4]

But this theme would not be taken up in *Le Cahier noir*. In 1943, the literary failure of the collaborators was an accepted fact. In his answer to Rebatet, Sartre would not have to demonstrate, but rather to merely observe the fact that "these big names of *La Gerbe* or *Je suis partout* are almost all devoid of talent."[5] Why did these different attempts to subvert the power relations that had structured the prewar literary field definitively fail? If the monopolization of key positions by the writers of the Collaboration did not suffice to topple them, it's first of all because, in a world where positions are not preexisting but have to be created, and where relationships are highly personalized, individuals are not interchangeable: Drieu La Rochelle's *NRF* was not that of Jean Paulhan. Did the hijacking of symbolic capital undertaken by Drieu's *NRF* have any chance of succeeding? I am tempted to respond negatively. By suppressing their adversaries, that is to say, by reducing them to silence, they suppressed the raison d'être of their own position. Isn't this what Drieu was expressing when, in March 1944, he asked himself in his diary: "What does Malraux think? Deprived of his attitude, he seems unnecessary?"[6] But it was Drieu himself who, deprived of the "attitude" of Malraux with respect to which he defined himself, suddenly appeared unnecessary in his own eyes: "[...] I am exasperated by the role I have to maintain until the end,"[7] he was writing as early as December 1942 in his journal. "His voice fell silent just because of that," Sartre explained about him. "You cannot write, you cannot speak in a desert."[8] Drieu was sufficiently initiated to the rules of the game to know this, and that is why in 1942 he showed more lucidity than Lucien Rebatet, still blinded by his aggression in 1944.

Through their claim of legitimacy, through their will to appropriate renowned writers, the agents of heteronomy ultimately pledged allegiance to the principle that founded the autonomy of the literary field, like a tribute from vice to virtue. However, the crisis conjuncture, by loosening the constraints that the peer community habitually imposed on the writers most inclined to heteronomy from the standpoint of respect for the rules of literary debate, revealed precisely the disposition of the latter to sacrifice literary interests to external causes.

If the stigmatization of the recognized writers of the interwar period would prove powerless to lastingly transform the hierarchy of literary values, it is also because the denounced group benefited from a level of cohesion superior to that of the denouncers, united only by their resentment. This was a cohesion that relied not only on a principle of seniority,[9] as the young age of most of the resisting writers proves, but on a principle of solidarity that formed the foundation upon which the literary field rebuilt itself, first in order to resist the loss of its autonomy, then to regain it, and which was none other than the very condition of its survival.

The crisis would thus reduce the internal struggles within the field to the opposition between forces of autonomy and forces of heteronomy. This dynamic derived from the "bad masters quarrel" and from institutional struggles. The war and the defeat favored the imposition of the problematic of national moralism in the literary field: it was in its name that the most legitimate writers, particularly Gide in the Southern zone and Mauriac in the Northern zone, were rendered responsible for the defeat by their competitors, whether they were dethroned elders like Bellessort or Bordeaux, or old adversaries like Massis, or young pretenders in a hurry to make a place for themselves on the literary scene like Brasillach, Rebatet, or Laubreaux. But this escalation in the designation of the "culprits," which drew on the rhetoric of contrition and the culture of disavowal, exposed, by contrast, the dissociation between nationalism and conservatism that the foreign occupation brought about, and which the Collaboration extremists brought to their climax. It reveals the priority that these moralists gave the defense of the social order to the detriment of patriotic sentiment, and to the struggle against the agents of "disorder" rather than the fight against the invader and against Nazism.

At first, the defenders of the literature of the interwar period settled for denying the accusations leveled against it in the name of the principle of art for art's sake. But the use of the argument of art for art's sake by Drieu La Rochelle's NRF to attract writers and legitimize its venture helped discredit this option in the new conditions imposed upon cultural production. Conjointly, the turn toward denunciation that the quarrel took in the Northern zone (including in La NRF, with the attacks against Mauriac and Aragon) led to a redefinition of the stakes. By accrediting the idea of an equivalence between "literary treason" and "national treason," it accelerated the process of converting personal indignation into universal indignation, which was, as we saw in the case of François Mauriac, one of the motivations for evolving from an attitude of "refusal" to an active engagement in the underground struggle. The violence of the attacks also contributed to the reworking of alliances between the group of marginalized founders of La NRF and the dissidents of the French Academy on one side, and between these elders and the young generation that emerged during this period on the other, alliances that would allow for the symbolic reunification of the fragmented literary field around the struggle to regain its dignity and its autonomy. This struggle now coincided with the fight to regain national independence. Using literary means, from the practice of contraband orchestrated by Aragon in the Southern zone, to the underground writings, it took the form of a struggle to reappropriate "the French spirit" and reaffirm its national particularism as a universalism. The poet's song became a cry; the rhyme embraced the saga of the shadow soldiers; the panting of the constricted country clipped the verse; the sonnet became "the expression of freedom under constraint, the embodiment of thought in fetters,"[10] as François La Colère alias Aragon wrote in reference to the *33 Sonnets* that Jean Noir (Jean Cassou) had composed while in custody. Through these practices, literature regained all its subversive charge. "Once again, poetry, put to the test, regroups, finds a specific meaning for its latent violence, cries out, accuses, hopes," Paul Eluard wrote in the preface to *L'Honneur des poètes*.[11]

It was only once the oppressive regime had been defeated that the true struggles to redefine the power relations would be engaged, between the generation born of the Resistance and its elders, and within the new generation. These struggles, associated with the disillusions of the Liberation, heightened the "nostalgia" for underground solidarity. This theme of "paradise lost," which had its referent in the complicity born of the principle of cohesion mentioned earlier, emerged very quickly. It figured in one of the first public statements by Vercors who, at the Liberation, perceived the "coldness" of those whose friendship he sought, Sartre and Camus:

> Mourning, destitution, life in the bottom of caves, tears, anger, the anxiety of each day ... and yet happiness. Yes. Should we be ashamed to admit it [...] We were happy. Will you deny it, Claude, Jacques, Pierre, and you, Paul, and you, Yvonne, and you, all my friends met in secret? [...] What did we have to offer each other? If not our devotion and our faith,—and in the end, perhaps, death [...] This bareness, this purity, see how they disappear with our struggle and our anonymity. Each returns to a social position along with his name [...] For whom will nobility endure? For whom will it weaken? Oh my friends, my friends, who among you will we keep or lose? [...].[12]

It would be taken up again by François Mauriac, at the time when he again drew closer to the CNE:

> My comrades, don't you ever happen to think sometimes about those dark days with a secret nostalgia? Who would have said then that, in liberated France, we would be tempted to say: "Those were the good days ... ?" No, of course not, the good days weren't that time of horror. But it was the time of

friendship and trust [...] We weren't unhappy, because we were overflowing with hope, because we trusted each other, because we felt we were brothers and we actually were. It is not too late to steal a little bit of that happiness in the midst of misfortune from the past . . .[13]

This theme of "paradise lost" can be compared to that of "freedom" introduced by Sartre in the famous opening sentence of his article "The Republic of Silence," published on the first page of the first legal issue of *Les Lettres françaises*: "We have never been so free as under the German occupation."[14] Both refer to the conditions of opposition, the first placing emphasis on brotherhood in the struggle, on trust,[15] on shared hope, while for its part the Sartrian theme of "freedom" referred to the position of refusal. Both also referred to disinterest: "purity" for Vercors, the "authenticity" of choice in the presence of death for Sartre. It was because it gave a simultaneously existential and universal content to the two founding values of the intellectual's autonomy, disinterest and critical examination (which founded refusal), even as it made literary practice itself into a means of action (which normally contradicts the ethos of disinterest), that the underground struggle constituted a privileged moment in the experience of these writers as such. Claude Roy would moreover combine the two preceding themes into one, insisting for his part on the good faith and good conscience that lay beneath the themes of "happiness" and "freedom":

> Why were we never so *happy* as during the Resistance and so *free* as under the occupation? It's because the cruelty and dumb bestiality of the Nazis made us lighter. It was possible to hate without remorse, to fight without reservations. In the great theological myths, God *needs* Satan [...] When Manichaeism is not an illusion of bad faith, when it has an objective reality, when the enemy is really a ferocious, stubborn, and negating enemy—what peace! Here I am talking about inner peace.[16]

The Effects of the Crisis

While the crisis situation revealed the founding principles of the autonomy of the literary field through the resistance mechanisms that it opposed to external constraints, the analysis of its functioning in the 1940s contributes, in return, to the study of crisis phenomena. Thanks to the heteronomous conditions of production and the upheaval of the rules of the game, the generalization of recourse to extraliterary arms to perpetrate "literary assassinations" was a first result of the crisis logic. While the divisions within the organized groups (the academies, *La NRF*) were exacerbated, the restriction of possibles which is typical of times of crisis conversely inspired unlikely alliances, such as the intergenerational alliance, or the alliance of the Communists and non-Communists. The progressive concentration of internal struggles around the opposition between forces of autonomy and forces of heteronomy actually led legitimate writers, like Gide, Valéry, Mauriac, and Duhamel, to ally themselves with the most subversive fractions of the literary field. Finally, the crisis favored the crystallization of a new literary generation, which established itself thanks to the reversal of the old/young relationship in the literary Resistance—it was only after the CNE had attained literary and national legitimacy that the elders would join its ranks—and the ensuing acceleration of careers.

On the other hand, the retranslation of political stakes into literary stakes, the persistence of protracted inner struggles, the homology that we have been able to observe between positions and position-takings, just like the survival logics of the institutions, show what behaviors in a time of crisis owe to the history proper to the literary field and its constants, namely the opposition between autonomy and heteronomy and intergenerational struggles.

From this point of view, the crisis had, as we saw, a revelatory effect, not only at the level of individuals, but also on the level of institutions. To ensure their survival, and thanks to the forms of dependency that they maintained with respect to the different social spheres close to them, the institutions were each involved in their own way with the literary field's process of losing autonomy. The comparison of the different modes of survival of the French Academy, the Goncourt Academy, and *La NRF* is revealing in this respect (and in the case of the CNE, of course, it only appeared as the Liberation approached). The crisis exacerbated internal divisions and favored the assumption of power by those members most disposed to respond to external demand. The most official among them, the two academies, ensured the mediation between Paris and Vichy, not without unleashing violent internal struggles concerning the definition of the institution's role. These struggles that, at the French Academy, were kept secret according to the state logic and "good taste," took on the form of scandal at the Goncourt Academy, thus ensuring, through their media coverage, the survival of an institution threatened with marginalization.

Through an apparent paradox, the reversal of the power relations in favor of the defenders of autonomy was most precocious in the most heteronomous of the three institutions, the French Academy. This is an apparent paradox because the Academy was also the best protected due to its status as an official body and its history: had it not survived every regime and every historical upheaval? But it was also too linked, by this same history, with the constitution of national identity to alienate that identity in favor of the "hereditary enemy" represented by

Germany. The degree of adaptation required to survive in a time of crisis grew in inverse proportion to the social foundations and means at the institution's disposal: we saw how, despite the rebalancing of power relations at the Goncourt Academy beginning at the turning point in the war, the opposing side could not impose their views until after the Liberation.

This speaks to the fragility of the most autonomous enterprises of the literary field under an authoritarian regime: the "taking" of *La NRF*, for which it would have to pay with its existence at the Liberation, serves as proof. Of course, the harnessing of *La NRF* by the "distinguished" pole of the Collaboration occurred, as in the other authorities, according to the principles of internal divisions (generational divisions, tensions between autonomy and heteronomy, ideological differences), and the failure of the venture, which was unable to endow itself with a true literary project, hastened a decline that was partially due to the process of social aging. But twice sacrificed to the interests of the Gallimard house, it would not be able to effect the necessary readjustments: not from lack of trying, as demonstrated by the dissidents' maneuvers to reappropriate it starting in 1942. And it was precisely these dissidents, led by the former director of the review, Jean Paulhan, who would form the Comité national des écrivains.

One of the effects of the crisis was precisely the birth of this new authority that, faced with the failure of the old institutions, claimed both the principle of literary autonomy and the defense of "the French spirit." It embodied the subversive logic that prevailed at the temporally dominated pole of the literary field, and which often led the avant-gardes to give their protest a political bearing. The CNE was representative of the dominated pole in the very principle that presided over its birth, given the position of its members in a literary field besieged by temporal forces: ex-surrealists, young debut poets, Communists, writers banned because of their origins or their ideological convictions.

Opposition to the occupying forces or the Vichy regime is not, in itself, a sufficient reason to turn to action or for the specific form of that action. Belief in the struggle was inextricably linked to the form of action specifically proposed to writers, to the fusion of this belief with the literary *illusio* that it made possible,[17] to the sociability (even, in certain cases, to socialization in the field) that it implied, to the reconversions that it allowed (Claude Roy), to the symbolic profits that it promised (the connection with Paulhan, Aragon, or Eluard). The solidarity of professional and literary interests, founded by the affinity of positions, would temporarily allow writers to overcome the generational, literary, and ideological divisions that would not fail to resurface when the Liberation approached.

But if, through its fight to safeguard "the French spirit," conceived as a means to struggle against oppression, the CNE reaffirmed literary autonomy, it was linked by the conditions of its birth to the underground Communist Party that provided it with the material means for this fight. Its mode of institutionalization at the Liberation and the conflicts that it created would confirm this dependency.

The modes of survival of these institutions at the Liberation present similar characteristics to those observed under the Occupation, in an inverted political power relation. While the French Academy, impassible, returned to its role as a conservative force without yielding to political and media pressures, the Goncourt Academy made a spectacular reversal by adjusting, as in 1940, to the new dominant ideology of the moment. The institutionalization of the CNE that, cloaked in its double literary and national legitimacy, established itself as an authority of ethical arbitration by drawing up a "blacklist" of writers who had been "compromised" with the occupant, was one of the most immediate consequences of the crisis. But the reign of the authorities born of the Resistance would be short-lived. Starting in 1946, their legitimacy was contested, while the process of "normalization" began. As early as 1948, the CNE lost its power of excommunication and soon looked like an imposter in the literary field. Torn apart by the struggles it experienced that would defeat the unity of the literary Resistance, it helped, just like the traditional authorities, to empty the underground heritage of its subversive charge, due to its academicization and its political neutralization. This neutralization, imposed (in the name of its survival) to prevent its original subversive vocation from turning against the Communist Party, destined it for a purely professional role.

The generation that emerged from the Resistance would, however, durably impose the notion of the writer's "responsibility." While the CNE largely contributed to this, it was *Les Temps modernes* that now occupied the place that had belonged to *La NRF* during the interwar period, at the symbolically dominant pole. "Art for art's sake," long condemned by the extreme right in the name of "action," was definitively discredited under the Occupation. It would be reappropriated after the Liberation by the reconverted losers. Registering the gains of the Resistance camp, Sartre "can overthrow it in a brilliant way: he can maintain that thinking and writing are not only themselves action, but the highest form of action," as Anna Boschetti has written.[18] This was a double reversal: with respect to the whole history of the debate on the responsibility of the writer, and also with respect to the literary Resistance's feeling of inferiority in comparison to armed struggle. What is more, by dissociating the notion of responsibility from the national moralism to which it had been historically linked in order to connect it to the notion of freedom, Sartre gave it a universal bearing, even as he ensured the writer an autonomy that was then threatened by the militant model embodied by Aragon and Eluard. It was the act of writing that engaged. Whether the "Hussards" like it or not, this conception would prevail at the pole of small-scale production until the *Nouveau Roman* group once again separated political commitment and literature, without, however, calling the principle of the writer's responsibility into question. They would give that principle a concrete content by signing the "Declaration on the Right to Insubordination in the Algerian War."[19]

Meanwhile, we still need to elucidate the question of the reversal of positions between the agents of moralism and the agents of "pure" literature at the Liberation. Wasn't Aragon the heir to Massis, as Paulhan suggested? Sartre to Paul Bourget, as Jacques Laurent would have us believe? Moralism would thus be the prerogative of the "victors," those who saw their principles triumph: Action française following the Great War, the Communist Party at the Liberation. Stopping there would mean aligning literary history with political history a bit too quickly, and above all underestimating the principles of division specific to the literary field. And so to wrap things up, we must return to the question of the status of moralism in literature.

Da Capo: On Moralism in Literature

The question of the writer's moral responsibility cannot be dissociated from the claim, inscribed in his professional practice, of universalism. This is why it is always taken seriously, even by the supporters of art's gratuitousness, and can never be definitively removed from the debate on the definition of literature and the social role of the writer.

In the Kantian tradition largely diffused by French secondary education in the nineteenth century, disinterest is supposed to found the superiority of judgment (ethical and aesthetic), even its universal value. As a result, it seems like a literary justification for the process of universalizing the "particular case, that is, of the privilege constituting the scholastic condition,"[20] in Pierre Bourdieu's words. This is all the more true among writers who, more than other intellectual fractions, have made a vocation out of the transubstantiation of the particular into the universal.

In an era characterized by the industrialization of the book market, the diversification of political options, and the multiplication of producers of symbolic goods with the expansion of education, disinterest as an ethical condition of a writer's professional practice took on a new meaning. As a result, its definition was the subject of internal struggles without it ever being called into question as the ethical foundation of the scholastic position.[21] While the absolute gratuity of the work of art, with the first romanticism or the theory of art for art's sake for example, could appear for a while as the supreme expression of this disinterest, it was no less condemned as a form of the intellectual's withdrawal to his "ivory tower" and the manifestation of his or her detachment from the "real."[22] This critique, regularly brandished by certain fractions of the intellectual field, owed its social efficacy to the fact that by showing itself for what it was, that is to say cut off from the world, the scholastic position risked losing in recognition of its universality what it won in autonomy. And it was at the time when they were led to take stock of their failure that writers most clearly expressed this injunction, which was more or less inscribed in their professional practice depending on the period. At the same time, this allowed them to attenuate their own responsibility, as this "confession" by Henry de Montherlant illustrates:

My mind is resistant to the political and the social [...] But my mind [...] does not manage, even if it has understood them (which is not always the case), to retain political and social data with precision and clarity [...] There is an intellectual infirmity that I have always deplored, although I have not excessively deplored it, because in the end, a musician, a sculptor, a painter, a scientist even, is not expected to have political ideas; why expect it of a literary man? We have other ways of serving both the country and society [...] That has been my error, to write books where I touched on these questions [...] And then, if I hadn't written them, couldn't the ivory tower have been brought up? I have preferred running the risk of talking rubbish, to an abstention that might have been taken for indifference.[23]

It is not by chance that the defenders of "pure" literature were led, in their polemics against the moralists, to minimize the importance of literature, its social impact, and/or deny writers the legitimacy of their competence in public affairs. Thus Jacques Rivière, in the debate that pitted him against the partisans of the primacy of national interest within the *NRF* team in the aftermath of the Great War, came to minimize the importance of literature and dissociate talent from the author's morality:

I agree with Jean [Schlumberger] also in thinking that a great writer is not necessarily a great character. I even go further. I claim that a great writer cannot be a great character. Several things prevent him: first, all of his preoccupations must rotate around himself; he is as poorly made as possible for devotion and sacrifice. Sacred egotism. Next, a certain falseness coming from a discrepancy with himself: he must separate a bit from his feelings in order to see them; and thus in him they are never completely true, or at least never as true as with others.

But I claim against Jean that just because the work that we have to do is less important than others, it is not a reason not to do it purely, to mix other ambitions in with it. Just because I am not a great character, it is not a reason, and on the contrary, not to seek to be a great writer.[24]

We find the same type of arguments among the defenders of the literature of the interwar period, François Mauriac for example, in response to the accusations leveled by his accusers who made him responsible for the defeat in 1940. Under the pen of Jean Paulhan after the Liberation, it further took on the form of the writer's "right to aberration," which the former director of *La NRF* opposed to his companions in the intellectual Resistance who intended to put their collaborationist colleagues on trial.

Conversely, it was through the claim of universalism that political passions acquired their privileges within this self-absorbed world, on the condition of presenting itself in the guise of moralism, whether it called itself "good," "truth," "justice," "general interest," or "state reason." It was in its name that intellectuals were regularly put on trial. These indictments have become a genre of their own, from the counterrevolutionary attacks aimed at Rousseau and Voltaire to Sartre's *Qu'est-ce que la littérature?* along with *La Trahison des clercs* (1927) by Julien Benda and *Les Chiens de garde* by Nizan (1932), the trials of intellectual responsibility for the defeat in 1940, or even the CNE "blacklist." The perpetuation of this genre, from right to left, is undeniably a means of reaffirming the symbolic power that intellectuals claim to hold, in the name of their charismatic legitimacy.[25]

But this genre, derived from the debate on the moral responsibility of the intellectual, whether it concerned the work or the prophetic position of its author, was also the legitimate mode of disqualifying adversaries. This process of universalizing passions, which exceeds the literary field in that it derives from the scholastic practice and can thus be generalized to other categories of intellectuals, was well described by Paul Bourget in *Le Disciple*, although Bourget used it in turn as a weapon in his critique of the position of the intellectual hidden in his ivory tower as embodied by Adrien Sixte: "So in his indignation against Dumoulin he sincerely believed that he was indignant at an obstacle to the public good."[26]

Politics, in an assumed or denied form, was thus one of the modes of universalizing passions in a period when the writer had to reaffirm his or her place in society and claims to the universal. But if this disposition for indignation was very widely shared, the modes by which passions tended to be universalized and the forms of politicization varied according to the degree and type of notoriety, as we saw through the discursive practices. While the degree of euphemization of passions (literary, political, or personal) increases as we move from the dominated to the dominant pole, the degree of stylization is a function of the symbolic capital held. According to the first principle, the discourse of the dominated is thus differentiated from that of the dominant because it takes on a more directly political form, whereas at the dominant pole, writers mark their distance with respect to political discourse by transposing it into the register of "academic" debate, whether we are speaking of the supporters of "good taste" who hide the political tone of their comments behind morality, or of writers endowed with a symbolic type of notoriety who sometimes reject it and sometimes relate it to superior universal concepts (like justice, freedom, etc.).

According to the second principle of differentiation, however, which opposes the autonomous and heteronomous logics, we must distinguish between two traditions of intellectual indictments. That for which, from the Dreyfusards to the members of the CNE and to Sartre, along with Benda and Nizan, the writers situated at the pole of small-scale production, each in his own way, blamed their colleagues, was above all the fact that they had put their pen in the service of the temporal forces and in so doing betrayed the elementary rules of the professional practice by alienating their ability for critical examination. The fact that these criticisms were able to be recuperated by a given party essentially changed nothing. In the other line that proceeds from the counterrevolutionary tradition up to the detractors of the "bad masters" under the Occupation, moralist discourse is a means of making competitors into "public enemies," enemies of the established order, of an order to reestablish, of an order to come, or more banally of the "public good." The adversaries are disqualified here in the name of extraliterary principles.

Indeed, we saw that the proponents of "good taste" (society authors, members of the French Academy) share with some of the literary men who were doubly dominated in the temporal and symbolic order (often journalists, like Henri Béraud or Alain Laubreaux), the propensity to privilege content over form and reduce literary judgment to a moral or social judgment. The former, who seek, like Henry Bordeaux, to make literature into an instrument to reproduce the dominant classes and maintain the social order, are normally declared enemies of the avant-gardes, whom they openly fight, while more secretly targeting symbolically dominant writers. It is these dominant writers that the latter, often reduced to relying on the logic of scandal and populist anti-intellectualism since they cannot handle the arms of the debate of ideas, more willingly denounce, which allows them to make their attitude appear subversive. The representatives of these two poles, which can be opposed in a dominant/dominated relationship, join in their common attempt to impose restrictions on critical thought. It was this secret alliance between the proponents of "good taste" and the populist extreme right that the crisis revealed.

This propensity to limit the exercise of critical thought favored in return, at the pole of autonomy, the alliance between symbolically dominant writers, like Gide, and the avant-gardes, who united to defend their professional practice. Under normal circumstances, these two groups confront each other according to the dynamic proper to the literary field, which has been evolving by revolutions since romanticism, namely through a perpetual overcoming of the relevant problematics at a given time. This confrontation masks what deeply unites them, namely respect for the rules of the game, and which is only revealed when those rules are threatened, as occurred under the Occupation. Such was the basis of the intergenerational alliance which allowed for the reconstruction of the literary field under oppression.

Collective mobilization thus occurs first through the defense of the autonomy of literature. This is a recurrent structural dynamic.[27] It is when their professional practice is threatened that the most legitimate writers—and intellectuals in general—tend to leave their ivory tower and enter the fray. Conversely, it is in their struggles against antiestablishment intellectuals that conservative writers make themselves into the guardians of a social order that is threatened or needs to be restored.[28] To the conception of literature as an instrument of the symbolic power of the forces of conservation, the guardians of autonomy oppose, as we saw, the bases of their professional ethics, namely the critical function of intellectual activity, the conception of literature as a quest, the universal values of the spirit, and this is why, at this pole, moralism tends, in opposition to the "common good" or state reason to be put forward by their adversaries, to take on the forms of a defense of truth, justice, and freedom.

Presentation of the Survey

The Population

The survey concerns a population of 185 writers who were active between 1940 and 1944, listed below. In order to arrive at a representation of all the relevant positions in the literary field under the Occupation, the sample has been created, combining both literary and political criteria, on the basis of different lists: members of the French Academy, of the Goncourt Academy, of the Comité national des écrivains, winners of the principal prizes for the novel (Goncourt, Renaudot, Femina, the French Academy's Prize for the Novel) between 1937 and 1944, contributors to the consecrated prewar literary reviews (*La NRF, Mercure de France*), to politico-literary weeklies (*La Gerbe, Je suis partout, Aujourd'hui*), critics for the major dailies *Le Figaro, Paris-Soir, Le Temps, Action française*). Except for the first three, these lists are not exhaustive and were combined with a criterion of visibility (based on participation in the debates of the period, like the "bad masters quarrel"). This criterion of visibility incited me to include some major authors in exile (Bernanos, Maritain, Saint-John Perse, Saint-Exupéry, Kessel, Maurois), who directly participated in these debates or who served as permanent references in the authorized, semi-legal, or clandestine press. On the other hand, I had to exclude a certain number of more obscure figures of the Collaboration, like Henri Poulain or Noël Bayon de la Mort, who entered the literary field thanks to the crisis situation, and for whom there is almost no biographical information (it is the same for some prizewinners). This difficulty of gathering biographical information on authors who were "erased" from literary history (either because they knew only very ephemeral success, or because of their political attitude during this period) leads to an underrepresentation of collaborationist writers, chiefly represented in my population by its most famous figures (Drieu La Rochelle, Brasillach), which creates a slight imbalance with respect to Resistance writers. Finally, women are also slightly underrepresented (they total eight) for similar reasons. In the Multiple Correspondence Analysis (MCA), seventeen writers were cast as illustrative individuals, either because the data was too incomplete or because they participated in the literary field solely due to the conjuncture (like the two priests, Maydieu and Bruckberger).

Sources

The biographical information was collected from documents, according to the prosopographical method (additional information was obtained, in some cases, through interviews). The notoriety of a part of the examined population allowed for significant recourse to printed sources. Aside from the numerous books and articles included in the bibliography—biographies, memoirs, essays or autobiographical fictions, commemorative collections, special tribute editions of reviews, manuals of literary history, anthologies, reception speeches at the French Academy, published obituaries—for those authors who received a lesser posthumous consecration, I used resources like the *Dictionnaire biographique du mouvement ouvrier français* by J. Maitron and C. Pennetier (Éditions ouvrières, 1964–1993), the *Dictionnaire des intellectuels français* edited by J. Julliard and M. Winock (Seuil, 1996), the *Dictionnaire des littératures de langue française*, edited by J.-P. Beaumarchais et al. (Bordas, 1984, reedited 1994, 4 vols.), and, in some cases, the biographical dictionaries established by Christophe Charle and Eva Telkes, *Les Professeurs du Collège de France* and *Les Professeurs de la faculté des sciences de Paris* (Paris: CNRS-INRP, 1988 and 1989). I also relied on biographical, literary, and political dictionaries like the *Dictionnaire de biographie française* (edited by Balteau, Prévost, and Barroux; Letouzé and Ané, 1932–1970); the *Dictionnaire biographique contemporain* (Pharos, 1951); *Qui êtes-vous?* (1908 and 1924); *Who's Who in France* (1953–); the *Dictionnaire de littérature française* (H. Lemaître, Bordas, 1986); the *Dictionnaire de la politique française* by H. Coston (1967, 3 vols.); the *Isographie de l'Académie française* by R. Didier (E. de Boccard, 1964); *L'Annuaire de l'Académie française: Documents et notices sur les membres de l'Académie* (Institut de France, 1966), and the *Dictionnaire des lettres françaises: XIXe siècle* by P. Moreau and Mgr. Pichard (Fayard, 1971–1972). In many cases, the father's profession was kindly communicated to me by the staff of the Public Records Office archives at the various town halls of the writers' birthplaces, based on the writer's birth certificate.

A systematic search in the catalogues of the Bibliothèque nationale allowed me to determine the publishers. For this purpose, I also used the *Bibliographie de la littérature française de 1800 à 1930* by H. Thième (Droz, 1933, 2 vols.), and the *Bibliographie des auteurs modernes de langue française* by H. Talvart and J. Place (Chronique des lettres françaises, 1928–1975). I systematically perused the periodicals I selected as indicators (*La Gerbe, La NRF, Poésie, Confluences,* the clandestine *Lettres françaises,* etc.) in order to establish contributor lists, a work I completed and cross-checked with the help of the publications of the *Annuaire de la presse française et étrangère* by M. Roux-Bluysen (1937, 1942–1943), and of invaluable works such as the index of contributors to *La NRF* drawn up by Claude Martin, the *Histoire politique de la revue* Esprit, by Michel Winock (Seuil, 1975), and *Les 700 rédacteurs de* Je suis partout, by P.-M. Dioudonnat (Sedopols, 1993). Jean-François Sirinelli's book, *Intellectuels et passions françaises: Manifestes et pétitions aux XXᵉ siècle* (Fayard, 1990), allowed me, along with other sources (essays, articles, and manifestos unearthed in the press), to establish the writers' political position-takings.

INDICATORS
Of the 128 variables that formed the original questionnaire, only 58 were retained for the factorial analysis, for reasons of readability, relevance, or lack of information, or to avoid redundancy. The Multiple Correspondence Analysis thus included 236 active and 12 illustrative modalities. [1] The variables I retained are divided into four main groups: social properties (age, social origin, geographical trajectory, educational trajectory, scholastic titles);[2] characteristics of the position in the field (preferred genre, places of publication, publishers and periodicals, prizes, membership in institutions, degree and type of recognition); aesthetic position-takings (literary schools, movements, or tendencies) and political ones (in the 1930s and under the Occupation).

While for some groups of variables, like political position-takings, periodicals, and membership in institutions, I only retained those that concerned the Occupation period and the 1930s, for others, like literary genres and tendencies, publishers, and prizes, the data refers to the entire trajectory. This has allowed me to connect a particular state of the field and long-term individual orientations.[3]

Social properties. Age is given for 1940. The age groups were divided according to several criteria, taking into account the stages of the literary career as well as the generational phenomena due to extraliterary causes, particularly World War I: I have thus been careful to isolate those writers who, very young and while their future was still undecided, had experienced war (and the front, for many of them); this is why I depart from the ten-year brackets for writers between forty-one and fifty-two years of age in 1940, and who therefore were twenty-six or younger in 1914 and eighteen or older in 1917 (those who were born in 1900 or later could not be mobilized); this time, in order to balance the numbers, I grouped together all the writers over the age of sixty, which presented no difficulty in terms of the evolution of the literary career.

Social origin (see table 1) was determined according to the profession of the father or guardian (if applicable). To regroup them, I used the categories established by Christophe Charle,[4] which allowed for comparison not only with the data collected by Rémy Ponton for 616 writers who were active in the second half of the nineteenth century (recoded by Christophe Charle), but also with other intellectual fractions, such as university professors, or with elites, such as senior civil servants. These categories are the following:

Wealthy fractions:	big property owner, industrialist, etc.
Senior civil servants:	diplomat, politician, high-ranking officer, etc.
Middle bourgeoisie:	engineer, entrepreneur, company head, stockbroker, retailer, architect, pharmacist, etc.
Legal professions:	lawyer, magistrate, notary, etc.
Intellectual and artistic fractions:	secondary and upper-level teacher, physician, literary man, journalist, artist, etc.
Mid-level civil service:	civil servant, subordinate officer
Petty bourgeoisie and working classes:[5]	primary school teacher, employee, minor retailer, farmer, artisan, laborer, peasant, etc.

In terms of social origins, the comparison of my population with the one studied by Rémy Ponton shows some differences, with the exception of the wealthy fractions (13 percent in both cases) and legal professions (8–9 percent). The underrepresentation, in his sample, of the sons of senior civil servants and politicians, as well as writers from the middle bourgeoisie (2.4 percent and 6 percent respectively, versus 6.5 percent and 13.5 percent for my sample), likely stems in part from the overselection of my population, and in part from the high rate of nonresponses that he obtained for authors born in Paris.[6] The sons of civil servants were, conversely, better represented there (13.3 percent versus 8.1 percent for my sample). The greater proportion of writers from intellectual fractions in my population (18.9 percent versus 13.7 percent) reflects, on the other hand, the growth of the liberal and intellectual professions at the end of the nineteenth century.[7] Similarly, the slightly higher rate of writers from the petty bourgeoisie and popular classes (27 percent versus 22.5 percent) is probably the expression of an evolution in the recruitment of the literary field, due in particular to the development of education.

For the coding of origin and geographical trajectory, the indicator of birthplace (see table 2) was supplemented by the geographical situation during childhood, adolescence (the age of secondary schooling, between ten and sixteen to seventeen years), and the transitional phase between the end of secondary schooling and entry into the literary field (between seventeen and twenty-two years, an age that corresponds to advanced studies for part of the population). These indicators allowed me to evaluate the significance of residential mobility in the conditions of access to the literary field. While one writer out of three was born in Paris, versus more than one out of two in the provinces, and about one out of ten in the colonies or abroad, which corresponds to the rates obtained by Rémy Ponton, the proportion of Parisians, already considerable at birth, increased twofold at the end of secondary education. This indicator of mobility also allowed me to evaluate the significance of familial resources and educational strategies for the orientation of the trajectory, since the writers who were best endowed in this respect were more likely to migrate to the capital during their secondary schooling, while the less endowed arrived there later.

The relatively privileged social origins of the writers of my population perhaps explain why few of them seem to have been educated in their community's public primary school, even after the law of 1882 which rendered it compulsory for children between seven and thirteen years of age (unless they had obtained a certificate of studies before that age).[8] The writers' rate of enrollment in secondary school bears an inverted relationship to that of the enrollment rate in France during the period they were in school: it went from 2.9 percent to 6.5 percent between 1887 and 1926, versus 78.4 percent for my whole population; 6.5 percent of writers attended upper primary school (EPS), which, even though they still belonged to the primary cycle, would be attached to the first secondary cycle in 1941 (see table 3).[9] The variable concerning secondary or postprimary education is a composite variable, based on attendance at two establishments (this is the case for two of five writers). In the relatively rare cases of a switch from public education to private Catholic education, or vice versa, I have privileged private education as an indicator of secondary education. It was important to expose the durable split engendered by the opposition between public and Catholic education under the Third Republic. For the most part, these consisted of collèges run by Marist or Marianite brothers, and more rarely by Jesuits: the banning of the Company of Jesus during a large part of the period when the writers of my population were educated partially explains this underrepresentation, but we might also suggest that Jesuit education, aimed at preparation for the grandes écoles, "produced" fewer writers. I have, moreover, dissociated the writers who were entirely educated in a major Parisian lycée from those who began their studies in a provincial lycée and finished them in the capital. This allowed me to confirm the significance of familial educational strategies on residential mobility, which is visible in the trajectories of the future "immortals," as opposed to their colleagues. Finally, it seemed pertinent to classify the École Alsacienne—attended by only three writers: Gide, Vercors, and Chevrillon, Taine's nephew, who finished his studies at Louis-le-Grand—among the major Parisian lycées rather than the private Catholic establishments.

My population differentiates itself the most clearly from the one studied by Rémy Ponton for the end of the nineteenth century by the rate of enrollment in higher education: 63.8 percent versus 36.9 percent, that is, a twofold higher rate (see table 4).[10] This difference chiefly reflects, as we saw, the overall increase in the number of students in France, which was multiplied by five between 1875 and 1924,[11] the period when almost all of my population was of age to undertake advanced studies.[12] The overall numbers having almost grown twofold just in the period between 1875 and 1882 (they went from 9,963 to 17,503 students), it is not surprising that the comparison of rates concerning the different areas of specialization for the writers of both populations reveals an average ratio of one to three. Only law constitutes an exception, since it was, along with medicine and pharmacology, the only course of study up until the reforms of the licence degree in arts and sciences between 1877 and 1888. It is thus overrepresented among writers' specializations in the nineteenth century.

Higher education is also a composite variable, since the cases of double or changed specialization affect almost a third of the sample. For categorization, I have privileged attendance at the grandes écoles, even for dropouts (I was able to reconstruct the dropout rate based on the gap between this variable and the highest diploma or title obtained, which is a separate variable). I proceeded with a different categorization than Rémy Ponton. It was more interesting, for the comparison between literary institutions, to tease out kinds of educational investments rather than the nature of the training.[13] I have therefore grouped, under the heading of "grandes écoles," the scientific grandes écoles (Polytechnique, Centrale, etc.) as well as the military ones (Saint-Cyr), the École des Chartes and the École libre des sciences politiques (which prepared students for careers in diplomacy). However I separated the École normale supérieure (letters) due to its less elitist social recruitment, on the one hand,[14] and the specificity of the position of normaliens in the literary field, on the other. The students at the grandes écoles and the normaliens represented 15.1 percent and 10.3 percent of my population, respectively, a rate that is three times higher than for the population studied by Rémy Ponton, if we reorganize his categories according to my code (5.5 percent and 2.9 percent). This is undoubtedly one of the major biases induced by the overselection of my population, and more particularly by the overrepresentation of French Academy members. But this difference can also be explained, for the first category, by the founding in 1872 of the École libre des sciences politiques (13 writers, or 7 percent of the population, attended it). Law studies, whether or not they were paired with a course of study in literature, were isolated. This specialization amounted to 14.1 percent of the courses of study for my overall population, a lower rate than that obtained by Rémy Ponton (20.8 percent). The difference grows further if we consider the relative weight of law in the training of only those writers who did postsecondary studies (the rate rose to 50 percent, then, for the nineteenth-century writers), which clearly reflects the development of literary studies from the 1880s (16.8 percent of our overall population of writers specialized in letters, versus 4.5 percent for the population studied by Rémy Ponton). The Hautes Études and the École des langues orientales, which do not represent more than 2 percent of specializations, were grouped with literary studies. Finally, I isolated medical studies, even though they were underrepresented in my sample as in that of Rémy Ponton (3.2 percent and 1.9 percent respectively), due to their specificity as a path for social ascension at the time, as Georges Duhamel described so well in the first volume of the *Chronique des Pasquier*.

The writers of my population were also twice as likely to finish their advanced studies as those studied by Rémy Ponton (51.3 percent versus 25.3 percent;[15] see table 5). This difference is, once again, the effect of both a morphological evolution and the overselection of my population. Conversely, 24.3 percent of writers' highest diploma was the baccalaureate, versus 37.8 percent of writers at the end of the nineteenth century who had reached "secondary level" or had not finished their postsecondary studies. The rate of writers in my population who had a level inferior to the baccalaureate (10 percent) corresponds to the sum of the rates obtained by Rémy Ponton for "primary level" and "unfinished secondary" (8 percent).

Finally, to the extent that it was possible, I coded the causes for the cessation of studies (which concerned, in total, 42.2 percent of my population) by distinguishing "incidents" in the educational career—academic failure (13 percent), which is, as we saw, a powerful factor in creating social resentment, and difficulties encountered due to a lack of financial resources, health problems, or the war (16.2 percent)—from dropout cases linked to orientation toward a literary career (4.9 percent).

Indicators of position in the field. The period of entry into the literary field was determined based on the first significant publication (work). Preferred literary genre (poetry, novel, theater, criticism, travel narrative, essay, political essay and lampoon, memoirs and autobiography) was assessed for three periods in the career. For publishing positions, I turned to a double coding, since it was very frequent for the writers to move from one main publisher to another. I grouped the publishers based on a combination of several criteria, namely age, size, structure of capital, type of publishing strategy from a commercial point of view (rapid sales versus long-term placement), and from the point of view of the trademark image of the house.[16] A first group includes the major publishing houses from the nineteenth century, which published successful authors and/or popular series at a low price: Calmann-Lévy, Albin Michel, Flammarion, Ferenczi, and Stock (the former publisher of the Dreyfusards was purchased in 1921 by Delamain and Boutelleau), to whom I had to add the conglomerate Hachette (which only concerns two cases). Under the heading of "right-wing publishers," I grouped, on one hand, houses from the nineteenth century like Fasquelle, Plon, Fayard, as well as the Librairie académique Perrin (which I situate among them because its only representative in my sample is the permanent secretary of the French Academy, André Bellessort, Action française member, who directed a series there); I also included the Éditions de France, founded in 1923 by Horace de Carbuccia with the support of the academician Marcel Prévost (editor of the *Revue de France*), and which launched the extreme-right weekly *Gringoire* in 1928. The publishing house Plon-Nourrit took on a Catholic-right hue (close to Action française), notably with the "Roseau d'or" series edited by Jacques Maritain and Henri Massis, and the creation in 1933 of a magazine bearing the name of the current year (*1933 . . .*), which included Robert Brasillach, Maurice Bardèche, Abel Bonnard, and Henri Massis among its contributors. The Librairie Arthème Fayard sealed its alliance with the ultra-nationalist right and with Action française by launching two extreme-right politico-literary weeklies: *Candide* in 1924 and *Je suis partout* in 1930. Under the heading "rear guard," I filed small houses that represented the pole of small-scale production at the turn of the century, like the Mercure de

France and Émile-Paul, but were closed to new tendencies during the interwar period. The Librairie G. Crès et Cie, which had established itself before the Great War and in the early 1920s, changed direction after the departure of Georges Crès in 1925 (its holdings were liquidated in 1932). The first three groups were thus composed of publishing houses from the nineteenth century that "were completely closed to all the avant-gardes," to borrow Pascal Fouché's expression.[17] I isolated Gallimard due to the overrepresentation of its authors in my population. It could have been filed with the fourth group, chiefly represented by Grasset. These two houses, founded before 1914, "very quickly imposed the literature of the day" following the victory, and competed for literary legitimacy during the interwar period. In this fourth category, I included Denoël et Steele, a publishing house born in 1928, which "specialized" in anti-conformism and the contestation of the established order. The publishers born under the Occupation were divided, for the Multiple Correspondence Analysis, between the Éditions de Minuit and the Éditions Seghers on one side (to which I added Le Seuil, which, after the Liberation, published Catholic left-wing writers who had taken part in the Resistance, like Pierre Emmanuel and Luc Estang, and published in the journal *Esprit*), and on the other, Julliard and Laffont. Finally, the Communist publishers (Éditions sociales internationales, Bibliothèque française, Éditeurs français réunis, Raison d'Être) were grouped together. For the factorial analysis, I added the Éditions Rieder (very little represented), due to their leftist orientation during the 1920s (they published the journal *Europe*) and the "populist" character of their series, "Prosateurs français contemporains."[18]

The chief literary prizes and membership in one of the two academies between 1940 and 1944 were taken as indicators of institutional consecration. The degree and type of recognition were constituted on the basis of several indicators. Contemporary and later notoriety, determined according to the inclusion, and length of entry, in literary histories (those of René Lalou, *Histoire de la littérature française contemporaine de 1870 à nos jours* [Paris: PUF, 1947], and Pierre de Boisdeffre, *Une histoire vivante de la littérature d'aujourd'hui 1939–1960* [Paris: Le Livre contemporain, 1959]), and in dictionaries (J.-P. Beaumarchais, D. Couty and A. Rey [eds.], *Dictionnaire des littératures de langue française* [Paris: Bordas, 1984, reedited 1994], and *Le Petit Robert* of proper names). Finally, a summary indicator, taking into account the information that it was impossible to code, like print runs, differentiates a worldly type of notoriety, sales successes, and the recognition of peers.

Aesthetic and political position-takings. Lists of the novelistic currents, schools, or poetic movements that were inventoried can be found in the key to figures

1.2 and 2.1; this data was assessed at two points in the career. Lists of the periodicals used in the Multiple Correspondence Analysis are also included. For the first set, categorizations could only be very rough (or risk obtaining one category per person in certain cases) and were made in function of their relevance with respect to the studied population. The lists of reviews, weeklies, and dailies are not, of course, exhaustive. I have retained only the most representative periodicals with respect to the studied population, and whose numbers were significant enough to not create a bias in the factorial analysis.

I have removed the variables concerning the successive militant position-takings from the 1920s up until the beginning of the 1950s from the Correspondence Analysis, in order to avoid redundancy. Aside from membership in the CNE between 1941 and the spring of 1944, I have only retained two other political variables: one concerning political tendency in the 1930s according to the pertinent political and ideological divisions of this period (privileging the anti-Fascism vs. neo-pacifism axis, while conserving political tendency; see the list in the key to figures 1.2 and 2.1); the other concerning tendency under the Occupation. For this last variable, the attitudes and position-takings were graduated so as to take evolutions into account. The categories are thus the following: résistants (with no distinction made between civil and active resistance, due to low numbers in the second case); Resistance sympathizers; writers who evolved from a Marshalist or Pétainist position to an attitude of sympathy toward the Resistance starting in 1942; die-hard Pétainists; collaborationists and those close to the Collaboration (closeness was determined according to publications in the collaborationist press, displays of sympathy with respect to the occupant, and participation in collaborationist society life); unlike exiled Vichyists, who were grouped with the Pétainists, the exiled opponents, such as Bernanos, Maritain, and Jules Romains, were coded separately, due both to their lesser exposure to the risks taken by the opponents who remained in France, and the specificity of their mode of intervention in the conjuncture; finally, a last category grouping undetermined positions.

The Social Recruitment of the Literary Field and of Its Institutions

The principle of constitution of the subpopulations for each institution was presented in the chapters devoted to them. The results concerning the twenty-eight regular contributors to *La* NRF before 1940 among my total population have only an indicative value. Let us also remember that among the forty contributors to the NRF of the "dark years," thirteen are not part of our total population. Finally, the writers elected to the two academies after the Liberation were included here to increase the numbers, but do not appear as such in the Correspondence Analysis, which only concerns the war years.

Table 1. Comparative recruitment of the authorities of the literary field according to the social origins of the writers

Social category of the father %	Writers 40–44	French Acad. 40–47	Gonc. Acad. 40–51	*NRF* before 1940	*NRF* 40–43	CNE 40–44
Wealthy fractions	13.0	12.9	20.0	14.3	7.5	8.0
Senior civil servants	6.5	12.9	5.0	7.1	5.0	4.0
Middle bourgeoisie	13.5	12.9	5.0	*21.4*	7.5	14.0
Legal professions	8.1	12.9	5.0	7.1	10.0	4.0
Intellectual fractions	18.9	9.7	20.0	10.7	10.0	*30.0*
Mid-level civil servants	8.1	*25.8*	5.0	14.3	12.5	4.0
Petty bourgeoisie / Working classes	27.0	12.9	*40.0*	21.4	*32.5*	22.0
NR	4.9	–	–	3.7	15.0	14.0
N =	185	31	20	28	40	50

Table 2. Comparative recruitment of the authorities of the literary field according to the geographical origins of the writers

Geographic Origin %	Writers 40–44	French Acad. 40–47	Gonc. Acad. 40–51	*NRF* before 1940	*NRF* 40–43	CNE 40–44
Paris	33.0	19.4	35.0	*46.5*	30.0	34.0
Province	52.4	*80.6*	45.0	39.3	*60.0*	46.0
Colonies/Abroad	10.8	–	20.0	7.1	–	14.0
NR	3.8	–	–	7.1	10.0	6.0
N =	185	31	20	28	40	50

Table 3. Comparative recruitment of the authorities of the literary field according to the secondary education of the writers

Secondary education %	Writers 40–44	French Acad. 40–47	Gonc. Acad. 40–51	*NRF* before 1940	*NRF* 40–43	CNE 40–44
Major lycée	20.0	19.4	25.0	*35.7*	20.0	20.8
Lycée/Major lycée	10.3	19.4	0.0	17.9	12.5	10.0
Catholic collège	18.4	*25.8*	15.0	3.6	10.0	18.0
Lycée/Collège	29.7	29.0	*40.0*	21.4	32.5	26.0
Higher primary school/none	6.5	3.2	5.0	10.7	10.0	4.0
Other/NR	15.1	3.2	15.0	10.7	15.0	20.0
N =	185	31	20	28	40	50

Table 4. Comparative recruitment of the authorities of the literary field according to the nature of the writers' higher education

Higher education	Writers 40–44	French Acad. 40–47	Gonc. Acad. 40–51	*NRF* before 1940	NRF 40–43	CNE 40–44
Grande école	15.1	*25.8*	5.0	14.3	10.0	14.0
ENS lettres	10.3	*25.8*	–	10.7	5.0	8.0
Medecine	3.2	3.2	5.0	3.6	2.5	2.0
Law	14.1	12.9	10.0	10.7	10.0	*18.0*
Literary studies	16.8	12.9	10.0	*32.1*	22.5	16.0
Art	4.3	3.2	10.0	3.6	2.5	4.0
Not relevant	29.7	9.7	*50.0*	17.9	*35.0*	32.0
Other/NR	6.5	6.5	10.0	7.1	12.5	6.0
N =	185	31	20	28	40	50

Table 5. Comparative recruitment of the authorities of the literary field according to the level of education reached

Highest diploma or title	Writers 40–44	French Acad. 40–47	Gonc. Acad. 40–51	NRF before 1940	NRF 40–43	CNE 40–44
Grande École/École	21.6	*45.1*	10.0	17.9	5.0	20.0
Licence/DES/ Doctorate	29.7	35.5	20.0	*50.0*	37.5	28.0
Baccalaureate	24.3	9.7	30.0	21.4	22.5	24.0
Inferior to bac	10.8	3.2	*20.0*	7.1	*17.5*	8.0
Other/NR	13.5	6.5	20.0	3.6	17.5	20.0
N =	185	31	20	28	40	50

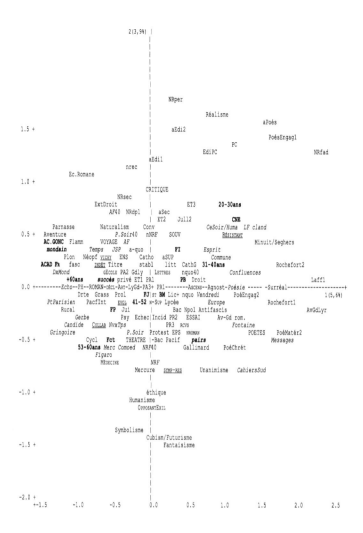

Fig. A.1 Literary positions under the Occupation. A Multiple Correspondence Analysis (partial presentation). Plane of the first and second axes of inertia: the space of the literary authorities and of aesthetic position-takings. Publishers are underlined. Institutions and periods of entry in the field are bold. Periodicals are in italics. Types of consecration in italics and bold. Genres in CAPITAL letters. *Note*: For the legibility of the graphs, I isolated, first of all, the variables relative to position in the field and to aesthetic position-takings. Thus the social properties and political position-takings are not included in this graph. Note that the emphases (bold, underlined, italics) do not correspond to the strongest contributions, which are detailed in chapter 1; they serve to facilitate the reading of the graph by grouping the modalities of a single variable.

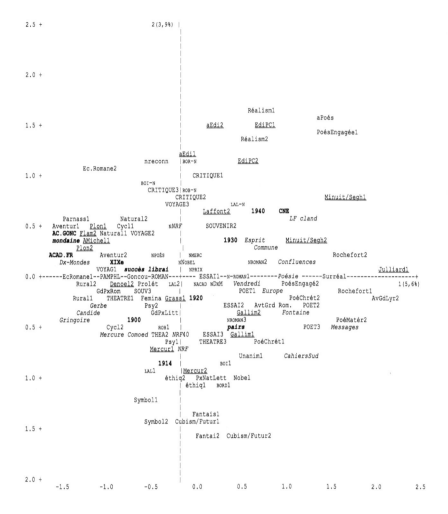

Fig. A.2 Positions and position-takings of the writers under the Occupation. Correspondence Analysis. Plane of the first and second axes of inertia: the space of properties (simplified presentation). Political position-takings under the Occupation are underlined; social origin, age, and forms of consecration are bolded; genres are in CAPS; periodicals are in italics. *Note:* This graph represents, in a simplified form, all of the variables, with the exception of literary prizes, anthologies, dictionaries, and certain modalities concerning nonparticipation in reviews, which appear in figure A.1. Moreover, when they were situated near each other, the first and second principal publisher, like the genres and the aesthetic position-takings at different times in the career, were grouped together (Symbol 1 and Symbol 2, for example, became symbolism).

Key

SOCIAL PROPERTIES

Age: in 1940: 20–30 years; 31–40 years; 41–52 years; 53–60 years; 60+ years.

Social category of the father: FP: wealthy fractions; **Fct:** senior and mid-level civil servants; **BM:** middle bourgeoisie; **FJ:** legal fractions **FI:** intellectual fractions; **PB:** petty bourgeoisie and working classes; **NRper:** no response.

Geographic trajectory: PA=Paris; PR=province; ET=foreign countries or colonies; 1=childhood; 2=adolescence; 3=age of entry into adult life (PA1=resides in Paris during childhood, etc.)

Secondary education: Gdlyc: major Parisian lycée (Louis-le-Grand, Henry IV, Condorcet...), and École Alsacienne; LycGd: provincial lycée, then major Parisian lycée; Lycée: (provincial) lycée; Catho: Catholic collège; EPS: upper primary school or no postprimary training.

Higher education: ENS: École normale supérieure, Letters; GÉcole: grandes écoles (Polytechnique, ENS sciences, etc.), École des Chartes, École libre des sciences politiques; Médeci: medical school; Law: law school (paired, or not, with Literature Studies); Lettres: formation in literature, philosophy, ethnology, etc.; Art: art school (Beaux-arts, Arts décoratifs); aSUP: other advanced formation; N-Sup: did not attend a higher education establishment.

Highest diploma or title: Title: graduated from a grande école (ENS included, with or without agrégation); Lic+: Diploma equivalent or higher than the licence (DES, doctoral degree), including agrégation (for the non-normaliens); Bac: baccalaureate; -Bac: diploma inferior to the baccalaureate (CEP, certificate or none); NRdpl: another diploma or no response.

Incident in educational career: Incid: incident due to material causes, to reasons of health, to war; Echec: relative academic failure (failed examinations, failed competitive examination); litt: dropped out to focus on literature; stabl: educational trajectory without incident.

Religion (illustrative): Catho: Catholic; Conv: converted Catholic; Protest: Protestant; Jui: Jewish; Agnost: agnostic (the nonresponses are not represented).

Social trajectory of the paternal family (illustrative): ASCENS: ascending familial trajectory; DECL: family in decline; RCVR: change of profession; ST: stability (the nonrespones are not represented).

POSITION IN THE LITERARY FIELD

Period of entry into the field (according to the date of first significant publication) XIXe: end of the nineteenth century; 1900: between 1900 and 1914; 1914: during World War I; 1920: 1920s; 1930: 1930s; 1940: 1940s.

Principal genre for three periods in the career (1=beginning of career; 2=peak of career; 3=end of career): POETES; ROMAN; CRITIQUE; VOYAGE: subgenres including travel narrative, biographies, versatility; ESSAI: philosophical, moral essay; PH: lampoon (pamphlet), political essay; SOUV(ENIRS): memoirs, autobiography.

Publishers (1=first principal publisher; 2=second principal publisher). The groups of publishers are represented by the publishers most characteristic of the group.

> Gallim: Gallimard; Grass: Grasset, Denoël, Corrêa; Flamm or A. Michel: old houses from the nineteenth century that gamble on rapid sales, with popular editions (Flammarion, Albin Michel, Ollendorf, Stock,Calmann-Lévy, Hachette, etc.); Plon: Plon, academic publishers (Perrin), editors on the right (Fayard); Mercur: small publishing houses now representing the rear guard (Mercure de France, Emile-Paul, Hartmann, Kra/Sagittaire, La Sirène, etc.); Minuit/Segh: small publishing houses started under the Occupation (Minuit, Seghers, Seuil); Jull or Laff: other young houses (Julliard, Laffont, etc.); EdiPC: Communist publishers and Rieder (ESI, Bibliothèque française, etc.); aEdi: another editor.

Prizes: Nobel; PxNatLett: national humanities prize; GPxLitt: Grand Prize for Literature given by the French Academy; GPxRom: Grand Prize for the Novel given by the French Academy; Goncou: Goncourt Prize; Femina: Femina Prize.

Institutional consecration (member of the French Academy, of the Goncourt Academy): ACAD.FR; AC.GONC; NACAD=belongs to neither of the two academies between 1940 and 1944.

Degree of recognition and of contemporary and later notoriety according to presence and place in anthologies, histories of contemporary literature, and dictionaries (1=long entry; 2=short entry; n=no entry):

> Lal: Lalou René, *Histoire de la littérature française contemporaine (de 1870 à nos jours)* (Paris: PUF, 1947).

> Boi: Boisdeffre Pierre de, *Une histoire vivante de la littérature d'aujourd'hui 1939–1960* (Paris: Le Livre contemporain, 1959).

Bor(das): Beaumarchais J.-P., Couty D., and Rey A. (eds.), *Dictionnaire des littératures de langue française* (Paris: Bordas, 1984, reedited 1994).

Rob: *Le Petit Robert*

Type of recognition: mondaine: worldly success; succès librai: sales success; pairs: peer recognition; nreconn: no recognition.

AESTHETIC AND POLITICAL POSITION-TAKINGS

Literary schools and movements, categories of classification (coded for two periods of the career: 1=beginning; 2=peak):

Novelistic genre: Aventur: adventure novel, exotic novel; Psy: legitimate novelistic genres, psychological novel, novel of manners, novel of analysis, Catholic novel; Cycl: cyclical novel; Réalism: social realism; Natural: naturalism and populism; Rural: rural, provincial, regional novel; Prolet: proletarian novel; Ethiq: "ethical generation" (G. Picon); AvGdR: avant-garde novels, existentialism, "realism of language" (usage of new novelistic techniques, oral language, etc.).

School or poetic movement: EcRomane: École romane; Parnasse: École du Parnasse; Unanim: Unanisme, Abbaye de Créteil; Fantais: Fantaisisme; Cubism/Futur: Cubism, futurism, epic poetry; Surréal: surrealism; PoésEngagée: engaged poetry, especially "national" poetry during the Occupation; Rochefort: École de Rochefort; AvGdLyr: "lyrical" avant-garde (*Messages* group); PoésMaterial: "materialist" poetry (objects, elements, etc.).

List of Weeklies and Magazines (contributed or did not contribute to the periodical; noncontribution is indicated by the first letters of the periodical preceded by an "n"):

Candide, Comoedia, La Gerbe, Gringoire, Je suis partout (*JSP*), underground *Lettres françaises* (*LF*), *Vendredi*.

Les Cahiers du Sud, Commune, Confluences, Esprit, Europe, Fontaine, Mercure de France, Messages, La Nouvelle Revue française (*NRF*), *La Nouvelle Revue française* from 1940 to 1943 (*NRF 40*), *Poésie 40,41*... , *Revue des deux mondes* (*DxMond*).

Dailies: *AF*: *L'Action française* (1930s); *AF40*: *L'Action française* (1940); *Echo*: *L'Écho de Paris*; *Temps*: *Le Temps* and *Le Matin* (1930s); *Le Figaro* (1930s) and *Le Figaro* 40 (1940); *Paris-Soir* (1930s) and *Paris-Soir* 40 (1940); *Ce Soir/L'Humanité*; *NvxTps*: collaborationist press (*Les Nouveaux Temps, La Révolution nationale, Aujourd'hui, Paris-Soir* Northern zone, *Cri du Peuple*); *PtParisien*: *Le Petit Parisien*; nquo: did not contribute to any periodical.

Political tendency:

1930s: PC: Communist/Communistic; Antifasc: anti-Fascist; Pacif: anti-Fascist pacifism; PacI: total pacifism; CathoG: progressive or anti-Fascist Catholics; Humanism: liberal humanism; Drte: right, conservativism; Néopf: neo-pacifist on the right; Extdroit: Action française, leagues; Fascis: Fascistic; npol: little interest in politics.

Occupation: Résistants: civil or active resistance; Symp.Résist: Resistance sympathizer; Evolu: evolved from Pétainism to support of the Resistance; Vichy: Pétainist; Collab: collaborationist or close to the Collaboration; Indét: indeterminate; Opposants exil: exiles opposed to the Vichy regime.

CNE: member of the CNE between 1941 and the spring of 1944.

List of Writers Included in the Statistical Inquiry

ACHARD Marcel (1900–1974)
ADAM Georges (1908–1963)
AJALBERT Jean (1863–1947)
ANGLÈS Auguste (1914–1983)
ANOUILH Jean (1910–1987)
ARAGON Louis (1897–1982)
ARLAND Marcel (1899–1986)
ARNOUX Alexandre (1884–1973)
AUDIBERTI Jacques (1899–1965)
AUDISIO Gabriel (1900–1978)
AVELINE Claude (1901–1992)
AYMÉ Marcel (1902–1967)
BATAILLE Georges (1897–1962)
BAUER Gérard (1888–1967)
BEAUVOIR Simone de (1908–1986)
BÉGUIN Albert (1901–1957)
BELLESSORT André (1886–1942)
BENDA Julien (1867–1956)
BENJAMIN René (1885–1948)
BENOIT Pierre (1886–1962)
BERNANOS Georges (1888–1948)
BERNARD Marc (1900–1983)
BERTRAND Louis (1866–1941)

BILLY André (1882–1871)
BLANZAT Jean (1906–1977)
BLECH René (1902–1953)
BONNARD Abel (1883–1968)
BORDEAUX Henry (1870–1963)
BORNE Alain (1915–1962)
BOULENGER Jacques (1879–1944)
BRASILLACH Robert (1909–1945)
BRUCKBERGER Raymond (1907–1998)
CADOU René Guy (1920–1951)
CAMUS Albert (1913–1960)
CARCO Francis (1886–1958)
CASSOU Jean (1897–1986)
CÉLINE Louis-Ferdinand (1894–1971)
CHAMPION Pierre (1880–1942)
CHAMSON André (1900–1983)
CHAR René (1907–1988)
CHARDONNE Jacques (1884–1968)
CHATEAUBRIANT Alphonse de (1877–1951)
CHAUMEIX André (1874–1955)

CHEVALLIER Gabriel (1895–1969)
CHEVRILLON André (1864–1957)
CLAUDEL Paul (1868–1955)
COCTEAU Jean (1889–1963)
COLETTE (1873–1954)
COMBELLE Lucien (1913–1994)
DAUDET Léon (1867–1942)
DEBÛ-BRIDEL Jacques (1902–1993)
DECOUR Jacques (1910–1942)
DEMAISON André (1883–1956)
DERÊME Tristan (1889–1941)
DESCAVES Lucien (1861–1949)
DESNOS Robert (1900–1945)
DESVIGNES Yvonne (1902–1981)
DONNAY Maurice (1859–1945)
DORGELÈS Roland (1885–1973)
DRIEU LA ROCHELLE Pierre
    (1893–1945)
DUHAMEL Georges (1884–1966)
DURAS Marguerite (1914–1996)
ELUARD Paul (1895–1952)
EMMANUEL Pierre (1916–1984)
ESTANG Luc (1911–1992)
ESTAUNIÉ Édouard (1862–1942)
FARGE Yves (1899–1953)
FARGUE Léon-Paul (1876–1947)
FARRÈRE Claude (1876–1957)
FERNANDEZ Ramon (1894–1944)
FOLLAIN Jean (1903–1971)
FOMBEURE Maurice (1906–1981)
FORT Paul (1872–1960)
FRENAUD André (1907–1997)
FUMET Stanislas (1896–1983)
GAILLARD Robert (1909–1975)
GENEVOIX Maurice (1890–1980)
GERMAIN José (1884–1964)
GHÉON Henri (1875–1944)
GIDE André (1869–1951)
GILLET Louis (1877–1943)

GIONO Jean (1895–1970)
GIRAUDOUX Jean (1882–1944)
GIRON Roger (1900–1990)
GUÉHENNO Jean (1890–1978)
GUILLEVIC Eugène (1907–1997)
GUILLOUX Louis (1899–1980)
GUITRY Sacha (1885–1957)
HAEDENS Kléber (1913–1976)
HALÉVY Daniel (1872–1962)
HAZARD Paul (1878–1944)
HENRIOT Emile (1889–1961)
HÉRIAT Philippe (1898–1971)
HERMANT Abel (1862–1950)
JACOB Max (1876–1944)
JALOUX Edmond (1878–1949)
JOUHANDEAU Marcel (1888–1979)
JOUVE Pierre Jean (1887–1976)
KESSEL Joseph (1898–1979)
LA VARENDE Jean de (1887–1959)
LACRETELLE Jacques de (1888–1985)
LARGUIER Léo (1878–1950)
LA TOUR DU PIN Patrice (1911–1975)
LAUBREAUX Alain (1899–1968)
LAVEDAN Henri (1859–1940)
LÉAUTAUD Paul (1872–1956)
LECOMTE Georges (1867–1958)
LEIRIS Michel (1901–1990)
LESCURE Jean (1912–2005)
LESCURE Pierre de (1891–1963)
LEYRIS Pierre (1907–2001)
MAC ORLAN Pierre (1882–1970)
MADAULE Jacques (1898–1993)
MALHERBE Henry (1886–1958)
MALRAUX André (1901–1976)
MARCEL Gabriel (1889–1973)
MARCENAC Jean (1913–1984)
MARITAIN Jacques (1882–1973)
MARTIN DU GARD Roger
    (1881–1958)

MARTIN-CHAUFFIER Louis
  (1894–1980)
MASSIS Henri (1886–1970)
MASSON Loys (1915–1969)
MAULNIER Thierry (1909–1988)
MAURIAC François (1885–1970)
MAUROIS André (1885–1967)
MAURRAS Charles (1868–1952)
MAYDIEU Jean (1900–1955)
MILLET Raymond (1899–1967)
MONTHERLANT Henry de
  (1896–1972)
MORAND Paul (1888–1976)
MORGAN Claude (1898–1980)
MOUSSINAC Léon (1890–1964)
OUDARD Georges (1889–1971)
PAGNOL Marcel (1895–1974)
PARROT Louis (1906–1948)
PAULHAN Jean (1884–1968)
PEISSON Édouard (1896–1963)
PELORSON Georges (1909–2008)
PESQUIDOUX Joseph de
  (1869–1946)
PETITJEAN Armand (1913–2003)
PLISNIER Charles (1894–1952)
PONGE Francis (1899–1988)
POULAILLE Henry (1896–1980)
POURRAT Henri (1887–1959)
POURTALÈS Guy de (1881–1941)
PRÉVOST Jean (1901–1944)
PRÉVOST Marcel (1862–1941)
QUENEAU Raymond (1903–1976)
REBATET Lucien (1903–1972)
REVERDY Pierre (1889–1960)
ROMAINS Jules (1885–1972)

ROSNY the Elder (1856–1940)
ROSNY the Younger (1859–1948)
ROUSSEAUX André (1896–1973)
ROY Claude (1915–1997)
SADOUL Georges (1904–1967)
SAINT-EXUPÉRY Antoine de
  (1900–1944)
SAINT-JOHN PERSE (1887–1975)
SALACROU Armand (1899–1989)
SALMON André (1881–1969)
SARRAUTE Nathalie (1900–1999)
SARTRE Jean-Paul (1905–1980)
SCHELER Lucien (1902–1999)
SCHLUMBERGER Jean (1877–1968)
SEGHERS Pierre (1906–1987)
SUPERVIELLE Jules (1884–1960)
TARDIEU Jean (1903–1995)
TAVERNIER René (1915–1989)
THARAUD Jean (1877–1952)
THARAUD Jérôme (1874–1953)
THÉRIVE André (1891–1967)
THIBON Gustave (1903–2001)
THOMAS Édith (1909–1970)
TORTEL Jean (1904–1993)
TRIOLET Elsa (1896–1970)
TROYAT Henri (1911–2007)
TRUC Gonzague (1877–1977)
VAILLAND Roger (1907–1965)
VALÉRY Paul (1871–1945)
VAUDAL Jean (1900–1945)
VERCORS (1902–1991)
VIALAR Paul (1898–1996)
VILDRAC Charles (1882–1971)
VIOLLIS Andrée (1879–1950)
WURMSER André (1899–1984)

Notes

Introduction

1 Thanks to the work of Gérard Loiseaux, Rita Thalmann, and Philippe Burrin, who utilize German archives, we have a better understanding of the Nazi propaganda machine in France and its mechanisms of repression as well as their effects on cultural production. Drawing on French archives, Pascal Fouché provides an exhaustive study of French publishers' activity during the Occupation. Stanley Hoffmann and Robert O. Paxton showed the specificity of a regime whose propaganda machine became the object of detailed studies; meanwhile, Christian Faure has analyzed the application of the Vichy cultural project, in the field of folklore. Through the lens of the construction of the "eternal feminine," Francine Muel-Dreyfus shed new light on those who participated in the "National Revolution." The conditions of underground production have also been the object of in-depth studies. Anne Simonin unearthed the literary and political stakes of the Éditions de Minuit's editorial policy. Among the recent studies devoted to Resistance movements, Daniel Virieux's thesis on the National Front offers a very complete portrait of the Communist organization of the intellectual Resistance. I am only referencing some of the principal works that have recently treated the ideological and cultural production of the "dark years"; I will continue to reference them throughout the book. For a list of general historical works or more specific studies, refer to the bibliography.

2 See especially Herbert R. Lottman, *The Left Bank: Writers, Artists, and Politics from the Popular Front to the Cold War* (Boston: Houghton Mifflin, 1982); *La Littérature française sous l'Occupation*, Actes du colloque de Reims, 1981 (Presses universitaires de Reims, 1989); Karl Kohut, *Literatur der Résistance und Kollaboration in Frankreich* (Tubingen: Gunter Narr Verlag, 1982–1984); Serge Added, *Le Théâtre dans les années Vichy 1940–1944* (Paris: Ramsay, 1992); Laurence Bertrand Dorléac, *The Art of the Defeat: France 1940–1944*, trans. Jane Marie Todd (Los Angeles: Getty, 2008).

3 In this perspective, we find the book by Claude Singer, *Vichy, l'Université et les juifs* (Paris: Les Belles Lettres, 1992). The work by Marc Olivier Baruch, *Servir l'État*

français: L'Administration en France de 1940 à 1944 (Paris: Fayard, 1997), is a two-fold contribution to the study of the Vichy regime and that of the civil servants under Vichy. For his part, Philippe Burrin shed new light on the question of collaboration by examining it through professional milieus in *France under the Germans: Collaboration and Compromise*, trans. Janet Lloyd (New York: New Press, 1996). An examination of the Resistance according to social and professional milieus can also be found in the special issue of *Le Mouvement social* 180, edited by Antoine Prost, "Pour une histoire sociale de la Résistance" (1997).

4 In this respect, my study, which emerged in part from a doctoral thesis, is linked to a series of work undertaken by Pierre Bourdieu (1971 and 1992), Rémy Ponton (1977), Christophe Charle (1979), Alain Viala (1985), Anna Boschetti (1985), and Anne-Marie Thiesse (1991) on the French literary field. See Gisèle Sapiro, *Complicités et anathèmes en temps de crise: Modes de survie du champ littéraire et de ses institutions, 1940–1953 (Académie française, Académie Goncourt, Comité national des écrivains).*

5 Pierre Bourdieu, "Le marché des biens symboliques," *L'Année sociologique* 22 (1971): 49–126, "The Market of Symbolic Goods," trans. R. Swyer, in Pierre Bourdieu, *The Field of Cultural Production: Essays on Art and Literature* (New York: Columbia University Press, 1993), 112–141, and *The Rules of Art: Genesis and Structure of the Literary Field*, trans. Susan Emanuel (Stanford, CA: Stanford University Press, 1995).

6 Max Weber, *Economy and Society*, trans. Ephraim Fischoff et al., vol. 1 (New York: Bedminster Press, 1968), 38–39.

7 Georges Duhamel, *Light on My Days*, trans. Basil Collier (London: J. M. Dent and Sons, 1948), 189. Note that this translation of *Lumières sur ma vie* includes only the first two volumes.

8 The 128 variables taken as indicators of the trajectories of these writers are divided into four main groups: social properties (age, social and geographical origins, education, etc.); indicators of position within the field: places of publication (publishers and periodicals), prizes, institutional memberships, degree and type of recognition; aesthetic and political position-takings. See the presentation of the survey in appendix 1.

9 Alain Viala, "Prismatic Effects," trans. Paola Wissing, in Philippe Desen, Priscilla Parkhust Ferguson, and Wendy Griswold (eds.), *Literature and Social Practice* (Chicago: University of Chicago Press, 1988), 260–261.

10 The statistical study formed the basis of the comparative analysis of these four institutions' social recruitment. The principal results, nuanced by qualitative studies of singular trajectories, will be presented in the chapters devoted to them. The summary tables can be found in appendix 2.

11 This research is bolstered by various sources, inventoried in the bibliography: press, reviews, essays, more or less "official" histories of the four institutions, written accounts (private journals, memoirs, autobiographies) and oral accounts (interviews), published and unpublished correspondence. I consulted the archives of the French Academy from 1914 to 1953 and those of the Goncourt Academy from its founding in 1903 up until the 1950s, as well as a press dossier concerning them at the National Archives. The analysis devoted to *La NRF* and the reviews that competed with it for

legitimacy is based on a study of content and on published and unpublished correspondence, the latter primarily from the Jean Paulhan collection (IMEC) and the Jacques Doucet collection. For the establishment of the underground Comité national des écrivains, I relied on the archives of the Comité d'histoire de la Deuxième Guerre mondiale (CHDGM), housed at the National Archives, and those of the Musée de la Résistance nationale (located by Daniel Virieux). The CNE archives (Fonds Aragon-CNRS), which were closed until recently, concern the legal period. The minutes only start in 1946. Supplemented by the press and by correspondence (published and unpublished), they allowed me to reconstruct the stakes of the committee's institutionalization at the Liberation. Finally, I consulted about a dozen files from the professional purge at the National Archives.

12 Priscilla Parkhurst Ferguson, *Literary France: The Making of a Culture* (Berkeley: University of California Press, 1987), translated into French as *La France, nation littéraire* (Brussels: Labor, 1991).

Chapter 1: Choices under Constraints

1 Vercors, *À dire vrai: Entretiens avec Gilles Plazy* (Paris: François Bourin, 1991), 76.

2 Christophe Charle, *Naissance des "intellectuels" 1880–1900* (Paris: Minuit, 1990), 231.

3 On the loss of reference points and the crisis of national identity engendered by the defeat, see Pierre Laborie, *L'Opinion française sous Vichy* (Paris: Seuil, 1990).

4 Roger Martin du Gard, *Journal*, t. 3, *1937–1949* (Paris: Gallimard, 1993), 347.

5 Robert O. Paxton, *Vichy France: Old Guard and New Order, 1940–1944* (New York: Columbia University Press, 2001), 38.

6 André Gide, *Journals*, vol. 4, *1939–1949*, trans. Justin O'Brien (Urbana: University of Illinois Press, 2000), 23 and 24.

7 Martin du Gard, *Journal*, t. 3, 367.

8 Paul Léautaud, *Journal littéraire*, t. 3 (Paris: Mercure de France, 1964, republished 1986), September 18, 1940, 172.

9 Account by André Rousseaux, December 2 and 14, 1949, Archives du Comité d'histoire de la Seconde Guerre mondiale, AN: 72AJ 78.

10 Yves Courrière, *Roger Vailland ou Un libertin au regard froid* (Paris: Plon, 1991), 253.

11 Comments by Henri Membré reported by Vercors, *À dire vrai*, 26.

12 Martin du Gard, *Journal*, t. 3, 376 and 377.

13 See Maria van Rysselberghe, *Les Cahiers de la Petite Dame*, t. 3, *1937–1945*, *Cahiers André Gide 6* (Paris: Gallimard, 1975), 217–218.

14 Léautaud, *Journal littéraire*, t. 3, 223–224 and 235–237.

15 Reported by Jean Grenier, *Sous l'Occupation [Propos recueillis]* (Paris: Éditions Claire Paulhan, 1997), 107.

16 Reported by Jean Grenier, ibid., 186.

17 Letter from François Mauriac to Georges Duhamel, December 18, 1940, *Nouvelles lettres d'une vie (1906–1970)* (Paris: Grasset, 1989) (216), 202–203.

18 Letter from François Mauriac to Jean Grenier, November 26, 1941, ibid. (226), 213.

19 Jean Lescure, *Poésie et liberté: Histoire de* Messages *(1939–1946)* (Paris: IMEC Éditions, 1998), 121.

20 Marc Bloch, "Réflexions d'un historien sur les fausses nouvelles de la guerre," in Marc Bloch, *Mélanges historiques*, vol. 1 (Paris: SEVPEN, 1963), 55.

21 Léautaud, *Journal littéraire*, t. 3, May 4, 1942, 577.

22 Alfred Fabre-Luce, *Journal de la France, août 1940–avril 1942* (Paris: Imprimerie JEP, 1942), 34.

23 See especially the study by Olivier Dard, *La Synarchie: Le mythe du complot permanent* (Paris: Perrin, 1998).

24 Norbert Elias and John L. Scotson, *The Established and the Outsiders* (London: Sage, 1994), chapter 7, "Observations on Gossip."

25 Raymond Queneau, *Journal 1939–1940* (Paris: Gallimard, 1986), 16.

26 Lescure, *Poésie et liberté*, 145.

27 Bloch, "Réflexions d'un historien sur les fausses nouvelles de la guerre," 54.

28 Quoted by Pascal Pia in a letter to Louis Parrot, January 16, 1941, in Lucien Scheler, *La Grande espérance des poètes (1940–1945)* (Paris: Temps Actuels, 1982), 53–54. Pia responded to Breton, as he explained to Louis Parrot in the same letter, that he was not aware of Aragon's current position: "If he has become something like 'marshalistic,' it goes without saying that he won't answer me," but he refrained from excluding Communists.

29 Letter from François Lachenal to Jean Lescure, quoted by Jean Lescure, *Poésie et liberté*, 236.

30 Interview with Jean Lescure (June 20, 1996) and Lescure, ibid., 170 and 212. As Anne Simonin has shown for the medical Resistance milieus, this kind of rumor fulfilled a social, even political function; see Anne Simonin, "Le comité médical de la résistance: Un succès différé," *Le Mouvement social* 180 (1997): 170–171. While in the case of the professor Robert Debré, which she discusses, the rumor that made him into an "honorary Aryan" was propagated by the Gaullist milieus, the Communists were at the root of the rumors concerning the duplicity of Sartre, Adamov, and probably Queneau.

31 Vercors, *À dire vrai*, 25–26.

32 Jean Guéhenno, *Journal des années noires* (Paris: Gallimard, 1947), 123.

33 Léautaud, *Journal littéraire*, t. 3, August 28, 1942, 687. See also 682.

34 Philippe Burrin, *France under the Germans: Collaboration and Compromise*, trans. Janet Lloyd (New York: New Press, 1996), 461–462.

35 Gérard Loiseaux, *La Littérature de la défaite et de la collaboration d'après* Phönix oder Asche? (Phénix ou cendres?) *de Bernhard Payr* (Paris: Publications de la Sorbonne, 1984, republished Fayard, 1995), 69.

36 Otto Abetz, "Politische Arbeit in Frankreich," July 30, 1940, quoted by Burrin, *France under the Germans*, 93. During the Phoney War, Abetz's team had worked on propaganda to demoralize French soldiers.

37 Loiseaux, *La Littérature de la défaite*, 29.

38 See Rita Thalmann, *La Mise au pas: Idéologie et stratégie sécuritaire dans la France occupée* (Paris: Fayard, 1991), 131.

39 Pascal Fouché, *L'Édition française sous l'Occupation 1940–1944*, vol. 1 (Bibliothèque de Littérature française contemporaine de l'Université de Paris VII, 1987), 22.

40 It completely controlled *Aujourd'hui*, *L'Appel*, perhaps *Les Nouveaux Temps*, and participated in the capital of *Paris-Soir*, *Paris-Midi*, *Le Petit Parisien*, *L'Œuvre*, and *Le Matin*. See Pascal Ory, *Les Collaborateurs 1940–1945* (Paris: Seuil, 1976, republished 1980), 65, Pierre-Marie Dioudonnat, *L'Argent nazi à la conquête de la presse française 1940–1944* (Paris: Éditions Jean Picollec, 1981), and Thalmann, *La Mise au pas*, 161.

41 Fouché, *L'Édition française*, vol. 1, 221.

42 Loiseaux, *La Littérature de la défaite*, 105.

43 Olivier Gouranton, *Comoedia pendant la Seconde Guerre mondiale* (MA thesis, Université de Paris I, 1992), 55.

44 Herbert Lottman, *The Left Bank: Writers, Artists, and Politics from the Popular Front to the Cold War* (Boston: Houghton Mifflin, 1982), 152.

45 According to the circulation figures established by Pascal Ory, based on the archives of the Paris prefecture of police dated January 23, 1943; Ory, *Les Collaborateurs*, 283. Pascal Ory also gives the figure of 33 percent unsold in September 1941 for *La Gerbe*, a relatively low rate with respect to the other collaborationist periodicals (38 percent for *Je suis partout*, 60 percent for *L'Appel*; ibid., 284). For his part, Philippe Burrin gives corroborating figures (without indicating the date): 130,000 copies, with 100,000 sold; Burrin, *France under the Germans*, 409.

46 Lucien Rebatet, *Les Mémoires d'un fasciste*, t. 2, *1941–1947* (Paris: J.-J. Pauvert, 1976), 101.

47 See G. Castelot, "Ce que nous voulons," *La Gerbe* 1 (July 11, 1940), and the box at the top of the newspaper starting on July 18, 1940. See also Alphonse de Chateaubriant, "Du peuple et de sa liberté," ibid., 3 (July 25, 1940).

48 A letter from Alphonse de Chateaubriant to Minister of Education Abel Bonnard, dated April 27, 1944, notes financial difficulties and asks for an annual subvention of 120,000 francs, informing him of the financing proposition of the RNP that he wants to be able to refuse in order to preserve his autonomy. AN: F21 8123.

49 Committee of the LVF, meeting of March 2, 1943, Dossier R.N.P.-P.P.F, AN: 72AJ 3 XV.

50 See Anne-Marie Thiesse, *Écrire la France: Le peuple régionaliste de langue française entre la Belle Époque et la Libération* (Paris: PUF, 1991), 154–156.

51 Lucien Combelle, *Péché d'orgueil* (Paris: Olivier Orban, 1978), 194–195.

52 Georges Montandon, "L'hérédité cautionne les lois raciales," *La Gerbe* 31 (February 6, 1941).

53 Combelle, *Péché d'orgueil*, 211.

54 The link between *La Gerbe* and the Grasset house is accredited by Grenier, *Sous l'Occupation*, 181–182. Let us note, in its support, that Bernard Grasset had just hired Robert de Chateaubriant, Alphonse's son, as his private secretary; see Jean Bothorel, *Bernard Grasset: Vie et passions d'un éditeur* (Paris: Grasset, 1989), 330.

55 Of the 28 writers of our population who contributed to *La Gerbe*, almost one in four had Grasset as a first or second principal editor, versus barely more than one

author out of ten for our total population of 185 writers who were active under the Occupation.

56 Pierre-Marie Dioudonnat, *Je suis partout 1930–1944: Les maurrassiens devant la tentation fasciste* (Paris: La Table Ronde, 1973), 109.

57 While Brasillach was a prisoner in Germany, Rebatet, Laubreaux, and Poulain had reached the Southern zone where they were named editors at the radio journal and received as such by Laval, head of information and vice president of the Council. Rebatet, on the other hand, was not received by Du Moulin de La Barthète, director of Pétain's civil cabinet, and ultimately did not get the job as director of Radio-Dakar that he had been offered; see Lucien Rebatet, *Les Mémoires d'un fasciste*, t. 1, *Les Décombres 1938–1940* (Paris: J.-J. Pauvert, 1976), 537 and 598; see also Dioudonnat, ibid., 342–343.

58 "Quand M. Thierry Maulnier s'en allait en guerre," *Le Cri du peuple*, November 26, 1940, and "Thierry Maulnier et *Je suis partout*," ibid., November 27, 1940; these attacks, revived in *Je suis partout* as soon as it resumed publication (498, February 7, 1941) can be attributed to Alain Laubreaux, who contributed to *Le Cri du peuple*.

59 This conception of literature was more often proclaimed than defined. We find a sketch of it in an article by Jean Turlais entitled, "Introduction à l'histoire de la littérature 'fasciste'" (*Les Cahiers français* 6 [May 1943]), in which Fascism is characterized more as a "morality" and especially an "aesthetic" than as a doctrine—"the sight of certain statues by Arno Breker has allowed us to reach the essence of national-socialism better than dozens of big tomes of doctrine could have done," he explained (25)—and "Fascist" literature as based on a "warrior morality," on the exaltation of youth, which is "the age of heroism" (31), and fueled by "[the] taste for superior individualities according to Gobineau's *Pléiades*, for recapturing man as a primitive animal, according to D. H. Lawrence, the call of race and the sense of national honor according to Péguy and Bernanos, virility according to Montherlant, the notion of Order according to Maurras" (32).

60 The fourteen writers of our population who contributed to *Je suis partout* were almost equally divided, from the viewpoint of their first or second principal editor, between Plon, where Brasillach was published (three), Grasset (between three and five depending on whether we count the authors who published there occasionally during the Occupation: Drieu La Rochelle and Abel Bonnard), Denoël (three), and Gallimard (three), but if we relate these figures to the level of representation of these editors in our total population, Denoël is very clearly overrepresented at *Je suis partout*, since three of the five writers of our total population who published in it under the Occupation belonged there.

61 See Jeannine Verdès-Leroux, *Refus et violences: Politique et littérature à l'extrême droite des années trente aux retombées de la Libération* (Paris: Gallimard, 1996), 151.

62 In fact, the schism was equally due to internal rivalries, Charles Lesca wanting to extend his power within the editorial staff; see Dioudonnat, *Je suis partout*, 365.

63 Ory, *Les Collaborateurs*, 117.

64 Charles Bettelheim, *Bilan de l'économie française 1919–1946* (Paris: PUF, 1947), 234.

65 Robert Belot, *Lucien Rebatet: Un itinéraire fasciste* (Paris: Seuil, 1994), 283.

66 Léautaud, *Journal littéraire*, t. 3, September 16, 1940, 170.

67 Jacques Isorni, *Le Procès de Robert Brasillach* (Paris: Flammarion, 1946), 67–68.

68 Micheline Dupray, *Roland Dorgelès: Un siècle de vie littéraire française* (Paris: Presses de la Renaissance, 1986), 362.

69 Olivier Gouranton, whose work I rely on here, has hypothesized that Jean Dubar, manager of the anonymous society, was a pseudonym for Gerhard Hibbelen; see *Comoedia pendant la Seconde Guerre mondiale*, 31.

70 See Thalmann, *La Mise au pas*, 158.

71 See the letter from Jean Paulhan to François Mauriac, January 26, 1944, Jean Paulhan collection, IMEC.

72 Of the twenty writers of our population who contributed to *Comoedia*, thirteen had Gallimard as their first or second principal publisher, that is, two-thirds, versus less than half the total of the population under review; eleven of the twenty-eight were contributors to *La Gerbe*, and only three of the fourteen were contributors to *Je suis partout* (Drieu La Rochelle, Marcel Aymé, and André Salmon).

73 See Michel Trebitsch, "Nécrologie: Les revues qui s'arrêtent en 1939–1940," *La Revue des revues* 24, "Des revues sous l'Occupation" (1997): 19–33.

74 Quotation excerpted from *Cahiers de Libération* 1 (September 1943), republished in Anne Simonin, "Les Éditions de Minuit: Littérature et politique dans la France des années sombres," *Bulletin de la* SHMC 3–4 (1994): 63.

75 Letter from Jean Paulhan to André Lhôte, [November 19, 1940], in Jean Paulhan, *Choix de lettres*, t. 2, *1937–1945. Traité des jours sombres* (Paris: Gallimard, 1992) (160), 200. Jean Paulhan affirmed to Jean Grenier that Pétain had submitted this request to Hitler during the meeting at Montoire (see Grenier, *Sous l'Occupation*, 159). This detail is unverifiable (in any case, I have not found any official traces).

76 See Léautaud, *Journal littéraire*, t. 3, 129, 139, 170, 219, and 197 on the rejection of the authorization request formulated by Combelle for the review *Contacts*. Pelorson, for his part, wanted to create a review within the Parisian section of the "Jeune France" association supported by Vichy; see Michel Leiris, *Journal, 1922–1989* (Paris: Gallimard, 1992), January 31, 1941, 335.

77 van Rysselberghe, *Les Cahiers de la Petite Dame*, t. 3, 198.

78 Jean Paulhan, manuscript belonging to the Jean Paulhan collection, IMEC; this text, which looks like a deposition, is attached to the copy of Paulhan's letter that was included in the file of statements for the Gallimard trial. On the version presented by Gallimard to André Gide, see van Rysselberghe, ibid., 199.

79 Fouché, *L'Édition française*, vol. 1, 70–71.

80 Comments reported by Grenier, *Sous l'Occupation*, 161.

81 Letter from the Propaganda-Staffel (signed by Kaiser) to Gaston Gallimard, November 28, 1940, confirming the agreement reached with Councilor Rahn of the embassy, republished based on a copy of the translation included in the file of the Commission interprofessionnelle, in Fouché, *L'Édition française*, vol. 1, 73.

82 Gerhard Heller, *Un Allemand à Paris: 1940–1944* (Paris: Seuil), 32 and 40.

83 On December 6, explaining to Léautaud about the censorship of Duhamel's book that this intransigence was due to the military authorities, rather than the civil

authorities (the embassy), Drieu implied that Kaiser would be called back to Germany. When he learned of Kaiser's departure in January, Léautaud could observe that Drieu was "well informed." See Léautaud, *Journal littéraire*, t. 3, 240 and 266.

84 On the "brilliant" career of Gerhard Heller, who was thirty-one years old upon his arrival in Paris, and was one of the few heads of cultural affairs to remain in office during the entire Occupation, whereas Epting, Bremer, and Abetz himself were called back to Berlin for a time, see Loiseaux, *La Littérature de la défaite*, 504.

85 Letter from Jean Paulhan to Franz Hellens, December 12, 1940, in Paulhan, *Choix de lettres*, t. 2, 208.

86 van Rysselberghe, *Les Cahiers de la Petite Dame*, t. 3, 197.

87 Denis Peschanski, "Une politique de la censure?," in Jean-Pierre Rioux (ed.), *La Vie culturelle sous Vichy* (Brussels: Complexe, 1990), 65.

88 This incident was at the root of the plan to create a French censorship "whose task would be to guide theater from a moral point of view." The system put in place consisted in submitting plays to the Association des directeurs de théâtres de Paris which, in case of uncertainty, referred them to Fernand de Brinon's office. In the case of non-respect of morality and public order, that office would warn the office of German censorship. This system, desired by the ADTP since it avoided useless financial expenditure, did not have an obligatory character. See Ingrid Galster, "Organisation des tâches de la censure théâtrale allemande à Paris, sous l'Occupation," in *La Littérature française sous l'Occupation*, Actes du colloque de Reims, 1981 (Presses Universitaires de Reims, 1989), 257, and Serge Added, *Le Théâtre dans les années de Vichy. 1940–1944* (Paris: Ramsay, 1992), 43.

89 Fabre-Luce, *Journal de la France*, 22–23.

90 Léautaud, *Journal littéraire*, t. 3, 447.

91 In chronological order, the order of doctors was created on October 7, 1940 (see Francine Muel-Dreyfus, *Vichy and the Eternal Feminine*, trans. Kathleen A. Johnson [Durham, NC: Duke University Press, 2001], the peasant corporation on December 2 (see Isabel Boussard, *Vichy et la corporation paysanne* [Paris: PFNSP, 1980]), and the order of architects on December 31 (see Danièle Voldman, *La Reconstruction des villes françaises de 1940 à 1954: Histoire d'une politique* [Paris: L'Harmattan, 1997], 247–248). The attempts to create an order of artists have been studied by Laurence Bertrand-Dorléac, "L'ordre des artistes et l'utopie corporatiste: Les tentatives de régir la scène artistique française, juin 1940–août 1944," *Revue d'Histoire moderne et contemporaine*, January–March 1990, 64–88.

92 Let us recall that the regulation of writers' rights and the state's acknowledgment of their professionalization are relatively recent. The Société des gens de lettres founded in 1837 at Balzac's initiative was only recognized as a public service in 1891, while its attempts to attain the status of an official body, like the French Academy, were unsuccessful. It was only in 1917 that the SGDL developed the plan for a union that would be able to file suit; its statutes were discussed in May 1919. See *Éphéméride de la Société des gens de lettres de France de 1888 à 1987*, compiled by Geneviève Py (Paris: SGDL, 1988), 16, 21, 125.

93 Alphonse Séché, "Et les lettres!," *Le Cri du peuple*, November 1, 1940.

94 André Billy, "La littérature de demain," *Le Figaro*, August 21, 1940.

95 As we can deduce from the responses to the question, "Does a reform [of literature] seem necessary to you? In what form?"; see the responses to the inquiry in *Le Figaro*, October 5–November 30, 1940. I will return to this inquiry in the next chapter.

96 According to the report made by Georges Duhamel, provisional permanent secretary of the French Academy, to the Company at the meeting of June 8, 1944; minutes of the French Academy, register 2 B 20 (1941–1951), 91, archives of the French Academy.

97 The "Caisse nationale des Lettres, arts et sciences" instituted by the 1928 Herriot plan would only be created—on paper—after the Liberation, by the law of October 11, 1946; it would not be operational until 1956. It was also only at the Liberation that an "office for literature" was created within the Direction générale des Arts et des Lettres, under the auspices of the Ministry of National Education. See Pascal Ory, "Le rôle de l'État: Les politiques du livre," in Roger Chartier and Henri-Jean Martin, *Histoire de l'édition*, t. 4, *Le livre concurrencé 1900–1950* (Paris: Fayard/Promodis, 1991), 51–67.

98 Quoted by Fouché, *L'Édition française*, vol. 1, 106.

99 Fouché, ibid., vol. 1, 174.

100 Ibid., vol. 2, 16.

101 Philippe Amaury, *Les Deux Premières Expériences d'un "ministère de l'information" en France* (Paris: Librairie générale de Droit et de Jurisprudence, 1969), 434–435.

102 Denis Peschanski, "Encadrer ou contrôler," in Laurent Gervereau and Denis Peschanski (ed.), *La Propagande sous Vichy* (Paris: Bibliothèque de Documentation Internationale Contemporaine, 1990), 1–31; see also Claude Lévy and Dominique Veillon, "Propagande et modelage des esprits," in Jean-Pierre Azéma and François Bédarida (eds.), *Le Régime de Vichy et les français* (Paris: Fayard), 184–203.

103 Claude Lévy and Dominique Veillon, "La Presse," in Gervereau and Peschanski, ibid., 164.

104 See Christian Faure, *Le Projet culturel de Vichy: Folklore et révolution nationale, 1940–1944* (Paris: Éditions du CNRS/Presses universitaires de Lyon, 1989).

105 Quoted by Thiesse, *Écrire la France*, 280.

106 See Jacques Duquesne, *Les Catholiques Français sous l'Occupation* (Paris: Grasset, 1966), 78.

107 Pierre Gaxotte, who also contributed to *Candide*, took refuge there after breaking with the team of *Je suis partout*.

108 In 1943, it benefited from an assistance of nearly 100,000 francs. See Amaury, *Les Deux Premières Expériences*, 787.

109 Marc Olivier Baruch, *Servir l'État français: L'Administration en France de 1940 à 1944* (Paris: Fayard, 1997), 202.

110 See Pierre Bourdieu, *The State Nobility*, trans. Lauretta C. Clough (Stanford, CA: Stanford University Press, 1996).

111 See Denis Peschanski, *Vichy 1940–1944: Archives de guerre d'Angelo Tasca* (Milan-Paris: Feltrinelli-CNRS, 1986), 661 (see also 517, n. 456).

112 See Bernard Comte, *Une utopie combattante: L'École des cadres d'Uriage, 1940–1942* (Paris: Fayard, 1991), 348.

113 Yves Urvoy, "Vitalité et sens de la grandeur," *Idées* 9 (July–August 1942).

114 See Géraud Poumarède, "Le Cercle Proudhon ou l'impossible synthèse," *Mil neuf cent* 12 (1994): 51–87.

115 Jean de Fabrègues, "Valeurs de la Révolution Nationale," *Idées* 10–11, "Construire la Révolution nationale" (September 1942): 41.

116 Armand Petitjean, "L'Appel de l'histoire," *Idées* 12 (October 1942): 20.

117 Maurice Gaït, "La Morale de l'Ordre contre 'l'Ordre Moral,'" *Idées* 10–11, "Construire la Révolution nationale" (September 1942): 33.

118 Jacques Bostan, "Prélude à heurter," ibid., 26.

119 Philippe Verdier, "L'État, forme politique de la Communauté," *Idées* 10–11, "Construire la Révolution nationale" (September 1942): 53.

120 Jean Maze, "Représentation populaire," *Idées* 10–11, "Construire la Révolution nationale" (September 1942): 66.

121 François Gravier, "Variations sur la Réforme de l'enseignement," *Idées* 4 (February 1942): 14–15.

122 See Paxton, *Vichy France*, 195.

123 Gravier, "Variations," 16.

124 See François Gravier, "Jeunesse et Révolution," *Idées* 2 (December 1941): 45.

125 Quoted by Marc Olivier Baruch, "Les revues de l'État français," *La Revue des revues* 24, "Des revues sous l'Occupation" (1997): 40.

126 Pierre Drieu La Rochelle, *Journal 1939–1945* (Paris: Gallimard, 1992), 246.

127 Baruch, "Les revues de l'État français," 41.

128 Jean Guéhenno, *Journal des années noires*, November 30, 1940, 59.

129 Ibid., *Journal*, February 16, 1941, 337.

130 [Claude Morgan], "Colette, la Bourgogne et M. Goebbels," the underground *Lettres françaises* 4 (December 1942).

131 "Notre Combat" (editorial), *La Pensée libre* 1 (February 1941): 4; and 1–2: "All the legal publications that exist in France are either directly emanate from the occupation authorities, or else they are only published under its control and its direction [. . .] one lone thought can be expressed legally in France: *propaganda* in favor of submission."

132 Leiris, *Journal*, January 31, 1941, 335.

133 Martin du Gard, *Journal*, t. 3, October 22, 1941, 450–451.

134 On these refusals, see Jean Lacouture, *André Malraux: Une vie dans le siècle* (Paris: Seuil, 1973), 273 and Olivier Todd, *Malraux: A Life* (New York: Knopf, 2005).

135 Account by François Mauriac in Jacques Debû-Bridel, *La Résistance intellectuelle* (Paris: Julliard, 1970), 96.

136 Leiris, *Journal*, November 4, 1941, 346.

137 Drieu La Rochelle, "Pierre Emmanuel," *La NRF* 344 (October 1, 1942): 473.

138 Jean Follain, *Agendas 1926–1971* (Paris: Seghers, 1993), 99.

139 André Gide, "Feuillets II," *La NRF* 324 (February 1, 1941): 348.

140 Pierre Seghers, "De P.C. 39 à Poésie 44," *Poésie 44* 20 (July–October 1944): 6

141 Letter from François Mauriac to Pierre Drieu La Rochelle, July 18, 1941, in François Mauriac, *Lettres d'une vie (1904–1969)* (Paris: Grasset, 1981) (244), 254.

142 Simone de Beauvoir, *The Prime of Life*, trans. Peter Green (Cleveland: World Publishing , 1962), 408; on Simone de Beauvoir's literary programs at Radio-Vichy, see Ingrid Galster, "Simone de Beauvoir et Radio-Vichy: À propos de quelques scénarios retrouvés," *Romanische Forschungen* 108, no. 1–2 (1996): 112–132.

143 Édith Thomas, *Le Témoin compromis: Mémoires* (Paris: Viviane Hamy, 1995), 100.

144 See the presentation by Dorothy Kaufmann, ibid., 19, and Édith Thomas, *Pages de journal 1939–1944* (Paris: Viviane Hamy), 120.

145 Jacques Debû-Bridel, *Les Éditions de Minuit: Historique* (Paris: Minuit, 1945), 15.

146 Opening text signed "Confluences," *Confluences* 1 (January–February 1945): 3.

147 La Girouette, "Aux Quatre Vents," *Le Figaro*, January 18, 1941.

148 François Mauriac, "Ne pas se renier," *Le Figaro*, July 23, 1940, republished in Jean Touzot, *Mauriac sous l'Occupation* (Paris: La Manufacture, 1990), 206.

149 Maurice Schumann's harangue is quoted at length by Jean Lacouture, *François Mauriac*, vol. 2, *Un citoyen du siècle 1933–1970* (Paris: Seuil, 1980), 118–119.

150 Jacques Maritain, *France My Country: Through the Disaster* (New York: Longmans, Green, 1941), 27. The first edition was published by the New York house Maison Française in January 1941, in the "Voix de France" [Voices of France] collection. The book revisited a talk that Maritain gave in November 1940 at the New School for Social Research, for French intellectuals in exile. See Michel Fourcade, "Jacques Maritain, inspirateur de la Résistance," *Cahiers Jacques Maritain* 32 (June 1996): 14–57. On the French intellectual milieus in the United States during the war, see Colin W. Nettelbeck, *Forever French: Exile in the United States 1939–1945* (New York: Berg, 1991).

151 René Lalou, "Le plus dur, ce va être de renoncer à Stendhal," *Le Figaro*, January 18, 1941.

152 Quoted by Pierre Seghers, *La Résistance et ses poètes: France 1940–1945* (Paris: Seghers, 1974), 64.

153 "Notre combat," 5.

154 "Manifeste du Front national des Écrivains," *Les Lettres françaises* 1 (September 1942).

155 James Steel, *Littérature de l'ombre: Récits et nouvelles de la Résistance 1940–1944* (Paris: PFNSP, 1991), 36 and 35.

156 "Les Éditeurs," "Avant-propos," *Deux Voix françaises: Péguy-Péri* (Éditions de Minuit, 1944).

157 François Mauriac, "From *The Black Notebook*," trans. Alastair Hamilton, in Germaine Brée and George Bernauer (eds.), *Defeat and Beyond: An Anthology of French Wartime Writing, 1940–1945* (New York: Pantheon, 1970), 64.

158 Anne Simonin, *Les Éditions de Minuit 1942–1955: Le devoir d'insoumission* (Paris: IMEC, 1994), 160.

159 Expression that Anne Simonin rightfully opposes to that of "*attentisme*" suggested by James Steel.

160 Henry de Montherlant, "Être de son époque," *Le Solstice de juin* (1941), in Henry de Montherlant, *Essais* (Paris: Gallimard, 1963), 901.

161 Marcel Arland, *Essais et Nouveaux essais critiques* (Paris: Gallimard, 1952), 31–32.

162 See Christophe Charle, *La Crise littéraire à l'époque du naturalisme: Roman, Théâtre, Politique* (Paris: PENS, 1979), 147.

163 See Norbert Bandier, *Sociologie du surréalisme (1924–1929)* (Paris: La Dispute, 1999), chapter 7.

164 On the regionalist movement, see Thiesse, *Écrire la France*; on the Catholic literary movement, see Hervé Serry, *Naissance de l'intellectuel catholique* (Paris: La Découverte, 2004); on the proletarian literature movement, see Jean-Michel Péru, "Une crise du champ littéraire français: Le débat sur la 'littérature prolétarienne,' 1925–1935," *Actes de la recherche en sciences sociales* 89 (September 1991): 47–65, and Jean-Charles Ambroise, "Écrivain prolétarien: Une identité paradoxale," *Sociétés contemporaines* 44 (2001): 41–56. For a more general approach, see Hervé Serry, "La littérature pour faire et défaire les groupes," *Sociétés contemporaines* 44 (2001): 5–14.

165 On the reviews born in the 1930s, see Jean-Louis Loubet del Bayle, *Les Nonconformistes des années 30: Une tentative de renouvellement de la pensée politique française* (Paris: Seuil, 1969).

166 Martyn Cornick, *The* Nouvelle Revue française *under Jean Paulhan, 1925–1940* (Amsterdam: Rodopi, 1995), 41.

167 The growth of production in publishing was translated less by an increase in the number of titles published annually—although the number of novels doubled, going from about 1,000 before 1914 to about 2,000 in the 1930s—than by the average print runs, which went from 5,500 in 1890 to 8,000 in 1923, and by the development of an intermediary sector between literary publishing and cheap popular publishing, which was characterized by relatively high printings (between 10,000 and 40,000 copies); see Isabelle de Conihout, "La conjoncture de l'édition," in Roger Chartier and Henri-Jean Martin (eds.), *Histoire de l'édition*, t. 4, 70–96. On the introduction of advertizing methods, see Fouché, "L'édition littéraire 1914–1950," in ibid., 210–264.

168 From 1891 to 1920, the number of students doubled, going from less than 23,000 to nearly 50,000; cf. Antoine Prost, *Histoire de l'enseignement en France 1800–1967* (Paris: Armand Colin, 1968), 243. Conjointly, the rate of enrollment for boys in secondary school also doubled from 1887 to 1921, the rate of access in sixth grade going from 2.9 percent to 6.5 percent of the age group, and the rate of bachelors from 1.7 percent to 5.4 percent, according to the calculations made by J.-P. Briand, J.-M. Chapoulie, and H. Peretz, "Les conditions institutionnelles de la scolarisation secondaire des garçons entre 1920 et 1940," *Revue d'histoire moderne et contemporaine* 26 (July–September 1979): 392. But it is women's enrollment that was particularly striking during this period. Secondary female enrollment was instituted by the law of December 21, 1880, leading to the creation of public and private establishments for girls. It first experienced great expansion at the upper primary level. Up until its integration with masculine instruction in 1924, feminine secondary instruction did not prepare students for the baccalaureate. At the Académie de Paris, the number of girls who took the "end of studies" diploma or the baccalaureate tripled between 1912 and 1921 (especially because of the increase in the number of baccalaureates, which went from 66 to 606); cf. Françoise Mayeur, *L'Enseignement secondaire des jeunes filles sous la IIIᵉ République* (Paris: PFNSP, 1977), and Francine Muel-Dreyfus, *Vichy and the Eternal Feminine*, 98–99.

169 For these circulation figures as well as some of the following, I rely notably on Marc Martin, *Médias et journalistes de la République* (Paris: Éditions Odile Jacob, 1997), 178–179.

170 Pierre Assouline, *Gaston Gallimard: Un demi-siècle d'édition française* (Paris: Balland, 1984), 216–220.

171 On this venture, see Bernard Laguerre, *Vendredi* (DEA thesis, Paris: FNSP, 1985). See also Géraldi Leroy and Anne Roche, *Les Écrivains et le Front populaire* (Paris: Presse de la FNSP, 1986).

172 Not far from half of the twenty contributors to *Candide* and the seventeen contributors to *Gringoire* were born in Paris, versus a third of our total population of writers, and almost two-thirds moved there during adolescence, versus less than half.

173 Between 1880 and 1910, the rate of literary *normaliens* who aimed for the literary field and journalism was twice as high as before (5.6 percent on average, with a peak of 6.9 percent for the decade from 1890 to 1899, versus 2.8 percent for the decade 1868–1879). This rate once again fell to less than 3.5 percent for the interwar classes, in favor of the new outlet that appeared at the turn of the century in diplomacy and cultural positions (its recruitment doubled between 1920 and 1930, going from 3.7 percent to 7.4 percent); cf. Robert J. Smith, *The École Normale Supérieure and the Third Republic* (Albany: SUNY, 1982), 52–54.

174 The chances of access to the ENS during the Belle Époque were higher for the sons of teachers, as Victor Karady has shown, and while the recruitment to the ENS was less "democratic" than it appeared, it remained more open to the middle and popular classes than the other grandes écoles. But the propensity to abandon teaching tended to decrease as social status increased. See Victor Karady, "Normaliens et autres enseignants à la Belle Époque: Note sur l'origine sociale et la réussite dans une profession intellectuelle," *Revue française de sociologie* 13: 1 (January–March 1972): 35–38; Christian Baudelot and Frédérique Matonti, "Le recrutement social des normaliens, 1914–1992," in Jean-François Sirinelli (ed.), *École normale supérieure: Le livre du bicentenaire* (Paris: PUF, 1994), 155–190, and Smith, *The École Normale Supérieure and the Third Republic*, 53.

175 See Diane Rubinstein, *What's Left? The École normale supérieure and the Right* (Madison: University of Wisconsin Press, 1990), 106.

176 See Dominique Kalifa, *L'Encre et le sang: Récits de crimes et société à la Belle Époque* (Paris: Fayard, 1995), 98–99.

177 Martin, *Médias et journalistes de la République*, 61.

178 Cf. ibid., 151.

179 See Antoine Prost, *Les Anciens combattants et la société française 1914–1939*, vol. 1, *Histoire* (Paris: PFNSP, 1977), 136.

180 Although he noted a relative overrepresentation of the generation following the "generation of fire" in *Vendredi*; Bernard Laguerre, "Marianne et Vendredi: Deux générations?," *Vingtième Siècle* 22 (April–June 1989): 39–45.

181 Antoine Prost, *Les Anciens combattants et la société française*, vol. 3, *Mentalités et idéologies*, 160–163; see also *Les Anciens combattants 1914–1940*, presented by Antoine Prost (Paris: Gallimard/Julliard, 1977), 161.

182 Robert Wohl, *The Generation of 1914* (Cambridge, MA: Harvard, 1979), 24.

183 Gaétan Picon has characterized what he has called "the ethical generation," that of the writers who revealed themselves between 1925 and 1930, by the search for a "salvation formula" through their novelistic works, which in that sense approached essay: "[The novel] becomes the means that the writer chooses to express his vision of things, his inner truth, the myths that exalt him: the equivalent of the confession, of the essay, of the moral treatise, of the poem." In this way, he establishes a filiation between this generation and the next, that of Sartre and Camus, which would, however, tend to pose the ethical problem in metaphysical terms; Gaétan Picon, *Panorama de la nouvelle littérature française* (Paris: Gallimard, 1976, reedited 1988), 53.

184 See Maurice Nadeau, *Histoire du surréalisme* (Paris: Seuil, 1945), 23.

185 Maurice Rieuneau, *Guerre et révolution dans le roman français 1919–1939* (Paris: Klincksieck, 1974); see also Prost, *Les Anciens combattants*, vol. 1, 132–136, and especially the graph, 133. Antoine Prost notes that the sales success of the translation of *All Quiet on the Western Front* by Erich Maria Remarque in 1929 confirmed, in the eyes of publishers, the general public's interest in war publications.

186 See Jean Norton Cru, *War Books: A Study in Historical Criticism*, trans. Hélène Vogel (San Diego: San Diego State University Press, 1988).

187 In a letter to Maria van Rysselberghe dated October 18, 1942, Roger Martin du Gard expressed, following a critical remark from Paulhan concerning *L'Été 14*, his regrets for having "slid" toward current events: "And I regret having slid, through a tangent (the similarity of the European situation in 1933, 1934, 1935 with that of 1913, 1914), in this trap of *current events*, of which I was so wary"; Martin du Gard, *Journal*, t. 3, 517.

188 See Rieuneau, *Guerre et révolution dans le roman français*, 313.

189 François Mauriac, "Les esthètes fascinés," *L'Écho de Paris*, September 16, 1932, quoted by Lacouture, *François Mauriac*, vol. 2, 24.

190 According to Henri Massis, *Les Idées restent* (Lyon: Lardanchet, 1941), 176.

191 Daniel Halévy, in "Hommage à François Mauriac," *La Revue du siècle* 4 (July–August 1933): 14; See also André Chaumeix, "Réponse," in François Mauriac, *Discours de réception à l'Académie française*, given November 16, 1933, at the French Academy (Paris: Grasset/Plon, 1934), 78.

192 Jean-Pierre A. Bernard, *Le Parti communiste français et la question littéraire 1929–1939* (Presses universitaires de Grenoble, 1972).

193 Nicole Racine-Furlaud, "L'AEAR." *Le Mouvement social* 54 (January–March 1966): 29–47; "Le Comité de vigilance des intellectuels antifascistes (1934–1939): Antifascisme et pacifisme," *Le Mouvement social* 101 (October–December 1977): 87–113; and Jean-Pierre Morel, *Le Roman insupportable: L'internationale littéraire et la France (1920–1932)* (Paris: Gallimard, 1985). On the Congrès pour la défense de la culture [Congress for Cultural Freedom], see Lottman, *The Left Bank*, 175–276, and Pascal Ory, *La Belle Illusion: Culture et politique sous le signe du Front populaire 1935–1938* (Paris: Plon, 1994), 188.

194 See especially Stéphane Courtois and Marc Lazar, *Histoire du Parti communiste français* (Paris: PUF, 1995), 124.

195 The Popular Front government would officialize this offer by calling on intellectuals to put its cultural politics into action; see Ory, *La Belle Illusion.*

196 It is not a matter of minimizing the specificity of Pétainist writers' support of the conservative revolution, but of proposing a minimal interpretation of the overrepresentation of the sons of civil servants among them, by pointing out an inherited form of allegiance to the state-guardian-of-order rather than a regime (the Republic) whose institutions they did not hesitate to disown. Moreover, we must remember that these sons of civil servants were all the more atypical with respect to their milieu of origin since the rate of writers who were recruited from it was proportionally low. It is therefore rather in the mode of redeployment of these dispositions in the literary field that we must search for the explanation of this phenomenon. I will return to this in chapter 4.

197 We cannot, however, deduce that there was a preestablished affinity between writers from the provinces and a regime that claimed decentralization: among the writers who were rather favorable to the Resistance but who didn't engage in its ranks (9 percent of our population), the distribution of geographic trajectories is similar; older than the *résistants* (more than a third among them were over fifty) but younger than the pro-Vichy faction, these Resistance sympathizers came, on the other hand, much more rarely from civil service backgrounds than their Pétainist colleagues and were most often recruited from the extremes of the social ladder, in the wealthy fractions (almost one out of five) or in the petty bourgeoisie and popular classes (more than one out of three); they were globally better endowed with educational capital than their colleagues who were close to the Collaboration (as was the case for the anti-Pétainist writers in exile, who represent 5 percent of our population). Among the writers initially favorable to the Vichy regime were, again, those who were the best endowed in educational capital and who would evolve toward a position favorable to the Resistance (6 percent of our population).

198 See Christophe Charle, *Les Élites de la République 1880–1900* (Paris: Fayard, 1987).

199 The data concerning incidents in the educational career, and particularly relative educational failure, are surely under-evaluated, this type of information being particularly difficult to gather (the common phrase, "abandoned his studies to devote himself to literature," product of an a posteriori reconstruction, could mask less respectable reasons). The statistical relationship between the different political tendencies is no less significant in this respect.

200 Rebatet, *Les Mémoires d'un fasciste*, t. 2, 126.

201 Bourdieu, *The State Nobility*, 282. This opposition is one of the axes of the pedagogical conception according to which private schools intended to assert themselves against "instruction" provided by public school, as Pierre Bourdieu has shown for the École des Roches. According to François Mauriac's account, these same values (sports, cult of the body) were to be found in the Marist brothers' education. Drieu La Rochelle was educated by the Marists, as well. He studied at the École libre des sciences politiques and failed the Foreign Affairs exam. After Janson-de-Sailly, Montherlant attended the Saint-Pierre de Neuilly school and the collège Sainte-Croix. Having struggled to pass his baccalaureate (he failed his first attempt

at the oral), he failed the exam for his first year in law school. I will return to Drieu La Rochelle's trajectory in chapter 6.

202 Combelle, *Péché d'orgueil*, 176 and 179.

203 Ibid., 131.

204 See the work that he devoted to him after the war: Lucien Combelle, *Je dois à André Gide* (Paris: Frédéric Chambriand, 1951).

205 Ory, *Les Collaborateurs*, 100.

206 Fifty-eight variables (including two supplementary variables) have been retained, or 236 active and 12 illustrative modalities. Out of the 185 individuals, 17 were projected as supplementary. The first factor of MCA summarizes 5.6 percent of the total inertia, versus 3.9 percent and 3.2 percent respectively for the second and third factor.

207 Pascal Fouché, "L'édition littéraire," in Chartier and Martin (eds.), *Histoire de l'édition*, t. 4, 224.

208 This bipolarization between résistants on one side, Vichyists and collaborationists on the other, appeared even when the latter two categories constituted distinct modalities.

209 The position in the field of power (or in the social space) does not entirely intersect with the position in the literary field, which founds its autonomy "on an inversion of the fundamental principles of the field of power and the economic field"; see Pierre Bourdieu, "Le champ littéraire," *Actes de la recherche en sciences sociales* 89 (September 1991): 7. Thus, economic profits that ensure a dominant position in the social space are not reconvertible into symbolic capital within the literary field, where the principle of internal hierarchization—the degree of specific consecration—wins out over the principle of external hierarchization—temporal success (the tensions between these two principles of hierarchization are specified in the opposition between a pole of small-scale production and a pole of large-scale production).

210 I will detail the social recruitment of these two authorities in the chapters devoted to them.

211 Interview with Jean Lescure, October 25, 1995; and Lescure, *Poésie et liberté*, 47.

212 Quoted by Emmanuel Souchier, *Raymond Queneau* (Paris: Seuil, 1991), 62.

213 Raymond Queneau, *Journal 1939–1940* followed by *Philosophes et voyous* (Paris: Gallimard, 1986), 31.

214 Letter from Jean Paulhan to Guillaume de Tarde, [October 1940], in Paulhan, *Choix de lettres*, t. 2 (156), 196. Jacques Boulenger, born in 1879 in Paris, former student at the École des Chartes, novelist, author of books on the sixteenth century and on the romantic era, on sports, on fashion, had been the director of *L'Opinion* from 1919 to 1928. Contributor to the *Revue des deux mondes*, *La Revue de Paris*, the *Revue universelle*, theater critic at *Nouveau siècle*, he was a war correspondent for *Le Temps* during the "Phoney War." After the defeat, he published in the collaborationist press, notably in *Le Cri du peuple*. In 1943, he would publish *Le Sang français* with Denoël, then from 1943 to 1944, would have a literary column in *Je suis partout*.

215 See the presentation of the study and figure A.1 in appendix 2.

216 Because it takes long-term recognition into account, this second axis is of course determined, in part, by the perception that we have today of the literature of that time, and especially by the very effects of the crisis that the field experienced under the Occupation because it helped exclude writers like Brasillach or Rebatet who were then at the beginning of their career; but it re-creates no less of an "indigenous" vision of the space of positions (moreover, the suppression of the variables indicating long-term recognition did not significantly modify the configuration of the graph).

217 I did not represent the period of entry into the field on figure 1.2, so as not to clutter it; this factor appears in figure A.1 in appendix 2.

218 The third axis of MCA opposes the generation of novelists who entered the field after the first war and who were launched, in particular, by Grasset—Montherlant, Malraux, Giono, and the proletarian novelists like Poulaille—to the consecrated poets who started to publish at the end of the nineteenth century, and who have, as their second main publisher, the Mercure de France or Gallimard: Valéry, Claudel, Paul Fort, L.-P. Fargue.

219 Christophe Charle, "Champ littéraire et champ du pouvoir, les écrivains et l'affaire Dreyfus," *Annales (ESC)* 2 (March–April 1977): 240–264.

220 See especially the article that Aragon devoted to him, "*Service inutile*—H. de Montherlant," *Europe* 156 (December 15, 1935), republished in Aragon, *L'Œuvre poétique*, 6 (Paris: Livre Club Diderot, 1975), 413–423.

221 The following quotation expresses this opposition: "(right now entire journals are read,—except, of course, the crap from the on-duty academician, in which he dilutes the statement; he would just as well do a theater column, or records, or gastronomy: it's all about pocketing money)"; Henry de Montherlant, "Le Solstice de juin" (July 1940), in Henry de Montherlant, *L'Équinoxe de septembre*, followed by *Le Solstice de juin* and *Mémoire* (Paris: Gallimard, 1976), 255. In what follows, I will refer to this edition, which contains the unpublished "memoir" of his attitude under the Occupation.

222 Montherlant, "Mémoire," in ibid., 278.

223 Typed manuscript joined to a letter from Montherlant addressed to Francisque Gay, director of *L'Aube*, September 13, 1944, Francisque Gay collection, Marc Sangnier collection.

224 The text of this manifesto is reproduced in Jean-François Sirinelli, *Intellectuels et passions françaises: Manifestes et pétitions au XXe siècle* (Paris: Fayard, 1990), 113.

225 He explains himself on this point in both of the previous versions of the "memoir," an explanation that he omitted from the published version: "I honestly confess here that I supported the armistice. I was unable to see that France's battle was lost, not its war. I deferred hope. I believed that, for a while, Pétain's politics were right. As for what was then called Gaullism, I unabashedly admit, since General de Gaulle himself has recognized (*Pages d'histoire*, 25) 'the reasons that might have led one to believe that this great movement could have been nipped in the bud,' I unabashedly admit that Gaullism seemed to me like a generous illusion. 'We were wrong again,' Louis XVI said"; typed manuscript dated September 1944, cited above, and typed manuscript sent to the Comité national d'épuration des gens de lettres, AN: F21 8124.

226 Henry de Montherlant, "L'avenir de la qualité humaine chez le Français moyen," *Le Solstice de juin*, republished in Montherlant, *L'Équinoxe*, 238 and 239; see also 244.

227 The reference to the two articles published in the review *Deutschland-Frankreich*, mentioned in the first two versions of the "memoir," was omitted from the published version.

228 Typed manuscript dated September 1944, cited above. This passage did not appear in the following two versions, the 1946 one and the published one. "L'État français" was the expression which replaced that of "French Republic" under the Vichy regime and became associated with it.

229 See Loiseaux, *La Littérature de la défaite*, 299.

230 Henry de Montherlant, "Mémoire," in Montherlant, *L'Équinoxe*, 280. This justification was also developed in the first versions of the "memoir."

231 Henry de Montherlant, "Le Solstice de juin," in ibid., 256; on "alternation," see also 264.

232 Ibid., 257. For a detailed analysis of *Solstice de juin* and Montherlant's positions during the war, see the article by Jean-Louis Garet, "Montherlant sous l'Occupation," *Vingtième Siècle* 31 (July–September 1991): 65–75.

233 Henry de Montherlant, "Au-delà du Solstice de juin," *Le Matin*, December 4, 1941.

234 Henry de Montherlant, "Mémoire," in Montherlant, *L'Équinoxe*, 305.

235 Martin du Gard, *Journal*, t. 3, October 10, 1940, 353–354.

236 Meanwhile, when Paul Léautaud received a 2,500 franc check in 1941 for the five articles of notes that he published in *Comoedia*, he couldn't get over it: "It's wonderfully paid." He was expecting 1,000 francs. At *La NRF*, he received 500 francs in February for a theater column. Léautaud, *Journal littéraire*, t. 3, 439; see also 446 and 283.

237 AN: F21 8124.

Chapter 2: *The Responsibility of the Writer*

1 Pierre Bourdieu, *The Field of Cultural Production*, ed. Randal Johnson (New York: Columbia University Press, 1993), 117.

2 See Pierre Bourdieu, *The Political Ontology of Martin Heidegger*, trans. Peter Collier (Stanford, CA: Stanford University Press, 1991).

3 See especially Yves Déloye, *École et citoyenneté: L'individualisme républicain de Jules Ferry à Vichy; Controverses* (Paris: PFNSP, 1994).

4 See Christophe Charle, *Naissance des "intellectuels" 1880–1900* (Paris: Minuit, 1990), 38.

5 Christophe Charle, *Les Intellectuels en Europe au XIXᵉ siècle: Essai d'histoire comparée* (Paris: Seuil, 1996).

6 Marc Fumaroli, "Le génie de la langue française," in Marc Fumaroli, *Trois institutions littéraires* (Paris: Gallimard, 1994), 211–314.

7 Charle, *Naissance des "intellectuels,"* 35; on the emergence of the figure of the scientist, see p. 28. On the intellectual magisterium of Taine, see Christophe Charle, *Paris fin de siècle: Culture et politique* (Paris: Seuil, 1998), 97.

8 Rémy Ponton, "Naissance du roman psychologique: Capital culturel, capital social et stratégie littéraire à la fin du 19ᵉ siècle," *Actes de la recherche en sciences sociales* 4 (1975): 66–81.

9 See Anna Boschetti, *The Intellectual Enterprise: Sartre and* Les Temps Modernes, trans. Richard C. McCleary (Evanston, IL: Northwestern University Press, 1988), 15–17.

10 Claude Digeon, *La Crise allemande de la pensée française (1870–1914)* (Paris: PUF, 1959), 186.

11 See, notably, Fritz Ringer, *Fields of Knowledge: French Academic Culture in Comparative Perspective, 1890–1920* (Cambridge: Cambridge University Press, 1992), 214.

12 Émile Durkheim, *The Division of Labor in Society*, trans. George Simpson (New York: Free Press, 1965), 42.

13 See especially the results of the Ribot Commission study (1899), as analyzed by Ringer, *Fields of Knowledge*, 122–124.

14 Such was the response made by the philosopher Alfred Fouillée, one of Durkheim's fiercest enemies, to the Ribot Commission study. See Francine Muel-Dreyfus, *Le Métier d'éducateur: Les instituteurs de 1900, les éducateurs spécialisés de 1968* (Paris: Minuit, 1983), 44.

15 Christophe Charle, "Situation du champ littéraire," *Littérature* 44 (1982): 9.

16 Pierre Bourdieu, *The State Nobility: Elite Schools in the Field of Power*, trans. Lauretta C. Clough (Stanford, CA: Stanford University Press, 1996), 287.

17 On the polemic inspired by *Le Disciple*, see notably Thomas Loué, "Les fils de Taine entre science et morale: À propos du *Disciple* de Paul Bourget (1889)," *Cahiers d'histoire* 65 (1996): 45–61.

18 René Benjamin, *Vérités et Rêveries sur l'éducation* (Paris: Plon, 1941), 186. See also Francine Muel-Dreyfus, *Vichy and the Eternal Feminine*, trans. Kathleen A. Johnson (Durham, NC: Duke University Press, 2001), 225.

19 Albert Thibaudet, *La République des professeurs* (Paris: Grasset, 1927), 127.

20 Ibid., 149.

21 Ferdinand Brunetière, "Éducation et instruction," *Revue des deux mondes* (February 1895): 931.

22 Edmond Goblot, *La Barrière et le niveau: Étude sociologique sur la bourgeoisie française moderne* (Paris: Alcan, 1930), 115.

23 Charle, *Naissance des "intellectuels,"* 38.

24 Ringer, *Fields of Knowledge*, 220–221. See also Vincent Duclert, "Anti-intellectualisme et intellectuels pendant l'affaire Dreyfus," *Mil neuf cent* 15 (1997): 69–83.

25 Ferdinand Brunetière, "Après le procès," *Revue des deux mondes* (March 1898): 443.

26 Ibid., 443, 445, and 446; see also 442, and Ringer, *Fields of Knowledge*, 222.

27 Émile Durkheim, "L'individualisme et les intellectuels," republished in Émile Durkheim, *La Science sociale et l'action*, introduced by J.-C. Filloux (Paris: PUF, 1987), 262 and 270.

28 Émile Durkheim, *The Evolution of Educational Thought: Lectures on the Formation and Development of Secondary Education in France*, trans. Peter Collins (London: Routledge, 1977), 308.

29 Hervé Serry, "Déclin social et revendication identitaire: la 'renaissance littéraire catholique' de la première moitié du XXe siècle," *Sociétés Contemporaines* 44 (2002): 91–109 and "Littérature et religion catholique (1880–1914): Contribution à une socio-histoire de la croyance," *Cahiers d'histoire* 87 (2002): 37–60. For a study of these conversions, see Frédéric Gugelot, *La Conversion des intellectuels au catholicisme en France 1885–1935* (Paris: CNRS Éditions, 1998).

30 "All *pions*, nothing but *pions*," Zola proclaimed, "and in truth, the former students of the École Normale today form a State within our literary State. They stand by, they have a freemasonery"; they have never produced poets and novelists, Bernard Lazard affirmed, and "from the pedants that they were, have become snobs"; Émile Zola, *Le Figaro* (April 4, 1881) and Bernard Lazare, *L'Événement* (August 4, 1892), quoted by Jean-François Sirinelli, *Génération intellectuelle: Khâgneux et Normaliens dans l'entre-deux-guerres* (Paris: Fayard, 1988), 117 and 118. [The word *pion* refers, often pejoratively, to a student monitor or hall monitor, as well as a pawn.—Trans.]

31 This permeability of discourse was especially apparent when these stigmatizing representations were transposed within the literary field. Jules Romains, who accumulated all the stigmas as an "upstart" normalien, thus became, as we will see later, the typical figure of the "bad master." We will also find these two discourses intertwined in Brasillach's attacks on *La NRF* in 1938 (see chapter 6).

32 On the development of scientific internationalism at the turn of the century, see Anne Rasmussen, *L'Internationale scientifique (1890–1914)* (PhD diss., EHESS, 1995).

33 See, notably, Anne Rasmussen, "Critique du progrès, 'crise de la science': Débats et représentations du tournant du siècle," *Mil neuf cent* 14 (1996): 89–113.

34 A competitor of Durkheim, Gabriel Tarde had developed a theory of social psychology that explained social events on the basis of two notions: invention and imitation, the first being of course reserved for certain individualities.

35 Particularly in reference to Durkheim: "Can he really be a true editor, he who treats the feeling and heart of the 'low and dark parts of ourselves,' and in the end doesn't see, conceive, imagine and revere anything in the world but that being, vague, monstrous, tyrannical, incomprehensible, and savage like the god of the Jews, the social Being..."; Agathon [Henri Massis and Alfred de Tarde], *L'Esprit de la Nouvelle Sorbonne: La Crise de la culture classique; La Crise du français* (Paris: Mercure de France, 1911), 112.

36 Thibaudet, *La République des professeurs*, 139–140.

37 Figures established by Victor Karady, *Relations inter-universitaires et rapports culturels en Europe (1871–1945)* (final report, ministère de la Recherche, 1992) and cited by Charle, *Paris fin de siècle*, 33.

38 Agathon, *L'Esprit de la Nouvelle Sorbonne*, 204–205.

39 Charles Péguy, "De la situation faite à l'histoire et à la sociologie dans les temps modernes," *Cahiers*, 8, 3 (1906) in Charles Péguy, *Œuvres en prose complètes*, t. 2 (Paris: Gallimard, 1988), 499.

40 Georges Sorel [*L'Indépendance*, April 15, 1911], quoted by René Benjamin, *La Farce de la Sorbonne* (Paris: Marcel Rivière, 1911), 7.

41 Ibid., 54. See also Wolf Lepennies, *Between Literature and Science: The Rise of Sociology*, trans. R. J. Hollingdale (Cambridge: Cambridge University Press; Paris: Éditions de la Maison des Sciences de l'Homme, 1988), 47–90.

42 Quoted by Pierre Lasserre, *La Doctrine officielle de l'Université: Critique du haut enseignement de l'État; Défense et théorie des humanités classiques* (Paris: Mercure de France, 1912), 235.

43 Agathon, *L'Esprit*, 77–78.

44 Quoted by Agathon, ibid., 115.

45 Agathon, ibid., 166–167.

46 Lasserre, *La Doctrine*, 326.

47 Pierre Lasserre, *Le Romantisme Français: Essai sur la Révolution dans les sentiments et dans les idées au XIXᵉ siècle* (Paris: Mercure de France, 1907), 343.

48 On Barrès's evolution during this period, and his rejection of Taine in favor of the psycho-physiological determinism of Jules Soury that led him to adopt racist doctrine, see Zeev Sternhell, *Maurice Barrès et le nationalisme français* (Paris: FNSP, 1974, republished Complexe, 1985), 254.

49 Quoted by Yehoshua Mathias, "Paul Bourget, écrivain engagé," *Vingtième siècle* 45 (January–March 1995): 15–16.

50 On Maurrassian "realism," which founded both his social philosophy and his scientific theory, see Colette Capitan Peter, *Charles Maurras et l'idéologie d'Action française* (Paris: Seuil, 1972), especially chapter 7.

51 Jacques Maritain, in Frédéric Lefèvre, *Une heure avec . . .* , second series (Paris: Gallimard, 1924), 58.

52 Marcel Raymond, *From Baudelaire to Surrealism*, trans. G. M. (New York: Wittenborn Schultz, 1949), 51–64 and 89–105; René Wellek, *A History of Modern Criticism.* Vol. 8, *French, Italian, and Spanish Criticism, 1900–1950* (New Haven, CT: Yale University Press, 1992), 4.

53 Albert Thibaudet, *Trente ans de vie française*, t. 1, *Les Idées de Charles Maurras* (Paris: Gallimard, 1919), 202.

54 Jacques Rivière, "La Nouvelle Revue française," *La NRF* 69 (June 1, 1919): 8.

55 Quoted by Wellek, *A History of Modern Criticism*, 19.

56 Lasserre, *Le Romantisme français*, 191 passim.

57 Ibid., 445 and 480.

58 Quoted by Victor Nguyen, *Aux origines de l'Action française: Intelligence et politique à l'aube du XXᵉ siècle* (Paris: Fayard, 1991), 801.

59 Pierre Bourdieu, "Le Nord et le Midi: Contribution à une analyse de l'effet Montesquieu," *Actes de la recherche en sciences sociales* 35 (November 1980): 21–25.

60 "[Woman], at her origins, discovered the aesthetic of Character that would later be opposed to that aesthetic of Harmony, which the Greeks invented and brought to perfection, because male intelligence dominated among them. The Greeks made the general and rational sense of the beautiful into the principle of their whole civilization, which was prolonged by Rome and Paris. The other peoples, from East and West, that is, all the barbarians, limited themselves to the principle of Character, such as feminine sentiment had revealed it"; Charles Maurras, "Le Romantisme

féminin," in Charles Maurras, *L'Avenir de l'intelligence*, suivi de *Auguste Comte, Le romantisme féminin, Mademoiselle Monk, L'invocation à Minerve* (Paris: Flammarion, 1905, republished 1927), 221; see also 218: "Instead of saying that Romanticism led to the degeneration of French souls or minds, wouldn't it be better to realize that it effeminated them?"

61 Digeon, *La Crise allemande de la pensée française*, 422.

62 Jules Renard, *Journal* (Paris: Gallimard, 1935), 58. Jean Carrère (1868–1932), born in Gontaud (Lot et Garonne), a seductive orator according to Jean Ajalbert's depiction, had met Charles Maurras in 1890. Won over to regionalism, he returned to the South in 1894. A correspondent for *Le Matin* and then *Le Temps* in Transvaal and Italy, where he would become a personal friend of the Duce, he contributed notably to *L'Ermitage* and, after the war, to Bainville and Massis's *Revue universelle*; see Jean Ajalbert, *Mémoires à rebours (1935–1870)*, t. 1, *Règlements de compte* (Paris: Denoël et Steele, 1936), 36; Léon Treich, *Almanach des lettres françaises et étrangères*, vol. 1 (Paris: Crès, 1924), 342; Hector Talvart, Joseph Place, and Georges Place, *Bibliographie des auteurs modernes de langue française (1801–1975)*, t. 2 (Éditions de la Chronique des lettres françaises, 1928–1975), 321–322; Nguyen, *Aux origines de l'Action française*, 498 and 506.

63 Jean Carrère, *Les Mauvais Maîtres* (Paris: Plon, 1922), 7.

64 Ibid., 11, 20, and 242.

65 Christophe Prochasson and Anne Rasmussen, *Au nom de la patrie: Les intellectuels et la Première Guerre mondiale, 1910–1919* (Paris: La Découverte, 1996), 272.

66 Abbé Delmont presented this series as a response to a demand from readers, who wished to see those writers mentioned in *L'Univers* "who have contributed the most, over the past century, to the intellectual and moral decomposition of our dear France." Abbé Th. Delmont, "Les malfaiteurs intellectuels: Madame de Staël," *L'Univers* 29 (March 17, 1918).

67 Pierre Lasserre, *Les Chapelles littéraires: Claudel, Jammes, Péguy* (Paris: Librairie Garnier, 1920), and Henri Brémond, *Pour le romantisme* (Paris: Bloud et Gay, 1923). See also Éliane Tonnet-Lacroix, *Après-guerre et sensibilités littéraires, 1919–1924* (Paris: Publications de la Sorbonne, 1991), 237, although her observation of a rehabilitation of romanticism during this period must be put into perspective.

68 Léon Daudet, *The Stupid XIXth Century*, trans. Lewis Galantière (New York: Payson and Clarke, 1928), 102, 122, and 127.

69 André Gide, *Journals*, vol. 2, *1914–1927*, trans. Justin O'Brien (Urbana: University of Illinois Press, 2000) 361.

70 According to a letter from Gaston Gallimard to Jacques Rivière, December 18, 1919, in Jacques Rivière and Gaston Gallimard, *Correspondance (1911–1924)* (Paris: Gallimard, 1994) (146), 160.

71 "Une heure avec Jacques Maritain et Henri Massis," *Les Nouvelles littéraires*, October 13, 1923, republished in Lefèvre, *Une heure avec . . .* , 50.

72 While *La NRF* had gained a maximum of 150 subscribers a month up to that point, it counted 750 new subscribers in 1923, 450 in 1924, and 875 in 1925, according to the letters that Jean Paulhan sent in August 1927 to André Gide and Jean Schlumberger;

see Jean Paulhan and André Gide, *Correspondance (1918–1951)* (Paris: Gallimard, 1998) (54), 72, and the letter to Schlumberger quoted by Martyn Cornick, *The Nouvelle Revue française under Jean Paulhan, 1925–1940* (Amsterdam: Rodopi, 1995), 13.

73 The first article, "Écrivains d'exportation," had appeared in *Les Cahiers d'aujourd'hui*, September 1, 1921. Eugène Montfort had rejected the second article, "M. André Gide et la Grammaire," that Béraud offered *Marges*, and in which he criticized Gide's supposedly improper usage of French grammar. "La Nature a horreur de Gide," meant for the review *L'Œuf dur*, was not published either. In February 1922, Béraud received a visit from Frédéric Lefèvre for an interview in *Les Nouvelles littéraires*. Henri Béraud, *La Croisade des longues figures* (Paris: Éditions du siècle, 1924).

74 See Pierre Assouline, *Gaston Gallimard: Un demi-siècle d'édition française* (Paris: Balland, 1984), 144. See also Assouline, *Gaston Gallimard: A Half-Century of French Publishing*, trans. Harold J. Salemson (San Diego: Harcourt Brace Jovanovich, 1988), 126 for a significantly abbreviated version of these events.

75 Béraud, *La Croisade*, 36.

76 Gide, *Journals*, vol. 2, 325.

77 Henri Massis, "L'influence de M. André Gide" [November 1921], in Henri Massis, *Jugements*, t. 2 (Paris: Plon, 1924), 21.

78 Henri Massis, *Évocations: Souvenirs 1905–1911* (Paris: Plon, 1931); *Maurras et notre temps: Entretiens et souvenirs* (Paris: Plon, 1961). See also Michel Toda, *Henri Massis: Un témoin de la droite intellectuelle* (Paris: La Table Ronde, 1987).

79 Letter from Henri Massis to Jacques Rivière, [n.d.], Jacques Rivière archives.

80 A candidate for the Henri-Robert chair to which Maurras would be elected two years later, he earned a good score, with ten votes in the fourth round. The election was inconclusive (minutes of the meeting of November 12, 1936, Register 2 B 19, archives of the French Academy); see also Roger Martin du Gard, *Journal*, t. 3, *1937–1949* (Paris: Gallimard, 1993), 134.

81 Jacques Maritain and Henri Massis, in Lefèvre, *Une heure avec . . .* , 54.

82 Massis, *Jugements*, t. 2, 8 and 34.

83 Ibid., 20.

84 Ibid., 76.

85 Peter, *Charles Maurras*, 44–45; see also Muel-Dreyfus, *Vichy and the Eternal Feminine*, 31–39.

86 Henri Massis, *Les Idées restent* (Lyon: Lardanchet, 1941), 147. Massis indicated young literature's interest in puberty in his critique of *Les Thibault* by Roger Martin du Gard, entitled "Le romantisme de l'adolescence" (see Massis, *Jugements*, t. 2, 114).

87 Maritain and Massis, in Frédéric Lefèvre, *Une heure avec . . .* , 48 and 51.

88 Henri Massis, "André Gide et son témoin" [1923], in Massis, *Jugements*, t. 2, 86.

89 Agathon, *Les Jeunes Gens d'aujourd'hui* (Paris: Plon, 1913), first chapter.

90 Jacques Rivière, "La Nouvelle Revue française," *La NRF* 69 (June 1, 1919): 4.

91 Notes prepared by Jacques Rivière for the meeting on July 3, 1919, of contributors to *La NRF*, in Henri Ghéon and Jacques Rivière, *Correspondance (1910–1925)* (Centre d'études gidiennes, Université de Lyon II, 1988), 200.

92 Ibid., 195.

93 Ibid., 199.

94 André Gide, "La Nouvelle Revue française: Un groupement d'esprits libres," *Le Gaulois du Dimanche. Supplément littéraire*, July 10, 1920, republished in Gide, Rivière, *Correspondance*, 780.

95 Jacques Laurent, *Histoire égoïste* (Paris: La Table Ronde, 1976), 117.

96 Jacques Maritain, in Lefèvre, *Une heure avec . . .* , 59.

97 Lasserre, *Le Romantisme français*, 453–454, and Massis, *Les Idées restent*, 16 and 36–37.

98 Robert Brasillach, *Before the War*, trans. Peter Tame (Lewiston, NY: Edwin Mellen, 2002), 31–32.

99 Jean-Jacques Becker and Serge Berstein, *Victoire et frustrations 1914–1929* (Paris: Seuil, 1990), 191.

100 "Déclaration d'indépendance de l'esprit," *L'Humanité*, June 26, 1919, republished in Jean-François Sirinelli, *Intellectuels et passions françaises: Manifestes et pétitions au XXe siècle* (Paris: Fayard, 1990), 42.

101 "Pour un parti de l'intelligence," *Le Figaro*, July 9, 1919, republished in ibid., 43–46.

102 On the debate inspired by this wave of orientalism in the intellectual milieus in the 1920s, and the stakes that grounded them, see Marguerite Bonnet, "L'Orient dans le surréalisme: Mythe et réel," *Revue de littérature comparée* 216 (October–December 1980): 411–424; and Michel Trebitsch, "L'image de l'Orient chez les intellectuels français et allemands au lendemain de la Première Guerre mondiale," in Étienne François et al. (eds.), *Deustch-Französischer Kulturtransfer 1790–1914* (Leipzig: Leipziger Universität-Verlag, 1998).

103 Jacques Maritain and Henri Massis, in Lefèvre, *Une heure avec . . .* , 60–61.

104 See René Guénon, *East and West*, trans. William Massey (London: Luzac, 1941).

105 Bonnet, "L'Orient," 417; see also 421–424; and Norbert Bandier, *Sociologie du surréalisme (1924–1929)* (Paris: La Dispute, 1999), chapter 7.

106 The manifesto "Aux travailleurs intellectuels: Oui ou non condamnez-vous la guerre ?," published in *L'Humanité* on July 2, 1925, has been republished in Sirinelli, *Intellectuels et passions françaises*, 62–64.

107 Pierre Drieu La Rochelle, *Mesure de la France* (Paris: Grasset, 1922, republished 1964), 67, and *Sur les écrivains* (Paris: Gallimard, 1964, new edition 1982), 46 and 47.

108 See Sirinelli, *Intellectuels et passions françaises*, 64–66.

109 Henri Massis, "La confession d'André Gide (à propos de son Dostoïevski)" [1923], in Massis, *Jugements*, t. 2, 63–64.

110 See Henri Massis, *Defence of the West*, trans. F. S. Flint (New York: Harcourt, Brace, 1927), 29 and 107 for the quotations.

111 Trebitsch, "L'image de l'Orient."

112 Paul Masson-Oursel, "Orient-Occident," *La NRF* 150 (February 1926): 267–279.

113 Ramon Fernandez, "Retour à l'Occident," *La NRF* 157 (April 1926): 487–492 (487, 488, 490 for the quotations).

114 André Malraux, "*Défense de l'Occident*, par Henri Massis," *La NRF*, 165 (August 1927): 813–818.

115 As its director, Jacques Raynaud, explained in "Latinité: Note préliminaire," *Latinité: Revue des Pays d'Occident* 1 (January 1929): 7.

116 Camille Mauclair, response to "L'enquête sur André Gide," *Latinité: Revue des pays d'Occident* 1 (January 1931): 109. For the favorable responses, see 101–107.

117 Massis, *Les Idées restent*, 182.

118 Camille Mauclair [*L'Éclaireur de Nice*, November 8, 1934], quoted by Cornick, *The Nouvelle Revue française*, 143, n. 95.

119 "Déclaration des intellectuels républicains au sujet des événements d'Espagne," *Commune*, December 1936.

120 "Pour la défense de la culture," *Commune* 40 (December 15, 1936), republished in Aragon, *L'Œuvre poétique*, 7 (Paris: Livre Club Diderot, 1977), 257–258. See also "La culture en danger," manifesto written and signed by members of the Association des écrivains pour la défense de la culture, present in Madrid in October 1936, and countersigned via telegram by the French leaders active in the international bureau of this organization, published in the same issue of *Commune* and republished in Aragon, *L'OP* 7, 267–270.

121 The two famous encyclicals, *Divini Redemptoris* and *Mit brenneder Sorge*, one widely diffused and condemning Communism; the other, addressed to the bishops of the Reich, condemning Nazism, were dated March 1937; see Étienne Fouilloux, *Les Chrétiens français entre crise et libération, 1937–1947* (Paris: Seuil, 1997), 19.

122 Anne Brassié, *Robert Brasillach ou Encore un instant de bonheur* (Paris: Laffont, 1987), 147.

123 Henri Massis, "Franco nous a dit," *Candide* 753 (August 18, 1938); "Franco et la France," *Occident* 21 (August 25, 1938).

124 See the "Manifeste pour la Justice et la Paix," *L'Aube*, October 18, 1935 and "Pour le peuple basque," *L'Aube*, May 8, 1937. See also Jean-François Sirinelli, *Intellectuels et passions françaises*, 103 and 110, and David Wingeate Pike, *Les Français et la guerre d'Espagne 1936–1939* (Paris: Publications de la Sorbonne, 1975).

125 On September 7, 1937, the very day when, in response to the July letter from the Spanish bishops, Cardinal Pacelli, future Pius XII, proposed to designate an official Vatican delegate to the Burgos government (a designation that was officialized a month later), a letter was published in the *Journal des débats* from Cardinal Verdier to Cardinal Goma, primate of Spain, which gave credence to the vision of a "struggle between Christian civilization and the so-called civilization of Soviet atheism." The reinstatement of religious teaching as a subject for the baccalaureate in nationalist Spain on October 8, 1937, would succeed in quelling any lingering resistance.

126 See Guy Hermet, *La Guerre d'Espagne* (Paris: Seuil, 1989), 197.

127 Louis Bertrand, "L'Espagne de toujours," *Revue universelle* 22 (February 15, 1937): 449–467), and *L'Espagne* (Paris: Flammarion, 1937), 64.

128 Bertrand, "L'Espagne de toujours," 466.

129 On Farrère's trip, see Alain Quella-Villéger, *Le Cas Farrère: Du Goncourt à la disgrâce* (Paris: Presse de la Renaissance, 1989), 330.

130 Claude Farrère, *Visite aux Espagnols (hiver 1937)* (Paris: Flammarion, 1937), 66.

131 Ibid., 50–52.

132 René Johannet, "Franco s'est adressé à des Français pour réorganiser l'enseignement en Espagne," *L'Époque*, November 16, 1937.

133 Montserrat Parra I Alba, "Fortune du *Journal d'un curé de campagne* et *Les Grands cimetières sous la lune*," in Monique Gosselin and Max Milner (eds.), *Bernanos et le monde moderne* (Colloque du centenaire de Georges Bernanos [1888–1988], Université Charles de Gaulle–Lille III, Presses universitaires de Lille, 1989).

134 Jean-Pierre Maxence, "Le voyage inutile," *Occident: Le Bi-mensuel franco-espagnol* 1 (October 25, 1937): 2; and " 'Espoir?' . . . Non; Désespoir," ibid. 7: 2.

135 "L'Espagne nationale d'après Claude Farrère" (interview), *Occident* 2 (November 10, 1937): 1, and Farrère, *Visite aux Espagnols*, 56.

136 Bernard Faÿ, "L'Espagne et son Destin," *Revue universelle* 16 (November 15, 1937): 385–398.

137 Henry Bordeaux, "L'Espagne dans notre littérature," *Occident* 6 (January 10, 1938): 4.

138 "Manifeste aux intellectuels espagnols," *Journal des débats*, December 9, 1937, and *Occident* 4 (December 10, 1937); see also the list of signers published on December 25, 1937, and January 10, 1938.

139 "Pour l'Espagne," *Occident* 9 (Februay 25, 1938): 8.

140 Eighteen doctors, nineteen university professors including six *agrégés*, a few "teachers" without any other precision, which I assume refers to private instruction, etc.

141 "Solidarité d'Occident," *Occident* 16 (June 10, 1938).

142 See the letter from Cardinal Baudrillart to Bernard Faÿ, in ibid.

143 Robert Havard de la Montagne, "Chronique de la quinzaine," *Revue universelle* 5 (June 1, 1938): 636.

144 Francis de Miomandre, "Maurras et l'Espagne," *Occident* 15 (May 25, 1938): 8.

145 See Pike, *Les Français et la guerre d'Espagne*, 241.

146 See Ralph Schor, *L'Antisémitisme en France pendant les années trente: Prélude à Vichy* (Brussels: Éditions Complexe, 1992), 42 and 51.

147 Ibid., 10.

148 "L'Action française," special issue, "Les juifs et la France," texts compiled by Lucien Rebatet, *Je suis partout* 430 (February 17, 1939).

149 Lucien Rebatet, *Les Mémoires d'un fasciste*, t. 1 (Paris: Pauvert, 1976), 19.

150 Brasillach, *Before the War*, 196.

151 Quoted by Wolfgang Babilas, "La querelle des mauvais maîtres," in *La Littérature française sous l'Occupation*, Reims conference proceedings, September 30–October 1 and 2, 1981 (Presses Universitaires de Reims, 1989), 199.

152 André Gide, *Journals*, vol. 4, *1939–1949*, trans. Justin O'Brien (Urbana: University of Illinois Press, 2000), 21–22.

153 Muel-Dreyfus, *Vichy and the Eternal Feminine*, 3 passim.

154 Alfred Fabre-Luce, *Journal de la France (août 1940–avril 1942)* (Paris: Imprimerie JEP, 1942), 30–31.

155 Thierry Maulnier, "Les 'Intellectuels' sont-ils responsables du désastre?," *Candide* 899 (June 4, 1941).

156 Babilas, "La querelle des mauvais maîtres."

157 Bourdieu, *The State Nobility*, 282.

158 "La jeunesse de France," *Le Temps*, July 9, 1940.

159 Guy de Pourtalès, "Après le désastre," *Le Journal de Genève*, July 28–29, 1940.

160 Although Guy de Pourtalès was far from an unknown in the literary world. Descended from a family of Protestants from the Cévennes who had taken refuge in Neuchâtel when the Edict of Nantes was revoked, son of Count Hermann de Pourtalès, officer in the service of the Prussian king, Guy de Pourtalès (1881–1941) had, after his father's death, adopted France as his "spiritual homeland" and asked to regain his rights as a French citizen. He was an NRF author starting in 1922.

161 André Billy, "Sur la responsabilité des écrivains et sur l'avenir du roman," *Le Figaro*, August 31, 1940.

162 André Rousseaux, "C'est la faute à Voltaire ou la querelle des mauvais Maîtres," *Le Figaro*, September 8, 1940; "Encore la querelle des mauvais maîtres," ibid., September 21, 1940.

163 "Matière et esprit," *Le Temps*, September 14, 1940 (my emphasis).

164 Henry Bordeaux, *Les Murs sont bons: Nos erreurs et nos espérances* (Paris: Fayard, 1940), 255.

165 Louis Madelin, "La mission des Lettres," *Le Petit Journal*, January 27, 1941, quoted by Wolfgang Babilas, "La querelle des mauvais maîtres," 202. Edmond Jaloux, "Les murs sont bons d'Henry Bordeaux," *Candide* 875 (December 18, 1940).

166 André Rousseaux, "La bonne littérature et la mauvaise," *Le Figaro*, November 26, 1940.

167 Born in 1881 in Bourbonne-les-Bains (Haute-Marne), son of a taxman, having lived in Canada, he participated in combat during the war of 1914 and then became a novelist and journalist. Editor in chief of *Paris-Centre* in Nevers and the *Journal de l'Ouest et du Centre* in Poitiers, in 1928 he won the Goncourt Prize for *Un homme se penche sur son passé*.

168 Maurice Constantin-Weyer, "Bien comprendre, bien choisir," *Le Journal*, January 2, 1941.

169 First by quoting Constantin-Weyer and Massis in his column (Charles Maurras, "La Politique," *L'Action française*, January 4, 1941), then by writing in response to François Mauriac (Charles Maurras, "La poitrine de la France," *Le Journal*, February 8, 1941; see infra).

170 Camille Mauclair, "Pour l'assainissement littéraire," *La Gerbe* 26 (January 2, 1941).

171 André Rousseaux, "Aux quatre vents," "Et voici que M. Mauclair assainit la littérature," *Le Figaro*, January 18, 1941.

172 François Mauriac, "L'honneur des Lettres," *Le Figaro*, January 25, 1941, republished in Jean Touzot, *Mauriac sous l'Occupation* (Paris: La Manufacture, 1990), 224 and 225.

173 Inquiry, "La littérature a-t-elle une part de responsabilité dans notre désastre ?" (by Adolphe Falgairolle): *Gringoire* 630, 638, and 639 (January 2, February 27, and March 8, 1941).

174 "La littérature a-t-elle une part de responsabilité dans notre désastre ?," *Gringoire* 638 (February 27, 1941).

175 Response by Henri Béraud to *Le Figaro* inquiry, November 16, 1940.

176 Henri Béraud, "Répétez-le," "Un homme de bonne volonté," *Gringoire* 632 (January 16, 1941).

177 André Bellessort, "Les lettres à l'épreuve de la guerre," *France 41: La Révolution nationale constructive, un bilan, un programme* (Paris: Éditions Alsatia, 1941), 276–277.

178 Response by Léon Daudet to the *Gringoire* inquiry.

179 Léon Daudet, "L'avenir des Lettres et la critique," *L'Action française*, October 18, 1940.

180 Bordeaux, *Les Murs sont bons*, 252–253.

181 Charles Maurras, "La poitrine de la France," *Le Journal*, February 8, 1941.

182 Maurras, *L'Avenir de l'intelligence*, 19.

183 See Paul Bourget, *Études et portraits*, t. 3, *Sociologie et littérature* (Paris: Plon-Nourrit, 1906), 14.

184 Bordeaux, *Les Murs sont bons*, 248–249.

185 Ibid., 250.

186 André Bellessort, "Les Lettres à l'épreuve de la guerre," *France 41*, 280, 281, 283.

187 Massis, *Les Idées restent*, 127–128 and 173.

188 Ibid., 125. See also Henri Massis, *Jugements*, t. 2, 6, and the letter he sent to Léon Daudet in reaction to the latter's position-taking in favor of Gide, in an article published by *Candide* on September 3, 1931: "It's not because Gide has the vices that are his that I attacked him, it's because he *justified* them. Poor kids invoke the 'theories' of *Corydon* even in the confessional; young beings have been radically perverted, existences ruined, depraved, lost by his example; and you know, as a psychologist and a doctor, what physical, intellectual, and moral miseries are the law of these depravations," republished in Massis, *Maurras et notre temps*, 247.

189 Edmond Jaloux, response to *Le Figaro* inquiry, November 30, 1940.

190 Henri Massis, *Les Idées restent*, xiv–xv; Robert Havard de La Montagne brandished this argument in reaction to Mauriac's article in *Le Figaro*, in which he contested the influence of literature on the masses. See "Revue de presse," *L'Action française*, January 28, 1941.

191 See Bourdieu, "Le Nord et le Midi."

192 Response by René Gillouin to the *Gringoire* inquiry, *Gringoire* 638 (February 27, 1941). See also the response by Henry Bordeaux, ibid. 639 (March 8, 1941), in which he returned to the arguments developed in his book.

193 Henry Bordeaux, "La responsabilité de l'écrivain," *Voici la France* 13 (March 1941): 1 and 4.

194 Francis Carco, response to *Le Figaro* inquiry, October 26, 1940.

195 Roland Dorgelès, response to *Le Figaro* inquiry, November 9, 1940.

196 André Gide, response to *Le Figaro* inquiry, October 12, 1940.

197 See *Poésie 40* 1 (October–November 1939): 38–39.

198 Jean Schlumberger, response to *Le Figaro* inquiry, October 12, 1940.

199 Paul Claudel, response to *Le Figaro* inquiry, October 5, 1940.

200 Kléber Haedens, response to *Le Figaro* inquiry, October 19, 1940. See also Kléber Haedens, "Revenir à la tradition?," *Le Figaro*, November 2, 1940. Claude Roy adopted a more distant position: evoking the polemic in the issue of *Voici la France* in which Henry Bordeaux's article on "The Responsiblity of the Writer" was also pub-

lished ([March 13, 1941]: 82), he contrasted him to François Mauriac and Henri Thomas, Gide's young imitator, who "align to respond: no, true writers actually do not hold the share in our misfortunes that is attributed to them," before deducing from the convergence of these accounts that they put an end to the debate.

201 Kléber Haedens, "La Révolution Nationale et la Littérature," *Le Figaro*, April 30, 1941.

202 Thierry Maulnier, "L'assaut des médiocres," *Voici la France* 14 (April 1941): 63.

203 Thierry Maulnier "L'avenir de la littérature [I–III]," *L'Action française*, August 28, September 18 and 25, 1941.

204 Jacques Bostan, "L'écrivain et l'état-civil," *Idées* 3 (January 1942): 29–30.

205 Jacques Bostan, "Assurances tous risques," *Idées* 5 (March 1942): 33–34.

206 For Thibon, they are "incomplete or misled Christians"; Gustave Thibon, "La pensée chrétienne," in *La France de l'esprit 1940–1943: Enquête sur les nouveaux destins de l'intelligence française* (Paris: Sequana, 1943), 36.

207 Marcel Arland, "Visages du Roman," *La France de l'esprit*, 51.

208 Thierry Maulnier, "La poésie française au XXᵉ siècle," *La France de l'esprit*, 62.

209 See Marc Angenot, *La Parole pamphlétaire: Typologie des discours modernes* (Paris: Payot, 1982), 73.

210 Paul Riche, "Gallimard et sa 'belle' Équipe," *Au pilori*, October 18, 1940, republished in Pascal Fouché, *L'Édition française sous l'Occupation 1940–1944*, vol. 1 (Bibliothèque de littérature française contemporaine de l'université Paris VII, 1987), 92.

211 "Couleur du Temps," *Messages* 1, "Éléments" (1942): 90.

212 Albert Janvier, "Pour l'épuration des livres," *Le Cri du peuple*, November 21, 1940.

213 Camille Mauclair, "Pour l'assainissement littéraire," *La Gerbe* 26 (January 2, 1941).

214 Riche, "Gallimard et sa 'belle' Équipe."

215 Mauclair, "Pour l'assainissement littéraire."

216 Angenot, *La Parole pamphlétaire*, 126.

217 Dr. Guillotin, "Petite tête de . . . François Mauriac," *L'Appel*, April 24, 1941, quoted by Babilas, "La querelle des mauvais maîtres," 204.

218 Such contradictions are frequent in anti-Semitic discourse, without troubling its propagators, as Ralph Schor has noted with regard to the two incompatible presuppositions of this discourse: on the one hand, the inassimilable character of Jews, illustrated by their endogamic behavior; on the other, the plot that was attributed to them—the will to "corrupt Aryan blood"—and which justified the sanctions applied to them; see Schor, *L'Antisémitisme en France*, 77.

219 Jacques Dyssord, "François Mauriac, le Greco de l'Uniprix," *La France au travail* 160 (December 6, 1940).

220 Jean Théroigne, "Giraudoux parfumier," *Au pilori* 104 (July 9, 1942).

221 Camille Mauclair, *La Farce de l'art vivant*, t. 2, *Les métèques contre l'art français* (Paris: La Nouvelle Revue critique, 1930).

222 See Gide's letter to Mauriac, in François Mauriac, *God and Mammon* (London: Sheed and Ward, 1946), 15.

223 Lucien Combelle, "Ses murs sont-ils bons?," *La Gerbe* 35 (March 6, 1941).

224 Lucien Combelle, "L'honneur de notre métier," *Je suis partout* 534 (August 11, 1941).

225 Jean Servière, "La littérature des bons sentiments," *Je suis partout* 508 (April 18, 1941).

226 Ibid.

227 See Lucien Rebatet, *Les Décombres* (Paris: Denoël, 1942), 30.

228 Jean-Pierre Maxence, "Journal de lectures," *La NRF*, July 1, 1941, 117–118.

229 See, for example, the preceding quote by Jean Servière, and Jean-Pierre Maxence, about Colette, ibid., 118.

230 In *Les Décombres*, Lucien Rebatet called Céline: "the genius, our only prophet"; in 1943, Robert Brasillach entitled an article, "Céline, Prophet," and Combelle wrote in his memoires: "And Céline, the prophet? Did you reread him? A bible should be reread!" See Rebatet, *Les Décombres*, 249; Robert Brasillach, "Céline, prophète," in Robert Brasillach, *Les Quatre Jeudis: Images d'avant-guerre* (Paris: Éditions Balzac, 1944), 223–236; Lucien Combelle, *Péché d'orgueil* (Paris: Olivier Orban, 1978), 166.

231 Lucien Combelle, "Céline et notre temps," *La Gerbe* 36 (March 13, 1941).

232 Ibid.

233 François de La Mésanchère, "En relisant Céline," *La Gerbe* 14 (October 10, 1940).

234 André Gaucher, "Céline, le Génie français et le Juif," *Au pilori* 25 (December 27, 1940).

235 André Gaucher, "Céline, le Génie français et le Juif," *Au pilori* 26 (January 3, 1941).

236 Robert Brasillach, "Céline, prophète," "Voyage au bout de la nuit" [1943], republished in Brasillach, *Les Quatre Jeudis*, 226.

237 Édouard Moreau de Bellain, alias Jacques Dyssord, born in 1880 in Oloron, in the Basses-Pyrénées, son of a property owner, had turned, after studying law in Toulouse, toward journalism and poetry in the wake of the Fantaisiste school.

238 The newspaper's declining circulation would lead to its discontinuation in the autumn of 1941 and its replacement by *La France socialiste*.

239 Jacques Dyssord, "François Mauriac le Greco de l'Uniprix," *La France au travail*, December 6, 1940.

240 Dr. Guillotin, "Le mauvais maître," *L'Appel*, April 24, 1941, quoted by Touzot, *Mauriac sous l'Occupation*, 38. Jean Touzot devotes a chapter to the attacks against Mauriac (ibid., 23–44). For the Nietzschean device, I refer to Friedrich Nietzsche, "The Problem of Socrates," *Twilight of the Idols and the Antichrist*, trans. Thomas Common (Mineola, NY: Dover, 1948), 9–13.

241 This is the title of an article that he had published four years earlier in the medical review *Le Courrier d'Epidaure*, quoted by Touzot, *Mauriac sous l'Occupation*, 38. Jean Touzot puts forth the hypothesis that Dr. Guillotin was the pseudonym of the same Fernand-Demeure. We know little about him, except that he would rival Camille Mauclair for the monopoly of racist art criticism in a series of articles that he would devote to "Israël contre le goût français" in the columns of *Au pilori* 175–182, December 9, 1943–February 10, 1944.

242 Rebatet, *Les Décombres*, 49. Mauriac did not have the privilege of this device, which Rebatet moreover applied to other representatives of the "Christian elite": "A few talents aside, but all so very specious, so equivocal, with each line zigzagging between sexual defects, obsessed impotents, masturbators choosing holy water fonts as latrine buckets, homosexuals seeking God in the asshole of boys. One single true

and healthy writer of Catholic persuasion, Paul Claudel, but politically a pyramidal imbecile" (ibid., 554).

243 Robert Brasillach, "François Mauriac ou le démon de midi," quoted by Lacouture, *François Mauriac*, vol. 2, *Un citoyen du siècle 1933–1970* (Paris: Seuil, 1980), 133. Let us recall that following Mauriac's support at the Liberation, Brasillach asked that this text be omitted from the republishing of his collection of critiques, *Les Quatre Jeudis*, first published by the Éditions Balzac in 1944 (it was not included in the 1951 edition at Sept Couleurs).

244 Report republished in Fouché, *L'Édition française sous l'Occupation*, vol. 1, 180.

245 Grasset had also intervened with Epting so that the print run would not be limited to 5,000 copies, a condition that was apparently imposed by the censors in the wake of pressures from the collaborationist press. See Touzot, *Mauriac sous l'Occupation*, 32.

246 Rebatet, *Les Mémoires d'un fasciste*, t. 2, 39.

247 Lucien Combelle, "Pitres ou traîtres?," *Je suis partout* 530 (September 20, 1941).

248 See Nicole Racine-Furlaud, "Bataille autour d'*intellectuel(s)* dans les manifestes et contre manifestes: De 1918 à 1939," in Danielle Bonnaud-Lamotte and Jean-Luc Rispail (eds.), *Intellectuel(s) des années trente: Entre le rêve et l'action* (Paris: Éditions du CNRS, 1989), 223–238.

249 Massis, *Les Idées restent*, xvi; René Benjamin, "Espoir," in *La France de l'esprit 1940–1943*, 190; Jean de Fabrègues, "Conscience de la France," *Idées* 8 (June 1942): 26: "A conquered country is never conquered solely by arms [...] A nation that has made a political error has made a mental error."

250 Ramon Fernandez, "Le devoir des clercs," *La Gerbe* 18 (November 7, 1940).

251 Lucien Combelle, "Faux témoins de notre temps," *La Gerbe* 33 (February 20, 1941).

252 Abel Bonnard, "Constitution d'une élite," "Les Conférences de la Gerbe," *La Gerbe* 29 (January 23, 1941).

253 Fernandez, "Le devoir des clercs."

254 Response by Jean-Pierre Maxence to the inquiry on "L'Intelligence et son rôle dans la cité," *Idées* 8 (June 1942): 55. On this inquiry, see infra.

255 de Fabrègues, "Conscience de la France," 27, 29, and 37.

256 François Navarre, "Jules Romains," *La Gerbe* 40 (April 10, 1941).

257 Pierre Drieu La Rochelle, *Journal 1939–1945* (Paris: Gallimard, 1992), 295 and 227.

258 Brasillach, *Before the War*, 193 and 196.

259 Fernandez, "Le devoir des clercs."

260 Charles Maurras, "L'Avenir de l'intelligence française," in *La France de l'esprit*, 12.

261 Albert Rivaud, "Regards sur le passé et l'avenir de la philosophie française," in *La France de l'esprit*, 30 and 33.

262 Gustave Thibon, "La pensée chrétienne," in ibid., 35.

263 Louis Madelin, "L'école historique française," in ibid., 77.

264 Alexis Carrel, "La science de l'homme," in ibid., 106. On Alexis Carrel and the Fondation pour l'étude des problèmes humains, see Alain Drouard, *Une inconnue des sciences sociales: La fondation Alexis-Carrel, 1941–1945* (Paris: INED/MSH, 1992), and Francine Muel-Dreyfus's reformulation in *Vichy and the Eternal Feminine*, 297–304.

265 René Benjamin, "Espoir," in *La France de l'esprit*, 190.

266 Jean Drault, "La faillite des grandes écoles prévue par Balzac," *La France au travail*, August 18, 1940.

267 Jacques Dyssord, "Appel aux travailleurs intellectuels," *La France au travail*, August 22, 1940.

268 Jacques Dyssord, "Le bonnet d'âne," *La France au travail*, September 24, 1940.

269 Drieu La Rochelle, *Journal 1939–1945*, 246.

270 Jacques Dyssord, "Jean Giraudoux, abstracteur de quintessence," *La France au travail*, December 2, 1940.

271 Pierre Drieu La Rochelle, "Pensées urgentes," *La Gerbe* 19 (November 14, 1940), republished in Pierre Drieu La Rochelle, *Ne plus attendre* (Paris: Grasset, 1941), 36.

272 "Matière et esprit," *Le Temps*, September 14, 1940.

273 Thierry Maulnier, "Les 'Intellectuels' sont-ils responsables du désastre?," *Candide* 899 (June 4, 1941).

274 Thierry Maulnier "L'avenir de la littérature II," *L'Action française* 218 (September 18, 1941).

275 Maulnier, "Les 'Intellectuels' sont-ils responsables du désastre?"

276 Response by Pierre Gaxotte, *Idées* 5 (March 1942): 56

277 Responses by Gabriel Boissy and Jacques Chardonne, *Idées* 6 and 7 (April and May 1942): 50 and 49.

278 Response by Henri Massis, *Idées* 9 (July–August 1942): 54.

279 Responses by Pierre Dominique and Daniel-Rops, *Idées* 6 (April 1942): 45–46, 48–49.

280 Response by René Gillouin, *Idées* 7 (May 1942): 47. See also the response by Edmond Jaloux, *Idées* 5 (March 1942): 53.

281 Response by Pierre Dominique, 46.

282 Response by Emmanuel Berl, *Idées* 5 (March 1942): 55.

283 Response by René Tavernier, *Idées* 8 (June 1942): 58.

284 Response by Jean-Pierre Maxence, *Idées* 8 (June 1942): 54–55.

285 Response by Edmond Jaloux, 54.

286 "L'Enquêteur," "Conclusions," *Idées* 9 (July–August 1942): 56 and 57.

287 In any case, no trace of it subsists in the archives of the Academy.

288 Letter from the leadership of Études générales to the Office of the State Secretary for Public Instruction, May 11, 1944, and plan for a joint press release, archives of the Académie française, Dossier pièces annexes 5 B 40.

289 de Fabrègues, "Conscience de la France," 31–32.

290 Ibid., 36.

291 Jean-Paul Sartre, "La République du silence," *Les Lettres françaises* 20 (September 9, 1944), published in English as "The Republic of Silence" in Jean-Paul Sartre, *The Aftermath of War (Situations III)*, trans. Chris Turner (London: Seagull, 2008), 3–7; Vercors, "La sédition humaine" [*Les Cahiers du Sud*, 1949], republished in Vercors, *Plus ou moins homme* (Paris: Albin Michel, 1950); Albert Camus, *The Rebel: An Essay on Man in Revolt*, trans. Anthony Bower (New York: Vintage, 1991).

292 I borrow this expression "the judges judged " from Jules Barbey d'Aurevilly, *La Critique ou les Juges jugés* (Paris: Frinzine, 1885).

293 François Mauriac, *Mémoires politiques* (Paris: Grasset, 1967), 19–20 (my emphasis).

294 [Jean-Paul Sartre], "La littérature, cette liberté!," *Les Lettres françaises* 15 (April 1944). See also, in the same issue, the article by François Mauriac, "Les faux calculs de Drieu": "Drieu saw the fires go out of a charming youth when everyone liked him; but no one read his books, no one took him seriously. Try as he might to come up with catchy titles, '*L'Homme couvert de femmes*' [The man covered in women] and other niceties, no one took him seriously. He saw Montherlant, Malraux's destinies take off and skyrocket. He didn't go anywhere, he already seemed outdated . . .

And, all of a sudden, swept by the defeat, the stage opens up [. . .].

We can understand why the 'iron-booted occupation' first seemed sweet to him, to this commensal of the German Embassy."

295 See Sartre's famous article, "Drieu La Rochelle ou la haine de soi," *Les Lettres françaises* 6 (April 1943), published in English as "Drieu La Rochelle, or Self-Hatred" in *The Writings of Jean-Paul Sartre*, vol. 2, *Selected Prose* (Chicago: Northwestern University Press, 1974); [Claude Morgan], "Le cas de Jean Giono," ibid. 7 (June 15, 1943); [Jean Vaudal], "Jacques Chardonne et 'Mein Kampf,'" ibid. 11 (November 1943); [Bernard Zimmer], "Rebatet dit Vinneuil," ibid. 15 (April 1944); [Charles Vildrac], "Dans le bourbier," ibid. 16 (June 1944).

296 Le Témoin des martyrs, *Le Crime contre l'esprit* (Éditions de Minuit, February 26, 1944).

297 [Sartre], "La littérature, cette liberté!"

Chapter 3: Literary Salvation and the Literature of Salvation

1 See Anne-Marie Thiesse, *Écrire la France: Le mouvement littéraire régionaliste de langue française entre la Belle Époque et la Libération* (Paris: PUF, 1991), 139 and 180.

2 René Lalou, *Histoire de la littérature française contemporaine (de 1870 à nos jours)*, vol. 2 (Paris: PUF, 1947), 749 (Mauriac's quotation was taken from this excerpt).

3 Let us recall that the "generational situation," such as Karl Mannheim has defined it, is only a potentiality that is more or less susceptible to crystallize under certain conditions, and that it can appear in opposing options. Karl Mannheim, "The Problem of Generations," *Essays on the Sociology of Knowledge*, ed. and trans. Paul Kecskemeti (New York: Oxford University Press, 1952), 288.

4 Henry Bordeaux, *Histoire d'une vie*, t. 1, *Paris aller et retour* (Paris: Plon, 1951), 73.

5 François Mauriac, *Commencements d'une vie*, in François Mauriac, *Œuvres autobiographiques* (Paris: Gallimard, 1990), 93; *La Rencontre avec Barrès*, in ibid. 170; *Nouveaux Mémoires intérieurs: More Reflections from the Soul*, trans. Mary Kimbrough (Lewiston, NY: Edwin Mellen, 1991), 106–107; *Souvenirs Retrouvés: Entretiens avec Jean Amrouche* (Paris: Fayard/INA, 1981), 16; Jean Lacouture, *François Mauriac*, vol. 1, *Le Sondeur d'abîmes 1885–1933* (Paris: Seuil, 1980), 22–23, 107, 206.

6 "... my father, more by wisdom than atavism, considered that the monarchy represented the best government for France. However, he had canceled his subscription to *Gazette de France* so as not to excite, with this daily reading, his five sons against a regime that they would perhaps be called to serve in their profession" (Bordeaux, *Histoire d'une vie*, t. 1, 84–85).

7 See Hervé Serry, "Le mouvement de 'renaissance littéraire catholique': Entre espoirs et désillusions," *Bulletin de l'Association Francis Jammes* 28 (December 1998): 11–50.

8 Mauriac, *La Rencontre avec Barrès*, 177.

9 Quoted by Lacouture, *François Mauriac*, vol. 1, 384; see also Mauriac, *Nouveaux Mémoires intérieurs*, 136.

10 Henry Bordeaux, *Histoire d'une vie*, t. 10, *Voyage d'un monde à l'autre* (Paris: Plon, 1964), 33; my emphasis.

11 Bordeaux, *Histoire d'une vie*, t.1, 85.

12 On the "sense of placement" as a "sense of social orientation" in the literary field, see Pierre Bourdieu, "Le champ littéraire: Préalables critiques et principes de méthode," *Lendemains* 36 (1984): 16. On the harmony or gap between dispositions and position, which is expressed subjectively in the feeling of being more or less "in one's place," see Pierre Bourdieu, "Le mort saisit le vif," *Actes de la recherche en sciences sociales* 32–33 (April–June 1980): 8.

13 Bordeaux, *Histoire d'une vie*, t. 1, 162; see also 259.

14 Henry Bordeaux, *Histoire d'une vie*, t. 8, *L'Enchantement de la victoire* (Paris: Plon, 1962), 285.

15 François Mauriac, *Mémoires politiques* (Paris: Grasset, 1967), 14.

16 See the letter from François Mauriac to Maurice Barrès, April 3, 1919, in François Mauriac, *Lettres d'une vie (1904–1969)* (Paris: Grasset, 1981) (74), 102; *Journal d'un homme de trente ans*, in *Œuvres autobiographiques*, 256.

17 In his memoirs, Mauriac projected his ambivalent relationship with the ecclesiastical authority onto his literary beginnings; it would be maintained in his later literary production: "From my first steps, I received the treatment from the ecclesiastical authority with which it always honored me: circumspection, often affectionate wariness. When I am cast aside, it is not in order to burn me. I am used, readers are warned. I can be useful as long as it is outside the fold"; Mauriac, *La Rencontre avec Barrès*, 176.

18 The contest program specified that "the disadvantages and ravages of Bolshevism should be exposed 'in light of the secular traditions engendered by Christian doctrine and morality'"; Henry Bordeaux, "Rapport du concours international de romans sur le bolchevisme," in Académie d'Éducation et d'Entr'aide Sociales, *Familles, Travail, Épargne*, public session held March 3, 1936 (Paris: Éditions Spes, 1936), 62. In his report, Bordeaux mentioned the objections he had made before accepting Mgr. Baudrillart's request: "A novelist myself, I have too often called for a freedom that we lose in the obsession with a subject to believe that the proposition of this subject is effective" (ibid., 57). On the contest, see also Paul Christophe, *1936: Les Catholiques et le Front populaire* (Paris: Desclée, 1979, republished by Éditions ou-

vrières, 1986), 34, and Henry Bordeaux, *Histoire d'une vie*, t. 11, *L'ombre de la guerre* (Paris: Plon, 1966), 55–58.

19 Bordeaux, *L'ombre de la guerre*, 81 and 126; Lacouture, *François Mauriac*, vol. 2, 36.

20 Bordeaux, *Histoire d'une vie*, t. 1, 197.

21 "[. . .] there can be no doctrinal harmony between communist materialism and Catholic spirituality," Henry Bordeaux wrote in his report for the international contest of novels on Bolshevism (66).

22 Bordeaux, *Histoire d'une vie*, t. 8, 285.

23 Mauriac, *Journal d'un homme de trente ans*, 229.

24 See his letter to Henri Guillemin, quoted in Henri Guillemin, *Parcours* (Paris: Seuil, 1989), 387.

25 Mauriac, *Journal d'un homme de trente ans*, 217.

26 Institut de France, Académie française, *Henry Bordeaux: Exposition du centenaire 1870–1970* (Paris: Bernard de Masclary Auteur-Éditeur, 1970), 32, and see Raphaël Gitton, *Henry Bordeaux, un conformiste? L'avocat bourgeois et l'écrivain classique 1870–1914* (DEA thesis, Paris, IEP, 1995), 2 and 110.

27 Henry Bordeaux, *La Crise de la famille française* (Paris: Flammarion, 1921).

28 Henri de Régnier, "Réponse," in Institut de France, Académie française, *Discours prononcés dans la séance publique du 27 mai 1920 pour la réception de M. Henry Bordeaux* (Paris: Firmin-Didot, 1920), 61 and 62; Pierre Benoit, *Henry Bordeaux* (Paris: Librairie Félix Alcan, 1931), 26 and 29.

29 Gonzague Truc, *Histoire de la littérature catholique contemporaine* (Paris: Casterman, 1961), 116.

30 "Henry Bordeaux" in Hector Talvart, Joseph Place, and Georges Place, *Bibliographie des auteurs modernes de langue française (1801–1975)*, t. 2 (Paris: Éditions de la Chronique des lettres françaises, 1930), 100.

31 Albert Thibaudet, "La Nouvelle Croisade des Enfants," republished in Albert Thibaudet, *Réflexions sur le roman* (Paris: Gallimard, 1938), 48–49; see also Henry Bordeaux, *Histoire d'une vie*, t. 3, *La Douceur de vivre menacée* (Paris: Plon, 1956), 286–305.

32 Mauriac, *Souvenirs retrouvés*, 124.

33 Mauriac, *La Rencontre avec Barrès*, 191–192 (my emphasis).

34 Quoted by Lacouture, *François Mauriac*, vol. 1, 177.

35 Mauriac, *La Rencontre avec Barrès*, 192.

36 Letter from François Mauriac to Madame F. Mauriac, February 8, 1922, *Lettres d'une vie* (92), 117.

37 *Génitrix* (1923) would succeed in establishing his celebrity. On the uncertain relations between Mauriac and Grasset, the publisher of *L'Enfant chargé de chaînes* (1913) and *La Robe prétexte* (1914), up until the publication of *Baiser au lépreux* (*La Chair et le Sang* and *Préséances* were published, in 1920 and 1921 respectively, by the Émile-Paul brothers), see Jean Bothorel, *Bernard Grasset: Vie et passions d'un éditeur* (Paris: Grasset, 1989), 78.

38 Mauriac, *Journal d'un homme de trente ans*, 227.

39 Mauriac, *La Rencontre avec Barrès*, 177, 178–179 and 203 (my emphasis).

40 Mauriac, *Souvenirs retrouvés*, 107–108.

41 Letter from François Mauriac to Jacques Rivière, March 28, 1923, *Lettres d'une vie* (99), 123–124.

42 Lacouture, *François Mauriac*, vol. 1, 283.

43 Ibid., 262.

44 Pierre Bourdieu, *The Logic of Practice* (Stanford: Stanford University Press, 1990), 64.

45 François Mauriac, *Mémoires intérieurs*, trans. Gerard Hopkins (New York: Farrar, Straus and Cudahy, 1961), 169.

46 "You torment the Christian. You want him to be not only attentive, but at the ready, on the lookout, trembling, and in permanent peril of perdition [...] You heap doubts and worries on him"; "You keep the faithful man in terror of what he will discover in himself. Salvation, which is the object of life, may as well painfully appear both necessary and inaccessible. Isn't there some Jansenism there?" André Chaumeix, "Response," in François Mauriac, *Discours de réception à l'Académie française*, speeches given November 16, 1933, at the French Academy (Paris: Grasset/Plon, 1934), 96 and 98. "It was necessary to speak of Jansenism with regard to this literature by François Mauriac"; Truc, *Histoire de la littérature catholique*, 172.

47 "My young father [...] I was not unaware that he had been Republican [...] and was, it seemed natural, anticlerical, perhaps even antireligious. This beloved absent one must have been the counterpart, within me, of everything that my mother and my masters ingrained in me. Our guardian, my father's brother, an irreligious magistrate as well, Republican and Dreyfusard, although he refrained from any intervention (our mother would not have tolerated it), must have acted on me through his silent opposition to everything that related to the Church" (Mauriac, *Mémoires politiques*, 8–9).

48 Mauriac, *Nouveaux Mémoires intérieurs*, 116, 104, and 113.

49 Mauriac, *Commencements d'une vie*, 85, and *Souvenirs retrouvés*, 57.

50 François Mauriac, *God and Mammon* (London: Sheed and Ward, 1946), 18.

51 Mauriac, *Souvenirs retrouvés*, 38, 40, 55, and 66. This may also explain his pronounced and persistent taste for Parisian society life, where, as an intellectual, he was immediately integrated.

52 Lacouture, *François Mauriac*, vol. 1, 307.

53 Mauriac, *God and Mammon*, 23–24.

54 Ibid., 23; the letter from Gide is reproduced on 14–15.

55 Mauriac, *Nouveaux Mémoires intérieurs*, 130. It was again with Charles Du Bos that Mauriac would try in vain to compete with *La NRF*—"It's a matter of balancing the NRF spirit"—by rallying Claudel, Maritain, and the new converts of the Gidian chapel around the Catholic review *Vigile*, first published by Grasset, then Desclée de Brouwer. Letter from François Mauriac to Paul Claudel, February 5, 1929, *Lettres d'une vie* (134), 153.

56 In 1938, he would hear the Socialist mayor of Bordeaux say to him, "Mr. Mauriac, you betray your class!" Mauriac, *Mémoires politiques*, 27.

57 Jean-Paul Sartre, "M. François Mauriac et la liberté," originally published in *La NRF*, February 1, 1939, published in English as "François Mauriac and Freedom" in *Liter-*

ary and Philosophical Essays, trans. Annette Michelson (New York: Criterion, 1955), 7–23, and as "Monsieur Mauriac and Freedom" in Critical Essays (Situations I), trans. Chris Turner (London: Seagull, 2010), 47–84.

58 "I wouldn't attach any importance to Gide's Bolshevism, if what attracted him were not precisely the antichrist, or, to be more exact, antireligion [...]"; Letter from François Mauriac to Jean Paulhan, 1932, Lettres d'une vie (174), 194.

59 Daniel Halévy has thus written: "What I see grow in him is militant virtue, the style of the combatant. Many of our master writers have ended their career in some great combat." La Revue du siècle 4, "Hommage à François Mauriac," July–August 1933, 14; see also André Chaumeix, "Réponse," in Mauriac, Discours de réception, 78.

60 Letter from François Mauriac to Paul Claudel, March 21, 1935, Lettres d'une vie (198), 215.

61 Mauriac, Mémoires politiques, 18.

62 Pierre Drieu La Rochelle, Journal 1939–1945 (Paris: Gallimard, 1992), p. 147.

63 François Mauriac, Journal 1932–1939 (Paris: La Table Ronde, 1947), 294.

64 Letter from François Mauriac to Georges Duhamel, September 14, 1940, Nouvelles lettres d'une vie (216), 202; letter to Henri Guillemin dated December 9, 1940, quoted by Guillemin, Parcours, 401.

65 Lacouture, François Mauriac, vol. 2, 119. Maurice Schumann would specify to Lacouture, in May 1979, that Mauriac had not been warned: "We needed all our weapons. Mauriac was one of them."

66 Pierre Bourdieu, "Genèse et structure du champ religieux," Revue française de sociologie 12 no. 3 (July–September 1971): 331.

67 Interview with François Mauriac in Jacques Debû-Bridel, La Résistance intellectuelle (Paris: Julliard, 1970), 97.

68 During his stay in Paris from October 22 to November 14, 1941, Mauriac frequently met Jean Blanzat, a member of the nascent committee of writers, and gave him the article "Dans l'état présent de la France," meant for the first issue of the underground Lettres françaises, which never saw the light of day (see chapter 7).

69 Jean-Paul Sartre, "François Mauriac and Freedom," 23; Pierre Drieu La Rochelle, "Mauriac," La NRF, September 1, 1941, 347.

70 Drieu La Rochelle, ibid., 346.

71 Letter from François Mauriac to Jean Paulhan, September 22, 1941, in Mauriac, Lettres d'une vie (246), 256.

72 Letter from François Mauriac to Louis Clayeux, December 10, 1941, Lettres d'une vie (249), 259.

73 In an interview with Pascal Mercier, Jacques Debû-Bridel affirmed that Mauriac's "endorsement" had great importance for the Comité national des écrivains, allowing certain authors to overcome their hesitations; see Pascal Mercier, Le Comité national des écrivains, 1941–1944 (MA thesis, Université de Paris III, 1980), 53.

74 Debû-Bridel, La Résistance intellectuelle, 77. Le Cahier noir was the first unpublished text by a great author that was published by the Éditions de Minuit, after the reedition of Jacques Maritain's À travers le désastre in November 1942.

75 Forez, Le Cahier noir (Paris: Éditions de Minuit, 1943), 6–8.

76 Ibid., 11–12.

77 On the successive versions of the manuscript, see Jacques Monférier, "La genèse du *Cahier noir*," *Travaux du centre d'études et de recherches sur François Mauriac* (Université de Bordeaux) 1, 1977, 3–14, and especially 5 for the vanishing use of the informal "tu." See also Jean Touzot, *Mauriac sous l'Occupation* (Paris: La Manufacture, 1990), 65–69 (especially on the "*we* of solidarity").

78 Forez, *Le Cahier noir*, 12 and 23.

79 "One could wonder, and we wondered for a long time, who could have written *Le Silence de la mer*. The question wasn't raised when, in August 1943, *Le Cahier noir* was published." Account from Jean Blanzat, in "François Mauriac Prix Nobel," *La Table ronde*, January 1953, 87.

80 Ibid., 23–24. On the suppression of the criticisms of Communism that appeared in the initial version of *Le Cahier noir*, see Monférier, "La genèse du *Cahier noir*," 12–13.

81 See Anne Simonin, *Les Éditions de Minuit 1942–1955: Le devoir d'insoumission* (Paris: IMEC, 1994), 153.

82 Debû-Bridel, *La Résistance intellectuelle*, 45. Debû-Bridel would bring up the same argument in response to a delegate who opposed Mauriac's reelection to the managing committee of the National Front during the Congress of February 1, 1945, invoking "what François Mauriac represent[ed] in the whole world" for having been the only academician to join the literary Resistance; quoted in Claude Mauriac, *Le Temps immobile*, t. 5, *Aimer de Gaulle* (Paris: Grasset, 1978), 132.

83 Louis Parrot, *L'Intelligence en guerre* (Paris: La Jeune Parque, 1945, republished by Le Castor astral, 1990), 33.

84 Henry Bordeaux, *Les Murs sont bons: Nos erreurs et nos espérances* (Paris: Fayard, 1940), 97–98.

85 Ibid., 212, 216, and 222.

86 See the translation of *Phönix oder Asche* by Dr. Payr in Gérard Loiseaux, *La Littérature de la défaite et de la Collaboration, d'après "Phonix oder Asche?" de Bernhard Payr* (Paris: Publications de la Sorbonne, 1984; Fayard, 1995), 151 and 153.

87 Henry Bordeaux, "Chaque maison, chaque chaumière doit être éclairée par ce visage," *Paris-Soir*, November 12, 1940.

88 Henry Bordeaux, *Images du Maréchal Pétain* (Paris: Sequana, 1941), 79 and 89.

89 Ibid., 105–106.

90 Mauriac, *Le Cahier noir*, 6.

91 Ibid., 31, 36–37, 43–44.

92 That is to say the modifications that the scholastic habitus is able to make the inherited dispositions undergo. The list would be eloquent, among writers who live on in posterity, of those who, descended from the upper bourgeoisie, broke away from their class of origin, from Flaubert to Gide. But this orientation is itself surely tributary of an experience of awkwardness during primary (familial) and/or secondary (educational) socialization: the conflictual relationship to religion (and likely to closeted homosexuality) for Mauriac, the contradiction between religious ethics and declared homosexuality that Gide assumed.

Part II: Literary Institutions and National Crisis

1 As Pierre Bourdieu has written, "the reason and the raison d'être of an institution . . . and its social effects is not in the 'will' of an individual or a group but in the field of antagonistic or complementary forces where, thanks to the interests associated with the different positions and habitus of their occupants, 'wills' emerge and where the reality of the institutions and their social effects, foreseen or unforeseen, are constantly being defined and redefined, in and through struggle." Pierre Bourdieu, "Le mort saisit le vif: Les relations entre l'histoire réifiée et l'histoire incorporée," *Actes de la recherche en sciences sociales* 32–33 (April–June 1980): 6.

2 On the contradictions between esprit de corps and field logics, see Pierre Bourdieu, "Effet de champ et effet de corps," *Actes de la recherche en sciences sociales* 59 (September 1985): 73.

Chapter 4: The Sense of Duty

The chapter epigraph is reprised in Jean Touzot (ed.), *François Mauriac* (Paris: Éditions de L'Herne [Cahiers de l'Herne no. 48], 1985), 406.

1 On the application of the Leibnizian conception of harmony preexisting the social fact and the concept of collective "adjustment" according to the principle of orchestration without a conductor, see Pierre Bourdieu, *The Logic of Practice* (Stanford, CA: Stanford University Press, 1990), 58–59.

2 Alain Viala, *Naissance de l'écrivain: Sociologie de la littérature à l'âge classique* (Paris: Minuit, 1985).

3 Marc Fumaroli, "La Coupole," *Trois institutions littéraires* (Paris: Gallimard, 1994), 9–110.

4 The expression is from Palissot, cited by Jacques Bainville, "L'Académie pendant la révolution," in *1635–1935: Trois siècles de l'Académie française* (Paris: Firmin-Didot et Cie, 1935), 281–282. See also Robert Darnton, *Bohème littéraire et révolution: Le monde des livres au XVIIIᵉ siècle* (Paris: Gallimard/Seuil, 1983), 34–35. An earlier and different version of the latter work was published in English as *The Literary Underground of the Old Regime* (Cambridge, MA: Harvard University Press, 1982).

5 Henry Bordeaux, *Charles Maurras et l'Académie française* (Paris: Éditions du Conquistador, 1955), 58.

6 René de La Croix de Castries, *La Vieille Dame du quai Conti: Une histoire de l'Académie française* (Paris: Perrin, 1978), 400.

7 Pierre Bourdieu, "Le marché des biens symboliques."

8 Paul Valéry, "Fonction et mystère," *1635–1935: Trois siècles de l'Académie française*, 509.

9 Georges Duhamel, interview with Henri Poulain, *Le Petit Parisien*, December 30, 1941.

10 With the exception of economic power, if we consider that the Academy did not include any representative of the industry and business world as such.

11 Jean-François Sirinelli, *Génération intellectuelle: Khâgneux et normaliens dans l'entre-deux-guerres* (Paris: Fayard, 1988), 124–125.

12 René de la Croix de Castries, *La Vieille Dame*, 377.

13 It was not until the very extensive worldly success of Bergson and his very favorable reception in Catholic milieus that a Jew was elected to the Academy, which had always contained a strong anti-Semitic current, and while the Dreyfus affair still troubled minds. And his entry raised strong opposition. His election in 1914 created a real precedent, unlike that of Ludovic Halévy, who had converted to Protestantism. Georges de Porto-Riche, whose candidacy "became a kind of academic Dreyfus Affair," was elected after twenty-four votes over twenty-four years. René Peter, *L'Académie française et le XXᵉ siècle* (Paris: Librairie des Champs Élysées, 1949), 134.

14 Louis Madelin, "Clio à l'Académie," in *1635–1935: Trois siècles*, 279.

15 Paul Bourget, "Le roman à l'académie," in *1635–1935: Trois siècles*, 216.

16 Rémy Ponton, "Naissance du roman psychologique," *Actes de la recherche en sciences sociales* 4 (1975): 66–81.

17 He would finally be approached at the Liberation by François Mauriac and Georges Duhamel, and would decline (see chapter 9). We might suppose that his real chances of getting in were limited.

18 René Lalou, *Histoire de la littérature française contemporaine (de 1870 à nos jours)*, 2 vols. (Paris: PUF, 1940, republished 1947), 725.

19 According to the data established for the recruitment of senior civil servants in 1901 by Christophe Charle, *Les Élites de la République 1880–1900* (Paris: Fayard, 1987), 74.

20 Out of the fifty-eight "immortals" studied, eight had at least one ancestor or relative by marriage who was a member of the Institute, including seven from the French Academy.

21 "Appearance-based capital" also entered into the qualities on which the representativity of the "immortals" was judged, according to Duke de Castries, who mentioned the case of the philosopher Gabriel Marcel, candidate in 1950, "whose intellectual value was appreciated but whose appearance was judged unacademic." See *La Vieille Dame*, 393.

22 Estimate based on my study of 185 writers active between 1940 and 1944 (see appendix); I compared these results with those obtained by Rémy Ponton for a population of 616 writers active during the second half of the nineteenth century (Ponton, *Le Champ littéraire de 1865 à 1906 (recrutement des écrivains, structures des carrières et production des œuvres)* (PhD diss., Université de Paris V, 1971), 46. The sample of writers from the French Academy (including critics) is composed of the 25 writers who were members in 1940 and the 6 writers elected between 1944 and 1947, for a total of 31. The writers elected after the Liberation were included in order to increase the sample size. Still, we should note that the elections of the immediate postwar were rather atypical with respect to the habitual recruitment of the Academy (I will come back to this.). The result of analyzing just the sample of 25 aca-

demic writers in 1940 thus accentuates the tendencies I have noted, and especially the difference with respect to the recruitment of the literary field.

23 Pierre Bourdieu, "Le champ littéraire: Préalables critiques et principes de méthode," *Lendemains* 36 (1984): 10.

24 Léon Daudet, *Souvenirs littéraires* (Paris: Grasset, 1933, republished 1968), 150.

25 The comparison with the sample of 665 senior civil servants constituted by Christophe Charle (*Les Élites de la République*, 74) for the end of the nineteenth century does not contain a real risk of historical discrepancy, for at least two reasons: first of all, two-thirds of the sample of Academy writers were older than sixty in 1940 and were already, for one part, active at the turn of the century; second, as I've said, the evaluation of the recruitment of the literary field is founded on the comparison of our sample to that of Rémy Ponton for the literary field in the second half of the nineteenth century.

26 Marked by a strong concentration around the capital in the seventeenth century, the geographical recruitment of the French Academy progressively "decentralized" starting in the eighteenth, with the momentum increasing during the nineteenth until the balance shifted in favor of the provinces. Daniel Oster, *Histoire de l'Académie française* (Paris: Vialetay, 1970), 188–190. See also Jacques Véron, "L'Académie française et la circulation des élites," *Population* 3 (May–June 1995): 461.

27 Archives of the *Revue des deux mondes* in the André Chaumeix collection at the IMEC; bio-bibliography of Jean Paulhan created by Claire Paulhan (Jean Paulhan collection, IMEC); Paul Léautaud, *Journal littéraire*, t. 3 (Paris: Mercure de France, 1964 and 1986), 657–658.

28 Pascal Fouché, "L'édition littéraire," in Roger Chartier and Henri-Jean Martin, *Histoire de l'édition*, t. 4, 218 and 268.

29 Quoted by M. B. "Quarante ans de succès pour Pierre Benoit," *Point de vue: Images du monde*, July 11, 1986, Press file for the Pierre Benoit centennial, archives of the French Academy.

30 Jean-Louis Curtis, "Pierre Benoit: De la gloire à la sortie du purgatoire," *Le Figaro littéraire*, June 23, 1986. See also Jacques-Henry Bornecque, *Pierre Benoit le magicien* (Paris: Albin Michel, 1986), 102–103.

31 On the career of Jules Romains, see Dominique Memmi, *Jules Romains ou la passion de parvenir* (Paris: La Dispute, 1998).

32 Jean-François Sirinelli credits him with the unsigned article that I cite below (see *Intellectuels et passions françaises: Manifestes et pétitions au XXᵉ siècle*. [Paris: Fayard, 1990], 163).

33 "Les élections à l'Académie française: Analyse d'un scrutin significatif; L'échec de M. Paul Morand," *Revue française de science politique* 8, no. 3 (September 1958): 647–648.

34 François Mauriac, "L'examen des titres" [1955], in Touzot (ed.), *François Mauriac* (Paris: Éditions de L'Herne [Cahiers de l'Herne no. 48], 1985), 403.

35 Pierre Bourdieu, *Distinction: A Social Critique of the Judgment of Taste*, trans. Richard Nice (Cambridge, MA: Harvard University Press, 1984), 175–207.

36 "Les élections à l'Académie," 648.

37 Peter, *L'Académie française et le XXᵉ siècle*, 19–20. The author notes another division into three groups: the "pions," or members of higher education, the "cabots," poets, dramaturges and other writers, and the "dukes," a group that also included the other lords and their "high commoner" friends.

38 Christophe Charle, *Naissance des "intellectuels" (1880–1900)* (Paris: Minuit, 1990).

39 Bourdieu, "Le champ littéraire," 10.

40 Christophe Charle, "Champ littéraire et champ du pouvoir, les écrivains et l'affaire Dreyfus," *Annales (ESC)* 2 (March–April 1977): 240–264.

41 Albert Thibaudet, *Réflexions sur le roman* (Paris: Gallimard, 1938), 235.

42 François Mauriac, "Histoire politique de l'Académie française," in Touzot (ed.), *François Mauriac*, 413.

43 André Gide and Jean Schlumberger, *Correspondance (1901–1950)* (Paris: Gallimard, 1993), 675, n. 2.

44 Albert Thibaudet, "La Nouvelle Croisade des Enfants," *La NRF* 66 (June 1914) and Benjamin Crémieux, *XXᵉ Siècle* (Paris: Gallimard, 1924), 188.

45 François Mauriac, "Histoire politique de l'Académie française (3)," in Touzot (ed.), *François Mauriac*, 413.

46 "Revue du mois," *La NRF* 186 (March 1, 1929): 428–429. See also Jean Paulhan and André Gide, *Correspondance (1918–1951)* (Paris: Gallimard, 1998) (70), 84 and n. 2.

47 Marcel Thomas, "Le cas Valéry," in Géraldi Leroy (ed.), *Les Écrivains et l'affaire Dreyfus* (Paris: PUF, 1983), 103–112.

48 "Les intellectuels aux côtés de la Patrie," *Le Figaro*, July 7, 1925, reproduced in Sirinelli, *Intellectuels et passions françaises*, 64–65.

49 See Denis Bertholet, *Paul Valéry 1871–1945* (Paris: Plon, 1995), 270.

50 Letter from Henry Bordeaux to René Doumic, October 10, 1927, archives of the *Revue des deux mondes* in the André Chaumeix collection, IMEC.

51 Comments related by Georges Duhamel, *Le Livre de l'amertume: Journal 1925–1956* (Paris: Mercure de France, 1983), 263.

52 Louis Bertrand, *Hitler* (Paris: Fayard, 1936).

53 François Mauriac, "Histoire politique de l'Académie française (1)," in Touzot (ed.), *François Mauriac*, 407.

54 Response speech by Pierre Benoit, in Institut de France, Académie française, *Discours prononcés dans la séance publique pour la réception de M. Claude Farrère*, April 23, 1936 (Paris: Firmin-Didot, 1936), 61.

55 "Manifeste d'intellectuels français pour la défense de l'Occident," published simultaneously in the *Journal des débats* and *Le Temps*, October 4, 1935; new signatures in both papers dated October 5; see also Sirinelli, *Intellectuels et passions françaises*, 93–94.

56 Letter to René Doumic, February 21, 1936, archives of the *Revue des deux mondes* in the André Chaumeix collection, IMEC.

57 See Anne Karakatsoulis, *La Revue des deux mondes de 1920 à 1940: Une revue française devant l'étranger* (PhD diss., Paris, EHESS, 1995), vol. 2, 510.

58 "Manifeste aux intellectuels espagnols," *Occident: Le bi-mensuel franco-espagnol*, December 10, 1937; see also the lists of signers that appeared in the December 25, 1937, and January 10, 1938, issues.

59 "Solidarité d'Occident," *Occident*, June 10, 1938.

60 Minutes of the meetings of February 16, 1939, and March 9, 1939, register 2 B 19 (1929–1941), 402 and 405, archives of the French Academy.

61 Letter from Henry Bordeaux to Charles Maurras, March 13, 1923, in Bordeaux, *Charles Maurras et l'Académie française*, 12.

62 Letter from René Doumic to Henry Bordeaux, quoted by Henry Bordeaux, ibid., 32.

63 According to an article entitled, "M. Maurras à l'Académie," *Aux Écoutes*, May 21, 1938, quoted by Henry Bordeaux, ibid., 43.

64 See Eugen Weber, *Action Française: Royalism and Reaction in Twentieth-Century France* (Stanford, CA: Stanford University Press, 1962), 394.

65 Letter reproduced in Bordeaux, *Charles Maurras*, 35.

66 Bordeaux, ibid., 36–37.

67 Alfred Baudrillart, *Les Carnets du Cardinal Baudrillart (1935–1939)* (Paris: Éditions du Cerf, 1996), 105, 636, and 743; Massis, *Maurras et notre temps: Entretiens et souvenirs* (Paris: Plon, 1961), 431; Weber, *Action Française*, 248–251. André Laudouze, *Dominicains français et Action française 1899–1940: Maurras au couvent* (Paris: Éditions ouvrières, 1989), 167–173.

68 François Mauriac, "Histoire politique," in Touzot (ed.), *François Mauriac*, 406.

69 According to the statements reported by Bordeaux, *Charles Maurras*, 38.

70 Bordeaux, ibid., 49–51 and *Histoire d'une vie*, t. 11 (Paris: Plon, 1966), 212–213. Minutes of the meeting of June 2, 1938, register 2 B 19, 373–374, archives of the French Academy.

71 Letter from Léon Daudet to Charles Maurras published in *L'Action française*, June 10, 1938, reproduced in *Cahiers Charles Maurras* 13 (1964): 14.

72 I am relying on the tally conducted by Weber (*Action française*, 412–413), and on the accounts of Henry Bordeaux (*Histoire d'une vie*, t. 11, 211) and Georges Duhamel (*Le Livre de l'amertume*, 281). Weber includes the votes of Jules Cambon and René Doumic, both of whom had died before the election, and omitted those of Edmond Jaloux and Gabriel Hanotaux. As Doumic's seat was only filled after the election of Maurras, the assembly only counted thirty-eight members at this point and there were only two absences: Bergson and Lavedan. The list of those present was verified in the minutes of the meeting of June 9, 1938, 375.

73 For the first, the tallies of Duhamel and Weber intersect. Duhamel did not mention the second.

74 Orion, "Édouard Estaunié," *L'Action française*, April 9, 1942.

75 Weber, *L'Action française*, 412–413.

76 Quoted by Weber, ibid., 409.

77 Gérard Bauer, quoted by Bordeaux, *Charles Maurras*, 98.

78 Laudouze, *Dominicains français et Action française*, 169.

79 Jean-Marie Guillon, "La philosophie politique de la Révolution nationale," in Jean-Pierre Azéma and François Bédarida (eds.), *Le Régime de Vichy et les Français* (Paris: Fayard, 1992), 174.

80 This was true of Pétain, Weygand, Franchet d'Espérey, Hanotaux, Maurras, Chaumeix, Émile Mâle, withdrawn to Vichy, Louis Gillet to Lyon, Pesquidoux to his

land in Armagnac, Edmond Jaloux to his property on the shores of Lake Geneva, as well as Maurois, exiled in the United States, and, among the academicians who had died in the first two years, Lavedan, Bergson, Marcel Prévost, Louis Bertrand (withdrawn to Antibes), Estaunié. The presence or absence of academicians was inventoried based on the minutes of the meetings of the French Academy from July 1940 to August 1944, registers 2 B 19 and 2 B 20, archives of the French Academy.

81 Noël B. de la Mort, "Immortalités actuelles. L'Académie en guerre," *Aujourd'hui*, February 7, 1942. Press file AN:72 AJ 1861.

82 Christian Faure, "Pétainisme et retour aux sources: Autour du tricentenaire Sully," *Cahiers d'Histoire* 28, no. 4 (1983): 3–32.

83 Claude Farrère, "Face au malheur," *La Gerbe*, April 10, 1941.

84 Henry Bordeaux, *Images du Maréchal Pétain* (Paris: Sequana, 1941), 6.

85 André Chaumeix, "La politique.—Six mois de restauration," *Revue des deux mondes*, December 15, 1940, 523–524.

86 Louis Madelin, "Conduire la France," *Revue des deux mondes*, June 1, 1941, 257.

87 Robert Bourget-Pailleron, "Le soldat de la dernière guerre," *Revue des deux mondes*, September 15, 1940, 161–169.

88 Farrère, "Face au malheur."

89 Joseph de Pesquidoux, "Le rôle social du paysan," *Revue des deux mondes*, December 15, 1941, 387, 394, 396.

90 Henry Bordeaux, "Le retour à la terre: Histoire d'un médecin de campagne," *Revue des deux mondes*, August 15, 1940, 273.

91 On the entanglement of these three themes in the rhetoric of the National Revolution ideologues, see Francine Muel-Dreyfus, *Vichy and the Eternal Feminine*, trans. Kathleen A. Johnson (Durham, NC: Duke University Press, 2001), 23 passim.

92 Robert O. Paxton, *Vichy France: Old Guard and New Order, 1940–1944* (New York: Columbia University Press, 2001).

93 André Chaumeix, "Pour le renouveau de l'esprit public," *Candide*, July 10, 1940; and Louis Madelin, "Tant d'hommes, et . . . pas d'Hommes," *Candide*, October 2, 1940.

94 Edmond Jaloux, "Les murs sont bons d'Henry Bordeaux," *Candide*, December 18, 1940.

95 Joseph de Pesquidoux, "Le retour à la terre: Les disciplines du sol," *Candide*, October 9, 1940.

96 Louis Madelin, "Les notables," *Candide*, December 25, 1940.

97 *France-Amérique* 343–348 (July–December 1940), and "Le comité France-Amérique en 1942," *Journal des nations américaines*, "La vie française" 711, war series 114. Musée de la Résistance nationale (MRN).

98 "Exposé des faits," in *Le Procès de Charles Maurras: Compte rendu sténographique* (Paris: Albin Michel, 1946), 8–16.

99 This is the title of a chapter in a work by Charles Maurras, *La Seule France, chronique des jours d'épreuve* (Lyon: Larchandet, 1941), which of course refers to the Gaullists.

100 Philippe Burrin, *France under the Germans: Collaboration and Compromise*, trans. Janet Lloyd (New York: New Press, 1996), 398.

101 "Cercle européen," document dated March 17, 1944, from the Georges Cogniot archives, MRN.

102 Gilles Ragache and Jean-Robert Ragache, *La Vie quotidienne des écrivains et des artistes sous l'Occupation* (1940–1944) (Paris: Hachette, 1988), 129.

103 Duhamel, *Le Livre de l'amertume*, 344–346. Paul Christophe, "Le Cardinal Baudrillat et ses choix pendant la Seconde Guerre mondiale," *Revue d'Histoire de l'Église de France* 200 (January–June 1992): 57–73.

104 According to Abel Bonnard, Cardinal Baudrillart received 200 to 300 insulting letters after his position-taking in November 1940 (see infra); reported by Ramon Fernandez to Jean Grenier, *Sous l'Occupation* (Paris: Éditions Claire Paulhan, 1997), 190.

105 Mgr. Chaptal, auxiliary of the archbishop of Paris, Cardinal Suhard, having failed to reason with Cardinal Baudrillart, the archbishop asked Mgr. Valeri, Vichy nuncio, to involve Rome. The request went unheeded: the Holy See decided not to respond; see Léon Papeleux, "Note à propos de l'affaire Baudrillart," *Revue d'Histoire ecclésiastique* 1 (January–April 1987): 50–53.

106 From the cardinal's *Carnets* dated June 23, 1940, quoted by Paul Christophe, "Le cardinal Baudrillart," 60.

107 From the cardinal's *Carnets* dated November 8, 1940, quoted by Paul Christophe, ibid., 63.

108 Cardinal Baudrillart, "Choisir, Vouloir, Obéir!," *La Gerbe*, November 21, 1940. See also *Le Testament politique d'un prince de l'Église*, text of the declaration made to Agence Inter-France, November 1, 1940, by Cardinal Baudrillat, preceded by a tribute from Abel Bonnard (Paris: Impr. Guillemot et Lamothe, 1942), 8–16. A private agency founded in 1938 by Dominique Sordet, Michel Alerme, and Xavier de Magallon, supported by the Germans and the Vichy regime, Inter-France had reached an agreement with the German agency Transozean in 1940 for the exchange and diffusion of information in the regional press of both zones; see Pascal Ory, *Les Collaborateurs* (Paris: Seuil, 1976 and 1980), 67–69 and Rita Thalmann, *La Mise au pas: Idéologie et stratégie sécuritaire dans la France occupée* (Paris: Fayard, 1991), 154.

109 Quoted by Jacques Duquesne, *Les Catholiques français sous l'Occupation* (Paris: Grasset, 1966), 167.

110 Abel Hermant, *Une vie, trois guerres (Témoignages et souvenirs)* (Paris: Pierre Lagrange, 1943), 16.

111 Ibid., 58.

112 Jacques Mièvre, "L'évolution politique d'Abel Bonnard (jusqu'au printemps 1942)," *Revue d'histoire de la Deuxième Guerre mondiale* 108 (October 1977): 1–26.

113 Muel-Dreyfus, *Vichy and the Eternal Feminine*, 215–220.

114 Abel Bonnard, "Constitution d'une élite," *La Gerbe*, January 23, 1941.

115 *Aux Écoutes*, May 21, 1938, quoted by Bordeaux, *Charles Maurras*, 45.

116 Jean Guéhenno, *Journal des années noires* (Paris: Gallimard, 1947), June 18, 1941, 123.

117 Louis Parrot, *L'Intelligence en guerre* (Paris: La Jeune Parque, 1945, republished by Le Castor astral, 1990), 35–36.

118 The speech was nonetheless published in 1942, without its author's permission, it seems, in *Paris au Maréchal*. See Bertholet, *Paul Valéry*, 371.

119 Paul Valéry, "Allocution prononcée à l'occasion de la mort de M. Henri Bergson," Thursday, January 9, 1941, in Institut de France, Académie française, *Publications diverses de l'année 1941* (Paris: Firmin-Didot, 1941). The order had been given to publish nothing in the Parisian press on the late philosopher; on this topic, see Duhamel's letter to Mauriac, January 13, 1941, in François Mauriac and Georges Duhamel, *Correspondance (1919–1966), Le Croyant et l'humaniste inquiet* (Paris: Klincksieck, 1997) (66), 123.

120 Georges Duhamel, *Positions françaises: Chronique de l'année 1939* (Paris: Mercure de France, 1940).

121 Claude Morgan, *Les Don Quichotte et les autres* (Paris: Roblot, 1979), 130.

122 Georges Duhamel, *Lumières sur ma vie*, t. 3, *Le temps de la recherche* (Paris: Mercure de France, 1944), 22.

123 Lucien Descaves, *Souvenirs d'un ours* (Paris: Éditions de Paris, 1946), 257. See also Georges Duhamel, "Pages inédites extraites du Journal de G. Duhamel," *Les Cahiers de l'Abbaye de Créteil* 2 (December 1980): 9–10.

124 François Mauriac, "Duhamel parmi nous," in *Georges Duhamel 1884–1966* (Paris: Mercure de France, 1967), 9–10.

125 Letter from Mauriac to Pierre Brisson, June 29, 1944, in Mauriac, *Lettres d'une vie (1904–1969)* (Paris: Grasset, 1981), 277.

126 Institut de France, Académie des sciences morales et politiques, "L'Académie des sciences morales et politiques et le redressement moral de la France après les événements de 1848," by M. le baron Seillière, *Séance solennelle du samedi 6 novembre 1941* (Paris: Firmin-Didot, 1941), 4.

127 Excerpted from the unpublished *Carnets* of Cardinal Baudrillart dated October 31, 1940, reproduced in Paul Christophe, *1939–1940: Les Catholiques devant la guerre* (Paris: Éditions ouvrières, 1989), 160. For more on this meeting, see also Duhamel, *Le Livre de l'amertume,* 358–360.

128 Cardinal Baudrillart, *Carnets.*

129 Letter from Bordeaux to Marshal Pétain dated November 20, 1940, reproduced in Henry Bordeaux, *Histoire d'une vie*, t. 12, *Lumière au bout de la nuit* (Paris: Plon, 1970), 89.

130 Letter from Mauriac to Duhamel, December 18, 1940, in Mauriac and Duhamel, *Correspondance* (64), 118.

131 Grenier, *Sous l'Occupation*, 191.

132 Thalmann, *La Mise au pas*, 172.

133 André Gide, *Journal*, vol. 4, *1939–1949*, trans. Justin O'Brien (Urbana: Illinois University Press, 2000), 221.

134 Léautaud, *Journal littéraire*, t. 3, 445.

135 Jacques Dyssord, "Baudruches," *La France au travail*, December 4–16, 1940 (see chapter 2).

136 Lucien Combelle, "André Maurois, plagiaire," *La Gerbe*, February 13, 1941; "Un bouffon académique," ibid., April 24, 1941.

137 Robert Jullien-Courtine, "Si nous parlions de l'Académie," *Au pilori*, November 19, 1942.

138 Jean Drault, "L'Académie Goncourt et les juifs," *Au pilori*, July 15, 1943.

139 "Suetone," "D'une académie à l'autre en passant par Xavier Vallat," *Au pilori*, October 23, 1941.

140 René Pernoud, *Paris-Midi*, February 14, 1942.

141 It is not one of the least ambiguities of the Vichy regime that the concentration of power was legitimated while the illusion of a cultural decentralization was given. "In theory, the strengthening of authority at the top was supposed to be accompanied by a deconcentration at regional and local levels. But in fact the power of the prefects was consolidated and 'administrators responsible for public order and supplies' were introduced." Jean-Pierre Azéma, *From Munich to the Liberation, 1938–1944*, trans. Janet Lloyd (Cambridge: Cambridge University Press, 1984), 62.

142 Abel Hermant, "La Province et les provincialismes," in Institut de France, Académie française, *Publications diverses de l'année 1941* (Paris: Firmin-Didot, 1941), 84.

143 Jérôme Tharaud, "Extrait du discours prononcé devant les cinq académies le 18 décembre 1941," in *Fumées de Paris et d'ailleurs* (Paris: Éditions de la Nouvelle France, 1946), 24. Duhamel found this speech "marvelous," as he wrote to Mauriac in a letter dated December 21, 1941, in Mauriac and Duhamel, *Correspondance* (83), 142.

144 Minutes of the meeting of January 11, 1940, register 2 B 19, 431, archives of the French Academy.

145 Roger Giron, "D'Alembert, Villemain, René Doumic précédèrent Georges Duhamel dans les fonctions de secrétaire perpétuel de l'Académie," *Paris-Soir*, February 14, 1942.

146 Léautaud, *Journal littéraire*, t. 3, 358.

147 Hector Talvart, Joseph Place, and Georges Place, *Bibliographie des auteurs modernes*, t. 2 (Paris: Éditions de la Chronique des lettres françaises, 1930), 349.

148 André Bellessort, "La Folie-Hubert de Robert Bourget-Pailleron," *Je suis partout*, January 26, 1940.

149 Institut de France, Académie française, "Rapport de M. André Bellessort, secrétaire perpétuel, sur les concours littéraires," annual public meeting held Thursday, December 18, 1941, *Publications diverses de l'année 1941* (Paris: Firmin-Didot, 1941), 41.

150 See the letters from François Mauriac to Blanche Duhamel, April 7, 1942, in Mauriac and Duhamel, *Correspondance* (85), 147, and from Jean Schlumberger to François Mauriac, June 13 and 19, 1942, François Mauriac collection, Jacques Doucet archives.

151 Letter from Schlumberger to Mauriac, June 19, 1942. Schlumberger had just refused to take part in the revamping of the NRF editorial staff and had explained himself to Mauriac, himself invited to participate in the new council, in a previous letter (May 25, 1942) in which he said he counted on him to prevent unwanted compromises (see chapter 6).

152 See the letter from Paulhan to Mauriac [1943], in Paulhan, *Choix de lettres*, t. 2, *1937–1945, Le Traité des jours sombres* (Paris: Gallimard, 1992) (255), 296.

153 Institut de France, Académie française, "Rapport de M. Georges Duhamel, secrétaire perpétuel, sur les concours littéraires," annual meeting held December 17, 1942,
Publications diverses de l'année 1942 (Paris: Firmin-Didot, 1942), 16.

154 Fouché, *L'Édition française sous l'Occupation 1940–1944* (Bibliothèque de littérature française contemporaine de l'université Paris VII, 1987) (64; Ragache and
Ragache, *La Vie quotidienne*, 241–242).

155 Letter from Mauriac to Duhamel, "Maundy Thursday" 1943, in Mauriac and Duhamel, *Correspondance* (95), 157.

156 Letter from Duhamel to Mauriac, ibid. (96), 158.

157 Minutes of the meeting of May 27, 1943, register 2 B 20, 55.

158 Henri Guillemin, *Parcours* (Paris: Seuil, 1989), 81.

159 Institut de France, Académie française, "Rapport de M. Georges Duhamel, secrétaire
perpétuel, sur les concours littéraires," annual meeting held December 16, 1943, *Publications diverses de l'année 1943* (Paris: Firmin-Didot, 1942), 8–9 (Renan's page, written in 1858, was taken from *Essais de morale et de critique*). In the same report,
Duhamel also referred to the execrated author of the regime, André Gide (ibid., 14).

160 See the letter from Mauriac to Duhamel, in Mauriac and Duhamel, *Correspondance*
(108), 173.

161 Minutes from the meeting of December 24, 1942, register 2 B 20, 39.

162 Georges Duhamel, *Éclaircissements* (Paris: Impr. P. Hartmann, 1947), 6.

163 [Jacques Debû-Bridel], "L'Académie Goncourt et les agents de l'ennemi," *Les Lettres
françaises*—underground 5 (January–February 1943).

164 Letter from Paulhan to Mauriac [April 12, 1943], in Paulhan, *Choix de lettres*, t. 2
(262), 302–303.

165 Letter from Mauriac to Paulhan, April 20, 1943, Jean Paulhan collection, IMEC.

166 The academicians who had died during this period were: in 1940, Henri Lavedan;
in 1941, Henri Bergson, Marcel Prévost, Louis Bertrand, Émile Picard; in 1942,
André Bellessort, Édouard Estaunié, Cardinal Baudrillart, Marshal Franchet
d'Espérey; in 1943, Louis Gillet; in 1944, Maurice Paléologue and Paul Hazard.

167 Henri Poulain, interview with Georges Duhamel, *Le Petit Parisien*, December 30, 1941.

168 Bordeaux, *Histoire d'une vie*, t. 12, 334.

169 This was, however, the solution that was adopted at the Liberation. On October 12,
1944, the planned date of the elections, the quorum had still not been met. Admiral
Lacaze, then acting director, recalled that in order to ensure its survival under the
Occupation, the Company had interpreted the spirit of its statute rather than conforming to its letter by proceeding with quarterly elections of the board members
despite the lack of quorum (which was fifteen members in this case). On this basis,
he proposed an interpretation of the statute that was adopted: arguing that the
twenty necessary to fill a chair represented half of the living members plus one, and
that the Academy currently counted only twenty-eight, he suggested bringing the
quorum down to fourteen. This solution allowed for the election of three new academicians. Minutes of the meeting of October 12, 1944, register 2 B 20, 114.

170 "Pas d'élection, dit l'Académie: Mais il y a cependant des candidatures," *Paris-Soir*,
July 16, 1942.

171 It was undated but was, according to Jean Touzot, completed in stages; see Touzot, *Mauriac sous l'Occupation* (Paris: La Manufacture, 1990), 101. I tend to think, however, that it was only drawn up after the Liberation (see chapter 9).

172 "Pour la première fois depuis la guerre, l'Académie annonce les candidatures aux fauteuils vacants," *Paris-Soir*, March 8, 1943.

Chapter 5: *The Sense of Scandal*

1 R. C. Sarmazeuilh, *Le Républicain du centre*, February 5, 1942. AN: 72 AJ 1861.

2 Testament of Edmond de Goncourt, reproduced in Jacques Robichon, *Le Défi des Goncourt* (Paris: Denoël, 1975), 333.

3 Ibid., 332.

4 Meeting held April 7, 1900, "Article premier," "Registre PV des réunions des membres de la Société littéraire des Goncourt," Goncourt archives, Geffroy collection, Municipal archives of Nancy, 2.

5 Quoted by Roger Gouze, *Les Bêtes à Goncourt: Un demi-siècle de batailles littéraires* (Paris: Hachette, 1973), 77.

6 See Jean Bothorel, *Bernard Grasset: Vie et passions d'un éditeur* (Paris: Grasset, 1989), 169.

7 Michel Caffier, *L'Académie Goncourt* (Paris: PUF, 1994), 69.

8 See Pierre Assouline, "Les dessous du Goncourt," *Lire* 194 (November 1991): 42, and my chapter 9.

9 Georges Ricou, *Inter-France*, October 9, 1941. AN: 72 AJ 1861.

10 Armand Salacrou, *Les Idées de la nuit* (Paris: Fayard, 1960), 190.

11 AFIP, October 12, 1941. AN: 72 AJ 1861 (AFIP: Agence française d'information de presse).

12 Quoted by Antoine Compagnon, *Connaissez-vous Brunetière? Enquête sur un anti-dreyfusard et ses amis* (Paris: Seuil, 1997), 113.

13 Maurice Barrès, *Discours de réception (Séance de l'Académie du 17 janvier 1907)* (Paris: Librairie Félix Juven, 1907), 21.

14 Christophe Charle, *La Crise littéraire à l'époque du naturalisme: Roman, Théâtre, Politique* (Paris: PENS, 1979), 83.

15 The data that follow were obtained through the study of the social properties of the thirty-four members who were elected to the Goncourt Academy from its foundation up to 1951, which I compare alternatively to the thirty-one writers of the French Academy, to the social recruitment of the literary field in the second half of the nineteenth century such as it has been established by Rémy Ponton (*Le Champ littéraire*), and to our population of 185 writers who were active in 1950. The jurors who died before 1940 were not included in our total population. They are thus taken into account here, but not in the tables that appear in the appendix, which includes only the twenty jurors who were members of the Goncourt Academy between 1940 and 1951.

16 Rémy Ponton, *Le Champ littéraire de 1865 à 1906 (recrutement des écrivains, structure des carrières et production des œuvres)* (PhD diss., Université Paris V, 1977), 43.

17 From this point forward we will only consider these twenty members, who constitute a subpopulation in our total sample of 185 writers who were active in 1940. See tables 1–5 in the appendix.

18 Let us recall that they grew from about 10,000 in 1869 to double that number in the 1880s, then nearly 50,000 at the beginning of the 1920s. See Antoine Prost, *Histoire de l'enseignement en France 1800–1967* (Paris: Armand Colin, 1968), 243.

19 François Broche, *Léon Daudet, le dernier imprécateur* (Paris: Laffont, 1992), 116–117; André Négis, *Mon ami Carco* (Paris: Albin Michel, 1953), 15; René Benjamin, *Mussolini et son peuple* (Paris: Plon, 1937), 141.

20 Letter from Lucien Descaves to Gustave Geffroy, dated [*illegible*] 9, 1917, box R.19, Gustave Geffroy collection.

21 Charle, *La Crise littéraire*, 167.

22 Lucien Descaves, *Souvenirs d'un ours* (Paris: Éditions de Paris, 1946), 241.

23 See chapter 2.

24 Descaves, *Souvenirs d'un ours*, 524.

25 Alain Laubreaux, "L'événement en littérature," *Le Petit Parisien*, August 19, 1941.

26 "Suetone," "D'une académie à l'autre, en passant par Xavier Vallat," *Au pilori*, October 23, 1941. See also Jean Drault, "L'académie Goncourt et les Juifs," *Au pilori*, July 15, 1943.

27 Jean Norton Cru, *Du témoignage* (Paris: Gallimard/NRF, 1930), trans. Hélène Vogel as *War Books: A Study in Historical Criticism* (San Diego: San Diego State University Press, 1988).

28 Maurice Rieuneau, *Guerre et révolution dans le roman français 1919–1939* (Paris: Klincksieck, 1974). See also Léon Riegel, *Guerre et littérature: Le bouleversement des consciences dans la littérature romanesque inspirée par la Grande Guerre (littératures française, anglo-saxonne et allemande) 1910–1939* (Paris: Klincksieck, 1978).

29 Micheline Dupray, *Roland Dorgelès: Un siècle de vie littéraire française* (Paris: Presses de la Renaissance, 1986), 196–197.

30 Minutes of the meeting of December 11, 1918, "Registre PV," 73.

31 Quoted by Gouze, *Les Bêtes à Goncourt*, 77.

32 Interview with François Nourrissier conducted by Pierre Assouline, "Les dessous du Goncourt," 36.

33 Estienne, "Le lauréat du prix Goncourt," *Gil Blas*, December 14, 1906.

34 For what follows, I rely on Jean Ajalbert, *Mémoires à rebours*, t. 1, *Règlements de compte* (Paris: Denoël and Steele, 1936), 203; Descaves, *Souvenirs d'un ours*, 267–269; and Robichon, *Le Défi des Goncourt*, 95–101.

35 Minutes of the meeting of February 22, 1933, "Registre PV," 144.

36 Quoted by Robichon, *Le Défi des Goncourt*, 97.

37 Minutes of the meeting of February 23, 1938, "Cahier chemises 38–39" and "Registre PV," 187.

38 Dupray, *Roland Dorgelès*, 389.

39 Léon Daudet, *L'Action française*, June 30, 1939.

40 Descaves, *Souvenirs d'un ours*, 276.

41 André Guérin, "du Grenier à l'Hôtel," *L'Œuvre*, January 22, 1942 (AN: 72 AJ 1861).

42 M[aurice] N[oël], "M. Sacha Guitry fait du mécénat," *Le Figaro*, November 18, 1944.

43 Léautaud, *Journal littéraire* (Paris: Mercure de France, 1964 and 1986), 690.

44 Alain Laubreaux, *Écrit pendant la guerre* (Paris: Éditions du Centre de l'agence Inter-France, 1944), 113.

45 Pierre-Marie Dioudonnat, *Je suis partout (1930–1944): Les maurrassiens devant la tentation fasciste* (Paris: La Table Ronde, 1973), 335, n. 101.

46 Quoted by Lacouture, *François Mauriac*, vol. 2, *Un citoyen du siècle 1933–1970* (Paris: Seuil, 1980), 351.

47 Broche, *Léon Daudet*.

48 Léon Daudet, "L'année du pire et du meilleur," *L'Action française*, December 24, 1940.

49 Léon Daudet, "Le retour de Dieu dans l'École," *L'Action française*, December 8–9, 1940.

50 Léon Daudet, "La médecine française aux français," *L'Action française*, August 29, 1940; see also "La médecine française et les métèques," ibid., September 18, 1940.

51 Léon Daudet, "La mauvaise conscience," *L'Action française*, October 12, 1940.

52 Pierre Gaxotte, *Candide*, July 10, 1942; Guillain de Bénouville in *L'Alerte* and Edmond Jaloux in *La Gazette de Lausanne*, quoted by Thierry Maulnier, "L'homme de la presse à Léon Daudet," *L'Action française*, July 6, 1942.

53 Lucien Descaves, *Souvenirs d'un ours*, and "Lucien Descaves," in Jean Maitron and Claude Pennetier (eds.), *Dictionnaire biographique du mouvement ouvrier français, 1971–1914*, t. 12 (Paris: Éditions ouvrières), 29–30; "Lucien Descaves," *Les Hommes du jour* 43 (November 14, 1908); (document kindly forwarded by Nicolas Offenstadt).

54 Charle, *La Crise littéraire*, 95; J.-P. Damour, "Rosny J.-H.," in J.-P. de Beaumarchais, D. Couty, and A. Rey, *Dictionnaire des littératures de langue française*, vol. 3 (Paris: Bordas, 1984, republished 1994), 2170.

55 Descaves, *Souvenirs d'un ours*, 287.

56 Anne-Marie Thiesse, *Écrire la France: Le mouvement littéraire régionaliste de langue française entre la Belle Époque et la Libération* (Paris: PUF, 1991), 208–210.

57 Ajalbert, *Mémoires à rebours*, t. 1, 20.

58 Léo Larguier, *Mes vingt ans et moi* (Paris: Albin Michel, 1944), 11–12.

59 See, for example, Léo Larguier, "Les menus de l' 'année terrible,'" *Paris-Soir*, January 29, 1943.

60 Dupray, *Roland Dorgelès*.

61 Roland Dorgelès, *Vive la liberté!* (Paris: Albin Michel, 1937), 310.

62 Gérard Loiseaux, *La Littérature de la défaite et de la Collaboration, d'après "Phonix oder Asche?" de Bernhard Payr* (Paris: Publications de la Sorbonne, 1984; Fayard, 1995), 511.

63 Quoted by Dupray, *Roland Dorgelès*, 340.

64 Négis, *Mon ami Carco*, 55.

65 Francis Carco, "Retour à la terre," *Le Figaro*, September 21, 1940.

66 Francis Carco, "Noir venin de la mélancolie," *Paris-Soir*, July 20, 1941.

67 Roman D'Amat, "René Benjamin," in J. Balteau and M. Barroux, continued by M. Prévost et. al. (eds.), *Dictionnaire de biographie française*, vol. 5 (Paris: Letouzey et Ané, 1951), col. 1415.

68 René Benjamin, *Vérités et rêveries sur l'éducation* (Paris: Plon, 1942), 38 and 22.

69 See, for example, Léon Daudet, "L'apparition de René Benjamin à Saint-Étienne," *L'Action française*, March 5, 1941.

70 René Benjamin, *Le Maréchal et son peuple* (Paris: Plon, 1941); *Les Sept Étoiles de France* (Paris: Plon, 1942), with a print run of 20,000; *Le Grand Homme seul* (Paris: Plon, 1943).

71 These comments were reported by Henri Guillemin, who attended the lunch in question, in *Parcours* (Paris: Seuil, 1989), 82–83.

72 Benjamin, *Vérités et rêveries*, 42.

73 Serge Added, *Le Théâtre dans les années Vichy 1940–1944* (Paris: Ramsay, 1992), 68–69, 146, 323–325. See also Sacha Guitry, *Quatre Ans d'occupations* (Paris: L'Élan, 1947), 194 and 260.

74 Sacha Guitry, ibid., 521; see also Gilles Ragache et Jean-Robert Ragache, *La Vie quotidienne des écrivains et des artistes sous l'Occupation (1940–1944)* (Paris: Hachette, 1988), 124 passim. In October 1941, Ernst Jünger met Sacha Guitry at the home of Fernand de Brinon. Guitry invited him, with Hans Speidel, to have lunch at his home, avenue Élysée-Reclus, a week later; see Ernst Jünger, *Journaux de guerre* (Paris: Julliard, 1990), 229 and 232.

75 Contributors to this volume included Colette, Father Sertillange, René Benjamin, Pierre Benoit, Louis Beydts, Maurice de Broglie, Pierre Champion, Jean Cocteau, Alfred Cortot, Maurice Donnay, Georges Duhamel, René Fauchois, Paul Fort, Jean Giraudoux, Abel Hermant, Léo Larguier, Jean de La Varende, Aristide Maillol, Paul Morand, J.-H. Rosny, Jean and Jérôme Tharaud, and Paul Valéry.

76 Guy Crouzet, "Erreur ou plaisanterie? Le prix Goncourt à Lyon," *Les Nouveaux Temps*, May 10, 1941.

77 "Qui sera choisi comme dixième par les 'Neuf'?," *Paris-Soir*, November 26, 1941, and A. N., *L'Œuvre*, November 21, 1941.

78 "L'histoire entre à l'académie Goncourt avec M. Pierre Champion, membre de l'Institut et conseiller national," *Paris-Soir*, December 22, 1941.

79 Lucien Descaves, "À propos des Goncourt. Voix au chapitre," *Comoedia*, December 20, 1941.

80 Ajalbert, quoted in *Le Petit Parisien*, January 6, 1942.

81 "L'agitation dans le grenier," *Le Cri du peuple*, January 8, 1942.

82 See Guitry, *Quatre Ans*, 300.

83 Henri Pourrat, *Vent de mars: Roman* (Paris: Gallimard, 1941), 189.

84 Thiesse, *Écrire la France*, 143.

85 Henri Pourrat, "Le chef français," *Revue des deux mondes*, February 15, 1941, 455. This long article, written on the occasion of the marshal's visit to Ambert, would be published with a postface and illustrations two years later; see Henri Pourrat, *Le Chef français* (Marseille: Laffont, 1942).

86 See Thiesse, *Écrire la France*, 123.

87 André Chaumeix, "Revue littéraire. Romans et prix littéraires," *Revue des deux mondes*, January 1, 1931, 223. John Charpentier, "Revue de la quinzaine: Les Romans," *Mercure de France*, February 1, 1938, 577.

88 Marcel Espiau, *Les Nouveaux Temps*, December 24, 1941.

89 Rosny the Younger, "Deux prix Goncourt en 1941 et l'élection du dixième Dix," *Le Petit Parisien*, December 5, 1941.

90 Interview with Rosny the Younger, conducted by Henri Poulain, *Le Petit Parisien*, December 16, 1941.

91 Jean Galtier-Boissière, *Mon journal pendant l'Occupation* (Paris: La Jeune Parque, 1944), 114.

92 "Treize candidats se disputeront mercredi prochain les deux 'Goncourt,'" *Paris-Soir*, December 5, 1941.

93 Karl Rauch, "Les éditeurs français et la collaboration," *Les Cahiers franco-allemands*, January–February 1941, quoted by Loiseaux, *La Littérature de la défaite*, 90–91.

94 René Benjamin, quoted by Marcel Espiau, *Les Nouveaux Temps*, December 24, 1941.

95 Christian Faure, "'Vent de mars' d'Henri Pourrat: Prix Goncourt 1941 ou la con-sécration d'une œuvre littéraire par le régime de Vichy," *Bulletin du centre Pierre Léon: Histoire Économique et Sociale de la Région Lyonnaise* 1 (1982): 8.

96 Bernhard Payr, *Phönix oder Asche?*, in Loiseaux, *La Littérature de la défaite*, 213; see also 111.

97 See Bothorel, *Bernard Grasset*, 363.

98 "L'agitation dans le grenier," *Le Cri du people*, January 8, 1942.

99 Interview with Fernand Plas, AFIP, January 1942 (AN: 72 AJ 1861); let us recall that the AFIP was controlled by the Germans.

100 Maurice Garçon, quoted in *Paris-Midi*, January 8, 1942.

101 AN: F21 8122.

102 See his response to the survey, "Ce que pense du départ de Jacques Doriot: Jean Ajalbert de l'Académie Goncourt," *L'Émancipation nationale*, April 10, 1943 and AN: F21 8122.

103 Jean Ajalbert, "L'Académie Goncourt continue," *Paris-Soir*, October 24, 1942.

104 Jean Ajalbert, "Vivent les vieux! Pour que vivent les jeunes," *Paris-Soir*, January 28, 1941.

105 Jean Ajalbert, "Pourquoi j'ai voté pour *Les Décombres*," *Notre Combat*, March 20, 1943, 16.

106 Minutes of the meeting of December 17, 1942, "Registre PV," 216.

107 René Benjamin, *La Galère des Goncourt*, with a préface by Sacha Guitry (Paris: L'Élan, 1948), 241–242.

108 Comments reported by Léautaud, *Journal littéraire*, t. 3, 853.

109 Quoted by Pierre Coulomb, *La Varende* (Paris: Dominique Wapler, 1951), 51. The biographical information on La Varende comes from this biography.

110 "It is unfortunate that Mr. de la Varende, a talented storyteller, writes with such a careless audacity," wrote Drieu La Rochelle, "Libéraux," *La NRF* 345 (November 1, 1942): 603.

111 Robert Brasillach, "La Varende, ou le dernier féodal" (1938), republished in *Les Quatre Jeudis: Images d'avant-guerre* (Paris: Éditions Balzac, 1944; Sceaux, Les Sept Couleurs, 1951), 424 and 432; Thierry Maulnier, "Causerie littéraire," *L'Action française*, September 10, 1942.

112 Robert Brasillach, ibid., 431.

113 Jean de La Varende, "L'immédiat," *Cahiers franco-allemands* 1 (1943): 10.

114 Quoted by Coulomb, *La Varende*, 143.

115 Pierre Coulomb, ibid., 143–144.

116 René de Lacroix de Castries, *La Vieille Dame du Quai Conti: Une histoire de l'Académie française* (Paris: Perrin, 1978), 397. His candidacy was supported by Pierre Benoit; see Bornecque, *Pierre Benoit le magicien*, 316.

117 Paul Fort, *Mes Mémoires: Toute la vie d'un poète 1872–1944* (Paris: Flammarion, 1944).

118 See Nicole Racine, "Marc Bernard," in Maitron and Pennetier (eds.), *Dictionnaire biographique du mouvement ouvrier français, 1914–1939*, t. 19, 25–26.

119 See Jean-Pierre Morel, *Le Roman insupportable: L'internationale littéraire et la France (1920–1932)* (Paris: Gallimard, 1985), 426.

120 According to the account Marc Bernard gave Jacques Robichon, *Le Défi des Goncourt*, 139.

121 Jean Grenier, *Sous l'Occupation* (Paris: Éditions Claire Paulhan, 1997), 101.

122 Letter from Marc Bernard to Jean Grenier, September 23, 1942, reproduced in Jean Grenier, ibid., 271.

123 "Le prix Théophraste-Renaudot à M. Robert Gaillard," *Paris-Soir*, December 21, 1942.

124 Robert Gaillard, *Le Choix vitaliste: Trois mois d'Activité Vitaliste* (Paris: Debresse, 1940), 1 and 2. See also "Trois mois de vitalisme" (9–16) for the history of the movement.

125 See Pierre Péan, *Une jeunesse française: François Mitterrand 1934–1947* (Paris: Fayard, 1994), 186, n. 2.

126 M. N., "De Jour en Jour," *Le Figaro*, December 30, 1941, and "Le Cours des livres est en hausse et le Tout-Paris écrit ses mémoires," *La Semaine*, February 11, 1943, quoted by Pascal Fouché, *L'Édition française 1940–1944*, vol. 1 (Bibliothèque de littérature française contemporaine de l'université Paris VII, 1987), 230.

127 Letter from the prefect, ministry delegate in the occupied territories, on the letterhead of the Ministry of the Interior, to Rosny the Younger, January 11, 1943, box "Dossiers AG 1902–1950," Goncourt Academy archives.

128 Léautaud, *Journal littéraire*, t. 3, 747.

129 Ibid., 759.

130 [Jacques Debû-Bridel], "L'Académie Goncourt et les agents de l'ennemi," *Les Lettres françaises* 5 (January–February 1943). It is in the same article that Debû-Bridel congratulated the French Academy for its attitude.

131 [Claude Morgan], "Quelques-uns des Goncourt," *Les Lettres françaises* 12 (December 1943).

132 Minutes of the meeting of December 11, 1943, "Registre PV," 219.

133 Letter from Jean de La Varende to Rosny the Younger, quoted by Robichon, *Le Défi des Goncourt*, 142.

134 Letter from René Benjamin to Roland Dorgelès, quoted by Dupray, *Roland Dorgelès*, 393.

135 Letter from André Billy to Paul Léautaud, December 22, 1943, reproduced in Léautaud, *Journal littéraire*, t. 3, 964–965.

136 Descaves, *Souvenirs d'un ours*, 288.

137 [Claude Morgan], "Quelques-uns des Goncourt."

138 Comments by Galtier-Boissière reported by Léautaud, *Journal littéraire*, t. 3, 922.

139 "Suetone," "D'une académie à l'autre, en passant par Xavier Vallat," *Au pilori!* 68 (October 23, 1941). For the meaning of the assimilation of women and Jews in the collective imaginary, refer to Francine Muel-Dreyfus, *Vichy and the Eternal Feminine*, trans. Kathleen A. Johnson (Durham, NC: Duke University Press, 2001).

140 Thierry Maulnier, "Causerie littéraire," *L'Action française* 136 (June 10, 1943).

141 Nathalie Sarraute and Marc Saporta, "Portrait d'une inconnue (conversation biographique)," in "Nathalie Sarraute," *L'Arc* 95 (1984): 16.

142 Instituted in 1880, women's secondary education experienced a significant expansion during this period, as I mentioned in the first chapter. If over 700 women are said to write at the end of the nineteenth century, it is most often a question of amateur activity rather than a professional activity for society women, or, on the opposite pole, a moneymaking task for women from modest backgrounds. Often forced to hide behind a masculine identity, women writers restricted themselves to didactic literature (for the Éditions de la Bonne presse), to children's literature, or to the popular novel. Those who achieved recognition were often from the aristocracy or the bourgeoisie, unless they established themselves through scandal, like Colette, a typical product of promotion via school who started as the "ghostwriter" for her first husband Willy before becoming independent. See Anne-Marie Thiesse, *Le Roman du quotidien: Lecteurs et lectures populaires à la Belle Époque* (Paris: Le Chemin vert, 1984), 183; Monique de Saint-Martin, "Les 'femmes écrivains' et le champ littéraire," *Actes de la recherche en sciences sociales* 83 (1990): 52–56. On the strategies of recognition of female intellectuals during this period, see Françoise Blum, "Itinéraires féministes à la lumière de l'Affaire," in *La Postérité de l'Affaire Dreyfus*, ten studies collected by Michel Leymarie (Villeneuve d'Ascq: Presses universitaires du Septentrion, 1998), 93–101.

143 On the denial of universality in the reception of women writers of the interwar period, see Jennifer E. Milligan, *The Forgotten Generation: French Women Writers of the Inter-war Period* (New York: Berg, 1996).

144 Thierry Maulnier, "Causerie littéraire," *L'Action française*, October 21, 1943.

145 Robichon, *Le Défi des Goncourt*, 140. The result of this vote was not recorded in the register of meeting minutes, either.

146 Document archived at the CDJC (Center of Contemporary Jewish Documentation), quoted by Francis Crémieux, "Arrêtez immédiatement la juive Elsa Kagan dite Triolet," *Faites entrer l'infini* 21 (June 1996): 15. Among the documents included

in this file is an article from *Le Petit Parisien* on the results of the Goncourt Prize elections, which mentions Elsa Triolet by name.

147 Simone de Beauvoir, *The Prime of Life*, trans. Peter Green (Cleveland, OH: World Publishing Company, 1962), 442.

148 Jean Ajalbert, "Du 'Goncourt' au 'Mallarmé,'" *Aujourd'hui* 1235 (July 30, 1944).

Chapter 6: The Sense of Distinction

1 Comments reported by Paul Léautaud, *Journal littéraire*, t. 3, November 6, 1940, 211.

2 Paul Léautaud, ibid., November 22, 1940, 223–224.

3 Letter from Paulhan to Arland [November 1940], in Jean Paulhan, *Choix de lettres*, t. 2, *1937–1945 Le Traité des jours sombres* (Paris: Gallimard, 1992) (163), 203.

4 This was expressed by authors as different as the Catholic novelist of the French Academy, the Hispanist writer and art critic close to the Popular Front, the young Christian poet, and the "organic" French Communist Party intellectual. François Mauriac, quoted by Jean Lacouture, *François Mauriac*, vol. 1, *Le Sondeur d'abîmes 1885–1933* (Paris: Seuil, 1980), 263; Jean Cassou, *Une vie pour la liberté* (Paris: Robert Laffont, 1981), 70; Pierre Emmanuel, in Alain Bosquet, *Pierre Emmanuel* (introduction) (Paris: Seghers, 1959, reprinted 1971), 15; André Wurmser, *Fidèlement vôtre: Soixante ans de vie politique et littéraire* (Paris: Grasset, 1979), 53.

5 On the routinization of charisma, see Max Weber, *Economy and Society*, trans. Ephraim Fischoff et al., t. 1 (New York: Bedminster Press, 1968), 246–254, and the application of this Weberian concept to literary history made by Rémy Ponton, "Programme esthétique et accumulation de capital symbolique: L'exemple du Parnasse," *Revue française de sociologie* 14 (1973): 202–220.

6 See Auguste Anglès, *André Gide et le premier groupe de* La Nouvelle Revue française, 3 vols. (Paris: Gallimard, 1978–1986).

7 See Pierre Assouline, *Gaston Gallimard: Un demi-siècle d'édition française* (Paris: Balland, 1984), abridged version trans. Harold J. Salemson as *Gaston Gallimard: A Half-Century of French Publishing* (San Diego: Harcourt Brace Jovanovich, 1988).

8 See the previously cited letter from Gaston Gallimard to Jacques Rivière, December 18, 1919, in Jacques Rivière and Gaston Gallimard, *Correspondance (1911–1924)* (Paris: Gallimard, 1994) (146), 160; see also Daniel Durosay, "La direction politique de Jacques Rivière à la 'Nouvelle Revue française' (1919–1925)," *Revue d'histoire littéraire de la France* (March–April 1977): 229, n. 6.

9 According to the anonymous author—who seems well informed—of "La faune de la collaboration," *La Pensée libre* 1 (February 1941): 79. On the rise in subscriptions under Paulhan's direction (1100 in 1926 and 950 between January and August 1927), see the previously cited letter from Jean Paulhan to André Gide [August 19, 1927], in Jean Paulhan and André Gide, *Correspondance (1918–1951)* (Paris: Gallimard, 1998) (54), 72.

10 Martyn Cornick, *The* Nouvelle Revue française *under Jean Paulhan 1925–1940* (Amsterdam: Rodopi, 1995), 12–14.

11 Lina Morino, La Nouvelle Revue française *dans l'histoire des Lettres (1908–1937)* (Paris, Gallimard, 1939), 26.

12 Letter from Jean Paulhan to Jean Schlumberger, July 1, 1935, quoted by Cornick, *The* Nouvelle Revue française, 38.

13 Quoted by Cornick, ibid., 41.

14 Pierre Drieu La Rochelle, "La véritable erreur des surréalistes," *La NRF*, August 1925, republished in *Sur les écrivains* (Paris: Gallimard, 1964, republished 1982), 45–49; André Rolland de Renéville, "Du temps que les surréalistes avaient raison," *La NRF* 265 (October 1, 1935): 612.

15 Jacques Rivière, "La Nouvelle Revue française," *La NRF* 69 (June 1, 1919): 10.

16 Letter from Paulhan to Jouhandeau, [April 1937], in Paulhan, *Choix de lettres*, t. 2 (7), 29.

17 Jean Paulhan, "Présentation de la *NRF* à Radio-37," quoted by Cornick, *The* Nouvelle Revue française, 37.

18 Letter from Jean Paulhan quoted by Frédéric Badré, *Paulhan le juste* (Paris: Grasset, 1996), 142.

19 Letter from Paulhan to Pierre Drieu La Rochelle, [October 1940], in Paulhan, *Choix de lettres*, t. 2 (153), 193. In 1934, he wrote to Ramuz that, as long as he directed it, *La NRF* would not be a "leftist review," "but rather—let's say with Gide: an extreme moderate" one; Badré, *Paulhan le juste*, 140.

20 This estimate was obtained from the analysis of the *NRF* subpopulation in my survey, which included a sample of seventy-seven active contributors in 1940, among which figured twenty-eight regular contributors (my observations are supported by the comparison of these two subsamples; see tables 1–5 in appendix 2 which present the same results for the latter, that is, the twenty-eight regular contributors). The inventory of contributors was chiefly based on the work of Claude Martin, La Nouvelle Revue française *de 1908 à 1943: Index des collaborateurs* (Lyon: Centre d'études gidiennes, Université Lyon II, 1981).

21 This observation would be accentuated if we accounted for the regular contributors to *La NRF* who were not included in our representative population for various reasons, such as Benjamin Crémieux and Brice Parain, both doctors ès Letters. [In France, this was the highest doctoral degree available in the humanities between 1808 and 1984–Trans.] (Parain was an ENS graduate), Robert Aron, *agrégé* in literature, Jacques Rivière, *licencié* in philosophy (but who failed the ENS entrance exam, as well as the philosophy agrégation), and so on.

22 *La NRF*, January 1, 1938, 132.

23 Robert Brasillach, "Vieilles Maisons, vieux Papiers," *Je suis partout*, January 14, 1938, quoted by Jeannine Kohn-Étiemble, *226 lettres inédites de Jean Paulhan: Contribution à l'étude du mouvement littéraire en France, 1933–1967* (Paris: Klincksieck, 1975), 156, n. 1.

24 Letters from Paulhan to René Daumal, April 11, 1938, in Paulhan, *Choix de lettres*, t. 2 (25), 48, and to René Étiemble, March 31, 1938, in Kohn-Étiemble, ibid., 156.

25 Letter from Paulhan to Gide, July 21, 1937, in Paulhan, ibid. (10), 33.

26 See Annie Cohen-Solal, *Sartre: A Life*, trans. Anna Cancogni (New York: Pantheon, 1987), 115–116.

27 Letter from Paulhan to René Daumal [April 1938], in Paulhan, *Choix*, t. 2 (28), 51.

28 Letter from Paulhan to Martin du Gard, [August] 13, [1938], in ibid. (34), 56; see also 456, n. 2.

29 Jean-Paul Sartre, "M. François Mauriac et la liberté," *La NRF*, February 1, 1939. Translated as "François Mauriac and Freedom" in *Literary and Philosophical Essays*, trans. Annette Michelson (New York: Criterion, 1955), 23.

30 Letter from Paulhan to Gide, April 2, [1940], in Paulhan, *Choix de lettres*, t. 2 (125), 161–162. On the refusal of Drieu La Rochelle, see especially the letter Paulhan sent him on May 23, 1939, ibid. (74), 98.

31 Letter from Paulhan to Schlumberger [autumn 1938], quoted by Cornick, *The* Nouvelle Revue française, 186. See also Cornick's analysis of this issue, 185–193.

32 The content of the article was developed in a letter from Jean Paulhan to Jean Grenier, [April 1940], in Paulhan, *Choix*, t. 2 (128), 167.

33 Jean Paulhan, "L'Espoir et le silence," *La NRF*, June 1, 1940; see also Paulhan, *Œuvres complètes*, t. 5 (Paris: Cercle du Livre précieux, 1970), 285–286.

34 See Jean Grenier, *Sous l'Occupation* (Paris: Éditions Claire Paulhan, 1997), 36.

35 Letter from Paulhan to Arland, October 20, [1939], in Paulhan, *Choix*, t. 2 (97), 125.

36 Letter from Paulhan to Petitjean, October 20, [1939], in ibid., 127.

37 Jean Paulhan, "Il ne faut pas compter sur nous," *La NRF*, December 1, 1939; see also *OC*, t. 5, 272–273.

38 Jean Paulhan, "Du pacifisme absolu," *La NRF* 304 (January 1, 1939): 167.

39 Letter from Paulhan to Petitjean, February 4, [1940], in Paulhan, *Choix*, t. 2 (118), 153.

40 Letter from Paulhan to Grenier, [April 1940], in ibid. (128), 166.

41 Letter from Paulhan to Schlumberger [August 20, 1940], in ibid. (144), 184.

42 See the letters from Drieu La Rochelle to Paulhan, February 10, 1940, and May 1, 1940, Jean Paulhan collection, IMEC.

43 Letter from Paulhan to Drieu La Rochelle, May 22, 1940, in Jean Paulhan, *Choix*, t. 2 (130), 169–170.

44 Quoted by Pierre Andreu and Frédéric Grover, *Drieu La Rochelle* (Paris: Hachette, 1979), 171, and further for the relationship between Aragon and Drieu.

45 Letter from Drieu La Rochelle to Paulhan, August 1925, in Pierre Drieu La Rochelle, *Textes retrouvés* (Monaco: Éditions du Rocher, 1992), 80.

46 Pierre Drieu La Rochelle, *Journal 1939–1945* (Paris: Gallimard, 1992), 381.

47 *Aragon parle avec Dominique Arban* (Paris: Seghers, 1968), 103; Drieu's phrase was quoted from Dominique Desanti, *Drieu La Rochelle: Le séducteur mystifié* (Paris: Flammarion, 1978), 17.

48 Letter from Drieu La Rochelle to Paulhan, 1931, in Drieu La Rochelle, *Textes retrouvés*, 84.

49 Drieu La Rochelle, *Journal*, 483.

50 Aragon, who witnessed this anger, related the episode in *Aragon parle*, 105.

51 Frédéric Lefèvre, "Une heure avec Pierre Drieu La Rochelle," *Les Nouvelles littéraires*, January 2, 1926.

52 Quoted in Andreu and Grover, *Drieu La Rochelle*, 191.

53 Ibid., 386.

54 Drieu La Rochelle, *Journal*, September 18 and January 3, 1940, 82 and 137.

55 Ibid., June 21, 1940, 246. Note that this phrase was written two months before Abetz offered him the direction of the new NRF.

56 Aragon, "Le Temps traversé," *Les Lettres françaises*, October 16, 1968, reprised in Louis Aragon, Jean Paulhan, and Elsa Triolet, *"Le Temps traversé": Correspondance 1920–1964* (Paris: Gallimard, 1994), 212.

57 See Philippe Olivera, "Le sens du jeu: Aragon entre littérature et politique (1958–1968)," *Actes de la recherche en sciences sociales* 111–112 (March 1996): 76–85.

58 Max Weber, "La sociologie compréhensive," *Essais sur la théorie des sciences* (Paris: Plon, 1965, republished 1992), 326.

59 Aragon, "Le Temps traversé," in Aragon, Paulhan, and Triolet, *"Le Temps traversé,"* 213.

60 Aragon, ibid., 214.

61 Letter from Paulhan to Aragon, [September] 7, [1939], ibid. (17), 49–50.

62 Letter from Paulhan to Elsa Triolet, March 26, 1939, ibid. (12), 44.

63 Pierre Seghers, *La Résistance et ses poètes: France 1940–1945* (Paris: Seghers, 1974), 119. "La rime en 40" was published in *Poètes casqués* 3 (April 20, 1940).

64 A first version of *Fleurs de Tarbes, ou La Terreur dans les lettres*, which was published in 1941 in the "Métamorphoses" series, had been published in *La NRF* from June to October 1936. Aragon was moreover aware, since his meeting with Paulhan in 1917, of the work that the latter was doing on proverbs. It fueled Aragon's reflections on rhyme that "associates words in an indestructible manner." Aragon, "Sur une définition de la poésie," *Poésie 41*, May–June 1941, reprised in Aragon, *L'Œuvre Poétique (OP)*, t. 9 (Paris: Livre Club Diderot, 1979), 315.

65 See the letters from Paulhan to Jean Blanzat, November 13, 1939, to Jules Supervielle, November 15, [1939], to Claude Gallimard, November 27, [1939], to Roger Caillois, November 25, 1939, in Paulhan, *Choix*, t. 2 (101, 102, 105, 106), 131–137.

66 Aragon, "Le Temps traversé," 215; "Les lilas et les roses" was published in *Le Figaro* on September 21, 1940, then in a corrected version on September 28.

67 Testimony of Elsa Triolet and Aragon for the Comité d'histoire de la Deuxième Guerre mondiale (CHDGM), dated October 2, 1949; January 4, 1950; and June 16, 1950; 3 (AN: AJ 72 45). See also *Aragon parle*, 137–138.

68 Letter from Paulhan to Petitjean, [October 1940], in Paulhan, *Choix,* t. 2 (151), 192, and 481, n. 3.

69 Text housed in the Gallimard publishing archives, quoted by Pierre Hebey, La NRF *des années sombres (juin 1940–juin 1941): Des intellectuels à la dérive* (Paris: Gallimard, 1992), 145.

70 Letters from Mauriac to Drieu La Rochelle, December 11 and 30, 1940, in François Mauriac, *Lettres d'une vie (1904–1969)* (Paris: Grasset, 1981) (234 and 235), 245.

71 Jean Guéhenno, *Journal des années noires* (Paris: Gallimard, 1947), 62.

72 Jacques Chardonne, "L'Été à la Maurie," *La NRF* 322 (December 1, 1940): 11 and 16. In reference to this tableau that "displeased readers," Chardonne criticized those readers' "prejudices" about Germans, whom even the most "independent" among them, "former friends of this review, where there was no consideration for stereotypes," "still

view […] following the tradition of their fathers"; Jacques Chardonne, "Voir la figure," *La NRF* 328 (June 1, 1941): 852–853.

73 See, for example, the articles by Alfred Fabre-Luce, "Lettre à un Américain," *La NRF* 322 (December 1, 1940): 67, and Drieu La Rochelle, "Le Fait," *La NRF* 328 (June 1, 1941): 855–859.

74 André Gide, "Feuillets," *La NRF* 322 (December 1, 1940): 85.

75 André Gide, "Feuillets," *La NRF* 324 (February 1, 1941): 343–344.

76 Henry de Montherlant, "Paternité et patrie," *La NRF* 326 (April 1, 1941): 610 and 611.

77 "All the good French writers have shown a political conviction, from the Middle Ages to our time," he wrote to Paulhan in his letter of resignation, May 1, 1940, Jean Paulhan collection, IMEC.

78 Henry de Montherlant, "La paix dans la guerre," *La NRF* 331 (September 1, 1941): 260 and 259.

79 Armand Robin, "Domaine terrestre," *La NRF* 323 (January 1, 1941): 208–209.

80 AN: F21 8125. He would also be criticized for having participated in the second Congress of Writers in Weimar in 1942, and for having signed a manifesto published in *Le Cri du peuple* following the bombing of the Renault factories in 1942 (he would say that this signature was applied without his knowledge). Thérive would nonetheless be charged, expelled from the Société des gens de lettres, and given the maximum professional sentence by the Comité d'épuration des gens de lettres: the totality of temporary bans lasting eighteen months.

81 Pierre Drieu La Rochelle, "Bilan," *La NRF* 347 (January 1, 1943): 104.

82 Quoted by Montherlant, "La paix dans la guerre," 262. It is clear that, of this article, republished in *Le Solstice de juin*, Montherlant only retained four pages (thus making the reference to Hitler disappear) in the reeditions of *Le Solstice*, in 1963 in the volume of essays published in the "Bibliothèque de la Pléiade," and in 1976 when he joined *L'Équinoxe de septembre* with *Le Solstice de juin*, followed by a "memoir" on his attitude under the Occupation.

83 Guéhenno, *Journal des années noires*, January 10, 1941, 73.

84 Drieu La Rochelle, *Journal*, 305.

85 Drieu La Rochelle, "Bilan," 104.

86 According to the comments Fernandez himself made to Jean Grenier, *Sous l'Occupation*, 189.

87 To Jean Grenier, Parain said that "he wishes that *La NRF* could not reappear. But his situation is delicate because he is Gallimard's secretary." Ibid., 172. After having submitted a short review for the first issue, Parain would abstain from contributing to the review.

88 André Gide, "Chardonne 40," *Le Figaro*, April 12, 1941. On the seduction that Drieu's *NRF* first exerted over Gide, see Maria van Rysselberghe, *Les Cahiers de la Petite Dame 1937–1945: Notes pour l'histoire authentique d'André Gide*, t. 3, *Cahiers André Gide*, no. 6 (Paris: Gallimard, 1976), 223.

89 André Blavier, "Chronologie de Raymond Queneau," *Europe* 650–651 (June–July 1983): 137.

90 Letter from Raymond Queneau to Jean Paulhan, November 10, 1940, in Raymond Queneau, *Lettres à Jean Paulhan* (Levallois-Perret: Les Cahiers Raymond Queneau, 1986), 39.

91 Letter from Jean Paulhan to Pierre Drieu La Rochelle [November 1940], in Paulhan, *Choix*, t. 2 (154), 194 and 482, n. 1. The "follow-up" referred to *Les Voyageurs de l'impériale*, which Aragon then agreed to submit to Drieu's NRF.

92 Letter from Jean Paulhan to Paul Eluard, in Paulhan, ibid. (258), 299–300.

93 Included on the blacklist of the CNE at the Liberation, Petitjean would in fact need to have it out with Paulhan, whose support he sought. In a letter dated November 16, 1944 (Jean Paulhan collection, IMEC), Petitjean wrote to him: "Yes, I should have asked for your advice before writing for Drieu's NRF. It wouldn't have changed anything. But I owed it to your friendship. I ask for your forgiveness." Paulhan would nonetheless intervene in his favor with the Commission d'épuration des gens de lettres—his case would be dismissed (AN: F21 Épuration 25)—and would ask the CNE, in the autumn of 1946, to remove Petitjean from the blacklist (see his letter to Jean Schlumberger, September 12, 1946, Jean Schlumberger collection, Jacques Doucet archives; see also chapter 8).

94 Armand Petitjean, *Combats préliminaires* (Paris, Gallimard, 1941), 19 passim. See also Délégation régionale de la jeunesse en Algérie, "Inventaire de la France," paper given at the École des cadres d'Algérie, April 21, 1942, by Mr. Armand Petitjean (Alger: Imp. La Typo-Litho and Jules Larborel), 17 and 12.

95 Letter from Paulhan to Drieu La Rochelle, [September 1941], in Paulhan, *Choix*, t. 2 (195), 235, and Drieu La Rochelle's response, September 15, 1941, Jean Paulhan collection, IMEC.

96 Armand Petitjean, "De 1938 à 1945: Un parcours singulier," *Esprit* 214 (August–September 1995): 222.

97 See Armand Petitjean, "L'Appel de l'histoire," *Idées* 12 (October 1942): 20, and "France-Allemagne 42," *La NRF* 342 (August 1, 1942): 129–148.

98 See Denis Peschanski, *Vichy 1940–1944: Archives de guerre d'Angelo Tasca* (Milan/Paris: Feltrinelli-CNRS, 1986).

99 Versus a bit more than half, and a quarter, respectively, before the war, for a sample of seventy-seven contributors (both regular and occasional; see above). The writers over fifty-three now represented only 22 percent of the total number of contributors to Drieu's review—inventoried based on a tally of *La NRF* from 1940 to 1943—that is to say, two times less than in the old NRF.

100 Marcel Jouhandeau, "Comment je suis devenu antisémite," *L'Action française*, October 8, 1936, republished in *Le Péril juif* (Sorlot, s.d. [1937]), 10. Quoted by Hebey, La NRF *des années sombres*, 351.

101 See Lucien Combelle, *Péché d'orgueil* (Paris: Olivier Orban, 1978), and the interview that Combelle granted David Pryce-Jones, *Paris in the Third Reich: A History of the German Occupation, 1940–1944* (London: Collins St James Place, 1981), 222–224.

102 On the ideological justification that *La NRF* brought the politics of collaboration through the defense of Fascism and "European" construction, see Lionel Richard,

"Drieu La Rochelle et *La Nouvelle revue française* des années noires," *Revue d'histoire de la Deuxième Guerre mondiale* 97 (January 1975): 67–84.

103 Letter from Drieu La Rochelle to Mauriac, December 23, 1940, in Drieu La Rochelle, *Textes retrouvés*, 106, and Mauriac's response, December 30, 1940, in Mauriac, *Lettres d'une vie* (235), 246. Confronted with strong reactions, Chardonne would have to make a clarification in "Voir la figure," *La NRF* 328 (June 1, 1941): 852–854. A number of those reactions, including those of Paulhan, Guéhenno, and Maurice Garçon, are known, and agree in finding him "abject." See Guéhenno, *Journal*, 62; letters from J. Paulhan to Franz Hellens and to Jouhandeau, Paulhan, *Choix*, t. 2 (168 and 169), 209; M. Garçon's comments were reported by Paul Léautaud, *Journal littéraire*, t. 3, 242. In reference to Drieu's article, Lucien Combelle told Paul Léautaud that the review had received tons of letters from former subscribers, "furious about Drieu la Rochelle's article" (Léautaud, *Journal littéraire*, 310). On Fabre-Luce's article, see Grenier, *Sous l'Occupation*, 109.

104 Pierre Drieu La Rochelle, "Le corps," *La NRF* 324 (February 1, 1941): 353.

105 Drieu La Rochelle, "Bilan," 105.

106 Pierre Seghers, "De *P.C. 39* à *Poésie 44*," *Poésie 44* 20 (July–October 1944): 5–6.

107 Letter from Drieu La Rochelle to Paulhan [1943], Jean Paulhan collection, IMEC.

108 The data concerning Drieu's NRF (see Tables 1–5 in appendix 2) were generated based on a population of forty authors who published in the review between 1940 and 1944, with no distinction made between the regular and occasional contributors that I differentiated in the qualitative analysis. I should mention that thirteen of the forty are not part of our total population of 185 writers who were active in 1940, and they were taken into account solely for the needs of this specific analysis of Drieu's NRF. The comparison with the old NRF was established on the basis of estimates I made based on twenty-eight regular contributors and forty-nine irregular contributors to the prewar review, for a total of seventy-seven (see supra). To ensure the validity of the comparison, in this instance I present figures concerning the totality of this population and not merely the regular contributors to the review. Let me note, however, that since the variations between the subpopulation of regular contributors and the totality of contributors are rather significant, the differences that I analyze are often increased, even doubled, if we compare the recruitment of Drieu's NRF with the first subpopulation, as the figures included in the table show.

109 See Jean Bouhier's introduction to the anthology *Les Poètes de l'École de Rochefort* (Paris: Seghers, 1983), 13–14.

110 See Herbert Lottman, *The Purge* (New York: William Morrow, 1986), 168. The French translation, *L'Épuration*, trad. Béatrice Vierne (Paris: Fayard, 1986), includes additional commentary on 294 and 418.

111 Letter from Paulhan to Supervielle, [1940], in Paulhan, *Choix de lettres*, t. 2 (148), 189.

112 Jean Lescure, *Poésie et liberté: Histoire de Messages* (Paris: IMEC, 1998), 115.

113 Eugène Guillevic and Raymond Jean, *Choses parlées: Entretiens* (Seyssel: Champ Vallon, 1982), 42.

114 Eugène Guillevic, *Avec Jean Follain* (Pully: PAP, 1993), 15.

115 See André Dhôtel, *Jean Follain* (Paris: Seghers, 1956, republished 1993).

116 Lescure, *Poésie et liberté*, 70; Jean Follain, *Agendas 1926–1971* (Paris: Seghers, 1993).

117 Rolland de Renéville, "L'activité poétique," *La NRF* 336 (February 1, 1942): 221.

118 Drieu La Rochelle, "Bilan," 103–104. Similarly, in an article that he devoted to young poets and in which he offered his reflections on the Celtic inspiration that he related to Nordic influence in reference to Armand Robin, Eugène Guillevic, and Jean Follain, Drieu did not cite any of those poets, although they were also from the West. See Drieu La Rochelle, "Notes vraiment peu politiques," *La NRF* 342 (August 1, 1942): 233–237.

119 Georges-Emmanuel Clancier, "Max-Pol Fouchet et les poètes de la revue *Fontaine*," in *La Littérature française sous l'Occupation*, 156.

120 Seghers, *La Résistance et ses poètes*, 260.

121 Letters from Jean Paulhan to Joë Bousquet, October 7, 1941, and to Roger Caillois, Christmas 1941, quoted by Alain Paire, "1941: Le journal de bord des *Cahiers du sud*," *La Revue des revues* 16 (1993): 90 and 91. See also Alain Paire, *Chronique des Cahiers du Sud 1914–1966* (Paris: IMEC, 1993), 294.

122 Max-Pol Fouchet, *Un jour je m'en souviens . . . Mémoire parlée* (Paris: Mercure de France, 1968), 121. See also Clancier, "Max-Pol Fouchet," 154–155.

123 Letters from Max-Pol Fouchet to Louis Parrot, February 12, 1941, in Lucien Scheler, *La Grande Espérance des poètes (1940–1945)* (Paris: Temps actuels, 1982), 56.

124 Fouchet, *Un jour*, 124.

125 Yves Ménager, "Les périodiques littéraires et la Résistance intellectuelle en France de 1940 à 1944," *Autour de la Seconde Guerre mondiale: Résistance, témoignages, fictions*, special issue, *L'École des Lettres* 2 (July 1991): 110.

126 See Pierre Seghers, *Pierre Seghers*, "Poètes d'aujourd'hui" (Paris: Seghers, 1967, re-published 1973), 9–28.

127 Thibault La Rochette de Rochegonde, *Poésie 40 . . . -44: Une revue littéraire contre Vichy* (MA thesis, Université Paris I, 1996), 30.

128 Pierre Daix, *Aragon, une vie à changer* (Paris: Seuil, 1975, updated edition by Flammarion, 1994), 382.

129 Account by René Tavernier, in Jacques Debû-Bridel, *La Résistance intellectuelle* (Paris: Julliard, 1970), 91.

130 André Gide, *Découvrons Henri Michaux* (Paris: Gallimard, 1941). On the conference that Gide decided to cancel after having received a letter signed by a group from the Legion, see van Rysselberghe, *Les Cahiers de la Petite Dame 1937–1945*, t. 3, 245–247.

131 See Colette Seghers, *Pierre Seghers: Un homme couvert de noms* (Paris: Robert Laffont, 1981), 113.

132 [Pierre Seghers], "Signaux et courrier," *Poésie 41* 6 (November–December 1941): 80.

133 [Pierre Seghers], "Signaux de Paris," *Poésie 41* 7 (December 1941–January 1942): 76.

134 See the critique of this issue by Gaston Baissette, "Sur le numéro spécial de *Fontaine* 'De la poésie comme exercice spirituel,'" *Poésie 42* 10 (July–August–September 1942): 62–65, and the article by Pierre Emmanuel, "D'une poésie armée," ibid., 59–61.

135 "*Confluences* instantly ranks at the level of the great reviews," Seghers wrote when it first appeared, in "Signaux et courrier," *Poésie 41* 5 (August–September 1941): 92. Note that in the first issue of *Confluences*, Marc Barbezat had praised *Fontaine* and *Poésie 41* (see 113–116), and that its second issue included poems by Seghers. *Poésie*

would continue to review it warmly, but without indulgence, as the review established itself.

136 Elsa Triolet, handwritten notes for a contribution to the history of the CNE, n.d., FETA.

137 Fouchet, *Un jour*, 54.

138 On "Jeune France," see Véronique Chabrol, "L'ambition de 'Jeune France,'" in Jean-Pierre Rioux (ed.), *La Vie culturelle sous Vichy* (Brussels: Éditions Complexe, 1990), 161–178, and Christian Faure, *Le Projet culturel de Vichy: Folklore et révolution nationale, 1940–1944* (Paris: Éditions du CNRS/Presses universitaires de Lyon, 1989), 57–65.

139 "Options et positions," *Confluences* 1 (July 1941): 1–2.

140 See Philippe Prudent, *Une revue culturelle dans les années noires: Confluences (1941–1944)* (MA thesis, Université Lyon II, 1994), 54 and 72.

141 Charles Boucaud, "Les revues," *Confluences* 1 (July 1941): 105 and 103; L. G. July 1941, 105 and 103; L. G. "Les livres," ibid., 79–82.

142 Max Fortuit, "Le mythe moderne," *Confluences* 4 (October 1941): 446–453, and René Tavernier, "Paroles aux Français," "Les livres," ibid. 6 (December 1941): 802–803.

143 René Tavernier, "Une expérience littéraire entre 1941 et 1944: *Confluences*," in *La Littérature française sous l'Occupation*, 132–133.

144 Yves Courrière, *Roger Vailland ou Un libertin au regard froid* (Paris: Plon, 1991), 259.

145 "Seek out new ones, above all; form them," he noted in his journal after the defeat, while he was drawing up an assessment of his enemies and those he wanted a closer relationship with (Céline, Giono, and Malraux); Drieu La Rochelle, *Journal*, 246.

146 According to the account of René Tavernier, "Quand Claudel rencontrait Aragon (Lyon 1944)," *Bulletin de la Société Paul Claudel* 119 (3rd trimester, 1990): 4.

147 Aragon, "Le vent d'Arles," *OP*, t. 7, 460.

148 André Gide, *Journals*, trans. Justin O'Brien, vol. 4, *1939–1949* (Urbana: University of Illinois Press, 2000), 78.

149 Daix, *Aragon, une vie à changer*, 368.

150 Vladimir Pozner, *Vladimir Pozner se souvient* (Paris: Julliard, 1972), 248.

151 Aragon, "La rime en 40," *P[oètes] C[asqués] 40* 3 (April 20, 1940), republished in Aragon, *OP*, t. 9, 164.

152 He also legitimated the use, traditionally forbidden, of hiatus, treated as a dipthong; ibid., 167.

153 Aragon, "Arma virumque cano," *Les Yeux d'Elsa* (Neuchâtel: La Baconnière, 1942), *OP*, t. 9, 174.

154 Aragon, *Pour expliquer ce que j'étais* [posthumous)](Paris: Gallimard, 1989), 62–63.

155 Aragon, "Arma virumque cano," *OP*, t. 9, 191.

156 *Aragon parle avec Dominique Arban*, 132.

157 Aragon, "Beautés de la guerre et leurs reflets dans la littérature," *Europe* 156 (December 15, 1935); *OP*, t. 6, 426–427, and 432 for the Barbusse quote.

158 The beginning of Brecht's text published in *Commune* 32 (April 1936) was quoted by Aragon in "Rolland et Brecht: Pour ne pas quitter avril," *OP*, t. 7, 95. On the late avowal of this inspiration and on Brecht's echo in the short stories that Aragon

wrote during the same period (collected in *Servitude et grandeur des Français*), see Renate Lance-Otterbein, "Jeanne, France, Harry et la guerre de 40," *Digraphe* 82/83 (autumn/winter 1997): 186. On the model that the Spanish poets constituted for Aragon, see Olivier Barbarant, *Aragon, la mémoire et l'excès* (Seyssel: Champ Vallon, 1997), 110–111.

159 Aragon, "La leçon de Ribérac ou l'Europe française," *Fontaine*, June 1941; republished in *OP*, t. 9, 308.

160 Jacques Gaucheron, *La Poésie, la Résistance: Du Front populaire à la Libération* (Paris: Les Éditeurs français réunis, 1979), 123.

161 Aragon, "Arma virumque cano," *OP*, t. 9, 180.

162 Aragon, "La leçon de Ribérac," *OP*, t. 9, 300, 294 and 309. Let us recall that the second volume in the anthology *L'Honneur des poètes*, published by the underground Éditions de Minuit, would significantly be entitled *Europe*.

163 Lionel Follet, *Aurélien: Le fantasme et l'Histoire* (Paris: Les Belles Lettres, 1988), 127.

164 Henry de Montherlant, "Les chevaleries," *La NRF* 323 (January 1, 1941): 157.

165 Aragon, "La leçon de Ribérac," *OP* 9, 298 and 306, n. 1. For the discourse of the National Revolution ideologues on women, see Francine Muel-Dreyfus, *Vichy and the Eternal Feminine*, trans. Kathleen A. Johnson (Durham, NC: Duke University Press, 2001).

166 Aragon, "Arma virumque cano," *OP* 9, 192.

167 Wolfgang Babilas, "'Contre la poésie pure': Lecture d'un poème poétologique d'Aragon," *Recherches Croisées Aragon/Triolet* 2 (1989): 233–252.

168 Aragon, "Arma virumque cano," *OP*, t. 9, 193–194.

169 Aragon, "La leçon de Ribérac," *OP*, t. 9, 298 and 307, n. 1.

170 "Signaux et courrier," *Poésie 41* 3 (February–March 1941): 68–71.

171 Henri Hell, "Sur la Nouvelle Revue française," *Fontaine* 14 (June 1941): 349.

172 Marc Barbezat, "Les revues," *Confluences* 1 (July 1941): 114.

173 Marc Beigbeder, "Les revues," *Confluences* 2 (August 1941): 247.

174 "Revues," *La NRF* 329 (July 1, 1941): 128. See also Michel Winock, *"Esprit": Des intellectuels dans la cité, 1930–1950*, revised and augmented edition (Paris: Seuil, 1996), 244–245. On Drieu La Rochelle's involvement in the circles that tried to form a single party during this time, see Pierre Drieu La Rochelle, *Fragment de mémoires, 1940–1941* (Paris: Gallimard, 1982), and the introduction by Robert O. Paxton, "Le parti unique et Pierre Drieu La Rochelle," ibid., 13–31.

175 "Revues," *La NRF* 329 (July 1, 1941): 128.

176 André Rolland de Renéville, "La poésie en 1941," *La NRF* 331 (September 1, 1941): 339.

177 Drieu La Rochelle, "Aragon," *La NRF* 332 (October 1, 1941): 483, 486 and 488.

178 Drieu La Rochelle, "Aragon," 485, n. 1. According to a letter from Drieu to Jean Paulhan dated October 17, 1941, in which he apologized for having forgotten to answer the letter Paulhan had sent him about Aragon's quotes, we might think that the objection came from Paulhan. See the Jean Paulhan collection, IMEC.

179 Daix, *Aragon, une vie à changer*, 385–386.

180 André Rolland de Renéville, "L'activité poétique," *La NRF* 336 (February 1, 1942): 221.

181 Maurice Chapelan, "*Tombeau d'Orphée* (éds. de Poésie 41) par Pierre Emmanuel," *La NRF* 338 (April 1, 1942): 488–489 and 490–491.

182 Pierre Drieu La Rochelle, "Pierre Emmanuel," *La NRF* 344 (October 1, 1942): 477 and 483.

183 Ibid., 471.

184 "Jean Paulhan was in contact with all the writers. He gave you news of André Verdet who struggled through long interrogations, as well as Jean Cayrol, the young poet from Bordeaux who spent long months in hiding," Claude Morgan would say. Quoted by Louis Parrot, *L'intelligence en guerre* (Paris: La Jeune Parque, 1945; Le Castor astral, 1990), 205.

185 This idea was only suggested at the end of his article "La démocratie fait appel au premier venu," *La NRF* 306 (March 1939), republished in Paulhan, *Œuvres complètes*, t. 5, 182. He would develop it mainly after the rise of the Vichy regime, among writers seduced by Fascism—in order to dissuade them with arguments that they could understand?—like Drieu. See, for example, the letters from Drieu [October 1940] and that of Rolland de Renéville [November 1940], in Paulhan, *Choix*, t. 2 (153, 154, 165), 193–194 and 205.

186 Divided, however, between a branch of ardent defenders of their faith, and a branch of "renegades" converted during the revocation of the Edict of Nantes; Paulhan had to justify himself to his lycée classmates in Nîmes who criticized his ancestry. See Christian Liger, *Histoire d'une famille nîmoise: Les Paulhan, Cahiers Jean Paulhan* 3 bis (Paris: Gallimard, 1984), 50 passim.

187 Pierre Vidal-Naquet, "Si Dieu le fit," *Esprit* 134 (January 1988): 7.

188 In 1912, Jean Paulhan had submitted two thesis topics at the Sorbonne, one on the "Semantics of the Proverb: Essay on the Variations of Malagasy Proverbs," under the direction of Lucien Lévy-Bruhl; the other, "Essay for a Linguistic Classification of Malagasy Proverbial Phrases," under the direction of Antoine Meillet. Interrupted in his research by the Great War, Paulhan would pursue his work assiduously after the end of hostilities, as his journal indicates. See Paulhan, *La Vie est pleine de choses redoutables: Textes autobiographiques* (Paris: Verdier, 1989, republished by Éditions Claire Paulhan, 1997), especially 198. If *Les Fleurs de Tarbes* is, in one sense, the culmination of his work, he would continue to work until the end of his life on the second part of this study, announced in 1943, which would remain unfinished.

189 Lescure, *Poésie et liberté*, 86.

190 According to a letter from Paulhan to Father Maydieu [August 11, 1946], quoted by Philippe Béguerie, *Jean-Augustin Maydieu* (Paris: Impr. Jouve, 1995) (819), 30. See also Jean Paulhan, "Une semaine de secret," *Le Figaro*, September 9, 1941, republished in *Écrivains en prison* (Paris: Seghers, 1945), 200–208, and the two letters from Paulhan to Drieu La Rochelle, May 20 and 22, 1941, in Paulhan, *Choix*, t. 2, (174 and 175), 214–215: "I really believe that it is thanks to you alone that I have returned to rue des Arènes tonight. So thank you" (214).

191 Letter from Paulhan to Drieu La Rochelle, [January 1942], in Paulhan, *Choix*, t. 2 (219), 262. *La NRF* would not publish any chapters from *Aminadab*.

192 Letter from Paulhan to Monique Saint-Hélier [December 22, 1941], in Jean Paulhan and Monique Saint-Hélier, *Correspondance (1941–1955)* (Paris: Gallimard, 1995) (24), 67.

193 See Philippe Mesnard, *Maurice Blanchot: Le sujet de l'engagement* (Paris: L'Harmattan, 1996), chapter 1, and Anne Simonin's review of this work, "Maurice Blanchot tel qu'on peut l'imaginer," *Art press* 218 (November 1996): 61–64.

194 Drieu La Rochelle, *Journal*, April 5, 1942, 292.

195 Jean Paulhan, "Les Fleurs de Tarbes," *Comoedia* 9 (August 16, 1941), and "Un primitif du roman, Duranty," ibid. 34 (February 14, 1942).

196 Letter from Rolland de Renéville to Paulhan, August 21, 1941, Jean Paulhan collection, IMEC.

197 Letter from Paulhan to Mauriac, [August 28, 1943], in Paulhan, *Choix*, t. 2 (286), 333.

198 See the letters from Paulhan to Monique Saint-Hélier [March 1942], in Paulhan and Saint-Hélier, *Correspondance* (53), 131, to Jean Guéhenno [March 11, 1942], to Paul Valéry, March 11, [1942], in Paulhan, *Choix*, t. 2 (223 and 224), 265–267.

199 "The Germans are afraid that the shop will close. This would be a new failure of the polit[ics] of collabor[ation] and my personal failure"; Drieu La Rochelle, *Journal*, April 5, 1942, 291.

200 Draft of a response by Jean Schlumberger (March 19, 1942) to the letter from Jean Paulhan dated March 11, 1942, Jean Schlumberger collection, Jacques Doucet archives.

201 See Gerhard Heller, *Un Allemand à Paris: 1940–1944* (Paris: Seuil, 1981), 96.

202 See the letter from Paulhan to Gide, March 15, 1942, in Jean Paulhan and André Gide, *Correspondance (1918–1951)* (Paris: Gallimard, 1998) (254), 258.

203 Letter from Duhamel to Paulhan, March 19, 1942, Jean Paulhan collection, IMEC.

204 Letters from André Gide to Jean Paulhan, March 16, 17, and 19, 1942, in Paulhan and Gide, *Correspondance* (255, 256 and 257), 260–262.

205 Letter from Paulhan to Drieu La Rochelle [April 17, 1942], in Paulhan, *Choix*, t. 2 (235), 276.

206 Letter from Paulhan to Valéry [April 16, 1942], in ibid. (234), 276.

207 Letter from Valéry to Gide, April 28, 1942, in André Gide and Paul Valéry, *Self Portraits: The Gide/Valéry Letters, 1890–1942*, trans. June Guicharnaud (Chicago: University of Chicago Press, 1966), 325.

208 Letter from Schlumberger to Mauriac, May 25, 1942, François Mauriac collection, Jacques Doucet archives.

209 Letter from Paulhan to Pourrat, [May] 27, [1943], in Paulhan, *Choix*, t. 2 (266), 306.

210 Aliette Armel, *Michel Leiris* (Paris: Fayard, 1997), 427.

211 Drieu La Rochelle, *Journal*, 269 and 316–317.

212 Pierre Drieu La Rochelle, "Pierre Emmanuel," *La NRF* 344 (October 1, 1942): 471 and n. 1.

213 "Mme Rousseaux brought back the first articles, and established for the following ones the relay of La Rochefoucauld where she had passed through, on a farm including land on both sides of the demarcation line," André Rousseaux continued. Account for the CHDGM, AN: 72 AJ 78.

214 Lescure, *Poésie et liberté*, 99.

215 Lescure, ibid., 87, and interview with Jean Lescure, June 26, 1996.

216 Interview with Jean Lescure, October 25, 1995.

217 Ibid.

218 Marcel Raymond, *From Baudelaire to Surrealism*, trans. G. M. (New York: Wittenborn Schultz, 1949), 5.

219 Jean Lescure, "Présentation," *Messages* 1 (1939): 3.

220 Quoted by Armel, *Michel Leiris*, 400. On Marcel Moré, see ibid., 366–367. This attempt to reconstitute the Collège de Sociologie was doomed to fail following the "violent fights between Pelorson, Queneau-Benda and Gide-Wahl," according to Jean Paulhan. See his letter to Roger Caillois, May 25, 1940, in Paulhan, *Choix*, t. 2 (133), 173.

221 Raymond Queneau, "Technique du roman," *Volontés* 1: 50–53. On Queneau's traditionalism, see Emmanuel Souchier, *Raymond Queneau* (Paris: Seuil, 1991), 28–30.

222 See Michel Leiris, *Journal, 1922–1989* (Paris: Gallimard, 1992), January 31, 1941, 335, and the letter sent by Georges Pelorson that told him of Queneau's agreement, 891, n. 5.

223 Comments reported by Leiris, ibid., February 16, 1941, 337.

224 See Michel Surya, *Georges Bataille: An Intellectual Biography*, trans. Krzysztof Fijalkowski and Michael Richardson (London: Verso, 2002), 316.

225 Interzonal card from Pierre Emmanuel to Jean Lescure, January 11, 1942, quoted by Lescure, *Poésie et liberté*, 86.

226 See the letter from Eugène Guillevic to Jean Lescure, quoted by Lescure, ibid., 115.

227 Lescure, ibid., 129.

228 Interview with Jean Lescure, October 25, 1995.

229 "Éléments," signed "les Cahiers," *Messages* 1 (March 1942): 1.

230 Lescure, *Poésie et liberté*, 119.

231 "Couleur du Temps," *Messages* 1 (March 1942): 90 and 91.

232 Letter from Jean Paulhan to Jean Lescure, quoted by Lescure, *Poésie et liberté*, 152.

233 Lescure, ibid., 158.

234 See Michel Fauré, *Histoire du surréalisme sous l'Occupation* (Paris: La Table Ronde, 1982), 159–164, and Anne Simonin, *Les Éditions de Minuit 1942–1955: Le devoir d'insoumission* (Paris: IMEC, 1994), 90–91.

235 Letter from Jean Paulhan to Jean Lescure, [December 42 or January 43], quoted by Lescure, *Poésie et liberté*, 160.

236 Armel, *Michel Leiris*, 396 and n. 5.

237 Lescure, *Poésie et liberté*, 185.

238 Anna Boschetti, *The Intellectual Enterprise: Sartre and* Les Temps Modernes, trans. Richard C. McCleary (Evanston, IL: Northwestern University Press, 1988).

239 See Jean-Paul Sartre, "A New Mystic," in *Critical Essays (Situations I)*, trans. Chris Turner (London: Seagull, 2010), 219–293; see 229 and 273 for the quotations.

240 Lescure, *Poésie et liberté*, 218–219.

241 See François Lachenal, *Éditions des Trois Collines: Genève-Paris* (Paris: IMEC, 1995), and Françoise Frey-Beguin (ed.), *Les Cahiers du Rhône: Refuge de la pensée libre* (La Chaux-de-Fonds: Éditions de la Baconnière, 1993), 49.

242 Pierre Seghers, "De *P.C. 39* à *Poésie 44*," *Poésie 44* 20 (July–October 1944): 5.

243 "We had to get around censorship, Swiss censorship first of all; it was extremely dif-
      ficult to found journals in Switzerland, whereas in order to import them to France,
      a periodical publication was, on the other hand, necessary." *Les Cahiers du Rhône*
      83; see also Olivier Cariguel, *Les Cahiers du Rhône dans la guerre 1941–1945* (Édi-
      tions de l'université de Fribourg, 1999).

244 Lescure, *Poésie et liberté*, 223.

245 Letter from Paul Claudel to Jean Lescure, quoted by Lescure, ibid., 242.

246 Ibid., 244 and 246.

247 Georges Meyzargues alias Aragon, "Un Prisonnier libéré: André Frénaud," *Poésie 42*
      10 (July–August–September 1942): 31. "André Frénaud is decidedly the revelation of
      this year's end," Seghers also wrote about the poems Frénaud published in *Fontaine* 24
      (October 1942), recalling that *Poésie 42* had already published his verses before in its
      fourth issue. See Pierre Seghers, "Les revues," *Poésie 43* 12 (January–February 1943).
      See also Georges-Emmanuel Clancier and Jean-Yves Debreuille, *André Frénaud*
      (Paris: Seghers, 1963), 12.

Chapter 7: The Sense of Subversion

1 See Christophe Prochasson, *Les Intellectuels, le socialisme et la guerre 1900–1938*
    (Paris: Seuil, 1993), 228–229.

2 Interview with Jean Lescure, October 25, 1995.

3 Rallying cry against oppression, the National Front was first of all a line of action,
    before becoming, in 1943, a resistance movement among others. See Daniel Virieux,
    *Le Front national de lutte pour la liberté et l'indépendance de la France: Un mouve-
    ment de Résistance—Période clandestine (mai 1941–août 1944)* (PhD diss., Paris
    VIII, Atelier de Lille, 1995).

4 The appeal of May 1941 is reproduced as an appendix in Stéphane Courtois, *Le PCF
    dans la guerre: De Gaulle, la Résistance, Staline* (Paris: Ramsay, 1980), 554–565; see
    also 189–192. Though it was the Communist International which rectified the
    wholesale strategy in the summer of 1940, illustrated by the negotiations with the
    occupant so that *L'Humanité* could reappear legally, Annie Kriegel has established
    that, at least from January 1941, Thorez played a "decisive role" with Dimitrov and
    Stalin to make them accept the principle of a national anti-Fascist resistance, de-
    spite the German-Soviet pact, even recognizing the "postive role" of de Gaulle's
    movement; see Annie Kriegel, "Le PCF, Thorez et la France," *Le Mouvement social*
    172 (July–September 1995): 99. On the evolution of PCF politics up to the call, see
    the first part of Virieux, *Le Front national*.

5 On the relations between these two great representatives of resistance legitimacy, the
    Communists and the Gaullists, see Pierre Nora, "Gaullistes et communistes," in Pierre
    Nora (ed.), *Realms of Memory: Rethinking the French Past*, vol. 1, *Conflicts and Divisions*
    (New York: Columbia University Press, 1996), 205–239. See also Henri Noguères,
    Marcel Degliame-Fouché, and Jean-Louis Vigier, *Histoire de la Résistance en France*, t.
    2, *L'armée de l'ombre: Juillet 1942–octobre 1942* (Paris: Robert Laffont, 1969), 52.

6 See Daniel Virieux, "Résistance-Professions. Un rapport sans histoire(s)?," in Antoine Prost (ed.), *La Résistance, une histoire sociale* (Paris: Éditions de l'Atelier, 1997), 116 passim. On the development of the armed branch, see Roger Bourderon, "Le PCF dans la lutte armée: conceptions et organisations," in *La Résistance et les Français: lutte armée et maquis*, colloque de Besançon, Annales littéraires de l'Université de Franche-Comté, 1996, 129–140.

7 Account by Pierre Villon in Jacques Debû-Bridel, *La Résistance intellectuelle* (Paris: Julliard, 1970), 248. See also Pierre Villon, *Résistant de la première heure*, interview with Claude Willard (Paris: Éditions sociales, 1983).

8 Jeanne Gaillard, who at that time was housing Solomon, denounced by Doriot, reported that Solomon "told [her] his plan to gather around *L'Université libre* [where he was editor in chief] all the patriotic intellectuals regardless of party or religious convictions, and he asked us to let him know about not only the reader, but also possible contributors in our lycées." Account by Jeanne Gaillard for the CHDGM, AN: 72 AJ 78.

9 "We had, actually, an organization that was completely ready to form committees of union, that is to say committees of the 'National Front': we had the Party that existed, that had its internal liaisons. It was enough, then, inside the C[ommunist] P[arty] to advance the idea that we had to assemble not only our comrades, but also gather non-Communists as it had asked in its May 13, 1941 appeal. The committes of the 'National Front' were to be propaganda centers to reinforce the wave of opposition against Pétain and of struggle against the occupying forces, and at the same time they were meant to help those that already existed and that formed the army of the 'National Front': the 'Francs-Tireurs and Partisans,'" Pierre Villon explained. Quoted by Noguères et al., *Histoire de la Résistance*, t. 2, 469.

10 See the account of Pierre Maucherat, head of production for the CHDGM (April 11, 1946), AN: 72 AJ 69.

11 On the evolution of the different intellectual committees, see Virieux, *Le Front national*; Anne Simonin, "Le Comité médical de la Résistance: Un succès différé," *Le Mouvement social* 180 (July–September 1997): 159–191; Olivier Barrot, *L'Écran français 1943–1953, histoire d'un journal et d'une époque* (Paris: EFR, 1979); Laurence Bertrand Dorléac, *Art of the Defeat: France 1940–1944*, trans. Jane Marie Todd (Los Angeles: Getty, 2008), 308–312.

12 Its origin was the call for a "sacred Union of Intellectuals in France," launched in mid-May 1943. The project of a French Union of Intellectuals was only abandoned in early 1944; see Virieux, *Le Front national*, 316, 416–421 and 589.

13 Account by Triolet and Aragon for the CHDGM, 8–9.

14 Interview with Jean Lescure, October 25, 1995. See also Simone de Beauvoir, *The Prime of Life*, trans. Peter Green (Cleveland, OH: World Publishing Company), 371–372: "[. . .] the German-Soviet pact, as far as I and many other people were concerned, had severely shaken our previous sympathy toward the U.S.S.R., and did not encourage us to place our trust in the Communist Party."

15 See Beauvoir, *The Prime of Life*, 396–397.

16 See Anne Simonin, *Les Éditions de Minuit 1942–1955: Le devoir d'insoumission* (Paris: IMEC, 1994), 71, which forms the basis of my analysis of the aborted project of openness of *La Pensée libre*.

17 The production network was supervised by the head of the PCF publishing house Jean Jérôme; see Roger Bourderon, "Politzer ou la passion des lumières," in *Politzer contre le nazisme*, clandestine texts presented by Roger Bourderon (Paris: Messidor/ Éditions sociales, 1984), 19. The distribution figure for the first issue, 1,625 copies, was established based on a handwritten sheet entitled "Diffusion from 25 June to 25 July 1942," signed "Denise," and dated July 27, 1942, MRN.

18 "Notre combat," *La Pensée libre* 1 (February 1941): 5.

19 "Après la mort de M. Bergson," *La Pensée libre* 1 (February 1941): 60 and 63.

20 In the Le Guyon network where he worked, it seems, with Fernand Holweck; see Simonin, *Les Éditions de Minuit*, 59–62 and 73. On the trajectory of Pierre Lescure, see ibid., 31.

21 Vercors, *The Battle of Silence*, trans. Rita Barisse (New York: Holt, Rinehart and Winston, 1968), 154. His account harmonizes with that of Jacques Debû-Bridel, *Les Éditions de Minuit: Historique* (Paris: Minuit, 1945), 18: "This is how, among others, we [Jacques Decour and he] decided to create *Les Lettres Françaises* to replace the discontinued review."

22 Debû-Bridel, ibid., 188: "[. . .] the collapse, starting with the second issue, of *La Pensée libre* was due to its thickness, which had required a material and printing personnel that exceeded security norms."

23 According to the sheet of July 27, 1942, 150 copies of this issue were distributed at that point, a figure increased to 200 according to a sheet from August 1942, mentioned by Virieux, *Le Front national*, 182.

24 Aragon, "Les Années Sadoul," *Europe* 590–591 (June–July 1978): 186–187 (my emphasis).

25 Elsa Triolet, handwritten notes for a contribution to the history of the CNE, n.d., FETA.

26 "Un manifeste des intellectuels de la zone non-occupée," *L'Université libre*, special issue (September–October 1941).

27 Notes by Georges Cogniot, reproduced by Virieux, *Le Front national*, vol. 5, 1642–1643.

28 "Les Allemands et les intellectuels de France," *Les Étoiles* 3 (March 1, 1943). Jean Ristat remembered that Aragon often spoke to him with indignation about this "Bergson affair." Aragon, *OP* 10 (Paris: Livre Club Diderot, 1979), 406, n. 33.

29 Aragon, "De l'exactitude historique en poésie," *OP* 10, 67.

30 "If need be, how do we lie to tell the truth?" It was in these terms that Aragon would evoke in *L'Œuvre poétique*, in reference to Brecht's 1936 article, the practice of "contraband" as a ruse to tell the truth; "Rolland et Brecht," *OP* 7, 97.

31 Aragon, "De l'exactitude historique en poésie," *OP* 10, 67. On the "epic sense" as a "national sense," see especially "Les poissons noirs ou de la réalité en poésie," introduction to the new edition of *Musée Grévin* (Minuit: 1946), *OP* 10, 152.

32 See the letter from Aragon to Albert Béguin, June 23, [1942], in Corinne Grenouillet, "Celui qui croyait au ciel et celui qui n'y croyait pas," *Recherches croisées Aragon/
Triolet* 4 (1992): 271.

33 Aragon, "La conjonction ET," *Les Cahiers du Rhône* 5, "Controverse sur le génie de
la France" (November 1942), *OP* 10, 37–52.

34 See Michel Apel-Muller, "L'édition de 1942 des *Voyageurs de l'impériale*: Une entreprise 'diabolique,'" *Recherches croisées Aragon/Elsa Triolet* 1 (1988): 167–208, and
Pierre Assouline, *Gaston Gallimard: Un demi-siècle d'édition française* (Paris: Balland, 1984), abridged version trans. Harold J. Salemson as *Gaston Gallimard: A Half-
Century of French Publishing* (San Diego: Harcourt Brace Jovanovich, 1988), 372.

35 Investment here is part of the economy of symbolic goods that, in a universe
founded on the denial of the market economy, opposes the act of seeking specific
symbolic profits, such as the recognition of peers, to the act of seeking material
profits. On the concept of "investment," see especially Pierre Bourdieu, "Is a Disinterested Act Possible?," trans. Randal Johnson, *Practical Reason* (Stanford, CA:
Stanford University Press and Polity Press, 1998), 75–91.

36 Georges Politzer, "Autobiographie," written at the request of the executive commission on November 26, 1933, Russian Center for the Conservation and Study of Documents in Contemporary History (Moscow). Claude Pennetier and Bernard Pudal
kindly referred me to this document. See also Nicole Racine, "Georges Politzer," in
Jean Maitron and Claude Pennetier (eds.), *Dictionnaire biographique du mouvement
ouvrier français, 1914–1939*, t. 39 (Paris: Éditions ouvrières, 1981–1992), 95–100, and
Michel Trebitsch, "Le groupe 'Philosophies,' de Max Jacob aux Surréalistes (1924–
1925)," *Cahiers de l'IHTP*, "Générations intellectuelles" 6 (November 1987): 29–38.

37 Claude Pennetier and Bernard Pudal, "La certification scolaire communiste dans les
années trente," *Politix* 35 (1996): 74.

38 Bourderon, "Politzer ou la passion des lumières," *Politzer contre le nazisme*, 11–31.

39 Virieux, *Le Front national*, 51.

40 Account by Jacques Debû-Bridel, in Henri Noguères, Marcel Degliame-Fouché,
and Jean-Louis Vigier, *Histoire de la Résistance en France*, t. 1, *La Première année:
Juin 1940–juin 1941* (Paris: Robert Laffont, 1967), 149 (my emphasis).

41 Jean Lescure, "Préface," in François Lachenal, *Éditions des Trois Collines* (Paris: IMEC,
1995), 12.

42 Jacques Debû-Bridel, "Naissance des 'Lettres françaises,'" *Les Lettres françaises* 20
(September 9, 1944; my emphasis).

43 Did the term seem indecent in the context of the struggle against the occupant?
Jacques Debû-Bridel (or Vercors?) would omit it from the version republished in
Les Éditions de Minuit, 17.

44 Debû-Bridel, *La Résistance intellectuelle*, 43 (my emphasis).

45 Édith Thomas, *Le Témoin compromis* (Paris: Viviane Hamy, 1995), 106.

46 Martin Blumenson, *The Vildé Affair: Beginnings of the French Resistance* (Boston:
Houghton Mifflin, 1977). See also Claude Aveline, "L'affaire du musée de l'Homme,"
Les Lettres françaises 44 (February 24, 1945).

47 Jean Paulhan, "Une semaine de secret," in *Écrivains en prison* (Paris: Seghers, 1945), 203.

48 Draft of a response to the questionnaire sent by Gerhard Heller to Jean Paulhan, April–May 1942, Paulhan collection, IMEC.

49 See Gerhard Heller, *Un Allemand à Paris: 1940–1944* (Paris: Seuil, 1981), 106. This is an affirmation that we can call into question based on the previously cited questionnaire, in which Heller questions Paulhan on his second arrest that, in reality, never took place (Paulhan having fled out the window), which would tend to relativize Heller's involvement in Paulhan's troubles with the Gestapo.

50 See Gérard Loiseaux, *La Littérature de la défaite et de la Collaboration, d'après "Phonix oder Asche?" de Bernhard Payr* (Paris: Publications de la Sorbonne, 1984; Fayard, 1995), 504.

51 Draft of a response to the questionnaire from Gerhard Heller, cited above.

52 Letter from Pierre Drieu La Rochelle to Jean Paulhan, September 15, 1941, Paulhan collection, IMEC: "I don't want to do anything for Wahl, who certainly does not *want* me to do anything for him."

53 According to Pierre Berger, Robert Desnos, imprisoned in Fresnes, was denounced as a "dangerous Communist" by the collaborationist journalist Alain Laubreaux who held onto an old grudge; we know what happened next, Desnos's deportation to Buchenwald and his death at Camp Dora; Pierre Berger, *Robert Desnos* (Paris: Seghers, 1949, republished 1970), 84–85.

54 Account by Jean Blanzat, May 8, 1946, CHDGM, AN: 72 AJ 45.

55 A. J. Maydieu, "L'appel des fusillés," in *Écrivains en prison*, 174. See also Édith Thomas, "Au Comité national des Écrivains (1941–1944)," in "Le père Maydieu," *La Vie intellectuelle* (August–September 1956): 67–70.

56 Account by Jean Guéhenno, in Debû-Bridel, *La Résistance intellectuelle*, 35.

57 François Mauriac, *Journal 1932–1939* (Paris: La Table Ronde, 1947), 294.

58 Letter from Mauriac to Blanche Duhamel, April 7, 1942, in Mauriac, *Nouvelles lettres d'une vie (1906–1970)* (Paris: Grasset, 1989) (231), 217.

59 See the letter from Blanzat to Paulhan [1945], Jean Paulhan collection, IMEC. See also Jean Bothorel, *Bernard Grasset: Vie et passions d'un éditeur* (Paris: Grasset, 1989), 400.

60 Letters from Paulhan to Blanzat, [April] 17, [1937], [September] 28, [1939], [November] 13, [1939], in Paulhan, *Choix*, t. 2, *1937–1945 Le Traité des jours sombres* (Paris: Gallimard, 1992) (4, 91, 101), 23, 117, 131.

61 Letter from Jean Blanzat to Jean Paulhan [1944], Jean Paulhan collection, IMEC.

62 According to the expression of Elsa Triolet in her handwritten notes for a history of the CNE.

63 See the letter from Georges Duhamel to Jean Paulhan, July 23, 1941, Jean Paulhan collection, IMEC, and the letter from Aragon to Paulhan, August 17, [1941], in Aragon, Paulhan, and Triolet, *"Le Temps traversé": Correspondance 1920–1964* (Paris: Gallimard, 1994) (72), 114–115 (he is definitely referring to Georges Duhamel here).

64 Comments reported by Claude Morgan, *Les Don Quichotte et les autres* (Paris: Roblot, 1979), 130.

65 According to Jacques Debû-Bridel's account in an interview with Annie Cohen-Solal, *Sartre: A Life*, trans. Anna Cancogni (New York: Pantheon, 1987), 177.

66 Debû-Bridel, "Naissance des 'Lettres françaises.'"

67 See Yves Courrière, *Roger Vailland ou Un libertin au regard froid* (Paris: Plon, 1991), 272.

68 See Pascal Mercier, *Le Comité national des écrivains 1941–1944* (MA thesis, Université de Paris III, 1980), 32.

69 On the double existence of social structures, simultaneously inscribed in things (institutions) and bodies (habitus), see Pierre Bourdieu, "Le mort saisit le vif," *Actes de la recherche en sciences sociales* 32/33 (April–June 1980): 4–14.

70 Morgan, *Les Don Quichotte*, 140. The author of the lampoon was, it seems, Jean Marcenac.

71 Cohen-Solal, *Sartre*, 177.

72 Anna Boschetti, *The Intellectual Enterprise: Sartre and* Les Temps Modernes, trans. Richard C. McCleary (Evanston, IL: Northwestern University Press, 1988), 75; see also 62–79.

73 Debû-Bridel, "Naissance des 'Lettres françaises.'"

74 Morgan, *Les Don Quichotte*, 131–132.

75 "Il y a trois ans au Mont-Valérien Jacques Decour," *Les Lettres françaises* 58 (June 2, 1945).

76 See the account by Pierre Villon in Debû-Bridel, *La Résistance intellectuelle*, 251–253, and Villon, *Résistant de première heure*, 63.

77 Debû-Bridel, "Naissance des 'Lettres françaises.'"

78 "'Nous sauverons l'honneur des Lettres françaises' proclaim the writers of the occupied zone," *La Pensée libre* 2 (February 1942): 3–4. The text is dated "February 1942."

79 "Sommaire du numéro préparé par Jacques Decour et qui fut détruit," the underground *Lettres françaises*, facsimile edition, 1947. Jean Blanzat had actually submitted a critique of Montherlant's *Le Solstice de juin* (account for the CHDGM).

80 Morgan, *Les Don Quichotte*, 132–33.

81 [Claude Morgan], "Haro sur Maupassant," *Les Lettres françaises* 2 (October 1942).

82 Letter from "François" [Georges Cogniot] to "Vidal," [Pierre Villon], November 23, 1942, Pierre Villon archives, MRN.

83 See Virieux, *Le Front national*, 217–222.

84 Handwritten letter from François (Georges Cogniot) to Vidal (Pierre Villon), December 30, 1942, Pierre Villon archives, MRN.

85 Morgan, *Les Don Quichotte*, 132 and 138.

86 Just as he tried to incite another conversion from the extreme right to Communism, that of Claude Roy, René Blech was surely instrumental in that of Morgan. See Claude Roy, *Moi je* (Paris: Gallimard, 1969 and 1978), 267–268.

87 [Claude Morgan], "Colette, la Bourgogne et M. Goebbels," *Les Lettres françaises* 4 (December 1942).

88 See Claude Morgan, "Vingt-trois mois d'action: Comment vécurent 'Les Lettres françaises,'" *Les Lettres françaises*, September 9, 1944.

89 Letter dated October 9 [1942], probably from Pierre Villon, handwritten notes by Georges Cogniot, quoted by Virieux, *Le Front national*, 276.

90 Encoded handwritten notes by Georges Cogniot on a letter from Vidal [Pierre Villon] to Fred [Jacques Duclos], December 23, 1942, Georges Cogniot archives, MRN, document decoded by Daniel Virieux.

91 "Notre ami Jacques Decour," by Paulhan, would not be published until June 1943, in *Les Lettres françaises* 7.

92 Personal handwritten notes by Georges Cogniot about a report on December 24, 1942, on the F.N. des intellectuels (by Villon?), Georges Cogniot archives, MRN.

93 Morgan, *Les Don Quichotte*, 135.

94 [Claude Morgan], "Dialogue sur l'action," *Les Lettres françaises* 1 (September 1942).

95 Jean Lescure, *Poésie et liberté: Histoire de* Messages (Paris: IMEC, 1998), 221.

96 Account by Jean Guéhenno, in Debû-Bridel, *La Résistance intellectuelle*, 35.

97 Quoted by Jean Lacouture, *François Mauriac*, vol. 2, *Un citoyen du siècle 1933–1970* (Paris: Seuil, 1980), 153–154.

98 Lescure, *Poésie et liberté*, 237.

99 Simonin, *Les Éditions de Minuit*, 87; see also 83.

100 Interview with Jean Lescure, October 25, 1995.

101 Vercors, *À dire vrai: Entretiens de Vercors avec Gilles Plazy* (Paris: François Bourin, 1991), 35.

102 Debû-Bridel, *Les Éditions de Minuit*, 43.

103 Robert Debré, *L'Honneur de vivre* (Paris: Hermann, 1974), 237.

104 Debû-Bridel, *Les Éditions de Minuit*, 31. See also Anne Simonin's analysis of this "secret" and the relationship that it would bring about between the writer and his identity, in *Les Éditions de Minuit*, 22–25.

105 See Pierre Bourdieu, "La production de la croyance: contribution à une économie des biens symboliques," *Actes de la recherche en sciences sociales* 13 (1977): 3–43.

106 Vercors, *The Battle of Silence*, 154.

107 Vercors, *Cent ans d'histoire de France*, t. 3, *Les Nouveaux Jours: Esquisse d'une Europe* (Paris: Plon, 1984), 31–32.

108 Debû-Bridel, *Les Éditions de Minuit*, 75. Oh how illusory was this affirmation, as Anne Simonin has shown in *Les Éditions de Minuit*, 101.

109 Quoted by Pierre Seghers, *La Résistance et ses poètes: France 1940–1945* (Paris: Seghers, 1974), 291.

110 Debû-Bridel, *Les Éditions de Minuit*, 34.

111 Comment by Claude Morgan in the facsimile of the underground *Lettres françaises*, 1947. The January issue could not be published, as the distribution service was too "congested" and the studio had been discovered by the Gestapo.

112 Morgan, *Les Don Quichotte*, 139.

113 Jean-Charles Gateau, *Paul Eluard ou Le frère voyant 1895–1952* (Paris: Robert Laffont, 1988), 233. See also Lucien Scheler, *La Grande Espérance des poètes (1940–1945)* (Paris: Temps actuels, 1982), 25.

114 Letter from Paul Eluard [December 17, 1936], in Paul Eluard, *Letters to Gala*, trans. Jesse Browner (New York: Paragon, 1989) (225), 221–222.

115 "For political reasons, each member of the surrealist group was supposed to commit to sabotaging Eluard's poetry by every means at his disposition. Any refusal led to exclusion. It seems to me that this act is the first to deserve inscription in the history of infamy," Max Ernst reported, quoted by Gateau, *Paul Eluard*, 257.

116 Jean Guérin [Jean Paulhan], "Bulletin," *La NRF* 297 (June 1, 1938): 1048, in reference to the publication of *Cours naturel* at Sagittaire.

117 Letter from Paul Eluard to Jean Paulhan, Monday [January 1941], Jean Paulhan collection, IMEC.

118 See Michel Fauré, *Histoire du surréalisme sous l'Occupation* (Paris: La Table Ronde, 1982), 215–240, and Lescure, *Poésie et liberté*, 209.

119 "Good riddance! (Between [you and me] I annoyed them on purpose)," Paul Eluard wrote to Louis Parrot on May 14, 1943, in Scheler, *La Grande Espérance des poètes*, 238.

120 See Scheler, ibid., 216 and his preface to Eluard's *Œuvres complètes*, 45.

121 Comments reported by Morgan, *Les Don Quichotte*, 139.

122 Encoded letter from François [Georges Cogniot] [to Jacques Duclos or to Pierre Villon], February 3, 1943, Pierre Villon archives, MRN, decoded by Daniel Virieux.

123 Encoded handwritten notes by Georges Cogniot on a letter from Vidal [Pierre Villon] to Fred [Jacques Duclos], December 23, 1942.

124 Morgan, *Les Don Quichotte*, 140.

125 Beauvoir, *The Prime of Life*, 424.

126 See Claude Morgan, "La vie cachée des 'Lettres françaises,'" *Les Lettres françaises*, September 16, 1944.

127 Interview with Jean Lescure, October 25, 1995.

128 See the account by René Tavernier, in Debû-Bridel, *La Résistance intellectuelle*, 88.

129 Scheler, *La Grande Espérance des poètes*, 221–223.

130 Account by François Mauriac, in Debû-Bridel, *La Résistance intellectuelle*, 98. Mauriac was likely confusing his support of the CNE, solicited by Blanzat, and his support of the National Front, which he gave to Debû-Bridel.

131 Encoded note by Georges Cogniot on the report by Vidal [Pierre Villon] n.d., distributed on May 4, 1943, decoded and reproduced by Virieux, *Le Front national*, appendix 3, vol. 5, 1481.

132 The Éditions de Minuit would publish two works for the CNE: *Jacques Decour, pages choisies* (February 20, 1944) and *Les Bannis* (July 14, 1944), an anthology of banned German poets and a reply to *L'Anthologie bilingue de la poésie allemande des origines à nos jours*, published by Stock in 1943.

133 Account by Édith Thomas, in Debû-Bridel, *La Résistance intellectuelle*, 62. On the relations between the CNE and the Éditions de Minuit, see Simonin, *Les Éditions de Minuit*, 122.

134 Interview with Vercors, April 30, 1991.

135 Yvonne Desvignes brought the package of books to Claude Morgan's office at the Louvre, where he was assigned to art security, and where he distributed them. See Morgan, *Les Don Quichotte*, 146 and Debû-Bridel, *Les Éditions de Minuit*, 61.

136 The first figure was given by Pierre Maucherat in his account for the CHDGM, AN: 72 AJ 69, the second by Claude Morgan, "La vie cachée des 'Lettres françaises.'"

137 Personal handwritten notes by Georges Cogniot in reference to a report on December 24, 1942, on the F.N. des intellectuels.

138 "Rapport général sur les intellectuels de Zone Sud," anonymous encoded document, annotated by René Roussel: "I don't know who wrote this report. 18/4/43," Pierre Villon archives, MRN, decoded and quoted by Virieux, *Le Front national*, 271–272.

139 "Rapport sur le travail chez les intellectuels de zone Sud, avril 1944," abbreviated notes by Georges Cogniot, Georges Cogniot archives, MRN.

140 Letter from Hubert Ruffe, December 5, 1943, quoted by Virieux, *Le Front national*, 594, n. 445.

141 Scheler, *La Grande Espérance des poètes*, 223.

142 Account by René Tavernier, in Debû-Bridel, *La Résistance intellectuelle*, 88–89.

143 See Stanislas Fumet, *Histoire de Dieu dans ma vie: Souvenirs choisis* (Paris: Fayard/ Mame, 1978), 463.

144 Louis Parrot, *L'Intelligence en guerre* (Paris: La Jeune Parque, 1945; Le Castor astral, 1990), 289.

145 See Eluard and Albert Béguin's correspondence with Louis Parrot, September–October 1942, in Scheler, *La Grande Espérance des poètes*, 152–169; see also Françoise Frey-Beguin, *Les Cahiers du Rhône: Refuge de la pensée libre*, fiftieth anniversary exhibit (September–December 1993) (La Chaux-de-Fonds: Éditions de la Baconnière, 1993), 78–79, Cariguel, Les Cahiers du Rhône *dans la guerre 1941–1945* (Éditions de l'université de Fribourg, 1999), and the correspondence between Aragon and Albert Béguin, published by Corinne Grenouillet, "Celui qui croyait au ciel et celui qui n'y croyait pas."

146 Account by René Tavernier, in Debû-Bridel, *La Résistance intellectuelle*, 89–90.

147 Ibid., 92.

148 Document given by Yvonne Paraf-Desvignes to the CHDGM, AN: 72 AJ 78.

149 *Aragon parle avec Dominique Arban* (Paris: Seghers, 1968), 148.

150 According to Yvonne Desvignes in the document given to the CHDGM, cited above. I was unable to consult this issue, as the first two issues of *Les Étoiles* were missing from the collections of the BDIC and the BNF. The third issue is dated March 1943.

151 "Aux intellectuels!," tract [late February 1943, Southern zone], MRN.

152 "Un document de première importance: Le manifeste du Comité national des écrivains," *Les Étoiles* 7 (June 7, 1943). This manifesto would be reprinted in 2,500 copies as a tract, with 500 copies meant for the Northern zone, according to a report by G[aillard *alias* Georges Ternet], "Mouvement des intellectuels," November 1, 1943, reproduced in Virieux, *Le Front national*, vol. 5, 1554–1560.

153 Account by Elsa Triolet and Aragon for the CHDGM.

154 The printing figures come from the report by G[aillard *alias* Georges Ternet], "Mouvement des intellectuels."

155 Letter from Eluard [January 1944] reproduced in Lescure, *Poésie et liberté*, 303.

156 On "seniority" as a value and principle of internal hierarchization within the Resistance, see Douzou, "L'entrée en résistance," in Prost (ed.), *La Résistance, une histoire sociale*, 9–20.

157 See Jean Marcenac, *Je n'ai pas perdu mon temps* (Paris: Messidor/Temps actuels, 1982), 323.

158 This list was established by cross-checking the two accounts of André Rousseaux, May 8, 1946 and December 2 and 14, 1949, for the CHDGM (AN: 72 AJ 45 and 72 AJ 78). André Rousseaux situated this meeting in October, but due to the arrest of Martin-Chauffier in late September 1943, it surely took place earlier. In addition to Claude Roy, Seghers also counted, for the first meeting in July 1943, Georges Mounin, Pierre Grappin, François Cuzin, and Jean Thomas; see Seghers, *La Résistance et ses poètes*, 233.

159 According to the report by G[aillard *alias* Georges Ternet], "Mouvement des intellectuels," November 1, 1943.

160 Ibid.

161 Roger Martin du Gard, *Journal*, t. 3, *1937–1949* (Paris: Gallimard, 1993), October 6, 1944, 703–705.

162 See "Rapport général sur les intellectuels de Zone Sud," cited above.

163 See Raymond-Léopold Bruckberger, *Nous n'irons plus au bois* (Paris: Amiot-Dumont, 1948), 32, and Herbert R. Lottman, *Albert Camus* (New York: Doubleday, 1979), 281.

164 Account by René Tavernier, in Debû-Bridel, *La Résistance intellectuelle*, 90–91.

165 Pierre Mazars, "Mort d'André Rousseaux," *Le Figaro*, November 29, 1973; see also the obituary published in *Le Monde*, November 30, 1973.

166 Account by André Rousseaux, December 2 and 14, 1949, for the CHDGM, 7.

167 The excerpt had been entitled, "Les Chrétiens trouvent Dieu dans ceux qui souffrent" [Christians find God in those who suffer], *Les Étoiles* 13 (November 1943).

168 Account by Elsa Triolet and Aragon, cited above. In fact, Aragon depended as much on Pierre Villon, director of Communist intellectuals, as Hubert Ruffe, via Georges Marane.

169 Quoted by Laurent Douzou, *La Désobéissance: Histoire d'un mouvement et d'un journal clandestins; Libération-Sud (1940–1944)* (Paris: Odile Jacob, 1995), 307; see also 306–310.

170 Letter from Hubert Ruffe, December 5, 1943, from the Duclos archives, quoted by Virieux, *Le Front national*, 619.

171 See [Georges Adam], "Les Cahiers de la Libération," *Les Lettres françaises* 18 (July 1944), which made a long inventory of the third issue of the *Cahiers* which included, among others, François La Colère-Aragon's preface to Jean Noir-Jean Cassou's *33 Sonnets*, published by the Éditions de Minuit on May 15, 1944, and le Juste-Jean Paulhan's parable entitled "L'Abeille." According to Pierre Seghers (*La Résistance et ses poètes*, 279), part of the publication of these issues of the *Cahiers*, delivered in sheets to Pierre Leyris in Paris, were bound at Georges Hugnet's bookstore.

172 Letter by Hubert Ruffe, cited above; see Virieux, *Le Front national*, 621.

173 I include the names listed in the September 16 correction.

174 Morgan, "La vie cachée des 'Lettres françaises.'"

175 Interview with Eugène Guillevic, July 1, 1991.

176 Ibid.

177 See Ingrid Galster, "Images actuelles de Sartre," *Cahiers d'Histoire des Littératures Romanes* (Heidelberg) 1–2 (1987): 215–44; "Les Mouches sous l'Occupation. À propos de quelques idées reçues," *Les Temps modernes* 531–533 (October–December 1990): 844–859.

178 "Rapport sur le travail chez les intellectuels de zone Sud, avril 1944," abbreviated notes by Georges Cogniot, cited above.

179 See Marcenac, *Je n'ai pas perdu mon temps*, 329–330.

180 Mercier, *Le Comité national des écrivains*, 75.

181 On the other hand, they are included in our total population, and in the statistical analysis of the subpopulation of Resistance writers (see chapter 1).

182 *Les Lettres françaises* 22 (September 23, 1944).

183 See Bruckberger, *Nous n'irons plus au bois*, 32, and Tavernier, "Quand Claudel rencontrait Aragon, Lyon 1944," *Bulletin de la société Paul Claudel* 199 (3rd trimester, 1990): 1–6. (See also chapter 8).

184 I refer to tables 1–5 in appendix 2.

185 This rate would have increased with the inclusion of Fathers Maydieu and Bruckberger, both sons of industrialists. Let us note, however, the relatively elevated rate of nonresponses for the social origins of the CNE members: 14 percent.

186 For the sake of comparison with the population studied by Rémy Ponton for the nineteenth century, senior civil service amounts to 16 percent of social origins in that group; intellectual fractions account for 13.7 percent. The increase in the rate of writers from intellectual backgrounds between these two periods is proportionate to the extension of education, which was accompanied by an important growth in the staff of liberal and intellectual professions, especially journalists and literary men. See Christophe Charle, *Naissance des "intellectuels" (1880–1900)* (Paris: Minuit, 1990), 41.

187 See Georges Bouquet and Pierre Menanteau, *Charles Vildrac* (Paris: Seghers, 1959), 23; Fumet, *Histoire de Dieu dans ma vie*, 12; Nicole Racine, "Louis Martin-Chauffier," in Maitron and Pennetier (eds.), *Dictionnaire biographique du mouvement ouvrier français*, t. 35, 397–400.

188 It is in fact less a matter of residing in the provinces that is at the origin of this difference for the CNE than it is a matter of residing in the colonies or abroad: while they were less likely to grow up outside of metropolitan France than the members of the Goncourt Academy (14 percent versus 20 percent), some of the members of the CNE in question, Camus, Elsa Triolet, Loys Masson, Georges Adam, stayed there longer (the rates balance out for the period of secondary education; at the age of entry into adult life, it is null at the Goncourt Academy, while it remains 8 percent for the members of the CNE). Albert Camus, living in Paris since 1937, had entered *Paris-Soir* thanks to the conjuncture of the Phoney War. His entry at Gallimard

through Pascal Pia, Jean Grenier, and Malraux occurred after the exodus. We cannot, however, affirm that in his case, the conjuncture of forced decentralization bene-fited the launching of the writer. See Lottman, *Albert Camus*, 245.

189 Pierre Emmanuel, *Autobiographies: Qui est cet homme (1947); L'Ouvrier de la onzième heure (1953)* (Paris: Seuil, 1970), 304.

190 Although here again, the two samples intersect for François Mauriac, educated by the Marianite brothers. Let us note that the two priests, who are not included, would have reinforced this overrepresentation of private instruction in the educational trajectories of the CNE members.

191 See Prost, *Histoire de l'enseignement en France 1800–1967* (Paris: Armand Colin, 1968), 192. Let us note that in 1879, only five congregations were authorized, including neither the Jesuits nor the Marists; see Laurent Laot, *Catholicisme, politique, laïcité* (Paris: Éditions ouvrières, 1990), 58.

192 Paul Duclos, "Introduction," in Jean-Marie Mayeur and Yves-Marie Hilaire, *Dictionnaire du monde religieux dans la France contemporaine*, t. 1, *Les Jésuites* (Paris: Beauschesne, 1985), 8–9. Half of the members of the CNE who had attended a Catholic establishment were born after 1906.

193 Vercors, "La résistance intellectuelle," in Jacques Meyer, *Vie et mort des Français 1939–1945* (Paris: Hachette, 1971; Tallandier, 1980), 291–292 (my emphasis).

194 Seghers, *La Résistance et ses poètes*, 271; see also 233.

195 On the question of literary genres, see chapter 1.

196 Julien Benda, *Exercice d'un enterré vif (juin 1940-août 1944)* (Geneva: Éditions des Trois Collines, 1944), 118. See also Louis-Albert Revah, *Julien Benda* (Paris: Plon, 1991), 242, and Maurice Joucla, "Benda sous l'occupation," *Europe* 389 (September 1961): 14–20.

197 See Nicole Racine, "Andrée Viollis," in Maitron and Pennetier (eds.), *Dictionnaire biographique du mouvement ouvrier français*, t. 43, 297–280.

198 Twenty-seven members of the CNE had or would have (after the Liberation) the Gallimard house as their chief publisher or second chief publisher; twenty-one contributed to the prewar *NRF*.

199 At least a quarter of the committee members contributed to *Europe* or *Vendredi*. Twenty-eight members out of fifty contributed to *Confluences*, twenty-five to *Poésie 40, 41 . . .* , sixteen to *Fontaine*, twenty-seven to the *Messages* anthology, *Domaine français* (out of a total of fifty-seven writers appearing in the table of contents).

200 After the Liberation, this unstable situation endured, while Debû-Bridel threw himself into a parliamentary career: during the wave of literature on the Resistance, Gallimard insisted on taking *Déroute*, which Debû-Bridel was saving for Vercors and the Éditions de Minuit, but later rejected *Sous la Cendre*; letters from Jacques Debû-Bridel to Jean Paulhan, February 23 and August 17, 1938, June 4, [1940] and August 17, [1950], Jean Paulhan collection, IMEC.

201 See Nicole Racine, "René Blech," in Maitron and Pennetier (eds.), *Dictionnaire biographique du mouvement ouvrier français*, t. 19, 259.

202 See Nicole Racine, "Jacques Decour," in ibid., t. 24, 176–177.

203 See Lomagne [Jean Paulhan], "Jacques Decour," in *Chroniques interdites* (Éditions de Minuit, 1943), 27–28, and his "préface" to Jacques Decour, *Pages choisies* (Éditions de Minuit, 1944), 7–8; Aragon would respond to Paulhan in his preface to *Comme je vous en donne l'exemple*, OP, t. 10, 388–389.

204 Jean Paulhan, "L'un des premiers de l'équipe," *Les Lettres françaises*, May 10, 1946.

205 Among the following cases, those who only made a brief pass through the house were not included in the totality of authors who had Gallimard as their main publisher or second main publisher.

206 Thus Aragon, deprived of his income as a journalist, continually demanded his advances from Gallimard before the party took responsibility for him, when he left Lyon for the Drôme in the summer of 1943.

207 Georges Sadoul found a job that paid ten francs per day at the Périgueux train station, and Francis Ponge earned 2,000 francs per month in an insurance office in the Southern zone. Jean Lescure, as we saw, lived off an income of 700 francs per month that his parents gave him. See Grenier, *Sous l'Occupation*, 158; letter from Francis Ponge to Jean Paulhan, October 10, 1940, in Jean Paulhan and Francis Ponge, *Correspondance (1923–1968)*, t. 1 (Paris: Gallimard, 1986), 242.

208 For short-term recognition, 43 percent of committee members appeared in the *Histoire de la littérature française contemporaine* by René Lalou, and 56 percent in *Une Histoire vivante de la littérature d'aujourd'hui 1939–1960* by Pierre Boisdeffre (Paris: Le Livre Contemporain, 1959). Keeping in mind the differences between these two books, due both to the chronological gap and the transformations of the literary field during the crisis period (the first, dated 1947, did not include the young authors who emerged in the 1940s, while the second, dated 1959, overrepresented Resistance writers), we can evaluate "literary legitimacy" at an average of 50 percent for the committee as a whole. This rate is confirmed by the signs of long-term recognition: twenty-six members, or half, of the committee appeared in the *Dictionnaire des littératures de langue française* (Paris: Bordas, 1994), but only 13 percent earned a long article. An average of one-third appeared in the *Petit Larousse* (1990) or the *Petit Robert* (1983).

209 Simonin, *Les Éditions de Minuit*, 201.

210 His signature can be found in Maurras's newspaper until April 1943.

211 I have already mentioned this exclusion of women from the authorities of consecration (see chapter 5). While the Resistance constituted a key moment in the entry of women into political life and while it ultimately helped legally inscribe them there (right to vote, eligibility, increased representativity in the authorities of power), recent studies agree that this inscription was not self-evident and that it remained limited (it rarely exceeded 8 percent in state and political organs); see especially William Guéraiche, "Les femmes politiques de 1944 à 1947: Quelle libération?," *Clio. Histoire, Femmes et Sociétés* 1 (1995), "Résistances et Libérations France 1940–1945": 165–186; Claire Andrieu, "Les résistantes, perspectives de recherche," in Prost (ed.), *La Résistance, une histoire sociale*, 69–96.

212 Édith Thomas remembered that she "kept quiet in [her] corner" during the underground meetings of the CNE that she hosted at her home; Thomas, *Le Témoin compromis*, 106–107.

213 See Simonin, *Les Éditions de Minuit*, 110–113.

214 It was Elsa Triolet's report that was published in *Les Lettres françaises* 16 (May 1944), while Édith Thomas's report would be published at the Liberation in the organ of the Union des femmes françaises; see *Femmes françaises* 2 and 3 (September 21 and 28, 1944). The tone with which Édith Thomas refers to the affair in her memoirs is unmistakable: "But Elsa Triolet was also preparing articles on the same subject and I wasn't sure that she wasn't looking for a way to be the only one to do them"; see Thomas, *Le Témoin compromis*, 122.

215 Alongside Action française supporters like René Benjamin and Henri Massis; see the text of this declaration in *Le Nouveau Siècle*, February 26, 1925, reproduced in Jean Plumyène and Raymond Lasierra, *Les Fascismes français 1923–1963* (Paris: Seuil, 1963), 35.

216 See ibid., 45–46 and 55–57. See also the entries for Roger Giron, Georges Oudard, and André Rousseaux in Henri Coston, *Dictionnaire de la politique française* (Paris: Publication Henri Coston, 1967), vols. 1 and 2; and "André Rousseaux" and "Georges Oudard," in Pierre-Marie Dioudonnat, *Les 700 rédacteurs de "Je suis partout" 1930–1944* (Paris: Sedopols, 1933), 70 and 78–79. Georges Oudard and Debû-Bridel would end up in the RPF group starting in 1947.

217 Jacques Duquesne, *Les Catholiques français sous l'Occupation* (Paris: Grasset, 1966), 130.

218 Interview with Jean Lescure, October 25, 1995.

219 Interview with Jean Lescure, May 26, 1996.

220 Lescure, *Poésie et liberté*, 125.

221 "La peur au ventre," *Les Lettres françaises* 10 (October 1943).

222 [Jacques Debû-Bridel], "L'Académie Goncourt et les agents de l'ennemi," The underground *Lettres françaises* 5 (January–February 1943).

223 [Georges Adam], "M. Haedens n'est pas content," *Les Lettres françaises* 12 (December 1943).

224 "Adresse au Comité Français de Libération nationale," *Les Lettres françaises* 11 (November 1943).

225 "La confusion sert les traîtres," *Les Étoiles* 13 (November 1943).

226 Letter from Jean Paulhan [1944], quoted by Lescure, *Poésie et liberté*, 327.

227 Claude Mauriac, *Le Temps immobile*, t. 4, *La Terrasse de Malagar* (Paris: Grasset, 1978), 186–187 (my emphasis).

228 Letter from Mauriac to Paulhan, [1942], Jean Paulhan collection, IMEC.

229 [Claude Morgan, Édith Thomas, Paul Eluard], "L'Agonie de la Nouvelle Revue française," *Les Lettres françaises* 8 (July 1943).

230 Letter from Paulhan to Édith Thomas, July 27, 1943, in Jean Paulhan, *Choix de lettres*, t. 2 (278), 323.

231 Letter from Guéhenno to Paulhan, July 30, 1943, Jean Paulhan collection, IMEC.

232 "La N.R.F. est morte: 'Vive la N.R.F.!,'" *Les Étoiles* 10 (August 1943). I attribute this article to Aragon, who alone could have such precise details on the censorship exerted by Drieu, and with good reason, since Paulhan had informed him about it in a letter on July 15, in Aragon, Paulhan, and Triolet, *"Le temps traversé"* (103), 161.

This desire to "spare" Paulhan is, I think, all the stronger since an incident had recently opposed Aragon and Paulhan, the former having unjustly suspected the latter of having been at the root of the rejection of Elsa Triolet's manuscript for *Les Amants d'Avignon* at the Éditions de Minuit. Paulhan explained himself directly to Aragon and Elsa Triolet; see Simonin, *Les Éditions de Minuit*, 111–112.

233 Letter from Mauriac to Paulhan, February 3, 1943, Jean Paulhan collection, IMEC.

234 Letter from Blanzat to Paulhan [1943], Jean Paulhan collection, IMEC.

235 Letter from Guéhenno to Paulhan, August 21, 1943, Jean Paulhan collection, IMEC.

236 Yvonne Desvignes, text written following the reception of Paulhan's book, *De la Paille et du Grain* [*Of Chaff and Wheat*] (1948), Jean Paulhan collection, IMEC.

237 Interview with Jean Lescure, October 25, 1995.

238 [Claude Morgan], "*Comoedia* comme les autres . . . ," *Les Lettres françaises* 11 (November 1943).

239 Letter from Paulhan to Mauriac, in Jean Paulhan, *Choix de lettres*, t. 2 (287), 333–334.

240 Letter from Mauriac to Paulhan, January 2, 1944, Jean Paulhan collection, IMEC.

241 Copy of the letter from Paulhan to Mauriac, Jean Paulhan collection, IMEC.

242 Letter from Mauriac to Paulhan, February 12, 1944, Jean Paulhan collection, IMEC.

243 Elsa Triolet, "Préface au désenchantement," in Aragon and Elsa Triolet, *Œuvres Romanesques Croisées*, t. 9 (Monaco/Paris: Jaspard, Polus et cie/Robert Laffont, 1964), 16.

244 Handwritten notes by Elsa Triolet for a contribution to the history of the CNE, FETA.

245 Interview with Lucien Scheler, June 24, 1991.

246 Interview with Jean Lescure, October 25, 1995.

247 Thomas, *Le Témoin compromis*, 108; see also her account in Debû-Bridel, *La Résistance intellectuelle*, 59–60.

248 Letter from Jean Paulhan to Jean Lescure, Friday [August 15, 1944], in Paulhan, *Choix de lettres*, t. 2 (321), 371. See also the letter to Jacques Debû-Bridel, ibid. (323), 373, which explicitly evoked the fears of a Communist censorship.

Part III: Literary Justice

1 "The acceleration of the social dynamic" is one of the determining causes of the actualization of potentialities inscribed in the "generational situation," as Karl Mannheim has explained in *Le Problème des générations* (Paris: Nathan, 1990), 65; see also 66–67.

Chapter 8: The Literary Court

The chapter epigraph poem, "Un petit nombre d'intellectuels français s'est mis au service de l'ennemi," was published anonymously in the underground *Lettres françaises* 10 (October 1943).

1 Herbert R. Lottman, *The Purge* (New York: William Morrow, 1986), 231–232, and Peter Novick, *The Resistance versus Vichy: The Purge of Collaborators in Liberated France* (New York: Columbia University Press, 1968), 117.

2 Jean Mottin, *Histoire politique de la presse 1944–1949* (Paris: Éditions Bilans hebdomadaires, 1949), 30–38.

3 Michel Winock, *Histoire politique de la revue "Esprit": Des intellectuels dans la cité, 1930–1950* (Paris: Seuil, 1975), 265; Denis Pelletier, *"Économie et Humanisme": De l'utopie communautaire au combat pour le tiers-monde, 1941–1966* (Paris: Éditions du Cerf, 1996), 113; and Anna Boschetti, *The Intellectual Enterprise: Sartre and* Les Temps Modernes, trans. Richard C. McCleary (Evanston, IL: Northwestern University Press, 1988), 105–106.

4 Letter from Blanzat to Paulhan [1944], Jean Paulhan collection, IMEC.

5 This figure is based on the CNE membership lists (dossiers "Associations 1945: Auteurs associés; Adhésions 44; Candidatures 45" and "CNE: Vente 1946; Bulletins d'adhésion et correspondance jointe," "Carnets d'adresse CNE: Premières années," CNE archives, FETA).

6 Comité national des écrivains, "Ce qu'on attendait," *Bulletin intérieur d'information* (n.d.), CNE archives, FETA. We can situate the publication of this issue between June 5 and 21, 1945. On the other hand, we are not able to specify whether other issues were published.

7 Comité national des écrivains, "Les moyens de vivre," *Bulletin intérieur d'information* (n.d.), CNE archives, FETA.

8 [Albert Camus], "Tout ne s'arrange pas," *Les Lettres françaises* 16 (May 1944); see also Herbert Lottman, *Albert Camus* (New York: Doubleday, 1979), 310–312, and Pascal Mercier, *Le Comité national des écrivains, 1941–1944* (MA thesis, Université Paris III, 1980), 70–71. On the motives for his resignation, see the letter from Claude Morgan to Jean Paulhan relating his conversation with Camus, October 1, 1944, Jean Paulhan collection, IMEC.

9 Letter from Camus to Paulhan, Tuesday, [September] 27, [1944], Jean Paulhan collection, IMEC.

10 Minutes from the meeting on February 10, 1946, register "CNE. Comptes rendus des assemblées générales," 30, CNE archives, FETA.

11 "Aux quatre vents," *Le Figaro*, September 9, 1944.

12 "Le Comité des Écrivains et l'Épuration," *Les Lettres françaises*, September 16, 1944.

13 Letters from Gabriel Marcel to Paulhan, September 17, 1944, Jean Paulhan collection, IMEC.

14 Letter from Paulhan to Jouhandeau, [September 7, 1944], in Jean Paulhan, *Choix de lettres*, t. 2, *1937–1945 Le Traité des jours sombres* (Paris: Gallimard, 1992) (324), 374.

15 Letter from Gabriel Marcel to Paulhan, September 26, 1944, Jean Paulhan collection, IMEC.

16 Jean Schlumberger, *Notes sur la vie littéraire* (Paris: Gallimard, 1999), 257.

17 Claude Mauriac, *Le Temps immobile*, t. 5, *Aimer de Gaulle* (Paris: Grasset, 1978), 65.

18 Press release published in *Les Lettres françaises* 24 (October 7, 1944).

19 There remains no trace of this list of "major offenders." It is likely that it was never drawn up, the project having been abandoned in the days following the meeting.

20 Letter from Paulhan to Mauriac [September 30, 1944], in Paulhan, *Choix de lettres*, t. 2 (327), 376.

21 Letter from Mauriac to Paulhan [1944], in François Mauriac, *Lettres d'une vie (1904–1969)* (Paris: Grasset, 1981) (270), 281.

22 Letter from Paulhan to Schlumberger, n.d., Jean Schlumberger collection, Jacques Doucet archives.

23 Letter from Morgan to Paulhan, October 1944, Jean Paulhan collection, IMEC archives; see also the copy of the letter from Paulhan to Morgan [October 2?] 1944, to which Morgan was responding.

24 Letter from Jean Paulhan to Jacques Debû-Bridel, Saturday [September 30? 1944], in Paulhan, *Choix de lettres*, t. 2 (325), 375.

25 Letter from Paulhan to Eluard, October 1, 1944, in Paulhan, *Choix de lettres*, t. 2 (328), 377.

26 "À la commission d'épuration du Comité national des Écrivains," *Les Lettres françaises*, October 7, 1944. The text was signed by the members of the commission: J. Debû-Bridel, P. Eluard, G. Marcel, R. Queneau, A. Rousseaux, L. Scheler, Vercors, Ch. Vildrac.

27 "Le Comité national des Écrivains et l'épuration des Lettres," *Les Lettres françaises*, October 21, 1944.

28 Letter from Paulhan to Mauriac [October 22, 1944], in Paulhan, *Choix de lettres*, t. 2 (334), 380. See also the copy of the letter that he sent to Claude Morgan, October 23, 1944, Jean Paulhan collection, IMEC.

29 Letter from Paulhan to Schlumberger [1944], Jean Schlumberger collection, Jacques Doucet archives (we can date this letter from October 22 or 23).

30 "Marcel appointed to the Commission, our actions as a body with regard to Justice [. . .] so here we are more judges and more denunciators than ever, in my opinion this is exactly what we shouldn't do [. . .]," Paulhan wrote to Aragon (October 3, 1944), in Aragon, Paulhan, and Triolet, *"Le Temps traversé": Correspondance 1920–1964* (Paris: Gallimard, 1994) (112), 176.

31 Letter from Paulhan to Schlumberger, October 12, 1944, Jean Schlumberger collection, Jacques Doucet archives.

32 Letter from Guéhenno to Paulhan, August 17, 1944, Jean Paulhan collection, IMEC.

33 See the letter from Blanzat to Paulhan [1944], Jean Paulhan collection, IMEC.

34 Letters from Guéhenno to Paulhan, [October 1944] and November 7, 1944, Jean Paulhan collection, IMEC.

35 In this light, these polemics were inscribed in continuity with the debates surrounding the formation of a corporation of writers, which I mentioned in chapter 2. The CNE opposed, however, the associative principle to the corporatist principle.

36 "Pierre Benoit rayé de la liste noire," *Les Lettres françaises*, November 22, 1946.

37 Vercors, *Petit Pamphlet des dîners chez Gazette* (Paris: Self-published, 1947), 3–4. A first version was published in *Les Lettres françaises* on April 4, 1947.

38 Herbert R. Lottman, *L'Épuration (1949–1953)* (Paris: Fayard, 1986); abridged version originally published as *The Purge* (New York: William Morrow 1986), 242.

39 CNE archives, FETA.

40 I rely here on the archives of the Comité d'épuration (AN: F21 8123–24); thirty individual files (F 21 8122–26) and Lottman, *The Purge*, 244–245.

41 AN: F21 8114. Some of the authors excluded from the associations, like Henri Massis, were probably reintegrated either following a dismissal, or thanks to the amnesty laws.

42 Letters from Audisio to the president of the CNE, November 19 and 29, 1946, to M. Forestier, secretary of the managing committee of the CNE, December 2, 1945, to Aragon, general secretary, March 19, 1946, and Aragon's response, March 25, 1946, CNE archives.

43 Minutes of the meeting on October 14, 1946, of the Comité d'épuration des gens de lettres (AN: F21 8114) and letter from Gabriel Audisio to the president of the CNE, November 29, 1946, CNE archives. Nothing allows us to reconstruct the conditions in which the work of the Comité d'épuration was interrupted. The minutes end on October 29, 1946. On April 20, 1948, Jacques Jaujard, general director of arts and letters, sent a note to the director of architecture, asking him to put a room on rue de Valois at the disposition of the Comité national des gens de lettres, which wished to resume its activities after a year's interruption. He assured him that the work of the committee would be finished within two or three months.

44 Minutes of the meeting of April 1, 1947, register "CNE. Comptes rendus du comité directeur," 19, CNE archives.

45 Interview with Lucien Scheler, June 24, 1991. The subject of the interview preferred that it not be recorded.

46 Lottman, *The Purge*, 246.

47 Jean Paulhan intervened in his favor and asked renowned writers, particularly André Gide and Georges Duhamel, to do the same.

48 Thus, the Comité d'épuration began proceedings in 1944 and froze them in 1946 while awaiting documents concerning the proceedings of legal purge to which the investigated author was subject, though it had still not ruled in 1949, when the author in question died (AN: F21 8122).

49 Peter Novick, *The Resistance versus Vichy*, 161–162. We must also take into account the complexity of the proceedings and the difficult situation of the magistrature during this period.

50 See Pierre Assouline, *L'Épuration des intellectuels* (Brussels: Éditions Complexe, 1985), 99.

51 On the publishing purge, see Pascal Fouché, *L'Édition française 1940–1944*, vol. 2 (Bibliothèque de littérature française contemporaine de l'université Paris VII, 1987), 153; on the comparison between the purge in the press and in publishing, see Pierre Assouline, *Gaston Gallimard: Un demi-siècle d'édition française* (Paris: Balland, 1984); abridged version trans. Harold J. Salemson as *Gaston Gallimard: A Half-Century of French Publishing* (San Diego: Harcourt Brace Jovanovich, 1988), 303.

52 "Adresse au C.N.R.," *Les Lettres françaises* 14 (March 1944); "Une initiative des écrivains concernant les éditeurs," *Les Étoiles* 17 (March 1944).

53 "Avertissement aux éditeurs," *Les Lettres françaises* 11 (November 1943).

54 Lottman, *The Purge*, 235.

55 See Pierre Bourdieu, "La production de la croyance: Contribution à une économie des biens symboliques," *Actes de la recherche en sciences sociales* 13 (1977): 3–45.

56 Letter from Schlumberger to Martin du Gard [August 1943], reproduced in Roger Martin du Gard, *Journal*, t. 3, *1937–1949* (Paris: Gallimard, 1993), 594–595.

57 Assouline, *Gaston Gallimard*, 309–314.

58 See especially the letter from François Mauriac to the president of the Bar, Maurice Ribet, June 9, 1948, in François Mauriac, *Nouvelles lettres d'une vie (1906–1970)* (Paris: Grasset, 1989) (260), 243–244. See Fouché, *L'Édition française*, vol. 2, 204 and 242. The publisher of Céline's pamphlets and Rebatet's *Décombres* was murdered in December 1945, in conditions that remain mysterious, after having been acquitted by the courts, as his business would be in 1948. Arrested and then released at the Liberation, Bernard Grasset, who publicly proclaimed his pro-German sentiments in his writing and correspondence, would be sentenced in absentia in 1948 to national degradation for life and five years of banishment, as well as the confiscation of his property. His business, condemned to dissolution, would benefit from the pardon of President Vincent Auriol: the sentence of confiscation was commuted to a fine, and Bernard Grasset would regain his place at the head of the house. He would receive amnesty in 1953. As for the file on the Gallimard booksellers, whose catalogue was not as compromising as that of its colleagues, it was shelved in October 1946, testimony having established the separation between Drieu's NRF and the house.

59 Assouline, *Gaston Gallimard*, 301.

60 Vercors, *Cent ans d'histoire de France, t. 3, Les Nouveaux jours, Esquisse d'une Europe* (Paris: Plon, 1984), 67. Vercors exposed his views on the publishing purge in an article called "La Gangrène"; article collected in Vercors, *Le Sable du temps* (Paris: Émile-Paul, 1946).

61 See Vercors, *À dire vrai: Entretiens de Vercors avec Gilles Plazy* (Paris: François Bourin, 1991), 102.

62 Anne Simonin, *Les Éditions de Minuit 1942–1955: Le devoir d'insoumission* (Paris: IMEC, 1994), 240.

63 Vercors, *Cent ans d'histoire de France*, t. 3, *Les Nouveaux jours*, 54.

64 Interview with Vercors, April 30, 1991.

65 Fouché, *L'Édition française*, vol. 2, 228. The commission resigned before obtaining legal recognition. It would be replaced by the Commission consultative de l'édition (ibid. 167 and 187).

66 Letter from Schlumberger to Gide, November 21, 1944, in André Gide and Jean Schlumberger, *Correspondance (1901–1950)* (Paris: Gallimard, 1993) (790), 962–963.

67 Letter from Benda to Paulhan, November 25, 1944, Jean Paulhan collection, IMEC archives.

68 Letter from Paulhan to Aragon [1943], in Paulhan, Aragon, and Triolet, *"Le Temps traversé,"* (107), 166.

69 Letter from Paulhan to Schlumberger, October 12, 1944, Jean Schlumberger collection, Jacques Doucet archives.

70 See Simone de Beauvoir, *Force of Circumstance*, trans. Richard Howard (New York: Putnam, 1965), 47.

71 He would, however, continue to contribute there under the pseudonym of Maast until late 1946, when he broke away from the CNE.

72 Interview with Vercors.

73 Aragon, "Retour d'André Gide," *Les Lettres françaises* 31 (November 25, 1944).

74 Galtier-Boissière, *Mon journal depuis la Libération* (Paris: La Jeune Parque, 1945), 65.

75 René Tavernier, "Quand Claudel rencontrait Aragon, Lyon 1944," *Bulletin de la société Paul Claudel* 199 (3rd trimester, 1990): 6. See also Mercier, *Le Comité national des écrivains*, 77.

76 Interview with Eugène Guillevic. See also, on this affair, Lottman, *La Rive gauche: Du Front populaire à la guerre froide* (Paris: Seuil, 1981); originally published as *The Left Bank: Writers, Artists, and Politics from the Popular Front to the Cold War* (Boston: Houghton Mifflin, 1982), 229–230.

77 Only Martin du Gard left the committee, to which he only belonged on paper, in March 1945. Not having been consulted about the inclusion of his name on the list—but he had, as we saw, given his theoretical support under the Occupation, and had been rather pleased at the Liberation to see his name figure in good company on this list (see Martin du Gard, *Journal*, t. 3, 703)—and not having attended any meetings, since he was still at Figeac, he sent a letter stating his refusal to belong to the legal CNE: "I am by nature rebellious to any kind of commitment. It has never been necessary for me to 'engage myself' to conduct my existence." Letter from Roger Martin du Gard to the CNE, Nice, March 14, 1945, Martin du Gard archives, BN: 1981 (518), 135; this source was kindly indicated to me by Pascal Mercier.

78 Letter from Jean Schlumberger to André Gide, November 27, 1944, in Gide and Schlumberger, *Correspondance* (791), 964–965. A lone voice rose up against Aragon's attack . . . in Brazil! Under the title "L'excommunication d'André Gide," Bernanos published a defense of the "great writer" in *O Jornal* on February 3, 1945. He spoke out against the opprobrium that was cast on Gide by a party, deploring the sight of "a great poet lowering himself to these lawyer's 'tricks.'" This text was republished under the title "Le Saint-Office communiste" in *Le Chemin de la Croix-des-Âmes* (Paris: Gallimard, 1948); see Georges Bernanos, *Essais et écrits de combat*, t. 2, (Paris: Gallimard, 1995), 669 and 673 for the quotes. See also Joseph Jurt, "Gide et Bernanos," *Bulletin des Amis d'André Gide* 94 (April 1992): 187–207.

79 Letter from Jean Paulhan to Jean Schlumberger [November 1944], Jean Schlumberger collection, Jacques Doucet archives.

80 Letter from Jean Paulhan to André Gide, December 6, [1944], in Paulhan, *Choix de lettres*, t. 2 (342), 389.

81 Claude Roy, *Nous* (Paris: Gallimard, 1972, republished 1980), 120.

82 See Victor Leduc, *Les Tribulations d'un idéologue* (Paris: Syros, 1985), 46.

83 Editorial, *Carrefour*, August 26, 1944.

84 Pierre Laborie, "Opinion et représentations: la Libération et l'image de la Résistance," *Revue d'histoire de la Deuxième Guerre mondiale* 131 (1983): 72.

85 Pierre Jean Jouve, "Les caractères sacrés de la révolution," excerpts from the introduction written for the first volume of the Swiss series "Le Cri de la France" devoted to the Revolution, reproduced in *Les Lettres françaises* 28 (November 4, 1944).

86 François Mauriac, "Servir la France ressuscitée," *Carrefour*, August 29, 1944. The article is reproduced in Jean Touzot, *Mauriac sous l'Occupation* (Paris: La Manufacture, 1990), 310–312 (312 for the quote).

87 François Mauriac, "La nation française a une âme," *Les Lettres françaises* 20 (September 9, 1944). Georges Bernanos, "Le message de la Révolution française," *Combat*, September 15, 1944; Jacques Debû-Bridel wrote, for his part, "It's a whole French tradition, that of 1789 and 1830 that was suddenly revived, reviving at the same time the hideous mask of the Marshal's France" ("Je reviens de Londres," *Les Lettres françaises* 28 [November 4, 1944]). Claude Morgan would respond to de Gaulle's speech at city hall: "But Paris was ready. Paris had regained its soul of 1793, 1830, 1848, the Commune" ("Paris était prêt," *Les Lettres françaises* 50 [April 7, 1945]).

88 Jean Cassou, "La Justice," *Les Lettres françaises* 65 (July 21, 1945).

89 Claude Morgan, "Les indulgents," *Les Lettres françaises* 68 (August 11, 1945).

90 Anne Simonin shows, meanwhile, that with the exception of currents that claim the counterrevolutionary tradition (particularly Action française), starting in 1947, the extreme right would assimilate the purge to the "White Terror" of the Bourbon Restoration. Comparing the 1945 purgers to the Committee of Public Safety would actually mean ennobling them. Anne Simonin, "1815 en 1945: Les formes littéraires de la défaite," *Vingtième Siècle* 59 (July–September 1998): 48–61. Let us note, moreover, that the assimilation of the Republican reestablishment to the Bourbon Restoration is the counterpart to the stigmatization of the Third Republic as the "Ancien Régime," a representation that was first circulated after the defeat by the Fascist "revolutionaries" in 1940.

91 Roger Lannes, unpublished journal, quoted by Touzot, *Mauriac sous l'Occupation*, 108.

92 Letter from Paul Léautaud to Jean Paulhan, October 20, 1944, Jean Paulhan collection, IMEC archives.

93 François Mauriac, "La nation française a une âme." The article is reproduced in Touzot, *Mauriac sous l'Occupation*, 297–306 (305 for the quote).

94 Letter from Paulhan to Mauriac [October 9, 1944], in Paulhan, *Choix de Lettres*, t. 2 (331), 379.

95 Raymond-Léopold Bruckberger, *Nous n'irons plus au bois* (Paris: Amiot-Dumont, 1948), 32–33.

96 One of Mauriac's famous adversaries, Michel Debré, would recognize the prophetic role that the writer played: "Of Mauriac's influence over public opinion, I retain three important and even remarkable examples on the part of the writer. During the Spanish Civil War, at the end of the Algerian War (what he said about it in 1956–1957 guided certain minds) and during the time when the Fourth Republic was disoriented, hesitant." Interview of Michel Debré with Jean Touzot, in Jean Touzot (ed.), *François Mauriac* (Paris: Éditions de L'Herne, *Cahiers de l'Herne* no. 48, 1985), 369.

97 Roger Lannes, unpublished journal, 2820, IMEC. Roger Lannes had acted as a censor under Vichy. He was among the censors who were complicit with the literary reviews, helping them avoid censorship (he worked with *Les Cahiers du sud*, in particular).

98 Mauriac, *Le Temps immobile*, t. 5, 65 and 86–87.

99 François Mauriac, "Révolution et révolution" (October 13, 1944), *Le Bâillon dé-noué: Après quatre ans de silence* (Paris: Grasset, 1945), 81.

100 Quoted by Lacouture, *François Mauriac*, vol. 2, *Un citoyen du siècle 1933–1970* (Paris: Seuil, 1980), 189.

101 François Mauriac, "Le sort tomba," *Le Figaro*, September 4, 1944.

102 Lacouture, *François Mauriac*, vol. 2, 194. "Nothing less political than his position, so sentimental," Claude Mauriac wrote in *Le Temps immobile*, t. 5, 71.

103 François Mauriac, "La justice et la guerre," *Le Figaro*, October 19, 1944, republished in Mauriac, *Le Bâillon dénoué*, 90.

104 François Mauriac, "La vraie justice," *Le Figaro*, September 8, 1944, republished in ibid., 27–28.

105 François Mauriac, "Révolution et révolution," 78.

106 Mauriac, "La justice et la guerre," 81 and 89.

107 Albert Camus, (editorial), *Combat*, October 20, 1944; see also October 25, 1944: "François Mauriac's allegations against the resistance press wounded us [...]." These texts have been translated into English and compiled in *Camus at Combat: Writing 1944–1947*, ed. Jacqueline Lévi-Valensi, trans. Arthur Goldhammer (Princeton, NJ: Princeton University Press), 80–81 and 88–90.

108 Albert Camus, (editorial), *Combat*, October 20, 1944; see *Camus at Combat*, 81 for the quotations.

109 François Mauriac, "Réponse à 'Combat,'" *Le Figaro*, October 22–23, 1944, *Le Bâillon dénoué*, 92–93.

110 Albert Camus, (editorial), *Combat*, October 25, 1944; see *Camus at Combat*, 89 for the quotations.

111 François Mauriac, "Le bilan de quatre-vingt jours" (November 14, 1944), *Le Bâillon dénoué*, 133–134.

112 Mauriac, "La Loterie," ibid., 205–208.

113 Mauriac, "Autour d'un verdict" (January 4, 1945), *Le Bâillon dénoué*, 221.

114 Albert Camus, "Justice et charité," *Combat*, January 11, 1945. See *Camus at Combat*, 168–170 for the complete article.

115 Letter from Camus to Marcel Aymé (January 27, 1945), quoted by Jeanyves Guérin, *Camus, portrait de l'artiste en citoyen* (Paris: François Bourin, 1993), 56.

116 Guérin, ibid., 59–60. See also Olivier Todd, *Albert Camus: A Life*, trans. Benjamin Ivry (New York: Knopf, 1997), 202.

117 François Mauriac, "Le mépris de la charité" (January 7–8, 1944), *Le Bâillon dénoué*, 223.

118 Claude Roy, "Ce n'est jamais une fois pour toutes," *Action*, October 27, 1944. Pascal Copeau, "Châtiment, épuration et politique," *Action*, January 19, 1945.

119 Jean Lacroix, "Charité chrétienne et justice politique," *Esprit* 3 (February 1945): 384, 385 and 387.

120 See Assouline, *L'Épuration des intellectuels*.

121 Galtier-Boissière, *Mon journal depuis la Libération*, 129.

122 Petition reproduced in Jean-François Sirinelli, *Intellectuels et passions françaises: Manifestes et pétitions au XXᵉ siècle* (Paris: Fayard, 1990), 151.

123 Interview with Lucien Scheler.

124 Vercors, *Les Nouveaux jours*, 66.

125 Louis-Ferdinand Céline, "Céline nous écrit," *Je suis partout*, October 29, 1943. Claude Morgan did not miss seeing a sign of weakness here: "Suddenly discovering the prospect of the Hitlerian catastrophe, the traitors are seized by fear." See [Claude Morgan], "L'innocent," *Les Lettres françaises* 11 (November 1943).

126 Jean Paulhan, *Of Chaff and Wheat: Writers, War, and Treason*, trans. Richard Rand (Urbana: University of Illinois Press, 2004), 37.

127 Jean-Paul Sartre, "Situation of the Writer in 1947," trans. Bernard Frechtman, *What Is Literature and Other Essays* (Cambridge, MA: Harvard University Press, 1988), 190–191.

128 Beauvoir, *Force of Circumstance*, 21–22.

129 Louis Parrot, "La responsabilité de l'écrivain," *Action*, September 9, 1944.

130 Charles Braibant, "Gavroche et les écrivains," *Gavroche*, November 9, 1944.

131 Simonin, *Les Éditions de Minuit*, 228–229.

132 Paul Eluard, "Les vendeurs d'indulgence," *Les Lettres françaises*, March 17, 1945, republished in Paul Eluard, *Au Rendez-vous allemand* (Paris: Minuit, 1945), 47.

133 Interview with Eugène Guillevic.

134 Simonin, *Les Éditions de Minuit*, 231.

135 Vercors, "Le Pardon," *Les Lettres françaises*, November 11, 1944.

136 Vercors's response to the survey on "The Responsibility of the Writer," *Carrefour*, February 10, 1945.

137 Letter from Jean Paulhan to Vercors and copy of his letter to Gérard Boutelleau, dated February 14, 1945, Vercors collection, Jacques Doucet archives.

138 Claude Aveline's response to the survey, *Carrefour*, March 3, 1945.

139 Max-Pol Fouchet's response to the survey, *Carrefour*, March 17, 1945.

140 Emmanuel Mounier's and Pierre Seghers's responses to the survey, *Carrefour*, March 3 and 17, 1945.

141 Émile Henriot's response to the survey, *Carrefour*, March 10, 1945.

142 Gabriel Marcel's and Georges Duhamel's responses to the survey, *Carrefour*, February 17 and March 17, 1945.

143 Georges Duhamel, *Les Nouvelles Épîtres*, XXᵉ épître, February 10, 1946 (BDIC).

144 René Lalou, "Le rôle social des écrivains," *Gavroche*, March 8, 1945.

145 Simonin, *Les Éditions de Minuit*, 230.

146 Lalou, "Le rôle social des écrivains."

147 Louis Martin-Chauffier, "L'engagement total," *Les Lettres françaises*, August 25, 1945. Earlier, I quoted an excerpt from Jean Cassou's article, "La justice" (*Les Lettres françaises* 65, July 21, 1945) where, responding to the "indulgents" and especially Mauriac, he invoked Camille Desmoulins and Saint-Just to call for the "traitors" to be treated as "enemies."

148 See Louis Martin-Chauffier, *L'Homme et la bête* (Paris: Gallimard, 1947). See also Nicole Racine, "Jean Cassou," in J. Maitron et C. Pennetier (eds.), *Dictionnaire biographique du mouvement ouvrier français 1971–1914* (Paris: Éditions ouvrières, 1984), t. 21, 270–273, and "Louis Martin-Chauffier," ibid., t. 35 (1989), 397–400.

149 [Jean Cassou], "Le mensonge en détresse," *Les Lettres françaises*, June 1944.

150 Simonin, *Les Éditions de Minuit*, 213 et 225.

151 André Chamson, *Il faut vivre vieux* (Paris: Grasset, 1984), 144.

152 I'm referring to "Situation of the Writer in 1947," *What Is Literature*, 141–238.

153 Julien Benda, *La France byzantine ou le triomphe de la littérature pure: Mallarmé, Gide, Proust, Valéry, Alain, Giraudoux, Suarès, les Surréalistes; Essai d'une psychologie originelle du littérateur* (Paris: Gallimard, 1945).

154 Julien Benda, "L'écrivain et le droit à l'erreur," *Les Lettres françaises*, March 8, 1946.

155 Julien Benda, "Les droits du 'talent,' " *L'Ordre*, October 7, 1947. See also "Psychologie des gens de Lettres," *L'Ordre*, December 8, 1946; "Le cas Paulhan," *L'Ordre*, October 27, 1947.

156 Léon-Pierre Quint, "Les écrivains devant la société," *Les Lettres françaises*, May 26, 1945.

157 Paulhan, *Of Chaff and Wheat*, 31, 34, 38–39, 40.

158 See Henry Rousso, *The Vichy Syndrome*, trans. Arthur Goldhammer (Cambridge, MA: Harvard University Press, 1991), 17.

159 Letter from Paulhan to Vercors, January 5, 1947, Vercors collection, Jacques Doucet archives.

160 "One does not do whatever one wants, and yet one is responsible for what one is: such are the facts. Man, who may be explained simultaneously by so many causes, is nevertheless alone in bearing the burden of himself. In this sense, freedom might appear to be a curse; it *is* a curse. But it is also the sole source of human greatness." Jean-Paul Sartre, "Introducing *Les Temps modernes*," trans. Jeffrey Mehlman, *"What Is Literature?" and Other Essays* (Cambridge, MA: Harvard University Press, 1988), 264.

161 [Jean-Paul Sartre], "La littérature, cette liberté!," *Les Lettres françaises* 15 (April 1944).

162 Jean-Paul Sartre, "The Nationalization of Literature," trans. Jeffrey Mehlman, *"What Is Literature,"* 285–286.

163 Boschetti, *The Intellectual Enterprise*, 112.

164 See Annie Cohen-Solal, *Sartre: A Life*, trans. Anna Cancogni (New York: Pantheon, 1987), 298–308, and Émile Copfermann, *David Rousset: Une vie dans le siècle* (Paris: Plon, 1991), 105.

165 Claude Morgan, "Ce que nous sommes," *Les Lettres françaises*, December 21, 1945. See also, for example, Laurent Casanova, "Le Parti et les intellectuels" [November 1, 1947], in *Le Parti communiste, les intellectuels et la nation* (Paris: Éditions Sociales, 1949), 16.

166 Jacques Laurent, "Paul and Jean-Paul," *La Table ronde*, February 1951, 22–53 (27 for the quote).

167 Jacques Laurent, "Le temps de *La Table ronde*," in Touzot (ed.), *François Mauriac, Cahiers de l'Herne*, 346.

168 Laurent, "Paul and Jean-Paul," 53.

169 This was the argument so frequently brandished by the "Hussards," to which Jacques Laurent belonged, against existentialism and Socialist realism; see Nicholas Hewitt, *Literature and the Right in Postwar France: The Story of the "Hussards"* (Washington, DC: Berg, 1996).

Chapter 9: Literary Institutions and National Reconstruction

1 Maurice Garçon, *Le Figaro*, November 4, 1944.

2 "Une élection avant l'épuration," *Les Lettres françaises* 36 (December 30, 1944).

3 A fragment of these "Cahiers," which were a report on the maquis, appeared under the title "Aux armes, citoyens!" in *Les Lettres françaises* 16 (May 1944).

4 In the chapter that he devotes to the image of women in literature, James Steel observes that they remain confined to a traditional role, defined in their relationship to the man (female characters are essentially wives of prisoners, widows, mothers, sisters, fiancées, or mistresses; see James Steel, *Littératures de l'ombre: Récits et nouvelles de la Résistance 1940–1944* [Paris: PFNSP, 1991], 143–158). However, the analysis that Amy Smiley has made based on the manuscripts of "Les Amants d'Avignon" offers a more nuanced view of this observation (*"Les Amants d'Avignon et la période de la Résistance"* [conference paper presented at "Elsa Triolet, un écrivain dans le siècle," Saint-Arnoult-en-Yvelines, November 15–17, 1996]): while the image of Juliette Noël, typist, remains heavily stereotyped, the evolution of the character in the different stages of the manuscript reflects the changes that occurred in the position of women, despite the arsenal deployed by the Vichy regime to reverse the course of events. This process is already noticeable in the work of a number of women writing during the interwar period; they call the dominant patriarchal values into question, as Jennifer Milligan has shown in *The Forgotten Generation: French Women Writers of the Inter-war Period* (New York: Berg, 1996).

5 C. G., *Appel des Femmes* (Toulouse), [n.d.], FETA press file.

6 See the analysis of Marie-Thérèse Eychart, "Réception du prix Goncourt 1944: Elsa Triolet ou la constitution d'une légende," *Recherches croisées Aragon/Elsa Triolet* 5 (1994): 203–211.

7 *L'Aurore*, July 4, 1945, FETA press file.

8 *Casablanca*, October 3, 1947, quoted by Micheline Dupray, *Roland Dorgelès: Un siècle de vie littéraire française* (Paris: Presses de la Renaissance, 1986), 400.

9 Louis Parrot, "Prix littéraires," *Les Lettres françaises*, December 18, 1947.

10 René Benjamin, *La Galère des Goncourt* (Paris: L'Élan, 1949), 247–250, and the minutes of the meetings on March 5 and December 24, 1947, archives of the Académie Goncourt. See also Jacques Robichon, *Le Défi des Goncourt* (Paris: Denoël, 1975), 168–177, and Robert Aron, *Histoire de l'épuration*, t. 3, vol. 2, *Le monde de la presse, des arts, des lettres . . . , 1944–1953* (Paris: Fayard, 1975), 51–55.

11 Article 13: "If one of the academicians commits an action unworthy of a man of honor, he will be censured or deposed according to the extent of his misdeed." Article 10 sets out the modalities for applying article 13. "Statuts et règlements de l'Académie française," February 22, 1935, reproduced in Institut de France, *Annuaire de l'Académie française: Documents et notices sur les membres de l'Académie* (Paris: Firmin-Didot, 1966), 25.

12 Speech by Jérôme Tharaud, minutes of the meeting on August 31, 1944, register 2 B 20, 108, archives of the French Academy. The deliberations concerning expulsions

were supposed to remain secret. They were not included in the minutes of the Academy. I will thus refer to the accounts that mention them.

13 Henry Bordeaux, *Histoire d'une vie*, t. 12, *Lumière au bout de la nuit* (Paris: Plon, 1970), 296.

14 Ibid.

15 However, due to his age, Hermant was freed from prison and admitted to the Chantilly hospice thanks to the intervention of Bordeaux; the Academy discreetly gave him subsidies until his death in 1950. As for Abel Bonnard, sentenced to death in absentia, he lived in exile in Spain. Having returned to France in 1958, he was judged in 1960 by the high court and was sentenced to ten years of banishment starting in 1945. Having learned that Abel Bonnard continued to sign articles in newspapers with the title "of the French Academy," the Company intervened to put this behavior to a stop. René de la Croix de Castries, *La Vieille Dame du quai Conti: Une histoire de l'Académie française* (Paris: Perrin, 1978), 395; the letter from Georges Lecomte to Henry Bordeaux about Abel Hermant, sent October 4, 1950, Dossier appendices 5 B 42, and the minutes of the meeting on January 8, 1953, register 2 B 21, 46, archives of the French Academy.

16 Georges Duhamel, *Éclaircissements* (Paris: P. Hartmann, 1947), 11.

17 Henry Bordeaux, *Histoire d'une vie*, t. 13, *La dernière ascension* (Paris: Plon, 1973), 43–50.

18 This message seems to have been an initiative by Duhamel, since its text was only approved by the Academy on May 17, 1945; minutes of the meeting of May 17, 1945, register 2 B 20, 139, archives of the French Academy.

19 Aron, *Histoire de l'épuration*, t. 3, vol. 2, 31.

20 Charles de Gaulle, *The Complete War Memoirs of Charles de Gaulle*, trans. Jonathan Griffin and Richard Howard, vol. 3, *Salvation*, trans. Richard Howard (New York: Carroll and Graf, 1998), 799.

21 Claude Mauriac reproduced this list in his journal on October 28, 1945; see Claude Mauriac, *Le Temps immobile*, t. 5, *Aimer de Gaulle* (Paris: Grasset, 1978), 212.

22 Letter from Jean Blanzat to Jean Paulhan [1944], Jean Paulhan collection, IMEC archives.

23 André Gide, *Journals*, vol. 4, *1939–1949*, trans. Justin O'Brien (Urbana: Illinois University Press, 2000), 256.

24 Letter from Paul Claudel to Paul Valéry, October 30, 1944. Reproduced in Paul Claudel, *Journal*, t. 2, *1933–1955* (Paris: Gallimard, 1969), 499.

25 *Le Procès de Charles Maurras: Compte rendu sténographique* (Paris: Albin Michel, 1946), 40.

26 Letter from Mauriac to Martin du Gard, October 27, [1944?], in François Mauriac, *Lettres d'une vie (1904–1969)* (Paris: Grasset, 1981), 286.

27 Letter from Martin du Gard to Duhamel, November 14, 1944, in Roger Martin du Gard, *Correspondance générale*, t. 8, *1940–1944* (Paris: Gallimard, 1997), 682–683.

28 Letter from Mauriac to Duhamel [February 1945], in François Mauriac, *Nouvelles Lettres d'une vie (1906–1970)* (Paris: Grasset, 1989), 230–231 (the letter was written after February 22, the date of the meeting that Mauriac references).

29 François Mauriac, "Histoire politique de l'Académie française (2)," in Jean Touzot (ed.), *François Mauriac* (Paris: Éditions de L'Herne [Cahiers de l'Herne no. 48], 1985), 408 and 409.

30 On the attitude of Jérôme Carcopino during the war and, in particular, as the director of the ENS, his rigorous application of the laws of exception and numerus clausus on the candidates and students of Jewish origin, see Stéphane Israël's study, "Jérôme Carcopino, directeur de l'École normale supérieure des années noires," in *Les Facs sous Vichy*, Actes du colloque des Universités de Clermont-Ferrand et de Strasbourg (November 1993), texts collected by André Gueslin (Clermont-Ferrand: Publications de l'Institut d'Études du Massif Central, Université Blaise-Pascal, 1994), 157–168; and Stéphane Israël, *Les Études et la guerre: Les normaliens et leur École face à la Seconde Guerre mondiale (1938–1946)* (Paris: Éditions rue d'Ulm, 2005).

31 "Les élections à l'Académie française: Analyse d'un scrutin significatif; L'échec de M. Paul Morand," *Revue française de science politique* 8, no. 3 (September 1958): 647 and 649 (this article is attributed to André Siegfried).

32 François Mauriac, "La bataille des bulletins blancs," *Le Figaro littéraire*, June 21, 1958, reproduced in Touzot (ed.), *François Mauriac*, 416.

33 Georges Cogniot, "Discours," in *Les Intellectuels et la Renaissance française* (Paris: Éditions du P.C.F., 1945), 21 and 23.

34 See Georges Ternet, "Notre journal restera au Front national," *Front national*, October 7–8, 1945; tract "Les Parisiens ne liront pas 'Front national' ce matin," signed "Front national"; "Arbitrage de conciliation rendu par la Fédération de la presse sur demande du 'Front national' et de M. Debû-Bridel," *Front national*, October 10, 1945, MRN.

35 Minutes from the assembly of February 10, 1946, register "CNE. Comptes rendus des assemblées générales," CNE archives, FETA, 30. This is the first general assembly for which minutes exist: actually, it seems that records were not kept for the year 1944–1945, and the CNE archives are incomplete with regards to this first year of the committee's existence.

36 Founded in 1929, *L'Ordre* was a journal with nationalist tendencies; it had adopted anti-Munich positions. Its contributors included Jacques Debû-Bridel, Pierre Loewel, and Léon Treich, among others. We have seen how, starting in late 1946, it published Julien Benda's attacks on Paulhan.

37 Jean Paulhan, *Of Chaff and Wheat*, trans. Richard Rand (Urbana: University of Illinois Press, 2004), 38.

38 Intervention by Aragon in the minutes of the assembly of February 10, 1946.

39 "Programme du CNE," *Les Lettres françaises*, March 8, 1946.

40 Aragon, "À l'un des Quarante," *Les Lettres françaises*, March 22, 1946. See also Stanislas Fumet, "L'Académie à relever," *Les Lettres françaises* 101 (March 29, 1946).

41 François Mauriac, "Le tournant académique," April 5, 1946, republished in François Mauriac, *Journal* t. 5 (Paris: Flammarion, 1953), 26.

42 Bernard Vargaftig, "Témoignage," in *Aragon 1956*, Actes du colloque d'Aix-en-Provence, September 5–8 1991 (Aix-en-Provence: Publications de l'Université de Provence, 1992), 53.

43 Letter from Blanzat to Paulhan [n.d.], Jean Paulhan collection, IMEC. We can date this letter to the beginning of October 1944.

44 Letter from Paulhan to Jouhandeau [April 2, 1944], ibid. (362), 410.

45 Card from Paulhan to Vercors, April 12, 1945, and draft of Vercors's response [n.d.], Vercors collection, Jacques Doucet archives.

46 Letter from Paulhan to Schlumberger, September 12, 1946, Jean Schlumberger collection, Jacques Doucet archives.

47 See the letter from Paulhan to Aragon, September 23, [1946], in Aragon, Paulhan, and Triolet, *"Le Temps traversé": Correspondance 1920–1964* (Paris: Gallimard, 1994) (131), 197.

48 See the letter from Paulhan to Aragon, November 23, [1946], in Aragon, Paulhan, and Triolet, *"Le Temps traversé"* (134), 200–201. According to Eugène Guillevic, Aragon argued in favor of Jouhandeau at the CNE (ibid., 200, n. 1). I have found no trace of an intervention by Aragon in this sense at the directive board, but it is possible that, not having met with unanimity, it was not transferred to the minutes.

49 Exceptional general assembly of May 28, 1946, 65. Shortly before voting the motion of exclusion, Aragon had published an article against the anthology published by René Lalou; Aragon, "M. René Lalou et notre honneur: Musique intérieure," *Les Lettres françaises* 106 (May 3, 1946). The motion to exclude was published in *Les Lettres françaises* on June 7, 1946.

50 "Pierre Benoit rayé de la liste noire," *Les Lettres françaises* 135 (November 22, 1946).

51 Letter from Paulhan to Schlumberger [November 23, 1946], Jean Schlumberger collection, Jacques Doucet archives.

52 Letter from Paulhan to Gallimard, July 19, 1946, in Jean Paulhan, *Choix de lettres*, t. 3, *1946–1968 Le don des langues* (Paris: Gallimard, 1996) (4), 31–32.

53 Letter from Gide to Paulhan, March 9, 1947, and response from Paulhan [March 10, 1947], in André Gide, Jean Paulhan, *Correspondance (1918–1951)* (Paris: Gallimard, 1998) (301 and 302), 302–303.

54 Letter from Jean Paulhan to Jean Schlumberger [December 1946], Jean Schlumberger collection, Jacques Doucet archives.

55 Jean Duché, interviews with Gabriel Marcel and Jean Schlumberger, *Cavalcade*, January 16, 1947.

56 Vercors, "Lettre ouverte," *Les Lettres françaises*, December 27, 1946.

57 Minutes of the meeting of January 26, 1948, register "CNE. Comptes rendus du comité directeur," 30 (double-sided). Mauriac's exclusion was made public three days later; "Au comité directeur du CNE," *Les Lettres françaises*, January 29, 1948.

58 François Mauriac, "Rue de l'Élysée," *Le Figaro*, May 9, 1949.

59 Louis Martin-Chauffier, "Le bonheur d'être libre," and "L'Allocution du Président de la République au Comité national des écrivains," *Les Lettres françaises*, October 28, 1948.

60 John and Carol Garrard, *Inside the Soviet Writers' Union* (New York: Macmillan, 1990).

61 Draft of a letter from Vercors to Paulhan, [January? 1947], Vercors collection, Jacques Doucet archives.

62 Pierre Daix, *J'ai cru au matin* (Paris: Laffont, 1976), 197.

63 Anne Simonin, *Les Éditions de Minuit 1942–1955: Le devoir d'insoumission* (Paris: IMEC, 1994), 280.

64 "M. Joxe évoque la crise du livre français," *Le Figaro*, April 25–26, 1948.

65 Marc Lazar, "Les 'Batailles du livre' du parti communiste français (1950–1952)," *Vingtième siècle* 10 (April–June 1986): 41.

66 Georges Duhamel (interview), "Le livre français d'abord," *Les Lettres françaises*, April 22, 1948.

67 Copy of the letter from Georges Lecomte, permanent secretary of the French Academy, to Louis Joxe, archives of the French Academy, Dossier appendices 5 B 41.

68 Aragon, "La culture et sa diffusion," speech given in April 1947 at the National Union of Intellectuals (Maison de la Pensée), *La Culture et les hommes* (Paris: Éditions sociales, 1947), 61 and 62.

69 Elsa Triolet, "Prenez exemple sur nos ennemis," *Les Lettres françaises*, March 25, 1948, republished in *L'Écrivain et le livre ou la suite dans les idées* (Paris: Éditions sociales, 1948), 67–68.

70 René Lacôte, "Le sabotage de la librairie française," *Les Lettres françaises*, April 1 and 15, 1948.

71 Triolet, *L'Écrivain et le livre*, 73.

72 André Wurmser, "Le livre français en Amérique du Sud," *Les Lettres françaises*, April 8, 1948.

73 "A crisis is raging in our literary production as in all artistic productions. The exorbitant prices that are demanded to transport books have brutally halted the circulation and diffusion of all the works of our mind. And here I am only considering one aspect of the dangerous problem that is posed and to which Elsa Triolet has devoted herself in all her generosity of spirit." Henry Malherbe, "Réflexions sur le déclin de la littérature commerciale: Les Français n'achètent plus les romans américains," *Les Lettres françaises*, March 24, 1949.

74 Jean Marcenac, "Les États généraux de la pensée française," *Les Lettres françaises*, March 31, 1949.

75 The directive board of the CNE, "Sur les conditions matérielles de la liberté d'expression," *Les Lettres françaises*, March 17, 1949.

76 Letter from François Billoux to Elsa Triolet dated "this November 1949" and published in *La Marseillaise* on March 9, 1950, quoted by Marc Lazar, "Les 'Batailles du livre,'" 40–41.

77 Elsa Triolet, "Se battre pour le livre," *Les Lettres françaises* 310 (May 4, 1950). See also the account of Dominique Desanti, *Les Staliniens: Une expérience politique 1944–1956* (Paris: Fayard, 1975), 238–241.

78 Previously cited interview with Vercors.

79 See the chapter that Jean-Pierre A. Bernard devotes to "La mondanité communiste" in *Paris rouge 1944–1964: Les communistes français dans la capitale* (Seyssel: Champs Vallon, 1991), 169–206.

80 In 1965, a sale would take place at the Palais des Sports; then, in 1968, it would come full circle, to the Palais d'Orsay.

81 Minutes from the meetings of October 28, 1948, and November 3, 1952, register "CNE. Comptes rendus du Comité directeur," 40 and 75; "CNE Journal 1945–1956," CNE archives, FETA.

82 Eluard's biographer estimates the sales figures: at the 1950 sale, Eluard sold 105,000 francs worth of books, three times less than Aragon, significantly less than André Wurmser or Jean Effel. The following year, the poet's sales figures triple: 330,000 francs. Jean-Charles Gateau, *Paul Eluard ou Le frère voyant 1895–1952* (Paris: Laffont, 1988), 350 and 356.

83 Minutes of the meeting of November 3, 1952, register "CNE. Comptes rendus du Comité directeur," 74.

84 See Aragon, *Chroniques du Bel Canto* (Geneva: Skira, 1947).

85 Aragon, *Journal d'une poésie nationale* (Lyon: Henneuse, Les Écrivains réunis, 1954).

86 Minutes of the meeting of December 1, 1950, register "CNE. Comptes rendus du Comité directeur," 59.

87 Charter of the Comité national des écrivains, CNE archives, FETA.

88 Louis Martin-Chauffier, "La Paix est notre affaire," opening speech of the CNE general assembly of May 7, 1949, reproduced in *Les Lettres françaises*, May 12, 1949.

89 "Extrait du rapport moral présenté par la secrétaire générale Elsa Triolet," *Les Lettres françaises*, March 16, 1950.

90 June 16, 1950 meeting, register "CNE. Comptes rendus du Comité directeur." Let us recall that the Stockholm Appeal, launched on March 19, 1950, by the Mouvement des partisans de la paix, and which notably demanded the banning of the atomic bomb, would collect 600 million signatures from around the world, including 14 million from France, according to official figures (in fact, French signers are estimated between 9 and 10 million). Stéphane Courtois and Marc Lazar, *Histoire du Parti communiste français* (Paris: PUF, 1995), 277–278.

91 André Wurmser, *Réponse à Jean Cassou* (Paris: Éditions de la Nouvelle Critique, 1950), 30.

92 Jean Cassou, "La révolution et la vérité," *Esprit* 12 (December 1949): 947 and 948.

93 Vercors, "Réponses," *Esprit* 12 (December 1949): 949.

94 Tony Judt, *Past Imperfect: French Intellectuals, 1944–1956* (Berkeley: University of California Press, 1992), 148.

95 "Des membres du CNE répondent à Serge Groussard," *Le Figaro littéraire*, February 28, 1950.

96 "Cinq nouvelles démissions," *Le Figaro littéraire*, March 7, 1953.

97 "Nouvelles démissions au CNE," *Le Figaro littéraire*, March 28, 1953.

98 Minutes of the meeting of January 26, 1953, register "CNE. Comptes rendus du Comité directeur," 80.

99 Press release published in *Les Lettres françaises* on January 29, 1953, and reproduced in *Le Figaro littéraire* on February 21, 1953.

100 Minutes of the meeting of February 19, 1953, register "CNE Comité directeur," 85.

101 Vercors, *Cent ans d'histoire de France*, t. 3, *Les Nouveaux jours, Esquisse d'une Europe* (Paris: Plon, 1984), 214.

102 A. A., "Les écrivains du CNE comptent leurs antisémites," *Le Figaro littéraire*, February 21, 1953.

103 "Des membres du CNE répondent."

104 Louis de Villefosse, *L'Œuf de Wyasma* (Paris: Julliard, 1962), 207.

105 Aside from short items in *Paroles françaises*, the first open attacks against Vercors appeared in *Combat* under the pen of Justin Saget, former contributor to the journal of Spinasse, *Le Rouge et le Bleu*, which represented the collaborationist left. Vercors was treated there as a "hysterical" and saw himself accused, among other things—and obviously wrongly—of plagiarism. See "Presse littéraire," *Les Lettres françaises* 146 (February 7, 1947). See also the analysis of Simonin, *Les Éditions de Minuit*, 326–327.

106 Vercors, *À dire vrai: Entretiens de Vercors avec Gilles Plazy* (Paris: François Bourin, 1991), 117.

107 "Des membres du CNE répondent à Serge Groussard."

108 Reported by Michel Apel-Muller in an interview with Lili Marcou, *Elsa Triolet: Les Yeux et la Mémoire* (Paris, Plon: 1994), 296.

109 See especially Dominique Berthet, *Le PCF, la culture et l'art* (Paris: La Table ronde, 1990), 223; Pierre Daix, *Aragon, une vie à changer* (Paris: Seuil, 1975; Flammarion, 1978), 456; Desanti, *Les Staliniens*, 241–244.

110 de Villefosse, *L'Œuf de Wyasma*, 210. On the 1956 crisis at the CNE, see Gisèle Sapiro, "Le CNE: Un héritage subversif détourné?," in Jacques Girault and Bernard Lecherbonnier (eds.), *Les Engagements d'Aragon*, Actes du colloque de l'Université Paris XIII, April 1, 1997 (Paris: L'Harmattan, 1998), 112–113.

111 See Pierre Grémion, *Intelligence de l'anticommunisme: Le Congrès pour la liberté de la culture à Paris 1950–1975* (Paris: Fayard, 1995), 246.

112 *Le Procès de Charles Maurras*, 371.

113 François Mauriac, "Réponse à 'Combat,'" in François Mauriac, *Le Bâillon dénoué: Après quatre ans de silence* (Paris: Grasset, 1945), 93.

114 André Rousseaux, "Épilogue à l'affaire Dreyfus," *Les Lettres françaises* 70 (August 25, 1945).

115 Charles Maurras, *Réponse à André Gide* (Paris: Éditions de La Seule France, 1948), 22 and 18.

116 Maurice Bardèche, *Lettre ouverte à François Mauriac* (Paris: La Pensée libre, 1947), 99, 101 and 58.

117 See Jeannine Verdès-Leroux, *Refus et violences: Politique et littérature à l'extrême droite des années trente aux retombées de la Libération* (Paris: Gallimard, 1996), 420, and Nicholas Hewitt, *Literature and the Right in Postwar France: The Story of the "Hussards,"* (Washington: Berg, 1996), 77.

118 In a letter to Mauriac on March 12, 1952, Paulhan expressly claimed filiation with the Dreyfusards; see the Jean Paulhan collection, IMEC archives. In his response, he made direct reference to Louis Martin-Chauffier, "To a Pharisian of the Resistance," *Le Littéraire*, March 15, 1952: "In *Les Morts*, I called for a new underground that would maintain, against politics, the mystique of the Resistance," before taking this theme up again later: "For we were not, résistants, a political party; [. . .] We were a mystique, Martin-Chauffier, and almost a religion. How did we fall from so high?

How did you not see that your tricks of justice and your forgeries belied our words of the time of occupation, and—as Péguy said—dejustify our conduct?"

119 Jean Paulhan, *Lettre aux directeurs de la Résistance* (Paris: Minuit, 1952, republished by Ramsay, 1987), 12.

120 See Anne Simonin, "La *Lettre aux directeurs de la Résistance* de Jean Paulhan: Pour une rhétorique de l'engagement," in Antoine de Baecque (ed.), *Les Écrivains face à l'histoire*, Actes du colloque organized at the BPI on March 22, 1997 (Paris: La BPI en actes, 1998), 45–69.

121 Letter from Mauriac to Paulhan, January 3, 1952, Jean Paulhan collection, IMEC archives. See also the letter from Jean Guéhenno, January 2, 1952.

122 Louis Martin-Chauffier, "Lettre à un transfuge de la résistance," *Le Littéraire*, February 2, 1952; response from Jean Paulhan, "À un pharisien de la Résistance," ibid., March 15, 1952; Martin-Chauffier, "Paulhan ne m'a pas répondu," ibid., March 29, 1952; Roger Stéphane, "Le renégat appliqué," *L'Observateur*, February 7, 1952; Elsa Triolet, "Jean Paulhan successeur de Drieu La Rochelle," *Les Lettres françaises*, February 7, 1952; Pierre de Lescure, "Le simple grammairien Jean Paulhan," *La Tribune des Nations*, March 21, 1952. Dossier of responses held in the Jean Paulhan collection, IMEC archives. Some of these articles are collected in Jean Paulhan, *Œuvres complètes*, t. 5, *Politique* (Paris: Cercle du Livre précieux, 1970), 429–438.

123 Martin-Chauffier, "Lettre à un transfuge de la Résistance."

124 Letter from Mauriac to Paulhan, March 20, 1952, Jean Paulhan collection, IMEC archives.

125 Two special issues of *La NRF* had preceded this launch: a tribute to André Gide in November 1951 and a tribute to Alain in September 1952. *Les Cahiers de la Pléiade* ceased publication in April 1952.

126 Quoted by Florent Brayard, *Comment l'idée vint à M. Rassinier: Naissance du révisionnisme* (Paris: Fayard, 1996), 259.

127 Jean Cassou, *La Mémoire courte* (Paris: Minuit, 1953), 73.

128 Reported by Henry Bordeaux, *Charles Maurras et l'Académie française* (Paris: Éditions du Conquistador, 1955), 156; see also the minutes of the meeting on November 20, 1952, register 2 B 21, 41.

129 Quoted by René de la Croix de Castries, *La Vieille Dame*, 396.

130 Aron, *Histoire de l'épuration*, t. 3, vol. 2, 37 and 39.

131 See Henry Rousso, *The Vichy Syndrome*, trans. Arthur Goldhammer (Cambridge, MA: Harvard University Press, 1991), 66.

Conclusion

1 Lucien Rebatet, "L'Académie de la dissidence ou la trahison prosaïque," *Je suis partout* 656 (March 10, 1944).

2 Ibid.

3 François Mauriac, "L'honneur des écrivains," *Le Figaro littéraire*, January 25, 1941, reproduced in Jean Touzot, *Mauriac sous l'Occupation* (Paris: La Manufacture, 1990), 225.

4 François Mauriac, unpublished underground text written in 1941 ("Dans l'état présent de la France"), published by Touzot, *Mauriac sous l'Occupation*, 228–230 (230 for this quote). The "sheets" refer to Céline's *Beaux-Draps*, or "Nice Sheets."

5 [Jean-Paul Sartre], "La littérature, cette liberté!," *Les Lettres françaises* 15 (April 1944).

6 Pierre Drieu La Rochelle, *Journal 1939–1945* (Paris: Gallimard, 1992), 373. By a strange coincidence, a few days after Drieu wrote this, Malraux would engage in the active Resistance.

7 Ibid., 317.

8 "Drieu La Rochelle, who was certainly one of the sincerest and perhaps one of the most pathetic among those who deceived themselves, had a review in which he regularly insulted muzzled men, men who could not answer back [. . .] Well, this man, who was not without insight, gradually became uneasy, and this showed in his writings; anger gave way to qualms of conscience, and finally he abandoned his review, just because he was speaking to people who could not answer back, just because he was speaking to people who were not free to pass judgment on what he wrote." Jean-Paul Sartre, "The Responsibility of the Writer," trans. Betty Askwith, in *Reflections on Our Age: Lectures delivered at the Opening Session of UNESCO at the Sorbonne University Paris* (New York: Columbia University Press, 1949), 74.

9 Although the principle of seniority was at work, at the margins of clandestinity, for all those who condemned the illicit practices of the agents of heteronomy, either openly, through the defense of writers stigmatized as "bad masters" for example, or even silently, like Roger Martin du Gard.

10 Aragon, preface to Jean Cassou, *33 Sonnets of the Resistance and Other Poems*, trans. Timothy Adès (Todmorden, UK: Arc, 2004), 17–18.

11 *L'Honneur des poètes*, Éditions de Minuit, July 14, 1943, republished 1945, 10.

12 Vercors, "Nous avons été heureux," *Les Lettres françaises* 23 (September 30, 1944).

13 François Mauriac, "Le parti de l'espérance," *Les Lettres françaises* 111 (June 7, 1946).

14 Jean-Paul Sartre, "The Republic of Silence," in *Defeat and Beyond: An Anthology of French Wartime Writing, 1940–1945*, ed. Germaine Brée, trans. Alastair Hamilton (New York: Pantheon Books, 1970), 331.

15 We should note that, probably because it was overselected and recruited from a network of acquaintances, perhaps also because it was the best protected due to the notoriety of its members, the underground literary organization was one of the few Resistance milieus, including within the intellectual Resistance, where there was no betrayal even though its elementary security rules were continually transgressed. It is also true that the printers, for their part, were more exposed. See Anne Simonin, *Les Éditions de Minuit 1942–1955: Le devoir d'insoumission* (Paris: IMEC, 1994), 189.

16 Claude Roy, *Moi je* (Paris: Gallimard, 1969), 139.

17 Pierre Bourdieu, *The Rules of Art: Genesis and Structure of the Literary Field*, trans. Susan Emanuel (Stanford, CA: Stanford University Press, 1995), 227.

18 Anna Boschetti, *The Intellectual Enterprise: Sartre and Les Temps Modernes*, trans. Richard C. McCleary (Evanston, IL: Northwestern University Press, 1988), 109.

19 See Anne Simonin, "La littérature saisie par l'Histoire: Nouveau Roman et guerre d'Algérie aux Éditions de Minuit," *Actes de la recherche en sciences sociales* 111–112 (March 1996): 69–71.

20 Pierre Bourdieu, *Pascalian Meditations*, trans. Richard Nice (Stanford, CA: Stanford University Press, 2000), 65.

21 "Disinterest" is, for example, as we have seen, the banner under which the turn-of-the-century struggles to defend the humanities against the "utilitarianism" of the sciences were led.

22 Heir to the first romanticism, the theory of art for art's sake was developed under the Second Empire by the second romantic generation against bourgeois art and social art, even though the evolution of the first romantics had led them to condemn pure art. Baudelaire himself, who would soon help impose the doctrine of art for art's sake, evoked the "puerile utopia of the school of art for art's sake" in 1852, and preached taking action against romantic melancholia. Albert Cassagne, *La Théorie de l'art pour l'art en France chez les derniers romantiques et les premiers réalistes* (Paris: Hachette, 1906, republished by Champ Vallon, 1997), 104. See also especially the chapter devoted to art for art's sake and morality, 217–244.

23 Henry de Montherlant, *Carnets (années 1930 à 1944)* (Paris: Gallimard, 1957), 330.

24 Notes prepared by Jacques Rivière for a meeting with the contributors to *La NRF* on July 3, 1919, in Henri Ghéon and Jacques Rivière, *Correspondance (1910–1925)* (Centre d'études gidiennes, Université de Lyon II, 1988), 201.

25 Christophe Charle, *Naissance des "intellectuels" (1880–1900)* (Paris: Minuit, 1990) and *Les Intellectuels en Europe au XIXᵉ siècle: Essai d'histoire comparée* (Paris: Seuil, 1996).

26 Paul Bourget, *The Disciple* (New York: Howard Fertig, 1976), 70.

27 Albert Cassagne observed this about Victor Hugo following the banning of *Le Roi s'amuse* under the July Monarchy: "It was to defend the freedom of art and even of art for art's sake that the poet became involved in politics." See Cassagne, *La Théorie de l'art pour l'art*, 86.

28 Pierre Bourdieu, "Le champ littéraire," *Actes de la recherche en sciences sociales* 89 (September 1991): 10, and Charle, *Naissance des "intellectuels."*

Appendix 1

Salah Bouhedja assisted me in the processing of the factorial analysis.

1 These 12 modalities correspond to two variables, religion and the paternal familial trajectory, which were treated as illustrative variables due to the high rate of non-responses.

 2 I have considered that the data concerning the original social trajectory was more reliable than indicators such as profession or the length of professional practice (which I coded, but don't use for the correspondence analysis). These indicators would have only been relevant as signs of social position if they were combined with assessments of literary and non-literary earnings and print numbers, impossible to establish. Similarly, the heterogeneity of "matrimonial" situations and the difficulty of obtaining in-

formation for a whole segment of the population (the *Who's Who* only started in 1953) did not allow me to process this type of information in a coherent manner. On the other hand, the atypical character of the population of writers overall and the relative heterogeneity of its social recruitment give the indicators of primary and secondary *habitus* a first-rate informational value to understand the relationships between social trajectory and position in the literary field. I have, for example, taken particular care in gathering data concerning geographical and educational trajectories, for which only a low rate of nonresponses subsists (including for the secondary). These data are all the more revealing, particularly for school, since they are almost systematically omitted from biographical entries of a literary nature (this phenomenon is, of course, an avatar of the traditional opposition between "creators" and "professors.")

3 We can thus verify, for example, that for the young poets who entered the field during this period, poetry was not a youthful choice characteristic of numerous literary careers following the "romantic" model, but actually a definitive choice since poets they would remain.

4 Christophe Charle, "Situation du champ littéraire," *Littérature* 44 (1982): 8–21, 9, and *La République des universitaires 1879–1940* (Paris: Seuil, 1994), 473.

5 They were grouped in one category, because of the relative rarity of writers from popular milieus.

6 Rémy Ponton, *Le Champ littéraire de 1865 à 1906 (recrutement des écrivains, structure des carrières et production des œuvres)*, PhD diss., Université Paris V, 1977, 21.

7 Especially journalists and literary men. See Christophe Charle, *Naissance des "intellectuels" (1880–1900)* (Paris: Minuit, 1990), 41.

8 Antoine Prost, *Histoire de l'enseignement en France 1800–1967* (Paris: Armand Colin, 1968), 192–193.

9 See J.-P. Briand, J.-M. Chapoulie and H. Peretz, "Les conditions institutionnelles de la scolarisation secondaire des garçons entre 1920 et 1940," *Revue d'histoire moderne et contemporaine* 26 (July–September 1979): 391–421; Jean-Pierre Briand and Jean-Michel Chapoulie, *Les Collèges du peuple: L'enseignement primaire supérieur et le développement de la scolarisation prolongée sous la Troisième République* (Paris: INRP, 1992), 367; Christian Baudelot and Roger Establet, *L'École capitaliste en France* (Paris: Maspero: 1971), 34–35.

10 Ponton, *Le Champ littéraire*, 46.

11 Prost, *Histoire de l'enseignement en France*, 243.

12 In the population studied by Rémy Ponton, only 13.3 percent were born after 1865, and 27.7 percent between 1855 and 1864; Ponton, *Le Champ littéraire*, 33. The gap also results in part from a difference between the coding criteria: whereas Rémy Ponton opted for a restrictive definition of higher education, even when it was unfinished (at least two years of study), I have chosen to keep the trace of initial orientations and first choices, even when they quickly came to an end.

13 Moreover, low numbers forced a rough categorization in order to expose the principal divisions.

14 See Christian Baudelot and Frédérique Matonti, "Le recrutement social des normaliens, 1914–1992," in Jean-François Sirinelli (ed.), *École normale supérieure: Le livre*

du bicentenaire (Paris: PUF, 1994), 155–190, and Pierre Bourdieu, *The State Nobility*, trans. Loretta. C. Clough (Stanford, CA: Stanford University Press, 1996).

15 Ponton, *Le Champ littéraire*, 43.

16 These criteria can nonetheless not be rigorously founded in the absence of in-depth investigations into the publishing space during the interwar period. In his work on the surrealist group, Norbert Bandier outlined the publishing field of the 1920s; see *Sociologie du surréalisme (1924–1929)* (Paris: La Dispute, 1999). I also relied a great deal on the synthesis by Pascal Fouché, "L'édition littéraire, 1914–1950," in Roger Chartier and Henri-Jean Martin (eds.), *Histoire de l'édition française*, vol. 4, *Le livre concurrencé* (Paris: Promodis, 1986).

17 Fouché, ibid., 227.

18 In 1937, they associated their commercial services with those of the Presses universitaires de France; see Fouché, ibid., 224 and 235.

Bibliography

I. Archives

French National Archives (AN)
72 AJ 3 XV: Dossier "R.N.P.-P.P.F."
72 AJ 45: Dossier "C.N.E."
72 AJ 69: Dossier "P.C."
72 AJ 78: Dossier "Résistance des intellectuels"
72 AJ 1861: Dossier "Académies" (press file)
F17 13331: Caisse nationale des lettres et caisse nationale des sciences
F17 13369: Abel Bonnard papers, dossier "Livres et écrivains"
F21 8114: Comité national d'épuration des gens de lettres, auteurs et compositeurs
F21 8122–26: Épuration professionnelle d'écrivains

ARCHIVES OF THE FRENCH ACADEMY

Registers of meeting minutes: 2B18 (1914–1928); 2B19 (1929–1941); 2B20 (1941–1951); 2B21 (1952–1961)
Supporting document files: 5B39 (1934–1938); 5B40 (1939–1943); 5B41 (1944–1947); 5B42 (1948–1951)
Individual files

ARCHIVES OF THE GONCOURT ACADEMY, FONDS
GEFFROY, MUNICIPAL ARCHIVES OF NANCY

2 registers of minutes for the meetings of members of the Goncourt literary society (1903–1954): B.H. 106 and B.H. 106 Bis
Box: Goncourt Academy Files 1902–1950
Box R.19: correspondence from Lucien Descaves to Gustave Geffroy
Box R.15: correspondence with the Daudets: from Léon Daudet to Gustave Geffroy

Box R.03: correspondence from Ajalbert to Gustave Geffroy
Box Br 01: correspondence from Henri Béraud to Gustave Geffroy
Unlabeled box: notebook BH 129: Pierre Champion "La paix sauvée?" September 1938;
Rosny the Elder's correspondence

ELSA TRIOLET-ARAGON COLLECTION (FETA-CNRS)

Archives of the Comité national des écrivains:
register "CNE. Comptes rendus des assemblées générales du 10 II 1946 au 15 V 1954"
register "CNE. Comptes rendus des comités directeurs du 27 II 1946 au 16 XI 1960"
Boxes: "Associations 1945. Auteurs associés. Adhésions 44. Candidatures 45," "Pièces
annexes, correspondance . . . ," "Premières assemblées générales 1946–1950," "CNE.
Activités," "CNE. Premières ventes 1945–1949," "CNE. Ventes 1946," "CNE. Adhé-
sions, démissions," "Comité du livre."
"CNE. Journal 1945–1956"
"Carnets d'adresse CNE. Premières années" (170x113, 229x177, 231x153), and directory.
Léon Moussinac Archives
Correspondence: from Jacques Debû-Bridel and Vercors to Aragon; from Georges Du-
hamel to Elsa Triolet.

BDIC ARCHIVES (BIBLIOTHÈQUE DE DOCUMENTATION
INTERNATIONALE CONTEMPORAINE)

Dossier France/Résistance/Front national
Documents published by the managing committee of the Front national

MUSÉE DE LA RÉSISTANCE NATIONALE (ARCHIVES LOCATED
BY DANIEL VIRIEUX)

Georges Cogniot collection
Pierre Villon collection
Biographical dossiers

IMEC ARCHIVES (INSTITUT MÉMOIRES DE L'ÉDITION CONTEMPORAINE)

Jean Paulhan collection:
letters from Louis Aragon, Jean Blanzat, Jacques Debû-Bridel, Pierre Drieu La Rochelle,
Georges Duhamel, Paul Eluard, Rolland de Renéville
correspondence between Jean Paulhan and Jean Guéhenno (critical edition edited by
Jean-Kély Paulhan)
correspondence between François Mauriac and Jean Paulhan (critical edition edited
by John Flower and published by Éditions Claire Paulhan)

ARCHIVES OF THE REVUE DES DEUX MONDES IN THE ANDRÉ
CHAUMEIX COLLECTION (CORRESPONDENCE)

Albert Camus collection: Combat dossier (articles 1944–1945; documentation). For a
translation of selected Combat articles by Camus, see *Camus at Combat: Writing
1944–1947*. Edited by Jacqueline Lévi-Valensi. Translated by Arthur Goldhammer.
Princeton, NJ: Princeton University Press, 2005.
Roger Lannes, unpublished journal

Fonds Jacques Doucet
Correspondence from Paul Eluard, Jean Paulhan
François Mauriac collection
Jean Schlumberger collection
Vercors collection

Jacques Rivière Archives: correspondence

Jacques Lecompte-Boinet Archives: Jacques Lecompte-Boinet, unpublished journal

Politzer, Georges. "Autobiographie." November 26, 1933. Russian Center for the Conservation and Study of Documents in Contemporary History (Moscow).

II. Oral Sources

Interview with Eugène Guillevic (July 7, 1991); Jean Lescure (October 25, 1995 and June
26, 1996); Jacques Nels (March 26, 1991); Lucien Scheler (June 24, 1991); Vercors
(April 30, 1991)

III. Print Sources

A. REFERENCE BOOKS

1. Anthologies, Literary History Manuals

Almanach des Lettres françaises. Comité national des écrivains, 1944.
Domaine français (Messages 1943). Geneva/Paris: Éditions des Trois Collines, 1943.
Le Paysan français à travers la littérature, texts selected and prefaced by Marcel Arland.
Paris: Stock, 1941.
Les Poètes de l'école de Rochefort, anthology introduced by Jean Bouhier. Paris: Seghers,
1983.

Billy, André. *La Littérature française contemporaine: Poésie, Roman, Idées*. Paris: Armand
Colin, 1928.
Boisdeffre, Pierre de. *Une histoire vivante de la littérature d'aujourd'hui 1939–1960*. Paris:
Le Livre contemporain, 1959.
Brée, Germaine, and Édouard Morot-Sir. *Littérature Française*, t. 9, *Du surrealisme à
l'empire de la critique*. Paris: Arthaud, 1984 and 1990.

Dumont, Jean, ed. *Histoire de la littérature française du XXe siècle.* Geneva: Éditions
Famot. T. 1, *De la Belle Époque aux années folles*, 1975; t. 2, *L'entre-deux-guerres*, 1976.

Huret, Jules. *Enquête sur l'évolution littéraire.* Paris: Les Éditions Thot, 1984.

Lalou, René. *Histoire de la littérature française contemporaine (de 1870 à nos jours).* 2 vols.
Paris: PUF, 1947.

Nadeau, Maurice. *Histoire du surréalisme.* Paris: Seuil, 1945.

———. *Le Roman français depuis la guerre.* Paris: Gallimard, 1963.

Paulhan, Jean, and Dominique Aury. *La Patrie se fait tous les jours: Textes français 1939–
1945.* Paris: Minuit, 1947.

Poulaille, Henry. *Nouvel Âge littéraire.* Paris: Valois, 1930; Bassac: Plein Chant, 1986.

Rousselot, Jean. *Les Nouveaux Poètes français: Panorama critique.* Paris: Seghers, 1959.

Sabatier, Robert. *Histoire de la poésie française*, t. 6, *La Poésie du vingtième siècle.* Paris:
Albin Michel. Vol. 2, *Révolution et conquêtes*, 1982; vol. 3, *Métamorphoses et Moder-
nité*, 1988.

Truc, Gonzague. *Histoire de la littérature catholique contemporaine.* Paris/Tournai: Casterman, 1961.

2. Underground Éditions de Minuit Collection (selection)

Deux Voix françaises: Péguy-Péri. Preface by Vercors, introduction by the Témoin des
Martyrs [Aragon]. Éditions de Minuit, June 22, 1944.

Les Bannis. Poems translated from the German by Armor (René Cannac). For the Comité national des écrivains. Minuit, July 14, 1944. *L'Honneur des poètes.* Minuit, July
14, 1943. *Chroniques interdites.* Minuit, "Easter 1943." *Nouvelles chroniques.* Minuit,
July 14, 1944.

Argonne [Jacques Debû-Bridel]. *Angleterre: D'Alcuin à Huxley.* Minuit, September 22,
1943.

Cévennes [Jean Guéhenno]. *Dans la prison.* Minuit, August 1, 1944.

Decour [Jacques]. *Pages choisies.* For the Comité national des écrivains. Minuit, 1944.

Forez [François Mauriac], *Le Cahier noir.* Minuit, August 15, 1943. Excerpts translated by
Alastair Hamilton as "From The Black Notebook" in *Defeat and Beyond: An Anthology
of French Wartime Writing, 1940–1945*, edited by Germaine Brée and George Bernauer.
New York: Pantheon, 1970.

Jean Noir [Jean Cassou], *Trente-Trois Sonnets composés au secret.* Presented by François
La Colère [Aragon]. Minuit, May 15, 1944. Translated by Timothy Adès as *33 Sonnets
of the Resistance and Other Poems.* Todmorden, UK: Arc, 2004.

Laurent Daniel [Elsa Triolet]. *Les Amants d'Avignon.* Minuit, October 25, 1943.

Le Témoin des martyrs. *Le Crime contre l'esprit.* Minuit, February 26, 1944

Maritain, Jacques. *À travers le désastre.* Minuit, November 12, 1942. Translated as *France
My Country: Through the Disaster.* New York: Longmans, Green, 1941.

Mortagne (Claude Morgan). *La Marque de l'homme.* Minuit, June 5, 1944.

Vercors. *Le Silence de la mer.* Minuit, February 20, 1942.

———. *La Marche à l'Étoile.* Minuit, Christmas 1943.

3. Correspondence

Aragon, Louis. *Lettres à Denise*. Presented by Pierre Daix. Paris: Maurice Nadeau, 1994.

Aragon, Louis, Jean Paulhan, and Elsa Triolet. *"Le Temps traversé": Correspondance 1920–1964*. Edition established, introduced, and annotated by Bernard Leuilliot. Paris: Gallimard, 1994.

Camus, Albert, and Jean Grenier. *Correspondance (1932–1960)*. Foreword and notes by Marguerite Dobrenn. Paris: Gallimard, 1981.

Céline et les Éditions Denoël (1932–1948). Correspondence and documents introduced and annotated by Pierre-Edmond Robert. Paris: IMEC, 1991.

Claudel, Paul, and Gaston Gallimard. *Correspondance (1911–1954)*. Edition established, introduced, and annotated by Bernard Delvaille. Paris: Gallimard, 1995.

Eluard, Paul. *Lettres à Gala (1924–1948)*. Edition established and annotated by Pierre Dreyfus, preface by Jean-Claude Carrière. Paris: Gallimard, 1984. Translated by Jesse Browner as *Letters to Gala*. New York: Paragon, 1989.

Ghéon, Henri, and Jacques Rivière. *Correspondance (1910–1925)*. Edition established, introduced, and annotated by Jean-Pierre Cap. Centre d'études gidiennes, Université de Lyon II, 1988.

Gide, André, and Jean Paulhan. *Correspondance (1918–1951)*. Edition established and annotated by Frédéric Grover and Pierrette Schartenberg-Winter. Paris: Gallimard, 1998.

Gide, André, and Jacques Rivière. *Correspondance (1909–1925)*. Edition established, introduced, and annotated by Pierre de Gaulmyn and Alain Rivière, with the collaboration of Kevin O'Neill and Stuart Barr. Paris: Gallimard, 1998.

Gide, André, and Jean Schlumberger. *Correspondance (1901–1950)*. Edition established, introduced, and annotated by Pascal Mercier and Peter Fawcett. Paris: Gallimard, 1993.

Gide, André, and Paul Valéry. *Correspondance (1890–1942)*. Preface and notes by Robert Mallet. Paris: Gallimard, 1955. Translated by June Guicharnaud as *Self Portraits: The Gide/Valéry Letters, 1890–1942*. Chicago: University of Chicago Press, 1966.

Giono, Jean, and Jean Guéhenno. *Correspondance (1928–1969)*. Edition established and annotated by Pierre Citron. Paris: Seghers, 1991.

Kohn-Étiemble, Jeannine. *226 lettres inédites de Jean Paulhan: Contribution à l'étude du mouvement littéraire en France, 1933–1967*. Paris : Klincksieck, 1975.

Martin du Gard, Roger. *Correspondance générale*, t. 8, *1940–1944*. Edition established, introduced, and annotated by Bernard Duchatelet. Paris: Gallimard, 1997.

Mauriac, François. *Lettres d'une vie (1904–1969)*. Edition introduced and annotated by Caroline Mauriac. Paris: Grasset, 1981.

———. *Nouvelles lettres d'une vie (1906–1970)*. Edition introduced and annotated by Caroline Mauriac. Paris: Grasset, 1989.

Mauriac, François, and Georges Duhamel. *Correspondance (1919–1966). Le Croyant et l'humaniste inquiet*. Edition introduced and annotated by J.-J. Hueber, preface by Jean Touzot. Paris: Klincksieck, 1997.

Paulhan, Jean. *Choix de lettres*. Established by Dominique Aury and Jean-Claude Zylberstein; revised, augmented, and annotated by Bernard Leuilliot. Paris: Gallimard. T. 1, *1917–1936. La littérature est une fête*, 1986; t. 2, *1937–1945. Le Traité des jours sombres*, 1992; t. 3, *1946–1968. Le don des langues*, 1996.

Paulhan, Jean, and Francis Ponge. *Correspondance (1923–1968)*. T. 1, *1923–1946*, critical edition annotated by Claire Boaretto. Paris: Gallimard, 1986.

Paulhan, Jean, and Monique Saint-Hélier. *Correspondance (1941–1955)*. Edition established and annotated by José-Flore Tappy. Paris: Gallimard, 1995.

Queneau, Raymond. *Lettres à Jean Paulhan*. Levallois-Perret: Les Cahiers Raymond Queneau, 1986.

Rivière, Jacques, and Gaston Gallimard. *Correspondance (1911–1924)*. Edition established, introduced, and annotated by Pierre-Edmond Robert with the collaboration of Alain Rivière. Paris: Gallimard, 1994.

Sartre, Jean-Paul. *Lettres au Castor et quelques autres (1940–1963)*. Edition established, introduced, and annotated by Simone de Beauvoir. Paris: Gallimard, 1983.

Scheler, Lucien. *La Grande Espérance des poètes (1940–1945)*. Paris: Temps actuels, 1982.

4. Essays

1635–1935: Trois siècles de l'Académie française, by the Forty. Paris: Imprimerie Firmin-Didot et Cie, 1935.

Assises nationales du peuple français pour la Paix et la Liberté, foreword by Jean Cassou. Paris: Les Combattants de la Liberté et de la Paix, 1949.

États généraux de la pensée française. Convened at the initiative of the Union nationale des intellectuels on March 25, 26, and 27 in Paris. Paris: Maison de la Pensée française, 1949.

L'Esprit NRF 1908–1940. Edition established and introduced by Pierre Hebey. Paris: Gallimard, 1990.

France 1941: La Révolution nationale constructive; Un bilan et un programme. Paris: Éditions Alsatia, 1941.

La France de l'esprit 1940–1943: Enquête sur les nouveaux destins de l'intelligence française. Paris: Sequana, 1943.

Institut de France, Académie française. *Publications diverses de l'année 1941*. Paris: Imprimerie Firmin-Didot, 1941.

———. *Publications diverses de l'année 1942*. Paris: Imprimerie Firmin-Didot, 1942.

———. *Publications diverses de l'année 1943*. Paris: Imprimerie Firmin-Didot, 1943.

Institut de France, Académie française, *Henry Bordeaux: Exposition du centenaire 1870–1970*. Paris: Bernard de Masclary Auteur-Éditeur, 1970.

Institut de France, Académie des sciences morales et politiques. "L'Académie des sciences morales et politiques et le redressement moral de la France après les événements de 1848," by M. le baron Seillière, *Séance solennelle du samedi 6 novembre 1941*. Paris: Firmin-Didot, 1941.

Nouveaux Destins de l'intelligence française. Éditions du ministère de l'Information, Union bibliophile de France, 1942.

Agathon [Henri Massis and Alfred de Tarde]. *L'Esprit de la Nouvelle Sorbonne: La Crise de la culture classique; La Crise du français.* Paris: Mercure de France, 1911.

———. *Les Jeunes Gens d'aujourd'hui.* Paris: Plon, 1913. Reedited with a presentation by Jean-Jacques Becker. Imprimerie nationale, 1995.

Anglès, Auguste. *Circumnavigations: Littérature, voyages, politique (1942–1983).* Lyon: Presses universitaires de Lyon, 1986.

Aragon, Louis. *Chroniques du bel canto.* Geneva: Skira, 1947.

———. *L'Homme communiste.* Paris: Gallimard. T. 1, *1946*; t. 2, *1953.*

———. *Journal d'une poésie nationale.* Lyon: Henneuse, Les Écrivains réunis, 1954.

Arland, Marcel. *Essais et Nouveaux Essais critiques.* Paris: Gallimard, 1952.

Arland, Marcel, Jean Mistler, Institut de France, and Académie française. *Discours prononcés dans la séance publique pour la reception de M. Marcel Arland.* April 24, 1969. Paris: Imprimerie Firmin-Didot, 1969.

Aron, Raymond. *Le Grand Schisme.* Paris: Gallimard, 1948.

———. *L'Opium des intellectuels.* Paris: Calmann-Lévy, 1955.

Aveline, Claude. *Les Devoirs de l'esprit.* Paris: Grasset, 1945.

Aveline, Claude, Jean Cassou, André Chamson, Georges Friedmann, Louis Martin-Chauffier, and Vercors. *L'Heure du choix.* Paris: Les Amis des Éditions de Minuit, 1947.

Aveline, Claude, Jean Cassou, Louis Martin-Chauffier, and Vercors. *La Voie libre.* Paris: Flammarion, 1951.

Barbey d'Aurevilly, Jules. *La Critique ou les Juges jugés.* Paris: Frinzine, 1885.

Bardèche, Maurice. Lettre ouverte à François Mauriac. Paris: La Pensée libre, 1947.

Barrès, Maurice. *Discours de reception de Maurice Barrès: Séance de l'Académie du 17 janvier 1907.* Paris: Librairie Félix Juven, 1907.

Baudrillart, Alfred. *Le Testament politique d'un prince de l'Église: Texte de la déclaration faite à l'agence Inter-France le 12 novembre 1940 par le cardinal Baudrillart, précédé d'un hommage de M. Abel Bonnard....* Paris: Imprimerie Guillemot et de Lamothe, 1942.

Beaunier, André. *Au service de la déesse.* Paris: Flammarion, 1923.

Béguin, Albert. *L'Âme romantique et le rêve. Essai sur le romantisme allemand et la poésie française.* Paris: José Corti, 1991.

Bellessort, André. *France 41: La Révolution nationale constructive, un bilan, un programme.* Paris: Éditions Alsatia, 1941.

Benda, Julien. *La Trahison des clercs.* Paris: Grasset, 1927.

———. *Un Antisémite sincère.* Toulouse: Comité national des écrivains, Centre des intellectuels, 1944.

———. *La France byzantine ou le triomphe de la littérature pure: Mallarmé, Gide, Proust, Valéry, Alain, Giraudoux, Suarès, Les Surréalistes; Essai d'une psychologie originelle du littérateur.* Paris: Gallimard, 1945.

Benjamin, René. *La Farce de la Sorbonne.* Paris: Marcel Rivière, 1911.

———. *Mussolini et son peuple.* Paris: Plon, 1937.

———. *Le Printemps tragique.* Paris: Plon, 1940.

————. *Le Maréchal et son peuple*. Paris: Plon, 1941.

————. *Vérités et rêveries sur l'éducation*. Paris: Plon, 1941.

————. *Les Sept Étoiles de France*. Paris: Plon, 1942.

————. *Le Grand Homme seul*. Paris: Plon, 1943.

Benoit, Pierre. *Henry Bordeaux*. Paris: Alcan, 1931.

Béraud, Henri. *La Croisade des longues figures*. Paris: Éditions du siècle, 1924.

Bernanos, Georges. *Essais et écrits de combat*. 2 vols. Paris: Gallimard, 1971 and 1995.

Bertrand, Louis. *Hitler*. Paris: Fayard, 1936.

————. *L'Espagne*. Paris: Flammarion, 1937.

Bordeaux, Henry. *La Crise de la famille française*. Paris: Flammarion, [1921].

————. "Rapport du concours international de romans sur le bolchevisme." In Académie d'éducation et d'entr'aide sociales, *Familles, Travail, Épargne*, public meeting held March 3, 1936. Paris: Éditions Spes, 1936.

————. *Les Murs sont bons: Nos erreurs et nos espérances*. Paris: Fayard, 1940.

————. *Images du Maréchal Pétain*. Paris: Sequana, 1941.

Bordeaux, Henry, Henri de Régnier, Institut de France, and Académie française. *Discours prononcés dans la séance publique du 27 mai 1920 pour la réception de M. Henry Bordeaux*. Paris: Imprimerie Firmin-Didot, 1920.

Boulenger, Jacques. *Le Sang français*. Paris: Denoël, 1943.

Bourget, Paul. *Études et portraits*. T. 3, *Sociologie et littérature*. Paris: Plon-Nourrit, 1906.

Brasillach, Robert. *Les Quatre Jeudis:Images d'avant-guerre*. Paris: Éditions Balzac, 1944; Sceaux, Les Sept Couleurs, 1951.

Brémond, Henri. *Pour le romantisme*. Paris: Bloud et Gay, 1923.

Camus, Albert. *Actuelles. Écrits politiques*. Paris: Gallimard, 1950.

————. *L'Homme révolté*. Paris: Gallimard, 1951. Translated by Anthony Bower as *The Rebel: An Essay on Man in Revolt*. New York: Vintage, 1991.

Carrère, Jean. *Les Mauvais Maîtres*. Paris: Plon, 1922.

Casanova, Laurent. *Le Parti communiste, les intellectuels et la nation*. Paris: Éditions sociales, 1949.

Cassou, Jean. *Pour la poésie*. Paris: Corrêa, 1935.

————. *La Mémoire courte*. Paris: Minuit, 1953.

Crémieux, Benjamin. *XXe Siècle*. Paris: Gallimard, 1924.

Chamson, André. *Retour d'Espagne, rien qu'un témoignage*. Paris: Grasset, 1937.

————. *Écrit en 1940*. Paris: Gallimard, 1945.

————. *Fragments d'un Liber Veritatis (1941–1942)*, in *Les Essais*. Paris: Gallimard, 1946.

Chamson, André, and Jean-Louis Vaudoyer. *Discours prononcé dans la séance publique tenue par l'Académie française pour la réception de M. André Chamson*. Paris: Imprimerie Firmin-Didot, 1957.

Cru, Jean Norton. *Du témoignage*. Paris: Gallimard/NRF, 1930. Translated by Hélène Vogel as *War Books: A Study in Historical Criticism*. San Diego: San Diego State University Press, 1988.

Daudet, Léon. *Le Stupide XIXe siècle* [1922]. Paris: Grasset, 1929. Translated by Lewis Galantière as *The Stupid XIXth Century*. New York: Payson and Clarke, 1928.

————. *Verts d'académie et vers de presse*. Paris: Éd. du Capitole, 1930.

Dorgelès, Roland. *Vive la Liberté!* Paris: Albin Michel, 1937.

Drieu La Rochelle, Pierre. *Mesure de la France*, suivi de *Écrits (1939–1940)*. Paris: Grasset, 1964 [first Grasset edition, 1922].

———. *Ne plus attendre*. Paris: Grasset, 1941.

———. *Notes pour comprendre le siècle*. Paris: Gallimard, 1941.

———. *Sur les écrivains*. Critical essays collected, prefaced, and annotated by Frédéric Grover. Paris: Gallimard, 1964 and 1982.

Duhamel, Georges. *Le Voyage à Moscou*. Paris: Mercure de France, 1927.

———. *Défense des lettres: Biologie de mon métier*. Paris: Mercure de France, 1937.

———. *Positions françaises: Chronique de l'année 1939*. Paris: Mercure de France, 1940.

———. *Éclaircissements*. Paris: Imprimerie Paul Hartmann, 1947.

———. *Tribulations de l'espérance*. Paris: Mercure de France, 1947.

Durkheim, Émile. *De la division du travail social*. Paris: Alcan, 1893; PUF, 1991. Translated by George Simpson as *The Division of Labor in Society*. New York: Free Press, 1965.

———. "L'individualisme et les intellectuels" in *La Science sociale et l'action*, 261–278. Introduction by J.-C. Filloux. Paris: PUF, 1987.

Fabre-Luce, Alfred. *Journal de la France (août 1940–avril 1942)*. Paris: Imprimerie JEP, 1942.

Farrère, Claude. *Visite aux Espagnols (hiver 1937)*. Paris: Flammarion, 1937.

Farrère, Claude, Pierre Benoit, Institut de France, and Académie française. *Discours prononcés dans la séance publique pour la réception de M. Claude Farrère*. April 23, 1936. Paris: Imprimerie Firmin-Didot, 1936.

Fernandez, Ramon. *Itinéraire français*. Paris: Éditions du Pavois, 1943.

Gaillard, Robert. *Le Choix vitaliste: Trois mois d'activité vitaliste*. Paris: Debresse, 1940.

Garaudy, Roger, and Georges Cogniot. *Les Intellectuels et la Renaissance française*. Paris: Éditions du P.C.F., 1945.

Germain, José. *Notre chef Pétain*. Preface by Abel Bonnard. Paris: La Technique du livre, 1942.

Gide, André. *Retour de l'U.R.S.S.* Paris: Gallimard, 1936.

———. *Découvrons Henri Michaux*. Paris: Gallimard, 1941 and 1998.

———. *Littérature engagée*. Texts collected and introduced by Yvonne Davet. Paris: Gallimard, 1950.

Gillouin, René. *Le Destin de l'Occident*, suivi de *Divers Essais critiques*. Paris: Éd. Prométhée, 1929.

Giono, Jean. *Écrits pacifistes*. Paris: Gallimard, 1937–1939 and 1978.

Giraudoux, Jean. *De pleins pouvoirs à sans pouvoirs*. Paris: Gallimard, 1950.

Groethuysen, Bernard. *Autres portraits*. Paris: Gallimard, 1995.

Guénon, René. *Orient et Occident*. Paris: Payot, 1924. Translated by William Massey as *East and West*. London: Luzac, 1941.

Lasserre, Pierre. *Le Romantisme français: Essai sur la Révolution dans les sentiments et dans les idées au XIXᵉ siècle*. Paris: Mercure de France, 1907.

———. *La Doctrine officielle de l'Université: Critique du haut enseignement de l'État; Défense et théorie des humanités classiques*. Paris: Mercure de France, 1912.

———. *Les Chapelles littéraires: Claudel, Jammes, Péguy*. Paris: Librairie Garnier, 1920.

Malraux, André. *La Tentation de l'Occident*. Paris: Grasset: 1926.

Martin-Chauffier, Louis. *L'Écrivain et la liberté*. Neuchâtel: La Baconnière, 1958.

Massis, Henri. *Jugements*. T. 2. Paris: Plon, 1924.

———. *Défense de l'Occident*. Paris: Plon, 1927. Translated by F. S. Flint as *Defence of the West*. New York: Harcourt, Brace, 1927.

———. *Les Idées restent*. Lyon: Lardanchet, 1941.

Mauclair, Camille. *La Farce de l'art vivant*. T. 2, *Les métèques contre l'art français*. Paris: Éditions de la Nouvelle Revue critique, 1930.

Mauriac, François. *Dieu et Mammon*, in *Œuvres romanesques et théâtrales complètes*. Vol. 2. Paris: Gallimard, 1979. Translated as *God and Mammon*. London: Sheed and Ward, 1946.

Mauriac, François, and André Chaumeix, *Discours de réception à l'Académie française et "Réponse" d'André Chaumeix* (speeches given on November 16, 1933, at the French Academy). Paris: Grasset/Plon, 1934.

Maurras, Charles. *L'Avenir de l'intelligence*, suivi de *Auguste Comte, Le romantisme féminin, Mademoiselle Monk, L'Invocation à Minerve*. Paris: Flammarion, 1905 and 1927.

———. *La Seule France, chronique des jours d'épreuve*. Lyon: Larchandet, 1941.

———. *Réponse à André Gide*. Éditions de la Seule France, 1948.

Merleau-Ponty, Maurice. *Humanisme et terreur: Essai sur le problème communiste*. Paris: Gallimard, 1947.

Montherlant, Henry de. *Essais*. Paris: Gallimard, 1963.

———. *L'Équinoxe de septembre*, suivi de *Le Solstice de juin* et de *Mémoire*. Paris: Gallimard, 1976.

———. *Essais critiques*. Paris: Gallimard, 1995.

Morgan, Claude. *Chronique des Lettres françaises*. T. 1, *À l'aube de la IV*; t. 2, *La fin d'un monde*. Paris: Éditions Raison d'être, 1946.

Nietzsche, Friedrich. *Le Crépuscule des idoles*. Paris: Mercure de France, 1948. Translated by Thomas Common as *Twilight of the Idols and the Antichrist*. Mineola, NY: Dover, 1948.

Nizan, Paul. *Les Chiens de garde*. Paris: Rieder, 1932.

Orion, [Jean Maze]. *Nouveau Dictionnaire des girouettes*, précédé de *L'Oubli en politique*. Paris: Éditions le Régent, 1948.

Parra I Alba, Montserrat. "Fortune du *Journal d'un curé de campagne* et *Les Grands cimetières sous la lune*." In *Bernanos et le monde moderne*. Edited by Monique Gosselin and Max Milner. Colloque du centenaire de Georges Bernanos [1888–1988]. Université Charles de Gaulle–Lille III, Presses universitaires de Lille, 1989.

Paulhan, Jean. *Les Fleurs de Tarbe ou la Terreur dans les Lettres*. Paris: Gallimard, 1941 and 1973.

———. *De la paille et du grain*. Paris: Gallimard, 1948. Translated by Richard Rand as *Of Chaff and Wheat: Writers, War, and Treason*. Urbana: University of Illinois Press, 2004.

———. *Lettre aux directeurs de la Résistance*. Paris, 1952; Ramsay, 1987.

———. *Œuvres complètes*. T. 5, *Politique*. Paris: Cercle du Livre précieux, 1970.

Péguy, Charles. "De la situation faite à l'histoire et la sociologie dans les temps modernes," *Cahiers* 8, 1, 1906, in *Œuvres en prose complètes*, 481–519. T. 2. Paris: Gallimard, 1957.

Péret, Benjamin. *Le Déshonneur des poètes*. Mexico: Poésie et révolution, 1945; Paris: J.-J. Pauvert, 1965.

Petitjean, Armand. *Combats préliminaires*. Paris: Gallimard, 1941.

———. "Inventaire de la France," paper given at the École des cadres d'Algérie, April 21, 1942. Algiers: Imp. La Typo-Litho and Jules Larborel, 1942.

———. *Mise à nu. Essais*. Paris: Jean Vigneau, 1946.

Pourrat, Henri. *Vent de mars: Roman*. Paris: Gallimard, 1941.

———. *Le Chef français*. Marseille: Laffont, 1942.

Pourtalès, Guy. *Vers l'affrontement ou Marianne, Wotan et la SDN: Receuil d'articles de Guy de Pourtalès (1933–1935)*. Selected and introduced by Doris Jakubec and Anne-Lise Delacrétaz. Cahiers Guy de Pourtalès, no. 2. Paris/Lausanne: H. Champion/Fondation Guy de Pourtalès, 1996.

Queneau, Raymond. *Bâtons, chiffres et lettres*. Paris: Gallimard, 1965 and 1985.

———. *Traité des vertus démocratiques*. Paris: Gallimard, 1993.

Quéval, Jean. *Première Page, cinquième colonne*. Paris: Fayard, 1945.

Raymond, Marcel. *De Baudelaire au surréalisme*. Paris: José Corti, 1940 and 1978. Translated by G. M. as *From Baudelaire to Surrealism*. New York: Wittenborn Schultz, 1949.

Rebatet, Lucien. *Les Décombres*. Paris: Denoël, 1942.

Rivière, Jacques, and Ramon Fernandez. *Moralisme et littérature*. Paris: Corrêa, 1932.

———. *Nouvelles Études*. Paris: Gallimard, 1947.

Rolland, Romain. *Au-dessus de la mêlée*. Paris: Ollendorf, 1915.

Sartre, Jean-Paul. *L'Existentialisme est un humanisme*. Paris: Nagel, 1946.

———. *Situations I: Critiques littéraires*. Paris: Gallimard, 1947 and 1993. Translated by Chris Turner as *Critical Essays (Situations I)*. London: Seagull, 2010.

———. *Situations II: Qu'est-ce que la littérature?* Paris: Gallimard, 1948 and 1975.

———. *Situations III: Lendemains de guerre*. Paris: Gallimard, 1949 and 1976. Translated by Chris Turner as *The Aftermath of War (Situations III)*. London: Seagull, 2008.

———. "The Responsibility of the Writer." Translated by Betty Askwith. In *Reflections on Our Age: Lectures delivered at the Opening Session of UNESCO at the Sorbonne University Paris* (New York: Columbia University Press, 1949), 74.

———. *Literary and Philosophical Essays*. Translated by Annette Michelson. New York: Criterion, 1955.

———. *Plaidoyer pour les intellectuels*. Paris: Gallimard, 1972.

———. *The Writings of Jean-Paul Sartre*. Vol. 2, *Selected Prose*. Chicago: Northwestern University Press, 1974.

———. *Qu'est-ce que la littérature?* Paris: Gallimard, 1985 and 1993.

———. *What Is Literature and Other Essays*. Cambridge, MA: Harvard University Press, 1988.

———. *La Responsabilité de l'écrivain [1946]*. Paris: Verdier, 1998.

Tharaud, Jérôme and Jean. *Fumées de Paris et d'ailleurs*. Paris: Éditions de la Nouvelle France, 1946.

Thibaudet, Albert. *Trente Ans de vie française*. T. 1, *Les Idées de Charles Maurras*. Paris: Gallimard, 1919.

———. *La République des professeurs*. Paris: Grasset, 1927.

———. *Réflexions sur le roman*. Paris: Gallimard, 1938.

———. *Réflexions sur la critique*. Paris: Gallimard, 1939.

Thibon, Gustave. *Diagnostics: Essai de physiologie sociale*. Preface by Gabriel Marcel. Paris: Librairie de Médicis, 1942.

———. *Retour au réel: Nouveaux diagnostics*. Lyon: Lardanchet, 1943.

Triolet, Elsa. *L'Écrivain et le livre ou la suite dans les idées*. Paris: Éditions sociales, 1948.

Valéry, Paul. *Regards sur le monde actuel*. Paris: Gallimard, 1945.

———. *Fonction et Mystère de l'Académie*. Iéna: Éditions Karl Rauch, 1948.

Vercors. *Le Sable du temps*. Paris: Émile-Paul, 1946.

———. *Petit Pamphlet des dîners chez Gazette*. Paris: Self-published, 1947.

———. *Plus ou moins homme*. Paris: Albin Michel, 1950.

———. *Pour prendre congé*. Paris: Albin Michel, 1957.

———. *Cent ans d'histoire de France, t. 3, Les Nouveaux jours, Esquisse d'une Europe*. Paris: Plon, 1984.

Wurmser, André. *Réponse à Jean Cassou*. Paris: Éditions de la Nouvelle Critique, 1950.

5. Journals, Memoirs, Accounts

Écrivains en Prison. Preface by Gabriel Audision. Paris: Seghers, 1945.

Georges Duhamel 1884–1966. Paris: Mercure de France, 1967.

Le Procès de Charles Maurras: Compte rendu sténographique. Paris: Albin Michel, 1946.

Ajalbert, Jean. *Les Mystères de l'Académie Goncourt*. Paris: Ferenczi, 1929.

———. *Mémoires à rebours (1935–1870)*. T. 1, *Règlements de comptes*. Paris: Denoël and Steele, 1936.

Anouilh, Jean. *La Vicomtesse d'Éristal n'a pas reçu son balai mécanique: Souvenirs d'un jeune homme*. Paris: La Table Ronde, 1987.

Aragon, Louis. *Entretiens avec Francis Crémieux*. Paris: Gallimard, 1964.

———. *Aragon parle avec Dominique Arban*. Paris: Seghers, 1968.

———. *Pour expliquer ce que j'étais* [posthumous]. Paris: Gallimard, 1989.

Arnoux, Alexandre. *Contacts allemands: Journal d'un demi-siècle*. Paris: Albin Michel, 1950.

Astruc, Alexandre. *Le Montreur d'ombres: Mémoires*. Paris: Bartillat, 1996.

Audisio, Gabriel. *Feuilles de Fresnes*. Minuit, 1946.

Baudrillart, Alfred. *Les Carnets du cardinal Baudrillart*. Text introduced, established, and annotated by Paul Christophe. 3 vols. Paris: Éditions du Cerf, 1994–1998.

Beauvoir, Simone de. *La Force de l'âge*. Paris: Gallimard, 1960. Translated by Peter Green as *The Prime of Life*. Cleveland, OH: World Publishing, 1962.

———. *La Force des choses*. Paris: Gallimard, 1963. Translated by Richard Howard as *Force of Circumstance*. New York: Putnam, 1965.

Benda, Julien. *Un Régulier dans le siècle*. Paris: Gallimard, 1937.

———. *Exercice d'un enterré vif (juin 1940–août 1944)*. Geneva: Éditions des Trois Collines, 1944.

Benjamin, René. *La Galère des Goncourt.* Preface by Sacha Guitry. Paris: L'Élan, 1948.

Bertrand, Louis, Institut de France, and Académie française. *Discours prononcés pour la réception de Louis Bertrand le 25 novembre 1906.* Paris: Imprimerie Firmin-Didot, 1926.

Bordeaux, Henry. *Histoire d'une vie.* 13 vols. Paris: Plon, 1951–1973.

———. *Charles Maurras et l'Académie française.* Paris: Éditions du Conquistador, 1955.

———. *Quarante Ans chez les Quarante.* Paris: Fayard, 1959.

Bouissounouse, Janine. *La Nuit d'Autun. Le Temps des illusions.* Paris: Calmann-Lévy, 1977.

Brasillach, Robert. *Notre Avant-Guerre: Mémoires.* Paris: Plon, 1941; Le Livre de proche, 1973. Translated by Peter Tame as *Before the War.* Lewiston, NY: Edwin Mellen, 2002.

Bruckberger, Raymond-Léopold. *Nous n'irons plus au bois.* Paris: Amiot-Dumont, 1948.

———. *Si Grande Peine (1940–1948).* Paris: Grasset, 1967.

Cassou, Jean. *Une vie pour la liberté.* Paris: Robert Laffont, 1981.

Chamson, André. *La Galère.* Paris: Gallimard, 1939.

———. *Le Chiffre de nos jours.* Paris: Gallimard, 1954.

———. *Il faut vivre vieux.* Paris: Grasset, 1984.

Claudel, Paul. *Journal.* 2 vols. Paris: Gallimard, 1968 and 1969.

Cocteau, Jean. *Journal (1942–1945).* Text established, introduced, and annotated by Jean Touzot. Paris: Gallimard, 1989.

Cogniot, Georges. *Parti pris: Cinquante-cinq ans au service de l'humanisme réel.* Paris: Éditions sociales, 1976.

Colette. *Journal à rebours.* Paris: Fayard, 1984.

Combelle, Lucien. *Je dois à André Gide.* Paris: Frédéric Chambriand, 1951.

———. *Prisons de l'espérance.* Paris: ETL, 1952.

———. *Péché d'orgueil.* Paris: Olivier Orban, 1978.

Daix, Pierre. *J'ai cru au matin.* Paris: Laffont, 1976.

Daudet, Léon. *Souvenirs littéraires.* Paris: Grasset, 1933 and 1968.

Debré, Robert. *L'Honneur de vivre.* Paris: Hermann, 1974.

Debû-Bridel, Jacques. *Les Éditions de Minuit: Historique.* Paris: Minuit, 1945.

———. *La Résistance intellectuelle.* Paris: Julliard, 1970.

Descaves, Lucien. *Souvenirs d'un ours.* Paris: Éditions de Paris, 1946.

Descaves, Pierre. *Mes Goncourt.* Paris: Calmann-Lévy, 1949.

Drieu La Rochelle, Pierre. *Fragment de mémoires, 1940–1941.* Preceded by a study on "Le parti unique et P. Drieu la Rochelle" by Robert O. Paxton. Paris: Gallimard, 1982.

———. *Journal 1939–1945.* Introduced and annotated by Julien Hervier. Paris: Gallimard, 1992.

———. *Textes retrouvés.* Monaco: Éditions du Rocher: 1992.

Duhamel, Georges. *Chronique des saisons amères (1940–1943).* Paris: Imprimerie Paul Hartmann, 1945.

———. *Lumières sur ma vie.* 5 vols. Paris: Imprimerie P. Hartmann and Mercure de France, 1944–1955. Excerpts translated by Basil Collier as *Light on My Days.* London: J. M. Dent and Sons, 1948.

———. *Le Livre de l'amertume: Journal 1925–1956.* Paris: Mercure de France, 1983.

Emmanuel, Pierre. *Discours de réception à l'Académie française.* Paris: Seuil, 1969.

————. *Autobiographies: Qui est cet homme? (1947); L'Ouvrier de la onzième heure (1953)*. Paris: Seuil, 1970.

Fabre-Luce, Alfred. *Hors d'atteinte*. Paris: L'auteur, impr. Edit. Ika, 1946.

Faÿ, Bernard. *De la prison de ce monde*. Paris: Plon, 1974.

Follain, Jean. *Agendas 1926–1971*. Edition established and annotated by Claire Paulhan. Paris: Seghers, 1993.

Fort, Paul. *Mes mémoires: Toute la vie d'un poète 1872–1944*. Paris: Flammarion, 1944.

Fouchet, Max Pol. *Un jour je m'en souviens*. Paris: Mercure de France, 1968.

————. *Les Poètes dans la guerre*. Offprint of the special issue "Les poètes de la revue Fontaine." *Poésie* 1 55/61 (September–November 1978).

Frénaud, André. *Notre inhabileté fatale: Entretiens avec Bernard Pingaud*. Paris: Gallimard, 1979.

Fumet, Stanislas. *Histoire de Dieu dans ma vie: Souvenirs choisis*. Paris: Fayard-Mame, 1978.

Galtier-Boissière, Jean. *Mon journal pendant l'Occupation*. Paris: La Jeune Parque, 1944.

————. *Mon journal depuis la Libération*. Paris: La Jeune Parque, 1945.

Gaulle, Charles de. *Mémoires de guerre*. 3 vols. Paris: Plon, 1954–1959. Translated by Jonathan Griffin and Richard Howard as *The Complete War Memoirs of Charles de Gaulle*. New York: Carroll and Graf, 1998.

Gide, André. *Journal*. 2 vols. Paris: Gallimard, 1948 and 1954; 1996 and 1997. Gide's journals translated in four volumes by Justin O'Brien as *Journals*. Urbana: University of Illinois Press, 2000.

————. *Journal 1939–1942*. Paris: Gallimard, 1946.

————. *Journal 1942–1949*. Paris: Gallimard, 1950.

Grenier, Jean. *Sous l'Occupation [Propos recueillis]*. Edition introduced and established by Claire Paulhan, annotated by Claire Paulhan and Gisèle Sapiro. Paris: Éditions Claire Paulhan, 1997.

Guéhenno, Jean. *Journal d'un homme de 40 ans*. Paris: Grasset, 1934.

————. *Journal des années noires*. Paris: Gallimard, 1947.

Guillemin, Henri. *Parcours*. Paris: Seuil, 1989.

Guillevic, Eugène, and Jean Raymond. *Choses parlées: Entretiens*. Seyssel: Champ Vallon, 1982.

————. *Avec Jean Follain*. Pully: PAP, 1993.

Guilloux, Louis. *Carnets (1921–1944)*. Paris: Gallimard, 1978.

————. *Carnets (1944–1974)*. Paris: Gallimard, 1982.

Guitry, Sacha. *Quatre Ans d'occupations*. Paris: L'Élan, 1947.

Heller, Gerhard. *Un Allemand à Paris: 1940–1944*. Paris: Seuil, 1981.

Hermant, Abel. *Une vie, trois guerres (Témoignages et souvenirs)*. Paris: P. Lagrange, 1943.

Isorni, Jacques. *Le Procès de Robert Brasillach*. Paris: Flammarion, 1946.

Jünger, Ernst. *Journaux de guerre*. Paris: Julliard, 1990.

Lachenal, François. *Éditions des Trois Collines*. Paris: IMEC, 1995.

Larguier, Léo. *Mes vingt ans et moi*. Paris: Albin Michel, 1944.

Laubreaux, Alain. *Écrit pendant la guerre*. Paris: Éditions du Centre de l'agence Inter-France, 1944.

Laurent, Jacques. *Histoire égoïste*. Paris: La Table Ronde, 1976.

Léautaud, Paul. *Journal littéraire*. 3 vols. Paris: Mercure de France, 1964 and 1986.

Leduc, Victor. *Les Tribulations d'un idéologue*. Paris: Syros, 1985.

Lefèvre, Frédéric. *Une heure avec . . .* 5 vols. Paris: Gallimard, 1924–1929. Excerpted new edition presented and annotated by Nicole Villeroux. 2 vols. Nantes: Siloë, 1996–1997.

Leiris, Michel. *Journal, 1922–1989*. Edition established, introduced, and annotated by Jean Jamin. Paris: Gallimard, 1992.

Lescure, Jean. *Poésie et liberté: Histoire de* Messages. Paris: IMEC, 1998.

Malaquais, Jean. *Journal de guerre, suivi de Journal du métèque, 1939–1942*. Paris: Phébus, 1997.

Malraux, André. *Antimémoires*. Paris: Gallimard, 1967.

Marcel, Gabriel. *En chemin, vers quel éveil?* Paris: Gallimard, 1971.

Marcenac, Jean. *Je n'ai pas perdu mon temps*. Paris: Messidor/Temps actuels, 1982.

Martin-Chauffier, Louis. *L'Homme et la bête*. Paris: Gallimard, 1947.

Martin du Gard, Roger. *Journal*. T. 3, *1937–1949*. Paris: Gallimard, 1993.

Massis, Henri. *Évocations: Souvenirs 1905–1911*. Paris: Plon, 1931.

———. *Maurras et notre temps: Entretiens et souvenirs*. Definitive edition augmented by unpublished texts. Paris: Plon, 1961.

Mauriac, Claude. *Le Temps immobile*. T. 4, *La Terrasse de Malagar*, 1977. T. 5, *Aimer de Gaulle*, 1978. Paris: Grasset.

Mauriac, François. *Journal*. T. 3. Paris: Grasset, 1940.

———. *Le Bâillon dénoué: Après quatre ans de silence*. Paris: Grasset, 1945.

———. *Journal 1932–1939*. Paris: La Table Ronde, 1947.

———. *Journal*. T. 4. Paris: Flammarion, 1950.

———. *Journal*. T. 5. Paris: Flammarion, 1953.

———. *Mémoires intérieurs*, translated by Gerard Hopkins. New York: Farrar, Straus and Cudahy, 1961.

———. *Mémoires politiques*. Paris: Grasset, 1967.

———. *Souvenirs retrouvés: Entretiens avec Jean Amrouche*. Paris: Fayard/INA, 1981.

———. *Œuvres autobiographiques*. Paris: Gallimard, 1990.

———. *Nouveaux mémoires intérieurs: More Reflections from the Soul*, translated by Mary Kimbrough. Lewiston, NY: Edwin Mellen, 1991.

Mazauric, Lucie. *Avec André Chamson*. T. 1, *Ah Dieu, que la paix est jolie!*, 1972. T. 2, *Vive le Front populaire (1934–1939)*, 1976. Paris: Plon.

Montherlant, Henry de. *Textes sous une occupation (1940–1944)*. Paris: Gallimard, 1953.

———. *Carnets (années 1930 à 1944)*. Paris: Gallimard, 1957.

Morgan, Claude. *Les Don Quichotte et les autres*. Paris: Roblot, 1979.

Moussinac, Léon. *Le Radeau de la medusa: Journal d'un prisonnier politique (1940–1941)*. Paris: Hier et aujourd'hui, 1945.

Nadeau, Maurice. *Grâces leur soient rendues: Mémoires littéraires*. Paris: Albin Michel, 1990.

Nels, Jacques. *Fragments détachés de l'oubli*. Paris: Ramsay, 1989.

Paulhan, Jean. *La Vie est pleine de choses redoutables: Textes autobiographiques*. Paris: Verdier, 1989; Éditions Claire Paulhan, 1997.

Pozner, Vladimir. *Vladimir Pozner se souvient*. Paris: Julliard, 1972.

Prévost, Jean. *Dix-Huitième Année*. Paris: Gallimard, 1929.

Queneau, Raymond. *Journal 1939–1940*, suivi de *Philosophes et voyous*. Paris: Gallimard, 1986.

———. *Journaux (1914–1965)*. Edition established, introduced, and annotated by Anne-Isabelle Queneau. Paris: Gallimard, 1996.

Rebatet, Lucien. *Les Mémoires d'un fasciste*. T. 1, *Les Décombres 1938–1940*. T. 2, *1941–1947*. Paris: Pauvert, 1976.

Renard, Jules. *Journal*. Paris: Gallimard, 1935.

Roy, Claude. *Moi je*. Paris: Gallimard, 1969 and 1978.

———. *Nous*. Paris: Gallimard, 1972 and 1980.

———. *La Conversation des poètes*. Paris: Gallimard, 1993.

Salacrou, Armand. *Les Idées de la nuit*. Paris: Fayard, 1960.

———. *Dans la salle des pas perdus*. T. 1, *C'était écrit*, 1974. T. 2, *Les Amours*, 1976. Paris: Gallimard.

Schlumberger, Jean. *Notes sur la vie littéraire*. Edition established, introduced, and annotated by Pascal Mercier. Paris: Gallimard, 1999.

Stéphane, Roger. *Chaque homme est lié au monde*. Preface by Emmanuel Astier. Paris: Le Sagittaire, 1946.

Thérive, André. *L'Envers du décor (1940–1944)*. Paris: La Clé d'or, 1948.

Thirion, André. *Révolutionnaires sans Révolution*. Paris: Laffont, 1972.

Thomas, Édith. *Pages de Journal 1939–1944*, suivies de *Journal intime de Monsieur Célestin Costedet*. Introduced by Dorothy Kaufmann. Paris: Viviane Hamy, 1995.

———. *Le Témoin compromis: Mémoires*. Introduced by Dorothy Kaufmann. Paris: Viviane Hamy, 1995.

Van Rysselberghe, Maria. *Les Cahiers de la Petite Dame: Notes pour l'histoire authentique d'André Gide*. 4 vols. *Cahiers André Gide*, no. 4–7. Paris: Gallimard, 1973–1977.

Vargaftig, Bernard. "Témoignage," in *Aragon 1956*. Actes du colloque d'Aix-en-Provence, September 5–8, 1991. Publications de l'université de Provence, 1992.

Vercors. *La Bataille du silence: Souvenirs de minuit*. Paris: Presses de la Cité, 1967; Éditions de Minuit, 1992. Translated by Rita Barisse as *The Battle of Silence*. New York: Holt, Rinehart and Winston, 1968.

———. *Cent Ans d'histoire de France*. 3 vols. Paris: Plon, 1981–1984.

———. *À dire vrai: Entretiens de Vercors avec Gilles Plazy*. Paris: François Bourin, 1991.

Vialar, Paul. *L'Enfant parmi les hommes, souvenirs*. Paris: Albin Michel, 1990.

Vildé, Boris. *Journal et lettres de prison (1941–1942)*. Paris: Allia, 1997.

Villefosse, Louis de. *L'Œuf de Wyasma*. Paris: Julliard, 1962.

Villon, Pierre. *Résistant de la première heure*. Interview by Claude Willard. Paris: Éditions sociales, 1983.

Werth, Léon. *Déposition: Journal (1940–1944)*. Text by Lucien Febvre, introduction by Jean-Pierre Azéma. Paris: Viviane Hamy, 1992.

Wurmser, André. *Fidèlement vôtre: Soixante ans de vie politique et littéraire*. Paris: Grasset, 1979.

6. Stories, Novels, Autobiographical Novels, Poetry (selection)

Aragon, Louis. *Les Voyageurs de l'impériale*. Paris: Gallimard, 1942, 1947, and 1975. Translated by Hannah Josephson as *The Century Was Young*. New York: Duell, Sloan and Pearce, 1941.

———. *Aurélien*. Paris: Gallimard, 1944. Republished in 1966, preceded by "Voici le temps enfin qu'il faut que je m'explique . . ." Translated by Eithne Wilkins as *Aurélien*. New York: Duelle, Sloan, and Pearce, 1947.

———. *Servitude et Grandeur des Français: Scènes des années terribles*. Paris: La Bibliothèque française, 1945.

———. *L'Œuvre poétique*. 15 vols. Paris: Livre Club Diderot, 1974–1981. Individual poetry books.

Barrès, Maurice. *Les Déracinés*. Paris: Fasquelle, 1898.

Béraud, Henri. *Le Martyre de l'obèse*. Paris: Albin Michel, 1922.

Bernard, Marc. *Pareil à des enfants*. Paris: Gallimard, 1942.

Bertrand, Louis. *Jean Perbal*. Paris: Fayard, 1925.

Blanchot, Maurice. *Thomas l'obscur*. Paris: Gallimard, 1941; new version, 1950; 1992. Translated by Robert Lamberton as *Thomas the Obscure*. Barrytown, NY: Station Hill Press, 1988.

———. *Aminadab*. Paris: Gallimard, 1942. Translated by Jeff Fort as *Aminadab*. Lincoln: University of Nebraska Press, 2002.

Bordeaux, Henry. *Le Pays natal*. Paris: Plon, 1900.

———. *Œuvres de jeunesse*. T. 1, *Vers et proses de mes vingt ans, poèmes de Villiers de l'Isle-Adam, Âmes modernes*. Paris: Plon, 1939.

Bory, Jean-Louis. *Mon village à l'heure allemande*. Paris: Flammarion, 1945. Translated as *French Village*. London: Dennis Dobson, 1948.

Bourget, Paul. *The Disciple*. New York: Howard Fertig, 1976.

Camus, Albert. *L'Étranger*. Paris: Gallimard, 1942 and 1971. Translated by Matthew Ward as *The Stranger*. New York: Vintage, 1988.

———. *La Peste*. Paris: Gallimard, 1947. Translated by Stuart Gilbert as *The Plague*. New York: Vintage, 1991.

Cayrol, Jean. *Je vivrai l'amour des autres (On vous parle: Les premiers jours)*. Paris/Neuchâtel, Seuil/La Baconnière, 1947.

Chamson, André. *Le Puits des miracles*. Paris: Gallimard, 1945.

Char, René. *Œuvres complètes*. Paris: Gallimard, 1983.

Curtis, Jean-Louis. *Les Forêts de la nuit*. Paris: Julliard, 1947 and 1974. Translated by Nora Wydenbruck as *The Forests of the Night*. London: John Lehmann, 1950.

Daudet, Léon. *Les Morticoles*. Paris: Fasquelle, 1894/1956.

Dorgelès, Roland. *Les Croix de bois*. Paris: Albin Michel, 1919 and 1931. Translated as *Wooden Crosses*. New York: G.P. Putnam's Sons, 1921.

Drieu La Rochelle, Pierre. *Rêveuse bourgeoisie*. Paris: Gallimard, 1937 and 1995.

———. *Gilles*. Paris: Gallimard, 1939.

Duhamel, Georges. *Civilisation 1914–1917*. Paris: Mercure de France, 1918 and 1944. Translated by E. S. Brooks as *Civilization, 1914–1917*. Columbia: University of South Carolina Press, 2009.

————. *Chronique des Pasquier*. T. 1, *Le Notaire du Havre*. Paris: Mercure de France, 1933. Translated by Béatrice de Holthoir as *News from Havre*. Leeds: Morely-Baker, 1969.

Eluard, Paul. *Au Rendez-vous allemand*, suivi de *Poésie et Vérité 1942*. Paris: Minuit, 1945 and 1992.

————. *Œuvres complètes*. 2 vols. Paris: Gallimard, 1968.

Frénaud, André. *Les Rois mages, poèmes 1938–1943*. New edition. Paris: Gallimard, 1977.

Gaillard, Robert. *Les Liens de chaîne*. Paris: Éditions Colbert, 1942.

Guillevic, Eugène. *Terraqué*, suivi d'*Exécutoire*. Paris: Gallimard, 1968 and 1991.

Leiris, Michel. *L'Âge d'homme*, précédé de *De la littérature considérée comme tauromachie*. Paris: Gallimard, 1939 and 1992. Translated by Richard Howard as *Manhood: A Journey from Childhood into the Fierce Order of Virility*. Chicago: University of Chicago Press, 1992.

Mauriac, François. *Œuvres romaneseques et théâtrales complètes*. 4 vols. Paris: Gallimard, 1978–1985.

Montherlant, Henry de. *Le Songe*. Paris: Gallimard, 1922 and 1954.

Mousset, Paul. *Quand le temps travaillait pour nous*. Paris: Grasset, 1941.

Queneau, Raymond. *Chêne et chien*. Paris: Gallimard, 1937 and 1969. Translated by Madeleine Velguth as *Raymond Queneau's Chêne et Chien: A Translation with Commentary*. New York: Peter Lang, 1995.

————. *Odile*. Paris: Gallimard, 1937 and 1964. Translated by Carol Sanders as *Odile*. Elmwood Park, IL: Dalkey Archive Press, 1988.

————. *Un rude hiver*. Paris: Gallimard, 1939. Translated by Betty Askwith as *A Hard Winter*. London: Lehmann, 1948.

Roy, Jules. *La Vallée heureuse*. Foreword by Pierre Jean Jouve. Paris: Éditions Charlot, 1947; Gallimard, 1947.

Triolet, Elsa. *Le premier accroc coûte deux cents francs*. Paris: Denoël, 1945. Translated as *A Fine of Two Hundred Francs*. New York: Penguin/Virago, 1986.

————. "Préface à la contrebande," "Préface à la clandestinité," and "Préface au désenchantement," in *Œuvres romanesques croisées d'Elsa Triolet et d'Aragon* by Aragon and Elsa Triolet. T. 3, 13–41; t. 5, 11–28; t. 9, 11–58. Monaco/Paris: Jaspard, Polus/Laffont, 1964.

Vailland, Roger. *Drôle de jeu*. Paris: Corrêa, 1945. Translated by Gerard Hopkins as *Playing with Fire: A Novel*. London: Chatto and Windus, 1948.

B. PERIODICALS

Action
Au pilori
Action française (L')
Art français (L')—underground
Cahiers français (Les)
Candide

Carrefour
Confluences
Cri du peuple (Le)
Étoiles (Les)
Figaro (Le)
Figaro littéraire (Le)
Fontaine
Gavroche
Gerbe (La)
Gringoire
Idées
Je suis partout
Latinité
Lettres françaises (Les)—underground
Lettres françaises (Les)
Messages
Mercure de France
Nouvelle Revue française (La) (La NRF)
Occident: Le bimensuel franco-espagnol
Paris-Soir
Pensée libre (La)
Revue des deux mondes
Revue universelle
Poésie 40, 41 . . .
Témoignage chrétien
Temps Modernes (Les)
Voici la France
Volontés

Tributes, recollections, special issues:
"Aragon poète." *Europe* 754 (May 1991).
"François Mauriac Prix Nobel." *La Table Ronde* (January 1953).
"Hommage à François Mauriac." *La Revue du siècle* 4 (July–August 1933).
"Hommage à Georges Sadoul." *Les Lettres françaises* 1021 (October 18–24, 1967).
"Jean Paulhan 1884–1968." *La NRF* 197 (May 1, 1969).
"Jean Schlumberger." *La NRF* 195 (March 1, 1969).
"Jean Tardieu." *Europe* 688–699 (August--September 1986).
"Julien Benda." *Europe* 389 (September 1961).
"La poésie et la Résistance." *Europe* 543–544 (July–August 1974).
"Le père Maydieu." *La Vie intellectuelle* (August–September 1956).
"Léon Moussinac." *Les Lettres françaises* 1021 (March 19–25, 1964).
"Paulhan." *L'Infini* 55 (Autumn 1996).
"Pierre de Lescure notre ami." *Brèches, Arts et Lettres* (Spring 1963).
"Raymond Queneau." *Europe* 650–651 (June–July 1983).

Aragon, Louis. "Les années Sadoul." *Europe* 590–591 (June–July 1978): 184–188.

Blanzat, Jean. "Les débuts des 'Lettres françaises' et du CNE." *Les Lettres françaises* 1082 (May 27, 1965).

Debû-Bridel, Jacques. "Naissance des 'Lettres françaises.'" *Les Lettres françaises* 20 (September 9, 1944).

Duhamel, Georges. "Pages inédites extraites du Journal de G. Duhamel." *Les Cahiers de l'Abbaye de Créteil* 2 (December 1980): 9–10.

Fumet, Stanislas. "Les Étoiles sous la nuée." *Les Étoiles* 81 (December 3, 1946).

Morgan, Claude. "La vie cachée des 'Lettres françaises.'" *Les Lettres françaises* 21–23 (September 16, 23, and 30, 1944).

———. "Les souvenirs sont vivants." *Les Étoiles* 81 (December 3, 1946).

Petitjean, Armand. "De 1938 à 1945: Un parcours singulier." *Esprit* 214 (August–September 1995): 218–224.

Sadoul, Georges. "Depuis quatre ans Les Étoiles . . ." *Les Étoiles* 81 (December 3, 1946).

Sarraute, Nathalie, and Marc Saporta. "Portrait d'une inconnue (conversation biographique)," in "Nathalie Sarraute." *L'Arc* 95 (1984): 5–23.

Schlumberger, Jean. "La vie spirituelle préservée: La Résistance dans la zone sud." *Revue de l'Alliance française*, new series, 1 (January 1945): 10–12.

Tavernier, René. "Quand Claudel rencontrait Aragon, Lyon 1944." *Bulletin de la société Paul Claudel* 199 (3rd trimester, 1990): 1–6.

Triolet, Elsa. "Contribution à une histoire du CNE." *Les Lettres françaises* 1082 (May 27, 1965).

Vidal-Naquet, Pierre. "Si Dieu le fit . . ." *Esprit* 134 (January 1988): 3–12.

Surveys:

"L'Académie française." *Le Crapouillot* (March 1939).

Ferlé, T. "L'Académie et le prix Goncourt." *La Documentation catholique* 867 (March 5, 1938): 305–314.

"Il ne faut pas tromper le peuple," "La Révolution et la Vérité," by Jean Cassou, and "Réponses" by Vercors. *Esprit* 12 (December 1949): 943–953. "L'intelligence et son rôle dans la cité." *Idées* (March-July 1942).

"La responsabilité de l'écrivain." *Carrefour* (February 10-March 17, 1945).

"Que sera demain la littérature?" *Le Figaro* (August 21–November 30, 1940).

"Tempête sur le C.N.E." *Le Figaro littéraire* (February 21, 1953–April 25, 1953).

IV. Tools

Almanach des gens de lettres 1908. Paris: E. Sansot et cie, 1908.

Annuaire de l'Académie française: Documents et notices sur les membres de l'Académie. Paris: Imprimerie Firmin-Didot, 1966.

Annuaire des lettres pour la zone libre. 2 vols. Aurillac: Éditions Romans et nouvelles, 1941 and 1942.

Dictionnaire biographique contemporain. Centre international de Documentation. Paris: Pharos, 1950.

Éphéméride de la Société des gens de lettres de France. Established by Geneviève Py. Paris: SGDL, 1988.

Guide des prix littéraires. Paris: Cercle de la librairie, 1955.

Institut de France and Académie française. *Les Titulaires des quarante fauteuils depuis la fondation de l'Académie française.* Paris: Imprimerie Firmin-Didot, 1967.

Qui êtes-vous? Annuaire des contemporains. 3 vols. Paris: Librairie Delagrave, 1908–1924.

Who's Who in France? Qui est qui en France? Paris: Éd. Jacques Laffitte S.A., 1953–1994.

Balteau, J. and M. Barroux, continued by M. Prévost et al., eds. *Dictionnaire de biographie française.* 18 vols. Paris: Letouzey et Ané, 1932–1995.

Beaumarchais, Jean Pierre de, Daniel Couty, and Alain Rey. *Dictionnaire des littératures de langue française.* 4 vols. Paris: Bordas, 1984 and 1994.

Charle, Christophe. *Les Professeurs de la faculté des lettres de Paris: Dictionnaire biographique.* Paris: CNRS-INRP. T. 1, *1809–1908, 1985*; t. 2, *1909–1939, 1986.*

Charle, Christophe, and Eva Telkes. *Les Professeurs du Collège de France: Dictionnaire biographique; 1901–1939.* Paris: CNRS-INRP, 1988.

———. *Les Professeurs de la faculté des sciences de Paris: Dictionnaire biographique; 1901–1939.* Paris: CNRS-INRP, 1989.

Coston, Henry, ed. *Partis, journaux et hommes politiques d'hier et d'aujourd'hui: Lectures françaises,* special issue (December 1960).

———. *Dictionnaire de la politique française.* 3 vols. Paris: Publication Henri Coston, 1967.

Dansel, Michel. *Les Nobel français de littérature.* Paris: André Bonne, 1967.

Didier, Robert. *Isographie de l'Académie française: Liste alphabétique illustrée des 125 facsimilés de signatures (1906–1963).* Paris: E. de Boccard, 1964.

Dioudonnat, Pierre-Marie. *Les 700 rédacteurs de 'Je suis partout' 1930–1944.* Paris: Sedopols, 1993.

Julliard, Jacques, and Michel Winock, eds. *Dictionnaire des intellectuels français.* Paris: Seuil, 1996.

Lacroix, Jean-Yves. *Bibliographie 1903–1995 des écrits de Jean Paulhan.* Paris: IMEC éditions, 1995.

Lemaître, Henri, ed. *Dictionnaire de littérature française.* Paris: Bordas, 1985 and 1986.

Maitron, Jean, and Claude Pennetier, eds. *Dictionnaire biographique du mouvement ouvrier français, 1971–1914.* 43 vols. Paris: Éditions ouvrières, 1964–1993.

Martin, Claude. La Nouvelle Revue française *de 1908 à 1943: Index des collaborateurs.* Lyon: Centre d'études gidiennes, Université de Lyon II, 1981.

Mayeur, Jean-Marie, and Yves-Marie Hilaire. *Dictionnaire du monde religieux dans la France contemporaine.* T. 1, *Les Jésuites.* Paris: Beauchesne, 1985.

Moreau, Pierre, and L. Pichard, eds. *Dictionnaire des lettres françaises: XIXᵉ siècle.* 2 vols. Paris: Fayard, 1971–1972.

Paulhan, Claire. "Chronologie bio-bibliographique de Jean Paulhan." Document dactylographié. IMEC.

Roux-Bluysen, Maurice. *Annuaire de la presse française et étrangère.* Paris: Annuaire de la Presse, 1937, 1942–1943, and 1946.

Talvart, Hector, Joseph Place, and Georges Place. *Bibliographie des auteurs modernes de langue française (1801–1975).* 22 vols. Paris: Éditions de la Chronique des lettres françaises, 1928–1975.

Temerson, Henri. *Biographies des principales personnalités décédées au cours de l'année 1956 . . . 1963.* 6 vols. Paris: Imprimerie centrale de l'Ouest, 1968.

Thième, Hugo. *Bibliographie de la littérature française de 1800 à 1930.* 2 vols. Paris: Droz, 1933.

Treich, Léon. *Almanach des lettres françaises et étrangères.* T. 1. Paris: Crès, 1924.

V. General Bibliography

A. THESES AND DISSERTATIONS

Gitton, Raphaël. *Henry Bordeaux, un conformiste? L'avocat bourgeois et l'écrivain classique 1870–1914.* DEA thesis, Paris: IEP, 1995.

Gouranton, Olivier. *Comoedia pendant la Seconde Guerre mondiale.* MA thesis, Université Paris I, 1992.

Laguerre, Bernard. *Vendredi.* DEA thesis, Paris: FNSP, 1985.

La Rochette de Rochegonde, Thibault. *Poésie 40 . . . –44: Une revue littéraire contre Vichy.* MA thesis, Université Paris I, 1996.

Mercier, Pascal. *Le Comité national des écrivains, 1941–1944.* MA thesis, Université de Paris III, 1980.

Olivera, Philippe. *Louis Aragon entre littérature et politique: Ses articles dans les Lettres françaises de 1960 à 1972.* MA thesis, Université Paris I, 1991.

Ponton, Rémy. *Le Champ littéraire de 1865 à 1906 (recrutement des écrivains, structure des carrières et production des œuvres).* PhD diss., Université de Paris V, 1977.

Prudent, Philippe. *Une revue culturelle dans les années noires: Confluences (1941–1944).* MA thesis, Université Lyon II, 1994.

Rasmussen, Anne. *L'Internationale scientifique (1890–1914).* 3 vols. PhD diss. Paris: EHESS, 1995.

Sapiro, Gisèle. *Complicités et anathèmes en temps de crise: Modes de survie du champ littéraire et de ses institutions, 1940–1953 (Académie française, Académie Goncourt, Comité national des écrivains).* PhD diss., EHESS, 1994.

Virieux, Daniel. *Le Front national de lutte pour la liberté et l'indépendance de la France: Un mouvement de Résistance—Période clandestine (mai 1941–août 1944).* 5 vols. PhD diss., Paris VIII, 1995. Atelier de reproduction des thèses de Lille.

B. REFERENCE WORKS

1. General Works

Amaury, Philippe. *Les Deux Premières Expériences d'un "ministère de l'information" en France.* Paris: Librairie générale de Droit et de Jurisprudence, 1969.

Aron, Robert. *Histoire de l'épuration.* T. 3. V. 2, *Le monde de la presse, des arts, des lettres . . . , 1944–1953.* Paris: Fayard, 1975.

Azéma, Jean-Pierre. *De Munich à la Libération 1938–1944*. Paris: Seuil, 1979. Translated by Janet Lloyd as *From Munich to the Liberation, 1938–1944*. Cambridge: Cambridge University Press, 1984.

Azéma, Jean-Pierre, and François Bédarida, eds. *Le Régime de Vichy et les Français*. With the collaboration of Denis Peschanski and Henry Rousso. Paris: Fayard, 1992.

———. *La France des années noires*. 2 vols. Paris: Seuil, 1993.

Baruch, Marc Olivier. *Servir l'État français: L'Administration en France de 1940 à 1944*. Paris: Fayard, 1997.

Babilas, Wolfgang. "La querelle des mauvais maîtres." In *La Littérature française sous l'Occupation*. Reims proceedings, September 30–October 2, 1981. Presses Universitaires de Reims, 1989.

Baudelot, Christian, and Roger Establet. *L'École capitaliste en France*. Paris: Maspero, 1971.

Baudelot, Christian, Roger Establet, and Jacques Malemort. *La Petite Bourgeoisie en France*. Paris: Maspero, 1974.

Baudelot, Christian, and Frédérique Matonti. "Le recrutement social des normaliens, 1914–1992." In *École normale supérieure: Le livre du bicentenaire*. Edited by Jean-François Sirinelli. Paris: PUF, 1994.

Becker, Jean-Jacques, and Serge Berstein. *Victoire et frustrations 1914–1929*. Paris: Seuil, 1990.

Béguerie, Philippe. *Jean-Augustin Maydieu*. Paris: Impr. Jouve, 1995.

Bellanger, Claude. *Presse clandestine (1940–1944)*. Paris: Armand Colin, 1961.

Bellanger, Claude, Jacques Godechot, Pierre Guiral, and Fernand Terrou. *Histoire générale de la presse française*. T. 4, *De 1940 à 1959*. Paris: PUF, 1975.

Berstein, Serge, and Pierre Milza. *Histoire de la France au XXe siècle (1930–1945)*. Brussels: Éditions Complexe, 1991.

Bettelheim, Charles. *Bilan de l'économie française 1919–1946*. Paris: PUF, 1947.

Bloch, Marc. "Réflexions d'un historien sur les fausses nouvelles de la guerre." In *Mélanges historiques*. Vol. 1. Paris: SEVPEN, 1963. 41–57.

———. *L'Étrange Défaite*. Paris: Gallimard, 1990. Translated by Gerard Hopkins as *Strange Defeat: A Statement of Evidence Written in 1940*. New York: Norton, 1968.

Blumenson, Martin. *Le Réseau du musée de l'Homme: Les débuts de la Résistance en France*. Paris: Seuil, 1979. Originally published as *The Vildé Affair: Beginnings of the French Resistance*. Boston: Houghton Mifflin, 1977.

Borne, Dominique, and Henri Dubief. *La Crise des années 30 (1929–1938)*. Paris: Seuil, 1976 and 1989.

Bourdieu, Pierre. *La Distinction: Critique sociale du jugement*. Paris: Minuit, 1979. Translated by Richard Nice as *Distinction: A Social Critique of the Judgment of Taste*. Cambridge, MA: Harvard University Press, 1984.

———. *Le Sens pratique*. Paris: Minuit, 1980. Translated by Richard Nice as *The Logic of Practice*. Stanford, CA: Stanford University Press, 1990.

———. *Ce que parler veut dire: L'économie des échanges linguistiques*. Paris: Fayard, 1982. Translated by Gino Raymond and Matthew Adamson as *Language and Symbolic Power*. Cambridge, MA: Harvard University Press, 1991.

———. *La Noblesse d'État: Grandes écoles et esprit de corps*. Paris: Minuit, 1989. Translated by Loretta. C. Clough as *The State Nobility*. Stanford, CA: Stanford University Press, 1996.

———. *The Field of Cultural Production*. Edited by Randal Johnson. New York: Columbia University Press, 1993.

———. *Raisons pratiques: Sur la théorie de l'action*. Paris: Seuil, 1994 and 1996. Translated by Randal Johnson, Gisèle Sapiro, et. al. as *Practical Reason*. Stanford, CA: Stanford University and Polity Press, 1998.

———. *Méditations pascaliennes*. Paris: Seuil, 1997. Translated by Richard Nice as *Pascalian Meditations*. Stanford, CA: Stanford University Press, 2000.

Boussard, Isabel. *Vichy et la corporation paysanne*. Paris: PFNSP, 1980.

Briand, Jean-Pierre, and Jean-Michel Chapoulie. *Les Collèges du peuple: L'enseignement primaire supérieur et le développement de la scolarisation prolongée sous la Troisième République*. Paris: INRP, 1992.

Burrin, Philippe. *La France à l'heure allemande*. Paris: Seuil, 1995. Translated by Janet Lloyd as *France under the Germans: Collaboration and Compromise*. New York: New Press, 1996.

Charle, Christophe. *Les Élites de la République 1880–1900*. Paris: Fayard, 1987.

Christophe, Paul. *1936: Les Catholiques et le Front populaire*. Paris: Desclée de Brouwer, 1979; Éditions ouvrières, 1986.

———. *1939–1940: Les Catholiques devant la guerre*. Paris: Éditions ouvrières, 1989.

Clancier, Georges-Emmanuel. "Max-Pol Fouchet et les poètes de la revue *Fontaine*." In *La Littérature française sous l'Occupation*. Reims proceedings, September 30–October 2, 1981. Presses Universitaires de Reims, 1989.

Comte, Bernard. *Une utopie combattante: L'École des cadres d'Uriage, 1940–1942*. Paris: Fayard, 1991.

Cotta, Michèle. *La Collaboration (1940–1944)*. Paris: Armand Colin, 1964.

Courtois, Stéphane. *Le PCF dans la guerre: De Gaulle, la Résistance, Staline . . .* Paris: Ramsay, 1980.

Courtois, Stéphane, and Marc Lazar. *Histoire du parti communiste français*. Paris: PUF, 1995.

Dard, Olivier. *La Synarchie: Le mythe du complot permanent*. Paris: Perrin, 1998.

Déloye, Yves. *École et citoyenneté: L'individualisme républicain de Jules Ferry à Vichy; Controverses*. Paris: PFNSP, 1994.

Desanti, Dominique. *Les Staliniens: Une expérience politique 1944–1956*. Paris: Fayard, 1975.

———. *Drieu La Rochelle: Le séducteur mystifié*. Paris: Flammarion, 1978.

Douzou, Laurent. *La Désobéissance: Histoire d'un mouvement et d'un journal clandestins: Libération-Sud (1940–1944)*. Paris: Odile Jacob, 1995.

Drouard, Alain. *Une inconnue des sciences sociales: La fondation Alexis-Carrel, 1941–1945*. Paris: INED/MSH, 1992.

Duquesne, Jacques. *Les Catholiques français sous l'Occupation*. Paris: Grasset, 1966.

Durand, Yves. *La France dans la 2ᵉ Guerre mondiale (1939–1945)*. Paris: Armand Colin, 1989.

Durkheim, Émile. *L'Évolution pédagogique en France*. Paris: PUF, 1938 and 1990. Translated by Peter Collins as *The Evolution of Educational Thought: Lectures on the Formation and Development of Secondary Education in France*. London: Routledge, 1977.

Elgey, Georgette. *La République des illusions (1945–1951) ou la vie secrète de la IVᵉ République*. Paris: Fayard, 1965.

Faure, Christian. *Le Projet culturel de Vichy: Folklore et révolution nationale, 1940–1944*. Paris: Éditions du CNRS/Presses universitaires de Lyon, 1989.

Fauvet, Jacques. *La IVᵉ République*. Paris: Fayard, 1959.

Fontaine, André. *Histoire de la guerre froide*. T. 1, *De la révolution d'Octobre à la guerre de Corée (1917–1950)*. Paris: Fayard, 1965; Seuil, 1983. Translated by D. D. Paige as *History of the Cold War: From the October Revolution to the Korean War, 1917–1950*. New York: Vintage, 1970.

Fouilloux, Étienne. *Les Chrétiens français entre crise et libération, 1937–1947*. Paris: Seuil, 1997.

Gervereau, Laurent, and Denis Peschanski, eds. *La Propagande sous Vichy*. Paris: Bibliothèque de Documentation internationale contemporaine, 1990.

Girardet, Raoul. *Le Nationalisme français: Anthologie (1871–1914)*. Paris: Seuil, 1983.

Goblot, Edmond. *La Barrière et le niveau: Étude sociologique sur la bourgeoisie française moderne*. Paris: Alcan, 1930.

Gueslin, André, ed. *Les Facs sous Vichy*. Actes du colloque des universités de Clermont-Ferrand et de Strasbourg (November 1993). Publications de l'Institut d'études du Massif central, Université Blaise-Pascal (Clermont II), 1994.

Hacquard, Georges. *Histoire d'une institution française: L'École alsacienne*. T. 1, *Naissance d'une école libre 1871–1891*. Paris: J.-J. Pauvert aux Éditions Garnier, 1982. T. 2, *L'École de la légende 1891–1922*. Paris: J.-J. Pauvert aux Éditions Suger, 1987.

Hermet, Guy. *La Guerre d'Espagne*. Paris: Seuil, 1989.

Hoffmann, Stanley. *Essais sur la France: Déclin ou renouveau?* Paris: Seuil, 1974.

Jäckel, Eberhard. *La France dans l'Europe de Hitler*. Paris: Fayard, 1968.

Julliard, Jacques. *La IVᵉ République (1947–1958)*. Paris: Calmann-Lévy, 1968.

Kedward, Harry Roderick. *Naissance de la Résistance dans la France de Vichy (1940–1942)*. Paris: Champ Vallon, 1989.

Kedward, Harry Roderick, and Roger Austin, eds. *Vichy France and the Resistance: Culture and Ideology*. Towota, NJ: Barnes and Noble Books, 1985.

Kedward, Harry Roderick, and Nancy Wood, eds. *The Liberation of France: Image and Event*. Washington, DC: Berg, 1995.

Laborie, Pierre. *L'Opinion française sous Vichy*. Paris: Seuil, 1990.

Lacouture, Jean. *Jésuites*. T. 2, *Les Revenants*. Paris: Seuil, 1992. A condensed version of the original two-volume work was translated by Jeremy Leggatt as *Jesuits: A Multibiography*. Washington, DC: Counterpoint, 1995.

Laot, Laurent. *Catholicisme, politique, laïcité*. Paris: Éditions ouvrières, 1990.

Laudouze, André. *Dominicains français et Action française 1899–1940: Maurras au couvent*. Paris: Éditions ouvrières, 1989.

Lottman, Herbert R. *L'Épuration (1949–1953)*. Paris: Fayard, 1986. Abridged version originally published as *The Purge*. New York: William Morrow, 1986.

Madjarian, Gérard. *Conflits, pouvoirs et société à la Libération*. Paris: UGE, 1980.

Mannheim, Karl. *Le Problème des générations*. Introduction and preface by Gérard Mauger. Paris: Nathan, 1990. Translated by Paul Kecskemeti as "The Problem of Generations," in *Essays on the Sociology of Knowledge*. Edited by Paul Kecskemeti. New York: Oxford University Press, 1952.

Marcot, François, ed. *La Résistance et les Français: Lutte armée et maquis*. Colloque de Besançon. Annales littéraires de l'Université de Franche-Comté, 1996.

Marrus, Michaël R., and Robert O. Paxton. *Vichy et les juifs*. Paris: Calmann-Lévy, 1981; Le Livre de poche, 1990. Translated as *Vichy France and the Jews*. Stanford, CA: Stanford University Press, 1995.

Martin, Marc. *Médias et journalistes de la République*. Paris: Odile Jacob, 1997.

Mauss, Marcel. *Sociologie et anthropologie*. Paris: PUF, 1950. Translated by Ben Brewster as *Sociology and Psychology*. London: Routledge, 1979.

Mayeur, Françoise. *L'Enseignement secondaire des jeunes filles sous la IIIᵉ République*. Paris: PFNSP, 1977.

———. *De la Révolution à l'école républicaine (1789–1930)*, in *Histoire générale de l'enseignement et de l'éducation en France*. Paris: Nouvelle Librairie de France, 1981.

Meyer, Jacques, ed. *Vie et mort des Français 1939–1945*. Paris: Hachette, 1971; Tallandier, 1980.

Michel, Henri, and Boris Mirkine-Guetzévitch, eds. *Les Idées politiques et sociales de la Résistance (documents clandestins 1940–1944)*. Paris: PUF, 1954.

Mottin, Jean. *Histoire politique de la presse 1944–1949*. Paris: Éditions Bilans hebdomadaires, 1949.

Muel-Dreyfus, Francine. *Le Métier d'éducateur: Les instituteurs de 1900, les éducateurs spécialisés de 1968*. Paris: Minuit, 1983.

———. *Vichy et l'éternel féminin: Contribution à une sociologie politique de l'ordre des corps.* Paris: Seuil, 1996. Translated by Kathleen A. Johnson as *Vichy and the Eternal Feminine*. Durham, NC: Duke University Press, 2001.

Noguères, Henri, Marcel Degliame-Fouché, and Jean-Louis Vigier. *Histoire de la Résistance en France*. 4 vols. Paris: Laffont, 1972.

Nora, Pierre, "Gaullistes et communistes," in *Les Lieux de mémoire III, Les France*, edited by Pierre Nora. T. 1, *Conflits et partages*. Paris: Gallimard, 1993. 347–393. Translated by Arthur Goldhammer as "Gaullists and Communists" in *Realms of Memory: Rethinking the French Past*. Vol. 1, *Conflicts and Divisions*. New York: Columbia University Press, 1996.

Novick, Peter. *L'Épuration française (1944–1949)*. Paris: Balland, 1985. Originally published as *The Resistance versus Vichy: The Purge of Collaborators in Liberated France*. New York: Columbia University Press, 1968.

Ory, Pascal. *Les Collaborateurs*. Paris: Seuil, 1976 and 1980.

———. La France allemande. Paroles du collaborationnisme français (1933–1945). Paris: Gallimard, 1977.

———. *La Belle Illusion: Culture et politique sous le signe du Front populaire 1935–1938*. Paris: Plon, 1994.

Paxton, Robert O. *La France de Vichy (1940–1944)*. Preface by Stanley Hoffmann. Paris: Seuil, 1973. Originally published as *Vichy France: Old Guard and New Order, 1940–1944*. New York: Columbia University Press, 2001.

Peschanski, Denis. *Vichy 1940–1944: Archives de guerre d'Angelo Tasca.* Milan/Paris: Fel-trinelli-CNRS, 1986.

——. *Vichy 1940–1944: Contrôle et exclusion.* Brussels: Éditions Complexe, 1997.

Pike, David Wingeate. *Les Français et la guerre d'Espagne 1936–1939.* Paris: Publications de la Sorbonne, 1975.

Plumyène, Jean, and Raymond Lasierra. *Les Fascismes français 1923–1963.* Paris: Seuil, 1963.

Prost, Antoine. *Histoire de l'enseignement en France 1800–1967.* Paris: Armand Colin, 1968.

——. *Les Anciens Combattants et la société française 1914–1939.* 3 vols. Paris: PFNSP, 1977. Abridged version translated by Helen McPhail as *In the Wake of War: Les anciens combattants and French Society.* Providence: Berg, 1992.

——. *Les Anciens Combattants 1914–1940.* Paris: Gallimard/Julliard, 1977.

——, ed. *La Résistance, une histoire sociale.* Paris: Éditions de l'Atelier, 1997.

Pryce-Jones, David. *Paris in the Third Reich: A History of the German Occupation, 1940–1944.* London: Collins St James Place, 1981.

Pudal, Bernard. *Prendre parti.* Paris: PFNSP, 1989.

Ringer, Fritz. *Fields of Knowledge: French Academic Culture in Comparative Perspective (1890–1920).* Cambridge/Paris: Cambridge University Press/Éditions de la MSH, 1992.

Rioux, Jean-Pierre. *La France de la Quatrième République.* Paris: Seuil. T. 1, *L'Ardeur et la nécessité,* 1980. T. 2, *L'Expansion et l'impuissance, 1983.* Translated by Godfrey Rogers as *The Fourth Republic, 1944–1958.* Cambridge: Cambridge University Press, 1987.

Rioux, Jean-Pierre, Antoine Prost, and Jean-Pierre Azéma. *Les Communistes français de Munich à Châteaubriant (1938–1941).* Paris: PFNSP, 1987.

Rouquet, François. *L'Épuration dans l'administration française: Agents de l'État et collaboration ordinaire.* Paris: Éditions du CNRS, 1993.

Rousso, Henry. *Le Syndrome de Vichy (1944–1987).* Paris: Seuil, 1987. Translated by Arthur Goldhammer as *The Vichy Syndrome.* Cambridge, MA: Harvard University Press, 1991.

Rubinstein, Diane. *What's Left? The École normale supérieure and the Right.* Madison: University of Wisconsin Press, 1990.

Schor, Ralph. *L'Antisémitisme en France pendant les années trente: Prélude à Vichy.* Brussels: Éditions Complexe, 1992.

Shennan, Andrew. *Rethinking France: Plans for Renewal (1940–1946).* Oxford: Clarendon Press, 1989.

Singer, Claude. *Vichy, l'Université et les juifs.* Paris: Les Belles Lettres, 1992.

Sirinelli, Jean-François. *Histoire des droites en France.* 3 vols. Paris: Gallimard, 1992.

——, ed. *École normale supérieure: Le livre du bicentenaire.* Paris: PUF, 1994.

Smith, Robert J. *The École Normale Supérieure and the Third Republic.* Albany: State University of New York Press, 1982.

Sternhell, Zeev. *La Droite révolutionnaire: Les origines françaises du fascisme (1885–1914).* Paris: Seuil, 1978 and 1984.

——. *Ni droite ni gauche: L'idéologie fasciste en France.* Paris: Seuil, 1983; Brussels: Éditions Complexe, 1987. Translated as *Neither Right nor Left: Fascist Ideology in France.* Berkeley: University of California Press, 1986.

Tartakowsky, Danielle. *Une histoire du* PCF. Paris: PUF, 1982.

Thalmann, Rita. *La Mise au pas: Idéologie et stratégie sécuritaire dans la France occupée.* Paris: Fayard, 1991.

Tournoux, Raymond. *Le Royaume d'Otto.* Paris: Flammarion, 1982.

Veillon, Dominique. *La Collaboration.* Paris: Le Livre de poche, 1984.

Voldman, Danièle. *La Reconstruction des villes françaises de 1940 à 1954: Histoire d'une politique.* Paris: L'Harmattan, 1997.

Weber, Eugen. *L'Action française.* Paris: Fayard, 1985. Originally published as *Action Française: Royalism and Reaction in Twentieth-Century France.* Stanford, CA: Stanford University Press, 1962.

Weber, Max. *Essais sur la théorie de la science.* Paris: Plon, 1965 and 1992.

———. *Économie et société.* 2 vols. Paris: Plon, 1971 and 1995. Translated by Ephraim Fischoff et al. as *Economy and Society.* New York: Bedminster Press, 1968.

2. Works about Intellectuals and the Literary World

La Littérature française sous l'Occupation. Reims conference proceedings. September 30–October 2, 1981. Presses universitaires de Reims, 1989.

Abraham, Pierre, and Roland Desné, eds. *Histoire littéraire de la France.* Vol. 2. Paris: Éditions sociales, 1979.

Added, Serge. *Le Théâtre dans les années Vichy 1940–1944.* Paris: Ramsay, 1992.

Alméras, Philippe. *Les Idées de Céline: Mythe de la race, politique et pamphlets.* Paris: Berg International, 1992.

Angenot, Marc. *La Parole pamphlétaire: Typologie des discours modernes.* Paris: Payot, 1982.

Anglès, Auguste. *André Gide et le premier groupe de* La Nouvelle Revue française. T. 1, *La formation du groupe et les années d'apprentissage.* T. 2, *L'âge critique (1911–1912).* T. 3, *Une inquiétante maturité (1913–1914).* Paris: Gallimard, 1978–1986.

Assouline, Pierre. *L'Épuration des intellectuels.* Brussels: Éditions Complexe, 1985.

Atack, Margaret. *Literature and the French Resistance: Cultural Politics and Narrative Forms 1940–1950.* Manchester, UK: Manchester University Press, 1989.

Bandier, Norbert. *Sociologie du surréalisme (1924–1929).* Paris: La Dispute, 1999.

Barbarant, Olivier. *Aragon, la mémoire et l'excès.* Seyssel: Champ Vallon, 1997.

Barrot, Olivier. *L'Écran français 1943–1953, histoire d'un journal et d'une époque.* Paris: EFR, 1979.

Bénichou, Paul. *Le Sacre de l'écrivain (1750–1830): Essai sur l'avènement d'un pouvoir spirituel laïque dans la France moderne.* Paris: José Corti, 1973; Gallimard, 1996. Translated by Mark K. Jensen as *The Consecration of the Writer, 1750–1830.* Lincoln: University of Nebraska Press, 1999.

Bernard, Jean-Pierre Arthur. *Le Parti communiste français et la question littéraire 1921–1939.* Presses universitaires de Grenoble, 1972.

———. *Paris rouge 1944–1964: Les communistes français dans la capitale.* Paris: Champ Vallon, 1991.

Berthet, Dominique. *Le* PCF, *la culture et l'art.* Paris: La Table Ronde, 1990.

Bertrand Dorléac, Laurence. *L'Art de la défaite* (1940–1944). Paris: Seuil, 1993. Translated by Jane Marie Todd as *The Art of the Defeat: France 1940–1944.* Los Angeles: Getty, 2008.

Bonnaud-Lamotte, Danielle, and Jean-Luc Rispail, eds. *Intellectuels des années trente: Entre le rêve et l'action.* Paris: Éditions du CNRS, 1990.

Boschetti, Anna. *Sartre et "Les Temps modernes": Une entreprise intellectuelle.* Paris: Minuit, 1985. Translated by Richard C. McCleary as *The Intellectual Enterprise: Sartre and* Les Temps Modernes. Evanston, IL: Northwestern University Press, 1988.

Bourderon, Roger. *Politzer contre le nazisme.* Underground texts introduced by Roger Bourderon. Paris: Messidor/Éditions sociales, 1984.

Bourdieu, Pierre. *Homo academicus.* Paris: Minuit, 1984. Translated by Peter Collier as *Homo Academicus.* Stanford, CA: Stanford University Press, 1988.

———. *L'Ontologie politique de Martin Heidegger.* Paris: Minuit, 1988. Translated by Peter Collier as *The Political Ontology of Martin Heidegger.* Stanford, CA: Stanford University Press, 1991.

———. *Les Règles de l'art: Genèse et structure du champ littéraire.* Paris: Seuil, 1992. Translated by Susan Emanuel as *The Rules of Art: Genesis and Structure of the Literary Field.* Stanford, CA: Stanford University Press, 1995.

Brenner, Jacques. *Tableau de la vie littéraire en France: D'avant-guerre à nos jours.* Paris: Luneau Ascot, 1982.

Broglie, Gabriel de. *Histoire politique de la Revue des Deux Mondes.* Paris: Perrin, 1979.

Brayard, Florent. *Comment l'idée vint à M. Rassinier: Naissance du révisionnisme.* Preface by Pierre Vidal-Naquet. Paris: Fayard, 1996.

Cabanis, José. *Dieu et la NRF (1909–1949).* Paris: Gallimard, 1994.

Caffier, Michel. *L'Académie Goncourt.* Paris: PUF, 1994.

Capitan Peter, Colette. *Charles Maurras et l'idéologie d'Action française: Étude sociologique d'une pensée de droite.* Paris: Seuil, 1972.

Cardahi, Choucri. *Regards sous la Coupole: Histoire et petite histoire de l'Académie française.* Preface by Jean Guitton. Paris: Mame, 1966.

Cariguel, Olivier. Les Cahiers du Rhône *dans la guerre 1941–1945.* Preface by Claire Andrieu. Éditions de l'université de Fribourg, 1999.

Casanova, Pascale. *La République mondiale des letters.* Paris: Seuil, 1999. Translated by M. B. DeBevoise as *The World Republic of Letters.* Cambridge, MA: Harvard University Press, 2004.

Cassagne, Albert. *La Théorie de l'art pour l'art en France chez les derniers romantiques et les premiers réalistes.* Paris: Hachette, 1906; Champ Vallon, 1997.

Castries, René de La Croix de. *La Vieille Dame du quai Conti: Une histoire de l'Académie française.* Paris: Perrin, 1978.

Caute, David. *Le Communisme et les intellectuels français (1914–1966).* Paris: Gallimard, 1964 and 1967.

———. *Les Compagnons de route (1917–1968).* Paris: Laffont, 1973 and 1979.

Charle, Christophe. *La Crise littéraire à l'époque du naturalisme: Roman, Théâtre, Politique.* Paris: PENS, 1979.

———. *Naissance des "intellectuels" (1880–1900).* Paris: Minuit, 1990.

————. *La République des universitaires 1870–1940.* Paris: Seuil, 1994.

————. *Les Intellectuels en Europe au XIXᵉ siècle: Essai d'histoire comparée.* Paris: Seuil, 1996.

————. *Paris fin de siècle: Culture et politique.* Paris: Seuil, 1998.

Chartier, Roger, and Henri-Jean Martin, eds. *Histoire de l'édition française.* T. 3, *Le temps des éditeurs: Du romantisme à la Belle Époque.* T. 4, *Le livre concurrencé 1900–1950.* Paris: Promodis, 1985; Fayard, 1990.

Chebel d'Appollonia, Ariane. *Histoire politique des intellectuels en France 1944–1954.* T. 1, *Des lendemains qui déchantent.* T. 2, *Le temps de l'engagement.* Brussels: Éditions Complexe, 1991.

Conley, Verena A. *Lire* Les Lettres françaises *(1942–1972): Perimètres et limites d'une idéologie.* PhD diss., University of Wisconsin-Madison, 1973. Revised and published as *Littérature, politique, et communisme: Lire* Les Lettres françaises *(1942–1972).* New York: Peter Lang, 2005.

Compagnon, Antoine. *La Troisième République des Lettres, de Flaubert à Proust.* Paris: Seuil, 1983.

————. *Connaissez-vous Brunetière? Enquête sur un antidreyfusard et ses amis.* Paris: Seuil, 1997.

Cornick, Martyn. *The* Nouvelle Revue française *under Jean Paulhan, 1925–1940.* Amsterdam: Rodopi, 1995.

Darnton, Robert. *Bohème littéraire et revolution: Le monde des livres au XVIIIᵉ siècle.* Paris: Gallimard/Seuil, 1983. Abridged version originally published in English as *The Literary Underground of the Old Regime.* Cambridge, MA: Harvard University Press, 1982.

David, Jean. *Le Procès de l'intelligence dans les lettres françaises au seuil de l'entre-deux-guerres (1919–1927).* Paris: Nizet, 1966.

Delporte, Christian. *Les Journalistes en France (1880–1950): Naissance et construction d'une profession.* Paris: Seuil, 1999.

Digeon, Claude. *La Crise allemande de la pensée française (1870–1914).* Paris: PUF, 1959.

Dioudonnat, Pierre-Marie. *Je suis partout (1930–1944): Les maurrassiens devant la tentation fasciste.* Paris: La Table Ronde, 1973.

————. *L'Argent nazi à la conquête de la presse française 1940–1944.* Paris: Éditions Jean Picollec, 1981.

Drouard, Alain. *Une inconnue des sciences sociales: La fondation Alexis-Carrel, 1941–1945* Paris: INED/MSH, 1992.

Fabiani, Jean-Louis. *Les Philosophes de la république.* Paris: Minuit, 1988.

Fauré, Michel. *Histoire du surréalisme sous l'Occupation.* Paris: La Table Ronde, 1982.

Fayolle, Roger. *La Critique littéraire en France du XVIᵉ siècle à nos jours.* Paris: Armand Colin, 1964.

Ferguson, Patricia Parkhurst. *La France, nation littéraire.* Brussels: Labor, 1991. Originally published as *Literary France: The Making of a Culture.* Berkeley: University of California Press, 1987.

Follet, Lionel. *Aurélien: Le fantasme et l'Histoire.* Paris: Les Belles Lettres, 1988.

Fouché, Pascal. "L'édition littéraire, 1914–1950." In *Histoire de l'édition française*. Vol. 4, *Le livre concurrencé*. Edited by Roger Chartier and Henri-Jean Martin. Paris: Promodis, 1986.

———. *L'Édition française sous l'Occupation 1940–1944*. 2 vols. Bibliothèque de littérature française contemporaine de l'université Paris VII, 1987.

Frey-Beguin, Françoise. *Les Cahiers du Rhône: Refuge de la pensée libre*. Fiftieth anniversary exhibit (September–December 1993). La Chaux-de-Fonds: Éditions de la Baconnière, 1993.

Fumaroli, Marc. *Trois Institutions littéraires*. Paris: Gallimard, 1994.

Galster, Ingrid. *Le Théâtre de Sartre devant ses premier critiques*. Paris/Tubingen: J.-M. Place/G. Narr Verlag, 1986.

Garrard, John, and Carol Garrard. *Inside the Soviet Writers' Union*. New York: Macmillan, 1990.

Gaucheron, Jacques. *La Poésie, la Résistance: Du Front populaire à la Libération*. Paris: Les Éditeurs français réunis, 1979.

Gerbod, Françoise, and Paul Gerbod. *Introduction à la vie littéraire du XXᵉ siècle*. Paris: Bordas, 1986.

Girault, Jacques, and Bernard Lecherbonnier, eds. *Les Engagements d'Aragon*. Actes du colloque de l'université Paris XIII (April 1, 1997). Paris: L'Harmattan, 1998.

Gouze, Roger. *Les Bêtes à Goncourt: Un demi-siècle de batailles littéraires*. Paris: Hachette, 1973.

Grémion, Pierre. *Intelligence de l'anticommunisme: Le Congrès pour la liberté de la culture à Paris 1950–1975*. Paris: Fayard, 1995.

Guérin, Jeanyves, ed. *Camus et la politique*. Actes du colloque de Nanterre (June 5–7, 1985). Paris: L'Harmattan, 1986.

Gugelot, Frédéric. *La Conversion des intellectuels au catholicisme en France 1885–1935*. Preface by Étienne Fouilloux. Paris: Éditions du CNRS, 1998.

Hanrez, Marc. *Les Écrivains et la guerre d'Espagne*. Dossiers H/Panthéon Press France, 1975.

Hebey, Pierre. La NRF *des années sombres (juin 1940–juin 1941): Des intellectuels à la derive*. Paris: Gallimard, 1992.

Hewitt, Nicholas. *Literature and the Right in Postwar France: The Story of the "Hussards."* Washington, DC: Berg, 1996.

Hollier, Denis, ed. *A New History of French Literature*. Cambridge, MA: Harvard University Press, 1989.

Hugues, H. Stuart. *The Obstructed Path: French Social Thought in the Years of Desperation (1930–1960)*. New York: Harper Torchbooks, 1966 and 1969.

Israël, Stéphane. *Les Études et la guerre: Les normaliens dans la tourment (1938–1946)*. Paris: Éditions rue d'Ulm, 2005.

Jennings, Jeremy, ed. *Intellectuals in Twentieth-Century France: Mandarins and Samurais*. New York: St. Martin Press, 1993.

Joubert, Marie Agnès. *La Comédie-Française sous l'Occupation*. Paris: Tallandier, 1998.

Judt, Tony. *Un passé imparfait: Les intellectuels en France (1944–1956)*. Paris: Fayard, 1992. Originally published as *Past Imperfect: French Intellectuals, 1944–1956*. Berkeley: University of California Press, 1992.

Kalifa, Dominique. *L'Encre et le sang: Récits de crimes et société à la Belle Époque*. Paris: Fayard, 1995.

Kohut, Karl, ed. *Literatur der Résistance und Kollaboration in Frankreich*. Vol. 2, *Geschichte und Wirkung II (1940–1950)*. Wiesbaden/Tubingen: Akademische Verlagsgesellschaft Athenaion/Gunter Narr Verlag, 1982. Vol. 3, *Texte und Interpretationen*. Tubingen: Gunter Narr Verlag, 1984.

Lepennies, Wolf. *Les Trois Cultures: Entre science et littérature, l'avènement de la sociologie*. Paris: Éditions de la MSH, 1990. Translated by R. J. Hollingdale as *Between Literature and Science: The Rise of Sociology*. Cambridge: Cambridge University Press, 1988.

Leroy, Géraldi, ed. *Les Écrivains de l'affaire Dreyfus*. Actes du colloque organisé par l'université d'Orléans et le centre Péguy (October 29–31, 1981). Paris: PUF, 1983.

Leroy, Géraldi, and Anne Roche. *Les Écrivains et le Front populaire*. Paris: PFNSP, 1986.

Leymarie, Michel, dir. *La Postérité de l'affaire Dreyfus*. Preface by Antoine Prost. Villeneuve d'Asq: Presses universitaires du Septentrion, 1998.

Lidsky, Paul. *Les Écrivains contre la Commune*. Paris: Maspero, 1982.

Lindenberg, Daniel. *Les Années souterraines (1937–1947)*. Paris: La Découverte, 1990.

Loiseaux, Gérard. *La Littérature de la défaite et de la Collaboration, d'après "Phonix oder Asche?" de Bernhard Payr*. Paris: Publications de la Sorbonne, 1984; Fayard, 1995.

Lottman, Herbert R. *La Rive gauche: Du Front populaire à la guerre froide*. Paris: Seuil, 1981. Originally published as *The Left Bank: Writers, Artists, and Politics from the Popular Front to the Cold War*. Boston: Houghton Mifflin, 1982.

Loubet del Bayle, Jean-Louis. *Les Non-Conformistes des années 30: Une tentative de renouvellement de la pensée politique française*. Paris: Seuil, 1969.

Mehlman, Jeffrey. *Genealogies of the Text: Literature, Psychoanalysis and Politics in Modern France*. Cambridge: Cambridge University Press, 1995.

Milligan, Jennifer E. *The Forgotten Generation: French Women Writers of the Inter-war Period*. New York: Berg, 1996.

Mollier, Jean-Yves. *L'Argent et les lettres: Histoire du capitalisme d'édition (1880–1920)*. Paris: Fayard, 1988.

Morel, Jean-Pierre. *Le Roman insupportable: L'internationale littéraire et la France (1920–1932)*. Paris: Gallimard, 1985.

Morel, Robert. *La Littérature clandestine*. Périgueux: Pierre Fanlac, 1945.

Morino, Lina. La Nouvelle Revue française *dans l'histoire des lettres (1908–1937)*. Paris: Gallimard, 1939.

Nadeau, Maurice. *Histoire du surréalisme*. Paris, Seuil: 1945.

Nettelbeck, Colin W. *Forever French: Exile in the United States 1939–1945*. New York: Berg, 1991.

Nguyen, Victor. *Aux origines de l'Action française: Intelligence et politique à l'aube du XXe siècle*. Paris: Fayard, 1991.

Ory, Pascal, ed. *Dernières Questions aux intellectuels*. Paris: Orban, 1990.

Ory, Pascal, and Jean-François Sirinelli. *Les Intellectuels en France, de l'affaire Dreyfus à nos jours*. Paris: Armand Colin, 1986.

Oster, Daniel. *Histoire de l'Académie française*. Paris: Vialetay, 1970.

Paire, Alain. *Chronique des* Cahiers du Sud *1914–1966*. Preface by Jean Duvignaud. Paris: IMEC éditions, 1993.

Parra I Alba, Montserrat. "Fortune du *Journal d'un curé de campagne* et *Les Grands cimetières sous la lune.*" In Monique Gosselin and Max Milner (eds.), *Bernanos et le monde moderne* (Colloque du centenaire de Georges Bernanos [1888–1988], Université Charles de Gaulle–Lille III, Presses universitaires de Lille, 1989).

Parrot, Louis. *L'Intelligence en guerre*. Paris: La Jeune Parque, 1945; Le Castor astral, 1990.

Pelletier, Denis. *Économie et Humanisme: De l'utopie communautaire au combat pour le tiers-monde, 1941–1966*. Paris: Éditions du Cerf, 1996.

Peter, René. *Vie secrète de l'Académie française, Cinquième période: Au seuil d'un monde nouveau*. Paris: Librairie des Champs-Élysées, 1940.

―――. *L'Académie française et le XXᵉ siècle*. Paris: Librairie des Champs-Élysées, 1949.

Picon, Gaétan. *Panorama de la nouvelle littérature française*. Paris: Gallimard, 1976 and 1988.

Pinto, Louis. *Les Neveux de Zarathoustra: La réception de Nietzsche en France*. Paris: Seuil, 1995.

Prochasson, Christophe. *Les Années électriques (1880–1910)*. Paris: La Découverte, 1991.

―――. *Les Intellectuels, le socialisme et la guerre (1900–1938)*. Paris: Seuil, 1993.

Prochasson, Christophe, and Anne Rasmussen. *Au nom de la patrie: Les intellectuels et la Première Guerre mondiale, 1910–1919*. Paris: La Découverte, 1996.

Ragache, Gilles, and Jean-Robert Ragache. *La Vie quotidienne des écrivains et des artistes sous l'Occupation (1940–1944)*. Paris: Hachette, 1988.

Ravon, Georges. *L'Académie Goncourt en dix couverts*. Avignon: E. Aubard, 1946.

Reynaud Paligot, Carole. *Parcours politique des surréalistes (1919–1969)*. Paris: Éditions du CNRS, 1995.

Riegel, Léon. *Guerre et littérature: Le bouleversement des consciences dans la littérature romanesque inspirée par la Grande Guerre*. Paris: Klincksieck, 1978.

Rieuneau, Maurice. *Guerre et révolution dans le roman français 1919–1939*. Paris: Klincksieck, 1974.

Rioux, Jean-Pierre, ed. *La Vie culturelle sous Vichy*. Brussels: Éditions Complexe, 1990.

Robichon, Jacques. *Le Défi des Goncourt*. Paris: Denoël, 1975.

Seghers, Pierre. *La Résistance et ses poètes: France 1940–1945*. Paris: Seghers, 1974.

Sérant, Paul. *Le Romantisme fasciste . . . ou l'œuvre politique de quelques écrivains français*. Paris: Fasquelle, 1959.

Serry, Hervé. *Naissance de l'intellectuel catholique*. Paris: La Découverte, 2004

Simonin, Anne. *Les Éditions de Minuit 1942–1955: Le devoir d'insoumission*. Paris: IMEC, 1994.

―――. "La Lettre aux directeurs de la Résistance de Jean Paulhan: Pour une rhétorique de l'engagement," in *Les Écrivains face à l'histoire*, edited by Antoine de Baecque. Actes du colloque organisé à la BPI (March 22, 1997). Paris: La BPI en actes, 1998. 45–69.

Sirinelli, Jean-François. *Génération intellectuelle: Khâgneux et normaliens dans l'entre-deux-guerres*. Paris: Fayard, 1988.

―――. *Intellectuels et passions françaises: Manifestes et pétitions au XXᵉ siècle*. Paris: Fayard, 1990.

Steel, James. *Littératures de l'ombre: Récits et nouvelles de la Résistance 1940–1944*. Paris: PFNSP, 1991.

Sternhell, Zeev. *Maurice Barrès et le nationalisme français*. Paris: PFNSP, 1974; Éditions Complexe, 1985.

Suleiman, Susan Rubin. *Le Roman à thèse ou l'autorité fictive*. Paris: PUF, 1983. Published in English as *Authoritarian Fictions: The Ideological Novel as a Literary Genre*. New York: Columbia University Press, 1983.

Thiesse, Anne-Marie. *Le Roman du quotidien: Lecteurs et lectures populaires à la Belle Époque*. Paris: Le Chemin vert, 1984.

———. *Écrire la France: Le mouvement littéraire régionaliste de langue française entre la Belle Époque et la Libération*. Paris: PUF, 1991.

Tonnet-Lacroix, Éliane. *Après-guerre et sensibilités littéraires, 1919–1924*. Paris: Publications de la Sorbonne, 1991.

Trebitsch, Michel. "L'image de l'Orient chez les intellectuels français et allemands au lendemain de la Première Guerre mondiale." In *Marianne-Germania: Deustch-Französischer Kulturtransfer 1790–1914*, edited by Étienne François, Marie-Claire Hoock-Demarle, Reinhart Meyer-Kalkus, and Michael Werner. Leipzig: Leipziger Universität-Verlag, 1998. 531–553.

Verdès-Leroux, Jeannine. *Au service du Parti: Le parti communiste, les intellectuels et la culture (1944–1956)*. Paris: Fayard/Minuit, 1983.

———. *Refus et violences: Politique et littérature à l'extrême droite des années trente aux retombées de la Libération*. Paris: Gallimard, 1996.

Viala, Alain. *Naissance de l'écrivain: Sociologie de la littérature à l'âge classique*. Paris: Minuit, 1985.

Wellek, René. *Une histoire de la critique moderne: La critique française, italienne et espagnole (1900–1950)*. Paris: José Corti, 1996. Originally published as *A History of Modern Criticism*. Vol. 8, *French, Italian, and Spanish Criticism, 1900–1950*. New Haven, CT: Yale University Press, 1992.

Wilkinson, James D. *The Intellectual Resistance in Europe*. Cambridge, MA: Harvard University Press, 1981.

Williams, Raymond. *Culture and Society (1780–1950)*. New York: Columbia University Press, 1958 and 1983.

Winock, Michel. *"Esprit": Des intellectuels dans la cité, 1930–1950*. Revised and expanded edition of *Histoire politique de la revue "Esprit."* Paris: Seuil, 1996 [first edition 1975].

———. *Le Siècle des intellectuels*. Paris: Seuil, 1997.

Wohl, Robert. *The Generation of 1914*. Cambridge, MA: Harvard University Press, 1979.

4. Biographies

Andreu, Pierre, and Frédéric Grover. *Drieu La Rochelle*. Paris: Hachette, 1979.

Armel, Aliette. *Michel Leiris*. Paris: Fayard, 1997.

Assouline, Pierre. *Gaston Gallimard: Un demi-siècle d'édition française*. Paris: Balland, 1984. Abridged version translated by Harold J. Salemson as *Gaston Gallimard: A Half-Century of French Publishing*. San Diego: Harcourt Brace Jovanovich, 1988.

Badré, Frédéric. *Paulhan le juste*. Paris: Grasset, 1996.

Bair, Deirdre. *Simone de Beauvoir*. Paris: Fayard, 1990. Originally published as *Simone de Beauvoir: A Biography*. New York : Summit Books, 1990.

Balvet, Marie. *Itinéraire d'un intellectual vers le fascisme: Drieu La Rochelle*. Paris: PUF, 1984.

Belot, Robert. *Lucien Rebatet: Un itinéraire fasciste*. Paris: Seuil, 1994.

Berger, Pierre. *Robert Desnos*. Paris: Seghers, 1949 and 1970.

Bertholet, Denis. *Paul Valéry 1871–1945*. Paris: Plon, 1995.

Bornecque, Jacques-Henry. *Pierre Benoit le magicien*. Paris: Albin Michel, 1986.

Bosquet, Alain. *Pierre Emmanuel*. Paris: Seghers, 1959 and 1971.

Bothorel, Jean. *Bernard Grasset: Vie et passions d'un éditeur*. Paris: Grasset, 1989.

Bouquet, Georges, and Pierre Menanteau. *Charles Vildrac*. Paris: Seghers, 1959.

Brassié, Anne. *Robert Brasillach ou Encore un instant de bonheur*. Paris: Laffont, 1987.

Broche, François. *Léon Daudet, le dernier imprécateur*. Paris: Laffont, 1992.

Butin, Jean. *De la Gerbe d'or au pain noir. La longue marche d'Henri Béraud*, s. 1. Éditions Horvath, 1979.

Citron, Pierre. *Giono (1895–1970)*. Paris: Seuil, 1990.

Clancier, Georges-Emmanuel, and Jean-Yves Debreuille. *André Frénaud*. Paris: Seghers, 1963 and 1989.

Cohen-Solal, Annie. *Sartre (1905–1980)*. Paris: Gallimard, 1985. Translated by Anna Cancogni as *Sartre: A Life*. New York: Pantheon, 1987.

Copfermann, Émile. *David Rousset: Une vie dans le siècle*. Paris: Plon, 1991.

Coulomb, Pierre. *La Varende*. Paris: Dominique Wapler, 1951.

Courrière, Yves. *Roger Vailland ou Un libertin au regard froid*. Paris: Plon, 1991.

Daix, Pierre. *Aragon, une vie à changer*. Paris: Seuil, 1975; Flammarion, 1978.

Desanti, Dominique. *Les Clés d'Elsa: Aragon-Triolet*. Paris: Ramsay, 1983.

Dhôtel, André. *Jean Follain*. Paris: Seghers, 1956 and 1993.

Dupray, Micheline. *Roland Dorgelès: Un siècle de vie littéraire française*. Paris: Presses de la Renaissance, 1986.

Garcin, Jérôme. *Pour Jean Prévost*. Paris: Gallimard, 1994.

Gateau, Jean-Charles. *Paul Eluard ou Le frère voyant 1895–1952*. Paris: Laffont, 1988.

Gleize, Jean-Marie. *Francis Ponge*. Paris: Seuil, 1988.

Guérin, Jeanyves. *Camus, portrait de l'artiste en citoyen*. Paris: François Bourin, 1993.

Joseph, Gilbert. *Une si douce occupation: Simone de Beauvoir et Jean-Paul Sartre (1940– 1944)*. Paris: Albin Michel, 1991.

Jouet, Jacques. *Raymond Queneau*. Paris: La Manufacture, 1988.

Kopp, Robert, and Dominique de Roux, eds. *Pierre Jean Jouve*. Paris: Éditions de l'Herne, 1972.

Lacouture, Jean. *André Malraux: Une vie dans le siècle*. Paris: Seuil, 1973. Translated by Alan Sheridan as *André Malraux*. New York: Pantheon, 1975.

———. *François Mauriac*. T. 1, *Le Sondeur d'abîmes 1885–1933*. Vol. 2, *Un citoyen du siècle 1933–1970*. Paris: Seuil, 1980.

———. *Une adolescence dans le siècle: Jacques Rivière et La NRF*. Paris: Seuil, 1994.

Lepape, Pierre. *André Gide le messager*. Paris: Seuil, 1997.

Leuwers, Daniel. *Jouve avant Jouve ou la naissance d'un poète (1906–1928)*. Paris: Klincksieck, 1984.

Liger, Christian. *Histoire d'une famille nîmoise: Les Paulhan*. Paris: Gallimard, 1984.

Lottman, Herbert R. *Albert Camus*. Paris: Seuil, 1979. Originally published as *Albert Camus*. New York: Doubleday, 1979.

Marcou, Lilly. *Elsa Triolet: Les Yeux et la Mémoire*. Paris: Plon, 1994.

Martin, Claude. *André Gide ou la vocation du bonheur*. T. 1, *1869–1911*. Paris: Fayard, 1998.

Marty, Éric. *André Gide*. Paris: La Manufacture, 1987.

Meizoz, Jérôme. Ramuz. *Un passager clandestin des Lettres françaises*. Genève: Éditions Zoé, 1997.

Memmi, Dominique. *Jules Romains ou la passion de parvenir*. Paris: La Dispute, 1998.

Mesnard, Philippe. *Maurice Blanchot: Le sujet de l'engagement*. Paris: L'Harmattan, 1996.

Moi, Toril. *Simone de Beauvoir: Conflits d'une intellectuelle*. Preface by Pierre Bourdieu. Paris: Diderot éditeur, 1995. Originally published as *Simone de Beauvoir: The Making of an Intellectual Woman*. Oxford: Blackwell, 1994.

Négis, André. *Mon ami Carco*. Paris: Albin Michel, 1953.

Péan, Pierre. *Une jeunesse française: François Mitterand 1934–1947*. Paris: Fayard, 1994.

Pierre-Quint, Léon. *André Gide: L'homme, sa vie, son oeuvre, entretiens avec Gide et ses contemporains*. Paris: Stock, 1952. Translated by Dorothy M. Richardson as *André Gide: His Life and His Work*. New York: Knopf, 1934.

Quella-Villéger, Alain. *Le Cas Farrère: Du Goncourt à la disgrâce*. Paris: Presse de la Renaissance, 1989.

Revah, Louis-Albert. *Julien Benda*. Paris: Plon, 1991.

Sadoul, Georges. *Aragon*. Paris: Seghers, 1967.

Seghers, Colette. *Pierre Seghers: Un homme couvert de noms*. Paris: Laffont, 1981.

Seghers, Pierre. *Pierre Seghers*. Paris: Seghers, 1967 and 1973.

Souchier, Emmanuel. *Raymond Queneau*. Paris: Seuil, 1991.

Sipriot, Pierre. *Montherlant sans masque*. T. 1, *L'enfant prodigue 1895–1932*. T. 2, *"Écris avec ton sang."* Paris: Laffont, 1990.

Surya, Michel. *Georges Bataille, la mort à l'œuvre*. Paris: Gallimard, 1992.

Tacou, Constantin, and Françoise Dax-Boyer. *Jean Tardieu*. Paris: Éditions de L'Herne (Cahiers de l'Herne no. 59), 1991.

Toda, Michel. *Henri Massis: Un témoin de la droite intellectuelle*. Paris: La Table ronde, 1987.

Todd, Oliver. *Albert Camus, une vie*. Paris: Gallimard, 1996. Abridged and edited version translated by Benjamin Ivry as *Albert Camus: A Life*. New York: Knopf, 1997.

———. *André Malraux, une vie*. Paris: Gallimard, 2001. Translated by Joseph West as *Malraux: A Life*. New York: Knopf, 2005.

Tortel, Jean. *Guillevic*. Paris: Seghers, 1954 and 1990.

Touzot, Jean, ed. *François Mauriac*. Paris: Éditions de L'Herne (*Cahiers de l'Herne* no. 48), 1985.

———. *Mauriac sous l'Occupation*. Paris: La Manufacture, 1990.

Vircondelet, Alain. *Duras: Biographie*. Paris: François Bourin, 1991. Translated by Thomas Buckley as *Duras: A Biography*. Normal, IL: Dalkey Archive Press, 1994.

Vitoux, Frédéric. *La Vie de Céline*. Paris: Grasset, 1988. Translated by Jesse Browner as *Céline : A Biography*. New York: Paragon, 1992.

C. PERIODICALS

"Les élections à l'Académie française: Analyse d'un scrutin significatif; L'échec de M. Paul Morand." *Revue française de science politique* 8, no. 3 (September 1958): 646–654.

Ambroise, Jean-Charles. "Écrivain prolétarien: Une identité paradoxale." *Sociétés contemporaines* 44 (2001): 41–56

Andrieu, Claire. "Les résistantes, perspectives de recherche." In "Pour une histoire sociale de la Résistance." Edited by Antoine Prost. Special issue of *Le Mouvement social* 180 (July–September 1997): 69–96.

Apel-Muller, Michel. "L'édition de 1942 des *Voyageurs de l'impériale*: Une entreprise 'diabolique.'" *Recherches croisées Aragon/Triolet* 1 (1988): 167–209.

———. "Aragon devant le texte de Barbusse." *Recherches croisées Aragon/Triolet* 2 (1989): 135–158.

Assouline, Pierre. "Les dessous du Goncourt." *Lire* 194 (November 1991): 33–47.

Babilas, Wolfgang. "'Contre la poésie pure': Lecture d'un poème poétologique d'Aragon." *Recherches croisées Aragon/Triolet* 2 (1989): 233–252.

———. "La querelle des mauvais maîtres," in *La Littérature française sous l'Occupation*, Reims conference proceedings, September 30–October 1 and 2, 1981 (Presses Universitaires de Reims, 1989), 199.

Balmand, Pascal. "L'anti-intellectualisme dans la culture politique française." *Vingtième Siècle* 36 (October–December 1992): 31–42.

Baruch, Marc Olivier. "Les revues de l'État français," in "Des revues sous l'Occupation." *La Revue des revues* 24 (1997): 35–43.

Belot, Robert. "Les lecteurs des Décombres de Lucien Rebatet: un témoignage inédit du sentiment fasciste sous l'Occupation." *Guerres mondiales et conflits contemporains* 163 (July 1991): 3–33.

Bertrand-Dorléac, Laurence. "L'ordre des artistes et l'utopie corporatiste: Les tentatives de régir la scène artistique française (juin 1940–août 1944)." *Revue d'histoire moderne et contemporaine* (January–March 1990): 64–88.

Blavier, André. "Chronologie de Raymond Queneau." *Europe* 650–651 (June–July 1983): 130–148.

Bonnet, Marguerite. "L'Orient dans le surréalisme: Mythe et réel," in "Littérature et Nation au XXᵉ siècle." *Revue de littérature comparée* 216 (October–December 1980): 411–424.

Boschetti, Anna. "Les Temps modernes dans le champ littéraire." *La Revue des revues* 7 (spring 1989): 6–13.

———. "Des revues et des hommes." *La Revue des revues* 18 (1994): 51–65.

Bourdieu, Pierre. "Champ du pouvoir, champ intellectual et habitus de classe." *Scolies* 1 (1971): 7–26.

———. "Genèse et structure du champ religieux." *Revue française de sociologie* 12 (July–September 1971): 295–334. Translated as "Genesis and Structure of the Religious Field." *Comparative Social Research* (1991) 13, no. 1 (1991): 1–44.

———. "Une interprétation de la théorie de la religion selon Max Weber." *Archives européennes de sociologie* 12, no. 1 (1971): 3–21. Revised and translated as "Legitimation and Structured Interests in Weber's Sociology of Religion" in Scott Lash and Sam Whimster (eds.), *Max Weber, Rationality and Modernity.* London: Allen and Unwin, 1987, 119–136.

———. "Le marché des biens symboliques." *L'Année sociologique* 22 (1971): 49–126. Abridged and translated by Rupert Swyer as "The Market of Symbolic Goods" in Randal Johnson (ed.), *The Field of Cultural Production: Essays on Art and Literature.* Cambridge: Polity Press, 1993, 112–141.

———. "Sur le pouvoir symbolique." *Annales ESC* (May–June 1977): 405–412. Translated by Richard Nice as "Symbolic Power." *Critique of Anthropology* 4, no. 13–14 (January 1979): 77–85.

———. "La production de la croyance: Contribution à une économie des biens symboliques." *Actes de la recherche en sciences sociales* 13 (1977): 3–45. Translated by Richard Nice as "The Production of Belief: Contribution to an Economy of Symbolic Goods." *Media Culture Society* 2, no. 3 (July 1980): 261–293.

———. "Le mort saisit le vif: Les relations entre l'histoire réifiée et l'histoire incorporée." *Actes de la recherche en sciences sociales* 32–33 (April–June 1980): 3–14.

———. "Le Nord et le Midi: Contribution à une analyse de l'effet Montesquieu." *Actes de la recherché en sciences sociales* 35 (November 1980): 21–25.

———. "Sartre." *London Review of Books* 2 (November 20–December 3, 1980): 11–12.

———. "Le champ littéraire: Préalables critiques et principes de méthode." *Lendemains* 36 (1984): 5–20.

———. "L'Illusion biographique." *Actes de la recherche en sciences sociales* 62–63 (June 1986): 69–73. Translated by Yves Winkin and Wendy Leeds-Hurwitz as "The Biographical Illusion." *Working Papers and Proceedings of the Centre for Psychosocial Studies* 14 (1987): 1–7.

———. "Intérêt et désintéressement." *Cahiers de recherche* 7 (September 1989).

———. "Le champ littéraire." *Actes de la recherche en sciences sociales* 89 (September 1991): 4–46.

Briand, Jean-Pierre, Jean-Michel Chapoulie, and Henri Peretz. "Les conditions institutionnelles de la scolarisation secondaire des garçons entre 1920 et 1940." *Revue d'histoire moderne et contemporaine* 26 (July–September 1979): 391–421.

Charle, Christophe. "Champ littéraire et champ du pouvoir, les écrivains et l'affaire Dreyfus." *Annales (ESC)* 2 (March–April 1977): 240–264.

———. "Situation du champ littéraire." *Littérature* 44 (1982): 8–21.

———. "Le champ universitaire parisien à la fin du 19e siècle." *Actes de la recherche en sciences sociales* 47–48 (June 1983): 77–90.

———. "Savoir durer: la nationalisation de Sciences-Po, 1936/45." *Actes de la recherche en sciences sociales* 86–87 (March 1991): 99–105.

———. "Le Temps des hommes doubles." *Revue d'histoire moderne et contemporaine* 39, no. 1 (January–March 1992): 73–86.

Chartier, Roger. "Pouvoir(s) et culture(s)." *Cahiers de recherche* 11 (1993): 5–56.

Christophe, Paul. "Le cardinal Baudrillart et ses choix pendant la Seconde Guerre mondiale." *Revue d'histoire de l'Église de France* 200 (January–June 1992): 57–73.

Cornick, Martyn. "Les années Paulhan à La Nouvelle Revue française." *La Revue des revues* 18 (1994): 33–42.

Crémieux, Francis. "Arrêtez immédiatement la juive Elsa Kagan dite Triolet." *Faites entrer l'infini* 21 (June 1996): 15–16.

Delmont, Abbé Th. "Les malfaiteurs intellectuels: Madame de Staël." *L'Univers* 29 (March 17, 1918).

Dobry, Michel. "Février 1934 et la découverte de l'allergie de la société française à la 'Révolution fasciste.'" *Revue française de sociologie* 30, no. 3/4 (July–December 1989): 511–533. Translated as "February 1934 and the Discovery of French Society's Allergy to the 'Fascist Revolution.'" In Brian Jenkins (ed.), *France in the Era of Fascism: Essays on the Authoritarian Right*. New York: Berghahn Books, 2005, 129–150.

Douzou, Laurent. "L'entrée en résistance." In "Pour une histoire sociale de la Résistance." Edited by Antoine Prost. Special issue, *Le Mouvement social* 180 (July–September 1997): 9–20.

Duclert, Vincent. "Anti-intellectualisme et intellectuels pendant l'affaire Dreyfus." *Mil Neuf Cent: Revue d'histoire intellectuelle* 15 (1997): 69–83.

———. "La Ligue de 'l'époque héroïque': La politique des savants." In "La Ligue des droits de l'homme." Edited by Madeleine Rebérioux. Special issue, *Le Mouvement social* 183 (April–June 1998): 25–34.

Durosay, Daniel. "La direction politique de Jacques Rivière à la 'Nouvelle revue française' (1919–1925)." *Revue d'histoire littéraire de la France* (March–April 1977): 227–245.

Elias, Norbert. "Remarques sur le commérage." Translated by Francine Muel-Dreyfus. *Actes de la recherche en sciences sociales* 60 (November 1985): 23–29. Published in English as "Observations on Gossip" in Norbert Elias and John Scotson, *The Established and the Outsiders*. London: Sage, 1994.

Even-Zohar, Itamar. "Polysystem Studies." *Poetics Today* 11, no. 1 (1990).

Eychart, Marie-Thérèse. "Réception du prix Goncourt 1944: Elsa Triolet ou la constitution d'une légende." *Recherches croisées Aragon/Triolet* 5 (1994): 197–228.

Faure, Christian. "Vent de mars d'Henri Pourrat: Prix Goncourt 1941 ou la consécration d'une œuvre littéraire par le régime de Vichy." *Bulletin du centre Pierre Léon: Histoire économique et sociale de la région lyonnaise* 1 (1982): 5–25.

———. "Pétainisme et retour aux sources: Autour du tricentenaire Sully." *Cahiers d'histoire* 28, no. 4 (1983): 3–32.

Fourcade, Michel. "Jacques Maritain, inspirateur de la Résistance." *Cahiers Jacques Maritain* 32 (June 1996): 14–57.

Galster, Ingrid. "Images actuelles de Sartre." *Cahiers d'histoire des littératures romanes* 1–2 (1987): 215–244.

———. "Les Mouches sous l'Occupation: À propos de quelques idées reçues." *Les Temps modernes* 531–533 (October–December 1990): 844–859.

———. "Simone de Beauvoir et Radio-Vichy: À propos de quelques scénarios retrouvés." *Romanische Forschungen* 108, no. 1–2 (1996): 112–132.

Garet, Jean-Louis. "Montherlant sous l'Occupation." *Vingtième Siècle* 31 (July–September 1991): 65–75.

Grenouillet, Corinne. "Celui qui croyait au ciel et celui qui ny croyait pas." *Recherches croisées Aragon/Triolet* 4 (1992): 221–290.

Guéraiche, William. "Les femmes politiques de 1944 à 1947: Quelle libération?" In "Résistances et Libérations France 1940–1945." Coordinated by F. Thébaud. Special issue, *Clio: Histoire, Femmes et Sociétés* 1 (1995): 165–186.

Joucla, Maurice. "Benda sous l'occupation." *Europe* 389 (September 1961): 14–20.

Jurt, Joseph. "Autonomie ou hétéronomie: le champ littéraire en France et en Allemagne." *Regards sociologiques* 4 (1992): 3–16.

———. "Gide et Bernanos." *Bulletin des Amis d'André Gide* 94 (April 1992): 187–207.

Karady, Victor. "Normaliens et autres enseignants à la Belle Époque: Note sur l'origine sociale et la réussite dans une profession intellectuelle." *Revue française de sociologie* 13, no. 1 (January–March 1972): 35–38.

———. "Les professeurs de la République: le marché scolaire, les réformes universitaires et les transformations de la fonction professorale à la fin du 19e siècle." *Actes de la recherche en sciences sociales* 47–48 (June 1983): 90–113.

Karakatsoulis, Anne. "La Revue des Deux Mondes à travers ses archives." *La Revue des revues* 14 (1992): 37–47.

———. "Une revue-entreprise: La Revue des Deux Mondes pendant l'entre-deux-guerres." *La Revue des revues* 22 (1996): 17–44.

Kid, William. "Un dialogue interrompu. Jacques Rivière et Ramon Fernandez," followed by letters from Ramon Fernandez to Jacques Rivière. *Bulletin des amis de Jacques Rivière et Alain-Fournier* 14 (first trimester 1979).

Kriegel, Annie. "Le PCF, Thorez et la France." *Le Mouvement social* 172 (July–September 1995): 95–99.

Laborie, Pierre. "Opinion et représentations: la Libération et l'image de la Résistance." *Revue d'histoire de la Deuxième Guerre mondiale* 131 (1983): 65–91.

Lafay, Arlette. "'La Résistance à visage découvert' de Georges Duhamel (1940–1945)." *Les Cahiers de l'abbaye de Créteil* 7 (December 1985): 60–71.

Laguerre, Bernard. "Marianne et Vendredi: Deux générations?" *Vingtième Siècle* 22 (April–June 1989): 39–45.

Lance-Otterbein, Renate. "Jeanne, France, Harry et la guerre de 40." *Digraphe* 82–83 (autumn/winter 1997): 161–190.

Lazar, Marc. "Les 'batailles du livre' du parti communiste français (1950–1952)." *Vingtième Siècle* 10 (April–June 1986): 37–49.

Leymarie, Michel. "Les Frères Tharaud, René Doumic et la Revue des Deux Mondes." *La Revue des revues* 22 (1996): 45–64.

Loué, Thomas. "Les fils de Taine entre science et morale: À propos du Disciple de Paul Bourget (1889)." In "Littérature politique." Edited by P. Olivera. Special issue, *Cahiers d'histoire: Revue d'histoire critique* 65 (1996): 45–61.

———. "'Les Barbares lettrés': Esquisse d'un temps long de l'anti-intellectualisme en France (1840–1900)." *Mil Neuf Cent: Revue d'histoire intellectuelle* 15 (1997): 69–85.

Mathias, Yehoshua. "Paul Bourget, écrivain engagé." *Vingtième Siècle* 45 (January–March 1995): 14–29.

Meizoz, Jérôme. "Queneau, les linguistes et les écrivains. 'Faute' de français et littérature." *Poétique* 115 (September 1998): 351–367.

Memmi, Dominique. "Les déplacés: Travail sur soi et ascension sociale; La promotion littéraire de Jules Romains." *Genèses* 24 (September 1996): 57–80.

———. "L'ascension sociale vue de l'intérieur: Les postures de la conquête." *Cahiers internationaux de sociologie.* Vol. C (1996): 33–58.

Ménager, Yves. "Les périodiques littéraires et la Résistance intellectuelle en France de 1940 à 1944." In *Autour de la Seconde Guerre mondiale: Résistance, témoignages, fictions.* Special issue, *L'École des Lettres* 2 (July 1991): 101–116.

Mièvre, Jacques. "L'évolution politique d'Abel Bonnard, jusqu'au printemps 1942." *Revue d'histoire de la Deuxième Guerre mondiale* 108 (October 1977): 1–26.

Monférier, Jacques. "La genèse du *Cahier noir.*" Travaux du centre d'études et de recherches sur François Mauriac (Université de Bordeaux) 1 (1977): 3–14.

Olivera, Philippe. "Le sens du jeu: Aragon entre littérature et politique (1958–1968)." In "Littérature et politique." Special issue, *Actes de la recherche en sciences sociales,* 111–112 (March 1996): 76–85.

Paire, Alain. "Les Cahiers du Sud et Le Grand Jeu (1927–1944)." *La Revue des revues* 14 (1992): 25–37.

———. "1941: Le journal de bord des *Cahiers du Sud.*" *La Revue des revues* 16 (1993): 71–98.

Papeleux, Léon. "Note à propos de l'affaire Baudrillart." *Revue d'histoire ecclésiastique* 1 (January–April 1987): 50–53.

Pennetier, Claude, and Bernard Pudal. "La certification scolaire communiste dans les années trente." *Politix* 35 (1996): 69–88.

Péru, Jean-Michel. "Une crise du champ littéraire français: Le débat sur la 'littérature prolétarienne' (1925–1935)." *Actes de la recherche en sciences sociales* 89 (September 1991): 47–65.

Ponton, Rémy. "Programme esthétique et accumulation de capital symbolique: L'exemple du Parnasse." *Revue française de sociologie* 14 (1973): 202–220.

———. "Naissance du roman psychologique: capital culturel, capital social et stratégie littéraire à la fin du 19ᵉ siècle." *Actes de la recherche en sciences sociales* 4 (1975): 66–81.

Poumarède, Géraud. "Le cercle Proudhon ou l'impossible synthèse." *Mil neuf cent: Revue d'histoire intellectuelle* 12 (1994): 51–87.

Pudal, Bernard. "Nizan: l'homme et ses doubles." *Mots* 32 (September 1992): 29–47.

Racine-Furlaud, Nicole. "L'AEAR." *Le Mouvement social* 54 (January–March 1966): 29–47.

———. "Le Comité de vigilance des intellectuels antifascistes, 1934–1939: Antifascisme et pacifisme." *Le Mouvement social* 101 (October–December 1977): 87–113.

———. "Une cause: l'antifascisme des intellectuels." *Politix* 17 (1992): 79–85.

Racine, Nicole, and Michel Trebitsch, eds. "Sociabilités intellectuelles. Lieux, milieux, réseaux." *Cahiers de l'IHTP* 20 (March 1992).

Rasmussen, Anne. "Critique du progress, 'crise de la science': Débats et représentations du tournant du siècle." In "Progrès et décadence." Special issue, *Mil Neuf Cent: Revue d'histoire intellectuelle* 14 (1996): 89–113.

Richard, Lionel. "Drieu La Rochelle et *La Nouvelle Revue française* des années noires." *Revue d'histoire de la Deuxième Guerre mondiale* 97 (January 1975): 67–84.

Rivière, Jacques. "Histoire abrégée de La Nouvelle Revue française." Introduced by Claire Paulhan. *La Revue des revues* 21 (1996): 73–96.

Saint-Martin, Monique de. "Les 'femmes écrivains' et le champ littéraire." *Actes de la recherche en sciences sociales* 83 (1990): 52–57.

Sapiro, Gisèle. "Académie française et Académie Goncourt dans les années 1940: Fonction et fonctionnement des institutions de la vie littéraire en période de crise nationale." In "Texte et histoire littéraire." Special issue, *Texte* 12 (1992): 151–197.

———. "La raison littéraire. Le champ littéraire français sous l'Occupation (1940–1944)." In "Littérature et politique." Special issue, *Actes de la recherche en sciences sociales* 111–112 (March 1996): 3–35.

———. "Salut littéraire et littérature du salut: Deux trajectoires de romanciers catholiques: François Mauriac et Henry Bordeaux." In "Littérature et politique." Special issue, *Actes de la recherche en sciences sociales* 111–112 (March 1996): 36–58.

———. "Les conditions professionnelles d'une mobilisation réussie: Le Comité national des écrivains." In "Pour une histoire sociale de la Résistance." Edited by Antoine Prost. Special issue, *Le Mouvement social* 180 (July–September 1997): 179–191.

Serry, Hervé. "Déclin social et revendication identitaire: la 'renaissance littéraire catholique' de la première moitié du XXe siècle." *Sociétés Contemporaines* 44 (2002): 91–109.

———. "Les écrivains catholiques dans les années 20." *Actes de la recherche en sciences sociales* 124 (September 1998): 80–87.

———. "La littérature pour faire et défaire les groupes." *Sociétés contemporaines* 44 (2001): 5–14.

———. "Littérature et religion catholique (1880–1914): Contribution à une socio-histoire de la croyance." *Cahiers d'histoire* 87 (2002): 37–60.

———. "Le mouvement de 'renaissance littéraire catholique': Entre espoirs et désillusions." *Bulletin de l'Association Francis Jammes* 28 (December 1998): 11–50.

Simonin, Anne. "Les Éditions de Minuit: Littérature et politique dans la France des années sombres." *Bulletin de la SHMC* 3–4 (1994): 63–68.

———. "La littérature saisie par l'Histoire: Nouveau roman et guerre d'Algérie aux Éditions de Minuit." In "Littérature et politique." Special issue, *Actes de la recherche en sciences sociales* 111–112 (March 1996): 69–71.

———. "Maurice Blanchot tel qu'on peut l'imaginer." *Art Press* 218 (November 1996): 61–64.

———. "Le Comité médical de la Résistance: Un succès différé." In "Pour une histoire sociale de la Résistance." Edited by Antoine Prost. *Le Mouvement social* 180 (July–September 1997): 159–191.

———. "1815 en 1945: Les formes littéraires de la défaite." *Vingtième Siècle* 59 (July–September 1998): 48–61.

Sirinelli, Jean-François, ed. "Générations intellectuelles." *Cahiers de l'IHTP* 6 (November 1987).

Thiesse, Anne-Marie. "Les infortunes littéraires: Carrières des romanciers populaires à la Belle Époque." *Actes de la recherche en sciences sociales* 60 (1985): 31–46.

Trebitsch, Michel. "Le groupe 'Philosophies,' de Max Jacob aux surréalistes (1924–1925)." In "Générations intellectuelles." Edited by Jean-François Sirinelli. Special issue, *Cahiers de l'IHTP* 6 (November 1987): 29–38.

———. "Nécrologie: Les revues qui s'arrêtent en 1939–1940." In "Des revues sous l'Occupation." *La Revue des revues* 24 (1997): 19–33.

Véron, Jacques. "L'Académie française et la circulation des élites." *Population* 3 (May–June 1995): 455–471.

Viala, Alain. "Effets de champ, effets de prisme." *Littérature* 70 (May 1988): 64–72. Translated by Paola Wissing as "Prismatic Effects" in Philippe Desen, Priscilla Parkhust Ferguson, and Wendy Grisvold (eds.), *Literature and Social Practice*. Chicago: University of Chicago Press, 1988, 260–261.

———. "Du caractère de l'écrivain à l'âge classique." *Textuel* 22 (1989): 49–58.

Virieux, Daniel. "L'Homme résistant." *Faites entrer l'infini* 23 (June 1997): 24–25.

———. "Résistance-Professions. Un rapport sans histoire(s)?" In "Pour une histoire sociale de la Résistance." Edited by Antoine Prost. Special issue, *Le Mouvement social* 180 (July–September 1997): 113–146.

Name Index

Ardenne de Tizac, Henri d' (pseudonym of Jean Viollis), 420
Arland, Marcel, 25, 32, 54, 75, 133, 295–96, 297, 304, 305, 319, 321, 325, 348, 349, 389, 432, 433–34, 470, 535, 570
Arnoux, Alexandre, 130, 150, 261, 262, 273, 281, 415, 448, 493, 498, 528, 530, 570
Aron, Robert, 502, 536, 629n21
Artaud, Antonin, 313
Assouline, Pierre, 460
Astier de la Vigerie, Emmanuel d', 410
Astorg, Bertrand d', 356
Astruc, Alexandre, 355, 469
Aubenque, Jacques, 334
Aubry, Octave, 39
Auclair, Marcelle, 529
Audiberti, Jacques, 72, 281, 285, 305, 313, 323, 324, 326, 327, 464, 470, 570
Audin, Maurice, 331
Audisio, Gabriel, 356, 414, 456–58, 570
Augier, Marc, 27
Aulard, Ernest (printer), 396
Auric, Georges, 367
Auriol, Vincent, 479, 519, 659n58
Aury, Dominique, 515
Autrand, Charles, 329
Aveline, Claude (pseudonym of Evgen Avtsine), 375–76, 403, 408, 410, 445, 482, 483, 526–28, 530, 570
Avtsine, Evgen. See Aveline, Claude
Aymé, Jacques d' (pseudonym of Léon Moussinac), 399
Aymé, Marcel, 28, 30, 46, 76, 477, 481, 518, 537, 570, 579n72

Babilas, Wolfgang, 121
Bachelard, Gaston, 353, 357
Bainville, Jacques, 56, 101, 208, 211, 212, 594n62
Ballard, Jean, 238, 329
Balzac, Honoré de, 98, 128, 150, 197, 213, 219, 236, 245–46, 580n92
Barbey d'Aurevilly, Jules, 248
Barbezat, Marc, 334, 335, 340, 341, 635n135

Barbusse, Henri, 109, 205, 207, 229, 256, 284, 337, 362, 525
Bardéche, Maurice, 56, 107, 236, 354, 518, 533, 558
Bargone, Frédéric-Charles. See Farrére, Claude
Baroncelli, Jean de, 275
Barraine, Elsa, 367
Barrés, Maurice, 89–91, 95, 101, 110, 111, 117, 128, 133, 143, 153, 160, 163, 165, 169–71, 198, 204, 206, 211, 248, 264, 270, 301, 533
Baruch, Marc Olivier, 45, 573–74n3
Bastard, Lucien. See Estang, Luc
Bataille, Georges, 71, 305, 353–58, 360, 570
Baudelaire, Charles, 98, 307, 322, 357, 674n22
Baudrillart, Henri-Marie-Alfred (Alfred Baudrillart), 114, 118, 165, 209–10, 213, 214, 216, 220, 221, 222–23, 225, 231, 234–35, 283, 606n18, 617n104, 617n105, 620n166
Bauer, Gérard, 130, 250, 499, 570
Bauer, Henry, 250, 499
Baumann, Émile, 246
Bazin, René, 117, 165, 170, 198, 204, 211
Béalu, Marcel, 324, 326
Béarn, Pierre, 28, 274
Beaufret, Jean, 107, 335
Beaumarchais, Jean-Pierre de, 552, 559, 569
Beaumont, Germaine, 284
Beauvoir, Simone de, 49, 290–91, 393, 427, 430, 469, 480, 570
Bedel, Maurice, 389
Bédier, Joseph, 214
Béguin, Albert, 330, 353, 359, 399, 570
Beigbeder, Marc, 145, 335, 340
Bellain, Édouard Moreau de. See Dyssord, Jacques
Bellessort, André, 30, 39, 57, 73, 107, 126, 128, 133, 199, 203, 208–9, 211, 213, 215–16, 220, 225, 231, 233–35, 540, 558, 570, 620n166
Bénard, Pierre, 367

Benda, Julien, 19, 35, 37, 54, 56, 99, 105, 254, 298, 305, 308, 312, 318, 321, 340, 360, 403, 420–21, 423, 464, 469, 485–87, 503, 525, 548, 549, 570, 667n36

Benjamin, René, 41, 71, 90, 94, 96, 115, 145, 149, 251, 252, 256, 260–63, 264, 266–67, 269, 271, 271–74, 276, 279–81, 283–84, 287–89, 437, 448, 457, 494–95, 498–99, 570

Benoist-Méchin, Jacques, 275

Benoit, Pierre, 16, 25, 31, 74, 133, 198, 199, 202, 206, 208, 213, 216, 221, 222, 226, 232, 256, 262, 283, 384, 448, 454, 457, 497, 500, 505, 513–14, 536, 570, 624n75, 626n116

Bérard, Léon, 209–10, 214, 217, 220

Béraud, Henri, 56, 84, 100–103, 112, 124, 125, 136–37, 141, 206, 280, 281, 302, 448, 459, 474, 476, 478, 483, 537, 549, 595n73

Berger, Pierre, 375n53

Bergerat, Émile, 250

Bergson, Henri, 95, 149, 196, 200, 228, 241, 358, 369, 371, 374, 395, 402, 505, 612n13, 615n72, 615–16n80, 620n166

Bérimont, Luc, 324, 326, 327

Berl, Emmanuel, 56, 152

Bernanos, Georges, 1, 35, 52, 73, 77, 114, 116, 140, 177, 330, 357, 470, 471, 474, 503, 504, 537, 551, 560, 570, 578n59, 660n78

Bernard, Elsé, 284

Bernard, Jacques, 17, 33

Bernard, Marc, 281, 284–86, 570

Bernard, Tristan (pseudonym of Paul Bernard), 255, 261, 271, 503

Bernoville, Gaëtan, 112

Bertheau, Julien, 367

Bertrand, Adrien, 256

Bertrand, Louis, 66, 71, 115, 198, 199, 208, 209, 213, 222, 225, 241, 356, 570, 615–16n80, 620n166

Besson, Georges, 469

Betz, Maurice, 275

Beydts, Louis, 624n75

Bidault, Georges, 221

Billoux, François, 393, 522

Billy, André, 38, 119, 123, 129, 154, 238, 251, 252, 273–74, 279, 281, 283, 288–90, 331, 340, 481, 494–96, 570

Blake, William, 353

Blanchard, Pierre, 367

Blanche, Jacques-Émile, 117

Blanchot, Maurice, 275, 347, 350, 354

Blanloeil, Abbé, 173

Blanzat, Jean, 178, 236, 239, 319, 349, 358, 365, 376, 377–79, 381, 382, 394–95, 421, 423, 426, 429, 432, 434, 444, 445, 449, 453, 503, 513, 570, 609n68, 648n130

Blanzat, Marguerite, 376

Blech, René, 367, 369, 385, 421, 570, 646n86

Blin, Georges, 330

Bloch, Jean-Richard, 58, 76, 177, 523

Bloch, Marc, 2, 18, 20, 120, 149

Blond, Georges, 30, 31, 275

Blondin, Antoine (printer), 396

Bloy, Léon, 135, 353

Blum, Léon, 92, 119, 145, 294

Bodin, Paul, 355

Bœx, Joseph-Henri Honoré. See Rosny, J.-H., the Elder

Bœx, Séraphin Justin François. See Rosny, J.-H., the Younger

Boileau, Nicolas, 483

Boisdeffre, Pierre de, 559, 568

Boissy, Gabriel, 152

Bonald, Louis-Gabriel-Ambroise, vicomte de, 95

Bonnard, Abel, 16, 28–30, 41, 42, 45, 56–57, 71–72, 141, 146, 153, 157, 176, 199, 206–7, 209, 211, 213, 215, 216, 217, 221–26, 231–32, 234–35, 242, 270, 279, 283, 322, 347, 356, 429, 448, 456, 500–502, 504, 537, 558, 570, 577n48, 578n60, 617n104, 617n108, 666n15

Bonnefoy, René, 40

Clemenceau, Georges, 257, 270

Cocteau, Jean, 28, 36, 76, 125, 169, 310, 321, 433, 459, 481, 506, 571, 624n75

Cogniot, Georges (François Cogniot), 367, 371, 383–84, 386–87, 392, 397, 507, 643n27, 647n92, 651n178

Cohen, Gustave, 525

Colette (Sidonie Gabrielle Colette), 43, 46, 271, 290–91, 375, 386, 481, 495–96, 571, 624n75, 627n142

Combelle, Lucien, 27, 28, 30, 33, 64–65, 138–39, 141, 144, 146, 184, 233, 321, 354, 448, 476, 478, 571, 602n230, 633n101, 644n103

Commandant Lauter. *See* Chamson, André

Constantin, Yves de, 529, 531

Constantin-Weyer, Maurice, 124, 126

Copeau, Jacques, 172, 175, 503

Copeau, Pascal, 477

Cortot, Alfred, 624n75

Coston, Henri, 552

Coty, François, 285, 426

Courriére, Yves, 335

Courtade, Pierre, 469

Courteline, Georges (pseudonym of Georges Victor Marcel Moineaux), 250, 253, 255, 267

Courthion, Pierre, 359

Cousteau, Pierre-Antoine, 30

Couty, Daniel, 559, 569

Crayencour, Marguerite Antoinette Jeanne Marie Ghislaine Cleenewerck de (Marguerite Yourcenar), 291

Crémieux, Benjamin, 17, 206, 321, 629n21

Crémieux, Francis, 17

Cros, Charles, 404

Crouzet, Guy, 272

Curtis, Jean-Louis, 498

Curtius, Ernst Robert, 108

Cuzin, François, 335, 650n158

Dabit, Eugéne, 284

Daix, Pierre, 332, 336, 343, 509

Daladier, Édouard, 534

Daniel, Arnaud, 338

Daniel, Laurent (pseudonym of Ella Kagan Triolet), 403

Daniel-Rops (pseudonym of Henri Petiot), 152, 386, 506

Dante, 338

Daquin, Louis, 367

Darboy, Georges, 180

Darien, Georges, 266

Darnand, Joseph, 268, 426

Darquier, Louis (Louis Darquier de Pellepoix), 118, 220

Daudet, Alphonse, 127, 161, 248, 250, 265, 499

Daudet, Léon, 58, 60, 99, 112, 125, 127, 131, 140, 201, 210, 213, 230, 250, 252, 254, 256, 259–65, 270, 273–74, 279–82, 571

Daudet, Lucien, 281

Daudet, Mrs., 163

Daumal, René, 19, 313, 330, 356

David, André, 511

Déat, Marcel, 16, 27, 431

Debré, Michel, 661n96

Debré, Professor Robert, 389, 576n50

Debû-Bridel, Jacques (Argonne), 50, 181–82, 358, 365, 374–75, 377, 380–82, 386–91, 394–95, 407, 419, 421–22, 426, 434, 445, 448, 450–51, 453, 456–57, 471, 508–9, 514, 571, 609n73, 610n82, 643n21, 643n22, 644n43, 648n130, 649n135, 652n100, 654n115, 657n16, 661n87, 667n36

Decour, Jacques (pseudonym of Daniel Decourdemanche), 8, 246, 346, 365–68, 370, 374–75, 377, 379–83, 385, 387, 394, 422, 450, 508, 571, 643n21

Deharme, Lise, 528

Delange, René, 32, 433

Delétang-Tardif, Yanette, 324–27

Delmont, Théodore, 99, 594n66

Deloncle, Eugène, 65

Demaison, André, 66, 456–57, 459, 571

Dumas, Alexandre, 255
Dumas, Georges, 352
Dumesnil, René, 238
Du Moulin de La Barthéte, Henri, 578n57
Dupanloup, Félix, 213
Durand, Pierre. *See* Pia, Pascal
Duranty, Louis, 348
Duras, Marguerite (pseudonym of Marguerite Donnadieu), 39, 290, 469, 571
Durkheim, Émile, 2, 87–88, 88fn, 90–91, 93, 591n14, 592n34, 592n35
Duval, Colette, 375
Duval, Jean, 375
Dyssord, Jacques (pseudonym of Édouard Moreau de Bellain), 138–39, 143, 150, 233, 448, 602n237

Eckermann, Johann Peter, 146
Effel, Jean, 670n82
Ehrenburg, Ilya, 523
Elias, Norbert, 19
Eluard, Paul (pseudonym of Eugène Émile Paul Grindel), 1, 20, 35, 58, 66, 70, 73, 236, 296, 299, 319, 324, 328, 330, 332, 335–37, 359–360, 375, 376, 384, 390–99, 402–4, 410, 413, 419–20, 423, 424–26, 428, 430, 433, 435, 437, 439, 442, 445, 448, 450, 451, 453, 458, 462–63, 466–67, 481, 486, 489, 503, 512, 519, 523, 525, 541, 544, 546, 571, 648n115, 648n119, 657n26, 670n82. *See also* Haut, Jean du
Emié, Louis, 356
Émile-Paul, the brothers, 375, 559, 568, 607n36
Emmanuel (pseudonym of Claude Morgan), 393
Emmanuel, Pierre (pseudonym of Noël Mathieu), 66, 236, 296, 329–30, 332, 333, 335, 344, 351, 352, 355, 359–60, 386, 389, 399, 403, 405–8, 416–17, 419, 423–24, 425, 462, 482, 559

Epting, Dr. Karl, 23, 24, 35, 77, 144, 580n84, 603n245
Ernst, Max, 648n115
Espiau, Marcel, 275
Estang, Luc (pseudonym of Lucien Bastard), 238, 403, 408, 417, 422, 423, 426, 515, 559
Estaunié, Édouard, 198, 207, 209, 213–14, 615–16n80, 620n166
Estelrich, Joan, 116
Estienne, 258

Fabrégues, Jean de, 41, 43, 145, 147, 154
Fabre-Luce, Alfred, 19, 36, 120, 315, 317, 322, 347, 351, 448
Fadeïev, Aleksandr (Alexandre) Aleksandrovitch, 519
Fardoulis-Lagrange, Michel, 354, 357
Fargue, Léon-Paul, 22, 46, 324, 326, 349, 503, 571, 589n218
Farrére, Claude (pseudonym of Frédéric-Charles Bargone), 66, 115–16, 176, 198, 199, 208–9, 213, 216, 218, 237, 258, 270, 291, 481, 511, 571
Faulkner, William, 304
Faure, Christian, 573
Faure, Gabriel, 235
Faÿ, Bernard, 27, 39–40, 116, 117
Fayard, Jean, 558
Febvre, Lucien, 149
Fegy, Camille, 28
Fernand Demeure (Fernand-Demeure), 144, 602n241. *See also* Guillotin, Dr.
Fernand-Laurent, 126
Fernandez, Ramon, 28–29, 40, 60, 75, 110, 141, 145, 146, 232, 301, 317, 318, 321, 323, 347, 351, 382, 427, 460, 571, 617n104
Feuillet, Octave, 305
Fichte, Johann Gottlieb, 106, 110, 533
Fieschi, Pascal, 327
Finbert, Elian J., 528
Flaubert, Gustave, 98, 238, 248, 610n92
Fleg, Edmond, 528
Flers, Robert de, 207

Flory, Jean, 355
Foch, Ferdinand, 196, 211
Follain, Jean, 48, 324–27, 355–56, 571, 635n118
Fombeure, Maurice, 324, 326–27, 571
Fondane, Benjamin, 355
Forestier, L., 445, 658n41
Forez (pseudonym of François Mauriac), 53, 181, 404, 409, 473
Fort, Paul, 283, 288, 289, 324, 327, 448, 457, 459, 589n218, 624n75
Fortuit, Max, 334
Fouché, Max-Pol, 329–30, 333, 335, 414, 445, 482–83
Fouché, Pascal, 34, 463, 559, 573n1, 588n107
Fouillée, Alfred, 591n14
Fouquet, Jean, 367
Fouquier-Tinville, Antoine, 471fn, 471–73
Fournier, Henri Alban, 170, 375. *See also* Alain-Fournier
Fraigneau, André, 17–18, 28, 433, 448, 518
France, Anatole, 94, 110, 133, 198
Franchet d'Esperey, Louis, 196, 214, 215, 220, 615n80, 620n166
Franco, Francisco, 113–18, 184, 210
François-Poncet, André, 528, 536
Fréche, Gérard, 456, 458
Frénaud, André, 66, 330, 332, 357, 360, 394, 417, 419, 422, 426, 528, 641n247
Freud, Sigmund, 128, 373
Fumet, Stanislas, 145, 330, 333, 398–99, 401, 405, 407, 408, 416, 417, 425, 445, 508, 529, 571
Fustel de Coulanges, Numa Denis, 164

Gadenne, Paul, 322
Gaillard, Jeanne, 367, 642n8
Gaillard, Robert, 285–86, 571
Gaït, Maurice, 42
Gallimard, Gaston, 34, 35, 55, 227, 257, 284, 286, 300, 303, 314, 318, 345, 348, 376, 431, 461–62, 464, 513

Galtier-Boissiére, Jean, 260, 276, 286, 289, 466, 478, 497
Gamarra, Pierre, 523
Gamon, Julien (printer), 355
Garas, Félix, 469
Garaudy, Roger, 469
Garçon, Maurice, 278–79, 494–95, 504, 506, 634n103
Gaucher, André, 141–42
Gaucheron, Jacques, 338
Gaulle, Charles de, 1, 15, 51, 178, 194, 232, 268, 335, 359, 365, 385, 391, 428, 449, 463, 473–75, 478, 493, 502–4, 507–8, 532, 537, 589n225, 641n4, 661n87
Gautier, Estelle, 250
Gautier, Jean-Jacques, 497
Gautier, Judith, 247, 250, 266, 291
Gautier, Théophile, 250
Gaxotte, Pierre, 29, 56, 152, 506, 581n107
Gay, Francisque, 462
Geffroy, Gustave, 287
Genevoix, Maurice, 198, 255, 258, 273, 281, 571
Germain, José, 41, 222, 457
Ghéon, Henri Vangeon, 103, 104, 126, 172
Gide, André, 1, 4, 6, 15–19, 34, 35, 48, 54–56, 59, 60, 64–65, 72–76, 82, 86, 97, 99–105, 109, 110–13, 120–39, 143, 154, 155, 160, 167, 169, 170–76, 182, 205–7, 232, 239, 269, 295–305, 312, 315, 318, 321, 329, 330, 332, 336, 340, 345, 349, 358, 360, 362, 363, 389, 423, 437, 464–68, 483, 485, 503, 504, 505, 512, 515, 518, 533, 537, 540, 543, 550, 556, 594–95n72, 600n188, 601n200, 609n58, 610n92, 629n19, 660n78, 672n125
Gilber-Lecomte, Roger, 357
Gillet, Louis, 143, 199, 208, 213, 220, 227, 233, 615n80, 620n166
Gillet, Martin-Stanislas, 212, 215, 241
Gillouin, René, 41, 125, 129, 152, 153
Gilson, Étienne, 502
Ginsburger, Roger. *See* Villon, Pierre

Heller, Gerhard, 23, 24, 34, 35, 144, 222, 268, 349, 350, 376, 580n84, 645n49
Helleu, Yves, 469
Hennezel, Henri d', 334
Hennique, Léon, 249, 254, 260
Henriot, Émile, 97, 199, 482, 483
Henriot, Philippe, 291–92, 481
Henri-Robert, 595n80
Hérédia, José-Maria de, 163
Hériat, Raymond-Gérard Payelle dit Philippe, 263, 493, 499, 509
Hermant, Abel, 16, 57, 71, 72, 198, 199, 209, 213, 216, 221, 222, 224, 231, 233–38, 448, 457, 475, 500, 501, 502, 504, 666n15
Herriot, Édouard, 197, 504, 581n97
Hervé, Pierre, 469
Herzog, Émile Salomon Wilhelm. *See* Maurois, André
Hesse, Hermann, 108
Hibbelen, Gerhard, 579n69
Hitler, Adolf, 24, 27, 34, 61, 118, 183, 184, 208, 212, 222, 223, 227, 261, 263, 294, 300, 317, 480, 579n75, 632n82
Hoffmann, Stanley, 573n1
Holweck, Fernand, 369, 643n20
Huc, Philippe (Tristan Deréme), 126, 571
Hugnet, Georges, 650n171
Hugo, Victor, 99, 134, 142, 264, 336, 674n27
Humbert, Agnès, 375–76
Humeau, Edmond, 413
Husserl, Edmund, 70
Husymans, Joris-Karl (pseudonym of Charles-Marie-Georges Huysmans), 254

Jacob, Max, 66, 326
Jacquier, Claude (pseudonym of de Georges Sadoul), 335, 399
Jaloux, Edmond, 124, 126, 129, 152, 153, 199, 203, 214, 219, 325, 500, 518, 615n71, 616n80
Jammes, Francis, 99, 116, 169

Janet, Pierre, 505
Janvier, Alain, 136
Jaujard, Jacques, 658
Jeanne d'Arc, 53, 271
Jeanneret-Gris, Charles-Édouard (Le Corbusier), 354
Jeantet, Claude, 29
Jérôme, Jean, 643n17
Johannet, René, 112, 117
Jonnart, Charles Célestin, 211
Jou, Louis (printer), 331
Jouglet, René, 522
Jouhandeau, Marcel, 75, 300, 316, 319, 321, 348, 349, 351, 447, 448, 452, 459, 464, 513, 514, 515, 518, 537, 668n48
Jouve, Pierre Jean, 66, 72, 300, 353, 355, 359, 471
Jouvenel, Bertrand de, 518
Jouvenel, Renaud de, 385
Joxe, Louis, 520
Joyce, James, 227
Judt, Tony, 527
Julliard, Jacques, 552
Julliard, René, 499
Jullien-Courtine, Robert, 233
Junger, Ernst, 624n74

Kaestner, Erich, 386
Kahn, family, 355
Kahnweiler family, 355
Kaiser, Friedhelm, 23
Kant, Emmanuel, 90, 533
Katz, Pierre, 356
Kemp, Robert, 506
Kessel, Joseph, 57, 298, 410, 551
Keyserling, Hermann von, 108, 110
Kistemaeckers, Henry, 265
Kojève, Aleksandr (Alexandre) Kojevnikov, 71, 355
Kostrowitzky, Wilhelm Apollinaris de. *See* Apollinaire, Guillaume
Koyré, Alexandre, 71, 355
Kriegel, Annie, 641n4
Kriegel-Valrimont, Maurice, 469

Labé, Louise, 290
Laborie, Pierre, 470
Lacaze, Jean-Lucien, 196, 209, 214, 216,
    220, 234, 235, 237, 240, 481, 500,
    620n169
Lachenal, François, 20, 359, 141
La Colére, François (pseudonym of Louis
    Aragon), 403, 541, 650n171
Lacôte, René, 521
Lacouture, Jean, 165, 172, 475
Lacretelle, Jacques de, 198, 199, 203, 213,
    216, 237, 304, 462, 470, 506
Lacroix, Jean, 477
Lafayette, Marie-Madeleine Pioche de La
    Vergne, comtesse de, 290
La Force, Auguste-Armand-Ghislain-
    Marie-Joseph Nompar de Caumont,
    duc de, 197, 209, 214, 481, 501
Lagarde, Pierre, 238
Lagneau, Jules, 90
Laguerre, Bernard, 58
La Hire, Jean de, 408
Lahr, Father, 173
Lahy-Hollebecque, Marie, 529
Lalou, René, 51, 159, 482–83, 514,
    559
Lambrichs, Georges, 357
La Mésanchè, François de, 602n233
Landsberg, Paul-Louis, 353
Langevin, Paul, 196, 231, 301
Langle, Camille de, 281
Lannes, Roger, 473, 474, 661n97
Lanson, Gustave, 87, 88
Lanza del Vasto, Joseph Jean (Giuseppe
    Giovanni Luigi Maria Enrico Lanza di
    Trabia-Branciforte), 356
Laporte, René, 413
Larguier, Léo, 251, 261, 263, 267, 273, 274,
    282, 283, 284, 288, 495, 496, 499
Lasserre, Pierre, 93, 94, 95, 97, 99, 254
La Tour du Pin, Patrice de, 20, 43
Laubreaux, Alain, 29–30, 254, 263,
    280, 448, 456, 540, 549, 578n57,
    645n53

Laurent, Jacques (Jacques Laurent-Célly;
    Jacques Bostan), 42, 105, 132, 133, 403,
    489, 490, 546, 664n196
Lauter, Commandant (pseudonym of
    André Chamson), 413
Lautréamont, comte de (pseudonym of
    Isidore Lucien Ducasse), 337
Laval, Pierre, 40, 45, 221, 224, 226, 228,
    279, 354, 536, 578n57
La Varende, Jean Balthazar Mallard, 26,
    30, 31, 43, 66, 71, 251, 252, 281–89, 448,
    452, 494, 495, 537, 624n75
Lavedan, Henri, 20, 198, 207, 210, 240,
    241, 615n71, 616n80, 620n166
Lazar, Marc, 592n30
Léautaud, Paul, 15, 17, 19, 22, 31, 36, 48, 65,
    202, 232, 235, 239, 262, 281, 286, 289, 294,
    471, 579–80n83, 590n236, 634n103
Le Bel, Philippe. See Decour, Jacques
Lebesque, Maurice (Morvan-Lebesque),
    30
Leblond, Marius, 261
Le Bon, Gustave, 129
Lebrun, Albert, 194, 211
Lécavelé, Roland. See Dorgelés, Roland
Lecherbonnier, Bernard, 671n110
Leclerc, Philippe de Hautecloque, 320
Lecœur, Auguste, 531
Lecomte, Georges, 63, 176, 198, 199, 209,
    213, 216, 228, 233, 234, 235, 237, 259, 384,
    416, 481
Le Corbusier (Charles-Édouard
    Jeanneret-Gris), 354
Leduc, Victor, 469
Leenhardt, Roger, 333
Lefèvre, Frédéric, 96, 100
Legendre, Maurice, 116, 117
Léger, Albine (Albine Loisy), 291
Léger, Alexis (Saint-John Perse; Saint-
    Léger Léger), 72, 73, 194, 238, 329, 400,
    551
Léger, Fernand, 442
Le Guern, Jean (pseudonym of Édith
    Thomas), 403

Michaux, Henri, 313, 328, 332
Michelet, Jules, 99
Miévre, Jacques, 225
Milhac, 459
Miller, Henry, 353, 521
Millet, Raymond, 423, 426
Milligan, Jennifer E., 665n4
Miomandre, Francis de, 117, 118
Mirbeau, Octave, 254
Mistral Frédéric, 533
Mitterand, François, 286
Mohrt, Michel, 44
Moineaux, Georges Victor Marcel. *See*
    Courteline, Georges
Moineaux, Jules, 250
Molière, Jean-Baptiste Poquelin, 131, 133
Mondor, Henri, 241, 281, 462, 470
Monnier, Thyde, 291
Montaigne, Michel Eyquem de, 422
Montand, Yves (Yvo Livi), 524
Montandon, Georges, 27
Montesquieu, 97, 129
Montfort, Eugène, 595n73
Montherlant, Henry de, 572
Morand, Paul, 25, 28, 29, 39, 40, 57, 76,
    108, 110, 194, 207, 220, 241, 298, 309,
    321, 351, 382, 383, 427, 452, 457, 506, 507
Moré, Marcel, 353
Morellet, André, 211
Morgan Claude (Emmanuel), 393
Morin, Edgar, 469
Mornet, Daniel, 384
Mort, Noël Bayon de la, 30, 216, 551
Morvan-Lebesque, Maurice Lebesque, 30
Moselly, Émile, 275
Mounier, Emmanuel, 333, 341, 399, 413,
    462, 482, 483
Mousset, Paul, 275, 277
Moussinac, Léon, 37, 373, 399, 424, 445,
    529. *See also* Aymé, Jacques d'
Muel-Dreyfus, Francine, 573
Mühlefeld, Madame, 163
Murat, Caroline Bonaparte, comtesse
    Joachim, 270

Musset, Alfred de, 98, 99
Mussolini, Benito, 31, 114, 176, 177, 208,
    235, 261, 287, 385

Nadeau, Maurice, 498
Naegelen, Marcel, 509, 510
Napoléon I, 167, 194
Napoléon II, 227
Navarre, François, 28
Nels, Jacques, 498
Neveux, Pol, 259, 261, 262
Nicolas, André, 29
Nizan, Paul, 92, 362, 363, 380, 548, 549
Noailles, Anna de, 169
Nodier, Charles, 211
Noël, Marie-Mélanie Rouger, 525
Noël, Maurice, 184, 262, 286, 410
Noir, Jean (pseudonym of Jean Cassou),
    541
Nolhac, Pierre de, 209, 235
Nordmann, Joë, 367
Nourissier, François, 258
Novalis (pseudonym of Georg Philipp
    Friedrich Freiherr, baron von
    Hardenberg), 353

Obey, André, 528
Oddon, Yvonne, 376
Oltramare, Georges, 456
Orion (pseudonym of André Rousseaux),
    408
Ormesson, Wladimir Olivier Lefèvre d',
    506
Ory, Pascal, 577n45
Oudard, Georges, 407, 423, 426

Pacelli, Cardinal Eugenio Maria Giuseppe
    Giovanni, 212, 215, 597n125. *See also*
    Pius XII, Pope
Pagnol, Marcel, 201, 241, 505
Paléologue, Maurice, 207, 209, 214, 215,
    216, 231, 234, 235, 237
Palewski, Gaston, 503
Palhan, Jean (Jean Guérin), 392, 353

Papadiamantopoúlos, Joánnis, 119

Paraf, Yvonne, 390, 395. *See also*
Desvignes, Yvonne

Parain, Brice, 40, 300, 318, 462, 629n21,
632n87

Parrot, Louis, 182, 227, 330, 332, 345, 392,
410, 424, 469, 480, 498

Pasteur, Louis, 86

Pasteur Vallery-Radot, Louis, 503, 504,
506

Paulhan, Jean (Maast), 1, 8, 16, 18, 19,
32–35, 47, 66, 70, 72, 75, 126, 147, 152,
178, 180, 202, 236–37, 239, 274,
293–314, 317–26, 329, 331, 334, 336, 340,
344, 355–61, 365, 370, 373–87, 389–96,
400, 405, 406, 410, 412, 419–35, 440,
441, 443–54, 462–69, 472, 474,
479–83, 486–90, 493, 496, 503–5, 508,
509, 513–17, 520, 533–35, 539, 544, 546,
548, 575n11, 586n187, 594n72, 631n64,
632n77, 633n93, 633n95, 634n103,
638n184, 638n188, 645n49, 650n171,
654n232, 658n47, 661n92, 661n94,
667n36, 671n118

Paxton, Robert O., 15, 573

Payr, Bernhard, 183, 277

Pécaut, Félix, 93

Péguy, Charles, 28, 30, 36, 43, 50, 53, 92,
94, 95, 99, 101, 104, 128, 256, 328, 331,
340, 402, 533, 578n59, 672n118

Peisson, Édouard, 284

Pellepoix, Louis Darquier de (pseudonym
of Louis Darquier), 118, 220

Pelorson, Georges, 33, 353, 354, 448,
579n76, 640n220

Pennetier, Claude, 552

Péquignot, 173

Péret, Benjamin, 486

Pergaud, Louis, 275

Pernoud, René, 233

Pérochon, Ernest, 275

Perroux, François, 44

Pesquidoux, Joseph de, 41, 66, 198, 199,
213, 217, 218, 219, 241, 277, 281, 615n80

Petain, Philippe, 15, 29, 30, 33, 41–43, 120,
122, 134, 139, 145, 149, 154, 158, 178, 181,
184, 196, 200, 204, 210, 214–28, 231–33,
236, 241, 265, 270, 271, 275, 277, 287,
334, 342–44, 369, 408, 449, 450, 452,
471, 478, 480, 500, 502, 506, 528, 532,
534, 536, 560, 578n57, 579n75, 587n196,
587n197, 589n22, 615n80, 642n9

Peter, René, 240

Petiot, Henri Jules Charles. *See* Daniel-
Rops

Petitjean, Armand, 17, 43, 64, 305, 307,
308, 317, 320, 447, 457, 513, 633n93

Petitot, Romain (François Bruel), 354

Peyrefitte, Roger, 496

Philipe, Gérard, 524

Philippon, René, 39

Pia, Pascal (pseudonym of Pierre
Durand), 20, 319, 405, 576n28, 652n188

Picard, Émile, 196, 214, 216, 231, 232, 235

Picasso, Pablo, 442, 531

Picon, Gaétan, 569, 586n183

Pignon, Édouard, 370

Pillement, Georges, 469

Pilon, Edmond, 452

Pius XII, Pope, 426. *See also* Pacelli,
Cardinal Eugenio Maria Giuseppe
Giovanni

Plas, Fernand, 278, 279

Plisnier, Charles, 152, 255

Poincaré, Raymond, 257

Politzer, Georges, 155, 366–73, 381, 383,
644n36

Ponchon, Raoul, 261

Ponge, Francis, 66, 74, 332, 352, 355, 360,
404, 407, 419, 421, 456, 469, 653n207

Pontigny, 298

Ponton, Rémy, 87, 554–58, 612n22,
613n25, 621n15, 651n186, 675n12

Porto-Riche, Georges de, 612n13

Poulaille, Henry, 28, 55, 284, 589n218

Pourrat, Henri, 1, 41, 76, 126, 230, 236, 241,
273–77, 280, 281, 286, 319, 330, 334, 350,
495, 496

Rosny, J.-H., the Younger (pseudonym of Séraphin Justin François Boex), 251, 252, 261, 263, 266, 267, 273–75, 278, 281, 283, 284, 287–90, 494–96, 499, 572

Röthke, Heinz, 291

Rougemont, Denis de, 305, 470

Rousseau, Jean-Jacques, 98, 99, 134, 206, 548

Rousseaux, André, 16, 81, 123–25, 132, 154, 184, 304, 351, 360, 396, 399, 401, 403, 405, 407–10, 426, 434, 446, 450, 466, 532, 650n158. *See also* Orion

Rousseaux, Mrs., 639n213

Roussel, Raymond, 298

Roussel, Romain, 275

Rousset, David, 489, 498

Roussy, Gustave, 506

Roux, François de, 284

Roy, Jules, 498

Ruffe, Hubert, 397, 398, 410, 650n168

Rysselberghe, Maria von, 15, 586n187

Sadoul, Georges, 37, 60, 335, 367, 373, 397, 399, 401, 403–6, 416, 419, 424, 469, 653n207. *See also* Jacquier, Claude

Saget, Justin, 671n105

Saint-Clair, Simone, 456

Sainte-Beuve, Charles-Augustin, 199

Saint-Exupéry, Antoine de, 35, 237, 358, 503, 551

Saint-Hélier, Monique, 347

Saint-John Perse. *See* Léger, Alexis

Saint-Just, Louis Antoine, 471, 663n147

Saint-Léger Léger. *See* Léger, Alexis

Saint-Roman, Arnaud de (pseudonym of Louis Aragon), 403

Saint-Simon, Louis de Rouvroy, 322

Salacrou, Armand, 246, 462, 493, 499, 528, 540

Salazar, 334

Salleron, Louis, 43

Salmon, André, 69, 324, 326, 327, 394, 457, 470

Sangnier, Marc, 162, 165, 176

Sarraute, Nathalie, 290

Sartre, Jean-Paul, 32, 50, 57, 60, 74, 75, 131, 143, 154–56, 175, 179, 290, 291, 303, 304, 313, 319, 357–58, 360, 367, 368, 380–81, 393, 394, 408, 413, 419, 421, 424, 425, 427, 430, 433, 438–40, 443, 462–64, 466, 469, 474, 480, 481, 483, 485, 486, 488–90, 515, 518, 530, 531, 537, 539, 541, 542, 545, 546, 548, 549, 576n30, 586n183, 664n160, 673n8

Sauger, André, 401

Sauvage, Marcel, 285

Savignon, André, 254

Scapini, Georges, 382

Scheler, Lucien, 392, 394, 396, 398, 424, 434, 448, 458, 478

Schlumberger, Jean, 17, 72, 73, 104, 130, 131, 236, 239, 298, 299, 301, 305, 308, 318, 321, 349, 350, 360, 389, 437, 448–53, 461, 464, 467, 468, 481, 503, 505, 513–18, 547

Schor, Ralph, 118, 601n218

Schumann, Maurice, 51, 178, 410, 583n149, 609n65

Séché, Alphonse, 38

Seghers, Pierre, 49, 66, 236, 239, 326, 328, 330–35, 343, 351, 352, 359, 360, 371, 389, 402, 403, 405, 406, 410–11, 416, 417, 419–21, 423, 462, 463, 480, 482, 483, 522, 559, 568, 635n135, 650n158, 650n171

Segonzac, André Dunoyer, 39

Seignobos, Charles, 87, 149, 252

Seillère, 505

Sertillange, Antonin-Dalmace, 624n75

Serviére, Jean, 139

Séverine, 265

Sicard, Maurice-Ivan, 260

Silvaire, André, 352, 353

Simonin, Anne, 53, 424, 425, 463, 481, 483, 485, 583n159, 661n90

Simonov, Kirill Mikhailovitch, 523

Singer, Claude, 573

Sirinelli, Jean-François, 553, 613n32

Slansky, Rudolf, 527
Smiley, Amy, 665n4
Smith, Robert J., 57
Socrates, 536
Solier, René de, 516
Solomon, Jacques, 366, 367, 369, 373, 383,
  642n8
Sonnier, Georges, 355
Sordet, Dominique, 617
Sorel, Georges, 43, 94, 311, 592n40
Soubiran, André, 291
Souday, Paul, 83
Soury, Jules, 593n48
Spencer, Herbert, 91
Spengler, Oswald, 108
Spire, André, 529
Starobinski, Jean, 359
Steeg, Jules, 93
Steel, James, 52, 665n4
Steinbeck, John, 523
Stendhal, Henri Beyle, 51, 98, 237,
  422
Stéphane, Roger Worms, 245, 534
Suarés, André, 35, 37, 300, 321
Suhard, Emmanuel, 617n105
Supervielle, Jules, 324, 330, 353, 400
Szabo, Zoltan, 523
Szyfer, Joseph, 456

Tagore, Rabindranath, 108
Taine, Hyppolite, 86, 87, 95, 164, 198, 556,
  593n48
Talagrand Jacques Louis. See Maulnier,
  Thierry
Talvart, Hector, 553
Tarde, Alfred de, 6, 93, 95, 101. See also
  Agathon
Tarde, Gabriel, 93, 129, 592n34
Tarde, Guillaume de, 72, 588n14
Tardieu, Jean, 66, 74, 319, 352, 356–58,
  419, 421
Tasca, Angelo, 320
Tavernier, René, 152, 332, 334–35, 394,
  398–404, 407, 410, 415, 435, 466

Ternet, Georges, 397, 403, 405, 407
Téry, Gustave, 101, 256
Tessier, Roland, 255
Thalmann, Rita, 573n1
Thaon, Mara, 354
Theuriet, André, 198
Thévenin, Denis. See Duhamel, Georges
Thibaudet, Albert, 89, 90, 93, 96, 126, 169,
  205, 206, 256, 259
Thibon, Gustave, 41, 134, 149, 601n206
Thiers, Adolphe, 198
Thiesse, Anne-Marie, 275, 574n4
Thomas, Édith, 49, 69, 73, 383, 386, 387,
  391, 394, 395, 403, 419, 421, 424, 430,
  434, 445, 451, 534, 653n212, 654n214.
  See also Le Guern, Jean
Thomas, Henri, 327, 356, 601n100
Thomas, Jean, 650n158
Thomas, Marcel, 614n47
Thorez, Maurice, 336, 365, 369, 371, 373,
  374, 531, 641n4
Toucas, Fernand, 310
Touchar, Pierre-André, 353
Touzot, Jean, 182, 241, 503, 602n241,
  621n171
Treich, Léon, 667n36
Triolet, Ella Kagan (Elsa Triolet), 49, 281,
  284, 290–92, 313–14, 333, 368, 370–71,
  389, 392, 395, 403, 405, 416, 424–25,
  430, 434, 435, 445, 446, 458, 462, 493,
  495–97, 510, 512, 518, 519, 521–29, 531,
  534, 627n146, 645n62, 651n188,
  654n214, 669n73. See also Daniel,
  Laurent
Truc, Gonzague, 28, 168
Turlais, Jean, 578n59

Ubac, Raoul, 354
Uhl, Walter, 352, 353
Urvoy, Yves, 43

Vailland, Roger, 16, 57, 107, 335, 380, 469,
  497
Valeri, Valerio, 617n105

66101065R00448

Made in the USA
Lexington, KY
03 August 2017